Mastering™

AutoCAD® 2007
and AutoCAD LT® 2007

Mastering™
AutoCAD® 2007
and AutoCAD LT® 2007

George Omura

Wiley Publishing, Inc.

Acquisitions Editor: Willem Knibbe

Development Editor: Heather O'Connor

Technical Editor: Jon McFarland

Production Editor: Martine Dardignac

Copy Editor: Pat Coleman

Production Manager: Tim Tate

Vice President and Executive Group Publisher: Richard Swadley

Vice President and Executive Publisher: Joseph B. Wikert

Vice President and Publisher: Dan Brodnitz

Media Development Specialist: Steven Kudirka

Permissions Specialist: Shannon Walters

Book Designers: Maureen Forys, Happenstance Type-O-Rama; Judy Fung

Illustrator: Jeffrey Wilson, Happenstance Type-O-Rama

Compositor: Craig Woods, Happenstance Type-O-Rama

Proofreader: Nancy Riddiough

Indexer: Ted Laux

Cover Designer: Design Site

Cover Image: Jack T. Myers, Design Site

Copyright © 2006 by Wiley Publishing, Inc., Indianapolis, Indiana

Published simultaneously in Canada

ISBN-13: 978-0-470-00876-8

ISBN-10: 0-470-00876-8

For general information on our other products and services or to obtain technical support, please contact our Customer Care Department within the U.S. at (800) 762-2974, outside the U.S. at (317) 572-3993 or fax (317) 572-4002.

Wiley also publishes its books in a variety of electronic formats. Some content that appears in print may not be available in electronic books.

Library of Congress Cataloging-in-Publication Data is available from the publisher.

10 9 8 7 6 5 4 3 2 1

Dear Reader,

Thank you for choosing Mastering AutoCAD 2007and AutoCAD LT 2007. This book is part of a family of premium quality Sybex graphics books, all written by outstanding authors who combine practical experience with a gift for teaching.

Sybex was founded in 1976. Thirty years later, we're still committed to producing consistently exceptional books. With each of our graphics titles we're working hard to set a new standard for the industry. From the paper we print on, to the writers and CAD professionals we work with, our goal is to bring you the best books available.

I hope you see all that reflected in these pages. I'd be very interested to hear your comments and get your feedback on how we're doing. To let us know what you think about this or any other Sybex book, please send me an email at: sybex_publisher@wiley.com. Please also visit us at www.sybex.com to learn more about the rest of our growing graphics line.

Best regards,

Dan Brodnitz
Vice President and Publisher
Sybex, an Imprint of Wiley

To my two wonderful sons, Arthur and Charles, and to
Susan, who helps me to laugh when I most need it.

Acknowledgments

Many talented and hardworking folks gave their best effort to produce Mastering AutoCAD 2007 and AutoCAD 2007 LT. I offer my sincerest gratitude to those people who helped bring this book to you.

Heartfelt thanks go to the editorial and production teams at Sybex for their efforts. Willem Knibbe made sure things got off to a great start and was always there for support. Martine Dardignac kept a watchful eye on the progress of the book and offered some great assistance with scheduling. Heather O'Connor kept things running smoothly and always had a positive attitude. Pat Coleman made sure I wasn't trying out new uses of the English language. Jon McFarland did an excellent job of ensuring that I didn't make any glaring mistakes and offered suggestions based on his own training experience.

You can see the handiwork of Paul Richardson and Christine Merredith of Technical Publications in the sidebars that discuss the San Francisco Main Library. Thanks also go to the architectural firms of Pei Cobb Freed & Partners and Simon Martin-Vegue Winkelstein Morris Associated Architects for generously granting permission to reproduce drawings from their design of the San Francisco Main Library.

At Autodesk, a special thanks goes to Eric Stover for taking the time from his busy schedule to write the foreword. Thanks for the kind words, Eric. Thanks also go to Denis Cadu, who has always given his steadfast support of my efforts over many projects. Jim Quanci, as usual, gave his generous and thoughtful assistance to us author types. Finally, a big thanks to Shaan Hurley for generously allowing us to have a look at the pre-release software.

And as usual, a great big thank you to my family and friends, who have always been a source of inspiration and support.

Foreword

AutoCAD and AutoCAD LT are the world's top-selling computer-aided design applications. As a user, you belong to special club of designers, drafters, engineers, and teachers numbering in the millions worldwide. You speak a special "AutoCAD" language with your colleagues and are passionate about your work. You've made this product line the success it is today, and we continually strive to make it better each year. As product manager, my role is to listen to AutoCAD and AutoCAD LT customers like you to help shape each new release. Autodesk is focused on improving day-to-day productivity of AutoCAD customers while at the same time making the software more flexible and easier to learn. As a development team, we work directly with thousands of customers to improve productivity in the areas that count. I am sure you will agree that AutoCAD and AutoCAD LT 2007 are the most productive AutoCADs yet.

I often get asked by customers what the best tool to help learn AutoCAD or AutoCAD LT is, and after spending many years teaching AutoCAD to hundreds of new and experienced users, I have seen a lot of approaches. *Mastering AutoCAD* is a fantastic way to learn no matter what your skill level. It starts with the basics and progressively turns you into an AutoCAD or AutoCAD LT expert. You can skip chapters you know and focus on what you need to learn with in-depth explanations and step-by-step exercises. Whether you are learning the ropes from scratch or getting up to speed on the latest product features such as 3D modeling, sheet sets, or dynamic blocks, it's all here in George's new book, *Mastering AutoCAD 2007 and AutoCAD LT 2007*.

Mastering AutoCAD 2007 and AutoCAD LT 2007 has been fully updated to cover all AutoCAD 2007 new or enhanced features, including modeling, visual styles, lights and materials, rendering and animation, and changes you asked for in commonly used commands. This excellent revision to the best-selling Mastering AutoCAD series features concise explanations, focused examples, step-by-step instructions, and hands-on projects for both AutoCAD and AutoCAD LT.

Award-winning author George Omura has been writing about AutoCAD almost as long as we've been making it, and the depth of his knowledge shows.

—*Eric Stover*
AutoCAD Product Manager

Contents at a Glance

Contents

Introduction

Welcome to *Mastering AutoCAD 2007 and AutoCAD LT 2007*. As many readers have already discovered, this book is a unique blend of tutorial and reference that includes everything you need to get started and stay ahead with AutoCAD. With this edition, you get coverage of the latest features of both AutoCAD 2007 and AutoCAD LT 2007, plus the latest information on new features.

How to Use This Book

Rather than just showing you how each command works, this book shows you AutoCAD 2007 in the context of a meaningful activity. You will learn how to use commands while working on an actual project and progressing toward a goal. This book also provides a foundation on which you can build your own methods for using AutoCAD and become an AutoCAD expert. For this reason, I haven't covered every single command or every permutation of a command response. You should think of this book as a way to get a detailed look at AutoCAD as it is used on a real project. As you follow the exercises, I encourage you to also explore AutoCAD on your own, applying the techniques you learn to your own work.

Both experienced and beginning AutoCAD users will find this book useful. If you are not an experienced user, the way to get the most out of this book is to approach it as a tutorial—chapter by chapter, at least for the first two parts of the book. You'll find that each chapter builds on the skills and information you learned in the previous one. To help you navigate, the exercises are shown in numbered steps. To address the needs of all readers worldwide, the exercises provide both U.S. (feet/inches) and metric measurements.

After you've mastered the material in Parts 1 and 2, you can follow your interests and explore other parts of the book in whatever order you choose. Part 3 takes you to a more advanced skill level. There, you'll learn more about storing and sharing drawing data and how to create more complex drawings. If you're interested in 3D, check out Part 4. If you want to start customizing right away, go to Part 5. You can check out Chapters 27 and 28 at any time because they give you general information on sharing AutoCAD files with your coworkers and consultants. Chapter 28 focuses on AutoCAD's Sheet Set Manager, which offers a way to organize your multisheet projects.

You can also use this book as a ready reference for your day-to-day problems and questions about commands. Optional exercises at the end of each chapter will help you review and look at different ways to apply the information you've learned. Experienced users will also find this book a handy reference tool.

Finally, if you run into problems using AutoCAD, see the "When Things Go Wrong" section in Appendix B. You'll find a listing of the most common issues that users face when first learning AutoCAD.

AutoCAD 2007 and AutoCAD LT 2007

Autodesk has released both AutoCAD 2007 and AutoCAD LT 2007 simultaneously. Not surprisingly, they are nearly identical in the way they look and work. You can share files between the two programs with complete confidence that you won't lose data or corrupt files. The main differences are that LT does not support all the 3D functions of AutoCAD 2007, nor does it support the customization tools of AutoLISP and VBA. But LT still has plenty to offer in both the productivity and customization areas. And because they are so similar, I can present material for both programs with only minor adjustments.

When a feature is discussed that is available only in AutoCAD 2007, you will see the AutoCAD Only icon.

You'll also see warning messages when tutorials vary between AutoCAD 2007 and LT. If only minor differences occur, you will see either a warning message or directions embedded in the tutorial indicating the differences between the two programs.

In the few instances in which LT has a feature that is not available in AutoCAD 2007, you will see the LT Only icon.

I've also provided work-around instructions wherever possible when LT does not offer a feature found in AutoCAD 2007.

Getting Information Fast

I've included plenty of tips and warnings:

TIP   Tips are designed to make practice easier.

WARNING   Warnings steer you away from pitfalls.

Also, in each chapter you will find more extensive tips and discussions in the form of sidebars set off from the main text. To encourage you along the way, some of the sidebars show you how topics in each chapter were applied to a real-world project, the San Francisco Main Library. Together, the tips, warnings, and sidebars provide a wealth of information I have gathered over years of using AutoCAD on a variety of projects in different office environments. You might want to browse through the book, just reading these notes, to get an idea of how they might be useful to you.

Another quick reference you'll find yourself turning to often is Appendix C, which contains tables of all the system variables and dimension variables with comments on their uses. If you experience any problems, you can consult the "When Things Go Wrong" section in Appendix B.

What to Expect

Mastering AutoCAD 2007 and AutoCAD LT 2007 is divided into five parts, each representing a milestone in your progress toward becoming an expert AutoCAD user. Here is a description of those parts and what they will show you.

Part 1: The Basics

As with any major endeavor, you must begin by tackling small, manageable tasks. In this first part, you will become familiar with the way AutoCAD looks and feels. Chapter 1, "Exploring the AutoCAD and AutoCAD LT Interface," shows you how to get around in AutoCAD. In Chapter 2, "Creating Your First Drawing," you will learn how to start and exit the program and how to respond to AutoCAD commands. Chapter 3, "Setting Up and Using AutoCAD's Drafting Tools," tells you how to set up a work area, edit objects, and lay out a drawing. In Chapter 4, "Organizing Objects with Blocks and Groups," you will explore some tools unique to CAD: symbols, blocks, and layers. As you are introduced to AutoCAD, you will also get a chance to make some drawings that you can use later in the book and perhaps even in future projects of your own. Chapter 5, "Keeping Track of Layers, Blocks, and Files" shows you how to use layers to keep similar information together and object properties such as linetypes to organize things visually.

Part 2: Mastering Intermediate Skills

After you have the basics down, you will begin to explore some of AutoCAD's more subtle qualities. Chapter 6, "Reusing Data to Work Efficiently" tells you how to reuse drawing setup information and parts of an existing drawing. In Chapter 7, "Mastering Viewing Tools, Hatches, and External References," you will learn how to use viewing tools and hatches and how to assemble and edit a large drawing file. Chapter 8, "Introducing Printing, Plotting, and Layouts," shows you how to get your drawing onto hard copy. Chapter 9, "Understanding Plot Styles," discusses methods for controlling lineweights and shading in your printer output. Chapter 10, "Adding Text to Drawings," tells you how to annotate your drawing and edit your notes. Chapter 11, "Using Fields and Tables," shows you how to add spreadsheet functionality to your drawings. Chapter 12, "Using Dimensions," gives you practice in using automatic dimensioning (another unique CAD capability).

Part 3: Mastering Advanced Skills

At this point, you will be on the verge of becoming a real AutoCAD expert. Part 3 is designed to help you polish your existing skills and give you a few new ones. Chapter 13, "Using Attributes," tells you how to attach information to drawing objects and how to export that information to database and spreadsheet files. In Chapter 14, "Copying Pre-existing Drawings into AutoCAD," you will learn techniques for transferring paper drawings to AutoCAD. In Chapter 15, "Advanced Editing and Organizing," you will complete the apartment building tutorial. During this process you will learn how to integrate what you've learned so far and gain some tips on working in groups. Chapter 16, "Laying Out Your Printer Output," shows you the tools that let you display your drawing in an organized fashion. Chapter 17, "Using Dynamic Blocks," shows you how you can create blocks that can be edited with grips without having to redefine them. Chapter 18, "Drawing Curves and Solid Fills," gives you an in-depth look at some special drawing objects, such as splines and fitted curves. In Chapter 19, "Getting and Exchanging Data from Drawings," you will practice getting information about a drawing and learn how AutoCAD can interact with other applications, such as spreadsheets and desktop-publishing programs. You'll also learn how to copy and paste data. If you need to link your drawing data to a database, the companion CD contains "Working with External Databases," a chapter that focuses on AutoCAD's dbConnect Manager. dbConnect offers a way to link objects and text in a drawing to a database manager so you can keep track of anything from assembly parts to equipment in a floor plan.

Part 4: 3D Modeling and Imaging

Although 2D drafting is AutoCAD's workhorse application, AutoCAD's 3D capabilities give you a chance to expand your ideas and look at them in a new light. Chapter 20, "Introducing 3D Drawings," covers AutoCAD's basic features for creating three-dimensional drawings. Chapter 21, "Using Advanced 3D Features," introduces you to some of the program's more powerful 3D capabilities. Chapter 22, "Rendering 3D Drawings," shows how you can use AutoCAD to produce lifelike views of your 3D drawings. Chapter 23, "Editing and Visualizing 3D Solids," takes a closer look at 3D solids and how they can be created, edited, and displayed in AutoCAD 2007. On the CD, you'll find "Architectural Solid Modeling," which takes you deeper into the world of 3D solid modeling as you model a classic building to learn the finer points of AutoCAD 3D. "Advanced Surface Modeling," also on the CD, shows you how to make full use of AutoCAD's surface-modeling tools to create more complex, free-form shapes.

Part 5: Customization and Integration

One of AutoCAD's greatest strengths is its openness to customization. Chapter 24, "Using the Express Tools," gives you a gentle introduction to the world of AutoCAD customization. You'll learn how to load and use existing Express tools that expand AutoCAD's functionality, and you'll be introduced to AutoLISP as a tool to create macros. Chapter 25, "Introducing AutoLISP," is a primer to AutoCAD's popular macro language. You'll learn how you can create custom "commands" built on existing ones and how you can retrieve and store locations and other data. Chapter 26, "Customizing Toolbars, Menus, Linetypes, and Hatch Patterns," shows you how to customize menus, toolbars, linetypes, and hatch patterns. Chapter 27, "Managing and Sharing Your Drawings," shows you how to adapt AutoCAD to your own work style. You'll learn about the tools that help you exchange drawings with others and how to secure your drawings to prevent tampering. Chapter 28, "Using Sheet Sets," shows you how to use the new Sheet Set Manager to simplify your file management. By using the Sheet Set Manager, you can automate some of the more tedious drawing coordination tasks.

If you're really serious about customization, you'll want to take a look at additional bonus chapters on the CD that offer in-depth coverage of customization topics. "Exploring VBA" covers the basic concepts of Visual Basic Automation for AutoCAD. Visual Basic lets you build custom applications that work with AutoCAD and other Windows programs. Two more chapters about VBA and ActiveX are also on the CD.

The Appendices

Finally, this book has three appendices. Appendix A, "Installing and Setting Up AutoCAD," contains an installation and configuration tutorial. If AutoCAD is not already installed on your system, follow the steps in this tutorial before starting Chapter 1. Appendix B, "Hardware and Software Tips," provides information on hardware related to AutoCAD. It also provides tips on improving AutoCAD's performance and troubleshooting and provides more detailed information on setting up AutoCAD's plotting feature. Appendix C, "System and Dimension Variables," provides a reference to system and dimension variables, as well as detailed information regarding dimension style settings. Finally, Appendix D, "New Features," summarizes the new features in AutoCAD 2007, as well as new and revised commands.

The Minimum System Requirements

This book assumes you have an IBM-compatible computer with at least a Pentium IV or equivalent CPU. Your computer should have at least one CD drive and a hard disk with 2GB or more of free space for the AutoCAD program files and about 120MB of additional space for sample files and workspace. In addition to these requirements, you should also have enough free disk space to allow for a Windows virtual memory page file that is about 1.5 times the amount of installed RAM. Consult your Windows manual or Appendix B of this book for more on virtual memory.

AutoCAD 2007 runs best on systems with at 2GB or more of RAM though you can get by with 512MB. Your computer should also have a high-resolution monitor and an up-to-date display card.

An SVGA display with a resolution of 1024 × 768 or greater will work fine with AutoCAD, but if you want to take full advantage of AutoCADs new 3D features, you'll want a 128MB or greater, OpenGL®-capable workstation class graphics card. If you intend to use a digitizer tablet, you'll want one free USB, or serial, port available. I also assume you are using a mouse and have the use of a printer or a plotter. A CD or DVD reader is needed to install AutoCAD and the software from this book. Finally, you'll want an Internet connection to take full advantage of the support offerings from Autodesk.

If you want a more detailed explanation of hardware options with AutoCAD, see Appendix B. You will find a general description of the available hardware options and their significance to AutoCAD.

TIP If you intend to use a digitizer tablet in place of a mouse, Autodesk also provides you with a digitizer template in the form of a drawing file called `Tablet.dwg`. You can open and print this file and then place it on your tablet. After the digitizer template is properly configured, you can select commands directly from the template. See Appendix B for instructions on configuring the digitizer template.

Doing Things in Style

Much care has been taken to see that the stylistic conventions in this book—the use of uppercase or lowercase letters, italic or boldface type, and so on—will be the ones most likely to help you learn AutoCAD. On the whole, their effect should be subliminal. However, you might find it useful to be conscious of the following rules:

◆ Drop-down menu selections are shown by a series of options separated by the ➤ symbol (for example, choose File ➤ New).

◆ Keyboard entries are shown in boldface (for example, enter **Rotate**).

◆ Command-line prompts are shown in a monospaced font (for example, `Select objects:`).

For most functions, this book describes how to select options from toolbars and the menu bar. In addition, where applicable, I include related keyboard shortcuts and command names in parentheses. These command names provide continuity for readers accustomed to working at the Command prompt.

What's on the CD?

A CD included with this book contains the drawing files from all the exercises throughout this book so that you can pick up an exercise anywhere in the book, without having to work through the book from front to back. You can also use these sample files to repeat exercises or to just explore how files are organized and put together.

Further, the CD even includes a trial version of AutoCAD 2007, in case you don't have access to the software. For readers who want to learn more about customization, you'll find three chapters that cover ActiveX and additional information on VBA.

WARNING AutoCAD now allows side-by-side installation of AutoCAD 2007 with earlier releases. However, if you purchase an upgrade version of AutoCAD 2007, you must remove the previous version of AutoCAD within 60 days.

New Features of AutoCAD 2007

If you've been a little shy about trying your hand at 3D, this is the version of AutoCAD you've been waiting for. Autodesk has completely revamped AutoCAD's 3D construction and rendering tools to make it much easier to build your ideas in 3D. At the same time, they've added some great features that give you the freedom to create just about any shape you can dream up. Rendering 3D models has also been improved to give you greater flexibility in the style of rendering you can produce. Everything from loose sketches to photorealistic renderings are supported. Here are some of the 3D modeling highlights:

◆ New tools such as Loft and Sweep let you create complex shapes with less effort.

◆ You can quickly extrude 2D drawings into 3D models using Presspull.

◆ You can move effortlessly between 3D surface orientations using Dynamic UCS.

◆ Editing solids is much easier using graphical grip tools.

◆ Visual Styles let you quickly change the display mode of your model.

◆ Rendering has been greatly improved with the addition of the mental ray rendering engine.

◆ You can visualize your model in real time using the Walk and Fly tools.

◆ Camera controls are now more robust and offer more controls through grips.

◆ You can now create MPEG animations quickly and easily using the Anipath command.

◆ Cut-away drawings are now possible using the Sectionplane command.

◆ You can see what's going on inside your models with the new Xray view tool.

◆ Improved support for 3D DWF lets you share your ideas more easily.

◆ Support for PDF is built into AutoCAD.

Contact the Author

I hope that *Mastering AutoCAD 2007 and AutoCAD LT 2007* will be of benefit to you and that, after you have completed the tutorials, you will continue to use the book as a reference. If you have comments, criticisms, or ideas about how the book can be improved, you can e-mail me at the following address:

george.omura@yahoo.com

If you find errors, please let my publisher know. At www.sybex.com, navigate to the catalog page for this book, and click the Errata link to find a form on which you can identify the problem. And thanks for choosing *Mastering AutoCAD 2007 and AutoCAD LT 2007*.

Part 1

The Basics

In this part:

Chapter 1

Exploring the AutoCAD and AutoCAD LT Interface

Before you can start to use AutoCAD 2007's new capabilities, you'll need to become familiar with the basics. If you are completely new to AutoCAD, you'll want to read this first chapter carefully. It introduces you to many of AutoCAD's basic operations, such as opening and closing files, getting a close-up look at part of a drawing, and changing a drawing. If you are familiar with earlier versions of AutoCAD, you will want to review this chapter anyway to get acquainted with features you haven't already used.

Autodesk has recently changed its AutoCAD update strategy to release new versions on a yearly basis. Part of this strategy is to introduce new items that are focused on a particular category of features. This latest version, AutoCAD 2007, includes several new features focused on 3D modeling. In fact, with these new 3D modeling features, AutoCAD has something of a split personality. The familiar and reliable 2D drawing features are still there, but AutoCAD's 3D feature set has changed so extensively that using them almost makes AutoCAD feel like an entirely different program.

You'll get a chance to explore these new 3D features in Part 4 of this book, but for now, let's get started with some basics!

Topics in this chapter include the following:

◆ Using the AutoCAD Window

◆ Opening an Existing File

◆ Getting a Closer Look with the Zoom Command

◆ Saving a File as You Work

◆ Making Changes and Opening Multiple Files

TIP In this chapter, and throughout the rest of the book, when I say AutoCAD, I mean both AutoCAD and AutoCAD LT. Some topics will apply only to AutoCAD. In those situations, you'll see an icon indicating that the topic applies only to AutoCAD and does not apply to AutoCAD LT. If you are using AutoCAD 2007 LT, these icons can help you focus on the topics that are more relevant to your work.

Taking a Guided Tour

In this section, you will get a chance to familiarize yourself with the AutoCAD screen and how you communicate with AutoCAD. As you do the exercises in this chapter, you will also get a feel for how to work with this book. Don't worry about understanding or remembering everything you see in this chapter. You will get plenty of opportunities to probe the finer details of the program as you work through the later chapters. To help you remember the material, you will find a brief exercise at the end of each chapter. For now, just enjoy your first excursion into AutoCAD.

WARNING   AutoCAD 2007 is designed to run on Windows 2000 and Windows XP. This book was written using AutoCAD 2007 on Windows XP Professional with a Windows Classic desktop theme.

If you already installed AutoCAD and are ready to jump in and take a look, proceed with the following steps to launch the program:

1. Choose Start ➢ Programs ➢ Autodesk ➢ AutoCAD 2007 ➢ AutoCAD 2007. You can also double-click the AutoCAD 2007 icon on your Windows Desktop. LT users will use AutoCAD LT 2007 in place of AutoCAD 2007.

2. The opening greeting, called a *splash screen,* tells you which version of AutoCAD you are using, to whom the program is registered, and the AutoCAD dealer's name and phone number, should you need help. If this is the first time you've started AutoCAD after installing it, you will also see a dialog box asking you to register the product.

3. After the splash screen closes, you see the Workspace screen. (You won't see this in LT.) This screen allows you to select between the 2D drawing workspace called AutoCAD Classic and the 3D workspace called 3D Modeling. Workspaces are saved arrangements of the AutoCAD window. Click AutoCAD Classic. You'll get a chance to explore the 3D Modeling workspace in Part 4.

4. You may also see the New Features Workshop screen, which offers a set of tutorials showing you the new features of AutoCAD 2007. Click the No, Don't Show Me This Again or Maybe Later radio button and click OK. You can always get to the New Features Workshop screen from the AutoCAD help menu by choosing Help ➢ New Features Workshop.

5. Next you see the AutoCAD window with a blank default document named `Drawing1.dwg`, as shown in Figure 1.1. AutoCAD users may see the Sheet Set Manager palette to the left of the AutoCAD window, which does not appear in Figure 1.1, to show more of the drawing area. LT users may see the Info palette in the left of the AutoCAD window.

NOTE   If you see the Startup dialog box after step 3, click Cancel. AutoCAD displays a default document, as shown in Figure 1.1. You'll learn more about the Startup dialog box in Chapter 2.

If this is the first time you've started AutoCAD since you installed it, you will be asked to register and authorize AutoCAD at step 2. If you are using the Trial version, you can use the default serial number of 000-00000000 for the one-month trial. After you've entered the registration information, you see the New Features Workshop window described in step 4.

Let's take a look at the AutoCAD window in detail. Don't worry if it seems like a lot of information. You don't have to memorize it all, but by looking at all the parts, you'll be aware of what is available in a general way.

IF YOUR AUTOCAD WINDOW DOESN'T LOOK LIKE FIGURE 1.1

As you saw in step 3 in the opening exercise, you have a choice between two workspaces when you start AutoCAD. If you did not see the Workspace screen, and your drawing opens to a 3D Modeling workspace (see Figure 1.2 later in this chapter), do the following to get to the AutoCAD Classic workspace.

1. Click the Workspace list in the upper-left corner of the AutoCAD window and select AutoCAD Classic. LT users can select AutoCAD LT from a floating Workspaces toolbar.

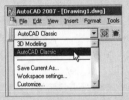

2. AutoCAD users should choose File ➢ New. Then in the Select Template dialog box, choose acad.dwt and click Open. LT users can skip this step.

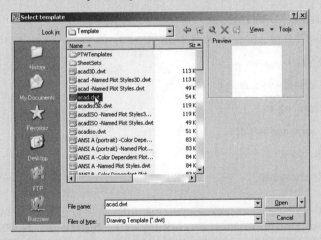

If you did step 2, the default file name will be Drawing2.dwg instead of Drawing1.dwg. Aside from that, your AutoCAD window will look similar to Figure 1.1, which shows AutoCAD in a moderate resolution screen.

FIGURE 1.1

A typical arrangement of the elements in the AutoCAD window. The Sheet Set Manager palette (and Info Palette for LT) is closed for clarity.

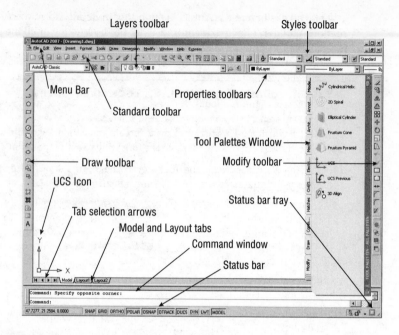

The AutoCAD Window

The AutoCAD program window is divided into six parts:

◆ Menu bar

◆ Docked and floating toolbars

◆ Drawing area

◆ Command window

◆ Status bar

◆ Tool palettes

TIP A seventh hidden component, the Properties palette (not to be confused with the Properties toolbar), gives you detailed information about the objects in your drawing. You can also use it to modify some of those properties. You'll learn more about the Properties palette in Chapter 4.

Figure 1.1, shown earlier in this chapter, shows a typical layout of the AutoCAD program window. Along the top is the *menu bar*, and at the bottom are the *Command window* and the *status bar*. Just below the menu bar and to either side of the window are the *toolbars*. The *drawing area* occupies the rest of the screen.

TIP Your screen might show the drawing area in black. You can set the drawing area background color by using the Options dialog box. Appendix A describes how to do this. The figures in this book show the drawing area background in white for clarity.

You can easily move and reshape many of the elements in the AutoCAD window. Figure 1.2 shows AutoCAD's 3D Modeling workspace, which looks for all the world like a completely different program. But the 3D Modeling workspace is really the same AutoCAD shown in Figure 1.1 with a different set of menus, palettes, and toolbars open. Figure 1.2 also shows a standard AutoCAD drawing file with a few setting changes to give it a 3D appearance.

TIP   You'll learn more about workspaces later in this chapter and in Chapter 26.

For a less radical change in appearance, you can move currently open toolbars from their default locations to any location on the screen. When toolbars are merged into the border of the AutoCAD window, like the ones shown in Figure 1.1, they are in their *docked* position. When they are moved to a location where they are free-floating, they are *floating*. Palettes can also be docked if you find you use them frequently.

The menu bar at the top of the drawing area (as shown in Figure 1.3) includes drop-down menus from which you select commands in a typical Windows fashion. The toolbars provide a variety of commands through tool buttons and drop-down lists. For example, the name or number of the layer that you are currently working on is displayed in a drop-down list in the Layers toolbar. To the right of the layer name are icons for tools you can use to work with the layer. The tools and lists on the toolbar are plentiful, and you'll learn more about all of them later in this chapter and as you work through this book.

TIP   A layer is like an overlay that enables you to separate different types of information. AutoCAD allows an unlimited number of layers. On new drawings, the default layer is 0. You'll get a detailed look at layers and the meaning of the Layer tools in Chapter 5.

The Draw and Modify toolbars, which are normally docked on either side of the drawing area, contain commands that create new objects and edit existing ones. These are just two of many toolbars available to you. Figure 1.4 shows these two toolbars in their floating state.

FIGURE 1.2
The 3D Modeling workspace offers an alternative arrangement of the elements in the AutoCAD window.

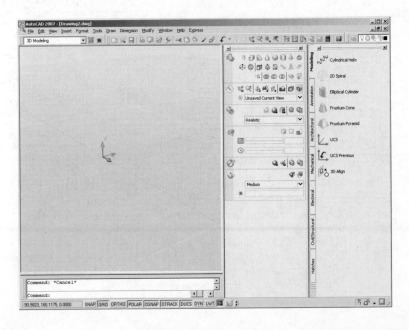

Using the Tool palettes (see figure 1.5) is a quick way to gain access to frequently used symbols, known as *block* in AutoCAD (refer to Figure 1.1). You can create your own symbols and add them to the palettes. You can also add your frequently used commands and tools to palettes as a way of customizing AutoCAD to better suit your way of working. You'll get a closer look at the Tool palettes in Chapter 2.

FIGURE 1.3
The menu bar, the Standard toolbar, and the Properties toolbar. LT users may see a floating Workspaces toolbar instead of the docked version shown in the far right side.

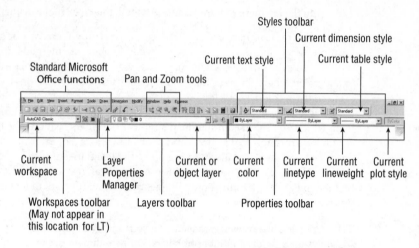

FIGURE 1.4
The Draw and Modify toolbars as they appear when floating

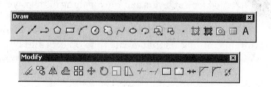

FIGURE 1.5
The Tool palettes for AutoCAD. LT users will see a different set of tools.

The drawing area occupies most of the screen. Everything you draw appears in this area. As you move your mouse around, crosshairs appear to move within the drawing area. This is the drawing cursor that lets you point to locations in the drawing area.

At the bottom of the drawing area, you'll see a set of tabs. These tabs give you access to the Layout views of your drawing. These views let you lay out your drawing as in a desktop publishing program. You'll learn about the Layout tabs in Chapter 8. The arrows to the left of the tabs let you navigate the tabs when there are more tabs than can fit in the AutoCAD window.

The Command window, located just below the Layout tabs, gives you feedback about AutoCAD's commands as you use them. You can move and resize this window just as you move and resize toolbars. By default, the Command window is in its docked position, as shown in Figure 1.6.

FIGURE 1.6

The Command window and the status bar

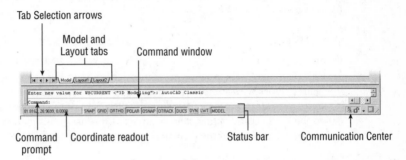

Tab Selection arrows

Model and Layout tabs

Command window

Command prompt | Coordinate readout

Status bar

Communication Center

Below the Command window is the status bar (see Figure 1.6). The status bar gives you information at a glance about the state of the drawing. For example, the coordinate readout toward the far left of the status bar tells you the location of your cursor.

TIP   In the default setup of AutoCAD, you will see a message balloon attached to the status bar. This message balloon alerts you to the latest news and information regarding AutoCAD through a feature called the Communication Center. You'll learn more about the Communication Center in Chapter 2.

PICKING POINTS IN THE DRAWING AREA

Let's practice using the coordinate readout and the drawing cursor:

1. Move the cursor around in the drawing area. As you move it, notice how the coordinate readout changes to tell you the cursor's location. It shows the coordinates in an X, Y, Z format.

2. Place the cursor in the middle of the drawing area and click the left mouse button. Move the cursor, and a rectangle follows. This is a *window selection;* you'll learn more about this window in Chapter 2. You'll also see a coordinate readout follow the cursor and a message asking you to Specify opposite corner:. This display at the cursor is called the *dynamic input*. You'll learn more about it a little later in this chapter.

Specify opposite corner: 20.1856   13.2404

TIP   If you don't see the dynamic input display, click the button labeled DYN in the status bar to turn it on.

3. Move the cursor a bit in any direction; then click the left mouse button again. Notice that the window selection disappears as does the dynamic input display.

4. Try picking several more points in the drawing area. Notice that as you click the mouse, you alternately start and end a window selection.

If you happen to click the right mouse button, a shortcut menu appears. A right-click frequently opens a menu containing options that are *context sensitive*. This means that the contents of the shortcut menu depend on the location where you right-click as well as the command that is active at the time of your right-click. If there are no appropriate options at the time of the right-click, AutoCAD treats the right-click as an ↵. You'll learn more about these options as you progress through the book. For now, if you happen to open this menu by accident, press the Esc key to close it.

THE UCS ICON

In the lower-left corner of the drawing area, you see an L-shaped arrow. This is the *User Coordinate System (UCS)* icon, which tells you your orientation in the drawing. This icon becomes helpful as you start to work with complex 2D drawings and 3D models. The X and Y arrows indicate the X and Y axes of your drawing. The little square at the base of the arrows tells you that you are in what is called the *World Coordinate System*. Chapter 21 discusses this icon in detail. For now, you can use it as a reference to tell you the direction of the axes.

> **IF YOU CAN'T FIND THE UCS ICON**
>
> The UCS icon can be turned on and off, so if you are on someone else's system and you don't see the icon, don't panic. If you don't see the icon or it doesn't look as it does in this chapter, see Chapter 21 for more information.

THE COMMAND WINDOW

At the bottom of the screen, just above the status bar, is a small horizontal window called the *Command window*. Here AutoCAD displays responses to your input. By default, it shows two lines of text. The bottom line shows the current messages, and the top line shows messages that have scrolled by or, in some cases, components of the current message that do not fit in a single line. Right now, the bottom line displays the message Command (see Figure 1.6 earlier in this chapter). This *prompt* tells you that AutoCAD is waiting for your instructions. As you click a point in the drawing area, you'll see the message Specify opposite corner:. At the same time, the cursor starts to draw a window selection that disappears when you click another point. The same message appears in the dynamic input display at the cursor.

As a new user, pay special attention to messages displayed in the Command window and the dynamic input display because this is how AutoCAD communicates with you. Besides giving you messages, the Command window records your activity in AutoCAD. You can use the scroll bar to the right of the Command window to review previous messages. You can also enlarge the window for a better view. (Chapter 2 discusses these components in more detail.)

Now let's look at AutoCAD's window components in detail.

TIP The Command window and the dynamic input display allow AutoCAD to provide text feedback to your actions. You might think of these features as a chat window to AutoCAD—as you enter commands, AutoCAD responds with messages. As you become more familiar with AutoCAD, you might find you don't need to rely on the Command window and dynamic input display as much. For new and casual users, however, the Command window and dynamic input display can be quite helpful in understanding what steps to take as you work.

The Drop-Down Menus

As in most Windows programs, the drop-down menus on the menu bar provide an easy-to-understand way to access the general controls and settings for AutoCAD. Within these menus you'll find the commands and functions that are the heart of AutoCAD. By clicking menu items, you can cut and paste items to and from AutoCAD, change the settings that make AutoCAD work the way you want it to, set up the measurement system you want to use, access the help system, and much more.

TIP To close a drop-down menu without selecting anything, press the Esc key. You can also click any other part of the AutoCAD window or click another drop-down menu.

The drop-down menu options perform three basic functions:

◆ Display a dialog box that contains settings you can change.

◆ Issue a command to create or modify your drawing.

◆ Offer an expanded set of the same tools found in the Draw and Modify toolbars.

As you point to commands and options in the menus or toolbars, AutoCAD provides additional help for you in the form of brief descriptions of each menu option, which appear in the status bar.

Here's an exercise to let you practice with the drop-down menus and get acquainted with the way you issue AutoCAD commands:

1. Click View in the menu bar. The list of items that appears includes the commands and settings that let you control the way AutoCAD displays your drawings. Don't worry if you don't understand them yet; you'll get to know them in later chapters.

WARNING LT users will not see the Render option in the View menu.

2. Move the highlight cursor slowly down the list of menu items. As you highlight each item, notice that a description of it appears in the status bar at the bottom of the AutoCAD window. These descriptions help you choose the menu option you need.

TIP If you look carefully at the command descriptions in the status bar, you'll see an odd word at the end. This is the keyboard command equivalent to the highlighted option in the menu or toolbar. You can actually type these keyboard commands to start the tool or menu item that you are pointing to. You don't have to memorize these command names, but knowing them will be helpful to you later if you want to customize AutoCAD.

3. Some of the menu items have triangular pointers to their right. This means the command has additional choices. For instance, highlight the Zoom item, and you'll see another set of options appear to the right. This second set of options is called a *cascading menu*. Whenever you see a drop-down menu item with the triangular pointer, you know that this item opens a cascading menu offering a more detailed set of options.

4. Other drop-down menu options are followed by an ellipsis (…). This indicates that the option displays a dialog box. For instance, move the highlight cursor to the Tools option in the menu bar.

TIP If you prefer, you can click and drag the highlight cursor over the drop-down menu to select an option.

5. Click the Options item at the bottom of the menu to open the Options dialog box. (LT users will not see a Profiles tab.) This dialog box contains several "pages," indicated by the tabs across the top, that contain settings for controlling what AutoCAD shows you on its screens, where you want it to look for special files, and other "housekeeping" settings. You needn't worry about what these options mean at this point. Appendix A describes the Options dialog box in more detail.

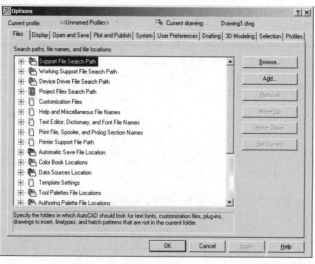

TIP The list in the Files tab of the Options dialog box works much like Windows Explorer. Clicking the plus sign to the left of the items in the list expands the option to display more detail.

6. In the Options dialog box, click the Open And Save tab. The options change to display new options. (LT users will not see the ObjectARX Applications group, and the Allow Other Users To Refedit Current Drawing option in the External References (Xrefs) group is also not available.)

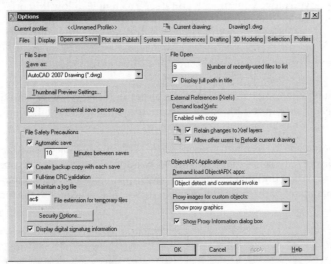

7. In the middle-left side of the dialog box, you'll see the Automatic Save check box, with the Minutes Between Saves input box set to 10 minutes. This setting controls how frequently AutoCAD performs an automatic save. Change the 10 to 20, and then click OK. You have just changed AutoCAD's Automatic Save feature to automatically save files every 20 minutes instead of every 10.

TIP If you want to know more about the settings in the Options dialog box, check out Appendix A.

The third type of item you'll find on drop-down menus is a command that directly executes an AutoCAD operation. In the next steps you'll explore these commands.

8. Click the X in the upper-right corner of the Tool Palettes window to close it. You won't be using the palettes for a while.

9. Click the Draw option from the menu bar and then click the Rectangle command. Notice that the Command window now shows the following prompt:

```
Specify first corner point or [Chamfer/Elevation/Fillet/Thickness/Width]:
```

AutoCAD is asking you to select the first corner for the rectangle, and, in brackets, it is offering a few options that you can take advantage of at this point in the command. Don't worry about those options right now. You'll have an opportunity to learn about command options in Chapter 2. You'll also see the same prompt, minus the bracketed options, in the dynamic input display at the cursor.

10. Click a point roughly in the lower-left corner of the drawing area, as shown in Figure 1.7. Now as you move your mouse, you'll see a rectangle follow the cursor, with one corner fixed at the position you just selected. You'll also see the following prompt in the Command window with a similar prompt in the dynamic input display:

```
Specify other corner point or [Area/Dimensions/Rotation]:
```

11. Click another point anywhere in the upper-right region of the drawing area. A rectangle appears (see Figure 1.8). You'll learn more about the different cursor shapes and what they mean in Chapter 2.

At this point, you've seen how most of AutoCAD's commands work. Many drawing and editing functions display messages in the Command window. They are also displayed in the dynamic input display. You'll find that dialog boxes are displayed when you want to change settings. Also, be aware that many of the drop-down menu items are duplicated in the toolbars, which you will explore next.

FIGURE 1.7
Selecting the first
point of a rectangle

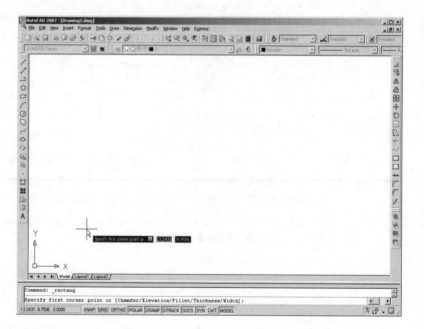

FIGURE 1.8

After you've selected your first point of the rectangle, you see a rectangle follow the motion of your mouse.

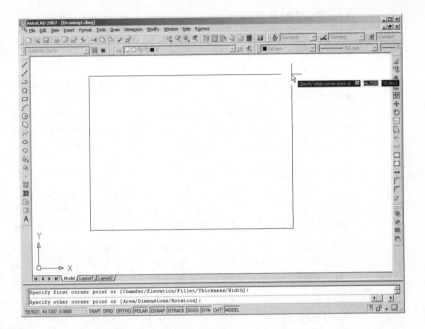

COMMUNICATING WITH THE COMMAND WINDOW AND DYNAMIC INPUT DISPLAY

AutoCAD is the perfect servant: it does everything you tell it to, and no more. You communicate with AutoCAD by using the drop-down menus and the toolbars. These devices invoke AutoCAD commands. A *command* is a single-word instruction you give to AutoCAD telling it to do something, such as draw a line (the Line tool in the Draw toolbar) or erase an object (the Erase tool in the Modify toolbar). Whenever you invoke a command, by either typing it or selecting a menu or toolbar item, AutoCAD responds by presenting messages to you in the Command window and the dynamic input display or by displaying a dialog box.

The messages in the Command window often tell you what to do next, or they display a list of options, usually shown within square brackets. A single command often presents a series of messages, which you answer to complete the command. These messages serve as an aid to new users who need a little help. If you ever get lost while using a command or forget what you are supposed to do, look at the Command window for clues. As you become more comfortable with AutoCAD, you will find that you won't need to refer to these messages as frequently.

As an additional aid, you can right-click to display a context-sensitive shortcut menu. If you are in the middle of a command, this menu displays a list of options specifically related to that command. For example, if you right-click your mouse before picking the first point for the rectangle command in the previous exercise, a menu opens, displaying the same options that are listed in the Command prompt, plus some additional options.

Finally, the dynamic input display allows you to enter dimensional data of objects as you draw them. Besides echoing the command line messages, the dynamic input display shows the coordinates and angles of objects you are drawing and editing. As you enter coordinate or angle values through the keyboard, they appear in the dynamic input display. If you are used to earlier versions of AutoCAD, you can easily turn the dynamic input display off by clicking the DYN button in the status bar. When the dynamic input display is turned off, your keyboard input appears in the Command window.

The Toolbars

Although the drop-down menus provide a full range of easy-to-understand options, they require some effort to navigate. The toolbars, on the other hand, give you quick, single-click access to the most commonly used AutoCAD features. In the default AutoCAD window arrangement, you see only the most commonly used toolbars. Other toolbars are available, but they are hidden from view until you open them.

Just like the drop-down menu commands, the tools in the toolbars perform three types of actions: they display further options, open dialog boxes, and issue commands that require keyboard or cursor input.

USING THE TOOLBAR TOOL TIPS

AutoCAD's toolbars contain tools that represent commands. To help you understand each tool, a *tool tip* appears just below the arrow cursor when you rest the cursor on a tool. Each tool tip helps you identify the tool with its function. A tool tip appears when you follow these steps:

1. Move the arrow cursor onto one of the toolbar tools and leave it there for a moment. Notice that a brief description of the tool appears nearby—this is the tool tip. In the status bar, a more detailed description of the tool's purpose appears (see Figure 1.9).

FIGURE 1.9

Tool tips show you the function of each tool in the toolbar. AutoCAD also displays a description of the tool in the status bar.

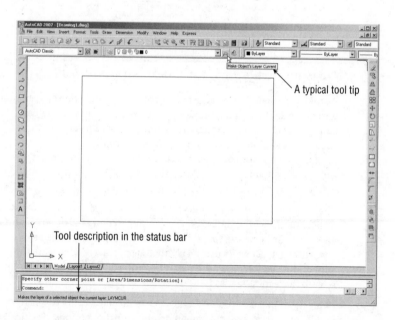

2. Move the cursor across the toolbar. As you do, notice that the tool tips and status bar descriptions change to describe each tool. The keyboard command equivalent of the tool is also shown in the status bar at the end of the description.

WORKING WITH FLYOUTS

Most toolbar tools start a command as soon as you click them, but a few tools display a set of additional tools (similar to the cascading menus in the menu bar) that are related to the tool you selected. This set of additional tools is called a toolbar *flyout*. If you've used other Windows graphics programs, chances are you've seen flyouts. Look closely at the tools just below the Express or Dimension drop-down menu options on your screen or in Figure 1.8 earlier in this chapter. You'll be able to identify which toolbar tool has a flyout; it has a small right-pointing arrow in the lower-right corner of the tool.

The following steps show you how a flyout works:

1. Move the cursor to the Zoom Window tool in the Standard toolbar. Click and hold the left mouse button to display the flyout. Don't release the mouse button.

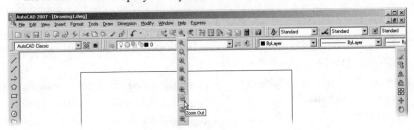

2. Still holding down the left mouse button, move the cursor over the flyout; notice that the tool tips appear here as well. Also, notice the description in the status bar.

3. Move the cursor to the Zoom Window tool at the top of the flyout and release the mouse button.

4. You don't need to use this tool yet, so press the Esc key to cancel it.

As you can see from this exercise, you get a lot of feedback from AutoCAD!

MOVING THE TOOLBARS

One characteristic of AutoCAD's toolbars is their mobility. They can float anywhere in the AutoCAD window or in a docked position. As stated earlier, *docked* means the toolbar is placed against the top, side, or bottom borders of the AutoCAD window so that the toolbar occupies a minimal amount of space. If you want to, you can move the toolbar to any location on your desktop, thus turning it into a floating toolbar.

Later in this section you'll find descriptions of all AutoCAD's toolbars, but first try the following exercise to move the Standard toolbar away from its current position in the AutoCAD window:

1. Move the arrow cursor so that it points to the vertical bars, called *grab bars*, to the far left of the Standard toolbar, as shown here:

2. Click and hold down the left mouse button. Notice that a dotted gray rectangle appears around the toolbar.

3. Still holding down the mouse button, move the mouse downward. The dotted gray box follows the cursor.

4. When the dotted gray box is over the drawing area, release the mouse button. The Standard toolbar—now a floating toolbar—moves to its new location.

You can now move the Standard toolbar to any location on the screen that suits you. You can also change the shape of the toolbar. Try the following steps:

1. Place the cursor on the bottom-edge border of the Standard toolbar. The cursor becomes a double-headed arrow, as shown here:

2. Click and drag the border downward. The dotted gray rectangle jumps to a new, taller rectangle as you move the cursor.

3. When the dotted gray rectangle changes to the shape you want, release the mouse button to reshape the toolbar.

4. To move the toolbar back into its docked position, place the arrow cursor on the toolbar's title bar, and slowly click and drag so that the cursor is in position in the upper-left corner of the AutoCAD window. Notice how the dotted gray outline of the toolbar changes as it approaches its docked position.

5. When the outline of the Standard toolbar is near its docked position, release the mouse button. The toolbar moves back into its previous position in the AutoCAD window.

TIP You can also move a toolbar from a docked position to a floating one by double-clicking the toolbar's grab bar. Double-click the title bar of a floating toolbar to move the toolbar to a docked position, though not necessarily its original docked position.

You can move and reshape any of AutoCAD's toolbars to place them out of the way and still have them ready to give you quick access to commands. You can also put them away altogether when you don't need them and bring them back at will, as shown in the following steps:

1. Click and drag the Draw toolbar from its position at the left of the AutoCAD window to a point near the center of the drawing area. Remember to click and drag the grab bars at the top of the toolbar.

2. Click the Close button in the upper-right corner of the Draw floating toolbar. This is the small square button with the X in it. The toolbar disappears.

3. To recover the Draw toolbar, right-click the border or grab bar of any toolbar—but not a toolbar button. A shortcut menu of toolbars appears.

4. Locate and select Draw in the shortcut menu. The Draw toolbar reappears.

5. Click and drag the Draw toolbar back to its docked position in the far-left side of the AutoCAD window.

TIP If you do not want the toolbar to dock but instead want it to appear "floating" near the border of the AutoCAD window, you can do the following: Change the shape of the toolbar to a vertical one, then press and hold the Ctrl key as you click and drag the toolbar into position. This prevents toolbars from automatically falling into a docked position.

AutoCAD remembers your toolbar arrangement between sessions. When you exit and then reopen AutoCAD later, the AutoCAD window appears just as you left it.

You might have noticed several other toolbars listed in the toolbar shortcut menu that don't appear in the AutoCAD window. To keep the screen from becoming cluttered, many of the toolbars are not placed on the screen by default. The toolbars you'll be using most often are displayed first; others that are less frequently used are kept out of sight until you need them and select them from the list.

You'll get a chance to work with all the toolbars over the course of this book. If you use the book simply as a reference, be sure to read through the exercises for explanations of which tools to use for specific operations.

MENUS VERSUS THE KEYBOARD

Throughout this book, you will be told to select commands and command options from the drop-down menus and toolbars. For new and experienced users alike, menus and toolbars offer an easy-to-remember method for accessing commands. If you are an experienced AutoCAD user who is used to the earlier versions of AutoCAD, you can still type commands directly from the keyboard. Most of the keyboard commands you know and love still work as they did.

Another method for accessing commands is to use *accelerator keys,* which are special keystrokes that open and activate drop-down menu options. You might have noticed that the commands in the menu bar and the items in the drop-down menus all have an underlined character. By pressing the Alt key followed by the key corresponding to the underlined character, you activate that command or option, without having to engage the mouse. For example, to choose File ➢ Open, press Alt, then F, and then finally O (Alt+F+O).

Many tools and commands have keyboard shortcuts; *shortcuts* are one-, two-, or three-letter abbreviations of a command name. As you become more proficient with AutoCAD, you might find these shortcuts helpful. As you work through this book, the shortcuts will be identified for your reference.

Finally, if you are feeling adventurous, you can create your own accelerator keys and keyboard shortcuts for executing commands by adding them to the AutoCAD support files. Chapter 25 discusses how to customize menus, toolbars, and keyboard shortcuts.

SAVING YOUR PREFERRED WORKSPACE

You may find that you prefer a specific arrangement of toolbars that you would like to be able to recall at will. You can rearrange the toolbars and then save the arrangement as a named *workspace*. This can be useful if you must share your AutoCAD workstation with someone else who prefers their own AutoCAD window layout or if you just want to set up different arrangements for different types of work. For example, you might want to save the current AutoCAD window layout with the Tool palettes out of the way while someone else prefers the default AutoCAD setup. To save the current setup under a new name, do the following:

1. In the Workspaces toolbar, click in the drop-down list and select Save Current As to open the Save Workspace dialog box.

2. Enter My Custom Layout in the text box, and then click Save. The current arrangement of AutoCAD components is saved under the name My Custom Layout.

3. To recall a workspace, select the name of the saved workspace from the drop-down list in the Workspaces toolbar.

You might notice a house icon in the Workspaces toolbar. This is the My Workspace tool, which offers a quick way to restore your favorite workspace. You can customize the My Workspace tool to recall any AutoCAD window layout you like. You'll learn more about creating and customizing workspaces in Chapter 26.

Working with AutoCAD

Now that you've been introduced to the AutoCAD window, you're ready to try using a few AutoCAD commands. First, you'll open a sample file and make a few simple modifications to it. In the process, you'll become familiar with some common methods of operation in AutoCAD.

Opening an Existing File

In this exercise, you will get a chance to see and use a typical Select File dialog box. To start with, you will open an existing file:

1. From the menu bar, choose File ➤ Close. A message appears asking whether you want to save the changes you've made to the current drawing. Click No.

2. Choose File ➤ Open to open the Select File dialog box. This is a typical Windows file dialog box, with an added twist. The large Preview box on the right lets you preview a drawing before you open it, thereby saving time while searching for files. To the left is a panel known

as the Places List in which you can find frequently used locations on your computer or the Internet.

TIP If you don't see a Preview box in the Select File dialog box, click the word Views in the upper-right corner and then select Preview from the list that appears.

3. In the Select File dialog box, open the Look In drop-down list and locate the `c:\acad2007\samplefiles\Mastering AutoCAD 2007\Projects\Chapters 01` folder. (You might need to explore the list to find it.) The file list changes to show the contents of the `\AutoCAD 2007\Projects\Chapter 01` folder.

4. Move the arrow cursor to the `clip.dwg` file and click it. Notice that the `clip.dwg` filename now appears in the File Name input box above the file list. Also, the Preview box now shows a thumbnail image of the file. Be aware that files from older versions of AutoCAD may not show a thumbnail.

TIP The `clip.dwg` drawing is included on the companion CD. If you cannot find this file, be sure you installed the sample drawings from the companion CD. See the Readme file on the CD for installation instructions.

5. Click the Open button at the bottom of the Select File dialog box. AutoCAD opens the `clip.dwg` file, as shown in Figure 1.10.

The `clip.dwg` file opens to display a Layout tab view of the drawing. You will know this by looking at the tabs at the bottom of the AutoCAD window. Currently, the Layout1 tab is highlighted.

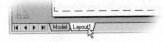

FIGURE 1.10

The Layout1 view of the clip.dwg file

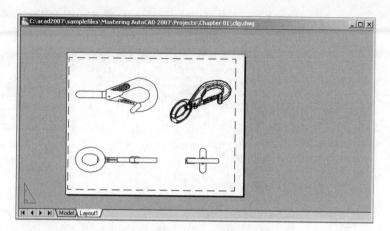

You might recall that a layout is a type of view that lets you lay out different views of your drawing in preparation for printing. Also notice that the AutoCAD window's title bar displays the name of the drawing. This offers easy identification of the file.

This particular file contains both 2D drawings and a 3D model of a typical locking clip. The Layout1 tab view shows a top, front, and right side view as well as an isometric view.

Getting a Closer Look

One of the most frequently used commands is Zoom, which gives you a closer look at a part of your drawing. It offers a variety of ways to control your view. In this section, you'll enlarge a portion of the clip drawing to get a more detailed look. To tell AutoCAD which area you want to enlarge, you use what is called a *zoom window*.

You'll start by switching to a Model Space view of the drawing. The Model tab places you in a workspace where you do most of your drawing creation and editing. Follow these steps:

1. Click the Model tab at the bottom of the AutoCAD window.

Your view changes to show the full 3D model with the 2D representations of the model.

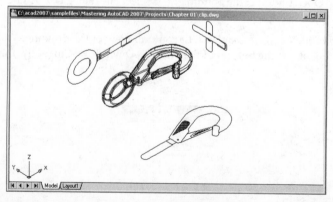

2. Choose View ➤ 3D Views ➤ Plan View ➤ World UCS. You can also type **PLAN↵W↵**. Your display changes to a two-dimensional view looking down on the drawing, as shown in the top image of Figure 1.11.

Click the Zoom Window button on the Standard toolbar.

You can also choose View ➤ Zoom ➤ Window from the drop-down menu or type the command **Z↵W↵**.

3. The Command window and the dynamic input display show the `Specify first corner:` prompt. Look at the top image in Figure 1.11. Move the crosshair cursor to a location similar to the one shown in the figure; then left-click the mouse. Move the cursor, and the rectangle appears, with one corner fixed on the point you just picked, while the other corner follows the cursor.

4. The Command window and dynamic input display now show the `Specify first corner:` and `Specify opposite corner:` prompts. Position the other corner of the zoom window so it encloses the lower image of the clip, as shown in the top image in Figure 1.11, and left-click the mouse again. The clip enlarges to fill the screen (see the bottom image in Figure 1.11).

FIGURE 1.11

Placing the zoom window around the clip

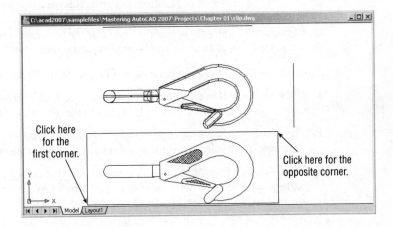

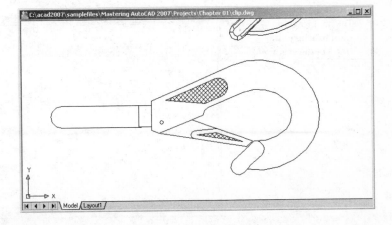

TIP If you decide that you don't like the position of the first point you pick while defining the zoom window, you can right-click the mouse and re-select the first point. This works when you enter **Z↵W↵** to issue the Zoom Window command or when you choose View ➤ Zoom ➤ Window from the Standard toolbar.

In this exercise, you used the Window option of the Zoom command to define an area to enlarge for your close-up view. You saw how AutoCAD prompts you to indicate first one corner of the window selection and then the other. These messages are helpful for first-time users of AutoCAD. You will use the Window option frequently—not just to define views, but also to select objects for editing.

Getting a close-up view of your drawing is crucial to working accurately, but you'll often want to return to a previous view to get the overall picture. To do so, click the Zoom Previous button on the Standard toolbar.

Do this now, and the previous view—one showing the entire clip—returns to the screen. You can also get there by choosing View ➤ Zoom ➤ Previous.

You can quickly enlarge or reduce your view by clicking the Zoom Realtime button on the Standard toolbar.

TIP You can also zoom in and out by clicking the Zoom In and Zoom Out buttons in the Zoom Window flyout of the Standard toolbar. The Zoom In button shows a magnifying glass with a plus sign; the Zoom Out button shows a minus sign. If you have a mouse equipped with a scroll wheel, you can zoom in and out just by turning the wheel. The location of the cursor at the time you move the wheel will determine the center of the zoom. A click-and-drag of the scroll wheel will let you pan your view.

Follow these steps to change your view with the Zoom Realtime button:

1. Click the Zoom Realtime button on the Standard toolbar. You can also right-click and choose Zoom from the shortcut menu. The cursor changes to a magnifying glass.

2. Place the Zoom Realtime cursor slightly above the center of the drawing area, and then click and drag downward. Your view zooms out to show more of the drawing.

3. While still holding the left mouse button, move the cursor upward. Your view zooms in to enlarge your view. When you have a view similar to the one shown in Figure 1.12, release the mouse button. (Don't worry if you don't get *exactly* the same view as the figure. This is just for practice.)

FIGURE 1.12

The final view you want to achieve in step 3 of the exercise

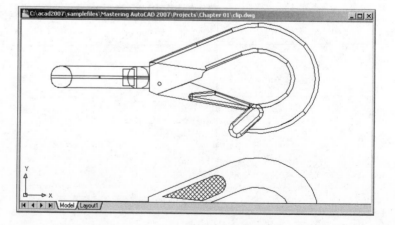

4. You are still in Zoom Realtime mode. Click and drag the mouse again to see how you can further adjust your view. To exit, you can select another command besides a Zoom or Pan, press the Esc key, or right-click your mouse and choose Exit from the shortcut menu.

5. Right-click now, and choose Exit from the shortcut menu to exit the Zoom Realtime command.

As you can see from this exercise, you have a wide range of options for viewing your drawings, just by using a few buttons. In fact, these buttons are all you need to control the display of 2D drawings.

MESSAGE TO VETERAN AUTOCAD USERS

AutoCAD, like many popular programs, is continually evolving. Quite often, that evolution forces us to change some old and cherished habits. If you've been using AutoCAD for a while, and you've grown accustomed to certain behaviors, you can take steps to make AutoCAD 2007 a more familiar environment.

You can, for example, restore the Enter (↵) function to the mouse right-click instead of using the newer shortcut menu. Follow these steps:

1. Choose Tools ➤ Options to open the Options dialog box.

2. Click the User Preferences tab.

3. In the Windows Standard Behavior group, click the Right-Click Customization button to open the Right-Click Customization dialog box.

4. Click the Enter radio button in the Command Mode group, and then click the Apply & Close button.

Another option is to turn on the time-sensitive right-click option at the top of the Right-Click Customization dialog box. With this option, a quick right-click is the same as pressing the Enter (↵) key, but you can still access the right-click shortcut menus by holding down the right mouse button a bit longer. You can even set the duration required to open the right-click shortcut menus.

If you prefer to enter commands and command options through the keyboard instead of using dialog boxes, you can do so for many commands.

Just add a minus sign (–) to the beginning of the command name as you enter the command through the keyboard. For example, to use the old Layer command, type **–layer** at the Command prompt. To use the old Pan command, type **–pan** at the Command prompt. (By the way, when you type **–pan** from the Command prompt, the command reverts to the "classic" method of panning in AutoCAD, in which you click two points to indicate the direction and displacement, instead of the "realtime" pan. This "classic" method is useful when you want to pan your view a specific distance because it lets you enter the pan distance and direction.)

Even if you don't care to enter commands from the keyboard, knowing about the use of the minus sign can help you create custom macros. See Chapter 26 for more on AutoCAD customization.

Saving a File as You Work

It is a good idea to save your file periodically as you work on it. You can save it under its original name (choose File ➢ Save) or under a different name (choose File ➢ Save As), thereby creating a new file.

By default, AutoCAD automatically saves your work at 10-minute intervals under a name that is a combination of the current file name plus a number and ending with the .sv$ file name extension; this is known as the *Automatic Save* feature. Using settings in the Options dialog box or system variables, you can change the name of the autosaved file and control the time between autosaves. See Chapter 3 for details.

TIP By default, in Windows XP, the Automatic Save file is stored in C:\Documents and Settings*User Name*\Local Settings\Temp\. You can find the exact location for your system by typing **Savefilepath**.⌐ at the Command prompt. This file location is often set as a hidden folder so you may need to set up Windows Explorer to display hidden folders before you can get to the Automatic Save file. See Appendix A for information on how to do this.

Let's first try the Save command. This quickly saves the drawing in its current state without exiting the program.

Choose File ➢ Save. You will notice some disk activity while AutoCAD saves the file to the hard disk, and you'll see a progress indicator in the status bar. As an alternative to choosing File ➢ Save, you can press Ctrl+ S. This is the accelerator key combination, also called *shortcut key*, for the File ➢ Save command.

Now try the Save As command. This command displays a dialog box that lets you save the current file under a new name:

1. Choose File ➢ Save As or type **Saveas**⌐ at the Command prompt to open the Save Drawing As dialog box. Notice that the current filename, clip.dwg, is highlighted in the File Name input box.

2. Type **Myfirst**. As you type, the name clip.dwg disappears from the input box and is replaced by Myfirst. You don't need to enter the .dwg filename extension. AutoCAD adds it to the filename automatically when it saves the file.

3. Click the Save button. The dialog box closes, and you will notice some disk activity.

You now have a copy of the clip file under the name Myfirst.dwg. The name of the file displayed in the AutoCAD window's title bar has changed to Myfirst. From now on, when you choose File ➢ Save, your drawing will be saved under its new name. Saving files under a different name can be useful when you are creating alternatives or when you just want to save one of several ideas you have been trying out.

TIP If you are working with a small monitor, you might want to consider closing the Draw and Modify toolbars. The Draw and Modify drop-down menus offer the same commands, so you won't lose any functionality by closing these toolbars. If you really want to maximize your drawing area, you can also turn off the scroll bars and reduce the Command window to a single line. Appendix A shows how to do this. You can also gain some extra drawing space by clicking the Maximize button in the upper-right corner of the drawing area.

Making Changes

You will frequently make changes to your drawings. In fact, one of AutoCAD's primary advantages is the ease with which you can make changes. The following exercise shows you a typical sequence of operations involved in making a change to a drawing:

1. From the Modify toolbar, click the Erase tool (the one with a pencil eraser touching paper). This activates the Erase command. You can also choose Modify ➤ Erase from the drop-down menu.

   Notice that the cursor has turned into a small square; this square is called the *pickbox*. You also see `Select objects:` in the Command window and the dynamic input display. This message helps remind new users what to do.

2. Move the pickbox over the drawing, placing it on various parts of the clip. Don't click anything yet. Notice that as you hover over objects with the pickbox, they are highlighted. This helps you see the objects the pickbox is likely to select should you click the left mouse button.

3. Place the pickbox on the crosshatch pattern of the clip (see Figure 1.13) and click it. The crosshatch changes in appearance from a dark highlight to a light highlight. The pickbox and the `Select objects:` prompt remain, indicating that you can continue to select objects.

4. Now press ↵. The crosshatch disappears. You have just erased a part of the drawing.

In this exercise, you first issued the Erase command, and then you selected an object by using a pickbox to click it. The pickbox tells you that you must select items on the screen, and it shows you what you are about to select by highlighting objects as you hover over them. Once you've clicked an object or a set of objects, press ↵ to move on to the next step. This sequence of steps is common to many of the commands you will work with in AutoCAD.

TIP   You can also click an object or a set of objects and then press the Delete key without using the Erase tool.

FIGURE 1.13
Erasing a portion of the clip

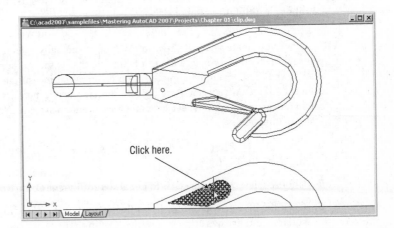

Click here.

Opening Multiple Files

You can have multiple documents open at the same time in AutoCAD. This can be especially helpful if you want to exchange parts of drawings between files or if you just want another file open for reference. Try the following exercise to see how multiple documents work in AutoCAD:

1. Choose File ➢ New to open the Select Template dialog box.

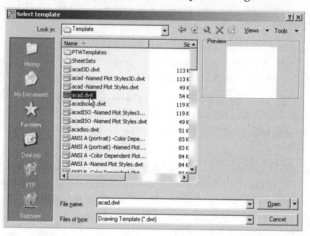

NOTE If you see the Create New Drawing dialog box after step 1, click the Start From Scratch button and select Imperial; then click OK and AutoCAD will display a default document. You'll learn more about the Create New Drawing dialog box in Chapter 2.

2. Make sure acad.dwt is selected and then click Open.

3. Choose Window ➢ Tile Vertically to get a view of both drawing files. The options in the Window drop-down menu act just like their counterparts in other Windows programs that allow multiple-document editing.

TIP When you create a new file in AutoCAD, you are actually opening a copy of a template file as you saw in step 1. A template file is a blank file that is set up for specific drawing types. The acad.dwt file is a generic template set up for Imperial measurements. Another template file called acadiso.dwt is a generic template useful for metric measurements. Other templates are set up for specific drawing sheet sizes and measurement systems. You'll learn more about templates in Chapter 6.

4. Now let's see what can be done with these two files. Click in the window with the clip drawing to make it active.

5. Choose View ➢ Zoom ➢ All to get an overall view of the drawing.

6. Click the 2D version of the clip at the bottom of the clip drawing to select it. A series of squares and arrows appears on the drawing. These are called *grips,* and you'll learn more about them in the next chapter.

7. Click and hold the mouse button on the selected object, but avoid clicking any of the blue squares. Also avoid dragging the object. You'll see a small rectangle appear next to the cursor.

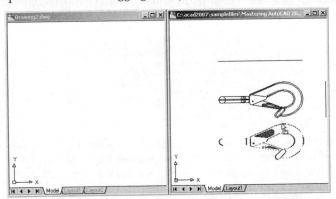

8. While still holding the left mouse button, drag the cursor to the new file window. When you see the clip appear in the new drawing window, release the mouse button. You've just copied part of a drawing from one file to another.

Now you have two files open at once. You can have as many files open as you want, as long as your computer has adequate memory to accommodate them. You can control the individual document windows as you would any window, using the Window drop-down menu or the window control buttons in the upper-right corner of the document window.

Adding a Pre-drawn Symbol with the Tool Palette

In the preceding exercise, you saw how you can easily copy an object from one file to another by using a click-and-drag method. Now let's take a look at another tool that lets you click and drag symbols into your drawings:

1. Click the Tool Palettes Window tool in the Standard toolbar to open the Tool palettes.

2. Make sure the Mechanical tab is selected in the Tool palettes, and then click and drag the Hex Socket Bolt (Side) - Metric symbol from the Tool palettes into the new file window.

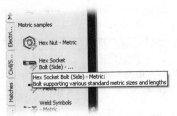

3. The bolt symbol appears in the window.

While you have the Tool palettes open, let's look at some of its unique features. Try these steps:

1. Right-click the Tool palettes title bar, and then choose Transparency from the shortcut menu to open the Transparency dialog box.

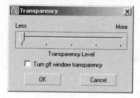

2. Move the Transparency Level slider to the middle of the dialog box and then click OK. You now see objects that are "behind" the Tool palettes. If the slider is grayed out, make sure the Turn Off Window Transparency option is not checked.

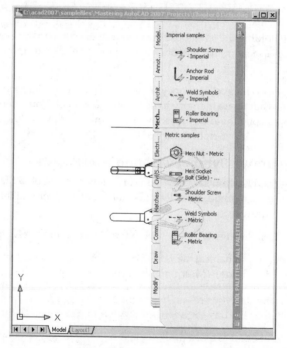

You can't actually select points that are "behind" the palettes as you draw, but the Transparency feature can help you visualize your drawing more easily while the palettes are open.

TIP The Command window also has a Transparency option. To use it, you must first move the Command window to an undocked position toward the middle of the AutoCAD window. You can then right-click the Command window title bar and choose Transparency. You will see the same Transparency dialog box you see when you right-click the Tool palettes and choose Transparency.

Let's take another look at a display feature of the Tool palettes:

1. Right-click the Tool palettes again and choose Auto-Hide.

2. Move the cursor away from the Tool palettes. The Tool palettes close so that just the Tool palettes title bar is visible.

3. Move the cursor on top of the Tool palettes title bar. The palette opens to reveal the palettes.

4. Turn the Auto-Hide feature off by right-clicking the Tool palettes and choosing Auto-Hide.

5. Click the X in the upper-right corner of the Tool palettes.

The Tool palettes offer a way to quickly add fill patterns and pre-drawn symbols to your drawing. It is a great tool to help you manage your library of custom, pre-drawn symbols. You've just had a taste of what it can do, but to make full use of its capabilities, you'll need to learn about blocks, hatch patterns, and the AutoCAD DesignCenter. You won't see much of this tool in the beginning of this book, but keep it in the back of your mind as you begin to learn more about AutoCAD. After finishing the first part of this book, you can skip ahead to Chapter 25 to learn how to use and customize the Tool palettes.

Closing AutoCAD

When you are finished with your work on one drawing, you can open another drawing, temporarily leave AutoCAD, or close AutoCAD entirely. To close all the open files at once and exit AutoCAD, choose File ➢ Exit.

Follow these steps to practice closing AutoCAD:

1. Choose File ➢ Exit, the last item in the File menu. A dialog box appears, asking whether you want to save changes to Myfirst.dwg and offering three buttons labeled Yes, No, and Cancel.

2. Click the No button.

3. AutoCAD displays another message asking whether you want to save Drawing2.dwg, which is the new drawing you opened in a preceding exercise. Click the No button again. AutoCAD closes both the clip drawing and the new drawing and exits without saving your changes.

Whenever you attempt to exit a drawing that has been changed, you get this same inquiry box. This request for confirmation is a safety feature that lets you change your mind and save your changes before you exit AutoCAD. In the previous exercise, you discarded the changes you made, so the clip drawing reverts to its state before you erased the grip. The new drawing is completely discarded, and no file is saved.

If you want to exit AutoCAD only temporarily, you can minimize it so it appears as a button on the Windows XP or Windows 2000 taskbar. You do this by clicking the Minimize button in the upper-right corner of the AutoCAD window; the Minimize button is the title-bar button that looks like an underscore (_). Alternatively, you can use the Alt+Tab key combination to switch to another program.

TIP The AutoCAD Express tools offer the Close All Drawings and Quick Exit tools that let you close multiple .dwg files at one time. See Chapter 24 for more on the Express tools.

If You Want to Experiment

Try opening and closing some of the sample drawing files on the accompanying CD:

1. Start AutoCAD by choosing Start ➢ Programs ➢ Autodesk ➢ AutoCAD 2007 ➢ AutoCAD 2007.

2. Once AutoCAD is open, choose File ➢ Open.

3. Use the dialog box to open the Myfirst file again. Notice that the drawing appears on the screen with the grip enlarged. This is the view you had onscreen when you used the Save command in the earlier exercise.

4. Erase the crosshatch, as you did in the earlier exercise then close the file.

5. At the Save changes message, click No.

6. Choose File ➢ Open again. This time, open the Dhouse file from the \Projects\Chapter 01 folder. The 3D Dhouse drawing opens.

7. Choose File ➢ Exit. Notice that you exit AutoCAD without opening the Save changes message box for the Dhouse drawing. This is because you didn't make any changes to the Dhouse file.

Chapter 2

Creating Your First Drawing

This chapter examines some of AutoCAD's basic functions. You will get a chance to practice with the drawing editor by building a simple drawing to use in later exercises. You'll learn how to give input to AutoCAD, interpret prompts, and get help when you need it. This chapter also covers the use of coordinate systems to give AutoCAD exact measurements for objects. You'll see how to select objects you've drawn and how to specify base points for moving and copying.

If you're not a beginning AutoCAD user, you might want to move on to the more complex material in Chapter 3. You can use the files supplied on the companion CD to continue the tutorials at that point.

Topics in this chapter include the following:

- ◆ Getting to Know the Draw Toolbar
- ◆ Starting Your First Drawing
- ◆ Specifying Distances with Coordinates
- ◆ Interpreting the Cursor Modes and Understanding Prompts
- ◆ Selecting Objects and Editing with Grips
- ◆ Using Dynamic Input
- ◆ Getting Help
- ◆ Displaying Data in a Text Window
- ◆ Displaying the Properties of an Object

Getting to Know the Draw Toolbar

Your first task in learning how to draw in AutoCAD is simply to draw a line. But before you begin drawing, take a moment to familiarize yourself with the toolbar you'll be using more than any other to create objects with AutoCAD: the Draw toolbar. Try these steps:

1. Start AutoCAD just as you did in the first chapter, by choosing Start ➤ Programs ➤ Autodesk ➤ AutoCAD 2007 ➤ AutoCAD 2007. If you see the Workspace dialog box, select AutoCAD Classic and click OK. If you see the Startup dialog box, click Cancel to go directly to the default Drawing1 document. You'll get a chance to work with the Startup dialog box later in this chapter. If the default Drawing1.dwg file shows a gray 3D workspace, choose File ➤ New, then select acad.dwt from the Select Template dialog box and click Open.

2. Make sure the Workspace toolbar shows AutoCAD Classic. If it doesn't, click the Workspace toolbar and select AutoCAD Classic.

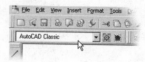

3. Close any open palettes.

4. In the AutoCAD window, move the arrow cursor to the top icon in the Draw toolbar, which is the vertical toolbar at the far left of the AutoCAD window, and rest it there so that the tool tip appears.

5. Slowly move the arrow cursor downward over the other tools in the Draw toolbar and read each tool tip.

In most cases, you'll be able to guess what each tool does by looking at its icon. The icon with an arc, for instance, indicates that the tool draws arcs; the one with the ellipse shows that the tool draws ellipses; and so on. For further clarification, the tool tip gives you the name of the tool. In addition, the status bar at the bottom of the AutoCAD window gives you information about a tool. For example, if you point to the Multiline Text tool at the bottom of the Draw toolbar, the status bar reads `Creates a multiple-line text object`. It also shows you the actual AutoCAD command name: MTEXT. This command is what you can type in the Command window to invoke the Multiline Text tool if you prefer not to click toolbar icons. You also use MTEXT if you are writing a macro or creating your own custom tools.

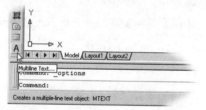

Figure 2.1 will aid you in navigating the two main toolbars, Draw and Modify. You'll get experience with many of AutoCAD's tools as you work through this book.

As you saw in Chapter 1, clicking a tool issues a command. Clicking and dragging some tools opens a flyout. A flyout provides further options for that tool. If a tool has a flyout, you'll see a small triangle in the lower-right corner of the tool.

In this exercise, you'll get some practice with the toolbar flyouts:

1. Click and drag downward on the Zoom Window tool on the Standard toolbar. A flyout appears with an additional set of tools. You can use these tools to adjust your view in various ways.

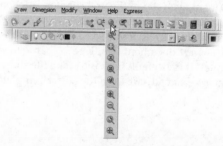

2. Move the cursor down the flyout to the last tool, until the tool tip reads *Zoom Extents*; then let go of the mouse button. Notice that the icon representing the Zoom Window tool now changes and becomes the icon from the flyout that represents Zoom Extents.

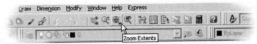

By selecting the Zoom Extents tool, you also issue the Zoom Extents command. This command adjusts the view of the drawing so that it fills the drawing area. Because nothing is currently in the drawing, the view doesn't change. You'll use Zoom Extents in Chapter 3 to see how it behaves when the drawing contains objects.

3. For now, you'll want to keep the Zoom Window tool visible in the Standard toolbar, so click and drag downward on the Zoom Extents tool, and then select Zoom Window from the top of the flyout. Press the Esc key to cancel the Zoom Window command. You'll get a chance to use Zoom Window in Chapter 3.

By making the most recently selected option on a flyout the default option for the toolbar tool, AutoCAD gives you quick access to frequently used commands. A word of caution, however: this feature can confuse the first-time AutoCAD user. Also, the grouping of options on the flyout menus is not always self-explanatory—even to a veteran AutoCAD user.

TIP If you find you are working a lot with one particular flyout, you can easily open a version of the flyout as a floating toolbar so that all the flyout options are readily available with a single click. For example, to open the Zoom flyout you just used as a toolbar, right-click any toolbar and choose Zoom from the shortcut menu.

FIGURE 2.1
The tools on the Draw and Modify toolbars

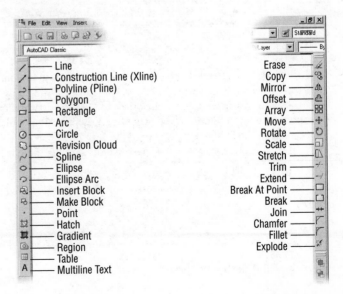

WORKING WITH TOOLBARS

As you work through the exercises, this book will show you the tools to choose, along with the toolbar or flyout that contains the tool. Don't be alarmed, however, if the toolbars you see in the examples don't look exactly like those on your screen. To save page space, in some places I have oriented the toolbars and flyouts horizontally for the illustrations; the ones on your screen might be oriented vertically, like the Draw and Modify toolbars to the left and right of the AutoCAD window. Although the shape of your toolbars and flyouts might differ from the ones you see in this book, the contents are the same. So when you see a graphic showing a tool, focus on the tool icon itself with its tool tip name, along with the name of the toolbar in which it is shown.

Starting Your First Drawing

In Chapter 1, you looked at a preexisting sample drawing. This time you will begin to draw on your own drawing, by creating a door that will be used in later exercises. First, though, you must learn how to tell AutoCAD what you want, and, even more important, you must understand what AutoCAD wants from you.

TIP In this chapter, you'll start to see instructions for both Imperial and metric measurement. In general, you will see the instructions for Imperial measurement first, followed by the metric instructions. You won't be dealing with inches or centimeters yet, however. You're just getting to know the AutoCAD system.

You will start by opening the Create New Drawing dialog box. This dialog box helps new users set up drawings quickly. Follow these steps:

1. Choose Tools ➢ Options to open the Options dialog box.

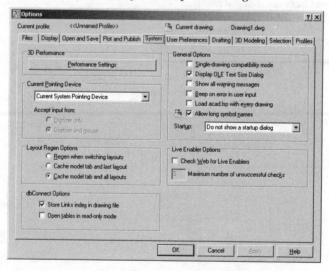

2. Click the System tab.

3. In the General Options group, click the Startup drop-down list and select Show Startup Dialog Box.

4. Click OK to apply the new setting and exit the dialog box.

When you select the Show Startup Dialog Box option, AutoCAD opens the Create New Drawing dialog box whenever you start a new drawing. You'll use this dialog box in the early stages of the book. If you decide you don't need the wizard as you become more comfortable with AutoCAD, you can easily turn it off by taking the previous steps again, and instead of choosing Show Startup Dialog Box in step 3, choose Do Not Show A Startup Dialog.

NOTE   With the Show Startup Dialog Box option turned on, you will also see the Startup dialog box when you first open AutoCAD. The Startup dialog box is basically the same as the Create New Drawing dialog box.

Now let's create a new file:

1. Choose File ➤ Close to close the current file. In the Save Changes dialog box, click No. Notice that the toolbars disappear and the AutoCAD drawing window appears blank when no drawings are open.

2. Choose File ➤ New to open the Create New Drawing dialog box.

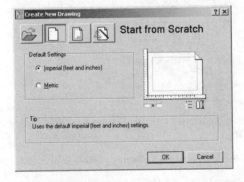

3. Click the Use A Wizard button in the dialog box. Two options appear in the Select A Wizard list box: Advanced Setup and Quick Setup.

4. Click the Quick Setup option, and then click OK to open the QuickSetup dialog box at the Units screen.

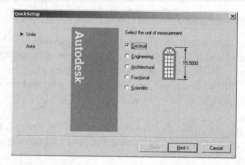

5. For now, you'll use the default Decimal units as indicated by the radio buttons. You'll learn more about these options in the next chapter. Click Next to open the QuickSetup dialog box at the Area screen.

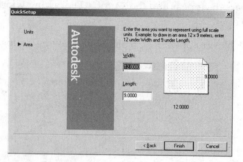

6. If the Width text box doesn't already show 12, double-click it and enter **12**. Metric users should enter **40**.

7. Press the Tab key to move to the Length text box and enter **9**. Metric users should enter **30**.

8. Click Finish. A new drawing file appears in the AutoCAD window.

9. From the menu bar, choose View ➤ Zoom ➤ All. This ensures that your display covers the entire area you specified in steps 5 and 6.

10. To give your new file a unique name, choose File ➢ Save As to open the Save Drawing As dialog box.

11. Type **Door**. As you type, the name appears in the File Name text box.

12. Save your file in the My Documents folder, or if you prefer, save it in another folder of your choosing. Just remember where you put it as you will use it later.

13. Click Save. You now have a file called Door.dwg, located in the My Documents folder. Of course, your drawing doesn't contain anything yet. You'll take care of that next.

The new file shows a drawing area roughly 12 inches wide by 9 inches high. Metric users will have a file that shows an area roughly 40 mm wide by 30 mm high. This area is your workspace, though you're not limited to it in any way. No visual clues indicate the size of the area. To check the area size for yourself, move the crosshair cursor to the upper-right corner of the screen and observe the value in the coordinate readout. This is the standard AutoCAD default drawing area for new drawings.

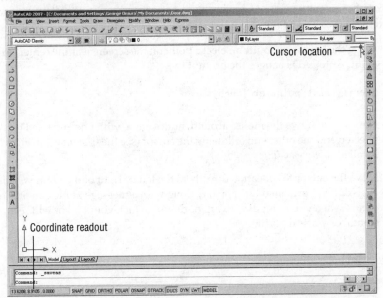

WARNING The coordinate readout won't show exactly 12 inches by 9 inches, or 40 mm by 30 mm for metric, because the proportions of your drawing area are not likely to be exactly 12 × 9 or 40 × 30. AutoCAD does try to optimize the display for the drawing area when you choose View ➢ Zoom ➢ All.

You're almost ready to do some drawing. Before you begin, turn off the Dynamic Input display. The Dynamic Input display is a great tool, but while you are learning how to enter coordinates, it can be a distraction.

1. To turn off Dynamic Input display, locate the DYN button in the status bar.

2. Click the DYN button so it is in the up, or off, position.

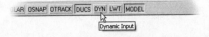

You'll get a chance to work with Dynamic Input display a bit later in this chapter. Now you can begin to explore the drawing process. To begin a drawing, follow these steps:

1. Click the Line tool on the Draw toolbar, or type L↵.

You've just issued the Line command. AutoCAD responds in two ways. First, you see the message

```
Specify first point:
```

in the Command prompt, asking you to select a point to begin your line. Also, the cursor has changed its appearance; it no longer has a square in the crosshairs. This is a clue telling you to pick a point to start a line.

TIP Throughout this book, you'll be given the option to use the keyboard shortcuts for commands. For example, in step 1, you were given the option to type L↵ in the Command window to start the Line command.

2. Using the left mouse-button, select a point on the screen near the center. After you select the point, AutoCAD changes the prompt to

```
Specify next point or [Undo]:
```

Now as you move the mouse around, notice a line with one end fixed on the point you just selected and the other end following the cursor (see the first image in Figure 2.2). This action is called *rubber-banding*.

3. Move the cursor to a location directly to the left or right of the point you clicked, and you'll see a dotted horizontal line appear, along with a message at the cursor. This action also occurs when you point directly up or down. In fact, your cursor will seem to jump to a horizontal or vertical position.

This feature is called *Polar Tracking*. Like a T-square or triangle, it helps to restrict your line to an exact horizontal or vertical direction. You can turn Polar Tracking on or off by clicking the Polar button in the status bar. If you don't see it, chances are it's just been turned off. You'll learn more about Polar Tracking in Chapter 3.

4. Now continue with the Line command: move the cursor to a point below and to the right of the first point you selected, and click the left mouse button again. The first rubber-banding line is now fixed between the two points you selected, and a second rubber-banding line appears (see the second image in Figure 2.1).

5. If the line you drew isn't the exact length you want, you can back up during the Line command and change it. To do this, type U↵. Now the line you drew previously will rubber-band as if you hadn't selected the second point to fix its length.

FIGURE 2.2
A rubber-banding line

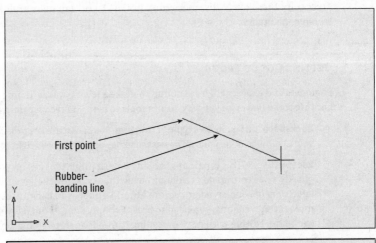

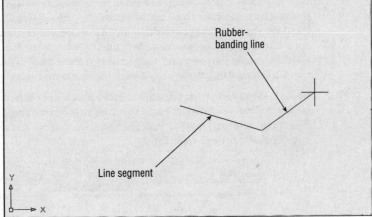

TIP   The Undo tool in the Standard toolbar offers an Undo drop-down list from which you can select the exact command that you want to undo. See the "Getting Out of Trouble" sidebar in this chapter for more information.

You've just drawn, and then undrawn, a line of an arbitrary length. The Line command is still active. Two onscreen clues tell you that you are in the middle of a command. If you don't see the word Command in the bottom line of the Command window, a command is still active. Also, the cursor will be the plain crosshair without the box at its intersection.

TIP   From now on, I will refer to the crosshair cursor without the small box as the Point Selection mode of the cursor. If you look ahead to Figure 2.8, you'll see all the modes of the drawing cursor.

Specifying Distances with Coordinates

Next, you will continue with the Line command to draw a plan view (an overhead view) of a door, to no particular scale. Later, you will resize the drawing to use in future exercises. The door will be 3.0 units long and 0.15 units thick. For metric users, the door will be 9 units long and 0.5 units thick.

To specify these exact distances in AutoCAD, you can use either relative polar coordinates or Cartesian coordinates.

GETTING OUT OF TROUBLE

Beginners and experts alike are bound to make a few mistakes. Before you get too far into the tutorial, here are some powerful yet easy-to-use tools to help you recover from accidents.

Backspace If you make a typing error, press the Backspace key to back up to your error, and then retype your command or response. The Backspace key is in the upper-right corner of the main keyboard area.

Escape (Esc) This is perhaps the single most important key on your keyboard. When you need to quickly exit a command or a dialog box without making changes, just press the Esc key in the upper-left corner of your keyboard. Before AutoCAD 2000, you had to press Esc twice in some instances. In more recent versions, you need to press Esc only once, though it won't hurt to press it twice. (Press Esc before editing with grips or issuing commands through the keyboard.)

U↵ If you accidentally change something in the drawing and want to reverse that change, click the Undo tool in the Standard toolbar (the left-pointing curved arrow). You can also type **U↵** at the Command prompt. Each time you do this, AutoCAD undoes one operation at a time, in reverse order. The last command performed is undone first, then the next-to-last command, and so on. The prompt displays the name of the command being undone, and the drawing reverts to its state prior to that command. If you need to, you can undo everything back to the beginning of an editing session.

Undo↵ If you decide that you want to back up a few steps of an operation you just performed, you can use the Undo tool (the left-pointing curved arrow) in the Standard toolbar. Or type Undo↵. Each click of the Undo tool steps you back one operation. You can also select the exact command to undo by using the Undo drop-down list.

You can open the Undo drop-down list by clicking the downward-pointing arrow found to the right of the Undo tool.

Redo↵ If you accidentally undo one too many commands, you can redo the last undone command by clicking the Redo tool (the right-pointing curved arrow) in the Standard toolbar. Or type **Redo↵**. In AutoCAD 2007, you can redo several operations that you might have undone with the Undo command. You can also select the exact command to redo by using the Redo drop-down list. To open the Redo drop-down list, click the downward-pointing arrow found to the right of the Redo tool.

WARNING   The Imperial and metric distances are not equivalent in the exercises in this chapter. For example, 3 units in the Imperial-based drawing is not equal to 9 metric units. These distances are arbitrary and based on how they will appear in the figures in this chapter.

Specifying Polar Coordinates

To enter the exact distance of 3 (or 9 metric) units to the right of the last point you selected, do the following:

1. Type @3<0. Metric users should type @9<0. As you type, the letters appear at the Command prompt.

2. Press ↵. A line appears, starting from the first point you picked and ending 3 units to the right of it (see Figure 2.3). You have just entered a relative polar coordinate.

The "at" sign (@) you entered tells AutoCAD that the coordinate you are specifying is from the last point you selected. The 3 (or 9 metric) is the distance, and the less-than symbol (<) tells AutoCAD that you are designating the angle at which the line is to be drawn. The last part is the value for the angle, which in this case is 0 for 0° . This is how to use polar coordinates to communicate distances and directions to AutoCAD.

TIP   If you are accustomed to a different method for describing directions, you can set AutoCAD to use a vertical direction or downward direction as 0° . See Chapter 3 for details.

Angles are given based on the system shown in Figure 2.4, in which 0° is a horizontal direction from left to right, 90° is straight up, 180° is horizontal from right to left, and so on. You can specify degrees, minutes, and seconds of arc if you want to be that exact. I'll discuss angle formats in more detail in Chapter 3.

FIGURE 2.3

Notice that the rubber-banding line now starts from the last point selected. This indicates that you can continue to add more line segments.

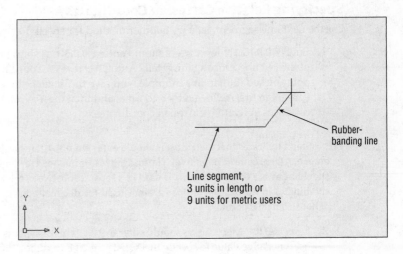

FIGURE 2.4
AutoCAD's default
system for specifying
angles

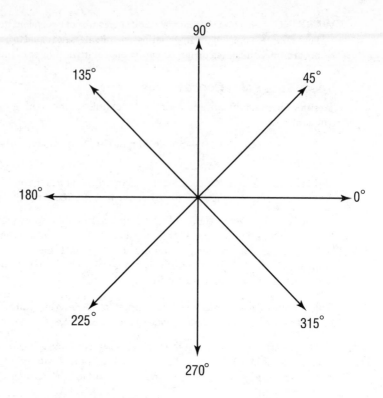

Specifying Relative Cartesian Coordinates

For the next line segment, let's try another method for specifying exact distances:

1. Enter **@0,0.15↵** . Metric users should enter **@0,0.5↵** . A short line appears above the endpoint of the last line. Once again, @ tells AutoCAD that the coordinate you specify is from the last point picked. But, in this example, you give the distance in X and Y values. The X distance, 0, is given first, followed by a comma, and then the Y distance, 0.15. This is how to specify distances in relative Cartesian coordinates.

TIP Step 1 indicates that metric users should enter **@0,0.5↵** for the distance. Instead, you could enter 0,.5 (zero comma point five). The leading zero is included for clarity. European metric users should be aware that the comma is used as a separator between the X and Y components of the coordinate. In AutoCAD, commas are not used for decimal points; you must use a period to denote a decimal point.

2. Enter **@-3,0↵** . Metric users should enter @-9,0↵ . This distance is also in X,Y values, but here you use a negative value to specify the X distance. The result is a drawing that looks like Figure 2.5.

Positive values in the Cartesian coordinate system are from left to right and from bottom to top (see Figure 2.6). (You might remember this from your high school geometry class!) If you want to draw a line from right to left, you must designate a negative value. It is also helpful to know where the origin of the drawing lies. In a new drawing, the origin, or coordinate 0,0, is in the lower-left corner of the drawing.

FIGURE 2.5

These three sides of the door were drawn by using the Line tool. Points are specified by using either relative Cartesian or polar coordinates.

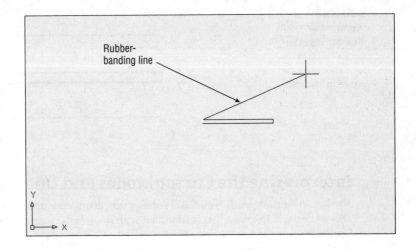

FIGURE 2.6

Positive and negative Cartesian coordinate directions

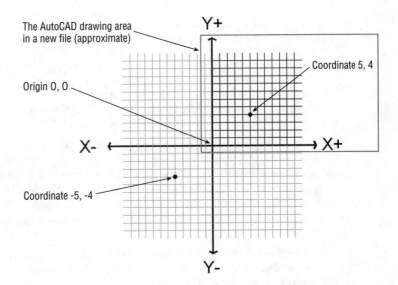

3. Type **C↵**. This C stands for the Close command. It closes a sequence of line segments. A line connecting the first and last points of a sequence of lines is drawn (see Figure 2.7), and the Line command terminates. The rubber-banding line also disappears, telling you that AutoCAD has finished drawing line segments. You can also use the rubber-banding line to indicate direction while simultaneously entering the distance through the keyboard. See the upcoming sidebar "A Fast Way to Enter Distances."

TIP To finish drawing a series of lines without closing them, you can press Esc, ↵, or the spacebar.

FIGURE 2.7

Distance and direction input for the door. Distances for metric users are shown in brackets.

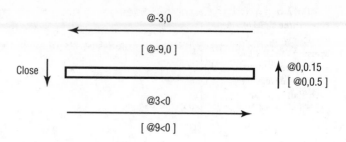

Interpreting the Cursor Modes and Understanding Prompts

The key to working with AutoCAD successfully is understanding the way it interacts with you. This section will help you become familiar with some of the ways AutoCAD prompts you for input. Understanding the format of the messages in the Command window and recognizing other events on the screen will help you learn the program more easily.

A FAST WAY TO ENTER DISTANCES

A third method for entering distances is to simply point in a direction with a rubber-banding line and then enter the distance through the keyboard. For example, to draw a line 3 units long from left to right, click the Line tool on the Draw toolbar, click a start point, and then move the cursor so the rubber-banding line points to the right at some arbitrary distance. While holding the cursor in the direction you want, type **3**↵. The rubber-banding line becomes a fixed line 3 units long.

Using this method, called the Direct Distance method, along with the Ortho mode or Polar Snap described in Chapter 3, can be a fast way to draw objects of specific lengths. Use the standard Cartesian or polar coordinate methods when you need to enter exact distances at angles other than those that are exactly horizontal or vertical. If you have the Dynamic Input display turned on, you can set the angle of the rubber-banding line using the angle display as a guide and then enter the distance you want through the keyboard followed by a ↵. Lines are drawn to the nearest whole degree shown in the Dynamic Input display.

On some systems, the AutoCAD Blipmode setting might be turned on. This causes tiny cross-shaped markers, called *blips*, to appear where you've selected points. These blips can be helpful to keep track of the points you've selected on the screen.

Blips aren't actually part of your drawing and do not print. Still, they can interfere with your work. To clear the screen of blips, choose View ➤ Redraw or type **R**↵. The screen quickly redraws the objects, clearing the screen of the blips. As you will see later in this book, Redraw can also clear up other display problems.

Another command, Regen, does the same thing as Redraw, but it also updates the drawing display database—which means it takes a bit longer to restore the drawing. Regen is used to update certain types of changes that occur in a drawing. You will learn about Regen in Chapter 6.

To turn Blipmode on and off, type **blipmode**↵ at the Command prompt, and then enter **on**↵ or **off**↵.

Understanding Cursor Modes

As the Command window aids you with messages, the cursor also gives you clues about what to do. Figure 2.8 illustrates the various modes of the cursor and gives a brief description of the role of each mode. Take a moment to study this figure.

FIGURE 2.8

The drawing cursor's modes

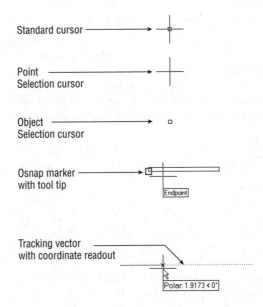

The **Standard cursor** tells you that AutoCAD is waiting for instructions. You can also edit objects by using grips when you see this cursor. *Grips* are squares that appear at endpoints and at the midpoint of objects when they are selected. (You might know them as *workpoints* from other graphics programs.)

The **Point Selection cursor** appears whenever AutoCAD expects point input. It can also appear in conjunction with a rubber-banding line. You can either click a point or enter a coordinate through the keyboard.

The **Object Selection cursor** tells you that you must select objects—either by clicking them or by using any of the object selection options available.

The **Osnap (object snap) marker** appears along with the Point Selection cursor when you invoke an osnap. Osnaps let you accurately select specific points on an object, such as endpoints or midpoints.

The **tracking vector** appears when you use the Polar Tracking or Object Snap Tracking feature. Polar Tracking aids you in drawing orthogonal lines, and Object Snap Tracking helps you align a point in space relative to the geometry of existing objects. Object Snap Tracking works in conjunction with Osnap. You'll learn more about the tracking vector in Chapters 3 and 4.

TIP If you are an experienced AutoCAD user, you might prefer to use the old-style crosshair cursor that crosses the entire screen. Choose Tools ➢ Options to open the Options dialog box, and then click the Display tab. Set the Crosshair Size option near the bottom left of the dialog box to 100. The cursor then appears as it did in previous versions of AutoCAD. As the option name implies, you can set the crosshair size to any percentage of the screen you want. The default is 5 percent.

Choosing Command Options

Many commands in AutoCAD offer several options, which are often presented to you in the Command window in the form of a prompt. This section uses the Arc command to illustrate the format of AutoCAD's prompts.

Usually, in a floor-plan drawing in the United States, an arc is drawn to indicate the direction of a door swing. Figure 2.9 shows some of the other standard symbols used in architectural-style drawings. This is a small sampling of the symbols available on the CD included with this book.

FIGURE 2.9

Samples of standard symbols used in architectural drawings

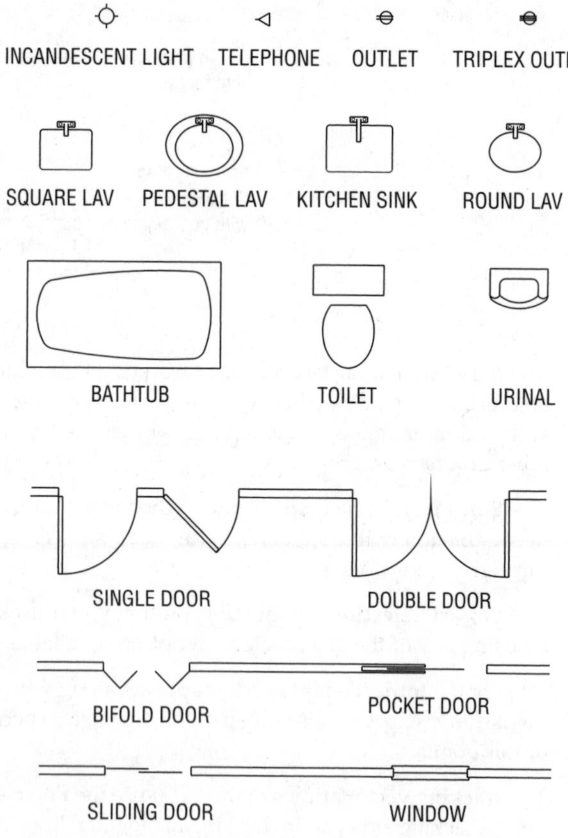

INCANDESCENT LIGHT   TELEPHONE   OUTLET   TRIPLEX OUTLET

SQUARE LAV   PEDESTAL LAV   KITCHEN SINK   ROUND LAV

BATHTUB   TOILET   URINAL

SINGLE DOOR   DOUBLE DOOR

BIFOLD DOOR   POCKET DOOR

SLIDING DOOR   WINDOW

Here you'll draw the arc for the door you started in the previous exercise:

1. Click the Arc tool in the Draw toolbar. The prompt Specify start point of arc or [Center]: appears, and the cursor changes to Point Selection mode.

Examine this `Specify start point of arc or [Center]:` prompt. The start point contains two options. The default option is the one stated in the main part of the prompt. In this case, the default option is to specify the start point of the arc. If other options are available, they will appear within square brackets. In the Arc command, you see the word `Center` within brackets telling you that if you prefer, you can also start your arc by selecting a center point instead of a start point. If multiple options are available, they appear within the brackets and are separated by slashes (/). The default is the option AutoCAD assumes you intend to use unless you tell it otherwise.

2. Type **C↵** to select the Center option. The prompt `Specify center point of arc:` appears. Notice that you had to type only the *C* and not the entire word *Center.*

TIP When you see a set of options in the Command window, note their capitalization. If you choose to respond to prompts by using the keyboard, these capitalized letters are all you need to enter to select that option. In some cases, the first two letters are capitalized to differentiate two options that begin with the same letter, such as `LAyer` and `LType`.

3. Now pick a point representing the center of the arc near the upper-left corner of the door (see the first image in Figure 2.10). The prompt `Specify start point of arc:` appears.

4. Type **@3<0↵** . Metric users should type **@9<0↵** . The prompt `Specify end point of arc or [Angle/chord Length]:` appears.

5. Move the mouse, and a temporary arc appears, originating from a point 3 units to the right of the center point you selected and rotating about that center, as in the middle image in Figure 2.10. (Metric users will see the temporary arc originating 9 units to the right of the center point.)

As the prompt indicates, you now have three options. You can enter an angle, a chord length, or the endpoint of the arc. The prompt default, to specify the endpoint of the arc, picks the arc's endpoint. Again, the cursor is in Point Selection mode, telling you it is waiting for point input. To select this default option, you only need to pick a point on the screen indicating where you want the endpoint.

6. Move the cursor so that it points in a vertical direction from the center of the arc. You'll see the Polar Tracking vector snap to a vertical position.

7. Click any location with the Polar Tracking vector in the vertical position. The arc is now fixed in place, as in the bottom image in Figure 2.10.

This exercise has given you some practice working with AutoCAD's Command window prompts and entering keyboard commands—skills you will need when you start to use some of the more advanced AutoCAD functions.

As you can see, AutoCAD has a distinct structure in its prompt messages. You first issue a command, which in turn offers options in the form of a prompt. Depending on the option you select, you get another set of options, or you are prompted to take some action, such as picking a point, selecting objects, or entering a value.

As you work through the exercises, you will become intimately familiar with this routine. After you understand the workings of the toolbars, the Command window prompts, and the dialog boxes, you can almost teach yourself the rest of the program!

FIGURE 2.10
Using the Arc command

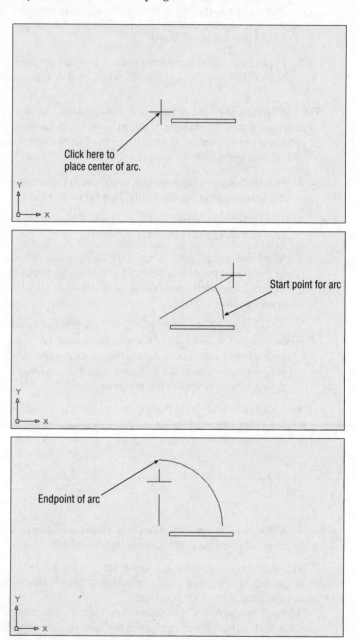

SELECTING OPTIONS FROM A SHORTCUT MENU

Now you know that you can select command options by typing them. You can also right-click at any time during a command to open a shortcut menu containing those same options. For example, in step 2 in the previous exercise, you typed **C**↵ to tell AutoCAD that you wanted to select the center of the arc. Instead of typing, you can also right-click the mouse to open a menu of options applicable to the Arc command at that time.

Notice that in addition to the options shown in the Command prompt, the shortcut menu also shows you a few more options, namely Enter, Cancel, Pan, and Zoom. The Enter option is the same as pressing ↵. Cancel cancels the current command. Pan and Zoom let you adjust your view as you are working through the current command.

The shortcut menu is context sensitive, so you'll see only those options that pertain to the command or activity that is currently in progress. Also, when AutoCAD is expecting a point, an object selection, or a numeric value, right-clicking does not display a shortcut menu. Instead, AutoCAD treats a right-click as ↵.

The location of your cursor when you right-click determines the contents of the shortcut list. You've already seen that you can right-click a toolbar to get a list of other toolbars. A right-click in the Command window displays a list of operations you can apply to the command line, such as repeating one of the last several commands you've used or copying the most recent history of command activity to the Clipboard.

A right-click in the drawing area when no command is active displays a set of basic options for editing your file, such as Cut, Paste, Undo, Repeat the last command, Pan, and Zoom, to name a few.

If you're ever in doubt over what to do in AutoCAD, you can right-click to see a list of options. You'll learn more about these options later in this book. For now, let's move on to the topic of selecting objects.

TIP If you're a veteran AutoCAD user, and you prefer to have the right-click issue an ↵ at all times instead of opening the shortcut menu (as in versions prior to AutoCAD 14), you can configure AutoCAD to do just that. See Appendix A for details on how to set up the mouse's right-click action. Be aware, however, that the tutorials in this book assume that AutoCAD is configured for the shortcut menu.

Selecting Objects

In AutoCAD you can select objects in many ways. This section has two parts: the first part covers object selection methods unique to AutoCAD, and the second part covers the more common selection method used in most popular graphic programs, the Noun/Verb method. Because these two methods play a major role in working with AutoCAD, it's a good idea to familiarize yourself with them early on.

TIP If you need to select objects by their characteristics rather than by their location, see Chapter 15, which describes the Quick Select and Object Selection Filters tools. These tools let you easily select a set of objects based on their properties, including object type, color, layer assignment, and so on.

Selecting Objects in AutoCAD

Many AutoCAD commands prompt you to `Select objects:`. Along with this prompt, the cursor changes from crosshairs to a small square (look back at Figure 2.8). Whenever you see the `Select objects:` prompt and the square Object Selection cursor, you have several options while making your selection. Often, as you select objects on the screen, you will change your mind about a selection or accidentally select an object you do not want. Let's take a look at most of the selection options available in AutoCAD and learn what to do when you make the wrong selection.

Before you continue, you'll turn off two features that, while extremely useful, can be confusing to new users. These features are called Running Osnaps and Osnap Tracking. You'll get a chance to explore these features in depth later in this book, but for now follow these steps to turn them off:

1. Check to see if either Running Osnaps or Osnap Tracking is turned on. Look at the Osnap and Otrack buttons in the status bar at the bottom of the AutoCAD window. If they are turned on, they look like they are pressed.

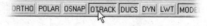

2. To turn off Running Osnaps or Osnap Tracking, click the Osnap or Otrack button in the status bar. When turned off, they will look like they are not pressed.

Now let's go ahead and see how to select an object in AutoCAD:

1. Choose Move from the Modify toolbar or type **M**↵ .

2. At the `Select objects:` prompt, click each of the two horizontal lines that constitute the door. As you know, whenever AutoCAD wants you to select objects, the cursor turns into the small square pickbox. This tells you that you are in Object Selection mode. As you place the cursor over an object, it appears thicker to give you a better idea of what you are about to select. As you click an object, it is highlighted, as shown in Figure 2.11.

WARNING   If objects do not become "thicker" as you roll over them with your selection cursor, the Selectionpreview system variable may be turned off. You can turn it back on by entering selection-preview⏎ 3⏎. This setting can also be found in the Selection tab of the Options dialog box. See Appendix A for more on the Options dialog box and Appendix C for more on System Variables.

FIGURE 2.11
Selecting the lines of the door and seeing them highlighted

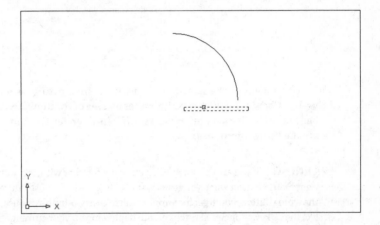

3. After making your selections, you might decide to deselect some items. Enter U⏎ from the keyboard. Notice that one line is no longer highlighted. When you type U⏎, objects are deselected, one at a time, in reverse order of selection.

4. You can deselect objects in another way. Hold down the Shift key and click the remaining highlighted line. It reverts to a solid line, showing you that it is no longer selected for editing.

5. By now you have deselected both lines. Let's try another method for selecting groups of objects. To select objects with a window selection, type **W**⏎ . The cursor changes to a Point Selection cursor, and the prompt changes to

   `Specify first corner:`

6. Click a point below and to the left of the rectangle representing the door. As you move your cursor across the screen, a selection window appears and stretches across the drawing area. You'll also notice that the window has a blue tint.

7. After the selection window completely encloses the door but not the arc, click this location to highlight the entire door. This window selects only objects that are completely enclosed by the window, as shown in Figure 2.12.

FIGURE 2.12
Selecting the door
within a selection
window

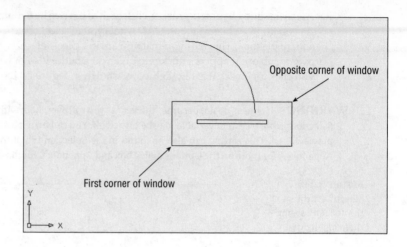

FIGURE 2.12
Selecting the door
within a selection
window

TIP Don't confuse the selection window you are creating here with the zoom window you used in Chapter 1, which simply defines an area of the drawing you want to enlarge. Remember that the Window option works differently under the Zoom command than it does for other editing commands.

WARNING If you are using a mouse you're not familiar with, it's quite easy to accidentally click the right mouse button when you really want to click the left mouse button, and vice versa. If you click the wrong button, you'll get the wrong results. On a two-button mouse, the right button will either act like the ↵ key or open a shortcut menu, depending on your current operation. An ↵ will be issued if you are selecting objects, but otherwise the shortcut menu appears.

8. Now that you have selected the entire door but not the arc, press ↵. This tells AutoCAD you have finished selecting objects. It is important to remember to press ↵ as soon as you finish selecting the objects you want to edit. A new prompt, `Specify base point or [Displacement]` `<Displacement>:`, appears. The cursor changes to its Point Selection mode.

Now you have seen how the selection process works in AutoCAD—but you're in the middle of the Move command. The next section discusses the prompt that's now on your screen and describes how to enter base points and displacement distances.

PROVIDING BASE POINTS

When you move or copy objects, AutoCAD prompts you for a base point, which is a difficult concept to grasp. AutoCAD must be told specifically *from* where and *to* where the move occurs. The *base point* is the exact location from which you determine the distance and direction of the move. After the base point is determined, you can tell AutoCAD where to move the object in relation to that point.

Follow these steps to practice using base points:

1. To select a base point, hold down the Shift key and right-click. A menu appears displaying the Object Snap (Osnap) options.

```
━o  Temporary track point
┌°  Erom
    Mid Between 2 Points
    Point Filters              ▶
⁄°  Endpoint
⁄   Midpoint
╳   Intersection
╳   Apparent Intersect
┄   Extension
⊙   Center
◇   Quadrant
○   Tangent
⊥   Perpendicular
//  Parallel
∘   Node
⟐   Insert
⁄°  Nearest
ℝ   None
∏□  Osnap Settings…
```

WARNING   When right-clicking the mouse, make sure the cursor is within the AutoCAD drawing area; otherwise, you will not get the results described in this book.

2. Choose Intersection from the Osnap menu. The Osnap menu closes.

3. Move the cursor to the lower-right corner of the door. Notice that as you approach the corner, a small x-shaped graphic appears on the corner. This is called an *Osnap marker*.

4. After the x-shaped marker appears, hold the mouse motionless for a second or two. A tool tip appears, telling you the current Osnap point AutoCAD has selected.

5. Now click the left mouse button to select the intersection indicated by the Osnap marker. Whenever you see the Osnap marker at the point you want to select, you don't have to point exactly at the location with your cursor. Just left-click the mouse to select the exact Osnap point (see Figure 2.13). In this case, you selected the exact intersection of two lines.

6. At the `Specify second point of displacement or <use first point as displacement>:` prompt, hold down the Shift key and click the right mouse button again. You'll use the Endpoint Osnap this time, but instead of clicking the option with the mouse, type **E↵**.

7. Now pick the lower-right end of the arc you drew earlier. (Remember that you only need to move your cursor close to the endpoint until the Osnap marker appears.) The door moves so that the corner of the door connects exactly with the endpoint of the arc (see Figure 2.14).

As you can see, the Osnap options let you select specific points on an object. You used Endpoint and Intersection in this exercise, but other options are available. Chapter 3 discusses some of the other Osnap options. You might have also noticed that the Osnap marker is different for each of the options you used. You'll learn more about osnaps in Chapter 3. Now let's continue with our look at point selection.

FIGURE 2.13
Using the Point Selection cursor and Osnap marker

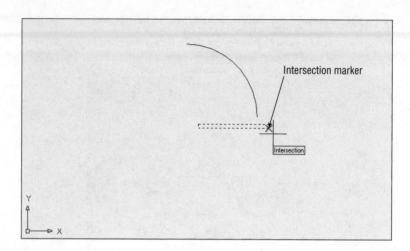

FIGURE 2.14
Moving the rectangle to its new position using the Endpoint Osnap

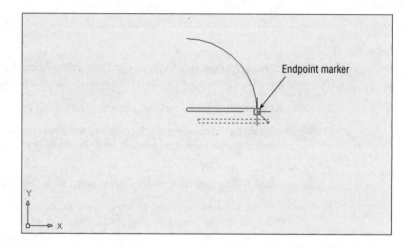

TIP You might have noticed the statement Use first point as displacement in the prompt in step 6. This means that if you press ↵ instead of clicking a point, the object will move a distance based on the coordinates of the point you selected as a base point. If, for example, the point you click for the base point is at coordinate 2,4, the object will move 2 units in the X axis and 4 in the Y axis.

If you want to specify an exact distance and direction by typing a value, select any point on the screen as a base point. Or you can just type @ followed by ↵ at the base point prompt; then enter the second point's location in relative coordinates. Remember that @ means the last point selected. In the next exercise, you'll try moving the entire door an exact distance of 1 unit in a 45° angle. Metric users will move the door 3 units in a 45° angle. Here are the steps:

1. Click the Move tool on the Modify toolbar.

2. Type **P**↵. The set of objects you selected in the previous exercise is highlighted. P is a selection option that selects the previously selected set of objects.

CONTROLLING THE STATUS BAR DISPLAY

To the far right of the status bar, you'll see a downward-pointing arrow. This arrow opens a menu that controls the display of the status bar. You use this menu to turn the items in the status bar on or off. A checkmark by an item indicates that it is currently on. If for some reason you do not see all the buttons mentioned in the previous exercise, check this menu to make sure that all the status bar options are turned on. Note that LT does not have an Otrack option in the status bar.

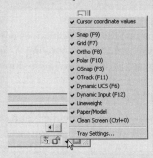

3. You're still in Object Selection mode, so click the arc to include it in the set of selected objects. Now the entire door, including the arc, is highlighted.

4. Press ↵ to tell AutoCAD that you have finished your selection. The cursor changes to Point Selection mode.

5. At the `Specify base point or [Displacement] <Displacement>:` prompt, choose a point on the screen between the door and the left side of the screen (see Figure 2.15).

FIGURE 2.15
The highlighted door and the base point just to the left of the door. Note that the base point does not need to be on the object that you are moving.

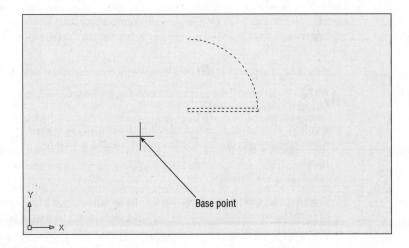

Base point

6. Move the cursor around slowly, and notice that the door moves as if the base point you selected were attached to the door. The door moves with the cursor, at a fixed distance from it. This demonstrates how the base point relates to the objects you select.

7. Now type @1<45↵ . (Metric users should type @3<45↵ .) The door moves to a new location on the screen at a distance of 1 unit (or 3 for metric users) from its previous location and at an angle of 45°.

TIP If AutoCAD is waiting for a command, you can repeat the last command used by pressing the spacebar or by pressing ↵. You can also right-click in the drawing area and select the option at the top of the list. If you right-click the Command window, a shortcut menu offers the most recent commands.

This exercise illustrates that the base point does not have to be on the object you are manipulating; it can be virtually anywhere on your drawing. You also saw how to re-select a group of objects that were selected previously, without having to duplicate the selection process.

Using "Noun/Verb" Selection

Nearly all graphics programs today allow the Noun/Verb method for selecting objects. This method requires you to select objects before you issue a command to edit them—that is, you identify the "noun" (the object you want to work on) before the "verb" (the action you want to perform on it). The exercises in this section show you how to use the Noun/Verb method in AutoCAD.

You have seen that when AutoCAD is waiting for a command, it displays the crosshair cursor with the small square. As mentioned, this square is actually a pickbox superimposed on the cursor. It indicates that you can select objects, even while the Command prompt appears at the bottom of the screen and no command is currently active. The square momentarily disappears when you are in a command that asks you to select points.

OTHER SELECTION OPTIONS

There are several other selection options you haven't tried yet. You'll see how these options work in exercises later in this book. Or if you are adventurous, try them now on your own. To use these options, type their keyboard abbreviations (shown in brackets in the following list) at any Select objects: prompt.

Add [add ↵]   Switches from the Remove mode to the Add mode. See Remove later in this sidebar.

All [all↵]   Selects all the objects in a drawing except those in frozen or locked layers. (See Chapter 4 for information on layers.)

Box [r↵]   Forces the standard selection window whereby a left to right selection uses a standard window and a right to left selection uses a crossing window.

Crossing [c↵]   Similar to the Window Selection option but selects anything that crosses through the window you define.

Crossing Polygon [cp↵]   Acts exactly like Window Polygon (see later in this sidebar) but, like the Crossing Selection option, selects anything that crosses through a polygon boundary.

Fence [f↵]   Selects objects that are crossed by a temporary line called a fence. This operation is like using a line to cross out the objects you want to select. After you invoke this option, you can then pick points, as when you are drawing a series of line segments. After you finish drawing the fence, press ↵, and then go on to select other objects or press ↵ again to finish your selection.

Group [r↵]   Allows you to select a group by name.

Last [l⏎]   Selects the last object you entered.

Multiple [m⏎]   Lets you select several objects first, before AutoCAD highlights them. In a large file, selecting objects individually can cause AutoCAD to pause after each selection, while it locates and highlights each object. The Multiple option can speed things up by letting you first select all the objects quickly and then highlight them all by pressing ⏎. This has no menu equivalent.

Previous [p⏎]   Selects the last object or set of objects that was edited or changed.

Remove [r⏎]   Switches to a selection mode whereby the objects you click are removed from the selection set.

Window [w⏎]   Forces a standard Window selection. This option is useful when your drawing area is too crowded to use the Autoselect feature to place a window around a set of objects. (See the Auto entry later in this sidebar.) It prevents you from accidentally selecting an object with a single pick when you are placing your window.

Window Polygon [wp⏎]   Lets you select objects by enclosing them in an irregularly shaped polygon boundary. When you use this option, you see the prompt First polygon point:. You then pick points to define the polygon boundary. As you pick points, the prompt Specify endpoint of line or [Undo]: appears. Select as many points as you need to define the boundary. You can undo boundary line segments as you go by pressing the U⏎ key. With the boundary defined, press ⏎. The bounded objects are highlighted and the Select objects: prompt returns, allowing you to use more selection options.

The following two selection options are also available, but seldom used. They are intended for use in creating custom menu options or custom toolbar tools.

Auto [au⏎]   Forces the standard automatic window or crossing window when a point is picked and no object is found. (See the "Using Autoselect" section later in this chapter.) A standard window is produced when the two window corners are picked from left to right. A crossing window is produced when the two corners are picked from right to left. After this option is selected, it remains active for the duration of the current command. Auto is intended for use on systems on which the Automatic Selection feature has been turned off.

Single [si⏎]   Forces the current command to select only a single object. If you use this option, you can pick a single object; then the current command acts on that object as if you had pressed ⏎ immediately after selecting the object. This has no menu equivalent.

TIP   In addition to Noun/Verb selection, AutoCAD offers other selection options that let you use familiar GUI techniques. See Appendix B to learn how you can control object selection methods. This appendix also describes how to change the size of the standard cursor.

Now try moving objects by first selecting them and then using the Move command:

1. Press the Esc key twice to make sure AutoCAD isn't in the middle of a command you might have accidentally issued. Then click the arc. The arc is highlighted, and you might also see squares appear at its endpoints, center point, and midpoint. As stated earlier, these squares are called *grips*. You'll get a chance to work with them a bit later.

2. Choose Move from the Modify toolbar. The cursor changes to Point Selection mode. Notice that the grips on the arc disappear, but the arc is still selected.

3. At the `Specify base point or [Displacement] <Displacement>:` prompt, pick any point on the screen. The following prompt appears:

```
Specify second point or
<use first point as displacement>:
```

4. Type **@1<0↵**. Metric users should type **@3<0↵**. The arc moves to a new location 1 unit (3 units for metric users) to the right.

WARNING　If you find that this exercise does not work as described here, chances are the Noun/ Verb setting has been turned off on your copy of AutoCAD. To turn on the Noun/Verb setting, choose Tools ➢ Options to open the Options dialog box, and click the Selection tab. In the Selection Modes group, place a checkmark in the check box next to the Noun/Verb Selection option and click OK.

In this exercise, you picked the arc *before* issuing the Move command. Then, when you clicked the Move tool, you didn't see the `Select objects:` prompt. Instead, AutoCAD assumed you wanted to move the arc that you selected and went directly to the `Specify base point or [Displacement] <Displacement>:` prompt.

USING AUTOSELECT

Next you will move the rest of the door in the same direction by using the Autoselect feature:

1. Pick a point just above and to the left of the rectangle representing the door. Be sure not to pick the door itself. A selection window appears that you can drag across the screen as you move the cursor. If you move the cursor to the left of the last point selected, the window appears dotted with a green tint (see the first image of Figure 2.16). If you move the cursor to the right of that point, it appears solid with a blue tint (see the second image of Figure 2.16).

2. Pick a point below and to the right of the door so that the door is completely enclosed by the window but not the arc, as shown in the bottom image in Figure 2.16. The door is highlighted (and again, you might see grips appear at the lines' endpoints and midpoints).

3. Click the Move tool again. Just as in the preceding exercise, the `Specify base point or [Displacement] <Displacement>:` prompt appears.

4. Pick any point on the screen; then enter **@1<0↵**. Metric users should enter **@3<0↵**. The door joins with the arc.

The two selection windows you have just seen—the blue solid one and the dotted green one— represent a standard window and a crossing window. If you use a *standard window,* anything completely within the window is selected. If you use a *crossing window,* anything that crosses through the window is selected. These two types of windows start automatically when you click any blank portion of the drawing area with a Standard cursor or a Point Selection cursor; hence the name *Autoselect.*

Next, you will select objects with an automatic crossing window:

1. Pick a point below and to the right of the door. As you move the cursor left, the crossing (dotted) window appears.

2. Select the next point so that the window encloses the door and part of the arc (see Figure 2.17). The entire door, including the arc, is highlighted.

3. Click the Move tool.

4. Pick any point on the screen; then enter **@1<180⏎** . Metric users should type **@3<180⏎** . The door moves back to its original location.

FIGURE 2.16
The dotted window (first image) indicates a crossing selection; the solid window (second image) indicates a standard selection window.

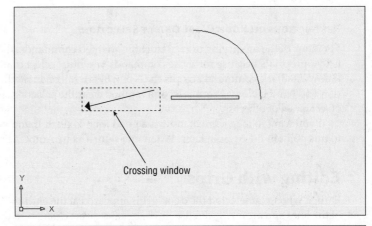

Crossing window

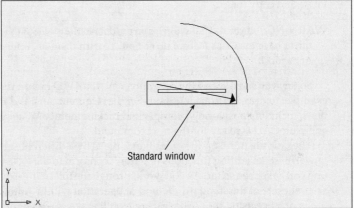

Standard window

FIGURE 2.17
The door enclosed by a crossing window

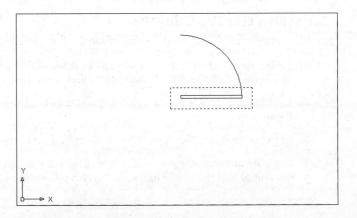

You'll find that in most cases, the Autoselect standard and crossing windows are all you need when selecting objects. They really save you time, so you'll want to become familiar with these features.

Before continuing, you need to choose File ➤ Save to save the Door file. You won't want to save the changes you make in the next section, so saving now stores the current condition of the file on your hard disk for safekeeping.

RESTRICTIONS ON NOUN/VERB OBJECT SELECTION

For many of the modifying or construction-oriented commands, the Noun/Verb selection method is inappropriate because for those commands you must select more than one set of objects. You'll know whether a command accepts the Noun/Verb selection method right away. Commands that don't accept the Noun/Verb selection method clear the selection and then ask you to select an object or set of objects.

If you want to take a break, now is a good time to do it. If you want, exit AutoCAD and return to this point in the tutorial later. When you return, start AutoCAD and open the Door file.

Editing with Grips

Earlier, when you selected the door, grips appeared at the endpoints, center points, and midpoints of the lines and arcs. You can use grips to make direct changes to the shape of objects or to quickly move and copy them.

WARNING   If you did not see grips on the door in the previous exercise, your version of AutoCAD might have the Grips feature turned off. To turn them on, refer to the information on grips in Appendix B.

So far, you have seen how operations in AutoCAD have a discrete beginning and ending. For example, to draw an arc, you first issue the Arc command and then go through a series of operations, including answering prompts and picking points. When you are finished, you have an arc, and AutoCAD is ready for the next command.

The Grips feature, on the other hand, plays by a different set of rules. Grips offer a small yet powerful set of editing functions that don't conform to the lockstep command/prompt/input routine you have seen so far. As you work through the following exercises, it is helpful to think of grips as a "subset" of the standard method of operation within AutoCAD.

To practice using the Grips feature, you'll make some temporary modifications to the door drawing.

Stretching Lines by Using Grips

In this exercise, you'll stretch one corner of the door by grabbing the grip points of two lines:

1. Press the Esc key to make sure you're not in the middle of a command. Click a point below and to the left of the door to start a selection window.

2. Use the Zoom tool to adjust your view so the size of the door is similar to what is shown in Figure 2.18.

3. Click above and to the right of the rectangular part of the door to select it.

4. Place the cursor on the lower-left corner grip of the rectangle, *but don't press the mouse button yet*. Notice that the cursor jumps to the grip point and that the grip changes color.

FIGURE 2.18

Stretching lines by using hot grips. The first image shows the rectangle's corner being stretched upward. The next image shows the new location of the corner at the top of the arc.

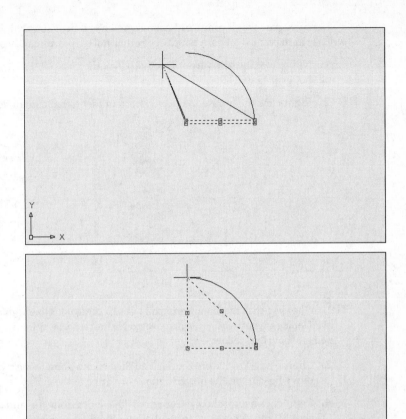

5. Move the cursor to another grip point. Notice again how the cursor jumps to it. When placed on a grip, the cursor moves to the exact center of the grip point. This means, for example, that if the cursor is placed on an endpoint grip, it is on the exact endpoint of the object.

6. Move the cursor to the upper-left corner grip of the rectangle and click it. The grip becomes a solid color and is now a *hot grip*. The prompt displays the following message:

```
**STRETCH**
Specify stretch point or [Base point/Copy/Undo/eXit]:
```

This prompt tells you that the Stretch mode is active. Notice the options in the prompt. As you move the cursor, the corner follows, and the lines of the rectangle stretch (see Figure 2.18).

TIP You can control the size and color of grips by using the Selection tab in the Options dialog box; see Appendix B for the details.

7. Move the cursor upward toward the top end of the arc and click that point. The rectangle deforms, with the corner placed at your pick point (see Figure 2.18).

Here you saw that a command called Stretch is issued simply by clicking a grip point. As you will see in these next steps, a handful of other hot-grip commands are also available:

1. Notice that the grips are still active. Click the grip point that you moved before to make it a hot grip again.

2. Right-click the mouse to open a shortcut menu that contains a list of grip edit options.

TIP When you click the joining grip point of two contiguous line segments, AutoCAD selects the overlapping grips of two lines. When you stretch the corner away from its original location, the end-points of both lines follow.

3. Choose Base Point from the list, and then click a point to the right of the hot grip. Now as you move the cursor, the hot grip moves relative to the cursor.

4. Right-click again, choose Copy from the shortcut menu, and enter @1<-30↵ . (Metric users should enter @3<-30↵ .) Instead of moving the hot grip and changing the lines, copies of the two lines are made, with their endpoints 1 unit (or 3 units for metric users) below and to the right of the first set of endpoints.

5. Pick another point just below the last. More copies are made.

6. Press ↵ or enter X↵ to exit the Stretch mode. You can also right-click again and choose Exit from the shortcut menu.

In this exercise, you saw that you can select a base point other than the hot grip. You also saw how you can specify relative coordinates to move or copy a hot grip. Finally, you saw that with grips selected on an object, right-clicking the mouse opens a shortcut menu that contains grip edit options.

Moving and Rotating with Grips

As you've just seen, the Grips feature is an alternative method for editing your drawings. You've already seen how you can stretch endpoints, but you can do much more with grips. The next exercise demonstrates some other options. You will start by undoing the modifications you made in the preceding exercise:

1. Type U↵. The copies of the stretched lines disappear.

2. Press ↵ again. The deformed door snaps back to its original form.

TIP   Pressing ↵ at the Command prompt causes AutoCAD to repeat the last command entered—in this case, U.

3. Select the entire door by first clicking a blank area below and to the right of the door.

4. Move the cursor to a location above and to the left of the rectangular portion of the door, and click. Because you went from right to left, you created a crossing window. Recall that the crossing window selects anything enclosed and crossing through the window.

5. Click the lower-left grip of the rectangle to turn it into a hot grip. Just as before, as you move your cursor, the corner stretches.

6. Right-click and then choose Move from the shortcut menu. The Command window displays the following:

```
**MOVE**
Specify move point or [Base point/Copy/Undo/eXit]
```

Now as you move the cursor, the entire door moves with it.

7. Position the door near the center of the screen and click. The door moves to the center of the screen. Notice that the Command prompt returns, yet the door remains highlighted, indicating that it is still selected for the next operation.

8. Click the lower-left grip again, right-click, and choose Rotate from the shortcut menu. The Command window displays the following:

```
**ROTATE**
Specify rotation angle or [Base point/Copy/Undo/Reference/eXit]:
```

As you move the cursor, the door rotates about the grip point.

9. Position the cursor so that the door rotates approximately 180° (see Figure 2.19). Then Ctrl+click the mouse (hold down the Ctrl key and press the left mouse button). A copy of the door appears in the new rotated position, leaving the original door in place.

10. Press ↵ to exit Grip Edit mode.

FIGURE 2.19
Rotating and copying the door by using a hot grip. Notice that more than one object is being affected by the grip edit, even though only one grip is "hot."

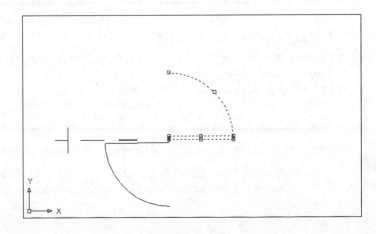

TIP You've seen how the Move command is duplicated in a modified way as a hot-grip command. Other hot-grip commands (Stretch, Rotate, Scale, and Mirror) also have similar counterparts in the standard set of AutoCAD commands. You'll see how those work in Chapters 12 and 14.

After you complete any operation by using grips, the objects are still highlighted with their grips still active. To clear the grip selection, press the Esc key.

In this exercise, you saw how hot-grip options appear in a shortcut menu. Several other options are available in that menu, including Exit, Base Point, Copy, and Undo. You can also adjust an object's properties by using the Properties option.

You can access many of these grip edit options by pressing the spacebar or ↵ while a grip is selected. With each press, the next option becomes active. The options then repeat if you continue to press ↵. The Ctrl key acts as a shortcut to the Copy option. You have to use it only once; then each time you click a point, a copy is made.

A QUICK SUMMARY OF THE GRIPS FEATURE

The exercises in this chapter include only a few of the grips options. You'll get a chance to use other hot-grip options in later chapters. Meanwhile, here is a summary of the Grips feature:

◆ Clicking endpoint grips stretches those endpoints.

◆ Clicking midpoint grips of lines moves the entire line.

◆ If two objects meet end to end and you click their overlapping grips, both grips are selected simultaneously.

◆ You can select multiple grips by holding down the Shift key and clicking the desired grips.

◆ When a hot grip is selected, the Stretch, Move, Rotate, Scale, and Mirror options are available to you; just right-click the mouse.

◆ You can cycle through the Stretch, Move, Rotate, Scale, and Mirror options by pressing ↵ while a hot grip is selected.

◆ All the hot-grip options let you make copies of the selected objects by either using the Copy option or holding down the Ctrl key while selecting points.

◆ All the hot-grip options let you select a base point other than the originally selected hot grip.

Using Dynamic Input

Earlier in this chapter, you turned off the Dynamic Input display so you could get an uncluttered view of what was going on in AutoCAD's display. In this section you'll get a chance to explore the Dynamic Input display through grip editing.

Start by going back to the original version of the Door.dwg drawing that you saved earlier.

1. Choose File ➢ Close.

2. When you are asked if you want to save changes, click No.

3. Choose File ➢ Open, and then locate and select the door.dwg file you saved earlier. You can also open the doorsample.dwg file from the sample files you installed from this book's companion CD.

4. The door appears in the condition you left it when you last saved the file.

5. Turn on Dynamic Input display by clicking the DYN button in the status bar. It should look like it is in the "down" position.

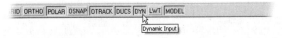

6. Click the arc to expose its grips.

7. Place the cursor on the outward-pointing arrow grip at the middle of the arc, but don't click it. (This is called "hovering" over a grip.) You will see the dimensions of the arc appear. This feature is useful when you need to check the size of objects you've drawn.

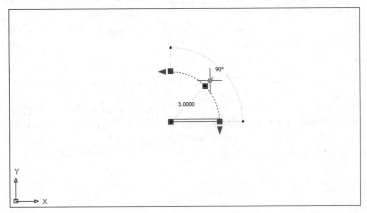

8. Now click the arrow you are hovering over. The Command prompt appears at the cursor, and the radius dimension changes to a text box.

9. Move the cursor toward the upper-right corner of the drawing area. The radius dimension changes as you move the cursor.

10. Enter 4↵. Metric users enter 130↵. As you type, the new value appears in the radius dimension. When you press ↵, the arc changes to the new radius.

11. Click the Undo button to revert to the original arc size.

Here you saw the basic methods for using the Dynamic Input display. You can hover over an object's grip to display its dimensions. Click the grip, and, if available, those dimensions can be edited directly through the keyboard. In this example, you were able to change the radius of the arc to an exact value. Depending on the grip you click, you can change a dimension through direct keyboard input. For example, if you want to change the degrees the arc covers instead of its radius, you can click the arrow grip at either end of the arc.

Next, try Dynamic Input display on a line.

1. Click the bottommost line of the door as shown in Figure 2.20; then hover over the rightmost grip on the selected line. Just as with the arc, you can see the dimensions of the line, including its length and directional angle.

2. Click the grip you are hovering over, and then move the cursor upward and to the right. You see two dimensions: one indicates the overall length, and the other shows the change in length of the line. You also see the Command prompt at the cursor. Notice that the dimension that indicates the change in length is highlighted.

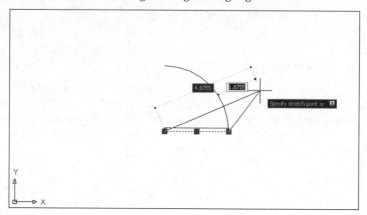

3. Enter **1** and press the Tab key to increase the length of the line by 1 unit. Metric users should enter **30** and press the Tab key. Now as you move the cursor, the line is locked at a new length that is 1 or 30 units longer than its original length. Also notice that the overall dimension is now highlighted. You'll also see a lock icon on the length dimension.

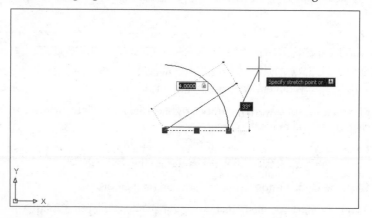

4. Press the Tab key again. Now the angle value is highlighted.

5. Enter **45** and press the Tab key to lock the angle of the line at 45°.

6. Make sure the cursor is not too close to the locked endpoint of the line, and then click the left mouse button. The line is now in its new orientation with a length of 4 (130 for metric users) and an angle of 45°, as shown in Figure 2.21.

You can see that the Dynamic Input display lets you enter specific dimensions for the selected object, making precise changes in an object's size possible.

FIGURE 2.20
Selecting a line on
the door

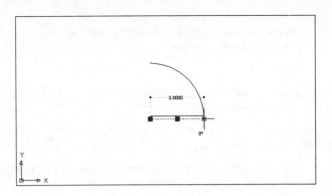

FIGURE 2.21
The line's new length
and orientation

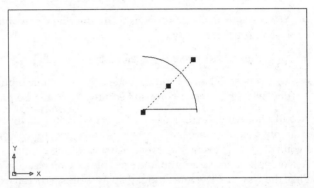

You can also use the Dynamic Input display while using other grip-editing features. Try the following exercise to see how the Dynamic Input display works while moving objects.

1. Click above and to the right of the door drawing to start a crossing selection window.

2. Click below and to the left to select the entire door drawing.

3. Click the middle grip of the arc.

4. Right-click and choose Move. Now you see the Command prompt at the cursor with the distance value highlighted. As you move the cursor, you can see the distance and angle values in the Dynamic Input display change.

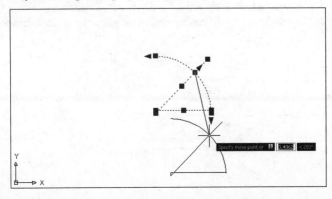

5. Enter **4**, and then press the Tab key. Now as you move the cursor, the distance from the original location of the arc's midpoint is locked at 4 units. The angle value is now highlighted and available for editing.

6. Enter **225**, and then press the Tab key to lock the angle at 225°.

7. Click a location away from the door drawing. The door moves to its new location exactly 4 units from its original location.

As you can see from these exercises, the Dynamic Input display adds some helpful methods for editing objects. To summarize, here is a rundown of the basic Dynamic Input display features:

♦ You can easily turn the Dynamic Input display on or off by clicking the DYN button in the status bar.

♦ You can quickly check the dimensions of an object by selecting it and then hovering over a grip.

♦ You can alter an object's dimension by entering values into the highlighted dimension of the Dynamic Input display.

♦ To highlight a different dimension, press the Tab key.

♦ To accept any changes you've made using Dynamic Input display, click the mouse at a location away from the grip you are editing. You can also press ↵ or the spacebar.

Not all grips will offer dimensions that can be edited. If you click the midpoint grip on the line, for example, you won't see the dimensions of the line, though you will see the Command prompt and you will be able to enter a new coordinate for the midpoint.

As you've seen in the arc and line examples, each object offers a different set of dimensions. If you like the way that Dynamic Input display works, you can experiment on the other types of objects. AutoCAD offers a number of settings that let you control the behavior of the Dynamic Input display. You'll learn about those settings later in Appendix A.

Getting Help

Eventually, you will find yourself somewhere without documentation, and you will have a question about an AutoCAD feature. AutoCAD provides an online help facility that gives you information on nearly any topic related to AutoCAD. Here's how to find help:

1. Choose Help ➢ Help from the menu bar to open the AutoCAD 2007 Help window.

2. If it isn't already selected, click the Contents tab. This tab contains a table of contents. The other two tabs—Index and Search—provide assistance in finding specific topics.

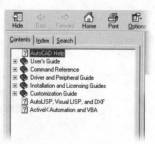

3. Scan down the screen until you see the topic Command Reference, and double-click it. Both panels of the Help window change to show more topics.

4. In the panel on the right, click the item labeled C just to the right of the Commands listing. The panel expands to display a list of command names that start with the letter *C*.

5. Look down the list and click the word *Copy*. A description of the Copy command appears in the panel to the right.

TIP   You can also press F1 to open the AutoCAD Help window.

You also have the Concepts and Procedures tabs along the top of the panel on the right. These options provide more detailed information on the use of the selected item. If you want to back up through the steps you have just taken, click the Back button on the toolbar.

Using the Search Tab

If you want to find information on a topic based on a keyword, you can use the Search tab of the Help window. Follow these steps:

1. Click the Search tab in the left panel of the Help window. If this is the first time you've selected the Search tab, you might see a message telling you that AutoCAD is setting up an index for searches.

2. Type **change** in the text box at the top of the Search tab, and then click Ask or press ↵. The list box displays all the items in the Help system that contain the word *change*.

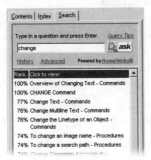

This list is a bit overwhelming. You can use Boolean AND, OR, NEAR, and NOT in conjunction with other keywords to help filter your searches, just as in a typical search engine that you might use in your web browser. After you've found a topic you want, select it from the Select Topic list and then click the Display button to display information related to the topic in the panel on the right.

Besides using a keyword for searches, you can also use phrases or questions. Try the following steps to see how you might use a question:

1. In the top text input box, type **How do I zoom into my view**↵. The list below the text box changes to show several items that relate to adjusting views in AutoCAD.

2. Click Pan or Zoom a View - Concepts. The right panel changes to display a description of how the Zoom command works.

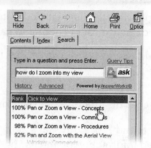

You'll notice three tabs in the right panel: Concepts, Procedures, and Commands. Concepts covers the general description of the topic. Procedures shows you methods for using the command, and Commands provides more detailed information about the command and its options.

If you scroll down to the bottom of the Search tab, you'll find a Search The Web For option. This does just what it says. If you don't find a satisfactory answer in the AutoCAD help system, you can select this option to open a web search page in the panel on the right. (Make sure you are connected to the Internet if you use this option.)

The Index tab lets you locate specific topics in the AutoCAD help system by entering a word in a list box. The Contents tab displays a listing of the help's contents in a table of contents format.

Using Context-Sensitive Help

AutoCAD also provides *context-sensitive help* to give you information related to the command you are currently using. To see how this works, try the following:

1. Close or minimize the Help window and return to the AutoCAD window.

2. Click the Move tool in the Modify toolbar to start the Move command.

3. Press the F1 function key, or choose Help from the menu bar to open the Help window. A description of the Move command appears in the panel on the right.

4. Click the Help window's Close button or minimize the Help window.

5. Press the Esc key to exit the Move command.

Finding Additional Sources of Help

The Help Topics tool is the main online source for reference material, but you can also find answers to your questions through the other options in the Help menu. Here is a brief description of them:

Info Palette A pop-up window that provides immediate feedback on the command that you are using. LT users will have the Info Palette window open by default. If you are a first-time user, this option might be helpful, but some users find it annoying. If you want to turn it off, click the X in the upper-left corner of the palette. You can always bring it back by choosing Help ➤ Info Palette.

New Features Workshop Descriptions and tutorials focused on the new features in AutoCAD 2007. You can update this unique support tool through the Autodesk website.

Help for Autodesk Subscription Users If you are a member of the Autodesk Subscription service, several options are available under the Help menu that are specifically designed for you. The Subscription e-Learning Catalog lists many interactive tutorials. The Create Support

Request option gives you direct access to a technical support person. View Support Requests lets you track your support issues, and the Edit Subscription Center Profile lets you track your subscription account. If you do not have a subscription account, you can ignore these options.

Online Resources Additional options that start your default web browser and open pages in the Autodesk website. You can find the most up-to-date information regarding AutoCAD support and training by using these options.

About Information about the version of AutoCAD you are using.

Staying Informed with the Communication Center

Another feature that can help you stay informed about the latest news on AutoCAD is the Communication Center. To the far right of the status bar, you'll see the Communication Center icon. You might also see a balloon message pointing to it.

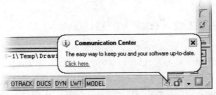

Click the Communication Center icon to open the Communication Center welcome dialog box.

As the Communication Center welcome dialog box explains, the Communication Center offers a way to stay informed about the latest software updates and support issues for AutoCAD. Click the Settings button to open the Configuration Settings dialog box.

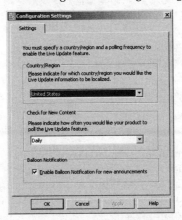

Here you can select your country from the Country/Region drop-down list to ensure that the information is correct for your country. The Check For New Content option lets you select the frequency at which the Communication Center checks for new information. You can choose Daily, Weekly, Monthly, or On Demand. If you want to turn off the balloon message, clear the Enable Balloon Notification For New Announcements check box at the bottom of the dialog box.

After you've selected a country for the first time, the Communication Center displays the Refresh Content button to the left of the Settings button in the Communication Center dialog box. If you are connected to the Internet, you can click this button at any time to check for updates from Autodesk. If any new information is available, a message alerting you to the new information is displayed in the dialog box.

The Communication Center works best if you use an "always on" Internet connection such as DSL or high-speed cable. If you don't have such a connection, you can set the Check For New Content option to On Demand. You can then check for updates when you connect to the Internet.

Displaying Data in a Text Window

You might have noticed that as you work in AutoCAD, the activity displayed in the Command window scrolls up. Sometimes it is helpful to view information that has scrolled past the view shown in the Command window. For example, you can review the command activity from your session to check input values or to recall other data entry information. Try the following exercise to see how the Text window works:

1. Choose Tools ➤ Inquiry ➤ List.

2. At the Select objects: prompt, click the arc and press⏎. Information about the arc is displayed in the AutoCAD Text Window (see Figure 2.22). Toward the bottom is the list of the arc's properties. Don't worry if the meaning of some listed properties isn't obvious yet. As you work through this book, you'll learn what the properties of an object mean.

FIGURE 2.22

The AutoCAD Text Window showing the data displayed by the List tool

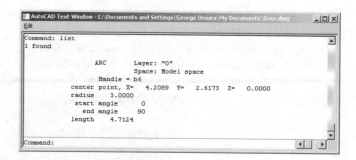

3. Press F2 to close the AutoCAD Text Window.

TIP Pressing F2 is a quick way to switch between the drawing editor and the AutoCAD Text Window.

The scroll bar to the right of the AutoCAD Text Window lets you scroll to earlier events. You can even set the number of lines AutoCAD retains by using the Options dialog box, or you can have AutoCAD record the AutoCAD Text Window information in a text file.

When you have more than one document open, the AutoCAD Text Window displays a listing for the drawing that is currently active.

Displaying the Properties of an Object

While we're on the subject of displaying information, you'll want to know about the Properties palette. In the preceding exercise, you saw how the List command showed some information regarding the properties of an object, such as the location of an arc's center and endpoints. You can also double-click an object to display a Properties palette that shows similar information. (In fact, you might accidentally display the Properties palette from time to time!)

To see what this palette is for, try the following exercise:

1. Double-click the arc in the drawing to open the Properties palette, which displays a list of the arc's properties. Don't worry if many of the items in this palette are undecipherable. You'll learn more about this palette as you work through the early chapters of this book. For now, just be aware that this palette appears whenever you double-click an object and that it displays the object's properties. You can also use it to modify many of the properties listed.

2. Click the small Auto-Hide box at the bottom left of the Properties palette. It is the icon that looks like a double arrow. The icon changes to a single arrow. The Auto-Hide option in the Properties palette lets you keep the palette open without having it take up too much of the drawing area. This can be useful when you need to edit the properties of many objects.

3. Move the cursor away from the Properties palette. The Properties palette collapses so that only the title bar remains.

4. Hover the cursor on the Properties palette title bar. The Properties palette opens to display all the options again.

5. Click the Auto-Hide box again to restore the "always open" mode of the palette.

6. Close the Properties palette by clicking the X in its upper corner. (The X will appear in the upper left or upper right, depending on the placement of the palette in the AutoCAD window.) You can also right-click the title on the side of the Properties palette and then choose Close from the shortcut menu.

7. Now you are finished with the door drawing, so choose File ➤ Close.

8. In the Save Changes dialog box, click the No button. (You've already saved this file just as you want it, so you do not need to save it again.)

TIP   You can also open the Properties palette by right-clicking an object and choosing Properties from the shortcut menu.

If You Want to Experiment

Earlier you were shown how you can use the Dynamic Input display to edit an object using grips. You can also use Dynamic Input display while you are drawing new objects. Try drawing the latch shown in Figure 2.23 using the Dynamic Input display as an aid.

FIGURE 2.23
Try drawing this latch. Dimensions are provided for your reference.

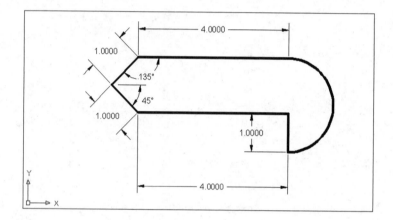

1. Start AutoCAD, open a new file, and name it Latch.

2. Click the DYN button in the status bar, if required, to turn on Dynamic Input display. Also make sure that the Polar mode is on, click the Line tool in the Draw toolbar, and start the line as shown in Figure 2.23.

3. Point the cursor directly to the left, and then enter 4↵ to draw a 4-unit-long line segment.

4. Enter 1 and press the Tab key. The next line segment is locked at 1 unit long. As you move the cursor, the line segment length remains locked while the angle changes.

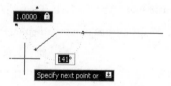

5. Place the cursor a little below the line you just drew, enter **135,** and press the Tab key. Now the angle is locked at 135° from 0° measured in a clockwise direction. Had you placed the cursor above the last point, AutoCAD would have locked the angle at 135° in a counterclockwise direction from 0°.

6. Click anywhere away from the endpoint. A 1-unit-long line segment appears at an angle of 135° from the last line segment.

7. Enter **1**, press Tab, enter **45**, press Tab, and then click a point away from the fixed line segment. Another segment is drawn.

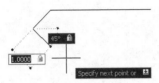

8. Point the cursor directly to the right and enter **4**↵.

9. Point the cursor directly downward and enter **1**↵.

10. Press ↵ again to exit the Line command. You've drawn the straight segments of the latch drawing using the Dynamic Input display.

Next, draw the arc portion of the latch.

1. Click the Arc tool on the Draw toolbar to begin drawing an arc for the curved part.

2. To start your arc, use the Endpoint Osnap to pick the endpoint indicated in Figure 2.23. To issue the Endpoint Osnap, Shift+right-click and then enter **E**↵.

3. Type **E**↵ to issue the End option of the Arc command.

4. Using the Endpoint Osnap again (Shift+right-click and press **E**↵), click the endpoint above where you started your line. A rubber-banding line and a temporary arc appear.

5. Type **D**↵ to issue the Direction option for the Arc command.

6. Position your cursor to the right so the arc looks like the one in Figure 2.23, and then click the mouse button to draw in the arc.

In this exercise, you used the Dynamic Input display to draw a series of lines. Instead of using the standard AutoCAD input notation of distance and angle, you used the Tab key to move between the distance and angle values in the Dynamic Input display.

Chapter 3

Setting Up and Using AutoCAD's Drafting Tools

Chapters 1 and 2 covered the basic information you need to understand the workings of AutoCAD. Now you will put this knowledge to work. In this architectural tutorial, which begins here and continues through Chapter 15, you will draw an apartment building composed of studios. The tutorial illustrates how to use AutoCAD commands and gives you a solid understanding of the basic AutoCAD package. With these fundamentals, you can use AutoCAD to its fullest potential, regardless of the kinds of drawings you intend to create or the enhancement products you might use in the future.

In this chapter you will start drawing an apartment's bathroom fixtures. In the process, you will learn how to use AutoCAD's basic tools. You'll also be introduced to the concept of drawing scale and how the size of what you draw is translated into a paper sheet size.

Topics in this chapter include the following:

- ◆ Setting Up a Work Area
- ◆ Using the AutoCAD Modes as Drafting Tools
- ◆ Exploring the Drawing Process
- ◆ Planning and Laying Out a Drawing

Setting Up a Work Area

Before beginning most drawings, you should set up your work area. To do this, determine the *measurement system*, the *drawing sheet size*, and the *scale* you want to use. The default work area is roughly 16″ × 9″ at full scale, given a decimal measurement system in which 1 unit equals 1 inch. Metric users will find that the default area is roughly 550 mm × 300 mm, in which 1 unit equals 1 mm. If these are appropriate settings for your drawing, you don't have to do any setting up. It is more likely, however, that you will make drawings of various sizes and scales. For example, you might want to create a drawing in a measurement system in which you can specify feet, inches, and fractions of inches at 1″ = 1′ scale and print the drawing on an 8$\frac{1}{2}$″ × 11″ sheet of paper.

In Chapter 2, you used the Create New Drawing dialog box to set up a drawing file. The Create New Drawing Wizard is a great tool, but it hides many of the drawing setup tools you'll need to know to work with AutoCAD. In this section, you will learn how to set up a drawing exactly the way you want.

Specifying Units

You will start by creating a new file called Bath and then you'll set up the unit style.
Use these steps to create the file:

1. If you haven't done so already, start AutoCAD. If AutoCAD is already running, choose File ➢ New.

2. In the Startup or Create New Drawing dialog box, select the Start From Scratch option, and then select Imperial from the list just below the button options. Metric users can select Metric. Click OK.

TIP If you don't see the Create New Drawing dialog box in step 2, but see the Select Template dialog box instead, select Acad.dwt and click Open. Metric users should select Acadiso.dwt and then click Open. To set up AutoCAD to display the Create New Drawing dialog box for new drawings, right-click in the drawing area and select Options. In the Options dialog box, select the System tab and then select Show Startup Dialog Box from the Startup drop-down list in the General Options group.

3. Choose View ➢ Zoom ➢ All.

4. Choose File ➢ Save As.

5. In the Save Drawing As dialog box, enter **Bath** for the filename.

6. Check to make sure you are saving the drawing in the My Documents folder or in the folder you have chosen to store your exercise files, and then click Save.

USING THE IMPERIAL AND METRIC EXAMPLES

Many of the exercises in this chapter are shown in both the metric and Imperial measurement systems. Be sure that if you start with the Imperial system, you continue with it throughout this book.

The metric settings described in this book are only approximations of their Imperial equivalents. For example, the drawing scale for the metric example is 1:10, which is close to the 1″=1′-0″ scale used in the Imperial example. In the grid example, you are asked to use a 30-unit grid, which is close to the 1′ grid of the Imperial example. Dimensions of objects will be similar, but not exact. For example, the Imperial version of the tub will measure 2′-8″×5′-0, and the metric version of the tub will be 81 cm×152 cm. The actual metric equivalent of 2′-8″×5′-0″ is 81.28 cm×152.4 cm. Measurements in the tub example are rounded to the nearest centimeter.

Metric users should also be aware that AutoCAD uses a period as a decimal point instead of the comma used in most European nations, South Africa, and elsewhere. Commas are used in AutoCAD to separate the X, Y, and Z components of a coordinate.

The next thing you want to tell AutoCAD is the *unit style* you intend to use. So far, you've been using the default, which is decimal inches. In this unit style, whole units represent inches, and decimal units are decimal inches. If you want to be able to enter distances in feet, you must change the unit style to a style that accepts feet as input. You'll do this through the Drawing Units dialog box, shown in Figure 3.1.

FIGURE 3.1

The Drawing Units
dialog box

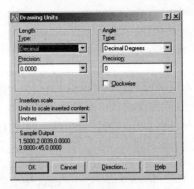

TIP If you are a civil engineer, you should know that the Engineering unit style lets you enter feet and decimal feet for distances. For example, the equivalent of 12´-6˝ is 12.5´. If you use the Engineering unit style, you will ensure that your drawings conform to the scale of drawings created by your architectural colleagues. And you will have the ability to enter decimal feet.

Follow these steps to set a unit style:

1. Choose Format ➤ Units or type **Un.**⏎ to open the Drawing Units dialog box.

2. Let's look at a few of the options available. Click the Type drop-down list in the Length group. Notice the unit styles in the list.

3. Click Architectural. The Sample Output section of the dialog box shows you what the architectural style looks like in AutoCAD. Metric users should keep this setting as Decimal.

TIP You can also control the Drawing Units settings by using several system variables. To set the unit style, you can type **lunits.**⏎ at the Command prompt. (The apostrophe lets you enter this command while in the middle of other commands.) At the Enter new value for Lunits <2>: prompt, enter **4** for Architectural. See Appendix C for other settings.

4. Click the Precision drop-down list just below the Type list. Notice the options available. You can set the smallest unit AutoCAD will display in this drawing. For now, leave this setting at its default value of ¹⁄₁₆˝. Metric users will keep the setting at 0.0000.

5. Press the Esc key to close the drop-down list, and then click the Direction button at the bottom of the Drawing Units dialog box to open the Direction Control dialog box. The Direction Control dialog box lets you set the direction for the 0° angle. For now, don't change these settings—you'll read more about them in a moment.

6. Click the Cancel button.

7. Now click the drop-down list in the Insertion Scale group. The list shows various units of measure.

8. Click Inches, or if you are a metric user, choose Centimeters. This option lets you control how AutoCAD translates drawing scales when you import drawings from outside the current drawing. You'll learn more about this feature in Chapter 27.

9. Click OK in the Drawing Units dialog box to return to the drawing.

If you use the Imperial system of measurement, you selected Architectural measurement units for this tutorial, but your own work might require a different unit style. You saw the unit styles available in the Drawing Units dialog box. Table 3.1 shows examples of how the distance 15.5 is entered in each of these styles.

In the previous exercise, you needed to change only two settings. Let's take a look at the other Drawing Units settings in more detail. As you read, you might want to refer to Figure 3.1.

TABLE 3.1:   Measurement Systems Available in AutoCAD

MEASUREMENT SYSTEM	AUTOCAD'S DISPLAY OF MEASUREMENT
Scientific	1.55E+01 (inches or metric)
Decimal	15.5000 (inches or metric)
Engineering	1´-3.5˝ (input as 1´3.5˝)
Architectural	1´-3 1/2˝ (input as 1´3-1/2˝)
Fractional	15 1/2˝ (input as 15-1/2˝)

Fine-Tuning the Measurement System

Most of the time, you will be concerned only with the units and angles settings of the Drawing Units dialog box. But as you saw from the preceding exercise, you can control many other settings related to the input and display of units.

TIP   To measure the distance between two points, choose Tools ➢ Inquiry ➢ Distance from the menu bar, or type **Di**↵, and then click the two points. (Di is the shortcut for entering Dist↵.) But if you find that this command doesn't give you an accurate distance measurement, examine the Precision option in the Drawing Units dialog box. If it is set too high, the value returned by the Dist command might be rounded to a value greater than your tolerances allow, even though the distance is drawn accurately.

The Precision drop-down list in the Length group lets you specify the smallest unit value that you want AutoCAD to display in the status line and in the prompts. If you choose a measurement system that uses fractions, the Precision list includes fractional units. You can also control this setting with the Luprec system variable.

The Angle group lets you set the style for displaying angles. You have a choice of five angle styles: Decimal Degrees, Degrees/Minutes/Seconds, Grads, Radians, and Surveyor's Units. In the Angle group's Precision drop-down list, you can specify the degree of accuracy you want AutoCAD to display for angles. You can also control these settings with the Aunits and Auprec system variables.

TIP You can find out more about system variables in Appendix C.

You can also tell AutoCAD which direction is positive, either clockwise or counterclockwise. This book uses the default, which is counterclockwise. You can also control these settings with the Angbase and Angdir system variables. The Direction Control dialog box lets you set the direction of the 0 base angle. The default base angle (and the one used throughout this book) is a direction from left to right. However, at times you might want to designate another direction as the 0 base angle.

The Insertion Scale setting in the Drawing Units dialog box lets you control how blocks from the Tool palettes or DesignCenter are scaled as they are imported into your current drawing. A *block* is a collection of drawing objects that form a single object. Blocks are frequently used to create standard symbols. You'll learn more about blocks in Chapter 4. The Insertion Scale setting lets you compensate for drawings of different scale by offering an automatic scale translation when importing blocks from an external file. The Insunits system variable also controls the Insertion Scale setting. You'll learn more about this setting in Chapter 27.

TIP If you're new to AutoCAD, don't worry about the Insertion Scale setting right now. Make a mental note of it. It might come in handy in your work in the future.

Setting Up the Drawing Limits

One of the big advantages in using AutoCAD is that you can draw at full scale; you aren't limited to the edges of a piece of paper the way you are in manual drawing. But you still have to consider what will happen when you want a printout of your drawing. When you start a new drawing, it helps to limit your drawing area to one that can be scaled down to fit on a standard sheet size. Although this is not absolutely necessary with AutoCAD, the limits give you a frame of reference between your work in AutoCAD and the final printed output.

THINGS TO WATCH FOR WHEN ENTERING DISTANCES

When you are using Architectural units, you should be aware of two points:

♦ Use hyphens only to distinguish fractions from whole inches.

♦ You cannot use spaces while specifying a dimension. For example, you can specify eight feet, four and one-half inches as 8´4-½″ or 8´4.5, but not as 8´-4½″.

These idiosyncrasies are a source of confusion to many architects and engineers new to AutoCAD because the program often displays architectural dimensions in the standard architectural format but does not allow you to enter dimensions that way.

Here are some tips for entering distances and angles in unusual situations:

♦ When entering distances in inches and feet, you can omit the inch (″) sign. If you are using the Engineering unit style, you can enter decimal feet and forgo the inch sign entirely.

♦ You can enter fractional distances and angles in any format you like, regardless of the current unit style. For example, you can enter a distance as **@1/2<1.5708r**, even if your current unit system is set for decimal units and decimal degrees (1.5708r is the radian equivalent of 90°).

◆ If you have your angle units set to degrees, grads, or radians, you do not need to specify g, r, or d after the angle. You do have to specify g, r, or d, however, if you want to use these units when they are not the current default angle system.

◆ If your current angle system is set to something other than degrees, but you want to enter angles in degrees, you can use a double less-than symbol (<<) in place of the single less-than symbol (<) to override the current angle system of measure. The << also assumes the base angle of 0° to be a direction from left to right and the positive direction to be counterclockwise.

◆ If your current angle system uses a different base angle and direction, and you want to specify an angle in the standard base direction, you can use a triple less-than symbol (<<<) to indicate angle. Note that this only works if Dynamic Input is turned off.

◆ You can specify a denominator of any size when specifying fractions. However, be aware that the value you have set for the maximum number of digits to the right of decimal points (under the Precision setting in the Length group of the Drawing Units dialog box) will restrict the actual fractional value AutoCAD uses. For example, if your units are set for a maximum of two digits of decimals and you give a fractional value of 5/32, AutoCAD rounds this value to 3/16, or 0.1875.

◆ You can enter decimal feet for distances in the Architectural unit style. For example, you can enter 6´-6˝ as **6.5´**.

To set up the drawing work area, it helps to understand how standard sheet sizes translate into full-scale drawing sizes. Tables 3.2 and 3.3 list widths and heights of drawing areas in inches, according to scales and final printout sizes. The scales are listed in the far-left column; the output sheet sizes are listed across the top.

Let's take an example. To find the area needed in AutoCAD for your bathroom drawing, look across from the scale 1˝ = 1´ to the column that reads 8 ½˝ × 11˝ at the top of Table 3.2. You'll find the value 102 × 132. This means the drawing area needs to fit within an area 102˝ × 132´ (8.5 feet × 11 feet) in AutoCAD in order to fit a printout of a 1˝ = 1´-0˝ scale drawing on an 8 ½˝ 11˝ sheet of paper. You might want the drawing area to be oriented horizontally, so that the 11 feet will be in the X axis and the 8.5 feet will be in the Y axis.

WARNING Note that the sheet sizes in tables 3.2 and 3.3 do not take into account the nonprintable margins of the paper. Make sure you take your printer margins into account.

TABLE 3.2: Work Area in Drawing Units (Inches) by Scale and Plotted Sheet Size from 8¹/₂˝ x 11˝ to 18˝ x 24˝

SCALE	8 ½ ˝ × 11˝	11˝ × 17	17˝ × 22˝	18˝ × 24˝
3˝ = 1´	34 × 44	44 × 68	68 × 88	72 × 96
1¹/₂˝ = 1´	68 × 88	88 × 136	136 × 176	144 × 192
1˝ = 1´	102 × 132	132 × 204	204 × 264	216 × 288
³/₄ ˝ = 1´	136 × 176	176 × 272	272 × 352	288 × 384
¹/₂˝ = 1´	204 × 264	264 × 408	408 × 528	432 × 576

TABLE 3.2: Work Area in Drawing Units (Inches) by Scale and Plotted Sheet Size from 8½″ x 11″ to 18″ x 24″ *(CONTINUED)*

SCALE	8½″ × 11″	11″ × 17	17″ × 22″	18″ × 24″
¼″ = 1′	408 × 528	528 × 816	816 × 1056	864 × 1152
⅛″ = 1′	816 × 1056	1056 × 1632	1632 × 2112	1728 × 2304
1/16″ = 1′	1632 × 2112	2112 × 3264	3264 × 4224	3456 × 4608
1/32″ = 1′	3264 × 4224	4224 × 6528	6528 × 8448	6912 × 9216
1″ = 10′	1020 × 1320	1320 × 2040	2040 × 2640	2160 × 2880
1″ = 20′	2040 × 2640	2640 × 4080	4080 × 5280	4320 × 5760
1″ = 30′	3060 × 3960	3960 × 6120	6120 × 7920	6480 8640
1″ = 40′	4080 5280	5280 × 8160	8160 × 10,560	8640 × 11,520
1″ = 50′	5100 × 6600	6600 × 10,200	10,200 × 13,200	10,800 × 14,400
1″ = 60′	6120 × 7920	7920 × 12,240	12,240 × 15,840	12,960 × 17,280

TABLE 3.3: Work Area in Drawing Units (Inches) by Scale and Plotted Sheet Size from 22″ x 34″ to 36″ x 48″

SCALE	22″ × 34″	24″ × 36″	30″ 42″	36″ × 48″
3″ = 1′	88 × 136	96 × 144	120 × 168	144 × 192
1½″ = 1′	176 × 272	192 × 288	240 × 336	288 × 384
1″ = 1′	264 × 408	288 × 432	360 × 504	432 × 576
¾″ = 1′	352 × 544	384 × 576	480 × 672	576 × 768
½″ = 1′	528 × 816	576 × 864	720 × 1008	864 × 1152
¼″ = 1′	1056 × 1632	1152 × 1728	1440 × 2016	1728 × 2304
⅛″ = 1′	2112 × 3264	2304 × 3456	2880 × 4032	3456 × 4608
1/16″ = 1′	4224 × 6528	4608 × 6912	5760 × 8064	6912 × 9216
1/32″ = 1′	8448 × 13,056	9216 × 13,824	11,520 × 16,128	13,824 × 18,432
1″ = 10′	2640 × 4080	2880 × 4320	3600 × 5040	4320 × 5760
1″ = 20′	5280 × 8160	5760 × 8640	7200 × 10,080	8640 × 11,520

TABLE 3.3: Work Area in Drawing Units (Inches) by Scale and Plotted Sheet Size from 22″ x 34″ to 36″ x 48″ *(CONTINUED)*

SCALE	22″ × 34″	24″ × 36″	30″ 42″	36″ × 48″
1″ = 30′	7920 × 12,240	8640 × 12,960	10,800 × 15,120	12,960 × 17,280
1″ = 40′	10,560 × 16,320	11,520 × 17,280	14,400 × 20,160	17,280 × 23,040
1″ = 50′	13,200 × 20,400	14,400 × 21,600	18,000 × 25,200	21,600 × 28,800
1″ = 60′	15,840 × 24,480	17,280 × 25,920	21,600 × 30,240	25,920 × 34,560

If you're a metric user, you'll be drawing the bathroom at a scale of 1 to 10. This scale is close to the 1″ = 1′-0″ scale used for the Imperial measurements in the exercises. So for an A4 sheet, your work area should be 297 cm × 210 cm. This is the equivalent of an A4 sheet (210 mm × 297 mm) enlarged by a factor of 10.

Now that you know the area you need, you can use the Limits command to set up the area:

1. Choose Format ➢ Drawing Limits.

2. At the Specify lower left corner or [ON/OFF] <0′-0″,0′-0″>: prompt, specify the lower-left corner of your work area. Press ↵ to accept the default.

3. At the Specify upper right corner <1′0″,0′9″>: prompt, specify the upper-right corner of your work area. (The default is shown in brackets.) Enter **132,102**. Or if you prefer, you can enter **11′,8′6**, because you've set up your drawing for architectural units. Metric users should enter **297,210**.

4. Next, choose View ➢ Zoom ➢ All. You can also select the Zoom All tool from the Zoom Window flyout on the Standard toolbar, or type **Z↵A↵**. Although it appears that nothing has changed, your drawing area is now set to a size that will enable you to draw your bathroom at full scale.

TIP You can toggle through the Coordinate Readout modes by repeatedly pressing Ctrl+I or by clicking the coordinate readout on the status bar. For more on the Coordinate Readout modes, see Chapter 1 and the "Using Grid and Snap Modes Together" section later in this chapter.

5. Move the cursor to the upper-right corner of the drawing area and watch the coordinate readout. Notice that now the upper-right corner has a Y coordinate of approximately 8′-6″, or 210 for metric users. The X coordinate depends on the proportion of your AutoCAD window. The coordinate readout also displays distances in feet and inches.

In step 5, the coordinate readout shows you that your drawing area is larger than before, but no visual clues tell you where you are or what distances you are dealing with. To help you get your bearings, you can turn on the Grid mode, which you will learn about shortly. The Grid mode displays an array of dots that help you visualize distances and the limits of your drawing. Before you get to grids, let's take a closer look at scale factors and how they work.

TIP As an alternative to setting up the drawing limits, you can draw a rectangle that outlines the same area used to define the drawing limits. For example, in the previous exercise you could use the Rectangle tool to draw a rectangle that has its lower-left corner at coordinate 0,0 and its upper-right corner at 132,102 (297,210 for metric users).

The steps you've just taken to set up your drawing are duplicated in the Advanced Setup option of the Create New Drawing Wizard. This section showed you the detailed method of setting up your drawing so you'll understand exactly what is going on, but if you prefer, you can use the Create New Drawing Wizard to set up future drawings. You can then use the Drawing Units dialog box to fine-tune your drawing or make adjustments later.

Understanding Scale Factors

When you draft manually, you work on the final drawing directly with pen and ink or pencil. With a CAD program, you are a few steps removed from the actual finished product. Because of this, you need a deeper understanding of your drawing scale and how it is derived. In particular, you need to understand scale factors. For example, one of the more common uses of scale factors is in translating text size in your CAD drawing to the final plotted text size. When you draw manually, you simply draw your notes at the size you want. In a CAD drawing, you need to translate the desired final text size to the drawing scale.

When you start adding text to your drawing (see Chapter 10), you have to specify a text height. The scale factor helps you determine the appropriate text height for a particular drawing scale. For example, you might want your text to appear $1/2$″ high in your final plot. But if you draw your text to $1/8$″ in your drawing, it appears as a dot when plotted. The text has to be scaled up to a size that, when scaled back down at plot time, appears $1/8$″ high. So, for a $1/4$″ scale drawing, you multiply the $1/8$″ text height by a scale factor of 48 to get 6″. Your text should be 6″ high in the CAD drawing in order to appear $1/8$″ high in the final plot. So where did the number 48 come from?

The scale factor for fractional inch scales is derived by multiplying the denominator of the scale by 12 and then dividing by the numerator. For example, the scale factor for $1/4$″ = 1′-0″ is $(4 \times 12)/1$, or 48/1. For $3/16$″ = 1′-0″ scale, the operation is $(16 \times 12)/3$, or 64. For whole-foot scales such as 1″ = 10′, multiply the feet side of the equation by 12. Metric scales require simple decimal conversions.

All the drawing sizes in Tables 3.2 and 3.3 were derived by using scale factors. Table 3.4 shows scale factors as they relate to standard drawing scales. These scale factors are the values by which you multiply the desired final printout size to get the equivalent full-scale size. For example, if you have a sheet size of 11″ × 17″, and you want to know the equivalent full-scale size for a $1/4$″-scale drawing, you multiply the sheet measurements by 48. In this way, 11″ becomes 528″ (48″ × 11″), and 17″ becomes 816″ (48″ × 17″). Your work area must be 528″ × 816″ if you intend to have a final output of 11″ × 17″ at $1/4$″ = 1′. You can divide these inch measurements by 12″ to get 44′ × 68′.

TABLE 3.4:   Scale Conversion Factors

Scale Factors for Engineering Drawing Scales							
$n = 1$″ 10′	20′	30′	40′	50′	60′	100′	200′
Scale factor 120	240	360	480	600	720	1200	2400

Scale Factors for Architectural Drawing Scales							
$n = 1′{-}0$″ $1/16$″	$1/8$″	$1/4$″	$1/2$″	$3/4$″	1″	$1\,1/2$″	3″
Scale factor 192	96	48	24	16	12	8	4

TIP   If you get the message `**Outside limits`, you selected a point outside the area defined by the limits of your drawing, and the Limits command's limits-checking feature is on. (Some third-party programs might use the limits-checking feature.) If you must select a point outside the limits, issue the Limits command, and then enter **off** at the `Specify lower left corner or [ON/OFF] <Lower left corner>:` prompt to turn off the limits-checking feature.

If you are using the metric system, you can use the drawing scale directly as the scale factor. For example, a drawing scale of 1:10 has a scale factor of 10; a drawing scale of 1:50 has a scale factor of 50; and so on. Table 3.5 shows drawing areas based on scale and sheet size. The sheet sizes are shown across the top, and the scales are shown in the column to the far left.

TABLE 3.5:   Work Area in Metric Units (Centimeters) by Scale and Plotted Sheet Size. Multiply Work Area Sizes by 10 for Millimeter Equivalents.

SCALE	A0 OR F 841 MM × 1189 MM (33.11″ × 46.81″)
1:5	420 cm × 594 cm
1:10	841 cm × 1189 cm
1:20	1682 cm × 2378 cm
1:25	2102.5 cm × 2972.5 cm
1:33⅓	2803 cm × 3962 cm
1:40	3360 cm × 4756 cm
1:50	4200 cm × 5940 cm
1:75	6307 cm × 8917 cm
1:100	8410 cm × 11,890 cm
1:125	10,512 cm × 14,862 cm
Scale	**A or D 594 mm × 841 mm (23.39″ × 33.11″)**
1:5	297 cm × 420 cm
1:10	594 cm × 841 cm
1:20	1188 cm × 1682 cm
1:25	1485 cm × 2102.5 cm
1:33⅓	1980 cm × 2803 cm
1:40	2376 cm × 3360 cm
1:50	2970 cm × 4200 cm

TABLE 3.5: Work Area in Metric Units (Centimeters) by Scale and Plotted Sheet Size. Multiply Work Area Sizes by 10 for Millimeter Equivalents. *(CONTINUED)*

SCALE	A0 OR F 841 MM × 1189 MM (33.11″ × 46.81″)
1:75	4455 cm × 6307 cm
1:100	5940 cm × 8410 cm
1:125	7425 cm × 10512 cm
Scale	**A2 or C 420 mm × 594 mm (16.54″ × 23.39″)**
1:5	210 cm × 297 cm
1:10	420 cm × 594 cm
1:20	840 cm × 1188 cm
1:25	1050 cm × 1485 cm
1:33$^1/_3$	1399 cm × 1980 cm
1:40	1680 cm × 2376 cm
1:50	2100 cm × 2970 cm
1:75	3150 cm × 4455 cm
1:100	4200 cm × 5940 cm
1:125	5250 cm × 7425 cm
Scale	**A3 or B 297 mm × 420 mm (11.70″ × 16.54″)**
1:5	148 cm × 210 cm
1:10	297 cm × 420 cm
1:20	594 cm × 840 cm
1:25	742.5 cm × 1050 cm
1:33$^1/_3$	990 cm × 1399 cm
1:40	1188 cm × 1680 cm
1:50	1480 cm × 2100 cm
1:75	2227 cm × 3150 cm
1:100	2970 cm × 4200 cm
1:125	3712 cm × 5250 cm

TABLE 3.5:   Work Area in Metric Units (Centimeters) by Scale and Plotted Sheet Size. Multiply Work Area Sizes by 10 for Millimeter Equivalents. *(CONTINUED)*

SCALE	A0 OR F 841 MM × 1189 MM (33.11″ × 46.81″)
Scale	A4 or A 210 mm × 297 mm (8.27″ × 11.70″)
1:5	105 cm × 148 cm
1:10	210 cm × 297 cm
1:20	420 cm × 594 cm
1:25	5250 cm × 742.5 cm
1:33$^1/_3$	700 cm × 990 cm
1:40	840 cm × 1188 cm
1:50	1050 cm × 1480 cm
1:75	1575 cm × 2227 cm
1:100	2100 cm × 2970 cm
1:125	2625 cm × 3712 cm

Metric users need to take special care regarding the base unit. The examples in this book will use centimeters as a base unit, which means that if you enter a distance as 1, you can assume the distance to be 1 cm. If you want to use millimeters as the base unit, multiply the sheet-size values in Table 3.5 by 10.

TIP   Metric users should note that the scale factor depends on whether you are using millimeters, centimeters, or meters as the basis for the final plot size. For example, a drawing that uses millimeters as its base unit of drawing measure (1 drawing unit = 1 millimeter) uses a scale factor of 1 to 500 if the final output is to be at a scale of 1:50 centimeters.

You will use scale factors to specify text height and dimension settings, so understanding them now will pay off later. Plotting to a particular scale will also be easier with an understanding of scale factors.

Using the AutoCAD Modes as Drafting Tools

After you set up your work area, you can begin the plan of a typical bathroom in your studio. You will use this example to learn about some of AutoCAD's drawing aids. These tools might be compared to a background grid (*Grid mode*), scale (*Coordinate Readout mode*), and a T-square and triangle (*Object Snap Tracking mode* and *Polar Tracking mode*). These drawing modes can be indispensable tools when used properly. The Drafting Settings dialog box helps you visualize the modes in an organized manner and simplifies their management.

Using the Grid Mode as a Background Grid

Using the Grid mode is like having a grid under your drawing to help you with layout. In AutoCAD, the Grid mode can also let you see the limits of your drawing because the grid can be set to display only within the limits setting of your drawing. The Grid mode also helps you visually determine the distances you are working with in any given view. In this section, you will learn how to control the grid's appearance. The F7 key toggles the Grid mode on and off; you can also click the Grid button in the status bar.

In this exercise, you'll set the grid spacing and display the grid:

1. Choose Tools ➢ Drafting Settings, or type **Ds**↵ to open the Drafting Settings dialog box, showing all the mode settings.

2. Click the Snap And Grid tab. You see five groups: Snap Spacing, Grid Spacing, Polar Spacing, Grid Behavior, and Snap Type.

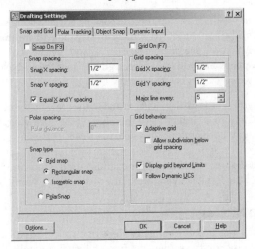

3. Let's start with the Grid Spacing group. Notice that the Grid X Spacing text box contains a value of $1/_2$″. Metric users see a value of 10.

4. Double-click the Grid X Spacing text box to highlight the entry. You can now type a new value for this setting.

TIP   You can use the Gridunit system variable to set the grid spacing. Enter **Gridunit**↵, and at the `Enter new value for GRIDUNIT <0´-0 1/2″,0´-0 1/2″>:` prompt, enter **12,12** (30,30 for metric users). You must enter the Gridunit value as an X,Y coordinate.

5. Type **12** for 12″, and then press Tab to move to the Grid Y Spacing text box. Metric users should type **30** and then press Tab. Notice that the Grid Y Spacing text box automatically changes to the same value as the Grid X Spacing value you just entered. In the case of the Imperial measurement, the value also changes from 12 to 1´. AutoCAD assumes you want the X and Y grid spacing to be the same, unless you specifically ask for a different Y setting.

6. In the Grid Behavior group, make sure that the "Display grid beyond limits" setting is not checked. If this setting is turned on, the grid will display outside the limits of the drawing.

7. Click the Grid On check box to make the grid visible. Notice the F7 in parentheses. This tells you that the F7 function key also controls the Grid On/Off function.

8. Click OK. The grid now appears as an array of dots with 12″ spacing in your drawing area (30 cm if you are following the metric version of this tutorial). The grid dots will not print with your drawing.

   With this spacing, you can see your work area more clearly. It also gives you a visual reference for your drawing. You can see what a 1-foot (or 30-cm) distance looks like in your drawing. Because the grid appears only within the drawing limits, you are better able to see your work area.

9. Press F7, or click Grid in the status bar. (You can also hold down the Ctrl key and press G.) The grid disappears.

10. Press F7 again to turn the grid back on.

WARNING If your view is such that the grid spacing appears quite small and the "Display grid beyond limits" setting is off, AutoCAD will not display the grid, in order to preserve the readability of the drawing. You will see the message Grid too dense to display in the Command window. If this happens, and you want to see a grid, change the grid spacing upward until the grid is visible in your view.

In this exercise, you set the grid spacing equal to the scale factor of your drawing. This makes the grid spacing equivalent to 1″ intervals of the final plotted drawing. For example, if your drawing is ¼″ = 1′-0″ scale, you can set your grid spacing to 48. The grid spacing then reflects the 1-inch spacing for a ¼″ scale drawing. If you're a metric user, you can keep the grid spacing at 10 to display the equivalent distance of 10 cm. This exercise used 30 for the metric grid spacing simply to match the display of the Imperial version. In the next section, you'll see how the Snap mode works.

Using the Snap Modes

The *Snap mode* forces the cursor to move in steps of a specific distance. Snap mode is useful when you want to select points on the screen at a fixed interval. Actually, two snap modes are available in AutoCAD: *Grid Snap* and *Polar Snap*. Let's start by looking at the Grid Snap mode. The F9 key toggles the Grid Snap mode on and off, or you can click the Snap button in the status bar. Follow these steps to access the Grid Snap mode:

1. Choose Tools ➢ Drafting Settings, or type **Ds.**↵ to open the Drafting Settings dialog box.

2. In the Snap Spacing group of the dialog box, double-click the Snap X Spacing text box and type **4**. (Metric users should enter **10**.) Then press the Tab key to move to the next option. As with the grid setting, AutoCAD assumes you want the X and Y snap spacing to be the same, unless you specifically ask for a different Y setting.

3. Click the Snap On check box to turn it on.

4. Click OK and start moving the cursor around. Notice how the cursor seems to move in "steps" rather than in a smooth motion. Also notice that the Snap button in the status bar appears pressed, indicating that the Snap mode is on.

5. Press F9 or click Snap in the status bar (you can also hold down the Ctrl key and press B); then move the cursor slowly around the drawing area. The Snap mode is now off.

6. Press F9 again to turn the Snap mode back on.

TIP You can use the Snapunit system variable to set the snap spacing. Enter **'Snapunit.**⌐. Then, at the Enter new value for SNAPUNIT <0´0˝,0´0˝>: prompt, enter **4,4** (10,10 for metric users). You must enter the Snapunit value as an X,Y coordinate.

Take a moment to look at the Drafting Settings dialog box. The other option in the Snap Spacing group enables you to force the X and Y spacing to be equal (Equal X and Y Spacing).

In the Snap Type group, you can change the snap and grid configuration to aid in creating 2D isometric drawings by clicking the Isometric Snap radio button. The PolarSnap option enables you to set a snap distance for the Polar Snap feature. When you click the PolarSnap radio button, the Polar Distance option at the middle left of the dialog box changes from gray to black and white to allow you to enter a Polar Snap distance. The next exercise discusses these features.

TIP You can use the Snaptype system variable to set the snap to either the Grid Snap or Polar Snap, and the Snapstyl system variable turns the isometric Grid Snap on and off. The Polardist system variable controls the snap distance for the Polar Snap feature.

Using Grid and Snap Modes Together

You can set the grid spacing to be the same as the snap setting, enabling you to see every snap point. Let's take a look at how Grid and Snap modes work together:

1. Open the Drafting Settings dialog box.

TIP You can take a shortcut to the Drafting Settings dialog box by right-clicking the Snap or Grid button in the status bar and then choosing Settings from the shortcut menu.

2. Make sure the Snap And Grid tab is selected; then double-click the Grid X Spacing text box in the Grid group and type **0**.

3. Click OK. Now the grid spacing has changed to reflect the 4˝ (or 10 cm) snap spacing. Move the cursor and watch it snap to the grid points.

4. Open the Drafting Settings dialog box again.

5. Double-click the Snap X Spacing text box in the Snap group, and type **1**⌐ (3 for metric users).

6. Click OK then choose View ➢ Redraw. The grid automatically changes to conform to the new snap setting. However, at this density, the grid is overwhelming.

7. Open the Drafting Settings dialog box again.

8. Double-click the Grid X Spacing text box in the Grid group, and type **12** (30 for metric users).

9. Click OK. The grid spacing is now at 12 (or 30) again, which is a more reasonable spacing for the current drawing scale.

With the snap spacing set to 1 (3 for metric users), it is difficult to tell whether the Snap mode is turned on based on the behavior of the cursor, but the coordinate readout in the status bar gives you a clue. As you move your cursor, the coordinates appear as whole numbers with no fractional distances. Metric users will notice the coordinate readout displaying values that are multiples of 3.

As you move the cursor over the drawing area, the coordinate readout in the lower-left corner of the AutoCAD window dynamically displays the cursor's position in absolute Cartesian coordinates. This enables you to find a position on your drawing by locating it in reference to the drawing origin—0,0— that is in the lower-left corner of the drawing. You can also set the coordinate readout to display relative coordinates by clicking the readout itself or by pressing Ctrl+I. Throughout these exercises, coordinates will be provided to enable you to select points by using the dynamic coordinate readout. (If you want to review the discussion of AutoCAD's coordinate display, see Chapter 1.)

Next, you'll learn how to use the snap tools as your virtual drawing scale, T-square, and triangle.

Using Polar Tracking and Snap as Your Scale, T-Square, and Triangle

In this section, you will draw the first item in the bathroom: the toilet. It is composed of a rectangle representing the tank and a truncated ellipse representing the seat. To construct the toilet, you'll use the Polar Tracking and Polar Snap tools to learn about them firsthand. Polar Tracking helps you align your cursor to exact horizontal and vertical angles, much like a T-square and triangle. Polar Snap is similar to Grid Snap in that it forces the cursor to move in exact increments. The main difference is that Polar Snap snaps to distances from a previously selected point rather than to a fixed grid. Polar Snap also works only in conjunction with Polar Tracking.

Start by setting up Polar Snap:

1. Open the Drafting Settings dialog box again.

2. Make sure the Snap And Grid tab is selected; then click the PolarSnap radio button in the Snap Type group.

3. Double-click the Polar Distance setting, and type **.5** for a ¹/₂-inch Snap setting. Metric users should type **1** for a 1 cm Polar Snap setting.

4. Click OK to close the Drafting Settings dialog box.

You've just set the Polar Snap setting to .5 or one-half (1 cm for metric users). As you move the cursor over the drawing area, notice that the Snap mode seems to be off. When Polar Snap is active, you'll have the snap in effect only when you are actually drawing an object.

You can, however, switch between Grid Snap and Polar Snap on the fly. Right-click on the Snap button in the status bar and select Grid Snap On or Polar Snap On to switch between the two modes. This is the same as selecting the PolarSnap or Grid Snap radio buttons in the Snap and Grid tab of the Drafting Settings dialog box.

Next you'll see how Polar Tracking can be used to draw lines.

1. Start your line at the coordinate 5′-7″, 6′-3″ by entering **5′7″,6′3″** . Metric users should enter **171,189**⏎ as the starting coordinate. This starting point is somewhat arbitrary, but by entering a specific starting location, you are coordinated with the figures and instructions in this book.

2. Right-click the Snap button again, and then choose PolarSnap On from the shortcut menu.

3. Make sure that Polar Tracking is on (the POLAR button in the status bar should be in the on position), and then move the cursor directly to the right. The Polar Tracking cursor appears, along with the Polar Tracking readout. Notice that the readout shows distances in ¹/₂″ increments (or 1-unit increments for metric users). It also shows you the angle in the standard AutoCAD distance and angle format. Even though Grid Snap is set to 1 (3 for metric users),

the snap distance changes to the value you set for Polar Distance when Polar Tracking is active and Polar Snap is on.

4. Move the cursor until the Polar Snap readout lists 1′-10″ < 0° and pick this point. Metric users should use a Polar Tracking readout of 56.0000 < 0°. As in Chapter 2, when you move the cursor around, the rubber-banding line follows it at any angle.

5. Move the cursor downward until the coordinate readout lists 0′-9″ < 270° and click this point. Metric users should use a readout of 23.0000 < 270°.

6. Continue drawing the other two sides of the rectangle by using the Polar Tracking readout. After you've completed the rectangle, press ↵ or the Esc key to exit the Line tool. You should have a drawing that looks like Figure 3.2.

FIGURE 3.2
A plan view of the toilet tank

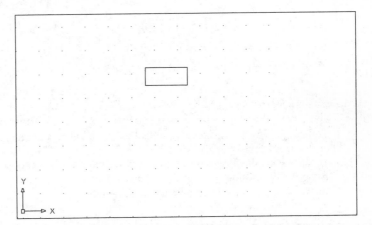

As you can see from the exercise, you can use Polar Tracking to restrain your cursor to horizontal and vertical positions, just like a T-square and triangle. Later, you'll learn how you can set up Polar Tracking to set the angle to any value you want in a way similar to an adjustable triangle.

In some situations, you might find that you do not want Polar Tracking on. You can turn it off by clicking the Polar button in the status bar. You can also press the F10 function key to turn Polar Tracking on or off.

TIP   In step 4, the coordinate readout displayed some extra values. The third coordinate that you see at the end of the coordinate readout listing indicates the Z value of the coordinate. This extra coordinate is significant only when you are doing 3D modeling; so for the time being, you can ignore it. If you'd like to know more about the additional Z-coordinate listing in the coordinate readout, see Chapter 20.

Although this exercise tells you to use the Line tool to draw the tank, you can also use the Rectangle tool. The Rectangle tool creates what is known as a *polyline,* which is a set of line or arc segments that acts like a single object. You'll learn more about polylines in Chapter 18.

By using the Snap modes in conjunction with the coordinate readout and Polar Tracking, you can locate coordinates and measure distances as you draw lines. This is similar to the way you draw when using a scale. The smallest distance registered by the coordinate readout and Polar Tracking readout depends on the area you have displayed on your screen. For example, if you are displaying an area the size of a football field, the smallest distance you can indicate with your cursor might be 6″ or 15 cm. On the other hand, if your view is enlarged to show an area of only one square inch or centimeter, you can indicate distances as small as $1/1000$ of an inch or centimeter by using your cursor.

Setting the Polar Tracking Angle

You've seen how Polar Tracking lets you draw exact vertical and horizontal lines. You can also set Polar Tracking to draw lines at other angles, such as 30° or 45°. To change the angle Polar Tracking uses, you use the Polar Tracking tab in the Drafting Settings dialog box.

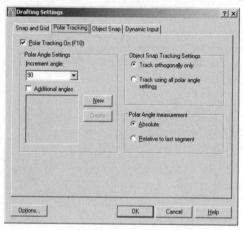

Right-click the Polar button in the status bar and then choose Settings from the shortcut menu to open the Drafting Settings dialog box. Or you can choose Tools ➢ Drafting Settings from the menu bar and then click the Polar Tracking tab.

THE ORTHO MODE

In addition to using the Polar Tracking mode, you can further restrain the cursor to a vertical or horizontal direction by using the Ortho mode. To use the Ortho mode, hold down the Shift key while drawing. You can also press F8 or click Ortho in the status bar to keep the Ortho mode on while you draw. When you move the cursor around while drawing objects, the rubber-banding line moves only vertically or horizontally. With the Ortho mode turned on, Polar Tracking is automatically turned off.

To change the Polar Tracking angle, enter an angle in the Increment Angle text box, or select a predefined angle from the drop-down list. You can do this while drawing a series of line segments, for example, so that you can set angles on the fly.

Numerous other settings are available in the Polar Tracking tab. Here is a listing of their functions for your reference:

Additional Angles This setting lets you enter a specific angle for Polar Tracking. For example, if you want Polar Tracking to snap to 12°, click the New button next to the Additional Angles list box and enter **12**. The value you enter appears in the list box, and when the Additional Angles check box is selected, Polar Tracking snaps to 12°. To delete a value from the list box, highlight it and click the Delete button.

The Additional Angles option differs from the Increment Angle setting in that the Increment Angle setting causes Polar Tracking to snap to every increment of its setting, whereas Additional Angles snaps only to the angle specified. You can enter as many angles as you want in the Additional Angles list box.

Object Snap Tracking Settings   These settings let you control whether Object Snap Tracking uses strictly orthogonal directions (0°, 90°, 180°, and 270°) or the angles set in the Polar Angle Settings group in this dialog box. (See the "Aligning Objects by Using Object Snap Tracking" section later in this chapter.)

Polar Angle Measurement   These radio buttons let you determine the zero angle on which Polar Tracking bases its incremental angles. The Absolute option uses the current AutoCAD setting for the 0° angle. The Relative To Last Segment option uses the last drawn object as the 0° angle. For example, if you draw a line at a 10° angle and the Relative To Last Segment option is selected with the Increment Angle set to 90°, Polar Tracking snaps to 10, 100°, 190°, and 280°, relative to the actual 0° direction.

Exploring the Drawing Process

This section presents some of the more common AutoCAD commands and shows you how to use them to complete a simple drawing. As you draw, watch the prompts and notice how your responses affect them. Also notice how you use existing drawing elements as reference points.

While drawing with AutoCAD, you create simple geometric forms to determine the basic shapes of objects, and you can then modify the shapes to fill in detail.

AutoCAD offers 14 basic 2D drawing object types: lines, arcs, circles, text, dimensions, traces, polylines, points, ellipses, elliptical arcs, spline curves, regions, hatches and multiline text. All drawings are built on these objects. In addition, there are five 3D meshes, which are three-dimensional surfaces composed of 3D Faces. You are familiar with lines and arcs; these, along with circles, are the most commonly used objects. As you progress through the book, you will learn about the other objects and how they are used. You'll also learn about 3D objects in the section on AutoCAD 3D.

Locating an Object in Reference to Others

To define the toilet seat, you will use an ellipse. Use these steps:

1. Click the Ellipse tool in the Draw toolbar or type **El**.↵. You can also choose Draw ➢ Ellipse ➢ Axis, End.

2. At the `Specify axis endpoint of ellipse or [Arc/Center]:` prompt, pick the midpoint of the bottom horizontal line of the rectangle. Do this by opening the Osnap pop-up menu and selecting Midpoint; then move the cursor toward the bottom line. (Remember, Shift+click the right mouse button to open the Osnap menu.) When you see the Midpoint Osnap marker on the line, click the left mouse button.

3. At the `Specify other endpoint of axis:` prompt, move the cursor down until the Polar Tracking readout lists 1′-10″ < 270°. Metric users should use a readout of 55.0000 < 270.

4. Pick this as the second axis endpoint.

5. At the `Specify distance to other axis or [Rotation]:` prompt, move the cursor horizontally from the center of the ellipse until the Polar Tracking readout lists 0′-8″ < 180°. Metric users should use a readout of 20.0000 < 180°.

6. Pick this as the axis distance defining the width of the ellipse. Your drawing should look like Figure 3.3.

TIP As you work with AutoCAD, you will eventually run into NURBS. NURBS stands for *Non-Uniform Rational B-Splines*—a fancy term meaning that curved objects are based on accurate mathematical models. When you trim the ellipse in a later exercise, it becomes a NURBS curve known as a spline in AutoCAD. You'll learn more about polylines and spline curves in Chapter 18.

FIGURE 3.3
The ellipse added to the tank

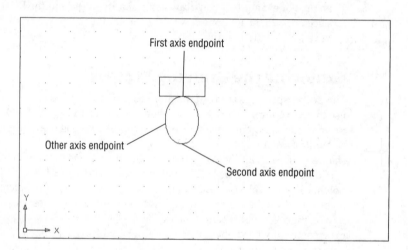

Getting a Closer Look

During the drawing process, you will often want to enlarge areas of a drawing to edit its objects. In Chapter 1, you saw how to use the Zoom capability for this purpose. Follow these steps to enlarge the view of the toilet:

1. Click the Zoom Window tool on the Standard toolbar or type **Z⏎W⏎**. You can also choose View ➢ Zoom ➢ Window.

2. At the `Specify first corner:` prompt, pick a point below and to the left of your drawing, at or near coordinate 5′-0″, 3′-6″. Metric users should use the coordinate of 150.0000,102.0000.

3. At the `Specify opposite corner:` prompt, pick a point above and to the right of the drawing, at or near coordinate 8′-3″, 6′-8″ (246.0000,195.0000 for metric users). The toilet should be completely enclosed by the zoom window. To obtain this view, use the Zoom Window tool. You can also use the Zoom Realtime tool in conjunction with the Pan Realtime tool. The toilet enlarges to fill more of the screen. Your view should look similar to Figure 3.4.

TIP To start the Zoom Realtime tool from the keyboard, type **Z**↵ ↵. If you have a mouse with a scroll wheel, you can avoid using the zoom command altogether; just place the cursor on the toilet and turn the wheel to zoom into the image.

Modifying an Object

Now let's see how editing commands are used to construct an object. To define the back edge of the seat, let's put a copy of the line defining the front of the toilet tank 3″ (7 cm for metric users) toward the center of the ellipse:

1. Click the Copy tool in the Modify toolbar or type **co**↵. You can also choose Modify ➢ Copy from the drop-down menu.

TIP You can also use the Grip Edit tools to make the copy. See Chapter 2 for more on grip editing.

2. At the Select objects: prompt, pick the horizontal line that touches the top of the ellipse. The line is highlighted. Press ↵ to complete your selection.

3. At the Specify base point or [Displacement} <Displacement>: prompt, pick a base point near the line. Then move the cursor down until the Polar Tracking readout lists 0′-3″ < 270° or 7.0000 < 270° for metric users.

4. Pick this point and then press ↵ to exit the Copy command. Your drawing should look like Figure 3.4.

FIGURE 3.4
The line copied down

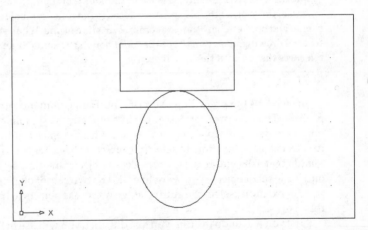

Notice that the Copy command acts exactly like the Move command you used in Chapter 2, except that Copy does not alter the position of the objects you select and you must press ↵ to exit Copy.

TRIMMING AN OBJECT

Now you must delete the part of the ellipse that is not needed. You will use the Trim command to trim off part of the ellipse:

1. Turn off the Snap mode by pressing F9 or clicking Snap in the status bar. Snap mode can be a hindrance at this point in your editing session because it can keep you from picking the points you want. Snap mode forces the cursor to move to points at a given interval, so you will have difficulty selecting a point that doesn't fall exactly at one of those intervals.

2. Click the Trim tool in the Modify toolbar. You will see this prompt:

```
Current settings: Projection=UCS Edge=None
Select cutting edges ...
Select objects or <select all>:
```

3. Click the line you just created—the one that crosses through the ellipse—and press ↵ to finish your selection.

4. At the `Select object to trim or shift-select to extend or [Fence/Crossing/ Project/Edge/eRase/Undo]`: prompt, pick the topmost portion of the ellipse above the line. This trims the ellipse back to the line.

5. Press ↵ to exit the Trim command.

TIP By holding down the Shift key in step 4, you can change from trimming an object to extending an object. You'll learn about the Extend command in Chapter 18.

ARCHITECTS AND THEIR SYMBOLS

You might be asking if there is a set of standard architectural measurements for common items, such as the aforementioned toilet tank. Some items, such as doors and kitchen appliances, do have "standard" sizes that architects learn in the course of their professional training. In this particular example, the 3-inch offset is arbitrary because the toilet symbol is just that, a symbol representing a toilet and not necessarily an exact representation of one. When you see a toilet symbol in an architectural drawing, it's saying "put the toilet here." The actual brand of toilet is specified in the written specs that go with the drawings.

In step 2 of the preceding exercise, the Trim command produces two messages in the prompt. The first prompt, `Select cutting edges...`, tells you that you must first select objects to define *the edge to which you want to trim an object*. In step 4, you are again prompted to select objects, this time to select the *objects to trim*. Trim is one of a handful of AutoCAD commands that asks you to select two sets of objects: the first set defines a boundary, and the second is the set of objects you want to edit. The two sets of objects are not mutually exclusive. You can, for example, select the cutting-edge objects as objects to trim. The next exercise shows how this works.

First you will undo the trim you just did; then you will use the Trim command again in a slightly different way to finish the toilet:

1. Click the Undo button in the Standard toolbar, or enter **U**↵ at the command prompt. The top of the ellipse reappears.

2. Start the Trim tool again by clicking it in the Modify toolbar.

3. At the `Select objects or <select all>`: prompt, click the ellipse and the line crossing the ellipse. (See the first image in Figure 3.5.)

FIGURE 3.5

Trimming the ellipse and the line

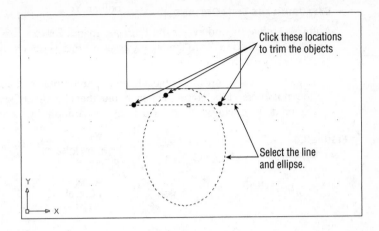

Click these locations to trim the objects

Select the line and ellipse.

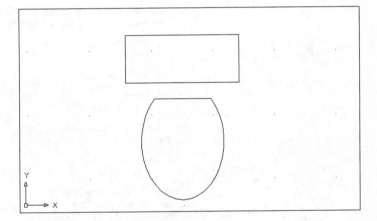

4. Press ↵ to finish your selection and move to the next step.

TIP These Trim options—Fence, Crossing, Project, Edge, eRase, and Undo—are described in the section "Exploring the Trim Options" next in this chapter.

5. At the Select object to trim or [Fence/Crossing/Project/Edge/eRase/Undo]: prompt, click the top portion of the ellipse, as you did in the previous exercise. The ellipse trims back.

6. Click a point near the left end of the trim line, past the ellipse. The line trims back to the ellipse.

7. Click the other end of the line. The right side of the line trims back to meet the ellipse. Your drawing should look like the second image in Figure 3.5.

8. Press ↵ to exit the Trim command.

9. Choose File ➢ Save to save the file in its current state but don't exit the file. You might want to get in the habit of doing this every 20 minutes.

Here you saw how the ellipse and the line are both used as trim objects, as well as the objects to be trimmed.

EXPLORING THE TRIM OPTIONS

AutoCAD offers six options for the Trim command: Fence, Crossing, Project, Edge, eRase, and Undo. As described in the following paragraphs, these options give you a higher degree of control over how objects are trimmed.

Edge [E]   Lets you trim an object to an apparent intersection, even if the cutting-edge object does not intersect the object to be trimmed. (See the top of Figure 3.6.) Edge offers two options: Extend and No Extend. You can also set these options by using the Edgemode system variable.

FIGURE 3.6

The Trim command's options

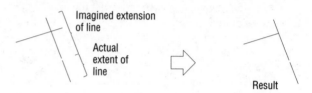

Imagined extension of line

Actual extent of line

Result

With the Extend option, objects will trim even if the trimmed object doesn't actually intersect with the object to be trimmed.

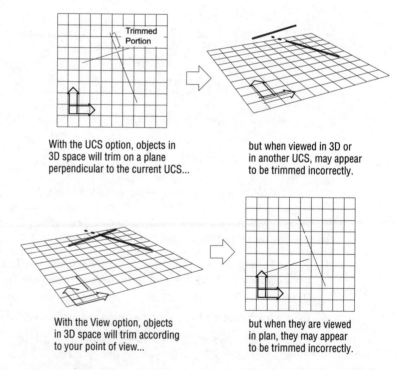

Trimmed Portion

With the UCS option, objects in 3D space will trim on a plane perpendicular to the current UCS...

but when viewed in 3D or in another UCS, may appear to be trimmed incorrectly.

With the View option, objects in 3D space will trim according to your point of view...

but when they are viewed in plan, they may appear to be trimmed incorrectly.

Project [P]   Useful when working on 3D drawings. It controls how AutoCAD trims objects that are not coplanar. Project offers three options: None, UCS, and View. The None option causes Trim to ignore objects that are on different planes so that only coplanar objects will be trimmed. If you choose

UCS, the Trim command trims objects based on a Plan view of the current UCS and then disregards whether the objects are coplanar. (See the middle of Figure 3.6.) View is similar to UCS but uses the current view's "line of sight" to determine how non-coplanar objects are trimmed. (See the bottom of Figure 3.6.)

eRase [R]   Allows you to erase an object while remaining in the Trim command.

Fence/Crossing [F or C]   Lets you use a Fence or Crossing window to select objects.

Undo [U]   Causes the last trimmed object to revert to its original length.

You've just seen one way to construct the toilet. However, you can construct objects in many ways. For example, you can trim only the top of the ellipse, as you did in the first Trim exercise, and then use the Grips feature to move the endpoints of the line to meet the endpoints of the ellipse. As you become familiar with AutoCAD, you will start to develop your own ways of working, using the tools best suited to your style.

If you'd like to take a break, now is a good time. You can exit AutoCAD and then come back to the Bath drawing file when you are ready to proceed.

SELECTING CLOSE OR OVERLAPPING OBJECTS

At times, you will want to select an object that is in close proximity to or lying underneath another object, and AutoCAD won't obey your mouse click. It's frustrating when you click the object you want to select, and AutoCAD selects the one next to it instead. To help you make your selections in these situations, AutoCAD provides Object Selection Cycling. To use it, hold down the Ctrl key while simultaneously clicking the object you want to select. If the wrong object is highlighted, press the left mouse button again (you do not need to hold down the Ctrl key for the second time), and the next object in close proximity is highlighted. If several objects are overlapping or close together, just continue to press the left mouse button until the correct object is highlighted. When the object you want is finally highlighted, press ⏎ and continue with further selections.

Planning and Laying Out a Drawing

For the next object, the bathtub, you will use some new commands to lay out parts of the drawing. This will help you get a feel for the kind of planning you must do to use AutoCAD effectively. You'll begin the bathtub by using the Line command to draw a rectangle 2′-8″ × 5′-0″ (81 cm × 152 cm for metric users) on the left side of the drawing area. For a change this time, you'll use a couple of shortcut methods built into AutoCAD: the Line command's keyboard shortcut and the Direct Distance method for specifying distance and direction.

First, though, you'll go back to the previous view of your drawing and arrange some more room to work. Follow these steps:

1. Return to your previous view, the one in Figure 3.7. A quick way to do this is to click the Zoom Previous tool on the Standard toolbar, or choose View ➤ Zoom ➤ Previous. Your view returns to the one you had before the last Zoom command (see Figure 3.7).

2. Turn on the Grid Snap mode by right-clicking the Snap button on the status bar and choosing Grid Snap On from the shortcut menu.

FIGURE 3.7

The view of the finished toilet after using the Zoom Previous tool. You can also obtain this view by using the Zoom All tool from the Zoom Window flyout.

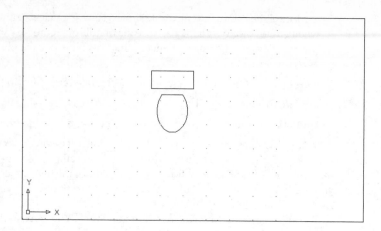

3. Type **L**↵ and pick the coordinate location 0´-9↵,0´-10↵ at the Specify first point: prompt. Metric users use the coordinate 24.0000,27.0000. You can either use the cursor in conjunction with the coordinate readout or enter the coordinate from the keyboard. (Metric users can leave off the zero decimal values while entering coordinates through the keyboard.)

4. Place your cursor to the right of the last point selected so that the rubber-banding line is pointing directly to the right and type **2´8**↵; then press ↵ for the first side of the tub. Metric users should enter **81**↵. Notice that the rubber-banding line is now fixed at the length you typed.

5. Now point the rubber-banding line upward toward the top of the screen and type **5´**; then press ↵ for the next side. Metric users should enter **152**↵.

6. Point the rubber-banding line directly to the left of the last point and type **2´8**↵ (**81** for metric users); then press ↵ for the next side.

7. Type **C**↵ to close the rectangle and exit the Line command.

TIP Instead of pressing ↵ during the Direct Distance method, you can press the spacebar or right-click and choose Enter from the shortcut menu.

Now you have the outline of the tub. Notice that when you enter feet and inches from the keyboard, you must avoid hyphens or spaces. Thus, 2 feet 8 inches is typed as **2´8˝**. Also notice that you didn't have to enter the at sign (@) or angle specification. Instead, you used the Direct Distance method for specifying direction and distance. You can use this method for drawing lines or moving and copying objects at right angles. The Direct Distance method is less effective if you want to specify exact angles other than right angles.

Some of the keyboard shortcuts for tools or commands you've used in this chapter are CO (Copy), E (Erase), EL (Ellipse), F (Fillet), M (Move), O (Offset), and TR (Trim). Remember that you can enter keyboard shortcuts, such as keyboard commands, only when the Command prompt is visible in the Command window.

Making a Preliminary Sketch

In this section, you'll see how planning ahead will make your use of AutoCAD more efficient. When drawing a complex object, you will often have to do some layout before you do the actual drawing. This is similar to drawing an accurate pencil sketch using construction lines that you later trace over to produce a finished drawing. The advantage of doing this in AutoCAD is that your drawing doesn't lose any accuracy between the sketch and the final product. Also, AutoCAD enables you to use the geometry of your sketch to aid you in drawing. While planning your drawing, think about what you want to draw and then decide which drawing elements will help you create that object.

You will use the Offset command to establish reference lines to help you draw the inside of the tub. This is where the Osnap overrides are quite useful. (See "The Osnap Options" sidebar later in this chapter.)

You can use the Offset tool on the Modify toolbar to make parallel copies of a set of objects, such as the lines forming the outside of your tub. Offset is different from the Copy command; Offset allows only one object to be copied at a time, but it can remember the distance you specify. The Offset option does not work with all types of objects. Only lines, arcs, circles, ellipses, splines and 2D polylines can be offset.

Standard lines are best suited for the layout of the bathtub in this situation. In Chapter 6 you will learn about two other objects, construction lines (Xlines) and rays, which are specifically designed to help you lay out a drawing. In this exercise, you will use standard lines:

1. Click the Offset tool in the Modify toolbar or type **O**↵. You can also choose Modify ➢ Offset from the drop-down menu.

2. At the `Specify offset distance or [Through/Erase/Layer] <Through>:` prompt, enter **3**↵. This specifies the distance of 3″ as the offset distance. Metric users should enter **7** for 7 cm, which is roughly equivalent to 3 inches.

3. At the `Select object to offset or [Exit/Undo] <Exit>:` prompt, click the bottom line of the rectangle you just drew.

4. At the `Specify point on side to offset or [Exit/Multiple/Undo]:` prompt, pick a point inside the rectangle. A copy of the line appears. You don't have to be exact about where you pick the side to offset; AutoCAD wants to know only on which side of the line you want to make the offset copy.

5. The prompt `Select object to offset or [Exit/Undo] <Exit>:` appears again. Click another side to offset; then click again on a point inside the rectangle.

6. Continue to offset the other two sides; then offset these four new lines inside the rectangle toward the center. You will have a drawing that looks like Figure 3.8.

7. When you are done, exit the Offset command by pressing ↵.

FIGURE 3.8
The completed layout

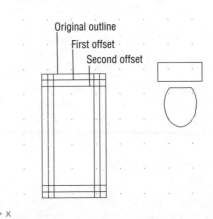

Using the Layout

Now you will begin to draw the inside of the tub, starting with the narrow end. You will use your offset lines as references to construct the arcs that make up the tub. Also in this exercise, you'll set up some of the Osnap tools to be available automatically whenever AutoCAD expects a point selection. Here are the steps:

1. Choose Tools ➢ Drafting Settings and then click the Object Snap tab. You can also type **Ds↵**, or right-click the Osnap button on the status bar and then choose Settings from the shortcut menu.

2. Click the Clear All button to turn off any options that might be selected.

TIP Take a look at the graphic symbols next to each of the Osnap options in the Object Snap tab. These are the Osnap markers that appear in your drawing as you select Osnap points. Each Osnap option has its own marker symbol. As you work with the Osnaps, you'll become more familiar with how they work.

3. Click the Endpoint, Midpoint, and Intersection check boxes so that a checkmark appears in the boxes, and make sure the Object Snap On option is selected; then click OK.

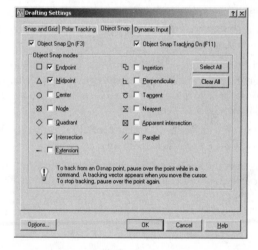

You've just set up the Endpoint, Midpoint, and Intersection Osnaps to be on by default. This is called a *Running Osnap*; AutoCAD automatically selects the nearest Osnap point without your intervention. Now let's see how a Running Osnap works:

1. In the Draw toolbar, click the Arc tool or type **a↵**. See Figure 3.9 for other Arc options available when you choose Draw ➢ Arc.

FIGURE 3.9

If you look at the Arc cascading menu, you'll see some additional options for drawing arcs. These options provide "canned" responses to the Arc command so that you only have to select the appropriate points as indicated in the drop-down menu option name.

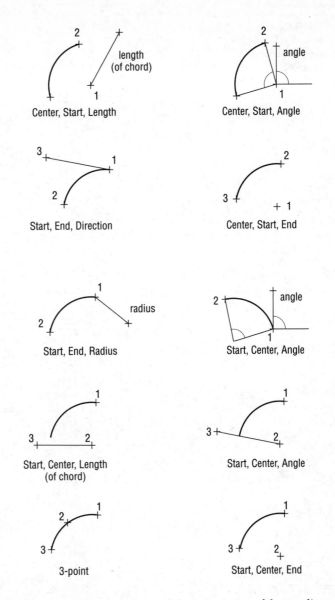

Center, Start, Length

Center, Start, Angle

Start, End, Direction

Center, Start, End

Start, End, Radius

Start, Center, Angle

Start, Center, Length (of chord)

Start, Center, Angle

3-point

Start, Center, End

2. For the first point of the arc, move the cursor toward the intersection of the two lines as indicated in the top image in Figure 3.10. Notice that the Intersection Osnap marker appears on the intersection.

FIGURE 3.10
Drawing the top, left
side, and bottom of
the tub

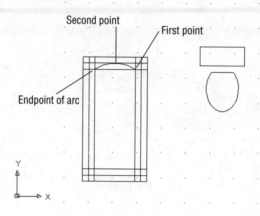

Second point

First point

Endpoint of arc

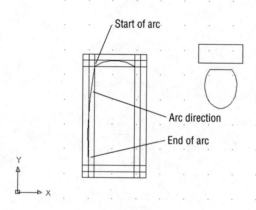

Start of arc

Arc direction

End of arc

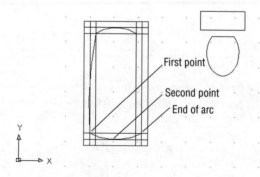

First point

Second point

End of arc

3. With the Intersection Osnap marker on the desired intersection, click the left mouse button.

4. Now move the cursor to the midpoint of the second horizontal line near the top. When the Midpoint Osnap marker appears at the midpoint of the line, click the left mouse button.

5. Finally, use the Intersection Osnap marker to locate and select the intersection of the two lines at the upper-left side of the bathtub.

The top image in Figure 3.10 shows the sequence I just described.

TIP When you see an Osnap marker on an object, you can have AutoCAD move to the next Osnap point on the object by pressing the Tab key. If you have several Running Osnap modes on (Endpoint, Midpoint, and Intersection, for example), pressing the Tab key cycles through those Osnap points on the object. This feature can be especially useful in a crowded area of a drawing.

ADJUSTING THE AUTOSNAP FEATURE

When you click the Options button in the Object Snap tab of the Drafting Settings dialog box, you'll see the Drafting Settings tab of the Options dialog box. This tab offers a set of options pertaining to the AutoSnap feature. AutoSnap looks at the location of your cursor during Osnap selections and locates the Osnap point nearest your cursor. AutoSnap then displays a graphic called a marker showing you the Osnap point it has found. If it is the one you want, you simply left-click your mouse to select it.

The AutoSnap settings enable you to control its various features:

Marker turns the graphic marker on or off.

Magnet causes the Osnap cursor to "jump to" inferred Osnap points.

Display AutoSnap Tooltip turns the Osnap tool tip on or off.

Display AutoSnap Aperture Box turns the old-style Osnap cursor box on or off.

AutoSnap Marker Size controls the size of the graphic marker.

Color controls the color of the AutoSnap marker. This option opens the Drawing Window Colors dialog box which lets you select a color.

Next, you will draw an arc for the left side of the tub:

1. In the Draw toolbar, click the Arc tool again.

2. Type @↵ to select the last point you picked as the start of the next arc.

WARNING It's easy for new users to select points inadvertently. If you accidentally select additional points after the last exercise and prior to step 1, you might not get the results described here. If this happens, issue the Arc command again, then use the Endpoint Osnap, and select the endpoint of the last arc.

3. Type **E**↵ to tell AutoCAD that you want to specify the other end of the arc, instead of the next point. Or you can right-click anywhere in the drawing area and choose End from the shortcut menu.

4. At the Specify end point of arc: prompt, use the Intersection Osnap to pick the intersection of the two lines in the lower-left corner of the tub. See the middle image in Figure 3.10 for the location of this point.

5. Type **D**↵ to select the Direction option. You can also right-click anywhere in the drawing area and then choose Direction from the shortcut menu. The arc drags as you move the cursor, along with a rubber-banding line from the starting point of the arc.

6. Move the cursor to the left of the dragging arc until it touches the middle line on the left side of the tub. Then pick that, as shown in the middle image in Figure 3.10.

TIP In step 3, the rubber-banding line indicates the direction of the arc. Be sure Ortho mode is off, because Ortho mode forces the rubber-banding line and the arc in a direction you don't want. Check the status bar; if the Ortho button looks like it's pressed, press F8 or click the Ortho button to turn off Ortho mode.

Now you will draw the bottom of the tub:

1. Click the Arc tool in the Draw toolbar again. You can also press ↵ to replay the last command.

2. Using the Endpoint Osnap marker, pick the endpoint of the bottom of the arc just drawn.

3. Using the Midpoint Osnap marker, pick the middle horizontal line at the bottom of the tub.

4. Finally, pick the intersection of the two lines in the lower-right corner of the tub (see the image at the bottom in Figure 3.10).

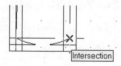

Now create the right side of the tub by mirroring the left side:

1. Click the Mirror tool on the Modify toolbar. You can also choose Modify ➤ Mirror or enter **mi**↵ at the Command prompt.

2. At the Select objects: prompt, pick the long arc on the left side of the tub to highlight the arc. Press ↵ to indicate that you've finished your selection.

3. At the `Specify first point of mirror line:` prompt, pick the midpoint of the top horizontal line. By now, you should know how to use the automatic Osnap modes you set up earlier.

4. At the `Specify second point of mirror line:` prompt, use the Polar Tracking mode to pick a point directly below the last point selected.

5. At the `Erase source objects? [Yes/No] <N>:` prompt, press ↵ to accept the default, No. A mirror image of the arc you picked appears on the right side of the tub. Your drawing should look like Figure 3.11.

FIGURE 3.11
The inside of the tub completed with the layout lines still in place

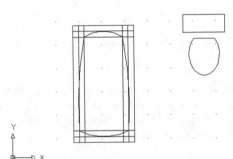

In this exercise, you were able to use the osnaps in a Running Osnap mode. You'll find that you will use the osnaps nearly all the time as you create your drawings. For this reason, you might want Running Osnaps on all the time. Even so, at times Running Osnaps can get in the way. For example, they might be a nuisance in a crowded drawing when you want to use a zoom window. The osnaps can cause you to select an inappropriate window area by automatically selecting osnap points.

Fortunately, you can turn Running Osnaps on and off quite easily by clicking the Osnap button in the status bar. This toggles the Running Osnaps on or off. If you don't have any Running Osnaps set, clicking the Osnap button opens the Object Snap settings in the Drafting Settings dialog box, enabling you to select your osnaps.

Erasing the Layout Lines

Next, you will erase the layout lines you created using the Offset command. But this time, you'll try selecting the lines *before* issuing the Erase command.

TIP If the following exercise doesn't work as described, be sure you have the Noun/Verb selection setting turned on. See Appendix A for details.

Follow these steps:

1. Click each internal layout line individually.

   If you have problems selecting just the lines, try using a selection window to select single lines. (Remember, a window selects only objects that are completely within the window.) You might also try the Object Selection Cycling option, as explained earlier in this chapter in the "Selecting Close or Overlapping Objects" sidebar.

2. After all the layout lines are highlighted, enter **E.**⏎ to use the keyboard shortcut for the Erase command, or right-click and choose Erase from the shortcut menu. Your drawing will look like Figure 3.12.

FIGURE 3.12
The drawing after erasing the layout lines

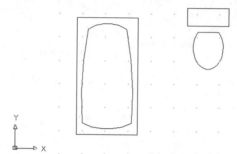

If you right-click to use the shortcut menu in step 2, you'll notice that you have several options besides Erase. You can move, copy, scale, and rotate the objects you selected. These options act just like the standard Modify toolbar options. Be aware that these commands act somewhat differently from the hot-grip options described in Chapter 2.

TIP If you need more control over the selection of objects, you will find the Add/Remove Selection Mode setting useful. This setting lets you deselect a set of objects within a set of objects you've already selected. While in Object Selection mode, enter **R.**⏎; then proceed to use a window or other selection tool to remove objects from the selection set. Enter **A.**⏎ to continue to add options to the selection set. Or if you need to deselect only a single object, Shift+click it.

TIP When preparing to erase an object that is close to other objects, you might want to select the object first, using the Noun/Verb selection method. This way you can carefully select objects you want to erase before you actually invoke the Erase command.

THE OSNAP OPTIONS

In the previous exercise, you made several of the Osnap settings automatic so that they were available without having to select them from the Osnap pop-up menu. Another way to invoke the Osnap options is by typing their keyboard equivalents while selecting points or by Shift+right-clicking while selecting points to open the Osnap shortcut menu.

Here is a summary of all the available Osnap options, including their keyboard shortcuts. You've already used many of these options in this chapter and in the previous chapter. Pay special attention to those options you haven't yet used in the exercises but might find useful to your style of work. The full name of each option is followed by its keyboard shortcut name in brackets. To use these options, you can enter either the full name or the abbreviation at any point prompt. You can also select these options from the pop-up menu obtained by Shift+clicking the right mouse button.

Tip: Sometimes you'll want one or more of these Osnap options available as the default selection. Remember that you can set Running Osnaps to be on at all times. Choose Tools ➢ Drafting Settings from the menu bar, and then click the Object Snap tab. You can also right-click the Osnap button in the status bar and choose Settings from the shortcut menu.

Available Osnap options (in alphabetic order):

Apparent Intersection [app]   Selects the apparent intersection of two objects. This is useful when you want to select the intersection of two objects that do not actually intersect. You will be prompted to select the two objects.

Center [cen]   Selects the center of an arc or a circle. You must click the arc or circle itself, not its apparent center.

Endpoint [endp or end]   Selects all the endpoints of lines, polylines, arcs, curves, and 3D Face vertices.

Extension [ext]   Selects a point that is aligned with an imagined extension of a line. For example, you can pick a point in space that is aligned with an existing line but is not actually on that line. To use that point, type **ext.** during point selection or select Extension from the Osnap pop-up menu; then move the cursor to the line whose extension you want to use and hold it there until you see a small, cross-shaped marker on the line. The cursor also displays a tool tip with the word *extension* letting you know that the Extension Osnap is active.

From [fro]   Selects a point relative to a picked point. For example, you can select a point that is 2 units to the left and 4 units above a circle's center. This option is usually used in conjunction with another Osnap option, such as From Endpoint or From Midpoint.

Insert [ins]   Selects the insertion point of text, blocks, Xrefs, and overlays.

Intersection [int]   Selects the intersection of objects.

Mid Between 2 Points [m2p]   Selects a point that is midway between two other points.

Midpoint [mid]   Selects the midpoint of a line or an arc. In the case of a polyline, it selects the midpoint of the polyline segment.

Nearest [nea]   Selects a point on an object nearest the pick point.

Node [nod]   Selects a point object.

None [non]   Temporarily turns off Running Osnaps.

Parallel [par]   Lets you draw a line segment that is parallel to another existing line segment. To use this option, type **par.** during point selection or select Parallel from the Osnap pop-up menu; then move the cursor to the line you want to be parallel to and hold it there until you see a small, cross-shaped marker on the line. The cursor also displays a tool tip with the word *parallel* letting you know that the Parallel Osnap is active.

Perpendicular [per]   Selects a position on an object that is perpendicular to the last point selected. Normally, this option is not valid for the first point selected in a string of points.

Point Filters   Not really object snaps but point selection options that let you filter X, Y, or Z coordinate values from a selected point. (See Chapter 20 for more on point filters.)

Quadrant [qua]   Selects the nearest cardinal (north, south, east, or west) point on an arc or a circle.

Tangent [tan]   Selects a point on an arc or a circle that represents the tangent from the last point selected. Like the Perpendicular option, Tangent is not valid for the first point in a string of points.

Temporary Track Point   Provides an alternate method for using the Object Snap Tracking feature described later in this chapter. (See Chapter 15 for more on Temporary Track Point.)

Putting On the Finishing Touches

The inside of the tub still has some sharp corners. To round out these corners, you can use the versatile Fillet command on the Modify toolbar. Fillet enables you to join lines and arcs end to end, and it can add a radius where they join, so there is a smooth transition from arc to arc or line to line. Fillet can join two lines that do not intersect, and it can trim two crossing lines back to their point of intersection:

1. Click the Fillet tool on the Modify toolbar or type **f↵**. You can also choose Modify ➢ Fillet from the menu bar.

2. At the prompt

   ```
   Current settings: Mode = TRIM, Radius = 0'-0½
   Select first object or [Undo/Polyline/Radius/Trim/Multiple]:
   ```

   enter **R↵**, or right-click and choose Radius from the shortcut menu.

3. At the Specify fillet radius <0'-0½">: prompt, enter **4↵**. This tells AutoCAD that you want a 4″ radius for your fillet. Metric users will see a value of <10.0000> for the default radius. Go ahead and keep this value, but keep in mind that you can alter the radius value at this prompt.

4. Pick two adjacent arcs. The fillet arc joins the two larger arcs.

5. Press ↵ again and fillet another corner. Repeat until all four corners are filleted. Your drawing should look like Figure 3.13.

6. Save and close the Bath file.

FIGURE 3.13
A view of the finished toilet and tub with the tub corners filleted

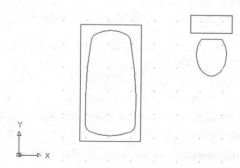

Aligning Objects by Using Object Snap Tracking

You saw how to use lines to construct an object such as the bathtub. In many situations, using these *construction lines* is the most efficient way to draw, but they can also be a bit cumbersome. AutoCAD 2007 offers another tool that helps you align locations in your drawing to existing objects without having to draw intermediate construction lines. The tool is called *Object Snap Tracking* or *Osnap Tracking*.

Osnap Tracking is like an extension of Object Snaps that enables you to *align* a point to the geometry of an object instead of just selecting a point on an object. For example, with Osnap Tracking, you can select a point that is exactly at the center of a rectangle.

In the following exercises, you will draw a Plan view of a bathroom sink as an introduction to the Osnap Tracking feature. This drawing will be used as a symbol in later chapters.

WARNING   The Object Snap Tracking feature is not available in AutoCAD LT 2007. If you are using LT, follow along with the tutorial until you are asked to draw the ellipse to represent the bowl of the sink. Go ahead and draw an ellipse approximating the shape and size of the one in the tutorial. In Chapter 15, you will learn about the Temporary Tracking feature, which is available in LT as well as AutoCAD and is similar to the Object Snap Tracking feature.

A QUICK SETUP

First, as a review, you'll open a new file by using the Create New Drawing Wizard. Because this drawing will be used as a symbol for insertion in other CAD drawings, don't worry about setting it up to conform to a sheet size. Chances are, you won't be printing individual symbols. Here are the steps:

1. Choose File ➢ New to create a new drawing for your bathroom sink.

2. Click the Use A Wizard button in the Create New Drawing dialog box, select Quick Setup from the list that appears below the buttons, and then click OK.

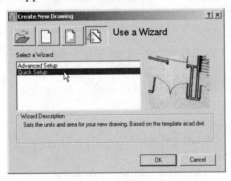

3. In the Units screen, choose Architectural; then click Next. Metric users can use the Decimal option. This option performs the same operation as the Drawing Units dialog box you saw earlier in this chapter.

4. In the Area screen, enter **48** for the width and **36** for the length. Metric users should enter **122** for the width and **92** for the length. Then click Finish. This option performs the same operation as choosing Format ➢ Drawing Limits from the menu bar.

5. Click the Grid button in the status bar, and then choose View ➢ Zoom ➢ All from the menu bar. This enables you to see your entire work area.

6. Choose File ➢ Save As to save the file under the name **Sink**.

As you saw in steps 3 and 4, the Create New Drawing Wizard simplifies the drawing setup process by limiting the options you need to work with.

TIP If you find that you use the same drawing setup over and over, you can create template files that are already set up to your own, customized way of working. Templates are discussed in Chapter 5.

USING AUTOCAD'S AUTOMATIC SAVE FEATURE

As you work with AutoCAD, you might notice that AutoCAD periodically saves your work for you. Your file is saved not as its current filename, but as a file with the .sv$ file name extension. The.sv$ file is really an AutoCAD .dwg file with the .sv$ filename extension added to make it distinguishable from other files you might be using. You can find this file in the `C:\Documents and Settings\User Name\Local Settings\Temp folder`. If you prefer, you can specify another location by modifying the information in the Files tab of the Options dialog box. See Appendix A for details.

In Chapter 1, you used the Options dialog box to change the interval between automatic saves to 20 minutes. You can also change this interval by doing the following:

1. Enter **Savetime.** at the Command prompt.

2. At the `Enter new value for SAVETIME <20>:` prompt, enter the desired interval in minutes. Or, to disable the automatic save feature entirely, enter **0** at the prompt.

DRAWING THE SINK

Now you're ready to draw the sink. First, you'll draw the sink countertop. Then you'll make sure Running Osnaps and Osnap Tracking are turned on. Finally, you'll draw the bowl of the sink.
Here are the steps for drawing the outline of the sink countertop:

1. Click the Grid button in the status bar to turn off the grid. It was helpful to let you see the work area, but you don't need it now.

2. Click the Rectangle tool in the Draw toolbar or type **rec.**.

3. At the prompt

   `Specify first corner point or [Chamfer/Elevation/Fillet/Thickness/Width]:`

   enter **0,0.**. This places one corner of the rectangle in the origin of the drawing.

4. At the `Specify other corner point or [Area/Dimensions/Rotation]:` prompt, enter @2′4,1′6.. Metric users should enter @71,46.. This makes the rectangle 2′-4″ wide by 1′-6″ deep, or 71 cm by 46 cm for metric users. The rectangle appears in the lower half of the drawing area.

5. Choose View ➢ Zoom ➢ Extents to enlarge the view of the sink outline. Then use the Zoom Realtime tool in the Standard toolbar to adjust your view so it looks similar to the one shown in Figure 3.14.

   When you draw the bowl of the sink, the bowl will be represented by an ellipse. You'll want to place the center of the ellipse at the center of the rectangle you've just drawn. To do this, you will use the midpoint of two adjoining sides of the rectangle as alignment locations. This is where the Osnap Tracking tool will be useful.

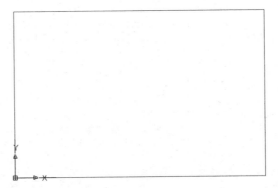

Therefore, you need to make sure Running Osnaps are turned on and that they are set to the Midpoint option. Then you'll make sure Osnap Tracking is turned on. Use these steps:

1. Right-click the Otrack button in the status bar and choose Settings from the shortcut menu to open the Drafting Settings dialog box at the Object Snap tab.

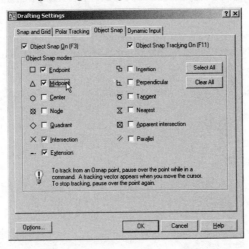

2. Make sure that the Midpoint check box in the Object Snap Modes group is selected.

3. Make sure also that Object Snap On and Object Snap Tracking On are both selected. Click OK. You'll notice that the Osnap and Otrack buttons in the status bar are now in the on position.

Finally, you are ready to draw the ellipse:

1. Click the Ellipse tool in the Draw toolbar or enter **El**↵.

2. At the `Specify axis endpoint of ellipse or [Arc/Center]:` prompt, type **C** or right-click and choose Center from the shortcut menu.

3. Move your cursor to the top, horizontal edge of the rectangle, until you see the midpoint tool tip.

4. Now move the cursor directly over the Midpoint Osnap marker. Without clicking the mouse, hold the cursor there for a second until you see a small cross appear. Look carefully because the cross is quite small. This is the Osnap Tracking marker.

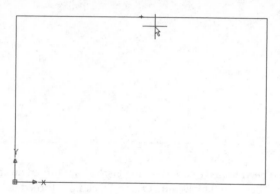

TIP You can alternately insert and remove the Osnap Tracking marker by passing the cursor over the Osnap marker.

5. Now as you move the cursor downward, a dotted line appears, emanating from the midpoint of the horizontal line. The cursor also shows a small X following the dotted line as you move it.

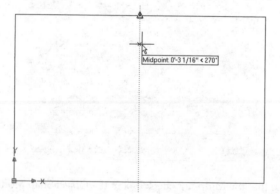

6. Move the cursor to the midpoint of the left vertical side of the rectangle. Don't click, but hold it there for a second until you see the small cross. Now as you move the cursor away, a horizontal dotted line appears with an X following the cursor.

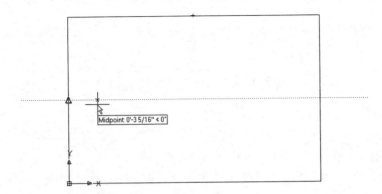

7. Move the cursor to the center of the rectangle. The two dotted lines appear simultaneously, and a small X appears at their intersection.

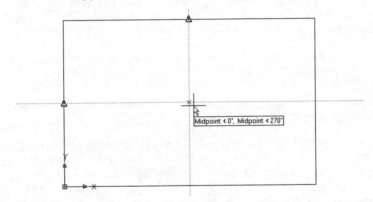

8. With the two dotted lines crossing and the X at their intersection, click the left mouse button to select the exact center of the rectangle.

9. Point the cursor to the right and enter **8.⏎** to make the width of the bowl 16″. Metric users should enter **20.⏎** for a bowl 400 cm wide.

10. Point the cursor downward and enter **6.⏎** to make the length of the bowl 12″. Metric users should enter **15.⏎** for a bowl with a length of 30 cm. The basic symbol for the sink is complete (see Figure 3.15).

FIGURE 3.15
The completed bath-
room sink

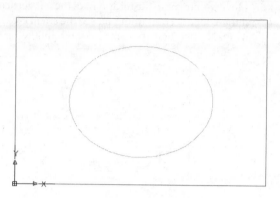

11. Choose File ➢ Save. You can exit AutoCAD now and take a break.

In this exercise, you saw how Osnap Tracking enabled you to align two locations to select a point in space. Although you used only the Midpoint Osnap setting in this exercise, you are not limited to only one Osnap setting. You can use as many as you need to in order to select the appropriate geometry. You can also use as many alignment points as you need, although in this exercise, you used only two. If you like, erase the ellipse and repeat this exercise until you get the hang of using the Osnap Tracking feature.

TIP As with all the other buttons in the status bar, you can turn Osnap Tracking on or off by click-ing the Otrack button.

ALIGNING WITH GRIPS

Osnaps, in conjunction with grips, offer a feature similar to Osnap Tracking that lets you align a grip with the direction of a line or an arc. Here's how it works. Select the line to which you want to be aligned so that its grips are displayed. Select the grip of another object that you want to edit, and then hover over the endpoint grip of the first line you selected. As you move your cursor away from the grip, an align-ment vector appears that is aligned with the first line. Your cursor will then "snap" to the line and the vector it describes. As you move the cursor, it will stay along the vector described by the line.

You can also hover over the endpoint grips of two lines or a line and an arc to find their intersection. Or you can quickly extend the length of a line or an arc using this method. Click the endpoint grip of a line, for example, hover over it until a cross appears, and then drag the endpoint along the direction of the line to lengthen or shorten it. This also works with grips in a polyline.

If You Want to Experiment

As you draw, you will notice that you are alternately creating objects and then copying and editing them. This is where the difference between hand drafting and CAD really begins to show.

Try drawing the wide flange beam shown in Figure 3.16. The figure shows you what to do, step by step. Notice how you apply the concepts of layout and editing to this drawing. Of course, this is just one way to draw a wide flange. Think of other ways you might construct this item.

FIGURE 3.16
Drawing a wide
flange beam

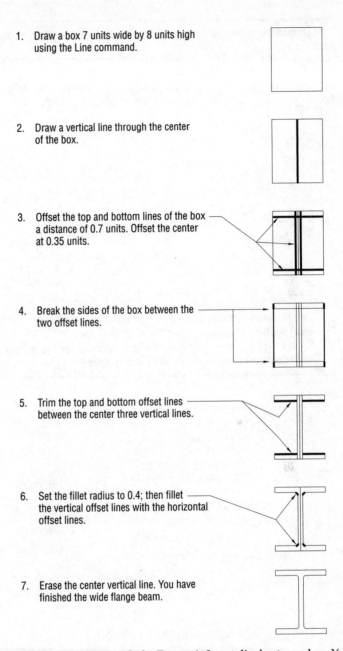

1. Draw a box 7 units wide by 8 units high using the Line command.

2. Draw a vertical line through the center of the box.

3. Offset the top and bottom lines of the box a distance of 0.7 units. Offset the center at 0.35 units.

4. Break the sides of the box between the two offset lines.

5. Trim the top and bottom offset lines between the center three vertical lines.

6. Set the fillet radius to 0.4; then fillet the vertical offset lines with the horizontal offset lines.

7. Erase the center vertical line. You have finished the wide flange beam.

Try drawing the wide flange a second time with the Dynamic Input display turned on. You can turn on the Dynamic Input display by clicking the DYN button in the status bar. Remember that command selection and input still work the same while Dynamic Input display is turned on. The difference is that you can watch the prompts (minus the bracketed list of options) at the cursor instead of having to look at the Command window. You'll also see the dimension of objects as you draw them.

USING OSNAP TRACKING AND POLAR TRACKING TOGETHER

In addition to selecting as many tracking points as you need, you can also use different angles besides the basic orthogonal angles of 0°, 90°, 180°, and 270°. For example, you can have AutoCAD locate a point that is aligned vertically to the top edge of the sink and at a 45° angle from a corner.

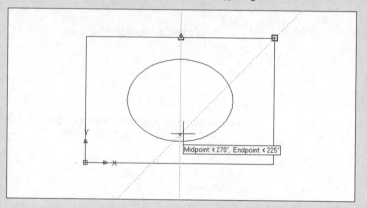

This can be accomplished by using the settings in the Polar Tracking tab of the Drafting Settings dialog box. (See the "Setting the Polar Tracking Angle" section earlier in this chapter.) If you set the increment angle to 45° and turn on the Track Using All Polar Angle Settings option, you will be able to use 45° in addition to the orthogonal directions. You'll see firsthand how this works in Chapter 5.

Chapter 4

Organizing Objects with Blocks and Groups

Drawing the tub, toilet, and sink in Chapter 3 might have taken what seemed to you an inordinate amount of time. As you continue to use AutoCAD, however, you will learn to draw objects more quickly. You will also need to draw fewer of them because you can save drawings as symbols and use them like rubber stamps, duplicating drawings instantaneously wherever they are needed. This saves a lot of time when you're composing drawings.

To make effective use of AutoCAD, begin a *symbol library* of drawings you use frequently. A mechanical designer might have a library of symbols for fasteners, cams, valves, or any type of parts for their application. An electrical engineer might have a symbol library of capacitors, resistors, switches, and the like. A circuit designer will have yet another unique set of frequently used symbols. This book's companion CD contains a variety of ready-to-use symbol libraries. Check them out—you're likely to find some you can use.

In Chapter 3, you drew three objects—a bathtub, toilet, and sink—that architects often use. In this chapter, you will see how to create symbols from those drawings.

This chapter includes the following topics:

◆ Creating and Inserting a Symbol

◆ Modifying a Block

◆ Inserting Symbols with Drag-and-Drop

◆ Grouping Objects

Creating a Symbol

To save a drawing as a symbol, you use the Block tool. In word processors, the term *block* refers to a group of words or sentences selected for moving, saving, or deleting. You can copy a block of text elsewhere within the same file, to other files, or to a separate file or disk for future use. AutoCAD uses blocks in a similar fashion. Within a file, you can turn parts of your drawing into blocks that can be saved and recalled at any time. You can also use entire existing files as blocks.

You'll start by opening the file you worked on in the last chapter and selecting the objects that will become a block.

1. Start AutoCAD, and open the existing Bath file. Use the one you created in Chapter 3, or open 04-bath.dwg on the companion CD. Metric users can use the 04-bath-metric.dwg file. The drawing appears just as you left it in the last session.

2. In the Draw toolbar, click the Make Block tool or type **B.**↵, the keyboard shortcut for the Make Block tool, to open the Block Definition dialog box. You can also choose Draw ➢ Block ➢ Make.

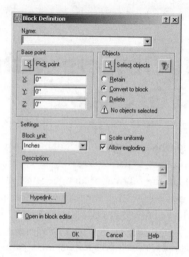

3. In the Name text box, type **Toilet**.

4. In the Base Point group, click the Pick Point button. This option enables you to select a base point for the block by using your cursor. (The insertion base point of a block is a point of reference on the block that is used like a grip.) When you've selected this option, the Block Definition dialog box temporarily closes.

TIP   Notice that the Block Definition dialog box gives you the option to specify the X, Y, and Z coordinates for the base point, instead of selecting a point.

5. Using the Midpoint Osnap, pick the midpoint of the back of the toilet as the base point. Remember that you learned how to set up some Running Osnaps in Chapter 3; all you need to do is point to the midpoint of a line to display the Midpoint Osnap marker and then left-click your mouse.

After you've selected a point, the Block Definition dialog box reappears. Notice that the X, Y, and Z values in the Base Point group now display the coordinates of the point you picked. For two-dimensional drawings, the Z coordinate should remain at 0.

Next, you need to select the actual objects you want as part of the block.

1. Click the Select Objects button in the Objects group. Once again, the dialog box momentarily closes. You now see the familiar object selection prompt in the Command window, and the cursor becomes an Object Selection cursor. Click a point below and to the left of the toilet. Then use a selection window to select the entire toilet. The toilet is now highlighted.

WARNING Make sure you use the Select Objects option in the Block Definition dialog box to select the objects you want to turn into a block. AutoCAD lets you create a block that contains no objects. If you try to proceed without selecting objects, you will get a warning message. This can cause some confusion and frustration, even for an experienced user.

2. Press ↵ to confirm your selection. The Block Definition dialog box opens again.

3. Select Inches from the Block Unit drop-down list. Metric users should select Centimeters.

4. Click the Description list box and enter **Standard Toilet**.

5. Make sure the Retain radio button in the Objects group is selected, and then click OK. The toilet drawing is now a block with the name Toilet.

6. Repeat the blocking process for the tub, but this time use the upper-left corner of the tub as the insertion base point and give the block the name Tub. Enter **Standard Tub** for the description.

SYMBOLS FOR PROJECTS LARGE AND SMALL

A symbol library was a crucial part of the production of the San Francisco Main Library construction documents. Shown here is a portion of an AutoCAD floor plan of the library in which some typical symbols were used.

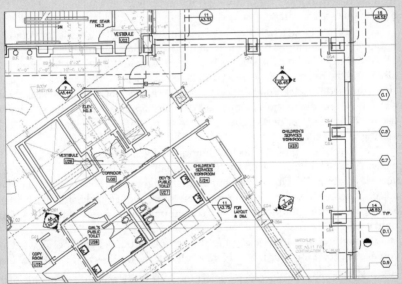

Notice the familiar door symbols, such as the door you created in Chapter 2. And, yes, there are even toilets in the lower half of the plan in the public restrooms. The method for drawing the wide flange demonstrated at the end of Chapter 3 is similar to the one that was used to create the I-beam column symbols shown here.

Symbol use isn't restricted to building components. Room number labels, diamond-shaped interior elevation reference symbols, and the hexagonal column grid symbols are all common to an architectural drawing, regardless of the project's size. As you work through this chapter, keep in mind that all the symbols used in the library drawing were created using the tools presented here.

TIP You can press ⏎ or right-click the mouse and choose Repeat Block from the shortcut menu to start the Make Block tool again.

When you turn an object into a block, it is stored within the drawing file, ready to be recalled at any time. The block remains part of the drawing file even when you end the editing session. When you open the file again, the block will be available for your use. In addition, you can access blocks from other drawings by using the AutoCAD DesignCenter and the Tool palettes. You'll learn more about the DesignCenter and the Tool palettes in Chapter 27.

A block acts like a single object, even though it is really made up of several objects. One unique characteristic of a block is that when you modify it, all instances of that block are updated to reflect the modifications. For example, if you insert several copies of the toilet into a drawing and then later decide the toilet needs to be of a different shape, you can edit the Toilet block, and all the other copies of the toilet are updated automatically.

You can modify a block in a number of ways after it has been created. In this chapter, you'll learn how to make simple changes to individual blocks by modifying the block's properties. For more detailed changes, you'll learn how to redefine a block after it has been created. Later, in Chapter 17, you'll learn how to use the Block Editor to make changes to blocks.

Understanding the Block Definition Dialog Box

The Block Definition dialog box offers several options that can help make the use of blocks easier. If you're interested in these options, take a moment to review the Block Definition dialog box as you read the descriptions of the options. Or if you prefer, you can continue with the tutorial and come back to this section later.

You've already seen how the Name option lets you enter a name for your block. AutoCAD does not let you complete the block creation until you enter a name.

You've also seen how to select a base point for your block. The base point is like the grip of the block. It is the reference point you use when you insert the block back into the drawing. In the exercise, you used the Pick Point option to indicate a base point, but you also have the option to enter X, Y, and Z coordinates just below the Pick Point option. In most cases, however, you will want to use the Pick Point option to indicate a base point that is on or near the set of objects you are converting to a block.

The Objects group of the Block Definition dialog box lets you select the objects that make up the block. You use the Select Objects button to visually select the objects you want to include in the block you are creating. The QuickSelect button to the right of the Select Objects button lets you filter out objects based on their properties. You'll learn more about QuickSelect in Chapter 15. Once you select a set of objects for your block, you will see a thumbnail preview of the block's contents in the upper right corner of the Block Definition dialog box.

Other options in the Objects group and Settings group let you specify what to do with the objects you are selecting for your block. Here is a list of the options and what they mean:

Retain Keeps the objects you select for your block as they are, unchanged.

Convert To Block Converts the objects you select into the block you are defining. It then acts like a single object after you've completed the Block command.

Delete Deletes the objects you selected for your block. This is what AutoCAD did in earlier versions. You might also notice that a warning message appears at the bottom of the Objects group. This warning appears if you have not selected objects for the block. After you've selected objects, the warning changes to tell you how many objects you've selected.

Block Unit   Lets you determine how the object is to be scaled when it is inserted into the drawing using the DesignCenter feature discussed in Chapter 27. By default, this value will be the same as the current drawing's insert value.

Scale Uniformly   By default, blocks can have a different X, Y, or Z scale. This means that they can be stretched in any of the axes. You can lock the X, Y, and Z scale of the block by placing a checkmark next to this option. That way, the block will always be scaled uniformly and cannot be stretched in one axis.

Allow Exploding   By default, blocks can be exploded or reduced to their component objects. You can lock a block so that it cannot be exploded by turning off this option. You can always turn this option on later if you decide that you need to explode a block.

Hyperlink   Lets you assign a hyperlink to a block. This option opens the Insert Hyperlink dialog box that lets you select a location or file for the hyperlink.

Description   Lets you include a brief description or keyword for the block. This option is helpful when you need to find a specific block in a set of drawings. You'll learn more about searching for blocks later in this chapter and in Chapter 27.

Open in Block Editor   If you turn on this option, the block will be created and then opened in the block editor described in Chapter 17.

Inserting a Symbol

You can recall the Tub and Toilet blocks at any time, as many times as you want. In this section, you'll first draw the interior walls of the bathroom, and then you'll insert the tub and toilet. Follow these steps to draw the walls:

1. Delete the original tub and toilet drawings. Click the Erase tool in the Modify toolbar, and then enter **All**↵↵ to erase the entire visible contents of the drawing. (Doing so has no effect on the blocks you created previously.)

2. Draw a rectangle 7′-6″ × 5′. Metric users should draw a 228 cm × 152 cm rectangle. Orient the rectangle so the long sides go from left to right and the lower-left corner is at coordinate 1′-10″,1′-10″ (or coordinate 56.0000,56.0000 for metric users).

   If you use the Rectangle tool to draw the rectangle, make sure you explode it by using the Explode tool. This is important for later exercises. (See the "Unblocking and Redefining a Block" section later in this chapter if you aren't familiar with the Explode tool.) Your drawing should now look like Figure 4.1.

TIP   The Insert Block tool is also on the Insert toolbar, which you can open by right-clicking any open toolbar and choosing Insert.

FIGURE 4.1
The interior walls of
the bathroom

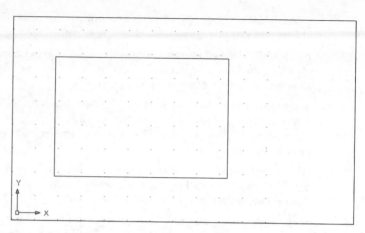

Now you're ready to place your blocks. Start by placing the tub in the drawing:

1. In the Draw toolbar, click the Insert Block tool or type I↲ to open the Insert dialog box.

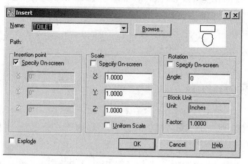

2. Click the Name drop-down list to display a list of the available blocks in the current drawing.

3. Click the block name Tub.

4. In the Rotation group, click the Specify On-Screen check box. This option lets you specify the rotation angle of the block graphically as you insert it.

5. Click OK, and you see a preview image of the tub attached to the cursor. The upper-left corner you picked for the tub's base point is now on the cursor intersection.

6. At the `Specify insertion point or [Basepoint/Scale/X/Y/Z/Rotate]:` prompt, pick the upper-left intersection of the room as your insertion point.

7. At the Specify rotation angle <0>: prompt, notice that you can rotate the block. This lets you visually specify a rotation angle for the block. You won't actually use this feature at this time, so press ↵ to accept the default of 0. The tub should look like the one in Figure 4.2.

FIGURE 4.2

The bathroom, first with the tub and then with the toilet inserted

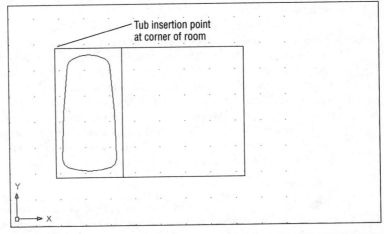

Tub insertion point at corner of room

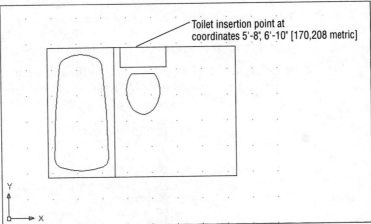

Toilet insertion point at coordinates 5'-8", 6'-10" [170,208 metric]

You've got the tub in place. Now place the Toilet block in the drawing:

1. Open the Insert dialog box again, but this time select Toilet in the Name drop-down list.

2. Clear the Specify On-Screen check box in the Rotation group.

3. Place the toilet at the midpoint of the line along the top of the rectangle representing the bathroom wall, as shown in the bottom image in Figure 4.2. Notice that after you select the insertion point, the toilet appears in the drawing; you are not prompted for a rotation angle for the block.

Scaling and Rotating Blocks

In step 7, you can see the tub rotate as you move the cursor. You can pick a point to fix the block in place, or you can enter a rotation value. This is the result of selecting the Specify On-Screen option in the Insert dialog box. You might find that you want the Rotation's Specify On-Screen option turned on most of the time to enable you to adjust the rotation angle of the block while you are placing it in the drawing.

The other options in the Insert dialog box that you did not use are the Scale group options. These options let you scale the block to a different size. You can scale the block uniformly, or you can distort the block by individually changing its X, Y, or Z scale factor. With the Specify On-Screen option unchecked, you can enter specific values in the X, Y, and Z text boxes to stretch the block in any direction. If you turn on the Specify On-Screen option, you'll be able to visually adjust the X, Y, and Z scale factors in real time. Although these options are not used often, they can be useful in special situations when a block needs to be stretched one way or another to fit in a drawing.

You aren't limited to scaling or rotating a block when it is being inserted into a drawing. You can always use the Scale or Rotate tools or modify an inserted block's properties to stretch it in one direction or another. This exercise shows you how this is done:

1. Click the Toilet block to select it.

2. Right-click and choose Properties from the shortcut menu to open the Properties palette. Take a moment to study the Properties palette. Toward the bottom, under the Geometry heading, you'll see a set of labels that show Position and Scale. These labels might appear as Pos… and Sca… if the width of the palette has been adjusted to be too narrow to show the entire label. Remember that you can click and drag the left or right edge of the palette to change its width. You can also click and drag the border between the columns in the palette.

3. If the first item label under the Geometry heading is not visible, place the cursor on the label. A tool tip displays the full wording of the item, which is Position X.

4. Move the cursor down one line to display the next tool tip for Position Y. This shows how you can view the label even if it is not fully visible.

5. Continue to move the cursor down to the Scale X label. The tool tip displays the full title.

6. Now let's try making some changes to the toilet properties. Double-click the Scale X value in the column just to the right of the Scale X label.

7. Enter **1.5.⌡**. Notice that the toilet changes in width as you do this.

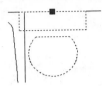

8. You don't really want to change the width of the toilet, so click the Undo tool in the Standard toolbar or enter **U⌡**.

9. Close the Properties palette by clicking the X in the upper-left corner.

WARNING   If a block is created with the Scale Uniformly option turned on in the Block Definition dialog box, you won't be able to scale the block in just one axis, as shown in the previous exercise. You will only be allowed to scale the block uniformly in all axes.

You've just seen how you can modify the properties of a block by using the Properties palette. In the exercise, you changed the X scale of the Toilet block, but you could have just as easily changed the Y value. You might have noticed other properties available in the Properties palette. You'll learn more about those properties as you work through this chapter.

You've seen how you can turn a drawing into a symbol, known as a block in AutoCAD. Now let's see how you can use an existing drawing file as a block.

Using an Existing Drawing as a Symbol

Now you need a door into the bathroom. Because you have already drawn a door and saved it as a file, you can bring the door into this drawing file and use it as a block:

1. In the Draw toolbar, click the Insert Block tool or type **I⌡**.

2. In the Insert dialog box, click the Browse button to open the Select Drawing File dialog box.

3. This is a standard Windows file browser dialog box. Locate the Door file and double-click it. If you didn't create a door file, you can use the door file from the Chapter 04 project files that you installed from the companion CD.

TIP   You can also browse your hard disk by looking at thumbnail views of the drawing files in a folder.

4. When you return to the Insert dialog box, make sure the Specify On-Screen options for the Scale and Rotation groups are checked, and then click OK. As you move the cursor around, notice that the door appears above and to the right of the cursor intersection, as in Figure 4.3.

5. At this point, the door looks too small for this bathroom. This is because you drew it 3 units long, which translates to 3˝. Metric users drew the door 9 cm long. Pick a point near coordinates 7´-2˝,2´-4˝, so that the door is placed in the lower-right corner of the room. Metric users should use the coordinate 210,70.

FIGURE 4.3
The door drawing being inserted in the Bath file

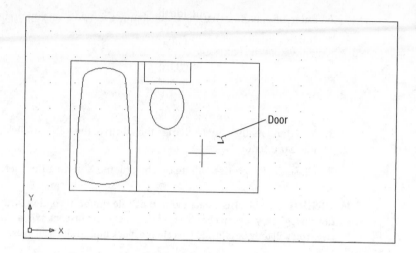

6. If you take the default setting for the X scale of the inserted block, the door will remain 3″ long, or 9 cm long for metric users. However, as mentioned earlier, you can specify a smaller or larger size for an inserted object. In this case, you want a 3′ door. Metric users want a 90 cm door. To get that from a 3″ door, you need an X scale factor of 12, or 10 for metric users. (You might want to look again at Table 3.3 in Chapter 3 to see how this is determined.) At the Enter X scale factor, specify opposite corner, or [Corner/XYZ] <1>: prompt, enter **12.**↵. Metric users should enter **10.**↵.

7. Press ↵ twice to accept the default Y = X and the rotation angle of 0°.

Now the Command prompt appears, but nothing seems to happen to the drawing. This is because when you enlarged the door, you also enlarged the distance between the base point and the object. This brings up another issue to be aware of when you're considering using drawings as symbols: all drawings have base points. The default base point is the absolute coordinate 0,0, otherwise known as the *origin*, which is located in the lower-left corner of any new drawing. When you drew the door in Chapter 2, you didn't specify the base point. So when you try to bring the door into this drawing, AutoCAD uses the origin of the door drawing as its base point (see Figure 4.4).

FIGURE 4.4
By default, a drawing's origin is also its insertion point. You can change a drawing's insertion point by using the Base command.

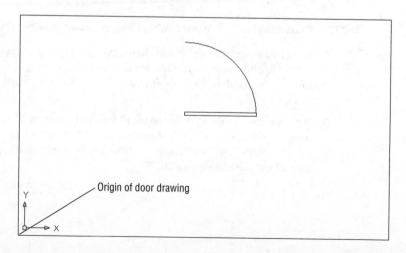

Because the door appears outside the bathroom, you must first choose Zoom ≻ All to show more of the drawing and then use the Move command on the Modify toolbar to move the door to the right-side wall of the bathroom. Let's do this now:

1. Choose View ≻ Zoom ≻ All from the menu bar drop-down menu to display the area set by the limits of your drawing (choose Format ≻ Drawing Limits), plus any other objects that are outside those limits. The view of the room shrinks, and the door is displayed. Notice that it is now the proper size for your drawing (see Figure 4.5).

FIGURE 4.5
The enlarged door

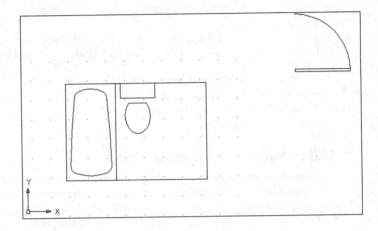

2. Choose Modify ≻ Move, or type **M**↵.

3. To pick the door you just inserted, at the `Select objects:` prompt, click a point anywhere on the door and press ↵. Notice that now the entire door is highlighted. This is because a block is treated like a single object, even though it might be made up of several lines, arcs, and so on.

4. At the `Specify base point or [Displacement] <Displacement>:` prompt, turn the Running Osnaps on and pick the lower-left corner of the door. Remember that pressing the F3 key or clicking Osnap in the status bar toggles the Running Osnaps on or off.

5. At the `Specify second point or <use first point as displacement>:` prompt, use the Nearest Osnap override, and position the door so that your drawing looks like Figure 4.6.

FIGURE 4.6
The door on the right-side wall of the bathroom

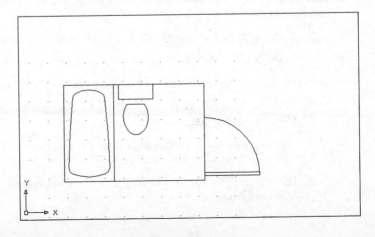

Because the door is an object that you will use often, it should be a common size so you don't have to specify an odd value every time you insert it. It would also be helpful if the door's insertion base point were in a more convenient location—that is, a location that would let you place the door accurately within a wall opening. Next, you will modify the Door block to better suit your needs.

Modifying a Block

You can modify a block in two ways. One way is to completely redefine the block. In earlier versions of AutoCAD, this was the only way to make changes to a block. A second way is to use the Block Editor.

In this chapter, you'll learn how to redefine a block by making changes to the door symbol. Later, in Chapter 17, you'll see how the Block Editor lets you add adjustability to blocks.

TIP   Double-clicking most objects displays the Properties palette. Double-clicking a block opens the Edit Block Definition dialog box, which gives you another way to edit blocks. The Edit Block Definition dialog box is not available in AutoCAD LT. You'll learn more about the Edit Block Definition dialog box in Chapter 17.

Unblocking and Redefining a Block

One way to modify a block is to break it down into its components, edit them, and then turn them back into a block. This is called *redefining* a block. If you redefine a block that has been inserted in a drawing, each occurrence of that block within the current file changes to reflect the new block definition. You can use this block redefinition feature to make rapid changes to a design.

To separate a block into its components, use the Explode command:

1. Choose Explode from the Modify toolbar. You can also type **X**↵ to start the Explode command.

2. Click the door and press ↵ to confirm your selection.

TIP   You can simultaneously insert and explode a block by clicking the Explode check box in the lower-left corner of the Insert dialog box.

Now you can edit the individual objects that make up the door, if you so desire. In this case, you want to change only the door's insertion point because you have already made it a more convenient size. So now you'll turn the door back into a block, this time using the door's lower-left corner for its insertion base point:

1. In the Draw toolbar, select Make Block or type **B**↵. You can also choose Draw ➢ Block ➢ Make.

2. In the Block Definition dialog box, select Door from the Name drop-down list.

3. Click the Pick Point button and pick the lower-left corner of the door.

4. Click the Select Objects button and select the components of the door. Press ↵ when you've finished making your selection.

5. Select the Convert To Block option in the Objects group to automatically convert the selected objects in the drawing into a block.

6. Select Inches from the Block Unit drop-down list, and then enter **Standard door** in the Description box.

7. Now click OK. You'll see a warning message that reads "Door is already defined. Do you want to redefine it?" You don't want to redefine an existing block accidentally. In this case, you know you want to redefine the door, so click the Yes button to proceed.

TIP The Select Objects and Pick Point buttons appear in other dialog boxes. Make note of their appearance, and remember that when you select them, the dialog box temporarily closes to let you select points or objects and otherwise perform operations that require a clear view of the drawing area.

In step 7, you received a warning message that you were about to redefine the existing Door block. But originally, you inserted the door as a file, not as a block. Whenever you insert a drawing file by using the Insert Block tool, the inserted drawing automatically becomes a block in the current drawing. When you redefine a block, however, you do not affect the drawing file you imported. AutoCAD changes only the block within the current file.

You've just redefined the door block. Now place the door in the wall of the room:

1. Choose Erase from the Modify toolbar and then click the door. Notice that the entire door is one object instead of individual lines and an arc. Had you not selected the Convert To Block option in step 5, the components of the block would have remained as individual objects.

2. Now insert the door block again, by using the Insert Block tool in the Draw toolbar or by choosing Insert ➢ Block. This time, however, use the Nearest Osnap override and pick a point on the right-side wall of the bathroom, near coordinate 9′-4″,2′-1″. Metric users should insert the door near 284,63.4.

3. Use the Grips feature to mirror the door, using the wall as the mirror axis so that the door is inside the room. Your drawing will look like Figure 4.7.

TIP To mirror an object using grips, first be sure that the Grips feature is on. (It is usually on by default.) Select the objects to mirror, click a grip, and then right-click. Select Mirror from the shortcut menu; then indicate a mirror axis with the cursor.

Next, you'll see how you can update an external file with a redefined block.

FIGURE 4.7
The bathroom floor
plan thus far

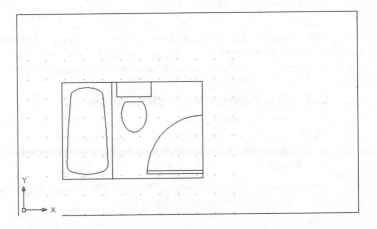

Saving a Block as a Drawing File

You've seen that, with little effort, you can create a symbol and place it anywhere in a file. Suppose you want to use this symbol in other files. When you create a block by using the Block command, the block exists within the current file only until you specifically instruct AutoCAD to save it as a drawing file on disk. For an existing drawing that has been brought in and modified, such as the door, the drawing file on disk associated with that door is not automatically updated. To update the Door file, you must take an extra step and use the Export option on the File menu. Let's see how this works.

TIP You can extract blocks that are embedded in other drawings by using a feature called the DesignCenter. See Chapter 27.

Start by turning the Tub and Toilet blocks into individual files on disk:

1. Choose File ➤ Export to open the Export Data dialog box, which is a simple file dialog box.

2. Open the Files Of Type drop-down list and select Block (*.dwg).

TIP If you prefer, you can skip step 2, and instead, in step 3, enter the full filename, including the .dwg extension, as in Tub.dwg.

3. Double-click the File Name text box and enter **Tub**.

4. Click the Save button to close the Export Data dialog box.

5. At the `[= (block=output file)/* (whole drawing)]` `<define new drawing>`: prompt, enter the name of the block you want to save to disk as the tub file—in this case, also **Tub↵**. The Tub block is now saved as a file.

6. Repeat steps 1 through 5 for the Toilet block. Give the file the same name as the block.

TIP AutoCAD gives you the option to save a block's file under the same name as the original block or with a different name. Usually you will want to use the same name, which you can do by entering an equal sign (=) after the prompt.

TIP Normally, AutoCAD saves a preview image with a file. This enables you to preview a drawing file before opening it. Preview images are not included with files that are exported with the File ➤ Export option or the Wblock command, which is discussed in the next section.

Replacing Existing Files with Blocks

The Wblock command does the same thing as choosing File ➤ Export, but output is limited to AutoCAD .dwg files. (Veteran AutoCAD users should note that Wblock is now incorporated into the File ➤ Export option.) Let's try using the Wblock command this time to save the Door block you modified:

1. Issue the Wblock command by typing **Wblock↵**, or use the keyboard shortcut by typing **w** to open the Write Block dialog box.

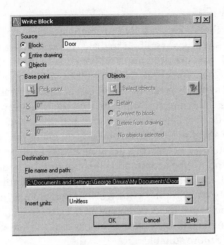

2. In the Source group, click the Block radio button.

3. Select Door from the drop-down list. Notice that the options in the Destination group change to reflect the location of the old `Door.dwg` file from which the Door block was originally inserted. You can keep the old name or enter a different name if you prefer.

4. In this case, you want to update the door you drew in Chapter 2, so click OK.

5. You'll see a warning message telling you that the `Door.dwg` file already exists. Go ahead and click Yes to confirm that you want to overwrite the old door drawing with the new door definition.

In this exercise, you typed the Wblock command at the Command prompt instead of choosing File ➢ Export. The results are the same, regardless of which method you use. If you are in a hurry, the File ➢ Export command is a quick way to save part of your drawing as a file. The Wblock option might be easier for new users because it offers options in a dialog box.

UNDERSTANDING THE WRITE BLOCK DIALOG BOX OPTIONS

The Write Block dialog box offers a way to save parts of your current drawing as a file. As you can see from the dialog box shown in the previous exercise, you have several options.

In that exercise, you used the Block option of the Source group to select an existing block as the source object to be exported. You can also export a set of objects by choosing the Objects option. If you choose this option, the Base Point and Objects groups become available. These options work the same way as their counterparts in the Block Definition dialog box that you saw earlier when you created the Tub and Toilet blocks.

The other option in the Source group, Entire Drawing, lets you export the whole drawing to its own file. This might seem to duplicate the File ➢ Save As option in the menu bar, but saving the entire drawing from the Write Block dialog box actually performs some additional operations, such as stripping out unused blocks or other unused components. This has the effect of reducing file size. You'll learn more about this feature later in this chapter.

Other Uses for Blocks

So far, you have used the Make Block tool to create symbols, and you have used the Export and Wblock commands to save those symbols to disk. As you can see, you can create symbols and save them at any time while you are drawing. You have made the tub and toilet symbols into drawing files that you can see when you check the contents of your current folder.

However, creating symbols is not the only use for the Insert Block, Block, Export, and Wblock commands. You can use them in any situation that requires grouping objects (though you might prefer to use the more flexible Object Group command discussed later in this chapter). You can also use blocks to stretch a set of objects along one axis by using the Properties palette. Export and Wblock also enable you to save a part of a drawing to disk. You will see instances of these other uses of the Block, Export, and Wblock commands throughout the book.

Make Block, Export, and Wblock are extremely versatile commands and, if used judiciously, can boost your productivity and simplify your work. If you are not careful, however, you can also get carried away and create more blocks than you can keep track of. Planning your drawings helps you determine which elements will work best as blocks and recognize situations in which other methods of organization are more suitable.

Another way of using symbols is to use AutoCAD's external reference capabilities. External reference files, known as *Xrefs*, are files inserted into a drawing in a way similar to blocks. The difference is that Xrefs do not actually become part of the drawing's database. Instead, they are loaded along with the current file at startup time. It is as if AutoCAD opens several drawings at once: the main file you specify when you start AutoCAD, and the Xrefs associated with the main file.

By keeping the Xrefs independent from the current file, you make sure that any changes made to the Xrefs automatically appear in the current file. You don't have to update each inserted copy of an Xref, as you must for blocks. For example, if you use the External References option on the Reference toolbar (discussed in Chapter 7) to insert the Tub drawing, and later you make changes to the tub, the next time you open the `Bath` file, you will see the new version of the tub. Or if you have both the tub and the referencing darwing open, and you change the tub, AutoCAD will notify you that a change has been made to an external reference. You can then update the tub Xref using the External Reference palette.

Xrefs are especially useful in workgroup environments, in which several people are working on the same project. One person might be updating several files that have been inserted into a variety of other files. Before Xrefs were available, everyone in the workgroup had to be notified of the changes and had to update all the affected blocks in all the drawings that contained them. With Xrefs, the updating is automatic. Many other features are unique to these files, and they are discussed in more detail in Chapters 7 and 12.

AN ALTERNATIVE TO BLOCKS

Another way to create symbols is by creating shapes. *Shapes* are special objects made up of lines, arcs, and circles. They can regenerate faster than blocks, and they take up less file space. Unfortunately, shapes are considerably more difficult to create and are less flexible to use than blocks.

You create shapes by using a coding system developed by Autodesk. The codes define the sizes and orientations of lines, arcs, and circles. You first sketch your shape, convert it into the code, and then copy that code into a text file. To learn more about shapes, see your *Customization Guide* in the AutoCAD 2007 Help window. You can get to it by choosing Help ➢ Additional Resources ➢ Developer Help.

Inserting Symbols with Drag-and-Drop

If you prefer to manage your symbol library by using Windows Explorer or to use another third-party file manager for locating and managing your symbols, you'll appreciate AutoCAD's support for drag-and-drop. With this feature, you can click and drag a file from Windows Explorer into the AutoCAD window. You can also drag and drop from the Windows Search tool. AutoCAD automatically starts the Insert command to insert the file. Drag-and-drop also works with a variety of other AutoCAD support files.

AutoCAD supports drag-and-drop for other types of data from applications that support Microsoft's ActiveX technology. Table 4.1 lists the files that you can drag and drop and the functions associated with them.

TIP You can also drag and drop from folder shortcuts placed on your Desktop or even from a website.

TABLE 4.1:   AutoCAD Support for File Drag-and-Drop

FILE TYPE	COMMAND ISSUED	FUNCTION PERFORMED WHEN FILE IS DROPPED
.cui	Cuiload	Loads CUI customization files
.dxf	Dxfin	Imports .dxf files
.dwg	Insert	Imports drawing files
.txt	Dtext	Imports text via Dtext
.lin	Linetype	Loads linetypes
..cui. mnu, .mns, .mnc	Menu	Loads menus
.psb, .shp,	Style	Loads fonts or shapes
.scr	Script	Runs script
.lsp	(Load)	Loads AutoLISP routine
.exe, .exp	(Xload)	Loads ADS application

Grouping Objects

Blocks are extremely useful tools, but for some situations, they are too restrictive. At times, you will want to group objects so they are connected yet can still be edited individually.

For example, consider a space planner who has to place workstations in a floor plan. Though each workstation is basically the same, some slight variations in each station could make the use of blocks unwieldy. For instance, one workstation might need a different configuration to accommodate special equipment, and another workstation might need to be slightly larger than the standard size. Using a block, you would need to create a block for one workstation, and then for each variation, explode the block, edit it, and then create a new block. A better way is to draw a prototype workstation and then turn it into a group. You can copy the group into position and then edit it for each individual situation, without losing its identity as a group. AutoCAD LT offers a different method for grouping objects. If you are using LT, skip this exercise and continue with the following section, "Grouping Objects for LT Users."

The following exercise demonstrate how grouping works:

1. Save the Bath file then open the drawing Office1.dwg from the companion CD. Metric users should open Office1-metric.dwg.

2. Use the Zoom command to enlarge just the view of the workstation, as shown in the first image in Figure 4.8.

FIGURE 4.8

A workstation in an office plan

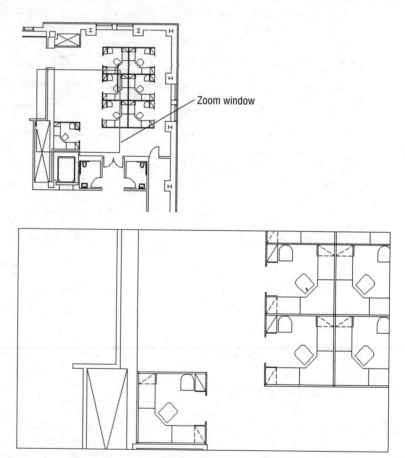

3. Type **G**↵ or **Group**↵ to open the Object Grouping dialog box.

4. Type **Station1**. As you type, your entry appears in the Group Name text box.

5. Click New in the Create Group group, about midway in the dialog box. The Object Grouping dialog box temporarily closes to let you select objects for your new group.

6. At the Select objects: prompt, window the entire workstation in the lower-left corner of the plan and press ↵ to display the Object Grouping dialog box. Notice that the name Station1 appears in the Group Name box at the top of the dialog box.

7. Click OK. You have just created a group.

Now, whenever you want to select the workstation, you can click any part of it to select the entire group. At the same time, you can still modify individual parts of the group—the desk, partition, and so on—without losing the grouping of objects.

Grouping Objects for LT Users

LT users will have to use a slightly different method to create a group. If you are using AutoCAD 2007 LT, do the following:

1. Open Office1.dwg from the companion CD. Metric users should open Office1-metric.dwg.

2. Use the Zoom command to enlarge just the view of the workstation, as shown in the first image in Figure 4.8.

3. Type **G**↵ or **Group**↵ to open the Group Manager dialog box.

4. Move the dialog box so that you have a clear view of the workstation; then use a selection window to select all the objects of the workstation. You can also click the individual objects of the workstation to make the selection.

5. In the Group Manager dialog box, click the Create Group button. A new listing appears in the Group Manager list box.

6. Type **Station1↵** in the text box that appears in the group list.

7. Close the Group Manager dialog box.

Now, whenever you want to select the workstation, you can click any part of it to select the entire group. At the same time, you can still modify individual parts of the group—the desk, partition, and so on—without losing the grouping of objects.

Modifying Members of a Group

Next, you will make copies of the original group and modify the copies. Figure 4.9 is a sketch of the proposed layout that uses the new workstations. Look carefully, and you'll see that some of the workstations in the sketch are missing a few of the standard components that exist in the Station1 group. One pair of stations has a partition removed; another station has no desk.

The exercises in this section show you how to complete your drawing to reflect the design requirements of the sketch.

FIGURE 4.9
A sketch of the new
office layout

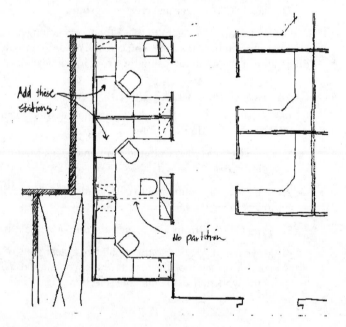

Start by making a copy of the workstation:

1. Click Copy on the Modify toolbar or type **Co**↵, and click the Station1 group you just created. Notice that you can click any part of the station to select the entire station. If only a single object is selected, press Shift+Ctrl+A and try clicking another part of the group.

2. Press↵ to finish your selection.

3. At the `Specify base point or [Displacement] <Displacement>:` prompt, enter **@**↵. Then enter **@8´2˝ <90** to copy the workstation 8´-2˝ vertically. Metric users should enter **@249<90**. Press ↵ to exit the Copy command.

TIP In step 3, you can also use the Direct Distance method by typing **@**↵ and then pointing the rubber-banding line 90° and typing **8´2˝** . Metric users should type **249**↵.

4. Issue the Copy command again, but this time click the copy of the workstation you just created. Notice that it too is a group.

5. Copy this workstation 8´-2˝ (249 cm for the metric users) vertically, just as you did the original workstation. Press ↵ to exit the Copy command.

Next, you'll use grips to mirror the first workstation copy:

1. Click the middle workstation to highlight it, and notice that grips appear for all the entities in the group.

2. Click the grip in the middle-left side, as shown in Figure 4.10.

FIGURE 4.10
Mirroring the new
group by using grips

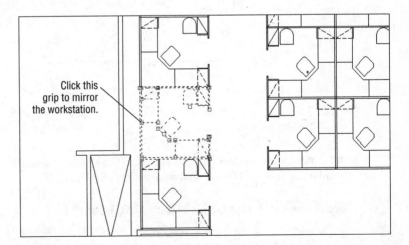

Click this
grip to mirror
the workstation.

3. Right-click the mouse and choose Mirror from the shortcut menu. Notice that a temporary mirror image of the workstation follows the movement of your cursor.

4. Turn on the Ortho mode and pick a point directly to the right of the hot grip you picked in step 2. The workstation is mirrored to a new orientation.

5. Press the Esc key twice to clear the grip selection. Also, turn off the Ortho mode.

Now that you've got the workstations laid out, you need to remove some of the partitions between the new workstations. If you had used blocks for the workstations, you would first need to explode the workstations that have partitions you want to edit. Groups, however, let you make changes without undoing their grouping.

Use these steps to remove the partitions:

1. At the Command prompt, press Shift+Ctrl+A. You should see the `<Group off>` message in the command line. If you see the `<Group on>` message instead, press Shift+Ctrl+A until you see `<Group off>`. This turns off groupings so you can select and edit individual objects within a group.

2. Using a window, erase the short partition that divides the two copies of the workstations, as shown in Figure 4.11.

FIGURE 4.11
Remove the partitions between the two workstations.

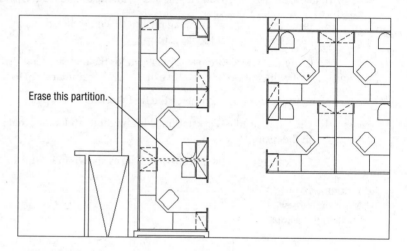

Erase this partition.

3. Press Shift+Ctrl+A again to turn groupings back on.

4. To check your workstations, click one of them to see whether all its components are highlighted together.

TIP Pickstyle is a system variable that controls how groups are selected. See Appendix C for more information about Pickstyle and other system variables.

Working with the Object Grouping Dialog Box

Each group has a unique name, and you can also attach a brief description of the group in the Object Grouping dialog box. When you copy a group, AutoCAD assigns an arbitrary name to the newly created group. Copies of groups are considered unnamed, but you can still list them in the Object Grouping dialog box by clicking the Include Unnamed check box. You can click the Rename button in the Object Grouping dialog box to name unnamed groups appropriately.

Objects within a group are not bound solely to that group. One object can be a member of several groups, and you can have nested groups.

Here are the options available in the Object Grouping dialog box:

GROUP IDENTIFICATION

Use the Group Identification group to identify your groups, using unique elements that let you remember what each group is for.

Group Name This text box lets you create a new group by naming it first.

Description This text box lets you include a brief description of the group.

Find Name Click this button to find the name of a group. The Object Grouping dialog box temporarily closes so you can click a group.

Highlight Click this button to highlight a group that has been selected from the Group Name list. This helps you locate a group in a crowded drawing.

Include Unnamed This check box determines whether unnamed groups are included in the Group Name list. Check this box to display the names of copies of groups for processing by this dialog box.

CREATE GROUP

Here's where you control how a group is created.

New Click this button to create a new group. The Object Grouping dialog box closes temporarily so that you can select objects for grouping. To use this button, you must have either entered a group name or selected the Unnamed check box.

Selectable This check box lets you control whether the group you create is selectable. See the description of the Selectable button in the Change Group group in the section that follows.

Unnamed This check box lets you create a new group without naming it.

CHANGE GROUP

These buttons are available only when a group name is highlighted in the Group Name list at the top of the dialog box.

Remove   Click this button to remove objects from a group.

Add   Click this button to add objects to a group. While using this option, grouping is temporarily turned off to allow you to select objects from other groups.

Rename   Click this button to rename a group.

Re-Order   Click this button to change the order of objects in a group. The order refers to the order in which you selected the objects to include in the group. You can change this selection order for special purposes such as tool path machining.

Description   Click this button to modify the description of a group.

Explode   Click this button to separate a group into its individual components.

Selectable   Click this button to turn individual groupings on and off. When a group is selectable, it is selectable only as a group. When a group is not selectable, the individual objects in a group can be selected, but not the group.

TIP   If a group is selected, you can remove individual items from the selection with a Shift+click. In this way, you can isolate objects within a group for editing or removal without having to temporarily turn off groups.

Working with the LT Group Manager

LT only

If you are using AutoCAD LT, you use the Group Manager to manage groups. Here is a rundown of the tools that are available in the Group Manager.

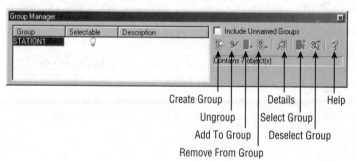

Create Group   Lets you convert a set of objects into a group. Select a set of objects and then click Create Group.

Ungroup   Removes the grouping of an existing group. Select the group name from the list and then select Ungroup.

Add To Group   Lets you add an object to a group. At least one group and one additional object must be selected before this option is available.

Remove From Group   Lets you remove one or more objects from a group. To isolate individual objects in a group, first select the group, and then Shift+click to remove individual objects from the selection set. After you isolate the object you want to remove, click Remove From Group.

Details   Lists detailed information about the group, such as the number of objects in the group and whether it is in Model Space or a layout. Select the group name from the group list and then click Details.

Select Group   Lets you select a group by name. Highlight the group name in the group list and then click Select Group.

Deselect Group   Removes a group from the current selection set. Highlight the group name in the group list and then click Deselect Group.

Help   Opens the AutoCAD LT Help dialog box and displays information about the Group Manager.

TIP   You've seen how you can use groups to create an office layout. You can also use groups to help you keep sets of objects temporarily together in a complex drawing. Groups can be especially useful in 3D modeling when you want to organize complex assemblies together for easy selection.

If You Want to Experiment

If your application is not architecture, you might want to experiment with creating other types of symbols.

Open a new file called Mytemp. Draw each screw or bolt head shown in Figure 4.12, and turn each part into a file on disk by using Export (choose File ➢ Export) or the Wblock command. When specifying a filename, use the name indicated for each part in the figure. For the insertion point, also use the points indicated in the figure. Use the Osnap modes (see Chapter 2) to select the insertion points. You can use the Experiment04-1.dwg sample file as a reference.

FIGURE 4.12
A typical set
of symbols

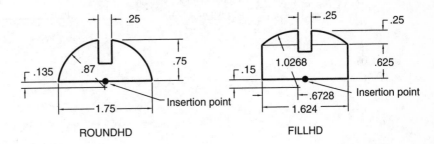

ROUNDHD   FILLHD

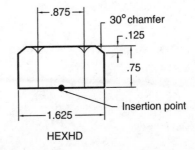

HEXHD

After you create the parts, exit the file by choosing File ➤ Exit, and then open a new file. Set up the drawing as an engineering drawing with a scale of $^1/_4\,''=1''$ on an 11″ × 17″ sheet. Create the drawing in Figure 4.13, using the Insert Block command to place your newly created parts. You can use the Experiment04-2.dwg file as a reference.

FIGURE 4.13
Draw this part using the symbols you create.

1. Set the snap mode to .125 and be sure it is on. Draw the figure at right using the dimensions shown as a guide.

2. Insert the HEXHD drawing at the location shown in the figure at right. Enter .25 for a scale value and when you are asked for a rotation angle, visually orient it as shown.

3. Insert the ROUNDHD drawing at the location shown in the figure at right. This time use a scale factor of .125 and when you are asked for a rotation angle, visually orient it as shown.

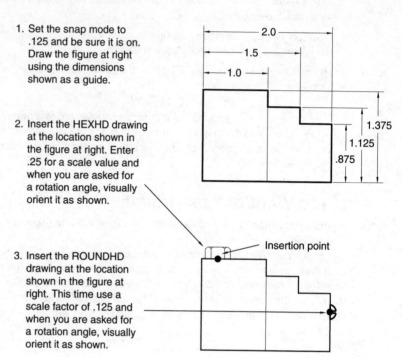

Chapter 5

Keeping Track of Layers, Blocks, and Files

Imagine a filing system that has only one category into which you would put all your records. For a handful of documents, such a filing system might work, but as soon as you start to accumulate more documents, you would want to start separating them into meaningful categories, perhaps alphabetically or by their use, so you can find them more easily.

The same is true for drawings. If you have a simple drawing with only a few objects, you can get by without using layers. But as soon as your drawing gets the least bit complicated, you'll want to start sorting your objects into layers to keep track of what's what. Layers don't restrict your editing of objects such as blocks or groups, and you can set layers up so that you can easily identify which object belongs to which layer.

In this chapter, you'll learn how to create and use layers to keep your drawings organized. You'll learn about how color can play an important role while working with layers, and you'll also learn how to include linetypes such as dashes and center lines through the use of layers.

This chapter includes the following topics:

◆ Organizing Information with Layers

◆ Controlling Line Weights

◆ Keeping Track of Blocks and Layers

Organizing Information with Layers

You can think of layers as overlays on which you keep various types of information (see Figure 5.1). In a floor plan of a building, for example, you want to keep the walls, ceiling, plumbing fixtures, wiring, and furniture separate so that you can display or plot them individually or combine them in different ways. It's also a good idea to keep notes and reference symbols, as well as the drawing's dimensions, on their own layers. As your drawing becomes more complex, you can turn the various layers on and off to allow easier display and modification.

For example, one of your consultants might need a plot of just the dimensions and walls, without all the other information; another consultant might need only a furniture layout. Using manual drafting, you would have to redraw your plan for each consultant or use overlay drafting techniques, which can be cumbersome. With AutoCAD, you can turn off the layers you don't need and plot a drawing containing only the required information. A carefully planned layering scheme helps you produce a document that combines the types of information needed in each case.

Using layers also lets you modify your drawings more easily. For example, suppose you have an architectural drawing with separate layers for the walls, the ceiling plan, and the floor plan. If any change occurs in the wall locations, you can turn on the ceiling plan layer to see where the new wall locations will affect the ceiling and then make the proper adjustments.

FIGURE 5.1

Placing drawing
elements on separate
layers

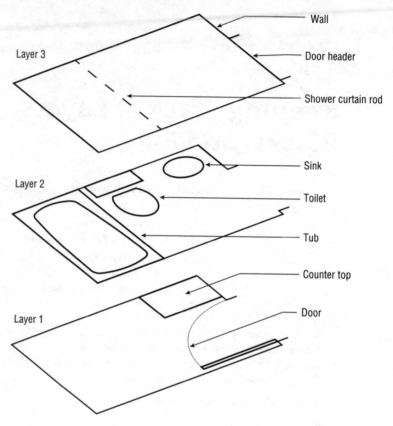

AutoCAD allows an unlimited number of layers, and you can name each layer anything you want.

Creating and Assigning Layers

You'll start your exploration of layers by using a dialog box to create a new layer, giving it a name
and assigning a color. Then you'll look at alternate ways of creating a layer through the command
line. Then you'll assign the new layer to the objects in your drawing. Start by getting familiar with
the Layer Properties Manager dialog box.

1. Open the Bath file you created in Chapter 4. (If you didn't create one, use the file
   04b-bath.dwg or 04b-bath-metric.dwg from the Chapter 4 project files that you
   installed from the companion CD.)

2. To display the Layer Properties Manager dialog box, click the Layer Properties Manager tool
   in the Layers toolbar, or choose Format ➢ Layer from the drop-down menu. You can also
   type **LA.⏎** to use the keyboard shortcut.

TIP   The Layer Properties Manager dialog box shows you at a glance the status of your layers. Right now, you have only one layer, but as your work expands, so will the number of layers. You will then find this dialog box indispensable.

3. Click the New Layer button at the top of the dialog box. The button has an icon that looks like a star next to a sheet.

A new layer named Layer1 appears in the list box. Notice that the name is highlighted. This tells you that by typing you can change the default name to something better suited to your needs.

4. Type **Wall**. As you type, your entry replaces the Layer1 name in the list box.

5. With the Wall layer name highlighted, click the Color icon in the Wall layer listing to display a dialog box in which you can assign a color to the Wall layer. The Color icon can be found under the Color column and currently shows White as its value. The icon is just to the left of the word *white*.

The Select Color dialog box opens.

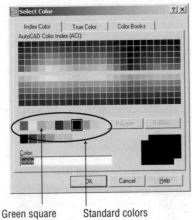

Green square   Standard colors

6. In the row of Standard Colors next to the ByLayer button, click the green square and then click OK. Notice that the color swatch in the Wall layer listing is now green.

7. When the Layer Properties Manager dialog box returns, click OK to close it.

From this point on, any object assigned to the Wall layer will appear green unless the object is specifically assigned a different color.

USING TRUE OR PANTONE COLORS

In the preceding exercise, you chose a color from the Index Color tab of the Select Color dialog box. Most of the time, you'll find that the Index Color tab includes enough colors to suit your needs. But if you are creating a presentation drawing in which color selection is important, you can choose colors from either the True Color or the Color Books tab of the Select Color dialog box.

The True Color tab offers a full range of colors through a color palette similar to one found in Adobe Photoshop and other image-editing programs.

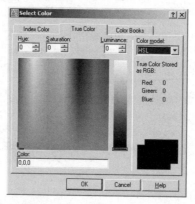

You have the choice of using hue, saturation, and luminance, which is the HSL color model, or you can use the RGB (red, green, blue) color model. You can select HSL or RGB from the Color Model drop-down list in the upper-right corner of the dialog box.

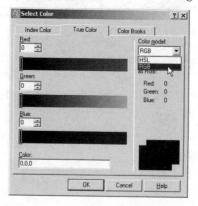

You can also select from a PANTONE "color book" by using the Color Books tab. The Color Book option lets you match colors to a PANTONE color book for offset printing.

TIP The Files tab of the Options dialog box (choose Tools ➢ Options) contains the Color Book Locations option, which tells AutoCAD where to look for the Color Book settings.

Now let's continue with our look at layers in AutoCAD.

UNDERSTANDING THE LAYER PROPERTIES MANAGER DIALOG BOX

The Layer Properties Manager dialog box conforms to the Windows interface standard. The most prominent feature of this dialog box is the Layer list box, as you saw in the preceding exercise. Notice that the bar at the top of the list of layers offers several buttons for the various layer properties. Just as you can adjust Windows Explorer, you can adjust the width of each column in the list of layers by clicking and dragging either side of the column head buttons. You can also sort the layer list based on a property simply by clicking the property name at the top of the list. And, just as with other Windows list boxes, you can Shift+click names to select a block of layer names, or you can Ctrl+click individual names to select multiples that do not appear together. These features will become helpful as your list of layers enlarges.

 Above the layer list, you'll see a box displaying the current layer. Just to the left of the current layer name are three tool buttons.

You've already seen how the New Layer tool works. That's the tool that has a star and sheet icon. The tool with the X icon is the Delete Layer tool. You select a layer or group of layers and then click this button to delete layers. Be aware that you cannot delete layer 0, locked layers, or layers that contain objects. The tool with the checkmark icon is the Set Current tool. It enables you to set the current layer on which you want to work. You can also see at a glance which layer is current by the green checkmark under the Status column of the layer list.

GETTING MULTIPLE USES FROM A DRAWING USING LAYERS

Layering lets you use a single AutoCAD drawing for multiple purposes. A single drawing can show both the general layout of the plan and more detailed information such as equipment layout or floor-paving layout.

The following two images are reproductions of the San Francisco Main Library's lower level and show how one floor plan file was used for two purposes. The first view shows the layout of furnishings, and the second view shows a paving layout. In each case, the same floor plan file was used, but in the first panel, the paving information is on a layer that is turned off. Layers also facilitate the use of differing scales in the same drawing. Frequently, a small-scale drawing of an overall plan will contain the same data for an enlarged view of other portions of the plan, such as a stairwell or an elevator core. The detailed information, such as notes and dimensions, might be on a layer that is turned off for the overall plan.

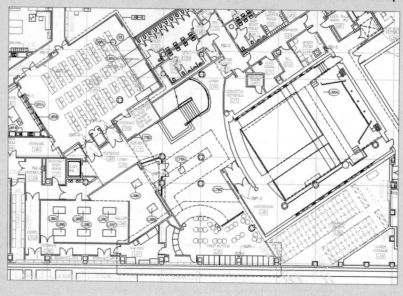

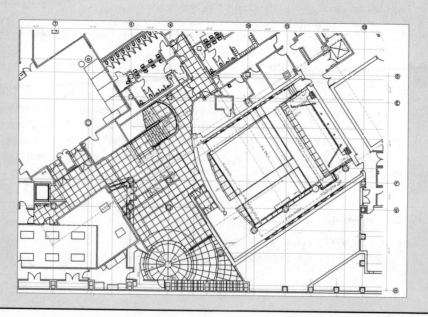

TIP   Another way to create or delete layers is to select a layer or set of layers from the list box and then right-click. A menu appears offering the same functions as the tools above the layer list.

You'll also notice another set of three tools farther to the left of the Layer Properties Manager dialog box. Those tools offer features to organize your layers in a meaningful way. You'll get a closer look at those tools a little later in this chapter.

CONTROLLING LAYERS THROUGH THE LAYER COMMAND

You have seen how the Layer Properties Manager dialog box makes it easy to view and edit layer information and how you can easily select layer colors from an on-screen toolbar. But you can also control layers through the Command prompt.

WARNING   LT users will not see the Pstyle option in the Layer prompt or the Truecolor/True Color/Color Books

WARNING   Books options in the Color option prompt.

Use these steps to control layers through the Command prompt:

1. Press the Esc key to make sure any current command is canceled.

2. At the Command prompt, enter **-Layer**↵. Make sure you include the minus sign in front of the word *Layer*. The following prompt appears:

```
Enter an option
[?/Make/Set/New/ON/OFF/Color/Ltype/LWeight/MATerial/Plot/PStyle/Freeze/Thaw/
LOck/Unlock/stAte]:
```

You'll learn about many of the options in this prompt as you work through this chapter.

3. Enter **N**↵ to select the New option.

4. At the Enter name list for new layer(s): prompt, enter **Wall2**↵. The [?/Make/Set/ New/ON/ OFF/Color/Ltype/LWeight/MATerial/Plot/PStyle/Freeze/Thaw/LOck/ Unlock /stAte]: prompt appears again.

5. Enter **C**↵.

6. At the New color [Truecolor/COlorbook]: prompt, enter **Yellow**↵. Or you can enter **2**↵, the numeric equivalent of the color yellow in AutoCAD.

7. At the Enter name list of layer(s) for color 2 (yellow) <0>: prompt, enter **Wall2**↵. The [?/Make/Set/New/ON/OFF/Color/Ltype /LWeight/MATerial/ Plot/ Pstyle/Freeze/Thaw/LOck/Unlock/stAte]: prompt appears again.

8. Press ↵ to exit the Layer command.

Each method of controlling layers has its own advantages. The Layer Properties Manager dialog box offers more information about your layers at a glance. On the other hand, the Layer command offers a quick way to control and create layers if you're in a hurry. Also, if you intend to write custom macros, you will want to know how to use the Layer command as opposed to using the Layer Properties Manager dialog box, because dialog boxes cannot be controlled through custom toolbar buttons or scripts.

TIP You can recall previously entered commands and keyboard entries by using the Up and Down arrow keys. For example, to recall the layer command and N option you entered in step 2 and 3 in the previous exercise, press the Up arrow key until –layer appears in the prompt. This saves time when you are performing repetitive operations such as creating multiple layers.

ASSIGNING LAYERS TO OBJECTS

When you create an object, that object is assigned to the current layer. Until now, only one layer has existed—layer 0—which contains all the objects you've drawn so far. Now that you've created some new layers, you can reassign objects to them by using the Properties palette:

1. Select the four lines that represent the bathroom walls. If you have problems singling out the wall to the left, use a window to select the wall line.

2. With the cursor in the drawing area, right-click and choose Properties from the shortcut menu to open the Properties palette. This palette lets you modify the properties of an object or a set of objects. (See the upcoming "Understanding Object Properties" sidebar for more on the properties of objects.)

3. Click the Layer option from the listing in the Properties palette. Notice that an arrow appears in the layer name to the right of the Layer option.

4. Click the downward-pointing arrow to the far right of the Layer option to display a list of all the available layers.

5. Select the Wall layer from the list. Notice that the wall lines you selected change to a green color. This tells you that the objects have been assigned to the Wall layer. Remember that you assigned a green color to the Wall layer.

6. Close the Properties palette by clicking the X button in the upper-left corner.

The bathroom walls are now on the new layer called Wall, and the walls are changed to green. Layers are more easily distinguished from one another when you use colors to set them apart.

Next, you will practice the commands you learned in this section and try some new ones by creating some new layers and changing the layer assignments of the rest of the objects in your bathroom:

1. Open the Layer Properties Manager dialog box (choose Format ➤ Layer or click the Layer Properties Manager button in the Layers toolbar). Create a new layer called Fixture and give it the color blue.

TIP You can change the name of a layer by clicking it in the Layer Properties Manager dialog box. After it is highlighted, click it again so that a box surrounds the name or press the F2 function key. You can then rename the layer. This works in the same way as renaming a file or folder in Windows.

2. Click the Tub and Toilet blocks, and then right-click and choose Properties from the shortcut menu to open the Properties palette.

3. Click Layer in the list of properties, and then select Fixture from the drop-down list to the right of the Layer listing.

4. Click the X in the top corner of the Properties palette to dismiss it, and then press the Esc key to clear your selection.

5. Now create a new layer for the door, name the layer Door, and make it red.

TIP Within a block, you can change the color assignment and linetype of only those objects that are on layer 0. See the sidebar "Controlling Colors and Linetypes of Blocked Objects" later in this chapter.

6. Just as you have done with the walls and fixtures, use the Properties palette to assign the door to the Door layer.

7. Use the Layer Properties Manager dialog box to create three more layers for the ceiling, door jambs, and floor, as shown in Table 5.1. Remember that you can open the Select Color dialog box by clicking the color swatch of the layer listing.

TABLE 5.1:   Create These Layers and Set Their Colors as Indicated

LAYER NAME	LAYER COLOR (NUMBER)
Ceiling	Magenta (6)
Jamb	Green (3)
Floor	Cyan (4)

UNDERSTANDING OBJECT PROPERTIES

It helps to think of the components of an AutoCAD drawing as having properties. For example, a line has geometric properties, such as its length, and coordinates that define its endpoints. An arc has a radius, a center, and beginning and ending coordinates. And even though a layer is not an object you can grasp and manipulate, it can have properties such as color, linetypes, and line weights.

By default, objects take on the color, linetype, and line weight of the layer to which they are assigned, but you can also assign these properties directly to individual objects. These general properties can be manipulated through both the Properties palette and the Properties toolbar.

Although many of the options in the Properties palette might seem cryptic, don't worry about them at this point. As you work with AutoCAD, these properties will become more familiar. You'll find that you really won't be too concerned with the geometric properties, because you'll be manipulating them with the standard editing tools in the Modify toolbar. The other properties will be explained in the rest of this chapter and in other chapters.

In step 3 of the previous exercise, you used the Properties palette, which offered several options for modifying the block. The options displayed in the Properties palette depend on the objects you have selected. With only one object selected, AutoCAD displays options that apply specifically to that object. With several objects selected, you'll see a more limited set of options because AutoCAD can change only those properties that are common to all the objects selected.

CONTROLLING COLORS AND LINETYPES OF BLOCKED OBJECTS

Layer 0 has special importance to blocks. When objects assigned to layer 0 are used as parts of a block, and that block is inserted on another layer, those objects take on the characteristics of their new layer. On the other hand, if those objects are on a layer other than layer 0, they maintain their original layer characteristics even if you insert or change that block to another layer. For example, suppose the tub is drawn on the Door layer, instead of on layer 0. If you turn the tub into a block and insert it on the Fixture layer, the objects the tub is composed of will maintain their assignment to the Door layer, although the Tub block is assigned to the Fixture layer.

It might help to think of the block function as a clear plastic bag that holds together the objects that make up the tub. The objects inside the bag maintain their assignment to the Door layer even while the bag itself is assigned to the Fixture layer. This might be a bit confusing at first, but it should become clearer after using blocks for a while.

AutoCAD also enables you to have more than one color or linetype on a layer. For example, you can use the Color and Linetype buttons in the Properties palette (the Properties button on the Standard toolbar) to alter the color or linetype of an object on layer 0. That object then maintains its assigned color and linetype—no matter what its layer assignment. Likewise, objects specifically assigned a color or linetype are not affected by their inclusion into blocks.

Working on Layers

So far you have created layers and then assigned objects to those layers. In this section, you'll learn how to use the Layer drop-down list in the Properties toolbar to assign layers to objects. In the process, you'll make some additions to the drawing.

The current layer is still layer 0, and unless you change the current layer, every new object you draw will be on layer 0. Here's how to change the current layer:

1. Click the arrow button next to the layer name on the Layers toolbar. A drop-down list opens, showing you all the layers available in the drawing.

    Notice the icons that appear next to the layer names; these control the status of the layer. You'll learn how to work with these icons later in this chapter. Also notice the box directly to the left of each layer name. This shows you the color of the layer.

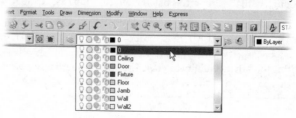

TIP Momentarily placing the cursor on an icon in the Layer drop-down list displays a tool tip that describes the icon's purpose.

2. Click the Jamb layer name. The drop-down list closes, and the name Jamb appears in the toolbar's layer name box. Jamb is now the current layer.

TIP You can also use the Layer command to reset the current layer. To do this here, enter **–Layer** (be sure to include the minus sign) at the Command prompt, and at the `?/Make/Set/New/ON/ OFF/Color/Ltype/LWeight/MATerial/Plot/PStyle/Freeze/Thaw/LOck/Unlock/ stAte]:` prompt, enter **S** for Set. At the `Enter layer name to make current or <select object>:` prompt, enter **Jamb** and then press ↵ twice to exit the Layer command.

3. Zoom in on the door and draw a 5″ line; start at the lower-right corner of the door and draw toward the right. Metric users should draw a 13 cm line.

4. Draw a similar line from the top-right end of the arc. Your drawing should look like Figure 5.2.

FIGURE 5.2
Door at wall with door jamb added

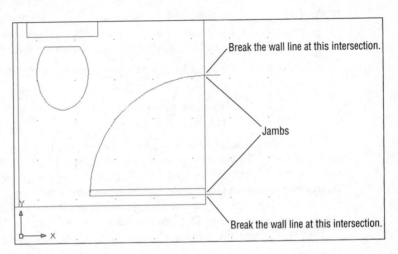

Because you assigned the color green to the Jamb layer, the two lines you just drew to represent the door jambs are green. This gives you immediate feedback about which layer you are on as you draw.

Now you will use the part of the wall between the jambs as a line representing the door header (the part of the wall above the door). To do this, you will have to cut the line into three line segments and then change the layer assignment of the segment between the jambs:

1. In the Modify toolbar, click the Break At Point tool.

2. At the `Select object:` prompt, click the wall between the two jambs.

3. At the `Specify first break point:` prompt, use the Endpoint Osnap override to pick the endpoint of the door's arc that is touching the wall, as shown in Figure 5.2, earlier in this chapter.

4. Click Break At Point on the Modify toolbar, and then repeat steps 2 and 3, this time using the jamb near the door hinge location to locate the break point (see Figure 5.2).

Though it may not be obvious, you've just broken the right-side wall line into three line segments: one at the door opening and two more on either side of the jambs. You can also use the Break tool (below the Break At Point tool) to produce a gap in a line segment.

TIP   The Break At Point tool will not work on a circle. You can, however, use the Break tool to place a small gap in the circle. If you create a small enough gap, the circle will still appear as a full circle.

Next, you'll change the Layer property of the line between the two jambs to the Ceiling layer. But instead of using the Properties tool, as you've done in earlier exercises, you'll use a shortcut method:

1. Click the line between the door jambs to highlight it. Notice that the layer listing in the Layers toolbar changes to Wall. Whenever you select an object to expose its grips, the Color, Linetype, Line Weight, and Plot Style listings in the Properties toolbar change to reflect those properties of the selected object.

2. Click the layer name in the Layers toolbar to open the layer drop-down list.

3. Click the Ceiling layer. The list closes, and the line you selected changes to the magenta color, showing you that it is now on the Ceiling layer. Also notice that the color list in the Properties toolbar also changes to reflect the new color for the line.

4. Press the Esc key twice to clear the grip selection. Notice that the layer returns to Jamb, the current layer.

5. Click the Zoom Previous tool in the Standard toolbar, or choose View ➢ Zoom ➢ Previous to return to the previous view.

In this exercise, you saw that by selecting an object with no command active, the object's properties are immediately displayed in the Properties toolbar under the Color Control, Linetype Control, Lineweight Control, and Plot Style Control boxes. Using this method, you can also change an object's color, linetype, line weight, and plot style independent of its layer. Just as with the Properties palette, you can select multiple objects and change their layers through the layer drop-down list. These options in the Properties toolbar offer a quick way to edit some of the properties of objects.

Now you'll finish the bathroom by adding a sink to a layer named Casework:

1. Open the Layer Properties Manager dialog box and create a new layer called Casework.

2. With the Casework layer selected in the Layer list, click the Set Current button at the top of the dialog box.

3. Click the color swatch for the Casework layer listing, and then select Blue from the Select Color dialog box. Click OK to exit the dialog box.

4. Click OK in the Layer Properties Manager dialog box. Notice that the layer listing in the Layers toolbar indicates that the current layer is Casework.

   Now you'll add the sink. As you draw, the objects will appear in blue, the color of the Casework layer.

5. Choose View ➢ Zoom ➢ All.

6. Click the Insert Block tool on the Draw toolbar, and then click the Browse button in the Insert dialog box to open the Select Drawing File dialog box.

7. Locate the Sink file and double-click it.

8. In the Insert dialog box, make sure that the Specify On-Screen options in both the Scale and Rotation groups are not selected; then click OK.

9. Place the sink roughly in the upper-right corner of the bathroom plan, and then use the Move command to place it accurately in the corner, as shown in Figure 5.3.

FIGURE 5.3

The bathroom with sink and countertop added

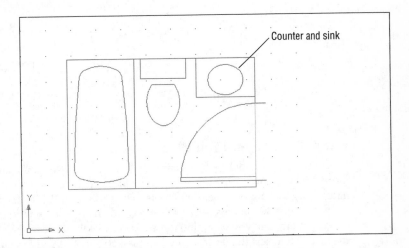

Counter and sink

Controlling Layer Visibility

I mentioned earlier that you'll sometimes want to display only certain layers to work with in a drawing. In this bathroom is a door header that would normally appear only in a reflected ceiling plan. To turn off a layer so that it becomes invisible, you click the Off button in the Layer Properties Manager dialog box, as shown in these steps:

1. Open the Layer Properties Manager dialog box by clicking the Layer Properties Manager button in the Layers toolbar.

2. Click the Ceiling layer in the layer list.

3. Click the lightbulb icon in the layer list, next to the Ceiling layer name. The lightbulb icon changes from yellow to gray to indicate that the layer is off.

4. Click the OK button to exit the Layer Properties Manager dialog box. When you return to the drawing, the door header (the line across the door opening) disappears because you have made it invisible by turning off its layer.

You can also control layer visibility by using the Layer drop-down list on the Layers toolbar.

1. On the Layers toolbar, click the Layer drop-down list.

2. Find the Ceiling layer and notice that its lightbulb icon is gray. This tells you that the layer is off and not visible.

3. Click the lightbulb icon to make it yellow.

4. Now click the drawing area to close the Layer drop-down list, and the door header reappears.

Figure 5.4 explains the role of the other icons in the Layer drop-down list.

FIGURE 5.4

The Layer drop-down list icons

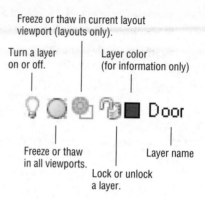

Freeze or thaw in current layout viewport (layouts only).

Turn a layer on or off.

Layer color (for information only)

Freeze or thaw in all viewports.

Lock or unlock a layer.

Layer name

Finding the Layers You Want

With only a handful of layers, it's fairly easy to find the layer you want to turn off. It becomes much more difficult, however, when the number of layers exceeds 20 or 30. The Layer Properties Manager dialog box offers some useful tools to help you find the layers you want fast.

Now suppose you have several layers whose names begin with *C*, such as C-lights, C-header, and C-pattern, and you want find those layers quickly. You can click the Name button at the top of the layer list to sort the layer names in alphabetic order. (You can click the Name button again to reverse the order.) To select those layers for processing, click the first layer name that starts with *C*; then scroll down the list until you find the last layer of the group and Shift+click it. All the layers between those layers will be selected. If you want to deselect some of those layers, hold down the Ctrl key while clicking the layer names you don't want to include in your selection. Or Ctrl+click other layer names you do want selected.

The Color and Linetype buttons at the top of the list let you control which layers appear in the list by virtue of their color or linetype assignments. Other buttons sort the list by virtue of the status: On/Off, Freeze/Thaw, Lock/Unlock, and so forth. (See the "Other Layer Options" sidebar later in this chapter.)

Now try changing the layer settings again, turning off all the layers except Wall and Ceiling and leaving just a simple rectangle. In this exercise, you'll get a chance to experiment with the On/Off options of the Layer Properties Manager dialog box:

1. Click the LayerProperties Manager button in the Layers toolbar or choose Format ➤ Layer.

2. Click the topmost layer name in the list box; then Shift+click the bottommost layer name. All the layer names are highlighted.

TIP   Another way to select all the layers at once in the Layer Properties Manager dialog box is to right-click the layer list and then choose the Select All option from the shortcut menu. And if you want to clear your selections, right-click the layer list and choose Clear All.

3. Ctrl+click the Wall and Ceiling layers to deselect them and thus exempt them from your next action.

4. Click the lightbulb icon of any of the highlighted layers.

5. A message appears warning you that the current layer will be turned off. Click NO in the message box. The lightbulb icons turn gray to show that the selected layers have been turned off.

6. Click OK. The drawing now appears with only the Wall and Ceiling layers displayed. It looks like a simple rectangle of the room outline.

7. Open the Layer Properties Manager dialog box again, select all the layers as you did in step 2, and then click any of the gray lightbulbs to turn on all the layers at once.

8. Click OK to return to the drawing.

In this exercise, you turned off a set of layers with a single click on a lightbulb icon. You can freeze/thaw, lock/unlock, or change the color of a group of layers in a similar manner by clicking the appropriate layer property. For example, clicking a color swatch of one of the selected layers opens the Select Color dialog box, in which you can set the color for all the selected layers.

Taming an Unwieldy List of Layers

Chances are, you will eventually end up with a fairly long list of layers. Managing such a list can become a nightmare, but AutoCAD provides some tools to help you organize layers so that you can keep track of them more easily.

On the left side of the Layer Properties Manager dialog box, you'll see a set of tools and a list box designed to help you with your layer management tasks.

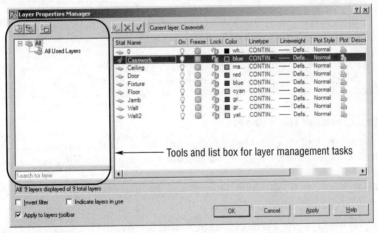

In the upper-left corner of the dialog box, you see a toolbar with three tools:

The New Property Filter tool lets you filter your list of layers to display only layers with certain properties, such as specific colors or names.

The New Group Filter tool lets you create named groups of layers that can be quickly recalled at any time. This tool is helpful if you often work with specific sets of layers. For example, you might have a set of layers in an architectural drawing that pertains to the electrical layout. You could create a group filter called Electrical that filters out all layers except those pertaining to the electrical layout. The filters don't affect the layers in any way; they just limit which layers are displayed in the main layer list.

The Layer States Manager tool lets you create sets of layer states. For example, if you want to save the layer settings that have only the wall and door layer turned on, you can do so by using this tool.

OTHER LAYER OPTIONS

You might have noticed the Freeze and Thaw buttons in the Layer Properties Manager dialog box. These options are similar to the On and Off buttons. However, Freeze not only makes layers invisible; it also tells AutoCAD to ignore the contents of those layers when you use the All response to the Select objects: prompt. Freezing layers can save time when you issue a command that regenerates a complex drawing. This is because AutoCAD ignores objects on frozen layers during Regen. You will get first-hand experience with Freeze and Thaw in Chapter 6.

Another pair of Layer Properties Manager options, Lock and Unlock, offer a function similar to Freeze and Thaw. If you lock a layer, you can view and snap to objects on that layer, but you can't edit those objects. This feature is useful when you are working on a crowded drawing and you don't want to accidentally edit portions of it. You can lock all the layers except those you intend to edit and then proceed to work without fear of making accidental changes.

Three more options—Lineweight, Plot Style, and Plot—offer control over the appearance of printer or plotter output. Lineweight lets you control the width of lines in a layer. Plot Style lets you assign plotter configurations to specific layers. (You'll learn more about plot styles in Chapter 9.) Plot lets you determine whether a layer gets printed in hard-copy output. This can be useful for setting up layers you might use for layout purposes only. The Linetype option lets you control the line patterns such as dashed or center lines.

Finally, you can save layer settings for later recall by using the Layer States Manager tool in the upper-left corner of the Layer Properties Manager dialog box. This feature is extremely useful when you want to save different layer combinations. Chapter 15 shows you how to use this feature. This option is also accessible from the State option in the command-line version of the Layer command.

FILTERING LAYERS BY THEIR PROPERTIES

Below these three tools is a filter list, which is a hierarchical list displaying the different sets of layer properties and group filters. Right now, you don't have any filters in place so you see only the All and All Used Layers.

In this section, you'll learn how the tools and the filter list box work. You'll start with a look at the New Property Filter tool:

1. Open the Layer Properties Manager dialog box by clicking the Layer Properties Manager button in the Layers toolbar. You can also choose Format ➤ Layer from the toolbar.

2. Click the New Property Filter tool in the upper-left corner of the dialog box to open the Layer Filter Properties dialog box. You see two list boxes. The Filter Definition list box at the top is where you enter your filter criteria. The Filter Preview list box below is a preview of your layer list based on the filter options. Right now, there are no filter options, so the Filter Preview list shows all the layers.

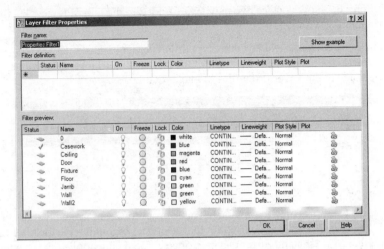

3. In the Filter Definition list box, click the blank box just below the Color label. A button appears in the box.

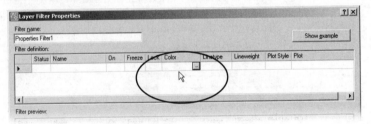

Click the box under the Color column.

4. Click in the blank box again; then enter **red**↵. The Filter Preview changes to show only layers that are red. In the current drawing, only one layer has been assigned the color red.

5. Click twice in the blank box below the one you just edited. Again you see a button appear.

6. This time, enter **green**↵. Now the layers that are green appear in the Filter Preview list.

TIP You can also select a color from the Select Color dialog box by clicking the button that appears in the box.

7. In the Filter Definition list, click in the Name column in the third row down. Notice that a cursor appears followed by an asterisk.

8. Enter **F↵**. Now you see two new layers added to the Filter Preview list that have names beginning with F.

9. In the Filter Name text box at the upper-left corner of the dialog box, change the name Properties Filter 1 to My List. Then click OK. Now you see the My List filter in the list box on the left side of the Layer Properties Manager dialog box.

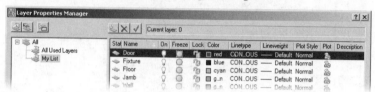

The layer list shows only the layers that have properties conforming to those you selected in the Layer Filter Properties dialog box. Notice that My List is highlighted in the filter list to the left. This tells you that My List is the current layer property filter being applied to the layer list to the right. You can change the layer list display by selecting different options in the filter list. Try these steps:

1. Click the All option in the filter list at the left side of the dialog box. The layer list to the right changes to display all the layers in the drawing. Also note that a brief description of the current layer filter is displayed at the bottom of the dialog box.

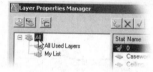

2. Click the All Used Layers option in the filter list. Now only layers that contain objects are displayed.

3. Click My List. The layer list changes back to the limited set of layers from your filter list.

4. Double-click My List. The Layer Filter Properties dialog box opens and displays the list of layer properties you set up earlier for My List. You can edit the criteria for your filter by making modifications in this dialog box.

5. Click Cancel to exit the Layer Filter Properties dialog box.

CREATING LAYER GROUPS

The preceding exercise shows how you can filter out layer names based on the properties you specify in the Layer Filter Properties dialog box. But suppose you want to create a layer filter list by graphically selecting objects on the screen. You can use the New Group Filter tool to do just that:

1. Click the New Group Filter tool in the upper-left corner of the Layer Properties Manager dialog box, and then press ↵ to accept the default name for the group. You see a new listing appear called Group Filter1.

2. Right-click the Group Filter1 listing, and then choose Select Layers ➤ Add from the shortcut menu. The Layer Properties Manager dialog box temporarily closes to

enable you to select objects in your drawing. Notice that your cursor is now an Object Selection cursor.

3. Click a line representing a wall of the bathroom; then click the door. Press ↵ when you are finished with your selection. The Layer Properties Manager dialog box reappears, and now you see the layers of the two objects you selected displayed in the layer list. Also note that Group Filter1 is highlighted in the filter list to the left.

TIP You might have noticed the Select Layers ➢ Replace option in the shortcut menu in step 2. This option lets you completely replace an existing group filter with a new selection set. It works just like the Select Layers ➢ Add option.

Earlier, you saw how you can double-click a properties filter to edit a properties filter list. But group filters work in a slightly different way. If you want to add layers to your group filter, you can click and drag them from the layer list to the group filter name. Here's how it's done:

1. In the Layer Properties Manager dialog box, select All from the filter list to the left.

2. Click the Fixture layer in the layer list; then Ctrl+click the Jamb layer in the list. These are layers you'll add to the Group Filter1 layer group.

3. Click and drag the Fixture layer to the Group Filter1 listing in the filter list to the left.

4. To check the addition to the Group Filter1, click it in the filter list. The Fixture and Jamb layers have been added to the Group Filter1 list.

If you want to delete a layer from a group filter, you can use the shortcut menu, as shown in these steps:

1. With the Group Filter1 list selected, select the Jamb layer from the layer list, and then right-click it.

2. Select Remove From Group Filter in the shortcut menu. (Make sure you do not select Delete Layer.) Jamb is removed from the Group Filter1 list.

TIP You can also convert a layer property filter into a group filter. Select the layer property filter from the filter list, right-click, and then select Convert To Group Filter. The icon for the layer property filter will change to a group filter icon, indicating that it is now a group filter.

You've seen how you can add property and group filters to the Layer Properties Manager dialog box by using the tools on the left side of the dialog box. One tool you haven't explored yet is the Layer States Manager. To understand how this tool works, you'll need to learn a little more about AutoCAD, so look for a discussion of the Layer States Manager in Chapter 15.

Before you move on, you'll want to know about the options just below the filter list.

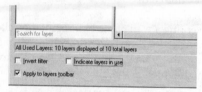

The Invert Filter check box changes the list of layers to show all layers *excluding* those in the selected filter. For example, if the My List filter contains layers that are red, and you select Invert Filter, the layer list will display all layers *except* those that are red.

The Indicate Layers In Use check box changes the icon in the status column of the list of layers to indicate layers that have no objects assigned to them. If you turn this option on, "empty" layers will display a gray icon in the Status column.

The Apply To Layers Toolbar check box, when selected, will apply the selected filter to the Layer drop-down list found in the Layers toolbar.

A text box directly below the filter list enables you to enter portions of a layer name to apply additional filters to the layer list currently displayed. For example, you can enter **F*** in the text box to display only layers from the current list that have names beginning with *F*. In this example, the text box contains the words *Search for Layer*.

In the next section, you'll find some tips for how to use layer names so that you can use text filters more effectively.

NAMING LAYERS TO STAY ORGANIZED

In the previous section, you saw how to create a layer property filter by using the name of a layer. If you name layers carefully, you can use them as a powerful layer management tool. For example, suppose you have a drawing whose layer names are set up to help you easily identify floor-plan data versus ceiling-plan data, as in the following list:

A-FP-WALL-JAMB

A-FP-WIND-JAMB

A-FP-WIND-SILL

A-CP-WIND-HEAD

A-CP-DOOR-HEAD

L-FP-CURB

C-FP-ELEV

The first character in the layer name designates the discipline related to that layer: *A* for architectural, *L* for landscape, *C* for civil, and so on. In this example, layers with names containing the two characters *FP* signify floor-plan layers. *CP* designates ceiling-plan information.

TIP   These layer examples are loosely based on a layer-naming convention devised by the American Institute of Architects (AIA). As you can see from this example, careful naming of layers can help you manage them.

If you want to isolate only those layers that have to do with floor plans, regardless of their discipline, enter **??FP*** in the Name column of the Layer Filter Properties dialog box. You can then give this layer property filter the name Floor Plan by entering **Floor Plan** in the Filter Name text box.

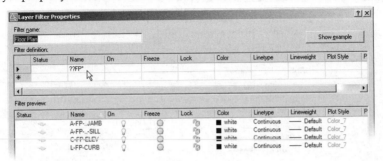

After you've created the Floor Plan layer properties list, you can then pick Floor Plan from the filter list on the right side of the Layer Properties Manager dialog box, and only those layers with names containing the letters *FP* as their third and fourth characters will appear in the list of layers. You can turn all these layers off, change their color assignment, or change other settings quickly, without having to wade through layers you don't want to touch. You can further create other filter properties to isolate other groups of layers. AutoCAD keeps these filter lists for future use until you delete them by using the Delete option in the shortcut menu. (Right-click the name of the properties filter and choose Delete.)

In the ??FP* example, the question marks (??) tell AutoCAD that the first two characters in the layer name can be anything. The *FP* tells AutoCAD that the layer name must contain *F* and *P* in these two places of the name. The asterisk (*) at the end tells AutoCAD that the remaining characters can be anything. The question marks and asterisk are known as *wildcard characters*. They are commonly used filtering tools for both the Unix and Windows operating systems.

As the number of layers in a drawing grows, you will find layer filters an indispensable tool. But bear in mind that the successful use of the layer filters can depend on a careful layer-naming convention. If you are producing architectural plans, you might want to consider the AIA layering guidelines.

TIP   Check out Chapter 24 for some additional tools that will help you manage layer settings.

Assigning Linetypes to Layers

You will often want to use different linetypes to show hidden lines, center lines, fence lines, or other noncontinuous lines. You can assign a color and a linetype to a layer. You then see ISO (International Organization for Standardization) and complex linetypes, including lines that can be used to illustrate gas and water lines in civil work or batt insulation in a wall cavity.

AutoCAD comes with several linetypes, as shown in Figure 5.5. ISO linetypes are designed to be used with specific plotted line widths and linetype scales. For example, if you are using a pen width of 0.5 mm, set the linetype scale of the drawing to 0.5 as well. (See Chapter 16 for more information on plotting and linetype scale.) The complex linetypes at the bottom of the figure are industry-specific, such as gas and water lines for civil work and a linetype that can be used to symbolize batt insulation in a wall cavity. You can also create your own linetypes (see Chapter 26).

FIGURE 5.5

Standard, ISO, and complex AutoCAD linetypes

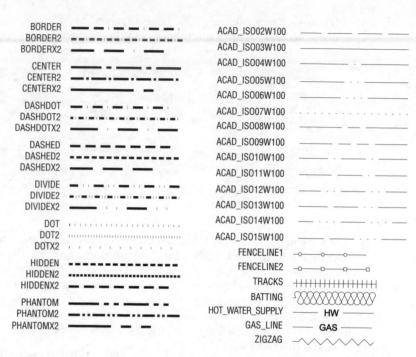

Linetypes that contain text, such as the gas line sample at the bottom of Figure 5.5, use the current text height and font to determine the size and appearance of the text displayed in the line. A text height of zero displays the text properly in most cases. See Chapter 10 for more on text styles.

AutoCAD stores linetype descriptions in an external file named Acad.lin, or Acadiso.lin for metric users. You can edit this file in a word processor to create new linetypes or to modify existing ones. You will see how this is done in Chapter 26.

Adding a Linetype to a Drawing

To see how linetypes work, add a dash-dot line in the bathroom plan to indicate a shower curtain rod:

1. Open the Layers Properties Manager dialog box and then select All from the filter list.

2. Click New and then type **Pole** to create a new layer called Pole.

TIP If you are in a hurry, you can simultaneously load a linetype and assign it to a layer by using the Layer command. In this exercise, you enter **–Layer↵** at the Command prompt. Then enter **L↵, dashdot↵, pole↵,** and press ↵ to exit the Layer command.

3. In the Pole layer listing, under the Linetype column, click the word *Continuous* to open the Select Linetype dialog box. To find the Linetype column, you might need to scroll the list to the right by using the scroll bar at the bottom of the list.

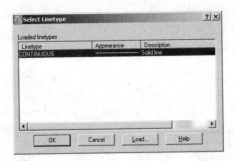

WARNING   The word *Continuous* truncates to *Contin* when the Linetype column is at its default width and the Continuous option is selected.

4. The Select Linetype dialog box offers a list of linetypes to choose from. In a new file such as the Bath file, only one linetype is available by default. You must load any additional linetype you want to use. Click the Load button at the bottom of the dialog box to open the Load Or Reload Linetypes dialog box. Notice that the list of linetype names is similar to the Layer drop-down list. You can sort the names alphabetically or by description by clicking the Linetype or Description heading at the top of the list.

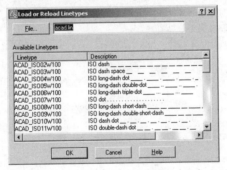

5. In the Available Linetypes list, scroll down to locate the Dashdot linetype, click it, and then click OK.

6. Notice that the Dashdot linetype is now added to the linetypes available in the Select Linetype dialog box.

7. Click Dashdot to highlight it; then click OK. Now Dashdot appears in the Pole layer listing under Linetype.

8. With the Pole layer still highlighted, click the Set Current button to make the Pole layer current.

9. Click OK to exit the Layer Properties Manager dialog box.

10. Turn off the Running Osnap mode; then draw a line across the opening of the tub area, from coordinate 4´-4˝,1´-10˝ to coordinate 4´-4˝,6´-10˝. Metric users should draw a line from coordinate 133,56 to 133,208.

CONTROLLING LINETYPE SCALE

Although you have designated this as a dashdot line, it appears solid. Zoom in to a small part of the line, and you'll see that the line is indeed as you specified.

Because you are working at a scale of 1″ = 1′, you must adjust the scale of your linetypes accordingly. This too is accomplished in the Linetype Manager dialog box. Here are the steps:

1. Choose Format ➤ Linetype from the drop-down menu. You can also select Other from the Linetype Control drop-down list in the Properties toolbar.

2. The Linetype Manager dialog box opens. Click the Show Details button in the upper-right corner of the dialog box. You'll see some additional options appear at the bottom.

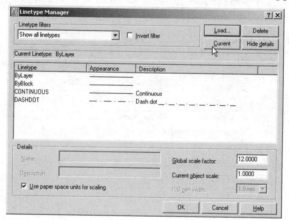

TIP The Linetype Manager dialog box offers the Load and Delete buttons that let you load or delete a linetype directly without having to go through a particular layer's linetype setting.

3. Double-click the Global Scale Factor text box and then type **12** (metric users type **30**). This is the scale conversion factor for a 1″ = 1′ scale (see Chapter 3).

4. Click OK. The drawing regenerates, and the shower curtain rod is displayed in the linetype and at the scale you designated.

5. Click the Zoom Previous tool so your drawing looks like Figure 5.6.

TIP You can also use the Ltscale system variable to set the linetype scale. Type **Ltscale.⏎**, and at the Enter new linetype scale factor <1.0000>: prompt, enter **12.⏎**.

FIGURE 5.6
The completed
bathroom

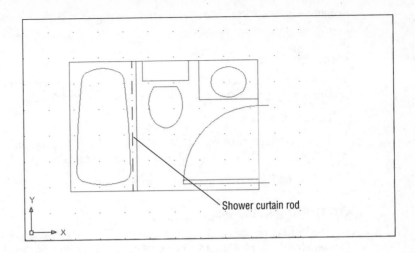

Shower curtain rod

TIP If you change the linetype of a layer or an object, but the object remains a continuous line, check the Ltscale system variable. It should be set to your drawing scale factor. If this doesn't work, set the Viewres system variable to a higher value (see Appendix C). (Viewres can also be set by the Arc And Circle Smoothness option in the Display tab of the Options dialog box.) The behavior of linetype scales depends on whether you are in Model Space or in a drawing layout. If your efforts to control linetype scale have no effect on your linetype's visibility, you might be in a drawing layout. See Chapter 16 for more on Model Space and layouts.

Remember that if you assign a linetype to a layer, everything you draw on that layer will be of that linetype. This includes arcs, polylines, circles, and traces. As explained in the "Setting Individual Colors, Linetypes, and Linetype Scales" sidebar later in this chapter, you can also assign different colors and linetypes to individual objects, rather than relying on their layer assignment to define color and linetype. However, you might want to avoid assigning colors and linetypes directly to objects until you have some experience with AutoCAD and a good grasp of your drawing's organization.

In the previous exercise, you changed the global linetype scale setting. This affects all noncontinuous linetypes within the current drawing. You can also change the linetype scale of individual objects by using the Properties button on the Properties toolbar. Or you can set the default linetype scale for all new objects, with the Current Object Scale option in the Linetype Manager dialog box.

When individual objects are assigned a linetype scale, they are still affected by the global linetype scale set by the Ltscale system variable. For example, say you assign a linetype scale of 2 to the curtain rod in the previous example. This scale is then multiplied by the global linetype scale of 12, for a final linetype scale of 24.

TIP You can also set the default linetype scale for individual objects by using the Celtscale system variable. After it is set, only newly created objects are affected. You must use the Properties palette to change the linetype scale of individual existing objects.

If the objects you draw appear in a different linetype from that of the layer they are on, check the default linetype by using the Linetype Control drop-down list on the Properties toolbar. You can also choose Format ➤ Linetype. Then, in the Linetype Manager dialog box, highlight ByLayer in the Linetype list, and click the Current button. In addition, check the linetype scale of the object itself, by using the Properties palette. A different linetype scale can make a line appear to have an assigned linetype that might not be what you expect. (See the sidebar "Setting Individual Colors, Linetypes, and Linetype Scales.")

ADDING THE FINAL DETAIL

If you are working through the tutorial, your final task here is to set up an insertion point for the current drawing, to facilitate its insertion into other drawings in the future. Follow these steps:

1. Type **Base** ↵.

2. At the Enter base point <0'-0",0'-0",0'-0">: prompt, pick the upper-left corner of the bathroom. The bathroom drawing is now complete.

3. Choose File ➢ Save to record your work up to now.

Controlling Line Weights

You might have noticed an option in the Layer Properties Manager dialog box called *Lineweight*. This option lets you control the thickness of your lines by adjusting the Lineweight setting, either through layer assignments or through direct object property assignment. This setting lets you view line weights as they will appear in your final plot.

With the Lineweight option, you have greater control over the look of your drawings. This can save time because you don't have to print your drawing just to check for lineweights. You'll be able to see how thick or thin your lines are as you edit your drawing. You'll get a chance to delve into line weights in Chapter 8.

Keeping Track of Blocks and Layers

The Insert and the Layer Properties Manager dialog boxes let you view the blocks and layers available in your drawing, by listing them in a window. The Layer Properties Manager dialog box also includes information about the status of layers. However, you might forget the layer on which an object resides. You've seen how the Properties option on the shortcut menu shows you the properties of an object. The List option in the Tools ➢ Inquiry menu also enables you to get information about individual objects.

Use these steps to see an alternate way to view the properties of a block:

1. Choose Tools ➢ Inquiry ➢ List from the menu bar.

TIP If you just want to quickly check which layer an object is on, click it. Its layer will appear in the Layer list of the Layers toolbar.

2. At the Select objects: prompt, click the Tub block and then press ↵ to open the AutoCAD Text Window.

3. In the AutoCAD Text Window, a listing appears that shows not only the layer that the tub is on, but also its space, insertion point, name, rotation angle, and scale.

The information you see in the Text window is duplicated in the Properties palette that you see when you right-click and choose Properties. But having the data in the AutoCAD Text Window gives you the flexibility to record the data in a text file, in case you need to store data about parts of your drawing. You can also use the AutoCAD Text Window to access and store other types of data regarding your drawings.

TIP The Space property you see listed for the Tub block designates whether the object resides in Model Space or Paper Space. You'll learn more about these spaces in Chapters 8 and 16.

Using the Log File Feature

Eventually, you will want a permanent record of block and layer listings. This is especially true if you work on drawing files that are being used by others. Here's a way to get a permanent record of the layers and blocks within a drawing by using the Log File option under the Environment Preferences:

1. Minimize the AutoCAD Text Window.

2. Choose Tools ➤ Options or type **op**↵ to open the Options dialog box. You can also right-click the drawing area and choose Options from the shortcut menu.

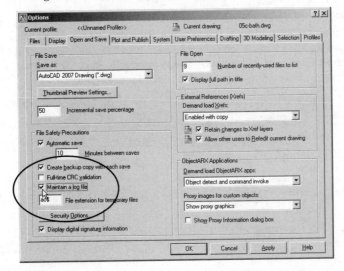

3. Click the Open And Save tab.

4. Click the Maintain A Log File check box on the bottom-left side of the dialog box.

5. Click OK, type **–LAYER**↵ (don't forget the minus sign) at the Command prompt, and then type **?**↵.

6. At the `Enter layer name(s) to list <*>:` prompt, press ↵ again. The AutoCAD Text Window appears, and a listing of all the layers scrolls into view.

7. Press F2 to return to the AutoCAD drawing screen, press Esc, and then open the Options dialog box again.

8. Click the Open And Save tab, click the Maintain A Log File check box again, and then click OK.

9. Use Windows Notepad to open the AutoCAD log file located in the `C:\Documents and Settings\YourSettings\Local Settings\Application Data\Autodesk\AutoCAD 2007 \R17 \enu\` folder. The name of the log file will start with the name of the current drawing, followed by a series of numbers and the .log filename extension, as in `04c-bath-metric_1_ 1_6500.log`. Notice that the layer listing is recorded there.

WARNING   The location of the AutoCAD log file is typical for AutoCAD running on Windows XP Professional on a simple workgroup network. The location of the AutoCAD log file depends on your operating system, the type of network you are using, and your user profile. If you are using Windows 2000, for example, change `\Documents and Settings` to `\Winnt\Profiles`. If you have difficulty finding the log file, you can enter **(getvar "logfilepath")** at the AutoCAD Command prompt to get a listing of the log file location. The log file may also be in a hidden folder so you may have to turn off the hidden folder setting in Windows Explorer. See Appendix A for instruction on how to do this.

With the Log File feature, you can record virtually anything that appears in the Command prompt. You can even record an entire AutoCAD session. The log file can also be helpful in constructing script files to automate tasks. (See Chapter 20 for more information on scripts.) If you want a hard copy of the log file, print it from an application such as Windows Notepad or your favorite word processor.

WARNING   If you want, you can arrange to keep the AutoCAD log file file in a folder other than the default AutoCAD subfolder. This setting is also in the Options dialog box under the Files tab. Locate the Log File Location listing in the Search Paths, File Names, And File Locations list box. Click the plus sign next to this listing, which expands to show the location for the log file. See Appendix A for more on the AutoCAD Options dialog box settings.

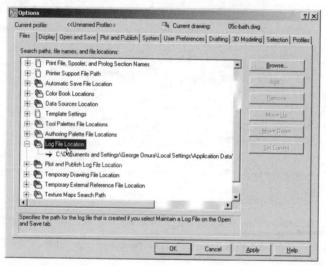

You can double-click the file location listing to open a Browse For Folder dialog box and specify a different location and filename for your log file.

TIP   After you've settled on a location on disk for the log file, use Windows Explorer to associate the log file with the Windows Notepad or WordPad application. Then click and drag the file to the AutoCAD program group. This gives you quick access to your log file by simply double-clicking its icon in the AutoCAD program group.

If You Want to Experiment

If your application is not architecture, you might want to experiment with creating other types of symbols. You might also start thinking about a layering system that suits your particular needs.

SETTING INDIVIDUAL COLORS, LINETYPES, AND LINETYPE SCALES

If you prefer, you can set up AutoCAD to assign specific colors and linetypes to objects, instead of having objects take on the color and linetype settings of the layer on which they reside. Normally, objects are given a default color and linetype called ByLayer, which means each object takes on the color or linetype of its assigned layer. (You've probably noticed the word *ByLayer* in the Object Properties toolbar and in various dialog boxes.)

Use the Properties tool on the Standard toolbar to change the color or linetype of existing objects. This tool opens a palette that lets you set the properties of individual objects. For new objects, use the Color control drop-down list on the Properties toolbar to set the current default color to red (for example), instead of ByLayer. Then everything you draw will be red, regardless of the current layer color. The Color control drop-down list also offers a "Select Color" option that opens the Select Color dialog box that you saw earlier in this chapter.

For linetypes, you can use the Linetype Control drop-down list in the Properties toolbar to select a default linetype for all new objects. The list shows only linetypes that have already been loaded into the drawing, so you must first load a linetype before you can select it.

Another possible color and linetype assignment is ByBlock, which you also set with the Properties toolbar. ByBlock makes everything you draw white, until you turn your drawing into a block and then insert the block on a layer with an assigned color. The objects then take on the color of that layer. This behavior is similar to that of objects drawn on layer 0. The ByBlock linetype works similarly to the ByBlock color.

Finally, if you want to set the linetype scale for each individual object, instead of relying on the global linetype scale (the Ltscale system variable), you can use the Properties palette to modify the linetype scale of individual objects. In place of using the Properties button, you can set the Celtscale system variable to the linetype scale you want for new objects.

As mentioned earlier, stay away from assigning colors and linetypes to individual objects until you are comfortable with AutoCAD; and even then, use color and linetype assignments carefully. Other users who work on your drawing might have difficulty understanding your drawing's organization if you assign color and linetype properties indiscriminately.

Open the file called Mytemp that you created from the previous chapter. In it, create layers numbered 1 through 8, and assign each layer the color that corresponds to its number. For example, give Layer 1 the color 1 (red), Layer 2 the color 2 (yellow), and so on. Draw each part shown in Figure 5.7, and turn each part into a file on disk by using Export (choose File ➤ Export) or the Wblock command. When specifying a filename, use the name indicated for each part in the figure. For the insertion point, also use the points indicated in the figure. Use the Osnap modes (see Chapter 2) to select the insertion points. You can use the Experiment05-1.dwg sample file as a reference.

After you create the parts, exit the file by choosing File ➤ Exit, and then open the MyAssembly drawing from the Chapter 5 projects folder. Use the Insert Block command to place your newly created parts as shown in Figure 5.8. You can use the Experiment05-2.dwg file as a reference.

FIGURE 5.7
A typical set of
symbols

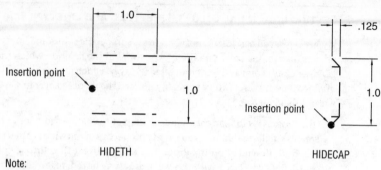

HIDETH   HIDECAP

Note:
Give layer 3 the HIDDEN linetype.
Put all of HIDETH and HIDECAP on layer 3.
Don't draw dimensions, just use them for reference.

FIGURE 5.8
Draw this part
using the symbols
you create

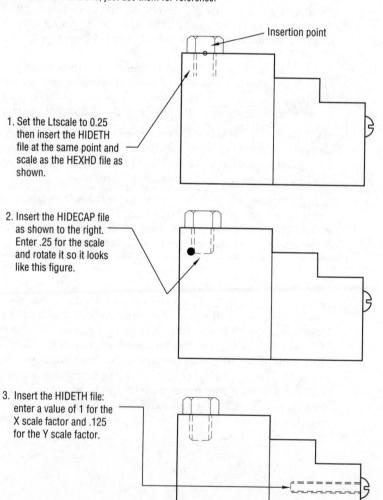

1. Set the Ltscale to 0.25
   then insert the HIDETH
   file at the same point and
   scale as the HEXHD file as
   shown.

2. Insert the HIDECAP file
   as shown to the right.
   Enter .25 for the scale
   and rotate it so it looks
   like this figure.

3. Insert the HIDETH file:
   enter a value of 1 for the
   X scale factor and .125
   for the Y scale factor.

Part 2

Mastering Intermediate Skills

In this part:

Chapter 6

Editing and Reusing Data to Work Efficiently

At least five AutoCAD commands are devoted to duplicating objects, ten if you include the Grips options. Why so many? If you're an experienced drafter, you know that you frequently have to draw the same item several times in many drawings. So AutoCAD offers a variety of ways to reuse existing geometry, thereby automating much of the repetitive work usually associated with manual drafting.

In this chapter, as you finish drawing the studio apartment unit, you will explore some of the ways to exploit existing files and objects while constructing your drawing. For example, you will use existing files as prototypes for new files, eliminating the need to set up layers, scales, and sheet sizes for similar drawings. With AutoCAD you can also duplicate objects in multiple arrays. In Chapter 3 you saw how to use the Object Snap (Osnap) overrides on objects to locate points for drawing complex forms. This chapter describes other ways of using lines to aid your drawing.

And, because you will begin to use the Zoom command more in the exercises in this chapter, you will review this command as you go along. You'll also discover the Pan command—another tool to help you get around in your drawing.

You're already familiar with many of the commands you will use to draw the apartment unit. So, rather than going through every step of the drawing process, the exercises will sometimes ask you to copy the drawing from a figure, using notes and dimensions as guides, and put objects on the indicated layers. If you have trouble remembering a command you've already learned, just go back and review the appropriate section of the book.

Topics in this chapter include the following:

- ◆ Creating and Using Templates
- ◆ Copying an Object Multiple Times
- ◆ Developing Your Drawing
- ◆ Finding an Exact Distance along a Curve
- ◆ Changing the Length of Objects
- ◆ Creating a New Drawing by Using Parts from Another Drawing
- ◆ Drawing Parallel Lines

Creating and Using Templates

Most programs today include what are called templates. A *template* is a file that is already set up for a specific application. For example, in your word processor, you might want to set up letters with a logo, a return address, and a date so you don't have to add these elements each time you create a letter. You might also want to format invoices in a slightly different way. You can set up a template for the needs of each type of document. That way, you don't have to spend time reformatting each new document you create.

Similarly, AutoCAD offers templates, which are drawing files that contain custom settings designed for a particular function. Out of the box, AutoCAD has templates for ISO, ANSI, DIN, GB, and JIS standard drawing formats that include generic title blocks. But you aren't limited to these "canned" templates. You can create your own templates for your particular style and method of drawing.

If you find that you use a particular drawing setup frequently, you can turn one or more of your typical drawings into a template. For example, you might want to create a set of drawings with the same scale and sheet size as an existing drawing. By turning a frequently used drawing into a template, you can save a lot of setup time for subsequent drawings.

Creating a Template

The following exercise guides you through creating and using a template drawing for your studio's kitchenette. Because the kitchenette will use the same layers, settings, scale, and sheet size as the bathroom drawing, you can use the Bath file as a prototype. Follow these steps:

1. Start AutoCAD in the usual way.

2. Choose File ➢ Open to open the Select File dialog box.

3. Locate the Bath file you created in the last chapter. You can also use the file 06-bath.dwg from the companion CD.

4. Click the Erase button on the Modify toolbar or enter e↵; then type all.↵↵. This erases all the objects that make up the bathroom, but other elements, such as layers, linetypes, and stored blocks, remain in the drawing.

5. Choose File ➢ Save As to open the Save Drawing As dialog box. Open the File Of Type drop-down list and select AutoCAD Drawing Template (*.dwt). The file list window changes to display the current template files in the \Template\ folder.

TIP When you choose the AutoCAD Drawing Template option in the Save Drawing As dialog box, AutoCAD automatically opens the folder containing the template files. The standard AutoCAD installation creates the folder named Template to contain the template files. If you want to place your templates in a different folder, you can change the default template location by using the Options dialog box (choose Tools ➢ Options). Click the Files tab, double-click to expand Template Settings, and then double-click Template Drawing File Location in the list. Double-click the folder name that appears just below Template Drawing File Location; then select a new location from the Browse For Folder dialog box that appears.

6. In the File Name text box, enter the name **Arch8x11h**. If you're a metric user, enter the name **A4plan**.

7. Click Save to open the Template Description dialog box.

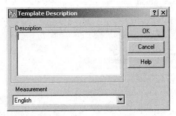

8. Enter the following description: **Architectural one inch scale drawing on** $8\frac{1}{2}$ **by 11 inch media**. Metric users should enter the description **Architectural 1:10 scale drawing on A4 media**.

9. Select English or Metric from the Measurement drop-down list, depending on the unit system you're using.

10. Click OK to save your new file and create a template. The template file you saved becomes the current file. (As with other Windows programs, choosing File ➢ Save As makes the saved file current.) This also shows that you can edit template files just as you would regular drawing files.

11. Close the template file.

Using a Template

Now let's see how a template is used. You'll use the template you just created as the basis for a new drawing you will work on in this chapter:

1. Choose File ➢ New to open the Create New Drawing dialog box. Alternately, you might see the Select Template dialog box. The dialog box that appears depends on the setting for the Startup option in the System tab of the Options dialog box. (See Appendix A for more on the System tab in the Options dialog box.)

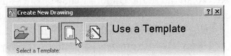

TIP If the Create New Drawing dialog box does not appear, do the following: Choose Tools ➢ Options. Select the System tab. In the General Options group, choose Show Startup Dialog Box from the Startup drop-down list. Click OK to close the Options dialog box.

2. In the Create New Drawing dialog box, click the Use A Template button to display a list box and a preview window. If AutoCAD displays the Select Template dialog box, skip to step 3.

3. In the Select A Template list box, click the filename `Arch8x11h.dwt`. Metric users should click the filename `A4plan.dwt`. Because this file is blank, you won't see anything in the preview window. Notice that the description you entered earlier in the Template Description dialog box appears in the Template Description area below the list.

4. Click OK. It might not be obvious, but your new file is set up with the same architectural units and drawing limits as the bathroom drawing. It also contains the Door, Toilet, and Tub blocks.

5. Now you need to give your new file a name. Choose File ➤ Save As to open the Save Drawing As dialog box. (Make sure you choose Save As or you won't get the Save Drawing As dialog box.) Enter **Kitchen** for the filename, and select the appropriate folder in which to save your new kitchen file.

6. Click Save to create the `Kitchen` file and close the dialog box.

TIP In Chapter 2, you were asked to select the Show Startup Dialog Box option in the General Options of the System tab, found in the Options dialog box. If you decide to turn off the Show Startup Dialog Box option, you can still select a template file when you start a new file. However, instead of the Startup dialog box, you will see the Select Template dialog box, which is a standard AutoCAD file dialog box complete with preview panel. From there, you can select a template file. To create a drawing from scratch by using templates, choose the `Acad.dwt` template file for Imperial units or the `Acadiso.dwt` file for metric units.

You've created and used your own template file. Later, when you have established a comfortable working relationship with AutoCAD, you can create a set of templates that are custom-made to your particular needs.

However, you don't need to create a template every time you want to reuse settings from another file. You can use an existing file as the basis or prototype for a new file without creating a template. Open the prototype file, and then choose File ➤ Save As to create a new version of the file under a new name. You can then edit the new version without affecting the original prototype file.

OPENING A FILE AS READ-ONLY

At times you will want to open an important file and view it while ensuring that it is protected from accidental changes. Or you might want to use a file as a starting point for a new project while leaving the original file unchanged. You can protect an open file by using the Open Read-Only option in the Select File dialog box.

Choose File ➤ Open to open the Select File dialog box. Click the downward-pointing arrow to the right of the Open button in the lower-right corner to display a menu that includes the Open Read-Only option.

Choose Open Read-Only to open the selected file. You can still edit the open file any way you please, but if you attempt to choose File ➤ Save, you will get the message "Drawing file is write protected." You can, however, save your changed file under another name by choosing File ➤ Save As.

The Open Read-Only option provides a way to protect important files from accidental corruption. It also offers another method for reusing settings and objects from existing files by letting you open a file as a prototype and then save the new file under another name.

Copying an Object Multiple Times

Now let's explore the tools that let you quickly duplicate objects. In this section, you will begin to draw parts of a small kitchen. The first exercise introduces the Array command, which you can use to draw the gas burners of a range top.

As you'll see, an array can be in either a circular pattern, called a *polar array,* or a matrix of columns and rows, called a *rectangular array.*

Making Circular Copies

To start the range top, first set the layer on which you want to draw, and then draw a circle representing the edge of one burner:

1. Set the current layer to Fixture.

TIP Because you used the Bath file as a template, Running Osnaps for Endpoint, Midpoint, and Intersection are already turned on and available in this new file.

2. Click the Circle tool on the Draw toolbar or type **C⏎**.

3. At the Specify Center point for circle or [3P/2P/Ttr (tan tan radius)]: prompt, pick a point at coordinate 4´, 4´. Metric users should pick a point at coordinate 120,120.

4. At the Specify radius of circle or [Diameter]: prompt, enter **3⏎**. Metric users should enter **7.6⏎**. The circle appears.

Now you're ready to use the Array command to draw the burner grill. You will first draw one line representing part of the grill and then use the Array command to create the copies:

1. Turn off both the PolarSnap and Grid Snap modes by clicking the Snap button in the status bar, and draw a 4˝ [inch] line starting from the coordinate 4´-1˝, 4´-0˝ [4´-1˝ and 4´-0˝ – 4 feet, 1 inch, 4 feet, 0 inches] and ending to the right of that point. Metric users should draw a 9 cm line starting at coordinate 122,120 and ending to the right of that point.

2. Zoom into the circle and line to get a better view. Your drawing should look like Figure 6.1.

FIGURE 6.1

A close-up of the circle and line

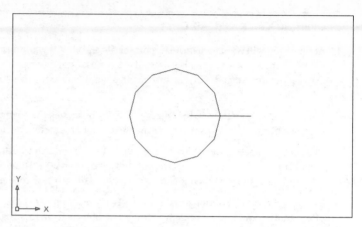

You've got the basic parts needed to create the burner grill. Now you're ready to make multiple copies of the line. For this part, you'll use the Array dialog box:

1. Click Array on the Modify toolbar or type **AR.⏎** to open the Array dialog box.

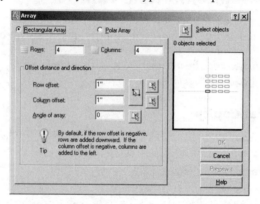

2. Click the Select Objects button. The dialog box temporarily closes, enabling you to select objects.

3. Type **L.⏎** to select the last object drawn, or click the object you want to array.

4. Press ⏎ to confirm your selection. The Array dialog reopens.

5. Click the Polar Array radio button at the top of the dialog box to tell AutoCAD you want a circular array. The Array dialog box displays the Polar Array options.

6. Click the Pick Center Point button to temporarily close the Array dialog box.

7. Pick the point that represents the center of the circular array. Use Center Osnap to select the center of the circle. After you've indicated a point, the Array dialog box returns.

TIP Remember that to access osnaps other than those set up as Running Osnaps, you Shift+right-click the mouse and then select the osnap you want to use from the resulting menu.

WARNING If you use Center Osnap, you must place the cursor on the circle's circumference, not on the circle's center point.

At this point, you've selected an object to array, and you've indicated the center location of the array. If you've selected the wrong object or the wrong center point, you can go back and specify these options again.

Now, to complete the process, tell AutoCAD the number of copies in the array and the extent of the array through the circle:

1. In the Array dialog box, enter **8** in the Total Number Of Items text box. This tells AutoCAD to make eight copies including the original.

2. Accept the default of 360 for the Angle To Fill text box. This tells AutoCAD to spread the copies evenly over the full 360°of the circle. Of course, you can enter other values here. For example, if you enter 180, the array will fill half the circle.

TIP You can click the Pick Angle To Fill button to the right of the Angle To Fill text box to graphically select an angle in the drawing.

3. Make sure the Rotate Items As Copied check box in the lower-left corner of the dialog box is selected. This ensures that the arrayed object is rotated about the array center. If you clear this option, the copies will all be oriented in the same direction as the original object.

4. Click the Preview button. AutoCAD shows you the results of your array settings plus a dialog box that offers Accept, Modify, and Cancel.

5. Click Accept. The circular array appears in the drawing, as shown in Figure 6.2.

In step 5, you could have selected the Modify option to return to the Array dialog box and change settings before committing to a final array pattern, or you could click Cancel to cancel the whole process. The Array dialog box gives you a lot of leeway in creating your array copies.

TIP If you're a veteran AutoCAD user and you prefer the command-line version of the Array command, you can type –Array↵ or –Ar↵ at the Command prompt, and then answer the prompts as you would in earlier versions of AutoCAD.

FIGURE 6.2
The completed
gas burner

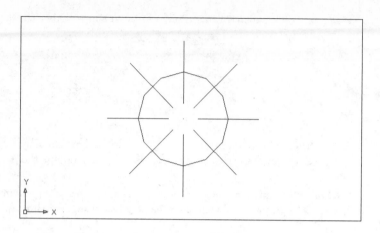

Making Row and Column Copies

Now you will draw the other three burners of the gas range by creating a rectangular array from the burner you just drew. You will first zoom back a bit to get a view of a larger area. Then you will proceed with the Array command.

Follow these steps to zoom back:

1. Choose View ➢ Zoom ➢ Scale, or type **Z↵ S↵**.

2. Enter **.5x↵**. Your drawing will look like Figure 6.3.

TIP If you're not too fussy about the amount you want to zoom out, you can choose View ➢ Zoom ➢ Out to quickly reduce your view, or you can click the Zoom Realtime tool on the Standard toolbar.

Entering .5x for the Zoom Scale factor tells AutoCAD you want a view that reduces the width of the current view to fill half the display area, enabling you to see more of the work area. If you specify a scale value greater than 1 (5, for example), you will magnify your current view. If you leave off the *x*, your new view will be in relation to the drawing limits rather than the current view.

FIGURE 6.3
The preceding
view reduced by
a factor of 0.5

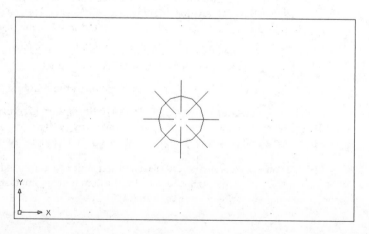

Now you will finish the range top. Here you will get a chance to use the Rectangular Array option to create three additional burners:

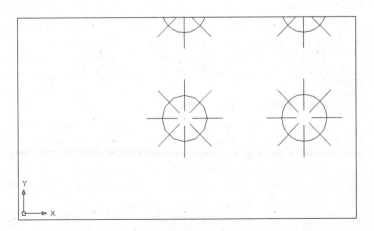

1. Click the Array tool on the Modify toolbar again or type **AR**↵ to open the Array dialog box.

2. Click the Select Objects button to temporarily close the Array dialog box.

3. Select the entire burner, including the lines and the circle, and then press ↵ to confirm your selection.

4. In the Array dialog box, click the Rectangular Array radio button.

5. Change both the Rows and Columns text boxes to 2.

6. Change the Row Offset text box value to 1´-2″ [1´-2″] (35.5 for metric users) and the Column Offset text box value to 1´-4″ [1´-4″] (or 40.6 for metric users).

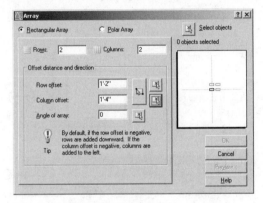

7. Click OK. Your screen will look like Figure 6.4.

AutoCAD usually draws a rectangular array from bottom to top and from left to right. You can reverse the direction of the array by giving negative values for the distance between columns and rows.

FIGURE 6.4
The burners arrayed

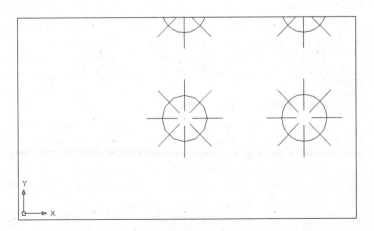

TIP At times, you might want to create a rectangular array at an angle. To accomplish this, enter the desired angle in the Angle Of Array text box of the Array dialog box. You can also select the angle graphically by clicking the Pick Angle Of Array button just to the right of the Angle Of Array text box.

If you need to graphically indicate an array cell, you can do so by using options in the Offset Distance And Direction group of the Array dialog box (see the bottom image in Figure 6.5). An *array cell* is a rectangle defining the distance between rows and columns (see the top image in Figure 6.5). You might want to use this option when objects are available to use as references from which to determine column and row distances. For example, you might have drawn a crosshatch pattern, as on a calendar, within which you want to array an object. You use the intersections of the hatch lines as references to define the array cell, which is one square in the hatch pattern.

FIGURE 6.5

An array cell and the Array dialog box options that let you graphically indicate array cells

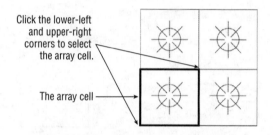

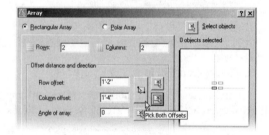

In the Offset Distance And Direction group, the Pick Both Offsets button lets you indicate the row and column distance by placing an array cell graphically in the drawing, as shown in the bottom image in Figure 6.5. You can also indicate a row or column distance graphically by using the Pick Row Offset or Pick Column Offset buttons to the right of the Pick Both Offsets button.

Fine-Tuning Your View

Back in Figure 6.4, you might have noticed that parts of the burners do not appear on the display. To move the view over so you can see all the burners, use the Pan command. Pan is similar to Zoom in that it changes your view of the drawing. However, Pan does not alter the magnification of the view the way Zoom does. Rather, Pan maintains the current magnification while moving your view across the drawing, just as you would pan a camera across a landscape.

QUICK ARRAY COPIES WITH GRIPS

Sometimes the Array tool can be overkill if you only need to make a few evenly spaced copies. Fortunately, grip editing offers a feature that lets you quickly make evenly spaced copies. Here's how it's done.

1. Press the Esc key to make sure you are not in the middle of a command; then select the objects you want to copy.

2. Click a grip point as your base point.

3. Right-click your mouse and select Move.

4. Ctrl+click a location to place a copy of the selected object. This first copy will determine the interval distance for additional copies.

5. Continue to hold down the Ctrl key and select additional points to make copies at regularly spaced intervals.

The copies snap to the distance you indicate with the first Ctrl+click point in step 4. You can use osnaps to select a distance based on the position of another object. Once you've made the first copy with the Ctrl+click, you can release the Ctrl key to make multiple copies at random intervals. Another option is to use PolarSnap while making grip edit copies. With PolarSnap, you can enter a specific distance for the intervals. See Chapter 3 for more on PolarSnap.

To activate the Pan command, follow these steps:

1. Click the Pan Realtime tool on the Standard toolbar, choose View ➢ Pan ➢ Realtime, or type **P** ↵. You can also right-click and choose Pan from the shortcut menu. A small hand-shaped cursor appears in place of the AutoCAD cursor.

2. Place the hand cursor in the center of the drawing area, and then click and drag it downward and to the left. The view follows the motion of your mouse.

3. Continue to drag the view until it looks similar to Figure 6.6; then release the mouse button.

FIGURE 6.6
The panned view of the range top

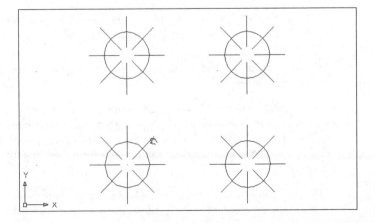

4. To finish the kitchen, you will want a view that shows more of the drawing area. Right-click to open the Zoom/Pan shortcut menu, and then choose Zoom. The cursor changes to the Zoom Realtime cursor. The Zoom/Pan shortcut menu also appears when you right-click during the Zoom Realtime command.

5. Place the cursor close to the top of the screen, and click and drag the cursor downward to zoom out until your view looks like the top panel of Figure 6.7. You might need to click and drag the Zoom Realtime cursor a second time to achieve this view.

FIGURE 6.7

The final view of the range top burners (top image) and the finished kitchen (bottom image). Metric dimensions are shown in brackets.

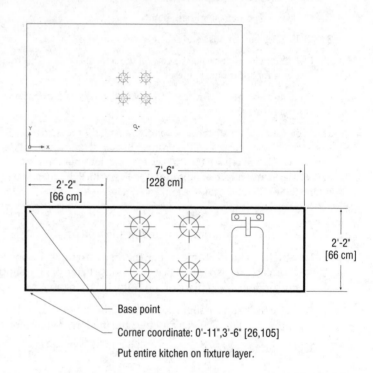

Base point

Corner coordinate: 0'-11",3'-6" [26,105]

Put entire kitchen on fixture layer.

6. Right-click the mouse again, and choose Exit from the shortcut menu. You're now ready to add more information to the kitchen drawing.

TIP To exit the Pan Realtime or Zoom Realtime command without opening the shortcut menu, press the Esc key.

This exercise showed how you can fine-tune your view by easily switching between Pan Realtime and Zoom Realtime. After you get the hang of these two tools working together, you'll be able to quickly access the best view for your needs. The other options in the shortcut menu—Zoom Window, Zoom Original, and Zoom Extents—perform the same functions as the options in the View drop-down menu.

TIP The Zoom Window option in the Zoom/Pan shortcut menu functions in a slightly different way from the standard Zoom Window option. Instead of clicking two points, you click and drag a window across your view.

While we're on the subject of display tools, don't forget the scroll bars to the right and bottom of the AutoCAD drawing area. They work like any other Windows scroll bars, offering a simple way to move up, down, left, or right in your current view. They also come in handy for quickly panning your view in one direction or another.

If for some reason the scroll bars do not appear in AutoCAD, or if you prefer to turn them off, open the Options dialog box (choose Tools ➢ Options), click the Display tab, and make sure that Display Scroll Bars In Drawing Window option is either selected to turn them on or cleared to turn them off.

Finishing the Kitchenette

Before you save and close the `Kitchen` file, you need to do one more thing. You will be using this drawing as a symbol and inserting it into the overall plan of the studio apartment unit. To facilitate accurate placement of the kitchen, you will want to change the location of the base point of this drawing to the upper-left corner of the kitchen. This will then be the *grip* of the drawing.

1. Complete the kitchenette as indicated in the bottom panel of Figure 6.7, shown earlier in this chapter. As the figure indicates, make sure you put the kitchenette on the Fixture layer. This will help you control the visibility of the kitchenette in future edits of this file. Draw the sink roughly as shown in the figure.

2. Choose Draw ➢ Block ➢ Base from the drop-down menu.

3. At the `Enter base point:` prompt, pick the upper-left corner of the kitchen, as indicated in the bottom image of Figure 6.7. The kitchen drawing is complete.

4. Choose File ➢ Save and exit the file.

Developing Your Drawing

As mentioned briefly in Chapter 3, when using AutoCAD, you first create the basic geometric forms used in your drawing; and then you refine them. In this section, you will create two drawings—the studio apartment unit and the lobby—that demonstrate this process in more detail.

First, you will construct a typical studio apartment unit by using the drawings you have created thus far. In the process, you will explore the use of lines as reference objects.

You will also further examine how to use existing files as blocks. In Chapter 4, you inserted a file into another file. The size and number of files you can insert are limitless. As you might already have guessed, you can also *nest* files and blocks; that is, you can insert blocks or files within other blocks or files. Nesting can help reduce your drawing time by enabling you to build one block out of smaller blocks. For example, you can insert your door drawing into the bathroom plan. In turn, you can insert the bathroom plan into the studio unit plan, which also contains doors. Finally, you can insert the unit plan into the overall floor plan for the studio apartment building.

Importing Settings

In this exercise, you will use the `Bath` file as a prototype for the studio unit plan. However, you must make a few changes to it first. After the changes are made, you will import the bathroom and thereby import the layers and blocks contained in the bathroom file.

As you go through this exercise, observe how the drawings begin to evolve from simple forms to complex, assembled forms.

Use these steps to modify the Bath file:

1. Open the Bath file. If you skipped drawing the Bath file in Chapter 5, use the file 05c-bath.dwg (or 05c-bath-metric.dwg) from the companion CD.

2. Use the Base command and select the upper-left corner of the bathroom as the new base point for this drawing, so you can position the Bath file more accurately.

3. Save the Bath file. If you use the file from the CD, choose File ➢ Save As and save it as Bath.

4. Choose File ➢ Close to close the Bath drawing.

Next, you will create a new file. But this time, instead of using the Start From Scratch or Use A Template option in the Create New Drawing dialog box, you'll try the Use A Wizard option:

1. Choose File ➢ New to open the Create New Drawing dialog box.

2. Click the Use A Wizard button to display two options below the drop-down list: Quick Setup and Advanced Setup.

3. Choose Quick Setup and click OK to open the QuickSetup dialog box.

4. Click the Architectural radio button. Metric users should use the default Decimal units.

5. Click Next to display the Area settings.

6. Enter **528** in the Width text box and **408** in the Length box. These are the appropriate dimensions for an $8^{1}/_{2}'' \times 11''$ [$8^{1}/_{2}$ inches × 11 inches] drawing at $^{1}/_{4}''$ [1/4 inches] = 1'-0 " [1 foot 0 inches] scale. Metric users should enter **1485** for the width and **1050** for the length. This is the work area for a 1:50 scale drawing on an A4 sheet.

7. Click Finish.

8. Choose Tools ➢ Drafting Settings to set the X and Y Snap Spacing to 1" [inch] and the X and Y Grid Spacing to 48 " [inches]. The grid spacing setting will change to 4´[feet]. This sets the grid spacing to display the equivalent of 1" intervals for a $^{1}/_{4}''$ = 1´-0" scale drawing. Metric users should set the snap spacing to 1 and the grid spacing to 120. Click OK when you are finished.

TIP If you need to find out the equivalent drawing area for a given sheet size and scale, see Chapter 3.

In prior sessions, you opened a blank file and chose Format ➢ Units And Format ➢ Drawing Limits to set up your drawing. This time, you used the QuickSetup Wizard to accomplish the same thing. In fact, the QuickSetup Wizard does nothing more than combine the Format ➢ Units And Format ➢ Drawing Limits options into one dialog box.

Now let's continue by laying out a typical studio unit. You'll discover how importing a file also imports a variety of drawing items such as layers and linetypes. Follow these steps:

1. Begin the unit by drawing two rectangles, one 14′ long by 24′ wide, and the other 14′ long by 4′ wide. Metric users should make the rectangles 426 cm wide by 731 cm long and 426 cm wide by 122 cm long. Place them as shown in Figure 6.8. The large rectangle represents the interior of the apartment unit, and the small rectangle represents the balcony. The size and location of the rectangles are indicated in the figure.

FIGURE 6.8

The apartment unit interior and balcony. Metric locations and dimensions are shown in brackets.

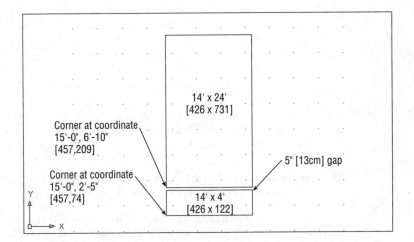

2. Click the Insert Block tool on the Draw toolbar to open the Insert dialog box.

3. Click the Browse button, and locate and select the bathroom drawing by using the Select Drawing File dialog box. Then click Open. If you haven't saved a Bathroom drawing from earlier exercises, you can use 05c-bath.dwg.

TIP If you used the Rectangle tool to draw the interior and balcony of the apartment unit, make sure you use the Explode tool on the Modify toolbar to explode the rectangles. The Rectangle tool draws a polyline rectangle instead of simple line segments, so you need to explode the rectangle to reduce it to its component lines. You'll learn more about polylines in Chapter 18.

TIP If you are using the 05c-bath.dwg file from the CD, do the following: After selecting 05c-bath.dwg in step 3, change the name that appears in the Block text box to Bath instead of 05c-bath before you click OK in step 4. This gives the inserted file a block name of Bath, even though its originating filename is 05c-bath.

4. Click OK in the Insert dialog box, and then click the upper-left corner of the unit's interior as the insertion point (see Figure 6.9). You can use the Endpoint Osnap to place the bathroom accurately. Use a scale factor of 1.0 and a rotation angle of 0°.

TIP If the Running Osnaps have not been set up in this file, you need to use the Osnap shortcut menu (Shift+right-click) to access the Endpoint Osnap. You can set up the Running Osnaps to take advantage of AutoCAD's AutoSnap functions by right-clicking the Osnap button in the status bar. Set the Running Osnaps as described in Chapter 3.

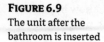

FIGURE 6.9

The unit after the bathroom is inserted

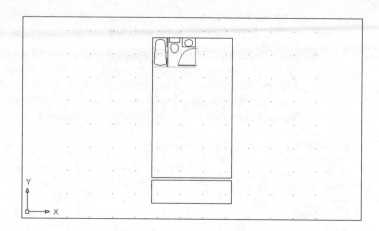

5. Assign the two rectangles that you drew earlier to the Wall layer. To do this, select the two rectangles so they are highlighted, and then open the Layer drop-down list in the Layers toolbar and select Wall. Press the Esc key twice to clear the selection.

TIP You can also use the Match Properties tool on the Standard toolbar to change layer settings of an object to those of another object in the drawing. See Chapter 7.

By inserting the bathroom, you imported the layers and blocks contained in the Bath file. You were then able to move previously drawn objects to the imported layers. If you are in a hurry, this can be a quick way to duplicate layers that you know exist in another drawing. This method is similar to using an existing drawing as a template, but it lets you start work on a drawing before deciding which template to use.

WARNING If two drawings contain the same layers and blocks, and one of these drawings is imported into the other, the layer settings and block definitions of the current file will take priority over those of the imported file. This is important to remember when the layer settings and block definitions are different in the two files.

Using Osnap Tracking to Place Objects

You will draw lines in the majority of your work, so it is important to know how to manipulate lines to your best advantage. In this section, you will look at some of the more common ways to use and edit these fundamental drawing objects. The following exercises show you the process of drawing lines, rather than just how individual commands work. While you're building walls and adding doors, you'll get a chance to become more familiar with Polar Tracking and Osnap Tracking.

ROUGHING IN THE LINE WORK

The bathroom you inserted in the preceding section has only one side of its interior walls drawn. (Walls are usually shown by double lines.) In this next exercise, you will draw the other side. Rather than trying to draw the wall perfectly the first time, you will "sketch" in the line work and then in the next section clean it up, in a way similar to manual drafting.

IMPORTING SETTINGS FROM EXTERNAL REFERENCE FILES

As explained in Chapter 4, you can use the External Reference (Xref) Attach DWG option to use another file as a background, or Xref, file. *Xref* files are similar to blocks except that they do not become part of the current drawing's database; nor do the settings from the externally referenced file automatically become part of the current drawing.

If you want to import layers, linetypes, text styles, and so forth from an Xref file, you must use the Xbind command, which you will learn more about as you work through this book. Xbind enables you to attach dimension style settings (discussed in Chapter 12 and in Appendix A), layers, linetypes, or text styles (discussed in Chapter 10) from an externally referenced file to the current file. You can also use Xbind to turn an externally referenced file into an ordinary block, thereby importing all the new settings contained in that file. See Chapter 15 for a more detailed description of how to use the External References (Xref) and Xbind commands.

Another tool for importing settings is the AutoCAD DesignCenter. You'll learn about the DesignCenter in Chapter 27.

Use these steps to rough in the wall lines:

1. Zoom into the bathroom so that the entire bathroom and part of the area around it are displayed, as in Figure 6.10.

FIGURE 6.10
The enlarged view of the bathroom

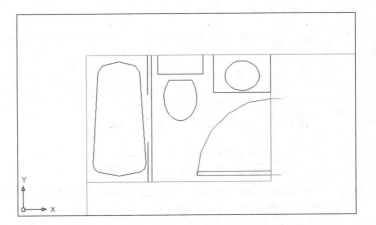

TIP   You might notice that some of the arcs in your bathroom drawing are not smooth. Don't be alarmed; this is how AutoCAD displays arcs and circles in enlarged views. The arcs will be smooth when they are plotted. If you want to see them now as they are stored in the file, you can regenerate the drawing by typing **Regen.⏎** at the Command prompt. Chapter 7 discusses regeneration in more detail.

2. Select Wall from the Layer drop-down list in the Layers toolbar to make Wall the current layer.

3. Make sure that the Otrack and Osnap buttons on the status bar are pressed, indicating that Osnap Tracking and Object Snap are turned on.

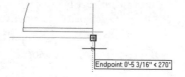

4. Choose Draw ➤ Line or type L↵.

5. At the Specify first point: prompt, move your cursor over the lower-right corner of the bathroom so that the Endpoint Osnap marker appears, but don't click it. As you move the cursor downward, the tracking vector appears. (If the tracking vector doesn't appear at first, move your cursor over the corner again until it does appear.)

TIP Remember that a little cross appears at the osnap location telling you that Osnap Tracking has "locked on" to that location.

6. With the tracking vector visible, point the cursor directly downward from the corner and then type 5↵. Metric users should type 13↵. Now a line starts 5″ (or 13 cm) below the lower-right corner of the bathroom.

7. Continue the line horizontally to the left, to slightly cross the left wall of the apartment unit, as illustrated in the top image in Figure 6.11. Press↵ .

8. Draw another line upward from the endpoint of the top door jamb to meet the top wall of the unit (see the second image in Figure 6.11). Use the Perpendicular Osnap to pick the top wall of the unit. This causes the line to end precisely on the wall line in perpendicular position, as in the bottom image in Figure 6.11.

TIP You can also use the Perpendicular Osnap override to draw a line perpendicular to a non-orthogonal line—one at a 45° angle, for instance.

9. Draw a line connecting the two door jambs. Then assign that line to the Ceiling layer. (See the first panel in Figure 6.12.)

10. Draw a line 6″ downward from the endpoint of the door jamb nearest the corner. (See the first panel in Figure 6.12.)

In the previous exercise, Osnap Tracking mode enabled you to specify a starting point of a line at an exact distance from the corner of the bathroom. In step 6, you used the Direct Distance method for specifying distance and direction.

TIP If you prefer, you can also choose From on the Osnap shortcut menu, and then open the shortcut menu again and select Endpoint. Select the corner and enter a polar coordinate such as @5<−90 to accomplish the same task as this exercise.

FIGURE 6.11

The corner of the bathroom wall and the filleted wall around the bathroom

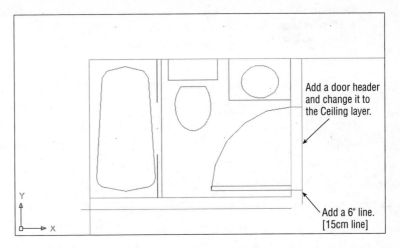

Add a door header and change it to the Ceiling layer.

Add a 6" line.
[15cm line]

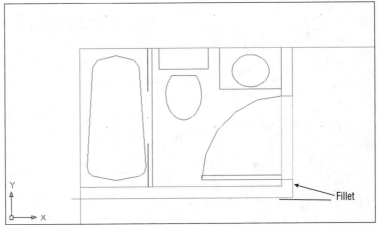

Fillet

UNDERSTANDING THE OSNAP TRACKING VECTOR

The Osnap Tracking vector comes into play only after you've placed an Osnap marker on a location, in this case, the corner of the bathroom. It won't appear at any other time. If you have both Running Osnaps and Osnap Tracking turned on, you'll get the tracking vector every time the cursor lands on an osnap location. This can be a bit confusing to novice users, so you might want to use Osnap Tracking sparingly until you become more comfortable with it.

And because Polar Tracking also uses a tracking vector, you can get the two confused. Remember that Polar Tracking lets you point the cursor in a specific direction while selecting points. If you're an experienced AutoCAD user, you can think of it as a more intelligent Ortho mode. On the other hand, Osnap Tracking lets you align points to osnap locations. Experienced AutoCAD users can think of Osnap Tracking as a more intelligent XYZ filter option.

FIGURE 6.12

The first wall line and the wall line by the door

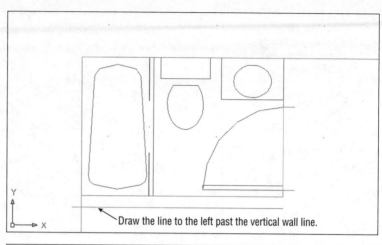

Draw the line to the left past the vertical wall line.

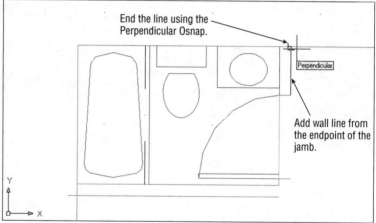

End the line using the Perpendicular Osnap.

Perpendicular

Add wall line from the endpoint of the jamb.

CLEANING UP THE LINE WORK

You've drawn some of the wall lines, approximating their endpoint locations. Next you will use the Fillet command to join lines exactly end to end and then import the Kitchen drawing.

Follow these steps to join the lines:

1. Click the Fillet tool on the Modify toolbar.

2. Type **R↵ 0↵** to make sure that the fillet radius is set to 0.

TIP The Chamfer command performs a similar function to the Fillet command. Unlike Fillet, the Chamfer command enables you to join two lines with an intermediate beveled line rather than with an arc. Chamfer can be set to join two lines at a corner in exactly the same manner as Fillet.

3. Fillet the two lines by picking the vertical and horizontal lines, as indicated in the second panel in Figure 6.12, shown earlier in this chapter. Notice that these points lie on the portion of the line you want to keep. Your drawing will look like the second panel in Figure 6.12.

4. Fillet the bottom wall of the bathroom with the left wall of the unit, as shown in Figure 6.13. Make sure the points you pick on the wall lines are on the side of the line you want to keep, not on the side you want to trimmed.

FIGURE 6.13

The cleaned-up wall intersections

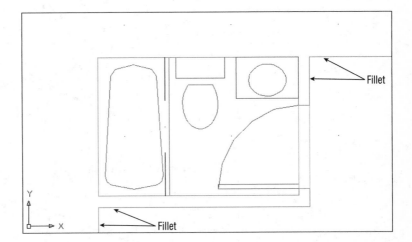

5. Fillet the top wall of the unit with the right-side wall of the bathroom, as shown in Figure 6.13.

TIP You can select two lines at once for the fillet operation by using a crossing window; type **C↵** at the Select first object or ...: prompt. The two endpoints closest to the fillet location are trimmed.

The location where you select the lines affects how the lines are joined. As you select objects for Fillet, the side of the line where you click is the side that remains when the lines are joined. Figure 6.14 illustrates how the Fillet command works and shows what the Fillet options do.

TIP If you select two parallel lines during the Fillet command, the two lines are joined with an arc.

Now import the Kitchen plan you drew earlier in this chapter:

1. Click Insert Block on the Draw toolbar, and then browse to locate the kitchen drawing you created earlier in this chapter. Make sure you leave the Specify On-Screen check box unselected under the Scale and Rotation groups of the Insert dialog box.

2. Place the kitchen drawing at the wall intersection below the bathtub. (See the top image in Figure 6.15.)

TIP If you didn't complete the kitchen earlier in this chapter, you can insert the 06a-kitchen.dwg file from the companion CD. Metric users can insert 05 kitchen-metric.dwg.

FIGURE 6.14

The place where you click the object to select it determines which part of an object gets filleted.

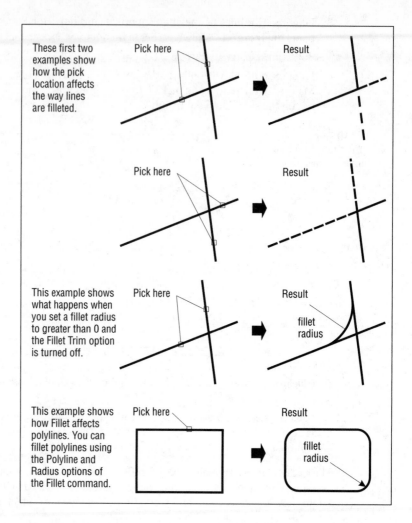

These first two examples show how the pick location affects the way lines are filleted.

This example shows what happens when you set a fillet radius to greater than 0 and the Fillet Trim option is turned off.

This example shows how Fillet affects polylines. You can fillet polylines using the Polyline and Radius options of the Fillet command.

3. Adjust your view with Pan and Zoom so that the upper portion of the apartment unit is centered in the drawing area, as illustrated in the top image in Figure 6.15.

PLACING THE DOOR ACCURATELY

The next step is to add the entry door shown in the bottom image in Figure 6.15. In doing that, you'll use a number of new tools together to streamline the drawing process.

In this exercise, you'll practice using the Osnap Tracking feature and the From Osnap option to place the entry door at an exact distance from the upper corner of the floor plan:

1. Right-click the Command window and choose Recent Commands ➢ Insert from the shortcut menu to open the Insert dialog box.

2. Select Door from the Name drop-down list.

3. Make sure the Specify On-Screen option is checked in the Rotation group but not in the Scale group, and then click OK. You'll see the door follow the cursor in the drawing window.

4. Shift+right-click the mouse to open the Osnap shortcut menu, and then choose From.

5. Make sure the Osnap and Otrack buttons on the status bar are on; then use the Endpoint Running Osnap to pick the corner where the upper horizontal wall line meets the bathroom wall.

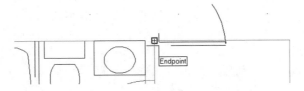

6. Move the cursor over the Osnap marker so that the Osnap Tracking vector appears from the corner. Now move the cursor to the right, and you'll see the Osnap Tracking vector extend from the corner.

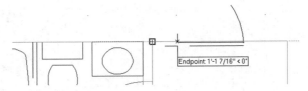

7. Continue to move the cursor to the right so that the tracking vector readout shows roughly 6″, or 15 cm for metric users.

8. With the cursor in this position, enter **5.↵**. Metric users should enter **13.↵**. The door is placed exactly 5 (or 13) units to the right of the corner.

9. At the `Specify rotation angle <0>:` prompt, enter **270.↵**. Or if you prefer, turn on Polar Tracking to orient the door so that it is swinging *into* the studio. You've now accurately placed the entry door in the studio apartment.

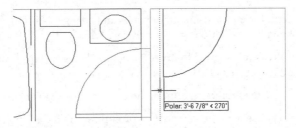

10. Make sure the door is on the Door layer.

TIP For a shortcut to setting an object's layer, you can select the object or objects, and then select a layer from the Layer drop-down list in the Layers toolbar.

FIGURE 6.15
The view after using Pan and Zoom, with the door inserted and the jamb and header added

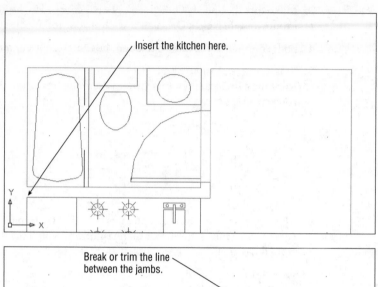

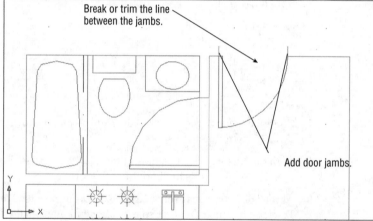

Now add the finishing touches to the entry door:

1. Add 5˝ (13 cm for metric users) door jambs and change their Layer property to the Jamb layer, as shown in the bottom image in Figure 6.15.

2. Choose the Break tool in the Modify toolbar, and then select the header over the entry door. (See the bottom image in Figure 6.15.)

3. Type **F⏎** to use the first-point option; then select the endpoint of one of the door jambs.

4. At the Specify second break point: prompt, select the endpoint of the other jamb as shown in the bottom image in Figure 6.15.

5. Draw the door header on the Ceiling layer, as shown in Figure 6.16.

FIGURE 6.16
The other side of the wall

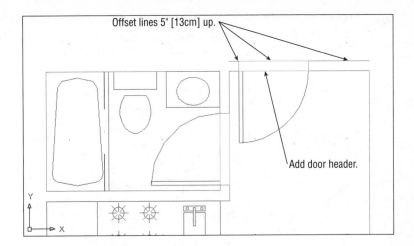

Offset lines 5" [13cm] up.

Add door header.

6. Click Offset on the Modify toolbar, and offset the top wall lines of the unit and the door header up 5″ (13 cm for metric users) so that they connect with the top end of the door jamb, as shown in Figure 6.16. Don't forget to include the short wall line from the door to the bathroom wall.

7. Choose File ➤ Save As to save your file as Unit.

OTHER METHODS FOR USING THE BREAK COMMAND

In the exercise for finishing the Unit plan, you used the Break command to accurately place a gap in a line over the entry door. In Chapter 4, you broke a line at a single point to create multiple, contiguous line segments.

In both cases you used the F option. You can also break a line without the F option with a little less accuracy. When you don't use the F option, the point at which you select the object is used as the first break point. If you're in a hurry, you can dispense with the F option and simply place a gap in an approximate location. You can then later use other tools to adjust the gap.

In addition, you can use locations on other objects to select the first and second points of a break. For example, you might want to align an opening with another opening some distance away. After you've selected the line to break, you can then use the F option and select two points on the existing opening to define the first and second break points. The break points will align in an orthogonal direction to the selected points.

USING POLAR AND OSNAP TRACKING AS CONSTRUCTION-LINE TOOLS

So far, you've been using existing geometry to accurately place objects in the plan. In this section, you will use the Polar and Osnap Tracking tools to extend the upper wall line 5″ (13 cm for metric users) beyond the right-side interior wall of the unit. You'll also learn how to use the Construction Line tool to accurately locate door jambs near the balcony.

Start by changing the Polar Tracking setting to include a 45° angle:

1. Right-click the Polar button in the status bar at the bottom of the AutoCAD window, and choose Settings to open the Drafting Settings dialog box at the Polar Tracking tab.

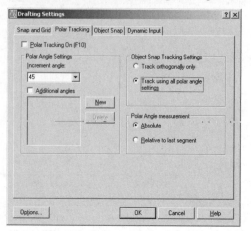

2. Select 45 from the Increment Angle drop-down list in the upper-left corner of the dialog box.

3. In the Object Snap Tracking Settings button group, make sure that the Track Using All Polar Angle Settings option is selected, and click OK.

You're ready to extend the wall line. For this operation, you'll use grip editing:

1. Click the wall line at the top of the plan, to the right of the door, to select the line and expose its grips.

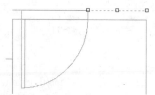

2. Click the Ortho button in the status bar to turn on Ortho mode. This keeps the wall line straight as you edit it.

3. Click the rightmost grip of the line to make it "hot."

4. Place the cursor on the upper-right corner of the plan until you see the Endpoint Osnap marker; then move the cursor away from the corner at a 45° angle. The Osnap Tracking vector appears at a 45° angle. Notice the small X that appears at the intersection of the Osnap Tracking vector and the line.

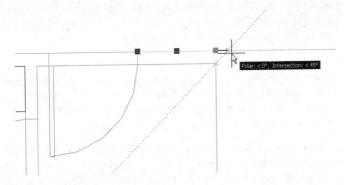

With the Osnap Tracking vector and the line intersecting, click the mouse button. The line changes to extend exactly 5 units beyond the vertical interior wall of the plan.

5. Press the Esc key twice to clear your selection. Then repeat steps 1 through 4 for the horizontal wall line to the left of the door, to extend that line to the left corner.

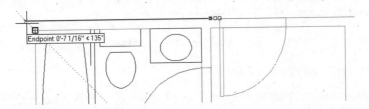

6. Choose View ➢ Zoom ➢ All to view the entire drawing. It will look like Figure 6.17.

FIGURE 6.17
The studio unit so far

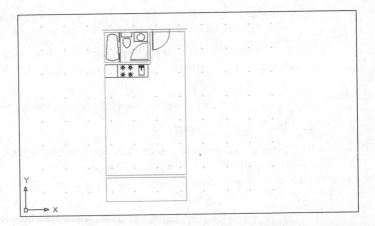

TIP With Polar Tracking set to 45 and Osnap Tracking turned on, you might find that you are selecting points that you don't really want to select in a crowded drawing. Just remember that if a drawing becomes too crowded, you can turn these options off temporarily by clicking the Otrack or Polar buttons in the status bar.

In this exercise, you used Polar Tracking and the Ortho mode to accurately position the two lines used for the exterior walls of the studio unit. This shows how you can take advantage of existing geometry with a combination of tools in the status bar.

TIP   If you prefer to use a standard line instead of a construction line as a construction tool, you can use the ray (choose Draw ➤ Ray from the menu bar). A ray is a line that starts from a point you select and continues off to an infinite distance. You specify the start point and angle of the ray. You can place a ray at the corner at a 45° angle and then fillet the ray to the horizontal wall line to shorten or lengthen the line to the appropriate length.

Now you will finish the balcony by adding a sliding glass door and a rail. This time, you will use lines for construction as well as for parts of the drawing. First, you'll add the door jamb by drawing an Construction Line. An *Construction Line* is a line that has an infinite length, but unlike the ray, it extends in both directions. After drawing the Construction Line, you'll use it to quickly position the door jambs.

Follow these steps:

1. Zoom into the balcony area.

2. Click the Construction Line tool on the Draw toolbar. You can also choose Draw ➤ Construction Line or type **XL**↵. You'll see this prompt:

```
Specify a point or [Hor/Ver/Ang/Bisect/Offset]:
```

3. Type **O**↵ to select the Offset.

4. At the `Specify offset distance or [Through] <0´-5″>:` prompt, type **4´**↵. Metric users should type **122**↵.

5. At the `Select a line object:` prompt, click the wall line at the right of the unit.

6. At the `Specify side to offset:` prompt, click a point to the left of the wall to display the Construction Line. (See the top image of Figure 6.18.)

7. At the `Select a line object:` prompt, click the left wall line, and then click to the right of the selected wall to create another Construction Line. Your drawing should look like the top image in Figure 6.18.

Next, you'll edit the Construction Lines to form the jambs.

8. Click Trim on the Modify toolbar.

9. Select the Construction Lines and the two horizontal lines representing the wall between the unit and the balcony, and press ↵. You can either use a crossing window or select each line individually. You have just selected the objects to trim to.

TIP   You can also use the Fence selection option to select the lines to be trimmed. For more information, see Chapter 2 or Chapter 15.

10. Click the horizontal lines at any point between the two Construction Lines. Then click the Construction Lines above and below the horizontal lines to trim them. Your drawing will look like the bottom image in Figure 6.18.

FIGURE 6.18
Drawing the
door opening

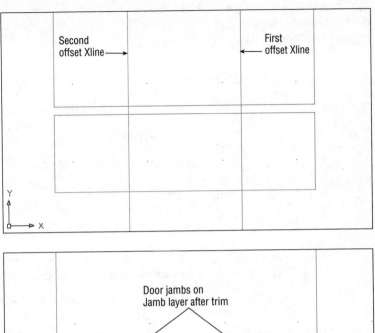

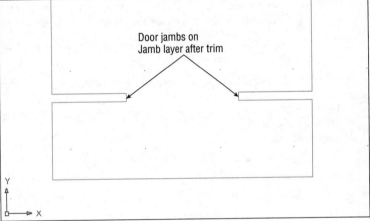

11. Assign the trimmed Construction Lines to the Jamb layer.

12. Add lines on the Ceiling layer to represent the door header.

13. Now draw lines between the two jambs (on the Door layer) to indicate a sliding glass door (see Figure 6.19).

The wall facing the balcony is now complete. To finish the unit, you need to show a handrail and the corners of the balcony wall:

1. Offset the bottom line of the balcony 3″ toward the top of the drawing. Metric users should offset the line 7.6 units.

2. Create a new layer called **F-rail** and assign this offset line to it.

3. Add a 5″ (13 cm for metric users) horizontal line to the lower corners of the balcony, as shown in Figure 6.19.

FIGURE 6.19
Finishing the sliding
glass door and the
railing

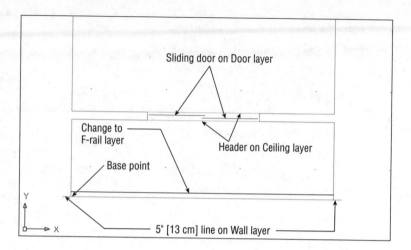

4. Now choose Draw ➤ Block ➤ Base from the drop-down menu to set the base point at the lower-left corner of the balcony, at the location shown in Figure 6.19.

5. Assign the lines indicating walls to the Wall layer, and put the sliding glass door on the Door layer (see Figure 6.19).

6. Zoom back to the previous view. Your drawing should now look like Figure 6.20.

FIGURE 6.20
The completed studio
apartment unit

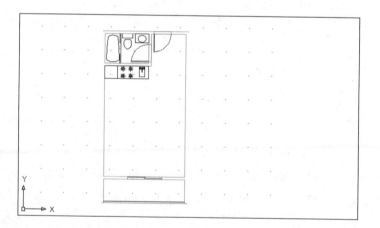

7. Choose File ➤ Save to save the drawing then close the file.

Your studio apartment unit plan is now complete. The exercises you've just completed demonstrate a typical set of operations you'll perform while building your drawings. In fact, nearly 80 percent of what you will do in AutoCAD is represented here.

Now, to review the drawing process, and to create a drawing you'll use later, you're going to draw the apartment building's lobby. As you follow the steps, refer to Figure 6.21.

As is usual in floor plans, the elevator shaft is indicated by the box with the large X through it, and the stair shaft is indicated by the box with the row of vertical lines through it. If you are in a hurry, use the finished version of this file called Lobby.dwg (Lobby-metric.dwg for metric users) in the Miscellaneous Samples folder that was installed from the companion CD.

THE CONSTRUCTION LINE OPTIONS

There is more to the Construction Line command than you have seen in the exercises in this chapter. Here is a list of the Construction Line options and their uses:

Hor   Draws horizontal Construction Lines as you click points.

Ver   Draws vertical Construction Lines as you click points.

Ang   Draws Construction Lines at a specified angle as you pick points.

Bisect   Draws Construction Lines bisecting an angle or a location between two points.

Offset   Draws Construction Lines offset at a specified distance from an existing line.

To draw the apartment building lobby, follow these steps:

1. Create a new file called Lobby, using the Unit file as a prototype. (Open the Unit file, choose File ➢ Save As, and enter **Lobby** for the new filename.)

2. Erase the entire unit (choose Erase ➢ All).

3. Begin by drawing the three main rectangles that represent the outlines of the stair shaft, the elevator shaft, and the lobby.

FIGURE 6.21

Drawing the lobby plan. Metric dimensions are shown in brackets

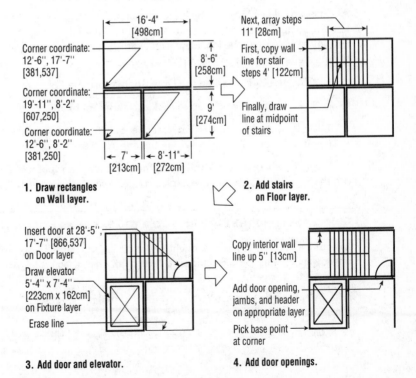

4. To draw the stairs, copy or offset the stair shaft's left wall to the right a distance of 4′ (122 cm). This creates the first line representing the steps.

5. Array this line in one row of 10 columns, using 11″ (28 cm) column offset.

6. Draw the center line dividing the two flights of stairs.

7. Draw the elevator, insert the door and assign the door to the Door layer. Practice using Construction Lines here.

8. Draw the door jambs. Edit the door openings to add the door jambs and headers.

9. Use the Base command to set the base point of the drawing. Your plan should resemble the one in Figure 6.21, step 4.

10. Save the Lobby file.

Finding Distances along Curves

You've seen how you can use lines to help locate objects and geometry in your drawing. But if you need to find distances along a curved object such as a spline, lines don't always help. This section describes two ways to find exact distances on spline curves. Try these exercises when you're not working through the main tutorial.

FINDING A STRAIGHT LINE DISTANCE ALONG A CURVED OBJECT

At times you'll need to find the location of a point on a curve that lies at a known straight-line distance from another point on the curve. Although there isn't a specific command to do this, you can employ a circle to do the job. Here's an example of how you might find the straight line distance from the endpoint of a spline curve:

1. Click the Circle tool on the Draw toolbar or type **C**↵.

2. Use the Endpoint Osnap to click the endpoint of an arc.

3. At the `Specify radius of circle or [Diameter]:` prompt, enter the length of the distance you want to locate along the curve.

The point where the circle intersects the curve is the endpoint of the chord (see Figure 6.22). You can then use the Intersection Osnap override to select the circle and curve intersection.

QUICKLY SETTING THE CURRENT LAYER TO THAT OF AN EXISTING OBJECT

As your list of layers grows, you might find it difficult to locate the exact layer you want quickly. You might want to draw objects on the same layer as an existing object in a drawing, but maybe you are not sure what that layer is.

AutoCAD offers the Make Object's Layer Current tool to help you easily set the current layer. This tool can be found on the Layers toolbar.

This tool lets you set the current layer by selecting an object in the drawing instead of selecting its name from a list. Click this tool and then click the object whose layer you want to make current.

Figure 6.22

Finding a chord distance along a curve by using a circle

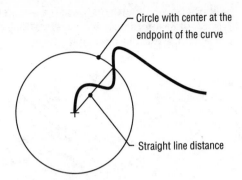

Circle with center at the endpoint of the curve

Straight line distance

Finding an Exact Distance along a Curve

To find an exact distance along a curve or to mark off specific distance increments along a curve, do the following:

1. Choose Format ➤ Point Style from the drop-down menu to open the Point Style dialog box.

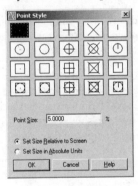

2. Click the X icon in the top row. Also be sure the Set Size Relative To Screen radio button is selected. Then click OK.

TIP   You can also set the point style by setting the Pdmode system variable to 3. See Appendix C for more on Pdmode.

3. Choose Draw ➤ Point ➤ Measure from the drop-down menu or type **me⏎**.

TIP   The Divide command (choose Draw ➤ Point ➤ Divide) marks off a line, an arc, or a curve into equal divisions, as opposed to divisions of a length you specify. You might use Divide to divide an object into 12 equal segments, for example. Aside from this difference in function, Divide works in exactly the same way as Measure.

4. At the Select object to measure: prompt, click the end of the curve that you want to use as the starting point for your distance measurement.

5. At the Specify length of segment or [Block]: prompt, enter the distance you want. A series of Xs appears on the curve, marking off the specified distance along the curve. You can select the exact location of the Xs by using the Node Osnap override (see Figure 6.23).

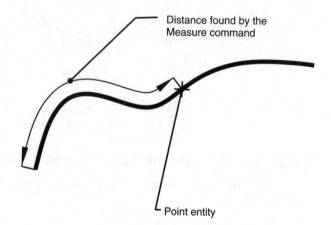

FIGURE 6.23

Finding an exact distance along a spline curve by using points and the Measure command

Distance found by the Measure command

Point entity

TIP The Block option of the Measure command enables you to specify a block to be inserted at the specified segment length, in place of the Xs on the arc. You can align the block with the arc as it is inserted. (This is similar to the polar array's Rotate Objects As They Are Copied option.)

The Measure command also works on most objects including arcs and polylines. You'll get a more detailed look at the Measure command in Chapter 18.

As you work with AutoCAD, you'll find that constructing temporary geometry such as the circle and points in the two previous examples will help you solve problems in new ways. Don't hesitate to experiment! Remember, you've always got the Save and Undo commands to help you recover from mistakes.

Changing the Length of Objects

Suppose that, after finding the length of an arc, you realize you need to lengthen the arc by a specific amount. Choosing Modify ➤ Lengthen lets you lengthen or shorten arcs, lines, polylines, splines, and elliptical arcs. As an example, here's how to lengthen an arc:

1. Choose Modify ➤ Lengthen or type **len**↵.

2. At the Select an object or [DElta/Percent/Total/DYnamic]: prompt, type **T**↵.

3. At the Specify total length or [Angle] <1.0000>: prompt, enter the length you want for the arc.

4. At the Select an object to change or [Undo]: prompt, click the arc you want to change. Be sure to click at a point nearest the end you want to lengthen. The arc increases in length to the size you specified.

The Lengthen command also shortens an object if it is currently longer than the value you enter.

In this short example, you have learned how to change an object to a specific length. You can use other criteria to change an object's length, using these options available for the Lengthen command:

DElta   Lengthens or shortens an object by a specific length. To specify an angle rather than a length, use the Angle suboption.

Percent   Increases or decreases the length of an object by a percentage of its current length.

Total   Specifies the total length or angle of an object.

DYnamic   Graphically changes the length of an object using your cursor.

Creating a New Drawing by Using Parts from Another Drawing

This section explains how to use the Wblock command (which you learned about in Chapter 4) to create a separate staircase drawing by using the staircase you've already drawn for the lobby. Although you haven't turned the existing stairs into a block, you can still use Wblock to turn parts of a drawing into a file.

Follow these steps:

1. If you closed the Lobby file, open it now. If you didn't create the lobby drawing, open the `Lobby.dwg` (or `Lobby-metric.dwg`) file from the companion CD.

2. Chose File ➢ Export or type **export**↵ to open the Export Data dialog box.

3. Enter **stair.dwg** in the File Name text box and click Save. By including the .dwg filename extension, you let AutoCAD know that you want to export to a drawing file and not some other format, such as a .dxf or .wmf file format.

4. At the `Enter name of existing block or [= (block=output file)/* (whole drawing)] <define new drawing>:` prompt, press ↵. When you export to a .dwg format, AutoCAD assumes you want to export a block. Bypassing this prompt by pressing ↵ tells AutoCAD that you want to create a file from part of the drawing, rather than from a block.

5. At the `Specify insertion base point:` prompt, pick the lower-right corner of the stair shaft. This tells AutoCAD the base point for the new drawing.

6. At the `Select objects:` prompt, use a window to select the stair shaft, as shown in Figure 6.24.

FIGURE 6.24
A selection window enclosing the stair shaft

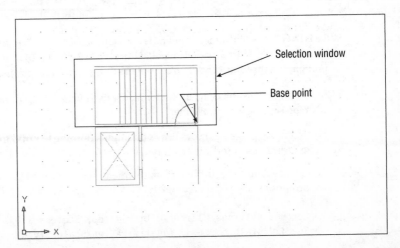

7. When the stair shaft, including the door, is highlighted, press ⏎ to confirm your selection. The stairs disappear.

8. Because you want the stairs to remain in the lobby drawing, click the Undo button to bring them back. Undo does not affect any files you might export by choosing File ➤ Export, by using Wblock, or by using the Make Block tool.

Drawing Parallel Lines

Frequently, when working on an architectural project, you will first do your schematic layout by using simple lines for walls. Then, as the design requirements begin to take shape, you can start to add more detailed information about the walls, for example, indicating wall materials or locations for insulation. AutoCAD provides multilines (the Multiline command and its equivalent tool on the Draw menu) for this purpose. *Multilines* are double lines that you can use to represent walls. You can also customize multilines to display solid fills, center lines, and additional linetypes, as shown in Figure 6.25. You can save your custom multilines as multiline styles, which are in turn saved in special files for easy access from other drawings.

FIGURE 6.25

Samples of multiline styles that users can create

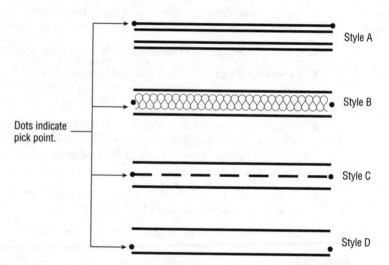

WARNING The Multiline command is not available in AutoCAD LT 2007. LT does offer the Dline command, which draws simple parallel lines. To use it, enter **DL**⏎ or **Dline**⏎ at the Command prompt. Use the Width option to control the distance between the parallel lines.

TIP Multilines are especially useful for metric users who need to draw cavity walls that are usually represented by multiple lines.

The following exercise shows how you might continue to build information into your drawings by using multilines to indicate wall types:

1. Choose Draw ➤ Multiline from the menu bar or type **ML**⏎. You'll see two lines in the prompt area:

```
Current settings: Justification = Top, Scale = 1.00, Style = STANDARD
Specify start point or [Justification/Scale/STyle]:
```

TIP The first line in the prompt area gives you the current settings for Multiline.

2. Type **S**⏎ (for Scale).

3. At the `Enter mline scale <1.00>`: prompt, type **5**⏎.

4. Pick a point to start the double line.

5. Continue to select points to draw more double-line segments, or type **C**⏎ to close the series of lines.

Let's take a look at the meaning of the multiline settings included in the prompt you saw in steps 1 and 2:

Justification Controls where the double lines are placed in relation to the points you pick. The default sets the double lines equidistant from the points you pick. By changing the justification value to be top or bottom, you can have AutoCAD draw double lines off center from the pick points.

Scale Lets you set the width of the double line.

Style Lets you select a style for multilines. You can control the number of lines in the multiline, as well as the linetypes used for each line in the multiline style, by using the Mledit command.

Close Closes a sequence of double lines, much as the Line command's Close option does.

Undo As you start to draw an Mline, you see the Undo option. This allows you to undo the last drawn Mline segment.

Customizing Multilines

In Chapter 4 you learned how to make a line appear dashed or dotted by using linetypes. In a similar way, you can control the appearance of multilines by using the Multiline Style dialog box. This dialog box enables you to do the following:

◆ Set the number of lines that appear in the multiline.

◆ Control the color of each multiline.

◆ Control the linetype of each multiline.

◆ Apply a fill between the outermost lines of a multiline.

◆ Control whether and how ends of multilines are closed.

To open the Multiline Style dialog box, choose Format ➢ Multiline Style or type **Mlstyle**⏎ at the Command prompt.

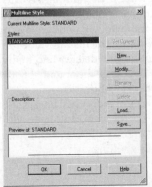

WARNING After you have drawn a multiline in a particular style, you cannot modify the style settings for that style in the Element Properties and Multiline Properties dialog boxes described later in this section. The Multiline Style dialog box enables you to set up styles only before they are used in a drawing.

A group of buttons and a list box enable you to create, edit, and select the multiline style you want to work with. The Styles list box shows all the multiline styles available. In a new file, there is just the Standard style. The New button lets you create a new style, and the Modify button lets you modify an existing one. The Standard style cannot be edited. The Load and Save buttons let you save multiline styles as files, allowing you to export your custom styles to other computers. The Preview Of box at the bottom of the dialog box shows you what the selected multiline style looks like.

CREATING A NEW STYLE

Click the New button to open the Create New Multiline Style dialog box. Here you can enter a name for a new style and click Continue to set up the new style. You must enter a name before you can click Continue.

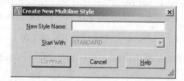

Once you click Continue, you see the New Multiline Style dialog box.

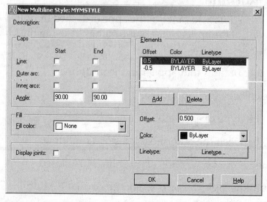

This is where you can set up your own multiline style to include additional lines, control the linetypes and color for the multiline, and add other features.

For example, click the Add button to add another line to your multiline. The offset distance of the new line appears in the list box. The default value for new lines is 0.0, which places the line at the center of the standard multiline. To delete a line, highlight its offset value in the Elements list box and click the Delete button. To change the amount of offset, highlight the element in the list box and enter a new value in the Offset text box.

To change the color and linetype of individual lines, use the Color drop-down list and Linetype button. The Caps and Fill groups of the New Multiline Style dialog box give you control over other features of the multiline such as end conditions and fills. Figure 6.26 contains some examples of multilines and their corresponding settings.

FIGURE 6.26

Samples of multiline styles you can create

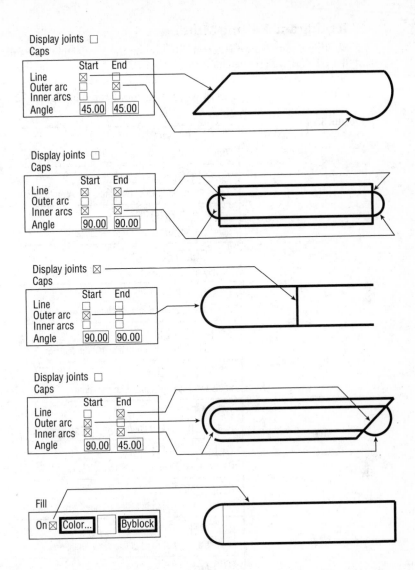

USING MULTILINES TO ADD WALL PATTERNS

You can easily indicate an insulated wall in an architectural drawing by adding a third center line (offset of 0.0) and giving that center line the Batting linetype. This linetype draws an S-shaped pattern typically used to represent fiberglass batt insulation in a floor plan. To see how other linetypes for wall patterns can be created, see Chapter 26.

You can also use a solid-filled multiline wherever you need to fill in a wall with a solid shade (or pouche, to use the drafting term). To quickly add a pouche, set one multiline offset to 0.0 and the other to the width of the wall. Make sure the Fill option is turned on for your Pouche style, and then use your Pouche style to trace either the inside or outside of the wall to be pouched.

Joining and Editing Multilines

Multilines are unique in their ability to combine several linetypes and colors into one entity. For this reason, you need special tools to edit them. AutoCAD provides the Modify menu's Object Multiline option and the command line's Mledit command; both have the sole purpose of enabling you to join multilines in a variety of ways, as demonstrated in Figure 6.27.

FIGURE 6.27

The Mledit options and their meanings

CLOSED CROSS Trims one of two intersecting multilines so that they appear overlapping.	
OPEN CROSS Trims the outer lines of two intersecting multilines.	
MERGED CROSS Joins two multilines into one multiline.	
CLOSED TEE Trims the leg of a tee intersection to the first line.	
OPEN TEE Joins the outer lines of a multiline tee intersection.	
MERGED TEE Joins all the lines in a multiline tee intersection.	
CORNER JOINT Joins two multilines into a corner joint.	
ADD VERTEX Adds a vertex to a multiline. The vertex can later be moved.	
DELETE VERTEX Deletes a vertex to straighten a multiline.	
CUT SINGLE Creeates an opening in a single line of a multiline.	
CUT ALL Creates a break across all lines in a multiline.	
WELD ALL Closes a break in a multiline.	

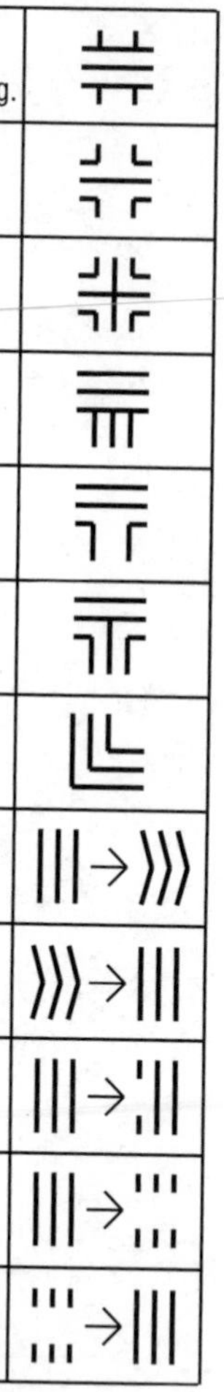

Here's how to edit multilines:

1. Type **Mledit** at the Command prompt or choose Modify ➢ Object ➢ Multiline to open the Multilines Edit Tools dialog box (see Figure 6.28), which provides a variety of ways to edit your multilines.

2. Click the graphic that best matches the edit you want to perform.

3. Select the multilines you want to join or edit.

TIP Besides the multiline editing tools, you can also use the Trim and Extend tools.

FIGURE 6.28
The Multilines Edit
Tools dialog box

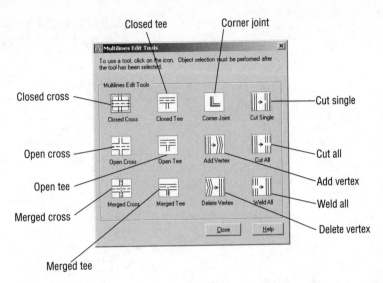

Closed tee

Corner joint

Closed cross

Cut single

Open cross

Cut all

Open tee

Add vertex

Merged cross

Weld all

Delete vertex

Merged tee

Another option is to explode multilines and edit them by using the editing tools you've used in this and previous chapters. When a multiline is exploded, it is reduced to its component lines. Linetype assignments and layers are maintained for each component.

Eliminating Unused Blocks, Layers, Linetypes, Shapes, and Styles and More

A template can contain blocks and layers you don't need in your new file. For example, the lobby you just completed contains the bathroom block because you used the Unit file as a prototype. Even though you erased this block, it remains in the drawing file's database. It is considered "unused" because it doesn't appear as part of the drawing. Such extra blocks can slow you down by increasing the amount of time needed to open the file. They will also increase the size of your file unnecessarily. You can eliminate unused elements from a drawing in two ways: by using the Purge command or by choosing File ➢ Export.

SELECTIVELY REMOVING UNUSED ELEMENTS

You use the Purge command to remove unused individual blocks, layers, linetypes, shapes, text styles, and other drawing elements from a drawing file. To help keep the file size small and to make layer maintenance easier, you will want to purge your drawing of unused elements. Bear in mind, however, that the Purge command does not delete certain primary drawing elements—namely, Layer 0, the Continuous linetype, and the Standard text style.

Use these steps to practice using the Purge command:

1. Choose File ➢ Open and open the Lobby file.

2. Choose File ➢ Drawing Utilities ➢ Purge to open the Purge dialog box (see Figure 6.29). You'll see a listing of drawing components that can be purged. If the drawing contains any of the types of components listed, you'll see a plus sign to the left of the component name.

3. Click the plus sign of the component you want to purge. In this exercise, click the plus sign next to the Blocks listing. The list expands to show the names of the items under the component category.

FIGURE 6.29

The Purge dialog box

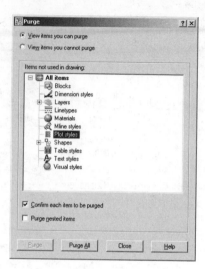

4. Select the name Bath from the expanded list. If you want to select more than one item, you can Ctrl+click individual names or Shift+click to select a group of names.

5. After the components are selected, click the Purge button in the lower-left corner of the dialog box. You then see a message box asking you to confirm that you want to purge the drawing.

REMOVING ALL UNUSED ELEMENTS

In the preceding exercise, you selected a single block for removal from the Lobby file. If you want to clear all the unused elements from a file at once, you can click the Purge All button at the bottom of the Purge dialog box (see Figure 6.29).

Here are the steps:

1. Choose File ➢ Drawing Utilities ➢ Purge to open the Purge dialog box.

2. Click the Purge Nested Items check box to turn on this option.

3. Click Purge All to open the Confirm Purge dialog box, which asks whether you want to purge a block.

4. Click Yes. The Confirm Purge dialog box displays the name of another block, asking you to confirm the purge. You can continue to click Yes, and AutoCAD will display the Confirm Purge dialog box for each unused element still in the drawing.

5. Click the Yes To All option to purge everything at once. The Confirm Purge dialog box closes.

6. At the Purge dialog box, click Close.

7. Close and save the Lobby file and exit AutoCAD.

The Lobby file is now trimmed down to the essential data it needs and nothing else. You might have noticed that when you returned to the Purge dialog box in step 6, the items in the list box no longer showed plus signs. This indicates that there are no longer any unused items in the drawing.

In this last exercise, you used the Purge Nested Items option at the bottom of the dialog box. The Purge Nested Items option automatically purges unused blocks, including those nested within other blocks. If this option is not checked, you might have to repeat the Purge operation to remove all unused elements in a drawing.

If You Want to Experiment

Try using the techniques you learned in this chapter to create new files. Use the files you created in Chapter 4 as prototypes to create the symbols shown in Figure 6.30.

The Make Object's Layer Current tool helps you easily set the current layer. This tool can be found on the Layers toolbar next to the Layers drop-down list.

This simple yet powerful tool lets you set the current layer by selecting an object in the drawing instead of selecting its name from a list. To use it, click the Make Object's Layer Current tool, and then click the object whose layer you want to make current. This reduces the three-step or four-step process of earlier AutoCAD versions to one click.

Remember this tool the next time you are faced with a drawing that has a long list of layers.

FIGURE 6.30

Mechanical symbols

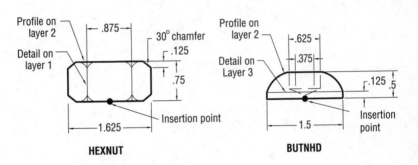

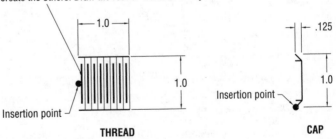

Note:
Create four layers named 1, 2, 3, and 4, if they do not already exist.
Give each layer the same color as its number.
Give layer 3 the HIDDEN linetype.
Don't draw dimensions, just use them for reference.

Chapter 7

Mastering Viewing Tools, Hatches, and External References

Now that you have created drawings of a typical apartment unit and the apartment building's lobby and stairs, you can assemble them to complete the first floor of the apartment building. In this chapter, you will take full advantage of AutoCAD's features to enhance your drawing skills, as well as to reduce the time it takes to create accurate drawings.

As your drawing becomes larger, you will find that you need to use the Zoom and Pan commands more often. Larger drawings also require some special editing techniques. You will learn how to assemble and view drawings in ways that will save you time and effort as your design progresses. Along the way, you'll see how you can enhance the appearance of your drawings by adding hatch patterns.

This chapter includes the following topics:

◆ Assembling the Parts

◆ Taking Control of the AutoCAD Display

◆ Using Hatch Patterns in Your Drawings

◆ Understanding the Boundary Hatch Options

◆ Using External References

Assembling the Parts

One of the best time-saving features of AutoCAD is its ability to quickly duplicate repetitive elements in a drawing. In this section, you'll assemble the drawings you've been working on into the complete floor plan of a fictitious apartment project. This will demonstrate how you can quickly and accurately copy your existing drawings in a variety of ways.

Start by creating a new file for the first floor:

1. Create a new file named Plan to contain the drawing of the apartment building's first floor. This is the file you will use to assemble the unit plans into an apartment building. If you want to use a template file, use Acad.dwt. Metric users can use the Acadiso.dwt template file. (These are AutoCAD template files that appear in the Create New Drawing dialog box when you choose File ➤ New.)

2. Set the Units style to Architectural (choose Format ➤ Units).

3. Set up the drawing for a $1/_8$″ = 1′-0″ scale on a 24″ × 18″ drawing area (choose Format ➤ Drawing Limits). If you look at Table 3.2 in Chapter 3, you'll see that such a drawing requires an area 2304 units wide × 1728 units deep. Metric users should set up a drawing at 1:100 scale

on an A2 sheet size. If you look at Table 3.4, you'll see that your drawing area should be 5940 cm × 4200 cm.

4. Create a layer called Plan1 and make it the current layer.

5. In the Drafting Settings dialog box, set the Snap Spacing to 1, and set Grid Spacing to 8′, which is the distance required to display 1″ divisions in a $\frac{1}{8}$″ = 1′-0″ scale drawing. Metric users can set the Grid mode to 250.

6. Turn on the grid if it isn't on already.

7. Choose View ➤ Zoom ➤ All or type Z↵A↵ to get an overall view of the drawing area.

Now you're ready to start building a floor plan of the first floor from the Unit plan you created in the previous chapter. You'll start by creating a mirrored copy of the apartment plan:

1. Make sure Running Osnaps are turned off, and then insert the Unit.dwg drawing at coordinate 31′-5″,43′-8″ (957,1330 for metric users). Accept the Insert defaults.

TIP If you prefer, you can specify the insertion point in the Insert dialog box by removing the checkmark from the Specify On-Screen check box. The Input options in the dialog box then become available to receive your input.

2. Zoom in to the apartment unit plan.

3. Click Mirror on the Modify toolbar, select the Unit plan, and press ↵.

4. At the Specify first point of the mirror line: prompt, Shift+right-click the mouse and choose From.

5. Shift+right-click again and choose Endpoint.

6. Select the endpoint of the upper-right corner of the apartment unit, as shown in Figure 7.1.

7. Enter @2.5<0↵. Metric users should enter @6.5<0↵. A rubber-banding line appears, indicating the mirror axis.

FIGURE 7.1
The unit plan mirrored

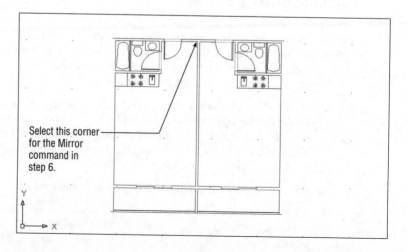

Select this corner for the Mirror command in step 6.

8. Turn on the Ortho mode and select any point to point the mirror axis in a vertical orientation.

9. At the `Erase Source Objects? [Yes/No] <N>:` prompt, press ⏎. You will get a 5″ wall thickness between two studio units. Your drawing should be similar to Figure 7.1.

You now have a mirror-image copy of the original plan in the exact location required for the overall plan. Now make some additional copies for the opposite side of the building:

1. Press ⏎ to reissue the Mirror command and select both units.

2. Use the From Osnap option again, and, using Endpoint Osnap, select the same corner you selected in step 5.

3. Enter **@24<90** to start a mirror axis 24″ directly above the selected point. Metric users should enter **@61<90**.

4. With the Ortho mode on, select a point so that the mirror axis is exactly horizontal.

5. At the `Erase source objects? [Yes/No] <N>:` prompt, press ⏎ to keep the two unit plans you selected in step 1 and complete the mirror operation.

With the tools you've learned about so far, you've quickly and accurately set up a fairly good portion of the floor plan. Continue with the next few steps to "rough in" the main components of the floor:

1. Choose View ➢ Zoom ➢ Extents or type **Z⏎E⏎** to get a view of the four plans. You can also use the Zoom Extents tool on the Zoom Window tool flyout. The Extents option forces the entire drawing to fill the screen at the center of the display area. Your drawing will look like Figure 7.2.

TIP If you happen to insert a block in the wrong coordinate location, you can use the Properties palette to change the insertion point for the block.

2. Copy the four units to the right at a distance of 28′-10″ (878 cm for metric users), which is the width of two units from center line to center line of the walls.

3. Insert the lobby at coordinate 89′-1″,76′-1″ (2713,2318 for metric users).

FIGURE 7.2
The unit plan, duplicated four times

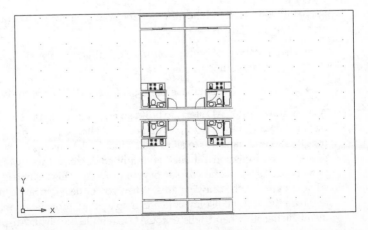

4. Copy all the unit plans to the right 74´-5″ (2267 cm for metric users), the width of four units plus the width of the lobby.

5. Choose View ➢ Zoom ➢ All or type Z↵A↵ to view the entire drawing, which should look like Figure 7.3. You can also use the Zoom All tool on the Zoom Window flyout.

FIGURE 7.3

The Plan drawing

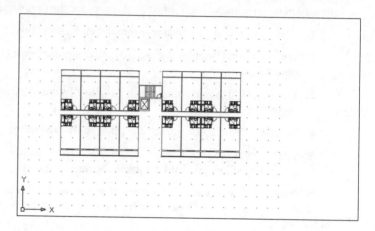

6. Choose File ➢ Save to save this Plan.dwg file to disk.

Taking Control of the AutoCAD Display

By now you should be familiar with the Pan and Zoom functions in AutoCAD. Many other tools can also help you get around in your drawing. In this section, you'll get a closer look at the ways you can view your drawing.

Understanding Regeneration and Redrawing

AutoCAD uses two commands for refreshing your drawing display: the drawing regeneration, or Regen, and the Redraw. Each command serves a particular purpose, though they may not be clear to a new user.

To better understand the difference between Regen and Redraw, it helps to know that AutoCAD stores drawing data in two ways:

◆ In a database of highly accurate coordinate information that is part of the properties of objects in your drawing

◆ In a simplified database used just for the display of the objects in your drawing

As you draw, AutoCAD starts to build an accurate, core database of objects and their properties. At the same time, it creates a simpler database that it uses just to display the drawing quickly. AutoCAD uses this second database to allow quick manipulation of the display of your drawing. For the purposes of this discussion, I'll call this simplified database the "virtual display" because it is like a computer model of the overall display of your drawing. This virtual display is in turn used as the basis for what is shown in the drawing area. When you issue a Redraw command, you are telling AutoCAD to reread this virtual display data and display that information in the drawing area. A Regen command, on the other hand, tells AutoCAD to rebuild the virtual display based on information from the core drawing database.

As you edit drawings, you might find that some lines in the display disappear or otherwise appear corrupted. Redraw will usually restore such distortions. In earlier versions of AutoCAD, the Blipmode system variable was turned on by default, causing markers called blips to appear wherever points were selected. Redraw was, and still is, useful in clearing the screen of these blips.

Regens are used less frequently and are brought to bear when you change settings and options that have a global effect on a drawing, such as a linetype scale, layer color, or text style. (You'll learn more about text styles in Chapter 10.) In fact, in many situations, regens are performed automatically when such changes occur. You usually don't have to issue the Regen command on your own, except in certain situations.

Regens can also occur when you select a view of a drawing that is not currently included as part of the virtual display. The virtual display contains display data for a limited area of a drawing. If you zoom or pan to a view outside that virtual display area, a regen occurs.

TIP   You might notice that the Pan Realtime and Zoom Realtime commands do not work beyond a certain area in the display. When you've reached a point where these commands seem to stop working, you've come to the limits of the virtual display data. To go beyond these limits, AutoCAD must rebuild the virtual display data from the core data; in other words, it must regenerate the drawing.

In the early days of AutoCAD, regens were to be avoided as much as possible, especially in large files. A regen on a very large file could take several minutes to complete. Today, regens are not the problem they once were. Still, they can be annoying when you're working with very large files, particularly if you are using an older Pentium-based computer. For these reasons, it pays to understand the finer points of controlling regens so you can reduce their impact on complex drawings.

You can control how regens affect your work in three ways:

◆   By taking advantage of AutoCAD's many display-related tools

◆   By setting up AutoCAD so that regens do not occur automatically

◆   By freezing layers that do not need to be viewed or edited

We'll explore these methods in the following sections.

Exploring Ways to Control AutoCAD's Display

Perhaps one of the easiest ways to avoid regens is by making sure you don't cross into an area of your drawing that falls outside the virtual display's area. If you use Pan Realtime and Zoom Realtime, you are automatically kept safely within the bounds of the display list. In this section, you'll be introduced to other tools that will help keep you within those boundaries.

CONTROLLING DISPLAY SMOOTHNESS

You can turn the virtual display on or off by using the Viewres command. The Viewres setting is on by default and, for the most part, should remain on. You can turn it off by typing **Viewres↵No↵** at the Command prompt. However, I don't recommend this. With Viewres off, a regen occurs every time you use Pan or Zoom to change your view.

The Viewres command also controls how smoothly linetypes, arcs, and circles are displayed in an enlarged view. With Viewres turned on, linetypes sometimes appear as continuous, even when they are supposed to be dotted or dashed. You might have noticed in previous chapters that onscreen arcs appear to be segmented lines, although they are always plotted as smooth curves. You can adjust the Viewres value to control the number of segments an arc appears to have: the lower the value, the fewer the segments and the faster the redraw and regeneration. However, a low Viewres value causes noncontinuous linetypes, such as dashes or center lines, to appear as continuous, especially in drawings that cover very large areas (for example, civil site plans). The default Viewres setting is 100.

TIP The Arc And Circle Smoothness setting in the Display tab of the Options dialog box has the same effect as the Viewres setting.

Another way to accelerate screen redraw is to keep your drawing limits to a minimum area. If the limits are set unnecessarily high, AutoCAD might slow down noticeably. Also, make sure the drawing origin falls within the drawing limits.

TIP A good value for the Viewres or Arc And Circle Smoothness setting is 500. At this setting, linetypes display properly, and arcs and circles have a reasonably smooth appearance. At the same time, redraw speed is not noticeably degraded. However, you might want to keep Viewres lower still if you have a limited amount of RAM. High Viewres settings can adversely affect AutoCAD's overall use of memory.

USING THE AERIAL VIEW

Let's take a tour of a tool that lets you navigate drawings representing very large areas. It's called the Aerial View:

1. Choose View ➤ Aerial View on the menu bar to open the Aerial View window, as shown in Figure 7.4.

FIGURE 7.4

The Aerial View window

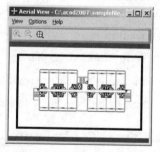

2. Click the Aerial View window. As you move your mouse, notice what happens in the AutoCAD window. Your view pans, following your motion in the Aerial View window. A bold rectangle in the Aerial View window representing your AutoCAD view moves with your cursor.

3. Click the Aerial View window again. Now as you move your cursor from left to right, the view in the AutoCAD window zooms in and out. This is the Zoom mode of the Aerial View. The rectangle in the Aerial View window now shrinks and expands as you move the cursor from left to right, indicating the size of the area being displayed in the AutoCAD window.

4. Move the cursor to the left so that the rectangle representing your AutoCAD view is about half the size of the overall view of the plan, and then right-click. Your AutoCAD view becomes fixed. Also notice that the magnification icon in the Aerial View toolbar becomes available.

CREATING MULTIPLE VIEWS

So far, you've looked at ways to help you get around in your drawing while using a single view window. You can also set up multiple views of your drawing, called viewports. With viewports, you can display more than one view of your drawing at one time in the AutoCAD drawing area. For example, one viewport can display a close-up of the bathroom, another viewport can display the overall plan view, and yet another can display the unit plan.

When viewports are combined with AutoCAD's Paper Space feature, you can plot multiple views of your drawing. Paper Space is a display mode that lets you "paste up" multiple views of a drawing, much like a page-layout program. To find out more about viewports and Paper Space, see Chapters 16 and 23.

As you can see from this exercise, you can cycle through the Pan and Zoom feature of the Aerial View by clicking the mouse. If you simply want to pan the view, you can right-click in step 2 of the previous exercise to fix your view in place. Or you can rapidly alternate between the Pan and Zoom modes by clicking the mouse until you've reached the location and view size you want.

The bold rectangle shows you exactly where you are in the overall drawing at any given time. This feature is especially useful in drawings of large areas that might take several pans to cross.

TIP Choosing View ➤ Zoom ➤ Dynamic performs a similar function to the Aerial View window, but instead of opening a separate window, the Dynamic option temporarily displays the overall view in the drawing area.

The Aerial View window is a great tool when you are working on a drawing that requires a lot of magnification in your zoomed-in views. It is also helpful when you need to maintain an overall view of a drawing as you work on closer detail. You might not find it helpful on drawings that don't require lots of magnification, such as the bathroom drawing you worked on in Chapters 3 and 4.

You were able to use the major features of the Aerial View in this exercise. Here are a few more features you can try on your own:

View ➤ Zoom In Zooms in on the view defined by the bold rectangle in the Aerial View.

View ➤ Zoom Out Zooms out of magnified view in the Aerial View.

View ➤ Global Displays an overall view of your drawing in the Aerial View window. Global is like a View ➤ Zoom ➤ Extents option for the Aerial View.

Options ➤ Auto Viewport Controls whether a selected viewport is automatically displayed in the Aerial View window. When this option is selected and a viewport becomes active, the Aerial View window automatically displays the contents of that viewport. (See Chapters 16 and 23 for more on viewports.)

Options ➤ Dynamic Update Controls how AutoCAD updates the Aerial View window. When this setting is on, AutoCAD updates the Aerial View in real time as changes in the drawing occur. When this setting is off, changes in the drawing will not appear in the Aerial View until you click the Aerial View window.

Options ➤ Realtime Zoom Controls whether the AutoCAD display is updated in real time as you zoom and pan in the Aerial View window.

SAVING VIEWS

Another way to control your views is by saving them. You might think of saving views as a way of creating a bookmark or a placeholder in your drawing.

For example, a few walls in the Plan drawing are not complete. To add the lines, you'll need to zoom in to the areas that need work, but these areas are spread out over the drawing. AutoCAD lets you save views of the areas you want to work on and then jump from saved view to saved view. This technique is especially helpful when you know you will often want to return to a specific area of your drawing.

You'll see how to save and recall views in the following set of exercises. Here's the first one:

1. Close the Aerial View window by clicking the Close button.

2. Choose View ➤ Zoom ➤ All or type **Z↵A↵** to get an overall view of the plan.

3. Choose View ➤ Named Views or type **V↵** to open the View Manager dialog box.

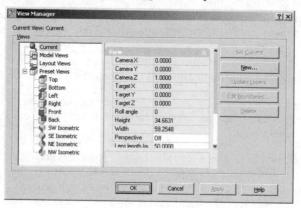

TIP In the View Manager dialog box, you can call up an existing view (Set Current), create a new view (New), or get detailed information about a view. You can also select from a set of pre-defined views that include orthographic and isometric views of 3D objects. You'll learn more about these options in Chapter 20.

4. Make sure the Current option is selected in the list to the left, and then click the New button to open the New View dialog box. You'll notice some options related to the User Coordinate System (UCS) plus an option called View Category. You'll get a chance to look at the UCS in Chapters 20 and 21. The View Category option relates to the Sheet Set feature described in Chapter 28. Other options, including Visual Style, Background, and Boundary, give you control over the appearance of the background and layout of a saved view. For now, you'll concentrate on creating a new view.

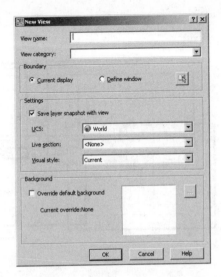

5. Click the Define Window radio button. The dialog boxes momentarily disappear and the Dynamic input display turns on.

6. At the Specify first corner: prompt, click near the coordinate 26´,40´ (1715,1150 for metric users). You don't have to be exact, because you are selecting view windows. Also, if you have Running Osnaps turned on, you might want to turn it off while selecting view windows.

7. At the Specify opposite corner: prompt, click a location near the coordinate 91´,82´ (2600,2500 for metric users). Your selected view area is indicated with a different background color. The Specify first corner: prompt appears again, allowing you to select another view window in case you didn't get it quite right the first time.

8. Press ↵ or right-click when you are satisfied with your view selection. The dialog boxes reappear.

9. Click the View Name input box and type **First** for the name of the view you just defined.

10. Click the OK button. The New View dialog box closes, and you see First listed in the Views list.

TIP If you need to make adjustments to a view after you've created it, you can do so by taking these steps: right-click the view name in the View Manager dialog box, select Edit Boundaries, and then select a window as you did in steps 6 and 7.

11. Repeat steps 3 through 9 to define five more views, named Second, Third, and so on. Use Figure 7.5 as a guide for where to define the windows. Click OK when you are done.

FIGURE 7.5

Save view windows in these locations for the Plan drawing.

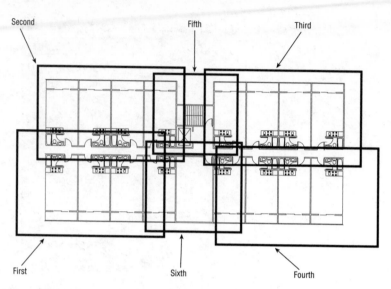

Second   Fifth   Third

First   Sixth   Fourth

Now let's see how to recall these views that you've saved:

1. Choose View ➢ Named Views or type **V**⏎ to open the View Manager dialog box again, and then click First in the list of views to the left of the dialog box. You'll see detailed information regarding the selected view in the panel in the middle of the dialog box.

TIP A quick way to restore saved views is to type **–V**⏎**R**⏎ and then enter the name of the view you want to restore.

2. Click the Set Current button and then click OK. Your screen displays the view you selected.

TIP To set the current view, you can also right-click the view name in the View Manager dialog box. You can then choose Set Current, New, Update Layers, Edit Boundaries, and Delete from a shortcut menu.

3. Set the current layer to Wall, and proceed to add the stairs and exterior walls of the building, as shown in Figure 7.6. (Remember that you exported the stairs from the Lobby drawing in the last chapter. You can also use the `stair.dwg` file from the companion CD.)

4. Use the View Manager dialog box again to restore the view named Second. Then add the wall, as shown in Figure 7.7.

TIP Remember that when no command is active, you can right-click the Command window and then select Recent Commands to repeat a recently issued command. You can also right-click the drawing area when AutoCAD is idle and repeat the last command.

Continue to restore the other views and add the rest of the exterior walls and plan components, as you have done with First and Second. Use the three panels in Figure 7.8 as a guide to completing the views.

FIGURE 7.6

The stairs and walls added to the restored First view

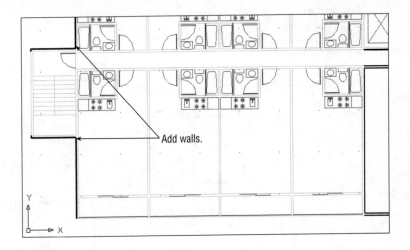

FIGURE 7.7

Walls added to the restored Second view

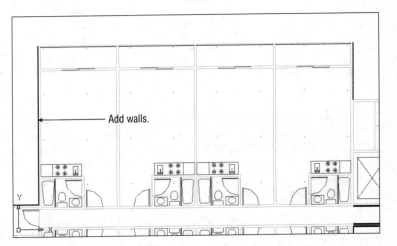

If you prefer, you can use the keyboard to invoke the View command and thus avoid all the dialog boxes:

1. Choose View ➤ Zoom ➤ Extents, or type **Z↵E↵**.

2. Enter **–View↵S↵** at the Command prompt or use the **–V↵S↵** shortcut. (Don't forget the minus sign in front of View or V.)

3. At the Enter view name to save: prompt, enter **Overall↵**.

4. Save the Plan file to disk.

As you can see, this is a quick way to save a view. With the name Overall assigned to this view, you can easily recall the Overall view at any time. (Choosing View ➤ Zoom ➤ All gives you an overall view too, but it might zoom out too far for some purposes, or it might not show what you consider an overall view.)

FIGURE 7.8
Walls, stairs, and doors added to the other views. Note that the image is foreshortened to fit on the page.

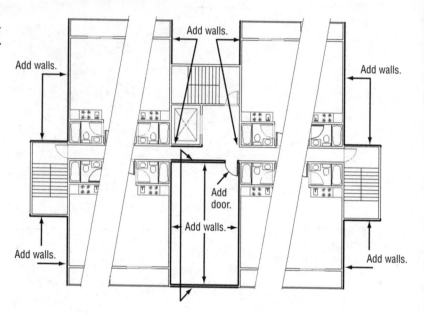

TIP Another useful tool for getting around in your drawing is the Zoom toolbar. It contains the Zoom Window, Dynamic, Scale, Center, Object In, Out, All, and Extents tools. To open the Zoom toolbar, right-click any toolbar and choose Zoom from the shortcut menu.

OPENING A FILE TO A PARTICULAR VIEW

The Select File dialog box contains a Select Initial View check box. If you open an existing drawing with this option selected, you are greeted with a Select Initial View dialog box just before the opened file appears on the screen. This dialog box lists any views saved in the file. You can then go directly to a view by double-clicking the view name. If you have saved views and you know the name of the view you want, using Select Initial View saves time when you're opening large files.

Understanding the Frozen Layer Option

As mentioned earlier, you might want to turn certain layers off altogether to plot a drawing containing only selected layers. But even when layers are turned off, AutoCAD still takes the time to redraw and regenerate them. The Layer Properties Manager dialog box offers the Freeze option; this acts like the Off option, except that Freeze causes AutoCAD to ignore frozen layers when redrawing and regenerating a drawing. By freezing layers that are not needed for reference or editing, you can reduce the time AutoCAD takes to perform regens. This can be helpful in very large, multi-megabyte files.

Be aware, however, that the Freeze option affects blocks in an unusual way. Try the following exercise to see firsthand how the Freeze option makes entire blocks invisible:

1. In the Layer Properties Manager dialog box, set the current layer to 0.

TIP You can freeze and thaw individual layers by clicking the Freeze/Thaw icon (which looks like a sun) in the layer list in the Layers toolbar.

2. Click the yellow lightbulb icon in the Plan1 layer listing to turn off that layer, and then click OK. Nothing changes in your drawing. Even though you turned off the Plan1 layer, the layer on which the unit blocks were inserted, the unit blocks remain visible.

3. Now use the Layer Properties Manager dialog box to turn off all the layers. You'll see a message warning you that the current layer will be turned off. Click No to turn off the current layer, then close the Layer Properties Manager by clicking OK. Now everything is turned off including objects contained in the unit blocks.

4. Open the Layer Properties Manager dialog box again, and turn all the layers back on.

5. Click the Plan1 layer's Freeze/Thaw icon. (You cannot freeze the current layer.) The yellow sun icon changes to a gray snowflake, indicating that the layer is now frozen.

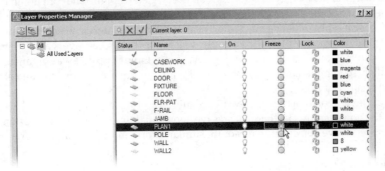

6. Click OK. Now only the unit blocks disappear.

Even though none of the objects within the unit blocks were drawn on the Plan1 layer, the entire contents of the blocks assigned to the Plan1 layer are frozen when Plan1 is frozen.

TIP Remember that to select all the layers at once, you can right-click a blank area of the Layer Properties Manager dialog box and then choose Select All from the shortcut menu.

You don't really need the Plan1 layer frozen. Do the following to turn it back on.

1. Issue the Regen command again and pay attention to the time it takes. The regen is faster this time.

2. Now, thaw layer Plan1 by opening the Layer Properties Manager dialog box and clicking the snowflake icon in the Plan1 layer listing.

3. Turn off the Ceiling layer. Exit the dialog box by clicking OK.

In this relatively small file, the differences between the regen times of the Off and Freeze states are insignificant. But in larger files, the difference can be quite significant. As your drawings become larger, try this exercise again to see how Off affects your regen speed compared with Freeze.

Making Good Use of Freeze and Off

The previous exercise showed the effect that freezing a layer has on blocks. When the layer of a block is frozen, the entire block is made invisible, regardless of the layer assignments of the objects contained in the block.

Keep in mind that when blocks are on layers that are not frozen, the individual objects that are a part of a block are still affected by the status of the layer to which they are assigned.

You can take advantage of this feature by using layers to store parts of a drawing that you might want to plot separately. For example, three floors in your apartment building plan might contain the same information, with some specific variation on each floor. In this case, one layer can contain blocks of the objects common to all the floors. Another layer contains the blocks and objects specific to the first floor, and additional layers contain information specific to the second and third floors. When you want to view or plot one floor, you can freeze the layers associated with the other floors. With respect to Freeze/Thaw visibility, external referenced files inserted by using the Xref command also act like blocks. For example, you can Xref several drawings on different layers. Then, when you want to view a particular Xref drawing, you can freeze all the layers except the one containing that drawing.

In larger projects, you might not want to combine all your floors into one file, but instead combine different types of data such as electrical, mechanical, interior, site, and lease data. When you want to plot an interior plan, for example, you turn off or freeze layers associated with other disciplines. In fact, this is how the San Francisco Main Library project was organized. However, you can still use common data such as structural grids, columns, elevator core, and staircase drawings as part of all your floor plan files.

Using layers and blocks in these ways requires careful planning and record keeping. If used successfully, however, this technique can save substantial time when you're working with drawings that use repetitive objects or that require similar information that can be overlaid.

Taking Control of Regens

If you work with extremely large files and regen times become a problem, you can control regeneration by setting the Regenmode system variable to 0 (zero). You can also use the Regenauto command to accomplish the same thing, by typing **Regenauto↵Off↵**.

If you then issue a command that typically triggers a regen, AutoCAD will give the message Regen queued. For example, when you globally edit attributes, redefine blocks, thaw frozen layers, change the Ltscale setting, or, in some cases, change a text style, you will get the Regen queued message. You can "queue up" regens and then, at a time you choose, issue a regen to update all the changes at once by choosing View ➤ Regen or by typing **Re↵**. This way, only one regen occurs instead of several over the course of an editing session.

By taking control of when regens occur, you can reduce the overall time you spend editing large files.

Using Hatch Patterns in Your Drawings

To help communicate your ideas to others, you will want to add graphic elements that represent types of materials, special regions, or textures. AutoCAD provides hatch patterns for quickly placing a texture over an area of your drawing. In this section, you will add a hatch pattern to the floor of the studio apartment unit, thereby instantly enhancing the appearance of one drawing. In the process, you'll learn how to quickly update all the units in the overall floor plan to reflect the changes in the unit.

Placing a Hatch Pattern in a Specific Area

It's always a good idea to provide a separate layer for hatch patterns. By doing so, you can turn them off if you need to. For example, in Chapter 3, you saw how the San Francisco Main Library floor plan displayed the floor paving pattern in one drawing, while in another drawing it was turned off so it wouldn't distract from other information.

In the following exercises, you will set up a layer for a hatch pattern representing floor tile and then add that pattern to your drawing. This will give you the opportunity to learn the different methods of creating and controlling hatch patterns.

Follow these steps to set up the layer:

1. Open the Unit file. Keep in mind that you still have the Plan file open as well.

2. Zoom into the bathroom and kitchen area.

3. Create a new layer called Flr-pat.

4. Make Flr-pat the current layer.

Now that you've set up the layer for the hatch pattern, you can place the pattern in the drawing:

WARNING If you are using LT, you will not see the Gradient tab in the Hatch And Gradient dialog box shown in step 1 of the next exercise.

1. Click the Hatch tool on the Draw toolbar or type **H↵**. Hatch is also located in the Draw drop-down menu. The Hatch And Gradient dialog box opens.

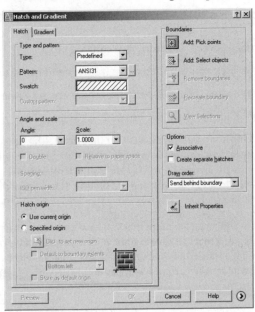

2. In the Type drop-down list box, select User-Defined. The User-Defined option lets you define a simple crosshatch pattern by specifying the line spacing of the hatch and whether it is a single- or double-hatch pattern. The Angle and Spacing input boxes become available, so you can enter values.

3. Double-click the Spacing text box near the bottom and enter **6** (metric users should enter **15**). This tells AutoCAD you want the hatch's line spacing to be 6 inches or 15 cm. Leave the Angle value at 0 because you want the pattern to be aligned with the bathroom.

4. Click the Double check box (on the right side of the dialog box). This tells AutoCAD you want the hatch pattern to run both vertically and horizontally. Also notice that the Swatch box displays a sample of your hatch pattern.

5. Click the Add: Pick Points button in the upper-right corner of the dialog box. The dialog box momentarily closes, enabling you to pick a point inside the area you want hatched.

6. Click a point anywhere inside the bathroom floor area, below the toilet. Notice that a highlighted outline appears in the bathroom. This is the boundary AutoCAD has selected to enclose the hatch pattern. It outlines everything, including the door swing arc.

TIP If you have text in the hatch boundary, AutoCAD will avoid hatching over it, unless the Ignore option is selected in the Island Display Style options of the Advanced Hatch settings. See the section "Using Additional Hatch Features" later in this chapter for more on the Ignore setting.

7. Press ↵ to return to the Hatch And Gradient dialog box.

8. Click the Preview button in the lower-left corner of the dialog box. The hatch pattern appears everywhere on the floor except where the door swing occurs. You also see this prompt:

```
Pick or press Esc to return to dialog or <Right-click to accept hatch>:
```

9. Press Esc or the spacebar to return to the dialog box.

10. Click the Add: Pick Points button again, pick a point inside the door swing, and press ↵.

11. Click Preview again. The hatch pattern now covers the entire floor area.

12. Right-click to place the hatch pattern in the drawing.

The Hatch And Gradient dialog box lets you first define the boundary within which you want to place a hatch pattern. You do this by simply clicking a location inside the boundary area, as in step 6. AutoCAD finds the actual boundary for you. Many options give you control over how a hatch boundary is selected. For details, see the section "Understanding the Boundary Hatch Options" later in this chapter.

TIP Say you want to add a hatch pattern that you have previously inserted in another part of the drawing. You might think that you have to guess at its scale and rotation angle. But with the Inherit Properties option in the Hatch And Gradient dialog box, you can select a previously inserted hatch pattern as a prototype for the current hatch pattern. However, this feature does not work with exploded hatch patterns.

Positioning Hatch Patterns Accurately

In the previous exercise, you placed the hatch pattern in the bathroom without regard for the location of the lines that make up the pattern. In most cases, however, you will want accurate control over where the lines of the pattern are placed.

TIP   You can also click the Swatch button in the upper half of the Hatch And Gradient dialog box to browse through a graphical representation of the predefined hatch patterns.

By default, hatch patterns use the drawing origin, 0,0 as the pattern origin. This means that the corner of the hatch pattern starts at the 0,0 coordinate, even though the pattern is only displayed in the area you select. The Hatch And Gradient dialog box offers a set of options that give you control over the hatch origin, thereby allowing you to control the exact positioning of the hatch pattern within the area you are hatching. This can be crucial for laying out tile patterns on a floor or ceiling, for example.

The following exercise guides you through the process of placing a hatch pattern accurately, using the example of adding floor tile to the kitchenette. You'll start by drawing the area of the tile pattern and then go on to select a pattern for the tile:

1. Pan your view so that you can see the area below the kitchenette, and using the Rectangle tool in the Draw toolbar, draw the 3´-0″ × 8´-0″ outline of the floor tile area, as shown in Figure 7.9. Metric users should create a rectangle that is 91 cm × 228 cm. You can also use a closed polyline.

FIGURE 7.9

The area below the kitchen showing the outline of the floor tile area

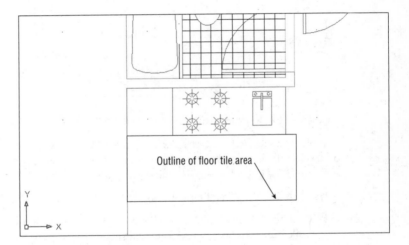

TIP   If you know the coordinates of the new snap origin, you can enter them in the Drafting Settings dialog box under the X Base and Y Base input boxes instead of using the Snapbase system variable.

2. Click the Hatch tool in the Draw toolbar.

3. In the Hatch And Gradient dialog box, make sure that Predefined is selected in the Type drop-down list box.

4. Click the button labeled with the ellipses (…) just to the right of the Pattern drop-down list.

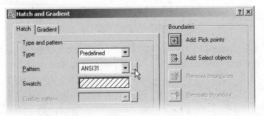

The Hatch Pattern Palette dialog box opens. This dialog box lets you select a predefined pattern from a graphic that shows what the pattern looks like.

TIP If you know the name of the pattern you want, you can select it from the Pattern drop-down list in the Hatch And Gradient dialog box.

5. Click the Other Predefined tab, and then locate and click AR-PARQ1.

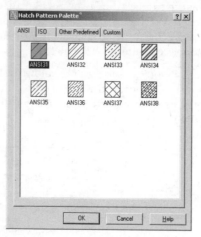

6. Click OK to exit the dialog box.

You've got the hatch pattern selected. The next thing is to place the pattern in the drawing. First, you'll select the location for the hatch pattern, and then you'll experiment with the origin settings to see how they affect the positioning of the pattern.

1. Click the Add: Pick Points button.

2. Click the interior of the area to be tiled and press ↵. Metric users should double-click the Scale input box and enter 2.54 to scale this pattern appropriately to match the proportions of the Imperial measurement example.

3. In the Hatch Origin group, make sure the Use Current Origin option is selected, and then click the Preview button. Notice that the hatch pattern does not fit evenly within the hatch area. Some of the tiles along the edges are only partially drawn, as if they were cut off.

4. Press the Esc key to return to the Hatch And Gradient dialog box.

5. In the Hatch Origin group, turn on the Specified Origin option and also turn on the Default To Boundary Extents option.

6. Click Preview again. This time the pattern fits completely within the boundary, with no incomplete tiles appearing around the edges.

7. Right-click the mouse to accept the hatch pattern location. A parquet-style tile pattern appears in the defined area.

8. Save the Unit file but keep it open.

TIP   You can use the Solid predefined hatch pattern at the top of the list to create solid fills. And don't forget that you can drag and drop solid fills and hatch patterns from the Tool palettes you saw in Chapter 1.

Notice that each tile is shown whole; none of the tiles are cut off as in the bathroom example. This is the result of using the Specified Origin option and the Default To Boundary Extents option in the Hatch And Gradient dialog box.

The Specified Origin option gives you access to a number of hatch pattern features. In the previous exercise, you used the Default To Boundary Extents feature, which is best suited to rectangular areas. This option assumes you are hatching a rectangular area, and it lets you place the boundary hatch origin in one of the four corners of a rectangle or directly in the center. The default option is Bottom Left as shown in the drop-down list. The graphic to the right of the list also shows a cross where the origin is located within a rectangular area.

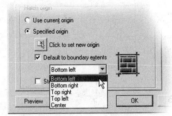

The Click To Set New Origin option lets you select a point within your drawing to specify the hatch origin. When you click this option, the dialog box temporarily closes to allow you to select a point.

Finally, the Store As Default Origin option lets you save your selected origin as the default origin for future hatch patterns in the current drawing.

In the previous exercise, you used a predefined hatch pattern. Figure 7.10 shows you all the patterns available. You can also create your own custom patterns, as described in Chapter 26.

In the next exercise, you'll use this updated Unit file to update all the units in the Plan file.

TIP   The predefined patterns with the AR prefix are architectural patterns that are drawn to full scale. In general, you will want to leave their Scale settings at 1. You can adjust the scale after you place the hatch pattern by using the Properties palette, as described later in this chapter.

Updating Blocks in the *Plan* File

As you progress through a design project, you make countless revisions. With traditional drafting methods, revising a drawing such as the studio apartment floor plan takes a good deal of time. If you change the bathroom layout, for example, you have to erase every occurrence of the bathroom and redraw it 16 times. With AutoCAD, on the other hand, revising this drawing can be a quick operation. You can update the studio unit you just modified throughout the overall plan drawing by replacing the current Unit block with the updated Unit file. AutoCAD can update all occurrences of the Unit block. The following exercise shows how this is accomplished:

1. Make sure you've saved the Unit file with the changes, and then return to the Plan file that is still open. Choose Window ➢ \directory path\Plan.dwg. Your full path to the Plan.dwg file will be shown in the Windows menu.

WARNING   This method does not update exploded blocks. If you plan to use this method to update parts of a drawing, do not explode the blocks you plan to update. See Chapter 4.

FIGURE 7.10
Predefined hatch patterns available in AutoCAD

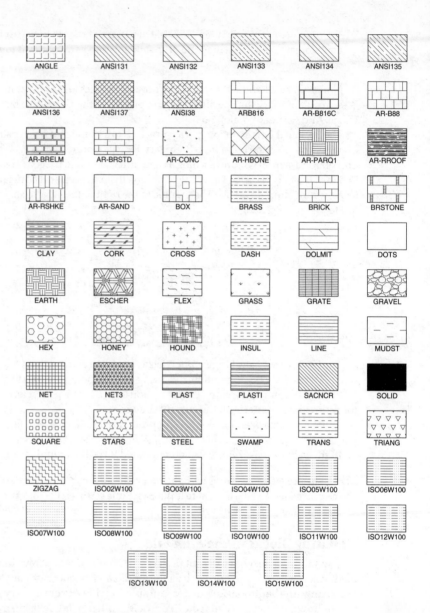

2. Click the Insert Block tool on the Draw toolbar.

3. Click the Browse button, and from the Select Drawing File dialog box, double-click the Unit filename.

4. Click OK at the Insert dialog box. A warning message tells you that a block already exists with the same name as the file. You can cancel the operation or redefine the block in the current drawing.

5. Click Yes. The drawing regenerates (unless you have Regenauto turned off).

6. At the `Specify insertion point or [Basepoint/Scale/X/Y/Z/Rotate]:` prompt, press the Esc key. You do this because you really don't want to insert the `Unit` file into your drawing, but rather are just using the Insert feature to update an existing block.

7. If Regenauto is turned off, type **Regen.⏎** to view the results of the Insert dialog box.

WARNING If Regenauto is turned off, you must use the Regen command to force a regeneration of the drawing before the updated Unit block appears on the display.

8. Now zoom in to one of the units. You will see that the floor tile appears in all the units as you drew it in the `Unit` file (see Figure 7.11).

FIGURE 7.11
The Plan drawing with the tile pattern

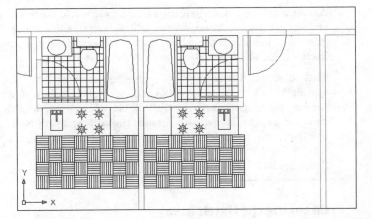

Nested blocks must be updated independently of the parent block. For example, if you modified the Toilet block while editing the `Unit` file and then updated the Unit drawing in the `Plan` file, the old Toilet block would not have been updated. Even though the toilet is part of the `Unit` file, it is still a unique, independent block in the `Plan` file, and AutoCAD will not modify it unless specifically instructed to do so. In this situation, you must edit the original Toilet block and then update it in both the `Plan` and `Unit` files.

TIP If you want to substitute one block for another within the current file, type –Insert.⏎. (Don't forget the minus sign in front of Insert.) At the `Block name:` prompt, enter the block name followed by an equal sign (=), and then enter the name of the new block or the filename. Do not include spaces between the name and the equal sign.

Also, block references and layer settings of the current file take priority over those of the imported file. For example, if a file to be imported has layers of the same name as the current file, but those layers have color and linetype assignments that are different from the current file's, the current file's layer color and linetype assignments will determine those of the imported file. This does not mean, however, that the actual imported file on disk is changed; only the inserted drawing is affected.

SUBSTITUTING BLOCKS

In the preceding example, you updated a block in your Plan file by using the Browse option in the Insert dialog box. In that exercise, the block name and the filename were the same. You can also replace a block with another block or file of a different name. Here's how to do this:

1. Open the Insert dialog box.

2. Click the Browse button next to the Name input box, locate and select the file you want to use as a substitute, and then click Open to return to the Insert dialog box.

3. Change the name in the Name input box to the name of the block you want replaced.

4. Click OK. A warning message appears, telling you that a block with this name already exists. Click OK to proceed with the block substitution.

You can use this method of replacing blocks if you would like to see how changing one element of your project can change your design. You might, for example, draw three different apartment unit plans and give each plan a unique name. You could then generate and plot three apartment building designs in a fraction of the time it would take you to do it by hand.

Block substitution can also reduce a drawing's complexity and accelerate regenerations. To substitute blocks, you temporarily replace large, complex blocks with schematic versions of those blocks. For example, you might replace the Unit block in the Plan drawing with another drawing that contains just a single-line representation of the walls and bathroom fixtures. You would still have the wall lines for reference when inserting other symbols or adding mechanical or electrical information, but the drawing would regenerate much faster. When doing the final plot, you reinsert the original Unit block showing every detail.

Changing the Hatch Area

You might have noticed the Associative option in the Hatch And Gradient dialog box. When this radio button is selected, AutoCAD creates an associative hatch pattern. Associative hatches adjust their shapes to any changes in their associated boundary, hence the name. The following exercise demonstrates how this works.

Suppose you want to enlarge the tiled area of the kitchen by one tile. Here's how it's done:

1. Return to the Unit file (choose Window ➢ *directory path*\\Unit.dwg); then click the outline border of the hatch pattern you created earlier. Notice the grips that appear around the hatch pattern area.

TIP You might need to zoom in closer to the pattern area or use the Object Selection Cycling feature to select the hatch boundary. For more on selection cycling, see Chapter 16.

2. Shift+click the grip in the lower-left corner of the hatch area.

TIP If the boundary of the hatch pattern consists of line segments, you can use a crossing window or polygon-crossing window to select the corner grips of the hatch pattern.

3. With the lower-left grip highlighted, Shift+click the lower-right grip.

4. Now click the lower-right grip again, but don't Shift+click this time.

5. Enter **@12<–90**↵ (**@30<–90** for metric users) to widen the hatch pattern by 1´. The hatch pattern adjusts to the new size of the hatch boundary.

6. Press the Esc key twice to clear any grip selections.

7. Choose File ➢ Save to save the Unit file.

8. Return to the Plan file (choose Window ➢ *directory path*\Plan.dwg) and repeat the steps in the exercise in the "Updating Blocks in the Plan File" section, earlier in this chapter, to update the units again.

The Associative feature of hatch patterns can save time when you need to modify your drawing, but you need to be aware of its limitations. A hatch pattern can lose its associativity when you do any of the following:

◆ Erase or explode a hatch boundary.

◆ Erase or explode a block that forms part of the boundary.

◆ Move a hatch pattern away from its boundary.

These situations frequently arise when you edit an unfamiliar drawing. Often, boundary objects are placed on a layer that is off or frozen, so the boundary objects are not visible. Or the hatch pattern might be on a layer that is turned off, and you proceed to edit the file, not knowing that a hatch pattern exists. When you encounter such a file, take a moment to check for hatch boundaries so you can deal with them properly.

Modifying a Hatch Pattern

Like everything else in a project, a hatch pattern might eventually need to be changed in some way. Hatch patterns are like blocks in that they act like single objects. You can explode a hatch pattern to edit its individual lines. The Properties palette contains most of the settings you'll need to make changes to your hatch patterns. Perhaps the most direct way to edit a hatch pattern is to use the Hatch Edit dialog box.

EDITING HATCH PATTERNS FROM THE HATCH EDIT DIALOG BOX

Follow these steps to modify a hatch pattern by using the Hatch Edit dialog box:

1. Return to the Unit drawing by choosing Window ➢ *directory path*\Unit.dwg.

2. Press the Esc key to clear any grip selections that might be active from earlier exercises.

3. Double-click the hatch pattern in the kitchen to open the Hatch Edit dialog box. It is the same as the Hatch And Gradient dialog box.

TIP When you double-click a hatch pattern, you don't get the typical Properties palette. Double-clicking complex objects such as text, blocks, attributes, and hatch patterns opens a dialog box in which you can edit the object in a more direct way. You can still access the Properties palette for any object by right-clicking the object and choosing Properties from the shortcut menu.

4. Click the ellipsis button to the right of the Pattern drop-down list to open the Hatch Pattern Palette dialog box at the Other Predefined tab.

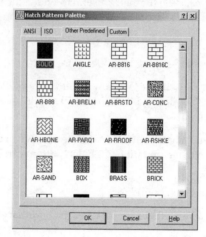

5. Locate and double-click the pattern named AR-BRSTD. It's the pattern that looks like a brick wall. The Hatch Pattern Palette dialog box closes, and you see the AR-BRSTD hatch pattern in the Swatch field.

6. Click OK to accept the change to the hatch pattern. The AR-BRSTD pattern appears in place of the original parquet pattern.

7. You want to keep the old pattern in your drawing, so at this point, exit the Unit file without saving it.

In this exercise, you were able to change the hatch just by double-clicking it. Although you changed only the pattern type, other options are available. You can, for example, modify a predefined pattern to a user-defined one by selecting User Defined from the Type listing in the Hatch Edit dialog box.

You can then enter angle and spacing values for your hatch pattern in the spaces provided in the Hatch Edit dialog box.

The other items in the Hatch Edit dialog box duplicate some of the options in the Hatch And Gradient dialog box. They let you modify the individual properties of the selected hatch pattern. The upcoming section "Understanding the Boundary Hatch Options" describes these other properties in detail.

If you create and edit hatch patterns frequently, you will find the Modify II toolbar useful. It contains an Edit Hatch tool that gives you ready access to the Hatch Edit dialog box. To open the Modify II toolbar, right-click any toolbar, and then click Modify II in the pop-up menu that opens.

EDITING HATCH PATTERNS FROM THE PROPERTIES PALETTE

If you prefer, you can still use the older method to edit a hatch pattern. To open the Properties palette, right-click a pattern and choose Properties from the shortcut menu. The Properties palette displays a Pattern category, which offers a Pattern Name option.

When you click this option, an ellipsis button appears, enabling you to open the Hatch Pattern Palette dialog box, just as in step 4 of the previous exercise. You can then select a new pattern from the dialog box. The Type option in the Properties palette lets you change the type of hatch pattern from Predefined to User Defined or Custom.

TIP   If you're working through the tutorial in this chapter, this would be a good place to take a break or stop. You can pick up the next exercise, which is in the "Attaching a Drawing as an External Reference" section, at another time.

Understanding the Boundary Hatch Options

The Hatch And Gradient dialog box offers many other options that you didn't explore in the previous exercises. For example, instead of selecting the area to be hatched by clicking a point, you can select the actual objects that bound the area you want to hatch by clicking the Add: Select Objects button. You can use Add: Select Objects to add boundaries to existing hatch patterns as well.

The Swatch box just below the Pattern drop-down list opens the Hatch Pattern Palette dialog box, which lets you select a predefined hatch pattern from a graphic window.

The Hatch Pattern Palette dialog box has several tabs that further divide the types of hatch patterns into four categories: ANSI, ISO, Other Predefined, and Custom. The Custom tab is empty until you create your own set of custom hatch patterns. See Chapter 26 for details on how to create custom hatch patterns.

Other options in the right column of the Hatch And Gradient dialog box include Remove Boundaries, Recreate Boundaries, View Selections, Associative, Create Separate Hatches, Draw Order, and Inherit Properties:

Remove Boundaries   Lets you remove a bounded area, or "island," within the area to be hatched. An example of this is the toilet seat in the bathroom. This option is available only when you select a hatch area by using the Add: Pick Points option and an island has been detected.

Recreate Boundaries Draws a region or polyline around the current hatch pattern. When this option is selected, the dialog box temporarily closes. You are then prompted to choose between a region or a polyline and to specify whether to reassociate the pattern with the recreated boundary. (See the Associative option discussed below.)

View Selections Temporarily closes the dialog box and then highlights the objects that have been selected as the hatch boundary by AutoCAD.

Associative Allows the hatch pattern to adjust to changes in its boundary. With this option turned on, any changes to the associated boundary of a hatch pattern will cause the hatch pattern to "flow" with the changes in the boundary.

Create Separate Hatches Creates separate and distinct hatches if you select several enclosed areas while selecting hatch areas. With this option off, separate hatch areas will behave as a single hatch pattern.

Draw Order Allows you to specify whether the hatch pattern appears "on top of" or underneath its boundary. This is useful when the boundary is of a different color or shade and must read clearly or when the hatch pattern must cover the boundary.

Inherit Properties Lets you select a hatch pattern from an existing one in the drawing. This is helpful when you want to apply a hatch pattern that is already used, but you do not know its name or its scale, rotation, or other properties.

Using Additional Hatch Features

AutoCAD's Boundary Hatch command has a fair amount of "intelligence." As you saw in an earlier exercise, it was able to detect not only the outline of the floor area, but also the outline of the toilet seat that represents an island within the pattern area. If you prefer, you can control how AutoCAD treats these island conditions and other situations by selecting options available when you click the More Options button in the lower-right corner of the Hatch And Gradient dialog box.

This button expands the dialog box to show additional hatch options.

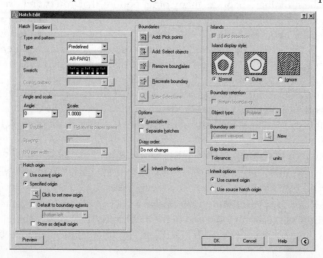

ISLANDS

The Islands group at the top of the dialog box controls how nested boundaries affect the hatch pattern. The graphics in this group show examples of the effect of the selected option. The Islands options include the following:

Island Detection   Turns on the Island Detection feature. This check box excludes closed objects within the boundary from being hatched. For example, when we were hatching the bathroom in an earlier exercise, the toilet seat was not hatched, because it was an island within the boundary.

Normal   Causes the hatch pattern to alternate between nested boundaries. The outer boundary is hatched; if there is a closed object within the boundary, it is not hatched. If *another* closed object is inside the first closed object, *that* object is hatched. This is the default setting.

Outer   Applies the hatch pattern to an area defined by the outermost boundary and a closed object within that boundary. Any boundaries nested within that closed object are ignored.

Ignore   Supplies the hatch pattern to the entire area within the outermost boundary, ignoring any nested boundaries.

BOUNDARY RETENTION

The Boundary Hatch command can also create an outline of the hatch area by using one of two objects: 2D regions, which are like 2D planes, or polyline outlines. Boundary Hatch creates such a polyline boundary temporarily, to establish the hatch area. These boundaries are automatically removed after the hatch pattern is inserted. If you want to retain the boundaries in the drawing, make sure the Retain Boundaries check box is selected. Retaining the boundary can be useful if you know you will be hatching the area more than once or if you are hatching a fairly complex area.

TIP   Retaining a hatch boundary is useful if you want to know the hatched area's dimensions in square inches or feet, because you can find the area of a closed polyline by using the List command. See Chapter 2 for more on the List command.

TIP   The Boundary command creates a polyline outline or region within a selected area. It works much like the Boundary Hatch command but does not add a hatch pattern.

BOUNDARY SET OPTIONS

The Boundary Hatch feature is view-dependent; that is, it locates boundaries based on what is visible in the current view. If the current view contains a lot of graphic data, AutoCAD can have difficulty finding a boundary or can be slow in finding a boundary. If you run into this problem, or if you want to single out a specific object for a point selection boundary, you can further limit the area that AutoCAD uses to locate hatch boundaries by using the Boundary Set options.

New (Select New Boundary Set)   Lets you select the objects from which you want AutoCAD to determine the hatch boundary, instead of searching the entire view. The screen clears and lets you select objects. This option discards previous boundary sets. It is useful for hatching areas in a drawing that contain many objects that you do not want to include in the hatch boundary.

Current Viewport   Tells you that AutoCAD will use the current view to determine the hatch boundary. After you select a set of objects by using the New button, you also see Existing Set as an option in this drop-down list. You can then use this drop-down list to choose the entire view or the objects you select for the hatch boundary.

The Boundary Set options are designed to give you more control over the way a point selection boundary is created. These options have no effect when you use the Add: Select Objects button to select specific objects for the hatch boundary.

GAP TOLERANCE

This group lets you hatch an area that is not completely enclosed. The Gap Tolerance value sets the maximum gap size in an area that you want to hatch. You can use a value from 0 to 5000.

INHERIT OPTIONS

This group controls the hatch origin of when the Inherit Properties option is used to create new hatch patterns. Select Use Current Origin when you want to use the current default hatch origin. Select Use Source Hatch Origin when you want to use the origin from the inherited hatch pattern.

Using Gradient Shading

You might have noticed that one of the hatch patterns offered is a solid. The solid hatch pattern lets you apply a solid color instead of a pattern to a bounded area. AutoCAD also offers a set of gradient patterns that let you apply a color gradient to an area.

You can apply a gradient to an area by using the same method you used to apply a hatch pattern, but instead of using the Hatch tab of the Hatch And Gradient dialog box, you use the Gradient tab to select a gradient pattern.

WARNING   The Gradient Shading feature is not available in AutoCAD LT.

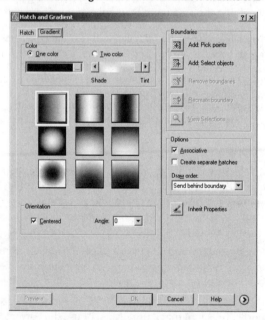

CHOOSING A GRADIENT COLOR

Instead of offering hatch patterns, the Gradient tab offers a variety of gradient patterns. It also lets you control the color of the gradient. For example, if you want to set the gradient between shades of blue, you can click the One Color radio button and then double-click the blue color swatch at the top of the dialog box.

When you double-click the color swatch, the Select Color dialog box opens, offering a palette of True Color options.

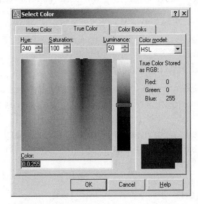

You can then select the color you want for the gradient. On the Gradient tab of the Hatch And Gradient dialog box, the Shade/Tint slider just below the Two Color radio button lets you control the shade of the single-color gradient.

USING TWO COLORS

You can choose a gradient that transitions between shades of a single color by clicking the One Color radio button, or you can transition between two entirely different colors by clicking the Two Color radio button. When you select Two Color, the slider below the Two Color option changes to a color swatch. You can double-click the swatch or click the ellipses button to the right of the swatch to open the Select Color dialog box.

SELECTING GRADIENT PATTERNS

Just below the One Color and Two Color options are the gradient pattern options. You can choose from nine patterns, plus you can select an angle for the pattern from the Angle drop-down list box. The Centered option places the center of the gradient at the center of the area selected for the pattern.

To place a gradient pattern, select a set of objects or a point within a bounded area, just as you would for a hatch pattern. You can then click the Preview button to preview your hatch pattern, or you can click OK to apply the gradient to the drawing.

Tips for Using the Boundary Hatch

Here are a few tips on using the Boundary Hatch feature:

- Watch out for boundary areas that are part of a very large block. AutoCAD examines the entire block when defining boundaries. This can take time if the block is quite large. Use the Boundary Set options to "focus in" on the set of objects you want AutoCAD to use for your hatch boundary.

- The Boundary Hatch feature is view dependent; that is, it locates boundaries based on what is visible in the current view. To ensure that AutoCAD finds every detail, zoom in to the area to be hatched.

- If the area to be hatched will be very large yet will require fine detail, first outline the hatch area by using a polyline. (See Chapter 18 for more on polylines.) Then use the Add: Select Objects option in the Hatch And Gradient dialog box to select the polyline boundary manually, instead of depending on Boundary Hatch to find the boundary for you.

- Consider turning off layers that might interfere with AutoCAD's ability to find a boundary.

- Boundary Hatch works on nested blocks as long as the nested block entities are parallel to the current UCS

Space Planning and Hatch Patterns

Suppose you are working on a plan within which you are constantly repositioning equipment and furniture, or you are in the process of designing the floor covering. You might be a little hesitant to place a hatch pattern on the floor because you don't want to have to rehatch the area each time you move a piece of equipment or change the flooring. You have two options in this situation: you can use the Boundary Hatch's associative capabilities to include the furnishings in the boundary set, or you can use the Display Order feature.

USING ASSOCIATIVE HATCH

Associative Hatch is the most straightforward method. Make sure the Associative option is selected in the Hatch And Gradient dialog box, and include your equipment or furniture in the boundary set. You can do this by using the Add: Select Objects option in the dialog box.

After the pattern is in place, the hatch pattern automatically adjusts to its new location when you move the furnishings in your drawing. One drawback, however, is that AutoCAD attempts to hatch the interior of your furnishings if they cross over the outer boundary of the hatch pattern. Also, if any boundary objects are erased or exploded, the hatch pattern no longer follows the location of your furnishings. To avoid these problems, you can use the method described in the next section.

OVERLAPPING OBJECTS WITH DRAW ORDER

The Draw Order feature lets you determine how objects overlap. In the space-planning example, you can create furniture by using a solid hatch to indicate horizontal surfaces (see Figure 7.12).

HOW TO QUICKLY MATCH A HATCH PATTERN AND OTHER PROPERTIES

Another tool to help you edit hatch patterns is Match Properties, which is similar to Format Painter in the Microsoft Office suite. This tool lets you change an existing hatch pattern to match another existing hatch pattern. Here's how to use it:

1. Click the Match Properties tool in the Standard toolbar.

2. Click the source hatch pattern you want to copy.

3. Click the target hatch pattern you want to change. The target pattern changes to match the source pattern.

The Match Properties tool transfers other properties as well, such as layer, color, and linetype settings. You can select the properties that are transferred by opening the Property Settings dialog box.

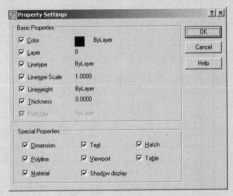

To open this dialog box, type **S.⏎** after selecting the object in step 2, or right-click and choose Settings from the shortcut menu. You can then select the properties you want to transfer from the options shown. All the properties are selected by default. You can also transfer text and dimension style settings. You'll learn more about text and dimension styles in Chapters 10 and 12.

You can then place the furniture "on top" of a floor-covering pattern, and the pattern will be covered and hidden by the furniture. Here's how to do that. (These steps are not part of the regular exercises of this chapter. They are shown here as general guidelines when you need to use the Draw Order feature.)

1. Draw the equipment outline and make sure the outline is a closed polygon.

2. Start the Hatch tool described earlier in this chapter to place a Solid hatch pattern inside the equipment outline.

3. In the Hatch And Gradient dialog box, make sure that Send Behind Boundary is selected in the Draw Order drop-down list.

FIGURE 7.12

Using Draw Order to create an overlapping effect over a hatch pattern

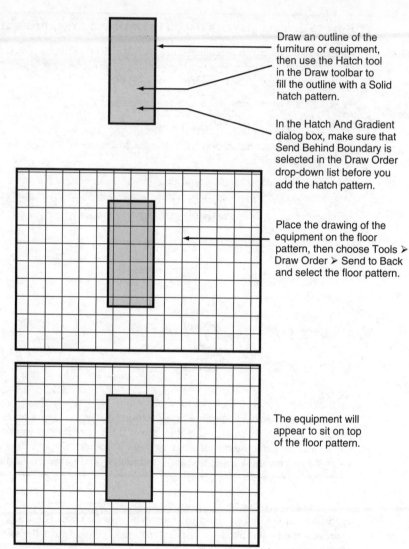

Draw an outline of the furniture or equipment, then use the Hatch tool in the Draw toolbar to fill the outline with a Solid hatch pattern.

In the Hatch And Gradient dialog box, make sure that Send Behind Boundary is selected in the Draw Order drop-down list before you add the hatch pattern.

Place the drawing of the equipment on the floor pattern, then choose Tools ➢ Draw Order ➢ Send to Back and select the floor pattern.

The equipment will appear to sit on top of the floor pattern.

4. Complete the rest of the hatch pattern.

5. After you've finished placing the hatch, turn the outline and solid hatch into a block, or use the Group command to group them.

6. Choose Tools ➢ Draw Order ➢ Bring To Front, and select the equipment. When you are done, the equipment will "cover" the floor hatch pattern (see the bottom panel in Figure 7.12).

After you take these steps, you can place the equipment over a hatched floor pattern, and the equipment will appear to rest on top of the pattern. If you create a floor pattern *after* you create the equipment, choose Tools ➢ Draw Order ➢ Send To Back to move the pattern to the back of the display order. You can also change the display order of objects relative to other objects.

The Draw Order options are all part of the Draworder command. As an alternative to the menu, you can type **Draworder.**↵ at the Command prompt, select an object, and then enter an option at the prompt:

```
Enter object ordering option
[Above object/Under object/Front/Back] <Back>:
```

For example, the equivalent of choosing Tools ➢ Draw Order ➢ Send To Back is entering **Draworder.**↵**B**↵. You can also select the object you want to edit, right-click, and then choose Draw Order from the shortcut menu.

If you need to "white out" an area of a hatch pattern to make text more readable, you can use a solid hatch along with the Display Order option to block out areas behind text.

TIP   Draworder settings are maintained through blocks and Xrefs.

You've had a detailed look at hatch patterns and fills in this section. Remember that you can also use the Tool palettes to help organize and simplify access to your favorite hatch patterns, or just use the patterns already available in the Tool palettes. The patterns in the Tool palettes can be edited and manipulated in the same way as described in this chapter. If you want to know how to make full use of the Tool palettes, check out the discussion on the AutoCAD DesignCenter in Chapter 27.

Using External References

This chapter's discussion about freezing layers mentioned that you can insert drawing files as external references, in a way similar to inserting blocks. To accomplish this, choose Insert ➢ External References (Xref). Chapter 4 briefly introduced external references. As discussed there, the difference between Xref files and blocks is that Xref files do not actually become part of the drawing's database. Instead, they are "loaded" along with the current file at startup time. It is as if AutoCAD were opening several drawings at once: the currently active file you specify when you start AutoCAD, and any file inserted as an Xref.

If you keep Xref files independent from the current file, any changes you make to the Xref automatically appear in the current file. You don't have to update the Xref file manually as you do blocks. For example, if you used Xref to insert the Unit file into the Plan file, and you later made changes to the Unit file, you would see the new version of the Unit file in place of the old the next time you opened the Plan file. If the Plan file is still open while edits are made, AutoCAD will notify you that a change has been made to an Xref.

TIP   You cannot Xref a file if the file has the same name as a block in the current drawing. If this situation occurs, but you still need to use the file as an Xref, you can rename the block of the same name by using the Rename command. You can also use Rename to change the name of various objects and named elements. See Chapter 10.

Another advantage of Xref files is that because they do not actually become part of a drawing's database, drawing size is kept to a minimum. This results in more efficient use of your hard disk space.

TIP Xref files, like blocks, can only be edited using special tools. You can, however, use osnaps to snap to a location in an Xref file, or you can freeze or turn off the Xref file's insertion layer to make it invisible.

Attaching a Drawing as an External Reference

The next exercise shows how to use an Xref in place of an inserted block to construct the studio apartment building. You'll start with creating a new unit file by copying the old one. Then you'll bring a new toolbar, the External References palette, to the screen.

Follow these steps to create the new file:

1. Return to the Unit file; choose File ➢ Save As to save it under the name Unitxref.dwg, and then close the Unitxref.dwg file. This will make a copy of the Unit.dwg file for the following steps. Or if you prefer, you can use the Unitxref.dwg file from the companion CD for the following steps.

2. Return to the Plan file, choose Save As, and save the file under the name Planxref. The current file is now Planxref.dwg.

3. Erase all the Unit plans (enter E↵All↵) and, as described in the next step, purge the Unit plans from the file. (By completing steps 2 and 3, you save yourself from having to set up a new file.)

4. Choose File ➢ Drawing Utilities ➢ Purge to open the Purge dialog box, and then click the Purge All button to open the Confirm Purge dialog box. This will purge blocks that are not in use in the drawing.

5. Click Yes To All.

Now you're ready to use the External References palette:

1. Choose Insert ➢ External References or type XR↵ to open the External References palette (see Figure 7.13).

2. Click the Attach DWG button in the upper-left corner of the palette to open the Select Reference File dialog box. This is a typical AutoCAD file dialog box complete with a preview window.

3. Locate and select the Unitxref.dwg file, and then click Open to open the External Reference dialog box (see Figure 7.14). Notice that this dialog box looks similar to the Insert dialog box. It offers the same options for insertion point, scale, and rotation.

4. You'll see a description of the options presented in this dialog box. For now, click OK.

5. Enter 31´-5″,43´-8″↵ (metric users enter **957,1330**) for the insertion point.

6. After the Unitxref.dwg file is inserted, re-create the same layout of the floor plan you created in the first section of this chapter by copying and mirroring the Unitxref.dwg external reference.

7. Save the Planxref file.

FIGURE 7.13
The External References palette

FIGURE 7.14
The External Reference dialog box

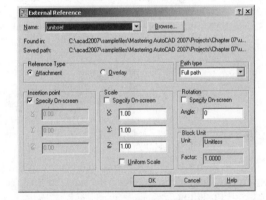

You now have a drawing that looks like the Plan.dwg file you created earlier in this chapter, but instead of using blocks that are detached from their source file, you have a drawing composed of Xrefs. These Xrefs are the actual Unitxref.dwg file, and they are loaded into AutoCAD at the same time that you open the Planxref.dwg file. An icon in the lower-right corner of the AutoCAD window tells you that the current drawing contains Xrefs.

This icon not only alerts you to Xrefs, but it also enables you to open the External References palette, as you'll see in the next exercise.

Next, you'll modify the Unitxref.dwg file and see the results in the Planxref.dwg file.

1. To open the Unitxref.dwg file, from the current Planxref file, select and then right-click the unit, and then choose Open Xref from the shortcut menu. You can also enter **Xopen.↵** at the Command prompt, and then select the unit plan Xref.

WARNING Xopen and the Open Xref option in the shortcut menu are not available in LT. If you are using LT, choose File ➤ Open, and use the Select File dialog box to open the Unitxref.dwg file.

2. Erase the hatch pattern and kitchen outline for the floors, and save the Unitxref.dwg file.

3. Choose Window ➤ Planxref.dwg to return to the Planxref.dwg file. You now see a message balloon pointing to the Xref icon in the lower-right corner of the AutoCAD window. The balloon warns you that an Xref has changed. Right-click the Manage Xrefs icon in the lower-right corner of the AutoCAD window, and then choose External References from the pop-up menu to open the External References palette.

4. Select the Unitxref name in the list box, click Reload, and then click OK. Notice that the units in the Planxref drawing have been updated to include the changes you made to the Unitxref file.

You can open multiple Xrefs at once by selecting more than one Xref while using the Xopen command.

TIP The Open option in the External References palette performs the same function as the Xopen command or the Open Xref option in the shortcut menu. To use this option, select and then right-click the Xref files from the list box in the External References palette, and then click Open.

You will want to be aware that when an Xref has been modified, the Manage Xrefs icon in the lower right of the AutoCAD window changes to show an exclamation point. This alerts you to changes in an Xref in the current drawing.

Click the Manage Xrefs icon to open the External References palette. The Xref that has been changed is indicated by a message in the Status column of the list box.

You can then select the Xref that needs to be updated, right-click, and choose the Reload option from the shortcut menu to reload the selected Xref. You can also select multiple Xrefs if more than one needs updating.

Here you saw how an Xref file is updated in a different way from blocks. Because Xrefs are loaded along with the drawing file that contains them, the containing file, which in this case was the Planxref file, automatically displays any changes made to the Xref when it is opened. Also, you avoid having to update nested blocks, because AutoCAD updates nested Xrefs, as well as non-nested Xrefs. When an Xref is modified while you are editing a file, you are alerted to the change through the Xref icon located in the lower-right corner of the AutoCAD window. You can click the balloon message that appears from that icon to update any modified Xrefs.

Other Differences between External References and Blocks

Here are a few other differences between Xrefs and inserted blocks that you will want to keep in mind:

◆ Any new layers, text styles, or linetypes brought in with cross-referenced files do not become part of the current file. If you want to import any of these items, you can use the Xbind command (described in Chapter 15).

IMPORTING BLOCKS, LAYERS, AND OTHER NAMED ELEMENTS FROM EXTERNAL FILES

You can use the Xbind command to import blocks and other drawing components from another file. First, use the External References palette to cross-reference a file; type **Xbind** at the Command prompt. In the Xbind dialog box, click the plus sign next to the Xref filename and then select Block. Locate the name of the block you want to import, click the Add button, and click OK. Finally, open the External References palette, select the Xref filename from the list, right-click, and select Detach to remove the Xref file. The imported block remains as part of the current file. (See Chapter 15 for details on importing drawing components.) You can also use the AutoCAD DesignCenter to import items from external files. DesignCenter is described in Chapter 27.

The Tool Palettes window give you access to frequently used blocks and hatch patterns that reside in other drawings. You can open the Tool palettes by clicking the Tool Palettes icon in the Standard toolbar.

In the standard AutoCAD installations, the Tool Palettes window is configured with sample 3D commands, blocks, and hatch patterns that you can drag and drop into your current drawing. Just select a tab for the Tool palette that contains the block or pattern you want, and then click and drag the item into your drawing. In the case of hatch patterns, click and drag the pattern into an area that is bounded on all sides by objects. When you are ready to customize the Tool Palettes window, you do so by clicking and dragging objects or tools into a new or existing palette. See Chapter 27 for more on customizing tool palettes.

♦ If you make changes to the layers of a cross-referenced file, those changes are not retained when the file is saved, unless you checked the Retain Changes To Xref Layers option in the Open And Save tab of the Options dialog box. This option, found in the External References (Xrefs) group, instructs AutoCAD to remember any layer color or visibility settings from one editing session to the next. In the standard AutoCAD settings, this option is on by default.

TIP Another way to ensure that layer settings for Xrefs are retained is to enter **Visretain.⏎** at the Command prompt. At the New value for VISRETAIN <0>: prompt, enter **1**.

♦ To segregate layers in Xref files from layers in the current drawing, the Xref file's layers are prefixed with their file's name. A vertical bar separates the filename prefix and the layer name when you view a list of layers in the Layer drop-down list or the Layer Properties Manager dialog box (as in Unitxref | wall).

♦ You cannot explode Xrefs. You can, however, convert an Xref into a block and then explode it. To do this, select the Xref in the External References palette to open another dialog box that offers two ways of converting an Xref into a block. See the section "The External References Palette" later in this chapter for more information.

♦ If an Xref is renamed or moved to another location on your hard disk, AutoCAD won't be able to find that file when it opens other files to which the Xref is attached. If this happens, you must select the path in the Found At field in the External References palette and then click the Browse button (the ellipses) to tell AutoCAD where to find the cross-referenced file.

WARNING Take care when retargeting an Xref file with the Browse button. The Browse button can assign a file of a different name to an existing Xref as a substitution.

♦ Xref files are especially useful in workgroup environments in which several people are working on the same project. For example, one person might be updating several files that are inserted into a variety of other files. Using blocks, everyone in the workgroup would have to be notified of the changes and would have to update all the affected blocks in all the drawings that contained them. With cross-referenced files, however, the updating is automatic; so you avoid confusion about which files need their blocks updated.

Other External Reference Options

Many other features are unique to external reference files. Let's briefly look at some of the other options in the External References palette.

EXTERNAL REFERENCES IN THE SAN FRANCISCO MAIN LIBRARY PROJECT

Although these exercises demonstrate how Xrefs work, you aren't limited to using them in the way shown here. Perhaps one of the more common ways of using Xrefs is to combine a single floor plan with different title block drawings, each with its own layer settings and title block information. In this way, single-drawing files can be reused in several drawing sheets of a final construction document set. This helps keep data consistent across drawings and reduces the number of overall drawings needed.

This is exactly how Xrefs were used in the San Francisco Main Library drawings. One floor-plan file contained most of the main information for that floor. The floor plan was then used as an Xref in another file that contained the title block, as well as additional information such as furnishings or floor finish reference symbols. Layer visibility was controlled in each title block drawing so only the data related to that drawing appeared.

Multiple Xref files were also used by segregating the structural column grid layout drawings from the floor-plan files. In other cases, portions of plans from different floors were combined into a single drawing by using Xrefs, as shown here.

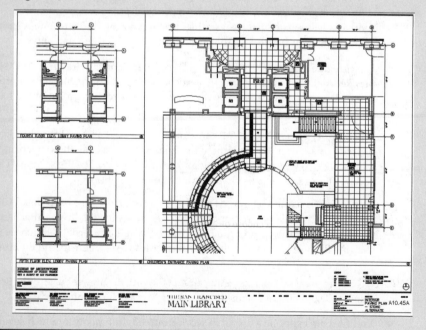

OPTIONS IN THE EXTERNAL REFERENCES PALETTE

Several options are available when you right-click an external reference name listed in the External References palette, shown in Figure 7.13 earlier in this chapter. You saw the Reload option in an earlier exercise. The following describes the other options that are available.

Attach   Opens the Select Reference dialog box, in which you can select a file to attach and set the parameters for the attachment.

Detach   Detaches an Xref from the current file. The file is then completely disassociated from the current file.

Reload   Restores an unloaded Xref.

Unload   Similar to Detach but maintains a link to the Xref file so that it can be quickly reattached. This has an effect similar to freezing a layer and can reduce redraw, regeneration, and file-loading times.

Bind   Converts an Xref into a block. Bind offers two options: Bind (again) and Insert. Bind's Bind option maintains the Xref's named elements (layers, linetypes, and text and dimension styles) by creating new layers in the current file with the Xref's filename prefix (see Chapter 15). The Insert option does not attempt to maintain the Xref's named elements but merges them with named elements of the same name in the current file. For example, if both the Xref and the current file have layers of the same name, the objects in the Xref are placed in the layers of the same name in the current file.

Open   Lets you open an Xref. Select the Xref from the list and then click Open. The Xref opens in a new window when you close the External References palette. This option is not available in AutoCAD LT.

Details   At the bottom of the External References palette, you will see a panel called Details. This panel is similar to the Properties palette in that it displays the properties of a selected external reference and also allows you to modify some of those properties. For example, the Reference Name option in the Details panel lets you give the external reference a name that is different from the Xref filename. Table 7.1 gives you a rundown on the options in the Details panel.

TABLE 7.1:   The Details Panel of the External References Palette

OPTION	FUNCTION
Reference Name	Lets you give the Xref a name that is different from the Xref's filename. This can be helpful if you want to use multiple external references of the same file.
Status	Tells you whether the Xref is loaded, unloaded, or not found (read only).
Size	Gives you the file size information (read only).
Type	Lets you choose between the Attach and Overlay attachment method for the Xref file. Xrefs attached as Overlays will not include nested Xrefs.
Date	Gives you the date and time the file was attached (read only).
Saved Path	Tells you where AutoCAD is expecting to find the Xref file (read only).
Found At	Lets you select the location of the Xref file. When you click the text box for this option, a Browse button appears to the right. You can click this button to locate a lost Xref or use a different file from the original attached Xref.

THE EXTERNAL REFERENCE DIALOG BOX

The External Reference dialog box, shown in Figure 7.14 earlier in this chapter, offers these options:

Browse Opens the Select Reference File dialog box to enable you to change the file you are importing as an Xref.

Attachment Tells AutoCAD to include other Xref attachments that are nested in the selected file.

Overlay Tells AutoCAD to ignore other Xref attachments that are nested in the selected file. This avoids multiple attachments of other files and eliminates the possibility of circular references (referencing the current file into itself through another file).

Path Type Xref files can be located anywhere on your system, including network servers. For this reason, links to Xrefs can be easily lost either by moving them or rearranging file locations. To help you manage Xrefs, the Path Type option offers three options for locating Xrefs: Full Path, Relative Path, and No Path. Full Path retains the current full path. Relative Path maintains paths in relation to the current drawing. The current drawing must be saved before using the Relative Path option. The No Path option is for drawings in which Xrefs are located in the same folder as the current drawing or in the Support File Search Path that is specified in the Files tab of the Options dialog box (choose Tools ➢ Options).

Specify On-Screen Appears in three places. It gives you the option to enter insertion point, scale factors, and rotation angles within the dialog box or in the Command window, in a way similar to inserting blocks. If you clear this option for any of the corresponding parameters, the parameters change to allow input. If they are selected, you are prompted for those parameters after you click OK to close the dialog box. With all three Specify On-Screen check boxes cleared, the Xref is inserted in the drawing using the settings indicated in the dialog box.

Clipping Xref Views and Improving Performance

Xrefs are frequently used to import large drawings for reference or backgrounds. Multiple Xrefs, such as a floor plan, column grid layout, and site plan drawing, might be combined into one file. One drawback to multiple Xrefs in earlier versions of AutoCAD is that the entire Xref is loaded into memory, even if only a small portion of the Xref is used for the final plotted output. For computers with limited resources, multiple Xrefs could slow the system to a crawl.

AutoCAD 2007 offers two tools that help make display and memory use more efficient when using Xrefs: the Xclip command and the Demand Load option in the Options dialog box.

CLIPPING VIEWS

The Xclip command lets you clip the display of an Xref or a block to any shape you want, as shown in Figure 7.15. For example, you might want to display only an L-shaped portion of a floor plan to be part of your current drawing. Xclip lets you define such a view. To access the command, choose Modify ➢ Clip ➢ Xref.

You can clip blocks and multiple Xrefs as well. And you can specify a front and back clipping distance so that visibility of objects in 3D space can be controlled. You can define a clip area by using polylines or spline curves, although curve-fitted polylines will revert to decurved polylines. (See Chapter 18 for more on polylines and spline curves.)

CONTROLLING XREF SETTINGS IN THE OPTIONS DIALOG BOX

The External References (Xrefs) group in the Open And Save tab of the Options dialog box offers some tools to help you manage memory use and other features related to Xrefs. If you're working on large projects with others in a workgroup, you'll want to be aware of these settings and what they do.

FIGURE 7.15

The first panel shows a polyline outline of the area to be isolated with Xclip. The second panel shows how the Xref appears after Xclip is applied. The last panel shows a view of the plan with the polyline's layer turned off.

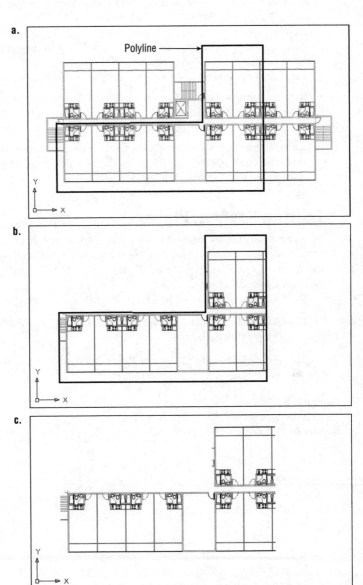

The Demand Load Xrefs drop-down list offers three settings: Disabled, Enabled, and Enabled With Copy. Demand Load is set to Enable With Copy by default in the standard AutoCAD drawing setup. Besides reducing the amount of memory an Xref consumes, Demand Load also prevents other users from editing the Xref while it is being viewed as part of your current drawing. This is done to help aid drawing version control and drawing management. The Enabled With Copy option creates a copy of the source Xref file and then uses the copy, thereby enabling other AutoCAD users to edit the source Xref file.

Demand loading improves performance by loading only the parts of the referenced drawing that are needed to regenerate the current drawing. You can set the location for the Xref copy in the Files tab of the Options dialog box under Temporary External Reference File Location.

Two other options are also available in the Options dialog box:

Retain Changes To Xref Layers   Instructs AutoCAD to remember any layer color or visibility settings of Xrefs from one editing session to the next. In the standard AutoCAD settings, this option is on by default.

Allow Other Users To Refedit Current Drawing   Lets others edit the current drawing by choosing Tools ➢ Xref And Block In-Place Editing ➢ Edit Reference In-Place (Refedit). You'll learn about this command in the next section.

Editing Xrefs in Place

You've seen different methods for editing blocks and Xrefs as external files. There is another way to edit a block or an Xref directly within a file, without having to edit an external file. You use the Xref And Block In-Place Editing option in the Tools drop-down menu. This option issues the Refedit command.

The following exercise demonstrates how Refedit works:

1. If it isn't already open, open the Planxref.dwg file. Also make sure that you have closed the Unitxref.dwg file.

2. Zoom into the unit plan in the lower-left corner of the drawing so you see a view similar to Figure 7.16.

FIGURE 7.16
The enlarged view of the Unit Xref in the Planxref file

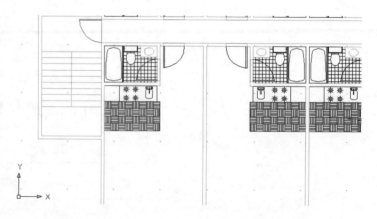

3. Double-click the the wall of the corner unit. You can also choose Tools ➤ Xref And Block In-Place Editing ➤ Edit Reference In-Place from the menu bar. Then, at the `Select reference:` prompt, click a wall of the corner unit to open the Reference Edit dialog box.

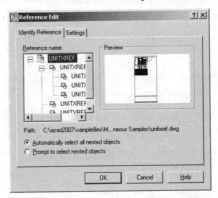

4. The Reference Edit dialog box contains two panels. The right panel shows a thumbnail view of the item that you are editing. The left panel shows a listing of the specific item you selected in the Xref. Notice that the listing shows the hierarchical relationship of the kitchenette block in relation to the Unitxref Xref.

5. In the left panel, click the unitxref | KITCHEN listing, and then click OK. The Reference Edit dialog box disappears, and the Refedit toolbar appears.

6. Use a selection window to select the entire lower-left corner unit. Notice that only the grips in the kitchenette appear, indicating that the objects in the kitchenette are selected. While the rest of the unit appears to be selected, they appear lighter in color. This shows you that only the kitchen is available for editing.

7. Press the Esc key to clear your selection.

TIP You can open the Refedit toolbar so that it stays on the screen by right-clicking any toolbar and choosing Refedit from the shortcut menu.

SPECIAL SAVE AS OPTIONS THAT AFFECT DEMAND LOADING

AutoCAD offers a few additional settings that boost the performance of the Demand Load feature. When you choose File ➤ Save As to save a file in the standard .dwg format, you see the Tools button in the upper-right corner. Choosing Tools ➤ Options opens the Save As Options dialog box. Using the options in the Index Type drop-down list in the DWG Options tab can help improve the speed of demand loading. The index options are as follows:

None   No index is created.

Layer   AutoCAD loads only layers that are both turned on and thawed.

Spatial   AutoCAD loads only portions of an Xref or raster image within a clipped boundary.

Layer & Spatial   Turns on both the Layer and Spatial options.

The Refedit command isolates the objects you select in step 5 for editing. You cannot edit anything else in the Xref until you exit the Refedit command and start over.

At this point, you can edit a block within an Xref. Now let's continue editing the kitchenette:

1. Zoom in on the kitchenette, and then move the four burners to the right 8″ (20 cm for metric users).

2. Erase the sink.

3. Click the Save Reference Edits button on the Refedit toolbar or choose Tools ➤ Xref And Block In-Place Editing ➤ Save Reference Edits.

4. A warning message appears, telling you that the changes you've made to the Xref will be saved. Click OK.

5. Zoom back to your previous view. Notice that the other units now reflect the changes you made to the Unitxref Xref (see Figure 7.17).

FIGURE 7.17
The Xrefs after being edited

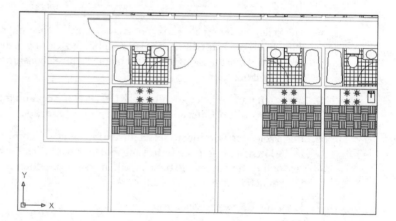

6. Open the Unitxref.dwg file. Notice that the kitchen now reflects the changes you made to the Xref of the unit in the Planxref file. This shows you that by choosing to save the reference edit in step 3, you actually save the changes back to the Xref's source file.

As you saw from these two exercises, it's possible to edit a specific block within an Xref, but to do that you must select the block name in the Reference Edit dialog box.

In these exercises, you edited a block contained within an Xref, but you could have just as easily edited a block within the current drawing. You can also edit nested blocks by using the Refedit command. Changes in blocks in the current file will not affect other files because blocks are not linked to external files. The changes to blocks remain within the current file until you explicitly export the changed block to a file, as you saw in earlier exercises.

Adding and Removing Objects from Blocks and Xrefs

In the previous exercises, you removed objects from the Kitchen block simply by using the Erase command. You can also move objects from a block or an Xref into the current drawing without erasing it. To do this, choose Tools ➤ Xref And Block In-Place Editing ➤ Remove From Working Set while in the Refedit command. This removes the object from the block or Xref without erasing it.

Likewise, you can add new objects to the block or Xref by choosing Tools ➢ Xref And Block In-Place Editing ➢ Add To Working Set. Both menu options invoke the Refset command, with different options applied.

To see how Refset works, try the following exercise:

1. Close the `Unitxref.dwg` file.

2. In the `Planxref` file, zoom into the kitchenette to get a view similar to the top panel of Figure 7.18.

3. Double-click the unit plan drawing. You can also choose Tools ➢ Xref And Block In-Place Editing ➢ Edit Reference In-Place and then click the unit plan.

4. Click the unitxref | KITCHEN listing in the Reference Edit dialog box and then click OK.

5. Use the Move tool to move the two burners on the right just to the right of the kitchenette, as shown in Figure 7.18.

6. Click the Remove From Working Set tool in the Refedit toolbar, or choose Tools ➢ Xref And Block In-Place Editing ➢ Remove From Working Set.

7. Select the two burners you just moved and then press ↵.

Notice that the burners become grayer to show that they are now removed from the working set. They remain as part of the Planxref drawing, but they are no longer part of the Kitchen block.

FIGURE 7.18
Moving the burners out of the Kitchen block and adding the rectangle.

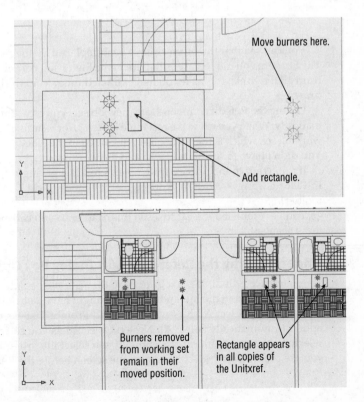

Now add a rectangle to the Kitchen block in place of the burners:

1. Draw a 7″ × 16″ (18 cm × 40 cm) rectangle in place of the moved burners, as shown in Figure 7.18. Anything you add to the drawing automatically becomes part of the working set.

2. Click Save Reference Edits on the Refedit toolbar or choose Modify ➢ Xref And Block In-Place Editing ➢ Save Reference Edits. You will see a warning message stating that "All reference edits will be saved". Click OK.

3. Zoom out enough to see the other units in the drawing (see Figure 7.19).

FIGURE 7.19

The Planxref drawing with the changes made to the Unitxref Xref

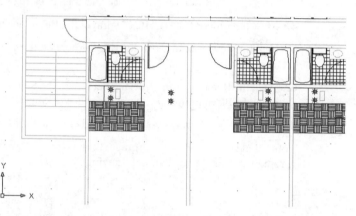

You can see that the burners have been replaced by the rectangle in all the other Xref units. The burners you moved are still there in the lower-left corner unit, but they have been removed from all the Xrefs. It is as if you had extracted them from the block and placed them in the Plan drawing.

During the Refedit command, any new objects you create are added to the working set automatically. When you drew the rectangle in step 1, for example, it was automatically included in the working set, which is the set of objects included in the block or Xref you are currently working on. You didn't have to specifically add it to the working set.

If you want to include existing objects in the working set, choose Tools ➢ Xref And Block In-Place Editing ➢ Add To Working Set, or choose Add To Working Set from the Refedit toolbar.

You've completed the exercises in this chapter so you can exit AutoCAD without saving these changes.

Understanding the Reference Edit Dialog Box Options

The Reference Edit dialog box offers you the option to isolate specific blocks within the Xref by selecting them from the hierarchy list. You might have also noticed the two radio button options: Automatically Select All Nested Objects and Prompt To Select Nested Objects. The default option, Automatically Select All Nested Objects, lets you select any object contained within the selected object in the hierarchy listing. If you select the Prompt To Select Nested Objects option, you are prompted to select objects on the screen before the Refedit toolbar appears.

ACAD only

In addition to the options you used in the exercises, the Reference Edit dialog box also offers the Settings tab with some additional options.

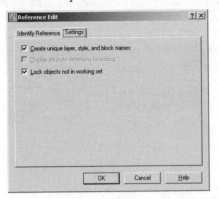

CREATE UNIQUE LAYER, STYLE, AND BLOCK NAMES

When you use the Refedit command with the Automatically Select All Nested Objects option turned on, you can import nested blocks into the current drawing. For example, if you selected the Bath block in the hierarchy list in the previous exercise, you would have access to the Tub and Toilet blocks in the Bath block. You can then copy either of those blocks into the current file.

When you make a copy of a block from an Xref, AutoCAD needs to assign that block a name. The Create Unique Layer, Style, And Block Names option tells AutoCAD to use the original block name and append a $#$ prefix to the name (# is a numeric value starting with zero). If you were to import the Bath block, for example, it would become 0bath in the current drawing. This ensures that the block will maintain a unique name when it is imported, even if there is a block with the same name in the current drawing. If you turn off the Create Unique Layer, Style, And Block Names option, the original name will be maintained. If the current drawing contains a block of the same name, the imported block will use the current file's definition of that block.

DISPLAY ATTRIBUTE DEFINITIONS FOR EDITING

If your drawing contains attributes (see Chapter 13 for more on attributes), this option is offered. If you turn on this option, you can then edit attribute definitions by using the Refedit command. If you select a block that contains an attribute definition while you are using the Refedit command, the attribute definition will be exposed, enabling you to make changes. Changes to attribute definitions affect only new attribute insertions. Except for the attribute of the edited block, existing attributes are not affected. If you want to update existing attributes to a newly edited definition, use the Sync option of the Block Attribute Manager (choose Modify ➤ Object ➤ Attribute ➤ Block Attribute Manager).

LOCK OBJECTS NOT IN WORKING SET

In the Refedit exercises, you saw that objects that are not selected in the Reference Edit dialog box are grayed out and are not selectable. The Lock Objects Not In Working Set option controls this feature and is turned on by default.

If You Want to Experiment

If you'd like to see firsthand how block substitution works, try doing the exercise in Figure 7.20. It shows how quickly you can change the configuration of a drawing by careful use of block substitution. As you work through the exercise, keep in mind that some planning is required to use blocks in this way. If you know that you will have to try various configurations in a drawing, plan to set up files to accommodate them.

FIGURE 7.20

An exercise in block substitution

1. Start a file called Part1 and draw the object shown at right.

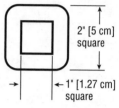

2" [5 cm] square

1" [1.27 cm] square

2. Next to that object, draw the object shown at right. Use the Wblock command and turn it into a file called Tab1.
(Note the insertion point location.)

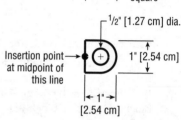

½" [1.27 cm] dia.

Insertion point at midpoint of this line

1" [2.54 cm]

1" [2.54 cm]

3. Draw the object shown at right and turn it into a file called Tab2.

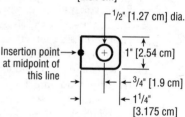

½" [1.27 cm] dia.

Insertion point at midpoint of this line

1" [2.54 cm]

¾" [1.9 cm]

1¼" [3.175 cm]

4. Insert Tab1 into the drawing in four places, as shown here. You can insert one and then use the Polar option under the Array command for the other three tabs.

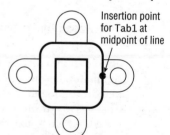

Insertion point for Tab1 at midpoint of line

5. Start the Insert command again but at the prompt

        Block name (or ?):

   enter Tab1=Tab2. The drawing regenerates and an alternative version of the part appears with Tab2 replacing Tab1. Cancel the Insert command.

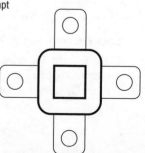

You might also want to try the exercise by using Xrefs instead of inserting files as blocks. After you've attached the Xref, try substituting the Tab1 Xref with the Tab2 Xref by using the Browse button in the External References palette. Highlight Tab1 in the list of Xrefs, and then click Browse and select Tab2. The current file still calls the Xref Tab1 by its original name, but instead loads Tab2 in its place.

TIP You can substitute Xrefs in a way similar to blocks, as shown in this example.

By now, you might be anxious to see how your drawings look on paper. In the next chapter, you will explore the use of AutoCAD's printing and plotting commands.

Chapter 8

Introducing Printing, Plotting, and Layouts

Getting hard-copy output from AutoCAD is something of an art. You'll need to be intimately familiar with both your output device and the settings available in AutoCAD. You will probably spend a good deal of time experimenting with AutoCAD's plotter settings and with your printer or plotter to get your equipment set up just the way you want.

With the huge array of output options available, this chapter can provide only a general discussion of plotting and printing. As a rule, the process for using a plotter isn't much different from those for a printer; you just have more media size options with plotters. Still, every output device is different. It's up to you to work out the details and fine-tune the way you and AutoCAD together work with your particular plotter or printer. This chapter describes the features available in AutoCAD and discusses some general rules and guidelines to follow when setting up your plots.

I'll start with an overview of the plotting features in AutoCAD and then delve into the finer details of setting up your drawing and controlling your plotter or printer.

Topics in this chapter include the following:

- ◆ Plotting the Plan
- ◆ Understanding the Plotter Settings
- ◆ WYSIWYG Plotting Using Layout Tabs
- ◆ Adding an Output Device
- ◆ Storing a Page Setup
- ◆ Plotter and Printer Hardware Considerations
- ◆ Sending Your Drawings to a Service Bureau
- ◆ Using Batch and Electronic Plots

Plotting the Plan

To see firsthand how the Plot command works, you'll plot the Plan file by using the default settings on your system. Start by getting a preview of your plot, before you commit to actually printing your drawing. As an introduction, you'll plot from the Model tab of an AutoCAD drawing, but be aware that typically you will want to plot from a Layout tab. The Layout tabs give you a greater degree of control over how your output will look. You'll be introduced to the Layout tab later in this chapter. Now let's get started!

First, try plotting your drawing to no particular scale:

1. Be sure your printer or plotter is connected to your computer and is turned on.

2. Start AutoCAD and open the Plan.dwg file.

3. Choose View ➢ Zoom ➢ All to display the entire drawing.

4. Choose File ➢ Plot to open the Plot dialog box. You can also right-click the Model tab at the bottom of the AutoCAD window and choose Plot.

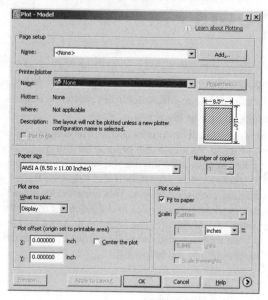

5. If the Name option in the Printer/Plotter group shows None, click the drop-down arrow and select your current Windows system printer.

6. In the Plot Area group, make sure the Display option is selected in the drop-down list. This tells AutoCAD to plot the drawing as it looks in the drawing window. You also have the option to plot the limits of the drawing or select an area to plot with a window. In addition, you can choose to plot the extents of a drawing or a saved view.

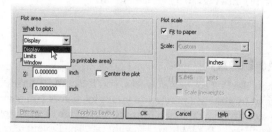

7. Make sure the Fit To Paper option is selected in the Plot Scale group.

8. Click the Preview button in the lower-left corner of the dialog box. AutoCAD works for a moment and then displays a sample view of how your drawing will appear when printed.

Notice that the view also shows the Zoom Realtime cursor. You can use the Zoom/Pan Realtime tool to get a close-up of your print preview.

9. Now go ahead and plot the file: right-click and choose Plot from the shortcut menu. AutoCAD sends the drawing to your printer.

10. Your plotter or printer prints the plan to no particular scale.

You've just plotted your first drawing to see how it looks on paper. You used the minimal settings to ensure that the complete drawing appears on the paper.

You might notice that a message bubble appears in the lower-right corner of the AutoCAD window.

If you click the text that reads Click to view plot and publish details..., the Plot And Publish Details dialog box opens to display some detailed information about your plot.

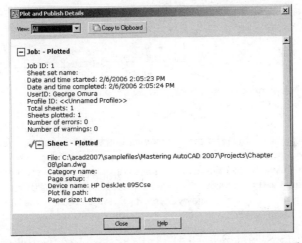

As you become more experienced with AutoCAD and your projects become more demanding, the information presented in the Plot And Publish Details dialog box might be useful to you. For now, make a mental note that this information is available should you need it.

Next, try plotting your drawing to an exact scale. This time you'll expand the Plot dialog box to show a few more options:

WARNING   It is important to make sure you use the appropriate unit settings in this chapter. If you've been using the metric measurements for previous exercises, make sure you use the metric settings in the exercises of this chapter; otherwise, your results will not coincide.

1. Choose File ➤ Plot again to open the Plot dialog box. If the Name option in the Printer/Plotter group shows None, click the drop-down arrow and select your current Windows system printer.

2. Click the More Options button; this is the round button with the > symbol in the lower-right corner of the dialog box. You'll see some additional options appear on the right side of the dialog box.

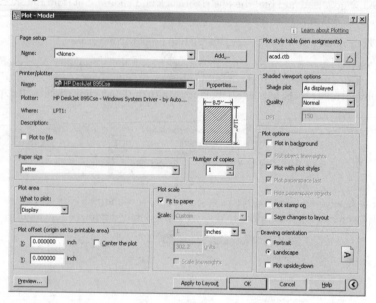

3. If your last printout was not oriented on the paper correctly, select the Landscape option in the Drawing Orientation group.

TIP   The appearance of the print preview depends on the type of output device you chose when you installed AutoCAD or when you last selected a Plotter Device option (described in the section "WYSIWYG Plotting Using Layout Tabs" later in this chapter). The print preview is also affected by other settings in the Plot dialog box, such as those in the Drawing Orientation, Plot Offset, and Plot Area groups. This example shows a typical preview view using the Windows default system printer in landscape mode.

4. In the Plot Scale group, clear the Fit To Paper check box. Then select $1/_{16}'' = 1$ -0″ from the Scale drop-down list. Metric users should select 1:20. As you can see, you have several choices for the scale of your output.

5. In the Paper Size group, select Letter. Metric users should select A4. The options in this drop-down list depend on your Windows system printer or the output device you configured for AutoCAD.

6. In the Plot Area group, select Limits from the drop-down list. This tells AutoCAD to use the limits of your drawing to determine which part of your drawing to plot.

7. Click the Preview button again to get a preview of your plot.

8. Right-click and choose Plot from the shortcut menu. This time, your printout is to scale.

Here, you were asked to specify a few more settings in the Plot dialog box. Several settings work together to produce a drawing that is to scale and that fits properly on your paper. This is where it pays to understand the relationship between your drawing scale and your paper's size, discussed in Chapter 3. You also saw how you can expand the options in the Plot dialog box.

TIP The next section is lengthy but doesn't contain any exercises. If you prefer to continue with the exercises in this chapter, skip to the section "WYSIWYG Plotting Using Layout Tabs." Be sure to come back and read the following section while the previous exercises are still fresh in your mind.

Understanding the Plotter Settings

In this section, you'll explore all the settings in the Plot dialog box. These settings give you control over the size and orientation of your image on the paper. They also let you control which part of your drawing gets printed. All these settings work together to give you control over how your drawing will fit on your printed output.

WARNING If you're a veteran AutoCAD user, be aware that AutoCAD 2007 relies mainly on the Windows system printer configuration instead of its own plotter drivers. It also remembers printer settings that are specific to AutoCAD so you don't have to adjust your printer settings each time you use AutoCAD. This gives you more flexibility and control over your output. Be aware that you'll need to understand the Windows system printer settings, in addition to those offered by AutoCAD.

Paper Size

You use the option in this group to select the paper size for your output. You can select a paper size from the Paper Size drop-down list. These sizes are derived from the sizes available from your currently selected system printer. You'll find out how to select a different printer later in this chapter.

AutoCAD 2007 offers sheet sizes in both Imperial and metric measurements with a drop-down list located in the Plot Scale group. AutoCAD assumes that if you pick a metric sheet size such as A4 or A5, you will want the sheet dimensions specified in metric measurements and adjusts the dialog box settings accordingly.

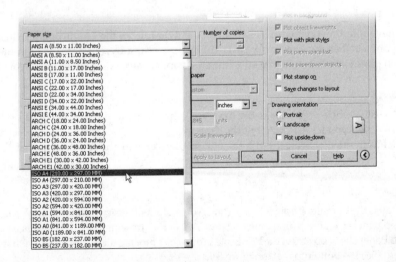

Drawing Orientation

When you used the Preview button in the first exercise in this chapter, you saw your drawing as it would be placed on the paper. In that example, it was placed in a *landscape orientation*, which places the image on the paper so that the width of the paper is greater than its height. You can rotate the image on the paper 90° into what is called a *portrait orientation* by selecting the Portrait radio button in the Drawing Orientation group. A third option, Plot Upside-Down, lets you change the orientation further by turning the landscape or portrait orientation upside down. These three settings let you print the image in any one of four orientations on the sheet.

In AutoCAD, the preview displays the paper in the orientation that it leaves the printer. So for most small-format printers, if you're printing in the portrait orientation, the image appears in the same orientation as you see it when you are editing the drawing. If you're using the landscape orientation, the preview image is turned sideways. For large-format plotters, the preview might be oriented in the opposite direction. The graphic in the Drawing Orientation group displays a capital *A* on a sheet showing the orientation of your drawing on the paper output.

TIP   Remember that you need to click the More Options button in the lower-right corner of the Plot dialog box to access the Drawing Orientation group. The More Options button looks like a circle with a greater-than sign. You can also press Alt+Shift+>.

Plot Area

The What To Plot drop-down list in the Plot Area group lets you specify which part of your drawing you want to plot. You might notice some similarities between these settings and the Zoom command options. Each Plot Area option is described next.

LIMITS

The Limits printing option (available in Model Space only) uses the limits of the drawing to determine what to print (see Figure 8.1). If you let AutoCAD fit the drawing onto the sheet (by selecting the Fit To Paper check box in the Plot Scale group), the plot displays exactly the same image that you would see on the screen had you selected View ➢ Zoom ➢ All.

LAYOUT

The Layout option (available in Layout tabs only) replaces the Limits option when you plot from a Layout tab. (See the section "WYSIWYG Plotting Using Layout Tabs" later in this chapter.) This option plots everything displayed within the paper margins shown in the Layout tab view.

EXTENTS

The Extents option draws the entire drawing, eliminating any space that borders the drawing (see Figure 8.2). If you let AutoCAD fit the drawing onto the sheet (that is, you select the Fit To Paper check box in the Plot Scale group), the plot displays exactly the same image that you would see on the screen if you choose View ➢ Zoom ➢ Extents.

DISPLAY

Display is the default option; it tells AutoCAD to plot what is currently displayed on the screen (see the top panel in Figure 8.3). If you let AutoCAD fit the drawing onto the sheet (that is, you select the Fit To Paper check box from the Plot Scale group), the plot is exactly the same as what you see on your screen. (See the bottom panel in Figure 8.3.)

VIEW

The View option is available when you have saved a view in the drawing by using the View command. When you select View from the What To Plot drop-down list, another drop-down list appears, offering a list of views available in the drawing. You can then select the view that you want to plot. (Figure 8.4 shows a typical result.)

FIGURE 8.1
The screen display and the printed output when Limits is chosen. The grid in the top image shows the limits of the drawing.

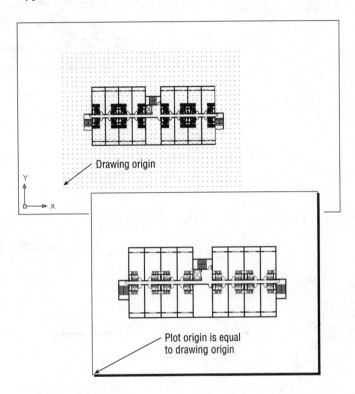

FIGURE 8.2
The printed output when Extents is chosen

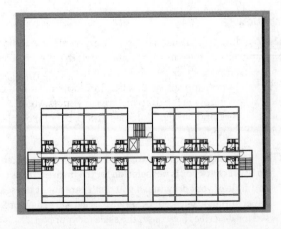

FIGURE 8.3

The screen display and the printed output when Display is chosen and no scale is used. (The drawing is scaled to fit the sheet.)

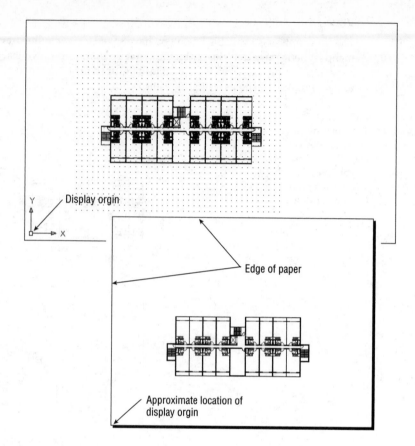

If you let AutoCAD fit the drawing onto the sheet (by selecting Fit To Paper from the Plot Scale group), the plot displays exactly the same thing that you would see on the screen if you had recalled the view you are plotting.

WINDOW

The Window option enables you to use a window to indicate the area you want to plot (see Figure 8.5). Nothing outside the window prints. To use this option, select it from the drop-down list. The Plot dialog box will temporarily close to allow you to select a window. After you've done this the first time, a Window button appears next to the drop-down list. You can then click the Window button and then indicate a window in the drawing area. If you let AutoCAD fit the drawing onto the sheet by using the Fit To Paper option in the Plot Scale group, the plot displays exactly the same thing that you enclose within the window.

TIP Do you get a blank printout, even though you selected Extents or Display? Chances are the Fit To Paper check box is not selected, or the Inches = Units setting is inappropriate for the sheet size and scale of your drawing. If you don't care about the scale of the drawing, make sure the Fit To Paper option is selected. Otherwise, make sure the Plot Scale settings are set correctly. The next section describes how to set the scale for your plots.

FIGURE 8.4

A comparison of the saved view and the printed output. Note how the printed image below is cut off at the top to conform to the AutoCAD view.

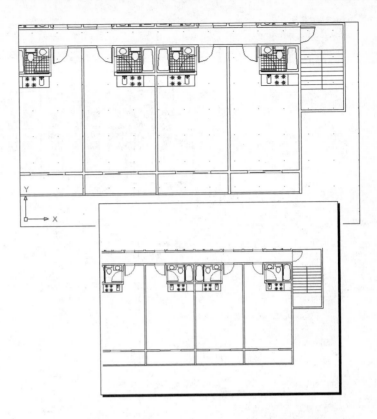

Plot Scale

In the previous section, the descriptions of several Plot Area options indicate that the Fit To Paper option can be selected. Bear in mind that when you instead apply a scale factor to your plot, it changes the results of the Plot Area settings, and some problems can arise. This is usually where most new users have difficulty.

For example, the apartment plan drawing fits nicely on the paper when you use Fit To Paper. But if you try to plot the drawing at a scale of 1″ = 1′, you will probably get a blank piece of paper because, at that scale, hardly any of the drawing fits on your paper. AutoCAD will tell you that it is plotting and then tell you that the plot is finished. You won't have a clue as to why your sheet is blank.

TIP   Remember that the Plan1.dwg file was set up for an 18′ × 24′ (A2, or 594 mm × 420 mm for metric users) sheet at a scale of $^1/_8$′ = 1″ -0′ (1:10 for metric users). If, when plotting from the Model tab, you select these settings from the Plot dialog box (provided your printer or plotter supports 18′ × 24′, or A2, paper) and you also select Limits for your plot area, your drawing will fit on the paper and will be at the appropriate scale.

If an image is too large to fit on a sheet of paper because of improper scaling, the plot image will be placed on the paper differently, depending on whether the plotter uses the center of the image or the lower-left corner for its origin. (See Figure 8.1 earlier in this chapter.) Keep this in mind as you specify scale factors in this area of the dialog box.

FIGURE 8.5

A selection window and the resulting printout

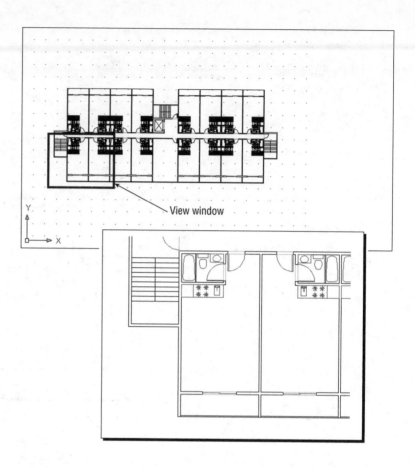

SCALE

You can select a drawing scale from a set of predefined scales in the Scale drop-down list. These options cover the most common scales you'll need to use.

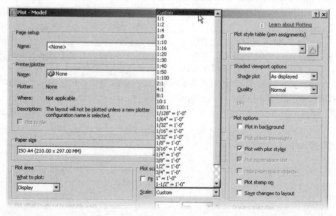

You've already seen how the Fit To Paper option enables you to avoid giving a scale altogether and forces the drawing to fit on the sheet. This works fine if you are plotting illustrations that are not to scale. If you select another option such as $1/8´ = 1˝ -0´$, you'll see the inches and units input boxes change to reflect this scale. The Inches = input box changes to 0.125, and the Units input box changes to 12.

CUSTOM SCALE

If you can't find the scale you want in the Scale drop-down list, you can select Custom from this list and then enter custom values in the Inches = and Units input boxes.

Through these input boxes, you can indicate how the drawing units within your drawing relate to the final plotted distance in inches or millimeters. For example, if your drawing is of a scale factor of 96, follow these steps:

1. Double-click the Inches = input box, enter **1**, and press the Tab key.

2. Double-click the Units input box, enter **96**, and press the Tab key.

   Metric users who want to plot to a scale of 1:10 should enter **1** in the MM input box and **10** in the Units input box.

If you are more used to the Architectural unit style in the Imperial measurement system, you can enter a scale as a fraction. For example, for a $1/8´$ scale drawing:

1. Double-click the Inches = input box, enter **1/8**, and press the Tab key.

2. Double-click the Units input box, enter **12**, and press the Tab key.

If you specify a different scale from the one you chose while setting up your drawing, AutoCAD will plot your drawing to that scale. You are not restricted in any way as to scale, but entering the correct scale is important: if it is too large, AutoCAD will think your drawing is too large to fit on the sheet, although it will attempt to plot your drawing anyway. See Chapter 3 for a discussion of unit styles and scale factors.

TIP   If you plot to a scale that is different from the scale you originally intended, objects and text will appear smaller or larger than would be appropriate for your plot. You'll need to edit your text size to match the new scale. You can do so by using the Properties palette. Select the text whose height you want to change, click the Properties tool on the Standard toolbar, and then change the Height setting in the Properties palette.

ADDING A CUSTOM SCALE TO THE SCALE DROP-DOWN LIST

If you have a custom scale you use frequently, you may find it annoying to have to input your scale every time you plot. AutoCAD offers the ability to add your custom scale to the Scale drop-down list shown earlier. You can then easily select your custom scale from the list instead of entering it through the text box.

Here are the steps you use to add a custom scale to the Scale drop-down list.

1. Choose Tools ➢ Options to open the Options dialog box.

2. Select the User Preferences tab, and then click the Edit Scale List button toward the bottom-center of the dialog box.

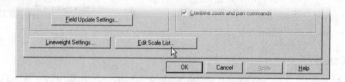

3. In the Edit Scale List dialog box, click the Add button.

4. In the Add Scale dialog box, enter a name for you custom scale in the Name Appearing In Scale List text box, and then enter the appropriate values in the Scale Properties text boxes.

5. Click OK at each dialog box to close them.

There are several options besides Add in the Edit Scale List dialog box. Clicking the Edit button lets you edit an existing scale in the list. Clicking the Move Up and Move Down buttons lets you change the location of an item in the list. Clicking Delete deletes an item or a set of items from the list. Clicking the Reset button restores the list to its default condition and removes any custom items you may have added.

TIP Instead of opening the Options dialog box and clicking Edit Scale List on the User Preferences tab, you can enter **Scalelistedit.**⏎ at the Command prompt to open the Edit Scale List dialog box directly.

SCALE LINEWEIGHTS

AutoCAD offers the option to assign line weights to objects either by their layer assignments or by directly assigning a line weight to individual objects. The line weight option, however, doesn't have any meaning until you specify a scale for your drawing. After you do specify a scale, the Scale Lineweights option is available. Select this check box if you want the line weight assigned to layers and objects to appear correctly in your plots. You'll get a closer look at line weights and plotting later in this chapter.

Shaded Viewport Options

Most of your plotting will probably involve 2D technical line drawings, but occasionally you might need to plot a shaded or rendered 3D view. You might need to include such 3D views combined with 2D or 3D Wireframe views. AutoCAD offers the Shaded Viewport Options that enable you to plot shaded or rendered 3D views of your AutoCAD drawing. These options give you control over the quality of your rendered output. (LT users will not have the Shaded Viewport Options.)

> **TIP** Remember that you need to click the More Options button in the lower-right corner of the Plot dialog box to get to the Shaded Viewport Options group. The More Options button looks like a circle with a greater-than sign. You also need to select a printer name in the Printer/Plotter group before these options are made available.

SHADE PLOT

The Shade Plot drop-down list lets you control how a Model Space view will be plotted. You can choose from As Displayed, Wireframe, Hidden, or Rendered.

As Displayed plots the Model Space view as it appears on your screen.

Wireframe plots the Model Space view of a 3D object as a wireframe view.

Hidden plots your Model Space view with hidden lines removed.

3D Hidden/3D Wireframe/Conceptual/Realistic plots the Model Space using one of these visual styles. These selections override the current Model Space visual style. See Chapter 20 for more on visual styles.

Rendered renders your Model Space view before plotting (see Chapter 22 for more on rendered views).

Draft/Low/Medium/High/Presentation sets the quality of the plot.

The Shade Plot options are not available if you are plotting from a Layout tab. You can control the way each layout viewport is plotted through the viewport's Properties settings. You'll learn more about layout viewport properties later in this chapter.

QUALITY AND DPI

The Quality drop-down list determines the dpi (dots per inch) setting for your output. These options are not available if you select Wireframe or Hidden from the Shade Plot drop down list:

Draft plots 3D views as wireframe.

Preview offers 150 dpi resolution.

Normal offers 300 dpi resolution.

Presentation offers 600 dpi resolution.

Maximum defers dpi resolution to the current output device's settings.

Custom lets you set a custom dpi setting. When Custom is selected, the DPI input box is made available for your input.

TIP If some of the terms discussed for the Shaded Viewport Options are unfamiliar, don't be alarmed. You'll learn about 3D Shaded and Rendered views in Part IV of this book. And when you start to explore 3D modeling in AutoCAD, come back and review the Shaded Viewport Options.

Plot Offset

Frequently, your first plot of a drawing shows the drawing positioned incorrectly on the paper. You can fine-tune the location of the drawing on the paper by using the Plot Offset settings. To adjust the position of your drawing on the paper, you enter the location of the view origin in relation to the plotter origin in X and Y coordinates (see Figure 8.6).

FIGURE 8.6
Adjusting the image location on a sheet

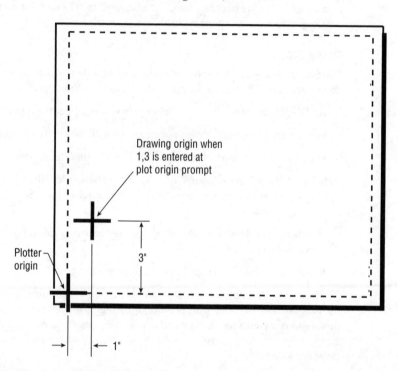

For example, suppose you plot a drawing, and then realize that it needs to be moved 1′ to the right and 3′ up on the sheet. You can replot the drawing by making the following changes:

1. Double-click the X input box, type **1**, and press the Tab key.

2. Double-click the Y input box, type **3**, and press the Tab key.

Now proceed with the rest of the plot configuration. With the preceding settings, the image is shifted on the paper exactly 1′ to the right and 3′ up when the plot is done.

You can also tell AutoCAD the location from which the offset is to occur. The Plot And Publish tab of the Options dialog box (choose Tools ➤ Options from the menu bar) offers the Specify Plot

Offset Relative To button group. This group offers two radio buttons: Printable Area and Edge Of Paper. You can select the option that makes the most sense for you.

Plot Options

The options in the Plot Options group offer a greater amount of control over your output and require some detailed instruction. Here is a brief description of these options. You'll learn more about them in the next section.

PLOT IN BACKGROUND

If you think that your plot will take some time to complete, this option will plot your drawing in the background so that after you begin a plot you can immediately return to your drawing work. This option can also be controlled through the Backgroundplot system variable.

PLOT OBJECT LINEWEIGHTS

As mentioned earlier, AutoCAD lets you assign line weights to objects either through their layer assignment or by directly assigning a line weight to the object itself. If you use this feature in your drawing, this option lets you turn line weights on or off in your output.

PLOT WITH PLOT STYLES

Plot styles give you a high degree of control over your drawing output. You can control whether your output is in color or black and white, and you can control whether filled areas are drawn in a solid color or a pattern. You can even control the way lines are joined at corners. You'll learn more about these options and how they affect your work in the next section.

PLOT PAPERSPACE LAST

When you are using a Layout tab, otherwise known as Paper Space, this option determines whether objects in Paper Space are drawn before or after objects in Model Space. You'll learn more about Model Space and Paper Space later in this chapter.

HIDE PAPERSPACE OBJECTS

This option pertains to 3D models in AutoCAD. When you draw in 3D, you see your drawing as a *Wireframe view*. In a Wireframe view, your drawing looks like it's transparent even though it is made up of "solid" surfaces. Using hidden line removal, you can view and plot your 3D drawings so that solid surfaces are opaque. To view a 3D drawing in the editor with hidden lines removed, use the Hide command. To plot a 3D drawing with hidden lines removed, use the Hidden option from the Shade Plot drop down list.

WARNING   Hide Paperspace Objects does not work for views in the Layout tab viewport described in the next section. Instead, you need to set the viewport's Shadeplot setting to Hidden. (Click the viewport, right-click, and choose Shade Plot ➢ Hidden from the shortcut menu.)

PLOT STAMP ON

The Plot Stamp feature lets you place pertinent data on the drawing in a location you choose. This data includes the drawing name, date and time, scale, and other data. When you click the Plot Stamp On check box to turn on this option, an additional button appears.

Click this button to gain access to the Plot Stamp dialog box. This dialog box offers many controls over the plot stamp. This is a fairly extensive tool, so rather than fill this chapter with a description of all its features, see Appendix B for a complete rundown of the Plot Stamp options.

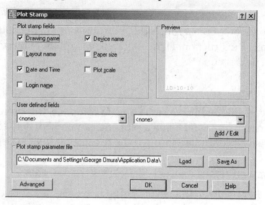

SAVE CHANGES TO LAYOUT

When this option is turned on, the changes you make to Plot dialog box settings are saved with the current layout. You'll learn more about layouts in the next section.

TIP In the Plot dialog box, you'll see the usual OK, Cancel, and Help buttons at the bottom. You'll also see the Apply To Layout button. This button lets you save the plot settings you make without actually sending your drawing to the printer or plotter for output. This option is convenient for those times when you decide halfway through your plot setup not to plot your drawing.

WYSIWYG Plotting Using Layout Tabs

You've probably noticed the tabs at the bottom of the drawing area labeled Model, Layout1, and Layout2. So far, you've done all your work in the Model tab, also known as Model Space. The other two tabs open views to your drawing that are specifically geared toward printing and plotting. The Layout views enable you to control drawing scale, add title blocks, and even set up different layer settings from those in the Model tab. You can think of the Layout tabs as page layout spaces that act like a desktop-publishing program.

You can have as many Layout tabs as you like, each set up for a different type of output. You can, for example, have two or three Layout tabs, each set up for a different scale drawing or with different layer configurations for reflected ceiling plans, floor plans, or equipment plans. You can even set up multiple views of your drawing at different scales within a single Layout tab. In addition, you can draw and add text and dimensions in Layout tabs just as you would in Model Space.

TIP When you create a new file, you see two Layout tabs. If you open a pre–AutoCAD 2000 file, you see only one Layout tab.

To get familiar with the Layout tabs, try the following exercise:

1. With the Plan file open, click the Layout1 tab at the bottom of the AutoCAD window. A view of your drawing appears on a gray background, as shown in Figure 8.7. This is a view

of your drawing as it will appear when plotted on your current default printer or plotter. The white area represents the printer or plotter paper.

2. Try zooming in and out using the Zoom Realtime tool. Notice that the entire image zooms in and out, including the area representing the paper.

Layout tabs give you full control over the appearance of your drawing printouts. You can print a Layout tab just as you did the view in the Model tab, by using the Plot option on the Layout1 tab's shortcut menu.

Let's take a moment to look at the elements in the Layout1 tab. As mentioned previously, the white background represents the paper on which your drawing will be printed. The dashed line immediately inside the edge of the white area represents the limits of your printer's margins. Finally, the solid rectangle that surrounds your drawing is the outline of the Layout viewport. A *viewport* is an AutoCAD object that works like a window into your drawing from the Layout tab. You might also notice the triangular symbol in the lower-left corner of the view. This is the UCS icon for the Layout tab. It tells you that you are currently in the Layout tab space. You'll see the significance of this icon in the following exercise:

1. Try selecting part of your drawing by clicking in the lobby area. Nothing is selected.

2. Click the viewport border, which is the solid rectangle surrounding the drawing, as shown in Figure 8.7. This is the viewport into the Model tab. Notice that you can select it.

FIGURE 8.7

A view of the Layout1 tab

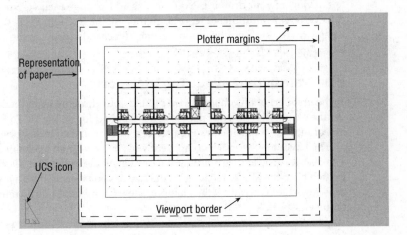

3. Right-click and choose Properties from the shortcut menu. You can see from the Properties palette that the viewport is just like any other AutoCAD object with layer, linetype, and color assignments. You can even hide the viewport outline by turning off its layer.

4. Close the Properties palette.

5. With the viewport still selected, click the Erase tool in the Modify toolbar. The view of your drawing disappears with the erasure of the viewport. Remember that the viewport is like a window into the drawing you created in the Model tab. After the viewport is erased, the drawing view goes with it.

6. Type **U**↵ or click the Undo button in the Standard toolbar to restore the viewport.

7. Double-click anywhere within the viewport's boundary. Notice that the UCS icon you're used to seeing appears in the lower-left corner of the viewport. The Layout UCS icon disappears.

8. Click the lobby of your drawing. You can now select parts of your drawing.

9. Try zooming and panning your view. Changes in your view take place only within the boundary of the viewport.

10. Choose View ➤ Zoom ➤ All or type **Z**↵**A**↵ to display the entire drawing in the viewport.

11. To return to Paper Space, double-click an area outside the viewport.

TIP   You can also type **PS**↵ to return to Paper Space and **MS**↵ to access the space within the viewport. Or click the Paper/Model button in the status bar at the bottom of the AutoCAD window.

This exercise shows you the unique characteristics of the Layout tab. The objects within the viewport are inaccessible until you double-click the interior of the viewport. You can then move about and edit your drawing within the viewport, just as you would while in the Model tab.

The Layout tabs can contain as many viewports as you like, and each viewport can hold a different view of your drawing. You can size and arrange each viewport in any way you like, or you can even create multiple viewports, giving you the freedom to lay out your drawing as you would a page in a desktop-publishing program. You can also draw in the Layout tab or import Xrefs and blocks for title blocks and borders.

Plot Scale in the Layout Tab Viewports

In the first part of this chapter, you plotted your drawing from the Model tab. You learned that to get the plot to fit onto your paper, you either had to use the Fit To Paper option in the Plot dialog box or indicate a specific drawing scale, plot area, and drawing orientation.

The Layout tab works in a different way: it is designed to enable you to plot your drawing at a 1-to-1 scale. Instead of specifying the drawing scale in the Plot dialog box, as you did when you plotted from the Model tab, you let the size of your view in the Layout tab viewport determine the drawing scale. You can set the viewport view to an exact scale by making changes to the properties of the viewport.

To set the scale of a viewport in a Layout tab, try the following exercise:

1. Press the Esc key to clear any selections. Then select the viewport border, right-click, and choose Properties from the shortcut menu. The Properties palette for the viewport appears.

2. Scroll down the Properties palette by using the scroll bar on the left side, and then locate the Standard Scale option under the Misc category. Click this option. The item to its right turns into a list box.

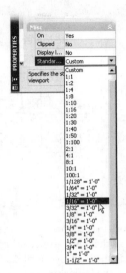

3. Open the list box and select $^1/_{16}' = 1''$ (metric users should select 1:20). The view in the drawing window changes to reflect the new scale for the viewport. Now most of the drawing fits into the viewport, and it is to scale.

TIP   The scale of $^1/_{16}' = 1'$ is similar to the metric 1:200 scale, but because you used centimeters instead of millimeters as the base unit for the metric version of the Plan file, you drop the second 0 in 200. The metric scale becomes 1:20.

4. Close the Properties palette.

5. Use the viewport grips to enlarge the viewport enough to display all of the drawing, as shown in Figure 8.8. You need to move only a single corner grip. As you move a corner grip, notice that the viewport maintains a rectangular shape.

6. Choose File ➢ Plot, and, in the Plot dialog box, make sure the Scale option is set to 1:1 and that your system printer is selected in the Printer/Plotter group; then click OK. Your drawing is plotted as it appears in the Layout tab, and it is plotted to scale.

7. After reviewing your plot, close the drawing without saving it.

In step 2, you saw that you can select a scale for a viewport by selecting it from the Properties palette. If you look just below the Standard Scale option, you'll see the Custom Scale option. Both options work like their counterpart, the Plot Scale group, in the Plot dialog box.

TIP   Veteran AutoCAD users can still choose View ➢ Zoom ➢ Scale to control the scale of the viewport view.

FIGURE 8.8

The enlarged viewport

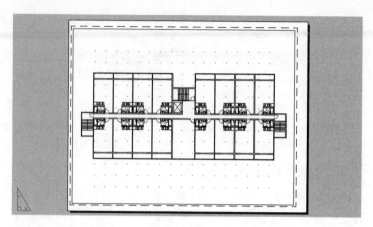

Layout tabs and viewports work in conjunction with your plotter settings to give you a better idea of how your plots will look. In fact, there are numerous plotter settings that can dramatically change the appearance of your Layout tab view and your plots. In the next section, you'll learn how some of the plotter settings can enhance the appearance of your drawings. You'll also learn how Layout tabs can display those settings, letting you see on your computer screen exactly what will appear on your paper output.

Adding an Output Device

This chapter mentioned that you can set up AutoCAD for more than one output device. You can do this even if you have only one printer or plotter connected to your computer. You might want multiple printer configurations in AutoCAD for many reasons. You might want to set up your system so that you can print to a remote location over a network or the Internet. Some printer configurations are strictly file-oriented, such as the AutoCAD .dwf format for Internet Web pages or raster file output. (See Chapter 27 for more on .dwf files.)

AutoCAD works best with printers and plotters configured as Windows system devices. Although you can add devices through the AutoCAD Plot Manager, Autodesk recommends that you set up your plotters and printers as Windows devices and then use the System Printer option in AutoCAD to select your output device. (In Windows XP, choose Start ➢ Control Panel ➢ Printers And Other Hardware ➢ Add A Printer to configure a new printer.)You can use the Add Printer Wizard to create predefined settings for your system printer so that you can quickly choose a printer or plotter setup.

You can also configure additional printers through the AutoCAD Plot Manager; this method also uses the Add-A-Plotter Wizard. Here's how it's done:

1. Choose File ➢ Plotter Manager to open the Plotters window. Your view of the Plotters window might look a little different depending on your operating system, but the same basic information is there.

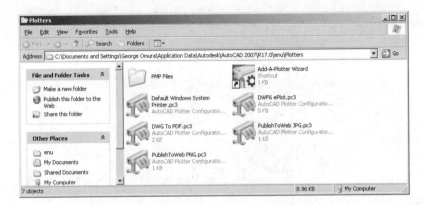

You can also open this window by clicking the Add Or Configure Plotters button in the Plot And Publish tab of the Options dialog box. It's just an Explorer window showing you the contents of the `Plotters` folder under the Documents and Settings folder for your Windows user profile.

2. Double-click the Add-A-Plotter Wizard icon to open the Add Plotter dialog box. You see the Introduction screen, which describes the purpose of the wizard.

3. Click Next. The next screen of the wizard lets you select the type of setup you want. Here you are offered three options: My Computer, Network Plotter Server, and System Printer. The My Computer and the Network Plotter Server options offer plotter options based on AutoCAD-specific drivers. The main difference between these two options is that the Network Plotter option asks you for a network server name. Otherwise, they both offer the same set of options. The System Printer option will use the existing Windows system printer as the basis for the setup.

4. If you click the My Computer radio button and then click Next, you see a listing of plotter models that are supported by AutoCAD directly through AutoCAD's own drivers. If you use a PostScript device, or if you want to convert drawings to raster formats, this is the place to select those options. You can select the plotter or printer manufacturer name from the Manufacturers list on the left and then select a specific model from the list to the right. If you have a driver for a specific plotter or printer that is not listed, you can click the Have Disk button to browse to your driver location.

5. After you've made a printer or plotter selection, click Next. You are then asked if you want to use an existing PCP or PC2 configuration file for the selected plotter. PCP and PC2 configurations files are plotter configuration files from earlier releases of AutoCAD.

6. Unless you plan to use one of those files, click Next on the Import PCP Or PC2 screen. If you selected My Computer in step 4, the Ports screen opens. With the Plot To A Port option selected, you can select a port from a list to which your printer or plotter is connected. The Configure Port button lets you set up the port if you have a specific requirement for the port. Or if you intend to plot to a file instead of to a port, you can select the Plot To File radio button at the top. An AutoSpool option is also offered if your printer requires this feature.

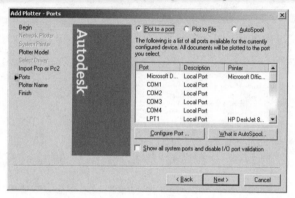

If you selected an option in step 4 that doesn't require a port setup, click the Next button to skip this option, and the Plotter Name screen opens. You can enter a descriptive name in the Plotter Name text box. This name will appear in the Printer Name drop-down list of the Plot Or Page Setup dialog box.

7. Enter a name for this configuration in the space provided; then click Next to open the Finish screen.

8. This screen gives you the option to make adjustments to the configuration you've just created by clicking the Edit Plotter Configuration button. Click Finish to exit the Add-a-Plotter Wizard. Your new configuration appears in the Plotters window.

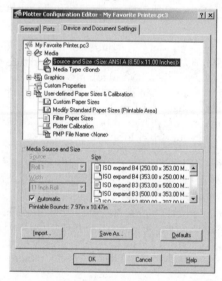

This editor lets you fine-tune your plotter settings. For example, you can calibrate your plotter for more accurate scaling of your plots, or if you're creating a raster file output configuration, you can create a custom page setting for extremely high resolution raster images.

After you've set up a plotter, the plotter information is stored as a file with the .pc3 filename extension in the `Plotters` subfolder under the Documents and Settings folder for your Windows user profile.

CONTROLLING THE APPEARANCE OF THE LAYOUT TABS

The Options dialog box offers a set of controls dedicated to the Layout tabs. If you don't like some of the graphics in the Layout tab, you can turn them off. Open the Options dialog box and click the Display tab to see a set of options in the Layout Elements group.

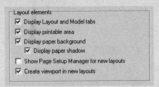

As you can see, you can control the display of the tabs themselves, the margins, the paper background, and the paper shadow. In addition, you can specify whether AutoCAD automatically creates a viewport or opens the Page Setup dialog box when you open a Layout tab for the first time.

Editing a Plotter Configuration

In step 7 of the previous exercise, you exited the Add-a-Plotter Wizard without editing the newly created plotter configuration. You can always go back and edit the configuration by opening the Plotters window (choose File ➤ Plotter Manager) and double-clicking the configuration you want to edit. You can recognize a plotter configuration file by its .pc3 file name extension.

Many users will use their Windows system printer or plotter for other applications besides AutoCAD, and frequently the AutoCAD settings for that printer will be different from the settings used for other applications. You can set up AutoCAD to automatically use its own settings so you don't have to reconfigure your Windows system printer every time you switch applications. To do so, take the following steps:

1. Choose File ➤ Page Setup Manager to open the Page Setup Manager dialog box.

2. Click the Modify button to open the Page Setup dialog box.

3. Select the printer that you want to configure in the Name drop-down list of the Printer/Plotter group.

4. Click the Properties button just to the right of the drop-down list to open the Plotter Configuration Editor dialog box. A list box displays all the properties of the printer or plotter. Not

all these properties are editable, however. Each time you click a property in the list box, the lower half of the dialog box displays the options associated with that property.

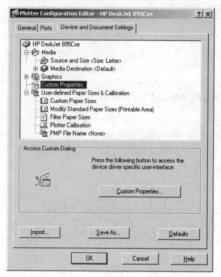

5. Click the Custom Properties item in the list box. The lower half of the dialog box displays the Custom Properties button.

6. Click the Custom Properties button. You'll see the Windows system printer options. These are the same options you see when you edit the properties of your printer by choosing Start ➤ Printers And Faxes or Start ➤ Control Panel ➤ Printers And Other Hardware.

7. Adjust these settings the way you want them when you plot from AutoCAD and click OK.

8. Back in the Plotter Configuration Editor dialog box, click the Save As button. A standard file dialog box appears.

9. Enter the name of the plot configuration you've set up, or accept the default name, which is usually the name of the Windows printer or plotter, and click Save.

10. Click OK in the Plotter Configuration Editor dialog box; then click OK in the Page Setup dialog box.

The Plotter Configuration Editor offers a wide variety of options that are fairly technical in nature. If you want to know more about the Plotter Configuration Editor, see Appendix B.

Storing a Page Setup

Unlike most other programs, AutoCAD offers hundreds of page setup options. It can be quite a chore keeping track of and maintaining all these options. But as you settle into using AutoCAD,

PLOTTING IMAGE FILES AND CONVERTING 3D TO 2D

If your work involves producing manuals, reports, or similar documents, you might want to add the Raster File Export option to your list of plotter configurations. The Raster File Export option lets you plot your drawings to a wide range of raster file formats including CALS, JPEG, PCX, Targa, Tiff, and BMP. You can then import your drawings into documents that accept bitmap images. Images can be up to 8000 × 8000 pixels (set through the Plotter Configuration Editor) and can contain as many colors as the file format allows. If you need several raster formats, you can use multiple instances of this or any plotter configuration.

If you want to convert your 3D wireframe models into 2D line drawings, add the AutoCAD DXB File output format. This format lets you plot a 3D image to a file. You can then import the resulting .dxb file by choosing Insert ➢ Drawing Exchange Binary.

Yet another option is to add an HPGL output device to your AutoCAD setup and then plot your 3D model to an HPGL file. You can then use the Convert PLT To DWG Express tool (choose Express ➢ File Tools ➢ Convert PLT To DWG) described in Chapter 24 to import an HPGL plot file into an AutoCAD drawing.

you'll probably find that you will set up a few plotter configurations and stick to them. AutoCAD 2007 lets you save a page setup under a name to help you store and manage those settings you use the most.

You've already seen the Page Setup Manager dialog box on your way to preparing a page for printing. In this section, you'll take a closer look at this useful tool.

Follow these steps to create a page setup.

1. In AutoCAD, choose File ➢ Page Setup Manager. You can also right-click a Layout tab and choose Page Setup Manager. The Page Setup Manager dialog box opens. So far, you've used only the Modify option in this dialog box to modify an existing page setup. Now you'll try creating a new setup.

2. Click the New button to open the New Page Setup dialog box.

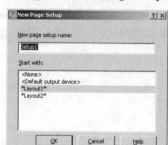

3. To create a new page setup, first enter a name in the New Page Setup Name input box and select a setup from the Start With list box. AutoCAD will use the setup you select as the basis for the new setup. Notice that AutoCAD offers the name of Setup1 as a default name for a new setup.

4. Click OK when you are finished. AutoCAD will open the Page Setup dialog box, where you can choose the settings for your new page setup.

5. Click OK to return to the Page Setup Manager. You'll see your new page setup listed in the Current Page Setup list box. From here, you can select a page setup from the list box, and then click the Set Current button to make it the current page setup for the layout.

You can also import other user-defined page setups by clicking the Import button. Because page setups are stored in the drawing, the Import button opens a standard file dialog box that displays drawing files. You can then select a file from which you would like to import a page setup.

The current page setup applies to the current Layout tab, but after you create a new page setup, it is offered as an option in the Page Setup Manager dialog box for all other Layout tabs. You can also select a page setup directly from the Plot dialog box by using the Name drop-down list in the Page Setup group.

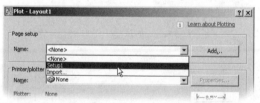

Page setups can be used with the Publish feature described in Chapter 27 to set up batch plots, or in the Sheet Set feature to quickly setup sheet layouts. If you decide that you want to create an entirely new page setup while in the Page Setup dialog box, you can click the Add button. This opens a simple dialog box that enables you to enter a name for your new setup. After you enter a new name and click OK, you can proceed to set up your page settings. Then click OK again, and the setup will be saved under the new name.

Plotter and Printer Hardware Considerations

Positioning an AutoCAD drawing on the printer output is something of an art. Before you face a deadline with hundreds of plots to produce, you might want to create some test plots and carefully refine your plotter settings so that you'll have AutoCAD set up properly for those rush jobs.

Part of the setup process will be to understand how your particular printer or plotter works. Each device has its own special characteristics, so a detailed description of printer hardware setup is beyond the scope of this section. However, here are a few guidelines that will make the process easier.

Understanding Your Plotter's Limits

If you're familiar with a word-processing or desktop-publishing program, you know that you can set the margins of a page, thereby telling the program exactly how far from each edge of the paper you want the text to appear. With AutoCAD, you don't have that luxury. To accurately place a plot on your paper, you must know the plotter's hard clip limits. The *hard clip limits* are like built-in margins, beyond which the plotter will not plot. These limits vary from plotter to plotter (see Figure 8.9).

It's crucial that you know your printer's or plotter's hard clip limits in order to place your drawings accurately on the sheet. Take some time to study your plotter manual and find out exactly what these limits are. Then make a record of them and store it somewhere, in case you or someone else needs to format a sheet in a special way.

FIGURE 8.9
The hard clip limits of
a plotter

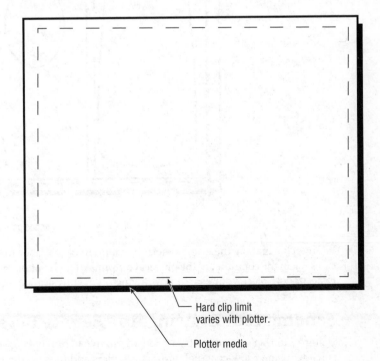

Hard clip limit
varies with plotter.

Plotter media

Hard clip limits for printers often depend on the software that drives them. You might need to consult your printer manual or use the trial-and-error method of plotting several samples to see how they come out.

After you've established the limits of your plotter or printer, you'll be better equipped to fit your drawing within those limits. You can then establish some standard drawing limits based on your plotter's limits. You'll also need to know the dimensions of those hard clip limits to define custom sheet sizes. Although AutoCAD offers standard sheet sizes in the Paper Size button group of the Page Setup and Plot dialog boxes, these sizes do not take into account the hard clip limits.

Knowing Your Plotter's Origins

Another important consideration is the location of your plotter's origin. For example, on some plotters, the lower-left corner of the plot area is used as the origin. Other plotters use the center of the plot area as the origin. When you plot a drawing that is too large to fit the sheet on a plotter that uses a corner for the origin, the image is pushed toward the top and to the right of the sheet (see Figure 8.10). When you plot a drawing that is too large to fit on a plotter that uses the center of the paper as the origin, the image is pushed outward in all directions from the center of the sheet.

FIGURE 8.10
Plotting an oversized image on a plotter that uses the lower-left corner for its origin

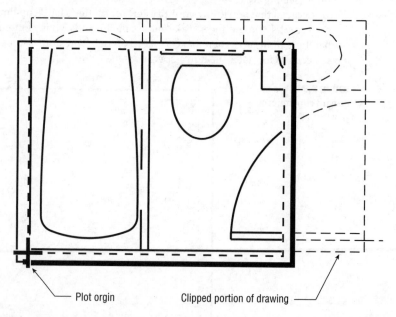

Plot orgin   Clipped portion of drawing

In each situation, the origin determines a point of reference from which you can relate your drawing in the computer to the physical output. After you understand this, you're better equipped to accurately place your electronic drawing on the physical medium.

Sending Your Drawings to a Service Bureau

Using a plotting service can be a good alternative to purchasing your own plotter. Or you might consider using a low-cost plotter for check plots and then sending the files to a service bureau for your final product. Most reprographic services, such as blueprinters, offer plotting in conjunction with their other services. Quite often you can send files over a high-speed connection, eliminating the need for using courier services or regular mail.

If you foresee the need for service bureaus, consider establishing a relationship with one or two service bureaus fairly early. Send them some sample plot files to make sure that they will produce the results you want. One of the greatest difficulties is miscommunication between what you want and what the service provides in the way of plotter output.

UNDERSTANDING THE PLOT AND PUBLISH TAB IN THE OPTIONS DIALOG BOX

I've mentioned the Plot And Publish tab in the Options dialog box earlier in this chapter. This tab contains several options related to plotting which can be useful. Here's a summary of those options and their purposes.

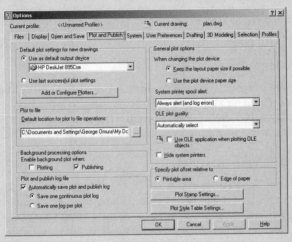

DEFAULT PLOT SETTINGS FOR NEW DRAWINGS

The settings in this group let you control the default plot settings for new drawings and for drawings from earlier versions of AutoCAD that are opened for the first time in AutoCAD 2007. The Use As Default Output Device radio button and drop-down list let you select the default plotter or printer to be used with new drawings. When selected, the Use Last Successful Plot Settings radio button uses the last successful plotter settings for subsequent plots. This is how earlier versions of AutoCAD worked. The Add Or Configure Plotters button opens the Plotters window. This is the same as choosing Files ➢ Plot Manager from the AutoCAD menu bar. From the Plotters window, you can launch the Add-A-Plotter Wizard to add new plotter configurations. You can also edit existing plotter configurations.

GENERAL PLOT OPTIONS

These options control some of the general plotter parameters. The Keep The Layout Paper Size If Possible radio button causes AutoCAD to attempt to plot to the paper size specified in the Plot dialog box, regardless of the actual paper size in the plotter. If the specified size is larger than the capacity of the plotter, a warning message is displayed. The Use The Plot Device Paper Size option causes AutoCAD to use the paper size specified by the system printer or the PC3 plot configuration file currently in use. Both settings are also controlled by the Paperupdate system variable.

The System Printer Spool Alert drop-down list offers control over printer spooling alert messages. The OLE Plot Quality drop-down list offers control over the quality of OLE objects embedded in or linked to a drawing. This setting can also be controlled through the Olequality system variable.

When the Use OLE Application When Plotting OLE Objects check box is selected, AutoCAD will launch any application that is associated with an OLE object embedded or linked to the AutoCAD drawing that is currently being plotted. This helps improve the plot quality of OLE objects. This option can also be set through the Olestartup system variable.

The Hide System Printers option affects the Printer/Plotter group's Name drop-down list in the Plot and Page Setup dialog boxes. With this option turned on, you will see only printers that have a .pc3 file associated with them. These include printers that have been set up using the Add-A-Plotter Wizard discussed earlier in this chapter.

PLOT TO FILE

You have the option to plot to a file that can be downloaded to your printer or plotter at a later date. The Plot To File group lets you specify the default destination for the plot files.

PLOT AND PUBLISH LOG FILE

You can maintain a plot log file that will record information about each plot you make. This can be helpful when you must keep records of hard-copy output for billing purposes. The location of the plot and publishing log file can be specified in the Files tab of the Options dialog box under the Plot And Publishing Log File Location listing. The log file will have a .csv filename extension.

BACKGROUND PROCESSING OPTIONS

AutoCAD will perform background plots so that after you begin a plot you can immediately return to your drawing work instead of waiting for the plot to be completed. The options in this group let you turn on this feature either for standard plotting or for the Publish feature discussed in Chapter 27. This option can also be controlled through the Backgroundplot system variable.

PLOT STAMP SETTINGS

This button opens the Plot Stamp dialog box which you saw earlier in the "Plot Options" section of this chapter. The Plot Stamp dialog box lets you determine what information is displayed in a plot stamp, which is a label placed on the print of a drawing to provide information about the source file.

PLOT STYLE TABLE SETTINGS

When you click this option, the Plot Style Table Settings dialog box opens. This dialog box controls the type of plot styles used in AutoCAD. In the case of named plot styles, you can also select a default plot style for Layer 0 and a default plot style for objects. Note that the Use Color Dependent Plot Styles and Use Named Plot Styles radio buttons do not have an effect on the current drawing; they affect only new drawings and pre–AutoCAD 2000 drawings being opened for the first time. The Default Plot Style Table drop-down list lets you select a default plot style table for new and pre–AutoCAD 2000 drawings. These settings are also controlled by the Pstylepolicy system variable.

The Add Or Edit Plot Style Tables button opens the Plot Styles dialog box. From there, you can double-click an existing plot style table file or start the Add-A-Plot Style Table Wizard to create a new plot style.

SPECIFY PLOT OFFSET RELATIVE TO

Here you can determine whether the plot offset is set in relation to the printable area of your printer or the edge of the paper. The printable area is determined by the printer margin.

You might be able to use the PC3 and other plotter setting files as part of your relationship with a service bureau. Plot configuration files and plot style table files can help communicate exactly what you're expecting. Chapter 9 discusses plot styles and plot style tables in detail.

Using Batch and Electronic Plots

The focus of this chapter so far has been printer or plotter hard-copy output. But a major part of your work will involve the transmission of electronic versions of your documents. More than ever, architects and engineers are using the Internet to exchange documents of all types, so AutoCAD offers several tools to make the process easier.

I've mentioned that you can control some of your output settings thorough the Plot And Publish tab of the Options dialog box. The Publish features includes items that enable you to "print" your drawings as a file that can be e-mailed to clients and consultants or posted on an FTP site or website. The Publish features enable you to create a single file that contains multiple pages so you can combine several drawing sheets into one file.

The Publish feature also enables you to plot several drawings at once without having to load and print each one individually. This can be helpful when you've finished a set of drawings and want to plot them during a break or overnight. Chapter 27 gives you a detailed look at the Publish feature.

If You Want to Experiment

At this point, because you aren't rushing to meet a deadline, you might want to experiment with some of the plotter and printer variables and see firsthand what each one does. Plot a drawing to scale from a Layout tab so you can get some practice. Chances are you'll do most of your final plotting from layouts, though you can get quick study prints by printing from the Model tab.

Chapter 9

Understanding Plot Styles

To gain full control over the appearance of your output, you'll want to know about plot style tables. By using *plot style tables*, you can control how colors are translated into plotted line weights and how area fills are converted into shades of gray or screened colors in your printer or plotter output. You can also control other aspects of how the plotter draws each object in a drawing.

If you don't use plot style tables, your plotter will produce output as close as possible to what you see in the drawing editor, including colors. With plot style tables, you can force all of the colors to print as black or you can also assign a fill pattern or a screen to a color. This can be useful for charts and maps that require area fills of different gradations. You can create multiple plot style tables to produce plots that fit the exact requirements of your project.

This chapter will show you firsthand how you can use plot style tables to enhance your plotter output. You'll look at how you can adjust the line weight of the walls in the Plan file and make color changes to your plotter output. Topics in this chapter include:

- ◆ Choosing between Color-Dependent and Named Plot Style Tables
- ◆ Creating a Color Plot Style Table
- ◆ Editing and Using Plot Style Tables
- ◆ Assigning Named Plot Styles Directly to Layers and Objects

Choosing between Color-Dependent and Named Plot Style Tables

You can think of a plot style as a virtual pen that has the attributes of color, width, shape, and screen percentage. A typical drawing may use several different line widths, so you would use a different plot style for each line width. Multiple plot styles are collected into *plot style tables* which allow you to control a set of plot styles from one dialog box.

AutoCAD offers two types of plot style tables: color and named. *Color plot style tables* enable you to assign plot styles to the individual AutoCAD colors. For example, you can assign a plot style with a 0.50 mm width to the color red so that anything that is red in your drawing is plotted with a line width of 0.50 mm. You can, in addition, set the plot style's color to black so that everything that is red in your drawing is plotted in black.

Named plot style tables let you assign plot styles directly to objects in your drawing, instead of assigning a plot style in a more general way through a color. Named plot style tables also enable you to assign plot styles directly to layers. For example, with named plot styles, you can assign a plot style that is black and has a 0.50 mm width to a single circle or line in a drawing, regardless of its color.

Named plot styles are more flexible than color plot styles, but if you already have a library of AutoCAD drawings set up for a specific set of plotter settings, the color plot styles would be a better choice when opening files that were created in AutoCAD 14 and earlier. This is because color plot styles are more similar to the older method of assigning AutoCAD colors to plotter pens. You might also want to use color plot style tables with files that you intend to share with an individual or office that is still using earlier versions of AutoCAD.

The type of plot style table assigned to a new drawing depends on the settings in the Plot Style Table Settings dialog box, which is accessed through the Plot And Publish tab of the Options dialog.

TIP You can change the type of plot style table assigned to a drawing. See the sidebar "Converting a Drawing from Color Plot Styles to Named Plot Styles" later in this chapter for more information on plot style conversions.

Here's how to set up the plot style type for new files:

1. Open the Options dialog box and click the Plot And Publish tab.

2. Click the Plot Style Table Settings button to open the Plot Style Table Settings dialog box.

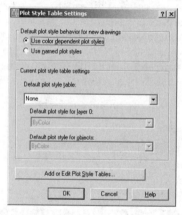

3. In the Default Plot Style Behavior For New Drawings button group, click the Use Color Dependent Plot Styles radio button. In a later exercise, you'll use the Use Named Plot Styles option.

4. Click OK. Then click OK again in the Options dialog box to return to the drawing.

After you've set up AutoCAD for color plot style tables, any new drawings you create are allowed to use only color plot style tables. You can change this setting at any time for new files, but after a file is saved, the type of plot style that is current when the file is created is the only type of plot style available to that file. If you find that you need to change a color plot style to a named plot style drawing, see the sidebar "Converting a Drawing from Color Plot Styles to Named Plot Styles" later in this chapter.

Next, you'll set up a custom color plot style table. Plot style tables are stored as files with the .ctb or .stb filename extension. The table filenames that end with .ctb are color plot style tables. The table filenames that end with .stb are named plot style tables.

TIP You can also select between color and named plot styles when selecting a new drawing template. When you choose File ➢ New, you'll see that many of the template files in the Select Template dialog box have "Color Dependent Plot Styles" or "Named Plot Styles" as part of their name. If you have AutoCAD set up to use the Startup dialog box, you'll see the color and named plot style template files when you select the Use A Template option from the Create New Drawing dialog box.

Creating a Color Plot Style Table

You can have several plot style table files on hand to quickly apply plot styles to any given plot or Layout tab. You can set up each plot style table to create a different look for your drawing. These files are stored in the `Plot Styles` folder of the `C:\Documents and Settings\`*Username*`\Application Data\Autodesk\AutoCAD 2007\R17.0\enu\` folder. Take the following steps to create a new plot style table. You'll use an existing file that was created in Release 14 as an example to demonstrate the plot style features.

TIP If you change your mind about a selection you make while using a wizard, you can move forward or backward by clicking the Next and Back buttons.

1. From the companion CD, open the sample file called `Plan-color.dwg`; then click the Layout1 tab.

2. Right-click the Layout tab and select Page Setup Manager; then in the Page Setup Manager dialog box, click Modify.

3. Notice that the Page Setup dialog box is similar to the Plot dialog box. The main difference is that the Page Setup dialog box does not have the Apply To Layout button at the bottom.

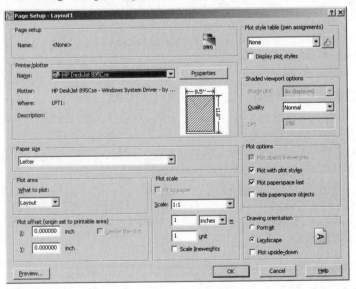

4. In the Plot Style Table (Pen Assignments) group in the upper right, open the drop-down list and select New to start the Add Color-Dependent Plot Style Table Wizard

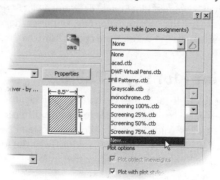

5. Click the Start From Scratch radio button and then click Next. The next screen of the wizard asks for a filename.

6. Enter **Mystyle** for the filename and click Next. The next screen of the wizard lets you edit your plot style and assign the plot style to your current, new, or old drawings. You'll learn about editing plot styles a bit later.

7. Click Finish to return to the Page Setup dialog box.

With the Add Color-Dependent Plot Style Table Wizard, you can create a new plot style table from scratch, or you can create one based on an AutoCAD R14 CFG, PCP, or PC2 file. You can also access the Add Color-Dependent Plot Style Table Wizard by choosing File ➢ Plot Style Manager and then double-clicking the Add-A-Plot Style Table Wizard icon.

The steps shown here are the same whether your drawing is set up for color plot styles or named plot styles.

Editing and Using Plot Style Tables

You now have your own plot style table. In this exercise, you'll edit the plot style and see firsthand how plot styles affect your drawing:

1. In the Page Setup dialog box, the filename `Mystyle.ctb` should appear in the drop-down list of the Plot Style Table (Pen Assignments) group. If not, open the drop-down list to select it.

2. Click the Edit button to open the Plot Style Table Editor. The Edit button is the one just to the right of the Plot Style Table drop-down list. Click the Form View tab, which is shown at the top of Figure 9.1.

TIP You can also open and edit existing plot style tables by choosing File ➢ Plot Style Manager to open the Plot Styles dialog box. You can then double-click the plot style you want to edit. A third option is to double-click the `Plot Style Table` file in `C:\Documents and Settings\`*Username*`\Application Data\Autodesk\AutoCAD 2007\R17.0\enu\Plot Styles`.

The Plot Style Table Editor dialog box has three tabs that give you control over how each color in AutoCAD is plotted. The Form View tab lets you select a color from a list box and then set the properties of that color by using the options on the right side of the tab.

TIP   The Table View tab displays each color as a column of properties. Each column is called a plot style. The property names are listed in a column to the far left. Although the layout is different, both the Table View tab and the Form View tab offer the same functions.

Next, you'll continue by changing the line width property of the color 3 (green) plot style. Remember that green is the color assigned to the Wall layer of your Plan drawing.

1. Click the Color 3 listing in the Plot Styles list box.

2. Click the Lineweight drop-down list and select 0.5000 mm.

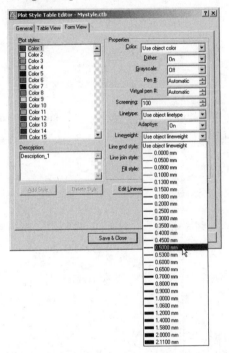

3. Click Save & Close to return to the Page Setup dialog box.

4. Click the Display Plot Styles check box in the Plot Style Table (Pen Assignments) group. Then click OK to close the Page Setup dialog box and click Close to close the Page Setup Manager dialog box.

FIGURE 9.1

The Plot Style Table
Editor dialog box,
open at the Form
View tab

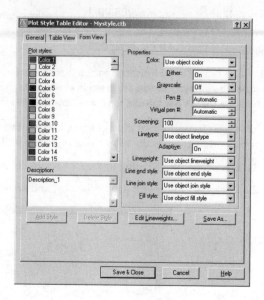

5. Zoom in to the plan to enlarge the view of a unit bathroom and entrance as shown in
   Figure 9.2.

FIGURE 9.2

Adjust your view to
look like this.

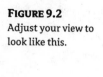

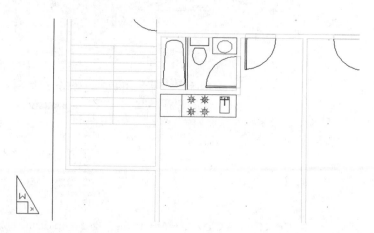

Making Your Plot Styles Visible

You won't see any changes in your drawing yet. You'll need to make one more change to your
drawing options:

1. Choose Format ➢ Lineweight to open the Lineweight Settings dialog box. The Lineweight
   Settings dialog box lets you control the appearances of line weights in the drawing. If line

weights are not showing up, this is the place to look to make them viewable. You can find out more about the Lineweight Settings dialog box in Chapter 16.

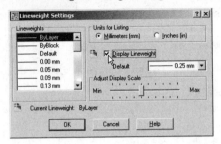

TIP You can also click the User Preferences tab in the Options dialog box and then click the Lineweight Settings button to open the Lineweight Settings dialog box.

2. Click the Display Lineweight check box to turn on this option.

3. Just below the Display Lineweight option, click the Default drop-down list and select 0.09 mm. This will make any unassigned or default line weight a very fine line.

4. Click Apply & Close. The layout will display the drawing with the line weight assignments you set up earlier (see Figure 9.3).

WARNING If your view does not reflect the Plot Style settings, make sure you have the Display Plot Styles option selected in the Plot Style Table (Pen Assignments) group of the Page Setup dialog box.

Making Changes to Multiple Plot Styles

Chances are, you'll want to plot your drawing in black and white for most of your work. You can edit your color plot style table to plot one or all of your AutoCAD colors as black instead of the AutoCAD colors.

FIGURE 9.3
The drawing with
new line weight
assignments

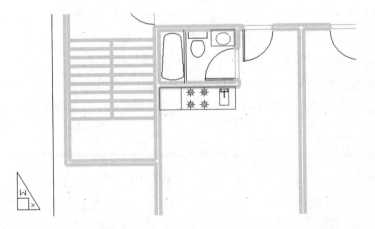

You saw how you can open the Plot Style Table Editor from the Page Setup dialog box to edit your color plot style table. In this exercise, you'll try a different route:

1. Choose File ➤ Plot Style Manager to open the Plot Styles window. This is a view to the Plot Styles folder under the C:\Documents and Settings*Username*\Application Data\Autodesk\AutoCAD 2007\R17.0 \enu\ folder.

2. Locate the file Mystyle.ctb and double-click it to open the Plot Style Table Editor dialog box.

3. Click the Form View tab.

4. Click Color 3 in the Plot Styles list box.

5. Click the Color drop-down list and select Black.

6. Click Save & Close; then close the Plot Styles window.

7. Choose View ➤ Regen All to view your drawing. Now the green objects appear black in the Layout tab.

8. Click the Model tab to view your drawing in Model Space. Notice that the objects are still in their original colors. This shows you that you haven't actually changed the colors of your objects or layers. You've only changed the color of the plotted output.

Next try changing all the output colors to black:

1. Repeat steps 1 and 2 of the previous exercise to open the Mystyle.ctb file.

2. Click the Form View tab; then click Color 1 in the Plot Styles list box.

3. Shift+click Color 9 in the Plot Styles list box to select all the plot styles from Color 1 to Color 9.

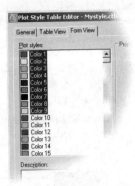

4. Click the Color drop-down list and select Black.

5. Click Save & Close, and close the Plot Styles window.

6. Click the Layout1 tab and then choose View ➢ Regen All. Now all the colors have changed to black.

Now when you plot your drawing, you will get a plot that is composed entirely of black lines. These exercises have shown that the Plot Style Table Editor lets you set the color of your printed output to be different from the colors you see in Model Space. In the exercises, you set the pen colors to black, but if you look down the Color drop-down list, you'll see that you can choose from any number of colors. The Select Color option in the Color drop-down list lets you select colors from the Select Color dialog box.

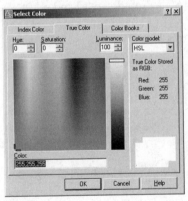

NOTE   To see the view shown here, make sure the True Color tab is selected and the HSL option is selected in the Color Model drop-down list. LT users will not see a Color Books tab.

In Chapter 4, you were introduced to the Select Color dialog box in the context of selecting colors for layers. Here, you can use it to assign colors to plot styles. The same three tabs are available: Index Color, True Color, and Color Books. (LT users will not see the Color Books tab.) The Index Color tab lets you select from the standard AutoCAD 255 index colors. The True Color tab lets you choose virtually any color you want. The Color Books tab lets you use PANTONE colors.

Setting Up Line Corner Styles

You might notice that the corners of the wall lines appear to be rounded, as shown in Figure 9.4, instead of having a crisp, sharp corner.

FIGURE 9.4
The corners of thick lines may appear rounded.

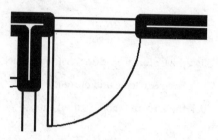

You can adjust the way AutoCAD draws these corners at plot time through the Plot Style Table Editor:

1. Open the `Mystyle.ctb` plot style table, as you did in the previous exercise.

2. Click the Form View tab, and then click Color 3 in the Plot Styles list box.

3. Click the Line End Style drop-down list and select Square.

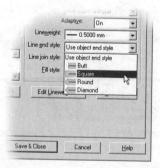

4. Click Save & Close; then click OK to close the Page Setup dialog box.

5. Choose View ➤ Regen All to view your changes. Notice that now the corners meet in a sharp angle, as shown in Figure 9.5.

NOTE   The Line join style setting can have an adverse affect on AutoCAD fonts. If you have text that appears distorted, check to see if the text is on a layer that used a line join style other than the default Use object end style setting.

FIGURE 9.5
The Line End Style set-
ting can alter the way
corners are drawn.

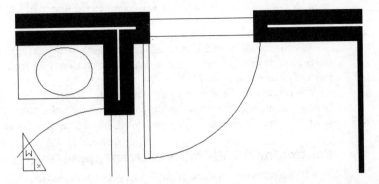

The Square option in the Line End Style drop-down list extends the endpoints of contiguous lines so that their corners meet in a clean corner instead of a notch. The Line Join Style drop-down list offers a similar set of settings for polylines. For example, you can round polyline corners by using the Round option in the Line Join Style drop-down list.

Setting Up Screen Values for Solid Areas

The last option you'll look at is how to change a color into a screened area. Frequently, you'll want to add a gray or colored background to an area of your drawing to emphasize that area graphically, as in a focus area in a map, or to designate functions in a floor plan. The setting you're about to use will enable you to create shaded backgrounds:

1. Open the Page Setup Manager and click Modify to open the Page Setup dialog box again, and then open the Plot Style Table Editor.

2. Select Color 3 from the Plot Styles list box.

3. In the Screening list box, click the number 100 to select it.

4. Type 50↵.

5. Click Save & Close; then click OK in the Page Setup dialog box. Click Close at the Page Setup Manager dialog box.

6. Choose View ➤ Regen All. Notice that now the walls are a shade of gray instead of solid black.

As you can see from this exercise, you turned a wide black line into a gray one. In this example, the Screening option lets you "tone down" the chosen color from a solid color to a color that has 50 percent of its full intensity.

You can use the Screening option in combination with color to obtain a variety of tones. If you need to cover large areas with color, you can use the Solid hatch pattern to fill those areas and then use the Screening option in the Plot Style Table Editor to make fine adjustments to the area's color.

Controlling the Visibility of Overlapping Objects

You'll also want to know about the Draworder command in conjunction with solid filled areas. This command lets you control how objects hide or overlap when displayed or plotted. If you find that your solid hatches are hiding text or other graphics, you need to learn about Draworder. See Chapter 14 for more information. Some output devices offer a Merge Control option that determines how overlapping graphics are plotted. For more information, see Appendix B.

Other Options in the Plot Style Table Editor

You've seen a lot of the plot style options so far, but there are many others that you might want to use in the future. This section describes those options that were not covered in the previous exercises.

TIP The options in the Plot Style Table Editor are the same regardless of whether you are editing a color plot style table or a named plot style table.

THE GENERAL TAB

You didn't really look at the General tab of the Plot Style Table Editor in the exercise presented earlier. The General tab offers information regarding the plot style you are currently editing. You can enter a description of the style in the Description box. This can be useful if you plan to include the plot style with a drawing you are sending to someone else for plotting.

The File Information group gives you the basic information on the file location and name, as well as the number of color styles included in the plot style table.

The Apply Global Scale Factor To Non-ISO Linetypes check box lets you specify whether ISO linetype scale factors are applied to all linetypes. When this item is selected, the Scale Factor input box becomes active, enabling you to enter a scale factor.

NOTE ISO (International Standards Organization) linetypes are special line types that conform to the ISO standards for technical drawings.

ISO PEN WIDTHS

You might have noticed a setting called ISO Pen Width in the detail view of the Linetype Manager dialog box discussed in Chapter 4 (choose Format ➢ Linetype and then click the Show Detail button). This setting is in the form of a drop-down list that is available when an ISO line type has been loaded into a drawing and is selected in the Linetype Manager dialog box. When you select a pen width from that list, the linetype scale is updated to conform to the ISO standard for that width. However, this setting has no effect on the actual plotter output. If you are using ISO standard widths, it is up to you to match the color of the lines to their corresponding widths in the Plot Style Table Editor.

COLORS AND LINE WEIGHTS IN THE SAN FRANCISCO MAIN LIBRARY

Technical drawings can have a beauty of their own, but they can also be deadly boring. What really sets a good technical drawing apart from a poor one is the control of line weights. Knowing how to vary and control line weights in both manual and CAD drawings can make a huge difference in the readability of the drawing.

In the San Francisco Main Library project, the designers at SMWM Associates were especially concerned with line weights in the reflected ceiling plan. The following graphic shows a portion of the reflected ceiling plan from the library drawings.

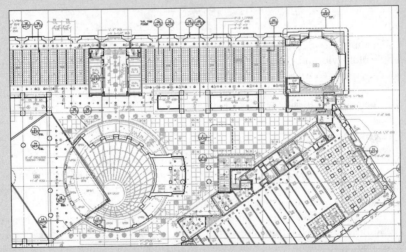

As you can see, it contains a good deal of graphical information, which, without careful line weight control, could become confusing. (Although you can't see it in the black-and-white print, a multitude of colors were used to vary line weight.) When the electronic drawings were plotted, colors were converted into lines of varying thickness. Bolder lines were used to create emphasis in components such as walls and ceiling openings, and fine lines were used to indicate ceiling tile patterns.

By emphasizing certain lines over others, visual monotony is avoided, and the various components of the drawing can be seen more easily.

THE TABLE VIEW TAB

The Table View tab offers the same settings as the Form View tab, only in a different format. Each plot style is shown as a column with the properties of each plot style listed along the left side of the tab. To change a property, click the property in the column.

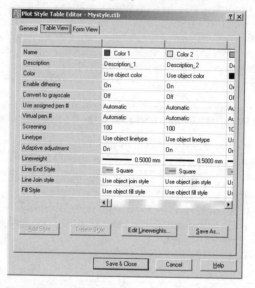

To apply the same setting to all plot styles at once, right-click a setting you want to use from a single plot style, and choose Copy from the shortcut menu. Right-click the setting again, and then choose Apply To All Styles from the shortcut menu.

Click the Edit Lineweights button to open the Edit Lineweights dialog box, which lets you adjust the line weight settings for the plot styles.

THE FORM VIEW TAB

You've already seen and worked with the Form View tab, shown in Figure 9.1 earlier in this chapter. This tab contains the same settings as the Table View tab but in a different format. Instead of displaying each color as a column of properties, the properties are listed as options along the right side, and the colors are listed in a list box.

To modify the properties of a color, you select the color from the list and then edit the values in the Properties group in the right side of the dialog box. So to change the screening value of the Color 3 style, highlight Color 3 in the Plot Styles list, and then double-click the Screening input box and enter a new value.

You've already seen what the Screening, Color, Lineweight, and Line Join Style options do. Here's a description of the other style properties.

TIP   The names of the properties in the Table View tab are slightly different from those in the Form View tab. The Table View property names are enclosed in brackets in this listing.

Description   This option enables you to enter a description for each color.

Dither [Enable Dithering]   Dithering is a method that enables your plotter to simulate colors beyond the basic 255 colors available in AutoCAD. Although this option is desirable when you want to create a wider range of colors in your plots, it can also create some distortions, including broken, fine lines and false colors. For this reason, dithering is usually turned off. This option is not available in all plotters.

[Convert To] Grayscale   This option converts colors to grayscale.

[Use Assigned] Pen #   This option lets you specify which pen number is assigned to each color in your drawing. This option applies only to pen plotters.

Virtual Pen #   Many ink-jet and laser plotters offer "virtual pens" to simulate the processes of the old-style pen plotters. Frequently, such plotters offer as many as 255 virtual pens. Plotters with virtual pens often let you assign AutoCAD colors to a virtual pen number. This is significant if the virtual pens of your plotter can be assigned screening, width, end style, and join styles. You can then use the virtual pen settings instead of using the settings in the Plot Style Table Editor. This option is most beneficial for users who already have a library of drawings that are set up for plotters with virtual pen settings.

You can set up your ink-jet printer for virtual pens under the Vector Graphics listing of the Device And Documents Setting tab of the Plotter Configuration Editor. See Appendix B for more on setting up your printer or plotter configuration.

Linetype   If you prefer, you can use this setting to control linetypes in AutoCAD based on the color of the object. By default, this option is set to Use Object Linetype. I recommend that you leave this option at its default.

Adaptive [Adjustment]   This option controls how noncontinuous linetypes begin and end. This option is on by default, which forces linetypes to begin and end in a line segment. With the option turned off, the same linetype is drawn without regard for its ending. In some cases, this can produce a line that appears incomplete.

Line End Style   This option lets you specify the shape of the end of simple lines that have a line weight greater than zero.

Line Join Style   This option lets you determine the shape of the corners of polylines.

Fill Style   This option lets you set up a color to be drawn as a pattern when used in a solid filled area. The patterns appear as follows:

Add Style   Clicking this button lets you add more plot styles or colors. This option is not available for color plot style tables.

Delete Style   Clicking this button deletes the selected style. This option is not available for color plot style tables.

Save As   Clicking this button lets you save the current plot style table with a different filename.

Assigning Named Plot Styles Directly to Layers and Objects

So far, you've learned that you can control how AutoCAD translates drawing colors into plotter output. You have been using a color plot style table, which assigns a plot style to each color in AutoCAD. You can also assign plot styles directly to objects or layers. To do this, you need to employ a named plot style table. As we said earlier, named plot style tables enable you to create plot styles that have names, rather than being assigned directly to colors in AutoCAD. You can then assign a plot style by name to objects or layers in your drawing. In this section you'll learn how to set up AutoCAD with a named plot style table to assign plot styles to objects; then you'll create a new plot style table.

Using Named Plot Style Tables

Out of the box, AutoCAD uses the color-dependent plot style table for all new drawings. You can create a new drawing that uses named plot style tables in two ways. The simpler way is to use any of the named plot style template files when you first create a new drawing. You'll see these templates under the Use A Template option in the Create New Drawing dialog box or in the Select Template dialog box.

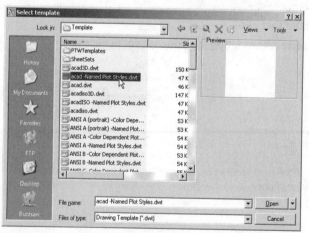

By offering both color and named plot style drawing templates, AutoCAD makes it easy to create and select the type of plot style for your drawing regardless of the current default style.

If you prefer, you can set up AutoCAD to use a named plot style by default when you create a drawing by using the Start From Scratch option in the Create New Drawing dialog box. To set up the default plot style table for new drawings, follow these steps:

1. Choose Tools ➢ Options to open the Options dialog box, and click the Plot And Publish tab. This tab offers a variety of settings geared toward your plotter or printer.

2. In the lower-right corner of the dialog box, click the Plot Style Table Settings button.

3. In the Plot Style Table Settings dialog box, click the Use Named Plot Styles radio button. Notice that the Default Plot Style For Layer 0 and Default Plot Style For Objects options become available. Click OK.

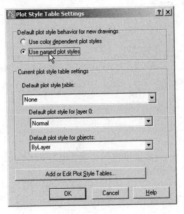

4. Click OK to close the Options dialog box.

To create and try out a new named plot style, you can open an existing file from an earlier version of AutoCAD. In the next few exercises, you'll use the `Plan-named.dwg` file from the companion CD. This is a Release 14 file that will be assigned the type of plot style table that is currently the default as determined by the Use Named Plot Styles option you just set in the previous exercise.

1. Open the `Plan-named.dwg` file from the companion CD.

2. Choose File ➢ Plot Style Manager to open a window to the `Plot Styles` folder.

3. Double-click the Add-A-Plot Style Table Wizard icon to start the Plot Style Table Wizard.

4. Click Next to open the Begin screen, choose Start From Scratch, and then click Next to open the Pick Plot Style Table screen.

5. Click the Named Plot Style Table radio button, and then click Next to open the File Name screen.

6. Enter **Mynamedstyle1** in the File Name input box, and click Next to open the Finish screen. Here you can exit, or you can edit the new plot style table. This time you'll edit the table from the wizard.

7. Click the Plot Style Table Editor button to open the Plot Style Table Editor dialog box.

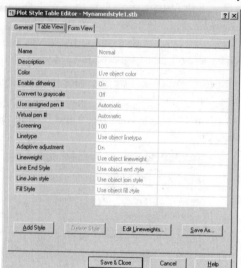

Notice that you have only one style named. Unlike the color plot style tables, you aren't assigning a style to each AutoCAD color; so you don't need a style for each of the 255 colors. Instead, you can create a limited set of styles, giving each style the characteristics you want to apply to objects or layers. Continue by adding some plot styles:

1. Click the Add Style button to display a new Style 1 column. If you choose, you can give the style a different name at this point simply by clicking in the Name box and typing a new name.

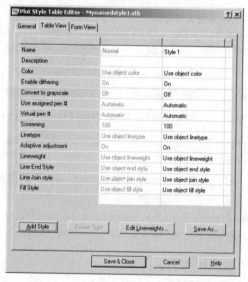

2. Click the Form View tab, and then select Style 1 from the Plot Styles list.

3. Click the Lineweight drop-down list and select 0.5000 mm.

4. Click the Add Style button, and then click OK in the Add Plot Style dialog box.

5. Select Style 2 from the Plot Styles list; then click the Lineweight drop-down list and select 0.7000 mm.

6. Click Save & Close to return to the Add Plot Style Table dialog box.

7. Click Finish to exit the wizard, and then close the Plot Styles window.

You might have noticed that the Add-A-Plot Style Table Wizard works in a slightly different way when you start it from the Plot Styles window. It adds an extra option (in step 5 of the exercise before the preceding one) that lets you choose between a color plot style table and a named plot style table.

You've just created a named plot style. Next, make `Mynamedstyle1.stb` the default plot style:

1. Open the Options dialog box and click the Plot And Publish tab.

2. Click the Plot Style Table Settings button. Then in the Default Plot Style Table drop-down list, select `Mynamedstyle1.stb`, the table you just created.

3. Click OK to exit the Plot Style Table Settings dialog box, and then click OK again to exit the Options dialog box.

Now you're ready to start assigning plot styles to the objects in your drawing.

Assigning Plot Styles to Objects

After you've set up AutoCAD to use named plot styles, you can begin to assign plot styles to objects through the Properties palette. Here are the steps to assign plot styles to objects:

1. Back in the `Plan-named.dwg` file, click the Layout1 tab.

2. Choose File ➤ Page Setup Manager; then click the Modify button in the Page Setup Manager dialog box.

WARNING If your plotter configuration is set up for a nonexistent printer, you will see a warning message telling you that a driver for you plotter assigned to this drawing cannot be found. This often occurs when you receive a file that has been set up to plot on a printer in another location. As the warning message explains, AutoCAD will set your plot device to "None." You must then make sure that your printer plotter is selected in the Printer/Plotter group of the Page Setup dialog box.

3. In the Page Setup dialog box, select `Mynamedstyle1.stb` from the drop-down list in the Plot Style Table (Pen Assignments) group.

4. Make sure the Display Plot Styles check box is checked; then click OK.

5. Click Close to close the Page Setup Manager dialog box.

You've assigned a named plot style table to Layout1. Note that you can assign different named plot styles to different layouts.

Next make sure the plot styles will be displayed in the drawing:

1. Choose Format ➤ Lineweight, make sure that the Display Lineweight check box is selected, and click OK.

2. Set up your view so you see a close-up of the lower-left corner unit.

3. Click the Model Or Paper Space button at the bottom of the AutoCAD window so that the word *Model* shows in the button. This will enable you to select objects in the drawing while in a Layout tab.

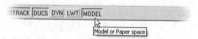

4. Select the line representing the outer wall of the unit at the bottom-left side of the plan, as shown in Figure 9.6; then right-click and choose Properties from the shortcut menu.

FIGURE 9.6
Select the line
shown here.

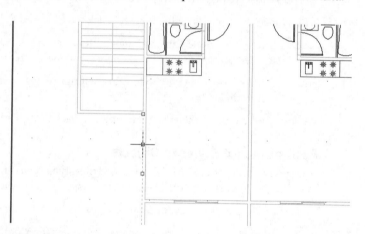

5. In the Properties palette, click the Plot Style option. The option turns into a drop-down list with a downward-pointing arrow to the far right.

6. Click the downward-pointing arrow, and then select Other from the list to open the Select Plot Style dialog box.

7. Select Style 1 and click OK. Notice that Style 1 now appears as the value for the Plot Style in the Properties palette.

8. Close the Properties palette.

9. Choose View ➢ Regen All. If you have the line weight visibility turned on, you'll see the results in the drawing editor (Depending on how your display is set up, you may need to zoom in further).

Another way to assign plot styles to individual objects is through the Plot Style Control drop-down list.

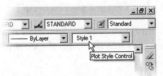

This enables you to select a plot style in a manner similar to the Layer & Linetype drop-down list. You can assign plot styles to individual objects by selecting the objects and then selecting a plot style from the Plot Style Control drop-down list. If you are using a color plot style table like the one you created in earlier exercises, the Plot Style Control drop-down list is unavailable.

Assigning Plot Style Tables to Layers

You can also assign named plot style tables to layers. This has a similar effect to using the color plot style tables. The main difference is that with named plot style tables, you assign the plot style tables directly to the layer instead of assigning a plot style to the color of a layer. Here's how to assign a plot style table to a layer.

1. In the Layers toolbar, click the Layer Properties Manager button to open the Layer Properties Manager dialog box.

2. Select the Wall layer.

3. Click the Normal label in the Plot Style column of the Wall layer listing. You might have to scroll to the right to see the Plot Style column.

The Select Plot Style dialog box opens.

4. Select Style 1 from the Plot Styles list.

5. Click OK. You return to the Layer Properties Manager dialog box, this time it shows the Plot Style property for the Wall layer listed as Style 1.

6. Click OK to close the Layer Properties Manager dialog box; then choose View ➢ Regen All. Your view of the plan changes to reflect the new plot style assignment to the Wall layer.

CONVERTING A DRAWING FROM COLOR PLOT STYLES TO NAMED PLOT STYLES

If you need to convert a color plot style drawing to a named plot style drawing, you can use the Convertctb and Convertpstyles commands. The conversion is a two-part process. In the first stage, which is needed only the first time you perform the conversion, you convert a color plot style table file into a named plot style table file. Then you actually convert the drawing file.

Here are the steps for the first part of the process:

1. Start AutoCAD, and, at the Command prompt, enter **Convertctb**↵. This command lets you convert a color plot style table file into a named plot style table file. A Select File dialog box opens to enable you to select a color plot style table file; these files have the filename extension .ctb. For this example, you can choose the Acad.ctb file.

2. Click Open to open the Create File dialog box, which enables you to provide a name for the converted file. If you opened the Acad.ctb file in step 1, you might want to give the new file the name AcadConvert so you know that it is a converted .ctb file. AutoCAD will automatically add the .stb filename extension.

3. After you click Save, AutoCAD creates a new Named Plot Style Table file, with the .stb filename extension, from the .ctb file you selected in step 1.

The next part is to actually convert the drawing file:

1. Open the file you want to convert and enter **Convertpstyles.⏎** at the Command prompt. You will see a warning message to make sure you've converted a .ctb file to a .stb file.

2. Click OK to open the Select File dialog box.

3. Select the converted .stb file you created using the Convertctb command. The current drawing is converted to use a named plot style table.

In the process shown here, I've suggested converting the Acad.ctb file, but if you have some custom settings saved in another .ctb file, you might want to convert your custom .ctb file instead.

To convert a drawing that uses a named plot style table to one that uses a color plot style table, just open the file in question and use the Convertpstyles command. You will see a warning message telling you that all the named plot styles will be removed from the drawing. Click OK to convert the drawing.

If You Want to Experiment

Plot styles can take a little time to master, but once you've gotten some practice, you'll find that they are not really that complicated. Try experimenting with a few new plot styles. If you work in a firm with lots of older drawings that need periodic changes, you'll want to become familiar with the color plot style tables. You can try experimenting with named plot styles to see which style you prefer.

Chapter 10

Adding Text to Drawings

One of the more tedious drafting tasks is applying notes to your drawing. Anyone who has had to manually draft a large drawing containing a lot of notes knows the true meaning of writer's cramp. AutoCAD not only makes this job go faster by enabling you to type your notes right into the same document as the corresponding drawing, but it also helps you to create more professional-looking notes by using a variety of fonts, type sizes, and type styles.

In this chapter, you will add notes to your apartment building plan. In the process, you will explore some of AutoCAD's text creation and editing features. You will learn how to control the size, slant, type style, and orientation of text and how to import text files.

Topics in this chapter include the following:

◆ Adding Text to a Drawing

◆ Understanding Text Formatting in AutoCAD

◆ Organizing Text by Styles

◆ What Do the Fonts Look Like?

◆ Adding Special Characters and Simple Text Objects

◆ Checking Spelling and Substituting Fonts

◆ Finding and Replacing Text

◆ Accelerating Zooms and Regens with Qtext

Adding Text to a Drawing

In this first section, you will add some simple labels to your Unit drawing to identify the general design elements: the bathroom, the kitchen, and the living room.

Start by setting up a drawing to which you can apply some text:

1. Start AutoCAD and open the Unit file. If you haven't created the Unit file, you can use the file called 10a-unit.dwg from the companion CD. Metric users should use 10a-unit-metric.dwg. After it is open, choose File ➢ Save As to save the Unit drawing to a file called Unit.dwg.

2. Create a layer called Notes and make it the current layer. Notes is the layer on which you will keep all your text information.

3. Turn off the Flr-pat layer. Otherwise, the floor pattern you added previously will obscure the text you enter during the exercises in this chapter.

TIP   It's a good idea to keep your notes on a separate layer, so you can plot drawings containing only the graphics information or freeze the Notes layer to save redraw/regeneration time.

4. Set up your view so it looks similar to the top image in Figure 10.1.

FIGURE 10.1

The top image shows the points to pick to place the text boundary window. The bottom image shows the completed text.

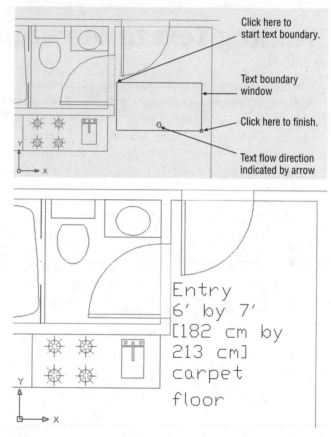

Click here to start text boundary.

Text boundary window

Click here to finish.

Text flow direction indicated by arrow

Entry
6′ by 7′
[182 cm by
213 cm]
carpet
floor

You've got the drawing ready. Now add some text:

1. Choose Draw ➤ Text ➤ Multiline Text from the menu bar, or type **MT↵**. You can also select the Multiline Text tool from the Draw toolbar. You'll see a prompt that tells you the current text style and height:

```
Current text style "STANDARD" Text height: 9 1/16"
Specify first corner:
```

2. Click the first point indicated in the top image in Figure 10.1 to start the text boundary window. This boundary window indicates the area in which to place the text. Notice the arrow near the bottom of the window. It indicates the direction of the text flow.

TIP   You don't have to be too precise about where you select the points for the boundary because you can adjust the location and size later.

3. At the `Specify opposite corner of [Height/Justify/Line spacing/Rotation/Style/Width]:` prompt, click the second point indicated in the top image in Figure 10.1. The Text Formatting toolbar appears with the Multiline Text Editor superimposed over the area you just selected.

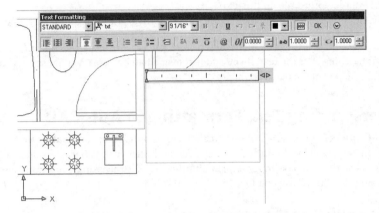

4. You could start typing the text for the room label, but first you need to select a size. Point to the Text Height drop-down list and click it. The default font size highlights.

5. Enter **6** to make the default height 6″. Metric users should enter **15** for a text height of 15 cm.

TIP Why make the text so tall? Remember that you are drawing at full scale, and anything you draw will be reduced in the plotted drawing. Text height is discussed in more detail later in this chapter.

6. Click the text panel and type **Entry**. As you type, the word appears in the text panel, just as it will appear in your drawing. As you will see later, the text also appears in the same font as the final text.

TIP The default font is a native AutoCAD font called `Txt.shx`. As you will see later, you can also use TrueType fonts and PostScript fonts.

7. Press ↵ to advance one line; then enter **6 by 7**.

8. Press ↵ to advance another line and enter [**182 cm by 213 cm**].

9. Press ↵ again to advance another line and enter **carpet floor**.

10. Click OK in the Text Formatting toolbar. The text appears in the drawing just as it did in the text editor. (See the bottom image in Figure 10.1.)

The Text Formatting toolbar and text editor work like any text editor, so if you make a typing error, you can highlight the error and then retype the letter or word. You can also perform other word processing functions such as search and replace, you can import text, and you can make font changes.

You also saw that the text editor shows you how your text will appear in the location you selected in steps 2 and 3. If your view of the drawing is such that the text is too small to be legible, the Text Formatting toolbar will enlarge the text so you can read it clearly. Likewise, if you are zoomed in too close to see the entire text, the Text Formatting toolbar will adjust the text in its text editor to enable you to see all the text.

In the next section, you'll look at some of the many options available for formatting text.

TIP If text is included in a selection where a hatch pattern is to be placed, AutoCAD automatically avoids hatching over the text. If you add text over a hatched area, you must rehatch the area to include the text in the hatch boundary.

Understanding Text Formatting in AutoCAD

AutoCAD offers a wide range of text-formatting options. You can control fonts, text height, justification, line spacing, and width. You can even include special characters such as degree symbols or stacked fractions. If you're familiar with other word processing programs, you should feel at home using the AutoCAD text feature.

Adjusting the Text Height and Font

Let's continue our look at AutoCAD text by adding a label for the living room of the studio apartment. You'll use the Multiline Text tool again, but this time you'll get to try out some of its other features.

In this first exercise, you'll see how you can adjust the size and font of text in the editor:

1. Pan your view so that the kitchen is just at the top of the drawing, as shown in the first image in Figure 10.2.

2. Click the Multiline Text tool again; then select a text boundary window, as shown in the first image in Figure 10.2.

3. In the text editor, type the following:

   ```
   Living Room
   14´-0˝ by 16´-5˝
   [427 cm by 500 cm]
   ```

   As you type, notice that the words *Living* and *Room* become two separate lines even though you did not press ↵ between them. AutoCAD uses word wrap to fit the text inside the text boundary area.

4. Highlight the text *14´-0˝ by 16´-5˝ [427 cm by 500 cm]* as you would in any word processor. For example, you can click the end of the line to place the cursor there; then Shift+click the beginning of the line to highlight the whole line.

5. In the Text Formatting toolbar, click the Text Height drop-down list and select 6. The highlighted text changes to a smaller size.

6. Highlight the words *Living Room*.

FIGURE 10.2
Placing the text
boundary window for
the living room label
and the final label

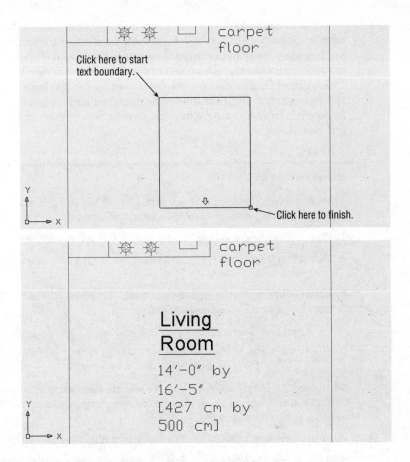

7. Click the Font drop-down list to display a list of font options.

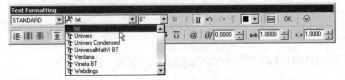

8. Scroll up the list until you find Arial. This is a standard TrueType font available in all installations of Windows 2000 and Windows XP. Notice that the text in the text editor changes to reflect the new font.

9. With the words *Living Room* still highlighted, click the Underline button in the Text Formatting toolbar.

10. Click OK in the Text Formatting toolbar. The label appears in the area you indicated in step 2 (see the bottom image in Figure 10.2).

11. Now to see how you might go back to the Text Formatting toolbar, double-click the text. The Text Formatting toolbar and text editor appear, enabling you to change the text.

12. Click OK to exit the Text Formatting toolbar.

While using the Multiline Text tool, you might have noticed the [Height/Justify/Line spacing/Rotation/Style/Width]: prompt immediately after you picked the first point of the text boundary. You can use any of these options to make on-the-fly modifications to the height, justification, line spacing, rotation style, or width of the multiline text.

For example, after clicking the first point for the text boundary, you can type **R↵** and then specify a rotation angle for the text window, either graphically with a rubber-banding line or by entering an angle value. After you've entered a rotation angle, you can resume selecting the text boundary.

USING POSTSCRIPT FONTS

If you have PostScript fonts that you would like to use in AutoCAD, you need to compile them into AutoCAD's native font format. To do so, follow these steps:

1. Type **Compile.↵** to open the Compile Shape Or Font File dialog box.

2. Select PostScript Fonts (*.pfb) from the Files Of Type drop-down list, and then browse to find the font you want to convert.

3. Double-click the PostScript font you want to convert into the AutoCAD format. AutoCAD will work for a moment; then you'll see this message:

   ```
   Compiling shape/font description file

   Compilation successful. Output file Program Files\AutoCAD2007\
   FONTS\fontname.shx contains 59578 bytes.
   ```

When AutoCAD is finished, you have a file with the same name as the PostScript font file but with the .shx filename extension. If you place your newly compiled font in AutoCAD's Fonts folder, it will be available in the Style dialog box.

When you work with AutoCAD's .shx font files, it is important to remember the following:

◆ License restrictions still apply to the AutoCAD-compiled version of the PostScript font.

◆ Like other fonts, compiled PostScript fonts can use up substantial disk space, so compile only the fonts you need.

Scaling Multiple Text Objects in a Hurry

Another way to quickly change the size of text is to use the Scaletext command. Choose Modify ➢ Object ➢ Text ➢ Scale, or type **Scaletext** at the Command prompt, and then select the text you want to scale. You can select multiple text objects. Press [↵? pc] when you've completed your selection. You see this prompt:

```
[Existing/Left/Center/Middle/Right/TL/TC/TR/ML/MC/MR/BL/BC/BR/]<Existing>:
```

Enter the letters corresponding to the justification option you want to use for the text. (See the section "Justifying Single-Line Text Objects" later in this chapter for a description of these options.) After you've entered an option, you see the next prompt:

```
Specify new height or [Match object/Scale factor] <Current height>:
```

At this prompt you have three options:

◆   Enter a new height.

◆   Type **M.⏎** and select another text object whose height you want to match.

◆   Type **S.⏎** and enter a scale factor to scale the text to a specific ratio.

Adding Color, Stacked Fractions, and Special Symbols

In the previous exercise, you were able to adjust the text height and font, just as you would in any word processor. You saw how you can easily underline portions of your text by using the tool buttons in the editor. Other tools enable you to set the color for individual characters or words in the text, create stacked fractions, or insert special characters. Here's a brief description of how these tools work:

To change the color of text, highlight it and then select the color from the Color drop-down list.

To turn a fraction into a stacked fraction, highlight the fraction and then click the Stack tool. Note that this option is grayed out unless you have a fraction selected.

To add a special character, place the cursor at the location where you want the character placed , and then click the Symbol tool. A menu appears from which you can select a symbol. You can also right-click, and then choose Symbol from the shortcut menu.

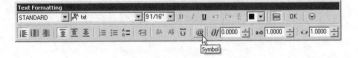

The Symbol option offers several commonly used symbols that you can add to your drawing. Also included is the nonbreaking space option, which adds a space that will not break into separate lines unless the text boundary is too narrow.

Degree	x°	Identity	≡
Plus/Minus	±	Initial Length	⌀⟶
Diameter	⌀	Monument Line	ℳ
Almost Equal	≈	Not Equal	≠
Angle	∠	Ohm	Ω
Boundary Line	℔	Omega	Ω
Center Line	℄	Property Line	ℙ
Delta	Δ	Subscript 2	x_2
Electrical Phase	φ	Squared	x^2
Flow Line	℔	Cubed	x^3

When you select these options, AutoCAD inserts the proper AutoCAD text code in the text that corresponds to these symbols. You'll get a more detailed look at special symbols later in this chapter.

Adjusting the Width of the Text Boundary Window

Although the font and height of your text are formatted correctly, the block of text appears too tall and narrow. The following steps will show you how to change the boundary to fit the text:

1. Click any part of the text you just entered to highlight it.

2. Click the upper-right grip.

3. Drag the grip to the right, to the location shown in Figure 10.3; then click that point.

FIGURE 10.3
Adjusting the text
boundary window

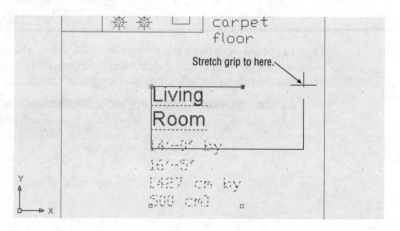

4. Click any grip, and then right-click and choose Move.

5. Move the text to a location that is more centered in the room.

AutoCAD's word-wrap feature automatically adjusts the text formatting to fit the text boundary. This feature is especially useful to AutoCAD users because other drawing objects often affect the placement of text. As your drawing changes, you will need to adjust the location and boundary of your notes and labels.

Adjusting the Text Alignment

The text is currently aligned on the left side of the text boundary. For a label such as the one in the living room, it is more appropriate to center the text.

Here's how you can change the text alignment:

1. Double-click the text to display the Text Formatting toolbar. You can also right-click the text after selecting it and then choose Mtext Edit from the shortcut menu. Or, from the menu bar, choose Modify ➤ Object ➤ Text ➤ Edit.

2. Right-click the text and then choose Justification ➤ Top Center from the shortcut menu. The living room label moves to a centered position above the second line (see Figure 10.4).

3. Click OK to accept the changes.

FIGURE 10.4
The text aligned using the Top Center alignment option

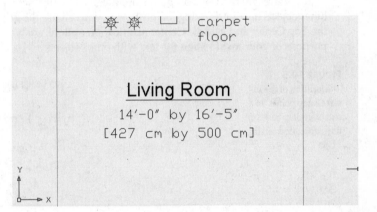

You can also change the justification of text through the text justification tools in the Text Formatting toolbar. Three tools let you set the justification to left, center, and right, while another set of tools let you set the top, middle, or bottom justification.

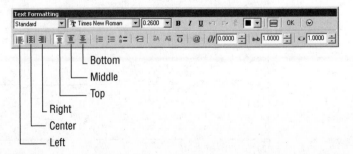

Yet another way to set justification is through the Properties palette. Select the multiline text you want to edit, and then right-click and choose Properties from the shortcut menu. Click the setting just to the right of the Justify option. It becomes a drop-down list. Open the list and select the justification style you want. The text changes as you select the justification style.

TIP You can open the Text Formatting toolbar from the Properties palette. Right-click the text after selecting it; then choose Properties to open the Properties palette. You can then select the Contents option and click the ellipsis button that appears to the far right of the option.

TEXT JUSTIFICATION AND OSNAPS

Although it's clear that the text is now aligned through the center of the text boundary, one important change occurred that is not so obvious. You might have noticed that the object justification list offered three centered options: Top Center, Middle Center, and Bottom Center. All three of these options have the same effect on the text's appearance, but they each have a different effect on how osnaps act on the text. Figure 10.5 shows where the osnap point occurs on a text boundary, depending on which justification option is selected. A multiline text object has only one insertion point on its boundary that you can access with the Insert Osnap.

The Osnap point also appears as an extra grip point on the text boundary when you click the text. If you click the text you just entered, you will see that a grip point now appears at the top center of the text boundary.

Knowing where the osnap points occur can be helpful when you want to align the text with other objects in your drawing. In most cases, you can use the grips to align your text boundary, but the Top Center and Middle Center justification options enable you to use the center and middle portions of your text to align the text with other objects.

FIGURE 10.5
The location of the Insert Osnap points on a text boundary based on its justification setting

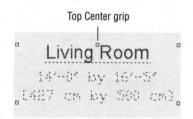

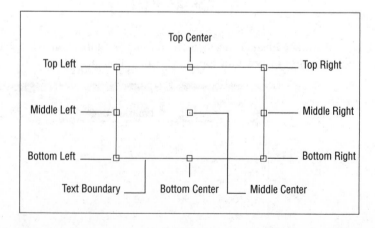

Changing Justification of Multiple Text Objects

You've seen how you can change the justification of an individual text object, but you will often find that you need to change the justification of several text objects at one time. AutoCAD offers the Justifytext command for this purpose. To use it, choose Modify ➢ Object ➢ Text ➢ Justify, or type **Justifytext** at the Command prompt. At the `Select objects:` prompt, select the text you want to change, and then press [↵? pc] to confirm your selection. You'll see the following prompt in the command line:

```
[Left/Align/Fit/Center/Middle/Right/TL/TC/TR/ML/MC/MR/BL/BC/BR] <BC>:
```

Enter the letters corresponding to the type of justification you want to use for the text. (See the section "Justifying Single-Line Text Objects" later in this chapter for a description of these options.) After you've entered an option, the selected text will change to conform to the selected justification option.

Setting Indents and Tabs

You'll also want to know about the indent and tab features of the Text Formatting toolbar's text window. You might have noticed the ruler at the top of the text editor. Figure 10.6 shows that ruler, including tab and indent markers.

FIGURE 10.6
The ruler at the top of the text editor lets you quickly set tabs and indents for text.

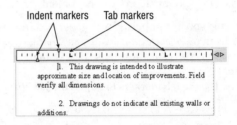

The indent markers let you control the indention of the first line and the rest of the paragraph. The tab markers give you control over tab spacing. For new text, the tab markers don't appear until you add them by clicking the ruler. The following exercises will demonstrate the use of these markers more clearly.

Start by practicing with the indent markers:

1. Save the Unit drawing, then open the `Indent.dwg` file from the companion CD. This file contains some text that you will experiment with.

2. Double-click the text at the top of the drawing to open the Text Formatting toolbar.

3. Press Ctrl+A to highlight all the text in the text editor. This is necessary to indicate the group of text to be affected by your indent settings.

4. Click and drag the top indent marker two spaces to the right. Notice that the indent of the first line moves with the marker. A note appears above the ruler showing you how much indent you are applying. Also notice that the text at the first tab remains at its starting location.

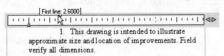

5. Click and drag the bottom indent marker two spaces to the left. Notice that the rest of the paragraph moves with the marker. Again, you see a note by the ruler showing you how much indent you are applying.

6. Click OK in the Text Formatting toolbar to exit.

Here you see how you can control the indents of the selected text with the indent markers. You can set paragraphs of a single Mtext object differently, giving you a wide range of indent-formatting possibilities. Just select the text you want to set and then adjust the indent markers.

Now try the tab markers. For this exercise you will try the text import feature to import a tab-delimited text file:

1. Click the Multiline Text tool on the Draw toolbar.

2. For the first corner, click the upper-left corner of the large rectangle in the drawing just below the paragraph.

3. For the opposite corner, click the lower-right corner of the rectangle.

4. Right-click in the text editor of the Text Formatting toolbar and select Import Text.

5. In the Select File dialog box, locate and select the `tabtest.txt` file from the Chapter 10 files from the companion CD. The contents of the `tabtest.txt` file are displayed in the text editor.

The file you just imported was generated from the Attribute Extraction feature of AutoCAD. You'll learn more about this feature in Chapter 13. This file contains tabs to align the columns of information. You can adjust those tabs in the Text Formatting toolbar, as you'll see in the next set of steps.

Now use the tab markers to adjust the tab spacing of the columns of text:

1. Press Ctrl+A to select all the text.

2. Click the ruler at a point that is at the 12th mark from the left (that's 3 of the taller tick marks in the ruler). An L-shaped marker appears, and the first tab column of text moves to this position.

3. Click the ruler again at the 20th mark. The second tab column aligns to this position.

4. Continue to click the ruler to add more tab markers so that the text looks similar to Figure 10.7. Don't worry about being exact. This is just for practice. After you've placed a marker, you can click and drag it to make adjustments.

5. Click OK on the Text Formatting toolbar. The text appears in the drawing as a door schedule.

FIGURE 10.7

Add tab markers so that your text looks similar to this figure.

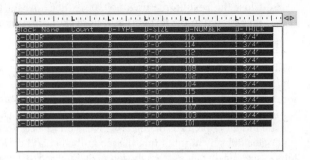

Here you saw how you can create a table or a schedule from an imported text file. You can also create a schedule from scratch by composing it directly in the text editor of the Text Formatting tool-bar. Prior to AutoCAD 2006, this was the only method available for creating this type of table, but AutoCAD now offers the Table feature specifically designed for creating tables (see Chapter 11). Still, this example offers a way to demonstrate the tab feature in the Multiline Text tool, and you may encounter a file in which a table is formatted in the way described here.

Besides using the indent and tab markers on the ruler, you can also control indents and tabs through the Indents And Tabs dialog box. Do the following to get a firsthand look:

1. Double-click the text at the top of the `Indent.dwg` drawing (the one you edited in the first part of this section) and then press Ctrl+A to select all the text.

2. Right-click the ruler above the text editor and then click Indents And Tabs to open the Indents And Tabs dialog box.

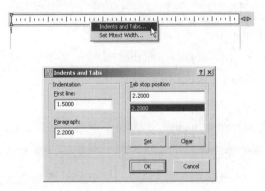

3. Change the value in the First Line input box to 1.5 and the Paragraph input box to 2.2.

4. Double-click the Tab Stop Position input box in the upper-right corner and enter **2.2**↵. You can also click the Set button instead of pressing ↵.

5. Click OK. Notice that the text now appears with the text indented from the numbers.

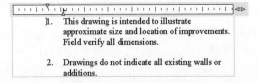

6. Close the Text Formatting toolbar. Notice how the text in the drawing is now formatted as it appeared in the text editor of the Text Formatting toolbar.

7. Exit the Indent.dwg file.

In this exercise, you used the Indents And Tabs dialog box to set the paragraph indent and the first tab marker to be the same value. This causes the text portion of the list to be aligned at a distance of 2.2 drawing units from the left text boundary, leaving the list number extended farther to the left. This gives the list a more professional appearance.

The Indents And Tabs dialog box gives you fine control over the formatting of your text. It lets you delete tabs by highlighting the tab in the list and clicking the Clear button. You can also add tabs at specific distances from the left margin of the text boundary by entering new tab locations in the Tab Stop Position input box and clicking the Set button.

You specify distances in drawing units. If your drawing is set up to use Architectural units, for example, you can enter values in feet and inches or just inches. The First Line and Paragraph input boxes let you enter a numeric value for paragraph indents. As you have just seen, you can use the First Line and Paragraph input boxes to create a numbered list by setting the Paragraph input box value to be the same as the first tab stop position.

TIP You might have noticed the Set Mtext Width right-click shortcut menu option in step 2 of the preceding exercise. This option opens a simple dialog box that enables you to enter a width for the text boundary. You can also click and drag the right inside edge of the ruler to change the text boundary width.

Adding Numbers, Bullets, or Letters for Lists

One of the more common types of text you'll create is a numbered, bulleted, or lettered list . AutoCAD can help you make quick work of such a list. Here's an example of how you can create a numbered list from existing text.

1. Open the textlist.dwg file from the Chapter 10 folder.

2. Double-click the text in the drawing.

3. Press Ctrl+A to select all the text.

4. In the Text Formatting toolbar, click the Numbering tool and then click OK.

5. Close but don't save the textlist.dwg file in case you want to use this tutorial again.

Each paragraph of the selected text is given a number, and it is formatted so that the number stands in a column to the left. You can then fine-tune the indent and line spacing, but most of the work is done for you.

The Bullets and Uppercase Letters tools work in the same way, but as their name implies, instead of numbers, you will get bullets and letters.

└ Uppercase Letters

└── Bullets

Adjusting Line Spacing

Another text-editing feature that is related to text indents and tabs is the Line Spacing option. You can adjust line spacing between the range of 0.5 and 4 times the height of the text. Here's how it works:

1. Go back to the Unit drawing, select the mtext object that contains the words *Living Room*, and then right-click.

2. Choose Properties from the shortcut menu to open the Properties palette.

3. Use the scroll bar at the left of the Properties palette to scroll down until you see all the entries in the Text group.

4. Click the Line Space Factor value in the Text group.

5. Enter **4.↵**. The value changes to reflect the spacing of the text at 4 times the height of the text.

6. Close the Properties palette. You see that the line spacing of the selected text has changed.

7. Type **U↵** or click the Undo button in the Standard toolbar. You don't need to save this change to the text.

In step 5 you entered **4** to indicate that you want a line-spacing value that is 4 times the text height. Below the Line Space Factor option in the Properties palette, you will see the Line Space Style option. This enables you to choose between an approximate spacing and an exact spacing.

Editing Text Content

It is helpful to think of text in AutoCAD as a collection of text documents. Each text boundary window you place is like a separate document. You've already seen how to change the formatting of text by using the Text Formatting toolbar. Now try changing the contents. This time, you'll try out the Ddedit command, which works in a slightly different way from the usual double-click method:

1. Choose Modify ➤ Object ➤ Text ➤ Edit, or type **Ddedit**↵ at the Command prompt.

2. Click the words *Living Room* to display the Text Formatting toolbar along with the text editor.

3. Place and click the text cursor on the end of the line that reads *Living Room,* and then type ↵ **230 square feet**.

4. Click OK. The text appears with the additional line in the drawing.

5. The Ddedit command is still active, so press ↵ to exit Ddedit.

In step 5, the Ddedit command remained active so that you could continue to edit other text objects. If you wanted to make additional changes, you could have selected another text object to change before pressing ↵ to exit the Ddedit command.

As with the previous exercise, you can change the formatting of the existing or new text while in the text editor of the Text Formatting toolbar. Notice that the formatting of the new text is the same as the text that preceded it. Just as in Microsoft Word, the formatting of text depends on the paragraph or word to which it is added. If you had added the text after the last line, it would appear in the AutoCAD Txt font and in the same 6″ height.

TIP You can highlight text in the text window and then click and drag to move it, or you can Ctrl+click and drag to copy it.

Converting Text to Lowercase or Uppercase

If you find that you need to change the case of existing text, you can do so with the Uppercase and Lowercase tools in the Text Formatting toolbar.

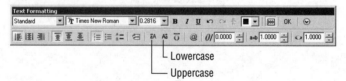

To use these tools, select the text you want to convert, and then click the tool you want to use. You can also use the right-click options while in the Text Formatting toolbar. Select the text, right-click, and then choose Change Case ➤ Uppercase or Change Case ➤ Lowercase.

Understanding Text and Scale

In the first few exercises of this chapter, you were asked to make the text height 6″. This is necessary to give the text the proper scale for the drawing. But where did we come up with the number 6? Why not 4 or 10? The 6″ height was derived by carefully considering the desired final height of the text in relation to the designated scale of the drawing. Just as in Chapter 3, where you applied a scale factor to a drawing's final sheet size to accommodate a full-scale drawing, you need to convert the scale of your text size so that the text conforms to the drawing's intended scale.

Text-scale conversion is a concept many people have difficulty grasping. As you discovered in previous chapters, AutoCAD lets you draw at full scale; that is, you can represent distances as values equivalent to the actual size of the object. When you later plot the drawing, you tell AutoCAD the scale at which you want to plot, and the program reduces the drawing accordingly. This allows you the freedom to enter measurements at full scale and not worry about converting them to various scales every time you enter a distance. Unfortunately, this feature can also create problems when you enter text and dimensions. Just as you had to convert the plotted sheet size to an enlarged size equivalent at full scale in the drawing editor, you must convert your text size to its equivalent at full scale.

To illustrate this point, imagine you are drawing the Unit plan at full size on a very large sheet of paper. When you are finished with this drawing, it will be reduced to a scale that enables it to fit on an 8.5″ × 11″ sheet of paper. So you have to make your text quite large to keep it legible after it is reduced. This means that if you want text to appear $\frac{1}{8}$″ high when the drawing is plotted, you must convert it to a considerably larger size when you draw it. To do this, you multiply the desired height of the final plotted text by a scale conversion factor.

If your drawing is at a $\frac{1}{8}$″ = 1′-0″ scale, you multiply the desired text height, $\frac{1}{8}$″, by the scale conversion factor of 96 to get a height of 12″. This is the height you must make your text to get $\frac{1}{8}$″-high text in the final plot. (Chapter 3 shows scale factors as they relate to standard drawing scales.) Table 10.1 shows you some other examples of text height to scale.

TABLE 10.1: $\frac{1}{8}$″-High Text Converted to Size for Various Drawing Scales

DRAWING SCALE	SCALE FACTOR	AUTOCAD DRAWING HEIGHT FOR 1/8-HIGH TEXT
$\frac{1}{16}$″ = 1′-0″	192	24.0″
$\frac{1}{8}$″ = 1′-0″	96	12.0″
$\frac{1}{4}$″ = 1′-0″	48	6.0″
$\frac{1}{2}$″ = 1′-0″	24	3.0″
$\frac{3}{4}$″ = 1′-0″	16	2.0″
1″ = 1′-0″	12	1.5″
$1\frac{1}{2}$″ = 1′-0″	8	1.0″
3″ = 1′-0″	4	0.5″

Organizing Text by Styles

If you understand the Text Formatting toolbar and text scale, you know all you need to know to start labeling your drawings. As you expand your drawing skills and your drawings become larger, you will want to start organizing your text into *styles*. You can think of text styles as a way to store your most common text formatting. Styles store text height and font information so that you don't have to reset these options every time you enter text. But styles also include some settings not available in the Text Formatting toolbar.

Creating a Style

In the previous examples, you entered text by using the AutoCAD default settings for text. Whether you knew it or not, you were also using a text style: AutoCAD's default style called Standard. The Standard style uses the AutoCAD Txt font and numerous other settings that you will learn about in this section. These other settings include width factor, oblique angle, and default height.

USING LAYOUT TABS FOR TEXT

Another way to deal with the text-scale issue is to avoid it altogether by adding your text in a layout tab. As you saw in Chapter 8, the layout tabs let you work on your drawings as they will appear when you print them. In the layout tabs, you work in sizes that relate to the printer output instead of full scale. This means that you can specify your text heights at the actual size that you want your text when it is printed. For example, you can specify a height of 0.25 if you want your text to appear ¼″ high instead of using a height of 6″.

Another advantage to adding text in a layout tab is that if you have multiple views of differing scales in your layout, you don't have to worry about adjusting the text size for each view. Since the text in the layout tab is independent of any viewport settings, you can add text on top of the viewport of your layout and just use one text height. This is especially significant for detail drawings in an architectural set.

There are a few drawbacks to adding your notes in a layout tab. Since the text is not in the model tab, you won't see where the text is located in relation to the rest of your drawing. As you edit the graphics of your drawing, you must take extra care to ensure that your text in the layout tabs is repositioned to match the changes in the graphics.

TIP If you don't like the way the AutoCAD default style is set up, open the Acad.dwt template file and change the Standard text style settings to your liking. You can also add other styles that you use frequently. Remember that the AutoCAD files that use the .dwt filename extension are just AutoCAD .dwg files with a slightly different extension to set them apart.

The previous exercises in this chapter demonstrate that you can modify the formatting of a style as you enter the text. But for the most part, after you've set up a few styles, you won't need to adjust settings such as fonts and text height each time you enter text. You'll be able to select from a list of styles you've previously created and just start typing.

To create a style, choose Format ➢ Text Style and then select from the available fonts. This next exercise will show you how to create a style:

1. Return to the Unit drawing (you can select it from the Windows menu), and then choose Format ➢ Text Style or type **St.↵** to open the Text Style dialog box.

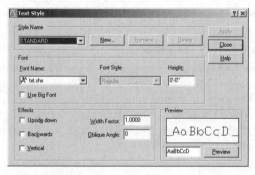

2. Click the New button in the Style Name group to open the New Text Style dialog box.

3. Enter **Note1 (Note one)** for the name of your new style; then click OK.

4. Now select a font for your style. In the Text Style dialog box again, click the Font Name drop-down list in the Font group.

5. Locate the Courier New TrueType font and select it.

6. In the Height input box, enter **6**.

7. Click Apply and then close the dialog box.

Using a Type Style

Now let's see how your new text style looks by adding more text to `Unit.dwg`:

1. Pan your view so that the balcony is centered in the AutoCAD drawing area, as shown in Figure 10.8.

2. Click the Multiline Text tool on the Draw toolbar.

3. Place the text boundary as shown in the top image in Figure 10.8. Notice that the font and height settings reflect the Note1 style you created earlier.

4. Enter the following text:

```
Balcony↵
14'-0" by 4'-0"↵
[427 cm by 122 cm]
```

FIGURE 10.8
Adding the balcony label using the Note1 text style

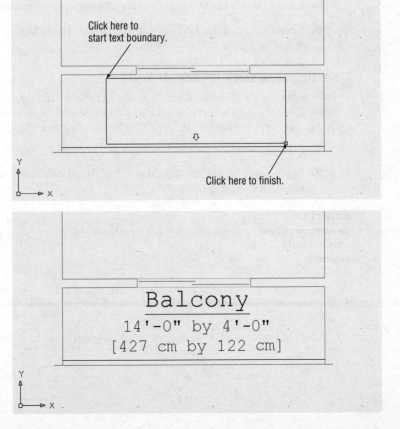

5. Highlight the word *Balcony* and then click the Underline button.

6. With *Balcony* still highlighted, click the Text Height drop-down list and enter **9**↵.

7. Highlight all the text.

8. Right-click and choose Justification ➢ Top Center.

9. Click OK. The text appears over the balcony in the style you selected.

A newly created style becomes the default style, and you don't have to explicitly select your new Note1 style in order to use it.

You can also change an existing piece of text to a different style. The following steps show you how:

1. Return to your previous view of the *Living Room* text.

2. Type **Ed**↵ and select the text.

3. Highlight one line of the text in the text window.

4. Click the Style drop-down list and select Note1. You see a warning message telling you that the style change can only be applied to the entire text object.

5. Click OK Notice that all the text is converted to the new style.

WARNING   When you change the style of a text object, it loses any custom formatting it might have, such as font or height changes that are different from those of the text's default style settings.

6. Click OK to exit the Text Formatting toolbar. The living room label is now in your Note1 style (see Figure 10.9).

Setting the Current Default Style

The previous exercise showed you how you can change the style of existing text. But suppose you want all the new text you create to be of a different style than the current default style. You can change the current style by using the Text Style dialog box. Here's how it's done:

1. Choose Format ➢ Text Style or type **St**↵ to open the Text Style dialog box.

2. Select a style name from the Style Name drop-down list. For this exercise, choose Standard to return to the Standard style.

FIGURE 10.9
The living room label
converted to the
Note1 style

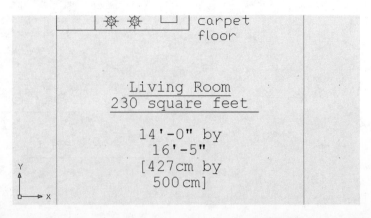

3. Click Close.

Or you can quickly select a style from the Styles toolbar, which is just to the right of the Standard toolbar.

After you've done this, the selected style will be the default until you select a different style. AutoCAD records the current default style with the drawing data when you choose File ➤ Save, so that the next time you work on the file you will still have the same default style.

Understanding the Text Style Dialog Box Options

Now you know how to create a new style. As mentioned, there are other settings in the Text Style dialog box that you didn't apply in an exercise. Here is a listing of those settings and their purposes. Some of them, such as the Width Factor, can be quite useful. Others, such as the Backwards and Vertical options, are rarely used.

STYLE NAME

In the Style Name group, you'll see a drop-down list showing the current style. This list also contains other styles that may be present in the drawing. You can use the drop-down list to select a default style. In addition, there are the following buttons:

New   Lets you create a new text style.

Rename   Lets you rename an existing style. This option is not available for the Standard style.

Delete   Deletes a style. This option is not available for the Standard style.

FONT

In the Font group, you have the following options:

Font Name   Lets you select a font from a list of available fonts. The list is derived from the font resources available to Windows 2000 or Windows XP, plus the standard AutoCAD fonts.

Font Style   Offers variations of a font, such as italic or bold, when they are available.

Height   Lets you enter a font size. A 0 height has special meaning when using the Dtext command to enter text, as described later in this chapter.

Use Big Font   The Use Big Font option is applicable to Asian fonts and is only offered with AutoCAD .shx fonts.

EFFECTS

In the Effects group, you have the following options:

Upside Down   Prints the text upside down.

Backwards   Prints the text backward.

Vertical   Prints text in a vertical column.

Width Factor Adjusts the width and spacing of the characters in the text. A value of 1 keeps the text at its normal width. Values greater than 1 expand the text, and values less than 1 compress the text.

> This is the Simplex font expanded by 1.4
> This is the simplex font using a width factor of 1
> This is the simplex font compressed by .6

Oblique Angle Skews the text at an angle. When this option is set to a value greater than 0, the text appears italicized. A value of less than 0 (–12, for example) causes the text to "lean" to the left.

> *This is the simplex font*
> *using a 12–degree oblique angle*

TIP You can also set the width factor and oblique angle directly to text using the Width Factor and Oblique Angle tools in the Text Formatting toolbar. These tools are located toward the lower right end of the toolbar.

Renaming a Text Style

You can use the Rename option in the Text Style dialog box to rename a style. This is a command that enables you to rename a variety of AutoCAD settings. Here's how to use it:

TIP This exercise is not part of the main tutorial. If you are working through the tutorial, make note of this exercise and then try it out later.

1. Choose Format ➢ Rename or enter **Ren.⏎** at the Command prompt to open the Rename dialog box.

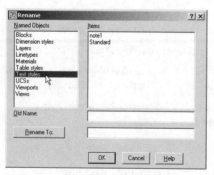

2. In the Named Objects list box, choose Text Styles.

3. Click the name of the style you want to change from the Items list on the right; the name appears in the Old Name input box below the list.

4. In the input box next to the Rename To button, enter the new name. Click the Rename To button and click OK.

TIP If you are an experienced AutoCAD user and accustomed to entering the Rename command at the Command prompt, you still can. Just remember to include the minus sign at the beginning as in –rename. Then answer the prompts that appear.

TIP If you need to change the style of one text object to match that of another, you can use the Match Properties tool. See Chapter 7 for details on how to use this tool.

What Do the Fonts Look Like?

You've already seen a few of the fonts available in AutoCAD. Chances are, you are familiar with the TrueType fonts available in Windows. You have some additional AutoCAD fonts from which to choose. In fact, you might want to stick with the AutoCAD fonts for all but your presentation drawings, as other fonts can consume more memory.

Figure 10.10 shows the basic AutoCAD text fonts. The Romans font is perhaps the most widely used because it offers a reasonable appearance while consuming little memory. Figure 10.11 lists some of the symbols and Greek fonts.

This section showed you samples of the AutoCAD fonts. You can see samples of all the fonts, including TrueType fonts, in the preview window of the Text Style dialog box. If you use a word processor, you're probably familiar with at least some of the TrueType fonts available in Windows and AutoCAD.

Adding Special Characters

Earlier in this chapter, you saw that you can add special characters by using the Symbol option from the Text Formatting toolbar. For example, you use the Degrees symbol to designate angles and the Plus/Minus symbol to show tolerance information. The Diameter characters are already available as special characters. AutoCAD also offers a nonbreaking space. You can use the nonbreaking space when you have a space between two words but do not want the two words to be separated by a line break.

FIGURE 10.10

Some of the standard AutoCAD text fonts

This is Txt	
This is Monotxt	
This is Simplex	(Old version of Roman Simplex)
This is Complex	(Old version of Roman Complex)
This is Italic	(Old version of Italic Complex)
This is Romans	(Roman Simplex)
This is Romand	(Roman double stroke)
This is Romanc	(Roman Complex)
This is Romant	(Roman triple stroke)
This is Scripts	(Script Simplex)
This is Scriptc	(Script Complex)
This is Italicc	(Italic Complex)
This is Italict	(Italic triple stroke)
Τηισ ισ Γρεεκσ	(This is Greeks - Greek Simplex)
Τηισ ισ Γρεεκχ	(This is Greekc - Greek Complex)
This is Gothice	(Gothic English)
This is Gothicg	(Gothic German)
This is Gothici	(Gothic Italian)

FIGURE 10.11
Some of the
AutoCAD symbols
and Greek fonts

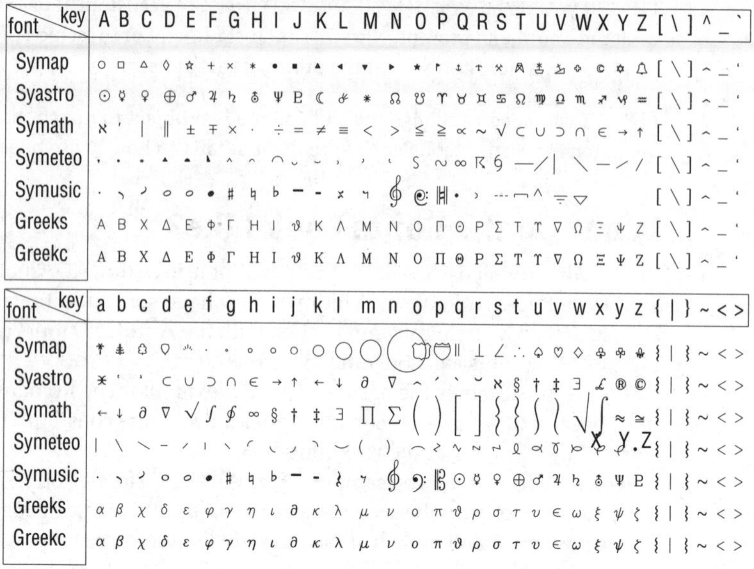

IMPORTING TEXT FILES

With multiline text objects, AutoCAD enables you to import ASCII text or Rich Text Format (RTF) files. RTF files can be exported from Microsoft Word and most other word processing programs and will retain most of their formatting in AutoCAD. Here's how you import text files:

1. With the Text Formatting toolbar open, right-click in the text panel and choose Import Text.

2. In the Select File dialog box, locate a valid text file. It must be either a file in a raw text (ASCII) format, such as a Notepad (.txt) file, or a Rich Text Format (.rtf) file. RTF files can store formatting information, such as boldface and varying point sizes.

3. After you've highlighted the file you want, double-click it or click Open. The text appears in the Edit Mtext window.

4. You can then click OK, and the text will appear in your drawing.

In addition, you can use the Windows Clipboard and the Cut and Paste functions to add text to a drawing. To do this, take the following steps:

1. Select some text and then choose Cut or Copy in any Windows program to place text on the Windows Clipboard.

2. Open AutoCAD. Choose Edit ➤ Paste and the pasted text appears in your drawing. It is not, however, editable within AutoCAD.

If the text is from a text editor like Windows Notepad, the text will be inserted as AutoCAD text. If the text contains formatting from a word processor like Microsoft Word, the text will be an OLE object.

Because AutoCAD is an OLE client, you can also attach other types of documents to an AutoCAD drawing file. See Chapter 19 for more on AutoCAD's OLE support.

THE TEXTFILL SYSTEM VARIABLE

Unlike the standard sticklike AutoCAD fonts, TrueType and PostScript fonts have filled areas. These filled areas take more time to generate; so if you have a lot of text in these fonts, your redraw and regen times will increase. To help reduce redraw and regen times, you can set AutoCAD to display and plot these fonts as outline fonts, even though they are filled in their true appearance.

To change its setting, type **Textfill**⏎ and then type **0**⏎. This turns off text fill for PostScript and TrueType fonts. (This is the same as setting the Textfill system variable to 0.)

By clicking the Other option in the Symbol shortcut menu, you can also add other special characters from the Windows Character Map dialog box. Characters such as the trademark (™) and copyright (©) symbols are often available. The contents of the Symbol drop-down list will depend on the font currently selected.

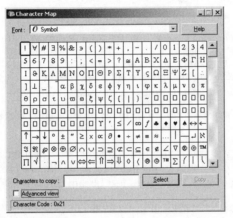

WARNING The Character Map dialog box is a Windows accessory. If it does not appear when you choose Other from the Text Formatting Symbol tool menu, you might need to install the Character Map from your Windows installation CD.

To use the characters from this dialog box, proceed with the following steps:

TIP This is not part of the regular tutorial in this chapter, but you can experiment with these steps on your own.

1. To open the Text Formatting toolbar, double-click a multiline text object.

2. Click the Symbol tool in the Text Formatting toolbar and select Other from the Symbol menu.

3. Highlight the character you want in the Character Map dialog box. Also make note of the font name. You'll need to use it when you add the symbol to AutoCAD.

4. Either double-click the character or click the Select button. The character appears in the box below the character field in the dialog box.

5. Click Copy to copy the character to the Clipboard.

6. Close the Character Map dialog box.

7. In the text editor, place the cursor where you want the special character to appear.

8. Press Ctrl+V to paste the character into your text. You can also right-click the mouse and choose Paste from the shortcut menu.

9. If the symbol does not appear correctly, highlight the character you just inserted, and then, from the font list in the Text Formatting toolbar, select the font name you noted in step 3.

Adding Simple Text Objects

You might find that you are entering a lot of single words or simple labels that don't require all the bells and whistles of the Multiline Text Editor. AutoCAD offers the *single-line text object* that is simpler to use and can speed text entry if you are adding only small pieces of text.

Continue the tutorial on the Unit.dwg file by trying the following exercise:

1. Adjust your view so it looks like Figure 10.12.

2. Enter **Dt**↵ or choose Draw ➤ Text ➤ Single Line Text. This issues the Dtext command.

3. .tifAt the Specify start point of text or [Justify/Style]: prompt, pick the starting point for the text you are about to enter, just below the kitchen at coordinate 16′-2″,21′-8″ (490,664 for metric users). Note that the prompt offers the Justify and Style options.

4. At the Specify height <0′-9 1/16″>: prompt, enter **6″** (**15** for metric users) to indicate the text height.

5. At the Specify rotation angle of text <0>: prompt, press ↵ to accept the default, 0. You can specify any angle other than horizontal (for example, if you want your text aligned with a rotated object). You'll see a text I-beam cursor at the point you picked in step 3.

6. Now as you type, the word appears directly in the drawing.

> **TIP** If you make a typing error, use the Right and Left arrow keys to move the text cursor in the drawing area to the error; then use the Backspace key to correct the error. You can also paste text from the Clipboard into the cursor location by using the Ctrl+V keyboard shortcut or by right-clicking in the drawing area to access the shortcut menu.

FIGURE 10.12
Adding simple labels to the kitchen and bath by using the Dtext command

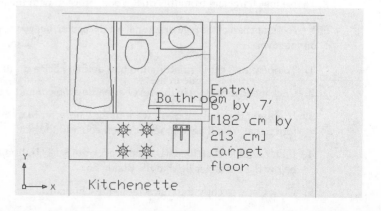

7. Press ↵ to move the cursor down to start a new line.

8. This time you want to label the bathroom. Pick a point to the right of the door swing at coordinate 19′-11″,26′-5″ (610,805 for metric users). The text cursor moves to that point.

9. Type **Bathroom**↵. Figure 10.12 shows how your drawing should look now.

10. Press ↵ again to exit the Dtext command.

TIP If for some reason you need to stop entering single-line text objects to do something else in AutoCAD, you can continue the text where you left off by pressing ↵ at the Specify start point of text or [Justify/Style]: prompt of the Dtext command. The text continues immediately below the last line of text entered.

Here you were able to add two single lines of text in different parts of your drawing fairly quickly. Dtext uses the current default text style settings (remember that earlier you set the text style to Standard), so the kitchen and bath labels use the Standard style.

Editing Single-Line Text Objects

You edit single-line text objects by using the same method as for multiline text, although you won't see the Text Formatting toolbar. In this exercise, you'll change the labels in both the kitchen and bath just by double-clicking them:

1. Double-click the Kitchenette label in the drawing to highlight it.

2. Using the cursor, highlight *ette* in *Kitchenette* and delete it.

3. Click the Bathroom label, and then click again.

4. Highlight *room* in *Bathroom* and delete it.

5. Press ↵ twice to return to the Command prompt.

As you can see, even the editing is simplified for single-line text. When you double-click single-line text, you invoke the Ddedit command. With this command, you are limited to editing the text only. This can be an advantage, however, when you need to edit several pieces of text. You don't have other options to get in the way of your editing.

You can change other properties of single-line text by using the Properties palette. For example, suppose you want to change the bath label to a height of 9″. Use these steps:

1. Click the Bath text, and then right-click and choose Properties to open the Properties palette.

2. Select the Height value in the Properties palette and change it to 9″.

3. Press ↵, and the text in the drawing increases in size to 9″ high.

4. Click the Undo tool on the menu bar to undo the change in text height.

5. Choose File ➢ Save to save the changes you've made thus far.

6. Close the Properties palette and the drawing.

The Properties palette lets you change the height, rotation, width factor, obliquing, justification, and style of a single-line text object. You can also modify the text content.

NOTE This is the end of the tutorial section of this chapter. The rest of this chapter offers additional information about text.

Justifying Single-Line Text Objects

Justifying single-line text objects works in a slightly different way from justifying multiline text. For example, if you change the justification setting to Center, the text moves so the center of the text is placed at the text insertion point. In other words, the insertion point stays in place while the text location adjusts to the new justification setting. Figure 10.13 shows the relationship between single-line text and the insertion point based on different justification settings.

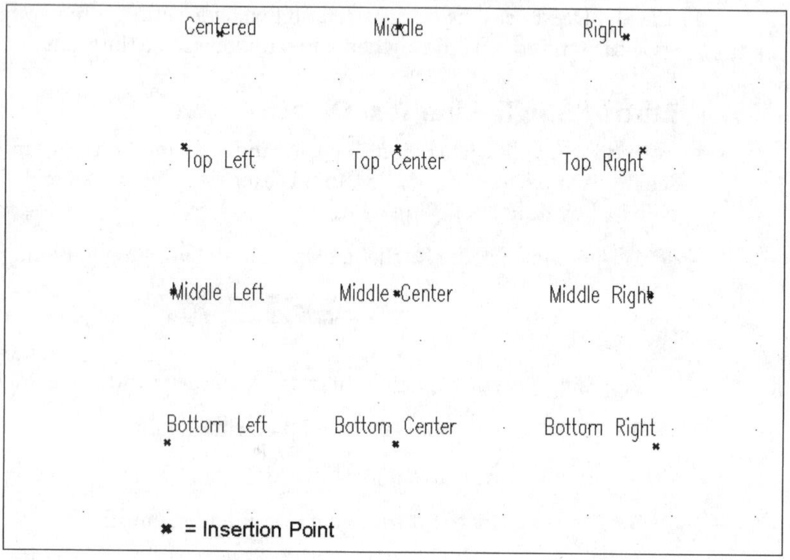

FIGURE 10.13

Text inserted using the various justification options

To set the justification of text as you enter it, you must enter **J↵** at the `Specify start point of text or [Justify/Style]:` prompt after issuing the Dtext command.

TIP You can also change the current default style by entering **S↵** and then the name of the style at the `Specify start point of text or [Justify/Style]:` prompt.

After you've issued the Dtext's Justify option, you get the following prompt:

```
Enter an option
[Align/Fit/Center/Middle/Right/TL/TC/TR/ML/MC/MR/BL/BC/BR]:
```

Here are descriptions of each of these options. (I've left Fit and Align until last, because these options require a bit more explanation.)

Center Centers the text on the start point, with the baseline on the start point.

Middle Centers the text on the start point, with the baseline slightly below the start point.

Right   Justifies the text to the right of the start point, with the baseline on the start point.

TL, TC, and TR   TL, TC, and TR stand for Top Left, Top Center, and Top Right. Text using these justification styles appears entirely below the start point, justified left, center, or right, depending on which option you choose.

ML, MC, and MR   ML, MC, and MR stand for Middle Left, Middle Center, and Middle Right. These styles are similar to TL, TC, and TR, except that the start point determines a location midway between the baseline and the top of the lowercase letters of the text.

BL, BC, and BR   BL, BC, and BR stand for Bottom Left, Bottom Center, and Bottom Right. These styles, too, are similar to TL, TC, and TR, but here the start point determines the bottommost location of the letters of the text (the bottom of letters that have descenders, such as *p*, *q*, and *g*).

Align and Fit   With the Align and Fit justification options, you must specify a dimension within which the text is to fit. For example, suppose you want the word *Refrigerator* to fit within the 26 -wide box representing the refrigerator. You can use either the Fit or the Align option to accomplish this. With Fit, AutoCAD prompts you to select start and end points and then stretches or compresses the letters to fit within the two points you specify. You use this option when the text must be a consistent height throughout the drawing and you don't care about distorting the font. Align works like Fit, but instead of maintaining the current text style height, the Align option adjusts the text height to keep it proportional to the text width, without distorting the font. Use this option when it is important to maintain the font's shape and proportion. Figure 10.14 demonstrates how Fit and Align work.

FIGURE 10.14

The word *Refrigerator* as it appears normally and with the Fit and Align options selected

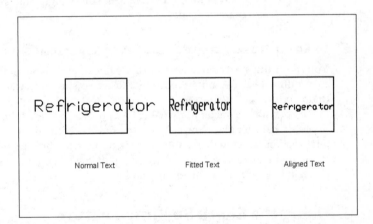

You can change the justification of single-line text by using the Properties palette, but the text will move from its original location while maintaining its insertion point. If you want to change the justification of text without moving the text, you can use the Justifytext command. Choose Modify ➤ Object ➤ Text ➤ Justify or type **Justifytext** at the Command prompt; then select the text you want to change. Justifytext works on both multiline and single-line text.

Using Special Characters with Single-Line Text Objects

Just as with multiline text, you can add a limited set of special characters to single-line text objects. For example, you can place the degree symbol (°) after a number, or you can *underscore* (underline) text. To accomplish this, you use double percent (%%) signs in conjunction with a special code. For example, to underscore text, you enclose that text with %% followed by the letter *u*, which is the underscore code. So, to create this text, "This is underscored text." you enter the following at the prompt:

This is %%uunderscored%%u text.

Overscoring (putting a line above the text) operates in the same manner. To insert codes for symbols, you just place the codes in the correct positions for the symbols they represent. For example, to enter 100.5°, you type **100.5%%d**.

Here is a list of the codes you can use:

Code	What It Does
%%o	Toggles overscore on and off.
%%u	Toggles underscore on and off.
%%d	Places a degree sign (°) where the code occurs.
%%p	Places a plus/minus sign where the code occurs.
%%%	Forces a single percent sign; useful when you want a double percent sign to appear or when you want a percent sign in conjunction with another code.
%%*nnn*	Allows the use of extended characters when these characters are used in a text-definition file; *nnn* is the three-digit value representing the ASCII extended character code.

USING THE CHARACTER MAP DIALOG BOX TO ADD SPECIAL CHARACTERS

You can add special characters to a single line of text in the same way you add special characters to multiline text. You might recall that to access special characters, you use the Character Map dialog box.

To open the Character Map dialog box, choose Start ➢ All Programs ➢ Accessories ➢ System Tools ➢ Character Map. You can then use the procedure discussed in the "Adding Special Characters" section earlier in this chapter to cut and paste a character from the Character Map dialog box. If you find that you use the Character Map dialog box often, create a shortcut for it and place the shortcut in your Start menu or on your Desktop.

Using the Check Spelling Feature

Although AutoCAD is primarily a drawing program, you will find that some of your drawings contain more text than graphics. Autodesk recognizes this and has included a spelling checker since AutoCAD Release 14. If you've ever used the spelling checker in a typical word processor, such as Microsoft Word, the AutoCAD spelling checker's operation will be familiar to you. These steps show you how it works:

1. Choose Tools ➢ Spelling from the drop-down menu or type **Sp**↵.

2. At the Select objects: prompt, select any text object you want to check. You can also enter **All**↵ to select everything in the drawing. AutoCAD will ignore nontext objects. You can

select a mixture of multiline and single-line text. When the spelling checker finds a word it does not recognize, the Check Spelling dialog box opens.

KEEPING TEXT FROM MIRRORING

At times you will want to mirror a group of objects that contain some text. This operation causes the mirrored text to appear backward. You can change a setting in AutoCAD to make the text read normally, even when it is mirrored:

1. At the Command prompt, enter **Mirrtext↵**.

2. At the `Enter new value for MIRRTEXT <1>:` prompt, enter **0↵**.

Now, any mirrored text that is not in a block will read normally. The text's position, however, will still be mirrored, as shown in the following graphic. Mirrtext is set to 0 by default.

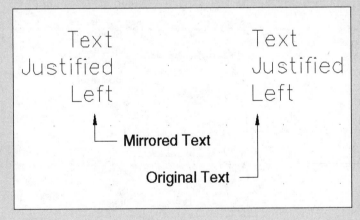

In the Check Spelling dialog box, you'll see the word in question, along with the spelling checker's suggested alternate word in the Suggestions input box. If the spelling checker finds more than one suggestion, a list of suggested alternate words appears below the input box. You can then highlight the desired replacement and click the Change button to change the misspelled word, or you can click Change All to change all occurrences of the word in the selected text. If the suggested word is inappropriate, choose another word from the replacement list (if any), or enter your own spelling in the Suggestions input box. Then choose Change or Change All.

Here is a list of the options available in the Check Spelling dialog box:

Ignore   Skips the word.

Ignore All   Skips all occurrences of the word in the selected text.

Change   Changes the word in question to the word you have selected (or entered) from the Suggestions input box.

Change All   Changes all occurrences of the current word when there are multiple instances of the misspelling.

Add   Adds the word in question to the current dictionary.

Lookup   Checks the spelling of the word in question. This option is for the times when you want to find another word that doesn't appear in the Suggestions input box.

Change Dictionaries   Lets you use a different dictionary to check spelling. This option opens the Change Dictionaries dialog box, described in the upcoming section.

The Check Spelling feature includes types of notation that are more likely to be found in technical drawings. It will also check the spelling of text that is included in block definitions.

Choosing a Dictionary

Clicking the Change Dictionaries button in the Check Spelling dialog box opens the Change Dictionaries dialog box, where you can select a particular main dictionary for foreign languages or create or choose a custom dictionary. Main dictionary files have the .dct extension. The main dictionary for the U.S. version of AutoCAD is Enu.dct.

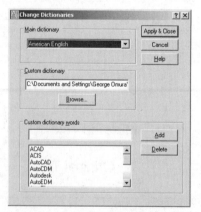

In the Change Dictionaries dialog box, you can also add or delete words from a custom dictionary. Custom dictionary files are ASCII files with the .cus extension. Because they are ASCII files, you can edit them outside AutoCAD. Click the Browse button to view a list of existing custom dictionaries.

If you prefer, you can also select a main or custom dictionary by using the Dctmain system variables. See Appendix C for more on Dctmain.

You can also select a dictionary from the Files tab of the Options dialog box (choose Tools ➤ Options). You can find the dictionary listing under Text Editor, Dictionary, And Font File Names. Click the plus sign next to this listing, and then click the plus sign next to the Main Dictionary listing to display the dictionary options.

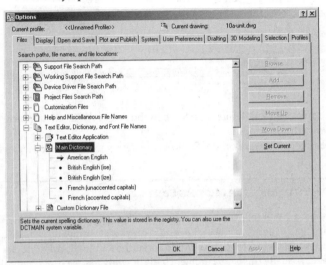

From here, you can double-click the dictionary you prefer.

Substituting Fonts

At times you'll want to change all the fonts in a drawing quickly. For instance, you might want to convert TrueType fonts into a simple Txt.shx font to help shorten redraw times while you are editing. Or you might need to convert the font of a drawing received from another office to a font that conforms to your own office standards. The Fontmap system variable works in conjunction with a font-mapping table, enabling you to easily substitute fonts in a drawing.

The font-mapping table is an ASCII file called Acad.fmp. You can also use a file you create yourself. You can give this file any name you choose, as long as it has the .fmp extension.

This font-mapping table contains one line for each font substitution you want AutoCAD to make. A typical line in this file would read as follows:

```
romant; C:\Program Files\Acad 2007\Fonts\txt.shx
```

In this example, AutoCAD is directed to use the txt.shx font in place of the romant.shx font. To execute this substitution, you type **Fontmap** *Fontmap_filename*.

Fontmap_filename is the font-mapping table you've created. This tells AutoCAD where to look for the font-mapping information. Then you issue the Regen command to view the font changes. To disable the font-mapping table, you type

Fontmap⏎ .⏎.

You can also specify a font-mapping file in the Files tab of the Options dialog box. Look for the Text Editor, Dictionary, And Font File Names listing. Click the plus sign next to this listing, and then click the plus sign next to the Font Mapping File listing to display the current default font-mapping filename. If you hold the cursor over the name, AutoCAD displays the full location of the file.

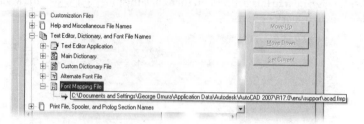

You can double-click this filename to open the Select A File dialog box. From there, you can select a different font-mapping file.

See Appendix C for more on the Fontmap system variable and other system variables.

MAKING SUBSTITUTIONS FOR MISSING FONTS

When text styles are created, the associated fonts do not become part of the drawing file. Instead, AutoCAD loads the needed font file at the same time that the drawing is loaded. So if a text style in a drawing requires a particular font, AutoCAD looks for the font in the AutoCAD search path; if the font is there, it is loaded. Usually this isn't a problem if the drawing file uses the standard fonts that come with AutoCAD or Windows. But occasionally you will encounter a file that uses a custom font.

In earlier versions of AutoCAD, you saw an error message when you attempted to open such a file. This missing-font message would often send the new AutoCAD user into a panic.

Fortunately, AutoCAD automatically substitutes an existing font for the missing font in a drawing. By default, AutoCAD substitutes the simplex.shx font, but you can specify another font by using the Fontalt system variable. Type **Fontalt.⏎** at the Command prompt and then enter the name of the font you want to use as the substitute.

You can also select an alternate font through the Files tab of the Options dialog box. Locate the Text Editor, Dictionary, And Font File Names listing, and then click the plus sign at the left. Locate the Alternate Font File listing and click the plus sign at the left. The current alternate is listed. You can double-click the font name to select a different font through a standard file dialog box.

Be aware that the text in your drawing will change in appearance, sometimes radically, when you use a substitute font. If the text in the drawing must retain its appearance, substitute a font that is as similar in appearance to the original font as possible.

Finding and Replacing Text

One of the most time-consuming tasks in drafting is replacing text that appears repeatedly throughout a drawing. Fortunately, you have a Find And Replace tool to help make this task a simple one. AutoCAD's Find And Replace works like any other find-and-replace tool in a word processing program. There are a few options that work specifically with AutoCAD. Here's how it works:

1. Choose Edit ➤ Find from the menu bar or enter **Find.⏎** at the Command prompt to open the Find And Replace dialog box.

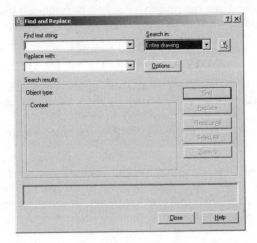

2. Enter the text you want to locate in the Find Text String input box.

3. Enter the replacement text in the Replace With input box.

4. Click Find. When AutoCAD finds the word, it appears in the Context window, along with any other text next to the word.

5. If you have any doubts, click the Zoom To button to display the text in the AutoCAD drawing area.

6. Finally, when you've made certain that this is the text you want to change, click Replace.

If you want to replace all occurrences of a word in the drawing, click Replace All. You can also limit your find-and-replace operation to a specific area of your drawing by clicking the Select Objects button in the upper-right corner of the Find And Replace dialog box.

When you click the Select Objects button, the Find And Replace dialog box closes temporarily to enable you to select a set of objects or a region of your drawing. Find And Replace will then limit its search to those objects or the region you select.

You can further control the types of objects that Find And Replace looks for by clicking the Options button to open the Find And Replace Options dialog box.

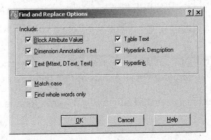

With this dialog box, you can refine your search by limiting it to blocks, dimension text, standard text, or hyperlink text. You can also specify whether to match case or find whole words only.

Accelerating Zooms and Regens with Qtext

If you need to edit a drawing that contains a lot of text, but you don't need to edit the text, you can use the Qtext command to help accelerate redraws and regenerations when you are working on the drawing. Qtext turns lines of text into rectangular boxes, saving AutoCAD from having to form every letter. This enables you to see the note locations so you don't accidentally draw over them.

TIP Selecting a large set of text objects for editing can be annoyingly slow. To improve the speed of text selection (and object selection in general), turn off the Highlight and Dragmode system variables. This disables certain convenience features but can improve overall performance, especially on large drawings. See Appendix C for more information on these system variables.

MANIPULATING TEXT BEYOND LABELS

This chapter concentrates on methods for adding labels to your drawing, but you also use text in other ways with AutoCAD. Many of the inquiry tools in AutoCAD, such as Dist and List, produce text data. You can use the Windows Clipboard to manipulate such data to your benefit.

For example, you can duplicate the exact length of a line by first using the List command to get a listing of its properties. After you have the property list in the AutoCAD Text window, you can highlight its length listing and then press Ctrl+C to copy it to the Windows Clipboard. Next, you can start the Line command and then pick the start point for the new line. Click the Command window and press Ctrl+V to paste the line-length data into the Command window; then add the angle data or use the Direct Distance method to draw the line.

You can copy any text data from dialog box input boxes or from the AutoCAD Text window to the Clipboard by using the Ctrl+C keyboard shortcut. You can likewise import that data into any part of AutoCAD that accepts text.

Consider using the Clipboard the next time you need to transfer data within AutoCAD or even when you need to import text from some other application.

The following steps tell you how to turn on Qtext:

1. Enter **Qtext**↵ at the Command prompt.

2. At the ON/OFF <OFF>: prompt, enter **ON**↵.

3. To display the results of Qtext, issue the Regen command from the prompt.

TIP You can also open the Options dialog box (choose Tools ➢ Options), click the Display tab, and then click the Show Text Boundary Frame Only option to display text as rectangular regions.

When Qtext is off, text is generated normally. When Qtext is on, rectangles show the approximate size and length of text.

If You Want to Experiment

At this point, you might want to try adding some notes to drawings you have created in other "If You Want to Experiment " sections of this book. Also, try the exercise shown in Figure 10.15. In addition, you might try importing a finish or door schedule from a word processor and practice using the AutoCAD tab settings. If your application is mechanical, you might try importing a parts list.

FIGURE 10.15
The sample mechanical drawing with notes added

1. Open the file called PART1 that you created in the last chapter. Using the Style command, create a style called Notes. Use the Romans font and give the style a height of .12 units and a width factor of .8.

2. Add the notes shown in this figure using the Dtext command. Place the notes approximately as shown.

3. When you've finished typing the note, press ↵ three times, then pick the point shown in this figure. Notice that the Dtext cursor moves to the point you pick. Press ↵ twice to continue.

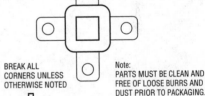

Pick this point.

4. Continue to add this second note to your drawing. Press return twice at the end of the last line to exit the Dtext command.

Note:
PARTS MUST BE CLEAN AND
FREE OF LOOSE BURRS AND
DUST PRIOR TO PACKAGING.

Note:
PARTS MUST BE CLEAN AND
FREE OF LOOSE BURRS AND
DUST PRIOR TO PACKAGING.

BREAK ALL
CORNERS UNLESS
OTHERWISE NOTED

Note:
PARTS MUST BE CLEAN AND
FREE OF LOOSE BURRS AND
DUST PRIOR TO PACKAGING.

Chapter 11

Using Fields and Tables

Adding text to a set of drawings can become a large part of your work. You'll find that you are edit-ing notes and labels almost as frequently as you are editing the graphics in your drawings. To make some of those editing tasks easier, AutoCAD provides a few special text objects.

In this chapter, you'll look at Fields and Tables, two features that can help automate some of the more common tasks in AutoCAD. Fields are a special type of text that can automatically update to reflect changes in the drawing. Tables are a tool that helps to automate the process of creating and editing tables and schedules. Tables are a common part of technical drawings and are similar to spreadsheets. In fact, AutoCAD Tables behaves much like a spreadsheet with the capability of add-ing formulas to cells.

You'll start this chapter with an introduction to Fields and then go on to learn about Tables. Toward the end, you'll revisit Fields to see how they can be used to add formulas to tables.

- ◆ Using Fields to Associate Text with Drawing Properties
- ◆ Adding Tables to Your Drawing
- ◆ Editing the Table Line Work
- ◆ Adding Formulas to Cells
- ◆ Importing and Exporting Tables
- ◆ Creating Table Styles

Using Fields to Associate Text with Drawing Properties

The text labels you worked with in Chapter 10 are static and do not change unless you edit them by using the tools described there. Another type of text object, called a field, behaves in a more dynamic way than the multiline text. A field can be linked to the properties of other objects and will update itself automatically as the associated properties change. For example, you can create a field that is associated with a block name. If the block name changes, the field text automatically changes as well.

Try the following exercise to see how this works:

1. Open the 11c-unit.dwg file from the companion CD. This file is similar to the drawing you worked on in Chapter 10.

2. Double-click the Kitchen text to highlight it and make it available for editing.

3. Right-click the highlighted Kitchen text and then choose Insert Field to open the Field dialog box. You see a list to the left that shows the types of fields available.

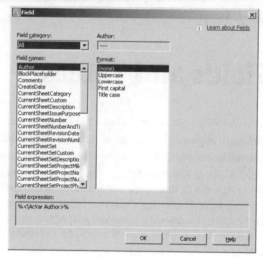

4. In the Field Category drop-down list, select Objects. This limits the display of field types to object fields.

5. In the Field Names list, select NamedObject.

6. Make sure that Block is selected in the Named Object Type drop-down list in the top of the dialog box; then select Kitchen. This associates the field with the Kitchen block name.

7. In the Format list to the far right, select First Capital. This causes the field text to be lowercase with a capital first letter, regardless of how the block name is actually spelled.

8. Click OK to exit the Field dialog box; then press ↵ twice to return to the Command prompt.

When you return to the drawing, you will see that the text appears in a gray background. This tells you that the text is a field rather than an Mtext or a Dtext object. The gray background is just a device to help you keep track of field text and will not plot.

You've converted existing text into a field that is linked to a block name. Now let's see how the field works:

1. Enter **Rename.↵** at the Command prompt to open the Rename dialog box.

2. Make sure Blocks is selected in the Named Objects list; then select Kitchen from the Items list. The word *Kitchen* appears in the Old Name input box near the bottom of the dialog box.

3. Enter **Kitchenette** in the input box just below the Old Name box; then click the Rename To button.

4. Click OK to close the Rename dialog box.

5. Choose View ➢ Regen. The field you created changes to reflect the new block name.

Fields can be associated with a wide variety of properties. You've just seen how a block name can be associated with a field. In this exercise, you'll use a field to display the area of an object:

1. Choose View ➤ Zoom ➤ Extents to view the entire plan.

2. Place a rectangle in the living room area so that it fills the area.

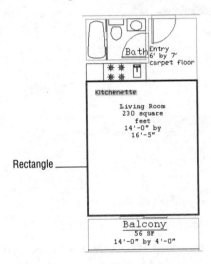

3. Double-click the Living Room text to open the Text Formatting toolbar.

4. Highlight the text that reads *230 square feet*, and then right-click the selected text and choose Insert Field from the shortcut menu.

5. In the Field dialog box, select Object from the Field Names list.

6. Click the Select Object button next to the Object Type input box at the top of the Field dialog box. The Field dialog box momentarily closes to enable you to select an object.

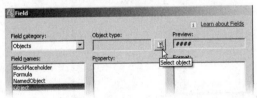

7. Select the rectangle you just added. The Field dialog box returns.

8. In the Property list just below the Object Type input box, select Area.

9. Select Architectural from the Format list to the far right.

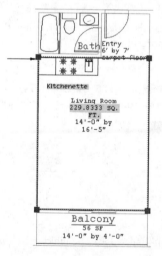

10. Click OK. The field you just added appears in the drawing as the area of the rectangle.

Next you'll alter the rectangle to see how it affects the field:

1. Click the rectangle to expose its grips. Then select the top two grips and move them upward so that they align with the bathroom wall. Remember to Shift+click to select multiple grips.

2. Choose View ➢ Regen. The field you just added updates to reflect the new area of the rectangle.

3. After reviewing the results, close 11c-unit.dwg.

TIP In previous exercises in this section, you changed existing text into fields. You can create new fields in either the Dtext or Mtext command by selecting Insert Field from the shortcut menu whenever you are typing the text content.

In this exercise, you used a rectangle, but you can use any closed polygon to create an area field. You've touched on just two of the many possible uses for fields. You can associate other types of properties including current layer, drawing name, linetypes, and more. You can include Diesel macros as part of fields. (You'll learn about Diesel macros in Chapter 26.) Fields can also be used in AutoCAD's Table feature, described in the next section, which enables you to quickly create tables and schedules. Fields are used to coordinate sheet labels with reference symbols in the AutoCAD Sheet Set feature described in Chapter 28.

For most of your work, the standard text objects will work just fine, but you might find fields useful when you know a label has to be associated with specific types of data in your drawing. In later chapters, you'll have more opportunities to work with fields.

Adding Tables to Your Drawing

One of the more common text-related tasks you'll do for your drawings is to create schedules, such as door and window schedules or parts schedules. Such schedules are tables used to provide more detailed information regarding the elements in your design.

In the past, AutoCAD users would use Mtext or Dtext to create the text for schedules and then use line-drawing tools to create the "cells" of the schedule. Since AutoCAD 2006 you can use Tables to help you generate schedules more quickly. Tables allow you to automatically format the columns and rows of text in a way similar to spreadsheet programs.

Creating a Table

The first step in creating a table is to determine the number of rows and columns you'll want. Don't worry if you are not certain of the exact number of rows and columns; you can always add or subtract them at any time. In this exercise, you'll create a table that contains 12 rows and 9 columns, as shown in Figure 11.1.

Start by creating the basic table layout:

1. Choose File New and use the standard Acad.dwt drawing template.

FIGURE 11.1
A sample table created with the Table tool

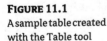

No.	Room	Finish				Ceiling Ht.	Area	Remarks
		Floor	Base	Walls	Ceiling			
110	Lobby	B	1	A	1	10'-0"	200sf	
111	Office	A	1	B	2	8'-0"	96sf	
112	Office	A	1	B	2	8'-0"	96sf	
113	Office	A	1	B	2	8'-0"	96sf	
114	Meeting	C	1	B	2	8'-0"	150sf	
115	Breakout	C	1	B	2	8'-0"	150sf	
116	Womens	D	2	C	3	8'-0"	50sf	
117	Mens	D	2	C	3	8'-0"	50sf	

Room Finish Schedule

2. Click Table from the Draw toolbar, or choose Draw ➢ Table from the menu bar to open the Insert Table dialog box.

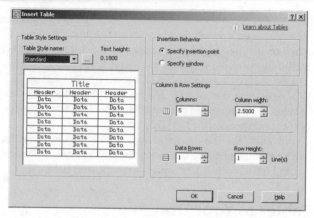

3. In the Column & Row Settings group, enter **9** for Columns and **12** for Column Rows.

4. Click OK. The dialog box closes, and you see the outline of a table follow your cursor.

5. Position the table in the center of your drawing area and click to place the table. The table appears with a cursor in the top cell of the table. You also see the Text Formatting toolbar above the table.

6. Enter **Room Finish Schedule** and press ↵. Notice that the cursor moves to the next cell.

7. Click OK to exit the Text Formatting toolbar.

Adding Cell Text

You've just created a table and added a title. Notice that the table actually contains 14 rows, including the title row at the top and an additional row for the headings of each column. You can delete these additional rows if you don't need them, but for now, you'll start to add some text to the table:

1. Adjust your view so that the table fills most of the drawing area.

2. Double-click in the first cell at the top left, just below the Room Finish Schedule label. The cell turns gray, and the Text Formatting toolbar opens. You also see labels across the top and left side showing the row and column addresses.

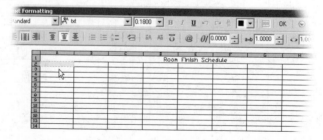

3. Enter **Number** for the room number column at the far left, and then press the Tab key to advance to the next cell to the right.

4. Enter **Room** and press the Tab key again.

5. Enter **Finish** and press the Tab key four times to advance four columns. You do this because the Finish heading shown in Figure 11.1 has four columns under it: Floor, Base, Walls, and Ceiling. In the next exercise, you'll learn how to format those four columns under the single heading.

6. Enter **Ceiling Ht.** and press the Tab key again.

7. Enter **Area**, press the Tab key, and enter **Remarks**.

8. Click OK in the Text Formatting toolbar to close it.

You have the column headings in place. Now you need to do a little extra formatting. In step 5, you left four cells blank because four of the columns will be combined under one heading. The Finish heading covers the Floor, Base, Walls, and Ceiling columns. Next you'll combine the blank headings with the Finish heading:

1. Click in the center of the cell with the Finish label to select it.

2. Shift+click in the third cell to the right of the Finish cell to select all four cells.

3. Right-click in the selected cells and choose Merge Cells ➤ All. The four selected cells merge into a single cell with the word *Finish*.

Now you need to add the subheads under the Finish header:

1. Double-click in the leftmost cell below the Finish cell to open the Text Formatting toolbar.

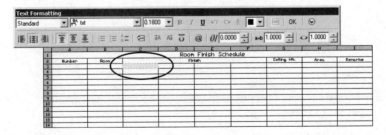

2. Enter **Floor** and press the Tab key.

3. Enter **Base**, **Wall**, and **Ceiling** in each of the following columns as you have been doing. Remember that the Tab key advances you to the next cell to the right. Your table should look like Figure 11.2.

FIGURE 11.2

The table so far

			Room Finish Schedule					
Number	Room		Finish			Ceiling Ht.	Area	Remarks
		Floor	Base	Wall	Ceiling			

4. Click OK in the Text Formatting toolbar to close it.

Adjusting Table Text Orientation and Location

You now have the basic layout of the table, with one difference. The Floor, Base, Walls, and Ceiling labels you've just added are oriented horizontally, but you want them oriented vertically, as in Figure 11.1. The following steps will show you how to rotate a set of labels in a table so that they appear in the orientation you want:

1. Click in the cell labeled Floor to select it.

2. Shift+click in the cell labeled Ceiling to select all four of the cells below the Finish heading. Notice that the combined cells have four grips, one on each side of the group.

Number	Room		Finish			Ceiling Ht.	Area	Remarks
		Floor	Base	Wall	Ceiling			

3. Click the grip at the bottom of the selected group and move it down about four rows. The entire row will become taller. This provides room for the text when you rotate it.

4. Right-click in the selected cells and choose Properties from the shortcut menu to open the Properties palette.

5. In the Properties palette, click the Text Rotation option under the Content group.

6. Click the drop-down list just to the right of the Text Rotation option and select 90. The text rotates into a vertical orientation.

With the text in this orientation, the columns are too wide, so you will want to change the cell width for the selected cells.

7. Move the right grip to the left to decrease the width of the cells.

Number	Room		Ceiling Ht.	Area	Remarks

8. For the final touch, you'll want to center the text in the cells. With the cells still selected, right-click in the selected cells and choose Cell Alignment ➤ Middle Left. The text becomes centered in the cells.

TIP You can also control the margin between the text and the cell border by using the Cell Margin options in the Properties palette. Select the entire table, right-click, and choose Properties. In the Properties palette, click the Vertical Cell Margin option or the Horizontal Cell Margin option in the Table group.

In this last exercise, you learned how you can adjust the text orientation and cell width through the Properties palette. You can also adjust the width of multiple cells by adjusting the grip location. For example, instead of changing the cell width value in step 7, you can move the left or right grip of the selected group of cells.

Now continue to add text to the cells and adjust their sizes:

1. Double-click in the cell in the Number column just below the row that contains the Floor, Base, Walls, and Ceiling cells. A text cursor appears in the cell, and the Text Formatting toolbar opens.

2. Enter **110** and press ↵. Notice that instead of advancing to the next cell to the right, you advance to the next cell below.

3. Enter **111** and press ↵ again. Continue to enter each room number in this way. When you've finished entering the room numbers, click OK in the Text Formatting toolbar to close it.

Now you'll want to reduce the width of the column to fit the text a bit better.

4. Click in the cell with the Number text label. It's the first column heading in the table.

5. Shift+click in the bottom cell of the Number column to select the entire column.

6. Click the grip to the left of the column and move the grip to the right so the column width is approximately half the width of the Room column. You can zoom in on the column to allow more control over the positioning of the grip.

7. Press Esc to exit the selection and view your table so far.

						Room Finish Schedule			
Number	Room	Finish				Ceiling Ht.	Area	Remarks	
		Floor	Base	Wall	Ceiling				
110									
111									
112									
113									
114									
115									
116									
117									

Now suppose you want to delete one of the extra rows of cells at the bottom of the table or to add a new row. Here's what to do:

1. Click the bottom left cell of the table to select it.

2. Right-click and choose Delete Rows from the shortcut menu. The row disappears.

3. To add a row: select a cell, right-click, and choose Insert Rows ➤ Above or Insert Rows ➤ Below depending on where you want the new row.

You might notice the Delete Columns and Insert Columns options in the shortcut menu that let you add or delete columns. These options function in a similar way to the Delete Rows and Insert Rows options.

Editing the Table Line Work

So far you've concentrated on how you can format text and cells in a table, but you'll also want some control over the lines in the table. Typically, heavier lines are used around the border of the table and between the title and the rest of the table.

The Cell Borders shortcut menu option lets you modify the outline of the border. When you select this option, the Cell Border Properties dialog box opens.

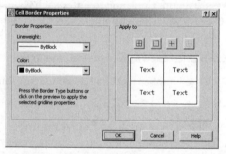

You can use this dialog box to fine-tune the appearance of the line work of the table. Try the following exercise to see firsthand how this dialog box works:

1. Turn on the display of line weights by choosing Format ➤ Lineweight.

2. In the Lineweight Settings dialog box, turn on the Display Lineweight setting; then click OK.

3. Click in the title cell at the very top of the table to select the cell, and then right-click and choose Cell Borders to open the Cell Border Properties dialog box.

4. Click the Lineweight drop-down list and select 0.30 mm.

5. Click the Outside Borders button in the Apply To group to tell AutoCAD to change the borders of the cell to the selected line weight.

6. Click OK. The title cell is now outlined in a heavier line.

You can also adjust the line weights that encircle a group of cells, as in the following exercise:

1. Click the cell in the upper-left corner with the Number label.

2. Shift+click the cell in the lower-right corner of the table so that all the cells from the second-from-the-top row down are selected.

3. Right-click and choose Cell Borders.

4. Select 0.30 mm from the Lineweight drop-down list again. Then click the Outside Borders button again as you did in step 5 of the previous exercise.

5. Click OK. The outline of the selected cells are given the new line weight setting.

6. Save this file for future reference.

Room Finish Schedule							
Number	Room	Finish				Ceiling Ht.	Area	Remarks
		Floor	Base	Wall	Ceiling			
110								
111								
112								
113								
114								
115								
116								
117								

TIP   In addition to the table borders, you can change the background color for the cells of the table through the Background Fill option in the Properties palette. Select a group of cells in the table that you want to affect (but don't select the entire table), right-click, and choose Properties. In the Properties palette, click the Background Fill option in the Cell group.

The Cell Border Properties dialog box also lets you set the line colors by selecting a color from the Color drop-down list before selecting an Apply To option.

In addition, the Apply To group offers four buttons: All Borders, Outside Borders (which you've already tried), Inside Borders, and No Borders. The All Borders option applies the changes to all borders. The Inside borders option applies the changes to just the inside borders. This option works only if you have selected multiple cells. The No Borders option lets you clear your border selections if you change your mind.

If you want to select only the vertical or horizontal inside borders, you can use the graphic in the Cell Border Properties dialog box to select either the vertical or horizontal inside border. You can also use the graphic to select individual sides of the outside border by clicking the sample border in the graphic. The sample will change to show you which border lines are affected.

Adding Formulas to Cells

In the beginning of this chapter, I mentioned that you can include formulas in cells of AutoCAD tables. This can be a great timesaver since you can set up a table with quantities that automatically adjust to changes in values within the table. You don't have to manually calculate the changes.

You may recall that formulas are actually a type of field and that a field can be linked with objects in a drawing so that the field displays the linked object's properties. The formula field can be linked to several numeric text values. The following example introduces you to the formula field and its use in tables. You'll see firsthand how a cell formula can display the sum of two other cells.

You'll start by opening a sample drawing file that already contains a table, and then you'll add a formula field to a blank cell.

1. Open the `FieldSample.dwg` from the sample files of the companion CD.

2. Double-click in the cell, as shown in Figure 11.3, to select the location for your formula.

3. Right-click the selected cell, and then choose Insert Field. You can also click the Insert Field tool in the Text Formatting toolbar. The Field dialog box opens.

FIGURE 11.3
Selecting the cell for your formula

Double-click this cell.

4. Select Objects from the Field Category drop down list in the upper left of the Field dialog box.

5. Select Formula in the Field Names list to the left. The next step is to build the formula to add the value of some of the cells.

6. Click the Cell button. The dialog box temporarily closes to allow you to select a cell.

7. Click the cell in the upper-left corner of the table, as shown in Figure 11.4. The Field dialog box reappears, and the cell's address appears in the Formula box near the bottom of the dialog box.

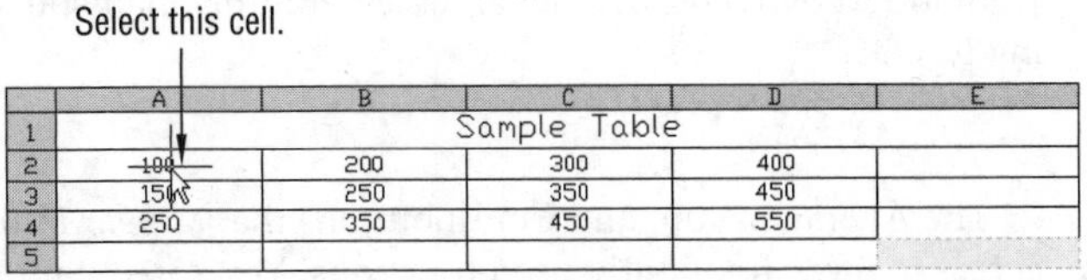

FIGURE 11.4

Selecting a cell to include in the formula

Select this cell.

	A	B	C	D	E
1			Sample Table		
2	100	200	300	400	
3	15	250	350	450	
4	250	350	450	550	
5					

In typical spreadsheet form, the cell address is an alphanumeric value with the column given as a letter and the row given as a number. A cell address of D4 is a cell in column D in row number 4, for example (see Figure 11.5).

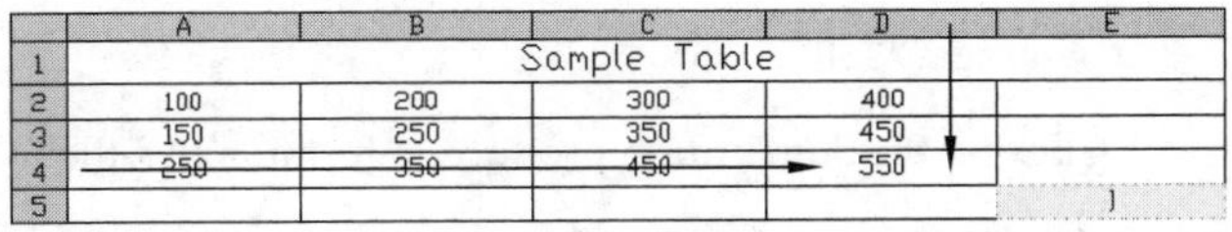

FIGURE 11.5

The value of 550 can be found in the cell in column D row 4, which is designated as D4.

	A	B	C	D	E
1			Sample Table		
2	100	200	300	400	
3	150	250	350	450	
4	250	350	450	550	
5					

1. Type + (plus sign) to add the value of the selected cell to the value of another cell. As you type, the plus sign appears in the Formula text box.

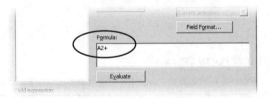

2. Click the Cell button again, and then click cell D4, the one with the value of 550. The address of the cell you select appears in the Formula box behind the plus sign you added in the previous step.

3. Click OK. The sum of the two cells appears in the cell you selected in step 1.

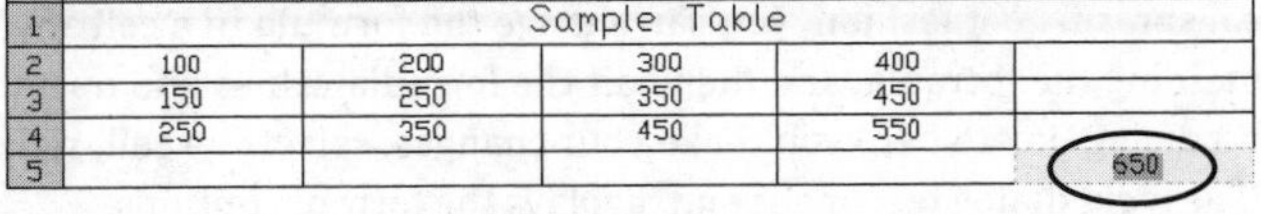

	A	B	C	D	E
1			Sample Table		
2	100	200	300	400	
3	150	250	350	450	
4	250	350	450	550	
5					650

4. Try changing the value in cell D4. The formula cell changes to reflect the new value.

Using Other Math Operations

In the previous exercise, the plus sign is used to add the value of two cells. You can string several cells addresses together to add multiple cells as in

    A2+A3+A4...

You can also subtract, multiply, or divide by using the – (subtract or minus), * (multiply or asterisk), or / (divide or hash) signs. To perform multiple operations on several cells, you can group operations with parentheses in a way similar to a typical spreadsheet formula. For example, if you want to add two cells together and then multiply their sum by another cell, you can use the following format:

    (A2+A3)*A4

The Average, Sum, and Count buttons that appear in the Field dialog box give you quick access to these frequently used functions. You can obtain the average value of a set of cells, quickly get the sum of a set of cells, or just get a count of the number of cells you select. When you click one of these buttons, the Field dialog box temporarily closes, allowing you to select several cells with a selection window. Once you've selected a set of cells, you'll see the appropriate formula in the Formula box. Clicking the Average button for example, produces a formula similar to the following:

    Average(A1:B5)

Clicking the Sum button produces a formula like the following:

    Sum(A1:B5)

In both cases, a range of cells is indicated using a colon as in A1:B5. You can use this format when entering formulas manually. You can also include a single cell with a range by using a comma as in

    Sum(A1:B5,C6)

USING FORMULAS DIRECTLY IN CELLS

You can also add a formula directly to a cell without using the Field dialog box. Double-click the cell, and then when the Text Formatting toolbar appears, enter the formula directly in the cell with the addition of an = (equal sign) at the beginning, as in the following:

    =A2+A3

The equal sign tells AutoCAD to convert the text into a formula field. When you start to edit a cell in a table, you'll see the row and column labels appear along the top and left side of the table. You can use these labels to determine the cell addresses for your formula.

TIP   In typical spreadsheet fashion, you can change the formula in a cell any time. Double-click the cell containing the formula, and then edit the formula values and operators. If you want to use the Field dialog box to help you make your changes, select the cell, right-click, and choose Edit Field. The Field dialog box opens and displays the formula options.

Importing and Exporting Tables

Frequently, tables will be created outside AutoCAD in a spreadsheet program such as Excel. You can import an Excel worksheet as an AutoCAD table by using the AutoCAD Entities option in the Paste Special feature. The ability to import tables lets other non-AutoCAD users create the table data while you concentrate on the drawing.

Try the following exercise to see how a table can be imported from a worksheet:

1. Open the Excel worksheet called `11a-plan.xls` from the companion CD and highlight the door data, as shown in Figure 11.6.
2. Choose Edit ➤ Copy to place a copy of the selected data into the Windows Clipboard; then switch back to AutoCAD.
3. Choose Edit ➤ Paste Special to open the Paste Special dialog box.
4. With the Paste radio button selected, click AutoCAD Entities from the list and then click OK.
5. At the `Specify insertion point or [paste as Text]:` prompt, click a point in the lower-right area of the drawing. The worksheet data appears in the drawing, though it is very small. You also see the Text Formatting toolbar.
6. Click OK in the Text Formatting toolbar to close it.
7. If needed, use the Scale tool to enlarge the table to a readable size.

In this exercise, the worksheet was imported by using the default standard table style. This gives you a simple-looking table using the AutoCAD Txt font. You can set up a custom table style, as described later in this chapter, with the fonts and borders you want and then import the table for a more custom appearance. Make sure your custom table style is the current style before you import the worksheet.

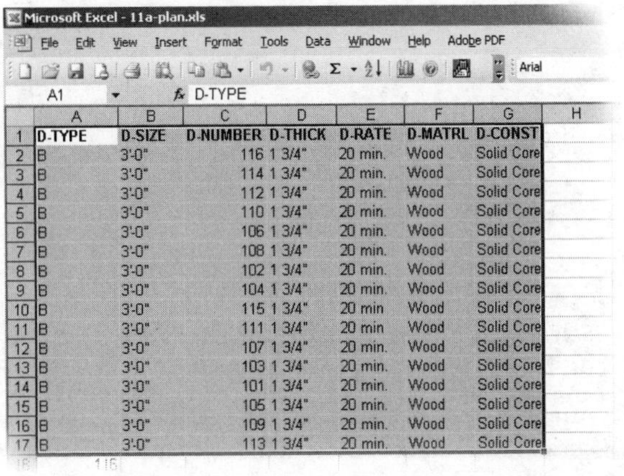

	A	B	C	D	E	F	G
1	D-TYPE	D-SIZE	D-NUMBER	D-THICK	D-RATE	D-MATRL	D-CONST
2	B	3'-0"	116	1 3/4"	20 min.	Wood	Solid Core
3	B	3'-0"	114	1 3/4"	20 min.	Wood	Solid Core
4	B	3'-0"	112	1 3/4"	20 min.	Wood	Solid Core
5	B	3'-0"	110	1 3/4"	20 min.	Wood	Solid Core
6	B	3'-0"	106	1 3/4"	20 min.	Wood	Solid Core
7	B	3'-0"	108	1 3/4"	20 min.	Wood	Solid Core
8	B	3'-0"	102	1 3/4"	20 min.	Wood	Solid Core
9	B	3'-0"	104	1 3/4"	20 min.	Wood	Solid Core
10	B	3'-0"	115	1 3/4"	20 min	Wood	Solid Core
11	B	3'-0"	111	1 3/4"	20 min	Wood	Solid Core
12	B	3'-0"	107	1 3/4"	20 min.	Wood	Solid Core
13	B	3'-0"	103	1 3/4"	20 min.	Wood	Solid Core
14	B	3'-0"	101	1 3/4"	20 min.	Wood	Solid Core
15	B	3'-0"	105	1 3/4"	20 min.	Wood	Solid Core
16	B	3'-0"	109	1 3/4"	20 min.	Wood	Solid Core
17	B	3'-0"	113	1 3/4"	20 min.	Wood	Solid Core

FIGURE 11.6
Selecting the door data in the `11a-plan.xls` spreadsheet.

Exporting Tables

You might some day want to export your AutoCAD table to a spreadsheet program or database. You can do this through a somewhat hidden option in a shortcut menu. Take the following steps:

1. Select the entire table. You can do so by clicking in a spot above and to the right of the table. With the crossing selection window, completely enclose the table and click.

2. Right-click anywhere in the table and choose Export from the shortcut menu to open the Export Data dialog box.

3. Specify a name and location for your exported table data and click Save.

Notice that the file is saved with a .csv filename extension. This type of file is a comma-delimited file and can be read by most spreadsheet programs, including Microsoft Excel. Unfortunately, the .csv file does not retain the AutoCAD table formatting.

To open the exported file from Excel, choose File ➢ Open in the Excel menu bar, and then in the Open dialog box, select Text File (*.prn, *.txt, *.csv) in the Files Of Type drop-down list. You can then locate the exported table and open it.

ADDING GRAPHICS TO TABLE CELLS

One of the more interesting features of the Table tool is its ability to include blocks in a cell. This can be useful if you want to include graphic elements in your table. Adding a block to a cell is a simple process. Here are the steps:

1. Click in a cell to select it.

2. Right-click and choose Insert Block from the shortcut menu to open the Insert A Block In A Table Cell dialog box.

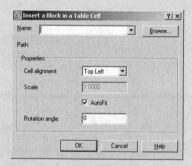

3. Select a block name from the Name drop-down list. You can also click the button to the right of the list to open a file dialog box that enables you to select a drawing file for import to the cell.

4. After you've selected a block and specified the settings in the Properties group of the dialog box, click OK. The block appears in the cell you've selected.

The Properties group in the dialog box enables you to specify the alignment and size of the inserted block. By default, the AutoFit option is turned on. This option adjusts the size of the block to make it fit in the current cell size.

Creating Table Styles

If you find that you are creating the same table layout over and over, you can set up predefined table styles. You can set up the properties of the title, column headings, and data in advance so you don't have to set them up each time you create a table. For example, if you prefer to use Arial bold at 0.25″ for the title and standard Arial at 0.125″ for the column headings, you can create a table style with those settings. The next time you need to create a table, you can select your custom table style and specify the number of columns and rows; then you'll be ready to add the data without having to format the text.

To create a table style, take the following steps:

1. Choose Format ➢ Table Style from the menu bar to open the Table Style dialog box. You see the Standard table style in the list box. This is the one you used in the previous exercises.

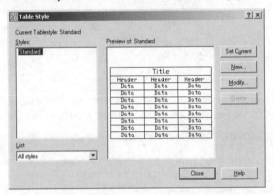

2. Click the New button to open the Create New Table Style dialog box. This is where you give your new table style a name.

3. Enter **My Table Style** and click Continue to open the New Table Style dialog box (see Figure 11.7).

4. Click the Column Heads tab and then click the Title tab at the top of the dialog box. Notice that options for these tabs are nearly identical to those for the Data tab.

5. You'll learn more about the options in this dialog box next. For now, click OK to close the dialog box.

6. Notice that your new table style now appears in the Styles list of the Table Style dialog box. If you want to edit an existing table style, you can select the style from the list and click the Modify button. The Modify Table Style dialog box will appear, enabling you to edit the existing style. The Modify Table Style dialog box is identical to the New Table Style dialog box shown in Figure 11.7.

7. Click Close to exit the dialog box.

FIGURE 11.7

The New Table Style dialog box

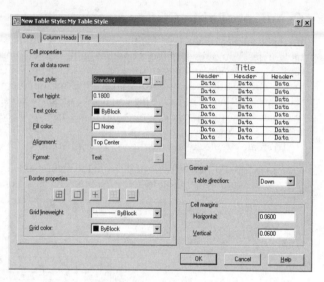

After you've created a style, you can select it from the Table Style Settings group of the Insert Table dialog box that you used to create the sample table (choose Draw ➢ Table).

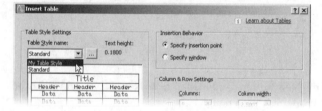

You can also open the New Table Style dialog box by clicking the Table Style Dialog button just to the right of the Table Style Name drop-down list in the Insert Table dialog box.

The Table Style Options

Let's take a closer look at the New Table Style dialog box in Figure 11.7. You saw in step 4 of the previous exercise that each of the three tabs at the top of the dialog box contains the same set of options. This enables you to specify the text-formatting options for these three table elements: Data, Column Heads, and Title. You also have the option to turn off the header row or the title row. As you make setting changes, the graphic to the right will show you how your changes affect your table style.

The dialog box includes these groups:

Cell Properties   The Cell Properties group lets you format the text of the table. You can choose the text style, height, color, alignment and cell format. A text style can be selected from the Text Style drop-down list, or you can click the button to the right of the drop-down list to open the Text Style dialog box. By offering this option, you can create a new text style if one doesn't exist to suit your needs. The Fill Color option lets you specify a background color for text cells.

TIP   You can control the cell background color for existing tables by using the Properties palette. Click a cell or group of cells, right-click, and choose Properties. In the Properties palette, select a color from the Background Fill option.

Border Properties   The Border Properties group lets you control the color and line weight of the table line work. The options in this group work just like the Cell Border Properties dialog box you saw in an earlier exercise.

General   The General group has only one option. The Table Direction option lets you specify whether the table reads from top to bottom or from the bottom up.

Cell Margins   Finally, the Cell Margins options let you specify the minimum distance between the text and the border of the cell. The Cell Margins options are useful when you find that the text is too close to one of the border lines.

TIP   You can edit the table direction and cell margins of an existing table by using the Properties palette. Select the entire table and then right-click and choose Properties from the shortcut menu. You'll find the Direction option and the Vertical and Horizontal Cell Margin options in the Table group of the Properties palette.

You've had the chance to see how the Table tool works with a small table in the previous exercise. Try experimenting with it to create some sample tables on your own.

If You Want to Experiment

As a final exercise, you might try importing a table of your own creation from Excel or other spreadsheet program to see how that works. If your application is mechanical, you might try importing a parts list.

Chapter 12

Using Dimensions

Before you determine the dimensions of a project, your design is in flux, and many questions might be unanswered. After you begin dimensioning, you will begin to see whether things fit or work together. Dimensioning can be crucial to how well a design works and how quickly it develops. The dimensions answer questions about code conformance if you are an architect; they answer questions about tolerances, fit, and interference if you are involved in mechanical applications. After you and your design team reach a design on a schematic level, communicating even tentative dimensions to others on the team can accelerate design development. Dimensions represent a point from which you can further develop your ideas.

With AutoCAD, you can easily add tentative or final dimensions to any drawing. AutoCAD gives you an accurate dimension without your having to take measurements. You simply pick the two points to be dimensioned and the dimension line location, and AutoCAD does the rest. AutoCAD's *associative dimensioning* capability automatically updates dimensions whenever the size or shape of the dimensioned object changes. These dimensioning features can save you valuable time and reduce the number of dimensional errors in your drawings.

Topics in this chapter include the following:

- ◆ Understanding the Components of a Dimension
- ◆ Creating a Dimension Style
- ◆ Drawing Linear Dimensions
- ◆ Editing Dimensions
- ◆ Dimensioning Non-orthogonal Objects
- ◆ Adding a Note
- ◆ Skewing Dimension Lines
- ◆ Applying Ordinate Dimensions
- ◆ Adding Tolerance Notation

Understanding the Components of a Dimension

Before you start the exercises in this chapter, it will help to know the names of the parts of a dimension. Figure 12.1 shows a sample of a dimension with the parts labeled. The *dimension line* is the line that represents the distance being dimensioned. It is the horizontal line with the diagonal tick marks on either end. The *extension lines* are the lines that originate from the object being dimensioned. They show you the exact location from which the dimension is taken. The *dimension text* is the actual dimension value, usually shown inside or above the dimension line.

The components of a
dimension

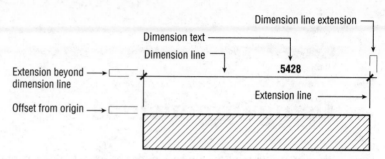

Another component of a dimension line is the *dimension line extension*. This is the part of the dimension line that extends beyond the extension line. Dimension line extensions are usually used only on architectural dimensions. The extension lines usually extend beyond the dimension lines in all types of dimensions. The extension line *offset from origin* is the distance from the beginning of the extension line to the object being dimensioned. The extension *beyond dimension line* is the distance the dimension line extends past the extension line and is most commonly used in architectural drawings.

You can control each of these components by creating or editing dimension styles. *Dimension styles* are the settings that determine the look of your dimensions. You can store multiple styles within a single drawing. The first exercise in this chapter will show you how to create a dimension style.

Creating a Dimension Style

Dimension styles are similar to text styles. They determine the look of your dimensions as well as the size of dimensioning features, such as the dimension text and arrows. You might set up a dimension style to have special types of arrows, for instance, or to position the dimension text above or in line with the dimension line. Dimension styles also make your work easier by enabling you to store and duplicate your most common dimension settings.

AutoCAD gives you one of two default dimension styles, *ISO-25* or *Standard*, depending on whether you use the metric or Imperial (also called English) measurement system. You will probably add many other styles to suit the types of drawings you are creating. You can also create variations of a general style for those situations that call for only minor changes in the dimension's appearance.

In this first section you'll learn how to set up your own dimension style based on the Standard dimension style (see Figure 12.2). For metric users, the settings will be different, but the overall methods will be the same.

Follow these steps to create a dimension style:

1. Open the Unit file you edited in the preceding chapter. If you didn't create one, use the 12a-unit.dwg file from the companion CD and rename it Unit.dwg. Metric users should open 12a-unit-metric.dwg and rename it Unit.dwg.

2. Issue Zoom All to display the entire floor plan.

3. Choose Format ➢ Dimension Style or type **D**⏎ at the Command prompt to open the Dimension Style Manager dialog box.

FIGURE 12.2
AutoCAD's Standard
dimension style
compared with an
architectural-style
dimension

A dimension using
the Standard default
settings

A dimension set
up for architectural
drawings

A sample of
other arrows

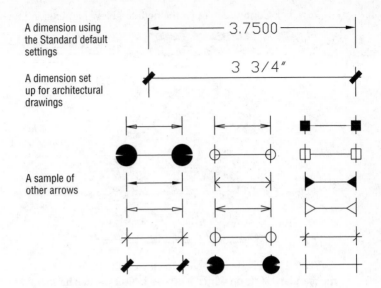

4. Select Standard from the Styles list box. Metric users should select ISO-25.

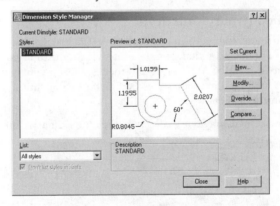

5. Click New to open the Create New Dimension Style dialog box.

6. With the Copy Of Standard or ISO-25 name highlighted in the New Style Name input box,
enter **My Architectural**.

7. Click Continue to open the detailed New Dimension Style dialog box.

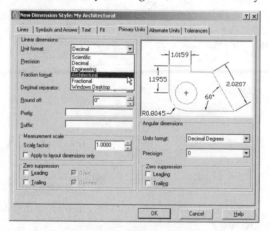

You've just created a dimension style called My Architectural, but at this point it is identical to the Standard style on which it is based. Nothing has happened to the Standard style; it is still available if you need to use it.

Setting Up the Primary Unit Style

Now you need to set up your new dimension style so that it conforms to the U.S. architectural style of dimensioning. Let's start by changing the unit style for the dimension text. Just as you changed the overall unit style of AutoCAD to a feet-and-inches style for your bath drawing in Chapter 3, you must do the same for your dimension styles. Setting the overall unit style does not automatically set the dimension unit style. Follow these steps:

1. In the New Dimension Style dialog box, click the Primary Units tab.

2. In the Linear Dimensions group, open the Unit Format drop-down list and choose Architectural. Notice that this drop-down list contains the same unit styles as the main Drawing Units dialog box (choose Format ➢ Units). Metric users can skip this option.

TIP You might notice the Decimal Separator option a few settings below the Unit Format option. The Decimal Separator option lets you choose between a period and a comma for decimal points. Metric users often use the comma for a decimal point, and U.S. users will use a period. This option doesn't have any meaning for measurements other than decimal, so it is dimmed when the Architectural unit format is selected.

3. Select 0´-0¼˝ from the Precision drop-down list, just below the Unit Format list. Metric users should select 0.00. The Precision option enables you to set the level of precision that is displayed in the dimension text. It doesn't limit the precision of AutoCAD's drawing database. This value is used to limit only the display of dimension text values.

TIP Every dimension style setting has an equivalent system variable. See Appendix C for more on system variables that are directly associated with dimensions.

4. Just below the Precision drop-down list, open the Fraction Format drop-down list and select Diagonal. Notice what happens to the graphic. The fractional dimensions change to show you how your dimension text will look. Metric users can skip this step, because it isn't available when the Decimal unit format is selected.

5. In the Zero Suppression group in the lower-left corner, click 0 Inches to turn off this check box. If you leave it turned on, indications of 0 inches will be omitted from the dimension text. (In architectural drawings, 0 inches are shown as in this dimension: 12´-0˝.) Metric users can ignore this option.

If you use the Imperial measurement system, you have set up My Architectural's dimension unit style to show dimensions in feet and inches, the standard method for U.S. construction documents. Metric users have just changed the Precision value and kept the Decimal unit system.

Setting the Height for Dimension Text

Along with the unit style, you will want to adjust the size of the dimension text. The Text tab of the New Dimension Style dialog box lets you set a variety of text options, including text location relative to the dimension line, style, and height.

Follow these steps to set the height of your dimension text:

1. Click the Text tab to display the text options.

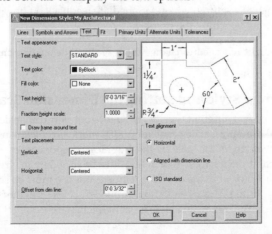

2. Highlight the contents of the Text Height input box.

3. Type **1/8.⏎** to make the text height ⅛″ high. Metric users should enter **0.3.⏎** for the text height.

Unlike the text you created in Chapter 10, you specify the text height by its final plot size. You then specify an overall dimension scale factor that affects the sizing of all the dimensioning settings such as text and arrows.

If you want to use a specific text style for your dimensions, select a text style in the Text Style drop-down list in the Text tab. If the style you select happens to have a height specification greater than 0, that height will override any text height settings you enter in the Text tab.

Setting the Location and Orientation of Dimension Text

AutoCAD's default setting for the placement of dimension text puts the text in line with the dimension line, as shown in the example at the top of Figure 12.2, earlier in this chapter. However, you want the new Architectural style to put the text above the dimension line, as is done in the center of Figure 12.2. To do that, you will use the Text Placement and Text Alignment options in the Text tab of the New Dimension Style dialog box:

1. In the Text Alignment group in the lower-right corner of the dialog box, click the Aligned With Dimension Line radio button.

2. In the Text Placement group, open the Vertical drop-down list and select Above. Notice how the appearance of the sample image changes to show you how your new settings will look.

3. Again in the Text Placement group, change the Offset From Dim Line value to ¹/₁₆. This setting controls the size of the gap between the dimension line and the dimension text.

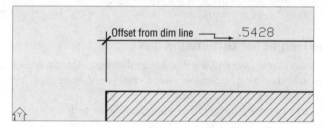

Each time you change a setting, you get immediate feedback on how your changes will affect your dimension style by watching the graphic.

TIP Metric users might not need to change these settings, depending on your preference for dimension styles.

Choosing an Arrow Style and Setting the Dimension Scale

Next, you want to specify a different type of arrow for your new dimension style. For linear dimensions in architectural drawings, a diagonal line, or *tick* mark, is typically used, rather than an arrow.

In addition, you want to set the scale for the graphical components of the dimension, such as the arrows and text. Recall from Chapter 10 that text must be scaled up in size in order to appear at the proper size in the final output of the drawing. Dimensions too must be scaled so they look correct when the drawing is plotted. The arrows are controlled by settings in the Symbols And Arrows tab, and the overall scale of the dimension style is set in the Fit tab.

Here are the steps for specifying the arrow type and scale:

1. Click the Symbols And Arrows tab to display the options for controlling the arrow style and dimension line extensions.

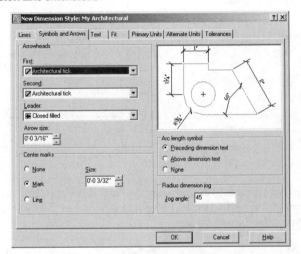

2. In the Arrowheads group, open the First drop-down list and choose Architectural Tick. The graphic next to the arrowhead name shows you what the arrowhead looks like.

TIP See Appendix C for details on how you can create your own arrowheads. Also, AutoCAD lets you set up a separate arrow style for leaders.

3. In the Arrowheads group, change the Arrow Size setting to $\frac{1}{8}$. Metric users should enter .3.

Next you'll need to set the behavior of the dimension line and extension lines:

1. Click the Lines tab to display the options for controlling the dimension and extension lines.

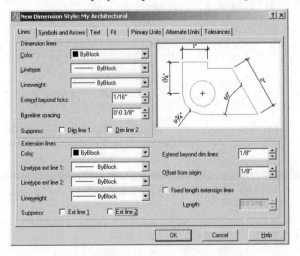

2. In the Dimension Lines group, highlight the value in the Extend Beyond Ticks input box and enter **1/16**. (Metric users should enter **0.15**.) This causes the dimension lines to extend past the tick arrows. This is a standard graphic practice used for dimensioning linear dimensions in architectural plans.

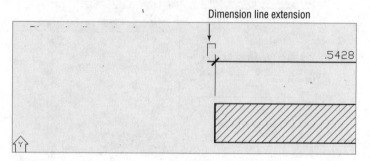

Dimension line extension

3. In the Extension Lines group, change the Extend Beyond Dim Lines setting to ¹/₈. Metric users should change this to .3. This setting determines the distance that the extension line extends past the dimension line.

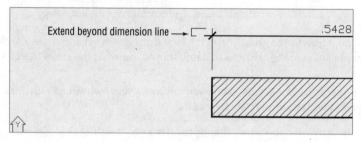

Extend beyond dimension line →

4. Again in the Extension Lines group, change the Offset From Origin setting to ¹/₈. Metric users should change this to .3. This sets the distance from the point being dimensioned to the beginning of the dimension extension line.

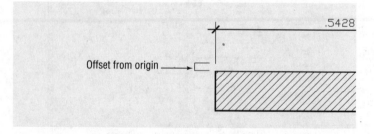

Offset from origin →

5. Click the Fit tab of the New Dimension Style dialog box to display the options for overall dimension scale and miscellaneous settings.

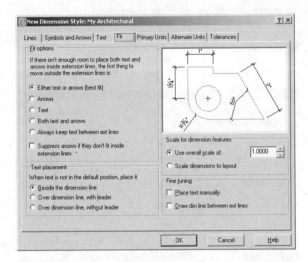

6. In the Scale For Dimension Features group, select the Use Overall Scale Of radio button.

7. Double-click the list box just to the right of the Use Overall Scale Of radio button and enter **48**. This is the scale factor for a $^1/_4$″ scale drawing. Metric users should enter **50**.

8. Click OK to close the New Dimension Style dialog box. The Dimension Style Manager dialog box opens again.

All the values that you enter for the various options in the New Dimension Style dialog box will be multiplied by this value to obtain the final size of the dimension components. For example, the text height you entered earlier, $^1/_8$″, will be multiplied by 48 for a dimension text height of 6″. For metric users, the text height of 0.3 will be multiplied by 50 for a text height of 15 cm.

TIP If you use the Scale Dimensions To Layout option in the Scale For Dimension Features group of the Fit tab, AutoCAD uses the layout viewport scale to size the dimension components. See Chapter 8 for more information on viewport scale settings. This can be useful if you have a drawing that you want to print at multiple scales.

Setting Up Alternate Units

You can use the Alternate Units tab of the New Dimension Style dialog box to set up AutoCAD to display a second dimension in centimeters or millimeters. Likewise, if you are a metric user, you can set up a second dimension to display feet and inches. The following exercise shows you how to set up alternate dimensions. You don't have to do this exercise now. It's here for your information. If you like, come back later and try it to see how it affects your dimensions. You can pick up the tutorial in the next section, "Setting the Current Dimension Style."

TIP If you decide later that you do not want the alternate units to be displayed, you can turn them off by returning to this dialog box and removing the checkmark from the Display Alternate Units check box.

Here are the steps for setting up alternate dimensions:

1. In the Dimension Style Manager, select a style, then click Modify. Or if you want to create a new style, click New.

2. In the New Dimension Style dialog box, click the Alternate Units tab.

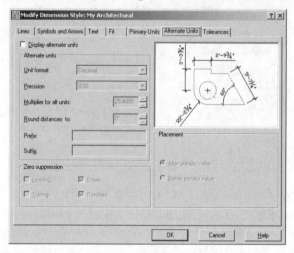

3. Click the Display Alternate Units check box. The options in the tab become available for your input.

4. Select the appropriate option from the Unit Format drop-down list. U.S. users should select Decimal to show metric alternate units. Metric users should select Architectural.

5. Select an appropriate precision value from the Precision drop-down list.

6. Enter a scale factor for your alternate dimension in the Multiplier For Alt Units input box. For U.S. users, the default value is 25.4. This value converts feet-and-inch dimensions to millimeters. In our metric examples, you've been using centimeters, so change this setting to 2.54. Metric users should enter **0.3937** to convert centimeters to feet and inches.

7. In the Placement group, select where you want the alternate dimension to appear in relation to the main dimension.

8. Click OK to close the New Dimension Style dialog box. The Dimension Style Manager dialog box opens again.

Setting the Current Dimension Style

Before you can begin to use your new dimension style, you must make it the current default.

1. Click My Architectural in the Styles list box in the Dimension Style Manager dialog box.

2. Click the Set Current button in the far-right side of the dialog box.

3. Click Close to exit the Dimension Style Manager dialog box.

You're now ready to use your new dimension style.

FITTING TEXT AND ARROWS IN TIGHT PLACES

Every now and then, you'll need to dimension a small gap or a small width of an object that won't allow dimension text to fit. The Fit tab includes a few other settings that control how dimensions act when the extension lines are too close. The Text Placement group contains three options to place the text in tight situations:

Beside The Dimension Line   Places text next to the extension line but close to the dimension line. You'll see how this affects your dimension later.

Over Dimension Line, With Leader   Places the dimension text farther from the dimension line and includes an arrow or a leader from the dimension line to the text.

Over Dimension Line, Without Leader   Does the same as the previous setting, but does not include the leader.

The options in the Fit Options group let you control how text and arrows are placed when there isn't enough room for both between the extension lines.

In the next set of exercises, you will be using the My Architectural style you just created. To switch to another style, open the Dimension Style Manager dialog box again, select the style you want from the Styles list, and click Set Current, just as you did in the previous exercise.

Modifying a Dimension Style

To modify an existing dimension style, open the Dimension Style Manager dialog box, highlight the style you want to edit, and then click Modify to open the Modify Dimension Style dialog box. This is virtually identical to the New Dimension Style dialog box you've been working with. You can then make changes to the different components of the selected dimension style. When you've finished making changes and closed both dialog boxes, all the dimensions associated with the edited style will update automatically in your drawing. For example, if you decide you need to change the dimension scale of a style, you can open the Modify Dimension Style dialog box and change the Scale value in the Fit tab.

This section introduces you to the various settings that let you set the appearance of a dimension style. This section doesn't discuss every option, so if you want to learn more about the other dimension style options, consult Appendix B. There you'll find descriptions of all the items in the New Dimension Style and Modify Dimension Style dialog box, plus reference material covering the system variables associated with each option.

TIP   If your application is strictly architectural, you might want to make these same dimension style changes to the Acad.dwt template file or create a set of template files specifically for architectural drawings of different scales.

Drawing Linear Dimensions

The most common type of dimension you'll be using is the *linear dimension*. The linear dimension is an orthogonal dimension measuring the width and length of an object. AutoCAD provides three dimensioning tools for this purpose: Linear (Dimlinear), Continue (Dimcont), and Baseline (Dimbase). These options are readily accessible from the Dimension toolbar or the Dimension drop-down menu.

WARNING In the following set of exercises, you'll see figures displaying dimensions in both Imperial and metric units. I've included both measurements so that both Imperial and metric users can more easily follow the tutorial. But in your own drawing you will see only one dimension value displayed above the dimension line.

Finding the Dimension Toolbar

Before you apply any dimension, you'll want to open the Dimension toolbar. This toolbar contains nearly all the commands necessary to draw and edit your dimensions. To open the Dimension toolbar, right-click any toolbar and choose Dimension from the shortcut menu. The Dimension commands are also available from the Dimension drop-down menu. Now you're ready to begin dimensioning.

TIP To help keep your screen organized, you might want to dock the Dimension toolbar on the right side of the AutoCAD window. You will lose the Dim Style Control drop-down list if you dock the toolbar on either side of the AutoCAD window. The drop-down list remains in place if you dock the toolbar at the top or bottom. See Chapter 1 for more on docking toolbars.

Placing Horizontal and Vertical Dimensions

Let's start by looking at the basic dimensioning tool, Linear Dimension. The Linear Dimension button (the Dimlinear command) on the Dimension toolbar accommodates both the horizontal and vertical dimensions.

In this exercise, you'll add a vertical dimension to the right side of the Unit plan:

1. To start either a vertical or horizontal dimension, click Linear Dimension on the Dimension toolbar or enter **Dli.⏎** at the Command prompt. You can also choose Dimension ➢ Linear from the drop-down menu.

2. The Specify first extension line origin or <select object>: prompt is asking you for the first point of the distance to be dimensioned. An extension line is the line that connects the object being dimensioned to the dimension line. Use the Endpoint Osnap override and pick the upper-right corner of the entry, as shown in Figure 12.3.

FIGURE 12.3
The dimension line added to the Unit drawing

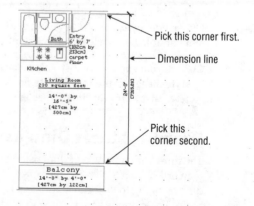

TIP   Notice that the prompt in step 2 gives you the option of pressing ⏎ to select an object. If you do this, you are prompted to pick the object you want to dimension, rather than the actual distance to be dimensioned. This method is discussed later in this chapter.

3. At the `Specify second extension line origin:` prompt, pick the lower-right corner of the living room, as shown in Figure 12.3.

4. In the next prompt, `Specify dimension line location or [Mtext/Text/Angle/ Horizontal/Vertical/Rotated]:`, the dimension line indicates the direction of the dimension and contains the arrows or tick marks. Move your cursor from left to right to display a temporary dimension. This enables you to visually select a dimension line location.

TIP   In step 4, you can append information to the dimension's text or change the dimension text altogether. You'll see how later in this chapter.

5. Enter @4'<0⏎ to tell AutoCAD you want the dimension line to be 4' to the right of the last point you selected. Metric users should enter @122<0⏎. (You could pick a point by using your cursor, but this doesn't let you place the dimension line as accurately.) After you've done this, the dimension is placed in the drawing, as shown in Figure 12.3.

Continuing a Dimension

You will often want to enter a group of dimensions strung together in a line. For example, you might want to continue dimensioning the balcony and align the continued dimension with the dimension you just entered.

To do this, use the Continue option found in both the Dimension toolbar and the Dimension drop-down menu:

1. Click the Continue Dimension option on the Dimension toolbar or enter **Dco**⏎. You can also choose Dimension ➤ Continue from the drop-down menu.

2. At the `Specify a second extension line origin or [Undo/Select] <Select>:` prompt, pick the upper-right corner of the balcony. (See the top image in Figure 12.4.)

3. Pick the right end of the rail on the balcony. See the bottom image in Figure 12.4 for the results.

4. Press ⏎ twice to exit the command.

TIP   If you select the wrong location for a continued dimension, you can click the Undo tool or press **U**⏎ to back up your dimension.

The Continue Dimension option adds a dimension from where you left off. The last drawn extension line is used as the first extension line for the continued dimension. AutoCAD keeps adding dimensions as you continue to pick points, until you press ⏎.

You probably noticed that the 5″ dimension is placed away from the dimension line with a leader line pointing to it. This is the result of the 5″ dimension's text not having enough space to fit between the dimension extension lines. You'll learn about dimension style settings that can remedy this problem. For now, let's continue adding dimensions to the plan.

FIGURE 12.4
The dimension
string continued
and completed

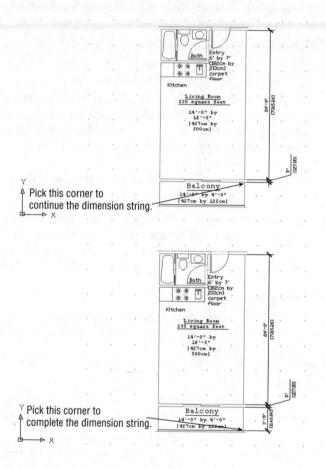

Continuing a Dimension from a Previous Dimension

If you need to continue a string of dimensions from an older linear dimension, instead of the most recently added one, press ↵ at the Specify a second extension line origin or [Undo/Select] <Select>: prompt you saw in step 2 of the previous exercise. Then, at the Select continued dimension: prompt, click the extension line from which you want to continue.

Drawing Dimensions from a Common Base Extension Line

Another way to dimension objects is to have several dimensions originate from the same extension line. To accommodate this, AutoCAD provides the Baseline option on the Dimension toolbar or Dimension drop-down menu.

To see how this works, you will start another dimension—this time a horizontal one—across the top of the plan:

1. Click Linear Dimension on the Dimension toolbar. Or, just as you did for the vertical dimension, you can type **Dli**↵ to start the horizontal dimension. This option is also on the Dimension drop-down menu.

DRAWING LINEAR DIMENSIONS

2. At the `Specify first extension line origin or <select object>:` prompt, use the Endpoint Osnap to pick the upper-left corner of the bathroom, as shown in Figure 12.5.

3. At the `Specify second extension line origin:` prompt, pick the upper-right corner of the bathroom, as shown in Figure 12.5.

4. At the `Specify dimension line location or [Mtext/Text/Angle/ Horizontal/ Vertical/Rotated]:` prompt, pick a point above the `Unit` plan, as shown in Figure 12.5. If you need to, pan your view downward to fit the dimension in.

TIP Because you usually pick exact locations on your drawing as you dimension, you might want to turn on Running Osnaps to avoid the extra step of selecting osnaps from the Osnap shortcut menu.

5. Now you're all set to draw another dimension continuing from the first extension line of the dimension you just drew. Click the Baseline Dimension option on the Dimension toolbar. Or you can type **Dba↵** at the Command prompt to start a baseline dimension.

6. At the `Specify a second extension line origin or [Undo/Select] <Select>:` prompt, click the upper-right corner of the entry, as shown in Figure 12.6.

7. Press ↵ twice to exit the Baseline Dimension command.

8. Pan your view down so it looks similar to Figure 12.6.

In this example, you see that the Baseline Dimension option is similar to the Continue Dimension option, except that the Baseline Dimension option enables you to use the first extension line of the previous dimension as the base for a second dimension. The distance between the two horizontal dimension lines is controlled by the Baseline Spacing setting in the Lines tab of the New Dimension Style and Modify Dimension Style dialog boxes.

FIGURE 12.5

The bathroom with horizontal dimensions

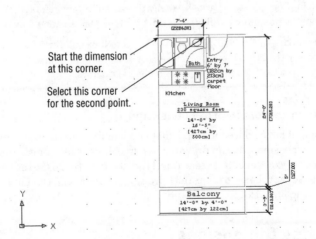

USING GRIDS IN ARCHITECTURAL DIMENSIONS

Common, if not essential, elements in architectural drawings are the *building grids*. These are the center lines of the main structural components, which are usually the columns and structural walls of the building. Grids are labeled similarly to map grids, with numeric labels placed horizontally and alphabetic labels placed vertically. A circle or hexagon is used at the end of the grid to label it. The grids are the first items dimensioned, and all other building components are dimensioned from the grid lines. The San Francisco Main Library made ample use of grids, incorporating both major and minor grid systems. There, a hexagon was used to label the grids.

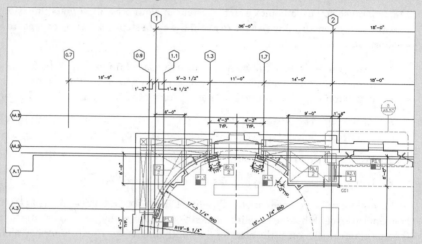

Because the structural components of a building are usually the first parts that are put in place, they play a crucial role in locating other components of the building during the construction process. When producing floor plans, the grid is usually the first thing an architect draws, mimicking to some degree the construction process. All other elements of the plan are then drawn in relation to that grid.

While working in AutoCAD, you can use a grid to start building your drawing. After the grid is in place, you can use the Offset tool to locate walls or other building components. Using AutoCAD's tracking feature, you can easily align drawing elements to grid lines.

CONTINUING FROM AN OLDER DIMENSION

You might have noticed in step 7 that you had to press ↵ twice to exit the command. As with Continue Dimension, you can draw the baseline dimension from an older dimension by pressing ↵ at the Specify a second extension line origin [Undo/Select] <Select>: prompt. You then get the Select base dimension: prompt, at which you can either select another dimension or press ↵ again to exit the command.

Editing Dimensions

As you begin to add more dimensions to your drawings, you will find that AutoCAD will occasionally place the dimension text or line in an inappropriate location, or you might need to modify the dimension text. In this section, you'll take an in-depth look at how you can modify dimensions to suit those special circumstances that always crop up.

FIGURE 12.6

The overall width dimension

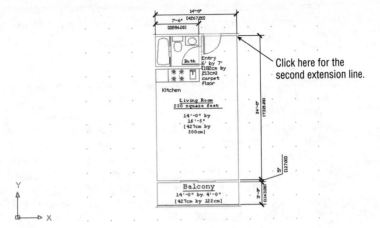

Click here for the second extension line.

Appending Data to Dimension Text

So far in this chapter, you've been accepting the default dimension text. You can append information to the default dimension value or change it entirely if you need to. At the point when you see the temporary dimension dragging with your cursor, enter **T↵**. Then, by using the less-than (<) and greater-than (>) symbols, you can add text either before or after the default dimension or replace the symbols entirely to replace the default text. The Properties button on the Properties toolbar lets you modify the existing dimension text in a similar way.

Let's see how this works by changing an existing dimension's text in your drawing:

1. Choose Modify ➢ Object ➢ Text ➢ Edit or type **ED↵**.

2. Click the last horizontal dimension you added to the drawing at the top of the screen to open the Text Formatting toolbar.

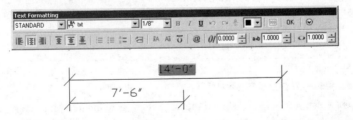

3. Press the End key to place the cursor at the end of the 14´-0˝ text, and then type **to face of stud**.

4. Click OK on the Text Formatting toolbar, and then press ↵ to exit the Ddedit command. The dimension changes to read 14´-0˝ to face of stud.

5. Because you don't really need the new appended text for the tutorial, click the Undo button in the Standard toolbar to remove the appended text.

TIP In this exercise, you were able to edit only a single dimension. To append text to several dimensions at once, you need to use the Dimension Edit tool. See the "Making Changes to Multiple Dimensions" sidebar in this chapter for more on this command.

If you need to restore the original dimension text for a dimension whose value has been completely replaced, you can use the steps shown in the previous exercise, but in step 3, replace the text with the <> bracket symbols.

You can also have AutoCAD automatically add a dimension suffix or prefix to all dimensions, instead of just a chosen few, by using the Suffix or Prefix option in the Primary Units tab of the New Dimension Style or Modify Dimension Style dialog box. See Appendix C for more on this feature.

AutoCAD provides the associative dimensioning capability to automatically update dimension text when a drawing is edited. Objects called *definition points* determine how edited dimensions are updated.

The definition points are located at the same points you pick when you determine the dimension location. For example, the definition points for linear dimensions are the extension line origin. The definition points for a circle diameter are the points used to pick the circle and the opposite side of the circle. The definition points for a radius are the points used to pick the circle, plus the center of the circle.

MAKING CHANGES TO MULTIPLE DIMENSIONS

You can use the Dimension Edit tool to quickly edit existing dimensions. It gives you the ability to edit more than one dimension's text at one time. One common use for the Dimension Edit tool is to change a string of dimensions to read *Equal* instead of showing the actual dimensioned distance. The following example shows an alternative to using the Properties palette for appending text to a dimension:

1. Click the Dimension Edit tool in the Dimension toolbar or type **Ded**↵.

2. At this prompt

   ```
   Enter type of dimension editing [Home/New/Rotate/Oblique]<Home>:
   ```

3. type **N**↵ to use the New option. The Multiline Text Editor opens, showing 0 in the text box.

4. Use the arrow keys to move the cursor behind or in front of the 0, and then enter the text you want to append to the dimension. Or you can replace the 0 entirely to replace the dimension with your text.

5. Click OK.

6. At the Select objects: prompt, pick the dimensions you want to edit. The Select objects: prompt remains, enabling you to select several dimensions.

7. Press ↵ to finish your selection. The dimension changes to include your new text or to replace the existing dimension text.

The Dimension Edit tool is useful in editing dimension text, but you can also use this tool to make graphical changes to the text. Here is a listing of the other Dimension Edit tool options:

Home Moves the dimension text to its standard default position and angle.

Rotate Rotates the dimension text to a new angle.

Oblique Skews the dimension extension lines to a new angle. (See the "Skewing Dimension Lines" section later in this chapter.)

Definition points are actually point objects. They are difficult to see because they are usually covered by the feature that they define. You can, however, see them indirectly by using grips. The definition points of a dimension are the same as the dimension's grip points. You can see them simply by clicking a dimension. Try the following:

1. Make sure the Grips feature is turned on. (See Chapter 2 to refresh your memory on the Grips feature.)

2. Click the longest of the three vertical dimensions you drew in the earlier exercise. You will see the grips of the dimension, as shown in Figure 12.7.

TIP   AutoCAD 2007 treats dimensions as fully associative. This means that dimensions are updated automatically whenever an object associated with the dimension is modified. See the section "Using Associative Dimensions" later in this chapter.

FIGURE 12.7
The grip points are the same as the definition points on a dimension.

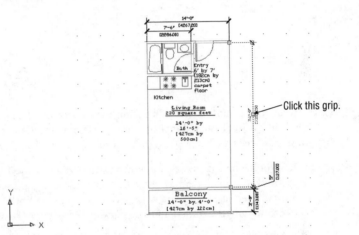

Click this grip.

Using Grips to Make Minor Adjustments to Dimensions

The definition points, whose location you can see through their grips, are located on their own unique layer called *Defpoints*. Definition points are displayed regardless of whether the Defpoints layer is on or off. To give you an idea of how these definition points work, try the following exercises, which show you how to directly manipulate the definition points.

In this exercise, you'll use coordinates to move a dimension line:

1. With the grips visible, click the grip near the dimension text.

TIP   Because the Defpoints layer has the unique feature of being visible even when turned off, you can use it as a layer for laying out your drawing. While Defpoints is turned off, you can still see objects assigned to it, but the objects won't plot.

2. Move the cursor around. Notice that when you move the cursor vertically, the text moves along the dimension line. When you move the cursor horizontally, the dimension line and text move together, keeping their parallel orientation to the dimensioned floor plan.

TIP Here the entire dimension line, including the text, moves. In a later exercise, you'll see how you can move the dimension text independently of the dimension line.

3. Enter **@9´<0**↵. Metric users should enter **@275<0**↵. The dimension line, text, and dimension extensions stretch to the new location to the right of the text (see Figure 12.8).

FIGURE 12.8
Moving the dimension
line by using its grip

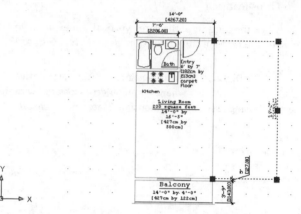

TIP If you need to move several dimension lines at once, select them all at the Command prompt; then Shift+click one set of dimension-line grips from each dimension. After you've selected the grips, click one of the hot grips again. You can then move all the dimension lines at once.

In step 3 of the previous exercise, you saw that you can specify an exact distance for the dimension line's new location by entering a relative polar coordinate. Cartesian coordinates work just as well. You can even use object snaps to relocate dimension lines.

Next, try moving the dimension line back by using the Perpendicular Osnap:

1. Click the grip at the bottom of the dimension line you just edited.

2. Shift+click the right mouse button and choose Perpendicular from the Osnap shortcut menu.

3. Place the cursor on the vertical dimension line that dimensions the balcony and click it.

The selected dimension line moves to align with the other vertical dimension, back to its original location.

Changing Style Settings of Individual Dimensions

In some cases, you will have to make changes to an individual dimension's style setting in order to edit that dimension. For example, if you try to move the text of a typical linear dimension, you might find that the text and dimension lines are inseparable. You need to make a change to the dimension style setting that controls how AutoCAD locates dimension text in relation to the dimension line. This section describes how you can change the style settings of individual dimensions to facilitate changes in the dimension.

TIP If you need to change the dimension style of a dimension to match that of another, you can use the Match Properties tool. See Chapter 7 for details on how to use this tool.

MOVING FIXED DIMENSION TEXT

Earlier in this chapter, you saw how dimension text is attached to the dimension line so that when the text is moved, the dimension line follows. You might encounter situations in which you want to move the text independently of the dimension line. The following exercises show you how you can separate dimension text from its dimension line. In the process, you'll learn how you can change a single dimension's style settings. Then you'll use grips to move the dimension text away from the dimension line.

Use these steps to change the necessary settings:

1. Press the Esc key twice to cancel the grip selection from the previous exercise.

2. Zoom in to the 24′ dimension so that you have a view similar to Figure 12.9.

3. Click the 24′-0″ dimension to expose its grips.

4. Right-click and choose Properties from the shortcut menu to open the Properties palette.

5. Scroll down the list of properties until you see the Fit category. If you do not see a list of options under Fit, click the downward pointing arrow to the right to display a new set of options.

6. Scroll down the list farther until you see the Text Movement option to the right of the Text Movement listing, and then click this option.

7. Click the arrow that appears next to the Keep Dim Line With Text listing to open the drop-down list; then select the Move Text, Add Leader option.

8. Close the Properties palette.

FIGURE 12.9

Selecting and then moving the 24-foot dimension

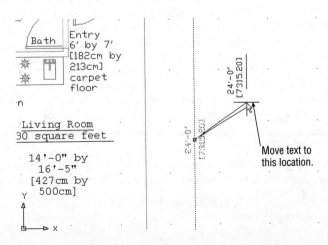

Let's see the effect of the changes you just made:

1. Click the grip of the 24′-0″ dimension text and move it up and to the right, and click again to place the text in a new location, as shown in Figure 12.9.

2. Review the changes that you made, and then click the Undo button twice to return to the state before you moved the dimension text.

Moving the text in step 1 demonstrates that the text is no longer tied to the dimension line. In the Properties palette, the Move Text, Add Leader option in the Fit category lets you move the dimension text independently of the dimension line. It also draws a leader from the dimension line to the text. Another option, Move Text, No Leader, does the same thing but doesn't include a leader. You can also set these options for a dimension style by using the Text Placement options in the Fit tab of the New Dimension Style or Modify Dimension Style dialog box.

As you can see from this exercise, the Properties palette gives you access to many of the settings that you saw for setting up dimension styles. The main difference here is that the Properties palette affects only the dimensions that you have selected.

In a previous exercise, you changed the format setting of a single dimension *after* it was placed. These settings can be made a standard part of your Architectural dimension style by using the Modify button in the Dimension Style Manager dialog box.

You need to make one more change to the drawing's dimension to set up for the next exercise:

1. Pan your view downward so you can see the 5″ dimension clearly, and then click the 5″ dimension and move it into a position in line with the dimension text.

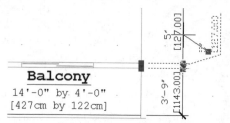

2. Choose View ➤ Zoom All, and then choose File ➤ Save to save this file in its current state.

In this short exercise, you were able to move the 5″ dimension without making any changes to its properties. AutoCAD automatically selects the appropriate Text Movement setting if the text is too large to fit between the dimension extension lines. In the case of the 5″ dimension text, AutoCAD automatically chose the Move Text, Add Leader setting when the dimension was placed in the drawing.

TIP   If you have multiple dimension styles and you want to change an existing dimension to the current dimension style, use the Dimension Update tool. Choose Dimension ➤ Update on the Dimension toolbar or choose Dimension Update from the drop-down menu. Then select the dimensions you want to change and press ↵. The selected dimensions will be converted to the current style.

ROTATING DIMENSION TEXT

Once in a while, dimension text works better if it is kept in a horizontal orientation, even if the dimension itself is not horizontal. If you need to rotate dimension text, here's the way to do it:

1. Click the Undo button twice in the toolbar or type U↵ to return the 5″ dimension to its original location.

2. Click the Dimension Edit tool in the Dimension toolbar.

3. At the `Enter type of dimension editing [Home/New/Rotate/Oblique] <Home>:` prompt, enter **R↵**.

4. At the `Specify angle for dimension text:` prompt, type **45↵** to rotate the text to a 45° angle.

5. At the `Select objects:` prompt, click the 5″ dimension text again. Press ↵.

6. Click the Undo button to undo the text rotation. You won't want to save this change to your drawing.

TIP You can also choose Dimension ➢ Align Text ➢ Angle, select the dimension text, and then enter an angle. A 0° angle returns the dimension text to its default angle.

The Dimension Text Edit tool (Dimtedit command) also enables you to align the dimension text to either the left or the right side of the dimension line. This is similar to the Alignment option in the Multiline Text Editor that controls text justification.

As you have seen in this section, the Grips feature is especially well suited to editing dimensions. With grips, you can stretch, move, copy, rotate, mirror, and scale dimensions.

UNDERSTANDING THE DIMENSION TEXT EDIT TOOL

One dimension text-editing tool you haven't used yet is the Dimension Text Edit tool. Although it might sound as though this tool enables you to edit dimension text, its purpose is to enable you to quickly position dimension text to the left, right, or center of the dimension line. To use it, choose Dimension Text Edit from the toolbar and then click the dimension text you want to move. You'll see the following prompts:

```
Select dimension:
Specify new location for dimension text or [Left/Right/Center/Home/Angle]:
```

You can then enter the letter of the option you want. For example, if you enter **L↵**, the dimension text moves to the left side of the dimension line.

Editing Dimensions and Other Objects Together

Certainly it's helpful to be able to edit a dimension directly by using its grips. But the key feature of AutoCAD's dimensions is their ability to *automatically* adjust themselves to changes in the drawing. As long as you include the dimension's definition points when you select objects to edit, the dimensions themselves will automatically update to reflect the change in your drawing.

To see how this works, try moving the living room closer to the bathroom wall. You can move a group of lines and vertices by using the Stretch command and the Crossing option:

1. Click the Stretch tool in the Modify toolbar, or type **S↵** and then **C↵**. You will see the following prompts:

```
At the Select objects to stretch by crossing-window or crossing-polygon...
Select objects: C
Specify first corner:
```

2. Pick a crossing window, as illustrated in Figure 12.10, and then press ↵ to confirm your selection.

FIGURE 12.10

The Stretch
crossing window

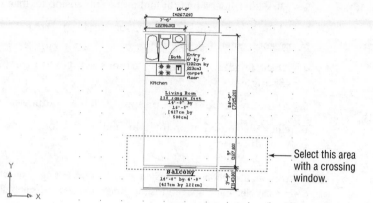

Select this area
with a crossing
window.

3. At the Specify base point or Displacement <Displacement>: prompt, pick any point on the screen.

4. At the Specify second point or <use first point as displacement>: prompt, enter **@2´<90** to move the wall 2´ in a 90° direction. The wall moves, and the dimension text changes to reflect the new dimensions, as shown in Figure 12.11.

5. After viewing the result of the stretch tool, click the Undo button in the toolbar or press U↵ to change the drawing back to it's previous state.

TIP   In some situations, a crossing window might select objects other than those you want to stretch. This frequently occurs when many objects are close together at the location of a vertex you want to stretch. To be more selective about the vertices you move and their corresponding objects, use a standard window instead of a crossing window to select the vertices. Then pick the individual objects whose vertices you want to move.

When you selected the crossing window corners, you included the definition points of both vertical dimensions. This enabled you to move the dimension extension lines along with the wall, thereby updating the dimensions automatically.

FIGURE 12.11

The moved wall,
with the updated
dimensions

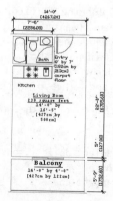

You can also use the Mirror, Rotate, and Stretch commands with dimensions. The polar arrays also work, and you can use Extend and Trim with linear dimensions.

When editing dimensioned objects, be sure to select the dimension associated with the object being edited. As you select objects, using the Crossing Window(C) or Crossing Polygon (CP) selection option helps you include the dimensions. For more on these selection options, see Chapter 2.

TIP If a hatch pattern or solid fill completely covers a dimension, you can use the Draworder command to have AutoCAD draw the dimension over the hatch or solid fill. See Chapters 7, 14, and 18 for more on various uses of the Draworder command.

MODIFYING THE DIMENSION STYLE SETTINGS BY USING OVERRIDE

In the "Moving Fixed Dimension Text" section, you used the Properties palette to facilitate the moving of the dimension text. You can also choose Dimension ➤ Override (Dimoverride command) to accomplish the same thing. The Override option enables you to change an individual dimension's style settings. Here's an example showing how you can use the Override option in place of the Properties palette in the first exercise of the "Moving Fixed Dimension Text" section.

1. Press the Esc key twice to make sure you are not in the middle of a command. Then choose Dimension ➤ Override from the drop-down menu.

2. At the next prompt

   ```
   Enter dimension variable name to override or [Clear overrides]:
   ```

3. type **Dimfit**↵.

4. At the Enter new value for dimension variable <3>: prompt, enter **4**↵. This has the same effect as selecting Move Text, Add Leader from the Fit option of the Properties palette.

5. The Enter dimension variable name to override: prompt appears again, enabling you to enter another dimension variable. Press ↵ to move to the next step.

6. At the Select objects: prompt, select the dimension you want to change. You can select a group of dimensions if you want to change several dimensions at once. Press ↵ when you have finished with your selection. The dimension settings will change for the selected dimensions.

As you can see from this example, the Dimoverride command requires that you know exactly which dimension variable to edit in order to make the desired modification. In this case, setting the Dimfit variable to 4 lets you move the dimension text independently of the dimension line. If you find the Dimoverride command useful, consult Appendix C to find which system variable corresponds to the Dimension Style dialog box settings.

Using Associative Dimensions

You've seen how you can edit dimensions by manipulating their definition points. For versions of AutoCAD prior to 2002, if you want to edit dimensions together with the objects, you need to use a crossing window because the dimension is not fully associated with the object it is dimensioning. In those versions, AutoCAD uses the dimension's definition point to simulate what is known as *associative dimensioning*. In AutoCAD 2002 and later, you can fully associate a dimension with an object so that you need only change the object and the dimension will follow.

To use *associative dimensioning,* you'll need to turn it on in the Options dialog box. Here's how it's done:

1. Choose Tools ➢ Options to open the Options dialog box, and then click the User Preferences tab.

2. In the Associative Dimensioning group, make sure the Make New Dimensions Associative option is turned on.

3. Click OK.

From now on, any dimension you place will be associated with the object you are dimensioning. Try the following exercise to see how it works:

1. Choose File ➢ New and create a new blank file from the Acad.dwt template.

2. Select the Rectangle tool from the Draw toolbar; then draw a rectangle roughly 12 units wide by 1 unit high.

3. Use the Zoom Window tool in the Standard toolbar to get a good view of your drawing so far.

4. Choose Dimension ➢ Linear, turn on the Object Snap mode, and then dimension the top of the rectangle.

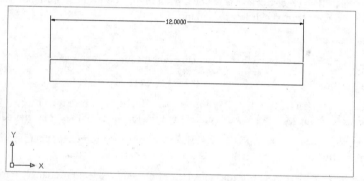

5. Click the rectangle to select it; then click the grip in the upper-right corner of the rectangle.

6. Move the grip to the right and upward and then click. The rectangle corner moves, and the dimension moves with it.

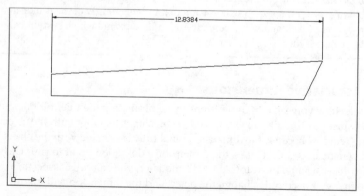

In this case, you had to change only the shape of the rectangle, and the dimension followed the change. The dimension in this example is fully associated with the rectangle.

Associative dimensioning also works with external references (see Chapter 15 for more on external references, or Xrefs) and blocks. This means that you can dimension an Xref, edit the source Xref file, and have the dimensions update in the current file. Such changes are not completely automatic; you need to issue the Dimregen command to update dimensions to the new Xref configuration.

You can use associative dimensioning on objects within blocks, and if the block is edited, those dimensions will update automatically. But be aware that nonuniform scaling of a block—that is, scaling along one axis and not the other—will not affect an associative dimension.

You can dimension a Model Space object in Paper Space, and the Paper Space dimension will be associated with the Model Space object. This means that even though the Paper Space dimension will not be visible in Model Space, the Paper Space dimension will reflect changes made to objects in Model Space. In some instances, you might need to use the Dimregen command to "refresh" Paper Space dimensions. See Chapter 16 for more on these features.

ASSOCIATING DIMENSIONS WITH OBJECTS

Now suppose you have a drawing from an older version of AutoCAD, and you want to create an association between an existing dimension and an object. The next exercise will show you how this is done. You'll use the Unit plan to associate one of the dimensions you've already created with a line representing a wall:

1. Close the rectangle drawing file. You don't have to save it.

2. Back in the Unit drawing, zoom in to the balcony area so your view looks similar to Figure 12.12.

3. Choose Dimension ➢ Reassociate Dimensions. You can also type **Dimreassociate**↵ at the Command prompt.

4. At the prompt

   ```
   Select dimension to reassociate…
   Select Objects:
   ```

   select the vertical dimension that dimensions the balcony (see Figure 12.12) and then press ↵.

FIGURE 12.12
Reassociating a
dimension to
an object

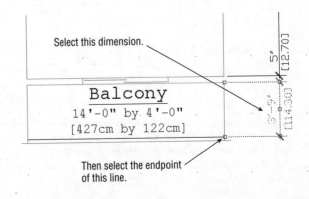

5. At the Specify first extension line origin or [Select object] <next>: prompt, you'll see an X at the top definition point of the dimension.

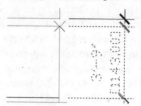

6. Press ↵. This tells AutoCAD to go to the next extension line origin. You'll see an X at the bottom definition point of the dimension.

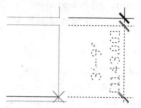

7. Use the Endpoint Osnap and click the end of the line representing the rail of the unit (see Figure 12.12). You now have the dimension associated with the endpoint of the line representing the rail of the balcony.

8. Try moving the rail to see what happens: use the Move tool in the Modify toolbar to move the balcony rail downward, as shown in Figure 12.13. The dimension follows the line.

9. Click the Undo button in the toolbar or enter U↵ to return the balcony to its original state.

FIGURE 12.13
The reassociated dimension follows the rail as it is moved.

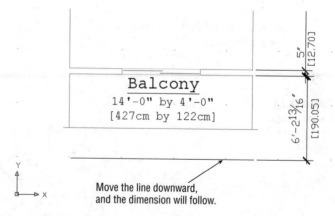

In step 5, you saw an X appear at the location of a dimension definition point. If the definition point is already associated with an object, the X will appear with a box around it. The box is a reminder that the definition point is already associated with an object and that you will be changing its association.

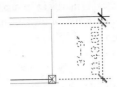

Also in step 5, you have the option to select an object. This option enables you to associate the dimension with an entire object instead of with just one endpoint. If you type **S**↵ at that prompt in step 5, you can then select the object that you want to associate with the dimension. The dimension will change so that its definition points coincide with the endpoints of the object. The dimension will remain in its original orientation. For example, a vertical dimension will remain vertical even if you associate the dimension with a horizontal line. In this situation, the dimension dutifully dimensions the endpoints of the line but will show a distance of zero.

TIP   You can remove a dimension's association with an object by using the Dimdisassociate command. Type **Dimdisassociate.**↵ at the Command prompt, select the dimension(s), and then press ↵.

Adding a String of Dimensions with a Single Operation

AutoCAD provides a method for creating a string of dimensions by using a single operation. The Qdim command lets you select a set of objects instead of having to select points. The following exercise demonstrates how the Qdim command works:

1. If you haven't done so already, zoom out so you have an overall view of the Unit floor plan.

2. Choose Dimension ➢ Quick Dimension or click Quick Dimension on the Dimension toolbar.

3. At the Select geometry to dimension: prompt, place a selection window around the entire left-side wall of the unit.

4. Press ↵ to finish your selection. The following prompt appears:

```
Specify dimension line position, or
[Continuous/Staggered/Baseline/Ordinate/Radius/Diameter/
datumPoint/Edit/seTtings] <Continuous>:
```

5. Click a point to the left of the wall to place the dimension. A string of dimensions appears, displaying all the dimensions for the wall.

6. When you have finished reviewing the results of this exercise, exit the file without saving it.

The prompt in step 4 indicates several types of dimensions you can choose from. For example, if you want the dimensions to originate from a single baseline, you can enter **B** in step 4 to select the Baseline option.

The Qdim command can be a time-saver when you want to dimension a wall quickly. It might not work in all situations, but if the object you're dimensioning is fairly simple, it can be all you need.

TIP   In this exercise, you used a simple window to select the wall. For more complex shapes, try using a crossing polygon selection window. See Chapter 2 for more on crossing polygons.

Removing the Alternate Dimensions

You may eventually encounter a drawing that contains alternate dimensions as shown in some of the figures earlier in this chapter. You can remove those alternate dimensions by turning off the alternate dimension features. Here's how it's done:

1. Choose Dimension ➤ Dimension Style or enter **D** to open the Dimension Style Manager dialog box.

2. Select the style that uses the alternate units. In the Styles list box, choose Modify.

3. Click the Alternate Units tab.

4. Click the Display Alternate Units check box to remove the checkmark.

5. Click OK, and then click Close to close the Dimension Style Manager dialog box.

The dimensions that use the style you just edited change to remove the alternate dimensions. You can also perform the reverse operation and add alternate dimensions to an existing set of dimensions. Follow the steps shown here, but instead of removing the checkmark in step 4, add the checkmark and make the appropriate setting changes to the rest of the Alternate Units tab.

Using Osnap While Dimensioning

When you pick intersections and endpoints frequently, as during dimensioning, it can be a bit inconvenient to use the Osnap shortcut menu. If you know you will be using certain osnaps frequently, you can use Running Osnaps. You can do so in the following two ways:

◆ Choose Tools ➤ Drafting Settings to open the Drafting Settings dialog box. In the Object Snap tab, make sure the Object Snap On check box is selected, and then select the desired default Osnap mode. You can pick more than one mode—for example, Intersection, Endpoint, and Midpoint—so that whichever geometry you happen to be nearest will be the point selected.

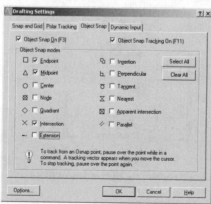

◆ Type **–osnap.**⏎ at the Command prompt, and then enter the name of the Osnap modes you want to use. If you want to use more than one mode, enter their names separated by commas; for example:

```
endpoint,midpoint,intersect
```

After you've designated your Running Osnaps, the next time you are prompted to select a point, the selected Osnap modes are automatically activated. You can still override the default settings by using the Osnap shortcut menu (Shift+click the right mouse button).

There is a drawback to setting a Running Osnap mode: when your drawing gets crowded, you can end up picking the wrong point by accident. However, you can easily toggle the Running Osnap mode off by clicking Osnap in the status bar or by pressing F3.

Dimensioning Non-orthogonal Objects

So far, you've been reading about how to work with linear dimensions. You can also dimension non-orthogonal objects, such as circles, arcs, triangles, and trapezoids. In this section, you will practice dimensioning non-orthogonal objects by drawing an elevation of a window in the set of plans for your studio apartment building.

You'll start by setting up the drawing:

1. Create a new file called Window.

2. In the Create New Drawing Wizard, click the Start From Scratch icon at the top, and then click the Imperial radio button if you are using feet and inches, or click the Metric radio button. This is important because, depending on which option you select, AutoCAD will set up the drawing with different dimension style defaults. AutoCAD will create a style called ISO-25 as the default style for metric users.

TIP If you don't see the Create New Drawing Wizard but instead see the Select Template dialog box, click the small button with the downward-pointing arrow to the right of the Open button in the lower-right corner of the dialog box. Then select Open With No Template Imperial or Open With No Template Metric, depending on which measurement system you are using.

3. Set the file up as an architectural drawing at a scale of $3'' = 1''-0''$ on an $8^1/_2'' \times 11''$ sheet. Metric users set up an A4 sheet at a scale of 1:4. See Chapter 3 for drawing areas and scales.

4. If you are using the Imperial measurement system, start by setting the dimension scale to 4. Normally, you use the Dimension Style Manager dialog box to set the dimension scale. A shortcut is to type **Dimscale.**⏎**4.**⏎. This changes the scale factor of the current dimension style to 4. Metric users can use the default setting.

5. Imperial system users should specify two more settings. Enter **Dimtih.**⏎**Off.**⏎. This turns off the setting that forces the dimension text located inside of the extension lines to be horizontal. Next type **Dimtad.**⏎**1.**⏎. This turns on the text-above-dimension feature. You'll want these two settings on to match the appearance of text in the metric ISO-25 style. Again, metric users do not have to change these settings.

WARNING In the following figures indicating the window dimensions, you'll see both Imperial and metric dimensions for the benefit of users of both systems. Your view will contain only the measurement in the system you've chosen.

Now you are ready to start drawing the window:

1. Click Polygon on the Draw toolbar or type **Pol**↵.

2. At the `Enter number of sides <4>:` prompt, enter **6**↵.

3. At the `Specify center of polygon or [Edge]:` prompt, pick the center of the polygon at coordinate 22,18. Metric users use 59,42 for the center coordinate.

TIP You can turn on the Snap mode to help you locate points for this exercise.

4. Enter **C**↵ at the `Enter an option [Inscribed in circle/circumscribed about circle]` `<I>:` prompt to select the Circumscribe option. This tells AutoCAD to place the polygon outside the temporary circle used to define the polygon.

5. At the `Specify radius of circle:` prompt, you will see the hexagon drag along with the cursor. You can pick a point with your mouse to determine its size.

6. Enter **8**↵ to get an exact size for the hexagon. Metric users enter **20.32**↵.

7. Draw a circle with a radius of 7″ and use 22,18 as its center. Metric users draw a circle with a radius of 17.78 and a center location of 59.42. Your drawing will look like Figure 12.14.

Dimensioning Non-orthogonal Linear Distances

Now you will dimension the window. The unusual shape of the window prevents you from using the horizontal or vertical dimensions you've used already. However, choosing Dimension ➤ Aligned enables you to dimension at an angle:

1. Click the Aligned Dimension tool on the Dimension toolbar. You can also enter **Dal**↵ to start the aligned dimension or choose Dimension ➤ Aligned.

2. At the `Specify first extension line origin or <select object>:` prompt, press ↵. You could have picked extension line origins as you did in earlier examples, but pressing ↵ shows you firsthand how the Select Object option works.

3. At the `Select object to dimension:` prompt, pick the upper-right face of the hexagon near coordinate 2′-5″,1′-10″ (75,55 for metric users). As the prompt indicates, you can also pick an arc or a circle for this type of dimension.

FIGURE 12.14
The window frame

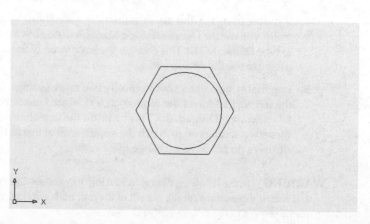

4. At the `Specify dimension line location or [Mtext/Text/Angle]`: prompt, pick a point near coordinate 2´-10˝,2´-2˝ (90,60 for metric users). The dimension appears in the drawing as shown in Figure 12.15.

TIP Just as with linear dimensions, you can enter **T.**⏎ at step 4 to enter alternate text for the dimension.

Next, you will dimension a face of the hexagon. Instead of its actual length, however, you will dimension a distance at a specified angle—the distance from the center of the face:

1. Click the Linear Dimension tool on the Dimension toolbar.

2. At the `Specify first extension line origin or <select object>`: prompt, press ⏎.

3. At the `Select object to dimension`: prompt, pick the lower-right face of the hexagon near coordinate 2´-6˝,1´-4˝ (77,33 for metric users).

4. At the `Specify dimension line location or [Mtext/Text/Angle/Horizontal/Vertical/Rotated]`: prompt, type **R.**⏎ to select the rotated option.

5. At the `Specify angle of dimension line <0>`: prompt, enter **30.**⏎.

6. At the `Specify dimension line location or [Mtext/Text/Angle/Horizontal/Vertical/Rotated]`: prompt, pick a point near coordinate 24´-11˝,0´-8˝ (88,12 for metric users). Your drawing will look like Figure 12.16.

Dimensioning Radii, Diameters, and Arcs

To dimension circular objects, you use another set of options from the Dimension menu:

1. Click the Angular Dimension tool on the Dimension toolbar. Or you can enter **Dan.**⏎ or choose Dimension ➤ Angular from the drop-down menu to start the angular dimension.

2. At the `Select arc, circle, line, or <specify vertex>`: prompt, pick the upper-left face of the hexagon near coordinate 1´-3˝,1´-10˝ (44,57 for metric users).

3. At the `Select second line`: prompt, pick the top face at coordinate 1´-9˝,2´-2˝ (54,62 for metric users).

FIGURE 12.15
A linear dimension using the Rotated option

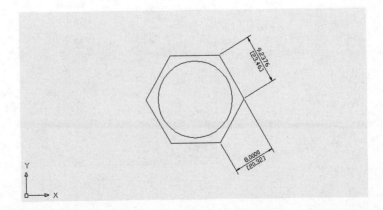

4. At the Specify dimension arc line location or [Mtext/Text/Angle]: prompt, notice that as you move the cursor around the upper-left corner of the hexagon, the dimension changes, as shown in the top images of Figure 12.17.

5. Pick a point near coordinate 1´-9˝, 1´-11˝(49,50 for metric users). The dimension is fixed in the drawing. (See the bottom image of Figure 12.17.)

TIP If you need to make subtle adjustments to the dimension line or text location, you can do so using grips, after you place the angular dimension.

FIGURE 12.16
The aligned dimen-
sion of a non-
orthogonal line

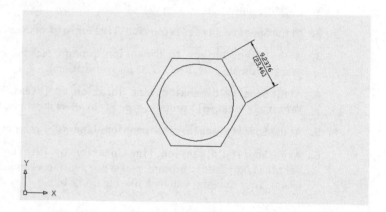

FIGURE 12.17
The angular dimen-
sion added to the
window frame

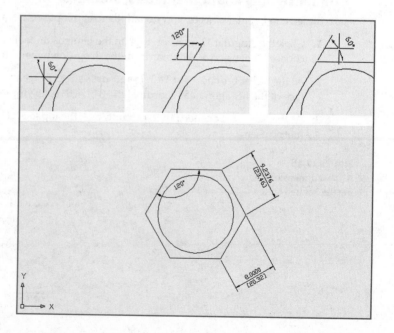

Now try the Diameter option, which shows the diameter of a circle:

1. Click the Diameter Dimension tool on the Dimension toolbar. Or you can enter **Ddi**↵ at the Command prompt.

2. At the `Select arc or circle:` prompt, pick the circle.

3. At the `Specify dimension line location or [Mtext/Text/Angle]:` prompt, you will see the diameter dimension drag along the circle as you move the cursor. If you move the cursor outside the circle, the dimension will change to display the dimension on the outside. (See the top image in Figure 12.18.)

TIP If the dimension text can't fit within the circle, AutoCAD gives you the option to place the dimension text outside the circle as you drag the temporary dimension to a horizontal position.

4. Place the cursor inside the circle so that the dimension arrow points in a horizontal direction, as shown in the bottom image of Figure 12.18.

5. With the text centered, click the mouse.

The Radius Dimension tool on the Dimension toolbar gives you a radius dimension just as the Diameter Dimension tool provides a circle's diameter.

FIGURE 12.18
Dimension showing
the diameter of a circle

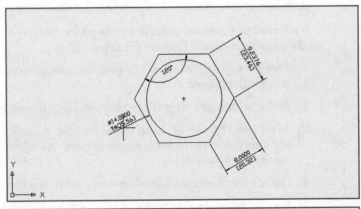

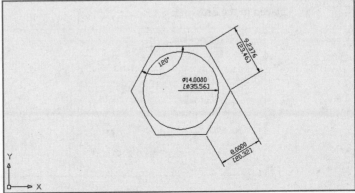

Figure 12.19 shows a radius dimension on the outside of the circle, but you can place it inside in a manner similar to the diameter dimension. The Center Mark tool on the Dimension toolbar just places a cross mark in the center of the selected arc or circle.

FIGURE 12.19
A radius dimension shown on the outside of the circle

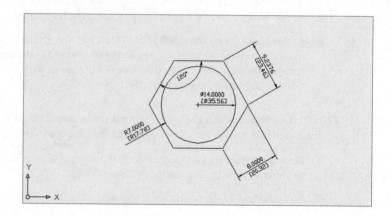

TIP   You can alter the format of diameter dimensions by changing the Dimtix and Dimtofl dimension variable settings. For example, if you want two arrows to appear across the diameter of the circle, turn on both Dimtix and Dimtofl. See Appendix C for more details.

If you need to dimension an arc or a circle whose center is not within the drawing area, you can use the jogged dimension. Here are the steps:

1. Click the Jogged Dimension tool from the Dimension toolbar, choose Dimension ➢ Jogged, or enter **Dimjogged**.

2. At the `Select arc or circle:` prompt, select the object you want to dimension.

3. At the `Specify center location override:` prompt, select a point that indicates the general direction to the center of the arc or circle. A dimension line appears and follows the movement of your cursor.

4. Position the dimension line where you want it, and then click.

5. Position the dimension line jog where you want it, and then click. The jogged dimension is placed in the drawing.

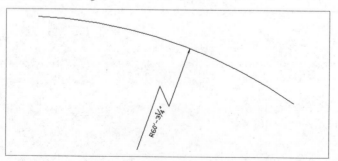

Arc lengths can also be given a dimension using the Arc Length tool. Choose the Arc Length tool from the Dimension toolbar, choose Dimension ➢ Arc Length, or enter Dimarc ↵ at the Command prompt. At the `Select Arc or polyline arc segment:` prompt, select the arc you want to dimension. It can be either a plain arc or a polyline arc. Once you've selected the arc, the arc dimension appears and moves with the cursor. You can then select the location for the dimension.

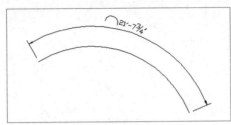

Adding a Note with an Arrow

Finally, there is the Dimension ➢ Leader option, which enables you to add a note with an arrow pointing to the object the note describes:

1. Click the Quick Leader tool on the Dimension toolbar, enter **Le**↵, or choose Dimension ➢ Leader from the drop-down menu.

2. At the `Specify first leader point, or [Settings] <Settings>:` prompt, pick a point near the top-left edge of the hexagon at coordinate 1´-4˝,2´-0˝ (45,59 for metric users).

3. At the `Specify next point:` prompt, enter **@6<110**↵. Metric users should enter **@15<110**↵.

4. At the `Specify next point:` prompt, you can continue to pick points just as you would draw lines. For this exercise, however, press ↵ to finish drawing leader lines.

TIP You can also add multiline text at the leader. See the next section, "Exploring the Leader Options."

5. At the `Specify text width <0 >:` prompt, press ↵.

6. At the `Enter first line of annotation text <Mtext>:` prompt, type **Window Frame**↵ as the label for this leader.

7. At the `Enter next line of annotation text:` prompt, press ↵ to finish the leader. Your drawing will look like Figure 12.20.

Exploring the Leader Options

The Leader tool is a deceptively simple tool with numerous options. In step 2 of the previous exercise, after choosing Dimension ➢ Leader from the menu bar, you can enter **S**↵ to open the Leader Settings dialog box.

From here, you can use the Leader tool to perform any number of functions, depending on the type of leader you want.

FIGURE 12.20
The leader with a
note added

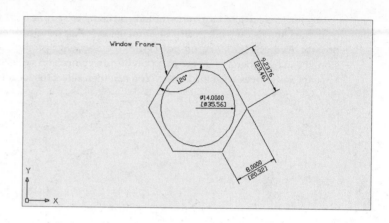

THE ANNOTATION TAB

The options in the Annotation tab let you control the type of annotation that is attached to the leader. AutoCAD uses the MText option by default, which places a multiline text object at the end of the leader.

In the Annotation Type button group are the following options:

Copy An Object Prompts you to select text, tolerance, or blocks to be copied to the endpoint of the leader.

Tolerance Opens the Tolerance dialog box when you've finished drawing the leader lines. See the section "Adding Tolerance Notation" later in this chapter.

Block Reference Lets you insert a block at the end of the leader.

None Ends the leader without adding a note.

In the MText Options button group are the following options:

Prompt For Width Asks you to select a width for multiline text.

Always Left Justify Left justifies multiline text.

Frame Text Draws a frame around the text.

In the Annotation Reuse button group are the following options:

None Always prompts you for annotation.

Reuse Next Reuses the annotation you enter for the next leader.

Reuse Current Reuses the current annotation text.

THE LEADER LINE & ARROW TAB

The options in the Leader Line & Arrow tab give you control over the leader line and arrow. You can select an arrow that is different from the default, or you can constrain the lines to follow a specific angle. The options are as follows:

Leader Line Lets you select from either a straight line or spline for your lines (see Figure 12.21).

FIGURE 12.21
Straight and spline
leader lines

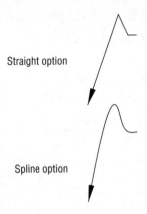

Straight option

Spline option

Number Of Points   Lets you constrain the number of points you select before the Command prompt prompts you for the annotation. The No Limit option lets you select as many points as you want. You then press ↵ when you've completed drawing the leader line and want to move on to entering the leader note.

Arrowhead   Lets you select an arrowhead from a list similar to the one in the New or Modify Dimension Style dialog box.

Angle Constraints   Lets you constrain the angle at which the leader line extends from the arrow and the second point.

THE ATTACHMENT TAB

The options in the Attachment tab (see Figure 12.22) let you control how the leader connects to MText annotation, depending on which side of the leader the annotation appears. The location of the leader endpoint in relation to the note is frequently a focus of drafting standards. These options let you customize your leader to produce results that conform to the standards you work with.

TIP   Just as with other dimensions, and objects in general, you can modify some of the properties of a leader by using the Properties palette. You can, for example, change a straight leader into a spline leader.

FIGURE 12.22
The Leader Settings
dialog box, open at the
Attachment tab

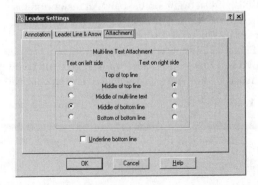

Skewing Dimension Lines

At times, you might need to force the extension lines to take on an angle other than 90° to the dimension line. This is a common requirement of isometric drawings, in which most lines are at 30° or 60° angles instead of 90°. To facilitate non-orthogonal dimensions like these, AutoCAD offers the Oblique option:

1. Choose Dimension ➢ Oblique or type **Ded.⌐O.⌐**. You can also select the Dimension Edit tool from the Dimension toolbar and then type **O.⌐**.

FIGURE 12.23

A dimension using the
Oblique option

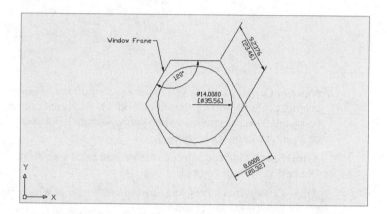

2. At the Select objects: prompt, pick the aligned dimension at the upper-right of the drawing and press ⌐ to confirm your selection.

3. At the Enter obliquing angle (Press ENTER for none): prompt, enter **60** for 60°. The dimension will skew so that the extension lines are at 60°, as shown in Figure 12.23.

4. Save the drawing and exit AutoCAD.

Applying Ordinate Dimensions

In mechanical drafting, *ordinate dimensions* are used to maintain the accuracy of machined parts by establishing an origin on the part. All major dimensions are described as X coordinates or Y coordinates of that origin. The origin is usually an easily locatable feature of the part, such as a machined bore or two machined surfaces.

Figure 12.24 shows a typical application of ordinate dimensions. In the lower-left corner, note the two dimensions whose leaders are jogged. Also note the origin location in the upper-right corner.

To use AutoCAD's Ordinate Dimension command, perform the following steps:

1. Choose Tools ➢ New UCS ➢ Origin or type **UCS.⌐Or.⌐**.

2. At the Specify new origin point <0,0,0>: prompt, click the exact location of the origin of your part.

3. Toggle the Ortho mode on.

FIGURE 12.24
A drawing using ordinate dimensions

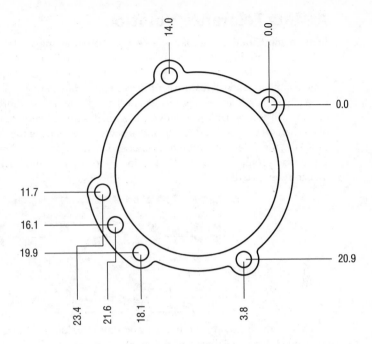

4. Click the Ordinate Dimension tool on the Dimension toolbar. You can also enter **Dor**⏎ to start the ordinate dimension.

5. At the `Specify feature location:` prompt, click the item you want to dimension.

TIP The direction of the leader determines whether the dimension will be of the Xdatum or the Ydatum.

6. At the `Specify leader endpoint or [Xdatum/Ydatum/Mtext/Text/Angle]:` prompt, indicate the length and direction of the leader. Do this by positioning the rubber-banding leader perpendicular to the coordinate direction you want to dimension and then clicking that point.

In steps 1 and 2, you used the UCS feature to establish a second origin in the drawing. The Ordinate Dimension tool then uses that origin to determine the ordinate dimensions. You will get a chance to work with the UCS feature in Chapter 21.

You might have noticed options in the Command window for the Ordinate Dimension tool. The Xdatum and Ydatum options force the dimension to be of the X or Y coordinate no matter what direction the leader takes. The MText option opens the Text Formatting toolbar, enabling you to append or replace the ordinate dimension text. The Text option lets you enter replacement text directly through the Command window.

TIP As with all other dimensions, you can use grips to adjust the location of ordinate dimensions.

If you turn Ortho mode off, the dimension leader will be drawn with a jog to maintain the orthogonal (look back at Figure 12.24).

Adding Tolerance Notation

In mechanical drafting, *tolerances* are a key part of a drawing's notation. They specify the allowable variation in size and shape that a mechanical part can have. To help facilitate tolerance notation, AutoCAD provides the Tolerance command, which offers common ISO tolerance symbols together with a quick way to build a standard feature control symbol. *Feature control symbols* are industry-standard symbols used to specify tolerances. If you are a mechanical engineer or drafter, AutoCAD's tolerance notation options will be a valuable tool. However, a full discussion of tolerances requires a basic understanding of mechanical design and drafting and is beyond the scope of this book.

To use the Tolerance command, choose Tolerance from the Dimension toolbar, type **Tol**↵ at the Command prompt, or choose Dimension ➤ Tolerance from the drop-down menu to open the Geometric Tolerance dialog box.

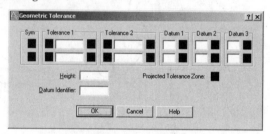

This is where you enter tolerance and datum values for the feature control symbol. You can enter two tolerance values and three datum values.

In addition, you can stack values in a two-tiered fashion.

Click a box in the Sym group to open the Symbol dialog box.

The top image in Figure 12.25 shows what each symbol in the Symbol dialog box represents. The bottom image shows a sample drawing with a feature symbol used on a cylindrical object. The symbols in the sample drawing show that the upper cylinder needs to be concentric within 0.0003″ of the lower cylinder.

In the Geometric Tolerance dialog box, you can click a box in any of the Datum groups or a box in the right side of the Tolerance groups to open the Material Condition dialog box. This dialog box contains standard symbols relating to the maximum and minimum material conditions of a feature on the part being dimensioned.

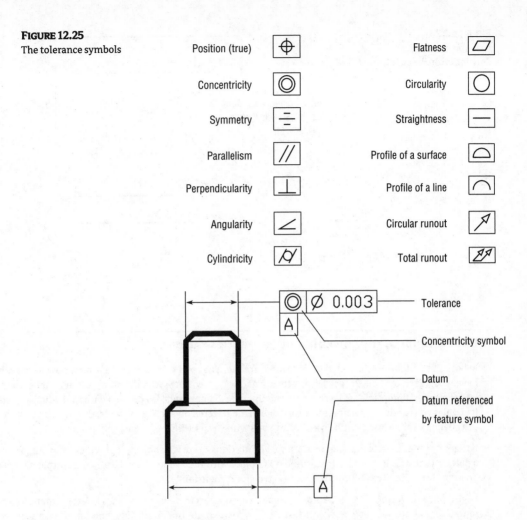

FIGURE 12.25

The tolerance symbols

If You Want to Experiment

At this point, you might want to experiment with the settings described in this chapter to identify the ones that are most useful for your work. You can then establish these settings as defaults in a prototype file or the Acad.dwt file. It's a good idea to experiment even with the settings you don't think you will need often—chances are you will have to alter them from time to time.

As an added exercise, try the steps shown in Figure 12.26. This exercise will give you a chance to see how you can update dimensions on a drawing that has been scaled down.

FIGURE 12.26

A sample mechanical drawing with dimensions

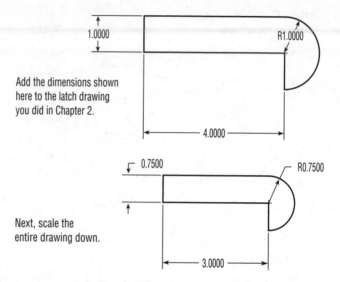

Add the dimensions shown here to the latch drawing you did in Chapter 2.

Next, scale the entire drawing down.

UNDERSTANDING THE POWER OF THE PROPERTIES PALETTE

In both this and the previous chapter, you made frequent use of the Properties palette. By now, you might have recognized that the Properties palette is a gateway to editing virtually any object. It enables you to edit the general properties of layer, color, and linetype assignments. When used with individual objects, it enables you to edit properties that are unique to the selected object. For example, through this tool, you can change a spline leader with an arrow into one with straight-line segments and no arrow.

If the Properties palette does not provide specific options to edit the object, it provides a button to open a palette that will. If you edit a multiline text object with the Properties palette, for example, you can open the Multiline Text Editor. The same is true for dimension text.

Beginning with AutoCAD 2000, Autodesk made a clear effort to make AutoCAD's interface more consistent. The text-editing tools now edit text of all types—single-line, multiline, and dimension text—so you don't have to remember which command or tool you need for a particular object. Likewise, using the Properties palette is a powerful way to edit all types of objects in your drawing.

As you continue with the rest of this tutorial, you might want to experiment with the Properties palette with new objects you learn about. In addition to enabling you to edit properties, the Properties palette can show you the status of an object, much like the List tool.

Part 3

Mastering Advanced Skills

In this part:

Chapter 13

Using Attributes

Early on in this book, you learned how to create blocks, which are assemblies of AutoCAD objects. Blocks enable you to form parts or symbols that can be easily reproduced. Furniture, bolts, doors, and windows are a few common items that you can create with blocks. And as you saw in later chapters, whole rooms and appliances can be made into blocks. There really is no limit to a block's size.

AutoCAD also offers a feature called *attributes* that allows you to store text information as a part of a block. For example, you can store the material specifications for a bolt or other mechanical part that you have converted into a block. If your application is architecture, you can store the material, hardware, and dimensional information for a door or window that has been converted into a block. By storing this information within a block, you can quickly gather information about that block that may not be obvious from just the graphics.

Attribute text can be set up to be invisible, or it can be displayed as text in the drawing. If it is invisible, you can easily view the attribute information by double-clicking the block that contains the attribute. The attribute information is displayed in a dialog box. This information can also be extracted to a database or spreadsheet, giving you the ability to keep an inventory of the blocks in your drawing. You can even convert attribute information into tables within an AutoCAD drawing. This can help you make quick work of parts lists or door and window schedules. By using attributes, you can keep track of virtually any object in a drawing or maintain textual information within the drawing that can be queried.

Keeping track of objects is just one way to use attributes. You can also use them in place of text objects when you must keep text and graphic items together. One common example of this is the reference symbol in an architectural drawing. Reference symbols are used to indicate the location of more detailed information in a drawing set such as the elevation views of a room or a cross-section of a wall or other part of a building. (See the "Common Uses for Attributes" sidebar later in this chapter for more examples.) In this chapter you will use attributes for one of their more common functions: maintaining lists of parts. In this case, the parts are doors. This chapter also describes how to import these attributes into a database management program. As you go through these exercises, think about the ways attributes can help you in your particular application.

This chapter covers the following topics:

◆ Creating Attributes

◆ Editing Attributes

◆ Extracting and Exporting Attribute Information

Creating Attributes

Attributes depend on blocks. You might think of an attribute as text information attached to a block. The information can be a description of the block or some other pertinent text. For example, you could include an attribute definition with the door block you created in Chapter 3. Then, every time you subsequently insert the door block, you would be prompted for a value associated with that door. The value can be a number, a height or width value, a name, or any type of text information you want. When you insert the door block, you are prompted for an attribute value. After you enter a value, it is stored as part of the door block within the drawing database. This value can be displayed as text attached to the door block, or it can be invisible. You can change the value at any time. You can even specify the actual prompts for the attribute value.

However, suppose you don't have the attribute information when you design the door block. As an alternative, you can add the attribute to a *symbol* that is later placed by the door when you know enough about the design to specify what type of door goes where. Figure 13.1 shows a sample door symbol and a table to which the symbol refers. The standard door type symbol suits this purpose nicely because it is an object that you can set up and use as a block independent of the actual door block.

TIP A door type symbol is a graphic code that indicates special characteristics of the associated door. The code refers to a note or detailed drawing on another drawing, or it can refer to a detailed description in a set of written specifications.

Adding Attributes to Blocks

In the following exercise, you will create a door type symbol, which is commonly used to describe the size, thickness, and other characteristics of any given door in an architectural drawing. The symbol is usually a circle, a hexagon, or a diamond with a number in it. The number is usually cross-referenced to a schedule that lists all the door types and their characteristics.

FIGURE 13.1

A door symbol tells you what type of door goes in the location shown. Usually the symbol contains a number or a letter that is keyed to a table that shows more information about the door.

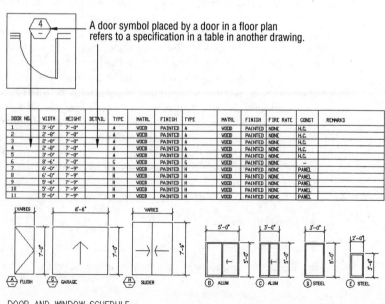

A door symbol placed by a door in a floor plan refers to a specification in a table in another drawing.

DOOR NO.	WIDTH	HEIGHT	DETAIL	TYPE	MATRL	FINISH	TYPE	MATRL	FINISH	FIRE RATE	CONST	REMARKS
1	3'-0"	7'-0"		A	WOOD	PAINTED	A	WOOD	PAINTED	NONE	H.C.	
2	2'-8"	7'-0"		A	WOOD	PAINTED	A	WOOD	PAINTED	NONE	H.C.	
3	2'-8"	7'-0"		A	WOOD	PAINTED	A	WOOD	PAINTED	NONE	H.C.	
4	2'-8"	7'-0"		A	WOOD	PAINTED	A	WOOD	PAINTED	NONE	H.C.	
5	3'-0"	7'-0"		A	WOOD	PAINTED	A	WOOD	PAINTED	NONE	H.C.	
6	8'-6"	7'-0"		G	WOOD	PAINTED	G	WOOD	PAINTED	NONE	-	
7	6'-0"	7'-9"		H	WOOD	PAINTED	H	WOOD	PAINTED	NONE	PANEL	
8	6'-0"	7'-9"		H	WOOD	PAINTED	H	WOOD	PAINTED	NONE	PANEL	
9	5'-6"	7'-9"		H	WOOD	PAINTED	H	WOOD	PAINTED	NONE	PANEL	
10	5'-0"	7'-9"		H	WOOD	PAINTED	H	WOOD	PAINTED	NONE	PANEL	
11	5'-0"	7'-9"		H	WOOD	PAINTED	H	WOOD	PAINTED	NONE	PANEL	

DOOR AND WINDOW SCHEDULE

In this exercise, you will create a new file containing attribute definitions. You could also include such definitions in blocks that you create by using the Make Block tool (the Block command) or in files that you create by using the Wblock command. Just create the attribute definitions as shown here, and then include them with the Block or Wblock selections.

Here are the steps for creating the attribute definition:

1. Create a new file and call it S-door (for *symbol-door*). The symbol will fit in the default limits of the drawing, so you don't have to change the Limits setting.

2. Draw a circle with its center at coordinate 7,5 and a radius of 0.125 (0.3 for metric users).

TIP Because this is a new drawing, the circle is automatically placed on Layer 0. Remember that objects in a block that are on Layer 0 take on the color and linetype assignment of the layer on which the block is inserted.

3. Next, zoom in to the circle so it is about the same size as that shown in Figure 13.2.

4. If the circle looks like an octagon, choose View ➢ Regen or type **Re↵** to regenerate your drawing.

5. Choose Draw ➢ Block ➢ Define Attributes or type **Att↵** to open the Attribute Definition dialog box.

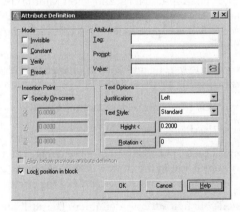

6. In the Attribute group, click the Tag input box and enter **D-TYPE**.

TIP The attribute tag is equivalent to a field name in a database. Or you can think of the tag as the name or ID of the attribute. It can help to identify the purpose of the attribute. The tag can be a maximum of 31 characters but cannot contain spaces. If you plan to use the attribute data in a database program, check that program's documentation for other restrictions on field names.

7. Press the Tab key or click the Prompt input box, and enter **Door type**. This is the text for the prompt that will appear when you insert the block containing this attribute. Often the prompt is the same as the tag, but it can be anything you like. Unlike the tag, the prompt can include spaces and other special characters.

TIP Use a prompt that gives explicit instructions so the user will know exactly what is expected. Consider including an example within the prompt. (Enclose the example in square brackets to imitate the way AutoCAD prompts often display defaults.)

FIGURE 13.2
The attribute
definition inserted
in the circle

8. Click the Value input box and enter a hyphen. This is the default value for the door type prompt.

TIP   If an attribute is to contain a number that will later be used for sorting in a database, use a default value such as 000 to indicate the number of digits required. The zeros can also serve to remind the user that values less than 100 must be preceded by a leading zero, as in 099.

9. Click the Justification drop-down list and select Middle. This enables you to center the attribute on the circle's center. You might notice several other options in the Text Options group. Because attributes appear as text, you can apply the same settings to them as you would to single-line text.

10. In the input box next to the Height < button, change the value to 0.125. (Metric users should enter **0.3**.) This makes the attribute text 0.125″ (0.3 cm) high.

11. In the Insertion Point group, make sure that the Specify On-Screen check box is checked.

12. Click OK to close the dialog box.

13. Using the Center Osnap, pick the center of the circle. You need to place the cursor on the circle's circumference, not in the circle's center, to obtain the center by using the Osnap. The attribute definition appears at the center of the circle (see Figure 13.2).

You have just created your first attribute definition. The attribute definition displays its tag in all uppercase letters to help you identify it. When you later insert this file into another drawing, the tag turns into the value you assign to it when it is inserted. If you want only one attribute, you can stop here and save the file. The next section shows how you can quickly add several more attributes to your drawing.

Adding Attribute Specifications

Next, you will add a few more attribute definitions, but instead of using the Attribute Definition dialog box, you will make an arrayed copy of the first attribute and then edit the attribute definition copies. This method can save you time when you want to create several attribute definitions that have similar characteristics. By making copies and editing them, you'll also get a chance to see firsthand how to change an attribute definition.

Follow these steps to make copies of the attribute:

1. Click Array on the Modify toolbar or type **Ar⏎** to open the Array dialog box.

2. Click the Rectangular Array radio button in the upper-left corner.

3. Click the Select Objects button and select the attribute definition you just created. Press ⏎ to confirm your selection.

4. In the Rows input box, enter **7** and in the Columns input box, enter **1**.

5. Enter **–0.18** in the Row Offset input box (**–0.432** for metric users) and **0** in the Column Offset input box. The Row Offset value is approximately 1.5 times the height of the attribute text height. The minus sign in the Row Offset value causes the array to be drawn downward.

6. Click OK.

7. Issue a Zoom Extents command or click the Zoom Realtime tool to view all the attributes.

Now you are ready to modify the copies of the attribute definitions:

1. Press Esc to clear any selections or commands, and click the attribute definition just below the original.

2. Right-click and choose Properties from the shortcut menu to open the Properties palette.

TIP You can double-click an attribute definition to change its Tag, Prompt, or Default value in the Edit Attribute Definition dialog box. However, this dialog box doesn't let you change an attribute definition's visibility mode.

3. Scroll down the list of properties until you see the Invisible option in the Misc category.

4. Select Yes from the Invisible option drop-down list.

5. Scroll back up the list of properties and locate the Tag option in the Text category.

6. Highlight the Tag value to the right and type **D-SIZE**↵. The attribute changes to reflect the change in the Tag value.

7. While still in the Text category, highlight the Prompt value and type **Door size**↵.

8. In the Value field, type **3´-0˝**↵. Metric users should type **90**↵.

TIP   Make sure you press ↵ after entering a new value for the properties in the Properties palette. Pressing ↵ confirms your new entry.

You've just learned how to edit an attribute definition. Now you'll make changes to the other attribute definitions:

1. Press Esc twice so that no attribute is selected, and then click the next attribute down so you can display its properties in the Properties palette.

2. Continue to edit this and the rest of the attribute definition properties by using the attribute settings listed in Table 13.1. To do this, repeat steps 4 through 8 of the preceding exercise for each attribute definition, replacing the Tag, Prompt, and Default Values with those shown in Table 13.1. Also, make sure all but the original attributes have the Invisible option selected.

3. When you've finished editing the attribute definition properties, close the Properties palette.

4. Choose Draw ➤ Block ➤ Base to change the base point of this drawing to the center of the circle. Use the Center Osnap to get the exact center.

5. Now you have finished creating your door type symbol with attributes. Save the S-door file.

When you later insert a file or a block containing attributes, the attribute prompts will appear in the order that their associated definitions were created. If the order of the prompts at insertion time is important, you can control it by editing the attribute definitions so their creation order corresponds to the desired prompt order. You can also control the order by using the Block Attribute Manager, which you'll look at later in this chapter.

TABLE 13.1:   Attributes for the Door Type Symbol

TAG	PROMPT	DEFAULT VALUE
D-NUMBER	Door number	–
D-THICK	Door thickness	–
D-RATE	Fire rating	–
D-MATRL	Door material	–
D-CONST	Door construction	–

Make sure the invisible option is selected for the attributes in this table.

Inserting Blocks Containing Attributes

In the preceding section, you created a door type symbol at the desired size for the actual plotted symbol. This means that whenever you insert that symbol, you have to specify an X and Y scale factor appropriate to the scale of your drawing. This enables you to use the same symbol in any drawing, regardless of its scale. (You could have several door type symbols, one for each scale you anticipate using, but this would be inefficient.)

The following steps demonstrate the process of inserting a block that contains attributes:

1. Open the Plan file you created in earlier exercises. Or you can use the 13a-plan.dwg file from the companion CD. Metric users can use the file 13a-plan-metric.dwg (from the CD's Chapter 6 folder).

2. Turn on the Attribute Dialog mode by entering **Attdia↵1↵** at the Command prompt. This enables you to enter attribute values through a dialog box in the next exercise.

3. Choose View ➢ Named Views, and then restore the view named First. Be sure the Ceiling and Flr-pat layers are off. Normally in a floor plan, the door headers are not visible, and they will interfere with the placement of the door reference symbol.

4. Click the Insert Block tool or type I↵ to open the Insert dialog box.

5. Click the Browse button.

6. Locate the S-door file in the file list and double-click it.

7. In the Insertion Point group, make sure that the Specify On-Screen option is turned on.

8. In the Scale group, make sure the Uniform Scale check box is selected; then enter **96** in the X input box. Metric users should enter **100** in the X input box.

9. In the Rotation group, make sure that the Specify On-Screen option is turned off; then Click OK.

You created the S-door file at the actual plotted size, so in step 9, you needed to scale it up by the drawing scale factor to make it the appropriate size for this drawing.

Now you're ready to place the file in your drawing and enter the attribute values for the symbol:

1. AutoCAD is waiting for you to select a location for the symbol. To place the symbol, click in the doorway of the lower-left unit, near coordinate 41´-3˝,72´-4˝. Metric users should use coordinate 1256,2202. When you click the location, the Enter Attributes dialog box opens.

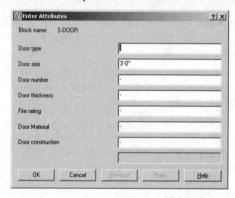

2. In the Door Type input box, enter **A**↵. Note that this is the prompt you created. Note also that the default value is the hyphen you specified.

TIP Attribute data is case sensitive, so any text you enter in all capital letters will be stored in all capital letters.

3. In the Door Number input box, change the hyphen to 116. Continue to change the values for each input box, as shown in Table 13.2.

TABLE 13.2: Attribute Values for the Typical Studio Entry Door

PROMPT	VALUE
Door type	A
Door Size	3´-0˝
Door number	(Same as room number; see figure 13.5)
Door thickness	1 ³/₄ ˝
Fire rating	20 min.
Door material	Wood
Door construction	Solid core

4. When you are finished changing values, click OK, and the symbol appears. The only attribute you can see is the one you selected to be visible: the door type.

TIP If the symbol does not appear, go back to the S-door.dwg file and make sure you set the base point to the center of the circle. After you have updated the file, Reinsert the file using the Browse button in the Insert dialog box (see step 5 of the previous exercise).

5. Add the rest of the door type symbols for the apartment entry doors by copying or arraying the door symbol you just inserted. You can use the previously saved views to help you get around the drawing quickly. Don't worry that the attribute values won't be appropriate for each unit. You'll see how to edit the attributes in the next section.

As a review exercise, you'll now create another file for the apartment number symbol (shown in Figure 13.3). This will be a rectangular box with the room number that you will place in each studio apartment.

Follow these steps:

1. Save the Plan file and then open a new file called S-apart (for the apartment number symbol).

2. Create an attribute definition and give it the tag name R-NUMBER, the prompt Room number, a default value of 000, and a text height of 0.125″.

3. Use the Base command (choose Draw ➢ Block ➢ Base) to set the base point of this drawing in the lower-left corner of the rectangle.

4. Save and close S-apart.

5. Go back to the Plan file again and insert the S-apart drawing you just created (using an X scale factor of 96) into the lower-left unit. Give this attribute the value 116.

6. Copy or array the room number symbol so that there is one symbol in each of the units. You'll learn how to modify the attributes to reflect their proper values in the following section, "Editing Attributes." Figure 13.4 shows what the view should look like after you've entered the door symbols and the apartment numbers.

FIGURE 13.3

The apartment number symbol

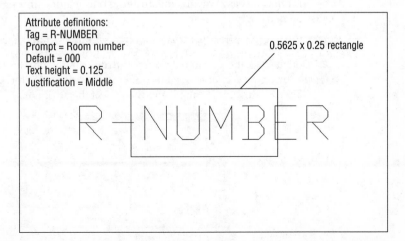

FIGURE 13.4
An overall view of the
plan with door sym-
bols and apartment
numbers added

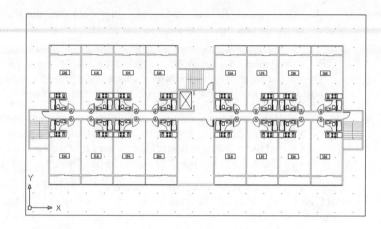

Editing Attributes

Because drawings are usually in flux even after actual construction or manufacturing begins, you will eventually have to edit previously entered attributes. In the example of the apartment building, many things can change before the final set of drawings is completed.

Attributes can be edited individually or *globally*—you can edit several occurrences of a particular attribute tag all at one time. In this section you will make changes to the attributes you have entered so far, using both individual and global editing techniques, and you will practice editing invisible attributes.

TIP If you prefer to start commands by using a toolbar, the Modify II toolbar in AutoCAD contains tools for the Enhanced Attribute Editor and the Block Attribute Manager discussed in this section.

Editing Attribute Values One at a Time

AutoCAD offers an easy way to edit attributes one at a time through a dialog box. The following exercise demonstrates this feature:

1. Choose View ➤ Named View, and then restore the First view.

2. Double-click the apartment number attribute in the unit just to the right of the first unit in the lower-left corner to open the Enhanced Attribute Editor. You can also choose Modify ➤ Object ➤ Attribute ➤ Single and then select the attribute.

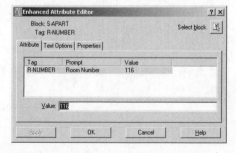

TIP LT users will see the Edit Attributes dialog box, which lists the attributes in a single column.

3. Change the value in the Value input box to 112 and then click OK to make the change.

4. Do this for each room number, using Figure 13.5 as a reference for assigning room numbers.

5. Now go back and edit the Door number attribute for the S-door attribute. Give each door the same number as the room number they are associated with. See Figure 13.5 for the room numbers.

FIGURE 13.5
Apartment numbers
for one floor of the
studio apartment
building

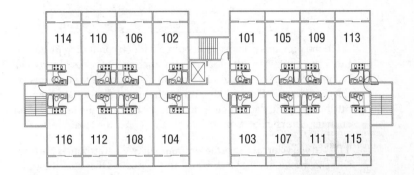

TIP If you're a veteran AutoCAD user, you can still use the Ddatte command (**Ate⏎** shortcut) to open the Edit Attributes dialog box. This dialog box is useful for reviewing attributes as well as editing them because both visible and invisible attributes are displayed in the dialog box.

Editing Attribute Text Formats and Properties

You might have noticed that the Enhanced Attribute Editor in the preceding exercise has three tabs: Attribute, Text Options, and Properties. When you double-click a block containing an attribute, the Enhanced Attribute Editor dialog box opens at the Attribute tab. You can use the other two tabs to control the size, font, color, and other properties of the selected attribute.

The Text Options tab lets you alter the attribute text style, justification, height, rotation, width factor, and oblique angle. (See Chapter 10 for more on these text options.)

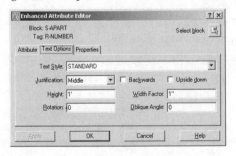

The Properties tab lets you alter the attribute's layer, linetype, color, line weight (effective only on AutoCAD fonts), and plot style assignments.

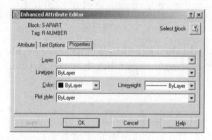

In the previous exercise, you edited a block containing just a single attribute. Double-clicking a block that contains multiple attributes, such as the S-door block, opens the Enhanced Attribute Editor dialog box at the Attribute tab. This tab displays all the attributes, regardless of whether they are visible, as shown in Figure 13.6. You can then edit the value, formats, and properties of the individual attributes by highlighting the attribute in the Attribute tab and then using the other tabs to make changes. The changes you make will affect only the attribute you've highlighted in the Attribute tab.

TIP If you want to change the location of individual attributes in a block, you can move attributes by using grips. Click the block to expose the grips and then click the grip connected to the attribute. Or if you've selected several blocks, Shift+click the attribute grips; then move the attributes to their new location. They will still be attached to their associated blocks.

The Enhanced Attribute Editor lets you change attribute values, formats, and properties one block at a time, but, as you'll see in the next section, you can also make changes to several attributes at once.

Making Global Changes to Attribute Values

At times you'll want to change the value of several attributes in a file to be the same value. You can use the Edit Attribute Globally option to make any global changes to attribute values.

Suppose you decide you want to change all the entry doors to a type designated as B, rather than A. Perhaps door type A was an input error, or type B happens to be better suited for an entry door. The following exercise demonstrates how this is done:

1. Choose View ➢ Named Views to open the View Manager dialog box and then restore the view named Fourth. Pan your view down so you can see the door reference symbol for all the rooms in this view of the drawing.

2. Choose Modify ➢ Object ➢ Attribute ➢ Global, or type **–Attedit**⏎ at the Command prompt. Make sure you include the dash at the beginning of –Attedit.

FIGURE 13.6
The Enhanced Attribute Editor showing the contents of a block that contains several attributes

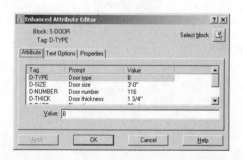

3. At the Edit Attributes one at a time? [Yes/No] <Y>: prompt, enter **N**↵ for No. You will see the message Performing global editing of attribute values. This tells you that you are in the Global Edit mode.

4. At the Edit only attributes visible on screen? [Yes/No] <Y>: prompt, press ↵. As you can see from this prompt, you have the option to edit all attributes, including those out of the view area. You'll get a chance to work with this option later in the chapter.

5. At the Enter block name specification <*>: prompt, press ↵. Optionally, you can enter a block name to narrow the selection to specific blocks.

6. At the Enter attribute tag specification <*>: prompt, press ↵. Optionally, you can enter an attribute tag name to narrow your selection to specific tags.

7. At the Enter attribute value specification <*>: prompt, press ↵. Optionally, you can narrow your selection to attributes containing specific values.

8. At the Select Attributes: prompt, select the door type symbols for units 103 to 115. You can use a window to select the attributes if you prefer.

9. At the Enter string to change: prompt, enter **A**↵.

10. At the Enter new string: prompt, enter **B**↵. The door type symbols all change to the new value.

In step 8, you were asked to select the attributes to be edited. AutoCAD limits the changes to those attributes you select. If you know you need to change every attribute in your drawing, you can do so by answering the series of prompts in a slightly different way, as in the following exercise:

1. Try the same procedure again, but this time enter **N** at the Edit only attributes visible on screen: prompt (step 4 in the previous exercise). The message Drawing must be regenerated afterwards appears. The AutoCAD Text Window appears.

2. Once again, you are prompted for the block name, the tag, and the value (steps 5, 6, and 7 in the previous exercise). Respond to these prompts as you did before. You then get the message 128 attributes selected. This tells you the number of attributes that fit the specifications you just entered.

3. At the Enter string to change: prompt, enter **A**↵ to indicate you want to change the rest of the A attribute values.

4. At the Enter new string: prompt, enter **B**↵. A series of Bs appears, indicating the number of strings that were replaced.

WARNING   If the Regenauto command is off, you must regenerate the drawing to see the change.

You might have noticed in the previous exercise that the Select Attribute: prompt is skipped and you go directly to the String to change: prompt. AutoCAD assumes that you want it to edit every attribute in the drawing, so it doesn't bother asking you to select specific attributes.

Making Invisible Attributes Visible

You can globally edit invisible attributes, such as those in the door reference symbol, by using the tools just described. You might, however, want to be a bit more selective about which invisible attribute you want to modify. Or you might simply want to make them temporarily visible for other editing purposes.

This exercise shows how you can make invisible attributes visible:

1. Enter **Attdisp**↵.

TIP You can also use the View menu to change the display characteristics of attributes. Choose View ➤ Display ➤ Attribute Display and then click the desired option on the cascading menu.

2. At the Enter attribute visibility setting [Normal/ON/OFF] <Normal>: prompt, enter **ON**↵. Your drawing will look like Figure 13.7. If Regenauto is turned off, you might have to issue the Regen command. At this point, you could edit the invisible attributes individually, as in the first attribute-editing exercise. For now, set the attribute display back to Normal.

FIGURE 13.7

The drawing with all the attributes visible. (Door type symbols are so close together that they overlap.)

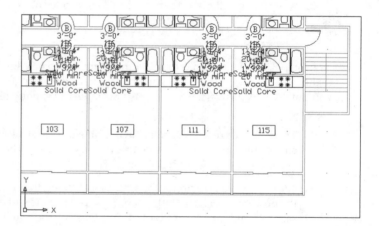

3. Enter **Attdisp**↵ again; then at the Enter attribute visibility setting [Normal/ON/ OFF] <ON>: prompt, enter **N**↵ for Normal.

TIP You've seen the results of the On and Normal options. The Off option makes all attributes invisible, regardless of the mode used when they were created.

Because the attributes were not intended to be visible, they appear to overlap and cover other parts of the drawing when they are made visible. Just remember to turn them back off when you are done reviewing them.

Making Global Format and Property Changes to Attributes

While we're on the subject of global editing, you'll want to know how to make global changes to the format and properties of attributes. Earlier in this section, you saw how to make format changes to individual attributes by using the Enhanced Attribute Editor dialog box. You can also use the Edit Attribute dialog box to make global changes, as the following exercise demonstrates.

USING SPACES IN ATTRIBUTE VALUES

At times, you might want the default value to begin with a blank space. This enables you to specify text strings more easily when you edit the attribute. For example, you might have an attribute value that reads 3334333. If you want to change the first 3 in this string of numbers, you have to specify 3334 when prompted for the string to change; then, for the new string, enter the same set of numbers again with the first 3 changed to the new number. If you only specify 3 for the string to change, AutoCAD will change all the 3s in the value. If you start with a space, as in _3334333 (I'm using an underline here only to represent the space; it doesn't mean you type an underline character), you can isolate the first 3 from the rest by specifying _3 as the string to change (again, type a space instead of the underline).

You must enter a backslash character (\) before the space in the default value to tell AutoCAD to interpret the space literally, rather than as a press of the spacebar (which is equivalent to pressing ↵).

TIP Although LT does not support the Edit Attribute dialog box, you can use the command-line version of the Attedit command to edit some of the format and property values of attributes. Enter **–Attedit**↵ at the command line and follow the prompts.

Follow these steps to make the global changes:

1. Choose Modify ➢ Object ➢ Attribute ➢ Block Attribute Manager to open the Block Attribute Manager dialog box.

TIP The Block Attribute Manager is often referred to as "Battman" by experienced AutoCAD users.

2. Select S-apart from the Block drop-down list at the top of the dialog box. This list displays all the blocks that contain attributes. The only attribute you've defined for the selected block is displayed in the list box below it.

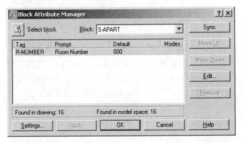

3. Click the attribute value in the list and click the Edit button to open the Edit Attribute dialog box. The Edit Attribute dialog box is nearly identical to the Enhanced Attribute Editor you saw earlier.

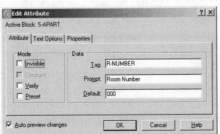

TIP If there is only one attribute in the attribute list box, you don't have to select it before clicking the Edit button.

4. Click the Properties tab, select Red from the Color drop-down list, and click OK.

5. Click OK to exit the dialog box.

The Edit Attribute dialog box you saw in this exercise offers a slightly different set of options from those in the Enhanced Attribute Editor dialog box. In the Attribute tab of the Edit Attribute dialog box, you can change some of the mode settings for the attribute, such as visibility and the Verify and Preset modes. You can also change the Tag, Prompt, and Default values. In contrast, the Attribute tab in the Enhanced Attribute Editor dialog box enables you to change the attribute value but none of the other attribute properties.

OTHER BLOCK ATTRIBUTE MANAGER OPTIONS

There are a few other options in the Block Attribute Manager dialog box that weren't covered in the exercises. Here's a rundown of the Settings, Move Up, Move Down, and Remove and Sync buttons:

Settings Click this button to open the Settings dialog box, which lets you control which attribute properties are displayed in the list box of the Block Attribute Manager dialog box.

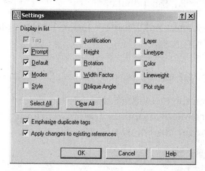

You can then select the properties to be displayed. The Emphasize Duplicate Tags option highlights duplicate tag names by showing them in red. The Apply Changes To Existing References option forces any changes you make to the attribute properties to be applied to existing attributes. If this setting is turned off, you have to use the Sync button in the Block Attribute Manager dialog box to update existing attributes, and the changes you make to attribute properties are applied only to new attributes added after the change. You can also enter **Attsync↵** at the Command prompt to synchronize older attributes.

Move Up and Move Down Clicking these buttons moves a selected attribute up or down the list of attributes in the list box. If you move an item down the list, the item will change its position when viewed using the Ddatte command or when viewing the attribute's properties in the Enhanced Attribute Editor dialog box. Of course, this has an effect only on blocks containing multiple attributes.

Remove Clicking this button removes the selected attribute from the block, so make sure you really mean it when you click this button.

Sync This option updates the attribute properties such as the attribute order, text formatting, mode, etc. It can also be used to globally update blocks that have had new attribute definitions added or deleted. It does not affect the individual attribute values.

Redefining Blocks Containing Attributes

Finally, be aware that attributes act differently from other objects when included in redefined blocks. Normally, blocks that have been redefined change their configuration to reflect the new block definition. But if a redefined block contains attributes, the attributes will maintain their old properties, including their position in relation to other objects in the block. This means that the old attribute position, style, and so on do not change even though you might have changed them in the new definition.

Fortunately, AutoCAD offers a tool specifically designed to let you update blocks with attributes. The following steps describe how to update attribute blocks:

1. Before you use the command to redefine an attribute block, you must first create the objects and attribute definitions that are going to make up the new replacement attribute block. The simplest way to do this is to explode a copy of the attribute block you want to update. This ensures that you have the same attribute definitions in the updated block.

2. Make your changes to the exploded attribute block.

WARNING Before you explode the attribute block copy, be sure that it is at a 1-to-1 scale. This is important, because if you don't use the original size of the block, you could end up with all your new attribute blocks at the wrong size. Also be sure you use a marker device, such as a line, to locate the insertion point of the attribute block before you explode it. This will help you locate and maintain the original insertion point for the redefined block.

3. Type **Attredef.⏎**.

4. At the Enter name of block you wish to redefine: prompt, enter the appropriate name.

5. At the Select objects: prompt, select all the objects, including the attribute definitions, you want to include in the revised attribute block.

6. At the Specify insertion base point of new Block: prompt, pick the same location used for the original block.

After you pick the insertion point, AutoCAD takes a few seconds to update the blocks. The amount of time depends on the complexity of the block and the number of times the block occurs in the drawing. If you include a new attribute definition with your new block, it too will be added to all the updated blocks, with its default value. Attribute definitions that are deleted from your new definition will be removed from all the updated blocks.

TIP You can also use the Refedit command (choose Tools ➢ Xref And Block In-Place Editing ➢ Edit Reference In-Place) to modify Attribute definitions. After editing, you must use the Sync option in the Block Attribute Manager to update all instances of the modified block.

Extracting and Exporting Attribute Information

After you enter the attributes in your drawing, you can extract the information contained in the attributes and use it to generate reports or to analyze the attribute data in other programs. You might, for example, want to keep track of the number and type of doors in your drawing through a database manager. This is especially useful if you have a project such as a large hotel that contains thousands of doors.

When you extract attribute data, AutoCAD creates a text file. You can choose to export the file in either comma-delimited or tab-delimited format. If you have Microsoft Excel or Access installed, you can also export the attribute data in a format compatible with these programs.

Performing the Extraction

In the past, extracting the attribute data from a drawing was an error-prone task requiring the creation of a template file. This template file had to contain a series of codes that described the data you wanted to extract. AutoCAD 2007 has a greatly improved system for attribute data extraction, in the form of the Attribute Extraction Wizard. The following exercises will walk you through a sample extraction.

NOTE LT does not offer the Attribute Extraction Wizard. Instead, you see the more simplified Attribute Extraction dialog box that offers the file format options (comma- or space-delimited or DXF output), the output filename, and template file options. For LT, the template file is used as an option to filter the attributes.

USING THE ATTRIBUTE EXTRACTION WIZARD

In this first exercise, you'll explore the Attribute Extraction Wizard:

TIP You can use the 13c-plan.dwg sample file if you haven't done the tutorials from the beginning of the chapter.

1. Go back to the Plan file and choose Tools ➤ Attribute Extraction to start the Attribute Extraction Wizard. In the Begin screen, you can choose to start an extraction from scratch or use a template you've created from previous extractions.

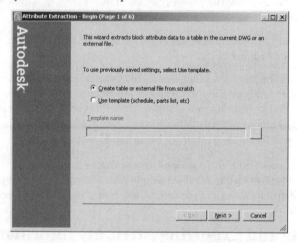

2. The Use Template option enables you to import extraction settings from an external file. Right now, it's not likely that you have any saved settings available, but in a later screen of the wizard, you will have a chance to save the options you select as a template file that you can import in later sessions. Click Next to open the Select Drawings screen. Here you can choose to extract attribute data from specific blocks, the entire current drawing, or different drawings.

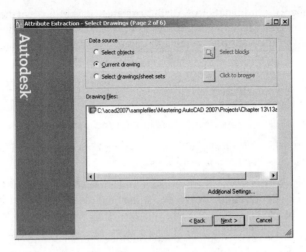

3. Click Additional Settings to view some other options. These options let you further refine the content of your extraction.

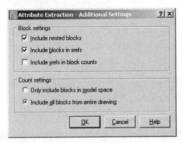

4. Click Cancel to close the Additional Settings dialog box; then click Next to open the Select Attributes screen.

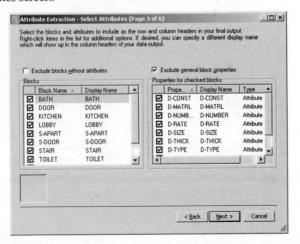

Take a moment to study the Select Attributes screen. It is the heart of the extraction process. Here you select the blocks that contain attributes as well as the specific attributes you want to extract. Notice that in the Blocks list box on the left, all the blocks in the drawing are displayed—not just those that contain user-defined attributes. The Properties For Checked Blocks list box to the right displays attribute and block properties.

SELECTING WHAT TO EXTRACT

Let's continue by selecting specific information for the extraction:

1. Turn on the Exclude Blocks Without Attributes option. Notice that the Blocks list now shows just the blocks that contain attributes.

2. In the Blocks list, turn off the S-apart block name to exclude it from the extraction. Though it isn't obvious, the attribute list changes to show just the values for the –DOOR block.

At the top of the Select Attributes screen, you'll see another option called Exclude General Block Properties. If you turn this option off, other types of data will be extracted besides the attribute data—information such as the layer of the attribute blocks, their insertion point, and orientation. These types of data may be useful for some applications, such as generating a list of datum points from a survey.

You won't need the general block properties, so you can leave that option turned on. Next, you'll get to see a preview of your current extraction settings.

1. Click Next to open the Finalize Output screen, which displays a listing of the attribute data that you selected in the previous screens. The attribute values are shown in a table, with each block listed as a row and the attributes of the block listed in columns. You can use the horizontal scroll bar at the bottom of the list to view all the columns.

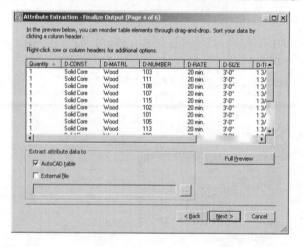

2. Click the Full Preview button to see a preview of how the extracted data will be formatted.

	Quantity	D-CONST	D-MATRL	D-NUMBER	D-RATE	D-SIZE	D-THICK	D-TYPE	Name
	1	Solid Core	Wood	103	20 min.	3'-0"	1 3/4"	B	S-DOOR
	1	Solid Core	Wood	111	20 min.	3'-0"	1 3/4"	B	S-DOOR
	1	Solid Core	Wood	108	20 min.	3'-0"	1 3/4"	B	S-DOOR
	1	Solid Core	Wood	107	20 min.	3'-0"	1 3/4"	B	S-DOOR
	1	Solid Core	Wood	115	20 min.	3'-0"	1 3/4"	B	S-DOOR
	1	Solid Core	Wood	102	20 min.	3'-0"	1 3/4"	B	S-DOOR
	1	Solid Core	Wood	101	20 min.	3'-0"	1 3/4"	B	S-DOOR
	1	Solid Core	Wood	105	20 min.	3'-0"	1 3/4"	B	S-DOOR
	1	Solid Core	Wood	113	20 min.	3'-0"	1 3/4"	B	S-DOOR
	1	Solid Core	Wood	109	20 min.	3'-0"	1 3/4"	B	S-DOOR
	1	Solid Core	Wood	112	20 min.	3'-0"	1 3/4"	B	S-DOOR
	1	Solid Core	Wood	116	20 min.	3'-0"	1 3/4"	B	S-DOOR
	1	Solid Core	Wood	106	20 min.	3'-0"	1 3/4"	B	S-DOOR
	1	Solid Core	Wood	104	20 min.	3'-0"	1 3/4"	B	S-DOOR
	1	Solid Core	Wood	110	20 min.	3'-0"	1 3/4"	B	S-DOOR
	1	Solid Core	Wood	114	20 min.	3'-0"	1 3/4"	B	S-DOOR

3. Close the Full Preview window to return to the Finalize Output screen.

COMMON USES FOR ATTRIBUTES

Using attributes is an easy way to combine editable text with graphic symbols without resorting to groups or separate text and graphic elements. One of the more common uses of attributes is in column grid symbols. Attributes are well suited for this purpose because they maintain their location in relation to the circle or hexagon shape usually used for grid symbols, and they can be easily edited.

Here is a portion of the San Francisco Main Library with a typical set of grid symbols. Each symbol contains an attribute similar to the one you created earlier for the room numbers. Other symbols in the figure, such as cut lines and detail bubbles, are also blocks with attributes for text.

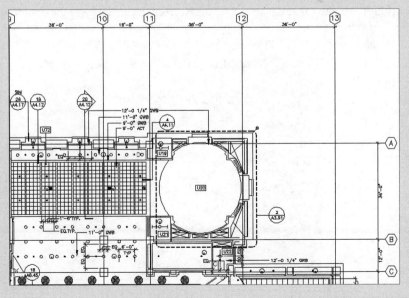

The Full Preview window showed that the attributes were not sorted by room number. You can set up the extraction to sort on a column by clicking the column head in the Finalize Output screen.

1. Click the D-NUMBER column head to sort the list based on room numbers.

2. Click Full Preview again. Notice that now the preview also shows the list sorted by room number.

3. Close the Full Preview window to return to the Finalize Output screen.

As you can see from the exercises so far, you can use the Attribute Extraction Wizard to quickly view attribute and block data without performing the entire extraction process.

SAVING THE ATTRIBUTE DATA TO A FILE

Now let's complete the extraction process.

1. In the Extract Attribute Data To group of the Finalize Output screen , make sure the External File option is turned on and the AutoCAD Table option is turned off. Once the External File option is turned on, you can enter a location for the external file in the text box below, or you can click the browse button to browse to a location.

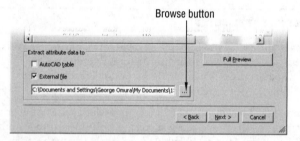

2. Click Next again to open the Finish screen. Here you have the option to save a template of your current settings. You might recall that earlier you had the option to recall a template file. This is where you can save a template file for subsequent recall.

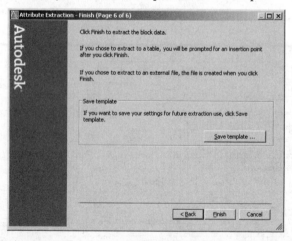

3. Click Finish. A file with the current drawing name and the `.csv` filename extension is created in the location specified in step 1.

You now have a file called `plan.csv` (`13a-plan.csv` if you used the sample file from the CD) that contains the data you saw earlier in the Full Preview window of the Attribute Extraction Wizard. You can import that data into any program that will accept a comma-delimited data file, including database, spreadsheet, and word-processing programs.

Extracting Attribute Data to an AutoCAD Table

You might have noticed the option to extract the attribute data to an AutoCAD table in the Finalize Output screen of the Attribute Extraction Wizard. This option lets you convert the attribute data directly into a table within the current drawing. Besides making it easy to create parts lists or other types of tables in your drawing, you get the added benefit of having tables update automatically whenever attribute data changes.

If you turn this option on and click Next, you will see the Table Style screen instead of the Finish screen.

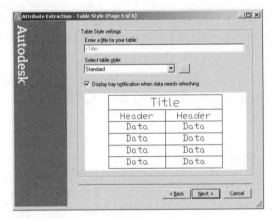

From here, you can take the following steps:

1. Select a table style for the extracted data, enter a title and click Next; you see the Finish screen.

2. Click Finish, and you see a warning message saying that changes made to the table will be lost if the table is refreshed.

3. Click OK, and you are prompted to select a point. Click in the drawing to place the table.

The table may appear at a small size depending on the scale of your drawing. Zoom into the location where you clicked, and you'll see the table.

Quantity	D-CONST	D-MATRL	D-NUMBER	D-RATE	D-SIZE	D-THICK	D-TYPE	Name
1	Solid Core	Wood	103	20 min.	3'-0"	1 3/4"	B	S-DOOR
1	Solid Core	Wood	111	20 min.	3'-0"	1 3/4"	B	S-DOOR
1	Solid Core	Wood	108	20 min.	3'-0"	1 3/4"	B	S-DOOR
1	Solid Core	Wood	107	20 min.	3'-0"	1 3/4"	B	S-DOOR
1	Solid Core	Wood	115	20 min.	3'-0"	1 3/4"	B	S-DOOR
1	Solid Core	Wood	102	20 min.	3'-0"	1 3/4"	B	S-DOOR
1	Solid Core	Wood	101	20 min.	3'-0"	1 3/4"	B	S-DOOR
1	Solid Core	Wood	105	20 min.	3'-0"	1 3/4"	B	S-DOOR
1	Solid Core	Wood	113	20 min.	3'-0"	1 3/4"	B	S-DOOR
1	Solid Core	Wood	109	20 min.	3'-0"	1 3/4"	B	S-DOOR
1	Solid Core	Wood	112	20 min.	3'-0"	1 3/4"	B	S-DOOR
1	Solid Core	Wood	116	20 min.	3'-0"	1 3/4"	B	S-DOOR
1	Solid Core	Wood	106	20 min.	3'-0"	1 3/4"	B	S-DOOR
1	Solid Core	Wood	104	20 min.	3'-0"	1 3/4"	B	S-DOOR
1	Solid Core	Wood	110	20 min.	3'-0"	1 3/4"	B	S-DOOR
1	Solid Core	Wood	114	20 min.	3'-0"	1 3/4"	B	S-DOOR

WARNING It is best to place your table in a layout tab of a drawing because the table will be drawn to a scale that may be too small for a full-size drawing in the Model tab. If you place the table in the Model tab and then scale it to a larger size, it will revert to its original smaller size when you update the table as described next.

You will also see the Attribute Extraction icon appear in the lower-right corner of the AutoCAD window.

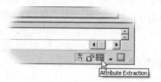

One unique characteristic of a table created from attributes is that you have the option to be notified whenever the table needs to be updated. For example, if the attribute values for the doors in the plan are changed in any way, you will see a balloon warning message in the lower-right corner of the AutoCAD window.

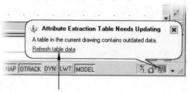

Click here to update the table.

You can then click the Refresh Table Data item in the balloon to update the table to the new attribute values. You can also dismiss the balloon warning and update the table later. When you are ready to update the table, right-click the Attribute Extraction icon in the lower-right corner of the AutoCAD window, and then select Update All Enabled Attribute Extraction Tables. The table will be updated to reflect the latest attribute values.

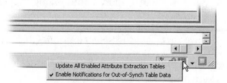

If You Want to Experiment

You can use attributes to help automate data entry into drawings. To demonstrate this, try the following exercise:

1. Create a drawing file called Record with the attribute definitions shown in Figure 13.8. Note the size and placement of the attribute definitions as well as the new base point for the drawing.

2. Save and exit the file, and then create a new drawing called Schedule containing the schedule shown in Figure 13.9.

3. Use the Insert command and insert the Record file into the schedule at the point indicated.

You are prompted for each entry of the record. Enter any value you like for each prompt. When you are finished, the information for one record is entered into the schedule.

FIGURE 13.8
The Record file with attribute definitions

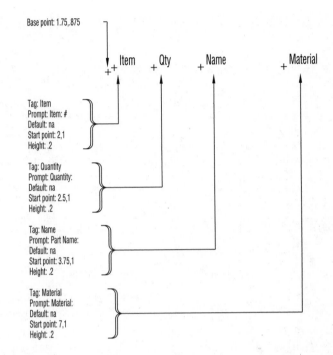

Base point: 1.75,.875

Item   Qty   Name   Material

Tag: Item
Prompt: Item: #
Default: na
Start point: 2,1
Height: .2

Tag: Quantity
Prompt: Quantity:
Default: na
Start point: 2.5,1
Height: .2

Tag: Name
Prompt: Part Name:
Default: na
Start point: 3.75,1
Height: .2

Tag: Material
Prompt: Material:
Default: na
Start point: 7,1
Height: .2

FIGURE 13.9
The Schedule drawing with the Record file inserted

Insert RECORD here.

Item	Qty	Name	Material
5	2	Washer, #10, flat	Steel

5 1/2"
\(1/2" spacing between lines\)

5/8" — 1 1/4" — 3 1/4" — 4 5/8"

Chapter 14

Copying Pre-existing Drawings into AutoCAD

At times you will want to turn a hand-drafted drawing into an AutoCAD drawing file. You might be modifying a design you created before you started using AutoCAD or converting your entire library of drawings for future AutoCAD use. Or perhaps you want to convert a sketch into a formal drawing. This chapter discusses three ways to enter a hand-drafted drawing: tracing, scaling, and scanning. Each method has its advantages and disadvantages.

This chapter covers the following topics:

◆ Converting Paper Drawings to AutoCAD Files

◆ Tracing a Drawing

◆ Importing and Tracing Raster Images

Converting Paper Drawings to AutoCAD Files

Tracing with a digitizing tablet is the easiest way to enter a hand-drafted drawing into AutoCAD, but a traced drawing usually requires some cleaning up and reorganizing. If dimensional accuracy is not too important, tracing is the best way to enter existing drawings into AutoCAD. It is especially useful for drawings that contain irregular curves, such as the contour lines of a topographical map.

TIP Even if you don't plan to trace drawings into AutoCAD, read the following section on tracing because some of the information presented here will help you with everyday editing tasks.

Scaling a drawing is the most flexible method because you don't need a tablet to do it, and, generally, you are faced with less cleanup afterward. Scaling also facilitates the most accurate input of orthogonal lines because you can read dimensions directly from the drawing and enter them into AutoCAD. The main drawback with scaling is that if the drawing does not contain complete dimensional information, you must constantly look at the hand-drafted drawing and measure distances with a scale. Also, irregular curves are difficult to scale accurately.

Scanning offers some unique opportunities with AutoCAD 2007, especially if you have a lot of RAM and a fast hard disk. Potentially, you can scan a drawing, save it on your computer as an image file, import the image into AutoCAD, and then trace over it. You still need to perform some cleanup work on the traced drawing, but because you can see your tracing directly on your screen, you have better control, and you won't have quite as much cleaning up to do as you do when tracing from a digitizer.

Programs are available that automatically convert an image file into a vector file of lines and arcs. These programs might offer some help, but they require the most cleaning up of the options presented here. Like tracing, scanning is best used for drawings that are difficult to scale, such as complex topographical maps containing more contours than are practical to trace on a digitizer, or nontechnical line art, such as letterhead and logos.

Tracing a Drawing

The most common way to enter a hand-drafted drawing into AutoCAD is tracing with a digitizer. If you are working with a large drawing and you have a small tablet, you might have to cut the drawing into pieces that your tablet can manage, trace each piece, and then assemble the completed pieces into the large drawing. However, the best solution is a large tablet. The following exercises are designed for a $4'' \times 5''$ (10 cm $\times$ 12.7 cm) or larger tablet. The sample drawings are small enough to fit completely on this size tablet. You can use either a stylus or a puck to trace them, but the stylus provides the most natural feel because it is shaped like a pen. A puck has crosshairs that you have to center on the line you want to trace, and this requires a bit more dexterity.

TIP If you don't have a digitizing tablet, you can use scaling to enter the utility room drawing used in this section's tracing exercise. (You will insert the utility room into your apartment building plan in Chapter 15.)

Reconfiguring the Tablet for Tracing

When you first installed AutoCAD, you configured the tablet to use most of its active drawing area for AutoCAD's menu template. (See Appendix A for more information.) Because you will need the tablet's entire drawing area to trace this drawing, you now need to reconfigure the tablet to eliminate the menu. Otherwise, you won't be able to pick points on the drawing outside the $4'' \times 3''$ (10 cm $\times$ 7.6 cm) screen pointing area AutoCAD normally uses (see Figure 14.1).

TIP You can save several AutoCAD configurations that can be easily set by using the Options dialog box.

Here are the steps to follow:

1. Start AutoCAD and create a new file called Utility.

2. Set up the file as an architectural drawing with a $1/4'' = 1'$ scale on an $8^1/_2'' \times 11''$ sheet (Limits set to 0,0 for the lower-left corner and 528,408 for the upper-right corner). Metric users should set up their drawing at a 1:50 scale on an A4 size sheet. (Limits for metric users should be 0,0 for the lower-left corner and 1480,1050 for the upper-right corner.)

3. Right-click and select Options from the shortcut menu to open the Options dialog box, then select the System tab.

4. In the Current Pointing Device group, make sure that the Wintab Compatible Digitizer is selected in the drop-down list.

5. Choose Tools ➢ Tablet ➢ Configure or type **Ta↵CFG↵**.

6. At the Enter number of tablet menus desired (0-4): prompt, enter **0↵**.

WARNING   When selecting points on the tablet, take care not to accidentally press the pick button twice, because this will give you erroneous results. Many tablets have sensitive pick buttons that can cause problems when you are selecting points.

7. At the `Do you want to respecify the Fixed Screen Pointing Area?:` prompt, enter **Y↵**.

8. At the `Digitize lower left corner of Fixed Screen pointing area:` prompt, pick the lower-left corner of the tablet's active drawing area.

TIP   On some tablets, a light shows you the active area; other tablets use a permanent mark, such as a corner mark. AutoCAD won't do anything until you have picked a point, so you don't have to worry about picking a point outside this area.

9. At the `Digitize upper right corner of Fixed Screen pointing area:` prompt, pick the upper-right corner.

10. At the `Do you want to specify the Floating Screen pointing area <N>:` prompt, press ↵.

Now as you move your stylus or puck, you'll notice a difference in the relationship between your hand movement and the screen cursor. The cursor moves more slowly and is active over more of the tablet surface.

FIGURE 14.1
The tablet's active drawing area

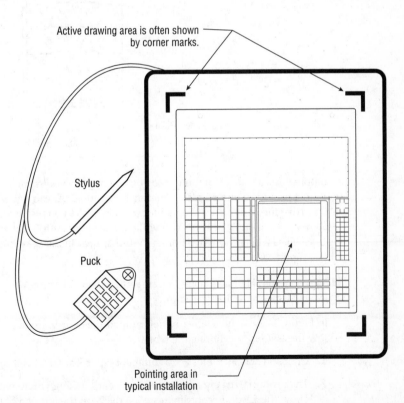

Active drawing area is often shown by corner marks.

Stylus

Puck

Pointing area in typical installation

Calibrating the Tablet for Your Drawing

Now make a photocopy of Figure 14.2, which represents a hand-drafted drawing of a utility room for your apartment building. Place the photocopied drawing on your tablet so that it is aligned with the tablet and completely within the tablet's active drawing area (see Figure 14.3).

FIGURE 14.2

The utility room drawing

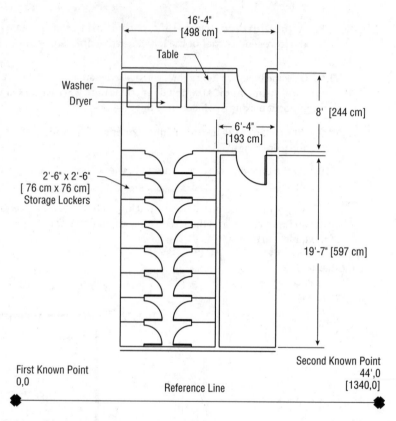

Before you can trace anything into your computer, you must calibrate your tablet. This means you must provide some points of reference so AutoCAD can know how distances on the tablet relate to distances in the drawing editor. For example, you might want to trace a drawing that was created at a scale of $1/8'' = 1'\text{-}0''$. You will have to show AutoCAD two specific points on this drawing, as well as where those two points should appear in the drawing editor. To do this, use the Tablet command's Cal option.

TIP When you calibrate a tablet, you are setting ratios for AutoCAD—for example, 2″ on your tablet equals 16′ in the drawing editor.

In Figure 14.2, we have already determined the coordinates for two points on a reference line. Follow these steps to calibrate the tablet:

1. Choose Tools ➢ Tablet ➢ Calibrate, or enter **Ta↵Cal↵** at the Command prompt.

2. The prompt Digitize point #1: appears, asking you to pick the first point for which you know the absolute coordinates. Pick the X on the left end of the reference line.

3. At the `Enter coordinates for point #1:` prompt, enter **0,0↵**. This tells AutoCAD that the point you just picked is equivalent to the coordinate 0,0 in your drawing editor.

4. Next, the `Digitize point #2:` prompt asks you to pick another point for which you know the coordinates. Pick the X on the right end of the reference line.

5. At the `Enter coordinates for point #2:` prompt, enter **44´,0↵**. Metric users should enter **1340,0↵**.

6. At the `Digitize point #3 (or RETURN to end):` prompt, press ↵. The tablet is now calibrated.

The word TABLET appears on the status bar to tell you that you are in Tablet mode. In this mode, you can trace the drawing, but you cannot access the menus in Windows with some digitizers. (Check your digitizer manual for further information.) If you want to choose a menu item, you must toggle the Tablet mode off by pressing the F4 function key. Or you can enter commands through the keyboard. (If you need some reminders of the keyboard commands, type **Help↵**, select the Contents tab, and click the Command reference listing in the Help dialog box to get a list.)

FIGURE 14.3
The drawing placed on the tablet

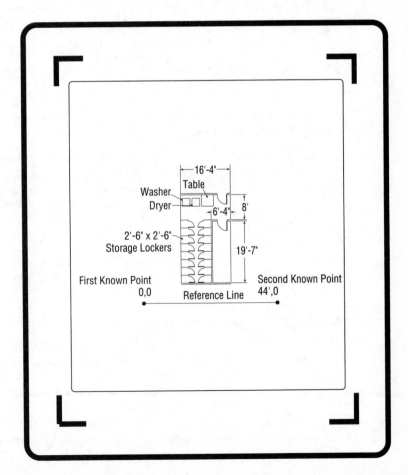

TRACING WITH TABLETS

If you're willing to try something different, another option is a tablet PC. These are portable notebook size PCs that use a stylus as an input device. With a tablet PC you could potentially trace a drawing directly onto the AutoCAD drawing area, as if you were tracing right over the monitor. Some computer monitor manufacturers also offer hand-held LCD monitors that use pens for input. These monitors are a kind of hybrid between a tablet PC and desktop PC, since they are really just a monitor with a tabletlike interface.

Tracing Lines from a Drawing

Now you are ready to trace the utility room. If you don't have a digitizer, you can skip this exercise. A traced file is included on the companion CD that you can use for later exercises. Here are the steps:

1. Make sure the Ortho and Polar buttons are off in the status bar.

2. Click the Line tool on the Draw toolbar or type L↵.

3. Trace the outline of all the walls except the storage lockers.

4. Add the doors by inserting the Door file at the appropriate points and then mirroring them. The doors might not fit exactly, but you'll get a chance to make adjustments later.

5. Trace the washer, and, because the washer and dryer are the same size, copy the washer over to the position of the dryer.

TIP   After a tablet has been calibrated, you can trace your drawing from the tablet, even if the area you are tracing is not displayed in the drawing editor.

At this point, your drawing should look something like the first image in Figure 14.4—a close facsimile of the original drawing, but not as exact as you might like. Zoom in to one of the doors. Now you can see the inaccuracies of tracing. Some of the lines are crooked, and others don't meet at the correct points. These inaccuracies are caused by the limited resolution of your tablet, coupled with the lack of steadiness in the human hand. The best digitizing tablets have an accuracy of 0.001″, which is actually not very good when you are dealing with tablet distances of $1/_8″$ and smaller. In the following section, you will clean up your drawing. (The raggedness of the door arc is the result of the way AutoCAD displays arcs when you use the Zoom command, but you can control this by using the Viewres command. See Chapter 7 for further explanation.)

Cleaning Up a Traced Drawing

In this section, you'll reposition a door jamb, straighten some lines, adjust a dimension, and add the storage lockers to the utility room. If you didn't have a chance to digitize your own Utility file, use the file 14a-util.dwg from the companion CD to do the following exercises.

MOVING THE END OF A WALL

In Figure 14.4, one of the door jambs is not in the right position (the second image gives you the best look). In this next exercise, you will use the Grips feature to fix this by repositioning a group of objects while keeping their vertices intact:

FIGURE 14.4

The traced drawing and a close-up of the door

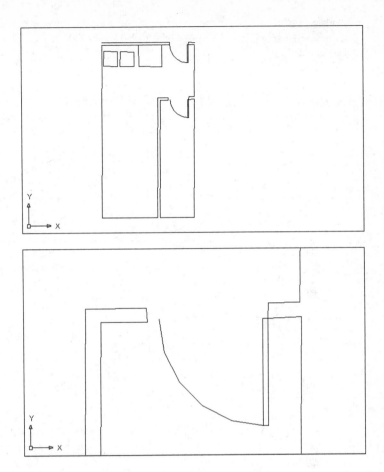

1. Enlarge your view so it looks similar to the second image in Figure 14.4.

2. Pick a crossing window, enclosing the door jamb to be moved. (See the top image in Figure 14.5.)

3. Shift+click one of the grips at the end of the wall and then Shift+click the other grip. You should have two hot grips at the door jamb.

4. Click the lower of the two hot grips and drag the corner away to see what happens. (See the bottom image in Figure 14.5.)

5. Use the Endpoint Osnap to pick the endpoint of the arc. The jamb repositions itself, and all the lines follow (see Figure 14.6).

TIP If AutoCAD doesn't respond in the way described in this section, make sure the Noun/Verb Selection setting and the Enable Grips feature are both turned on.

FIGURE 14.5
A window crossing
the door jamb,
and the door jamb
being stretched

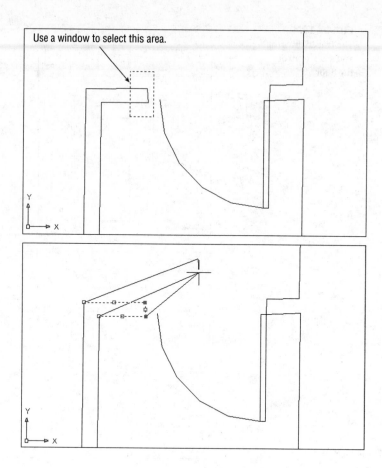

FIGURE 14.6
The repositioned
door jamb

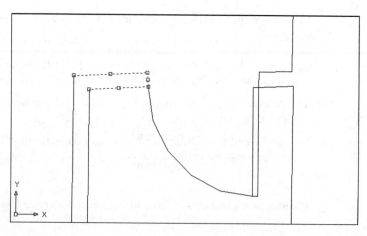

CALIBRATING MORE THAN TWO POINTS

In step 6 of the previous exercise, you bypassed the prompt that offered you the chance to calibrate a third point. In fact, you can calibrate as many as 31 points. Why would anyone want to calibrate so many points? Often the drawing or photograph you are trying to trace will be distorted in one direction or another. For example, blueline prints are usually stretched in one direction because of the way prints are rolled through a print machine.

You can compensate for distortions by specifying several known points during your calibration. For example, you could include a vertical distance on the utility room drawing to indicate a distance in the Y axis. You could then pick that distance and calibrate its point. AutoCAD would then have a point of reference for the y distance as well as the x distance. If you calibrate only two points, as you did in the previous exercise, AutoCAD will scale x and y distances equally. Calibrating three points causes AutoCAD to scale x and y distances separately, making adjustments for each axis based on their respective calibration points.

Now suppose you want to trace a perspective view of a building, but you want to "flatten" the perspective so that all the lines are parallel. You can calibrate the four corners of the building's facade to stretch out the narrow end of the perspective view to be parallel with the wide end. This is a limited form of what cartographers call rubber-sheeting, in which various areas of the tablet are stretched by specific scale factors.

When you select more than two points for calibration, you will get a message similar to that shown here. Let's take a look at the parts of this message.

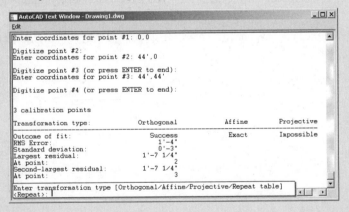

In the Text window, you see the labels Orthogonal, Affine, and Projective. These are the three major types of calibrations, or transformations. The orthogonal transformation scales the X axis and Y axis by using the same values. Affine transformation scales the X axis and Y axis separately and requires at least three points. How the projective transformation stretches the tablet coordinates depends on where you are on the tablet. It requires at least four calibration points.

For each transformation type you will see the Outcome Of Fit: either Success, Exact, or Impossible. This tells you whether any of these transformation types are available to you. Because this example shows what you see when you pick three points, you get Impossible for the projective transformation.

The far-left column tells you what is shown in each of the other three columns.

Finally, the prompt at the bottom of the screen lets you select which transformation type to use. If you calibrate four or more points, the projective transformation is added to the prompt. The Repeat Table option simply refreshes the table.

Take care when you calibrate points on your tablet. Here are some tips:

♦ Use only known calibration points.

♦ Try to locate calibration points that cover a large area of your image.

♦ Don't get carried away. Try to limit calibration points to those necessary to get the job done.

STRAIGHTENING LINES

Another problem in this drawing is that some of the lines are not orthogonal. To straighten them, you use the Change command, together with the Ortho mode. In the following exercise, you'll use the Change command keyboard shortcut:

1. Press the Esc key to clear any active grip selections.

2. Toggle the Ortho mode on.

3. Type **–Ch.⌐** at the Command prompt to start this operation. Make sure you include the minus sign.

4. At the Select objects: prompt, pick the four lines representing the walls just left of the door, and press ⌐ to confirm your selection.

5. At the Specify change point or [Properties]: prompt, click the corner where the two walls meet.

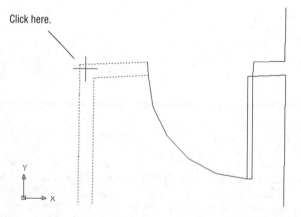

Click here.

The four lines straighten out, as shown in Figure 14.7.

6. Use the Fillet tool in the Modify toolbar to join the corners. You can also choose Modify ➢ Fillet.

WARNING The Change command's Change Point option changes the location of the endpoint closest to the new point location. This can cause erroneous results when you are trying to modify groups of lines.

FIGURE 14.7
The lines after using the Change Point option of the Change command

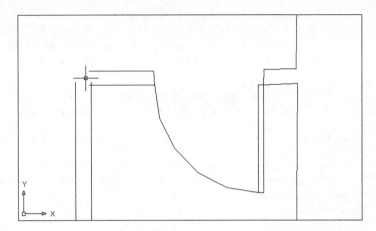

As you have just seen, you can use the Change command to quickly straighten a set of lines. When used carefully, this command can be a real time-saver.

WARNING   Be aware that the Change command moves the nearest endpoints of selected lines to the new location. This can cause unpredictable results in some situations. (See Figure 14.9 later in this chapter.) Note that the Change command does not affect polyline line segments.

In addition to straightening lines, you can use the Change command to align a set of lines with another line. For example, when you combine Change with the Perpendicular Osnap, you can align several lines at a perpendicular angle to another line. However, this works only with the Ortho mode on.

You also can extend several lines to be perpendicular to a non-orthogonal line. To do so, you must rotate the cursor to that line's angle. (See the top image in Figure 14.8.) To rotate the cursor, you can use the Snapang system variable: enter Snapang↵ and enter the rotation angle for your cursor. Then use the process just described to extend or shorten the other lines (see the bottom image in Figure 14.8).

When changing several lines to be perpendicular to another line, you must carefully choose the new endpoint location. Figure 14.9 shows what happens to the same line shown in the top image in Figure 14.8 when a perpendicular reference is placed in the middle of the set of lines. Some lines are straightened to a perpendicular orientation, while others have the wrong endpoints aligned with the reference line.

Before moving on to the next section, use the Change command to straighten the other lines in your drawing. Start by straightening the corner to the right of the door in Figure 14.7, earlier in this chapter:

1. Issue the Change command again.

2. Select the five lines that represent the walls to the right of the door and then press ↵.

3. Click a point near the corner.

4. Chances are, the two vertical lines are not aligned. Move the top line so that it aligns with the lower one. You can use the Perpendicular Osnap to help with the alignment.

5. Use the Change command on each of the other corners until all the walls have been straightened. You can also use Change in a similar way to straighten the door jambs.

6. After you've straightened the lines, use the Fillet tool on the Modify toolbar to join the corners end to end.

TIP When you confirm your selection to the Change command in step 4, you have the option to press **P↵** for the Properties option. This option lets you change the color, elevation, layer, linetype, linetype scale, line weight, and thickness of the selected object. It can be especially helpful in 3D work when you want to set the elevation of several objects to the same elevation.

TIP When using the Fillet tool to join lines, you can issue the Fillet command, type **C↵**, and enclose the two lines you want to fillet with a crossing window.

FIGURE 14.8

You can use the Change command to quickly straighten a set of nonparallel lines and to align their endpoints to another reference line.

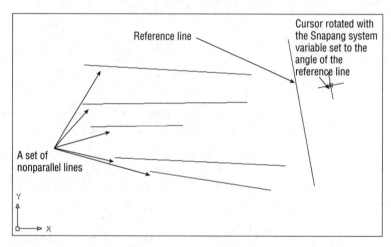

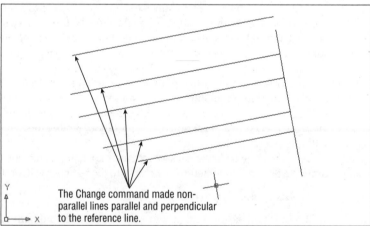

FIGURE 14.9

The results of the Change command can be unpredictable if the endpoint location is too close to the lines being changed.

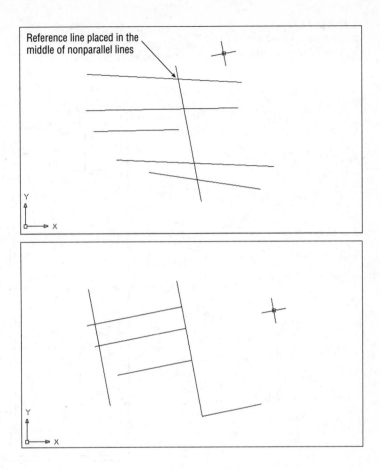

ADJUSTING THE ROOM SIZE

The overall interior dimension of the original utility room drawing is 16′-4″ × 28′-0″. Chances are that the dimensions of the drawing you traced will vary somewhat from these. You will need to adjust your drawing to fit these dimensions:

1. Draw a horizontal line 16′-4″ long (498 cm for metric users) from the left wall; then draw a vertical line 28′ long (856.6 cm for metric users) from the bottom wall line, as shown in Figure 14.10.

2. Use the two lines you drew in step 1 to adjust the walls to their proper positions (see Figure 14.10). You can either use the Grips feature or click Stretch on the Modify toolbar.

3. Choose Draw ➢ Block ➢ Base or type **Base**. Then make the upper-left corner of the utility room the base point.

4. To add the storage lockers, begin by drawing one 30″ × 30″ (76 cm × 76 cm for metric users) locker accurately.

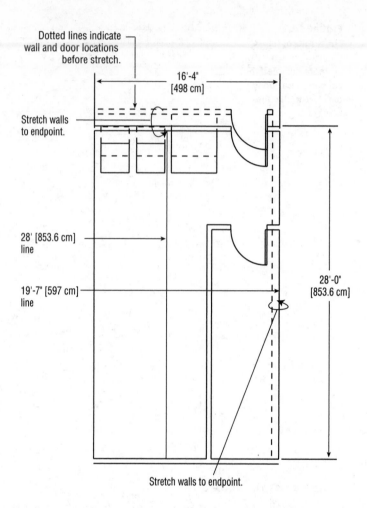

FIGURE 14.10

The walls stretched to the proper dimensions

Use the Mirror and Array commands to create the other lockers. Both commands are available on the Modify toolbar. (For entering objects repeatedly, this is actually a faster and more accurate method than tracing. If you traced each locker, you would also have to clean up each one.)

Finally, you might want to add the dimensions and labels shown earlier in Figure 14.2:

1. Create a layer called Notes to contain the dimensions and labels.

2. Set the Dimscale dimension setting to 48 (50 for metric users) before you start dimensioning. To do this, choose Dimension Style from the Dimension toolbar. Make sure the Standard dimension style is selected; then click Modify. In the Modify Dimension Style dialog box, click the Fit tab and click the Use Overall Scale Of radio button. Next, enter 48 (50 for metric users) in the input box to the right of the Use Overall Scale Of radio button. (See Chapter 12 for details on this process.)

TIP You can also set the Dimscale setting by typing **Dimscale.⅃** and then entering the desired scale of 48.

3. Click the Text tab and set Text Height to $1/8''$ (0.3 for metric users).

4. When you are finished, click OK. Then click Close, save the file, and exit AutoCAD.

TIP Make sure that the text style you are using with your dimension style is set to a height of 0 if you want the dimension style text height to take effect.

Working Smarter with Digitizers

Earlier in this chapter, you traced most of a drawing and used Mirror and Array to speed up the drawing re-creation. However, you could have just traced the major lines with the Ortho mode on and then used the Offset command to draw the wall thickness. You could then use the Fillet and Trim commands (see Chapter 6) to clean up the drawing where lines cross or where they don't meet.

SCANNING A DRAWING

No discussion of drawing input can be complete without mentioning scanners. Imagine how easy it would be to convert an existing library of drawings into AutoCAD drawing files by simply running them through a scanning device. Unfortunately, scanning drawings is not quite that simple.

In scanning, the drawing size can be a problem. Small-format scanners are cheap and nearly as common as printers. If you need to scan only letters, you can purchase a desktop "all-in-one" scanner/printer in the $8^{1}/_{2}'' \times 12''$ (or 26 cm $\times$ 30 cm) sheet size for about $100. Larger scanners up to $12'' \times 17''$ can be found in the $1000 range. But the price of larger scanners in the $24''$ range, the size needed for a typical architectural or engineering drawing, starts to climb dramatically.

After the drawing is scanned and saved as a file, you have two paths to importing it into AutoCAD. One path is to convert the scanned image into AutoCAD objects such as lines, arcs, and circles. This requires special software and is usually a fairly time-consuming process. Finally, the drawing typically requires some cleanup, which can take even longer than cleaning up a traced drawing. The poorer the condition of the original drawing, the more cleanup you'll have to do.

Another path is to import a scanned image directly into AutoCAD and then use all or part of the scanned image in combination with AutoCAD objects. You can use standard AutoCAD tools to trace over the scanned image and then discard the image when you are finished, or you can use the scanned image as part of your AutoCAD file. With AutoCAD's ability to import raster images, you can, for example, import a scanned image of an existing paper drawing and then mask off the area you want to edit. You can then draw over the masked portions to make the required changes.

Whether a scanner can help you depends on your application. If you have drawings that would be difficult to trace—large, complex topographical maps, for example—a scanner might well be worth a look. You don't necessarily have to buy one; some scanning services offer excellent value. And if you can accept the quality of a scanned drawing before it is cleaned up, you can save a lot of time. On the other hand, a drawing composed mostly of orthogonal lines and notes might be more easily traced by hand with a large tablet or entered directly by using the drawing's dimensions.

Scanning can be an excellent document management tool for your existing paper drawings. You might consider scanning your existing paper drawings for archiving purposes. Some blueprint companies even offer free large document scanning as an incentive to other digital reproduction services.

You can then use portions or all of your scanned drawings later, without committing to a full-scale, paper-to-AutoCAD scan conversion.

If you are a civil engineer, you would probably take a different approach. In laying out a road, for instance, you might first trace the center lines and then use the Offset option on the Modify toolbar to place the curb and gutter. You could trace curved features by using arcs (just to see what the radius of the curve is) and then redraw the arc accurately, joining straight-line segments. The digitizer can be a great tool if it is used with care and a touch of creativity.

Importing and Tracing Raster Images

If you have a scanner and you would like to use it to import drawings and other images into AutoCAD, you can use AutoCAD's raster image import capabilities. There are many reasons for wanting to import a scanned image. In architectural plans, a vicinity map is frequently used to show the location of a project. With the permission of its creator, you can scan a map into AutoCAD and incorporate it into a cover sheet. That cover sheet can also contain other images, such as photographs of the site, computer renderings and elevations of the project, and company logos.

WARNING LT users cannot import raster images. However, images placed in drawings can be viewed, moved, and scaled in LT, and their frames can be turned on or off.

Another reason for importing scanned images is to use the image as a reference to trace over. You can trace a drawing with greater accuracy by using a scanned image as opposed to a digitizing tablet. With the price of scanners falling to less than $100, a scanner is a cost-effective tool for tracing a wide variety of graphic material. In this section, you'll learn firsthand how you can import an image as a background for tracing.

Choose Insert ➤ External References to open the External References palette, which lets you import a full range of raster image files.

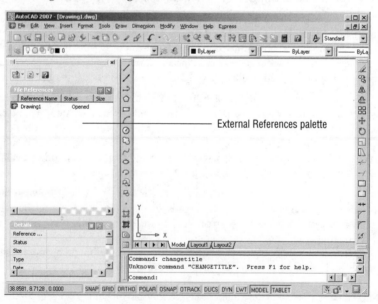

If you've read Chapter 7, this palette should look familiar. It is the same palette you use to manage external references. Just like external references (Xrefs), raster images are loaded when the current file is open, but they are not stored as part of the current file when the file is saved. This helps keep file sizes down, but it also means that you need to keep track of inserted raster files. You will need to make sure that they are kept together with the AutoCAD files in which they are inserted. For example, you might want to keep image files in the same folder as the drawing file to which they are attached.

TIP AutoCAD has a utility called eTransmit that will collect AutoCAD files and their related support files, such as raster images, external references, and fonts, into any folder or drive that you specify. See Chapter 27 for details.

Another similarity between Xrefs and imported raster images is that you can clip a raster image so that only a portion of the image is displayed in your drawing. Portions of a raster file that are clipped are not stored in memory, so your system won't get bogged down, even if the raster file is huge.

The following exercise gives you step-by-step instructions for importing a raster file. It also gives you a chance to see how scanned resolution translates into an image in AutoCAD. This is important for those of you interested in scanning drawings for the purpose of tracing over them. Here are the steps:

1. Create a new file called `Rastertrace`.

2. Set up the file as an architectural drawing with a $1/4'' = 1'$ scale on an $8^1/_2'' \times 11''$ sheet (Limits set to 0,0 for the lower-left corner and 528,408 for the upper-right corner). Make sure that the drawing units type is set to Architectural. Metric users should set up their drawing at a 1:50 scale on an A4 size sheet. (Limits for metric users should be 0,0 for the lower-left corner and 1480,1050 for the upper-right corner.)

3. Choose View ➤ Zoom ➤ All to make sure the entire drawing limits are displayed on the screen.

4. Draw a line across the screen from coordinates 0,20′ to 64′,20′. Metric users should draw the line from 0,600 to 1820,600. You will use this line in a later exercise.

5. Click the line you just drew, and then select Red from the Color Control drop-down list in the Properties toolbar. This will help make the line more visible.

6. Choose Insert ➤ Raster Image Reference or type **iat↵** to open the Select Image File dialog box. This is a typical AutoCAD file dialog box complete with a preview window.

 Locate and select the `raster1.jpg` project file you installed from the companion CD. Notice that you can see a preview of the file in the right side of the dialog box.

7. Click Open to open the Image dialog box. Click OK.

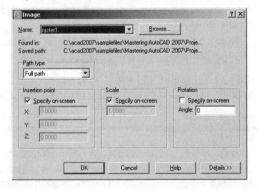

8. Press ↵ at the `Specify insertion point:` prompt to accept the 0,0 coordinates.

9. At the Specify scale factor <1>: prompt, use the cursor to scale the image so it fills about half the screen, as shown in Figure 14.11. Notice that the raster1.jpg filename appears in the External References palette.

FIGURE 14.11

Manually scaling the raster image

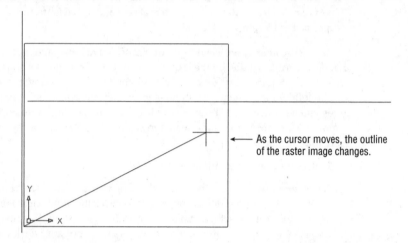

← As the cursor moves, the outline of the raster image changes.

TIPS FOR IMPORTING RASTER IMAGES

When you scan a document into your computer, you get a raster image file. Unlike AutoCAD files, *raster image files* are made up of a matrix of colored pixels that form a picture, which is why raster images are also sometimes called *bitmaps*. *Vector files*, like those produced by AutoCAD, are made up of instructions to draw lines, arcs, curves, and circles. The two formats, raster and vector, are so different that it is difficult to accurately convert one format to the other. It is easier to trace a raster file in AutoCAD than it is to try to have some computer program make the conversion for you.

But even tracing a raster image file can be difficult if the image is of poor quality. Here are a few points you should consider if you plan to use raster imports for tracing drawings:

◆ Scan in your drawing by using a grayscale or color scanner, or convert your black-and-white scanned image to grayscale by using your scanner software.

◆ Use a paint program or your scanner software to clean up unwanted gray or spotted areas in the file before importing it into AutoCAD.

◆ If your scanner software or paint program has a "de-speckle" or "de-spot" feature, use it. It can help clean up your image and ultimately reduce the raster image file size.

◆ Scan at a reasonable resolution. Remember that the human hand is usually not more accurate than a few thousandths of an inch, so scanning at 150dpi to 200dpi might be more than adequate.

◆ If you plan to make heavy use of raster imports, upgrade your computer to the fastest processor you can afford and don't spare the memory.

The raster import commands can incorporate paper maps or plans into 3D AutoCAD drawings for presentations. I know of one architectural firm that produces some impressive presentations with little effort by combining 2D scanned images with 3D massing models for urban design studies. (A *massing model* is a model that shows only the rough outline of buildings without giving too much detail. Massing models show the general scale of a project without being too fussy.) Raster images do not, however, appear in perspective views.

Scaling a Raster Image

The raster1.jpg file from the companion CD is a scanned image of Figure 14.2 that you saw earlier in this chapter. It was scanned as a grayscale image at 100dpi. This shows that you can get a reasonable amount of detail at a fairly low scan resolution.

Now suppose you want to trace over this image to start an AutoCAD drawing. The first thing you'll want to do is to scale the image to the appropriate size. You can scale an image file to full size. Try the following steps to see how you might begin the process:

1. Choose View ➢ Zoom ➢ Extents.

2. Click Scale on the Modify toolbar.

3. Click the edge of the raster image to select it.

4. Press ↵ to finish your selection.

5. At the Specify base point: prompt, click the X in the lower-left corner of the image—the one you used in the first exercise to calibrate your digitizing tablet.

6. At the Specify scale factor or [Copy/Reference]: prompt, enter **R**↵ to use the Reference option.

7. At the Specify reference length <1>: prompt, type @↵. This tells AutoCAD that you want to use the last point selected as one end of the reference length. After you enter the @ symbol, you'll see a rubber-banding line emanating from the X.

8. At the Specify second point: prompt, click the X at the lower-right corner of the image.

9. At the Specify new length or [Points]: prompt, enter **44'**↵. Metric users should enter **1341**↵. The image enlarges. Remember that this reference line is 44' or 1341 cm in length.

The image is now scaled properly for the plan it portrays. You can proceed to trace over the image. You can also place the image on its own layer and turn it off from time to time to check your trace work. Even if you don't trace the scanned floor plan line for line, you can read the dimensions of the plan from your computer monitor, instead of having to go back and forth between measuring the paper image and drawing the plan on the computer.

Controlling Object Visibility and Overlap with Raster Images

With the introduction of raster image support, AutoCAD inherited a problem fairly common to programs that use them. Raster images will obscure other objects that were placed before the raster image. The image you imported in the previous exercise, for example, obscures the line you drew when you first opened the file. In most cases, this overlap will not be a problem, but in some situations you will want AutoCAD vector objects to overlap an imported raster image. An example of this is a civil engineering drawing showing an AutoCAD drawing of a new road superimposed over an aerial view of the location for the road.

Paint and page-layout programs usually offer a "to front/to back" tool to control the overlap of objects and images. AutoCAD offers the Draworder command. Here's how it works:

1. Choose View ➢ Zoom ➢ Extents to get an overall view of the image.

2. Choose Tools ➢ Draw Order ➢ Bring Above Objects.

3. At the Select objects: prompt, select the horizontal line you drew when you first opened the file.

4. You could go on to select other objects. Press ↵ to finish your selection.

5. At the Select reference objects: prompt, click the edge of the raster image of the utility room and then press ↵.

The drawing regenerates, and the entire line appears, no longer obscured by the raster image.

TIP You can mask out areas of an imported raster image by creating a solid hatch area and using the Draworder command to place the solid hatch "on top" of the raster image. Such masks can be helpful as backgrounds for text that must be placed over a raster image.

The Draworder command you just used has four options:

Tools ➢ Draw Order ➢ Bring To Front Places an object or a set of objects at the top of the draw order for the entire drawing. The effect is that the objects are completely visible.

Tools ➢ Draw Order ➢ Send To Back Places an object or a set of objects at the bottom of the draw order for the entire drawing. The effect is that other objects in the drawing might obscure those objects.

Tools ➢ Draw Order ➢ Bring Above Objects Places an object or a set of objects above another object in the draw order. This has the effect of making the first set of objects appear above the second selected object.

Tools ➢ Draw Order ➢ Bring Under Objects Places an object or a set of objects below another object in the draw order. This has the effect of making the first set of objects appear underneath the second selected object.

You can also use the **Dr** keyboard shortcut to issue the Draworder command. If you do this, you see these prompts:

```
Select objects:
Enter object ordering option [Above objects/Under objects/Front/Back]<Back>:
```

You must then select the option by typing the capitalized letter of the option.

Finally, if you prefer to use a toolbar, the Draw Order toolbar appears in the lower-right corner of the AutoCAD window.

Although this section discussed the Draw Order tools in relation to raster images, they can also be invaluable in controlling visibility of line work in conjunction with hatch patterns and solid fills. See Chapter 7 for a detailed discussion of the Draw Order tools and hatch patterns.

Clipping a Raster Image

In Chapter 7, you saw how you can clip an external reference object so that only a portion of it appears in the drawing. You can also clip imported raster images in the same way. Just as with Xrefs, you can create a closed outline of the area you want to clip, or you can specify a simple rectangular area.

In the following exercise, you'll try out the Imageclip command to control the display of the raster image:

1. Choose Modify ➢ Clip ➢ Image or type **Icl**↵.

2. At the Select image to clip: prompt, click the edge of the raster image.

3. At the Enter image clipping option [ON/OFF/Delete/New boundary]<New>: prompt, press ↵ to create a new boundary.

THE IMAGE MANAGER DIALOG BOX OPTIONS

The Image Manager dialog box you saw in step 6 of the exercise before the previous one helps you manage your imported image files. It is especially helpful when you have a large number of images in your drawing. Its options are similar to the Xref Manager dialog box; you can temporarily unload images (to help speed up the editing of AutoCAD objects), reload, detach, and relocate raster image files. See Chapter 7 for a detailed description of these options.

---

4. At the Enter clipping type [Polygonal/Rectangular]<Rectangular>: prompt, enter **P↵** to draw a polygonal boundary.

5. Select the points shown in the top image in Figure 14.12 and then press ↵. The raster image is clipped to the boundary you created, as shown in the second image in Figure 14.12.

As the prompt in step 3 indicates, you can turn the clipping off or on, or you can delete an existing clipping boundary through the Clip Image option.

After you clip a raster image, you can adjust the clipping boundary by using its grips:

1. Click the boundary edge of the raster image to expose its grips.

2. Click a grip in the upper-right corner, as shown in the final image in Figure 14.12.

3. Drag the grip up and to the right, and then click a point. The image adjusts to the new boundary.

In addition to hiding portions of a raster image that are unimportant to you, clipping an image file reduces the amount of RAM the raster image uses during your editing session. AutoCAD loads only the visible portion of the image into RAM and ignores the rest.

Adjusting Brightness, Contrast, and Strength

ACAD only

AutoCAD offers a tool that enables you to adjust the brightness, contrast, and strength of a raster image. Try making some adjustments to the raster image of the utility room in the following exercise:

1. Choose Modify ➢ Object ➢ Image ➢ Adjust or type **Iad↵**.

2. At the Select image(s): prompt, click the edge of the raster image and press ↵ to open the Image Adjust dialog box.

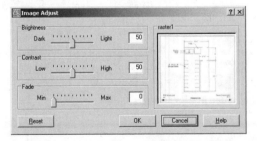

3. Click and drag the Fade slider to the right so that it is near the middle of the slider scale. Or enter **50** in the Fade input box that is just to the right of the slider. Notice how the sample image fades to the AutoCAD background color as you move the slider.

FIGURE 14.12

Adjusting the boundary of a clipped image

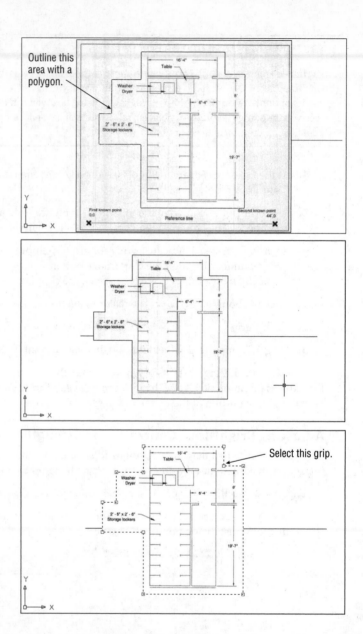

Outline this area with a polygon.

Select this grip.

4. Click OK. The raster image appears faded.

5. Save the file as Rasterimport.dwg.

You can adjust the brightness and contrast by using the other two sliders in the Image Adjust dialog box. Clicking the Reset button resets all the settings to their default values.

By using the Image Adjust option in conjunction with image clipping, you can create special effects. Figure 14.13 shows an aerial view with labels of downtown San Francisco. This view consists of two copies of the same raster image. One copy serves as a background, which was lightened using the method demonstrated in the previous exercise. The second copy is the darker area of the image with a roughly triangular clip boundary applied. You might use this technique to bring focus to a particular area of a drawing you are preparing for a presentation.

If the draw order of objects is incorrect after opening a file or performing a Pan or Zoom, issue a Regen to recover the correct draw order view.

FIGURE 14.13

Two copies of the same image can be combined to emphasize a portion of the drawing.

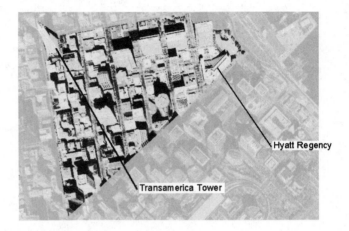

Turning Off the Frame, Adjusting Overall Quality, and Controlling Transparency

You can make three other adjustments to your raster image: frame visibility, image quality, and image transparency.

By default, a raster image displays an outline, or a frame. In many instances, this frame can detract from your drawing. You can globally turn off image frames by choosing Modify ➢ Object ➢ Image ➢ Frame (LT users should choose Modify ➢ Object ➢ Image Frame) and then entering **1 (on)** or 0 **(Off)**, depending on whether you want the frame visible or invisible (see Figure 14.14). You can also type **Imageframe.⌐0.⌐**. A third option, 2, leaves the frame visible but will not plot the frame.

WARNING If you turn off the frame of a raster image, you will not be able to select the image for editing. You can use this to your advantage if you don't want a raster image to be moved or otherwise edited. To make a raster image selectable, turn on the image frame setting.

ACAD only

If your drawing doesn't require the highest-quality image, you can set the image quality to Draft mode. You might use Draft mode when you are tracing an image or when the image is already of a high quality. To set the image quality, choose Modify ➢ Object ➢ Image ➢ Quality, and then enter **H** for High mode (high quality) or **D** for Draft mode. In Draft mode, your drawing will regenerate faster.

The High mode softens the pixels of the raster image, giving the image a smoother appearance. The Draft mode displays the image in a "raw," pixelated state. If you look carefully at the regions between the truck and the background in the second image in Figure 14.15, you will see that it appears a bit jagged. The first image in Figure 14.15 uses the High setting to soften the edges of the truck. You might need to look closely to see the difference.

FIGURE 14.14

A raster image with the frame on (top) and off (bottom)

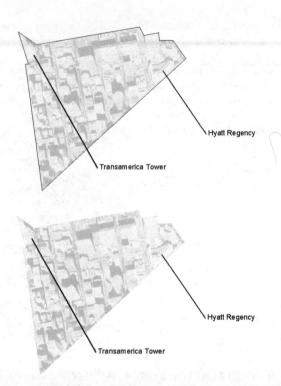

FIGURE 14.15

A close-up of a raster image with quality set to High (top) and Draft (bottom)

Finally, you can control the transparency of raster image files that allow transparent pixels. Some file formats, such as the CompuServe GIF 89a format, enable you to set a color in the image to be transparent (usually the background color). Most image-editing programs support this format because it is a popular one used on web pages.

When you turn on the Transparency setting, objects normally obscured by the background of a raster image might show through. Choose Modify ➤ Object ➤ Image ➤ Transparency, and then select the raster image that you want to make transparent. Press ↵ and enter **On** or **Off**, depending on whether you want the image to be transparent. Unlike the Frame and Quality options, Transparency works on individual objects rather than globally.

TIP   The Properties palette offers many of the same adjustments described in this section, and you can use it for quick access to the Transparency setting and other raster image settings. You can access the Image Adjust dialog box, hide or display clipped areas, or hide the entire raster image.

WARNING   In earlier versions of AutoCAD, you could import PostScript files. AutoCAD 2006 and 2007 no longer support this function. If you need to import a PostScript file, you will have to convert the file into a format that AutoCAD will accept. Most programs that generate PostScript files will also produce DXF files or Windows Metafile files (WMF). WMF files can be imported to AutoCAD by using the Insert menu and DXF files can be opened using the standard File ➤ Open menu option.

If You Want to Experiment

You've seen how you can import a scanned image of an existing drawing and scale it to full scale. Try tracing over that scanned image in this exercise:

1. If you have closed the `Rasterimport.dwg` file, open it again.

2. Use the Line tool and trace over the outline of the floor plan. As you draw, use the dimensions shown in the scanned image to determine the lengths of the lines. Use the Direct Distance method described in Chapter 2 to place the lines. You might also want to use the Ortho mode or the Polar Tracking mode to keep your lines straight.

3. Create a layer called Image, and change the layer assignment of the raster image to the Image layer.

4. Turn the Image layer off to view your floor plan.

Chapter 15

Advanced Editing and Organizing

Because you might not know all of a project's requirements when it begins, you usually base the first draft of a design on anticipated needs. As the plan goes forward, you adjust for new requirements as they arise. As more people enter the project, additional design restrictions come into play, and the design is further modified. This process continues throughout the project, from the first draft to the end product.

In this chapter, you will review much of what you've already learned. Throughout the process, you will look at some techniques for setting up drawings to help manage the continual changes a project undergoes. You will also be introduced to tools and techniques you can use to minimize duplication of work. AutoCAD can be a powerful time-saving tool if used properly. This chapter examines ways to harness that power.

This chapter includes the following topics:

◆ Editing More Efficiently

◆ Using Grips to Simplify Editing

◆ Using External References (Xrefs)

◆ Managing Layers

◆ Using Advanced Tools: Filter, Quick Select, and QuickCalc

◆ Using the QuickCalc Calculator

Editing More Efficiently

The apartment building plan you've been working on is incomplete. For example, you need to add the utility room you created in Chapter 14. In the real world, this building plan would also undergo numerous changes as the project developed. Wall and door locations would change, and more notes and dimensions would be added. However, in the space of this book's tutorials, you can't develop these drawings to full completion. But I can give you a sample of what is in store while using AutoCAD on such a project.

In this section, you will add a closet to the Unit plan. (You will update the Plan file later in this chapter.) In the editing you've already done, you've probably found that you use the following commands frequently: Move, Offset, Fillet, Trim, Grips, and the Osnap overrides. Now you will learn some ways to shorten your editing time by using them more efficiently.

QUICK ACCESS TO YOUR FAVORITE COMMANDS

As you continue to work with AutoCAD, you'll find that you use a handful of commands 90 percent of the time. You can collect your favorite commands into a single toolbar by using AutoCAD's toolbar customization feature. This way, you can have ready access to your most frequently used commands. Chapter 26 gives you all the information you need to create your own custom toolbars.

Editing an Existing Drawing

First, let's look at how you can add a closet to the Unit plan. You'll begin by copying existing objects to provide the basis for the closet:

1. Open the Unit file.

2. Make Wall the current layer by trying the following: click the Make Object's Layer Current tool on the Layers toolbar and then click a wall line.

3. Make sure the Notes and Flr-pat layers are frozen. This will keep your drawing clear of objects you won't be editing.

TIP If you didn't create a Unit plan, you can use 15a-unit.dwg from the companion CD.

4. If they are not already on, turn on Noun/Verb Selection and the Enable Grips features. Turn off Running Osnaps and Polar Tracking for now. They might get in the way of point selection in these exercises.

5. Click the right-side wall and then click its midpoint grip.

6. Enter **C↵** to start the Copy mode; then enter **@2´<180↵**. Metric users should enter **@60<180↵** (see Figure 15.1).

7. Press the Esc key to exit the Grip mode.

8. Zoom in to the entry area shown in Figure 15.2.

9. Click Offset on the Modify toolbar or type **O↵**.

10. At the Specify offset distance or [Through/Erase/Layer] <Through>: prompt, use the Nearest Osnap and pick the outside wall of the bathroom near the door, as shown in Figure 15.2.

11. At the Specify second point: prompt, use the Perpendicular Osnap override and pick the other side of that wall (see Figure 15.2).

12. Click the copy of the wall line you just created, and then click a point to the left of it.

13. Press ↵ to exit the Offset command.

FIGURE 15.1
Copying the wall to
start the closet

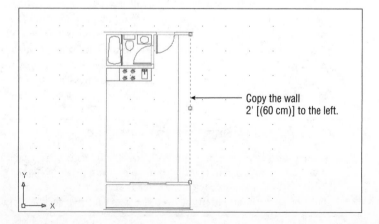

Copy the wall
2' [(60 cm)] to the left.

FIGURE 15.2

Using an existing wall as a distance reference for copying

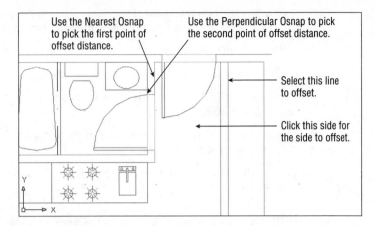

Use the Nearest Osnap to pick the first point of offset distance.

Use the Perpendicular Osnap to pick the second point of offset distance.

Select this line to offset.

Click this side for the side to offset.

In steps 10 and 11 of the previous exercise, you determined the offset distance by selecting existing geometry. If you know you want to duplicate a distance but don't know that distance, you can often use existing objects as references.

Next, use the same idea to copy a few more lines for the other side of the closet:

1. Click to highlight the two horizontal lines that make up the wall at the top of your view.

2. Shift+click the midpoint grips of these lines (see Figure 15.3).

3. Click one of the midpoint grips again, and then enter **C↵** to select the Copy option.

4. Enter **B↵** to select the Base Point option.

5. Use the upper-right corner of the bathroom for the base point and the lower-right corner of the kitchen as the second point (see Figure 15.3).

6. Press the Esc key twice to clear the grip selection.

TIP In these exercises, you are asked to enter the grip options through the keyboard. This can be a quicker method to access the Copy and Base grip options. You can also right-click your mouse and select the Copy and Base Point options from the shortcut menu.

FIGURE 15.3

Adding the second closet wall

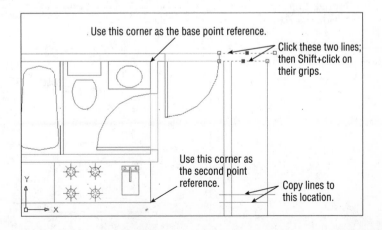

Use this corner as the base point reference.

Click these two lines; then Shift+click on their grips.

Use this corner as the second point reference.

Copy lines to this location.

Now you have the general layout of the closet. The next step is to clean up the corners. First, you'll have to do a bit of prep work and break the wall lines near the wall intersections:

1. Click Break on the Modify toolbar. This tool creates a gap in a line, an arc, or a circle.

2. Click the vertical wall to the far right at a point near the location of the new wall (see Figure 15.4).

3. Click the vertical line again near the point you selected in step 2 to create a small gap, as shown in Figure 15.4.

4. Use the Break tool again to create a gap in the horizontal line at the top of the unit, near the door, as shown in Figure 15.4.

5. Click Fillet on the Modify toolbar or type **F⏎**, and join the corners of the wall, as shown in Figure 15.5.

WARNING   As soon as you click the Fillet tool, you see the radius specification of 0 in the command line. If you don't check this setting before you start to fillet corners, you might end up with very small arcs joining your lines. To change the fillet radius, enter **R⏎** instead of selecting lines. You can then enter a fillet radius.

FIGURE 15.4
Breaking the wall lines

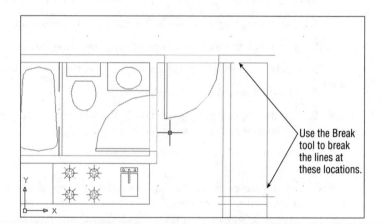

Use the Break tool to break the lines at these locations.

FIGURE 15.5
Filleting the corners

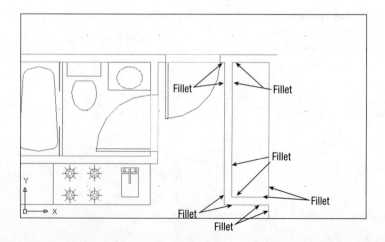

TIP If Fillet is not trimming lines, type **Trimmode**↵**1**↵. This sets the Trimmode system variable to 1, which causes the Fillet and Chamfer tools to "trim" objects back to their intersection points.

In steps 2, 3, and 4, you didn't have to be too exact about where to pick the break points because the Fillet tool takes care of joining the wall lines exactly. Now you are ready to add the finishing touches:

1. At the closet door location, draw a line from the midpoint of the interior closet wall to the exterior (see the top image in Figure 15.6). Make sure this line is on the Jamb layer.

2. Offset the new line 3′ in both directions (90 cm for metric users). These new lines are the closet door jambs.

3. Erase the first line you drew at the midpoint of the closet wall.

4. Click Trim on the Modify toolbar or type **Tr**↵.

5. Click the two jambs and then press ↵.

6. Type **F**↵ to invoke the Fence option; then click a point to the left of the wall, as shown in the bottom image in Figure 15.6.

FIGURE 15.6
Constructing the closet door jambs

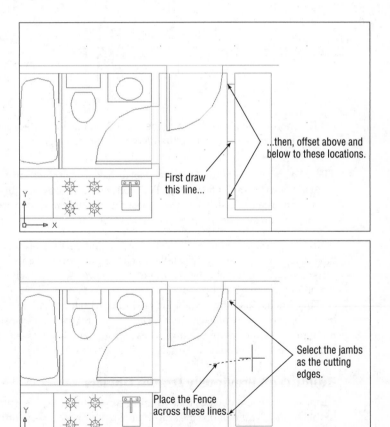

First draw this line...

...then, offset above and below to these locations.

Select the jambs as the cutting edges.

Place the Fence across these lines.

7. As you move the cursor, you see a rubber-banding line from the last point you picked. Click a point to the right of the closet wall so that the rubber-banding line crosses over the two wall lines, as shown in Figure 15.6.

8. Press ↵ to finish your Fence selection. The wall lines trim back to the jambs.

9. Press ↵ again to exit the Trim command.

10. As shown in Figure 15.7, add the door headers and the sliding doors, and assign these objects to their appropriate layers. Delete the line you drew in step 1.

Figure 15.7

The finished closet

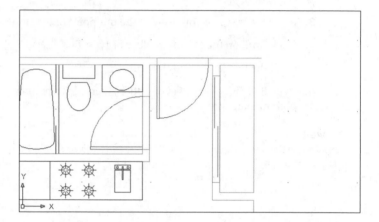

11. Choose File ➤ Save to save the file. If you used the file from the companion CD, choose File ➤ Save As and save the file under the name Unit.

TIP You can use the Match Properties tool to make a set of objects match the layer of another object. Click Match Properties on the Standard toolbar (it looks like a paintbrush), select the objects whose layer you want to match, and then select the objects you want to assign to the objects layer. See Chapter 7 for more on the Match Properties tool.

In this exercise, you used the Fence option to select the objects you wanted to trim. You could have selected each line individually by clicking it, but the Fence option provides a quick way to select a set of objects without having to be too precise about where they are selected. You'll get a closer look at the Fence option a bit later in this chapter.

This exercise also showed that it's easier to trim lines and then draw them back in than to try to break them precisely at each jamb location. At first this might seem counterproductive, but trimming the lines and then drawing in headers actually takes fewer steps and is a less tedious operation than some other routes. And the end result is a door that is exactly centered on the closet space.

Building on Previously Drawn Objects

Suppose your client decides that your apartment building design needs a few one-bedroom units. In this section, you will use the studio unit drawing as a basis for the one-bedroom unit. To do so, you will double the studio's size, add a bedroom, move the kitchen, rearrange and add closets, and move the entry doors. In the process of editing this new drawing, you will see how you can build on previously drawn objects.

As you work through this section, you'll be using commands that you've seen in previous exercises, so I won't describe every detail. But do pay attention to the process taking place, as shown in Figures 15.8 through 15.12.

Start by setting up the new file:

1. You've already saved the current Unit file. Now choose File ➢ Save As to save this file under the name of Unit2.dwg. This way, you can use the current file as the basis for the new one-bedroom unit.

2. Thaw the Notes layer and type **Z↵A↵** to get an overall view of the drawing.

3. Move the dimension string at the right of the unit, 14´-5″ (439 cm) farther to the right, and copy the unit the same distance to the right. Your drawing should look like Figure 15.8.

4. Now erase the bathroom, kitchen, doors, closet, room labels, and wall lines, as shown in Figure 15.9.

TIP Although you could be more selective in step 4 about the objects you erase and then add line segments where there are gaps in walls, this is considered bad form. When editing files, it's wise to keep lines continuous rather than fragmented. Adding line segments increases the size of the drawing database and slows down editing operations.

FIGURE 15.8
The copied unit

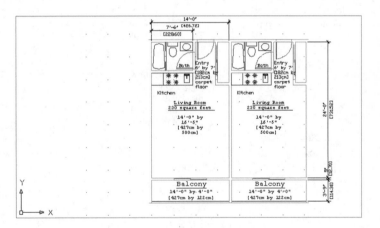

FIGURE 15.9
Objects to be erased

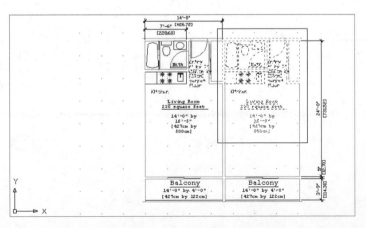

USING THE TEMPORARY TRACK POINT FEATURE

The living room of this one-bedroom unit will be on the right side. You will want to move the Living Room label from the left half to the right half. Normally, you would probably just move the label without worrying about accuracy, but I'll take this opportunity to show how the Temporary Track Point feature works.

In this exercise, you will place the Living Room label in the center of the living room area:

1. Make sure the Osnap and Polar buttons are off in the status bar; then click the Living Room label in the unit to the left.

2. Click the top-center grip in the label, as shown in the first image in Figure 15.10.

3. Shift+right-click to open the Osnap menu.

4. Choose Temporary Track Point. LT users should select Tracking.

5. Shift+right-click again and then choose Insert from the Osnap menu.

FIGURE 15.10

Using the Temporary Track Point feature to move the Living Room label to the center of the new living room

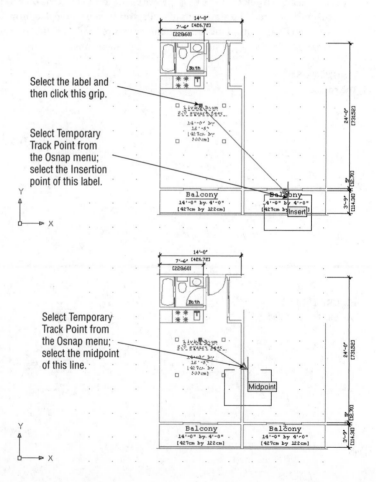

6. Click the insertion point of the Balcony label of the unit to the right, as shown in the first image in Figure 15.10. Notice a tracking vector emanating from the selected insertion point, as shown in the second image in Figure 15.10.

7. Shift+right-click and select Temporary Track Point. LT users should select Tracking.

8. Shift+right-click again and select Midpoint.

9. This time, click the midpoint of the vertical wall between the two units, as shown in the second image in Figure 15.10. Notice that a tracking vector now emanates from a point that represents the intersection of the text insertion point and the midpoint of the wall.

10. Move the text to the middle of the room on the right, as shown in Figure 15.11. Notice that two tracking vectors appear and converge in the middle of the room. (LT users will not see the tracking vectors.)

FIGURE 15.11

The tracking vectors intersect in the middle of the room.

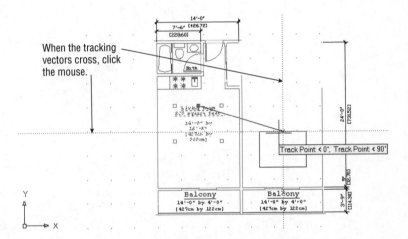

11. With the tracking vectors crossing and the text in the approximate location shown in Figure 15.11, click the mouse. (LT users can just press ↵ without clicking the mouse.) The text moves to the middle of the unit on the right.

In earlier chapters, you saw how to use the Object Snap Tracking feature with Running Osnaps. Here, you used Object Snap Tracking in a slightly different way through the Temporary Track Point feature (or Tracking in LT). The Temporary Track Point feature works by enabling you to select points that are aligned orthogonally, like the insertion point of the balcony text and the midpoint of the wall in the previous exercise. But unlike Object Snap Tracking with Running Osnaps, the Temporary Track Point feature lets you focus on specific object snap points.

The following exercise shows how you can use Temporary Track Point in conjunction with the Polar Tracking tool to move the endpoint of a line to align with the endpoint of another line:

1. Click the line at the top-right side of the unit to expose its grips, as shown in the top image in Figure 15.12.

2. Click the grip at the right end of the line.

3. As in the previous exercise, choose Temporary Track Point from the Osnap menu.

FIGURE 15.12

Stretching a line by using the Tracking function

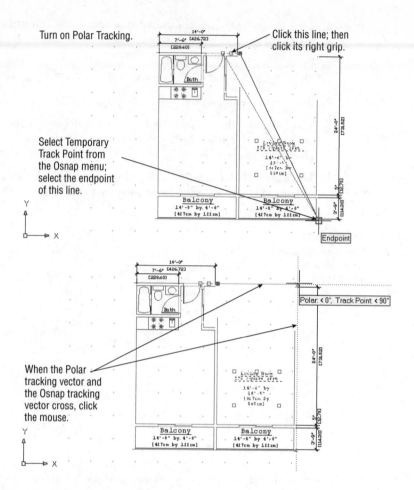

4. Open the Osnap menu again and choose Endpoint.

5. Click the Polar button in the status bar to turn it on.

6. Select the rightmost endpoint of the short line at the bottom-right corner of the unit, as shown in the top image in Figure 15.12.

7. Move the cursor so that the Polar Tracking vector crosses the Osnap Tracking vector in the upper-right corner of the drawing, as shown in the bottom image in Figure 15.12; then click that point.

8. Press the Esc key twice to clear the grip selection.

9. Move the kitchen to the opposite corner of the unit, as shown in Figure 15.13.

10. Click the Move tool and select the closet area, as shown in Figure 15.13.

11. Move the closet down 5´-5˝ (165 cm), as shown in Figure 15.14. You can use the corners of the bathroom as reference points.

FIGURE 15.13
Moving the closet and kitchen

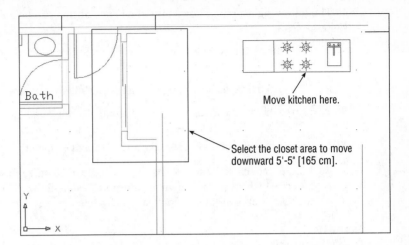

Move kitchen here.

Select the closet area to move downward 5'-5" [165 cm].

FIGURE 15.14
Using an existing door to create a door opening

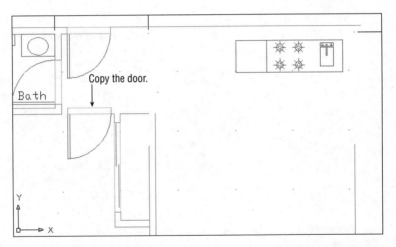

Copy the door.

When a drawing gets crowded, Running Osnaps might get in the way of your work. The Temporary Track Point feature lets you access the Osnap Tracking vector without having to turn on Running Osnaps.

The Temporary Track Point feature and the other tools that use tracking vectors take a little practice to use, but after you understand how they work, they are an indispensable aid in your drawing.

WORKING WITH THE FENCE OPTION

Next, you'll work on finishing the new bedroom door and entry. Once again, you will get a chance to work with the Fence option. Fence is a great tool for selecting locations on objects that would otherwise be difficult to select. With Fence, you can select objects by crossing over them with a rubber-banding line. It's like selecting objects by crossing them out. In addition, the point at which the rubber-banding line crosses the object is equivalent to a pick point. This is important when using commands that respond differently depending on where objects are selected.

The following exercise shows how the Fence option can be helpful in selecting objects in tight spaces:

1. Copy the existing entry door downward, including header and jambs (see Figure 15.14). Use the Endpoint override to locate the door accurately.

2. Clean up the walls by adding new lines and filleting others, as shown in Figure 15.15.

3. Mirror the door you just copied so it swings in the opposite direction.

TIP Use the midpoint of the door header as the first axis endpoint.

4. Use Stretch (click Stretch on the Modify toolbar) to move the entry door a distance of 8′ (244 cm) to the right, as shown in Figure 15.16. Remember to use a crossing window to select the objects and endpoints you want to stretch.

FIGURE 15.15
Cleaning up the wall

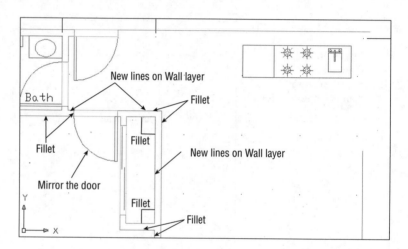

FIGURE 15.16
Moving the door

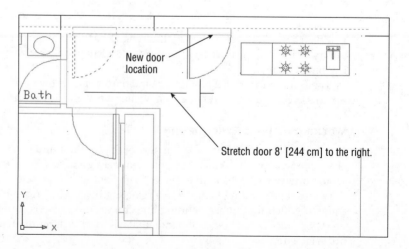

5. After you've moved the entry door, mirror it in the same way you mirrored the other door.

In this exercise, you once again used parts of a previous drawing instead of creating new parts. In only a few instances are you adding new objects.

Next, you'll use the Fence option to add a new closet wall:

1. Set the view of your drawing so it looks similar to the first image in Figure 15.17, and turn off Polar Tracking and Running Osnaps if they are on.

2. Click Extend on the Modify toolbar or type **Ex.⏎** at the Command prompt.

3. At the prompt

```
Select boundary edges ...
Select objects or <select all>:
```

pick the wall at the bottom of the screen, as shown in Figure 15.17, and press ⏎. Just as with Trim, the Extend command requires that you first select a set of objects to define the boundary of the extension and then select the objects you want to extend.

FIGURE 15.17
Adding walls for a second closet

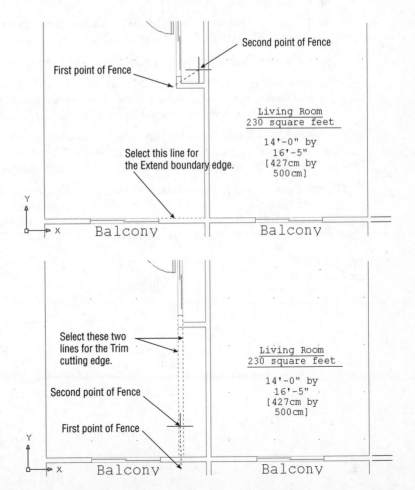

4. At the `Select object to extend or shift-select to trim or [Fence/Crossing/Project/Edge/Undo]:` prompt, you need to pick the two lines just below the closet door. To do this, first enter **F↵** to use the Fence option.

5. At the `Specify first fence point:` prompt, pick a point just to the left of the lines you want to extend.

6. Make sure the Ortho mode is off. Then at the `Specify next fence point or [Undo]:` prompt, pick a point to the right of the two lines so that the fence crosses over them (see the first image in Figure 15.17).

7. Press ↵. The two lines extend to the wall.

8. Press ↵ again to exit the Extend command.

You've extended the wall to form another closet space. The next step is to clean up the wall connections at the balcony:

1. Click Trim and then select the two lines you just extended.

2. Press ↵ to finish your selection.

3. Type **F↵**, and then pick two points to place a fence between the endpoints of the two selected lines (see the second image in Figure 15.17).

4. Use a combination of Trim and Fillet to clean up the other walls.

5. Add another closet door on the right side of the new closet space you just created. Use the same methods you've used for the other closets: place the door jams first, then break or trim wall to the door jambs. Your drawing should look like Figure 15.18.

The Extend tool works just like the Trim tool: first you select the boundary objects and then you select the objects you want to modify. Here again, you used the Fence option to select the object to extend. In this situation, the Fence option is crucial because it can be more difficult to select the lines individually.

TIP At times you need to trim and extend in a single operation. You can do so by using the Shift key with the Trim or Extend command. When you hold down the Shift key in the Extend command while selecting objects to extend, the Extend command trims the objects. Likewise, when you hold down the Shift key while selecting objects to trim in the Trim command, AutoCAD extends the objects.

FIGURE 15.18
The second closet

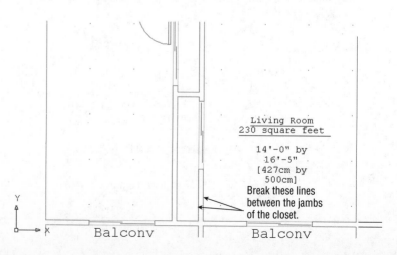

Using Grips to Simplify Editing

Throughout this book, I've shown you ways of using the Grips feature to edit drawings. When and how you use grips will really depend on your preference, but in some situations editing with grips makes more sense than editing without them. Here you'll explore some basic situations in which grips can be useful.

Now, suppose you want to change the location and orientation of the kitchen. In this exercise, you will use the Grips feature to do just that:

1. Set up a view similar to the one in Figure 15.19 and turn on Polar Tracking.

2. Add the horizontal line at the top of the kitchen, as shown in Figure 15.19.

3. Fillet the new line with the vertical wall line to the right of the unit.

4. Click the kitchen.

5. Click the grip in the upper-left corner to make it a hot grip. The grip changes color to indicate that it is selected.

6. Right-click and choose Rotate from the shortcut menu. (You can also press ↵ two times until you see the ** ROTATE ** message at the prompt.)

TIP   Remember that the spacebar acts the same as the ↵ key for most commands, including the Grips modes.

7. Enter **–90** or rotate the kitchen by pointing the cursor downward until the tracking vector appears, and then click the mouse.

8. Click the kitchen grip again; then, using the Endpoint Osnap, click the upper-right corner of the room.

9. Press the Esc key twice to clear the grip selection. Your drawing should look like Figure 15.20.

FIGURE 15.19
Finishing the kitchen wall and selecting the kitchen rotation base point

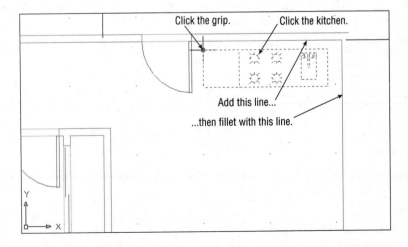

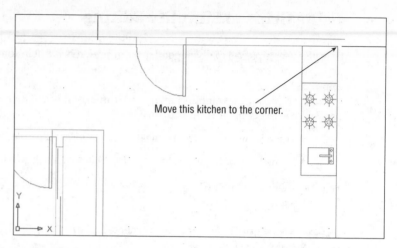

Move this kitchen to the corner.

Because the kitchen is a block, its grip point is the same as its insertion point. This makes the kitchen block—as are all blocks—a great candidate for grip editing. Remember that the door, too, is a block.

Now suppose you want to widen the entrance door from 36″ to 42″ (90 cm to 105 cm for metric users). Try the following exercise editing the location of a door in a wall:

1. Use a crossing window to select the door jamb to the left of the entry door, as shown in Figure 15.21.

2. Shift+click both of the door jamb's corner grips.

3. Click the bottom corner grip again. It is now a hot grip.

4. At the ** Stretch ** prompt, enter **@6<180** (metric users should enter **@15<180**). The door should now look like Figure 15.21. You can also use the Direct Distance method: with Polar Tracking on, point the cursor to the left and then type **6↵**.

TIP   The Stretch hot-grip command will ignore a block as long as you do not include its insertion point in the window selection.

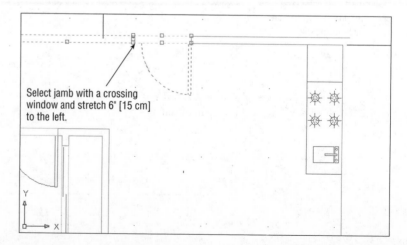

Select jamb with a crossing window and stretch 6" [15 cm] to the left.

DISPLAYING GRIPS OF OBJECTS WITHIN A BLOCK

You can set up AutoCAD to display the grips on all the entities within a block. This enables you to use those grips as handles for any of the grip operations such as Move, Rotate, or Scale. However, you cannot edit individual objects within the block.

To display all the grips within a block, type **Gripblock**⏎**1**⏎. You can also turn on the Enable Grips Within Blocks option in the Grips section of the Options dialog box's Selection tab (choose Tools ➤ Options).

Notice that in step 4 you didn't have to specify a base point to stretch the grips. AutoCAD assumes the base to be the original location of the selected hot grip (the grip selected in step 3).

Now you can enlarge the door by using the Grip command's Scale option. Scale enables you to change the size of an object or a group of objects. You can change the size by entering a scale value or by using an object for reference. In this exercise, you will use the current door width as a reference:

1. Press the Esc key twice to clear your selection set.

2. Click the door and then click the door's grip point at the hinge side.

3. Right-click and choose Scale.

4. At the `Specify scale factor or [Base point/Copy/Undo/Reference/eXit]:` prompt, enter **R**⏎ to select the Reference option.

5. At the `Specify reference length <0′-1″>:` prompt, type **@**⏎ to indicate that you want to use the door insertion point as the first point of the reference length.

6. At the `Specify second point:` prompt, click the endpoint of the door's arc at the wall line (see the first image in Figure 15.22). Now as you move the cursor, the door changes in size relative to the distance between the grip and the end of the arc.

7. At the `Specify new length or [Base point/Copy/Undo/Reference/eXit]:` prompt, use the Endpoint Osnap again and click the door jamb directly to the left of the arc endpoint. The door enlarges to fit the new door opening (see the second image in Figure 15.22).

8. To finish this floor plan, zoom out to get the overall view of the unit, thaw the Flr-pat layer, and then erase the floor pattern in the bedroom area just below the bathroom.

9. Save the file.

You could have used the Modify ➤ Scale option to accomplish the operation performed in this exercise with the Scale hot-grip command. The advantage to using grips is that you don't need to use the osnap to select exact grip locations, thereby reducing the number of steps.

In the next section, you will update the Plan file to include the revised studio apartment and the one-bedroom unit you have just created (see Figure 15.23). You will be making changes such as these throughout the later stages of your design project. As you have seen, the ability to make changes easily and quickly in AutoCAD can ease your work and help you test your design ideas more accurately.

FIGURE 15.22

The enlarged door

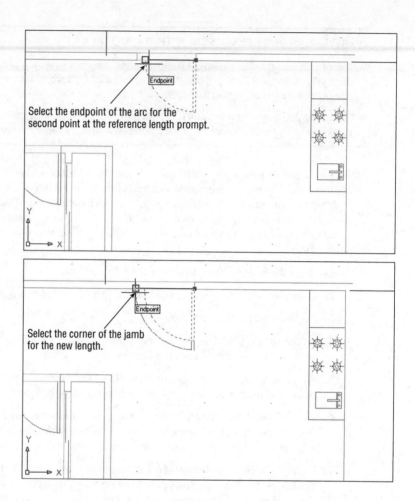

Select the endpoint of the arc for the
second point at the reference length prompt.

Select the corner of the jamb
for the new length.

FIGURE 15.23

The finished one-
bedroom unit

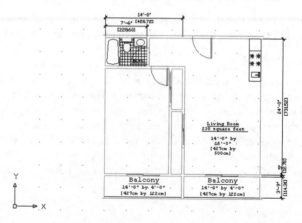

SINGLING OUT PROXIMATE OBJECTS

Chapter 3 mentioned that you will sometimes need to select an object that is overlapping or very close to another object. Often in this situation, you end up selecting the wrong object. To select the exact object you want, you can use the Selection Cycling tool and the Draworder command.

Selection Cycling lets you cycle through objects that overlap until you select the one you want. To use this feature, first enter Legacyctrlpick ↵ 1↵ . This changes the way the Ctrl-click functions in AutoCAD. Next, hold down the Ctrl key and click the object you want to select. If the first object highlighted is not the one you want, click again, but this time don't hold down the Ctrl key. When several objects are overlapping, just keep clicking until the correct object is highlighted and selected. When the object you want is highlighted, press ↵, and then go on to select other objects or press ↵ to finish the selection process. If you do a lot of work in 3D, make sure you set Legacyctrlpick back to 0 by entering Legacyctrlpick↵ 0↵.

Another way to gain access to an overlapped object is to use the Draworder command. You can select the overlapping object and then choose Tools ➤ Draw Order ➤ Send To Back. This has the effect of "moving" the overlapping object underneath the overlapped object. You can then click the previously overlapped object to select it. You can also use the Draw Order toolbar to gain access to the Draworder command.

Using External References (Xrefs)

Chapter 7 mentioned that careful use of blocks, external references (Xrefs), and layers can help improve your productivity. In this section you will see firsthand how to use these features to help reduce design errors and speed up delivery of an accurate set of drawings. You do this by controlling layers in conjunction with blocks and external references to create a common drawing database for several drawings.

TIP   You can also use AutoCAD DWF files as external references. See Chapter 27 for more on DWF files.

Preparing Existing Drawings for Cross-Referencing

Chapter 6 discussed how you can use Xrefs to assemble one floor of the apartment. In this section you will explore the creation and use of Xrefs to build multiple floors, each containing slightly different sets of drawing information. By doing so, you will learn how Xrefs enable you to use a single file in multiple drawings to save time and reduce redundancy. You'll see that by sharing common data in multiple files, you can reduce your work and keep the drawing information consistent.

You'll start by creating the files that you will use later as Xrefs:

1. Open the Plan file. If you didn't create the Plan file, you can use the 15a-plan.dwg file from the companion CD (see Figure 15.24).

2. Turn off the Ceiling, Notes and Flr-pat layers to get a clear, uncluttered view of the individual unit plans.

3. Use the Wblock command (enter W↵ at the Command prompt) and write the eight units in the corners of your plan to a file called Floor1.dwg (see Figure 15.25). When you select objects for the Wblock, be sure to include the door symbols and apartment number symbols for those units. Use 0,0 for the Wblock insertion base point. Also make sure that the Delete From Drawing check box is selected in the Write Block dialog box before you click OK.

4. Using Figure 15.26 as a guide, insert the Unit2 file into the corners where the other eight units were previously.

FIGURE 15.24

The overall plan

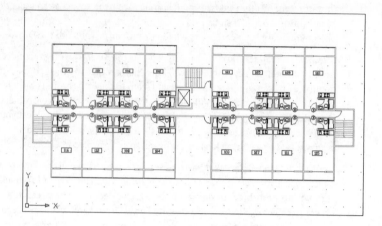

FIGURE 15.25

Units to be exported to the Floor1 file

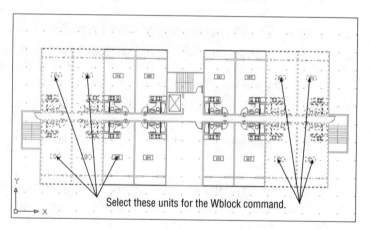

Select these units for the Wblock command.

FIGURE 15.26

Insertion information for Unit2. Metric coordinates are shown in brackets.

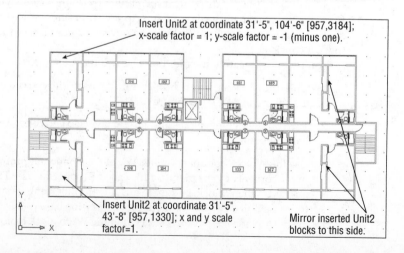

Insert Unit2 at coordinate 31'-5", 104'-6" [957,3184]; x-scale factor = 1; y-scale factor = -1 (minus one).

Insert Unit2 at coordinate 31'-5", 43'-8" [957,1330]; x and y scale factor=1.

Mirror inserted Unit2 blocks to this side.

TIP If you didn't create the Unit2 file earlier in this chapter, use the 15a-unit2.dwg file from the companion CD.

5. After you've accurately placed the corner units, use the Wblock command to write these corner units to a file called Floor2.dwg. Again, use the 0,0 coordinate as the insertion base point for the Wblock and make sure the Delete from drawing setting is turned on.

6. Choose File ➢ Save As to turn the remaining set of unit plans into a file called Common.dwg.

You've just created three files: Floor1, Floor2, and Common. Each of these files contains unique information about the building. Next, you'll use the Xref command to recombine these files for the different floor plans in your building.

Assembling External References to Build a Drawing

You will now create composite files for each floor, using external references of only the files needed for the individual floors. You will use the Attach option of the Xref command to insert all the files you exported from the Plan file.

Follow these steps to create a file representing the first floor:

1. Close the Common.dwg file, open a new file, and call it Xref-1.

2. Set up this file as an architectural drawing $8\frac{1}{2}'' \times 11''$ with a scale of $\frac{1}{16}'' = 1'$. The upper-right corner limits for such a drawing are 2112,1632. Metric users should set up a drawing at 1:200 scale on an A4 sheet size. Your drawing area should be 4200 cm by 5940 cm. Choose View ➢ Zoom ➢ All so your drawing area is adjusted to the window.

TIP In this exercise, you are asked to use a small paper size because it is the most common size available. Normally, you would specify a larger size and scale for architectural drawings.

3. Set the Ltscale value to 192. Metric users should set it to 200.

4. Open the Reference toolbar by right-clicking a toolbar and then choosing Reference from the shortcut menu.

5. Click Attach Xref on the Reference toolbar or type **Xa**↵ to open the Select Reference File dialog box.

6. Locate and select the Common.dwg file.

7. In the External Reference dialog box, make sure the Specify On-Screen check box in the Insertion Point group is not selected. Then make sure the X, Y, and Z values in the Insertion Point group are all 0.

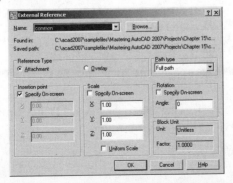

TIP   Because the insertion points of all the files are the same, namely 0,0, they will fit together perfectly when they are inserted into the new files.

8. Click OK. The Common.dwg file appears in the drawing.

9. Click the Attach Xref tool on the Reference toolbar again, and then click the Browse button to locate, select, and insert the Floor1 file.

10. Repeat step 9 to insert the Col-grid.dwg file as an Xref. The Col-grid.dwg file can be found on the companion CD. You now have the plan for the first floor.

11. Save this file.

Now use the current file to create another file representing a different floor:

1. Choose File ➢ Save As to save this file as Xref-2.dwg.

2. Click the External Reference tool in the Reference toolbar or type **Xr**↵.

3. In the External References palette, highlight Floor1 in the list of Xrefs and then right-click and select Detach from the shortcut menu.

4. Right-click in the blank portion of the list in the External References palette and then select Attach DWG from the shortcut menu.

5. Locate and select Floor2.dwg.

6. In the External Reference palette, make sure that the X, Y, and Z values in the Insertion Point group are all set to 0.

7. Click OK. The Floor2 drawing appears in place of Floor1. Turn off the notes layer to see the plan clearly.

LOCATING EXTERNAL REFERENCE FILES

If you move an external reference file after you insert it into a drawing, AutoCAD may not be able to find it later when you attempt to open the drawing. If this happens, you can click the Browse button of the Found At option at the bottom of the External References palette to tell AutoCAD the new location of the external reference file. The Browse button appears at the far right of the Found At text box when you click in the text box.

If you know that you will be keeping your project files in one place, you can use the Projectname system variable in conjunction with the Options dialog box to direct AutoCAD to look in a specific location for xref files. Here's what to do:

1. Choose Tools ➢ Options.

2. Click the File tab, then locate and select the Project File Search Path option.

3. Click Add, then enter a name for your project, or accept the default name of Project1.

4. Click Browse and locate and select the folder where you plan to keep your xref files.

5. Close the Options dialog box, then enter **Projectname** ↵ at the command prompt.

6. Enter the project name you used in step 3 then save your file so it remembers this setting.

Now when you need to make changes to Xref-1 or Xref-2, you can edit their individual external reference files. Then, the next time you open either Xref-1 or Xref-2, the updated Xrefs will automatically appear in their most recent forms.

External references do not need to be permanent. As you saw in the previous exercise, you can attach and detach them easily at any time. This means that if you need to get information from another file—to see how well an elevator core aligns, for example—you can temporarily attach as an external reference the other file to quickly check alignments and then detach it when you are finished.

Think of these composite files as final plot files that are used only for plotting and reviewing. You can then edit the smaller, more manageable external reference files. Figure 15.27 illustrates the relationship of these files.

FIGURE 15.27
A diagram of external reference file relationships

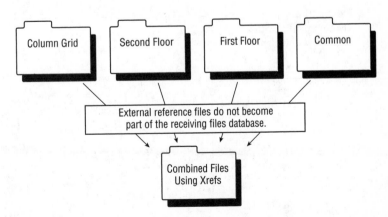

The combinations of external references are limited only by your imagination, but you should avoid multiple external references of the same file in one drawing.

TIP   Because Xref files do not become part of the file they are referenced into, you must take care to keep Xref files in a location where AutoCAD can find them when the referencing file is opened. This can be a minor annoyance when you need to send files to others outside your office. To help you keep track of external references, choose File ➤ eTransmit. See Chapter 27 for details.

UPDATING BLOCKS IN EXTERNAL REFERENCES

Several advantages are associated with using external reference files. Because the Xrefs don't become part of the drawing file's database, the referencing files remain quite small. Also, because Xref files are easily updated, work can be split up among several people in a workgroup environment or on a network. For example, in our hypothetical apartment building, one person can be editing the Common file while another works on Floor1, and so on. The next time the composite Xref-1.dwg or Xref-2.dwg file is opened, it automatically reflects any new changes made in the external reference files. Or if the xref is updated while you still have the receiving file open, you will receive a balloon message telling you that an Xref requires a reload.

Now let's see how to set this up:

1. Save and close the Xref-2 file and then open the Common.dwg file.

2. Update the Unit plan you edited earlier in this chapter. Click Insert Block on the Draw toolbar.

3. In the Insert dialog box, click the Browse button and then locate and select Unit.dwg. Click Open, and then click OK in the Insert dialog box.

4. At the warning message, click Yes.

5. At the Insertion point: prompt, press the Esc key.

6. Enter RE↵ to regenerate the drawing. You will see the new Unit plan in place of the old one (see Figure 15.28). You might also see all the dimensions and notes for each unit.

7. If the Notes layer is on, use the Layer drop-down list to turn it off.

FIGURE 15.28
The Common file with the revised Unit plan

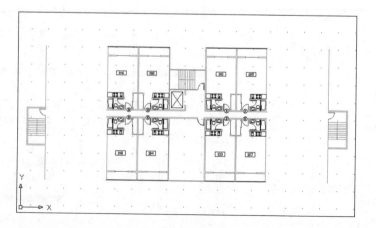

8. Using the Insert Block tool on the Draw toolbar again, replace the empty room across the hall from the lobby with the utility room you created in Chapter 14 (see Figure 15.29). If you didn't create the utility room drawing, use the `utility.dwg` file from the companion CD.

9. Save the Common file.

10. Now open the `Xref-1` file, right-click Common in the External References palette, and select Reload from the shortcut menu. You can also right-click the Manage Xrefs icon in the lower right corner of the AutoCAD Window and select Reload DWG Xrefs. You will see the utility room and the typical units in their new form. Your drawing should look like the top image in Figure 15.30.

FIGURE 15.29
The utility room installed

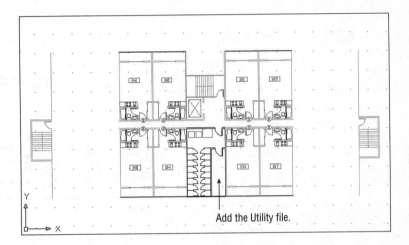

Add the Utility file.

11. Open `Xref-2` and reload the Common external reference as you did in step 8. You see that the utility room and typical units are updated in this file as well (see the bottom image in Figure 15.30).

Importing Named Elements from External References

Chapter 5 discussed how layers, blocks, linetypes, and text styles—called *named elements*—are imported along with a file that is inserted into another file. External reference files, on the other hand, do not import named elements. You can, however, review their names and use a special command to import the ones you want to use in the current file.

TIP You can set the Visretain system variable to 1 to force AutoCAD to remember layer settings of external reference files. Or turn on the Retain Changes To Xref Layers option in the Open And Save tab of the Options dialog box. You can also use the Layer States Manager in the Layer Properties Manager dialog box to save layer settings for later recall. The Layer States Manager is described in detail later in this chapter.

AutoCAD renames named elements from Xref files by giving them the prefix of the filename from which they come. For example, the Wall layer in the `Floor1` file will be called Floor1 | WALL in the `Xref-1` file; the Toilet block will be called Floor1 | TOILET. You cannot draw on the layer Floor1 | WALL, nor can you insert Floor1 | TOILET; but you can view external reference layers in the Layer Properties Manager dialog box, and you can view externally reference blocks by using the Insert dialog box.

FIGURE 15.30

The Xref-1 file with the units updated

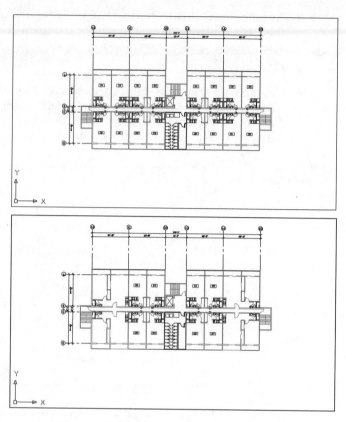

Next, you'll look at how AutoCAD identifies layers and blocks in external reference files, and you'll get a chance to import a layer from an Xref:

1. With the Xref-1 file open, open the Layer Properties Manager dialog box. Notice that the names of the layers from the external reference files are all prefixed with the filename and the vertical bar (|) character. Exit the Layer Manager Properties dialog box.

TIP You can also open the Layer Control shortcut menu to view the layer names.

2. Click the Xbind tool on the Reference toolbar or enter **Xb**↵ to open the Xbind dialog box. You see a listing of the current Xrefs. Each listing shows a plus sign to the left. This list box follows the Microsoft Windows format for expandable lists, much like the tree view in Windows Explorer.

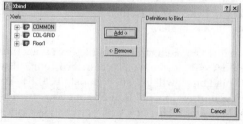

3. Click the plus sign next to the Floor1 Xref listing. The list expands to show the types of elements available to bind.

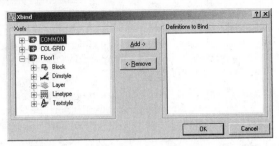

4. Now click the plus sign next to the Layer listing. The list expands further to show the layers available for binding.

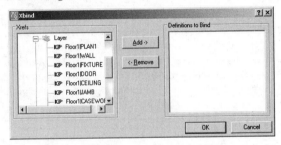

5. Locate Floor1 | WALL in the listing, click it, and then click the Add button. Floor1 | WALL is added to the list to the right: Definitions To Bind.

6. Click OK to bind the Floor1 | WALL layer.

7. Now open the Layer Properties Manager dialog box.

8. Scroll down the list and look for the Floor1 | WALL layer. You will not find it. In its place is a layer called Floor1$0$WALL.

TIP The AutoCAD DesignCenter lets you import settings and other drawing components from any drawing, not just Xref drawings. You'll learn more about the AutoCAD DesignCenter in Chapter 27.

As you can see, when you use Xbind to import a named item, such as the Floor1 | WALL layer, the vertical bar (|) is replaced by two dollar signs surrounding a number, which is usually zero. (If for some reason the imported layer name Floor1$0$WALL already exists, the zero in that name is changed to 1, as in Floor1$1$WALL.) Other named items are renamed in the same way, using the 0 replacement for the vertical bar.

You can also use the Xbind dialog box to bind multiple layers, as well as other items from Xrefs attached to the current drawing.

TIP You can bind an entire Xref to a drawing, converting it to a simple block. By doing so, you have the opportunity to maintain unique layer names of the Xref being bound or to merge the Xref's similarly named layers with those of the current file. See Chapter 7 for details.

NESTING EXTERNAL REFERENCES AND USING OVERLAYS

External references can be nested. For example, if the Common.dwg file created in this chapter used the Unit.dwg file as an external reference rather than an inserted block, you would still get the same result in the Xref-1.dwg file. That is, you would see the entire floor plan, including the unit plans, when you open Xref-1.dwg. In this situation, Unit.dwg is nested in the Common.dwg file, which is in turn externally referenced in the Xref-1.dwg file.

Though nested Xrefs can be helpful, take care in using external references in this way. For example, you might create an external reference by using the Common.dwg file in the Floor1.dwg file as a means of referencing walls and other features of the Common.dwg file. You might also reference the Common.dwg file into the Floor2.dwg file for the same reason. After you do this, however, you will have three versions of the Common plan in the Xref-1.dwg file, because each Xref now has Common.dwg attached to it. And because AutoCAD would dutifully load Common.dwg three times, Xref-1.dwg would occupy substantial computer memory, slowing your computer down when you edit the Xref-1.dwg file.

To avoid this problem, use the Overlay option in the External Reference dialog box. An overlayed external reference cannot be nested. For example, if you use the Overlay option when inserting the Common.dwg file into the Floor1.dwg and Floor2.dwg files, the nested Common.dwg files are ignored when you open the Xref-1.dwg file, thereby eliminating the redundant occurrence of Common.dwg. In another example, if you use the Overlay option to import the Unit.dwg file into the Common.dwg file and then attach the Common.dwg into Xref-1.dwg as an Xref, you do not see the Unit plan in Xref-1.dwg. The nested Unit.dwg drawing is ignored.

Controlling the Xref Search Path

One problem AutoCAD users have encountered in the past is a lost or broken link to an Xref. This occurs when an Xref file is moved from its original location or when you receive a set of drawings that includes Xrefs. The Xref links are broken because AutoCAD doesn't know where to look. Since AutoCAD 2005, you have better control over how AutoCAD looks for Xref files.

When you insert an Xref, the External Reference dialog box opens, offering you options for insertion point, scale, and rotation. This dialog box also offers the Path Type option, which enables you to select a method for locating Xrefs. You have three path type options to choose from:

Full Path   Lets you specify the exact filename and path for an Xref, including disk drive or network location. Use this option when you want AutoCAD to look in a specific location for the Xref.

Relative Path   Lets you specify a file location relative to the location of the current or host drawing. For example, if the host drawing is in a folder called C:\mycadfiles and the Xrefs are in a folder called C:\mycadfiles\xrefs, you can specify .\xrefs for the location of the Xref file. This option is useful when you know you will maintain the folder structure of the host and Xref files when moving or exchanging these files. Note that since this is a relative path, this option is valid only for files that reside on the same local hard disk.

No Path   Perhaps the most flexible option, this tells AutoCAD to use its own search criteria to find Xrefs. When No Path is selected, AutoCAD first looks in the same folder of the host drawing; then it looks in the project search path that is defined in the Files tab of the Options dialog box. (See Appendix A for more on the Options dialog box.) Last, AutoCAD looks in the Support File Search Path, also defined in the Files tab of the Options dialog box. If you plan to send your files to a client or a consultant, you might want to use this option.

Managing Layers

In a survey of AutoCAD users, Autodesk discovered that one of the most frequently used features in AutoCAD was the Layer command. You'll find that you are turning layers on and off to display and edit the many levels of information contained in your AutoCAD files. As your files become more complex, the control of layer visibility becomes more difficult. Fortunately, AutoCAD offers the Layer States Manager to make your work a little easier.

Saving and Recalling Layer Settings

The Layer States Manager lets you save layer settings. This can be crucial when you are editing a file that serves multiple uses, such as a floor plan and reflected ceiling plan. You can, for example, turn layers on and off to set up the drawing for a reflected ceiling plan view and then save the layer settings. Later, when you need to modify the ceiling information, you can recall the layer setting to view the ceiling data.

The following steps show you how the Layer States Manager works:

1. In AutoCAD, open the 15b-unit.dwg file. Open the Layer Properties Manager dialog box and turn on all the layers except the Notes and Flr-pat layers. Your drawing should look similar to the top image in Figure 15.31.

FIGURE 15.31
The view of the 15b-unit.dwg file, before and after changing layer settings

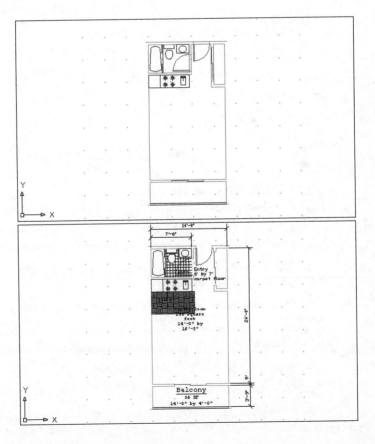

2. Open the Layer Properties Manager dialog box again, and click the Layer States Manager button to open the Layer States Manager dialog box. Take a moment to look at the options in this dialog box. This is where you can specify which layer settings you want saved with this layer state.

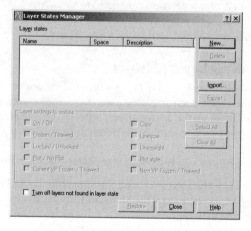

3. Now you're ready to save the current layer state. Click the New button in the Layer States Manager dialog box. The New Layer State To Save dialog box opens.

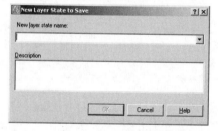

4. Enter **blank floor plan** in the New Layer State Name input box. Note that you can also enter a brief description of your layer state. Click OK to return to the Layer States Manager dialog box.

5. Make sure the On/Off check box is selected in the Layer States Manager dialog box; then click Close. Note that there are several other options available but you can leave them as they are.

6. Back in the Layer Properties Manager dialog box, turn on the Flr-pat and Notes layers and turn off the Ceiling layer.

7. Click OK. Your drawing will look like the bottom image in Figure 15.31.

You've just saved a layer state and then changed the layer settings to something different from the saved state. The following steps demonstrate how you can restore the saved layer state.

1. Reopen the Layer Properties Manager dialog box.

2. Click the Layer States Manager button to open the Layer States Manager dialog box.

3. Select blank floor plan from the list and then click Restore. You return to the Layer Properties Manager dialog box. Notice that the layer settings have changed back to the settings you saved.

4. Click OK. Your drawing reverts to the previous view with the Notes and Flr-pat layers turned off and the Ceiling layer on.

5. This brings you to the end of the xref tutorial so you can exit the file and save it.

The layer states are saved with the file so you can retrieve them at a later date. As you can see from the Layer States Manager dialog box, you have a few other options:

Delete   Deletes a layer state from the list.

Import   Imports a set of layer states that have been exported using the Export option of this dialog box.

Export   Saves a set of layer states as a file. By default, the file is given the name of the current file with the .las filename extension. You can import the layer state file into other files.

In addition to saving layer states by name, you can quickly revert to a previous layer state by clicking the Layer Previous tool in the right side of the Layers toolbar. This tool enables you to quickly revert to the previous layer settings without affecting other settings in AutoCAD. Note that the Layer Previous mode does not restore renamed or deleted layers, nor does it remove new layers.

After you become familiar with these layer state tools, you'll find yourself using them frequently in your editing sessions.

TIP   The Layerpmode command controls the tracking of layer states. It is normally turned on, but if it is turned off, the Layer Previous tool will not work. To turn it on, enter **Layerpmode.↵On.↵**.

Using Advanced Tools: Filter, Quick Select, and QuickCalc

Two other tools are extremely useful in your day-to-day work with AutoCAD: selection filters and QuickCalc. I have saved the discussion of these tools until this part of the chapter because you don't really need them until you've become accustomed to the way AutoCAD works. Chances are you've already experimented with some of the AutoCAD menu options not yet discussed in the tutorial. Many of the drop-down menu options and their functions are self-explanatory. Selection filters and QuickCalc, however, do not appear in any of the menus and require some further explanation.

Let's start with selection filters. There are actually two selection-filtering tools in AutoCAD. The *Quick Select tool* offers a quick way to locate objects based on their properties. The *Filter tool* lets you select objects based on a more complex set of criteria.

Filtering Selections

Suppose you need to isolate just the walls of your drawing in a separate file. One way to do this is to turn off all the layers except the Wall layer. You can then use the Wblock command and select the remaining walls, using a window to write the wall information to a file. Filters can simplify this operation by enabling you to select groups of objects based on their properties.

Follow these steps to select objects based on their layer assignment:

1. Open the Unit file.

2. Type **w.↵** to start the Wblock command. Then, in the Write Block dialog box, enter **Unitwall** in the File Name And Path input box.

3. Make sure the Objects and Retain radio buttons are selected in the dialog box, and then click the Select Objects button in the Objects group. The dialog box closes so that you can select objects.

4. At the `Select Objects:` prompt, type **Filter.⏎** to open the Object Selection Filters dialog box.

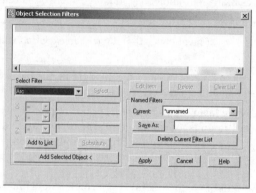

5. Open the drop-down list in the Select Filter group.

6. Scroll down the list, and find and highlight the Layer option.

7. Click the Select button next to the drop-down list to display a list of layers. Then highlight Wall and click OK.

8. In the Object Selection Filters dialog box, click the Add To List button toward the bottom of the Select Filter group to add Layer = Wall to the list box.

9. Click Apply to close the Object Selection Filters dialog box.

10. Type **all.⏎** to select everything in the drawing. Only the objects assigned to the Wall layer are selected. You'll see a message in the Command window indicating how many objects were found.

11. Press ⏎ and you'll see the message `Exiting Filtered selection Resuming WBLOCK command - Select objects: 29 found`.

12. Press ⏎ again to complete the selection and then click OK to complete the Wblock command. All the walls are written out to a file called `Unitwall`.

13. After reviewing the results of the exercise, type **U.⏎** or click the Undo button in the Standard toolbar to undo the Wblock command.

In this exercise, you filtered out a layer by using the Wblock command. After you designate a filter, you then select the group of objects you want AutoCAD to filter through. AutoCAD finds the objects that match the filter requirements and passes those objects to the current command.

As you've seen from the previous exercise, you can choose from many options in this utility. Let's take a closer look.

Working with the Object Selection Filters Dialog Box

To use the Object Selection Filters dialog box, first select the criterion for filtering from the drop-down list. If the criterion you select is a named item (layer, linetype, color, or block), you can then click the Select button to choose specific items from a list. If there is only one choice, the Select button is dimmed.

After you've determined what to filter, you must add it to the list by clicking the Add To List button. The filter criterion then appears in the list box at the top of the Object Selection Filters dialog box, and you can apply that criterion to your current command or to a later command. AutoCAD remembers your filter settings, so if you need to reselect a filtered selection set, you don't have to redefine your filter criteria.

Saving Filter Criteria

If you prefer, you can preselect filter criteria. Then, at any `Select objects:` prompt, you can click Selection Filters on the toolbar (or type **Filter**↵), highlight the appropriate filter criteria in the list box, and click Apply. The specifications in the Object Selection Filters dialog box remain in place for the duration of the current editing session.

You can also save a set of criteria by entering a name in the input box next to the Save As button and then clicking the button. The criteria list data is saved in a file called `Filter.nfl` in the current drawing's folder. You can then access the criteria list at any time by opening the Current drop-down list and choosing the name of the saved criteria list.

Filtering Objects by Location

Notice the X, Y, and Z drop-down lists just below the main Select Filter drop-down list in the Object Selection Filters dialog box. These lists become accessible when you select a criterion that describes a geometry or a coordinate (such as an arc's radius or center point). You can use these lists to define filter selections even more specifically, using greater than (>), less than (<), equal to or greater than (>=), Equal to or less than (<=), equal to (=), or not equal to (!=) comparisons (called *relational operators*).

For example, suppose you want to grab all the circles whose radii are greater than 4.0 units. To do this, choose Circle Radius from the Select Filter drop-down list. Then in the X list, select >. Enter **4.0** in the input box to the right of the X list, and click Add To List. You see the items

```
Circle Radius > 4.0000
Object = Circle
```

added to the list box at the top of the dialog box. You used the > operator to indicate a circle radius greater than 4.0 units.

Creating Complex Selection Sets

At times you'll want to create a specific filter list. For instance, say you need to filter out all the Door blocks on the layer Floor2 *and* all arcs with a radius equal to 1. To do this, you use the *grouping operators* found at the bottom of the Select Filter drop-down list. You'll need to build a list as follows:

```
** Begin OR
** Begin AND
Block Name = Door
Layer = Floor2
** End AND
** Begin AND
```

```
Entity = Arc
Arc Radius = 1.0000
** End AND
** End OR
```

Notice that the Begin and End operators are balanced; that is, for every Begin OR or Begin AND, there is an End OR or End AND.

This list might look rather simple, but it can get confusing. If criteria are bounded by the AND grouping operators, the objects must fulfill *both* criteria before they are selected. If criteria are bounded by the OR grouping operators, the objects fulfilling *either* criteria will be selected.

Here are the steps to build the previous list.

TIP   If you add the wrong option accidentally, select it from the list, then click the Delete button. If you need to insert an option in the middle of the list, select the item in the list that comes after the item you want to insert, then select and add the item:

1. In the Select Filter drop-down list, choose **Begin OR and then click Add To List. Then do the same for **Begin AND.

2. Click Block Name in the Select Filter drop-down list, click the Select button and select Door from the list that appears. Click Add To List.

3. For the layer, click Layer from the Select Filter drop-down list. Then click Select, choose the layer name, and click Add To List.

4. In the Select Filter drop-down list, choose **End AND and then click Add To List. Then do the same for **Begin AND.

5. Select Arc from the Select Filter drop-down list and click Add To List.

6. Select Arc Radius from the Select Filter list, and enter **1.0** in the input box next to the X drop-down list. Be sure the equal sign (=) shows in the X drop-down list and then click Add To List.

7. Choose **End AND and click Add To List. Then do the same for **End OR.

If you make an error in any step, simply highlight the item, select an item to replace it, and click the Substitute button instead of the Add To List button. If you need to only change a value, click Edit Item near the center of the dialog box.

Using Quick Select

The Filter command offers a lot of power in isolating specific types of objects, but in many situations, you might not need such an elaborate tool. The Qselect command can filter your selection based on the object properties, which are more common filter criteria. To access the Qselect command, choose Tools ➤ Quick Select, or right-click the drawing area when no command is active and choose Quick Select from the shortcut menu to open the Quick Select dialog box.

Quick Select is also offered as an option on a few dialog boxes. Try using the Wblock command again, this time using the QuickSelect option offered in its dialog box:

1. With the Unit file open, type **W**↵ to start the Wblock command, and then in the Write Block dialog box, enter **Unitwall2** in the File Name And Path input box.

2. Make sure the Objects radio button is selected in the top of the dialog box. Then click the QuickSelect button to the right of the Select Objects button in the Objects group to open the Quick Select dialog box.

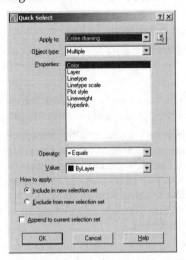

3. Select Layer from the Properties list.

4. Select Wall from the Value drop-down list near the bottom of the dialog box.

5. Click the Select Objects button in the upper-right corner of the dialog box. The dialog boxes close so that you can select objects.

6. Select the entire drawing by using a window and then press ↵ to finish your selection. The Quick Select dialog box returns.

7. Click OK, and then click OK in the Write Block dialog box. The walls disappear, indicating that they have been written to a file.

8. Click the Undo button to undo the deletion.

The Qselect command selects objects based on the object's properties, as shown in the Properties list box. You can apply the selection criteria based on the entire drawing, or you can use the Select Objects button in the upper-right corner of the dialog box to isolate a set of objects to which you want to apply the selection criteria.

In the previous exercise, you used Quick Select from within another dialog box. As mentioned earlier, you can also use Quick Select by choosing Tools ➢ Quick Select or by right-clicking the drawing area when no command is active and choosing Quick Select from the shortcut menu. Quick Select then makes use of the Noun/Verb selection method, so you select objects using Quick Select first, and then you apply editing commands to the selected objects.

TIP If you want to use Quick Select with a command that does not allow the Noun/Verb selection method, you can select objects by using Quick Select, start the command you want to use, and then use the Previous Selection option.

Here is a description of the Quick Select dialog box options:

Apply To Lets you determine the set of objects to which you want to apply the Quick Select filters. The default is the entire drawing, but you can use the Select Objects button to select a set of objects. If you select a set of objects before issuing the Quick Select command, you also see the Current Selection option in the Apply To drop-down list.

Object Type Lets you limit the filter to specific types of objects such as lines, arcs, circles, and so on. The Multiple option lets you filter your selection from all the objects in the drawing regardless of its type.

Properties After you select an object type, you can then select the property of the object type you want to filter. The Properties list changes to reflect the properties that are available to be filtered.

Operator Offers a set of criteria to apply to the property you select in the Properties list to make your selection. You can select objects that are *equal to* or *not equal to* the criteria you select in the Object Type and Properties lists. Depending on the property you select, you also might have the option to select objects that are *greater than* or *less than* a given property value. For example, you can select all lines whose X coordinate is less than 5 by choosing Line from the Object Type drop-down list and Start X from the Properties list. You then select < Less Than from the Operator drop-down list and enter **5** in the Value input box.

Value Displays the values of the property you select in the Properties list. For example, if you select Layer from the Properties list, the Value option lists all the layers available.

How To Apply Lets you specify whether to include or exclude the filtered objects in a new selection set.

Append To Current Selection Set Lets you append the filtered objects to an existing selection set or create an entirely new selection set.

Using the QuickCalc Calculator

You may have noticed a calculator icon in the Standard toolbar. This is the QuickCalc tool. If you click it, you'll see the QuickCalc calculator shown in Figure 15.32. At first glance, it looks like a typical calculator. It has both the standard math functions as well as scientific functions that are available when you click the More button. If your view of QuickCalc doesn't look like Figure 15.32, click the More/Less button, and then expand the Number Pad or Scientific sections by clicking the arrows in the section title. You'll also see a section for converting units, which comes in handy when you want to find the metric equivalent of an Imperial measurement.

At the bottom you'll see a section for variables. This area lets you store custom formulas and values that you want to refer to frequently.

Near the top, you'll see the display area. This is where QuickCalc keeps a running record of your calculation results. It also allows you to recall both the results and formulas you've used. Just below the display area is the input box. As you type or as you click the keys of QuickCalc, your input appears in this box. Pressing Enter displays the resulting value both in the input box and in the display area.

Above the display area is a set of tools in a toolbar. These tools let you obtain other types of data from the drawing, such as the coordinate of a point or the intersection of two lines (see Figure 15.33).

The function of these tools will become more clear as you become familiar with QuickCalc. Table 15.1 describes each tool. Next, you'll get a chance to try out QuickCalc on some typical AutoCAD tasks.

FIGURE 15.32

QuickCalc and its parts

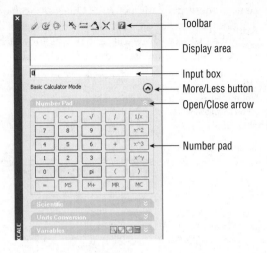

- Toolbar
- Display area
- Input box
- More/Less button
- Open/Close arrow
- Number pad

FIGURE 15.33

The QuickCalc toolbar

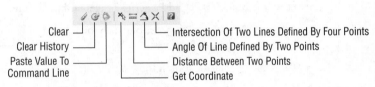

- Clear
- Clear History
- Paste Value To Command Line
- Get Coordinate
- Distance Between Two Points
- Angle Of Line Defined By Two Points
- Intersection Of Two Lines Defined By Four Points

TABLE 15.1:   The QuickCalc Tools

TOOL	PURPOSE
Clear	Clears value from input box.
Clear History	Clears the display area.
Paste Value To Command Line	Pastes data from the input box to the command line.
Get Coordinates	Temporarily closes QuickCalc and prompts you to pick a point or points. Coordinates of the point or the angle value are placed in the input area.
Distance Between Two Points	Temporarily closes QuickCalc and prompts you to enter a point. Select two points and the distance between the points is placed in the input area of QuickCalc.
Angle Of Line Defined By Two Points	Returns the angle of two points.
Intersection Of Two Lines Defined By Two Points	Returns the coordinate of the intersection of four points.

Adding Lengths and Finding the Sum of Angles

Although QuickCalc may look simple, it provides a powerful aid in your work in AutoCAD. Besides offering the typical calculator functions, QuickCalc also enables you to quickly add and subtract angle values, feet and inch lengths, and much more. You can paste the results from calculations into the command line so that you can easily include results as part of command line responses.

To get a full appreciation of what QuickCalc can do for you, try the following exercises. Imagine that you have a renovation project for which someone has taken dimensions in the field. You might be asked to draw a section of wall for which the overall dimension is not given, but portions of the wall are dimensioned in a sketch as shown in Figure 15.34.

FIGURE 15.34

A sketch of measurements taken from an existing building

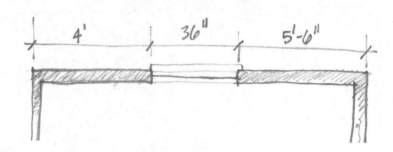

You can use QuickCalc to add a series of feet and inch dimensions:

1. Open the `QuickCalc.dwg` sample file, which contains some lines you can work with. It is set up to use architectural units.

2. Click the QuickCalc tool in the Standard toolbar.

3. Double-click in the input box of QuickCalc, and then enter **4′+36+5′6**. As you type, you see your entry appear in the input box.

4. Press ↵. The sum of the lengths, 12′-6″, appears in the input box and in the display area.

Notice that you only had to enter the foot (′) sign. QuickCalc assumes that a value is in inches unless you specify otherwise. You can also enter distances in the more traditional way using dashes and zeros as in 4′-0″ or 5′-6″. QuickCalc ignores the dashes.

Now suppose you want to use your new-found length to draw a line. You can quickly add the results from the input box to the command line as shown in the following exercise.

1. Click the Line tool, and then click a point in the left portion of the drawing area then enter @ in preparation for the inclusion of a coordinate.

2. In the QuickCalc toolbar, click the Paste Value To Command Line tool. Notice that the value in the input box appears in the command line after the @ symbol.

3. Click in the drawing area or command line to continue drawing the line.

4. With the Polar mode turned on in the status bar, press ↵ while pointing the rubber-banding line directly to the right. A horizontal line is drawn to the length of 12′-6″.

In this example, you made use of the Paste Value To Command Line tool in the QuickCalc toolbar. If you want to use a value that has scrolled up in the display area, you can select that value, right-click, and choose Paste To Command Line.

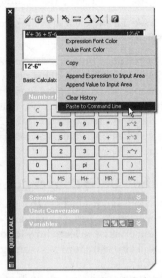

This is especially useful when you've used QuickCalc to add several strings of dimensions and you need to recall them individually from the display area. Besides adding feet and inches, you can also perform other math functions such as dividing a length by two or multiplying a length. If the input value is in feet and inches, the resulting value will also be returned in feet and inches. For example, if you divide 25′ by 6, the result will be 4′-2″.

Another useful QuickCalc tool is Angle Of Line Defined By Two Points, which allows you to obtain the angle defined by two points.

1. In QuickCalc, click the Angle Of Line Defined By Two Points tool. QuickCalc temporarily closes to allow you to select points.

2. With osnaps turned on, select the endpoints of the lower line, starting with the bottom endpoint, as shown in Figure 15.35.

FIGURE 15.35
Select these endpoints using the Angle Of Line Defined By Two Points option.

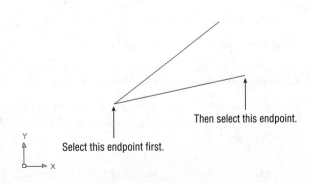

Then select this endpoint.

Select this endpoint first.

3. Back in QuickCalc, click the plus button in the number pad or enter +; then click the Angle Of Line Defined By Two Points tool again.

4. Select the endpoints of the upper line starting with the bottom end of the line.

5. Back in QuickCalc, you see the angle value of the second line added to the input box. Press ↵ to get the total angle value.

Here you added the angle of two lines, but you could just as easily have subtracted one angle from another or multiplied the value of a single angle. This can be useful if you need to find a fraction or a multiple of an angle. For example, you might need to find one-quarter of the angle described by a line, or you might want to find the angle that bisects two lines. You can do so by adding the value of two angles, as described in the exercise, and then divide by 2 using the number pad or by including /2 in the input box. Once you've obtained a value, you can paste it into the command line while specifying angles for drawing input.

Using the Display Area and Units Conversion

Besides performing math functions on distances and angles, you can also do some basic unit conversions. QuickCalc will perform length, area, volume, and angle conversions within its Units Conversion group. Try the following exercise to learn how to convert a length from centimeters to feet and inches. In the process, you'll also learn how you can move a value from the Units Conversion area to the input box of QuickCalc.

Suppose you have a paper drawing that was done in metric, and you need to turn it into an AutoCAD drawing in feet and inches. Here's an example of how you can convert centimeters to feet and inches.

1. In QuickCalc, expand the Units Conversion group by clicking the arrow to the right of the Units Conversion title bar.

2. Select Length from the Units Type drop-down list.

3. Select Centimeters from the Convert From drop-down list.

4. Select Feet from the Convert To drop-down list.

5. In the Value To Convert input box, enter 450↵ for 450 cm. You see the equivalent value in feet in the Converted Value box.

6. Click the Converted Value option and you'll also see QuickCalc icon to the far right. Click this icon to display the value in the input box at the top of QuickCalc.

The value is in feet and decimal feet. You can convert the value to feet and inches by doing the following.

1. Edit the value in the input box to read as follows: **14´ +(.763779527559*12)**

2. Press ↵. The value converts to a feet-and-inch value of 14´-9³⁄₁₆˝.

One limitation to the unit conversion feature is that it will not take feet and inch input when converting from feet. For example, if you want to convert 12´-4˝ to centimeters, you have to enter 12.334. In other words, you have to convert the inches to decimal feet. Since the Unit Conversion area is part of QuickCalc, this just means an extra step. You can quickly calculate the decimal feet equivalent of feet and inch values and then transfer them to the Units Conversion area.

Try the following to see how this might work:

1. Click the Clear button in the QuickCalc tolbar (it looks like an eraser), then double-click in the QuickCalc's input box.

2. Enter **12 + (4 / 12)** in QuickCalc's input box. The first 12 is the 12 feet. The 4/12 is for the 4 inches converted to decimal feet. Once you press ↵, the value of 12.333333 appears.

3. Click anywhere in the Units Conversion group. Notice that the value from the input box is automatically transferred to the Value To Convert input box.

4. Select Feet from the Convert From drop-down list, and select Centimeters from the Convert To drop-down list. You see the centimeter equivalent of 12.333333 feet appear in the Converted Value input box.

Here you saw how values from the input box automatically transfer to the Units Conversion area. You can also cut and paste values from other sources into either the main calculator input box or the Units Conversion input box.

Using QuickCalc to Find Points

You've seen how QuickCalc will let you add values of distances and angles and how it can perform unit conversions. You can also use it to calculate coordinate locations. To work with coordinates, you need to use a few special functions built into QuickCalc that let you select points and manipulate their value.

Before AutoCAD added the Midpoint Between Two Points osnap, the AutoCAD Cal command was the only way to find the midpoint between two points without drawing a temporary line. In the following example, you'll use QuickCalc to perform the same function as an example of how you can acquire point data and manipulate it to derive other coordinate locations.

1. Click the Clear button in the QuickCalc toolbar, then double click in the QuickCalc's input box.

2. In the QuickCalc input box, enter **(end + end)/2**↵. QuickCalc closes temporarily to allow you to select points.

3. Select the endpoints of the two lines, as shown in Figure 15.36.

4. QuickCalc returns and displays the coordinates of a point exactly between the two endpoints of the lines you selected in step 2.

FIGURE 15.36
The endpoints of the
two lines

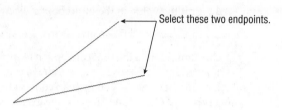

Select these two endpoints.

In step 1, you used the *end* function that is built into QuickCalc. As you saw, the end function lets you select the endpoint of an object. The end + end in the formula tells QuickCalc to add the two coordinates you select in step 2. The /2 in the formula divides the sum of the coordinates to find their average, which happens to be the midpoint between the two points.

If you were to perform this calculation using pencil and paper, you would add the X, Y, and Z coordinate values of each point separately and then divide each coordinate by two. Finally, you would combine the resulting X, Y, and Z coordinates back into a single point location.

USING OSNAP MODES IN QUICKCALC EXPRESSIONS

In the previous exercise, you used osnap modes as part of arithmetic formulas (or *expressions* as they are called in AutoCAD). QuickCalc treats osnap modes as temporary placeholders for point coordinates until you actually pick the points (at the prompts shown in steps 2 and 3 of the previous exercise).

The expression

```
(end + end)/2
```

finds the average of two values. In this case, the values are coordinates, so the average is the midpoint between the two coordinates. You can take this one step further and find the centroid of a triangle by using this expression:

```
(end + end + end)/3
```

Note that only the first three letters of the Osnap mode are entered in calculator expressions. Table 15.2 shows what to enter in an expression for Osnap modes. Table 15.2 includes two items that are not really osnap modes, although they work similarly when they are used in an expression. The first is Rad. When you include Rad in an expression, you get the following prompt:

```
Select circle, arc or polyline segment for RAD function:
```

You can then select an arc, a polyline arc segment, or a circle, and its radius is used in place of Rad in the expression.

The other item, Cur, prompts you for a point. Instead of looking for specific geometry on an object, it just locates a point. You could have used Cur in the previous exercise in place of the End and Cen modes to create a more general-purpose midpoint locator, as in the following formula:

```
(cur + cur)/2
```

TABLE 15.2:   The Geometry Calculator's Osnap Modes

CALCULATOR OSNAP	MEANING
End	Endpoint
Ins	Insert
Int	Intersection
Mid	Midpoint
Cen	Center
Nea	Nearest
Nod	Node
Qua	Quadrant
Per	Perpendicular
Tan	Tangent
Rad	Radius of object
Cur	Cursor pick

Pasting to the Command Line

Now that you have the coordinate for the midpoint, try the next exercise to apply that coordinate to a command. In this example, you will use the coordinate found in step 3 as the starting point for a line.

1. Click the Line tool in the Draw toolbar.

2. In QuickCalc, right-click the (end + end)/2 listing in the display area, and then select Paste To Command Line.

3. Notice that the coordinate value from the display area is pasted into the command line at the Line command's `Specify first point:` prompt. Press ⏎ to accept the input from Quick-Calc. You see a rubber-banding line beginning at a point midway between the two endpoints of the lines you selected in the previous exercise.

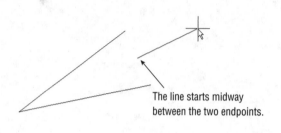

The line starts midway
between the two endpoints.

4. Click another point to place the line in the drawing, and then press ⏎ to exit the Line command.

Finding Fractional Distances between Two Points

Another common need that AutoCAD users have is the ability to find a location that is a fractional distance along a line. For example, users frequently need to find a point that is one-third the distance from the endpoint of a line. Here's how that can be accomplished using QuickCalc.

1. Enter **plt (end, end, 0.333).**⏎ in the QuickCalc input box. QuickCalc will close temporarily to allow you to select points.

2. Click the endpoints of the line shown in Figure 15.37. QuickCalc returns with the coordinates of a point that is 0.3333 percent of the length of the line from the first endpoint you selected.

FIGURE 15.37
Select these points
to find a point that is
one-third the distance
from an endpoint.

Click the endpoints of this line.

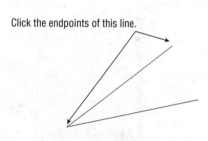

3. Click the Line tool.

4. Click in the QuickCalc display area on the last entry, right-click, and choose Paste To Command Line.

5. Press ↵, and you see a line start at a point that is one-third the distance from the endpoint.

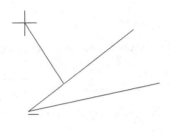

6. Press Esc to exit the Line command. You don't need to actually draw the line as this exercise is intended to show you how the formula in step 1 works.

In step 1, you used a formula that contained the Plt function. This function finds a point that is a particular percentage between two points. You specify the two points first, using the now-familiar end function, and then the percentage between the two endpoints is specified as a decimal value. The (end, end, 0.333) indicates the two endpoints you selected in step 2 and the percentage as a decimal value of 0.333.

TIP In the formulas you've seen so far, you have used the end function to select endpoints. If you prefer to select your own osnaps during the point selection process, you can use the cur function. Cur lets you use any osnap you want when selecting points. In the first example, you could use (cur + cur)/2 instead of (end + end)/2.

The Plt function is just one of several special functions you can use with QuickCalc. Table 15.3 lists other functions you can use to find points in your drawing and gather other data. In that table, 2D points are represented as pt1, pt2, and so on. 3D points or points describing a plane are indicated by ptp1, ptp3, and so on. The center of an arc or a circle is indicated with apex for a 2D location or apex1 and apex2 for a 3D axis.

TABLE 15.3:   Functions in QuickCalc and the Format for Their Use

FUNCTION AND FORMAT	DESCRIPTION
Getvar (*system variable name*)	Get the value of a system variable
Vec(*pt1,pt2*)	Vector described with distance between the two points
Vec1(*pt1,pt2*)	Vector described with 1 unit length

TABLE 15.3: Functions in QuickCalc and the Format for Their Use *(CONTINUED)*

FUNCTION AND FORMAT	DESCRIPTION
Abs(*vector*)	Absolute value of the length of a vector
Cur (no arguments required)	Get a point
@ (no arguments required)	Lastpoint
w2u(point) and u2w(point)	Convert world coordinates to current user coordinates [w2u] or user coordinates to world
Pld(pt1,pt2,distance)	Point on a line at a specified distance
Plt(pt1,pt2,percent)	Point on a line at a percentage (decimal) of line length
Rot(pt1,apex, angle) or Rot(Pt1,apex1, apex2, angle)	Rotation of a point pt1 about an apex
Ill(pt1, pt2, pt3, pt4)	Intersection between two lines
Ilp(pt1, pt2, ptp1, ptp2, ptp3)	Intersection between a line and a plane; 5 points required
Dist (pt1, pt2)	Distance between two points
Dpl (point,pt1,pt2)	Shortest distance between a point and a line
Dpp(point,ptp1,ptp2,ptp3)	Shortest distance between a point and a plane
Rad (no arguments required)	Returns a radius
Ang (vector or pt1,pt2 or apex, pt1, pt2 or apex1, pt1, pt2 ,apex2)	Returns an angle; can use up to 4 parameters when working in 3D
Nor (vector, or pt1,pt2 or ptp1, ptp2, ptp3)	Finds the normal of a vector or plane

Using QuickCalc While in the Middle of a Command

In all the previous examples, you've used QuickCalc as a stand-alone calculator. You've also seen how you can insert a calculation into the command line while a command is in progress. A third way to work with QuickCalc is to open it while in the middle of a command.

In a previous exercise, you used the (end + end)/2 formula to find the midpoint between two points, and then you inserted the resulting value into the Line command. Suppose you started the Line command before you opened QuickCalc. Try the following to see how you can use QuickCalc once a command has been initiated.

1. Close QuickCalc.

2. Start the Line command.

3. Click the QuickCalc tool in the Standard toolbar.

4. In the QuickCalc input box, enter **(end + end)/2** but don't press ↵. Instead, click the Apply button at the bottom of QuickCalc.

5. Select the endpoints of two lines. A line starts at the midpoint between the two points.

6. Click another point to draw the line, and then press ↵ to end the Line command.

In this exercise, you saw that an Apply option appears at the bottom of the QuickCalc window, along with Close and Help buttons. These buttons are not present when you open QuickCalc with no command active. The Apply button executes the formula and then immediately returns the resulting value to the command. Using QuickCalc this way eliminates a few steps.

FINDING A POINT RELATIVE TO ANOTHER POINT

Now suppose you want to start a line at a relative distance from another line. The following steps describe how to use the calculator to start a line from a point that is 2.5″ in the X axis and 5.0″ in the Y axis from the endpoint of another line:

1. Make sure QuickCalc is closed and start the Line command.

2. Click the QuickCalc tool in the Standard toolbar and enter **end + [2.5,5.0]** ↵ in the input box.

3. Click the Apply button at the bottom of QuickCalc.

4. Click the endpoint of the line you just drew. Another line starts at a location that is at a distance of 2.5 in the X axis and 5.0 in the Y axis from the endpoint you selected.

In this example, you used the Endpoint Osnap mode to indicate a point of reference. This is added to Cartesian coordinates in square brackets, describing the distance and direction from the reference point. You could have entered any coordinate value within the square brackets. You also could have entered a polar coordinate in place of the Cartesian coordinate, as in the following: **end + [5.59<63]**.

You can replace the end in the expression with the at sign (@) to continue from the last point you selected. Also, it's not necessary to include every coordinate in the square brackets. For example, to indicate a displacement in only one axis, you can leave out a value for the other two coordinates while leaving in the commas, as in the following examples:

```
[4,5] = [4,5,0]
[,1] = [0,1,0]
[,,2] = [0,0,2]
```

COMBINING COORDINATES AND EXPRESSIONS

In the previous two examples, you saw that you can use an expression or enter coordinates, but what if you wanted to combine an expression within a coordinate? For example, in the beginning of this section, you saw how you can add feet and inches and then transfer the result to the command line. In that example, you had to switch back and forth between QuickCalc and the command line to create the response for the Command prompt. If you prefer, you can create an expression that supplies the entire command input. Here are the steps to do this:

1. Close QuickCalc, and then start the Line command.

2. Click the QuickCalc tool in the Standard toolbar.

3. Enter the following in the input box:

```
End + [(4´+36+5´6)<45]
```

4. Click Apply.

5. In the drawing area, click the endpoint of a line. AutoCAD draws a line that begins at at distance of 12´-6˝ from and at a 45° angle to the endpoint you select.

In this exercise, you used the expression (4´+36+5´6) right in the middle of a coordinate value. As described earlier, the coordinate is within square brackets. By using this method, you can more easily calculate measurements and apply them to commands. The trick is to become familiar enough with the syntax QuickCalc requires so you can write these expressions without errors.

Storing Expressions and Values

The ability to create expressions to manipulate coordinates can be useful, but you may find it difficult to remember an expression once you've created it. Fortunately, QuickCalc offers the Variables group, which allows you to store frequently used expressions and values that you use frequently.

At the bottom of QuickCalc, you'll see the Variables group and its set of tools within its titlebar (see Figure 15.38).

These tools let you add, edit, or delete items from the list. A fourth option lets you send a variable to the main calculator input box.

TIP   You can also right-click in the Variables group list box and select these same options from a shortcut menu. The shortcut menu also lets you create a new category and rename an existing one.

The Variables group also contains a list of currently stored variables. Some sample variables are shown in the list. If you select a variable, you will see a description of that variable's function at the bottom of the group. You might need to click and drag the bottom edge of the QuickCalc window downward to see the description.

FIGURE 15.38

The Variables group

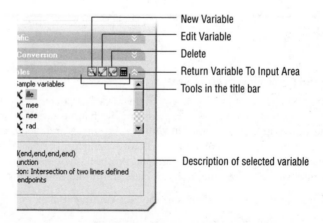

— New Variable
— Edit Variable
— Delete
— Return Variable To Input Area
— Tools in the title bar

— Description of selected variable

To use an existing variable, select it from the list and click the Return Variable To Input Area button; it's the one that looks like a calculator. To add a variable to the list, click the New Variable button, which opens the Variable Definition dialog box:

This dialog box lets you enter the properties of the variable and choose the type. In the Variable Properties group, you enter the name of the variable in the Name text box. In the Group With drop-down list, you select a category under which your formula will appear in the Variables list. You can also create a new category. The Value Or Expression input box is where you put your actual formula. It can also be a single value such as a number or a coordinate. At the bottom, you have a space to enter a description for the variable. This description will appear in the Variable group's detail box at the bottom of QuickCalc.

At the top, you see two options: Constant and Function. If you choose Function, your variable will behave as it normally does when you enter it in the input box. If you choose Constant and your variable is a formula, your variable will be executed when you close the Variable Definition dialog box. The resulting value will become the value for the variable.

If you want to edit an existing variable, highlight it in the Variables group list, and then click the Edit Variable button to open the Variable Definition dialog box.

Guidelines for Working with QuickCalc

You might be noticing some patterns in the way expressions are formatted for the calculator. Here are some guidelines to remember:

- Coordinates are enclosed in square brackets.

- Nested or grouped expressions are enclosed in parentheses.

- Operators are placed between values, as in simple math equations.

- Object snaps can be used in place of coordinate values.

Table 15.4 lists all the operators and functions available in QuickCalc. You might want to experiment with these other functions on your own. You can enter many of these operators using the keys in the number pad or in the scientific group.

TABLE 15.4: The Geometry Calculator's Functions

OPERATOR/FUNCTION	WHAT IT DOES	EXAMPLE
+ or −	Add or subtract numbers or vectors	2 − 1 = 1 [a,b,c] + [x,y,z] = [a+x, b+y, c+z]
* or /	Multiply or divide numbers or vectors	2 * 4.2 = 8.4 a*[x,y,z] = [a*x, a*y, a*z]
^	Exponentiation of a number	3^2 = 9
sin	Sine of an angle	sin (45) = 0.707107
cos	Cosine of an angle	cos (30) = 0.866025
tang	Tangent of an angle	tang (30) = 0.57735
asin	Arcsine of a real number	asin (0.707107) = 45.0
acos	Arccosine of a real number	acos (0.866025) = 30.0
atan	Arctangent of a real number	atan (0.57735) = 30.0
ln	Natural log	ln (2) = 0.693147
log	Base-10 log	log (2) = 0.30103
exp	Natural exponent	exp (2) = 7.38906
exp10	Base-10 exponent	exp10 (2) = 100
sqr	Square of a number	sqr (9) = 81.0
abs	Absolute value	abs (−3.4) = 3.4
round	Round to nearest integer	round (3.6) = 4
trunc	Drop decimal portion of real number	trunc (3.6) = 3
r2d	Convert radians to degrees	r2d (1.5708) = 90.0002
d2r	Convert degrees to radians	d2r (90) = 1.5708
pi	The constant pi	3.14159

The QuickCalc is capable of much more than the typical uses you've seen here. A description of its full capabilities extends beyond the scope of this text. Still, the processes described in this section will be helpful as you use AutoCAD. If you want to know more about QuickCalc, consult the AutoCAD Help User Documentation (choose Help ➤ Help).

If You Want to Experiment

Try storing an expression in the Variables group to see how this process works. In the following exercise, you'll store the expression you used to find the one-third distance along a line.

1. Open QuickCalc and open the Variables group.

2. Click the New Variable button to open the Variable Definition dialog box.

3. In the Variable Type group, select Function.

4. In the Name input box, enter OneThirdLine. You cannot use spaces, hyphens, or underscores in the name.

5. Open the Group With drop-down list and select New.

6. In the Category Definition dialog box, enter **My Variables** in the Name input box and click OK.

7. In the Value Or Expression input box, enter the expression **plt (end, end, 0.333)**.

8. In the Description input box, enter **Find a point 1/3 the distance between two points**, and then click OK.

You see the new category and variable in the Variables group list box. Your new variable will be available at any time you need it. Once you place the expression of the variable in the QuickCalc input box, you can edit it to customize it on the fly. For example, if you need to find a distance that is one-quarter the way between two points, change the 0.333 to 0.25 in the expression.

Chapter 16

Laying Out Your Printer Output

Your set of drawings for this studio apartment building would probably include a larger-scale, more detailed drawing of the typical unit plan. You already have the beginnings of this drawing in the form of the Unit file.

As you have seen, the notes and dimensions you entered into the Unit file can be turned off or frozen in the Plan file so that they don't interfere with the graphics of the drawing. The Unit file can be part of another drawing file that contains more detailed information on the typical unit plan at a larger scale. To this new drawing you can add notes, symbols, and dimensions. Whenever the Unit file is altered, you update its occurrence in the large-scale drawing of the typical unit as well as in the Plan file. The units are thus quickly updated, and good correspondence is ensured among all the drawings for your project.

Now suppose that you want to combine drawings having different scales in the same drawing file—for example, the overall plan of one floor plus an enlarged view of one typical unit. You can do so using the Layout tabs and a feature called Paper Space.

Topics in this chapter include the following:

◆ Understanding Model Space and Paper Space

◆ Working with Paper Space Viewports

◆ Creating Odd-Shaped Viewports

◆ Understanding Line Weights, Linetypes, and Dimensions in Paper Space

Understanding Model Space and Paper Space

So far, you've looked at ways to help you get around in your drawing while using a single view. This single view representation of your AutoCAD drawing is called the *Model Space* display mode. You can also set up multiple views of your drawing, called *floating viewports*. You create floating viewports by using the Layout tabs to work in *Paper Space* display mode.

To get a clear understanding of the Model Space and Paper Space modes, imagine that your drawing is actually a full-size replica or model of the object you are drawing. Your computer screen is your window into a "room" where this model is being constructed, and the keyboard and mouse are your means of access to this room. You can control your window's position in relation to the object through the use of Pan, Zoom, View, and other display-related commands. You can also construct or modify the model by using drawing and editing commands. Think of this room as your Model Space.

So far, you have been working on your drawings by looking through a single "window" into Model Space. Now suppose you have the ability to step back and add windows with different views looking into your Model Space. The effect is as if you have several video cameras in your

Model Space "room," each connected to a different monitor. You can view all your windows at once on your computer screen or enlarge a single window to fill the entire screen. Further, you can control the shape of your windows and easily switch from one window to another. This is what Paper Space is like.

Paper Space lets you create and display multiple views of Model Space. Each view window, called a *viewport*, acts like an individual virtual screen. One viewport can have an overall view of your drawing, while another can be a close-up. You can also control layer visibility individually for each viewport and display different versions of the same area of your drawing. You can move, copy, and stretch viewports and even overlap them.

TIP Another type of viewport, called the Tiled viewport, can be set up in Model Space. Chapter 21 discusses this type of viewport.

Perhaps one of the more powerful features of Paper Space is that you can plot several views of the same drawing on one sheet of paper. You can also include graphic objects such as borders and notes that appear only in Paper Space. In this function, Paper Space acts much like a page-layout program such as QuarkXPress or Adobe InDesign. You can "paste up" different views of your drawing and then add borders, title blocks, general notes, and other types of graphic and textural data. Figure 16.1 shows the Plan drawing set up in Paper Space mode to display several views.

Creating a Paper Space Layout

Your gateway to Paper Space is the Layout tabs at the bottom of the AutoCAD window. When the Model tab is selected, you are in Model Space. When you select a Layout tab, you are in Paper Space.

FIGURE 16.1
Different views of the same drawing in Paper Space

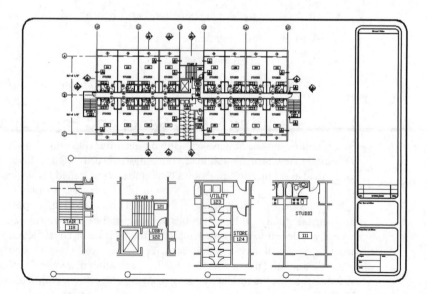

TIP You can also use a system variable to switch between tabs. When Tilemode is set to 1 (On), the default setting, you are in Model Space. When it is set to 0 (Off), you are in Paper Space.

Let's start with the basics of entering Paper Space:

1. Open the Xref-1 file you saved from the last chapter, and ensure that your display shows all the drawing. You can also use 16-xref1.dwg from the companion CD project files.

2. Click the Layout1 tab or click Model on the status bar, right-click the Layout1 tab, and then select Page Setup Manager to open the Page Setup Manager dialog box.

3. Click the Modify button to open the Page Setup dialog box.

4. Select the Letter paper size option from the Paper Size drop-down list. Metric users should select A4 (210 mm × 297 mm). The paper size you select here determines the shape and margin of the Paper Space layout area.

5. Select a printer from the Printer/Plotter name drop down list.

6. Click OK to close the Page Setup dialog box, and then click Close to close the Page Setup Manager dialog box. Note that the word PAPER replaces the word MODEL in the status bar; this tells you at a glance that you are in Paper Space.

AutoCAD bases the Paper Space work area on the paper size you specify. The area shown in Paper Space reflects the area of the paper size you select in step 4. If for some reason you need to change the paper size, repeat steps 2 through 5. You can also store the way you've set up your Paper Space layout using the Page Setup Manager you saw in step 2. See Chapter 8 for more on this feature.

Creating New Paper Space Viewports

As you saw in Chapter 8, the different look of the Layout tab tells you that you are in Paper Space. You also learned that a viewport is automatically created when you first open a Layout tab. The viewport displays an overall view of your drawing to no particular scale.

In this section, you will work with multiple viewports in Paper Space, instead of just the default single viewport you get when you open the Layout tab.

This first exercise shows you how to create three new viewports at once:

1. Right-click the Draw or Modify toolbar, and choose Viewports to open the Viewports toolbar. You'll use this toolbar a bit later in this exercise.

2. Click the viewport border to select it. The viewport border is the solid rectangle surrounding your drawing, just inside the dashed rectangle.

3. Click the Erase tool to erase the viewport. Your drawing disappears. Don't panic; remember that the viewport is like a window to Model Space. The objects in Model Space are still there.

4. Click Display Viewports Dialog in the Viewports toolbar to open the Viewports dialog box. You can also choose View ➤ Viewports ➤ New Viewports. This dialog box contains a set of predefined viewport layouts.

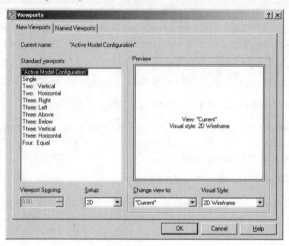

TIP You'll learn more about the Viewports dialog box and its options in Chapter 21.

5. Click the Three: Above option in the Standard Viewports list box. The box to the right shows a sample view of the Three: Above layout you selected.

6. Click OK. The `Specify first corner or [Fit] <Fit>:` prompt appears.

7. Press ↵ to accept the default Fit option. The Fit option fits the viewport layout to the maximum area allowed in your Paper Space view. Three rectangles appear in the formation, as shown in Figure 16.2. Each of these is a viewport to your Model Space. The viewport at the top fills the whole width of the drawing area; the bottom half of the screen is divided into two viewports.

FIGURE 16.2
The newly created viewports

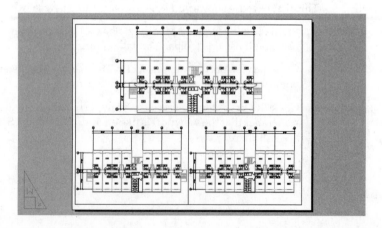

When you create new viewports, AutoCAD automatically fills the viewport with the extents of your Model Space drawing. You can specify an exact scale for each viewport, as you'll see later.

Notice that the dashed line representing your paper margin has disappeared. That's because the viewports are pushed to the margin limits, thereby covering the dashed line.

You could have kept the original viewport that appeared when you first opened the Layout1 tab and then added two new viewports. Completely replacing the single viewport is a bit simpler because the Viewports dialog box fits the viewports in the allowed space for you.

Reaching Inside Viewports

Now suppose you need access to the objects within the viewports in order to adjust their display and edit your drawing. Try these steps:

1. Click Paper on the status bar. This gives you control over Model Space even though you are in Paper Space. (You can also enter **MS↵** as a keyboard shortcut to enter Model Space mode.)

   The first thing you notice is that the UCS icon changes back to its L-shaped arrow form. It also appears in each viewport, as if you had three AutoCAD windows instead of just one.

2. Move your cursor over each viewport. Notice that in one of the viewports the cursor appears as the AutoCAD crosshair cursor, while in the other viewports it appears as an arrow pointer. The viewport that shows the AutoCAD cursor is the active one; you can pan and zoom, as well as edit objects in the active viewport.

TIP   If your drawing disappears from a viewport, you can usually retrieve it by choosing View ➤ Zoom ➤ Extents (type **Zoom↵E↵**).

3. Click in the lower-left viewport to activate it.

4. Choose View ➤ Zoom ➤ Window and place a window selection around the elevator area.

5. Click the lower-right viewport and choose View ➤ Zoom ➤ Window to enlarge your view of a typical unit. You can also use the Pan Realtime and Zoom Realtime tools.

TIP   If you don't see the UCS icon, it has been turned off. Type **UCSicon↵On↵** to turn it on. See Chapter 21 for more on the UCS icon.

When you click the Paper button on the status bar, the UCS icon again changes shape—instead of one triangular-shaped icon, you have three arrow-shaped ones, one for each viewport on the screen. Also, as you move your cursor into the currently active viewport, the cursor changes from an arrow into the usual crosshair. Another way to tell which viewport is the active one is by its bold border.

TIP   You can also switch between Model Space and Paper Space by double-clicking an area in either region. For example, to go to Model Space from Paper Space, double-click inside a viewport. To get back to Paper Space, double-click the area outside the viewport. If you have an enlarged view of a viewport and no portion of the Paper Space area is available to click, click the Paper button on the status bar.

You can move from viewport to viewport even while you are in the middle of most commands. For example, you can issue the Line command, pick the start point in one viewport, go to a different viewport to pick the next point, and so on. To activate a different viewport, you simply click it (see Figure 16.3).

FIGURE 16.3
The three viewports, each with a different view of the plan

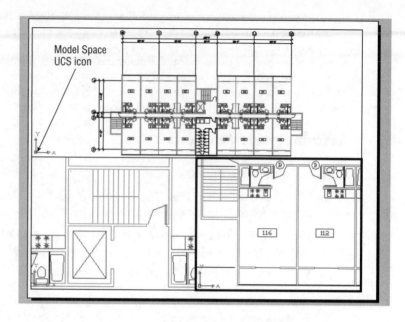

TIP   You might find it difficult to access the contents of overlapping viewports, especially if the viewports are the same size or if one is enclosed by another. In this situation, you can move between viewports by pressing Ctrl+R repeatedly until you get to the viewport you want.

You've seen how you can zoom into a viewport view, but what happens when you use the Zoom command while in Paper Space? Try the following exercise to find out:

1. Click the Model button on the status bar or double-click an area outside the viewports to return to Paper Space.

2. Click the Zoom Realtime tool in the Standard toolbar and then zoom in to the Paper Space view. The entire view enlarges, including the views in the viewports.

3. Right-click and select Exit, then choose View ➢ Zoom ➢ All or enter Z↵A↵ to return to the overall view of Paper Space.

This brief exercise shows that you can use the Zoom tool in Paper Space just as you would in Model Space. All the display-related commands are available, including the Pan Realtime command.

Getting Back to Full-Screen Model Space

After you've created viewports, you can then reenter Model Space through the viewport by clicking the Model/Paper button on the status bar. This button performs two functions: it shows you which space you are in, and it enables you to switch between the two spaces. But what if you want to quickly get back into the old, familiar, full-screen Model Space you were in before you entered Paper Space? The following exercise demonstrates how this is done:

1. Click the Model tab at the bottom of the drawing area or enter **Tm.↵1.↵**. Your drawing returns to the original full-screen Model Space view—everything is back to normal.

2. Click the Layout1 tab or enter **Tm.↵0.↵**. You are back in Paper Space. Notice that all the viewports are still there when you return to Paper Space. After you've set up Paper Space, it remains part

of the drawing until you delete all the viewports. Also notice that you didn't see the Page Setup dialog box this time. After you've chosen a sheet size, AutoCAD assumes that you will continue to use that sheet size and other page setup information until you tell it otherwise.

You might prefer using Model Space for doing most of your drawing and using Paper Space for setting up views for printing. Because viewport layouts are retained, you won't lose anything when you go back to Model Space to edit your drawing.

Working with Paper Space Viewports

Paper Space is intended as a page-layout or composition tool. You can manipulate viewports' sizes, scale their views independently of one another, and even set layering and linetype scales independently.

Let's try manipulating the shape and location of viewports by using the Modify toolbar options:

1. Turn off Running Osnaps if it is on.

2. Make sure you're in Paper Space. (The Paper button should appear to the right of the status bar buttons.) Then click the bottom edge of the lower-left viewport to expose its grips (see the top image in Figure 16.4).

FIGURE 16.4

Stretching, erasing, and moving viewports

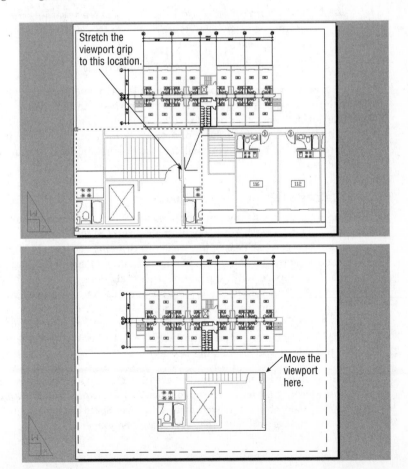

Stretch the viewport grip to this location.

Move the viewport here.

3. Click the upper-right grip, and then drag it to the location shown in the top image in Figure 16.4.

4. Press the Esc key, and then erase the lower-right viewport by selecting it and then clicking Erase in the Modify toolbar. Then click the bottom edge of the viewport.

5. Move the lower-left viewport so it is centered in the bottom half of the window, as shown in the bottom image in Figure 16.4.

In this exercise, you clicked the viewport edge to select it for editing. If, while in Paper Space, you attempt to click the image within the viewport, you will not select anything. Later you will see, however, that you can use the Osnap modes to snap to parts of the drawing image within a viewport.

Because viewports are recognized as AutoCAD objects, you can manipulate them by using all the editing commands, just as you would manipulate any other object. In the previous exercise, you moved, stretched, and erased viewports.

Next, you'll see how layers affect viewports:

1. Create a new layer called Vport.

2. In the Properties palette, change the viewport borders to the Vport layer.

3. Finally, turn off the Vport layer. You will see a warning message telling you that the members of the selected objects are on a layer that is off or frozen. Click OK and the viewport borders disappear.

4. After reviewing the results of step 3, turn the Vport layer back on.

You can assign a viewport's border a layer, a color, a linetype, and even a line weight. If you put the viewport's border on a layer that has been turned off or frozen, that border becomes invisible, just like any other object on such a layer. Making the borders invisible is helpful when you want to compose a final sheet for printing. Even when turned off, the active viewport has a heavy border around it when you switch to the floating model space, and all the viewports still display their views.

Scaling Views in Paper Space

Paper Space has its own unit of measure. You have already seen how you are required to specify a paper size when opening a Layout tab to a Paper Space view. When you first enter Paper Space, regardless of the area your drawing occupies in Model Space, you are given limits that are set by the paper size you specify in the Page Setup dialog box. If you keep in mind that Paper Space is like a paste-up area that is dependent on the printer you configured for AutoCAD, this difference of scale becomes easier to comprehend. Just as you might paste up photographs and maps representing several square miles onto an 11″ × 17″ board, so can you use Paper Space to paste up views of scale drawings representing city blocks or houses on an 8 1/2″ × 11″ sheet of paper. But in AutoCAD, you have the freedom to change the scale and size of the objects you are pasting up.

TIP While in Paper Space, you can edit objects in a Model Space viewport, but to do so, you must use Floating Model Space. You can then click a viewport and edit within that viewport. While in this mode, objects that were created in Paper Space cannot be edited. Choosing View ➢ Paper Space brings you back to the Paper Space environment.

DISAPPEARING VIEWPORTS

As you add more viewports to a drawing, some of them might blank out even though you know you haven't turned them off. Don't panic. AutoCAD limits the number of viewports that display their contents at any given time to 64. (A viewport that displays its contents is said to be *active*.) This limit is provided because too many active viewports can bog down a system.

If you are using a slow computer with limited resources, you can lower this limit to two or three viewports to gain some performance. Then only two or three viewports will display their contents. (All viewports that are turned on will still plot, regardless of whether their contents are visible.) Zooming in to a blank viewport restores its visibility, thereby enabling you to continue to work with enlarged Paper Space views containing only a few viewports.

The Maxactvp system variable controls this value. Type **Maxactvp** and then enter the number of viewports you want active at any given time.

If you want to be able to print your drawing at a specific scale, you must carefully consider scale factors when composing your Paper Space paste-up. Let's see how to put together a sheet in Paper Space and still maintain accuracy of scale:

1. Make sure you're in Paper Space. Check to see whether the Paper button appears on the status bar. If Model appears there, click that button to change it to Paper.

2. Click the topmost viewport's border to select it.

3. Right-click and then choose Properties from the shortcut menu to open the Properties palette.

4. Scroll down the list of properties until you see the Standard Scale listing.

5. Click the Custom setting next to the Standard Scale listing; then click the downward-pointing arrow that appears next to Custom to open the list.

6. Select $1/32'' = 1'-0''$ from the drop-down list. Notice how the view in the top viewport changes.

7. Press the Esc key twice to clear the selection of the viewport.

8. Click the lower viewport border. The information in the Properties palette changes to reflect the properties of the newly selected viewport.

9. Click the Standard Scale Custom listing and open the drop-down list as you did in step 5.

10. Select $3/16'' = 1'-0''$ from the list. Notice that the view in the viewport changes to reflect the new scale (see Figure 16.5).

It's easy to adjust the width, height, and location of the viewports so that they display only the parts of the unit you want to see. While in Paper Space, use the Stretch, Move, or Scale command to edit any viewport border, or just use the viewport's grips to edit its size. The view within the viewport itself remains at the same scale and location, while the viewport changes in size. You can move and stretch viewports with no effect on the size and location of the objects within the view.

If you need to overlay one drawing on top of another, you can overlap viewports. Use the Osnap overrides to select geometry within each viewport, even while in Paper Space. This enables you to align one viewport on top of another at exact locations.

FIGURE 16.5

Paper Space viewport views scaled to $^1/_{32}$″ = 1′-0″ and $^3/_{16}$″ = 1′-0″

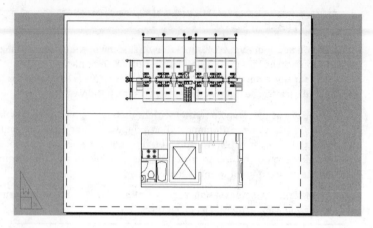

You can also add a title block in Paper Space at a 1:1 scale to frame your viewports and then plot this drawing from Paper Space at a scale of 1:1. Your plot appears just as it does in Paper Space, at the appropriate scale. Paper Space displays a dashed line to show you where the nonprintable areas occur near the edge of the paper.

While working in Paper Space, pay close attention to whether you are in Paper Space or Floating Model Space mode. It is easy to accidentally pan or zoom within a Floating Model Space viewport when you intend to pan or zoom your Paper Space view. This can cause you to lose your viewport scaling or alignment with other parts of the drawing. It's a good idea to save viewport views by choosing View ➤ Named Views in case you happen to accidentally change a viewport view.

Another way to prevent your viewport view from being accidentally altered is to turn on View Lock. To do this, while in Paper Space, click a viewport border. Right-click to open the shortcut menu, and then choose Display Locked ➤ Yes. After the view is locked, you cannot pan or zoom a viewport view. You also cannot change the size of the viewport. This setting is also available in the viewport's Properties palette.

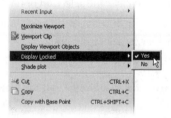

TIP   If your viewport views are automatically zooming to extents when you enter them, the Ucsfollow system variable has been changed from its default setting of 0 (zero). Change Ucsfollow back to 0 by typing **Ucsfollow.↓o.↓**. You can also use the UCS dialog box to change this setting. Choose Tools ➤ Named UCS. In the UCS dialog box, click the Settings tab and then make sure that the Update View To Plan When UCS Is Changed option is turned off.

Setting Layers in Individual Viewports

Another unique feature of Paper Space viewports is their ability to freeze layers independently. You could, for example, display the usual plan information in the overall view of a floor but show only the walls in the enlarged view of one unit.

You control viewport layer visibility through the Layer Properties Manager dialog box. You might have noticed that there are three sun icons for each layer listing.

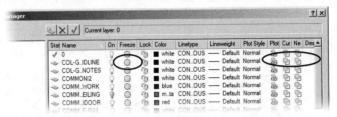

TIP   You might need to widen the Layer Properties Manager dialog box to view all the columns. Simply click and drag the right border of the dialog box to the right.

You're already familiar with the sun icon farthest to the left. This is the Freeze/Thaw icon that controls the freezing and thawing of layers globally. Several columns to the right of that icon are two sun icons with transparent rectangles. These icons control the freezing and thawing of layers in individual viewports. Of this pair, the one on the left controls existing viewports and the one on the right controls settings for newly created viewports.

This exercise shows you firsthand how the sun icon for existing viewports works:

1. Click the Paper button on the status bar to go to Floating Model Space.

2. Activate the lower viewport.

3. Open the Layer Properties Manager dialog box.

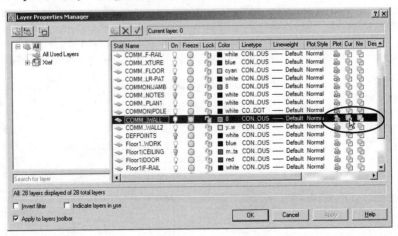

4. Locate the Common | WALL layer; then click its name to help you isolate this layer.

WARNING   You cannot use the Cur VP and New VP options in the Layer Properties Manager dialog box while you are in the Model tab.

5. Click the column labeled Current VP Freeze for the selected layer. You might need to widen the Layer Properties Manager dialog box to do this. The Current VP Freeze column is the third column from the right side of the dialog box. Click the icon, which looks like a transparent rectangle under a sun. The sun changes to a snowflake, telling you that the layer is now frozen for the current viewport.

6. Click OK. The active viewport regenerates, with the Wall layer of the Common Xref made invisible in the current viewport. However, the walls remain visible in the other viewport (see Figure 16.6).

7. After reviewing the effects of the Current VP Freeze setting, go back to the Layer Properties Manager dialog box and thaw the Common | WALL layer by clicking its Current VP Freeze icon again so that it turns back into a sun.

8. Click OK to exit the dialog box.

9. Take a moment to study the drawing, and then save the Xref-1 file.

You might have noticed another, identical sun icon next to the one you used in the previous exercise. This icon controls layer visibility in any new viewports you might create next, rather than controlling existing viewports.

If you prefer, you can also use the Layer drop-down list in the Layers toolbar to freeze layers in individual viewports. Double-click in the viewport you want to modify, select the layer from the list, and then click the same sun icon with the small rectangle beneath it.

This section concludes the apartment building tutorial. Although you haven't drawn the complete building, you've learned all the commands and techniques you need to do so. Figure 16.7 shows you a completed plan of the first floor; to complete your floor plans and get some practice using AutoCAD, you might want to add the symbols shown in this figure to your Plan file.

Because buildings like this one often have the same plans for several floors, the plan for the second floor can also represent the third floor. Combined with the first floor, this gives you a three-level apartment building. This project might also have a ground-level garage, which would be a separate file. You can use the Col-grid.dwg file from the companion CD in the garage file as a reference for dimensions. The other symbols can be blocks stored as files that can be retrieved in other files.

FIGURE 16.6
The drawing with the Common | WALL layer turned off in the active viewport

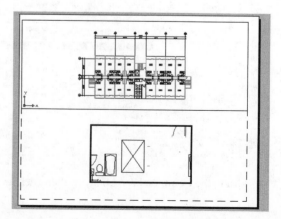

FIGURE 16.7
A completed floor of
the apartment building

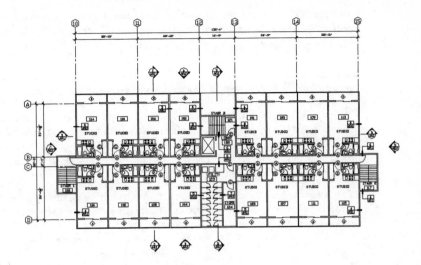

MASKING OUT PARTS OF A DRAWING

Chapter 7 described a method for using AutoCAD's Draw Order feature to hide floor patterns under equipment or furniture in a floor layout. You can use a similar method to hide irregularly shaped areas in a Paper Space viewport. This would be desirable for plotting site plans, civil plans, or floor plans that require portions of the drawing to be masked out. Or you might want to mask part of a plan that is overlapped by another to expose dimension or text data.

Creating and Using Multiple Paper Space Layouts

You're not limited to just one or two Paper Space layouts. You can have as many Paper Space layouts as you want, with each layout set up for a different sheet size containing different views of your drawing. You can use this feature to set up multiple drawing sheets based on a single AutoCAD drawing file. For example, a client requires full sets of plans in both $1/8'' = 1'$ scale and $1/16'' = 1''$ scale. You can set up two Layout tabs, each with a different sheet size and viewport scale.

You can also set up different Paper Space layouts for the different types of drawings. In the San Francisco Main Library project, a single drawing contained the data for mechanical layout, equipment and furnishing, floor plans, and reflected ceiling plans. Although that project used multiple files to set the layers for each plan, a single file with multiple Layout tabs can serve the same purpose in AutoCAD 2007.

To create new Layout tabs, do the following:

1. Right-click any tab.

2. Choose New Layout from the shortcut menu to add a new tab to those that already exist.

3. Click the new layout tab. The layout appears with a single default viewport.

In step 1, you may have noticed that the Layout tab shortcut menu includes the From Template option. The From Template option lets you create a Paper Space layout based on an AutoCAD template file. AutoCAD provides several standard layouts that include title blocks based on common sheet sizes.

PAPER SPACE AND THE SAN FRANCISCO MAIN LIBRARY PROJECT

The San Francisco Main Library project made extensive use of Paper Space. As you've seen in earlier chapters, the library project used multiple instances of the same file to show different types of information. Paper Space was instrumental in enabling the CAD specialists to manage large amounts of drawing data. One floor-plan drawing served as the basis for several sheets, including floor plans, reflected ceiling plans, equipment plans, exit plans, and others.

The following image shows a Paper Space view of a drawing from the San Francisco Main Library construction document set. This particular sheet shows the floor pattern layout of some of the main circulation areas.

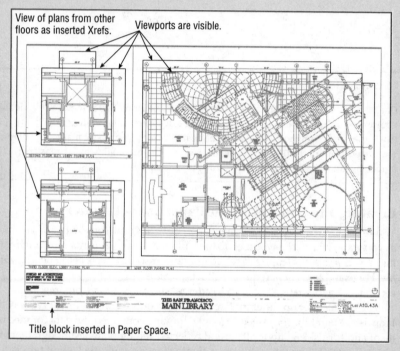

The title block is inserted in Paper Space as a block, rather than as an Xref. This was done because each drawing has unique drawing title information that is kept as attribute data in the title block. The attributes can be easily updated from a dialog box.

The plan drawings are Xrefs inserted into Model Space, with Paper Space viewports displaying selected areas. The viewport borders are turned on in this view to show how they are arranged. These borders are turned off when the drawing is plotted.

Notice that the grid reference symbols are in their own viewport adjacent to the main enlarged floor plan. These adjacent grid viewports display portions of the drawing that are actually some distance from the floor plan shown in the main viewport. The following image shows the overall floor plan with the viewport areas outlined. Here you can see that the column grid symbols are actually at the edge of the drawing.

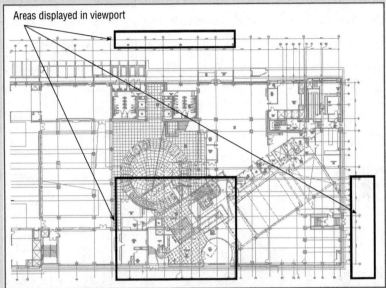

Areas displayed in viewport

This example shows how viewports helped the creator of this drawing reuse existing data. If a change is made to the overall plan, including the column grids, the enlarged plan of the entry is automatically updated.

The Layout tab shortcut menu also includes options that enable you to delete, rename, move, copy, or select all the tabs. If there are more tabs than can fit in the space provided, you can navigate the tabs by using the arrows just to the left of the tabs.

Creating Odd-Shaped Viewports

In many situations, a rectangular viewport will not provide a view appropriate for what you want to accomplish. For example, you might want to isolate part of a floor plan that is L-shaped or even circular. You can create viewports from virtually any shape you need, as the following exercise demonstrates.

WARNING   This feature is not available in AutoCAD LT.

Follow these steps to set up a Layout tab to show only the lower apartment units and the elevators and stairs:

1. Click the Clip Existing Viewport tool in the Viewports toolbar. You can also choose Modify ➢ Clip ➢ Viewport.

2. At the `Select viewport to clip:` prompt, click the viewport border.

3. At the `Select clipping object or [Polygonal] <Polygonal>:` prompt, press ↵.

4. Turn off Running Osnaps, and draw the outline shown in the top portion of Figure 16.8.

5. After you finish selecting points, press ↵. The viewport changes to conform to the new shape.

6. Click the viewport border to expose its grips.

7. Click a grip and move it to a new location. Notice that the viewport view conforms to the new shape.

FIGURE 16.8

Drawing a polygon outline for a viewport

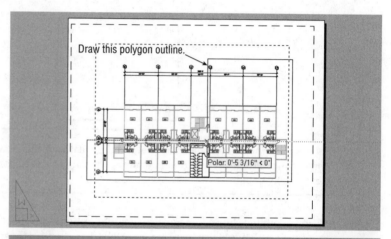

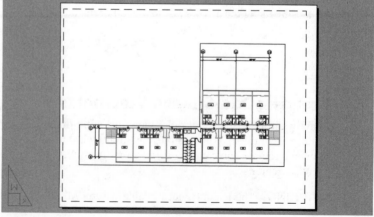

The new viewport shape gives you more flexibility in isolating portions of a drawing. This can be especially useful if you have a large project that is divided into smaller sheets. You can set up several Layout tabs, each displaying a different portion of the plan.

What if you want a viewport that is not rectilinear? This exercise shows you how to create a circular viewport:

1. Erase the viewport you just modified.

2. Draw a circle that roughly fills the Paper Space area.

3. Click the Convert Object To Viewport option on the Viewports toolbar or choose View ➢ Viewports ➢ Object.

4. Click the circle. The plan appears inside the circle, as shown in Figure 16.9.

To simplify this exercise, you were asked to draw a circle as the basis for a new viewport. However, you are not limited to circles; you can use any closed polyline or spline of any shape. (See Chapter 18 for a detailed discussion of polylines and splines.) You can also use the Polygon tool in the Draw toolbar to create a shape and then turn it into a viewport.

If you look carefully at the series of prompts for the previous exercise, you'll notice that the Convert Object To Viewport option invokes a command-line version of the Vports command (–vports). This command-line version offers some options that the standard Vports command does not. The following options are available with the command-line version of Vports:

```
-vports
[ON/OFF/Fit/Shadeplot/Lock/Object/Polygonal/Restore/2/3/4] <Fit>:
```

You used two of the options in the two previous exercises, Polygonal and Object. If you're an experienced AutoCAD user, you might notice that this command-line version of Vports is the same as the Mview command of earlier releases. You can still use the Mview command if you prefer.

Understanding Line Weights, Linetypes, and Dimensions in Paper Space

The behavior of several AutoCAD features depends on whether you are in Paper Space or Model Space. The most visible of these features are line weights, linetypes, and dimensions. In this section, you'll take a closer look at these features and see how to use them in conjunction with Paper Space.

FIGURE 16.9
A circular viewpoint

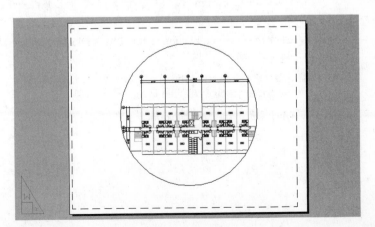

Controlling and Viewing Line Weights in Paper Space

Line weights can greatly improve the readability of technical drawings. You can make important features stand out with bold line weights while keeping the "noise" of smaller details from overpowering a drawing. In architectural floor plans, walls are traditionally drawn with heavier lines so that the outline of a plan can be easily read. Other features exist in a drawing for reference only, so they are drawn in a lighter weight than normal.

In Chapter 9, you saw how to control line weights in AutoCAD by using plot style tables. You can apply either a named plot style table or a color plot style table to a drawing. If you already have a library of AutoCAD drawings, you might want to use color plot style tables for backward compatibility. AutoCAD also enables you to assign line weights directly to layers or objects and to view the results of your line weight settings in Paper Space.

Here's an exercise that demonstrates how to set line weights directly:

1. Click the Layout1 tab; then open the Layer Properties Manager dialog box.

2. Right-click the Layer list; then choose Select All.

3. Click the Lineweight column to open the Lineweight dialog box.

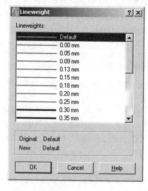

4. Select 0.13 mm from the list and then click OK. You've just assigned the 0.13 mm line weight to all layers.

5. Right-click the Layer list again and choose Clear All.

6. Click the Common | WALL layer and ctrl+click Floor1 | WALL layer to select these two layers.

7. Click the Lineweight column for either of the two selected layers to open the Lineweight dialog box again.

8. Select 0.40 mm from the dialog box; then click OK. You've just assigned the 0.4 mm line weight to the two selected layers.

9. Click OK in the Layer Properties Manager dialog box.

Although you set the line weights for the layers in the drawing, you need to make a few more changes to the file settings before they are visible in Paper Space:

1. Choose Format ➤ Lineweight to open the Lineweight Settings dialog box.

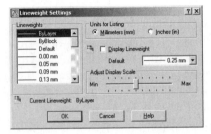

2. Click the Display Lineweight check box and then click OK.

3. Make sure you are in Paper Space and then zoom in to the drawing.

4. Choose View ➤ Regen All. The lines representing the walls are now thicker, as shown in Figure 16.10.

5. After reviewing the results of this exercise, close the file.

With the ability to display line weights in Paper Space, you have better control over your output. Instead of using a trial-and-error method to print your drawing and then checking your printout to see whether the line weights are correct, AutoCAD 2007 lets you see the line weights right on your screen.

This exercise showed you how to set line weights so that they appear in Paper Space as they will when you plot your drawing. If you normally plot your drawings in black, you can go one step further and set all your layer colors to black to really see how your plots will look. But you'll need to save your layer settings so you can restore the layers to their original colors. You'll learn more about saving and restoring layer settings later in this chapter. Another way to view your drawing in black and white without affecting your layer settings is to use the color plot style table described in Chapter 9.

FIGURE 16.10

An enlarged view of the plan with line weights displayed

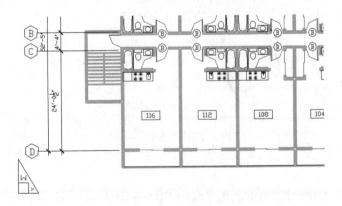

TIP When line weight display is turned on, you'll see line weights in Model Space as well as in Paper Space. Line weights can be distracting while you work on your drawing in Model Space, but you can quickly turn them off by entering **Lwdisplay⏎On⏎** at the Command prompt. Entering **Lwdisplay⏎Off⏎** turns the line weight display back on.

The Lineweight Settings Dialog Box

There are a few other settings in the Lineweight Settings dialog box that you didn't use in the previous exercise. Here is a description of those settings for your reference:

Units For Listing   You can choose between millimeters and inches for the unit of measure for lineweights. The default is millimeters.

Adjust Display Scale   This setting lets you control just how thick line weights appear in the drawing. Move the slider to the right for thicker lines and to the left for thinner lines. This setting affects only the display on your monitor. As you move the slider, you can see a sample of the results in the Lineweights list box.

Default Drop-Down List   This drop-down list lets you select the default line weight that you see in the Layer Properties Manager dialog box. It is set to 0.01″ (0.25 mm) by default. You might want to lower the default line weight to .005″ (.13 mm) just as a matter of course, because most printers these days can print lines to that size and even smaller.

Linetype Scales and Paper Space

As you have seen in previous exercises, you must carefully control drawing scales when creating viewports. Fortunately, this is easily done through the Properties palette. Although Paper Space offers the flexibility of combining images of different scale in one display, it also adds to the complexity of your task in controlling that display. Your drawing's linetype scale, in particular, needs careful attention.

In Chapter 5, you saw that you had to set the linetype scale to the scale factor of the drawing in order to make the linetype visible. If you intend to plot that same drawing from Paper Space, you will have to set the linetype scale back to 1 to get the linetypes to appear correctly. This is because AutoCAD faithfully scales linetypes to the current unit system. Remember that Paper Space units are different from Model Space units. When you scale a Model Space image down to fit within the smaller Paper Space area, the linetypes remain scaled to the increased linetype scale settings. In the Chapter 5 example, linetypes are scaled up by a factor of 48. This causes noncontinuous lines to appear as continuous in Paper Space because you see only a small portion of a greatly enlarged noncontinuous linetype.

The Psltscale system variable enables you to determine how linetype scales are applied to Paper Space views. You can set Psltscale so that the linetypes will appear the same, regardless of whether you view them directly in tiled Model Space or through a viewport in Paper Space. By default, this system variable is set to 1. This causes AutoCAD to scale all the linetypes uniformly across all the viewports in Paper Space. You can set Psltscale to 0 to force the viewports to display linetypes exactly as they appear in Model Space.

You can also control this setting in the Linetype Manager dialog box (choose Format ➤ Linetype). When you click the Show Details button, you see a setting called Use Paper Space Units For Scaling in the lower-left corner. When this check box is selected, Psltscale is set to 1. When it is not selected, Psltscale is set to 0.

Dimensioning in Paper Space Layouts

At times, you might find it more convenient to add dimensions to your drawing in Paper Space rather than directly on your objects in Model Space. This can be helpful when you are using Layout tabs to produce views of the same Model Space drawing at different scales. Or you might want to combine several drawings at different scales in one Layout tab as in a detail sheet.

You have two basic options when dimensioning Model Space objects in Paper Space. The Associative Dimensioning feature can make quick work of dimensions for Layout tabs containing drawings of differing scales. Or, if you prefer not to use Associative Dimensioning, you can adjust settings for individual dimension styles.

USING ASSOCIATIVE DIMENSIONING IN PAPER SPACE

Perhaps the simplest way to dimension in Paper Space is to use the Associative Dimensioning feature. With this feature turned on, you can dimension Model Space objects while in a Paper Space layout. Furthermore, Paper Space dimensions of Model Space objects will be automatically updated if the Model Space object is edited.

Try the following exercise to see how Associative Dimensioning works:

1. Choose File ➢ New and use the Start From Scratch option to create a new blank file. If you are using a template for new files, use the Acad.dwt template.

2. Draw a rectangle 12 units wide by 4 units high. If you're using a metric file, make the rectangle 480 units wide by 160 units high.

3. Click the Layout1 tab, right click the tab and select Page Setup Manager.

4. At the Page Setup Manager dialog box, click Modify and then in the Page Setup dialog box, choose the Letter paper size in the Printer/Plotter section

5. Click OK and then Close the Page Setup Manager dialog box.

6. Right-click in the drawing area and then choose Options from the shortcut menu.

7. In the Options dialog box, click the User Preferences tab and make sure the Make New Dimensions Associative option in the Associative Dimensioning group is turned on. Click OK to exit the dialog box.

Next, you'll use the rectangle you drew in Model Space to test the Associative Dimensioning feature in the Layout1 tab:

1. Choose Dimension ➢ Linear, and then using the Endpoint Osnap, dimension the bottom edge of the rectangle you drew in Model Space. The dimension shows 12.0000 (480 for metric drawings), the actual size of the rectangle.

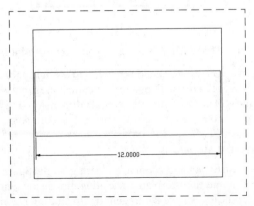

2. Double-click inside the viewport, and then use the Zoom Realtime tool to zoom out a bit so that the rectangle appears smaller in the viewport. After you exit the Zoom Realtime tool, the dimension follows the new view of the rectangle.

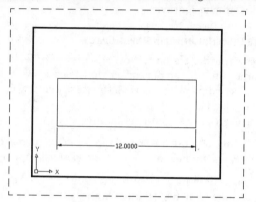

3. While you're in Floating Model Space, click the rectangle, and then click the grip in the lower-left corner and drag it upward and to the right.

4. Click again to place the corner of the rectangle in a new location. The dimension changes to conform to the new shape.

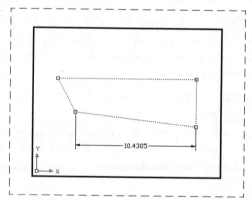

5. Close the rectangle file without saving it. You won't need it in the future.

You've just seen how you can dimension an object in Model Space while in Paper Space. You can also dimension Model Space Xrefs in Paper Space in much the same way. The only difference is that changes to the Xref file will not automatically update dimensions made in Paper Space. You'll need to employ the Dimregen command to refresh Paper Space dimensions of Xref objects.

UPDATING ASSOCIATIVE DIMENSIONS

If you use a wheel mouse to pan and zoom in a Floating Model Space viewport, you might need to use the Dimregen command to refresh an associative dimension. Simply type **Dimregen**↵ at the Command prompt. You can also use Dimregen to refresh dimensions from drawings that have been edited in earlier versions of AutoCAD or, as mentioned already, to refresh dimensions of objects contained in external references.

PAPER SPACE DIMENSIONING WITHOUT ASSOCIATIVE DIMENSIONING

In some situations, you might not want to use Associative Dimensioning although you still want to dimension Model Space objects in Paper Space. For example, you might be in an office that has different versions of AutoCAD, or you might be sharing your drawings with other offices that are not using AutoCAD 2007, and the use of Associative Dimensioning creates some confusion.

To dimension Model Space objects in Paper Space without Associative Dimensioning, you need to have AutoCAD adjust the dimension text to the scale of the viewport from which you are dimensioning. You can have AutoCAD scale dimension values in Paper Space so they correspond to a viewport zoom-scale factor. The following steps show you how this setting is made:

1. Open the Dimension Style Manager dialog box.

2. Select the dimension style you want to edit and click Modify.

3. Click the Primary Units tab.

4. In the Measurement Scale group, enter the scale factor of the viewport you intend to dimension in the Scale Factor input box. For example, if the viewport is scaled to a $\frac{1}{2}'' = 1'-0''$ scale, enter **24**.

5. Click the Apply To Layout Dimensions Only check box.

6. Click OK, and then click Close in the Dimension Style Manager dialog box. You are ready to dimension in Paper Space.

Remember that you can snap to objects in a floating viewport so you can add dimensions as you normally would in Model Space. If you are dimensioning objects in viewports of different scales, you'll need to set up multiple dimension styles, one for each viewport scale.

Other Uses for Paper Space

The exercises in this section should give you a sense of how you work in Paper Space. I've given examples that reflect the more common uses of Paper Space. Remember that Paper Space is like a page-layout portion of AutoCAD—separate yet connected to Model Space through viewports.

You needn't limit your applications to floor plans. Interior and exterior elevations, 3D models, and detail sheets can all take advantage of Paper Space. When used in conjunction with AutoCAD raster import capabilities, Paper Space can be a powerful tool for creating large-format presentations.

If You Want to Experiment

Try the following exercise to become more familiar with Paper Space. You will add two more viewports by choosing View ➤ Viewports. In the process, you'll find that editing Paper Space views requires frequent shifts from Model Space to Paper Space and back:

1. Open the Xref-1 file you used for the earlier Paper Space exercise. You can also use the 16-xref1 file from the Chapter 16 folder on the CD.

2. If you aren't already in Paper Space, click the Layout1 tab and make sure that Paper appears in the status bar.

3. Stretch the lower viewport so that it occupies the lower-right third of the screen (see the first image in Figure 16.11).

FIGURE 16.11
Creating new viewports in Paper Space

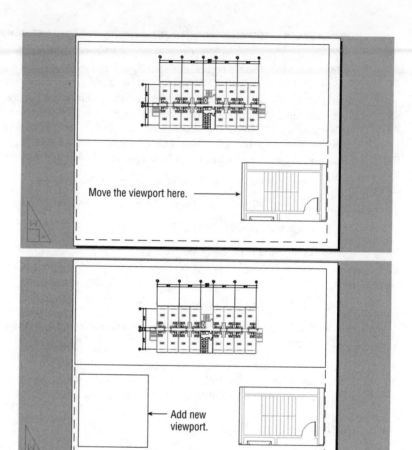

Move the viewport here. ──────▶

◀── Add new viewport.

4. Switch to Floating Model Space and click the lower viewport.

5. Pan the view so that the entire staircase is displayed.

6. Return to Paper Space to create a new viewport.

7. Choose View ➢ Viewports ➢ New Viewports, or type **vports↵**.

8. In the Viewports dialog box, make sure the New Viewports tab is selected and select Single from the list.

9. Click OK, and then click the lower-left corner of the screen.

10. At the Specify opposite corner: prompt, size the viewport so that it is similar to the viewport on the right, as shown in the bottom image in Figure 16.11.

11. Click the Paper button in the status bar to go to Floating Model Space; then click in the lower-left viewport.

12. Type **Regen↵**. Notice that only the current viewport regenerates.

13. Use the Zoom and Pan commands to display the stairway at the far left of the floor plan.

14. Return to Paper Space and copy the new viewport to the right.

15. Return to Floating Model Space, and use the Pan Realtime tool to pan the view in the new viewport to display the stairway to the far right of the floor plan. Notice that when you use the Pan Realtime tool, you can pan across the entire AutoCAD window; you're not limited to panning just inside the viewport area. You can also use the scroll bar to pan the active viewport.

16. Return to Paper Space to resize the viewports to display only the stairs in the lower half of the layout, as in Figure 16.12.

FIGURE 16.12
Copy viewport in Paper Space

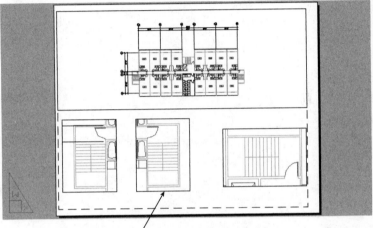

Copy viewport and change view to show other stair.

Chapter 17

Using Dynamic Blocks

Blocks are a great way to create and store ready-made symbols. They can be a great time-saver, especially when you have assemblies that you use often. Earlier in this book, you learned how to create a basic, no frills block. Once you've understood the basics of block creation, you can begin to work with *dynamic blocks*.

Dynamic blocks have properties that you can modify using grips. For example, you can create a dynamic block of a door and then easily grip edit its size and orientation. In another example, you can have a single block that is used to represent several versions of a similar object. You can have a single block of a bed that can be modified to show a single-, twin-, queen-, or king-sized shape.

In this chapter, you'll explore the use of dynamic blocks through a series of tutorials. Each tutorial will show you an example of how dynamic blocks can be used in different ways. This will help you become familiar with the methods involved in creating dynamic blocks. You'll start by looking at the Block Editor, which in itself makes editing blocks much easier. Then you'll be introduced to the tools used to create dynamic blocks.

- ◆ Exploring the Block Editor
- ◆ Creating a Dynamic Block
- ◆ Keeping an Object Centered
- ◆ Adding Scale and Stretch Actions to a Parameter
- ◆ Adding More Than One Parameter for Multiple Grip Functions
- ◆ Creating Multiple Shapes in One Block
- ◆ Rotating Objects in Unison
- ◆ Filling in a Space Automatically with Objects

Exploring the Block Editor

Before you start to add dynamic block features to blocks, you'll want to get familiar with the Block Editor. The Block Editor offers an easy way to make changes to existing blocks, and as you'll see a bit later, it is also the tool you'll use to give your blocks some additional capabilities.

As an introduction to the Block Editor, you'll be making changes to the now familiar unit plan from earlier tutorials. Start by editing the kitchen block in the unit.

1. Open the Unit.dwg file you've saved from earlier exercises. You can use the 17-unit.dwg file from the companion CD sample files.

2. Double-click the kitchenette in the plan to open the Edit Block Definition dialog box. Notice that all the blocks in the drawing are listed in the dialog box and that the kitchen block is highlighted. You also see a preview of the block in the preview panel.

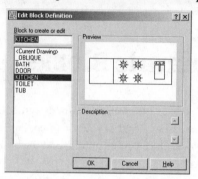

3. With the KITCHEN block name selected, click OK.

4. You'll see a message asking you if you want a demonstration of dynamic blocks in the New Features Workshop. Click No. You might also want to place a checkmark in the Do Not Display This Alert Again option. You can always get to the New Features Workshop through the Help menu bar option. Once you've clicked No, you'll see an enlarged view of the kitchenette in the drawing area with a yellow background (see Figure 17.1).

The yellow background tells you that you are in the Block Editor. You'll also see the Block Editor toolbar along the top of the drawing area, and the Block Authoring palettes, as shown in Figure 17.1.

FIGURE 17.1
The Block Editor and
its components

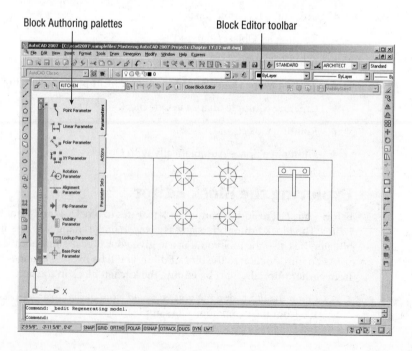

Take a moment to look over the Block Editor. The toolbar across the top offers several "house-keeping" tools that let you open, save, and exit the Block Editor. You can point to each tool to see a description of it. Figure 17.2 shows the toolbar and each tool's description.

FIGURE 17.2

The Block Editor toolbar

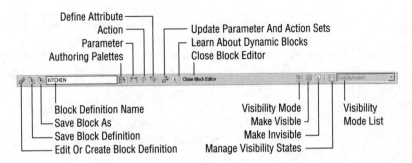

Both the toolbar and the Block Authoring palettes offer tools for adding dynamic block features that you will explore later in this chapter. For now, let's continue our look at the basic features of the Block Editor.

Editing a Block and Creating New Blocks

The Block Editor lets you edit a block using all the standard AutoCAD editing tools. In the following exercise, you'll modify the kitchen sink and save your changes to the drawing.

1. Delete the rectangle that represents the sink in the kitchen block.

2. Click the Close Block Editor button in the Block Editor toolbar.

3. A message appears asking if you want to save your changes to the kitchen block. Click Yes. Your view returns to the standard AutoCAD drawing area, and you can see the changes you made to the kitchen, as shown in Figure 17.3.

FIGURE 17.3

The unit plan with the edited kitchen block

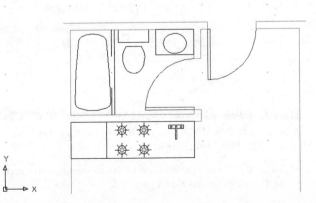

As you can see, editing blocks with the Block Editor is simple and straightforward. In this example, you deleted part of the block, but you can perform any type of drawing or editing to modify the block. The Block Editor also offers other block-saving options in its toolbar. You can save the block as you work by clicking the Save Block Definition tool. If you need to create a variation on the block you are currently editing, you can click the Save Block As button (see Figure 17.2 earlier in this chapter) to create a new block or overwrite an existing one with the drawing that is currently in the Block Editor.

If you want to edit a different block after editing the current one, you can click the Save Block Definition button to save your current block, and then click the Edit Or Create Block Definition tool.

This tool opens the Edit Block Definition dialog box that you saw earlier. You can then select another block to edit or create a new block by entering a name for your block in the Block To Create Or Edit input box.

Creating a Dynamic Block

Now that you've seen how the Block Editor works, you can begin to explore the creation of dynamic blocks. As an introduction, you'll create a simple rectangle that you will use to replace the sink in the kitchen. You'll add a dynamic block feature that will allow you to adjust the width of the sink using grips. In addition, you'll add a control that limits the size to 1-unit increments.

Start by creating a block from scratch using the Block Editor.

1. Click the Block Editor tool in the Standard toolbar.

2. In the Edit Block Definition dialog box, enter **Sink** in the Block To Create Or Edit input box, and then click OK. If you see the message asking if you want to see a demonstration, click No. The Block Editor opens with a blank screen.

3. Use the Rectangle tool in the Draw toolbar to draw a rectangle that is 12 units in the X axis and 15 units in the Y axis.

4. Zoom into the rectangle so your view looks similar to Figure 17.4.

FIGURE 17.4

The rectangle for the Sink block

You could just save this block now, and you'd have a simple, nondynamic block. Next, you'll add a couple of features called *parameters* and *actions*. As their names imply, parameters define the parameters or limits of what the dynamic block will do, and actions describe the particular action taken when the grips of the dynamic block are edited. For example, in the next section, you will add a Linear Parameter that tells AutoCAD that you want to restrain the grip editing to a linear direction. You will also add a Stretch Action that tells AutoCAD that you want the grip edit to behave like a Stretch command that pulls a set of vertices in one direction or another.

Adding a Parameter

The first parameter you will add establishes the base point for the block. This will let you determine the point used when inserting the block in your drawing.

1. In the Block Authoring palettes, select the Parameters tab.

2. Click the Base Point Parameter tool, Shift+right-click, select the Endpoint osnap, and then click the lower-left corner of the rectangle. This is how you determine the base point or insertion point of a block while using the Block Editor.

TIP You can also click the Parameter tool in the Block Editor toolbar and then enter **B** to insert a base point parameter.

Next, you'll add a parameter that will determine the type of editing you want to add to the block. In this case, you want to be able to grip edit the width of the block. For that you will use the Linear Parameter.

1. Click the Linear Parameter tool in the Parameters tab, or click the Parameter tool in the Block Editor toolbar and enter **L↵**.

2. At the prompt

```
Specify start point or [Name/Label/Chain/Description/Base/Palette/Value set]:
```

Shift+right-click and select the Midpoint osnap; then select the left side of the rectangle.

3. Shift+right-click again, select Midpoint from the Osnap menu, and select the right side of the rectangle.

4. At the `Specify label location:` prompt, you'll see the parameter name appear with the parameter label at the cursor. Click below the rectangle to place the label as shown in Figure 17.5.

NOTE If you use the Parameter tool, you will see an additional prompt asking if you want 0, 1, or 2 grips. Press ↵ to accept the default of 2.

The parameter you just added lets you modify the block in a linear fashion. In this particular case, it will allow you to change the width of the rectangle. As you will see, the location of the arrows of the parameter later become the grip locations for the dynamic block.

But just adding the parameter won't make the block dynamic. You need to include an Action before a parameter can be used. You may have noticed the warning symbol in the parameter you just added. It tells you that you need to take some further steps to make the parameter useful.

TIP When you see the warning symbol in a parameter, you can double-click the symbol to display a list of options.

Adding an Action

Next, add a Stretch Action that will enable you to use the Linear Parameter you just added. The Stretch Action will enable you to stretch the block horizontally using grips. As you add the Action, notice that it is similar to using the Stretch command. The only difference is that you don't actually stretch the object. You only specify the vertices to stretch and the object you want to stretch.

1. Click the Actions tab in the Block Authoring palettes and select Stretch Action.

2. At the `Select parameter:` prompt, click the left-pointing parameter arrow at the middle of the rectangle on the left side. You'll see a circle with an X through it showing the location of a parameter point.

FIGURE 17.5

Placing the Linear Parameter

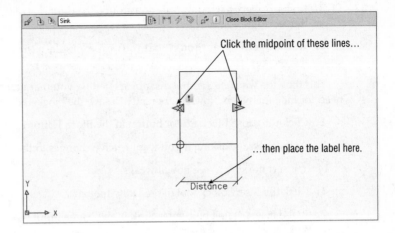

3. At the `Specify parameter point to associate with action or enter [sTart point/ Second point] <Second>:` prompt, point to the left-pointing arrow again.

4. Click the circle with the arrow.

5. At the `Specify first corner of stretch frame or [CPolygon]:` prompt, place a window selection around the entire left side of the rectangle. This selects the portion of the rectangle that is to be stretched when grip editing the block.

6. At the `Specify objects to stretch:` prompt, select the rectangle and the base point you added earlier; then press ⏎ to complete your selection.

7. At the `Specify action location [Multiplier/Offset]:` prompt, place the Action icon to the left of the rectangle.

You've just added an Action to the Linear Parameter that you added earlier. Notice that the warning symbol is still showing. You need to add another Action to the right side of the parameter, since the parameter expects that you will want to be able to grip edit both sides.

1. Repeat the previous set of steps, but instead of clicking the left arrow of the Linear Parameter in step 2, click the right arrow.

2. In steps 3 and 4, point to and click the right arrow of the Linear Parameter.

3. In step 5, place a window selection around the right side of the rectangle; then at step 6, select the rectangle again.

4. At the `Specify action location:` prompt, place the Action icon to the right of the rectangle.

This time the warning symbol disappears, telling you that you have completed the steps you need for the parameter. Now you're ready to save the block and try it out.

1. Click the Close Block Editor button in the Block Editor toolbar.

2. At the message asking if you want to save changes to the Sink block, click Yes.

Next, insert the sink to see how it works.

1. Click the Insert Block tool in the Draw toolbar.

2. In the Insert dialog box, enter **Sink** in the Name input box, and then click OK. You see the sink appear at the cursor.

3. Place the block at the location shown in Figure 17.6.

4. Make sure the Dynamic Input display is turned on by clicking the DYN button in the status bar; then click the newly inserted sink. You see two arrows at the vertical midpoints of the block.

5. Turn on the Ortho mode and click and drag the arrow on the right side of the block. The width of the block follows the arrow as you drag it. You also see the dimension of the sink as you drag the arrow.

6. Enter 3↵. The width of the block changes to 15 inches from the original 12.

While you entered a value in step 6 to change the width of the sink, you could have clicked the mouse to visually change the width of the sink. The rectangle is still a block. You didn't have to explode it to change its width. If you hover the cursor over the dynamic block grip, you see the width dimension of the block.

FIGURE 17.6
The Sink block in place

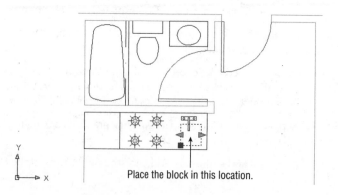

Place the block in this location.

Adding an Increment Value

You can grip edit your dynamic Sink block to modify its width, and as you've seen from the last exercise, you can enter a specific value for the width as well. But suppose you'd like to limit grip movement so that the sink only changes in 1-inch increments. Or you might have a dynamic block representing a bolt, and you want the bolt length to increment in $\frac{1}{16}$-inch steps.

Parameters can be set to have an increment value so that grip edits are limited to a specific distance. The following steps show how you can set up the Linear Parameter of the Sink block so that the sink width can be grip edited to 1-inch increments.

1. Double-click the Sink block; then in the Edit Block Definition dialog box, make sure Sink is selected and click OK.

2. Click the Distance label of the Linear Parameter, and then right-click and choose Properties.

3. In the Properties palette, scroll down to the Value Set group and click the Dist Type listing. The Dist Type option changes to a drop-down list.

4. Expand the list and then select Increment.

5. Click in the Dist Increment input box just below the Dist Type options and enter **1** for an increment distance of 1 inch.

6. Close the Properties palette, and then click Close Block Editor in the Block Editor toolbar.

7. Save the Sink block.

8. Click the Sink block to expose its grips.

9. Click and drag the right arrow grip to the left. As soon as you click the grip, you see a set of increment marks appear indicating the increment steps for the grip. As you move the grip, the sink width "jumps" to the increment marks, which are 1 inch apart as shown in Figure 17.7.

10. Set the width of the sink back to 12 inches.

TIP You can set the increment value of a Linear Parameter at the time you add it to your block. Click the parameter from the Parameters tab of the Block Authoring palettes; then before you click a location, enter **V**↵. You will see a prompt asking for a distance value. Type I ↵ to use the Increment option, then enter an increment value. Once you've done this, you will also be prompted for a minimum and maximum value.

Besides an increment distance, you can also set a range of movement for the Linear Parameter. You may have noticed the minimum and maximum input boxes in the Properties palette in steps 4 and 5. You can enter values for these settings that define the range of movement allowed for the grip edits.

TIP You can turn on the Cycling option in the Misc group of the Properties palette of any parameter grip. Cycling allows you to use the parameter grip as an insertion point. With this option turned on, you can press the Alt key to "cycle" between the standard insertion point and the cycle-enabled grip of a parameter while inserting the block.

The sink exercise is a simple demonstration of how you can create and use dynamic blocks. But as you can see from the Block Authoring palettes, you can add many other parameters and actions to a block.

Editing Parameters and Actions

In the previous exercises, you inserted parameters and actions using the default settings. These settings give you default names and labels for the parameters and actions, but you can always change these settings later. To change the label that appears for a parameter, double-click the label. The label will then appear within a rectangular box showing you that you can change its text. To edit an action's label, choose Modify ➤ Object ➤ Text ➤ Edit, and then select the action's label. The label will show a gray background, and you can then type changes.

If you want to include additional objects for an action, double-click the action. You'll see the prompt

```
Specify first corner of stretch frame or [Cpolygon]:
```

Press ↵ to skip this prompt. You then see the next prompt

```
Select object to add to action set or [Remove]:
```

You can then select additional objects or enter **R**↵ and select objects to remove from the selection set of the action.

FIGURE 17.7
Grip editing the Sink block with the Linear Parameter's increment value set to 1

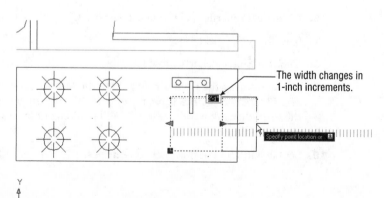

The width changes in 1-inch increments.

Keeping an Object Centered

Now suppose you want to add a drain to the sink, but to make things a little more complicated, you want to make sure the drain remains centered if the sink is widened or made narrower. You can add a Move action to the existing Linear Parameter and then use an option of the Move action to keep the drain centered. Here's how it works.

1. Double-click the Sink block to open the Edit Block Definition dialog box; make sure Sink is selected, and click OK.

2. Add a 3″ diameter circle in the center of the rectangle. This circle will represent the drain.

3. In the Actions tab of the Block Authoring palettes, click Move Action.

4. At the Select parameter: prompt, click the right Linear Parameter arrow shown in Figure 17.8.

FIGURE 17.8
Adding the Move Action to the sink drain

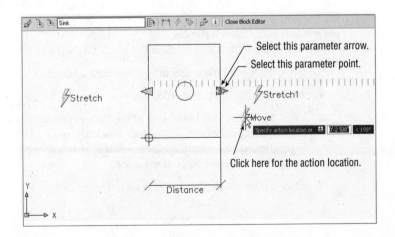

5. At the `Specify parameter point to associate with action or enter [sTart point/ Second point] <Second>:` prompt, click the parameter point on the right arrow as shown in Figure 17.8.

6. At the `Select objects:` prompt, select the circle and press ↵.

7. At the `Specify action location or [Multiplier/Offset]:` prompt, enter **M**↵ to use the Multiplier option.

8. At the `Enter distance multiplier <1.0000>:` prompt, enter **0.5**↵. This indicates that you want the move to occur at half the rate (0.5) of the Linear Parameter motion.

9. At the `Specify action location or [Multiplier/Offset]:` prompt, click the location shown in Figure 17.8.

10. Click the Close Block Editor button and save the sink block.

Now try grip editing the block to see how the Move Action affects the sink drain.

1. Click the sink to select it.

2. Click and drag the right arrow grip to the right. Notice how the drain stays centered in the sink.

You could have entered any value for the multiplier in step 7 of the previous exercise to alter the degree of motion that the sink drain would follow. For example, if you had entered 2, the drain would move twice the distance of the grip motion.

Adding Scale and Stretch Actions to a Parameter

In the sink example, you added two Stretch Actions to a Linear Parameter. This enabled the block to be stretched in both the left and right directions. But you aren't restricted to assigning one type of action to a parameter. In the next section, you'll turn a simple door block into a dynamic block. In the process, you will learn how to add two different actions to a single Linear Parameter.

At first, you might think that changing the scale of a door would be all you need for editing a door. But when you scale the door, all its features, including the door width, are scaled proportionally. You really only want to stretch the door width and scale the door swing, leaving the door thickness at the same dimension. This can be accomplished by adding a Linear Parameter with a scale action and a Stretch Action.

Start by opening the door block in the Block Editor and adding the Linear Parameter.

1. Click the Block Editor tool in the Standard toolbar.

2. In the Edit Block Definition dialog box, select DOOR, and then click OK.

3. Click the Linear Parameter tool in the Parameters tab of the Block Authoring palettes, and then click the endpoints of the door block as shown in Figure 17.9, starting with the hinge side. The order of selection is important as you'll see a bit later. Use the Endpoint osnaps to select the exact endpoints of the door.

4. Place the parameter label as shown in Figure 17.9.

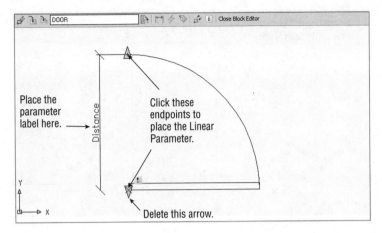

Figure 17.9 labels: Place the parameter label here. / Distance / Click these endpoints to place the Linear Parameter. / Delete this arrow.

Most likely, you will only need to scale the door based on the door opening, which is represented by the location and orientation of the Linear Parameter you just added. In addition, you will probably only be stretching the door from the end of the door swing arc, so you can remove the parameter arrow from the hinge side of the door.

1. Click the blue arrow on the hinge side of the door, as shown in Figure 17.9.

2. Press the Delete key to delete the arrow. You now have only one end of the parameter that needs an action. Earlier when you placed the Linear Parameter, you selected the hinge side first. This allows you to delete a single arrow. If you attempt to delete the arrow on the opening side of the door, both arrows are deleted.

Just as with the sink, you have a Linear Parameter for the door that describes the direction of the grip edit. Now you need to add the actions associated with the parameter. You'll add the Stretch Action first. You used the Stretch Action before for the sink, but this time, you'll need to modify the way the Stretch Action works. First, add the action, and then you'll make a change to the action to better suit the Door block.

1. Click the Actions tab in the Block Authoring palettes, and then select Stretch Action.

2. At the `Select parameter:` prompt, click the blue parameter arrow at the end of the arc.

3. At the `Specify parameter point to associate with action or enter [sTart point/ Second point] <Second>:` prompt, click the red marker on the same arrow.

4. At the `Specify first corner of stretch frame or [CPolygon]:` prompt, place a window selection around the right end of the door as shown in Figure 17.10.

5. At the `Specify objects to stretch:` prompt, select the lines that represent the length of the door and the door edge as shown in Figure 17.11. These are the parts of the door that you want to stretch.

6. At the `Specify action location or [Multiplier/Offset]:` prompt, type **O.⌐**. This lets you specify an angle for the Stretch Action.

FIGURE 17.10
Selecting the param-
eter and the stretch
frame

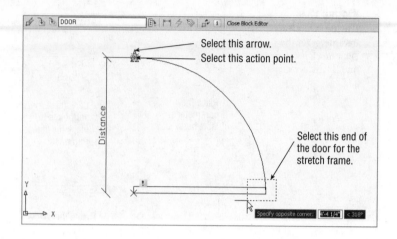

FIGURE 17.11
Selecting the lines of
the door

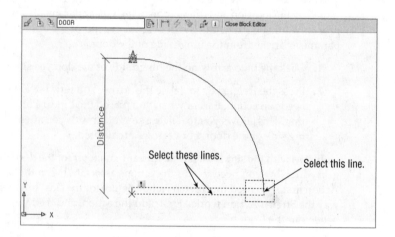

7. At the `Enter angle offset <0>:` prompt, enter –90↵.

8. Finally, at the `Specify action location or [Multiplier/Offset]:` prompt, click a location near the parameter arrow to place the action icon.

Normally, you would want the Stretch Action to move in the same direction as the arrow in the
Linear Parameter. But in this case, you want the door to stretch in a direction that is –90° from Linear
Parameter. Figure 17.12 shows how the Stretch Action needs to work. The Offset option you used in
steps 6 and 7 allows you to do just that. By using the Offset option, you were able to tell AutoCAD that
the Stretch Action is to work in a direction that is –90° from the direction of the grip edit motion. This
will become more clear once you've actually used the door blocks grip to change its size.

Besides stretching the door, you will want to scale the door arc in size as the door width is grip
edited. For this, you need to add a Scale Action.

1. Click Scale Action in the Actions tab of the Block Authoring palettes.

2. At the `Select parameter:` prompt, click the blue arrow of the Linear Parameter, the same
arrow you selected for the scale parameter earlier.

FIGURE 17.12

The Stretch Action works in a negative 90° direction to the grip movement direction.

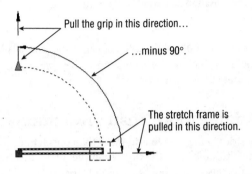

Pull the grip in this direction…

…minus 90°.

The stretch frame is pulled in this direction.

3. At the

```
Specify selection set for action
Select objects:
```

prompt, select the arc and press ↵ to finish your selection.

1. At the Specify action location or [Base type]: prompt, click a location near the midpoint of the arc to place the action icon.

2. Click the Close Block Editor tool in the Block Editor toolbar and save the door block.

Now you're ready to try the new Door block.

1. Pan your view so that you can see the entry door clearly, as shown in Figure 17.13.

2. Click the door to select it. You see the added Linear Parameter arrow appear as a grip on the right end of the Door block.

FIGURE 17.13

The Door block with its grips exposed

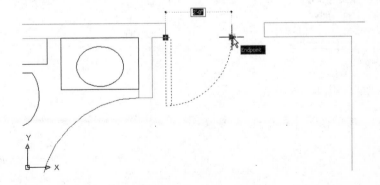

3. Click the arrow grip. The length dimension becomes available for your input, and as you move the mouse, the door changes in size. Note that the thickness of the door does not change as you alter its width.

4. Enter 24⏎ to change the door width to 24″.

Notice that besides being able to enter a door dimension directly to the block, you do not change the door thickness when the door size changes. Only the door swing and width change to accommodate the new door size.

Adding More Than One Parameter for Multiple Grip Functions

Besides being able to add more than one action to a parameter, you can also add multiple parameters to a block. In the door example, you added only the single Linear Parameter. Suppose you would also like a quick way to mirror, or "flip," the door so it changes from a left-hand door to a right-hand door and vice versa.

Including a Mirror Capability

In the next exercise, you'll add the flip parameter to the door, which does exactly that: it enables you to mirror the door at the click of a mouse.

1. Click the Block Editor tool in the Standard toolbar.

2. In the Edit Block Definition dialog box, select DOOR, and then click OK.

3. In the Block Authoring palettes, select the Parameters tab and then select Flip Parameter.

4. At the `Specify base point of reflection line or [Name/Label/Description/ Palette]:` prompt, use the Midpoint osnap and select the midpoint of the door, as shown in Figure 17.14.

5. At the `Specify endpoint of reflection line:` prompt, use the Endpoint osnap and select the lower-right corner of the door, as shown in Figure 17.14.

6. At the `Specify label location:` prompt, place the label as shown in Figure 17.14.

FIGURE 17.14
Adding a flip parameter

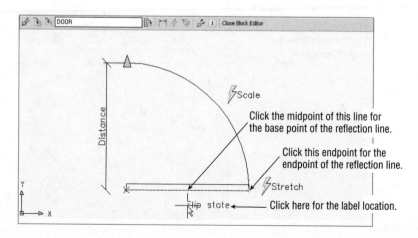

As you did with the Linear Parameter, you need to assign an action to the newly placed parameter. In this case, you will add the Flip Action.

1. In the Block Authoring palettes, select the Actions tab and select Flip Action.

2. At the `Select parameter:` prompt, click the blue arrow of the Flip parameter, as shown in Figure 17.15.

3. At the `Select objects:` prompt, select the entire block, including all the parameters and actions. Press ↵ when you've selected everything.

4. At the `Specify action location:` prompt, place the action icon as shown in Figure 17.15.

The Flip parameter and action are complete. Now you can try to use them.

1. Click the Save Block Definition tool in the Block Editor. A warning message appears telling you that changes to blocks containing parameters may not be obvious. Click Yes and then click the Close Block Editor tool.

2. Click the entry door.

3. Click the arrow pointing to the door, as shown in Figure 17.16. The door mirrors to point toward the bathroom.

4. Click the arrow again to return the door to its original position

Adding a Selectable List

Earlier you saw how you can add an increment value set to make a dynamic block stay within a set range of sizes. You can also set up a dynamic block to offer a range of sizes in a pop-up list. To do this, you need to employ two parameters: the Visibility parameter and the List parameter.

In the following exercise, you'll add these parameters to the Door block to allow the door size to be selected from a list. Start by adding the List parameter, which offers a way to define and name a set of parameter criteria.

1. Double-click the door to open the Edit Block Definition dialog box, select DOOR, and then click OK.

FIGURE 17.15
Adding the Flip action

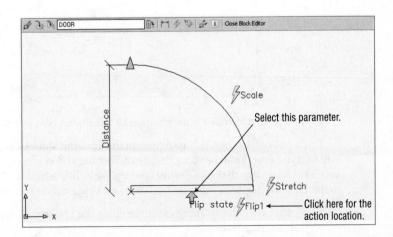

FIGURE 17.16
Click the arrow grip to
flip the door.

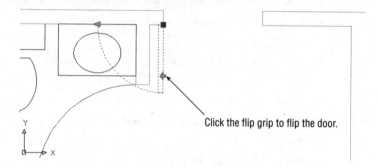

Click the flip grip to flip the door.

2. In the Block Authoring palettes, select Lookup Parameter from the Parameters tab.

3. Place the Lookup parameter in the location shown in Figure 17.17.

4. In the Actions tab, select Lookup Action.

5. At the `Select parameter` prompt, select the Lookup Parameter arrow that you just added in step 3.

6. At the `Specify location` prompt, place the Lookup Action in the location shown in Figure 17.17. The Property Lookup Table dialog box opens.

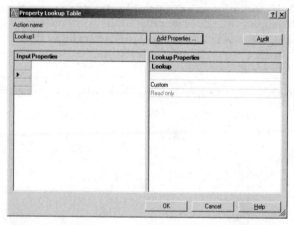

7. You'll need to make some changes to this dialog box, but for now, click OK to close it.

You'll notice that the Lookup Action in the drawing shows the exclamation point icon telling you that you need to make some changes before the action is complete. If you hover over the icon, you'll see a message that says Empty Lookup Table. In the next set of steps, you'll start to add items to the Property Lookup Table dialog box to make the action functional.

1. Double-click the warning exclamation on the Lookup Action to open the Property Lookup Table dialog box.

FIGURE 17.17
Adding the Lookup
parameter and action

FIGURE 17.17
Adding the Lookup
parameter and action

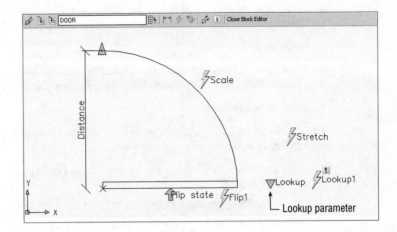

2. Click the Add Properties button at the top of the dialog box to open the Add Parameter Properties dialog box.

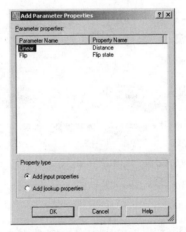

3. Select Linear, and then click OK. You'll see the Distance column appear.

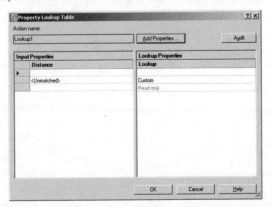

4. In the first input box just below the Distance column heading, enter **24**, and then press the Tab key. The cursor advances to the next input box under the Distance column.

5. Enter **36**.

6. Click the input box just under the Lookup column, and then enter **24″ wide door**↵. Once you press ↵, the cursor advances to the next input box just below the one you just edited.

7. Enter **36″ wide door**↵.

You've added the Linear Parameter to the Property Lookup Table. You need to make one last setting change to make the whole thing work.

1. Click the Read Only item at the bottom of the Lookup column, and then select Allow Reverse Lookup.

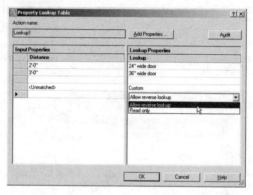

2. Click OK. Notice that the warning splat is gone, telling you that you've completed the Lookup action.

3. Click the Close Block Editor button in the Block Editor toolbar and save the Door block.

Now you can select from two door sizes in a pop-up list.

1. Click the door to select it.

2. Click the downward-pointing grip closest to the door, as shown in the left side of Figure 17.18.

3. Select 36″ door from the list that appears. The door changes to a 36″-wide door. (See the view to the far right in Figure 17.18.)

FIGURE 17.18
Selecting a door size from a list

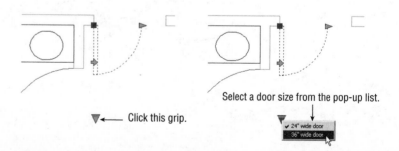

Click this grip.

Select a door size from the pop-up list.

Including Block Information with Attribute Extraction

In Chapter 13, you learned how you can attach data to blocks through attributes and then extract that data to spreadsheets or AutoCAD tables. You can also include dynamic block information that has been included in a property lookup table. This can be extremely useful for generating bill of material data or in other situations if you need to track the numbers and types of items in your drawing.

To see how this works, you'll continue to edit the Door block to include the flip state of the door. You can then use the flip state to determine if the door is a left- or right-hand door. You can extract this information as part of the attribute extraction process.

First, add the flip state to the property lookup table. By adding the flip state, you can track whether doors are left- or right-handed.

1. Double-click the door to open the Edit Block Definition dialog box, select DOOR, and then click OK.

2. In the Block Editor, double-click the Lookup action to open the Property Lookup Table dialog box.

3. Click the Add Properties button to open the Add Parameter Properties dialog box.

4. Select Flip and click OK.

5. Back in the Property Lookup Table dialog box, you see the Flip State column added in the Input Properties list. Double-click the top input box just below the Flip State column, and select Not Flipped from the drop-down list. Not Flipped is now a property that is included for a 24″-wide door.

6. In the top input box of the Lookup column, add the text RH (for right-hand) so that it reads 24″ wide door RH (see Figure 17.19).

7. Repeat steps 5 and 6 for the 36″ door input box, but change the lookup text to read 36″ wide door RH (see Figure 17.19).

8. Add two more rows as shown in Figure 17.19 to include the flipped condition for each door size. Note that the Lookup column includes the text LH for left-hand for the flipped state.

FIGURE 17.19
Adding additional items to the Property Lookup Table dialog box

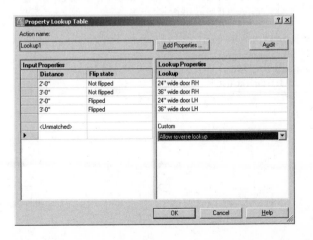

9. At the bottom of the Lookup column, make sure that Allow Reverse Lookup is selected, and then click OK.

10. Click Close Block Editor in the Block Editor toolbar, and save the door block.

You've added a property to the Properties Lookup Table dialog box. Now let's see how this has affected the block.

1. Copy the entry door upward so that it appears above the existing door. You may need to pan your view to make room for the copy. This will give you an additional door to experiment with.

2. Click the copy of the door to select it.

3. Click the downward-pointing grip closest to the door, as shown in Figure 17.20.

4. Select 24″ wide LH from the list that appears. The door changes to a 24″-wide door that is flipped.

Now use the Attribute Extraction command to see how the data you added will appear as an exported table or a spreadsheet.

1. Choose Tools ➢ Attribute Extraction to start the Attribute Extraction Wizard.

2. At the Begin screen, click Next.

3. At the Select Drawing screen, click Next again.

4. At the Select Attributes screen, remove the checkmark from all but DOOR in the left column.

5. Remove the checkmark from all but the Distance and Lookup options in the right column (see Figure 17.21).

6. Click Next. You now see the data that will be exported to a spreadsheet file or table (see Figure 17.22).

7. You don't really want to extract this data, so once you've gotten a good look at this screen, click Cancel. This is the end of the door example so you can exit this file. Save it for future reference if you like.

FIGURE 17.20
Click the lookup grip and select 24″ wide door LH from the list.

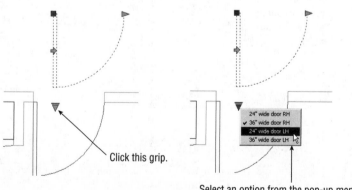

Click this grip.

| 24″ wide door RH |
| ✓ 36″ wide door RH |
| 24″ wide door LH |
| 36″ wide door LH |

Select an option from the pop-up menu.

FIGURE 17.21
Set up the Select
Attributes screen to
look like this.

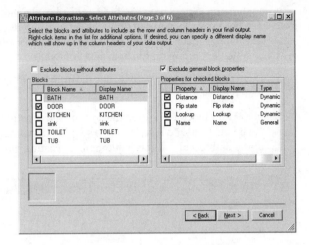

FIGURE 17.22
The resulting table to
be extracted as shown
in the Finalize Output
screen of the Attribute
Extraction Wizard

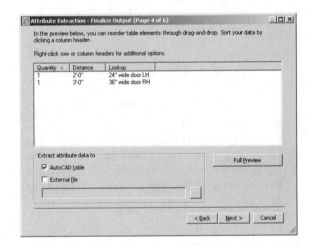

Notice that Figure 17.22 shows the three doors: one 24″ wide LH and two 36″ wide RH. If you had more doors, they would also show up in this screen. You can edit the bathroom block to gain access to its door, and it will also show the lookup data.

WARNING If you use the Mirror command to mirror a block that contains a flip action in a property lookup table, the Attribute Extraction command will still report the nonmirrored flip state of the door. Therefore, be sure that if you set up a block with parameters and actions, you use those actions to edit the door, and don't rely on standard editing tools. That way you will ensure the accuracy of your extracted data.

Creating Multiple Shapes in One Block

Depending on circumstances, you may need a block to display a completely different form. For example, you might want a single generic bath that can "morph" into a standard bath, a corner bath, or a large spa-style bath with jets.

Using dynamic blocks, you can hide or display elements of a block by selecting a *visibility state* from a list. For example, you can draw the three different bath sizes and then set up three visibility states for each size. Each visibility state displays only one bath size at a time. You can then select a visibility state depending on the bath size you want.

1. Open the `visibilitysample.dwg` file from the companion CD, and then click the Block Editor tool in the Standard toolbar.

2. In the Edit Block Definition dialog box, select bathtub from the list and then click OK. Click No if you are asked if you want to see how dynamic blocks are made. You'll see the contents of the Bathtub block. It is just the three existing blocks—Standard, Jetted, and Corner—inserted at the same origin.

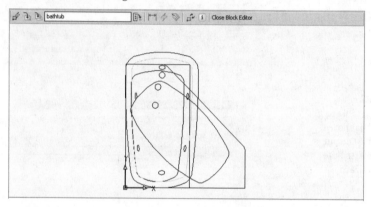

If you were to insert this block in a drawing, it would appear just as you currently see it with each bathtub type overlayed on another. Next you'll see how you can add control over the visibility of each bathtub type so that only one is displayed at a time.

The first thing you need to do is add a Visibility parameter.

1. In the Parameters tab of the Block Authoring palettes, click Visibility Parameter.

2. Click below the blocks to place the Visibility parameter as shown in Figure 17.23.

FIGURE 17.23
Adding the Visibility parameter

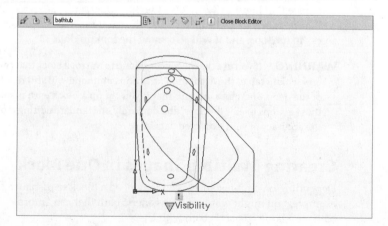

3. Double-click the Visibility parameter you just added to open the Visibility States dialog box. One visibility state, VisibilityState0, is already provided.

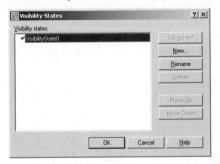

You'll need three visibility states: one for each type of bathtub whose visibility you want to control. You've already got one, but you want a name that is more appropriate to the application.

1. Click the Rename button. The existing visibility state in the list to the left becomes editable.

2. Enter **Standard.**↵. This will be the visibility state for your standard bathtub.

3. Click the New button to open the New Visibility State dialog box.

4. Enter **Jetted** in the Visibility State Name input box.

5. Make sure the Leave Visibility Of Existing Objects Unchanged In New State radio button is selected, and then click OK.

6. Click the New button again.

7. In the New Visibility State dialog box, enter **Corner** in the Visibility State Name input box.

8. Make sure Leave Visibility Of Existing Objects Unchanged In New State radio button is selected, and then click OK.

9. You've just created all the visibility states you need. Now select Standard from the list, and then click the Set Current button. You can also just double-click the Standard listing. A checkmark appears to the left of Standard showing you that it is now the current state.

10. Click OK to exit the Visibility States dialog box.

You've got the visibility states you need, and you have the objects whose visibility you want to control. Now you just need to determine which block is visible for each state.

Remember that in step 9 of the last set of steps, you made Standard the current visibility state. You'll want only the standard Bathtub block visible for this state. Do the following to "turn off" the other two Bathtub blocks for the current state.

1. Select the Jetted and Corner blocks (see Figure 17.24).

FIGURE 17.24
Locating the blocks

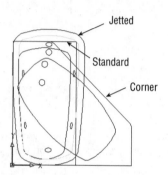

Jetted

Standard

Corner

2. Right-click and choose Object Visibility ➢ Hide For Current State. You can also click the Make Invisible tool on the right side of the Block Editor toolbar.

The selected blocks disappear. They didn't really go anywhere. Instead, they were just made invisible.

3. Click in the drop-down list in the far right of the Block Editor toolbar and select Jetted. The hidden blocks appear.

4. The current visibility state is now Jetted, so you want only the Jetted block to be visible. Select the Standard and Corner blocks, and then click the Make Invisible tool. You can also right-click and then choose Object Visibility ➢ Hide For Current State. Now only the Jetted block is visible.

5. In the Block Editor toolbar, click the drop-down list again and select Corner. All the blocks appear again.

6. Select the Standard and Jetted blocks, and then click the Make Invisible tool again. Now only the Corner block is visible.

You've created visibility states and set up the blocks so that they appear only when the appropriate visibility state is current. Now you can test the block.

1. Click Close Block Editor and save the changes you've made.

2. Click the Insert Block tool in the Draw toolbar, and in the Insert dialog box, select bathub from the Name drop-down list.

3. In the Insertion Point group, make sure Specify On Screen is checked, click OK, and then place the block to the right of the other three blocks.

4. Click the Bathtub block that you just inserted, and then click the Visibility grip (see Figure 17.25).

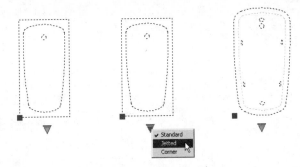

FIGURE 17.25

Using the Visibility grip to change the bathtub

5. Select Jetted from the list. The Jetted bathtub appears.

6. Click the Bathtub block again, and then click the Visibility grip and select Corner. Now the Corner tub appears.

TIP You can set up AutoCAD to display objects whose visibility has been turned off while editing them in the Block Editor. If you set the bvmode system variable to 1, objects will appear gray when their visibility has been turned off.

In this example, you used a set of bathtubs, but you can use the Visibility parameter for anything that requires a different appearance. AutoCAD comes with an example of a weldment symbol that can be changed using visibility states. As mentioned at the beginning of this chapter, another use might be a block of a bed that contains a double-, queen-, and king-sized bed.

You can also combine the Visibility parameter with the Lookup Property Table to produce preset variations of each type of bathtub. The possibilities are limited only by your imagination.

Rotating Objects in Unison

You've seen how actions and parameters can control the behavior of a single object in a block. You can also apply actions to multiple objects so that they move or change in unison. The following example shows how you can apply more than one Rotate Action to a single Rotation Parameter to control two objects.

1. Open the `gatesample.dwg` file from the companion CD.

2. Double-click the object in the drawing to open the Edit Block Definition dialog box, and then click OK. This opens the Gate block for editing.

3. In the Block Authoring palettes, select Rotation Parameter from the Parameters tab.

4. At the `Specify base point or [Name/Label/Chain/Description/Palette/Value set]:` prompt, use the Center osnap and select the center of the arc, as shown in Figure 17.26.

5. At the `Specify radius of parameter:` prompt, click a point to the right of the center as shown in Figure 17.26. You don't have to be to exact about the radius dimension as long as it is directly to the right of the center.

6. At the `Specify default rotation angle or [Base angle] <0>:` prompt, press ↵ to accept the default of 0° for the rotation angle.

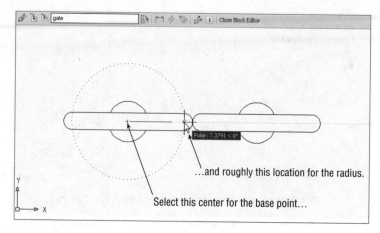

You have the Rotation parameter. Now you need to add an action. You'll add an action for each of the two gate objects in the drawing.

1. From the Action tab of the Block Authoring palettes, click Rotate Action.

2. At the `Select parameter:` prompt, click the blue dot of the Rotate Parameter, as shown in Figure 17.27.

3. At the `Select objects:` prompt, select the gate on the left as shown in Figure 17.27, and then press ↵.

4. At the `Specify action location or [Base type]:` prompt, click below the block you selected in step 3.

You've got enough now to rotate the block to the left with a rotation grip. Add another Rotate action to rotate the block to the right in unison with the one on the left.

1. From the Actions tab of the Block Authoring palettes, click Rotate Action.

2. At the `Select parameter:` prompt, click the same blue dot of the Rotate Parameter that you selected for the first Rotate action (see Figure 17.28).

FIGURE 17.27
Setting up the Rotate action

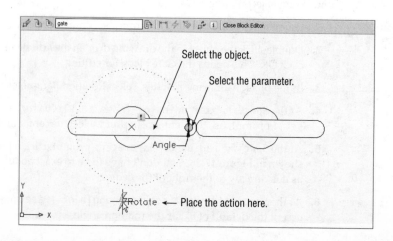

FIGURE 17.28
Adding the second
Rotate action

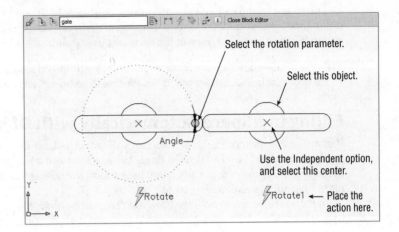

3. At the Select objects: prompt, select the gate on the right.

4. At the Specify action location or [Base type]: prompt, type **B**↵ for the Base type option.

5. At the Enter base point type [Dependent/Independent] <Dependent>: prompt, enter **I**↵ for the Independent option.

6. At the Specify base point location <xx.xxxx,yy.yyyy>: prompt, click the center of the block to the right as shown in Figure 17.28.

7. At the Specify action location or [Base type]: prompt, click below the block to the right to place the action icon.

Now you're ready to save the block and try it out.

1. Click the Close Block Editor button in the Block Editor toolbar and save the block.

2. Click the block to expose its grips.

3. Click and drag the blue dot grip downward. Both sides of the block rotate about their own centers (see Figure 17.29).

FIGURE 17.29
The two parts rotate
independently be-
cause the action for the
right side uses the In-
dependent base type.

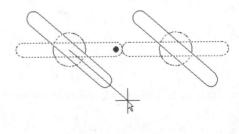

This example shows that you can specify a different base point for an action. You saw that you can use the same parameter for two different actions; one action uses the base point of the original parameter, and the other uses an independent base point.

TIP   You can set up a dynamic block to rotate in opposite directions using a lookup action similar to the door example earlier. See the "If You Want to Experiment" section at the end of this chapter.

Filling in a Space Automatically with Objects

Perhaps one of the more tedious tasks you will face is to draw the vertical bars of a hand railing for an elevation view. You can draw a single bar and then use the Array command to repeat the bars as many times as needed, but when you have to edit the railing, you may find that you are spending more time adding and erasing bars.

In the next example, you'll see how you can create a block that will automatically fill in vertical bars as the width of the railing changes. You'll start with an existing drawing of a single vertical bar and an outline of the railing opening around the bar.

1. Open the `railsample.dwg` file from the companion CD.

2. Double-click the object in the drawing to open the Edit Block Definition dialog box, and then click OK. This opens the Railvertical block for editing. When the Block Editor opens, you'll notice that the block already has a Linear Parameter and Stretch Action added. You'll recall from the sink example in the beginning of this chapter that the Linear Parameter and Stretch Action let you vary the width of an object. In this case, the outermost rectangle is being stretched.

3. In the Actions tab of the Block Authoring palettes, click Array Action.

4. At the `Select parameter:` prompt, click the blue arrow for the Linear Parameter, as shown in Figure 17.30.

5. At the `Select objects:` prompt, select the dark vertical rectangle representing the vertical bar of the railing, as shown in Figure 17.30, and then press ↵.

6. At the `Enter the distance between columns (|||):` prompt, enter 4↵.

FIGURE 17.30

Adding the Array action to the Railvertical block

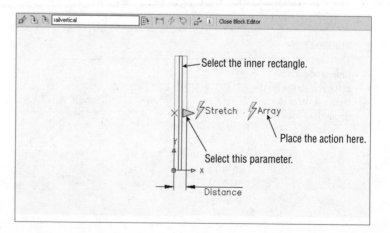

7. At the `Specify action location:` prompt, make sure the Ortho mode is turned off and place the action next to the arrow, as shown in Figure 17.30.

8. Click the Close Block Editor button in the Block Editor toolbar and save the block.

9. Click the block to expose its grips.

10. Click and drag the blue arrow grip to the right. As the rail expands, additional vertical bars are added at 4″ intervals (see Figure 17.31).

FIGURE 17.31
The Railvertical block adds vertical bars as its width expands.

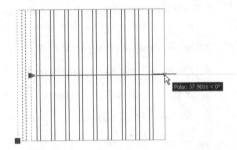

You can now use this block wherever you need to draw a simple railing with vertical bars. Another example of how the Array action might be used is in a side view of a bolt. You can show the threads of the bolt and use the array action to increase the number of threads as the bolt is lengthened (see Figure 17.31).

USING PARAMETER SETS

You probably noticed the Parameter Sets tab in the Block Authoring palettes. The options in this tab are pre-defined combinations of parameters and actions that are commonly used together. For example, the Polar Array set inserts a Polar parameter with an Array action. You only need to supply the object. The Polar Array set causes the associated object to rotate about a center point with a grip. You can also array the object by stretching the grip away from the rotation center.

To associate an object with a parameter set, double-click the action included in the set, and then select an object. If a stretch is employed, select the parameter point, and then select a stretch frame and an object to stretch.

If You Want to Experiment

By now you've tried using most of the parameters and actions available in the Block Editor. The dynamic block features have been presented in a simplified way so you can see clearly how each feature works, but as you become more expert at using dynamic blocks, you'll be able to combine the parameters and actions to create some more elaborate blocks. I encourage you to experiment with dynamic blocks and see how they might apply to your particular trade or profession. You might also want to examine how the sample dynamic blocks work that are provided in the tool palettes.

Earlier you saw how you can use the Independent Base Point option of the Rotate action to rotate an object in unison with another object. In that example, both objects rotate in the same direction. You can set up a block so that objects rotate in opposite directions using the lookup parameter. Try the following exercise to see how this works.

1. Open the `experiment17.dwg` file from the companion CD. This file uses the same objects as the objects for the rotation example earlier in this chapter.

2. Double-click the object in the drawing to open the Edit Block Definition dialog box, and then click OK. This opens the Gate block for editing. When the Block Editor opens, you'll notice that the block already has two Rotate parameters, one for each of the "dials" of the gate. It also has two Rotate actions labeled Left Rotate and Right Rotate.

3. In the Parameters tab of the Block Authoring palettes, click Lookup Parameter.

4. Place the Lookup Parameter in the location shown in Figure 17.32.

5. In the Actions tab of the Block Authoring palettes, click Lookup Action.

6. At the `Select parameter:` prompt, select the blue arrow of the Lookup parameter you just added.

7. Place the Lookup Action in the location shown in Figure 17.32. The Property Lookup Table dialog box opens.

8. Click the Add Properties button to open the Add Parameter Properties dialog box, select both parameter properties in the list box, and click OK. You can use the Shift or Ctrl keys to select multiple items in the list.

9. Back in the Property Lookup Table dialog box, fill in the columns and rows as shown in Figure 17.33:

10. Click the item at the bottom of the Lookup column labeled Read Only. It changes to a drop-down list.

11. Select Allow Reverse Lookup from the list, and then click OK.

Now try the added lookup parameter.

1. Click the Close Block Editor button in the Block Editor toolbar and save the block.

2. Click the block to expose its grips.

3. Click the blue lookup grip to the right of the block, and then select 30 Degrees. The two dials turn 30° in opposite directions.

4. Click the grip again and try another setting.

You've gotten a chance to try many of the parameters and actions that are available. You can also open the tool palettes window and experiment with the sample dynamic blocks that are available there in the architectural, mechanical, and electrical palettes. Open some of the sample blocks with the Block Editor to see how they work. You might get ideas for your particular applications by experimenting with these blocks.

FIGURE 17.32
Placing the Lookup
parameter and action

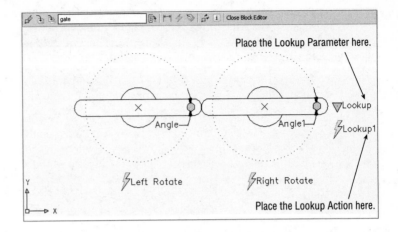

FIGURE 17.33
Fill in the Property
Lookup Table dialog
box as shown here.

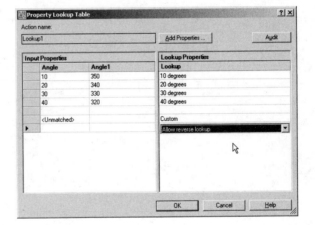

FIGURE 17.34
The Gate block with
different settings

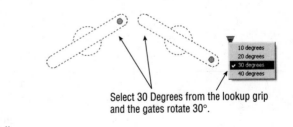

Chapter 18

Drawing Curves and Solid Fills

So far in this book, you've been using basic lines, arcs, and circles to create your drawings. Now it's time to add polylines and spline curves to your repertoire. Polylines offer many options for creating forms, including solid fills and free-form curved lines. Spline curves are perfect for drawing accurate, smooth, nonlinear objects.

Topics in this chapter include the following:

◆ Introducing Polylines

◆ Editing Polylines

◆ Creating a Polyline Spline Curve

◆ Using True Spline Curves

◆ Marking Divisions on Curves

◆ Sketching with AutoCAD

◆ Filling In Solid Areas

Introducing Polylines

Polylines are like composite line segments and arcs. A polyline might look like a series of line segments, but it acts like a single object. This characteristic makes polylines useful for a variety of applications, as you'll see in the upcoming exercises.

Drawing a Polyline

First, to introduce you to the polyline, you will begin a drawing of the top view of the joint in Figure 18.1.

FIGURE 18.1
A sketch of a metal joint

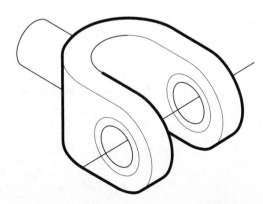

Follow these steps to draw the joint:

1. Open a new file and save it as Joint2d. Don't bother to make special setting changes, because you will create this drawing with the default settings.

2. Set the limits to 0,0 for the lower-left corner and 12,9 for the upper-right corner, and then choose View ≻ Zoom ≻ All or type **Z↵ A↵** .

3. Click the Polyline tool on the Draw toolbar or type **Pl↵** .

4. At the Specify start point: prompt, enter a point at coordinate 3,3 to start your polyline.

5. At the Specify next point or [Arc/Halfwidth/Length/Undo/Width]: prompt, enter @3<0↵ to draw a horizontal line of the joint.

TIP You can draw polylines just as you do with the Line command. Or you can use the other Pline options to enter a polyline arc, specify the polyline thickness, or add a polyline segment in the same direction as the previously drawn line.

6. At the Specify next point or [Arc/Close/Halfwidth/Length/Undo/Width]: prompt, enter **A↵** to continue your polyline with an arc.

TIP The Arc option enables you to draw an arc that starts from the last point you selected and then select additional options. Select the Arc option, then as you move your cursor, an arc follows it in a tangential direction from the first line segment you drew. You can return to drawing line segments by entering **L↵**.

7. At the prompt

```
Specify endpoint of arc or
[Angle/CEnter/CLose/Direction/Halfwidth/Line/Radius/Second pt/Undo/Width]:
```

enter @4<90↵ to draw a 180° arc from the last point you entered. Your drawing should now look similar to Figure 18.2.

FIGURE 18.2
A polyline line and arc

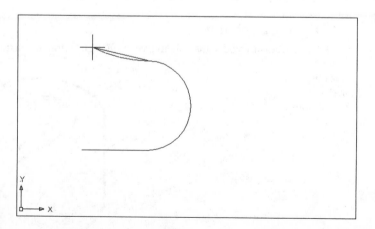

8. To continue the polyline with another line segment, enter **L**↵.

9. At the Specify next point or [Arc/Close/Halfwidth/Length/Undo/Width]: prompt, enter **@3<180**↵. Another line segment continues from the end of the arc.

10. Press ↵ to exit Pline.

You now have a sideways, U-shaped polyline that you will use in the next exercise to complete the top view of your joint.

Setting Polyline Options

Let's take a break from the tutorial to look at some of the Polyline options in the Polyline prompt that you didn't use:

Close   Draws a line segment from the last endpoint of a sequence of lines to the first point picked in that sequence. This works exactly like the Close option for the Line command.

Length   Enables you to specify the length of a line that will be drawn at the same angle as the last line entered.

Halfwidth   Creates a tapered line segment or an arc by specifying half its beginning and ending widths (see Figure 18.3).

Width   Creates a tapered line segment or an arc by specifying the full width of the segment's beginning and ending points.

Undo   Deletes the last line segment drawn.

If you want to break a polyline into simple lines and arcs, you can use the Explode option on the Modify toolbar, just as you would with blocks. After a polyline is exploded, it becomes a set of individual line segments or arcs.

FIGURE 18.3

A tapered line segment and an arc created with Halfwidth

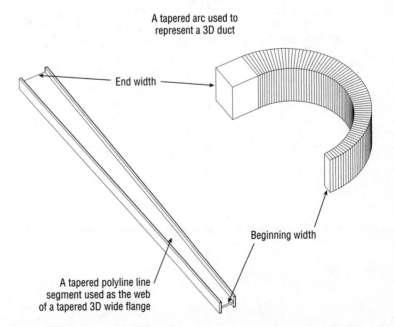

A tapered arc used to represent a 3D duct

End width

Beginning width

A tapered polyline line segment used as the web of a tapered 3D wide flange

To turn off the filling of solid polylines, open the Options dialog box and click the Display tab. Clear the Apply Solid Fill check box in the Display Performance group. (The options in the Display Performance group are explained in detail later in this chapter in the section on solid fills.)

TIP You can use the Fillet tool on the Modify toolbar to fillet all the vertices of a polyline composed of straight-line segments. Click Fillet, set your fillet radius, type **P.┘** to select the Polyline option, and then pick the polyline you want to fillet.

Editing Polylines

You can edit polylines with many of the standard editing commands. To change the properties of a polyline, double-click the polyline to open the Properties palette. You can use the Stretch command on the Modify toolbar to move vertices of a polyline, and the Trim, Extend, and Break commands on the Modify toolbar also work with polylines.

In addition, many editing capabilities are offered only for polylines. For instance, later in this section you will see how to smooth out a polyline by using the Fit option in the Pedit command.

 In this exercise, you'll use the Offset command on the Modify toolbar to add the inside portion of the joint:

1. Click the Offset tool in the Modify toolbar or type **O.┘**.

2. At the Specify offset distance or [Through/Erase/Layer] <THROUGH>: prompt, enter **1**.

3. At the Select object to offset or [Exit/Undo]<exit>: prompt, pick the U-shaped polyline you just drew.

4. At the Specify point on side to offset or [Exit/Multiple/Undo] <Exit>: prompt, pick a point toward the inside of the U. A concentric copy of the polyline appears (see Figure 18.4).

5. Press ┘ to exit the Offset command.

The concentric copy of a polyline made by choosing Modify ➤ Offset can be useful when you need to draw complex parallel curves like the ones in Figure 18.5.

FIGURE 18.4
The offset polyline

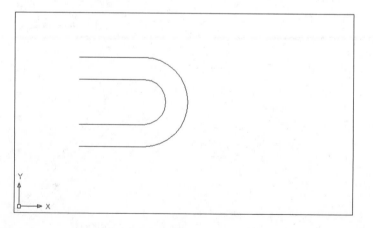

FIGURE 18.5

Sample complex
curves drawn by using
offset polylines

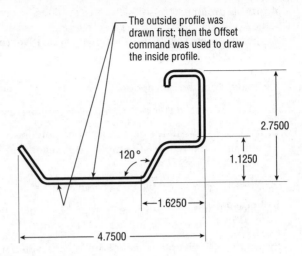

The outside profile was
drawn first; then the Offset
command was used to draw
the inside profile.

120°

2.7500

1.1250

1.6250

4.7500

Next, complete the top view of the joint:

1. Connect the ends of the polylines with two short line segments (see Figure 18.6).

WARNING If the objects to be joined don't touch, you can use the "fuzzy" join feature. Type **Pe⏎**
M⏎ to start the Pedit command with the Multiple option; then select all the objects you want to
join. If you see a convert message, enter **Y⏎**. At the Enter fuzzy distance or [Jointype]:
prompt, enter a distance that approximates the size of the gap between objects. By default,
AutoCAD extends the lines so they join end to end. You can use the Jointype option if you want
Pedit to join segments with an additional segment.

2. Choose Modify ➢ Object ➢ Polyline, type **Pe⏎**, or choose Edit Polyline from the Modify II
toolbar.

3. At the Select polyline or [Multiple]: prompt, pick the outermost polyline.

FIGURE 18.6

The drawing polyline

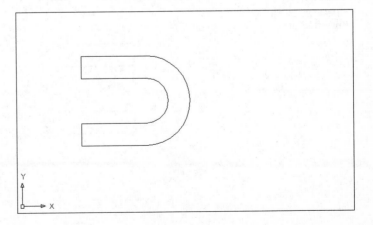

4. At the prompt

```
Enter an option [Close/Join/Width/Edit vertex/Fit/Spline/Decurve/Ltype
gen/Undo]:
```

enter **J**↵ for the Join option.

5. At the `Select objects:` prompt, select all the objects you have drawn so far.

6. Press ↵ to join all the objects into one polyline. It appears that nothing has happened, although you will see the message `5 segments added to polyline` in the Command window.

7. Press ↵ again to exit the Pedit command.

8. Click the drawing to expose its grips. The entire object is highlighted, indicating that all the lines have been joined into a single polyline.

By using the Width option under Edit Polyline, you can change the thickness of a polyline. Let's change the width of your polyline, to give some thickness to the outline of the joint:

1. Type **Pe**↵ or click the Edit Polyline tool on the Modify II toolbar again.

2. Click the polyline.

3. At the `Enter an option [Open/Join/Width/Edit vertex/Fit/Spline/Decurve/Ltypegen/Undo]:` prompt, enter **W**↵ for the Width option.

4. At the `Specify new width for all segments:` prompt, enter **.03**↵ for the new width of the polyline. The line changes to the new width (see Figure 18.7), and you now have a top view of your joint.

5. Press ↵ to exit the Pedit command.

6. Save this file.

FIGURE 18.7
The polyline with a new thickness

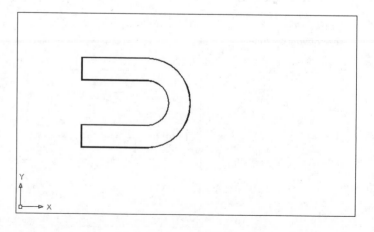

Setting Pedit Options

Now here's a brief look at a few of the Pedit options you didn't try firsthand:

Close   Connects the two endpoints of a polyline with a line segment. If the polyline you selected to be edited is already closed, this option changes to Open.

Open   Removes the last segment added to a closed polyline.

Spline/Decurve   Smooths a polyline into a spline curve (discussed in detail later in this chapter).

Edit Vertex   Lets you edit each vertex of a polyline individually (discussed in detail later in this section).

Fit   Turns polyline segments into a series of arcs.

Ltype Gen   Controls the way noncontinuous linetypes pass through the vertices of a polyline. If you have a fitted or spline curve with a noncontinuous linetype, turn on this option.

TIP   You can change the thickness of regular lines and arcs by using Pedit to change them into polylines and then using the Width option to change their width.

Smoothing Polylines

You can create a curve in AutoCAD in many ways. If you don't need the representation of a curve to be accurate, you can use a polyline curve. In the following exercise, you will draw a polyline curve to represent a contour on a topographical map:

1. Open the topo.dwg drawing from the companion CD. The first image in Figure 18.8 contains the drawing of survey data. Some of the contours have already been drawn in between the data points.

2. Zoom in to the upper-right corner of the drawing, so your screen displays the area shown in the second image in Figure 18.8.

3. Click the Polyline tool in the Draw toolbar. Using the Center Osnap, draw a polyline that connects the points labeled 254.00. Your drawing should look like the second image in Figure 18.8.

4. Press ↵.

TIP   If Running Osnaps are not set, you can choose Tools ➤ Drafting Settings or type **Os**↵ to open the Drafting Settings dialog box. From there, select the Object Snap tab and turn on the Center option. See Chapter 3 for more on this dialog box.

5. Next, you will convert the polyline you just drew into a smooth contour line. Choose Modify ➤ Object ➤ Polyline or type **Pe**↵.

6. At the Select polyline or [Multiple]: prompt, pick the contour line you just drew.

7. At the prompt

    Enter an option [close/Join/Width/Edit vertex/Fit/Spline/Decurve/Ltype gen/Undo]:

    press **F**↵ to select the Fit option. The polyline smooths out into a series of connected arcs that pass through the data points.

8. Press ↵ to end the Pedit command.

Your contour is now complete. The Fit option under the Pedit command causes AutoCAD to convert the straight-line segments of the polyline into arcs. The endpoints of the arcs pass through the endpoints of the line segments, and the curve of each arc depends on the direction of the adjacent arc. This gives the effect of a smooth curve. Next, you'll use this polyline curve to experiment with some of the editing options unique to the Pedit command.

TURNING OBJECTS INTO POLYLINES AND POLYLINES INTO SPLINES

At times you will want to convert regular lines, arcs, or even circles into polylines. You might want to change the width of lines or join lines to form a single object such as a boundary. Here are the steps to convert lines, arcs, and circles into polylines:

1. Choose Modify ➤ Object ➤ Polyline, or type **Pe**↵ at the Command prompt.

2. At the `Select polyline or [Multiple]:` prompt, pick the object you want to convert. If you want to convert a circle to a polyline, first break the circle (using the Break option on the Modify toolbar) so that it becomes an arc of approximately 359°.

3. At the prompt

   `Object selected is not a polyline. Do you want to turn it into one? <Y>:`

   press ↵. The object is converted into a polyline.

If you have several objects that you want to convert to polylines, type **M**↵ at the `Select polyline or [Multiple]:` prompt; then select the objects you want to convert. You will then see the `Convert Lines and Arcs to polylines [Yes/No]?:` prompt. Type **Y**↵, and all the selected objects will be converted to polylines. You can then go on to use other Pedit options on the selected objects.

To turn a polyline into a true spline curve, do the following:

1. Choose Modify ➤ Object ➤ Polyline or type **Pe**↵. Select the polyline you want to convert.

2. Type **S**↵ to turn it into a polyline spline; then press ↵ twice to exit the Pedit command.

3. Click the Spline tool in the Draw toolbar, type **Spl**↵, or choose Draw ➤ Spline from the drop-down menu.

4. At the `Specify first point or [Object]:` prompt, type **O**↵ for the Object option.

5. At the `Select objects:` prompt, click the polyline spline. Though it may not be apparent at first, the polyline is converted into a true spline.

You can also use the Spline Edit tool (choose Modify ➤ Object ➤ Spline or enter **Spe**↵) on a polyline spline. If you do, the polyline spline is automatically converted into a true spline.

If you know you will always want to convert an object into a polyline when using Pedit, you can turn on the Peditaccept system variable. Enter **peditaccept**↵ at the Command prompt, and then enter **1**↵.

FIGURE 18.8

The topo.dwg drawing shows survey data portrayed in an AutoCAD drawing. Notice the dots indicating where elevations were taken. The actual elevation value is shown with a diagonal line from the point.

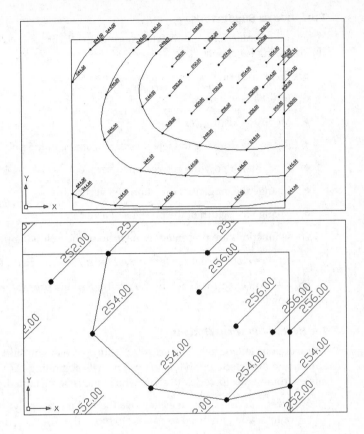

Editing Vertices

One of the Pedit options that I haven't yet discussed, Edit Vertex, is almost like a command within a command. Edit Vertex has numerous suboptions that enable you to fine-tune your polyline by giving you control over its individual vertices.

To access the Edit Vertex options, follow these steps:

1. First, turn off the Data and Border layers to hide the data points and border.

2. Issue the Pedit command again and then select the polyline you just drew.

3. Type E↵ to enter the Edit Vertex mode. An X appears at the beginning of the polyline, indicating the vertex that will be affected by the Edit Vertex options.

WARNING   When using Edit Vertex, you must be careful about selecting the vertex to be edited. Edit Vertex has six options, and you often have to exit the Edit Vertex operation and use Pedit's Fit option to see the effect of Edit Vertex's options on a curved polyline.

EDIT VERTEX SUBOPTIONS

After you've entered the Edit Vertex mode of the Pedit command, you have the option to perform the following functions:

◆ Break the polyline between two vertices.

◆ Insert a new vertex.

◆ Move an existing vertex.

◆ Regen the drawing to view the current shape of the polyline.

◆ Straighten a polyline between two vertices.

◆ Change the tangential direction of a vertex.

◆ Change the width of the polyline at a vertex.

These functions are presented in the form of the following prompt:

```
[Next/Previous/Break/Insert/Move/Regen/Straighten/Tangent/Width/eXit] <N>:
```

This section examines each of the options in this prompt, starting with the Next and Previous options.

The Next and Previous Options

These options let you select a vertex for editing. When you start the Edit Vertex option, an X appears on the selected polyline to designate its beginning. As you select Next or Previous, the X moves from vertex to vertex to show which one is being edited. Let's try this:

1. Press ↵ a couple of times to move the X along the polyline. (Because Next is the default option, you only need to press ↵ to move the X.)

2. Type P↵ for Previous. The X moves in the opposite direction. Notice that now the default option becomes P.

TIP To determine the direction of a polyline, note in which direction the X moves when you use the Next option. Knowing the direction of a polyline is important for some of the other Edit Vertex options.

The Break Option

The Break option breaks the polyline between two vertices:

1. Position the X on one end of the segment you want to break.

2. Enter B↵ at the Command prompt.

3. At the `Enter an option [Next/Previous/Go/eXit] <N>:` prompt, use Next or Previous to move the X to the other end of the segment to be broken.

4. When the X is in the proper position, enter G↵ to break the polyline (see Figure 18.9).

FIGURE 18.9
How the Break
option works

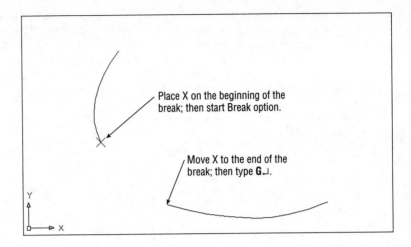

Place X on the beginning of the
break; then start Break option.

Move X to the end of the
break; then type **G↵**.

TIP You can also use the Break and Trim options on the Modify toolbar to break a polyline anywhere, as you did when you drew the toilet seat in Chapter 3.

The Insert Option

Next, try the Insert option, which inserts a new vertex:

1. Type **X↵** to temporarily exit the Edit Vertex option. Then type **U↵** to undo the break.

2. Type **E↵** to return to the Edit Vertex option.

3. Press ↵ to advance the X marker to the next point.

4. Enter **I↵** to select the Insert option.

5. When the prompt Specify location for new vertex: appears, along with a rubber-banding
line originating from the current X position (see Figure 18.10), pick a point indicating the new
vertex location. The polyline is redrawn with the new vertex.

FIGURE 18.10
The new vertex
location

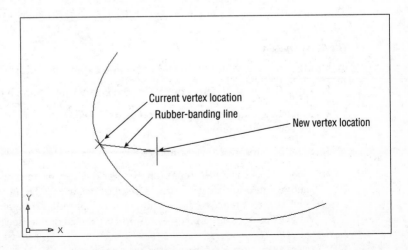

Current vertex location
Rubber-banding line
New vertex location

Notice that the inserted vertex appears between the currently marked vertex and the *next* vertex, so the Insert option is sensitive to the direction of the polyline. If the polyline is curved, the new vertex will not immediately be shown as curved. (See the first image in Figure 18.11.) You must smooth it out by exiting the Edit Vertex option and then using the Fit option, as you did to edit the site plan. (See the second image in Figure 18.11.) You can also use the Stretch command (on the Modify toolbar) to move a polyline vertex.

FIGURE 18.11

The polyline before and after the curve is fitted

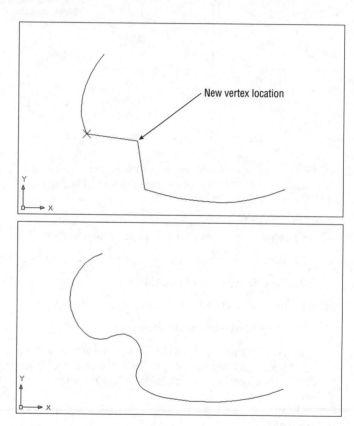

The Move Option

In this brief exercise, you'll use the Move option to move a vertex:

1. Undo the inserted vertex by exiting the Edit Vertex option (enter **X↵**) and typing **U↵**.

2. Restart the Edit Vertex option, and use the Next or Previous option to place the X on the vertex you want to move.

3. Enter **M↵** for the Move option.

4. When the Specify new location for marked vertex: prompt appears, along with a rubber-banding line originating from the X (see the first image in Figure 18.12), pick the new vertex. The polyline is redrawn (see the second image in Figure 18.12). Again, if the line is curved, the new vertex appears as a sharp angle until you use the Fit option (see the final image in Figure 18.12).

TIP   You can also move a polyline vertex by using its grip.

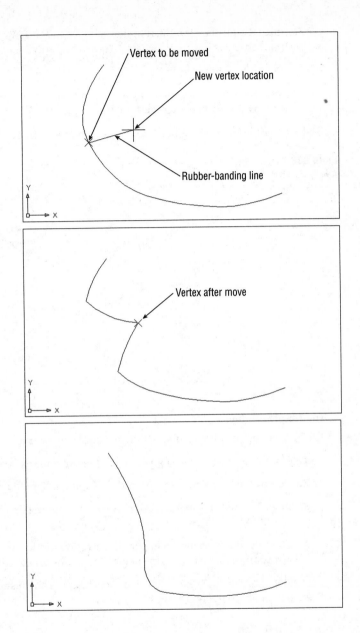

FIGURE 18.12

Picking a new location for a vertex, with the polyline before and after the curve is fitted

The Straighten Option

The Straighten option straightens all the vertices between two selected vertices, as shown in the following exercise:

1. Undo the moved vertex (from the previous exercise).

2. Start the Edit Vertex option again and select the starting vertex for the straight line.

3. Enter **S↵** for the Straighten option.

4. At the `Enter an option [Next/Previous/Go/eXit] <N>:` prompt, move the X to the location for the other end of the straight-line segment.

5. After the X is in the proper position, enter **G↵** for the Go option. The polyline straightens between the two selected vertices (see Figure 18.13).

TIP Using the Straighten option is a quick way to delete vertices from a polyline.

FIGURE 18.13
A polyline after
straightening

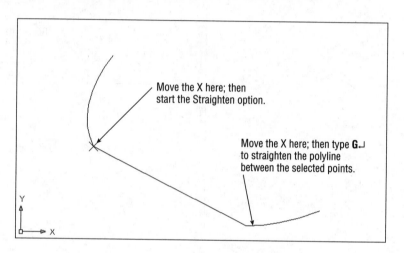

Move the X here; then
start the Straighten option.

Move the X here; then type **G↵**
to straighten the polyline
between the selected points.

The Tangent Option

The Tangent option alters the direction of a curve on a curve-fitted polyline:

1. Undo the straightened segment from the previous exercise.

2. Restart the Edit Vertex option and position the X on the vertex you want to alter.

3. Enter **T↵** for the Tangent option. A rubber-banding line appears. (See the top image in Figure 18.14.)

4. Point the rubber-banding line in the direction for the new tangent and click the mouse. An arrow appears, indicating the new tangent direction. (See the second image in Figure 18.14.)

Don't worry if the polyline shape does not change. You must use Fit to see the effect of Tangent. (See the final image in Figure 18.14.)

The Width Option

Finally, try out the Width option. Unlike the Pedit command's Width option, the Edit Vertex/ Width option enables you to alter the width of the polyline at any vertex. Thus, you can taper or otherwise vary polyline thickness. Try these steps:

1. Undo the tangent arc from the previous exercise.

2. Return to the Edit Vertex option and place the X at the beginning vertex of a polyline segment you want to change.

FIGURE 18.14

Picking a new tangent direction

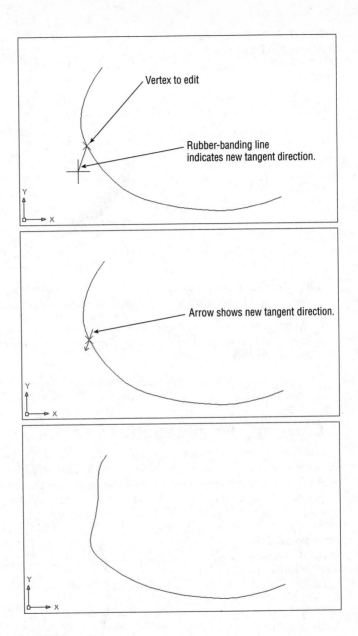

Vertex to edit

Rubber-banding line indicates new tangent direction.

Arrow shows new tangent direction.

3. Type **W**⏎ to issue the Width option.

4. At the Specify starting width for next segment <0.0000>: prompt, enter a value, **12** for example, indicating the polyline width desired at this vertex.

5. At the Specify ending width for next segment <12.0000>: prompt, enter the width, **24** for example, for the next vertex.

The width of the polyline changes to your specifications. (See Figure 18.15.)

FIGURE 18.15
A polyline with the
width of one segment
increased

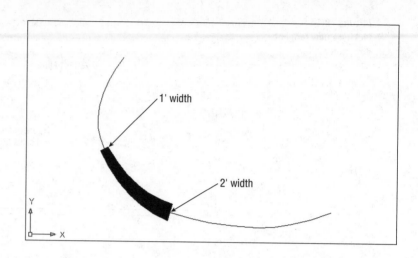

TIP The Width option is useful when you want to create an irregular or curved area in your drawing that is to be filled in solid. This is another option that is sensitive to the polyline direction.

As you have seen throughout these exercises, you can use the Undo option to reverse the last Edit Vertex option used. And you can use the Exit option to leave Edit Vertex at any time. Just enter **X↲** to display the Pedit prompt:

```
Enter an option [Close/Join/Width/Edit vertex/Fit/Spline/Decurve/Ltype
gen/Undo]:
```

Creating a Polyline Spline Curve

The Pedit command's Spline option (named after the spline tool used in manual drafting) offers you a way to draw smoother and more controllable curves than those produced by the Fit option. A polyline spline does not pass through the vertex points as a fitted curve does. Instead, the vertex points act as weights pulling the curve in their direction. The polyline spline touches only its beginning and end vertices. Figure 18.16 illustrates this concept.

FIGURE 18.16
The polyline spline
curve pulled toward
its vertices

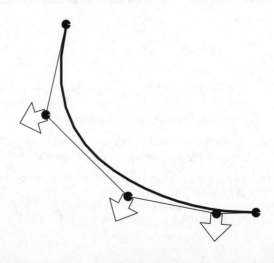

TIP   A polyline spline curve does not represent a mathematically true curve. See the next section, "Using True Spline Curves," to learn how to draw a more accurate spline curve.

Let's see how using a polyline spline curve might influence the way you edit a curve:

1. Undo the width changes you made in the previous exercise.

2. To change the contour into a polyline spline curve, choose Modify ➢ Object ➢ Polyline.

3. Pick the polyline to be curved.

4. At the prompt

```
Enter an option [Close/Join/Width/Edit vertex/Fit/Spline/Decurve/Ltypegen/Undo]:
```

enter S↵. Your curve changes to look like Figure 18.17.

FIGURE 18.17
A spline curve

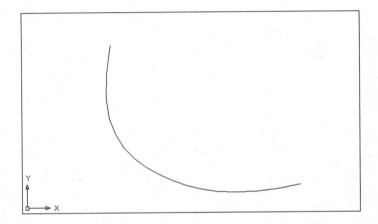

5. Press ↵ to exit Edit Polyline.

The curve takes on a smoother, more graceful appearance. It no longer passes through the points you used to define it. To see where the points went and to find out how spline curves act, do the following:

1. Make sure the Noun/Verb Selection mode and the Enable Grips feature are turned on.

2. Click the curve. You'll see the original vertices appear as grips. (See the first image in Figure 18.18.)

3. Click the grip that is second from the top of the curve, as shown in the first image in Figure 18.18, and move the grip around. Notice how the curve follows, giving you immediate feedback on how the curve will look.

4. Pick a point as shown in the second image in Figure 18.18. The curve is fixed in its new position.

TIP   You can set up AutoCAD to display both the curved and the straight segments defining the curve by turning on the Splframe system variable. Enter **splframe.**↵ **1**↵ and then issue a Regen command. You'll see a frame that connects the grips of the curve. To turn off the display of the straight segments, enter **splframe.**↵ **0**↵ .

FIGURE 18.18
The fitted curve changed to a spline curve, with the location of the second vertex and the new curve

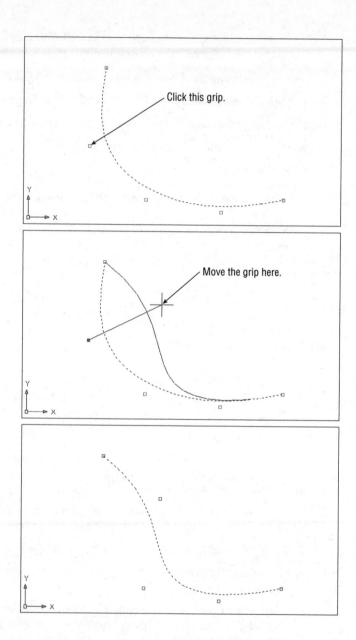

Using True Spline Curves

So far, you've been working with polylines to generate spline curves. The advantage to using polylines for curves is that they can be enhanced in other ways. You can modify their width, for instance, or join several curves. But at times you will need a more exact representation of a curve. The spline object, created by choosing Draw ➢ Spline, produces a more accurate model of a spline curve, as well as giving you more control over its shape.

The splines are true NURBS curves. *NURBS* stands for *Non-Uniform Rational B-Splines.* A full description of NURBS is beyond the scope of this book, but basically, NURBS are a standard mathematical form used to represent shapes.

Drawing a True Spline

The following exercise shows you how to create a spline curve:

1. Undo the changes made in the previous two exercises.

2. Turn the Data layer on so you can view the data points.

3. Adjust your view so you can see all the data points with the elevation of 250.00 (see Figure 18.19).

FIGURE 18.19

Starting the spline curve at the first data point

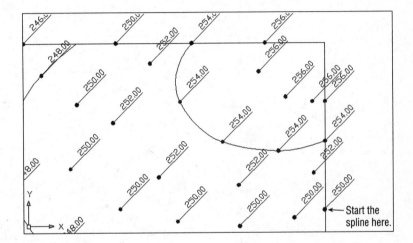

4. Choose Draw ➤ Spline or type **Spl**↵.

5. At the Specify first point or [Object]: prompt, use the Center Osnap to start the curve on the first data point in the lower-right corner. (See Figure 18.19.) The prompt changes to Specify next point:.

6. Continue to select the 250.00 data points until you reach the last one. Notice that as you pick points, a curve appears, and it bends and flows as you move your cursor.

7. After you've selected the last point, press ↵. Notice that the prompt changes to Specify start tangent:. Also, a rubber-banding line appears from the first point of the curve to the cursor. As you move the cursor, the curve adjusts to the direction of the rubber-banding line. Here, you can set the tangency of the first point of the curve. (See the first image in Figure 18.20.)

8. Press ↵. This causes AutoCAD to determine the first point's tangency based on the current shape of the curve. A rubber-banding line appears from the last point of the curve. As with the first point, you can indicate a tangent direction for the last point of the curve. (See the second image in Figure 18.20.)

9. Press ↵ to exit the Spline command without changing the endpoint tangent direction.

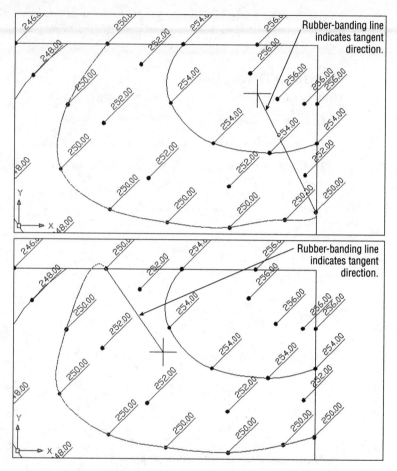

You now have a smooth curve that passes through the points you selected. These points are called the *control points*. If you click the curve, you'll see the grips appear at the location of these control points, and you can adjust the curve simply by clicking the grip points and moving them. (You might need to turn off the Data layer to see the grips clearly.)

TIP See Chapter 2 for more detailed information on grip editing.

You might have noticed two other options—Fit Tolerance and Close—as you were selecting points for the spline in the previous exercise. Here is a description of these options:

Fit Tolerance Lets you change the curve so that it doesn't actually pass through the points you pick. When you select this option, you get the prompt Specify fit tolerance <0.0000>. Any value greater than 0 causes the curve to pass close to, but not through, the points. A value of 0 causes the curve to pass through the points. (You'll see how this works in a later exercise.)

Close Lets you close the curve into a loop. If you choose this option, you are prompted to indicate a tangent direction for the closing point.

Fine-Tuning Spline Curves

Spline curves are different from other types of objects, and many of the standard editing commands won't work on splines. AutoCAD offers the Modify ➢ Object ➢ Spline option (Splinedit command) for making changes to splines. The following exercises will give you some practice with this command. You'll start by focusing on Splinedit's Fit Data option, which lets you fine-tune the spline curve.

CONTROLLING THE FIT DATA OF A SPLINE

The following exercise demonstrates how the Fit Data option lets you control some of the general characteristics of the curve:

1. Choose Modify ➢ Object ➢ Spline or type **Spe↵** at the Command prompt.

2. At the Select spline: prompt, select the spline you drew in the previous exercise.

3. At the prompt

   ```
   Enter an option [Fit data/Close/Move vertex/Refine/rEverse/Undo]:
   ```

   type **F↵** to select the Fit Data option.

TIP   Like the Edit Vertex option of the Pedit command, the Fit Data option offers a subset of options that let you edit certain properties of the spline.

Controlling Tangency at the Beginning Points and Endpoints

Next, let's see how you can adjust the tangency of the first and last points of a spline:

1. At the prompt

   ```
   [Add/Close/Delete/Move/Purge/Tangents/toLerance/eXit] <eXit>:
   ```

   type **T↵** to select the Tangents option. Move the cursor, and notice that the curve changes tangency through the first point, just as it did when you first created the spline. (See Figure 18.20, earlier in this chapter.)

2. Press ↵. You can now edit the other endpoint tangency.

3. Press ↵ again. You return to the prompt

   ```
   [Add/Close/Delete/Move/Purge/Tangents/toLerance/eXit] <eXit>:
   ```

Adding New Control Points

Now add another control point to the spline curve:

1. At the prompt

   ```
   [Add/Close/Delete/Move/Purge/Tangents/toLerance/eXit] <eXit>:
   ```

   type **A↵** to access the Add option.

2. At the Specify control point <exit>: prompt, click the second grip point from the bottom end of the spline (see the top image in Figure 18.21). A rubber-banding line appears from the point you selected. That point and the next point are highlighted. The two highlighted points tell you that the next point you select will fall between these two points. You also see the Specify new point <exit>: prompt.

FIGURE 18.21

Adding a new control point to a spline

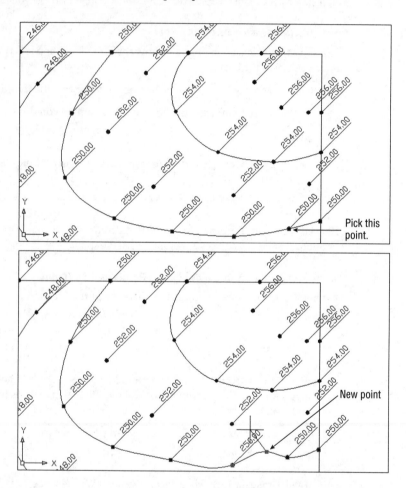

3. Click a new point. The curve changes to include that point. In addition, the new point becomes the highlighted point, indicating that you can continue to add more points between it and the other highlighted point. (See the bottom image in Figure 18.21.)

4. Press ↵. The Specify control point <exit>: prompt appears, enabling you to select another point if you so desire.

5. Press ↵ twice to return to the prompt

`[Add/Close/Delete/Move/Purge/Tangents/toLerance/eXit] <eXit>:`

Type **X**↵ to exit.

Adjusting the Spline Tolerance Setting

Before ending the description of the Fit Data options, let's look at how Tolerance works:

1. At the prompt

`[Add/Close/Delete/Move/Purge/Tangents/toLerance/eXit] <eXit>:`

type **L**↵ to select the Tolerance option. This option sets the tolerance between the control point and the curve.

2. At the `Enter fit tolerance <1.0000E-10>:` prompt, type **30**↵. Notice how the curve no longer passes through the control points, except for the beginning point and endpoints (see Figure 18.22). The fit tolerance value you enter determines the maximum distance the spline can be from any control point.

FIGURE 18.22
The spline after seting the control point tolerance to 30

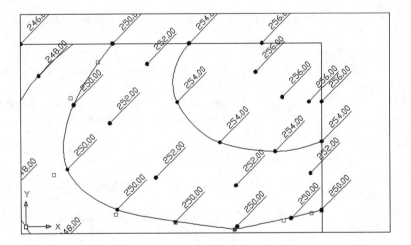

3. Type **X**↵ to exit the Fit Data option.

You've seen how you can control many of the shape properties of a spline through the Fit Data option. Here are descriptions of the other Fit Data options you didn't try in these exercises:

Close   Lets you close the spline into a loop.

Delete   Removes a control point in the spline.

Move   Lets you move a control point.

Purge   Deletes the fit data of the spline, thereby eliminating the Fit Data option for the purged spline.

When Can't You Use Fit Data?

The Fit Data option of the Splinedit command offers many ways to edit a spline; however, this option is not available to all spline curves. When you invoke certain of the other Splinedit options, a spline curve will lose its fit data, thereby disabling the Fit Data option. These operations are as follows:

◆ Fitting a spline to a tolerance (Spline/Fit Tolerance) and moving its control vertices

◆ Fitting a spline to a tolerance (Spline/Fit Tolerance) and opening or closing it

◆ Refining the spline

◆ Purging the spline of its fit data by using the Purge option of the Splinedit command. (Choose Modify ➢ Object ➢ Spline or enter **Splinedit**↵, and then select the spline and enter **F**↵ **P**↵.)

Also, note that the Fit Data option is not available when you edit spline curves that have been created from polyline splines. See the "Turning Objects into Polylines and Polylines into Splines" sidebar earlier in this chapter.

ADJUSTING THE CONTROL POINTS WITH THE REFINE OPTION

While you are still in the Splinedit command, let's look at another of its options, Refine, which you can use to fine-tune the curve:

1. Type **U**↵ to undo the changes you made in the previous exercise.

2. At the prompt

   ```
   Enter an option [Fit data/Close/Move vertex/Refine/rEverse/Undo]:
   ```

   type **R**↵. The Refine option lets you control the "pull" exerted on a spline by an individual control point. This isn't quite the same effect as the Fit Tolerance option you used in the previous exercise.

3. At the prompt

   ```
   Enter a refine option [Add control point/Elevate order/Weight/eXit] <eXit>:
   ```

   type **W**↵. The first control point is highlighted.

4. At the next prompt

   ```
   Enter new weight (current = 1.000) or [Next/Previous/Select Point/eXit] <N>:
   ```

   press ↵ three times to move the highlight to the fourth control point.

5. Type **25**↵. The curve not only moves closer to the control point, it also bends around the control point in a tighter arc (see Figure 18.23).

You can use the Weight value of Splinedit's Refine option to pull the spine in tighter. Think of it as a way to increase the "gravity" of the control point, causing the curve to be pulled closer and tighter to the control point.

Continue your look at the Splinedit command by adding more control points—without actually changing the shape of the curve. You do this using Refine's Add Control Point and Elevate Order options:

1. Type **1**⏎ to return the spline to its former shape.

2. Type **X**⏎ to exit the Weight option; then type **A**⏎ to select the Add Control Point option.

3. At the `Specify a point on the spline <exit>:` prompt, click the second-to-last control point toward the top end of the spline. (See the top image in Figure 18.24.) The point you select disappears and is replaced by two control points roughly equidistant from the one you selected. (See the bottom image in Figure 18.24.) The curve remains unchanged. Two new control points now replace the one control point you selected.

4. Press ⏎ to exit the Add Control Point option.

5. Now type **E**⏎ to select the Elevate Order option.

6. At the `Enter new order <4>:` prompt, type **6**⏎. The number of control points increases, leaving the curve itself untouched.

7. Type **X**⏎ twice to exit the Refine option and then the Splinedit command.

You will probably never edit the contour lines of a topographical map in quite the way these exercises have shown. But by following this tutorial, you have explored all the potential of AutoCAD's spline object. Aside from its usefulness for drawing contours, it can be a great tool for drawing free-form illustrations. It is also an excellent tool for mechanical applications, in which precise, nonuniform curves are required, such as drawings of cams or sheet metal work.

FIGURE 18.23

The spline after increasing the Weight value of a control point

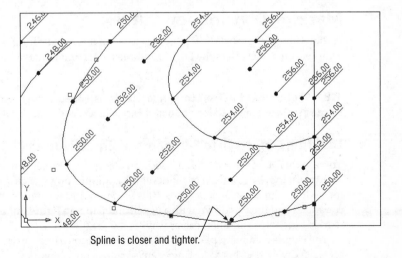

Spline is closer and tighter.

FIGURE 18.24
Adding a single control point by using the Refine option

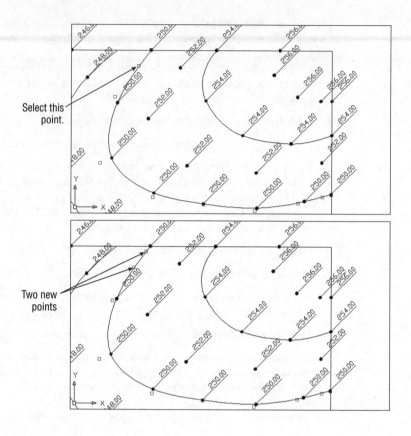

Marking Divisions on Curves

Perhaps one of the most difficult things to do in manual drafting is to mark regular intervals on a curve. AutoCAD offers the Divide and Measure commands to help you perform this task with speed and accuracy.

TIP The Divide and Measure commands are discussed here in conjunction with polylines, but you can use these commands on any object except blocks and text.

Dividing Objects into Segments of Equal Length

You use the Divide command to divide an object into a specific number of equal segments. For example, suppose you need to mark off the contour you've been working on in this chapter into nine equal segments. One way to do this is to first find the length of the contour by using the List command and then sit down with a pencil and paper to figure out the exact distances between the marks. But there is another, easier way.

The Divide command places a set of point objects on a line, an arc, a circle, or a polyline, marking off exact divisions. This following exercise shows how it works:

1. Open the 18a-divd.dwg file from the companion CD. This file is similar to the one you have been working with in the previous exercises.

2. Choose Draw ➢ Point ➢ Divide or type **Div**↵.

3. At the `Select object to divide:` prompt, pick the spline contour line that shows Xs in Figure 18.25.

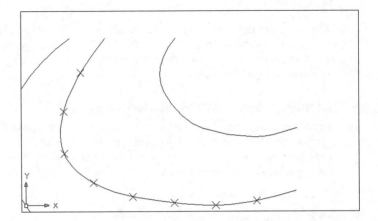

4. The `Enter the number of segments or [Block]:` prompt that appears next is asking for the number of divisions you want on the selected object. Enter **9**↵.

The Command prompt now returns, and it appears that nothing has happened. But AutoCAD has placed several points on the contour that indicate the locations of the nine divisions you requested. To see these points more clearly, follow these steps:

5. Choose Format ➢ Point Style to open the Point Style dialog box.

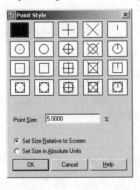

6. Click the X point style in the upper-right side of the dialog box, click the Set Size Relative To Screen radio button, and then click OK.

7. If the Xs don't appear, choose View ➢ Regen or enter **Re**↵. A set of Xs appears, showing the nine divisions (see Figure 18.25).

TIP You can also change the point style by changing the Pdmode system variable. When Pdmode is set to 3, the point appears as an X. See Appendix C for information on Pdmode.

The Divide command uses *point* objects to indicate the division points. You create point objects by using the Point command; they usually appear as dots. Unfortunately, such points are nearly invisible when placed on top of other objects. But, as you have seen, you can alter their shape by using the Point Style dialog box. You can use these X points to place objects or references to break the object being divided. (The Divide command does not actually cut the object into smaller divisions.)

TIP If you are in a hurry and you don't want to bother changing the shape of the point objects, you can do the following: Set the Running Osnaps to Node. Then, when you are in the Point Selection mode, move the cursor over the divided curve. When the cursor gets close to a point object, the Node Osnap marker appears.

Dividing Objects into Specified Lengths

The Measure command acts just like Divide; however, instead of dividing an object into segments of equal length, the Measure command marks intervals of a specified distance along an object. For example, suppose you need to mark some segments exactly 5″ apart along the contour. Try the following exercise to see how the Measure command is used to accomplish this task:

1. Erase the X-shaped point objects.

2. Choose Draw ➢ Point ➢ Measure or type **Me.**↵.

3. At the `Select object to measure:` prompt, pick the contour at a point closest to its lower endpoint. I'll explain shortly why this is important.

4. At the `Specify length of segment or [Block]:` prompt, enter **60**↵. The X points appear at the specified distance.

5. Exit this file.

TIP The Measure command is AutoCAD's equivalent of the divider tool in manual drafting. A divider is a V-shaped instrument, similar to a compass, used to mark off regular intervals along a curve or line.

Bear in mind that the point you pick on the object to be measured determines where the Measure command begins measuring. In the previous exercise, for example, you picked the contour near its bottom endpoint. If you picked the top of the contour, the results would be different because the measurement would start at the top, not the bottom.

MARKING OFF INTERVALS BY USING BLOCKS INSTEAD OF POINTS

You can also use the Block option under the Divide and Measure commands to place blocks at regular intervals along a line, a polyline, or an arc. Here's how to use blocks as markers:

1. Be sure the block you want to use is part of the current drawing file.

2. Start either the Divide or Measure command.

3. At the `Specify length of segment or [Block]:` prompt, enter **B**↵.

4. At the `Enter name of block to insert:` prompt, enter the name of a block.

5. At the `Align Block with Object? [Yes/No]:` prompt, press ↵ if you want the blocks to follow the alignment of the selected object. (Entering **N**↵ inserts each block at a 0 angle.)

6. At the `Enter the number of Segments:` prompt or the `Specify length of segment:` prompt, enter the number or length of the segments. The blocks appear at regular intervals on the selected object.

One example of using the Block option of Divide or Measure is to place a row of sinks equally spaced along a wall. Or you might use this technique to make multiple copies of an object along an irregular path defined by a polyline. In civil engineering projects, you can indicate a fence line by using Divide or Measure to place Xs along a polyline.

Sketching with AutoCAD

No discussion of polylines would be complete without mentioning the Sketch command. Though AutoCAD isn't a sketch program, you *can* draw "freehand" by using the Sketch command. With Sketch, you can rough in ideas in a free-form way and later overlay a more formal drawing using the usual lines, arcs, and circles. You can use Sketch with a mouse, but it makes more sense to use this command with a digitizing tablet that has a stylus. The stylus affords a more natural way of sketching.

Here's a step-by-step description of how to use Sketch:

1. Make sure the Ortho and Snap modes are turned off. Then type **Skpoly**↵ **1**↵. This sets the Sketch command to draw using polylines.

2. Type **Sketch**↵ at the Command prompt.

3. At the `Record increment <0.1000>:` prompt, enter a value that represents the smallest line segment you will want Sketch to draw, and then press ↵. This command approximates a sketch line by drawing a series of short line segments. The value you enter here determines the length of those line segments.

4. At the `Sketch.Pen eXit Quit Record Erase Connect:` prompt, click the Pick button and then start your sketch line. Notice that the message `<Pen down>` appears, telling you that AutoCAD is recording your cursor's motion.

TIP You can also start and stop the sketch line by pressing the P key.

5. Click the Pick button to stop drawing. The message `<Pen up>` tells you that AutoCAD has stopped recording your cursor motion. As you draw, notice that the line is green. This indicates that you have drawn a temporary sketch line and have not committed the line to the drawing.

6. A line drawn with Sketch is temporary until you use Record to save it, so turn the sketch line into a polyline now by typing **R**.

7. Type **X**↵ to exit the Sketch command.

Here are some of the other Sketch options:

Connect Enables you to continue a line from the end of the last temporary line drawn. Type **C** and then move the cursor to the endpoint of the temporary line. AutoCAD automatically starts the line, and you just continue to draw. This works only in the `<Pen up>` mode.

Period (.) Enables you to draw a single straight-line segment by moving the cursor to the desired position and then pressing the period key. This works only in the `<Pen up>` mode.

Record, Erase, Quit, and Exit Controls the recording of lines and exiting from the Sketch command. Record is used to save a temporary sketched line; after a line has been recorded, you must edit it as you would any other line. With Erase, you can erase temporary lines before you record them. Quit ends the Sketch command without saving unrecorded lines. On the other hand, the Exit option on the Sketch menu automatically saves all lines you have drawn and then exits the Sketch command.

Filling In Solid Areas

You have learned how to create a solid area by increasing the width of a polyline segment. But suppose you want to create a simple solid shape or a very thick line. AutoCAD provides the Solid, Trace, and Donut commands to help you draw simple filled areas. The Trace command acts just like the Line command (with the added feature of drawing wide line segments), so only the Solid fills and the Donut command are discussed here.

TIP You can create free-form, solid-filled areas by using the solid hatch pattern. Create an enclosed area by using any set of objects, and then use the Hatch tool to apply a solid hatch pattern to the area. See Chapter 7 for details on using the Hatch tool.

Drawing Solid Filled Areas

If you've ever played with a paint program, you know how to create a solid fill. It's usually accomplished with a paint bucket tool. This tool always looks like a paint bucket, and it seems to be universal among paint programs. In AutoCAD, creating solid fills is not quite so obvious. It's actually one of many hatch patterns offered with the Hatch tool. Here is a short exercise to demonstrate how to use the Hatch tool to create a solid fill:

1. Open the file 18a-htch.dwg from the companion CD.

2. Click the Hatch tool on the Draw toolbar.

3. In the Hatch And Gradient dialog box, click the Add: Pick Points button.

4. Click the area bounded by the border and contour line in the upper-right corner of the drawing, as shown in the first image in Figure 18.26. Then press ↵. If you need to, you can click more areas before you press ↵, but, for this example, you are only selecting one area.

5. Back in the Hatch And Gradient dialog box, click the Ellipsis button to the right of the Pattern drop-down list.

6. In the Hatch Pattern Palette dialog box, select the Solid box in the Other Predefined tab.

7. Click OK and then click OK again. A solid fill is applied to the selected area, as shown in the second image in Figure 18.26.

Overlapping Solid Lines and Shaded Fills

If you use an ink-jet plotter, a raster plotter, or a laser printer that can convert solid areas into screened or gray-shaded areas, you might encounter the problem of shading areas overlapping lines and hiding them. This problem might not be apparent until you plot the drawing; it frequently occurs when a gray-shaded area is bounded by lines. (See Figure 18.27.)

FIGURE 18.26
Locating the area to fill, and the final result of the solid hatch

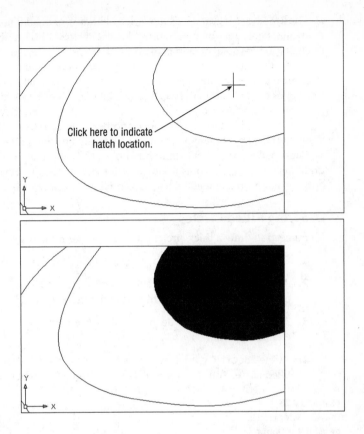

Click here to indicate hatch location.

FIGURE 18.27
Problems that occur with overlapping lines and gray areas

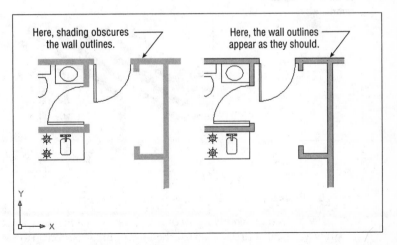

Here, shading obscures the wall outlines.

Here, the wall outlines appear as they should.

The left side of Figure 18.27 shows how shading or solid fills can cover line work. The outline of the walls is obscured by the shading. The right side of Figure 18.27 shows how the drawing was intended to be displayed and printed.

Most other graphics programs have specific tools to handle this overlapping difficulty. These tools are commonly named Move To Front or Move To Back, indicating that you move an object in front of or behind another object. AutoCAD offers the Draworder command to perform the same function as the Move To Back and Move To Front tools of other programs.

To force an object to appear above another, choose Tools ➤ Draw Order ➤ Bring To Front, and then select the object that you want to overlap all the others. Or choose Tools ➤ Draw Order ➤ Send To Back to place an object behind other objects. You can also select specific objects to overlay or underlay by using the Tools ➤ Draw Order ➤ Bring Above Objects and Send Under Objects options. For more detailed instructions on how to use Draworder, see Chapters 7 and 14.

Drawing Filled Circles

If you need to draw a thick circle, such as an inner tube or a solid filled circle, follow these steps:

1. Choose Draw ➤ Donut or type **Do**⏎ at the Command prompt.

2. At the `Specify inside diameter of donut <0˝-½˝>:` prompt, enter the desired diameter of the donut "hole." This value determines the opening at the center of your circle.

3. At the `Specify outside diameter of donut <0˝-1˝>:` prompt, enter the overall diameter of the circle.

4. At the `Specify center of donut or <exit>:` prompt, click the desired location for the filled circle. You can continue to select points to place multiple donuts (see Figure 18.28).

FIGURE 18.28
Drawing wide circles by using the Donut command

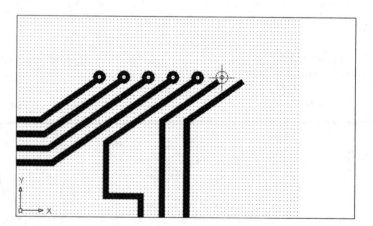

5. Press ⏎ to exit this process.

If you need to fill only a part of a circle, such as a pie slice, you can use the Donut command to draw a full, filled circle. Then use the Trim or Break option on the Modify toolbar to cut out the portion of the donut you don't need.

Toggling Solid Fills On and Off

After you have drawn a solid area with the Pline, Solid, Trace, or Donut command, you can control whether the solid area is actually displayed as filled in. Open the Options dialog box (choose Tools ➤ Options) and then click the Display tab. Locate the Display Performance group in the lower-right corner of the dialog box. The Apply Solid Fill option controls whether solid areas are displayed. If the Apply Solid Fill check box does not show a checkmark, thick polylines, solids, traces, and donuts appear as outlines of the solid areas (see Figure 18.29).

FIGURE 18.29
Two polylines with the Apply Solid Fill option turned on (top) and turned off (bottom)

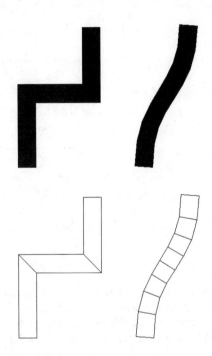

TIP   You can shorten regeneration and plotting time if solids are not filled in.

WARNING   If Regenauto is turned off, you have to issue the Regen command to display the effects of the Fill command.

The Apply Solid Fill option is an easy-to-remember way to control the display of solid fills. Or you can enter **Fill⏎** at the Command prompt; then, at the Enter Mode ON/OFF <ON>: prompt, enter your choice of **On** or **Off**.

If You Want to Experiment

There are many valuable uses for polylines beyond those covered in this chapter. I encourage you to become familiar with this unique object so you can take full advantage of AutoCAD.

To further explore the use of polylines, try the following exercise, illustrated in Figure 18.30. It will give you an opportunity to try some of the options discussed in this chapter that weren't included in exercises:

FIGURE 18.30

Drawing a simple plate with curved edges

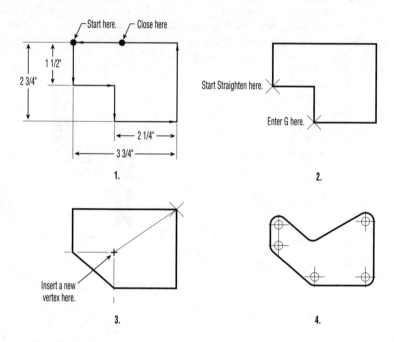

1.

2.

3.

4.

1. Open a new file called PART14. Set the Snap spacing to 0.25, and be sure that Snap mode is on. Use the Pline command to draw the object shown in step 1 of Figure 18.30. Draw it in the direction indicated by the arrows and start at the upper-left corner. Use the Close option to add the last line segment.

2. Start the Pedit command, select the polyline, and then type **E↵** to issue the Edit Vertex option. At the prompt

   ```
   [Next/Previous/Break/Insert/Move/Regen/Straighten/Tangent/ Width/eXit] <N>:
   ```

   press ↵ until the X mark moves to the first corner, shown in step 2 of Figure 18.30. Enter **S↵** for the Straighten option.

3. At the prompt

   ```
   Enter an option [Next/Previous/Go/eXit] <N>:
   ```

   press ↵ twice to move the X to the other corner shown in step 2 of Figure 18.30. Press **G** for Go to straighten the polyline between the two selected corners.

4. Press ↵ twice to move the X to the upper-right corner, and then enter **I**↵ for Insert. Pick a point as shown in step 3 of Figure 18.30. The polyline changes to reflect the new vertex. Enter **X**↵ to exit the Edit Vertex option, and then press ↵ to exit the Pedit command.

5. Start the Fillet command, use the Radius option to set the fillet radius to .30, and then use the Polyline option and pick the polyline you just edited. All the corners fillet to the .30 radius. Add the .15 radius circles as shown in step 4 of Figure 18.30 and exit the file with the End command.

Chapter 19

Getting and Exchanging Data from Drawings

AutoCAD drawings contain a wealth of data—graphic information such as distances and angles between objects, as well as precise areas and the properties of objects. But as you become more experienced with AutoCAD, you will also need data of a different nature. For example, as you begin to work in groups, the various settings in a drawing become important. You will need statistics on the amount of time you spend on a drawing when you are billing computer time. As your projects become more complex, file maintenance requires a greater degree of attention. To take full advantage of AutoCAD, you will want to exchange much of this data with other people and other programs.

In this chapter, you will explore the ways in which all types of data can be extracted from AutoCAD and made available to you, your coworkers, and other programs. First, you will learn how to obtain specific data about your drawings. Then you will look at ways to exchange data with other programs—such as word processors, desktop-publishing software, and even other CAD programs.

This chapter covers the following topics:

◆ Finding the Area of Closed Boundaries

◆ Getting General Information

◆ Using the DXF File Format to Exchange CAD Data with Other Programs

◆ Using AutoCAD Drawings in Desktop Publishing

◆ Combining Data from Different Sources

Finding the Area of Closed Boundaries

One of the most frequently sought pieces of data you can extract from an AutoCAD drawing is the area of a closed boundary. In architecture, you want to find the area of a room or the footprint of a building. In civil engineering, you want to determine the area covered by the boundary of a property line or the area of cut for a roadway. In this section, you'll learn how to use AutoCAD to obtain exact area information from your drawings.

TIP   To find absolute coordinates in a drawing, use the ID command. Choose Tools ➤ Inquiry ➤ ID Point or type **ID↵**. At the ID Point: prompt, use the Osnap overrides to pick a point, and its X, Y, and Z coordinates are displayed on the prompt line.

Finding the Area of an Object

Architects, engineers, and facilities planners often need to know the square footage of a room or a section of a building. A structural engineer might want to find the cross-sectional area of a beam. In this section, you will practice determining the areas of regular objects.

First, you will determine the square-foot area of the living room and entry of your studio unit plan:

1. Start AutoCAD. Open the Unit file you created earlier or use the 19a-unit.dwg file from the companion CD.

2. Enter **Blipmode⏎on⏎**. This turns on a marking feature that displays a tiny cross called a *blip* whenever you click in the drawing area. Blips do not print and can be cleared from the screen with a redraw. You'll use them to help keep track of your point selections in this exercise.

3. Zoom in to the living room and entry area so you have a view similar to Figure 19.1.

4. Choose Tools ➤ Inquiry ➤ Area or type **Area⏎** at the Command prompt.

TIP   You can also select the Area command from the Inquiry toolbar. Right-click any toolbar and choose Inquiry from the shortcut menu.

FIGURE 19.1
Selecting the points to determine the area of the living room and entry

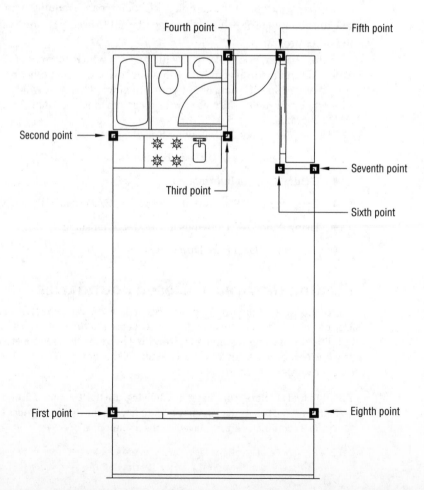

5. Using the Endpoint Osnap, start with the lower-left corner of the living room and select the points shown in Figure 19.1. You are indicating the boundary.

6. When you have come full circle to the eighth point shown in Figure 19.1, press ↵. You get the following message:

```
Area = 39570.00 square in. (274.7917 square ft), Perimeter = 76'-0"
```

7. Now turn off Blipmode by typing **Blipmode↵off↵**. Then choose View ➢ Redraw to clear the blips from the screen.

The number of points you can pick to define an area is limitless, so you can obtain the areas of very complex shapes. Use the Blipmode feature to keep track of the points you select so you know when you come to the beginning of the point selections.

Using Hatch Patterns to Find Areas

Hatch patterns are used primarily to add graphics to your drawing, but they can also serve as a means to finding areas. You can use any hatch pattern you want since you are only interested in the area it reports back to you. You can also set up a special layer devoted to area calculations and then assign the hatch patterns you use to find areas to this layer. That way, you can turn the hatch patterns off so they don't plot, or you can turn off the Plot setting for that layer to ensure that it doesn't appear in your final output.

To practice using hatch patterns to find an area, do the following:

1. Set the current layer to Floor.

2. Turn off the Door and Fixture layers. Also make sure the Ceiling layer is turned on. You want the hatch pattern to follow the interior wall outline, so you need to turn off any objects that will affect the outline, such as the door and kitchen.

3. Choose Draw ➢ Hatch or type **h↵** to open the Hatch And Gradient dialog box.

WARNING   If the area you're trying to measure has gaps, set the Gap Tolerance setting in the Hatch And Gradient dialog box to a value higher than the size of the gaps. If you don't see the Gap Tolerance setting, click the More Options button in the lower-right corner of the Hatch And Gradient dialog box.

4. Click the Add Pick Points button to close the dialog box.

5. At the `Pick internal point or [Select objects/remove Boundaries]:` prompt, click in the interior of the Unit plan. The outline of the interior is highlighted (see Figure 19.2).

6. Press↵; then in the Hatch And Gradient dialog box, click OK.

7. Choose Tools ➢ Inquiry ➢ Area again or type **Area↵** at the Command prompt. Then enter **O↵** for the Object option.

8. Click the hatch pattern you just created; when it is highlighted, press↵. Again you get the following message:

```
Area = 39570.00 square in. (274.7917 square ft), Perimeter = 76'-0"
```

TIP   If you need to recall the last area calculation value you received, enter ´**Setvar↵ Area↵**. The area is displayed in the prompt. Enter ´**Perimeter↵** to get the last perimeter calculated.

FIGURE 19.2

After you select a point on the interior of the plan by using the hatch pattern, an outline of the area is highlighted by a dotted line.

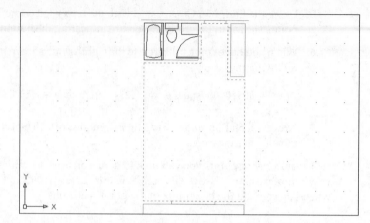

The Hatch command creates a hatch pattern that conforms to the boundary of an area. This feature, combined with the ability of the Area command to find the area of a hatch pattern, makes short work of area calculations. Another advantage to using hatch patterns is that, by default, hatch patterns avoid islands within the boundary whose area you are trying to find.

The area of a hatch pattern is also reported by the Properties palette. Select the hatch pattern whose area you want to find, and then click the Properties tool in the Standard toolbar. Scroll down to the bottom of the Geometry group, and you'll see the Area listing for the hatch pattern you selected. You can select more than one hatch pattern and find the cumulative area of the selected hatch patterns in the Properties palette.

Adding and Subtracting Areas with the Area Command

Hatch patterns work extremely well for finding areas, but if you find that, for some reason, you cannot use hatch patterns, you have another alternative. You can still use a command called Boundary to generate polyline outlines of enclosed boundaries and then obtain the area of the outline using the Area command. If islands are present within the boundary, you have to use the Subtract feature of the Area command to remove the area of the island from the overall boundary area. In this section, you'll use the example of the flange part, which contains two islands in the form of the two circles at the lower end (see Figure 19.3).

FIGURE 19.3

A flange to a mechanical device

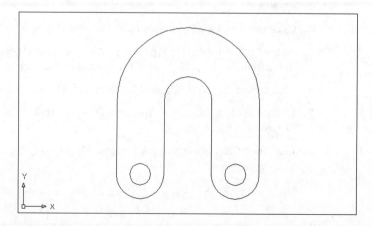

By using the Add and Subtract options of the Area command, you can maintain a running total of several separate areas being calculated. This gives you flexibility in finding areas of complex shapes. This section guides you through the use of these options.

For the following exercise, you will use a flange shape that contains circles. This shape is composed of simple arcs, lines, and circles. Use these steps to see how you can keep a running tally of areas:

1. Exit the Unit file and open the file Flange.dwg from the companion CD (see Figure 19.3). Don't bother to save changes in the Unit file.

2. Choose Draw ➢ Boundary to open the Boundary Creation dialog box.

3. Click Pick Points.

4. Click in the interior of the flange shape. Notice that the entire shape is highlighted, including the circle islands.

5. Press ↵. You now have a polyline outline of the shape, though it won't be obvious that polylines have been created since they are drawn over the boundary objects.

6. Now let's continue by using the Area command's Add and Subtract options. Choose Tools ➢ Inquiry ➢ Area.

7. Type A↵ to enter the Add mode, and then type O↵ to select an object.

8. Click a vertical edge of the flange outline. You see the following message:

```
Area = 27.7080, Perimeter = 30.8496
Total area = 27.7080
```

9. Press ↵ to exit the Add mode.

10. Type S↵ to enter the Subtract mode, and then type O↵ to select an object.

11. Click one of the circles. You see the following message:

```
Area = 0.6070, Perimeter = 2.7618
Total area = 27.1010
```

This shows you the area and perimeter of the selected object and a running count of the total area of the flange outline minus the circle.

12. Click the other circle. You see the following message:

```
Area = 0.6070, Perimeter = 2.7618
Total area = 26.4940
```

Again, you see a listing of the area and perimeter of the selected object along with a running count of the total area, which now shows a value of 26.4940. This last value is the true area of the flange.

13. Press ↵ twice to exit the Area command.

In this exercise, you first selected the main object outline and then subtracted the island objects. You don't have to follow this order; you can start by subtracting areas to get negative area values and then add other areas to come up with a total. You can also alternate between Add and Subtract modes, in case you forget to add or subtract areas.

You might have noticed that the Area Command prompt offered Specify first corner point or [Object/Add/Subtract]: as the default option for both the Add and Subtract modes. Instead of using the Object option to pick the circles, you can start selecting points to indicate a rectangular area, as you did in the first exercise of this chapter.

Whenever you press ↵ while selecting points for an area calculation, AutoCAD automatically connects the first and last points and returns the calculated area. If you are in the Add or Subtract mode, you can then continue to select points, but the additional areas are calculated from the *next* point you pick.

As you can see from these exercises, it is simpler to first outline an area with a polyline, wherever possible, and then use the Object option to add and subtract area values of polylines.

In this example, you obtained the area of a mechanical object. However, the same process works for any type of area you want to calculate. It can be the area of a piece of property on a topographical map or the area of a floor plan. For example, you can use the Object option to find an irregular area such as the one shown in Figure 19.4, as long as it is a polyline.

FIGURE 19.4
The site plan with an area to be calculated

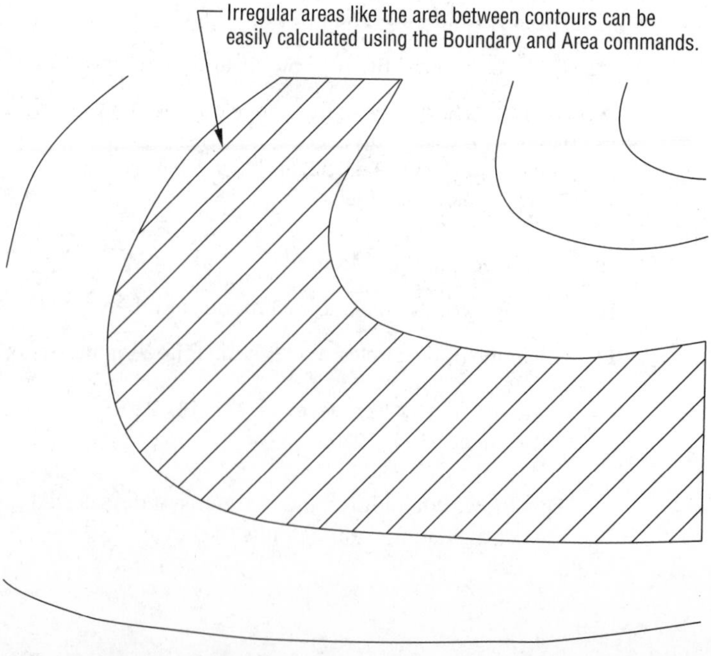

Irregular areas like the area between contours can be easily calculated using the Boundary and Area commands.

RECORDING AREA DATA IN A DRAWING FILE

After you find the area of an object, you'll often need to record it somewhere. You can write it down in a project logbook, but this is easy to overlook. A more dependable way to store area information is to use *attributes*.

Consider the following example: In a building project, you can create a block that contains attributes for the room number, room area, and the date when the room area was last measured. You might make the area and date attributes invisible, so only the room number appears. You can then insert this block into every room. After you find the area, you can easily add it to your block attribute with the Ddatte command. In fact, you can use such a block with any drawing in which you want to store area data. See Chapter 13 for more on attributes.

Getting General Information

So far in this book, you've seen how to get data about the geometry of your drawings. AutoCAD also includes a set of tools that you can use to access the general state of your drawings. You can gather information about the status of current settings in a file or the time at which a drawing was created and last edited.

In this section, you will practice extracting this type of information from your drawing, using the tools found in the Tools ➢ Inquiry option's cascading menu.

Determining the Drawing's Status

When you work with a group of people on a large project, keeping track of a drawing's setup becomes crucial. You can use the Status command to obtain some general information about the drawing you are working on, such as the base point, current mode settings, and workspace or computer memory use. The Status command is especially helpful when you are editing a drawing someone else has worked on, because you might want to identify and change settings for your own style of working. Choosing Tools ➢ Inquiry ➢ Status displays a list like the one shown in Figure 19.5.

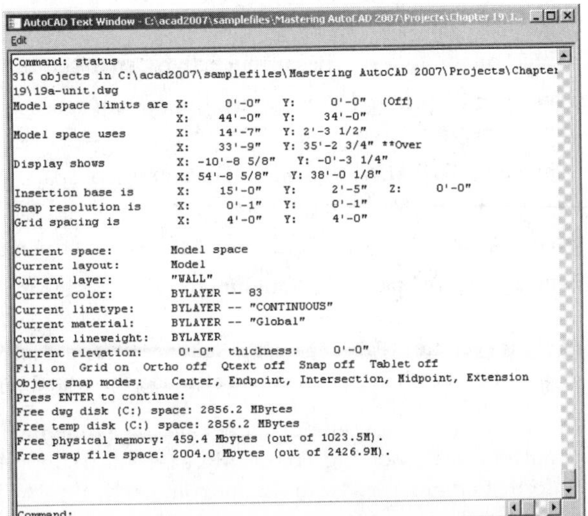

FIGURE 19.5

The Status screen of the AutoCAD Text Window

TIP If you have problems editing a file created by someone else, the difficulty can often be attributed to a new or different setting you are not used to working with. If AutoCAD is acting in an unusual way, use the Status command to get a quick glimpse of the file settings before you start calling for help.

Here is a brief description of each item on the Status screen. Note that some of the items you see on the screen will vary somewhat from what I've shown here, but the information applies to virtually all situations except where noted.

(*Number*) Objects In *Drive:\Folder\Subfolder\Name.dwg* The number of entities or objects in the drawing.

Model Space Limits Are The coordinates of the Model Space limits. Also indicates whether limits are turned off or on. (See Chapter 3 for more details on limits.)

Model Space Uses The area the drawing occupies; equivalent to the extents of the drawing.

**Over If present, this item means that part of the drawing is outside the limit boundary.

Display Shows The area covered by the current view.

Insertion Base Is, Snap Resolution Is, and Grid Spacing Is The current default values for these mode settings.

Current Space Model Space or Paper Space.

Current Layout The current tab.

Current Layer The current layer.

Current Color The color assigned to new objects.

Current Linetype The linetype assigned to new objects.

Current Material The material assigned to new objects.

Current Lineweight The current default Lineweight setting.

Current Elevation/Thickness The current default Z coordinate for new objects, plus the default thickness of objects; these are both 3D-related settings. (See Chapter 20 for details.)

Fill, Grid, Ortho, Qtext, Snap, and Tablet The status of these options.

Object Snap Modes The current active Osnap setting.

Free Dwg Disk (*Drive:*) Space The amount of space available to store drawing-specific temporary files.

Free Temp Disk (*Drive:*) Space The amount of space left on your hard drive for AutoCAD's resource temporary files.

Free Physical Memory The amount of free RAM available.

Free Swap File Space The amount of Windows swap file space available.

TIP When you are in Paper Space, the Status command displays information regarding the Paper Space limits. See Chapter 16 for more on Model Space and Paper Space.

In addition to being useful in understanding a drawing file, the Status command is an invaluable tool for troubleshooting. Frequently, a technical support person can isolate problems by using the information provided by the Status command.

TIP For more information on memory use, see Appendix B.

Keeping Track of Time

The Time command enables you to keep track of the time spent on a drawing, for billing or analysis purposes. You can also use the Time command to check the current time and find out when the drawing was created and most recently edited. Because the AutoCAD timer uses your computer's time, be sure the time is set correctly in Windows.

To access the Time command, enter **Time.**⏎ at the Command prompt or choose Tools ➢ Inquiry ➢ Time. You get a message like the one in Figure 19.6.

FIGURE 19.6

The Time screen in the AutoCAD Text Window

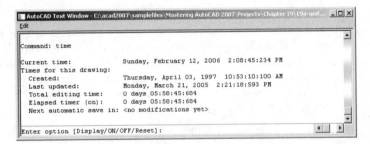

The first four lines of this message tell you the current date and time, the date and time the drawing was created, and the last time the drawing was saved or ended.

The fifth line shows the total time spent on the drawing from the point at which the file was opened. This elapsed timer lets you time a particular activity, such as changing the width of all the walls in a floor plan or redesigning a piece of machinery. The last line tells you when the next automatic save will be.

You can turn the elapsed timer on or off or reset it by entering **ON**, **OFF**, or **Reset** at the prompt shown at the bottom of the message. Or press ⏎ to exit the Time command.

Getting Information from System Variables

If you've been working through this book's ongoing studio apartment building tutorial, you'll have noticed occasional mentions of a *system variable* in conjunction with a command. You can check the status or change the setting of any system variable while you are in the middle of another command. To do this, you simply type an apostrophe (´), followed by the name of the system variable, at the Command prompt.

For example, if you start to draw a line and suddenly decide you need to rotate your cursor 45°, you can do the following:

1. At the Specify next point or [Undo]: prompt, enter ´**snapang.**

2. At the Enter new value for SNAPANG <0>: prompt, enter a new cursor angle. You are returned to the Line command with the cursor in its new orientation.

You can also recall information such as the last area or distance calculated by AutoCAD. Because the Area system variable duplicates the name of the Area command, you need to choose Tools ➢ Inquiry ➢ Set Variable and then type **Area.**⏎ to read the last area calculation. You can also type ´**Setvar.**⏎**Area.**⏎. The Tools ➢ Inquiry ➢ Set Variable option also lets you list all the system variables and their status, as well as access each system variable individually by entering a question mark (**?**). You can then indicate which variables to list using wildcard characters such as the asterisk or question mark. For example, you can enter **g*** to list all the system variables that start with the letter G.

Many of the system variables give you direct access to detailed information about your drawing. They also let you fine-tune your drawing and editing activities. In Appendix C you'll find all the information you need to familiarize yourself with the system variables. Don't feel that you have to memorize them all at once; just be aware that they are available.

TIP Many of the dialog box options you have been using throughout this book, such as the options in the Options dialog box, are actually system variable settings.

Keeping a Log of Your Activity

At times you might find it helpful to keep a log of your activity in an AutoCAD session. A *log* is a text file containing a record of your activities. It can also contain notes to yourself or others about how a drawing is set up. Such a log can help you determine how frequently you use a particular command, or it can help you construct a macro for a commonly used sequence of commands.

The following exercise demonstrates how to save and view a detailed record of an AutoCAD session by using the Log feature:

1. Choose Tools ➢ Options to open the Options dialog box. Click the Open And Save tab. A new set of options appears.

TIP As a shortcut, you can quickly turn the Maintain A Log File feature on and off by typing **Log-fileon**↵ and **Logfileoff**↵ at the Command prompt.

2. In the File Safety Precautions group, click the Maintain A Log File check box and then click OK.

3. Choose Tools ➢ Inquiry ➢ Status.

4. Return to the Open And Save tab of the Options dialog box, and turn off the Maintain A Log File option.

5. Click OK to exit the dialog box.

6. Switch to Windows and start the Notepad application or any text editor.

7. With the text editor, open the log file whose name starts with Flange in the folder listed here:

   ```
   C:\Documents and Settings\User Name\Local Settings\Application
   Data\Autodesk\AutoCAD 2007\R17\enu\
   ```

   This file stores the text data from the Command prompt whenever the Log File option is turned on. You must turn off the Log File option before you can actually view this file. When attempting to view the log file using the Windows Notepad, make sure you set the File Of Type in the Notepad Open dialog box to All Files.

As you can see in step 7, the log file is given the name of the drawing file from which the log is derived, with some additional numeric values. Since the Flange log file is a standard text file, you can easily send it to other members of your workgroup or print it for a permanent record.

TIP   If you cannot find the log file for the current drawing, you can enter **logfilename.**⏎ at the Command prompt, and AutoCAD will display the filename including the full path. If you want to change the default location for the log file, open the Options dialog box and click the Files tab. Click the plus sign to the left of the Log File Location option in the list box. A listing appears showing you where the drawing log file is stored. You can then modify this setting to indicate a new location. LT users enter **Modemacro.**⏎ and then **$(getvar, logfilepath)**.

Capturing and Saving Text Data from the AutoCAD Text Window

If you are working in groups, it is often quite helpful to have a record of the status, editing time, and system variables for particular files readily available to other group members. It is also convenient to keep records of block and layer information, so you can see whether a specific block is included in a drawing or what layers are normally on or off.

You can use the Windows Clipboard to capture and save such data from the AutoCAD Text Window. The following steps show you how it's done:

1. Move the arrow cursor to the Command prompt at the bottom of the AutoCAD Text Window.

2. Right-click and choose Copy History from the shortcut menu to copy the contents of the AutoCAD Text Window to the Clipboard.

If you want to copy only a portion of the AutoCAD Text Window to the Clipboard, perform the following steps:

1. Press the F2 function key to open the AutoCAD Text Window.

2. Using the I-beam text cursor, highlight the text you want to copy to the Clipboard.

3. Right-click and then choose Copy from the shortcut menu. You can also choose Edit ➤ Copy from the AutoCAD Text Window's menu bar. The highlighted text is copied to the Clipboard.

4. Open Notepad or another text-editing application and paste the information.

Although you used the AutoCAD Text Window to copy text in this exercise, you can also copy from the docked command line at the bottom of the AutoCAD window.

You might notice four other options on the shortcut menu: Recent Commands, Paste, Paste To CmdLine, and Options. Choosing Recent Commands displays a list of the most recent commands. For most activities, you'll use a handful of commands repeatedly. The Recent Commands option can save you time by giving you a shortcut to those commands you use the most. The Paste options paste the first line of the contents of the Clipboard into the command line or input box of a dialog box. This can be useful for entering repetitive text or for storing and retrieving a frequently used command. Choosing Options opens the Options dialog box.

TIP   Items copied to the Clipboard from the AutoCAD Text Window can be pasted into dialog box input boxes. This can be a quick way to transfer layers, linetypes, or other named items from the AutoCAD Text Window into dialog boxes. You can even paste text into the drawing area.

Storing Searchable Information in AutoCAD Files

As you start to build a library of AutoCAD files, you'll have to start thinking about how to manage those files. Keeping track of AutoCAD files can be a daunting task. Most AutoCAD users start to name files by their job number to keep things organized. But even the best organization schemes don't help if you need to find that one special file among thousands of files in your library. In this section, you'll learn how to include information in an AutoCAD file that you can use later to locate the file by using the Windows Search utility.

TIP   AutoCAD includes the DesignCenter, a tool that can help you locate a file more easily based on a keyword or description. Chapter 27 contains a complete discussion of the DesignCenter.

To add general information about your drawing file that is searchable, use the drawing Properties dialog box (choose File ➢ Drawing Properties).

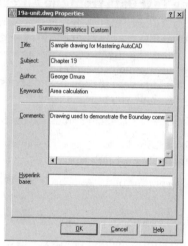

Here's a description of the four tabs in this dialog box:

General   The General tab gives you general information about the file. This information is similar to what you would see if you use the Properties options in Windows Explorer to view the properties of a file.

Summary   In the Summary tab, enter any text in the Title, Subject, Author, and Keywords fields that is appropriate to the drawing. The information you enter here is stored with the drawing and can be used to locate the file through the AutoCAD DesignCenter or the Windows Search utility (choose Start ➢ Search).

In addition, you can enter a base location for hyperlinks that are applied to objects in your drawing. This base location can be a folder on your computer or network or an Internet web address. See Chapter 27 for more information on hyperlinks.

Statistics   The Statistics tab contains the Windows username of the person who last saved the drawing, as well as the time spent on the file. This is the login name at the beginning of the Windows session.

Custom   The Custom tab contains two columns of input boxes. This tab lets you store additional custom data with the drawing that is also searchable. For example, you might enter **Job Number** in the Name column and then enter **9901** in the Value column. You might also include information such as project manager names, consultants, or revision numbers. You can then locate the file by using the AutoCAD DesignCenter or the Windows Search utility by doing a search for those keywords from the Name and Value columns.

Searching for AutoCAD Files

After you've included information in the Properties dialog box of a file, you can use the AutoCAD DesignCenter, the File dialog box, or the Windows Search function to locate your file.

A Find option is also located in the Tools menu in the upper-right corner of the AutoCAD Select File dialog box. To access it, choose File ➤ Open, and then in the Select File dialog box, choose Tools ➤ Find in the upper-right corner.

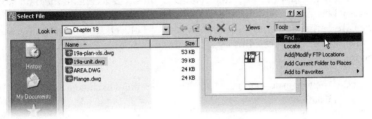

This option opens a Find dialog box that works just like the Windows XP Search Results window.

Recovering Corrupted Files

No system is perfect. Eventually, you will encounter a file that is corrupted in some way. Two AutoCAD tools can frequently salvage a corrupted file:

Audit   Enables you to check a file that you can open but suspect has some problem. Audit checks the currently opened file for any errors and displays the results in the AutoCAD Text Window.

Recover   Enables you to open a file that is so badly corrupted that AutoCAD is unable to open it in a normal way. A Select File dialog box appears, enabling you to select a file for recovery. After you select a file, it is opened and checked for errors.

You can access these tools from the File ➤ Drawing Utilities cascading menu. More often than not, these tools will do the job, although they aren't a panacea for all file-corruption problems. In the event that you cannot recover a file even with these tools, make sure your computer is running smoothly and that other systems are not faulty.

If for some reason, your computer shuts down while you're in the middle of editing a file, you will see the File Recovery Manager the next time you start AutoCAD. The Drawing Recovery Manager lets you recover the file you had been working on when AutoCAD unexpectedly shut down. This feature works just like the file recovery feature in Microsoft Office where a panel appears to the left of the AutoCAD Text Window showing you a list of recoverable files. You can then select the filename from the panel to open it. You can always get to the File Recovery Manager by choosing File ➤ Drawing Utilities ➤ Ddrawing Recovery Manager.

Using the DXF File Format to Exchange CAD Data with Other Programs

AutoCAD offers many ways to share data with other programs. Perhaps the most common type of data exchange is simply to share drawing data with other CAD programs. In this section, you'll see how to export and import CAD drawings using the DXF file format.

A *DXF (Drawing Exchange Format) file* is a plain-text file that contains all the information needed to reconstruct a drawing. It is often used to exchange drawings created with other programs. Many CAD and technical drawing programs, including some 3D perspective programs, can generate or read files in DXF format. You might want to use a 3D program to view your drawing in a Perspective view, or you might have a consultant who uses a different CAD program that accepts DXF files.

Be aware that not all programs that read DXF files will accept all the data stored therein. Many programs that claim to read DXF files will "throw away" much of the DXF file's information. Attributes are perhaps the most commonly ignored objects, followed by many of the 3D objects, such as meshes and 3D Faces. But DXF files, though not the perfect medium for translating data, have become something of a standard.

TIP AutoCAD no longer supports the IGES (Initial Graphics Exchange Specification) standard for CAD data translation.

Exporting DXF Files

To export your current drawing as a DXF file, follow these steps:

1. Choose File ➢ Save As to open the Save Drawing As dialog box.

2. Click the Files Of Type drop-down list. You can export your drawing under a number of formats, including three DXF formats.

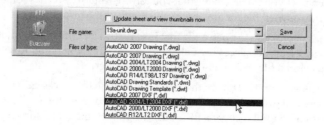

3. Select the appropriate DXF format and then enter a name for your file. You do not have to include the .dxf filename extension.

4. Select a folder for the file and then click Save.

In step 2, you can select from the following DXF file formats:

◆ AutoCAD 2007 DXF

◆ AutoCAD 2004/LT 2004 DXF

◆ AutoCAD 2000/LT 2000 DXF

◆ AutoCAD R12/LT2 DXF

Choose the format appropriate to the program you are exporting to. In most cases, the safest choice is AutoCAD R12/LT2 DXF if you are exporting to another CAD program, though AutoCAD will not maintain the complete functionality of AutoCAD 2007 for such files.

After you've selected a DXF format from the Files Of Type drop-down list, you can set more detailed specifications by choosing Tools ➢ Options in the upper-right corner of the Save Drawing As dialog box. Doing so opens the Saveas Options dialog box. For DXF files, select the DXF Options tab.

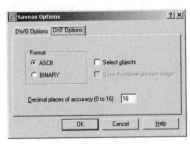

The DXF Options tab contains the following options:

Format   Lets you choose between ASCII (plain text) or binary file formats. Most other programs accept ASCII, so it is the safest choice. Some programs accept binary DXF files, which have the advantage of being more compact than the ASCII format.

Select Objects   Lets you select specific objects within the drawing for export. You can select objects after you close the Saveas Options dialog box and choose Save from the Save Drawing As dialog box.

Decimal Places Of Accuracy (0–16)   Enables you to determine the accuracy of the exported file. Keeping this value low helps reduce the size of the export file, particularly if it is to be in ASCII format. Some CAD programs do not support the high accuracy of AutoCAD, so using a high value here might have no significance.

TIP   You can also type **Dxfout.⏎** at the Command prompt to open the Create DXF File dialog box. This is a standard Windows file dialog box that includes the Options button described here.

Opening or Importing DXF Files

Some offices have made the DXF file format their standard for CAD drawings. This is most commonly seen in offices that use a variety of CAD software besides AutoCAD.

AutoCAD can be set up to read and write DXF files by default, instead of the standard DWG file format. Here's how it's done:

1. Choose Tools ➢ Options to open the Options dialog box.

2. Select the Open And Save tab.

3. In the File Save group, select any of the DXF formats from the Save As drop-down list.

4. Click OK.

After you do this, all your drawings are automatically saved in the DXF format of your choice.

You can also set the default AutoCAD file type by clicking the Options button in the Save Drawing As dialog box. As you saw in an earlier section, the Saveas Options dialog box includes the DWG Options tab. You can select a default file type from the Save All Drawings As drop-down list.

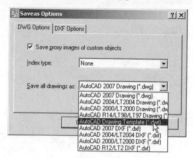

If you need to open a DXF file only once in a while, you can do so by selecting DXF from the Files Of Type drop-down list in the Select File dialog box. This is the dialog box you see when you choose File ➤ Open. You can also use the Dxfin command.

1. Type **Dxfin**↵ at the Command prompt to open the Select File dialog box.

2. Locate and select the DXF file you want to import.

3. Double-click the filename. If the drawing is large, the import might take several minutes to open.

If you want to import a DXF file into the current drawing, you can use the Insert dialog box (choose Insert ➤ Block). Click the Browse button to locate and select a file. Make sure the Files Of Type option is set to DXF.

Using AutoCAD Drawings in Desktop Publishing

As you probably know, AutoCAD is a natural for creating line art, and because of its popularity, most desktop-publishing programs are designed to import AutoCAD drawings in one form or another. Those of you who employ desktop-publishing software to generate user manuals or other technical documents will probably want to use AutoCAD drawings in your work. In this section, you'll examine ways to output AutoCAD drawings to formats that most desktop-publishing programs can accept.

You can export AutoCAD files to desktop-publishing formats in two ways: by using raster export and by using vector file export.

Exporting Raster Files

In some cases, you might need only a rough image of your AutoCAD drawing. You can export your drawing as a raster file that can be read in virtually any desktop-publishing and word-processing program. To do this, you must create a new plotter configuration that plots to an image file instead of an output device. (Chapter 8 describes how to use the Add-A-Plotter Wizard to add a plotter configuration to AutoCAD.)

Here is some additional information on how to use that wizard to set up AutoCAD for raster file output:

1. Start the Add-A-Plotter Wizard, and then choose Next at the Introduction screen.

2. On the Begin screen of the Add-A-Plotter Wizard, choose My Computer.

3. On the Plotter Model screen, select Raster File Formats from the Manufacturers list, and then select the type of raster file you want to use from the Models list. For example, you can choose Independent JPEG Group JFIF (JPEG Compression). This is one of the more universal file types. Click Next when you've made your selection.

4. Skip the Import PCP or PC2 screen and the Ports screen.

5. Enter a name for your raster output settings on the Plotter Name screen.

6. On the Finish screen, click the Edit Plotter Configuration button to open the Plotter Configuration Editor dialog box.

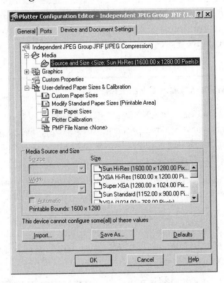

7. Click the Source And Size listing that appears in the large list box in the top of the dialog box. A list of options appears in the Size list box in the lower-right corner of the dialog box.

8. Click Custom Paper Sizes from the large list box at the top of the dialog box. The options change in the lower half of the dialog box.

9. Click the Add button to start the Custom Paper Size Wizard.

10. Click the Start From Scratch radio button, and then click Next to open the Media Bounds screen.

11. Enter a height and width in pixels for your image file, and then click Next to open the Paper Size Name screen. Enter a name that best describes the size of the image file, and then click Next to open the File Name screen.

12. Enter a name for the Plotter Model Parameters file. This file stores specific setting information about the plotter. Click Next when you are finished.

13. On the Finish screen, click Finish. The Plotter Configuration Editor dialog box reappears. Click OK, and then click Finish in the Add-A-Plotter Wizard.

After you've finished creating a plotter configuration, it appears as a file in the \R17.0\enu\ Plotters subfolder of the AutoCAD 2007 folder. You can access this file through Windows Explorer or from AutoCAD by choosing File ➤ Plotter Manager.

To create a raster file version of your drawing, choose File ➤ Plot, and then in the Plot dialog box select your raster file plotter configuration from the Name drop-down list of the Printer/Plotter group. You can then proceed to plot your drawing, but instead of paper output, you'll get a raster file. You can specify the filename and location when you click the OK button to plot the file.

If you need to make changes to your raster file configuration, choose File ➤ Plotter Manager, and then in the Plotters window, double-click your raster file configuration file. You will see the same Plotter Configuration Editor you used to set up the raster plotter configuration.

You can set up a different plotter configuration for each type of raster file you use. You can also set up plotter configurations for different resolutions, if you choose. To learn more about plotting in general, see Chapter 8. Appendix B provides detailed information on the Plotter Configuration Editor.

EXCHANGING FILES WITH EARLIER RELEASES

One persistent dilemma that has plagued AutoCAD users is how to exchange files between earlier versions of the program. In the past, if you upgraded AutoCAD, you were locked out from exchanging your drawings with people using earlier versions. Release 12 alleviated this difficulty by making Release 12 files compatible with Release 11 files.

With Release 13, the file structure was radically different from earlier versions of AutoCAD. Then AutoCAD 14 made it possible to freely exchange files between Release 13 and 14.

AutoCAD 2002 uses the AutoCAD 2000 file format, which has some features, such as multiple layouts and searchable properties, that do not translate to earlier versions. AutoCAD 2006 shares the same file format with AutoCAD 2004, but has some new features that make it incompatible with AutoCAD 2000 and 2002. AutoCAD 2007 also uses a unique file format that is not compatible with earlier versions.

If compatibility with earlier versions is more important than the new features of AutoCAD 2007, you can set up AutoCAD 2007 to read and write to AutoCAD 2006 or earlier. Or if you're willing to work with DXF files, you can set up AutoCAD 2007 to automatically write AutoCAD 2006 DXF files.

To set up AutoCAD to automatically write earlier versions, use the Options dialog box to set the default file type, as described earlier in the "Opening or Importing DXF Files" section, but instead of selecting a DXF file type, select the DWG file type you want to use.

Exporting Vector Files

If you need to preserve the accuracy of your drawing, or if you want to take advantage of TrueType or PostScript fonts, you can use either the DXF, WMF, or PostScript vector formats.

For vector format files, DXF is the easiest to work with, and with TrueType support, DXF can preserve font information between AutoCAD and desktop-publishing programs that support the DXF format. The WMF (Windows Metafile) format is also a commonly accepted file format for vector information, and it preserves TrueType fonts and line weights that are used in your drawings.

PostScript is a raster/vector hybrid file format that AutoCAD supports; unfortunately, AutoCAD dropped direct PostScript font support with Release 14. However, you can still use substitute fonts to stand in for PostScript fonts. These substitute fonts are converted to true PostScript fonts when AutoCAD exports the drawing. You won't see the true results of your PostScript output until you actually print your drawing on a PostScript printer.

The DXF file export was covered in the previous section of this chapter, so this section will concentrate on the WMF and PostScript file formats.

TIP If you are a circuit board designer or drafter, you might want to use the PostScript Out option to send your layout to PostScript typesetting devices. This saves time and reduces file size because the PostScript Out option converts AutoCAD entities into true PostScript descriptions.

WMF Output

The Windows Metafile (WMF) file type is one of the more popular vector file formats in Windows. It can be opened and edited by most illustration programs, including CorelDRAW and Adobe Illustrator. Most word-processing, database, and worksheet programs can also import WMF files. It's a great option for AutoCAD file export because it preserves TrueType fonts and line weight settings; you can export WMF files that preserve line weights as well.

To export WMF files, do the following:

1. Choose File ➤ Export to open the Export Data dialog box.

2. Enter a name and location for your WMF file, select Metafile (*.wmf) from the File Of Type drop down list, and then click OK. The dialog box closes, and you are prompted to select objects.

3. Select the objects you want to export to the WMF file and press ↵. The objects are saved to your WMF file.

PostScript Output

AutoCAD can export to the Encapsulated PostScript file format (EPS). If you are using AutoCAD 2007, you can obtain PostScript output in two ways: you can choose File ➤ Export, or you can enter **Psout**↵ at the command prompt. Another method is to install a PostScript printer driver and plot your drawing to an EPS file. LT users cannot export to EPS by choosing File ➤ Export. You must set up a PostScript plotter and use it to plot to a file.

To set up AutoCAD to plot your drawing to an EPS file, follow the steps described in the "Exporting Raster Files" section earlier in this chapter, but in step 2, select Adobe from the Manufacturers list and then select the appropriate PostScript level from the Models list.

WARNING AutoCAD does not preserve font information when creating EPS files from the printer option. It also produces larger files, especially if your drawing contains a lot of area fills and filled fonts.

PostScript Font Substitution

I mentioned earlier that AutoCAD substitutes its own fonts for PostScript fonts when you use the Export Data dialog box to export a file to an EPS file. If your work involves PostScript output, you will want to know these font names in order to make the appropriate substitution. Table 19.1 shows a list of AutoCAD font names and their equivalent PostScript names.

To take advantage of AutoCAD's ability to translate fonts, you need to create AutoCAD fonts that have the names listed in the first column of Table 19.1. You then need to use those fonts when creating text styles in AutoCAD. AutoCAD then converts the AutoCAD fonts into the corresponding PostScript fonts.

Creating the AutoCAD fonts can be simply a matter of copying and renaming existing fonts to those listed in Table 19.1. For example, you can make a copy of the Romans.shx font and name it Agd.shx. Better yet, if you have the PostScript PFB file of the font, you can compile it into an

AutoCAD font file and rename the compiled file appropriately. By compiling the PFB file, you get a close approximation of its appearance in AutoCAD. See Chapter 10 for a description of how to compile PostScript fonts.

TABLE 19.1: A Partial List of AutoCAD Font Filenames and Their Corresponding PostScript Fonts

AutoCAD Font Name	PostScript Font Name	AutoCAD Font Name	PostScript Font Name
agd	AvantGarde-Demi	agdo	AvantGarde-DemiOblique
agw	AvantGarde-Book	agwo	AvantGarde-BookOblique
bdps	Bodoni-Poster	bkd	Bookman-Demi
bkdi	Bookman-DemiItalic	bkl	Bookman-Light
bkli	Bookman-LightItalic	c	Cottonwood
cibt	CityBlueprint	cob	Courier-Bold
cobo	Courier-BoldOblique	cobt	CountryBlueprint
com	Courier	coo	Courier-Oblique
eur	EuroRoman	euro	EuroRoman-Oblique
fs	FreestyleScript	ho	Hobo
hv	Helvetica	hvb	Helvetica-Bold
hvbo	Helvetica-BoldOblique	hvn	Helvetica-Narrow
hvnb	Helvetica-Narrow-Bold	hvnbo	Helvetica-Narrow-BoldOblique
hvno	Helvetica-Narrow-Oblique	hvo	Helvetica-Oblique
lx	Linotext	ncb	NewCenturySchlbk-Bold
ncbi	NewCenturySchlbk-BoldItalic	nci	NewCenturySchlbk-Italic
ncr	NewCenturySchlbk-Roman	par	PanRoman
pob	Palatino-Bold	pobi	Palatino-BoldItalic
poi	Palatino-Italic	por	Palatino-Roman
rom	Romantic	romb	Romantic-Bold
romi	Romantic-Italic	sas	SansSerif
sasb	SansSerif-Bold	sasbo	SansSerif-BoldOblique

TABLE 19.1: A Partial List of AutoCAD Font Filenames and Their Corresponding PostScript Fonts *(CONTINUED)*

AUTOCAD FONT NAME	POSTSCRIPT FONT NAME	AUTOCAD FONT NAME	POSTSCRIPT FONT NAME
saso	SansSerif-Oblique	suf	SuperFrench
sy	Symbol	te	Technic
teb	Technic-Bold	tel	Technic-Light
tib	Times-Bold	tibi	Times-BoldItalic
tii	Times-Italic	tir	Times-Roman
tjrg	Trajan-Regular	vrb	VAGRounded-Bold
zcmi	ZapfChancery-MediumItalic	zd	ZapfDingbats

If you are using PostScript fonts not listed in Table 19.1, you can add your own AutoCAD-to-PostScript substitution by editing the Acad.psf file. This is a plain-text file that contains the font substitution information as well as other PostScript translation data.

TIP The HPGL plot file format is another vector format you can use to export your AutoCAD drawings. Use the method described earlier in the section "Exporting Raster Files" to add the HPGL plotter driver to your printer/plotter configuration.

USING AUTOCAD DWF FILES

The Autodesk DWF file format is another format you can use to exchange drawing data with others. It offers features that are geared toward AutoCAD users. You can import DXF files as external references and using a free DWF viewer, you can gather information about a drawing such as block information, attribute data, and distance measurements. See Chapter 27 for more on DWF.

Combining Data from Different Sources

Imagine being able to import and display worksheet data in an AutoCAD drawing. Further imagine that you can easily update that worksheet data, either directly from within the drawing or remotely by editing the source worksheet document. With a little help from a Windows feature called Object Linking and Embedding (OLE), such a scenario is within your grasp. The data is not limited to worksheets; it can be a word-processed document, a database report, or even a sound or video clip.

To import data from other applications, you use the Cut and Paste features found in virtually all Windows programs. You cut the data from the source document and then paste it into AutoCAD.

When you paste data into your AutoCAD file, you can link it to the source file or you can embed it. If you *link* it to the source file, the pasted data is updated whenever the source file is modified.

This is similar to an AutoCAD cross-referenced file. (See Chapter 15 for more on cross-referenced files.) If you *embed* data, you are pasting it into AutoCAD without linking it. You can still open the application associated with the data by double-clicking it, but the data is no longer associated with the source file. This is similar to a drawing inserted as a block; changes in the source drawing file have no effect on the inserted block.

Using OLE to Link a Worksheet to AutoCAD

Let's see firsthand how OLE works. The following exercise shows how to link an Excel worksheet to AutoCAD. You will need a copy of Microsoft Excel 2002 or later, but if you have another application that supports OLE, you can follow along.

Follow these steps:

1. Open the file called 19a-plan-xls.dwg from the companion CD. This is a copy of the plan you might have created in earlier exercises.

2. Open the Excel worksheet called 19a-plan.xls, also from the companion CD. You may see a security warning in Excel because the file contains macros. Go ahead and enable the macros for this file.

3. In Excel, highlight the door data, as shown in Figure 19.7, by clicking cell A1 and dragging to cell G17.

4. Choose Edit ➢ Copy to place a copy of the selected data into the Windows Clipboard.

5. Switch to AutoCAD, either by clicking a visible portion of the AutoCAD window or by clicking the AutoCAD button in the Taskbar at the bottom of the Windows Desktop. You can also press Alt+Tab.

6. Choose Edit ➢ Paste Special to open the Paste Special dialog box.

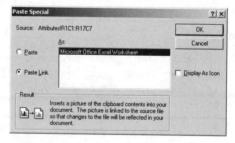

7. Click the Paste Link radio button to tell AutoCAD that you want this paste to be a link. Notice that the list of source types changes to show only one option: Microsoft Office Excel Worksheet.

8. Click OK. You are prompted to select an insertion point.

9. Click a point just above the UCS icon in the lower-left corner of the drawing. The worksheet data appears in the drawing, though it is so small that it appears as a dot (see Figure 19.8).

FIGURE 19.7

The Excel worksheet

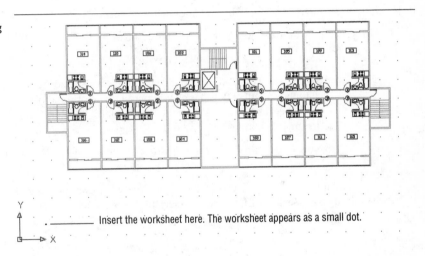

	A	B	C	D	E	F	G	H	I	J	K
1	D-TYPE	D-SIZE	D-NUMBER	D-THICK	D-RATE	D-MATRL	D-CONST				
2	B	3'-0"	116	1 3/4"	20 min.	Wood	Solid Core				
3	B	3'-0"	114	1 3/4"	20 min.	Wood	Solid Core				
4	B	3'-0"	112	1 3/4"	20 min.	Wood	Solid Core				
5	B	3'-0"	110	1 3/4"	20 min.	Wood	Solid Core				
6	B	3'-0"	106	1 3/4"	20 min.	Wood	Solid Core				
7	B	3'-0"	108	1 3/4"	20 min.	Wood	Solid Core				
8	B	3'-0"	102	1 3/4"	20 min.	Wood	Solid Core				
9	B	3'-0"	104	1 3/4"	20 min.	Wood	Solid Core				
10	B	3'-0"	115	1 3/4"	20 min.	Wood	Solid Core				
11	B	3'-0"	111	1 3/4"	20 min.	Wood	Solid Core				
12	B	3'-0"	107	1 3/4"	20 min.	Wood	Solid Core				
13	B	3'-0"	103	1 3/4"	20 min.	Wood	Solid Core				
14	B	3'-0"	101	1 3/4"	20 min.	Wood	Solid Core				
15	B	3'-0"	105	1 3/4"	20 min.	Wood	Solid Core				
16	B	3'-0"	109	1 3/4"	20 min.	Wood	Solid Core				
17	B	3'-0"	113	1 3/4"	20 min.	Wood	Solid Core				
18	116										
19	108										
20	112										
21	104										
22	115										
23	107										

FIGURE 19.8

The AutoCAD drawing with the worksheet pasted in

Insert the worksheet here. The worksheet appears as a small dot.

10. Click the inserted worksheet. Then click and drag the upper-right grip of the worksheet to the right until you can read the worksheet, as in Figure 19.9. You can use the Move tool to move the worksheet into a better position.

11. Zoom in to the worksheet so you can read its contents clearly.

As you saw in step 10, you can resize a pasted object by using the corner grips. The corner grips maintain the original proportion of the inserted object.

You now have a linked object inserted into the AutoCAD drawing. You can save this file and send it off to someone else, along with the pasted document, 19a-plan.xls. The other person will be able to open the AutoCAD file and view the drawing with the worksheet.

WARNING   Objects that are pasted into AutoCAD are maintained within AutoCAD until you use the Erase command to delete them. They act like other AutoCAD objects where layers are concerned. One limitation to pasted objects is that they do not appear in prints or plots unless you use the Windows system printer or plotter.

FIGURE 19.9
Resizing the work-
sheet within AutoCAD

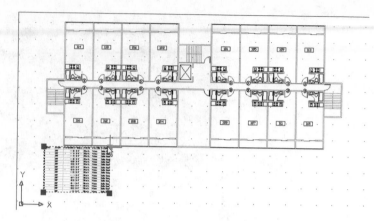

Now let's see how the Link feature works by making some changes to the worksheet data:

1. Go back to Excel by clicking the Excel button in the Windows Taskbar.

2. Click the cell just below the column heading D-RATE.

3. Change the cell's contents by typing **No Rating.**⏎.

4. Go back to AutoCAD and notice that the corresponding cell in the inserted worksheet has changed to reflect the change you made to the original document. Because you inserted the worksheet as a linked document, OLE updates the pasted copy whenever the original source document changes.

5. Now close both the Excel worksheet and the AutoCAD drawing. You can save the change if you like or just close them without saving.

In addition to using the Edit ➢ Paste Special option, you can also import an OLE object by choosing Insert ➢ OLE Object to open the Insert Object dialog box.

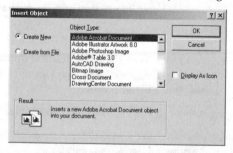

You can then select the type of object you want to import from the Object Type list box. Two radio buttons to the left of the list box let you import an existing object or create a new object of the type listed in the list box. If you choose the Create New radio button, the application associated with the object type will start and open a new file. If you choose the Create From File radio button, the dialog box changes to show a filename and a Browse button.

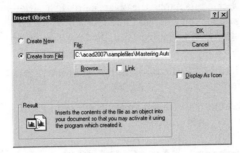

You can then browse for an existing file to import. The Link check box lets you specify whether the imported file is to be linked. If you choose Insert ➤ OLE Object to import an Excel worksheet, the entire worksheet is imported.

ADDING SOUND, MOTION, AND PHOTOS TO YOUR DRAWINGS

You've already seen how you can include scanned images in AutoCAD drawings through the Raster Image tools. Through OLE, you can also include sound files, video clips, and animation. Imagine how you might be able to enhance your AutoCAD files with these types of data. You can include voice annotation or, if the file is to go to a client, an animated walk-through of your building or mechanical design. The potential for this feature is enormous.

Editing Links

After you've pasted an object with links, you can control the links by choosing Edit ➤ OLE Links. If there are no linked objects in the drawing, this option is grayed out; otherwise it opens the Links dialog box.

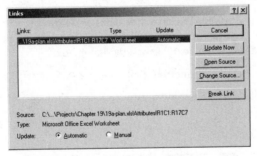

The options available in the Links dialog box are as follows:

Cancel   Cancels the link between a pasted object and its source file. After this option is used, changes in the source file have no effect on the pasted object. This is similar to using the Bind option in the Xref command.

Update Now   Updates an object's link when the Manual option is selected.

Open Source   Opens the linked file in the application associated with the object and lets you edit it.

Change Source Lets you change the object's link to a different file. When you select this option, AutoCAD opens the Change Link dialog box, which lets you select another file of the same type. For example, if you are editing the link to a sound file, the Change Link dialog box will display files with the .wav file extension.

Automatic and Manual Radio buttons that control whether linked objects are updated automatically or manually.

Break Link Disconnects the link between the inserted data and the source document. The inserted data then becomes embedded, rather than linked.

Importing Worksheets as AutoCAD Tables

Although it can be beneficial to import worksheets as linked OLE objects, you might prefer to import worksheets as AutoCAD entities. You might not need the direct link to the source material that OLE linking offers. The ability to edit the imported worksheet directly within AutoCAD might have a higher priority for you.

In Chapter 10, you saw how you could create tables in AutoCAD by using the Table tool. You can import an Excel worksheet as an AutoCAD table by using the AutoCAD Entities option in the Paste Special dialog box. By importing worksheets as tables, you have more control over the layout and appearance of the worksheet data.

Try the following exercise to see how a table can be created from a worksheet:

1. As in the earlier exercise, open the Excel worksheet called 19a-plan.xls from the companion CD and highlight the door data, as shown in Figure 19.7, earlier in this chapter.

2. Choose Edit ➤ Copy to place a copy of the selected data into the Windows Clipboard; then switch back to AutoCAD.

3. Choose Edit ➤ Paste Special to open the Paste Special dialog box.

4. With the Paste radio button selected, select AutoCAD Entities from the list and then click OK.

5. At the Specify insertion point or [paste as Text]: prompt, click a point in the lower-right area of the drawing. The worksheet data appears in the drawing, though it is very small. You also see the Text Formatting dialog box.

6. Click OK in the Text Formatting toolbar to close it.

7. Use the Scale tool to enlarge the table to a readable size and use the corner grips to adjust the width.

8. Close the Excel file.

D-TYPE	D-SIZE	D-NUMBER	D-THICK	D-RATE	D-MATRL	D-CONST
B	3'-0"	116	1 3/4"	no rating	Wood	Solid Core
B	3'-0"	114	1 3/4"	20 min	Wood	Solid Core
B	3'-0"	112	1 3/4"	20 min	Wood	Solid Core
B	3'-0"	110	1 3/4"	20 min	Wood	Solid Core
B	3'-0"	106	1 3/4"	20 min	Wood	Solid Core
B	3'-0"	108	1 3/4"	20 min	Wood	Solid Core
B	3'-0"	102	1 3/4"	20 min	Wood	Solid Core
B	3'-0"	104	1 3/4"	20 min	Wood	Solid Core
B	3'-0"	115	1 3/4"	20 min	Wood	Solid Core
B	3'-0"	111	1 3/4"	20 min	Wood	Solid Core
B	3'-0"	107	1 3/4"	20 min	Wood	Solid Core
B	3'-0"	103	1 3/4"	20 min	Wood	Solid Core
B	3'-0"	101	1 3/4"	20 min	Wood	Solid Core
B	3'-0"	105	1 3/4"	20 min	Wood	Solid Core
B	3'-0"	109	1 3/4"	20 min	Wood	Solid Core
B	3'-0"	113	1 3/4"	20 min	Wood	Solid Core

You can edit this imported worksheet using the editing methods for AutoCAD tables described in Chapter 10. In that chapter, you learned that you can edit the text format, border line weight and color, and the background of cells. You can add rows and columns and rotate text so that it fits more uniformly in a vertical column.

In this exercise, the worksheet was imported by using the default standard table style. This gives you a simple-looking table using the AutoCAD Txt font. You can set up a custom table style with the fonts and borders you want and then import the table for a more custom appearance. Make sure your custom table style is the current style before you import the worksheet.

Understanding Options for Embedding Data

The Paste Special dialog box offers several other options that might better suit your needs. Here is a brief description of each format that is available:

Picture (Metafile) Imports the data as vector or bitmap graphics, whichever is appropriate. If applicable, text is also maintained as text, though you cannot edit it within AutoCAD.

Bitmap Imports the data as a bitmap image, closely reflecting the appearance of the data as it appears on your computer screen in the source application.

Picture (Enhanced Metafile) Similar to the Picture (Metafile) option with support for more features.

AutoCAD Entities Converts the data into AutoCAD objects such as lines, arcs, and circles. Text is converted into AutoCAD single-line text objects. Worksheets are converted into AutoCAD tables.

Image Entity Converts the data into an AutoCAD raster image. You can then edit it by using the raster image–related tools found in the Modify ➢ Object ➢ Image cascading menu of the menu bar. See Chapter 14 for more on how to use raster images.

Text Converts the data into AutoCAD multiline text objects. Formatting is not imported with text.

Unicode Text Imports text data in the Unicode format. Unicode is an international standard for encoding text. If the Text option does not work, try Unicode Text.

The options you see in the Paste Special dialog box depend on the type of data being imported. You saw how the Microsoft Excel Worksheet option maintains the imported data as an Excel worksheet. If the contents of the Clipboard come from another program, you are offered that program as a choice in place of Excel.

TIP Choosing Edit ➢ Paste embeds OLE data objects into AutoCAD, as does the Paste From Clipboard tool in the Standard toolbar.

Using the Clipboard to Export AutoCAD Drawings

Just as you can cut and paste data into AutoCAD from applications that support OLE, you can also cut and paste AutoCAD images to other applications. This can be useful as a way of including AutoCAD images in word-processing documents, worksheets, or desktop-publishing documents. It can also be useful in creating background images for visualization programs such as Autodesk's 3ds Max or VIZ, or paint programs such as Corel Painter.

TIP If you cut and paste an AutoCAD drawing to another file by using OLE and then send the file to someone using another computer, they must also have AutoCAD installed before they can edit the pasted AutoCAD drawing.

The receiving application does not need to support OLE, but if it does, the exported drawing can be edited with AutoCAD and will maintain its accuracy as a CAD drawing. Otherwise, the AutoCAD image will be converted to a bitmap graphic.

To use the Clipboard to export an object or a set of objects from an AutoCAD drawing, choose Edit ➢ Copy. You are then prompted to select the objects you want to export. If you want to simultaneously export and erase objects from AutoCAD, choose Edit ➢ Cut.

If you want the AutoCAD image to be linked to AutoCAD, choose Edit ➢ Copy Link. You won't be prompted to select objects. The current visible portion of your drawing will be exported. If you want to export the entire drawing, choose View ➢ Zoom ➢ Extents before using the Copy Link option. Otherwise, set up AutoCAD to display the portion of your drawing you want to export, before using Copy Link.

In the receiving application, choose Edit ➢ Paste Special. You'll see a dialog box similar to AutoCAD's Paste Special dialog box. Select the method for pasting your AutoCAD image and then click OK. If the receiving application does not have a Paste Special option, choose Edit ➢ Paste. The receiving application converts the image into a format it can accept.

TIP You can copy multiple viewport views from Paper Space into the Clipboard by choosing Edit ➢ Copy Link.

If You Want to Experiment

With a little help from a Visual Basic macro and OLE, you can have Excel extract attribute data from a drawing and then display that data in a worksheet imported into AutoCAD. The following exercise uses a Visual Basic macro embedded in the 19a-plan.xls file you used in an earlier exercise:

1. Open the 19a-plan-xls.dwg file in AutoCAD again.

2. Open the 19a-plan.xls file in Excel.

3. Repeat the exercise in the "Using OLE to Link a Worksheet to AutoCAD" section of this chapter, but stop before exiting the two files.

4. In AutoCAD, choose Modify ➢ Object ➢ Attribute ➢ Single, and then click the door type symbol in room 114 (not the actual door).

5. Change the Fire Rating Attribute value to 1 hour and then click OK.

6. In Excel, choose Tools ➢ Macro ➢ Macros.

7. In the Macro dialog box, highlight the Extract macro and then click Run. Excel takes a moment to extract the attribute data from the open file; then it displays the data in the worksheet.

8. Return to AutoCAD and check the Fire Rating Attribute value for room 114 in the imported worksheet. It reflects the change you made in the attribute in step 4.

9. Close both files.

The macro you used in the Excel file is a small sample of what can be done using AutoCAD's implementation of Visual Basic Automation. You can learn more about VBA in Bonus Chapter 4, "Exploring VBA," on the CD.

In this chapter, you have seen how AutoCAD enables you to access information ranging from the areas of objects to data from other programs. You might never use some of these features, but knowing they are there could, at some point, help you to solve a production problem.

You've just completed Part III of our tutorial. If you've followed the tutorial from the beginning, this is where you get a diploma. You have reached Expert status in 2D drawing and have the tools to tackle any drawing project thrown at you. You only need to log in some time on a few real projects to round out your experience.

From now on, you won't need to follow the book's chapters in order. If you're interested in 3D, go ahead and continue to Part IV, where you'll get thorough instructions on 3D drawing and imaging with AutoCAD. Otherwise, you can skip to Part V to become a full-fledged AutoCAD power user.

Also, don't miss the appendices and the CD—they are packed with information that will answer many of your specific questions or problems. Of course, the entire book is a ready reference to answer questions as they arise or to refresh your memory about specific commands.

Good luck!

Part 4

3D Modeling and Imaging

In this part:

Chapter 20

Creating 3D Drawings

Viewing an object in three dimensions gives you a sense of its true shape and form. It also helps you conceptualize your design, which results in better design decisions. In addition, using three-dimensional objects helps you communicate your ideas to those who might not be familiar with the plans, sections, and side views of your design.

A further advantage to drawing in three dimensions is that you can derive 2D drawings from your 3D models, which might otherwise take considerably more time with standard 2D drawing methods. For example, you can model a mechanical part in 3D and then quickly derive its 2D top, front, and right-side views by using the techniques discussed in this chapter.

Getting to Know the 3D Modeling Workspace

Most of this book is devoted to showing you how to work in what is called the *AutoCAD Classic* workspace. This classic workspace is basically a 2D drawing environment although you can certainly work in 3D as well.

AutoCAD 2007 offers something called the 3D Modeling workspace, which gives you a set of tools to help ease your way into 3D modeling. This 3D Modeling workspace gives AutoCAD a different appearance , but don't worry. AutoCAD still behaves in the same basic way, and the AutoCAD files produced are the same regardless of whether they are 2D or 3D drawings.

You can get to the 3D Modeling workspace in two ways. The first is to select 3D Modeling from the Workspaces dialog box that you see when you start AutoCAD (see Figure 20.1).

FIGURE 20.1
Select 3D Modeling from the Workspaces dialog box when you start AutoCAD.

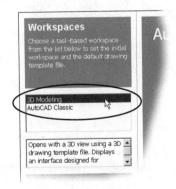

If you start AutoCAD in the AutoCAD Classic workspace, you can do the following to get to the 3D Modeling workspace.

1. Start AutoCAD, and then choose Tools ➢ Workspaces ➢ 3D Modeling. You'll see a new palette to the right of the AutoCAD window.

2. To start a new 3D model, choose File ➢ New to open the Select Template dialog box. Select the acad3D.dwt template file and click Open. Your screen will look similar to Figure 20.2.

Although AutoCAD now looks entirely different, it isn't really . The drawing area displays the workspace as a perspective view with a gray background and a grid. This is really just a typical AutoCAD drawing file with a couple of setting changes. The view has been set up to be a perspective view by default, and a new feature called *Visual Styles* has been set to show 3D objects as solid objects. You'll learn more about the tools that let you adjust the appearance of your workspace later in this chapter. For now, let's take a look at the tool palette to the right of the AutoCAD window.

Two pallets appear in the 3D Modeling workspace. To the far right is the AutoCAD Tool Palettes window that you've already seen, and it contains some shortcuts to various AutoCAD tools. To the left of the Tool Palettes window is the *Dashboard*. The Dashboard offers all the tools you'll need to create 3D models. It is divided into six sections called *control panels*. Each section is marked by an icon in the far left border of the dashboard (see Figure 20.3). The following list describes the function of each control panel.

TIP You can open the Dashboard at any time in any workspace by choosing Tools ➢ Palettes ➢ Dashboard or by entering **dashboard**↵ at the Command prompt.

3D Make Contains tools you'll use to create 3D objects. You'll also find tools that are specifically designed to edit 3D objects in this control panel.

FIGURE 20.2
The AutoCAD 3D
Modeling workspace

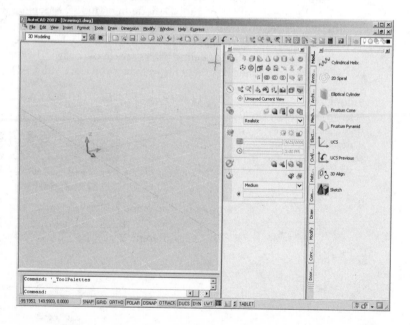

FIGURE 20.3
The Dashboard and its
components

3D Make

3D Navigate

Visual Style

Light

Materials

Render

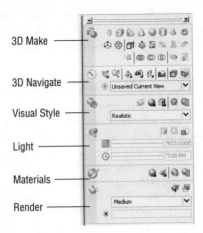

3D Navigate   Contains tools to help you get around in your 3D model. You'll find tools to change your view angle as well as your field of view when using a perspective view. You can switch between perspective views and isometric style views called parallel projection. With the tools in this control panel, you can even create an animation known as a "walkthrough," which allows you to move around as if you are walking through your model.

Visual Style   Gives you tools that change the way AutoCAD displays your 3D model. I mentioned earlier that the reason your drawing in the workspace looks different from what you are used to is that a different visual style is applied to the drawing. You can select from five visual styles in this control panel. You can even create your own visual style, though that is an advanced topic not discussed in this book.

Light   Lets you add lights to create presentation views of your model. You can set up point lights, which are like lightbulbs, or spotlights, which point a light in a specific direction. If your application is architecture, you can set up an accurate representation of sunlight to perform shadow studies for any location and time of day.

Materials   Lets you create and apply textures to your 3D objects. Textures can be anything from a shiny metallic texture to a brick pattern. The pattern emerges when you use the Render control panel to create a rendered view of your model. A crude representation of the material also appears when you use the default Realistic visual style in your workspace.

Render   Lets you generate a high-quality rendering of your model based on the lighting and materials you've used. The rendering appears in a separate window that opens when you start the render process. You can save a rendered view as an image file such as a TIFF or JPEG file.

Besides the Dashboard, the bottom of the AutoCAD window contains a few extra tools as shown in Figure 20.4. Using these tools is just a different way to get to the layout tabs. You'll also notice that the cursor and UCS icon are different. You'll learn more about these features in the "Rotating Objects in 3D Using Dynamic UCS" section later in this chapter.

FIGURE 20.4
Tools to switch from
model space to layouts

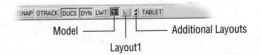

Model — Layout1 — Additional Layouts

In the next section, you'll gain some firsthand experience creating and editing some 3D shapes using the 3D Make, 3D Navigate, and Visual Style control panels. This way you will get a feel for how things work in the 3D Modeling workspace.

Drawing in 3D Using Solids

You can work with two types of 3D objects in AutoCAD: solids and surfaces. You can treat solid objects as if they were solid material. For example, you can create a box and then remove shapes from the box as if you were carving it, as shown in Figure 20.5.

With surfaces, you create complex surfaces shapes by building upon lines, arcs, or polylines. For example, you can quickly turn a series of curved polylines, arcs, or lines into a warped surface, as shown in Figure 20.6.

In the first section, you'll learn how to create a solid box and then make some simple changes to the box as an introduction to 3D modeling.

TIP If you have some experience with AutoCAD 3D already, note that the new surface modeling features are not the same as the surface objects you may have created in the older version of AutoCAD. The new surface objects can interact with solid primitive objects and can be converted into 3D solids. You can still create the old style 3D surface objects, but be aware that they are not the same type of object as the 3D surfaces in AutoCAD 2007. You can convert the old style surfaces into the new 3D surfaces using the Convtosurface command described in the sidebar "Converting Objects with Thickness into 3D Solids" later in this chapter.

FIGURE 20.5
Solid modeling lets you remove or add shapes.

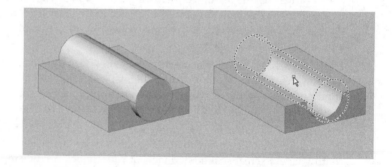

FIGURE 20.6
Using the Loft tool, you can use a set of 2D objects on the left to define a complex surface.

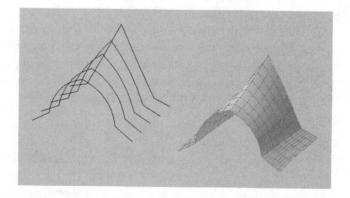

Creating a 3D Box

Start by creating a box using the Box tool in the 3D Make control panel:

1. Close the Tool Palettes window. You won't need it for this chapter.

2. Click the Box tool in the 3D Make control panel.

3. Click a point near the origin of the drawing shown in Figure 20.7 You can use the coordinate readout to select a point near 0,0. Once you've clicked, you see a rectangle follow the cursor.

4. Click another point near coordinate 20,15 as shown in the left image of Figure 20.7. Now as you move the cursor, the rectangle is fixed, and the height of the 3D box appears.

5. Enter 4↵ for a height of 4 units for the box. You can also click to fix the height of the box.

TIP When you start a 3D model using the acad3D.dwt template, the default layer 0 is set to a color that is a light gray instead of the white or black that is used in the standard acad.dwt template. The gray color is used so that you can see the 3D shapes clearly when the model is displayed using a shaded visual style. If you happen to start a 3D model using the acad.dwt template, you might want to change the default color to something other than white or black.

FIGURE 20.7
Drawing a
3D solid box

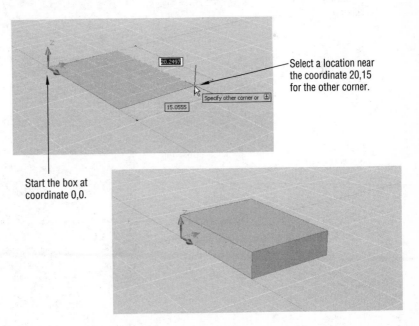

Select a location near
the coordinate 20,15
for the other corner.

Start the box at
coordinate 0,0.

You used three basic steps in creating the box. You first clicked one corner to establish a location for the box; then you clicked another corner to establish the base size. Finally, you selected a height. You use a similar set of steps to create any of the other 3D solid primitives found in the 3D Make control panel. For example, for a cylinder, you select the center, then the radius, and then a height. For a wedge, you select two corners as you did with the box, and then you select the height of the wedge. You'll learn more about these 3D solid primitives in Chapter 23.

Editing 3D Solids with Grips

Once you've created a solid, you can "fine-tune" its shape by using grips.

1. Click the solid to select it. You might see a message alerting you to the new editing options. Dismiss the message, and you will see that grips appear on the 3D solid, as shown in Figure 20.8.

The square grips at the base of the solid allow you to adjust the location of those grips in a way that is similar to adjusting the grips on 2D objects. The arrow grips let you adjust the length of the site to which the arrows are attached. If you click an arrow grip and you have Dynamic Input turned on, a dimension appears at the cursor, as shown in Figure 20.8. You can enter a new dimension for the length associated with the selected grip, or you can drag and click the arrow to adjust the length. Remember that you can press the Tab key to shift between dimensions shown in the Dynamic input display.

NOTE If your Ctrl+click does not work as described here, you may need to change the setting for the Legacyctrlpick system variable. At the command prompt, enter legacyctrlpick↵ then enter 0.↵.

FIGURE 20.8
Grips appear on a
3D solid.

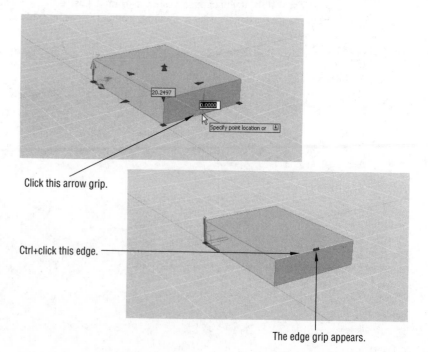

Click this arrow grip.

Ctrl+click this edge.

The edge grip appears.

2. Click the arrow grip toward the front of the box as shown in the upper left of Figure 20.8. Now as you move the cursor, the box changes in length.

3. Press Escape to clear the grip selection.

You can also move individual edges by using a Ctrl+click.

1. Ctrl+click the top-front edge as shown in the lower right of Figure 20.8. The edge is highlighted, and a grip appears at its midpoint.

2. Click the edge's grip and move the cursor. The edge follows the grip.

3. Hold down the Shift key, and "pull" the grip forward away from the box's center. The Shift key constrains the motion in the X, Y, or Z axis.

4. Click a point to fix the edge's new position.

5. Click the Undo button to return the box to its original shape.

As you can see, you have a great deal of flexibility in controlling the shape of the box. Using the shift key lets you constrain the motion of the grip.

Constraining Motion with the Grip Tool

Another handy tool for grip editing 3D objects is the *grip tool*. This is an icon that looks like the UCS icon, and it appears whenever you hover over a grip. Try the next exercise to see how the grip tool works firsthand.

1. Ctrl+click the front top edge of the box again to expose the edge's grip.

2. Place the cursor on the grip, but don't click. The grip tool appears, as shown in Figure 20.9.

3. Place the cursor on the blue Z axis of the grip tool, but don't click. A blue line appears that extends across the drawing area, and the Z axis of the grip tool changes color as shown in Figure 20.9.

4. Click the Z axis. Now as you move the cursor, the grip motion is constrained in the Z axis.

5. Click again to fix the location of the grip.

FIGURE 20.9
Using the grip tool to constrain motion

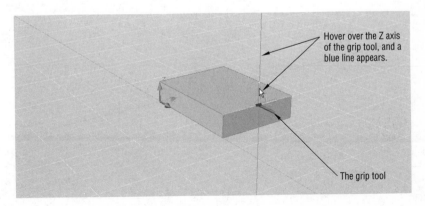

Hover over the Z axis of the grip tool, and a blue line appears.

The grip tool

6. Press the Escape key to clear your grip selection.

7. Click the Undo tool to undo the grip edit.

Here you see that you can use the grip tool to easily change the Z location of a grip. You can use the grip tool to modify the location of a single grip or the entire object.

Rotating Objects in 3D Using Dynamic UCS

Typically, you work in what is known as the *World Coordinate System,* or WCS. This is the default coordinate system that AutoCAD uses in new drawings, but you can also create your own coordinate systems that are subsets of the WCS. A coordinate system that you create is known as a User Coordinate System, or UCS.

UCSs are significant in 3D modeling because they can help you orient your work in 3D space. For example, you can set up a UCS that is on a vertical face of the 3D box you created earlier. You could then draw on that vertical face just as you would on the WCS of the drawing. Figure 20.10 shows a cylinder drawn on the side of a box. The vertical grid shows the orientation of the UCS. Also notice the orientation of the UCS at the center of the cylinder.

The UCS has always been an important tool for 3D modeling in AutoCAD. AutoCAD 2007 introduces the Dynamic UCS, which automatically changes the orientation of the X, Y, and Z axes to conform to the flat surface of a 3D object.

You might have noticed that when you created the new 3D file using the acad3D.dwt template, the cursor looked different. Instead of the usual cross, you saw three intersecting lines. If you look carefully, you'll see that each line of the cursor is a different color. In its default configuration, AutoCAD shows a red line for the X axis, a green line for the Y axis, and a blue line for the Z axis. This mimics the color scheme of the UCS icon as shown in Figure 20.11.

FIGURE 20.10

Drawing on the side of a box

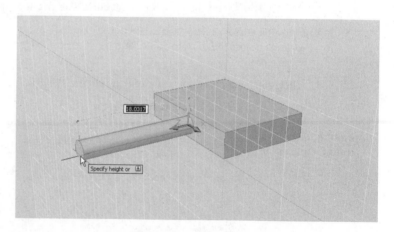

FIGURE 20.11

The UCS icon at the left and the cursor in 3D to the right are color matched.

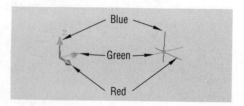

As you work with the Dynamic UCS, you'll see that the orientation of these lines changes when you point at a surface on a 3D object. The following exercise shows you how to use the Dynamic UCS to help you rotate the box about the X axis.

1. Be sure that the Osnap and Dynamic UCS features are turned on. Check the DUCS button at the bottom of the AutoCAD window. It should be in the "down," or "on," position. If it isn't, click it to turn it on.

2. Choose Modify ➢ Rotate.

3. At the `Select objects:` prompt, click the box, and then press ⏎ to finish your selection.

4. At the `Specify base point:` prompt, don't click anything, but move the cursor from one surface of the box to a side of the box. As you do this, pay attention to the orientation of the cursor. It changes depending on which surface you are pointing to.

5. Place the cursor on the left side as shown in Figure 20.12.

6. Place the osnap cursor on the lower-front corner of the box as shown in the left image of Figure 20.12. Click this corner. As you move the cursor, the box rotates about the Y axis.

7. Enter **–30** for the rotation angle. Your box should look like the image in the lower right of Figure 20.12

Here you see that you can hover over a surface to indicate the plane about which the rotation is to occur. Now suppose you want to add an object to one of the sides of the rotated box. The next section will show you another essential tool you can use to do just that.

FIGURE 20.12
Select a base point
and the resulting box
orientation

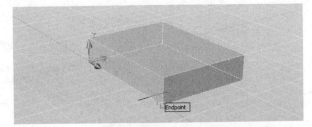

USING OBJECT SNAPS AND OSNAP TRACKING IN 3D SPACE

If you need to place objects in precise locations in 3D, such as endpoints or midpoints of other objects, you can do so using object snaps, just as you would in 2D. But some care must be taken when using object snaps where the Dynamic UCS is concerned.

In the exercise in the "Rotating Objects in 3D Using Dynamic UCS" section, you are asked to make sure that you place the cursor on the side of the box that coincided with the rotational plane *before* you select the Endpoint osnap. This ensures that the Dynamic UCS feature has selected the proper rotational plane; otherwise you may find that the box rotates in the wrong direction.

In some operations, you cannot use object snaps while in perspective mode. Osnap Tracking also does not work in perspective mode. Switch to a parallel projection view if you know you will want to use object snaps. (See the section "Changing from Perspective to Parallel Projection" later in this chapter.) If you need to snap to points that are in the back of an object, switch to 2D or 3D wireframe visual style. See the section "Getting a Visual Effect" later in this chapter for more on visual styles.

Drawing on a 3D Object's Surface

In the rotation exercise, you saw that you can hover over a surface to indicate the plane of rotation. You can use the same method to indicate the plane on which you want to place an object. Try the following exercise to see firsthand how it's done.

1. Choose Draw ➤ Circle ➤ Center, Radius.

2. Place the cursor on the top surface of the rectangle, as indicated in Figure 20.13, and hold it there for a moment. The cursor will align with the angle of the top surface.

FIGURE 20.13

Drawing circles on the surface of a 3D solid

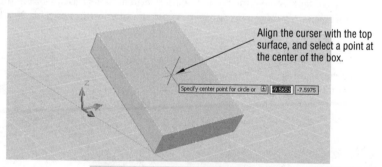

Align the curser with the top surface, and select a point at the center of the box.

Specify center point for circle or [-2.5653] [-7.5975]

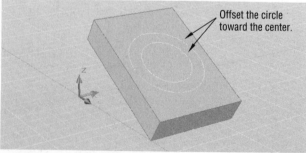

Offset the circle toward the center.

3. With the cursor aligned with the top surface of the box, click a point roughly at the center of the box. The circle appears on the surface, and as you move the cursor, the circle's radius follows.

4. Adjust the circle so it is roughly the same 6-unit radius as the one shown on the right in Figure 20.13, and then click to set the radius. You can also enter **6**↵.

5. Choose Modify ➢ Offset, and offset the circle 2 units inward, as shown in the second panel of Figure 20.13.

This demonstrates that you can use Dynamic UCS to align objects with the surface of an object. Note that the Dynamic UCS only works on flat surfaces. For example, you can't use Dynamic UCS to place an object on the curved side of the cylinder.

USING A "FIXED" UCS

If you're working in a crowded area of a drawing, or if you know you need to do a lot of work on one particular surface of an object, you can create a UCS that remains in a fixed orientation until you change it, instead of relying on the Dynamic UCS feature. Choose Tools ➢ New UCS ➢ Face, and then click the surface that defines the plane on which you want to work and press ↵. The UCS will align with the selected surface, and you won't have to worry about accidentally drawing in the wrong orientation. To return to the WCS, choose Tools ➢ New UCS ➢ World. You'll learn more about the UCS in Chapter 21.

Pushing and Pulling Shapes from a Solid

You've just added a 2D circle to the top surface of the 3D box. AutoCAD offers a tool that lets you use that 2D circle or any closed 2D shape to modify the shape of your 3D object. The Presspull tool in the 3D Make control panel lets you "press" or "pull" a 3D shape from the surface of a 3D object. The following shows you firsthand how this works.

1. Make sure the Polar button in the status bar is in turned on, and then click the Presspull tool in the 3D Make control panel. You can also enter **Presspull**↵ at the Command prompt.

2. Place the cursor over the center of the inner circle but don't click just yet. Notice that the circle is highlighted. (See the top-left panel of Figure 20.14.)

3. Move the cursor to the top surface of the box between both circles. Now the area between the circles is highlighted. (See the right panel of Figure 20.14.)

4. With the cursor between the two circles, click the mouse. Now as you move the mouse, the circular area defined by the two circles moves.

5. Adjust the cursor location so that the polar coordinate readout shows a minus Z (−Z) as shown in the top panel of Figure 20.15. Now enter **3**↵ to create a 3-unit indentation, as shown in the second panel of Figure 20.15.

FIGURE 20.14

Move the cursor over different areas of the box, and notice how the areas are highlighted.

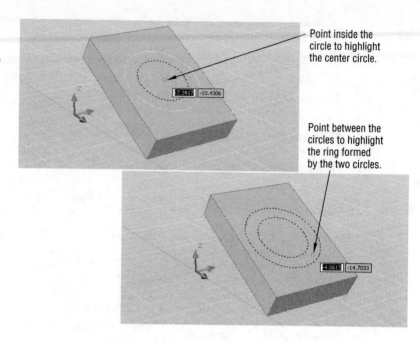

Point inside the circle to highlight the center circle.

Point between the circles to highlight the ring formed by the two circles.

FIGURE 20.15

Creating an indentation in the box using Presspull

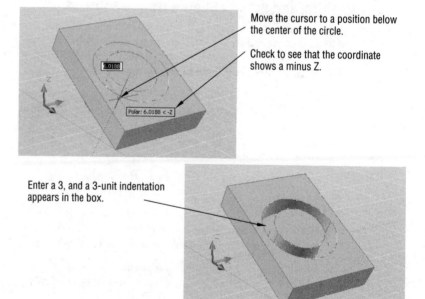

Move the cursor to a position below the center of the circle.

Check to see that the coordinate shows a minus Z.

Enter a 3, and a 3-unit indentation appears in the box.

Here you created a circular indentation in the box by "pressing" the circular area defined by the two circles. You could have "pulled" the area upward to form a circular ridge on the box. Pressing the circle into the solid is essentially the same as subtracting one solid from another. By pressing the shape into the solid, AutoCAD assumes you want to subtract the shape.

TIP   Presspull works with any closed 2D shape such as a circle, closed polyline, or other completely enclosed area. An existing 3D solid is not needed. For example, you can draw two concentric circles without the 3D box and then use Presspull to convert the circles into a 3D solid ring. In the previous exercise, the solid box showed that you can use Presspull to subtract a shape from an existing solid.

As you can see from this exercise, the Presspull tool can help you quickly subtract a shape to an existing 3D solid. Figure 20.16 shows some other examples of how you can use Presspull. For example, you can draw a line from one edge to another and then use Presspull to extrude the resulting triangular shape. You can also draw concentric shapes and extrude them, or you can even use offset spline curves to add a trough to a solid.

WARNING   If you use an open 2D object on a 3D surface, such as a curved spline or line, the endpoints must touch exactly on the edge of the surface before Presspull will work.

Making Changes to Your Solid

When you're creating a 3D model, you will hardly ever get the shape right the first time. Suppose you decide that you need to modify the shape you've created so far by moving the hole from the center of the box to a corner. This next exercise will show you how you can gain access to the individual components of a 3D solid to make changes.

The model you've been working with is composed of two objects: a box and a cylinder. These two components of the solid are referred to as *subobjects* of the main solid object. Faces and edges of 3D solids are also considered subobjects. When you use the Union, Subtract, or Intersect tool on a set of objects, the objects merge into a single solid, or at least that is how it seems at first. You can gain access and modify the shape of the subobjects from which the shape is constructed just by using the Ctrl key while clicking the solid. Try the following to see firsthand how this works.

1. Place the cursor on the solid that you've made so far. You'll see that the entire object is highlighted as if it were one object. If you were to click it (don't do it yet), the entire object would be selected.

FIGURE 20.16
Adding complex
shapes using the
Presspull tool

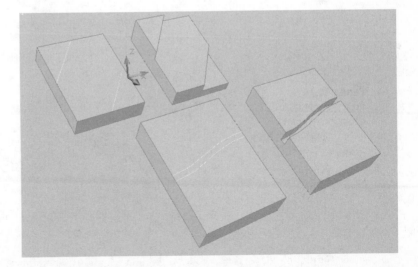

2. Hold down the Ctrl key and move the cursor over the circular indentation. As you do this, you will see that the indentation is highlighted (see the left image in Figure 20.17).

3. While still holding the Ctrl key down, click the indentation. The grips for the indentation appear, as shown on the right side in Figure 20.17. As you might guess, you can use these grips to change the shape and location of a feature of the selected solid.

4. Click the center square grip of the indentation and move your cursor around. If you find it a bit uncontrollable, turn off the Polar mode. As you move the cursor, you see that the indentation moves with the cursor.

5. Place the indentation in the location shown in Figure 20.18 and click. You've just moved the indentation from the center to the edge of the cylinder.

6. Press the Escape key to clear the selection.

FIGURE 20.17

You can select subobjects of a 3D solid when you hold down the Ctrl key.

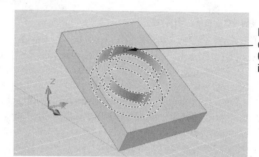

Hold down the Ctrl key, and hover over the circular indentation. Click the mouse when the indentation is highlighted.

Click the center square grip. The indentation will move with the mouse.

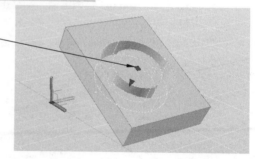

FIGURE 20.18

You can move the indentation to a new location using its grip.

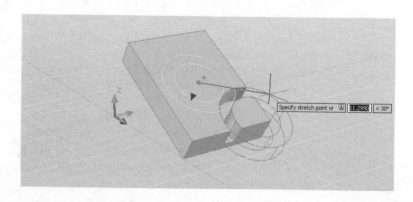

This example shows you that the Ctrl key can be an extremely useful tool when you have to edit a solid; it allows you to select the subobjects that form your model. Once the subobjects are selected, you can move them, or you can use the arrow grips to change their size.

Creating 3D Forms from 2D Shapes

The 3D solid primitives are great for creating some basic shapes, but in many situations, you will want to create a 3D form from a more complex shape. Fortunately, you can extrude 2D objects into a variety of shapes using additional tools found in the 3D Make control panel. For example, you can draw a shape like a star and then extrude it into a third dimension as shown in Figure 20.19. Or you can use several strategically placed 2D objects that can form a flowing surface like the wing of an airplane as shown on the right side of Figure 20.19.

FIGURE 20.19
The closed polyline on the left can be used to construct the 3D shape on the right.

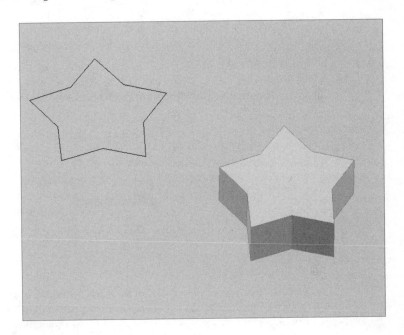

Extruding a Polyline

You can create a 3D solid by extruding a 2D closed polyline. This is a more flexible way to create shapes because you can create a polyline of any shape and extrude it to a fairly complex form.

In the following set of exercises, you'll turn the apartment room from previous chapters into a 3D model. I've created a version of the apartment floor plan that has a few additions to make things a little easier for you. Figure 20.20 shows the file you will use in the exercise. It is the same floor plan you've been working with in earlier chapters, but with the addition of closed polylines outlining the walls.

You'll also notice that the plan is not shaded as in the previous examples of this chapter. You'll see that you can work in 3D in this display mode just as easily as in a shaded mode.

1. Open the 20-unit.dwg file from the project files you installed from the companion CD. Metric users should open 20-unit-metric.dwg.

FIGURE 20.20

The Unit plan with closed polylines outlining the walls

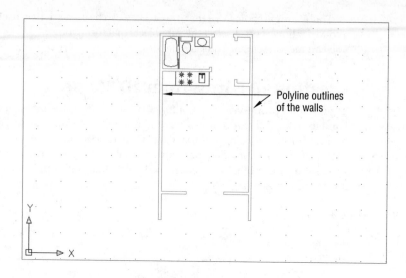

Polyline outlines of the walls

2. Choose Southwest Isometric from the 3D Navigate control panel drop-down list.

You can also choose View ➤ 3D Views ➤ SW Isometric. Your view now looks as if you are standing above and to the left of your drawing, rather than directly above it (see Figure 20.21). The UCS icon helps you get a sense of your new orientation.

3. Click the Extrude tool in the 3D Make control panel.

You can also choose Draw ➤ Modeling ➤ Extrude or enter **Extrude** at the Command prompt. You'll see a message Current wire frame density: ISOLINES=4 in the Command window, followed by the Select objects to extrude: prompt.

4. Select the wall outlines shown in Figure 20.21, and then press ↵.

5. At the Specify height of extrusion or [Direction/Path/Taper angle] <0.0000>: prompt, enter **8′**↵. Metric users should enter 224↵. The walls extrude to the height you entered, as shown in Figure 20.22.

FIGURE 20.21
A 3D view of the
floor plan

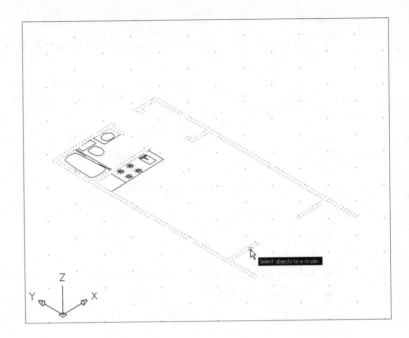

FIGURE 20.22
The extruded walls

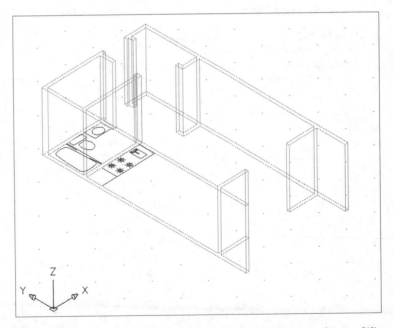

Unlike the earlier exercise with the box, you can see through the walls because this is a Wire-frame view. A *Wireframe view* shows the volumes of a 3D object by displaying the lines representing the edges of surfaces. Later in this chapter I'll discuss how to make an object's surfaces appear opaque like the box earlier in this chapter.

Next you will add door headers to define the wall openings:

1. Adjust your view so you get a close look at the door shown in Figure 20.23. You can use the Pan and Zoom tools in this 3D view as you would in a 2D view.

2. Turn off the Dynamic UCS mode by clicking the DUCS button in the status bar so that it looks like it's in the "up" position. This is to avoid accidentally orienting your cursor to the wall behind the door header.

3. Click the Box tool in the 3D Make control panel.

4. Use the endpoint osnaps, and click the two points shown in Figure 20.23.

5. At the `Specify height or [2Point] <8'-0">:` prompt, point the cursor downward from the points you just selected and enter **12**↵. Metric users should enter 30↵. The door header appears.

6. Repeat steps 2 and 3 to draw the other door headers shown in Figure 20.24.

FIGURE 20.23

Adding the door header to the opening at the balcony of the unit plan

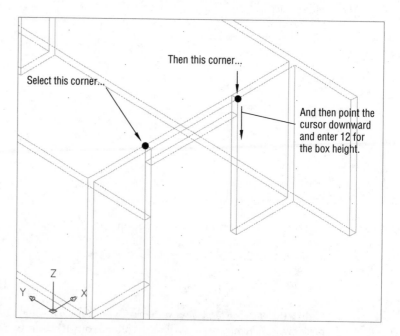

Select this corner...

Then this corner...

And then point the cursor downward and enter 12 for the box height.

FIGURE 20.24

Adding the remaining door headers

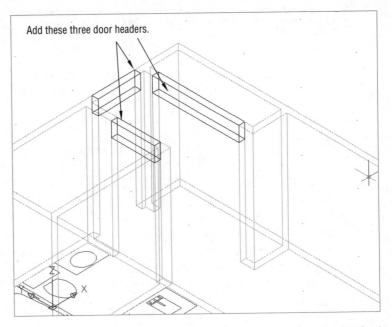

Add these three door headers.

The walls and door headers now give you a better sense of the space in the Unit plan. To further enhance the appearance of the 3D model, you can join the walls and door headers so they appear as seamless walls and openings.

1. Zoom out so you can see the entire unit, and then click the Union tool in the 3D Make control panel.

You can also choose Modify ➢ Solid Editing ➢ Union.

2. At the Select objects: prompt, select all the walls and headers, and then press ↵.

Now the walls and headers appear as one seamless surface without any distracting joint lines. You can really get a sense of the space of the Unit plan. You'll want to start to explore ways of viewing the unit in 3D, but before you do that, you'll want to know about one more 3D modeling feature—*Point Filters*.

Isolating Coordinates with Point Filters

AutoCAD offers a method for 3D point selection, called *point filters*, that can help you isolate the X, Y, or Z coordinate of a location in 3D. Point filters enable you to enter an x, y, or z value by picking a point on the screen and telling AutoCAD to use only the x, y, or z value of that point or any combination of

CONVERTING OBJECTS WITH THICKNESS INTO 3D SOLIDS

If you have worked with 3D in AutoCAD before, you probably know that you can give an object a thickness property greater than 0 to make it a 3D object. For example, a line with a thickness property greater than 0 will look like a vertical surface.

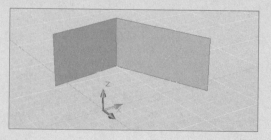

In the Unit plan exercise, you can do the same for the polylines used to draw the walls. Click the wall polylines, and then right-click and choose Properties. In the Properties palette, change the Thickness value to 8´ or 224 cm.

Close the Properties palette. The walls will appear in three dimensions. But be aware that these walls are not 3D solids. If you zoom in to a detail of the wall, you will see that they appear hollow.

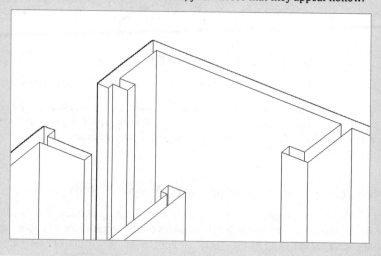

Fortunately, AutoCAD supplies a tool that will convert a closed polyline with thickness into a solid. Expand the 3D Make control panel by clicking the downward-pointing arrow in the 3D Make title bar, and then click the Convert To Solid tool in the 3D Make toolbar. You can also enter **convtosolid.**⏎.

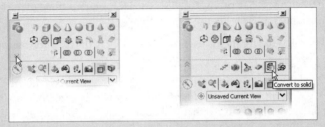

Select the polyline walls and press ⏎ when you've finished your selection. Once you do this, the walls will become 3D solids. This operation works with any closed polyline, providing an alternate way of creating a 3D solid. If you have existing 3D models that have been produced using the Thickness property, you can use the Convert To Solid tool to bring your 3D models up-to-date. The Convert To Solid tool can also convert open polylines that have a width and thickness greater than 0. (See Chapter 18 for more on polylines.)

Another tool called Convert To Surface will convert objects with thickness into 3D surface objects. You can use 3D surfaces to "slice" or "thicken" 3D solids into full 3D solids. You'll learn more about 3D surfaces in Chapter 23.

those values. For example, suppose you want to start the corner of a 3D box at the X and Y coordinates of the corner of the unit plan, but you want the Z location at 3′ instead of at ground level. You can use the point filters to select only the X and Y coordinates of a point and then specify the Z coordinate as a separate value. The following exercise demonstrates how this works.

1. Zoom into the balcony door again, and then turn on the F-Rail layer.

2. Click the Box tool on the 3D Make control panel.

3. At the Specify first corner or [Center]: prompt, Shift+right-click to display the Osnap menu; then choose Point Filters ➤ .XY. As an alternative, you can enter **.xy** . By doing this, you are telling AutoCAD that you are going to first specify the X and Y coordinates for this beginning point and then later indicate the Z coordinate.

TIP You might have noticed the .X, .Y, and .Z options on the Object Snap menu (Shift+right-click) in step 2. These are the 3D point filters. By choosing one of these options as you select points in a 3D command, you can filter an *x*, *y*, or *z* value, or any combination of values, from that selected point. You can also enter filters through the keyboard.

4. At the Specify first corner or [Center]: .XY of: prompt, pick the corner of the Unit plan as shown in Figure 20.25.

5. At the (need Z): prompt, enter **36**⏎ (the Z coordinate). Metric users enter **92**⏎. The outline of the box appears at the 36″ (or 92 cm) elevation and at the corner you selected in step 2.

6. At the `Specify other corner or [Cube/Length]:` prompt, Shift+right-click to display the Osnap menu again and choose Point Filters ➢ .XY. Select the other endpoint indicated in Figure 20.25.

7. At the `(need Z):` prompt: you'll see a temporary outline of the box appear at the 36″ height. Click the mouse to fix the base outline of the box.

8. Enter 4↵ (10↵ for metric users) for the height of the box. The box appears as the balcony rail.

In step 4, you selected the corner of the unit, but the box did not appear right away. You had to enter a Z value in step 5 before the outline of the box appeared. Then in step 6 you saw the box begin at the 36″ elevation. Using point filters allowed you to accurately place the box in the drawing even though there were no features that you could snap to directly.

Now that you've gotten most of the unit modeled in 3D, you'll want to be able to look at it from different angles. The next section shows you some of the tools available to control your views in 3D.

FIGURE 20.25
Constructing the rail using point filters.

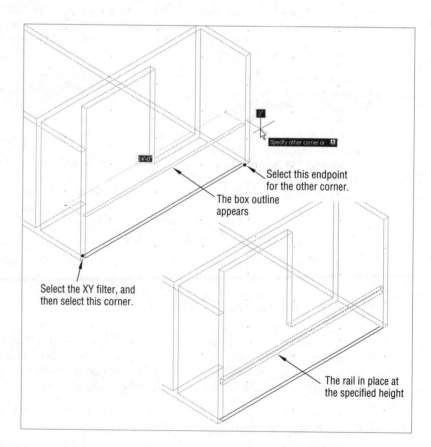

Select this endpoint for the other corner.

The box outline appears

Select the XY filter, and then select this corner.

The rail in place at the specified height

TIP   In my own work in 3D, point filters are a real lifesaver. Understanding this tool will greatly improve your ability to work in 3D.

Moving Around Your Model

AutoCAD offers a number of tools to help you view your 3D model. You've already used one to get the current 3D view. Choosing Southwest Isometric from the 3D Navigate control panel's drop-down list displays an Isometric view from a southwest direction. You might have noticed several other Isometric view options in that list. This section introduces you to some of the ways you can move around in your 3D model.

Finding Isometric and Orthogonal Views

Figure 20.26 illustrates the Isometric view options you saw earlier in the 3D Navigate control panel drop-down list: Southeast Isometric, Northeast Isometric, and Northwest Isometric. The cameras represent the different viewpoint locations. You can get an idea of their location in reference to the grid and UCS icon.

The 3D Navigate control panel's drop-down list also offers another set of options: Top, Bottom, Left, Right, Front, and Back. These are Orthogonal views that show the sides, top, and bottom of the model, as illustrated in Figure 20.27. In this figure, the cameras once again show the points of view.

When you use any of the View options described here, AutoCAD attempts to display the extents of the drawing. You can then use the Pan and Zoom tools to adjust your view.

TIP   If you don't have the Dashboard open, you can get to the Isometric and Orthogonal views by choosing View ➢ 3D Views.

FIGURE 20.26
This diagram shows the isometric viewpoints for the four Isometric views available from the View 3D Views cascading menu.

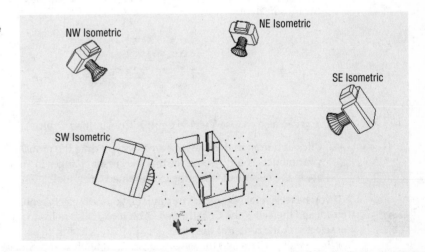

FIGURE 20.27
This diagram shows
the six viewpoints
of the Orthogonal
view options on
the View 3D Views
cascading menu.

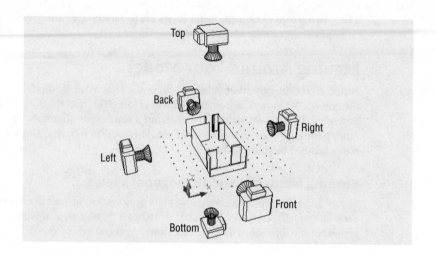

Rotating Freely Around Your Model

You might find the Isometric and Orthogonal views a bit restrictive. The Constrained Orbit tool lets you move around your model in "real time." You can fine-tune your view by clicking and dragging the mouse using this tool. Try the following to see firsthand how it works:

1. Zoom out so you see an overall view of your model.

2. Click the Constrained Orbit tool in the 3D Navigate control panel. If you don't see the Constrained Orbit tool, click and hold the mouse and select Constrained Orbit from the button flyout.

3. You can also choose View ➤ Orbit ➤ Constrained Orbit.

4. Click and drag in the drawing area. As you drag the mouse, the view will revolve around your model. You'll also notice that the cursor changes to an orbit icon to let you know you are in the middle of using the Constrained Orbit tool.

If you have several objects in your model, you can select an object that you want to revolve around, and then click the Constrained Orbit tool. It also helps to pan your view so that the object you select is in the center of the view.

When you have reached the view you want, right-click and choose Exit. You are then ready to make more changes or use another tool.

TIP   If you have a mouse with a scroll wheel, you can hold down the Shift key while clicking and dragging the wheel to get the same effect as using the Constrained Orbit tool.

Changing Your View Direction

AutoCAD uses a camera analogy for views in your 3D model. With a camera, you have a camera location and a target, and both can be fined-tuned in AutoCAD. The Constrained Orbit tool is a bit like moving a camera around an object. Using the Swivel tool is like keeping the camera stationary while pointing in a different direction.

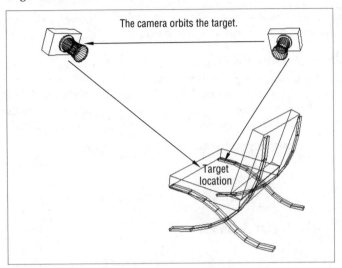

The camera orbits the target.

Target location

At first the Swivel tool may seem just like the Pan tool. But in the 3D world, Pan actually moves both the camera and target in unison. Pan is a bit like pointing a camera out the side of a moving car. If you don't keep the view in the camera fixed on an object, you are panning across the scenery. The Swivel tool is like standing in one spot and swiveling the camera to take in a panoramic view.

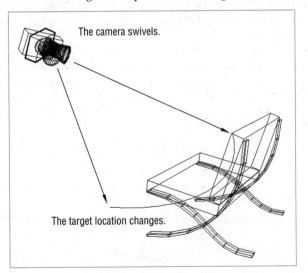

The camera swivels.

The target location changes.

To use Swivel, click the Swivel tool, and then click and drag the mouse across the view.

You'll notice that the icon changes to a camera with a swivel arrow. When you've adjusted your view to your liking, right-click and choose Exit.

Flying through Your View

Another tool for getting around in your model is the Walk/Fly tool. If you are familiar with computer games, this tool is for you. When you click the Walk tool in the 3D Navigate control panel, you might see a message asking if you want to change to perspective mode. Click Yes to proceed. You might then see a message box telling you how to use Walk and Fly.

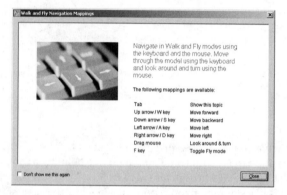

It tells you all you need to know about the Walk and Fly tools. Click the Close button, and you can use the arrow keys to move through your model. Click and drag the mouse to change the direction to which you are looking.

If you press the F key, Walk changes to Fly mode. The main difference between Walk and Fly is that in Walk, both your position in the model and the point to which you are looking move with the Up and Down arrow keys. Walk is a bit like Pan. When you are in the Fly mode, the arrow keys move you toward the center of your view, which is indicated by a crosshair.

In addition to the crosshair, you will see a palette that shows your position in the model from a top-down view.

You can use the palette to control your view by clicking and dragging the camera or the view target graphic. If you prefer, you can close the palette and continue to "walk" through your model. When you are finished using Walk, right-click and choose Exit.

Changing from Perspective to Parallel Projection

When you create a new drawing using the acad3D.dwt template, you are automatically given a perspective view of the file. If you need a more schematic parallel projection style of view, you can get one by selecting the Parallel Projection tool in the 3D Navigate control panel (see Figure 20.28).

You can return to a perspective view by clicking the Perspective Projection tool next to the Parallel Projection tool as shown in Figure 20.28.

Getting a Visual Effect

3D models are extremely useful in communicating your ideas to others, but sometimes you find that the default appearance of your model is not exactly what you want. If you are only in a schematic design stage, you might want your model to look more like a sketch instead of a finished product. Conversely, if you're trying to sell someone on a concept, you might want a realistic look that includes materials and even special lighting.

AutoCAD provides a variety of tools to help you get a visual style, from a simple wireframe to a fully rendered image complete with chrome and wood. In this section you will get a preview of what is available to control the appearance of your model. Later in Chapter 22, you'll get an in-depth look at rendering and camera tools that allow you to produce views from hand-sketched "napkin" designs to finished renderings.

FIGURE 20.28
The Parallel Projection and Perspective Projection tools

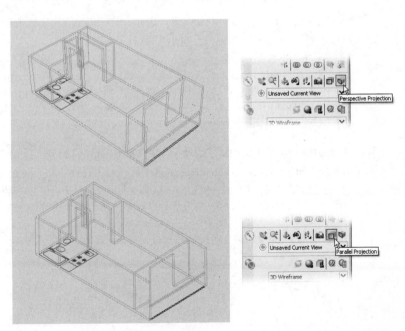

Using Visual Styles

In the earlier tutorials of this chapter, you drew a box that appeared to be solid. When you then opened an existing file to extrude the Unit plan into the third dimension, you worked in a Wireframe view. These views are known as visual styles in AutoCAD. You used the default 3D visual style called Realistic when you drew the box. The Unit plan used the default 2D Wireframe view that is used in the AutoCAD Classic style of drawing.

Sometimes it helps to use a different visual style depending on your task. For example, the 2D Wireframe view of your unit plan model can help you visualize and select things that are behind a solid. AutoCAD includes several shaded view options that can bring out different features of your model. Try the following exercises to explore some of the other visual styles.

1. Click the Visual Styles drop-down list in the Visual Style control panel. A set of graphic images appear that give you an idea of what each visual style shows you.

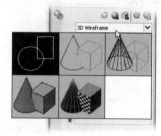

2. Select 3D Wireframe. You can also choose View ➤ Visual Styles ➤ Wireframe. Your model appears as a transparent wireframe object with a gray background.

3. To get to the shaded view of your model, choose Realistic from the Visual Styles drop-down list or chooseView ➤ Visual Styles ➤ Realistic.

You might have noticed a few other Visual Styles options. Figure 20.29 shows those options as they are applied to a sphere. From left to right they are 2D Wireframe, Hidden, 3D Wireframe, Conceptual, and Realistic. 2D Wireframe and 3D Wireframe may appear the same, but 3D Wireframe uses a perspective view and a background color, while 2D Wireframe uses a parallel projection view and no background color.

Creating a Sketched Look with Visual Styles

You might notice a blank in the visual styles options in the Visual Style control panel. This is a space to allow you to create a custom visual style. This is significant for designers because it gives you an opportunity to create a visual style that mimics a hand-drawn sketch. The following exercise will step you through the process.

1. Click the Visual Styles Manager tool in the Visual Style control panel.

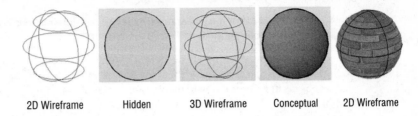

2D Wireframe   Hidden   3D Wireframe   Conceptual   2D Wireframe

The Visual Styles Manager palette appears. This palette looks similar to the Properties palette with the addition of thumbnail examples of the visual styles at the top of the palette.

2. Click the Create New Visual Style tool in the Visual Styles Manager palette toolbar.

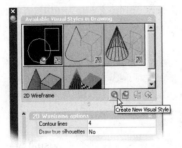

The Create New Visual Style dialog box opens.

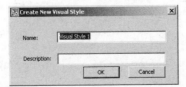

3. Enter **Sketch.⏎** in the Name input box.

4. Enter **Hand Drawn Appearance** in the Description input box, and then click OK. You see a new thumbnail in the bottom-right corner of the samples at the top of the palette.

You've just created a new visual style. This new style uses the default settings that are similar to the Realistic visual style but without the Material Display option turned on. The material setting causes objects in your drawing to display any material assignments that have been given to objects. You'll learn more about materials in Chapter 22.

Now that you have a new visual style, you can begin to customize it. But before you start your customization, make your new visual style the current one so you can see the effects of your changes as you make them.

1. Click the Apply Selected Visual Style To Current Viewport tool in the Visual Styles Manager toolbar.

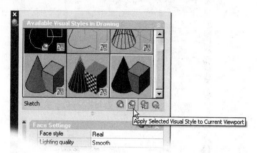

The display changes slightly, and you see the name Sketch appear in the Visual Style control panel drop-down list. Next you'll turn on the two features that will give your new visual style a sketchlike appearance.

2. Use the scroll bar to the left of the Visual Styles Manager toolbar to scroll down to the bottom of the list of options.

3. Locate the Edge Modifiers option group, and then click the Overhanging Edges tool in the Edge Modifiers title bar.

Notice that edges of your model now appear to be drawn with lines extending beyond the corners (see Figure 20.30).

FIGURE 20.30

The 3D unit plan with the Sketch visual style

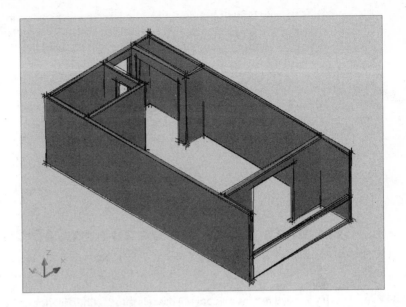

4. Click the Jitter Edges tool in the Edge Modifiers title bar.

5. Now the edges take on a sketched look as shown in Figure 20.30.

6. Close the Visual Styles Manager toolbar.

7. Save the unit plan file.

The 3D view takes on a hand-drawn appearance. Notice that the lines overhang the corners in a typical architectural sketch style. This is the effect of the Overhanging Edges option in step 3. The lines are made rough and broken by the Jitter Edges setting. You can control the amount of overhang and jitter in the Edge Modifiers group of the Visual Styles Manager to exaggerate or soften these effects.

The Jitter and Edges settings can also be turned on for an existing visual style by using the Edge Overhand and Edge Jitter tools in the expanded Visual Style control panel. The sliders to the right of these tools control the amount of overhang and jitter applied to the style.

Turning a 3D View into a 2D AutoCAD Drawing

Many architectural firms use AutoCAD 3D models to study their designs. After a specific part of a design is modeled and approved, they convert the model into 2D elevations, ready to plug in to their elevation drawing.

If you need to convert your 3D models into 2D line drawings, you can use the Flatshot tool in the 3D Make toolbar.

Set up your drawing view, and then click the Flatshot tool or enter **Flatshot.⌐** at the Command prompt to open the Flatshot dialog box:

PRINTING YOUR MODEL USING VISUAL STYLES

A drawing using Visual Styles can be printed either from the Model tab or from a Layout tab. If you are printing from the Model tab, choose File ➤ Plot. Then in the Plot dialog box, select the visual style from the Shade Plot drop-down list in the Shaded Viewport Options group. If you are plotting from a Layout tab, select the layout viewport border, right-click, and choose Shade Plot from the shortcut menu. You can select from a list of visual styles from a cascading menu. Once you've done this, plot your layout as you normally would.

Select the options you want to use for the 2D line drawing, and then click Create. Depending on the options you select, you will be prompted to select an insertion point or indicate a location for an exported drawing file.

Flatshot offers the ability to place the 2D version of your model in the current drawing as a block, to replace an existing block in the current drawing, or to save the 2D version as a DWG file. Table 20.1 describes the Flatshot options in more detail.

TABLE 20.1:   The Flatshot Options

DESTINATION	WHAT IT DOES
Insert As New Block	Inserts the 2D view in the current drawing as a block. You are prompted for an insertion point, scale, and rotation.
Replace Existing Block	Replaces an existing block with a block of the 2D view. You are prompted to select an existing block.
Select Block	If Replace Existing Block is selected, Select Block lets you select a block to be replaced. A warning is shown if no block is selected.
Export To A File	Exports the 2D view as a drawing file.
File Name And Path	Displays the location for the export file. Click the Browse button to specify a location.
Foreground Lines	
Color	Sets the overall color for the 2D view.
Linetype	Sets the overall linetype for the 2D view.
Obscured Lines	
Show	Displays hidden lines
Color	If Show is turned on, sets the color for hidden lines.
Linetype	If Show is turned on, sets the linetype for hidden lines. The Current Linetype Scale setting is used for linetypes other than continuous.

One very useful feature of Flatshot is that it can create a 2D drawing that displays the hidden lines of a 3D mechanical drawing. Turn on the Show option, and then select a line type such as Hidden for obscured lines to produce a 2D drawing like the one shown in Figure 20.31.

THINGS TO WATCH OUT FOR WHEN EDITING 3D OBJECTS

You have seen how you can use the Copy command on 3D objects. You can also use the Move and Stretch commands on 3D objects to modify their Z coordinate values—but you have to be careful with these commands when editing in 3D. Here are a few tips:

◆ If you want to move a 3D solid using grips, you will need to select the square grip at the bottom center of the solid. The other grips will only move the feature associated with the grip, like a corner or edge. Once that bottom grip is selected, you can switch to another grip as the base point for the move by doing the following: After selecting the base grip, right-click and select Base Point from the shortcut menu, then click on the grip you want to use.

◆ The Scale command will scale an object's Z coordinate value, as well as the standard X coordinate and Y coordinate. Suppose you have an object with an elevation of 2 units. If you use the Scale command to enlarge that object by a factor of 4, the object will have a new elevation of 2 units times 4, or 8 units. If, on the other hand, that object has an elevation of 0, its elevation will not change, because 0 times 4 is still 0.

◆ You can also use Array, Mirror, and Rotate (on the Modify toolbar) on 3D solid objects, but these commands won't affect their Z coordinate values. Z coordinates can be specified for base and insertion points, so take care when using these commands with 3D models.

◆ Using the Move, Stretch, and Copy commands (on the Modify toolbar) with object snaps can produce some unpredictable and unwanted results. As a rule, it is best to use point filters when selecting points with osnap overrides. For example, to move an object from the endpoint of one object to the endpoint of another on the same Z coordinate, invoke the .XY point filter at the Specify base point : and Specify second point : prompts before issuing the Endpoint override. Proceed to pick the endpoint of the object you want; then enter the Z coordinate, or just pick any point to use the current default Z coordinate.

◆ When you create a block, the block will use the currently active UCS to determine its own local coordinate system. When that block is later inserted, it will orient its own coordinate system with the current UCS. (The UCS is discussed in more detail in Chapter 21.)

If You Want to Experiment

You saw how you can create a visual style that mimics the appearance of a freehand sketch. Although such a visual style can be helpful to soften the look of your 3D models, you can also use it on 2D drawings to achieve a similar effect. In this last exercise, you'll see how you can apply the Sketch visual style you created earlier to a 2D plan.

1. Go to the unit plan file you used for the Sketch visual style.

2. Click the Visual Styles Manager tool in the Visual Style control panel.

FIGURE 20.31

A sample of a 2D drawing generated from a 3D model using Flatshot. Note the dashed lines showing the hidden lines of the view.

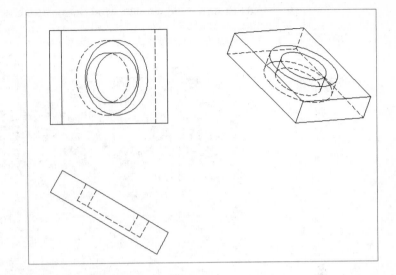

3. In the Visual Styles Manager palette, save the Sketch Visual Style to the Tool Palettes window by clicking the Export The Selected Visual Style To The Tool Palette tool in the Visual Styles Manager toolbar.

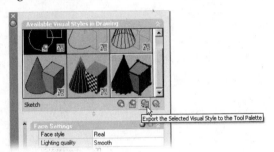

The Tool Palettes window opens and the Sketch visual style appears in the Modeling palette.

4. Open the `20-plan.dwg` file from the companion CD sample files.

5. Click the Sketch visual style in the Modeling palette.

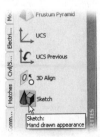

The plan changes to appear like a rough, hand-drawn sketch as shown in Figure 20.32.

FIGURE 20.32

FIGURE 20.32
The Sketch visual
style applied to a
2D drawing

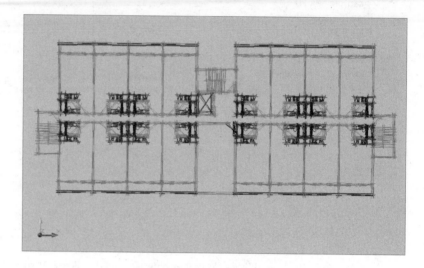

Chapter 21

Using Advanced 3D Features in AutoCAD 2007

AutoCAD 2007's extended set of tools for working with 3D drawings lets you create 3D objects with few limitations on shape and orientation. This chapter focuses on the use of these tools, which help you easily generate 3D forms and view them in both the Perspective and Orthogonal modes.

WARNING   AutoCAD LT does not support any of the features described in this chapter.

Topics in this chapter include the following:

◆ Setting Up AutoCAD 2007 for this Chapter

◆ Mastering the User Coordinate System

◆ Understanding the UCS Options

◆ Using Viewports to Aid in 3D Drawing

◆ Creating Complex 3D Surfaces

◆ Creating Spiral Forms

◆ Creating Surface Models

◆ Moving Objects in 3D Space

Setting Up AutoCAD 2007 for This Chapter

Before you actually start any work, I'd like you to set up AutoCAD in a way that will make your work a little easier. You'll use the AutoCAD Classic workspace, but you will also open the dashboard, which is the 3D palette you were introduced to in Chapter 20. To do so, follow these steps:

1. Open AutoCAD, and then when you see the Workspaces dialog box, select AutoCAD Classic. If for some reason, the Workspaces dialog box does not appear, choose AutoCAD Classic from the Workspaces toolbar.

2. Close the Tool Palettes window and the Sheet Set Manager palette to get a clear view of the drawing area.

3. Choose Tools ➢ Palettes ➢ Dashboard to open the Dashboard palette. Your screen should look similar to Figure 21.1.

With this setup, you can quickly select items from the Draw and Modify toolbars. You also have access to the Properties and Layers toolbars. Now you're ready to get to work.

FIGURE 21.1

The AutoCAD window
set up for this chapter

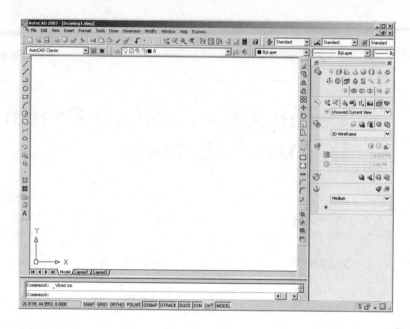

Mastering the User Coordinate System

The User Coordinate System (UCS) enables you to define a custom coordinate system in 2D and 3D space. In fact, you've been using a default UCS, called the *World Coordinate System (WCS)*, all along. By now you are familiar with the L-shaped icon in the lower-left corner of the AutoCAD screen, containing a small square and the letters X and Y. The square indicates that you are currently in the WCS; the X and Y indicate the positive directions of the X and Y axes. WCS is a global system of reference from which you can define other User Coordinate Systems.

It might help to think of these AutoCAD User Coordinate Systems as different drawing surfaces, or two-dimensional planes. You can have several User Coordinate Systems at any given time. By setting up these different UCSs, you can draw as you would in the WCS in 2D, yet draw a 3D image.

Suppose you want to draw a house in 3D with doors and windows on each of its sides. You can set up a UCS for each of the sides; then you can move from UCS to UCS to add your doors and windows (see Figure 21.2). Within each UCS, you draw your doors and windows as you would in a typical 2D drawing. You can even insert elevation views of doors and windows that you created in other drawings.

In this chapter, you will be experimenting with several views and UCSs. All the commands you will use are available both at the command line and via the menu bar. In addition, you can access a number of the UCS commands from the UCS toolbar.

Defining a UCS

In the first set of exercises, you will draw a chair that you can later add to your 3D unit drawing. In drawing this chair, you will be exposed to the use of the UCS, as well as to some of the other 3D capabilities available in AutoCAD.

1. Open the `barcelona1.dwg` file from the Projects files of the companion CD. Metric users should open `barcelona1_metric.dwg`. This file contains two rectangles that you'll use to create a chair.

2. Select Southwest Isometric from the 3D Navigate control panel or choose View ➤ 3D Views ➤ SW Isometric. This gives you a 3D view from the lower left of the rectangles, as shown in the bottom image in Figure 21.3. Zoom out a bit to give yourself some room to work.

3. Select the two rectangles, and then click the Properties tool on the Standard toolbar.

4. In the Properties palette, enter **3** in the Thickness setting and press ↵. This gives the seat and back a thickness of 3 . Metric users should make the thickness 7.6 cm.

FIGURE 21.2

Different User Coordinate Systems in a 3D drawing

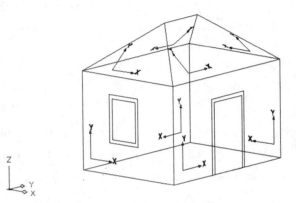

FIGURE 21.3

The chair seat and back in the Plan (top) and Isometric (bottom) views

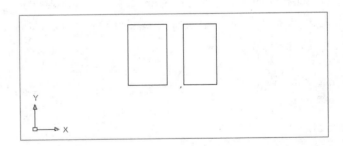

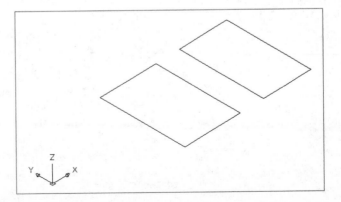

5. Press the Escape key and close the Properties palette. Click the Convert To Solid tool in the expanded 3D Make control panel. To expand the 3D Make control panel, point to the 3D Make title bar, and then click the downward-pointing arrow that appears.

Click here to expand the
3D Make control panel.

6. Select the two rectangles, and then press ↵.

Notice that the UCS icon appears in the same plane as the current coordinate system. The icon will help you keep track of which coordinate system you are in. Now you can see the chair components as 3D objects.

Next, you will define a UCS that is aligned with one side of the seat:

1. Right-click any toolbar and choose UCS from the shortcut menu to open the UCS toolbar.

Choose Tools ➢ Named UCS to open the UCS dialog box.

2. Select the Orthographic UCSs tab to view a set of predefined UCSs.

3. Select Front in the list box. Figure 21.4 shows the orientation of the Front UCS.

4. Click the Set Current button to make the Front UCS current.

5. Click OK to close the dialog box.

The Orthographic UCSs tab offers a set of predefined UCSs for each of the six standard orthographic projection planes. Figure 21.4 shows these UCSs in relation to the World Coordinate System.

FIGURE 21.4
The six predefined
UCS orientations

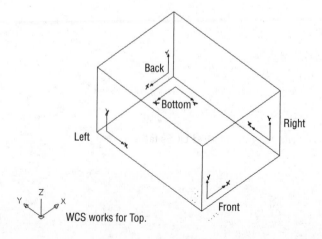

Because a good part of 3D work involves drawing in these orthographic planes, AutoCAD supplies these ready-made UCS orientations for quick access. But you aren't limited to these six orientations by any means. If you're familiar with mechanical drafting, you'll see that the orthographic UCSs correspond to the typical orthographic projection used in mechanical drafting. If you're an architect, the Front, Left, Back, and Right UCSs correspond to the south, west, north, and east elevations of a building. Before you continue building the chair model, you'll want to move the UCS to the surface on which you will be working. Right now, the UCS has its origin located in the same place as the WCS origin.

You can move a UCS so that its origin is anywhere in the drawing where it's needed:

1. Click the Origin UCS tool in the UCS toolbar or choose Tools ➤ New UCS ➤ Origin.

2. Use the Endpoint Osnap and click the bottom-front corner of the chair seat, as shown in Figure 21.5. The UCS icon moves to indicate its new origin's location.

FIGURE 21.5
Setting up a UCS

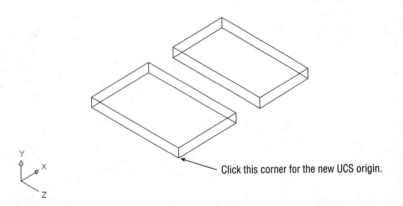

Click this corner for the new UCS origin.

You just created a new UCS based on the Front UCS you selected from the UCS dialog box. Now as you move your cursor, you'll see that the origin of the UCS icon corresponds to a 0,0 coordinate. Although you have a new UCS, the World Coordinate System still exists, and you can always return to it when you need to.

Saving a UCS

After you've gone through the work of creating a UCS, you might want to save it, especially if you think you'll want to come back to it later. Here's how to save a UCS:

1. Choose Tools ➤ Named UCS to open the UCS dialog box.

2. Make sure the Named UCSs tab is selected, and then highlight the Unnamed option in the Current UCS list box.

3. Right-click Unnamed and then choose Rename from the shortcut menu. The item changes to allow editing.

4. Type **3DSW**↵ for the name of your new UCS.

5. Click OK to exit the dialog box.

Your UCS is now saved with the name 3DSW. You'll be able to recall it from the UCS dialog box or by using other methods that you'll learn about later in this chapter.

Working in a UCS

Next, you will want to arrange the seat and back and draw the legs of the chair. Your UCS is oriented so that you can easily adjust the orientation of the chair components. As you work through the next exercise, notice that while you are manipulating 3D objects, you are really using the same tools you've used to edit 2D objects.

Follow these steps to adjust the seat and back and to draw legs:

1. Click the seat back to expose its grips.

2. Click the bottom grip, as shown in the first image in Figure 21.6.

3. Right-click the mouse to open the Grip Edit shortcut menu.

FIGURE 21.6
Moving the components of the chair into place

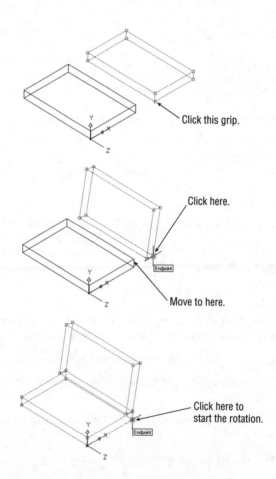

4. Choose Rotate from the menu. Notice how the seat back now rotates with the movement of the cursor. It rotates in the plane of the new UCS you created earlier.

5. Type **80.⅃** to rotate the seat back 80°. Your view will look like the second image in Figure 21.6.

6. Click the bottom grip, as shown in the second image in Figure 21.6.

7. Right-click the mouse again and choose Move.

8. Using the Endpoint Osnap, click the top corner of the chair seat to join the chair back to the seat, as shown in the second image in Figure 21.6.

9. Click both the chair seat and back; then click the bottom-corner grip of the seat, as shown in the third image in Figure 21.6.

10. Right-click the mouse and then choose Rotate from the Grip Edit shortcut menu.

11. Enter **–10.⅃** to rotate both the seat and back a minus 10 degrees. Press the Esc key to clear the grips. Your chair will look like Figure 21.7.

FIGURE 21.7
The chair after rotating and moving the components

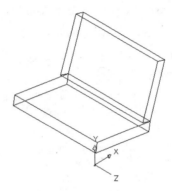

The new UCS orientation enabled you to use the grips to adjust the chair seat and back. All the grip rotation in the previous exercise was confined to the plane of the new UCS. Mirroring and scaling will also occur in relation to the current UCS.

Building 3D Parts in Separate Files

As you work in 3D, your models will become fairly complex. When your model becomes too crowded to see things clearly, it helps to build parts of a model and then import them instead of building everything in one file. In the next set of exercises, you'll draw the legs of the chair and then import them to the main chair file to give you some practice in the procedure.

I've prepared a drawing called legs.dwg, which consists of two polylines that describe the shape of the legs. This is done to save you some tedious work that is not related to 3D modeling. You'll use this file as a starting point for the legs, and then you'll import the legs into the barcelona1.dwg file.

1. Open the legs.dwg file from the project samples you installed from the companion CD. The file consists of two polyline splines that are in the shape of one set of legs. You'll turn these simple lines into 3D solids.

2. Choose Modify ➢ Object ➢ Polyline.

3. At the Select polyline or [Multiple]: prompt, enter **M** ↵ to select multiple polylines. Then select the two polylines and press ↵.

4. At the Enter an option [Close/Open/Join/Width/Fit/Spline/Decurve/Ltype gen/ Undo]: prompt, enter **W** ↵.

5. At the Specify new width for all segments: prompt, enter **0.5** to give the polylines a width of 0.5″. Metric users should enter **1.27**.

6. Press ↵ to exit the Pedit command.

Next you need to change the Thickness property of the two polylines to make them 2″ or 5 cm wide.

1. With the two polylines selected, open the Properties palette and set their Thickness to 2″. Metric users should make the thickness 5 cm.

2. Close the Properties palette when you are finished changing the Thickness property.

3. Click the Convert To Solid tool in the 3D Make control panel, choose Modify ➢ 3D Operations ➢ Convert To Solid, or enter **convtosolid** ↵ at the Command prompt.

4. Select the two polylines, and then press ↵. The lines become 3D solids as shown in Figure 21.8.

5. Click the Union tool in the 3D Make control panel, select the two legs, and press ↵. The two legs are now a single 3D solid.

As you've just seen, you can convert polylines that have both a width and a thickness into 3D solids. Now you're ready to add the legs to the rest of the chair.

FIGURE 21.8

Move the legs so they meet the chair seat at the corner indicated.

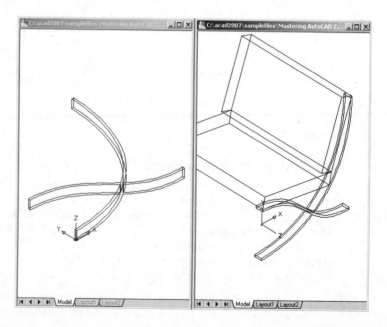

TIP   Polylines are the best objects to use for 3D, because you can generate complex shapes easily by giving the polylines thickness and width. But when you convert a polyline into a solid, you must be in the same UCS as the one on which the object was created. You can use the Object option of the UCS command to orient the UCS to the polyline before you use the Convert To Solid tool.

1. Choose Window ➤ Tile Vertically. You'll see the legs drawing on the left and the rest of the chair on the right.

2. Click in the barcelona1 drawing and choose View ➤ Zoom ➤ Extents to get an overall view of the chair so far.

3. Click in the Legs drawing, and then click the legs 3D solid to select it.

4. Click and hold the cursor on the legs until you see the arrow cursor with a small rectangle.

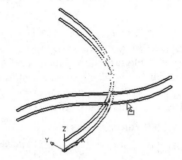

5. When you see the rectangle, drag the mouse into the barcelona1 drawing. You see the legs appear in the proper orientation.

6. Release the mouse to place the legs in the barcelona1 drawing. You don't need to be precise about placing the legs as you can move them into position next.

7. Use the Move tool to move the legs so that the endpoint of the upper leg joins the chair seat as shown in Figure 21.8.

8. Save and close the `legs.dwg` file, and expand the `barcelona1.dwg` file to fill the AutoCAD window.

In these last few exercises, you worked on the legs of the chair in a separate file and then imported them into the main chair file with a click-and-drag motion. By working on parts in separate files, you can keep your model organized and more manageable. You may have also noticed that although the legs were drawn in the WCS, they were inserted in the 3DSW UCS that you created earlier. This shows you that imported objects are placed in the current UCS. The same would have happened if you inserted an Xref or another file.

Understanding the UCS Options

You've seen how to select a UCS from a set of predefined UCSs. You can frequently use these preset UCSs and make minor adjustments to them to get the exact UCS you want.

You can define a UCS in other ways. You can, for example, use the surface of your chair seat to define the orientation of a UCS. In the following section, you will be shown the different ways you can

CONTROLLING THE UCS ICON

If the UCS icon is not behaving as described in the exercises of this chapter, chances are that its settings have been altered. You can control the behavior of the UCS icon through the UCS dialog box. To open the UCS dialog box, choose Tools ➤ Named UCS or click the Named UCS tool on the UCS II toolbar; then click the Settings tab.

The settings in the UCS Icon Settings group affect the way the UCS icon behaves. Normally, the On and Display At UCS Origin Point check boxes are selected. If On is not selected, you won't see the UCS icon at all. If the Display At UCS Origin Point check box is not selected, the UCS icon will remain in the lower-left corner of the drawing window, no matter where its origin is placed in the drawing.

If you have multiple viewports set up in a drawing, you can set these two options independently for each viewport. The third option, Apply To All Active Viewports, forces the first two settings to apply in all viewports.

Two more options appear in the UCS Settings group. If you have multiple viewports open, the Save UCS With Viewport option enables AutoCAD to maintain a separate UCS for each viewport. The Update View To Plan When UCS Is Changed option forces the display to show a Plan view of the current UCS. This means that if you change a UCS orientation, AutoCAD will automatically show a Plan view of the new UCS orientation. This option also forces viewport views to show the extents of Plan views; so if you find that your views are automatically zooming to extents when you don't want them to, turn this setting off.

Another tool for controlling the UCS icon is the UCS Icon dialog box. To open it, enter **Ucsicon.↵P.↵**.

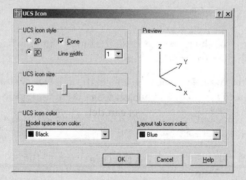

By using this dialog box, you can fine-tune the appearance of the UCS icon, including size and color. The 2D radio button in the UCS Icon Style group changes the UCS icon to the old-style UCS icon used in earlier versions of AutoCAD.

set up a UCS. Learning how to move effortlessly between UCSs is crucial to mastering the creation of 3D models, so you'll want to pay special attention to the command options shown in these examples.

Note that these examples are for your reference. You can try them out on your own model, but you don't need to use these examples as exercised for this chapter. These options are accessible from either the Tools ➤ New UCS cascading menu or the UCS toolbar.

UCS Based on Object Orientation

You can define a UCS based on the orientation of an object. This is helpful when you want to work on a predefined object to fill in details on its surface plane. Follow these steps to define a UCS in this way:

NOTE   These steps are for information only and are not part of the tutorial. You can try this out at another time when you are not working through an exercise.

1. Click the Object UCS tool on the UCS toolbar, choose Tools ➤ New UCS ➤ Object, or type **UCS↵OB↵**.

2. At the `Select object to align UCS:` prompt, pick the object that you want to use to define the UCS. For example, you could click on a polyline that you want to edit in 3D. The UCS icon shifts to reflect the new coordinate system's orientation. Figure 21.9 shows an example of using the OB option to select the edge of the chair seat.

FIGURE 21.9

Using the Object option of the UCS command to locate a UCS

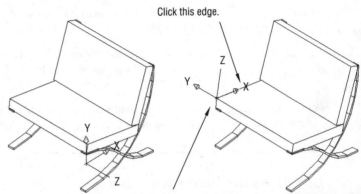

Click this edge.

The UCS will align to the select object using the Object option.

When you create a UCS using the Object option, the location of the UCS origin and its orientation depends on how the selected object was created.

Table 21.1 describes how an object can determine the orientation of a UCS.

TABLE 21.1:   Effects of Objects on the Orientation of a UCS

OBJECT TYPE	UCS ORIENTATION
Arc	The center of the arc establishes the UCS origin. The X axis of the UCS passes through the pick point on the arc.
Circle	The center of the circle establishes the UCS origin. The X axis of the UCS passes through the pick point on the circle.
Dimension	The midpoint of the dimension text establishes the origin of the UCS origin. The X axis of the UCS is parallel to the X axis that was active when the dimension was drawn.
Face (of a 3D solid)	The origin of the UCS will be placed on a quadrant of a circular surface or on the corner of a polygonal surface.
Line	The endpoint nearest the pick point establishes the origin of the UCS, and the x-z plane of the UCS contains the line.

TABLE 21.1:   Effects of Objects on the Orientation of a UCS *(CONTINUED)*

OBJECT TYPE	UCS ORIENTATION
Point	The point location establishes the UCS origin. The UCS orientation is arbitrary.
2D polyline	The starting point of the polyline establishes the UCS origin. The X axis is determined by the direction from the first point to the next vertex.
Solid	The first point of the solid establishes the origin of the UCS. The second point of the solid establishes the X axis.
Trace	The direction of the trace establishes the X axis of the UCS, and the beginning point sets the origin.
3D Face	The first point of the 3D Face establishes the origin. The first and second points establish the X axis. The plane defined by the 3D Face determines the orientation of the UCS.
Shapes, text, blocks, attributes, and attribute definitions	The insertion point establishes the origin of the UCS. The object's rotation angle establishes the X axis.

UCS Based on Offset Orientation

At times you might want to work in a UCS that has the same orientation as the current UCS but is offset. For example, you might be drawing a building that has several parallel walls offset with a sawtooth effect (see Figure 21.10).

FIGURE 21.10
Using the Origin option
to shift the UCS

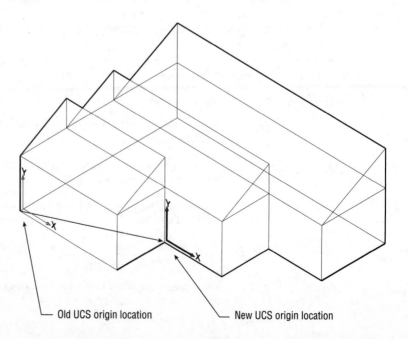

Old UCS origin location   New UCS origin location

You can easily hop from one UCS to a parallel UCS by using the Origin option. Click the Origin UCS tool on the UCS toolbar, choose Tools ➤ New UCS ➤ Origin, or type **UCS**↵**O**↵. At the Specify new origin point <0,0,0>: prompt, pick the new origin for your UCS.

Moving versus Creating a UCS Origin

The Origin UCS tool creates a new UCS that you can save under its own name. A similar option is Move UCS on the Tools drop-down menu. At first glance, these tools seem to do the same thing; that is, they create a new UCS by moving an existing UCS's origin. There is a subtle difference between the two, however. Choosing Tools ➤ Move UCS moves an existing named UCS to a new location. It doesn't actually create a new one. For example, if you use Move UCS to move the 3DSW UCS you created earlier in this chapter, 3DSW will appear in its new location when you recall it. On the other hand, if you use the Origin UCS tool to change the origin of the 3DSW UCS, AutoCAD creates an entirely different UCS and maintains the original location of 3DSW.

The Tools ➤ Move UCS option can also be found on the UCS II toolbar. You'll get a chance to work with the UCS II toolbar in the next section.

NOTE The steps in this section are for information only and are not part of the tutorial. You can try this out at another time when you are not working through an exercise.

UCS Rotated Around an Axis

Now suppose you want to change the orientation of the X, Y, or Z axis of a UCS. You can do so by using the X, Y, or Z Axis Rotate UCS options on the UCS toolbar. This is perhaps one of the most frequently used UCS options.

1. Click the Z tool on the UCS toolbar, choose Tools ➤ New UCS ➤ Z, or type **UCS**↵**Z**↵. This will enable you to rotate the current UCS around the Z axis.

2. At the Specify rotation angle about Z axis <90>: prompt, press ↵ to accept the default of 90°. The UCS icon rotates about the Z axis to reflect the new orientation of the current UCS (see Figure 21.11).

FIGURE 21.11
Rotating the UCS
about the Z axis

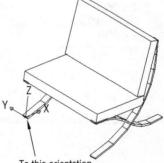

The UCS rotates 90° from this orientation...   To this orientation.

Similarly, the X and Y Axis Rotate UCS options enable you to rotate the UCS about the current X and Y axis, respectively, just as you did for the Z axis earlier. The X and Y Axis Rotate UCS tools are helpful in orienting a UCS to an inclined plane. For example, if you want to work on the plane of a sloped roof of a building, you can first use the Origin UCS tool to align the UCS to the edge of a roof and then use the X Axis Rotate UCS tool to rotate the UCS to the angle of the roof slope, as shown in Figure 21.12. Note that the default is 90°, so you only have to press ↵ to rotate the UCS 90°; but you can also enter a value at the Specify another rotation angle: prompt.

Finally, you align the Z axis between two points using the Z Axis Vector option. This is useful when you have objects in the drawing that you can use to align the Z axis. Here are the steps:

1. Click the Z Axis Vector tool on the UCS toolbar, choose Tools ➤ New UCS ➤ Z Axis Vector, or type **UCS↵ZA↵**.

2. At the Specify new origin point or [Object]<0,0,0>: prompt, press ↵ to accept the default, which is the current UCS origin, or you can select a new origin.

3. At the next prompt

   Specify point on positive portion of Z-axis <0′-0″, 0′- 0″, 0′-1″>:

   select another point to indicate the Z axis orientation. Figure 21.13 shows the resulting UCS if you use the bottom of the Barcelona1 chair leg to define the Z axis.

FIGURE 21.12
Moving a UCS to the plane of a sloping roof

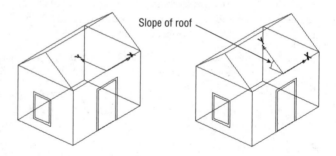

FIGURE 21.13
Picking points for the Z Axis Vector option

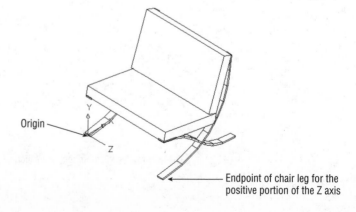

WARNING   Because your cursor location is in the plane of the current UCS, it is best to pick a point on an object by using either the Osnap overrides or the coordinate filters.

Orienting a UCS in the View Plane

Finally, you can define a UCS in the current view plane. This is useful if you want to switch quickly to the current view plane for editing or for adding text to a 3D view.

Click the View UCS tool on the UCS toolbar, choose Tools ➢ New UCS ➢ View, or type **UCS.⏎V⏎**. The UCS icon changes to show that the UCS is aligned with the current view.

AutoCAD uses the current UCS origin point for the origin of the new UCS. By defining a view as a UCS, you can enter text to label your drawing, just as you would in a technical illustration. Text entered in a plane created in this way appears normal.

Now you've finished your tour of the UCS command. Set the UCS back to the World Coordinate System and save the `Barcelon1.dwg` file.

You've explored nearly every option in creating a UCS, except for one. In the next section, you'll learn about the 3 Point option for creating a UCS. This is the most versatile method for creating a UCS, but it is a bit more involved than some of the other UCS options.

Saving a UCS with a View

AutoCAD has the ability to save a UCS with a view. Choose View ➢ Named Views to open the Views dialog box, and then click the Named Views tab. Click the New button to open the New View dialog box. Enter a name for your new view; then make sure the Save UCS With View check box is selected. By default, AutoCAD saves the current UCS with the view. You can also choose a UCS to save with a new view by using the UCS Name drop-down list.

Using Viewports to Aid in 3D Drawing

In Chapter 15, you worked extensively with AutoCAD's floating viewports in Paper Space. In this section, you will use *tiled* viewports to see your 3D model from several sides at the same time. This is helpful in both creating and editing 3D drawings because it enables you to refer to different portions of the drawing without having to change views.

Tiled viewports are created directly in Model Space, as you'll see in the following exercise:

1. Choose View ➢ Viewports ➢ Named Viewports to open the Viewports dialog box.

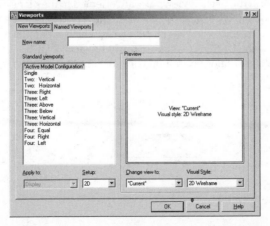

2. Make sure the New Viewports tab is selected, and then select Three: Right from the Standard Viewports list on the left. The window on the right changes to display a sample of the viewport configuration. It shows three rectangles, which represent the viewports, arranged with two on the left and one larger one to the right. Notice that each rectangle is labeled as Current. This tells you that the current view will be placed in each viewport.

3. Open the Setup drop-down list at the bottom of the dialog box and select 3D. Now notice that the labels in the viewport sample change to indicate Top, Front, and SE Isometric. This is close to the arrangement that you'll want, but you need to make one more adjustment. The viewport to the right, SE Isometric, will show the back side of the chair. You want an SW Isometric view in this window.

4. Click the SE Isometric viewport sample. Notice that the sample viewport border changes to a double border to indicate that it is selected.

5. Open the Change View To drop-down list just below the sample viewports and select SW Isometric. The label in the selected viewport changes to let you know that the view will now contain the SW Isometric view. Notice that the Change View To list contains the standard four Isometric views and the six Orthogonal views. By clicking a sample viewport and selecting an option from the Change View To drop-down list, you can arrange your viewport views in nearly any way you want.

6. To keep this viewport arrangement, enter **My Viewport Setup** in the New Name input box.

7. Now click OK. Your display changes to show three viewports arranged as they were indicated in the Viewports dialog box (see Figure 21.14).

You've set up your viewport. Let's check to see that your viewport arrangement was saved:

1. Choose View ➢ Viewports ➢ Named Viewports to open the Viewports dialog box again.

2. Click the Named Viewports tab. My Viewport Setup is listed in the Named Viewports list box. If you click it, a sample view of your viewport arrangement appears on the right.

3. After you've reviewed the addition to the Named Viewports list, close the dialog box.

Now take a close look at your viewport setup. Notice that the UCS icon in each of the two Orthogonal views in the two left viewports are oriented to the plane of the view. AutoCAD enables you to set up a different UCS for each viewport. The top view uses the WCS because it is in the same plane as the WCS. The side view has its own UCS, which is parallel to its view. The Isometric view to the right retains the UCS you saved—namely the 3DSW UCS.

Another Viewports dialog box option you haven't tried yet is the Apply To drop-down list in the New Viewports tab.

FIGURE 21.14

Three viewports, each displaying a different view

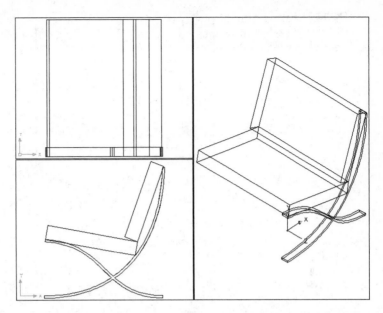

This list shows two options: Display and Current Viewport. When Display is selected, the option you choose from the Standard Viewports list applies to the overall display. When Current Viewport is selected, the option you select applies to the selected viewport in the sample view in the right side of the dialog box. You can use the Current Viewport option to build multiple viewports in custom arrangements.

You have the legs for one side. The next step is to mirror those legs for the other side:

1. Click the top view of the chair in the upper-left viewport.

2. Turn the Polar mode on, and then click the Mirror tool on the Modify toolbar.

3. In the upper-left viewport, click the 3D solid representing the chair legs, and then press ↵.

4. At the Specify first point of mirror line: prompt, use the Midpoint Osnap and select the midpoint of the chair seat, as shown in Figure 21.15.

5. At the Specify second point of mirror line: prompt, pick any location to the right of the point you selected so that the rubber-banding line is exactly horizontal.

6. Press ↵ at the Erase source objects? [Yes/No]: prompt. The legs are mirrored to the opposite side of the chair. Your screen should look similar to Figure 21.15.

Your chair is now complete. Let's finish by getting a better look at it:

1. Click the viewport to the right showing the Isometric view.

2. Choose View ➤ Viewports ➤ 1 Viewport..

3. Use the Zoom tool to adjust your view so that it looks similar to Figure 21.16.

FIGURE 21.15
Mirroring the legs from
one side to another

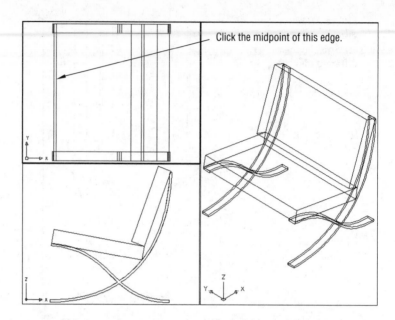

Click the midpoint of this edge.

FIGURE 21.16
The chair in 3D with
hidden lines removed

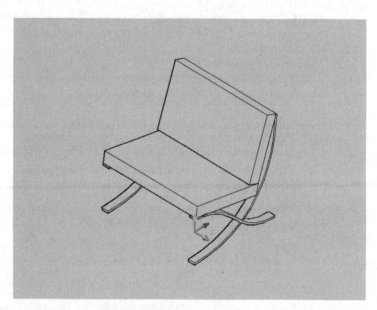

4. Click the drop-down list in the Visual Styles control panel and select 3D Hidden to get a view similar to Figure 21.16.

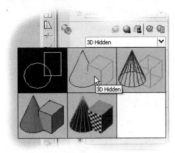

Creating Complex 3D Surfaces

In the previous example, you drew a chair composed of objects that were mostly straight lines or curves with a thickness. All the forms in that chair were defined in planes perpendicular to one another. For a 3D model such as this, you can get by using the orthographic UCSs. At times, however, you will want to draw objects that do not fit so easily into perpendicular or parallel planes. In this section, you'll create more-complex forms by using some of AutoCAD's other 3D commands.

Laying Out a 3D Form

In this next group of exercises, you will draw a butterfly chair. This chair has no perpendicular or parallel planes to work with, so you will start by setting up some points that you will use for reference only. This is similar in concept to laying out a 2D drawing. As you progress through the drawing construction, notice how the reference points are established to help create the chair. You will also construct some temporary 3D lines to use for reference. These temporary lines will be your layout. These points will define the major UCSs needed to construct the drawing. So the main point here is to show you some of the options for creating and saving UCSs.

To save some time, I've created the 2D drawing that you'll use to build your 3D layout. This drawing consists of two rectangles that are offset by 4″ or 10 mm for metric users. To make it more interesting, they are also off center from each other (see Figure 21.17).

1. Open the `Butterfly1.dwg` file from the Project files you installed from the companion CD.

2. Choose View ➢ 3D Views ➢ SW Isometric. This will give you a view from the lower-left side of the rectangles.

3. Zoom out so the rectangles occupy about a third of the drawing area window.

Now you need to move the outer rectangle in the Z axis so that its elevation is 30″(76 cm for metric users):

1. Click the outer rectangle and then click one of its grips.

2. Right-click to open the Grip Edit shortcut menu.

3. Choose Move and then enter @0,0,30⤶. Metric users should enter @0,0,76⤶. This tells AutoCAD to move the rectangle a 0 distance in both the X and Y axes and 30″ (or 76 cm) in the Z axis.

FIGURE 21.17

Setting up a layout for a butterfly chair

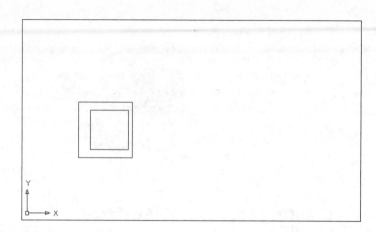

TIP As an alternate method in step 3, after choosing Move from the Grip Edit shortcut menu, you can also turn on the Ortho mode and point the cursor vertically so it shows a −Z in the coordinate readout; then enter **30↵** or **76↵** for metric users.

4. Pan your view downward so it looks similar to Figure 21.18.

5. Use the Line tool to draw lines from the corners of the outer square to the corners of the inner square. Use the Endpoint Osnap to select the exact corners of the squares. This is the layout for your chair—not yet the finished product.

Spherical and Cylindrical Coordinate Formats

In the previous exercise, you used relative Cartesian coordinates to locate the second point for the Move command. For commands that accept 3D input, you can also specify displacements by using the Spherical and Cylindrical Coordinate formats.

FIGURE 21.18

The finished chair layout

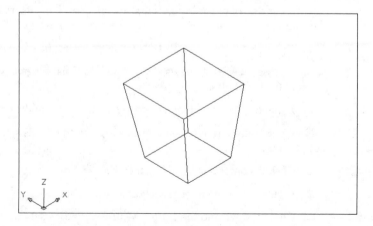

The *Spherical Coordinate format* lets you specify a distance in 3D space while specifying the angle in terms of degrees from the X axis of the current UCS and degrees from the x-y plane of the current UCS (see the top image in Figure 21.19). For example, to specify a distance of 4.5″ (11.43 cm) at a 30° angle from the X axis and 45° from the x-y plane, enter **@4.5<30<45** (or **@11.43<30<45** for metric users). This refers to the direct distance, followed by a < symbol; then the angle from the X axis of the current UCS followed by another < symbol; then the angle from the x-y plane of the current UCS. To use the Spherical Coordinate format to move the rectangle in the exercise, enter **@30<0<90** at the Second point: prompt, or **@76<0<90** for metric users.

FIGURE 21.19

The Spherical and Cylindrical Coordinate formats

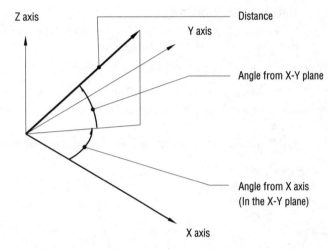

[Distance] < [Angle from X axis] < [Angle from X-Y plane]

The Spherical Coordinate Format

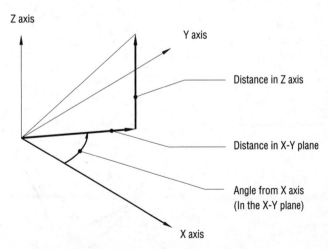

[Distance in X-Y plane] < [Angle from X axis] , [Distance in Z axis]

The Cylindrical Coordinate Format

The *Cylindrical Coordinate format,* on the other hand, lets you specify a location in terms of a distance in the plane of the current UCS and a distance in the Z axis. You also specify an angle from the X axis of the current UCS (see the bottom image in Figure 21.19). For example, to locate a point that is a distance of 4.5″ (11.43 cm) in the plane of the current UCS, at an angle of 30°from the X axis, and a distance of 3.3″ (8.38 cm) in the Z axis, enter **@4.5<30,3.3** (or **@11.43<30,8.38** for metric users). This refers to the distance of the displacement from the plane of the current UCS, followed by the < symbol; then the angle from the X axis, followed by a comma; then the distance in the Z axis. Using the cylindrical format to move the rectangle, you enter **@0<0,30** at the Second point: prompt, or **@0<0,76** for metric users.

Using a 3D Polyline

Now you will draw the legs for the butterfly chair by using a 3D polyline. This is a polyline that can be drawn in 3D space. Here are the steps:

1. Choose Draw ➢ 3D Polyline or type **3p↵**.

2. At the Specify start point of polyline: prompt, pick a series of points, as shown in Figure 21.20 (top), by using the Endpoint and Midpoint Osnap.

TIP   This would be a good place to use the Running Osnaps feature.

FIGURE 21.20
Using 3D polylines to
draw the legs of the
butterfly chair

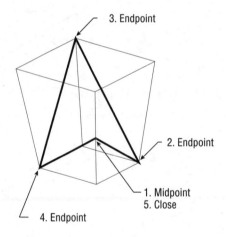

3. Endpoint

2. Endpoint

1. Midpoint
5. Close

4. Endpoint

Draw a polyline
in the sequence
shown to the left.
Use the Osnap
overrides indicated
in the figure.

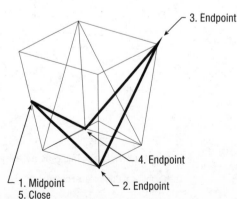

3. Endpoint

4. Endpoint

1. Midpoint
5. Close

2. Endpoint

Repeat the process
for the other part
of the chair legs.

3. Draw another 3D polyline in the mirror image of the first (see the lower image in Figure 21.20).

4. Erase the connecting vertical lines that make up the frame but keep the rectangles. You'll use them later.

All objects, with the exception of lines and 3D polylines, are restricted to the plane of your current UCS. Two other legacy 3D objects, 3D Faces and 3D Meshes, are also restricted. You can use the Pline command to draw polylines in only one plane, but you can use the 3DPoly command to create a polyline in three dimensions. 3Dpoly objects cannot, however, be given thickness or width.

Creating a Curved 3D Surface

Next, you will draw the seat of the chair. The seat of a butterfly chair is usually made of canvas and drapes from the four corners of the chair legs. You will first define the perimeter of the seat by using arcs, and then you'll use the Edge Surface tool on the Surfaces toolbar to form the shape of the draped canvas. The Edge Surface tool creates a surface based on four objects defining the edges of that surface. In this example, you will use arcs to define the edges of the seat.

To draw the arcs defining the seat edge, you must first establish the UCSs in the planes of those edges. In the previous example you created a UCS for the side of the chair before you could draw the legs. In the same way, you must create a UCS defining the planes that contain the edges of the seat.

Because the UCS you want to define is not orthogonal, you will need to use the three-point method. This lets you define the plane of the UCS based on three points:

1. Click the 3 Point UCS tool on the UCS toolbar, choose Tools ➤ New UCS ➤ 3 Point, or type UCS↵3↵. This option enables you to define a UCS based on three points that you select.

TIP Remember, it helps to think of a UCS as a drawing surface situated on the surface of the object you want to draw or edit.

2. At the Specify new origin point <0,0,0>: prompt, use the Endpoint Osnap to pick the bottom of the chair leg to the far left, as shown in the left image of Figure 21.21. This is the origin point of your new UCS.

3. At the Specify point on positive portion of X-axis: prompt, use the Endpoint Osnap to pick the bottom of the next leg to the right of the first one, as shown in the left image in Figure 21.21.

FIGURE 21.21
Defining and saving three UCSs

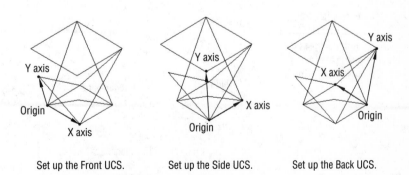

Set up the Front UCS.   Set up the Side UCS.   Set up the Back UCS.

4. At the `Specify point on positive-Y portion of the UCS XY plane:` prompt, pick the top corner of the butterfly chair seat, as shown in the left image in Figure 21.21. The UCS icon changes to indicate your new UCS.

5. Now that you have defined a UCS, you need to save it so that you can return to it later. Choose Tools ➢ Named UCS, or type **UC↵** to open the UCS dialog box.

6. With the Named UCSs tab selected, right-click the Unnamed item in the list box and choose Rename from the shortcut menu.

7. Enter **Front↵**.

8. Click OK to exit the UCS dialog box.

You've defined and saved a UCS for the front side of the chair. As you can see from the UCS icon, this UCS is at a non-orthogonal angle to the WCS. Continue by creating UCSs for two more sides of the butterfly chair:

1. Define a UCS for the side of the chair, as shown in the middle image in Figure 21.21. Use the UCS Control dialog box to rename this UCS Side, just as you did for Front in steps 5 through 8. Remember that you renamed the Unnamed UCS.

2. Repeat these steps for a UCS for the back of the chair, named Back. Use the right image in Figure 21.21 for reference.

3. Open the UCS dialog box again, and in the Named UCSs tab, highlight Front.

4. Click the Set Current button and then click OK. This activates Front as the current UCS.

5. Choose Draw ➢ Arc ➢ Start, End, Direction.

6. Draw the arc defining the front edge of the chair (see Figure 21.22). Use the Endpoint Osnap override to pick the top endpoints of the chair legs as the endpoints of the arc. (If you need help with the Arc command, refer to Chapter 3.)

7. Repeat steps 3 through 6 for the UCS named Back—each time using the top endpoints of the legs for the endpoints of the arc.

8. Restore the UCS for the side, but instead of drawing an arc, use the Polyline tool and draw a polyline spline similar to the one in Figure 21.22. If you need help with polyline splines, see Chapter 14.

FIGURE 21.22
Drawing the front and back seat edge using arcs and a polyline spline

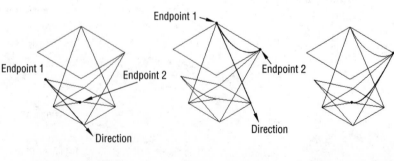

Drawing the front arc   Drawing the back arc   The polyline spline

Next, you will mirror the side-edge spline to the opposite side. This will save you from having to define a UCS for that side:

1. Click the World UCS tool on the UCS toolbar to restore the WCS. The reason for doing this is that you want to mirror the arc along an axis that is parallel to the plane of the WCS. Remember that you must use the coordinate system that defines the plane in which you want to work.

2. Click the polyline you drew for the side of the chair (the one drawn on the Side UCS).

3. Click the midpoint grip of the arc in the Side UCS; then right-click and choose Mirror from the shortcut menu.

4. Enter **C**↵ to select the Copy option.

5. Enter **B**↵ to select a new base point for the mirror axis.

6. At the `Specify base point:` prompt, use the Midpoint override to pick the midpoints of the rectangle at the bottom of the model. Refer to Figure 21.23 for help. The polyline should mirror to the opposite side, and your chair should look like Figure 21.24.

7. Press the Esc key twice to clear the grips.

FIGURE 21.23

Set your UCS to World, and then mirror the arc that defines the side of the chair seat.

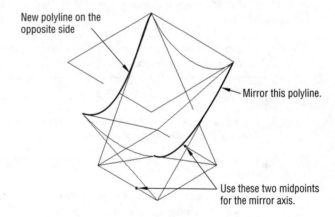

New polyline on the opposite side

Mirror this polyline.

Use these two midpoints for the mirror axis.

FIGURE 21.24

Your butterfly chair so far

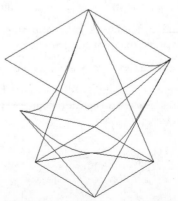

QUICK HOPS TO YOUR UCSS

If you find you're jumping from one saved UCS to another, you'll want to know about the UCS II toolbar. The UCS II toolbar has a drop-down list that contains the World and Previous UCS options as well as all the saved UCSs in a drawing. You can use this list as a quick way to move between UCSs that you've set up or even between the predefined orthogonal UCSs.

Two other tools on the UCS II toolbar give you access to the UCS dialog box and the Move UCS tool, which moves an existing UCS to another location. As with all toolbars, you can open the UCS II toolbar by right-clicking any toolbar and then choosing UCS II from the shortcut menu.

Another great way to jump quickly between UCSs is to use the UCS Face option. The Face option requires a 3D solid, but once you have one in place, you can choose Tools ➢ New UCS ➢ Face and then click the face of the solid to which you want to align your UCS. For example, you can use the Loft command (see the section "Shaping the Solid" later in this chapter) to create a solid similar to the solid shown in Figure 21.27 that connects the top and bottom rectangles of the butterfly chair. You can then use the UCS Face option to align to the sides of that solid to draw the arcs and polylines for the seat outline. This way, you are using the 3D solid as a layout tool.

Finally, let's finish this chair by adding the mesh representing the chair seat.

1. Click the Loft tool in the 3D Make control panel, choose Draw ➢ Modeling ➢ Loft, or enter **Loft.**↵ at the Command prompt.

2. At the `Select cross-sections in lofting order:` prompt, click the arc at the front of the layout.

3. At the `Select cross-sections in lofting order:` prompt, click the arc at the back of the layout, and then press ↵ to finish your selection of cross-sections.

4. At the `Enter an option [Guides/Path/Cross-sections only] <Cross-sections only>:` prompt, enter **G**↵ for the Guides option. You will use the other two arcs as guides.

5. At the `Select guide curves:` prompt, select the two polylines on the sides of the layout, and then press ↵ to complete your selection. Your chair begins to take form, as shown in Figure 21.25.

6. Choose File ➢ Save to save the chair so far.

You've got the beginnings of a butterfly chair with the legs drawn in schematically and the seat as a 3D surface. You can add some detail by using a few other tools as you'll see in the next set of exercise.

FIGURE 21.25
The butterfly chair
so far

FIGURE 21.25
The butterfly chair
so far

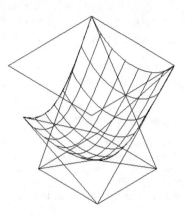

Converting the Surface into a Solid

In the previous example, you used the Loft tool to create a 3D surface. Once you have a surface, you can convert it to a solid to perform other modifications.

You'll want to round the corners of the seat surface to simulate the way a butterfly chair hangs off its frame. You'll also want to round the corners of the frame and turn the frame into a tubular form. Start by rounding the seat surface. This will involve turning the surface into a solid so you can use solid editing tools to get the shape you want.

1. Click the Thicken Surface tool in the 3D Make control panel.

You can also choose Modify ➤ 3D Operations ➤ Thicken or enter **Thicken**↵ at the Command prompt.

2. Select the seat surface and press ↵ to finish your selection.

3. At the Specify thickness <0'-0">: prompt, enter **0.01**↵ or **0.025** for metric users.

The seat surface appears to loose its webbing, but it has just been converted to a very thin 3D solid.

Shaping the Solid

The butterfly chair is in a fairly schematic state. The corners of the chair are sharply pointed whereas a real butterfly chair would have rounded corners. In this section you'll round the corners of the seat with a little help from the original rectangles you used to form the layout frame.

First, you'll use the Fillet command to round the corners of rectangles. Then you'll use the rounded rectangles to create a solid from which you will form a new seat.

1. Choose the Fillet tool from the Modify toolbar, choose Modify ➤ Fillet, or enter **F**↵ at the Command prompt.

2. At the `Select first object or [Undo/Polyline/Radius/Trim/Multiple]:` prompt, enter **R**↵.

3. At the `Specify fillet radius <0'-0">:` prompt, enter **3**↵.

4. At the `Select first object or [Undo/Polyline/Radius/Trim/Multiple]:` prompt, enter **P**↵ for the Polyline option.

5. At the `Select 2D polyline:` prompt, select the top rectangle as shown in Figure 21.26. The polyline corners become rounded.

6. Press ↵ to repeat the Fillet command.

7. Enter **P**↵ to use the Polyline option, and then click the bottom rectangle as shown in Figure 21.26. Now both polylines have rounded corners.

Next, create a 3D solid from the two rectangle using the Loft tool.

1. Click the Loft tool in the 3D Make control panel or choose Draw ➤ Modeling ➤ Loft.

2. At the `Select cross-sections in lofting order:` prompt, select the two rectangles, and then press ↵ to finish your selection.

3. At the `Enter an option [Guides/Path/Cross-sections only] <Cross-sections only>:` prompt, press ↵. The Loft Settings dialog box appears.

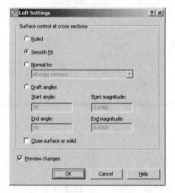

4. Click the Ruled option and click OK. The rectangles join to form a 3D solid (see Figure 21.27).

Finding the Interference Between Two Solids

In this next exercise, you will use a tool that is intended to find the interference between two solids. This is useful if you are working with very crowded 3D models and you need to check whether objects might be interfering with each other. For example, a mechanical designer might want to check to make sure that duct locations are not passing through a structural beam.

You'll use Interfere as a modeling tool to obtain a shape that is a combination of two solids: the seat and the rectangular solid you just created.

1. Click the Interference Checking tool in the 3D Make control panel.

You can also choose Modify ➢ 3D Operations ➢ Interference or enter **interfere**↵ at the Command prompt.

2. At the `Select first set of objects or [Nested selection/Settings]:` prompt, select the chair seat solid and then press ↵.

3. At the `Select second set of objects or [Nested selection/checK first set]` `<checK>:` prompt, click the rectangular solid you created in the previous exercise and then press ↵. The Interference Checking dialog box appears, and the drawing temporarily changes to a view similar to the Realistic visual style.

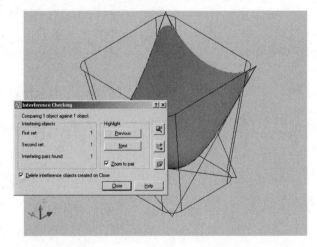

The view shows the interference of the two solids in red. Notice that the corners are rounded on the red interference.

4. In the Interference Checking dialog box, turn off the Delete Interference Objects Created On Close option, and then click Close. The display returns to the wireframe view. If you look carefully at the seat corners, you'll see that a new solid is overlayed on the seat (see Figure 21.28).

5. Delete the rectangular solid and the original seat as shown in Figure 21.28.

FIGURE 21.26
Round the corners
of the rectangles with
the Fillet command.

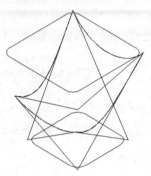

FIGURE 21.27
The lofted rectangles
form a 3D solid.

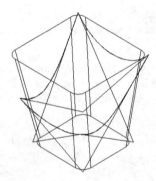

FIGURE 21.28
The Interference solid
appears on top of the
original seat.

Delete the rectangular solid.

Delete the original seat.

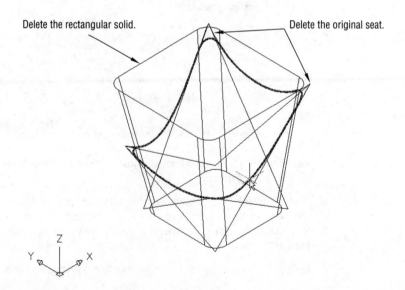

As mentioned earlier, the Interference Checking tool is really intended to help you find out if objects are colliding in a 3D model, but as you've just seen, it can be an excellent modeling tool that can help you derive a form that you might otherwise not have the ability to create.

A number of other options are available when using the Interference Checking tool. Table 21.2 lists the options you saw in the Interference Checking dialog box.

TABLE 21.2:   The Interference Checking Dialog Box Options

OPTION	WHAT IT DOES
First Set	Specifies the number of objects in the first set of selected objects
Second Set	Specifies the number of objects in the second set of selected objects
Interfering Pairs Found	Indicates the number of interferences found
Previous	Highlights the previous interference object
Next	Highlights the next interference object if multiple objects are present
Zoom To Pair	Zooms to the interference object while using the Previous and Next options
Zoom Realtime	Closes the dialog box to allow you to use Zoom Realtime
Pan Realtime	Closes the dialog box to allow you to use Pan
3D Orbit	Closes the dialog box to allow you to use 3D Orbit
Delete Interference Objects Created On Close	Deletes the interference object after the dialog box is closed

The prompt for the Interference Checking command also showed some options. The prompt in step 2 shows `Nested selection/Settings`. The `Nested selection` option lets you select objects that are nested within a block or an Xref. The `Settings` option opens the Interference Settings dialog box.

This dialog box offers settings for the temporary display of interference objects while in the Interference command. Table 21.3 lists the options for this dialog box.

TABLE 21.3: The Interference Settings Dialog Box Options

OPTION	WHAT IT DOES
Visual Style	Controls the visual style for interference objects
Color	Controls the color for interference objects
Highlight Interfering Pair	Highlights the interfering objects
Highlight Interference	Highlights the resulting interference objects
Visual Style	Controls the visual style for the drawing while displaying the interference objects

Creating Tubes with the Sweep Tool

One more element needs to be taken care of before your chair is complete. The legs are currently simple lines with sharp corners. In this section, you'll learn how you can convert lines into 3D tubes. To make it more interesting, you'll add some rounded corners to the legs.

Start by rounding the corners on the lines you've created for the legs.

1. Use the Explode tool to explode the 3D polyine legs into simple lines.

2. Choose the Fillet tool from the Modify toolbar, choose Modify ➤ Fillet, or enter **F↵** at the Command prompt.

3. At the `Select first object or [Undo/Polyline/Radius/Trim/Multiple]:` prompt, enter **R↵**.

4. At the `Specify fillet radius <0'-0">:` prompt, enter **2↵**.

5. At the `Select first object or [Undo/Polyline/Radius/Trim/Multiple]:` prompt enter **M↵**, and then select pairs of lines to fillet their corners.

6. When all the corners are rounded, press ↵ to exit the Fillet command.

7. Delete the two polyline splines you used to form the sides of the seat. Your drawing should look like Figure 21.29.

The chair is almost complete, but the legs are just wireframes. Next you will give them some thickness by turning them into tubes. Start by creating a set of circles. You'll use the circles to define the diameter of the tubes.

1. Draw a 3/4″ (19 mm) diameter circle in the location shown in Figure 21.29. Don't worry if your location is a little off; the placement of the circle is not important.

2. Use the Array command to make 16 copies of the circle. In Figure 21.29. A 4 × 4 array is used with the default 1″ spacing. Metric users should use a spacing of about 30 mm.

FIGURE 21.29

Drawing the circles for
the tubes

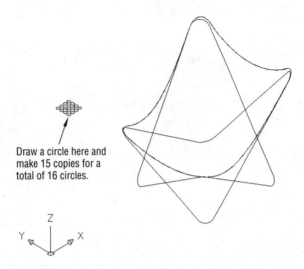

Draw a circle here and
make 15 copies for a
total of 16 circles.

Now you're ready to form the tubes.

1. Click the Sweep tool in the 3D Make toolbar.

2. You can also choose Draw ➢ Modeling ➢ Sweep or enter **sweep**↵ at the Command prompt.

3. At the `Select objects to sweep:` prompt, click one of the circles you just created. It doesn't matter which circle you use since they're identical. Press ↵ when you are finished.

4. At the `Select sweep path or [Alignment/Base point/Scale/Twist]:` prompt, select one of the lines or fillet arcs that make up the legs.

5. Press ↵ to repeat the sweep command, and then repeat steps 2 and 3 for each part of the leg segments, including the fillet arcs.

6. Continue with step 4 until all the lines in the legs have been converted into tubes.

7. Change the color of the solid representing the seat to cyan, and then select the Realistic visual style from the Visual Style control panel. Your drawing will look similar to the image on the left of Figure 21.30, which shows a perspective view. The image on the right is the chair with some materials assigned to the parts of the chair and a slight adjustment to the seat location.

FIGURE 21.30
A perspective view of
the butterfly chair
with tubes for legs

Using Sweep to Create Complex Forms

Although you used circles with the Sweep command to create tubes, you can use any closed polyline shape. Figure 21.31 gives some examples of other shapes that can be used with the Sweep command.

In step 3 of the previous exercise, you may have noticed some command line options. These options offer some additional control over the way Sweep works. Here is a rundown on these options and their function:

Alignment This option lets you determine whether the object to sweep is automatically set perpendicular to the sweep path. By default, this option is set to Yes, which means that the object to sweep is set perpendicular to the path. If set to no, Sweep assumes the current angle of the object, as shown in Figure 21.32.

Base Point By default, Sweep uses the center of the object to sweep as the location to align with the path as shown in Figure 21.33. Base point lets you set a specific location on the object.

FIGURE 21.31
You can use any closed
shape with the Sweep
command.

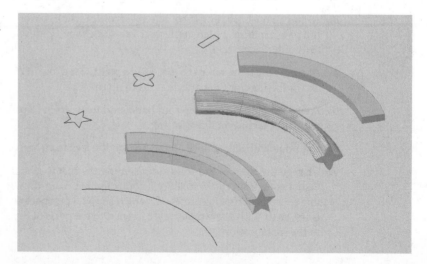

FIGURE 21.32
Alignment lets you set the angle between the object to sweep and the sweep path.

FIGURE 21.33
Base Point lets you set a point on the object to sweep that is aligned with the sweep path.

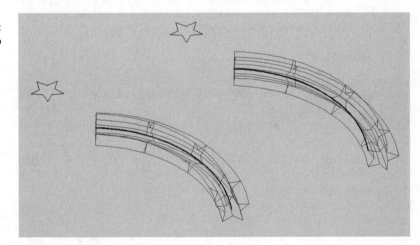

FIGURE 21.34
Scale lets you scale the object to sweep as it is swept along the path.

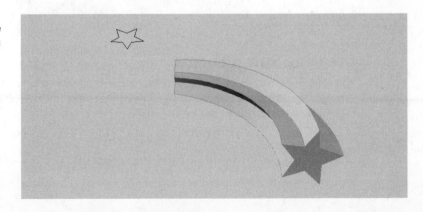

FIGURE 21.35
You can have the object to sweep twist along the path to create a spiral effect.

Scale You can have Sweep scale the sweep object from one end of the path to the other to create a tapered shape, as shown in Figure 21.34. This option requires a numeric scale value.

Twist You can have the object to sweep twist along the path to form a spiral shape as shown in Figure 21.35. This option requires a numeric value in the form of degrees of rotation.

These options are available to you as soon as you select the sweep object and before you select the path object. You can use any combination of options you need. For example, you can apply the Twist and Scale options together as shown in Figure 21.36.

FIGURE 21.36
The Scale and Twist options applied together

Creating Spiral Forms

You can use the Sweep tool in conjunction with the Helix tool to create a spiral form, such as a spring or the threads of a screw. You've already seen how the Sweep tool works. Try the following to learn how the Helix tool works firsthand.

In this exercise, you'll draw a helicoil thread insert. This is a device used to repair stripped threads and is basically a coiled steel strip that forms internal and external threads.

1. Open the `Helicoil.dwg` file from the sample project files you installed from the companion CD. This is a standard AutoCAD drawing containing a closed polyline in a stretched octagon shape.

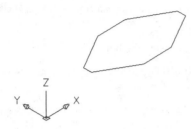

This is the cross-section of the helicoil thread, and you'll use it as an object to sweep after you've created a helix.

2. Click the Helix tool in the expanded 3D Make control panel.

You'll see the following prompt:

```
Number of turns = 3.0000    Twist=CCW
Specify center point of base:
```

3. Pick a point roughly in the center of the view. A rubber-banding line appears along with a circle.

4. At the `Specify base radius or [Diameter] <1.0000>:` prompt, enter .375↵.

5. At the `Specify top radius or [Diameter] <0.3750>:` prompt, press ↵ to accept the default, which is the same as the value you entered in step 4.

6. At the `Specify helix height or [Axis endpoint/Turns/turn Height/tWist]` `<1.0000>:` prompt, enter T↵ to use the Turns option.

7. At the `Enter number of turns <3.0000>:` prompt, enter 15↵ to create a helix with 15 turns total.

8. At the `Specify helix height or [Axis endpoint/Turns/turn Height/tWist] <1.0000>:` prompt, press ↵ to accept the default height of 1. The helix appears as a spiral drawn to the dimensions you have just specified for diameter, turns, and height (see Figure 21.37).

In step 6, you used the Turns option to specify the total number of turns in the helix. You also have other options that give you control over the shape of the helix. Figures 21.38 shows you the effects of the Helix command options. You might want to experiment with them on your own to get familiar with Helix.

TIP   If you find that you have created a helix with the wrong settings, you don't have to erase and re-create it. You can use the Properties palette to make adjustments to any of the helix options presented in Figure 21.38 even after a helix has been created. Select the helix, right-click, and then choose Properties. Look in the Geometry section of the Properties palette for the helix settings.

Now use the Sweep tool to complete the helicoil.

1. Click the Sweep tool in the 3D Make control panel, choose Draw ➢ Modeling ➢ Sweep or enter Sweep at the Command prompt.

2. At the `Select objects to sweep:` prompt, select the thread cross section in the lower-left corner of the drawing, and then press ↵.

FIGURE 21.37
The helix and the helicoil after using Sweep

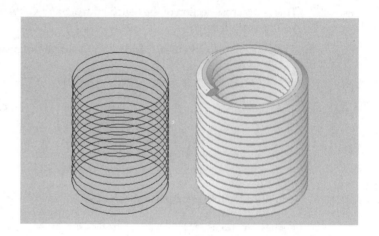

FIGURE 21.38
The Helix command options

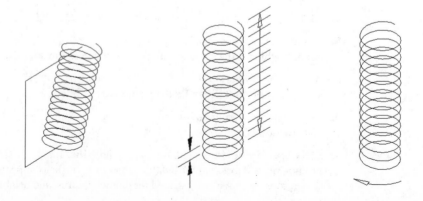

3. At the `Select sweep path or [Alignment/Base point/Scale/Twist]:` prompt, select the helix. After a moment, the helicoil appears.

4. To see the helicoil more clearly, choose the Realistic option from the Visual Styles drop-down list, and then change the helicoil to the helicoil layer.

WARNING If the space between the coils is too small for the cross section, you may get an error message. If you get an error message at step 3, make sure you created the helix exactly as specified in the previous exercise. You may also try to increase the helix height.

In step 3, instead of selecting the sweep path, you can select an option to apply to the object to sweep. For example, by default, Sweep aligns the object to sweep at an angle that is perpendicular to the path and centers the object to sweep. See "Using Sweep to Create Complex Forms" earlier in this chapter.

Creating Surface Models

In an earlier exercise, you used the Loft command to create the seat of a butterfly chair. In this section you'll return to the Loft command to explore some of its other uses. This time, you use it to create a 3D model of a hillside based on a set of site contour lines. You'll also see how a surface created from the Loft command can be used to slice a solid into two pieces, imprinting the solid with the surface shape.

WARNING If you have used earlier versions of AutoCAD to create 3D models, the surfaces created with the Loft command are not the same as those created with the Surfaces toolbar. You can convert those older "mesh" objects into the new surface objects using the Convert To Surface tool, which is next to the Convert To Solid tool in the 3D Make control panel.

1. Open the `contour.dwg` file from the sample project files folder.

2. Click the Loft tool from the 3D Make control panel.

3. Select each brown contour in consecutive order from right to left or left to right. It doesn't matter whether you start at the left end or the right end, but you must select the contours in order.

4. When you're finished selecting all the contours, press ↵.

5. At the `Enter an option [Guides/Path/Cross-sections only] <Cross-sections only>:` prompt, press ↵ and wait a moment. AutoCAD requires a bit of time to calculate the surface. Once it does, you'll see the Loft Settings dialog box and you'll see the surface.

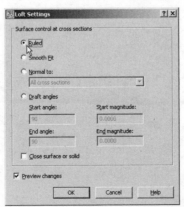

6. Click the Ruled radio button, and then click OK. You can now see the surface clearly as shown in Figure 21.39.

In the butterfly chair exercise, you used the Guides option in the Loft command prompt. This allowed you to use the polyline curves to "guide" the loft shape from the front arc to the back arc. In this exercise, you didn't use the command options and went straight to the Loft Settings dialog box. The Ruled setting that you used in step 6 generates a surface that connects the cross-sections in a straight line. You'll learn more about the options in this dialog box later in this section.

Slicing a Solid with a Surface

In the Barcelona chair example, you converted a surface into a solid using the Thicken command. Next you'll use a surface to create a solid in a slightly different way. This time, you'll use the surface to slice a solid into two pieces. This will give you a form that is more easily read and understood as a terrain model.

1. Click the Extrude tool in the 3D Make control panel.

2. At the `Select objects to extrude:` prompt, select the large rectangle below the contours and press ↵. The rectangle turns into a box whose height follows your cursor.

3. At the `Specify height of extrusion or [Direction/Path/Taper angle] <0'-0">:` prompt, move the cursor upward so that the box looks similar to the one in Figure 21.40. Then click the mouse to fix the box's height.

You may have noticed that as you raised the box height, you could see how it intersected the contour surface. Next you'll slice the box into two pieces.

1. Click the Slice tool in the expanded 3D Make control panel.

2. At the `Select objects to slice:` prompt, select the box and press ↵.

FIGURE 21.39
Creating a 3D surface from contour lines

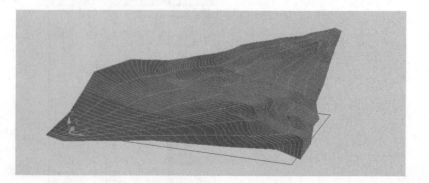

FIGURE 21.40
The box extruded
through the contours

3. At the `Specify start point of slicing plane or [planar Object/Surface/Zaxis/ View/XY/YZ/ZX/3points] <3points>:` prompt, enter **S↵**.

4. At the `Select a surface:` prompt, select the contour surface.

5. At the `Select solid to keep or [keep Both sides] <Both>:` prompt, click the part of the box that is below the surface. The top part of the box disappears, and you see the surface once again.

6. Delete the contour surface. The box remains with an imprint of the surface, as shown in Figure 21.41.

In step 3, you saw a prompt that offered a variety of methods for slicing the box. The Surface option allowed you to slice the box using an irregular shape, but most of the other options let you slice a solid by defining a plane or a series of planar objects.

Finding the Volume of a Cut

A question I hear frequently form civil engineers is, How can I find the volume of earth from an excavated area? This is often referred to as a "cut" from a "cut and fill" operation. To do this, you have to first create the cut shape. You can then use the Interfere command to find the intersection between the cut shape and the contour surface. You can then find the volume of the cut shape using one of AutoCAD's inquiry commands. The following exercise demonstrates how this is done.

Suppose that the contour model you've just created represents a site where you will excavate a rectangular area for a structure. You want to find the amount of earth involved in the excavation. A rectangle has been placed in the contour drawing representing such an area.

1. Select the 3D Wireframe option from the Visual Styles drop-down list. This will allow you to see the excavation rectangle more clearly.

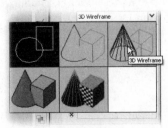

2. Click the Extrude tool in the 3D Make control panel.

3. Select the rectangle shown in Figure 21.42, and then press ↵.

4. Extrude the rectangle to the height of 10′.

With the excavation rectangle in place, you can use the Interfere command to find the shape of the excavation.

1. Click the Interference Checking tool in the 3D Make control panel.

2. At the Select first set of objects or [Nested selection/Settings]: prompt, click the contour and press ↵.

FIGURE 21.41
The box with the contour surface imprinted

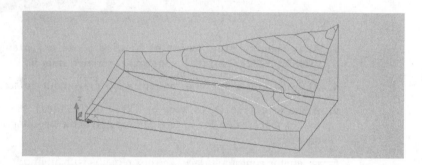

FIGURE 21.42
Selecting the rectangle representing the excavation area

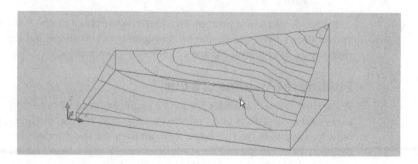

3. At the Select second set of objects or [Nested selection/checK first set] <checK>: prompt, select the box and press ↵. The Interference Checking dialog box appears.

4. At the Interference Checking dialog box turn off the Delete Interference Object Created On Close option and click Close.

5. Delete the box you used to represent the excavation area. The remaining shape contains the volume of the excavation.

6. Choose Tools ➢ Inquiry ➢ Region/Mass Properties.

7. At the Select Objects: prompt, select the excavation solid as shown in Figure 21.43, and then press ↵. The AutoCAD Text Window appears, and it displays the properties of the excavation area. At the top, you see the volume of the selected solid in cubic inches.

8. At the Write analysis to a file? [Yes/No] <N>: prompt, you can press ↵ to exit the command or enter Y↵ to save the information to a text file.

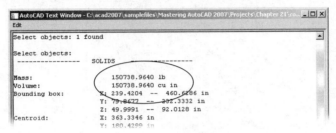

FIGURE 21.43

The 3D solid representing the excavation

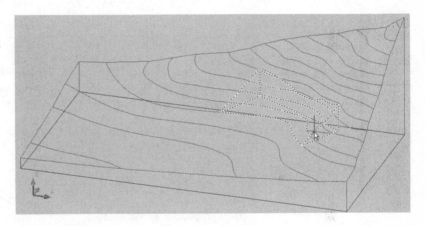

Understanding the Loft Command

As you've seen from the exercises in this chapter, the Loft command lets you create just about any shape you can imagine, from a simple sling to the complex curves of a contour map. If your loft cross sections are a set of closed objects like circles or closed polylgons, the resulting object is a 3D solid instead of a surface.

The order in which you select the cross-sections is important as Loft will follow your selection order to create the surface or solid. For example, Figure 21.44 shows a series of circles used for a lofted solid. The circles are identical in size and placement, but the order of selection is different. The solid on the left was created by selecting the circles in consecutive order from bottom to top, creating an hourglass shape. The solid on the right was created by selecting the two larger circles first from bottom to top; the smaller, intermediate circle was selected last. This selection order created a hollowed out shape with more vertical sides.

Besides the selection order, you have several other settings that affect the shape of a solid created by the Loft command. In the contour map example, you selected a setting in the Loft Settings dialog box. This dialog box appears when you select the Cross Section Only option after you've selected a set of cross sections.

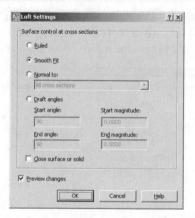

FIGURE 21.44
The order in which you select the cross-sections affects the result of the Loft command.

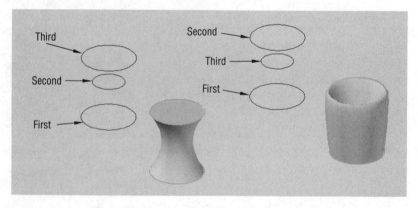

You can radically affect the way the Loft command forms a surface or a solid through the options in this dialog box, so it pays to understand what those settings do. Take a moment to study the following sections that describethe Loft Settings dialog box options.

RULLED AND SMOOTH FIT

The Ruled option connects the cross-sections with straight surfaces as shown in the sample to the left in Figure 21.45.

The Smooth Fit option connects the cross-sections with a smooth surface. It attempts to make the best smooth transitions between the cross-sections as shown in the right image of Figure 21.45.

NORMAL TO

Normal To is actually a set of four options presented in a drop-down list. To understand what this option does, you need to understand that a normal is a mathematical term referring to a direction that is perpendicular to a plane as shown in Figure 21.46. In these options, the Normal refers to the direction the surface takes as it emerges from a cross-section.

If you use the All Cross Sections option, the surfaces emerge in a perpendicular direction from all the cross-sections as shown in the first image of Figure 21.47. If you use the End Cross Section option, the surface emerges in a direction that is perpendicular to just the end cross-section as shown in the second image of Figure 21.47. The Start Cross Section option causes the surface to emerge in a direction perpendicular to the start cross-section. The Start And End Cross Sections option combines the effect of the Start Cross Section and End Cross Section options.

DRAFT ANGLES

The Draft Angles option affects only the first and last cross-sections. This option generates a smooth surface with the added control over the start and end angle. Unlike the Normal To option that forces a perpendicular direction to the cross-sections, Draft Angles allows you to set an angle for the surface direction. For example, if you set Start Angle to a value of 0, the surface will "bulge" outward from the start cross-section as shown in the first image of Figure 21.48.

FIGURE 21.45
Samples of a ruled loft at left and a Smooth Fit loft on the right

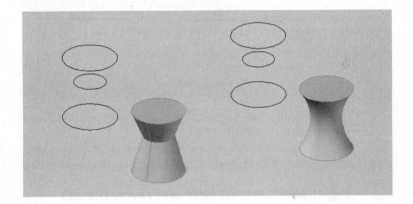

FIGURE 21.46
A normal is a direction perpendicular to a plane.

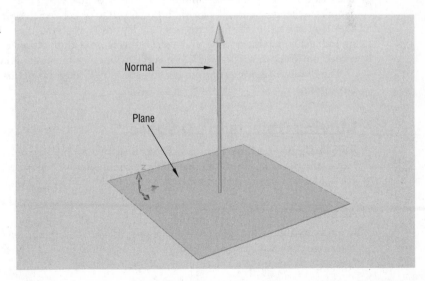

FIGURE 21.47
Samples of the Normal
To options applied to
the same set of cross
sections

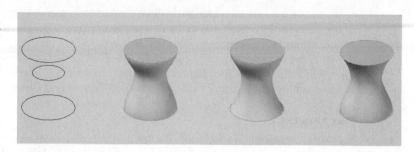

FIGURE 21.48
The Draft Angle
options

Likewise, the End Angle setting of 0 will cause the surface to bulge at the end cross-section (see the second image in Figure 21.48.

The Start and End Magnitude settings let you determine a relative strength of the bulge. The right image in Figure 21.48 shows a Draft Angle of zero and magnitude of 50 for the last cross-section.

CLOSE SURFACE OR CLOSE SOLID AND PREVIEW CHANGES

The Close Surface or Close Solid option is only available when the Smooth Fit option is selected, and it causes the first and last cross-section object to be connected so that the surface or solid loops back from the last to the first cross-section. Figure 21.49 shows the cross-sections at the left, a smooth version in the middle, and a smooth version with the Close Surface or Close Solid option turned on. You can see that the Close Surface option causes the solid to become a tube.

The Preview Changes option lets you see in real time the effects of the Loft Settings dialog box options.

Moving Objects in 3D Space

AutoCAD provides three tools specifically designed for moving objects in 3D space: Align, 3D Move, and 3D Rotate. You can find all three commands by choosing Modify ➢ 3D Operations. These tools help you perform some of the more common moves associated with 3D editing.

Aligning Objects in 3D Space

In mechanical drawing, you often create the parts in 3D and then show an assembly of the parts. The Align command can greatly simplify the assembly process. The following steps show how to use Align to line up two objects at specific points:

1. Open the Align drawing from the Chapter 21 folder of the sample files.

2. Choose Modify ➢ 3D Operations ➢ Align or type Al↓.

3. At the `Select objects:` prompt, select the 3D wedge-shaped object. (The *source object* is the object you want to move.)

4. At the `Specify base point or [Copy]:` prompt, pick a point on the source object that is the first point of an alignment axis, such as the center of a hole or the corner of a surface. For the Align drawing, use the upper-left corner of the wedge.

FIGURE 21.49
The Close Surface or Close Solid option connects the end and the beginning cross-section.

5. At the `Specify second point or [Continue] <C>:` prompt, pick a point on the source object that is the second point of an alignment axis, such as another center point or other corner of a surface. For this example, select the other top corner of the wedge.

6. At the `Specify third source point or [continue] <C>:` prompt, you can press ↵ if two points are adequate to describe the alignment. Otherwise, pick a third point on the source object that, along with the first two points, best describes the surface plane you want aligned with the destination object. Pick the lower-right corner of the wedge shown in Figure 21.50.

7. At the `Specify first destination point:` prompt, pick a point on the destination object to which you want the first source point to move. (The *destination object* is the object with which you want the source object to align.). This would be the top corner of the rectangular shape. (See the first destination point in Figure 21.50.)

8. At the `Specify second destination point or [eXit]:` prompt, pick a point on the destination object indicating how the first and second source points are to align in relation to the destination object. (See the second destination point in Figure 21.50.)

9. If you pick a third source point in step 6, you'll be prompted for a third destination point. Pick a point on the destination object that, along with the previous two destination points, describes the plane with which you want the source object to be aligned. (See the third destination point in Figure 21.50.) The source object will move into alignment with the destination object.

10. If you press ↵ at step 7, you see the `Scale objects based on alignment points? [Yes/No] <N>:` prompt. If you press ↵ to accept the default, the selected object(s) will move into alignment with the destination points without changing size. If you enter **Y**↵, the selected object(s) will be scaled up or down to align exactly with the two destination points.

FIGURE 21.50

Aligning two
3D objects

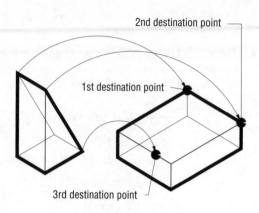

2nd destination point

1st destination point

3rd destination point

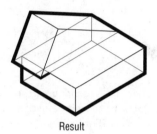

Result

Moving an Object in 3D

In Chapter 20, you saw how you can use the Grip tool to help restrain the motion of an object in the X, Y, or Z axis. AutoCAD offers a Move command specifically designed for 3D editing that includes a Grip tool to restrain motion. Here's how it works.

TIP   You don't need to perform these steps as an exercise. You can try the command on your own when you need to use it.

1. Click the 3D Move tool in the 3D Make control panel.

You can also choose Modify ➢ 3D Operations ➢ 3D Move. The Visual Style temporarily changes to Realistic.

2. Select the object or set of objects you want to move and press ↵. You'll see the Grip tool appear at the cursor.

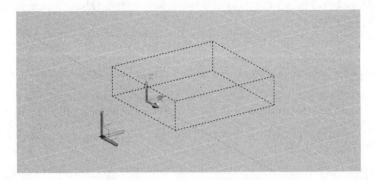

3. Select a base point for the move. The Grip tool remains fixed at the base point.

4. Point to the X, Y, or Z axis of the Grip tool and click it. Now as you move the cursor, the motion of your selected objects will be restrained to the selected axis.

5. Enter a distance along the axis or click a point to complete the move.

Rotating an Object in 3D

The 3D Rotate command is another command that is like an extension of its 2D counterpart. With 3D Rotate, a Rotate Grip tool appears that restrains the rotation about the X, Y, or Z axis. Here is how it works.

TIP You don't need to perform these steps as an exercise. You can try the command on your own when you need to use it.

1. Click the 3D Rotate tool in the 3D Make toolbar.

2. You can also choose Modify ➢ 3D Operations ➢ 3D Rotate.

3. Select the object or objects you want to rotate and then press ↵. The Rotate Grip tool appears at the cursor.

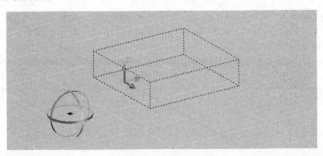

4. At the `Specify a base point:` prompt, select a point about which the selected objects are to be rotated.

5. Point to the colored circle that represents the axis of rotation for your objects. You'll see a line appear representing the axis of rotation. When you're happy with the selected axis, click the mouse.

6. At the `Specify angle start point:` prompt, you can enter an angle value or click a point. You can use the Shift key or the ortho mode to restrain the direction to 90°.

7. At the `Specify angle end point:` prompt, enter an angle value or click another point for the rotation angle.

If You Want to Experiment

You've covered a lot of territory in this chapter, so it might be a good idea to play with these commands to help you remember what you've learned. Perhaps the most important 3D feature to master is the UCS. Try your hand at manipulating the UCS to fit the different faces of the model shown in Figure 21.1. Use the file called `Experiment21.dwg` from the companion CD.

USING 3DMIRROR AND 3DARRAY

Two other commands, 3Dmirror and 3Darray are also available in the Modify ➤ 3D Operations menu. These are 3D Versions of the Mirror and Array commands. They work in a way similar to the standard mirror and array commands with a slight difference.

3Dmirror begins by asking you to select objects, then you are asked to specify a mirror plane instead of a mirror axis. You can then define a plane using the default 3 points or you can use one of the 7 other options of Object/Last/Zaxis/View/XY/YZ/ZX. By using a plane instead of an axis, you can mirror an object or set of objects anywhere in 3D space. One way to visualize this is to imagine holding a mirror up to your 3D model. The mirror is your 3D plane and the reflected image is the mirrored version of the object. You might imagine tilting the mirror to various angles to get a different mirror image. In the same way, you can tilt the plane in the 3Dmirror command to mirror an object in any number of ways.

3Darray works like the command line version of the Array command and offers the same prompts with a couple of additions. If you choose to do a rectangular array, you will be prompted for the usual row and column numbers, and then you are also prompted for the number of levels for the 3rd dimension. You are also prompted for the distance between rows, columns, and levels.

For polar arrays, you are prompted for the number of items to array and the angle to fill, just like the standard Array command, but instead of asking for a point to indicate the center of the array, you are prompted to select two points to indicate an axis. The axis can be defined in any direction in 3D space so your array can be tilted from the current UCS. One way to visualize this is to think of a bicycle wheel with the axle of the wheel as the array axis and the array objects as the spokes. You can align the axle in any direction and the array of spokes will be perpendicular to the axle.

Chapter 22

Rendering 3D Drawings

ACAD only

In this chapter, you'll learn how to use rendering tools in AutoCAD to produce rendered still images of your 3D models. With these tools, you can add materials, control lighting, and even add landscaping and people to your models. You also have control over the reflectance and transparency of objects, and you can add bitmap backgrounds to help set the mood.

WARNING   AutoCAD 2007 LT does not support any of the features described in this chapter.

Topics in this chapter include the following:

◆ Things to Do before You Start

◆ Creating a Quick-Study Rendering

◆ Simulating the Sun

◆ Adding a Distant Light

◆ Using Materials

◆ Adding a Background

◆ Using Materials and Lights to Create Effects

◆ Applying and Adjusting Texture Maps

◆ Simulating Trees and People with Opacity Maps

◆ Understanding the Rendering Options

◆ Adding Cameras for Better View Control

◆ Creating an Animated Walk-Through

◆ Printing Your Renderings

◆ Rendering Interior Views

Things to Do before You Start

Before you actually start any work, set up AutoCAD as you did for Chapter 21. You'll use the AutoCAD Classic workspace, but you will also open the Dashboard, which is the 3D palette you were introduced to in Chapter 20.

1. Open AutoCAD; then when you see the Workspaces dialog box, select AutoCAD Classic. If for some reason, the Workspaces dialog box does not appear, choose AutoCAD Classic from the Workspaces toolbar.

2. Close the Tool Palettes window and the Sheet Set Manager palette to get a clear view of the drawing area.

3. Choose Tools ➢ Palettes ➢ Dashboard to open the Dashboard palette.

With this setup, you can quickly select items from the Draw and Modify toolbars. You also have access to the Properties and Layers toolbars. Now you're ready to get to work.

Creating a Quick-Study Rendering

Throughout this chapter, you will work with a 3D model that was created using AutoCAD's 3D modeling tools. The model is of two buildings on a street corner. You'll start by using the default rendering settings to get a quick view of what you have to start with:

1. Open the `facade.dwg` file from the companion CD.

2. Click the Render tool in the Render control panel.

3. The Render window appears, and you see the rendering generated in the Render window display (see Figure 22.1).

FIGURE 22.1
The Render Window with your first rendered view

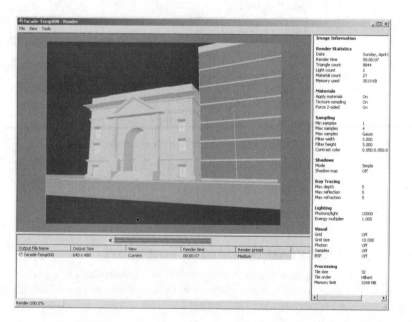

The Render window displays the render settings in a column to the right. At the bottom of the window, you see the name that AutoCAD gives to the rendering as well as the rendering resolution in pixels, the time it took, and the preset that was used for the rendering. You'll learn more about these options later in this chapter.

Simulating the Sun

AutoCAD allows you to create several types of light sources. If you don't add a light source, AutoCAD uses a default lighting source that has no particular direction or characteristic. The rendering you just did uses the default lighting to show your model.

You can add a point light that behaves like a lightbulb, a spot light, or a directed light that behaves like a distant light source such as the sun. AutoCAD also offers a sunlight option that can be set for the time of the year and the hour of the day. This sunlight option is especially important for shadow studies in architectural models.

Setting Up the Sun

So let's add the sun to our model to give a better sense of the building's form and relationship to its site. Start by making sure the sun is set for your location:

1. Minimize the Render window; then expand the Light control panel by clicking the downward-pointing arrows in the Light control panel title bar (see Figure 22.2).

2. Turn on the Sun Status tool by clicking the sun icon in the Light control panel.

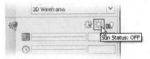

You see a message box warning you that the default lighting must be turned off when using other lights. Click Yes.

FIGURE 22.2
The Light control panel title bar arrows and the Geographic Location tool

Click here to expand the control panel.

The Geographic Location tool.

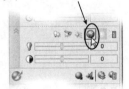

3. Click the Geographic Location tool in the expanded portion of the Light control panel as shown in Figure 22.2. The Geographic Location dialog box appears.

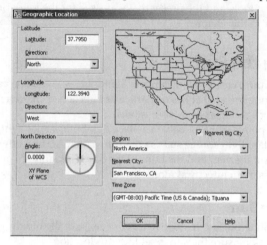

4. For the sake of this tutorial, suppose the Facade model is a building in San Francisco, California, USA. Select North America from the drop-down list below the map.

5. Locate and select San Francisco CA in the Nearest City drop-down list. Notice that the Latitude and Longitude input boxes in the upper left of the dialog box change to reflect the location of San Francisco. For locations not listed, you can enter values manually in those input boxes.

6. Click OK

7. Next you'll want to set the date and time of day for the rendering:

8. Click in the Date input box of the Light control panel, and then enter **9/21/2006**.

9. Click in the Time input box of the Light control panel, and enter **2:00 pm**.

10. Click the Render tool in the Render control panel. The Render window appears and begins to create a new rendering with the sunlight option turned on as shown in Figure 22.3.

Now that you've added the sun, you can see the shadows that the sunlight casts. You can turn off the shadows for the sun if you prefer, but they are on by default.

Setting Polar North

If you are including the sun as a light source in a drawing in order to run shade studies, it's essential to orient your drawing accurately. To set the direction of polar north in your drawing, you use the North Direction setting in the Geographic Location dialog box (see Figure 22.4).

FIGURE 22.3
The rendering with the sun turned on

FIGURE 22.4
The North Direction setting in the Geographic Location dialog box

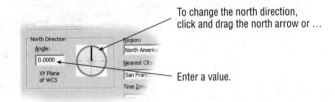

To change the north direction, click and drag the north arrow or …

Enter a value.

By using this setting, you can set true north in any of the following ways:

◆ Click and drag the north arrow in the graphic to point to the north direction.

◆ Enter a value directly in the input box.

IMPROVING THE SMOOTHNESS OF CIRCLES AND ARCS

You might notice that at times when using the Render, Hide, or Shade tool, solid or region arcs appear segmented rather than curved. This might be fine for producing layouts or backgrounds for hand-rendered drawings, but for final plots, you will want arcs and circles to appear as smooth curves. You can adjust the accuracy of arcs in your hidden, rendered, or shaded views through a setting in the Options dialog box.

You can modify the Rendered Object Smoothness setting in the Display tab of the Options dialog box to improve the smoothness of arcs. Its default setting is 0.5, but you can increase this to as high as 10 to smooth out faceted curves. In the Facade.dwg model, you can set Rendered Object Smoothness to 1.5 to render the arch in the entry as a smooth arc instead of a series of flat segments. You can also adjust this setting by using the Facetres system variable.

Adding a Distant Light

The rendering gives you a fairly accurate idea of how the shadows will fall. This might be all you need if you're doing a shadow study. For example, you could render a plan view of a 3D model to see where the shadow will fall on a street or a neighboring building, like the image in Figure 22.5:

But the current rendering needs more attention in order to show some of the building detail. One problem is that the shadows are too dark and hide some of the features of the building. To bring out those features, you'll want to add some ambient light.

In the real world, a good deal of light is reflected from the ground. You can simulate that reflected light by adding a distant light that shines from below the model. A distant light is like a cross between a point light and a spotlight. Like the sun, distant light is like a point source of light, but one that is so far away that its rays are essentially parallel (see Figure 22.6).

FIGURE 22.5

A series of simple renderings showing the way shadows fall from a set of buildings

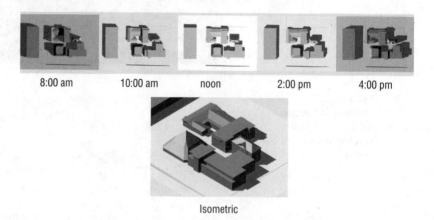

8:00 am 10:00 am noon 2:00 pm 4:00 pm

Isometric

FIGURE 22.6

A distant light is a source whose light "rays" are parallel, much like the sun's rays.

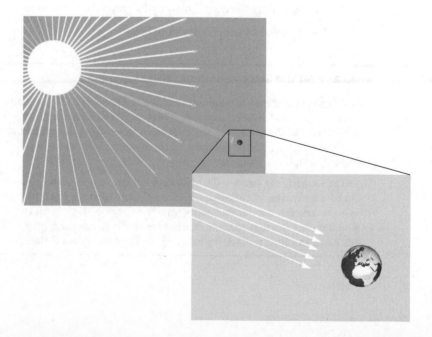

A distant light pointing straight up can simulate reflected light from the ground, so in the following set of exercise, you'll add a directed light to do just that. In the process, you'll see how you can quickly switch from a single view to a multi-viewport view using some tools in the Navigate control panel.

First change your single view into a four-viewport view.

1. Expand the 3D Navigate control panel by clicking the downward-pointing arrow in the 3D Navigate control panel title bar.

2. Click the Multiple Viewports tool in the expanded 3D Navigate control panel shown in Figure 22.7.

3. Expand the Light control panel as you did the 3D Navigate control panel; then click the Create A Distant Light tool in the Lights control panel to start the Distantlight command.

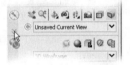

4. At the Specify light direction FROM <0,0,0> or [Vector]: prompt, click in the lower-left viewport; then click below the model as shown in Figure 22.8.

FIGURE 22.7
Expanding the 3D Navigate control panel to display the Multiple Viewports tool

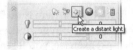

FIGURE 22.8
Add the directed light as shown in the lower-left viewport.

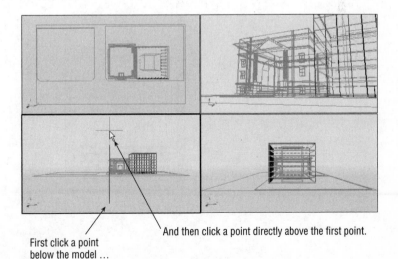

First click a point below the model …

And then click a point directly above the first point.

5. At the `Specify light direction TO <1,1,1>:` prompt, click a point to indicate an upward direction for the directed light as shown in Figure 22.8.

6. At the `Enter an option to change [Name/Intensity/Status/shadoW/Color/eXit]` `<eXit>:` prompt, press ⏎ to exit the directed light command.

7. Click the perspective view in the upper-right corner of the AutoCAD window to make it active; then open the 3D Navigate control panel and click the Single Viewport tool to return to a single view of the model.

You've just added a directed light though there is really nothing in the drawing to tell you that it's there. Even though it is not visible, you can gain access to the distant light you just added through the Light List tool. In the next exercise, you'll see how you can control the intensity of the directed light through the Light list.

1. Click the Light List tool in the Lights control panel or enter **Lightlist**⏎.

The Lights In Model palette appears.

2. Double-click Distantlight1 in the list. The Properties palette appears displaying the properties of the distant light you just added.

3. Locate the Intensity Factor setting in the General group of the Properties palette and change the value to 0.25.

4. Locate the Shadows setting and turn it off.

5. Close the Properties palette and the Lights In Model palette.

6. Click the Render tool in the Render control panel. Your rendering now shows more natural-looking shadows on the building to the left, as shown in Figure 22.9.

FIGURE 22.9
The model rendered with the distant light added.

Using Materials

The rendering methods you've learned so far can be of enormous help in your design effort. Simply being able to see how the sun affects your design can help sell your ideas or move plans through a tough planning board review. But the look of the building is still somewhat cartoonish. You can further enhance the rendering by adding materials to the objects in your model.

Adjusting the Global Material

AutoCAD uses a default material, called the global material, for objects in a drawing that don't have a specific material assigned to them. The global material is just like other materials you could use in your drawing, but it is set up in a way that is as generic as possible to produce simple renderings. For example, the global material uses the object's color to determine the rendered color.

As an introduction to materials, try the following exercise. You'll change the global material so that it applies a specific color to objects when they are rendered, rather than rely on the object's color.

1. Click the Materials tool in the Materials control panel. The Materials palette appears, as shown in Figure 22.10.

   At the top you see the Available Materials In Drawing panel, which currently shows only the global material. This is a default material that is applied to everything in the drawing that does not already have a material assignment.

2. Turn off the By Object option that appears in the Diffuse settings.

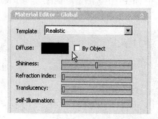

FIGURE 22.10

The Materials palette

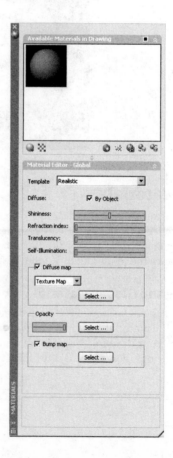

3. Click the Diffuse color swatch that appears next to the By Object check box. The Select Color dialog box appears.

4. Move the Luminance slider up until the Luminance value is set to 93, and then click OK to close the Select Color dialog box.

5. Click the Render tool in the Render control panel. This time you see a monochrome image in the Render window.

You've just changed the color of the global material to an off-white. so everything in the model now appears in shades of gray.

Creating a New Material and Changing Its Properties

Two of the most glaring problems in the rendering are the black background and the white glass in the building. You'll learn how to add a background later, but first you'll tackle the glass. To do this, you'll want to become familiar with the Materials dialog box.

1. Click the Create New Material button in the Materials palette toolbar.

2. In the Create New Material dialog box, enter **Glass1** for the name, and then click OK.

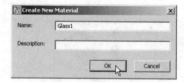

You've just created a new material, but it isn't assigned to anything, nor is it much different from the global material already in the drawing. To make this new Glass1 material appear as glass, you need to make some adjustments. You can make a material translucent or transparent, give it color, and even have it "glow" with self-illumination. You'll start by giving your new material a set of predefined values that will provide the basis for your glass.

1. In the Materials palette, select Glass - Clear from the Template drop-down list. The settings and options for your new material change to the default values you've just selected.

2. The sample image in the Materials Available In Drawing panel looks like a blank. To see the glass more clearly, click the Checkered Underlay button just below the samples. This provides a background in the sample so you can see transparent materials clearly.

3. Now add the glass to the building on the right. Click the Apply Material To Objects tool in the Materials palette toolbar.

4. Select the blue box in the drawing that represents the glass as shown in Figure 22.11, and then press ↵ to finish your selection.

5. Click the Render tool in the Render control panel. The building on the right now has the glass exterior.

The glass is too dark and ominous looking. You can lighten the glass and even add a fake reflection to give it a bit more life.

1. In the Diffuse Map group of the Materials palette, click the Select button (see Figure 22.12); then browse to the sample files folder for Chapter 22 and select sky.jpg. This is actually a copy of a file from an earlier version of AutoCAD.

2. Move the Diffuse Map slider all the way to the right to give the glass bitmap full strength.

FIGURE 22.11
Selecting the glass

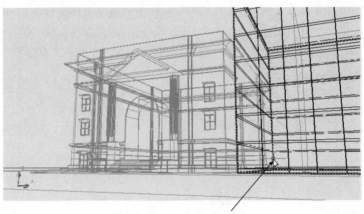

Click the blue box in the drawing.

FIGURE 22.12
The Diffuse Map and
Opacity groups

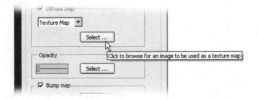

3. In the Opacity group, click and drag the slider to the right. As you do this, you see a numeric readout at the cursor. Set the slider so it reads 12 or 13. You'll now begin to see the clouds appear in the sample image at the top of the Materials palette.

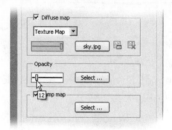

You've added a diffuse map to your glass, which is like adding a surface pattern to your material. More on that a bit later, but right now, you have one more thing you need to do to make the sky reflection work. The material has to be set up to fit the box representing the glass in the model. The Adjust Scale tool helps you do this.

1. Click the Adjust Scale tool in the Diffuse Map group of the Materials palette, as shown in the left image of Figure 22.13. The Adjust Bitmap dialog box appears (see the image to the right of Figure 22.13).

2. Click the Fit To Object radio button, and then click Close.

3. Click the Render tool in the Render control panel. Now the building to the right looks like it is reflecting a cloud-filled sky, as shown in Figure 22.14.

FIGURE 22.13
The Adjust Scale tool and the Adjust Bitmap dialog box

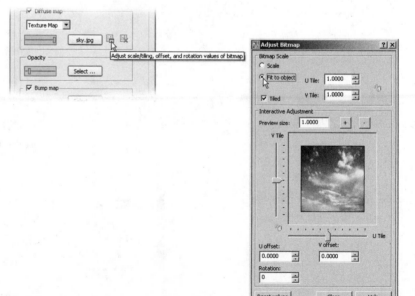

FIGURE 22.14
The rendering after
adding glass

With the Opacity slider set to 12, the glass is able to display the sky.jpg diffuse map you added earlier and still be transparent enough to show some of the interior of the building.

Adding a Background

You've got the glass looking a bit more like real glass. Next, add a background to your view so it doesn't render as black. Backgrounds are added through the View Manager dialog box.

1. In the 3D Navigate control panel, click the drop-down list and select Manage Views at the bottom of the list. The View Manager dialog box appears.

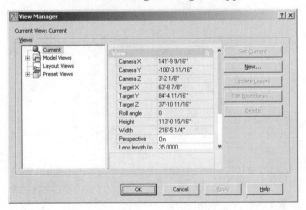

2. Click the New button toward the right of the dialog box. The New View dialog box appears.

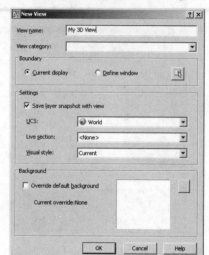

3. Enter the name My 3D View in the View Name input box.

4. In the Background group toward the bottom of the dialog box, turn on the Override default background option. The Background dialog box appears.

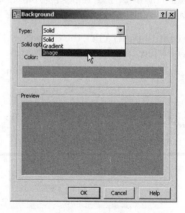

5. Select Image from the Type drop-down list at the top of the dialog box. You see that the options in the dialog box change.

6. In the Image Options group, click the Browse button.

7. Make sure the File of type setting is set to .JPG, and then browse to the Chapter 22 sample file folder and select and open the sky.jpg file. This is the same file you used for the glass earlier.

8. Click the Adjust Image button to open the Adjust Background Image dialog box.

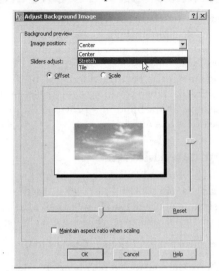

9. You see the sky.jpg file appear in the sample panel. Select Stretch from the Image Position drop-down list at the top of the dialog box. The image expands to fill the sample panel area.

10. Click OK in all the dialog boxes until you get to the View Manager dialog box.

11. In the View Manager dialog box, select My 3D View from the list to the left, and then click the Set Current button to the right.

12. Click OK to exit the View Manager dialog box. The background now appears in the drawing area.

13. Render the view to see the results. You should have something that looks similar to Figure 22.15.

FIGURE 22.15
The rendered model with a background added

Using Materials and Lights to Create Effects

Up to now, you've used only two light sources, a Distant Light and the Sun. You have two other light sources available to help simulate light: point-light sources and spotlights. This section will show you some examples of how to use these types of light sources, along with some imagination, to perform any number of visual tricks.

The office building on the right half of the rendering is still a bit cold looking. It's missing a sense of activity. You might notice that when you look at glass office buildings, you can frequently see the ceiling lights from the exterior of the building—provided the glass isn't too dark. In a subtle way, those lights lend a sense of life to a building.

Adding a Self-Illuminated Material

To help improve the image, you'll add some ceiling lights to the office building. I've already supplied the lights in the form of square 3D Faces arrayed just at the ceiling level of each floor, as shown in Figure 22.16. In this section, you will learn how to make the ceiling lights appear illuminated.

Follow these steps to assign a reflective, white material to the ceiling fixtures:

1. In the Materials control panel, click the Materials tool.

2. Click the Create New Material tool in the Materials palette, enter **Ceiling Light** in the Name input box of the Create New Material dialog box, and click OK.

3. Back in the Materials palette, move the Self-Illumination slider all the way to the right. Notice that the sample image at the top of the palette brightens to appear as if it were lighted.

4. Click the Diffuse color swatch just under the Template setting.

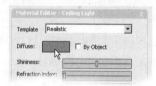

The Select Color dialog box appears.

5. Move the Luminance slider to the top to set the diffuse color to white, and then click OK.

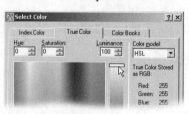

FIGURE 22.16

The 3D Face squares representing ceiling light fixtures

The ceiling lights appear as squares.

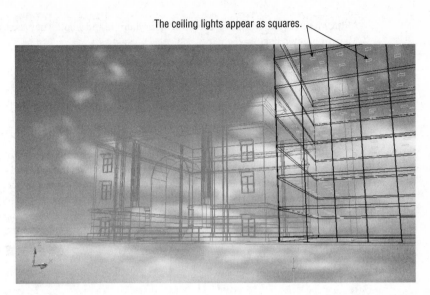

USING WOOD AND MARBLE PROCEDURAL MAPS

Procedural maps are texture maps that are derived mathematically rather than from a bitmap image. The advantage to a procedural map is that it gives a more natural representation of a material. For example, if you cut a notch out of a box that uses a wood procedural map, the notch will appear correctly with the appropriate wood grain. Do the same for a box that uses a bitmap texture map, and the grain does not appear correctly. With a bitmap texture map, the same image is placed on all four sides of the box, so cuts will not show the grain properly.

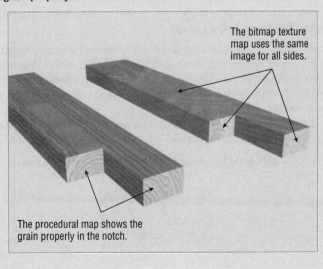

The bitmap texture map uses the same image for all sides.

The procedural map shows the grain properly in the notch.

AutoCAD offers two types of procedural maps: marble and wood. They can be selected from the Texture Map drop-down list.

If you select a procedural map, you can click the Edit Map button to the right of the drop-down list to open a dialog box that lets you control the map's properties. You can set the color and grain thickness of wood or the vein spacing and width of marble. These options let you customize a texture to your specifications. You might want to experiment with these settings on your own to see how they affect the appearance of an object.

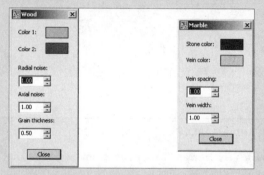

Procedural maps are not affected by the material map of an object (see "Applying and Adjusting Texture Maps" later in this chapter). Also, they do not appear in the Realistic visual style like other texture maps. You must render your view to see the results of a procedural map.

Assigning Materials by Layer

You've just created a self-illuminated material. The next step is to assign the material to the ceiling lights in the model. So far, you've used the Apply Material To Objects tool in the Materials palette toolbar, but it would be too time-consuming to have to select each light individually. You can assign materials to layers, which can save time as long as you've organized your model into layers that represent materials.

In the Facade drawing, I've already set up some layers for you. The ceiling lights are on a layer called Clglite. The next exercise shows you how to apply a material to a layer.

1. Click the Attach By Layer tool in the Materials control panel.

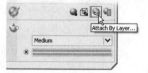

The Material Attachment Options dialog box appears. You see a list of materials on the left and a list of layers on the right.

Material Attachment Options	? X

Drag a material onto a layer:

Material Name		Layer	Material	
Ceiling Light		0	Global	
Glass1		CLGLITE	Ceiling Light	X
Global		DKGLASS	Global	
		GLASS	Global	
		CONCR...	Global	
		MULLION	Global	
		ASHADE	Global	

OK   Cancel   Help

2. Click and drag Ceiling Light from the left panel to the Clglite listing in the right panel. You see the name Ceiling Light appear next to the Clglite layer name along with an X.

3. While you are here, click and drag Glass1 from the left panel to the DKglass and Glass layers in the right panel.

4. Click OK to exit the dialog box.

5. Render your view. Now you see the lights appear in the ceiling of each of the floors (see Figure 22.17).

In this exercise you created a self-illuminated material that, when assigned to an object, appears to glow. It does not actually produce light in the model, however. To do that, you will have to add some light objects such as a distant light or spotlights.

FIGURE 22.17
The lights appear in the ceilings of the building to the right.

Simulating a Night Scene with Spotlights

Spotlights are lights that can be directed and focused on a specific area. They are frequently used to provide emphasis and are usually used for interior views or product presentations. In this exercise, you'll set up a night view of the Facade model by using spotlights to illuminate the facade.

You'll start by setting up a view to help place the spotlights. You'll also save this view because you'll be going back to it several times.

1. Select 2D Wireframe from the Visual Style control panel and Southeast Isometric from the 3D Navigate control panel.

2. Adjust your view so it looks similar to Figure 22.18.

3. In the 3D Navigate control panel, select New View from the drop-down list.

4. In the New View dialog box, enter **SE Isometric Wireframe** for the name, and then click OK.

FIGURE 22.18
Set up your view to look similar to this, and then add the spotlight.

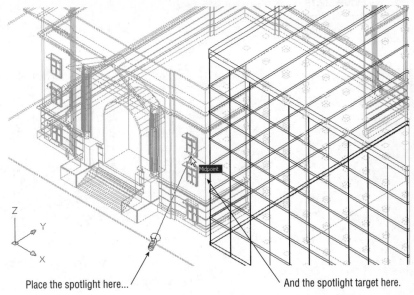

Place the spotlight here...   And the spotlight target here.

Now you're ready to add the lights.

1. Expand the Light control panel by clicking the downward-pointing arrow in the Light control panel title bar.

2. Click the Create A Spotlight tool or enter **spotlight**⤶ at the Command prompt.

3. At the `Specify source location <0,0,0>:` prompt, click the point shown in Figure 22.18. You don't have to be exact, but the idea is to place the spotlight in front of the windows on the right side of the entrance to the building.

4. At the `Specify target location <0,0,-10>:` prompt, use the Midpoint Osnap and select the bottom of the window sill of the upper window as shown in Figure 22.18. You see the prompt

   ```
   Enter an option to change
   [Name/Intensity/Status/Hotspot/Falloff/shadoW/Attenuation/Color/eXit] <eXit>:
   ```

5. Press ⤶ to accept the default settings. You can always change the optional settings for the light through the Properties dialog box.

6. Copy the spotlight you just created to the location shown in Figure 22.19. You can use the spotlight target to copy from the midpoint of one window sill to the other.

7. Since you're trying to produce a night-time rendering, turn off the sun by clicking the Sun Status tool in the Light control panel. The Sun Status tool looks just like the Light Glyphs tool lower down in the same control panel so make sure you click the right tool near the top of the Light control panel.

FIGURE 22.19
Copy the spotlight
to this location.

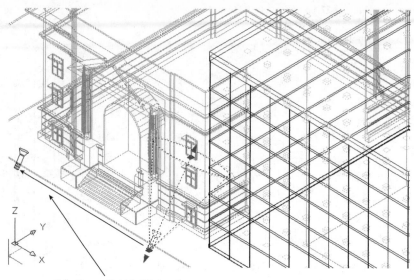

Copy the spotlight to this location.

8. Return to the original view by choosing My 3D View from the 3D Navigate control panel.

9. Click the Render tool in the Render control panel to see the results of your spotlight addition. Your rendering will look similar to Figure 22.20.

FIGURE 22.20
The rendered view
of the model with the
spotlights

Adding a Point Light

A few things still need to be added to improve this rendering. You can adjust the spotlight so it casts light over a wider area. You can also add a light in the entrance so it isn't quite so dark. The next section will show you how to make adjustments to your spotlight and how you can add a point light to obtain a different lighting effect.

1. Return to the view you used to add the spotlights by choosing SE Isometric Wireframe from the 3D Navigate control panel drop-down list.

2. Click the Create A Point Light tool in the Light control panel, or enter **Pointlight**↲.

3. At the `Specify source location <0,0,0>:` prompt, Shift+right-click and choose Point Filters ➢ .XZ or enter **.xz**↲. This will let you select just the X and Z coordinates for the location of the light.

4. Shift+right-click again and select Center. Then select the arch over the entrance, as shown in Figure 22.21.

5. At the `(need Y):` prompt, Shift+right-click and select Midpoint. Then select the midpoint of the base of the entrance wall, as shown in Figure 22.21. You see the prompt

   ```
   Enter an option to change [Name/Intensity/Status/shadoW/Attenuation/Color/eXit]
   <eXit>:
   ```

6. Press ↲ to accept the default settings for the point light.

7. The point light appears as a spherical glyph in the archway of the building.

FIGURE 22.21
Select the center of the arch.

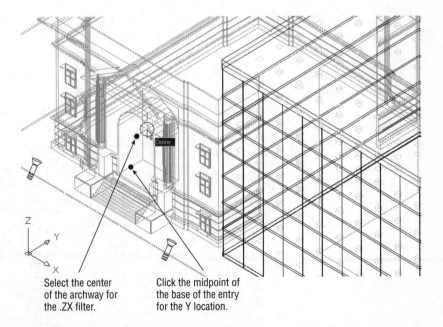

Select the center
of the archway for
the .ZX filter.

Click the midpoint of
the base of the entry
for the Y location.

Editing Lights

You've added the point light. Before you see the results in a rendering, you'll also want to change the spread of the spotlights. In this exercise, you'll edit the properties of the spotlight. Not all lights have the same properties, but the basic process for editing all lights is the same.

1. Click the two spotlights, and then right-click and choose Properties. The Properties palette appears.

TIP Another way to get to the Properties of lights is to click the Light List tool in the Light control panel, and then from the Lights In Model palette, select the lights whose properties you want to adjust. Right-click and select Properties. This method is useful if you have your light glyphs turned off.

2. Look for the Falloff angle setting in the General section of the palette and change the value from 50 to 90. Notice how the falloff cone changes in the drawing (see Figure 22.22).

3. Close the Properties palette.

4. Return to the original view by choosing My 3D View from the 3D Navigate control panel.

5. Click the Render tool in the Render control panel to see the results of your spotlight addition. Your rendering will look similar to Figure 22.23.

FIGURE 22.22

Adjust the falloff of the spotlight.

The falloff cones enlarge in the drawing when the Falloff angle value is increased to 90.

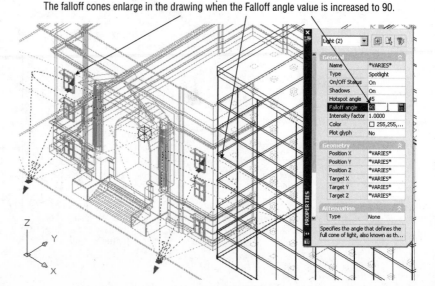

In step 2 you saw a list of options for the spotlight. Many of these options are available when you first insert the light. They appear as command line options. Often it is easier to place the light first and then play with the settings.

In this particular example, you adjusted the falloff of the spotlight. By increasing the falloff angle you broadened the spread of the light cast by the spotlight and also made the transition from light to dark appear smoother, as shown in Figure 22.24. The hotspot can also be adjusted to a narrow beam or a wide swath.

FIGURE 22.23
The rendered view of the model with the spotlights modified and the point light added

FIGURE 22.24
The hotspot and falloff of a spotlight at top produce the lighting shown in the bottom.

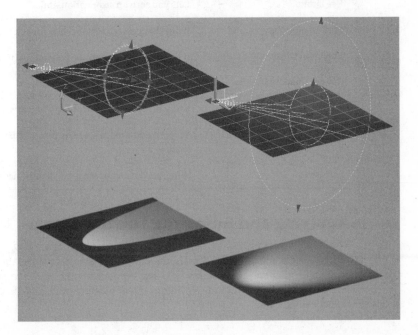

Notice that you have many other light properties available to you in the Properties dialog box. Table 22.1 describes them.

TABLE 22.1:   Properties Available for Lights

General	
Name	Name of light
Type	Type of light
On/Off Status	On or Off
Hotspot Angle	Spotlight hotspot angle
Falloff Angle	Spotlight falloff angle
Intensity Factor	Light intensity
Color	Light color
Plot Glyph	Allows the light glyph to be plotted
Attenuation	
Type	Selects the type of attenuation: inverse linear, inverse square, or none
Use Limits	Lets you turn on attenuation limits
Start Limit Offset	If Use lLmits is on, sets the distance to the beginning of attenuation
End Limit Offset	If Use Limits is on, sets the distance to the end of attenuation
Render Shadow Details	
Type	Lets you select between Sharp and Soft shadow edges
Map Size	When shadow maps are used, lets you determine the size of the shadow map
Softness	When shadow maps are used, determines the softness of shadows

Applying and Adjusting Texture Maps

You've already seen how to assign a material to an object by adding the glass materials to the buildings in the facade.dwg file. You used a sky bitmap image to simulate a reflection on the glass. You can create other surface textures by using bitmaps in other ways to help enhance your rendering. For example, you can include a photograph of existing buildings that might exist within the scene you are rendering.

Creating a Building from a Box

Figure 22.25 shows a bitmap image that was scanned into the computer and edited using a popular paint program.

I've added some blank white space to the bitmap image of the building so you can get some practice in fitting an image to an object. Now imagine that this building is across the street from the Facade model, and you want to include it in the scene to show its relationship to your building. The following exercise will show you how it's done:

1. Return to the view you used to add the spotlights by choosing SE Isometric Wireframe from the 3D Navigate control panel drop-down list, and then choose Southwest Isometric from the list. The Southwest view offers a clear view to your work.

2. Adjust your view so it looks similar to Figure 22.26, and then draw a box that is approximately 130´ square by 80 ´ tall (see Figure 22.26).

FIGURE 22.25

A bitmap image of a building you'll use in the model

The box you just added represents the building on the next block. Now create the material that you'll use to give this building some detail.

1. Click the Materials tool in the Materials control panel to open the Materials palette.

2. Click the Create New Material tool in the Materials palette toolbar and enter **Build1** for the material name.

3. In the Diffuse Map group of the Materials Palette, click the Select button.

4. Locate and select the MARKET1.tif file in the Chapter 22 sample files from the companion CD.

5. Click Open to exit this dialog box.

6. Click the Adjust Scale button to open the Adjust Bitmap dialog box and make sure the Fit To Object option is selected in the Bitmap Scale group. Click Close when you are finished.

FIGURE 22.26

Drawing the box representing the building on the next block

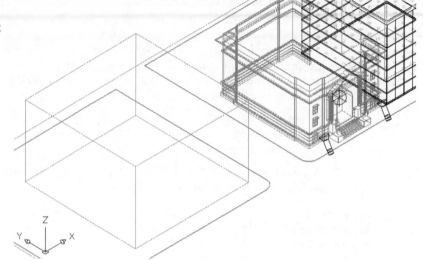

7. In the Materials palette, make sure Build1 is selected in the Materials list and then click the Apply Material To Objects button.

8. Select the box you added in step 2 of the previous exercise, and then press ⏎.

9. To see how the bitmap fits on the box, choose Realistic from the Visual Styles drop-down list.

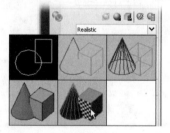

Adjusting a Material to Fit an Object

You can see that the entire image, including the blank white space, is placed on the box. You even see the image on the rooftop, though you won't see the rooftop in any of the renderings (You can hide it with another box or 3D surface if you want an aerial view). You can adjust the position and scale of the bitmap by using the Mapping tools in the Materials control panel.

1. Click and hold the Planar Mapping tool in the Materials control panel. The mapping flyout appears.

2. Select the Box Mapping tool from the flyout. You can also enter **Materialmap**⏎, and then enter **B**⏎ for the Box option.

3. At the Select faces or objects: prompt, click the box you just created and press ⏎. The box is outlined in yellow and you see a set of arrows around the box as shown in Figure 22.27.

FIGURE 22.27

The Material mapping appears as a yellow box around the selected box.

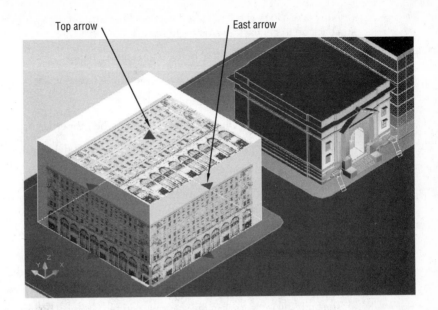

Top arrow

East arrow

4. Hover on the arrow at the top of the box (see Figure 22.27), and when it turns green, click it. Now as you move the cursor, the arrow follows, and the image stretches or compresses.

5. Stretch the image upward until the white space at the top of the building is gone and the building image fills the upper portion of the box. When you're satisfied, click the mouse.

6. Now hover over the arrow pointing to the east (see Figure 22.27), and when it turns green, click it.

7. Drag the arrow to the right until the white space of the image is gone and the image of the building fills the box.

8. Repeat steps 6 and 7 for the north side. Your box should look like Figure 22.28.

9. Press ↵ to exit the Materialmap command.

FIGURE 22.28

The box after adjusting the map

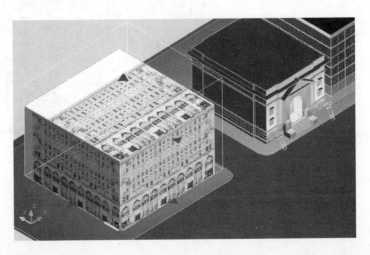

Now take a look at the rendered version. First turn off the spotlight and point light and turn the sun back on to get back to a daylight setting.

1. Click the Light List tool in the Light control panel.

2. Select the two spotlights and the point light from the list box of the Lights In Model palette.

3. Right-click and select Properties.

4. Select Off in the On/Off Status setting of the Properties palette.

5. Close the Properties palette and the Lights In Model palette.

6. Click the Sun Status tool in the Light control panel to turn the sun back on.

You've set the lighting for a daylight rendering. Notice that you were able to select several lights to turn them off all at once.

Next, render your view.

1. Choose My 3D View from the 3D Navigate control panel.

2. Click the Render tool in the Render control panel. The building appears to the left of the image (see Figure 22.29).

The building is too dark in the shadow. You can lighten it by increasing the Self Illumination setting in the Materials palette.

1. Open the Materials palette by clicking the Materials button in the Materials control panel.

2. Make sure the Building1 material is selected, and then move the Self-Illumination slider to the right. As you do this, you see a numeric value appear at the cursor. Set this value to 24 or 25.

3. Render the view again. This time the building on the next block begins to show up.

FIGURE 22.29
The rendering with
the new building

Another option is to use a paint program to refine the bitmap image before it is used in AutoCAD. AutoCAD attempts to place the bitmap accurately on a surface, so if the bitmap is fairly clean and doesn't have any extra blank space around the edges, you can usually place it on an object without having to make any adjustments other than its orientation. I purposely made the spaces in the image so you can practice using the Materialmap feature.

NOTE You briefly encountered the Template drop-down list in the Materials palette when you created a material. The settings of these templates depend on the kind of material you are trying to model.

Other Material Mapping Options

You may have notice several material mapping options in the previous exercise. You used the Box option because it was a natural fit for the box you created. But other options are offered for a planar surface, a cylinder, and a sphere. Figure 22.30 shows how these other options might be applied to the shapes for which they are intended.

You don't have to apply the map to the shape they describe. Later you'll see how you can apply a planar map to a box. You can apply a cylinder map to a thin box to achieve an interesting effect. Or a spherical map can be applied to a cube (see Figure 21.31).

Specifying the Size of a Bitmap

As you've just seen, the Material Map feature gives you a quick and intuitive way to set the location of a material map onto an object. There are several other ways to control the appearance of a material on an object. If you have a surface pattern that repeats over the surface, such as a tile pattern, you can set the frequency and size of the pattern. For example, you might have a brick pattern that repeats over a 12´ square area and you want that pattern reproduced accurately on a surface.

FIGURE 22.30
The planar, box, cylinder, and sphere material maps

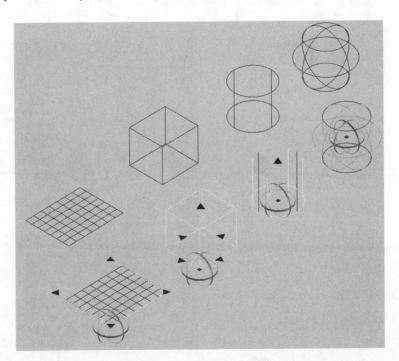

FIGURE 22.31
Material maps applied
to different shapes

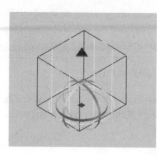

Imagine you need to apply a brick pattern to a wall that is 8 feet wide by 4 feet tall. The blocks are the standard 8″ by 16″ split face concrete masonry unit, and you have an image that shows 4 courses of blocks two blocks wide as shown in Figure 22.32. This is the `Masonry.Unit Masonry.CMU.Split-Face.Running.jpg` file in the Textures folder that is installed with AutoCAD 2007.

1. Open the `CMUwall.dwg` sample file from the projects folder. This file contains a simple box representing the 4′ by 8′ wall.

2. Click the Materials tool in the Materials control panel to open the Materials palette.

3. Click the Create New Material tool in the toolbar and give your new material the name CMU.

FIGURE 22.32
The bitmap image of a
set of blocks

4. Click the Select button in the Diffuse Map group, and then locate and select the `Masonry.Unit Masonry.CMU.Split-Face.Running.jpg` file in the AutoCAD Textures folder. This is typically found at `C:\Documents and Settings\All Users\Application Data\Autodesk\ AutoCAD 2007\R17.0\enu\`. You may also use `CMU.Split-Face.Running.jpg` in the sample project folder for chapter 22.

5. Click the Apply Material To Objects tool in the Materials palette toolbar, and then click the wall object and press ↵. The wall displays the material you've just created as shown in the left panel of Figure 22.33.

The wall has a texture, but it isn't what you would expect. You see the results of a material with the default settings. You need to adjust the bitmap options so the texture appears to the proper scale on the wall object.

1. In the Materials palette, click the Adjust Scale tool in the Diffuse Map group.

2. In the Adjust Bitmap dialog box, make sure the Scale option in the Bitmap Scale group is selected, and then select Inches from the Units drop-down list.

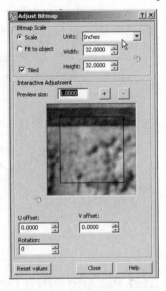

3. Change the Width and Height values to 32 inches. You use 32 inches because that is the actual width and height of the blocks shown in Figure 22.32. As you enter these values, the block wall changes to reveal the blocks at the proper size as shown in the image in the right side of Figure 22.33.

4. Close the Adjust Bitmap dialog box, then close and save the `CMUwall.dwg` file.

Now suppose that you want the blocks to appear 4″ high instead of 8″ high. You can go back to the Adjust Bitmap dialog box and change the Height setting to 16 or half the height you specified originally. The block wall changes to show a 4″ high block as shown in Figure 22.34.

You can use many other settings in the Adjust Bitmap dialog box to fine-tune the appearance of a material over an object. You've used the major settings in these exercises. The following is a run-down of all the settings for your reference.

FIGURE 22.33
The wall with the
material applied

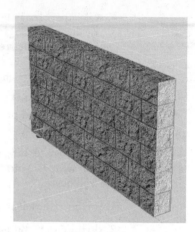

FIGURE 22.34
Change the Height set-
ting in the Adjust Bit-
map dialog box and
the wall also changes.

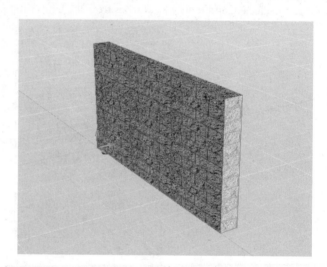

Simulating Trees and People with Opacity Maps

There's nothing like adding landscaping and people to a rendering to add a sense of life and scale. Computer images, in particular, need landscape props because they tend to appear cold and lifeless.

In the following set of exercise, you create a tree material and apply it to a 3D solid to simulate a tree. In doing so, you'll get a chance to explore some of the other features of the Materials palette. You'll use the same "Diffuse map" texture map option you've been using so far to create a tree material, but you'll also add something called an *opacity map*. An opacity map lets you control the transparency of a texture map through a black-and-white image file. For example, in the tree you'll be creating, you will apply a tree material to a simple rectangular 3D solid. You will want the area around the tree to be transparent, creating an illusion of a complex, tree-shaped outline.

The opacity map lets you determine transparency through black-and-white areas of an image. White areas are transparent, and black areas are opaque. You can use shade of gray to vary transparency. Figure 22.35 shows you an example of how an opacity map works.

FIGURE 22.35

A material using an opacity map can be applied to a 3D solid to create the illusion of a complex outline such as a tree.

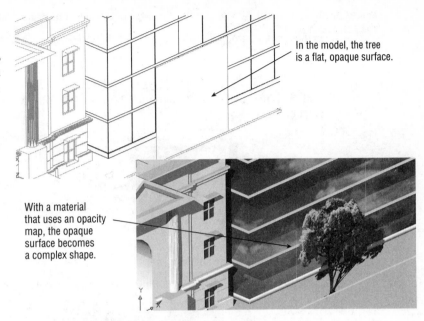

In the model, the tree is a flat, opaque surface.

With a material that uses an opacity map, the opaque surface becomes a complex shape.

To start your tree, create a new material in the Materials palette:

1. Open the Materials palette by clicking the Materials tool in the Materials control panel.

2. Click the Create New Material tool in the Materials palette toolbar.

3. Give the new material the name Tree1.

Next, add a texture map of a tree.

1. In the Diffuse Map group, click the Select button.

2. Use the Select Image File dialog box to browse to the Chapter 22 project folder from the companion CD.

3. Locate and select the file CamphorAM.tif.

4. Click the Adjust Scale tool to the right of the Select button in the Diffuse Map group.

5. In the Adjust Bitmap dialog box, turn on the Fit To Object radio button, and then click Close.

Finally, add an opacity map for the tree. The process is basically the same as adding a texture map.

1. In the Opacity Map group, click the Select button.

2. Use the Select Image File dialog box to browse to the Chapter 22 project folder from the companion CD.

3. Locate and open the file CamphorOP.tif.

4. Click the Adjust Scale tool to the right of the Select button in the Opacity group.

5. In the Adjust Bitmap dialog box, turn on the Fit To Object radio button, and then click Close.

To check your Tree1 material so far, make some adjustments to the sample image in the panel at the top of the Materials palette.

1. With the Tree1 material selected, click the Toggle Display Mode button at the top of the palette.

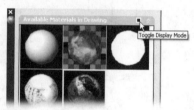

2. The image enlarges to fill the panel.

3. Click the Checkered Underlay Off tool in the lower left of the panel.

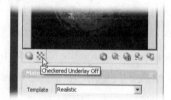

4. Click the Swatch Geometry tool that is just to the left of the Checkered Underlay Off tool and select the cube icon.

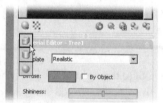

The sample shows the tree and the transparent area around it.

Finally, create an object representing a tree in the drawing, and then apply the Tree1 material to the object.

1. Adjust your view so it looks similar to Figure 22.36.

2. Set up a UCS that is vertical to the ground plane. Choose Tools ➢ New UCS ➢ Face, click the location shown in Figure 22.36, and then press ↵ to accept the new UCS.

3. Click the Box tool in the 3D Make control panel, and then draw a box that is approximately 30′ by 30′. Give the box a height of 0.01. You don't want it to be too thick.

4. Open the Materials palette, and then click the Apply Material To Objects tool.

5. Click the box you just created, and then press ↵.

6. Select My 3D View in the 3D Navigate control panel, and then click Render in the Render control panel to see the results of your work (see Figure 22.37).

The process of adding people is just the same. You create a material that includes a texture map and an opacity map and then apply the material to a flat box. Make sure you turn on the Fit To Object option in the Adjust Bitmap dialog box for both the texture and the opacity map. Figure 22.38 shows a rendering that includes some additional trees and people.

Understanding the Rendering Options

You actually have quite a few settings available to control the quality of the renderings. If you expand the Render control panel, several other options appear as shown in Figure 22.39.

The Save Rendering To File option lets you set up a file to which the renderings will be saved. If you turn this option on, each time you render your model, the rendering will be saved automatically to the file you designate.

FIGURE 22.36
Adding a tree

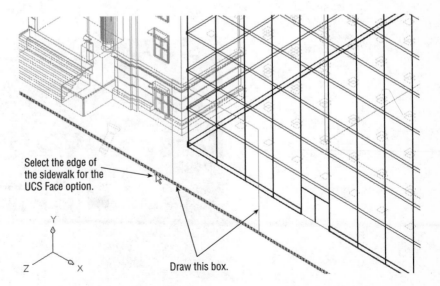

Select the edge of the sidewalk for the UCS Face option.

Draw this box.

WHAT IS A BUMP MAP

You may have noticed the Bump Map group just below the Opacity Map. The Bump Map option lets you add another image to add texture to a surface. For example, you can include a series of parallel lines to a material to simulate a corrugated surface.

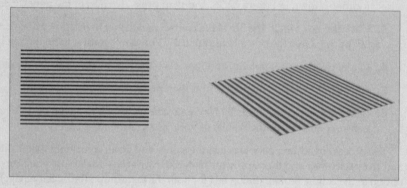

You can adjust the depth of the bump using the Bump Map slider in the Bump Map group. Move the slider to the right for a "deeper" bump.

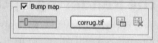

The Output Size option lets you set the vertical and horizontal resolution in pixels of the rendering. The default is 640 × 480. You can choose from a set of predetermined standard sizes or set a custom size.

FIGURE 22.37
The tree added to your rendering

FIGURE 22.38
A rendering with more trees and people

FIGURE 22.39
The expanded Render control panel

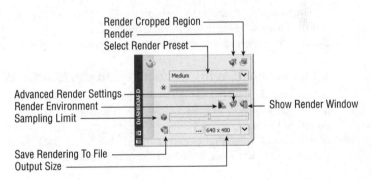

The Render Environment option lets you add a fog effect to your rendering (see Figure 22.40). Click this option to open the Render Environment dialog box. This dialog box offers a set of options to control how the fog appears in the rendering. For example, Enable Fog lets you turn the fog effect on or off. Fog Color lets you select a color for the fog. You can experiment with the Render Environment dialog box on your own: when you click an option name in the left column, you see a description of the option at the bottom of the dialog box.

The Select Render Preset is a drop-down list that gives you a set of options you can use to select the quality of the rendering. The default is Medium, which is the setting you've been using. This offers a decent quality rendering without taking a lot of time. When you want to produce a final, high-quality rendering, you can select Presentation from this list. The rendering will take longer, but more detail will be brought out in the rendering.

The Advanced Render Settings opens the Advanced Render Settings palette. These settings are for the advanced user, and most users won't need to work with them. The Rendering Presets are actually predetermined sets of the Advanced Render Settings. You can make adjustments to these settings if you need to (see "Rendering Interior Views" later in this chapter for more on the Advanced Rendering Settings).

FIGURE 22.40
The Render Environment option lets you add fog to a Rendering.

The Sampling Limit slider controls the level at which AutoCAD "samples" each pixel of the rendering. Move the slider to the left and the rendering will appear blocky as if it were a low-resolution image. Move the slider to the right and rendering becomes sharper and more detailed.

Checking and Saving Renderings in the Render Window

All your renderings appear in the Render window, which has a few options you'll want to know about. At the bottom of the window, you see a list of all the renderings you've done in the current AutoCAD Session. If you've done several renderings, you can go back to an earlier rendering by clicking it in the list. Right-click an item in the list to display a list of options that you can apply to the selected item . Table 22.2 describes these options.

TABLE 22.2: The Right-Click Options for Image Filenames in the Render Window

OPTION	WHAT IT DOES
Render Again	Renders the selected image again.
Save	Saves the selected image to a file. AutoCAD offers a choice of monochrome, 8-bit grayscale, 8-bit color, and 24-bit color. You can save your image as a BMP, PCX, TGA, TIFF JPEG, or PNG file.
Save Copy	If you've already saved a file once, this option lets you save it again under a different name.
Make Render Settings Current	If you've rendered several views and you want to return to the setting of a previous rendering, select the view whose settings you want to restore and select this option.
Remove From The List	Removes the selected rendering from the list.
Delete Output File	If you've saved a rendered view as a file, this option lets you delete the file.

Perhaps the most important of these options are the Save and Save Copy. These enable you to keep copies of your rendered view as bitmap images.

If you want to check a detail in the rendering, you can use the Tools menu to zoom in or zoom out of the image. When you zoom in, horizontal and vertical scroll bars are displayed to allow you to pan over the image.

To the right of the window is a listing of the rendering's statistics. You can make adjustments to many of these settings through system variables and the Advanced Render Settings palette.

Adding Cameras for Better View Control

You've seen how you can save and recall views throughout this chapter. Views can be a real time-saver, especially if you have several views you save and recall. Views will also save background and visual styles. Typically, you set up a view using the tools you've learned so far, but another tool can give you that extra level of control you may need for special circumstances.

1. What is not obvious is that your views are also represented as cameras. Right now, you can't see the cameras because a setting called *Camera Glyph* is turned off. Try the following to visualize your My 3D View as a camera. Return to the SE Isometric Wireframe view using the 3D Navigate control panel drop down list.

2. Adjust your view so it looks similar to Figure 22.41.

3. Expand the 3D Navigate control panel, and then click the Display Cameras tool. You see two cameras in the lower half of the drawing.

4. Click one of the cameras. A window appears that shows you what the camera sees.

5. Press the Escape key, and then click the other camera. The camera preview changes to show you samples of the other view.

USING THE RENDER CROPPED REGION TOOL FOR A QUICK CHECK

At times you may want to just check a part of your to see if it will render correctly without having to do a full blown rendering. You can use the Render Cropped Region tool in the Render control panel to do just that.

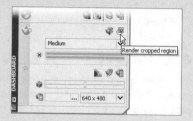

Click the Render Cropped Region tool, and then place a selection window around the area you want to check. AutoCAD will render just the selected area directly in the drawing area. Choose View ➢ Redraw to clear the screen of the rendered region.

When you select a camera, not only do you see the camera preview, but you also see a set of grips for the camera. You'll get a chance to work with some of those grips a little later. Next, try to create a view using the Camera tool.

The following exercise will show an example of adding a camera to the facade model. You'll not only add a camera, but you'll apply one of the options available for the camera:

1. Click the Create Camera tool in the 3D Navigate control panel.

You see the prompt

```
Current camera settings: Height=0' Lens Length=50.0000 mm
Specify camera location:
```

2. Click the point shown in Figure 22.41 to set the camera location.

3. At the `Specify target location:` prompt, use the Center Osnap and select the center of the arch. You'll see the prompt

```
Enter an option [?/Name/LOcation/Height/Target/LEns/Clipping/View/eXit]<eXit>:
```

4. You'll want to set the height of the camera to eye level, so type **H**⏎ for the Height option.

5. At the `Specify camera height <0">:` prompt, enter 5'⏎. The options prompt returns to allow you to enter more options.

6. Press ⏎ to complete the camera insertion. The camera appears at the location you selected in step 2.

FIGURE 22.41

Adding a new camera

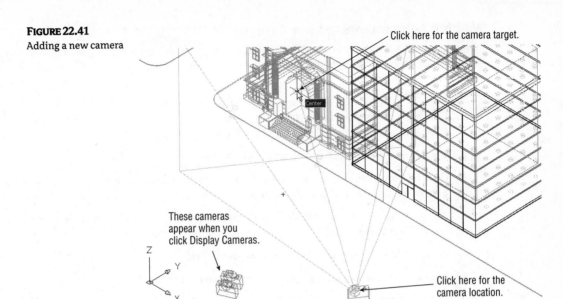

Click here for the camera target.

These cameras
appear when you
click Display Cameras.

Click here for the
camera location.

You were able to set the height of the camera independent of the location you selected in step 2 by using one of the options in the prompt. Table 22.3 gives you a description of the other options that are available.

TIP AutoCAD gives your camera the default name of Camera1, though you can rename it any time in the Properties palette or in the View Manager dialog box.

TABLE 22.3: The Camera Prompt Options

OPTION	WHAT IT DOES
?	Displays a list of cameras in the current drawing
Name	Lets you provide a name for your camera. No spaces are allowed
LOcation	Lets you change the location of the camera
Height	Lets you specify the height of the camera
Target	Lets you select a target location
LEns	Lets you specify a lens focal length in mm
Clipping	Lets you include a front and back clipping plane
View	Lets you go to the camera's view
eXit	Exits the command

Making Adjustments to Your Camera

Now that you've got the camera in place, you can see what the view looks like. You can use the 3D Navigate drop-down list to display the view from your new camera, or you can click the camera to open the camera preview window. Before you do any of that, try making some adjustments to your camera.

1. Click the camera you just created. You see the Camera Preview dialog box, which shows a sample of the view from your camera (see Figure 22.42).

2. You also see the camera view frame and target.

3. Click the camera grip and move the camera round. You can see the changes you make in real time in the Camera Preview dialog box.

4. Adjust the camera location back to its original location so your preview looks similar to the one in Figure 22.42.

Now turn on the clipping planes to see how they work.

1. With the camera still selected, right-click and select Properties.

2. At the bottom of the Properties palette, click the Clipping option and select Front And Back On.

Notice that the sample view changes.

3. Change the Front Plane value to 20′ and the Back Plane value to –20′ (minus twenty feet). The Camera Preview view now shows the view of just the entry.

FIGURE 22.42

The Camera Preview dialog box

The clipping planes hide objects either behind or in front of the target location. As you've just seen, you can indicate the clipping plane distance from the target in the Properties dialog box. You can also make adjustments to the clipping plane directly in the drawing using the camera's grips.

1. Hover over the Front Clip Plane grip shown in Figure 22.43 so you can see the tooltip describing the grip.

2. Click the grip, drag it back and forth, and watch the camera preview. You can see how the clipping plane hides more or less of the foreground as you move the grip.

3. Click the original location of the grip (the red grip) to keep it at 20´.

You can adjust the back grip in the same way so you can get direct feedback on how much of your view is being clipped.

Next, try adjusting one of the other grips.

1. Click the Lens Length grip on the left side, as shown in Figure 22.43, and then drag it to the left. This has the effect of shortening the lens length. The shorter the lens length, the more of the view the camera is able to take in. But past a certain point, the view begins to distort.

2. Click a point to the left, as shown in Figure 22.43, to fix the view at a lower lens length. You see the Lens Length value change in the Properties palette.

3. In the Properties palette, change the Lens Length value back to the default of 50.

As you can see in the Properties palette for the camera, you have a number of controls to affect the view. In fact, since cameras and user-created views are basically the same thing, the properties you see for cameras are the same as those you would see for views in the View Manager. (Open the 3D Navigate drop-down list and select Manage Views at the bottom of the list.) Obviously, the options we present here apply to other views as well.

FIGURE 22.43
Selecting the camera grips

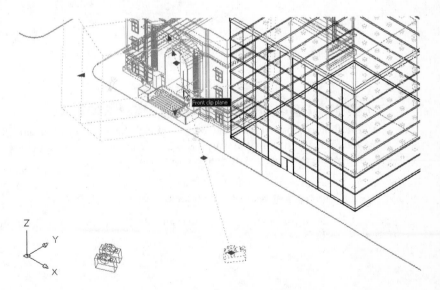

Now let's see the results of your work.

1. In the 3D Navigate control panel, select Camera1 from the drop-down list. You see the camera view you just set up.

2. Expand the Visual Style control panel and click the Edge Overhang option.

This last step gives your view a sketched appearance.

Creating an Animated Walk-Through

Another feature that is related to the camera is the *motion path animation*. This is a feature that allows you to create an animated walk-through of your design. Such animations can be a great aid in helping others to visualize your ideas more clearly.

1. Choose SE Isometric Wireframe from the 3D Navigate control panel drop-down list, and then adjust your view so it looks similar to Figure 22.44.

2. Draw the polyline shown in Figure 22.44, and then move the polyline in the Z axis so it is at the 5′ level.

FIGURE 22.44
Draw the polyline for the motion path.

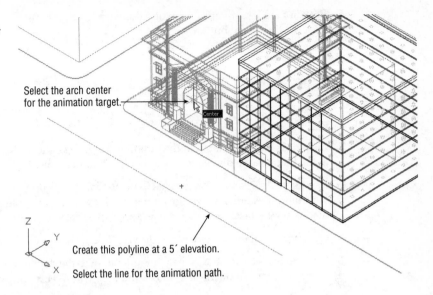

Select the arch center for the animation target.

Create this polyline at a 5´ elevation.

Select the line for the animation path.

3. Choose View ➢ Motion Path Animations. The Motion Path Animation dialog box appears.

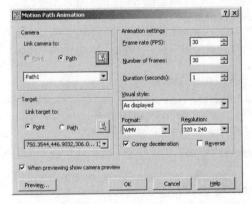

4. In the Camera group, select the Path option, and then click the Select Path button.

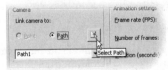

5. Select the polyline you just drew, and then click OK to accept the default path name.

6. Back in the Motion Path Animation dialog box, select Point in the Target group, and then click the Pick Point button.

7. Pick the center of the arch in the building entrance as shown in Figure 22.44 then click OK at the Point Name dialog box to accept the default name.

8. Make sure As Displayed is selected in the Visual Style drop-down list, and then click the Preview button. A preview window appears, and you see a sample of your animation. The animation is a bit fast, but you can make adjustments later.

9. Close the Animation Preview window, and then click OK.

10. In the Save As dialog box, save your animation to the default filename. AutoCAD will take a moment to generate the animation, and then you'll see a camera at the end of your animation path.

You were asked to go ahead and save the animation, even though it was in a fairly crude state and was too fast. The advantage to saving the animation right away is that you will then have access to the animation camera.

AutoCAD creates a new camera with default settings when an animation is created. You can then make adjustments to the camera and other animation settings to refine your animation.

Fine-Tuning the Animation

Once you've created and saved an animation, no matter how crude, you can edit the camera settings for that animation, as well as the speed, resolution, and visual style for the animation. To get a feel for how to edit an animation, try the following:

1. Click the camera at the end of the animation path, and then right-click and select Properties.

2. In the Properties palette, change the Lens Length setting to 35 to get a wider field of view. Close the Properties palette.

3. Choose View ➢ Motion Path Animation.

4. Change the Duration setting to 8 seconds.

5. Change the visual style to 3D Hidden.

6. Click OK and save the animation again. You can save it under a different name if you like, so you have a record of the original animation.

This time AutoCAD will take more time to process the animation since you've increased the duration. When it is done, locate your animation file using Windows Explorer and double-click it to view the results.

As you saw in step 5, you can use any visual style that is in the drawing. You can even create a fully rendered version of the animation, but be aware that the more complex the animation, the longer it will take AutoCAD to process.

You can also modify the polyline path by adding more segments or changing the location of the vertices of the path.

You've seen how a few of the options in the Motion Path Animation dialog box work. If you think you might find this tool useful, you will want to experiment with some of the other settings. Table 22.4 describes these options.

TABLE 22.4:   The Motion Path Animation, Camera, and Target Options

OPTION	WHAT IT DOES
Camera and Target Options	
Point/Path	Selects between a point or a path for the camera or target.
Select Path/Pick Point	Temporarily closes the dialog box to allow you to select a path or a point.
Drop-down list	Lets you choose from a point or a path that has already been selected.
Animation Settings Options	
Frame Rate (FPS):	Sets the frame rate in frames per second. 16 is the lowest you can go for a smooth animation. TV is usually around 30 fps.
Number Of Frames	Sets the total number of frames in the animation. The lower the number, the faster the animation. This setting is dependent on the Duration and Frame Rate settings.
Duration	Sets the duration of the animation. 10 seconds is a typical duration.
Visual Style	Sets the visual style for the animation. You can also select Rendered for a fully rendered animation.
Format	Lets you choose an animation file format. If you plan to use the Windows Movie Maker application to edit your animation, use WMV. Other options are AVI (Windows), MOV (QuickTime), and MPG (Mpeg 1 or 2).
Resolution	Sets the resolution of the animation. 320 × 240 is typical for computer video and VCD. 640 × 480 is typical for DVD quality.
Other Options	
Corner Deceleration	Automatically decelerates the animation motion at corners for smoother transitions.
Reverse	Reverses the animation.
When Previewing Show Camera Preview	Displays the preview in a window; otherwise the camera motion is shown along the animation path.
Preview	Shows you a preview of your animation.

Printing Your Renderings

When you've decided that your rendering is perfect, you can print a copy directly from AutoCAD. Through a Layout tab, you can also put together presentations that include 2D floor plans and elevations with your rendering on a single sheet. Or you can have several renderings on one sheet.

Try the following to set up a Layout tab to render the 3D model in both a rendered view and a hidden-line view:

1. Click the Layout1 tab.

2. Click the viewport border to expose its grips, and then use a grip to make the viewport smaller so it is about half the height of the Paper Space layout. Keep the height-to-width proportions of the viewport as close to the original as possible.

3. Double-click inside the viewport and then enter **V↵** to open the View Manager dialog box.

4. Select My 3D View from the Views list and then click Set Current. Click OK to exit the View Manager dialog box.

5. Turn on the Sun Status in the Light control panel.

6. Double-click outside the viewport, and then copy the viewport down so you have an identical viewport just below the original.

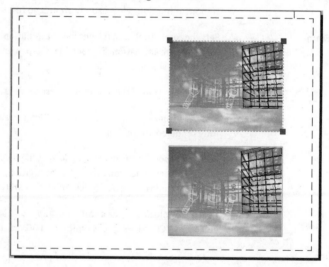

Now you're ready to set up the viewport to render the views in specific ways. For example, you can set one viewport to render as a fully rendered view while rendering another viewport as a hidden-line view:

1. Click the border of the top viewport, and then right-click and choose Shade Plot ➤ Rendered.

2. Click the border of the lower viewport, and then right-click and choose Shade Plot ➤ Hidden.

3. Right-click the Layout1 tab and select Plot.

4. Choose a printer name for the Printer/Plotter group, and then click Preview. After a moment, you see a preview of your plot showing a fully rendered view in the top viewport and a hidden-line view in the lower viewport.

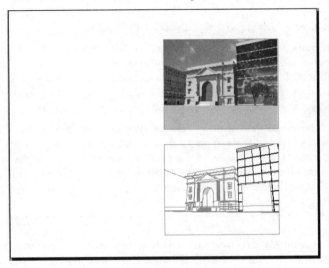

You can add viewports to include floor plans and elevations if needed. Or you can add Isometric views with labels that point out features of the drawing.

You also have control over the quality of the rendered viewport. If you right-click the Layout tab and choose Page Setup Manager, the Page Setup Manager dialog box opens. Click the Modify button to open the Page Setup dialog box. You can use the Shaded Viewport Options group to select from a set of viewport quality settings.

You can choose from Draft, Preview, Normal, Presentation, Maximum, and Custom. These options are described in detail in Chapter 8, so I won't go into detail here. Just remember that the options are available to help you get the most from your rendered printer output.

Rendering Interior Views

If you are more interested in rendering interior architectural views, you'll want to know about some of the advanced rendering settings that are available in AutoCAD 2007. Two groups of settings are particularly important to understand when rendering interior views.

Figure 22.45 is a rendering of a simple model using the material techniques described in this chapter. It also includes a sunlight source. As you can see, the rendering is fairly dark and not interesting.

GETTING A SKETCH PRESENTATION WITH VISUAL STYLES

This chapter has focused on getting a realistic rendering of your model, but frequently, you will want to show your model in a less realistic view. This is especially true in the early stages of a design when you don't want to give the impression that you've created a finished design.

In Chapter 21, you saw how you can create a custom visual style. You may find that for most of your work, a custom visual style is all you need to get your ideas across. You can plot visual styles from either the Model tab or the layout tab. If you choose a layout tab to plot a visual style, select the viewport border, right-click, and select the Shadeplot option. You'll see a cascading menu that contains a list of the visuals styles available. Select the visual style you want to use for your plot.

In addition, if you need to get a bitmap version of your plot file for use in Photoshop or another image-editing program, you can add a raster plotter to AutoCAD. Use the Add-A-Plotter Wizard as described in Chapter 7, and when you get to the part that asks for the plotter model, select Raster File Format and continue with the wizard. Once you've installed the raster plotter, you can select it as a plot device in the Plot Or Page Setup dialog box. The raster plotter will produce a bitmap image file. See Chapter 7 for more on plotting your drawing.

Figure 22.46 is the same model rendered using two advanced rendering features: Global Illumination and Final Gathering. Global Illumination is a feature that simulates the way light bounces off objects in a scene. When you turn on this option, AutoCAD calculates the reflection of light off the various surfaces in the model and applies that reflected light to neighboring objects. For example, the orange hue from the floor is reflected on the walls. The Final Gathering feature has the effect of refining the rendering by increasing the amount of detail the Global Illumination produces.

TIP   It helps to add a background view to simulate a view out of the window. After you've rendered your view using Global Illumination, go back to the image you used for a background and adjust its brightness to match the rendering's brightness.

FIGURE 22.45
An interior rendering
using just the sun

FIGURE 22.46
The same interior rendering with Global Illumination and Final Gathering turned on

These two features can be turned on and edited using the Advanced Render Settings tool in the Render control panel. This tool opens the Advanced Render Settings palette, which is shown in Figure 22.47.

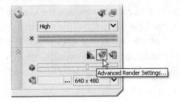

FIGURE 22.47
The Advanced Render Settings palette

Once you've opened the Advanced Render Settings palette, select the Render presets you want to use from the Select Render Preset drop-down list at the top. You can then turn on the Global Illumination feature by clicking the lightbulb icon in the Global Illumination title bar (see Figure 22.47). To turn on the Final Gathering feature, click the lightbulb icon in the Final Gather title bar.

Just turning these features on won't give you great results right away, however. You'll need to make some careful setting adjustments. First, you must set up your drawing units using the Drawing Units dialog box (choose Format ➤ Units). Once you've done this, you must stick to that unit style. If you choose architectural, for example, you don't want to change it to decimal.

Once you've set your units, turn on the Use Radius setting in the Global Illumination group (see Figure 22.47), and then set Radius to 36″. If you're working in metric, set Radius to a value similar to 36″. If this value is too small, the rendering will appear splotchy.

Next, scroll down to the Light Properties group and change the Energy Multiplier setting to a value around 0.008.

Once you've made these settings, you can render your interior view and see the results. If the direct sunlight is too bright, you can reduce the sun's intensity factor by clicking the Edit The Sun tool in the Light control panel and adjusting the intensity factor in the Sun Properties palette. If the interior appears too dark or too light, adjust the Energy Multiplier value in the Light Properties group of the Advanced Rendering Settings palette.

You can adjust the sun angle by setting the date and time for the sun in the Sun Properties palette. To do quick study renderings, you can turn off Final Gathering and increase the Global Lighting Radius setting to 100 inches or 2000 mm. You can also reduce the Global Illuminations Photons/Sample setting and the Light Properties Photons/Light setting while making your study rendering. You will likely end up making several renderings before you arrive at one that you like.

While not perfect, Global Illumination can greatly improve your interior views. You can save some time by getting a rendering close to what you want and then using an image-editing program to fine-tune the image.

TIP If you'd like to see how the file used in Figure 22.46 is set up, you can find it as 22-setting.dwg in the projects folder for this chapter.

If You Want to Experiment

In this chapter, you participated in a guided tour of AutoCAD's rendering tools and saw their main features. Because of space considerations, this chapter didn't go into the finer details of many features, but you now have the basic knowledge from which to build your rendering skills. Without too much effort, you can adapt much of what you've learned here to your own projects. If you need more detailed information, click the Help button found in all Render dialog boxes.

Computer rendering of 3D models is a craft that takes some time to master. Experiment with these rendering tools to see firsthand the types of results you can expect. You might want to try different types of views such as an Isometric or Elevation view, the latter of which is shown in Figure 22.48. With a bit more detail added, this rendered elevation could fit nicely into a set of renderings for a presentation.

FIGURE 22.48
An Elevation view of
the Facade model

MAKING YOUR OWN RENDERING PRESETS

If you want to create your own custom rendering presets so you have the default ones available, follow these steps:

1. In the Advanced Rendering Settings palette (see Figure 22.47), select Manage Render Presets from the drop-down list at the top of the palette. The Render Presets Manager dialog box opens.

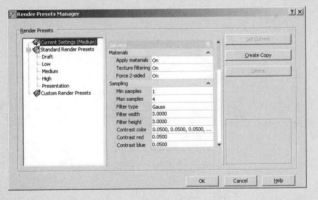

2. Select a preset that you'd like as your prototype from the list to the left, and then click the Create Copy button to the right.

3. In the Copy Render Presets dialog box, enter a name for your presets and a description if you like. Click OK.

4. You'll see your copy appear at the bottom of the list to the right under Custom Render Presets.

You can also edit the render presets from the Render Presets Manager using the settings in the middle column. Once you've created a set of custom render presets, you can select it from the Render control panel drop-down list.

Chapter 23

Editing and Visualizing 3D Solids

In the previous 3D chapters, you spent some time becoming familiar with the AutoCAD 3D modeling features. In this chapter, you'll focus on 3D solids and how they are created and edited. You'll also learn how you can use some special visualization tools to show your 3D solid in a variety of ways.

You'll create a fictitious mechanical part to explore some of the ways you can shape 3D solids. This will also give you a chance to see how you can turn your 3D model into a standard 2D mechanical drawing. In addition, you'll learn about the 3D solid editing tools that are available through the Solid Editing toolbar.

TIP   LT users do not have solid modeling capabilities. However, you can take advantage of the region objects and their related editing commands described in the section "Using 3D Solid Operations on 2D Drawings" in this chapter.

Topics in this chapter include the following:

◆   Understanding Solid Modeling

◆   Creating Solid Forms

◆   Creating Complex Solids

◆   Editing Solids

◆   Enhancing the 2D Drawing Process

◆   Finding the Properties of a Solid

◆   Taking Advantage of Stereolithography

Understanding Solid Modeling

Solid modeling is a way of defining 3D objects as solid forms. When you create a 3D model by using solid modeling, you start with the basic forms of your model—cubes, cones, and cylinders, for instance. These basic solids are called *primitives*. Then, using more of these primitives, you begin to add to or subtract from your basic forms.

For example, to create a model of a tube, you first create two solid cylinders, one smaller in diameter than the other. You then align the two cylinders so they are concentric and tell AutoCAD to subtract the smaller cylinder from the larger one. The larger of the two cylinders then becomes a tube whose inside diameter is that of the smaller cylinder, as shown in Figure 23.1. Several primitives are available for modeling solids in AutoCAD (see Figure 23.2).

FIGURE 23.1

Creating a tube by using solid modeling

Create two cylinder primitives, one for the outside diameter and one for the inside diameter.

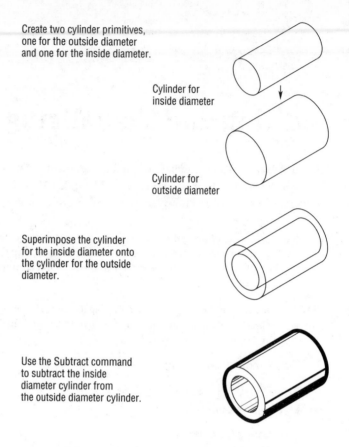

Cylinder for inside diameter

Cylinder for outside diameter

Superimpose the cylinder for the inside diameter onto the cylinder for the outside diameter.

Use the Subtract command to subtract the inside diameter cylinder from the outside diameter cylinder.

FIGURE 23.2

The solid primitives

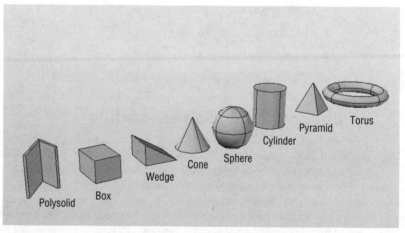

Polysolid Box Wedge Cone Sphere Cylinder Pyramid Torus

You can join these shapes—box, wedge, cone, cylinder, sphere, pyramid, polysolid, and donut (or *torus*)—in one of four ways to produce secondary shapes. The first three, demonstrated in Figure 23.3 using a cube and a cylinder as examples, are called *Boolean operations*. (The name comes from the 19th-century mathematician George Boole.)

FIGURE 23.3

The intersection, subtraction, and union of a cube and a cylinder

A solid box and a solid cylinder are superimposed.

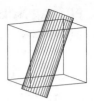

The intersection of the primitives creates a solid cylinder with the ends skewed.

The cylinder subtracted from the box creates a hole in the box.

The union of the two primitives creates a box with two round pegs.

The three Boolean operations are as follows:

Intersection   Uses only the intersecting region of two objects to define a solid shape.

Subtraction   Uses one object to cut out a shape in another.

Union   Joins two primitives so they act as one object.

The fourth option, *interference,* lets you find exactly where two or more solids coincide in space—similar to the results of a union. The main difference between interference and union is that interference enables you to keep the original solid shapes, whereas union discards the original solids, leaving only their combined form. With interference, you can have AutoCAD either show you the shape of the coincident space or create a solid based on the coincident space's shape.

Joined primitives are called *composite solids.* You can join primitives to primitives, composite solids to primitives, and composite solids to other composite solids.

Now let's take a look at how these concepts let us create models in AutoCAD.

TIP   To simplify the exercises in this chapter, the instructions don't specify inches or centimeters. This way, users of both the metric and Imperial measurement systems can use the exercises without having to read through duplicate information.

Creating Solid Forms

In this section, you will begin to draw the object shown in Figure 23.4. In the process, you will explore the creation of solid models by creating primitives and then setting up special relationships between them.

Creating Primitives

Primitives are the basic building blocks of solid modeling. At first, it might seem limiting to have only eight primitives to work with, but consider the varied forms you can create with just a few two-dimensional objects. Let's begin by creating the basic mass of our steel bracket.

First, prepare your drawing for the exercise:

1. Create a new file called Bracket using the acad.dwt template.

2. Right-click the Snap button on the status bar; then, in the Drafting Settings dialog box, set Snap Spacing to 0.5 and turn on the Grid and Snap modes.

3. Choose Tools ➢ Palettes ➢ Dashboard so you have the 3D modeling tools at the ready.

Now start building the solid model:

1. Click the Box tool in the 3D Make control panel, enter **BOX**↵, or choose Draw ➢ Modeling ➢ Box.

2. At the Specify first corner or [Center]: prompt, pick a point at coordinate 3,2.5.

3. At the Specify other corner or [Cube/Length]: prompt, enter **@7,4**↵ to create a box with a length of 7 and a width of 4.

4. The Specify height or [2Point]: prompt that appears next is asking for the height of the box in the Z axis. Enter **1**↵.

   Now, let's change the view so you can see the box more clearly. Use the Ddvpoint command to shift your view so you are looking at the WCS from the lower left.

5. Open the Viewpoint Presets dialog box (choose View ➢ 3D Views ➢ Viewpoint Presets), and then enter **225** in the From X Axis input box and **19.5** in From XY Plane.

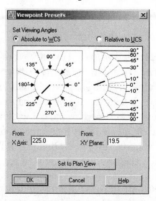

6. Click OK and then adjust your view so it looks similar to Figure 23.5.

You use the Viewpoint Presets dialog box here because it is the easiest way to duplicate the views used for this book.

FIGURE 23.4
The first stage of
the bracket

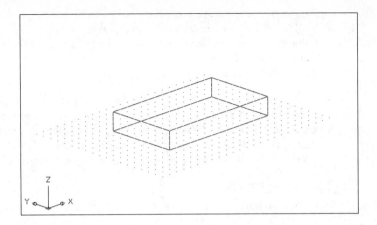

FIGURE 23.5
The converted
polyline box

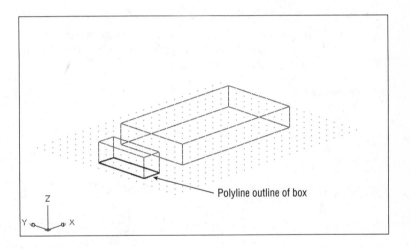

Polyline outline of box

Turning a 2D Polyline into a 3D Solid

Now let's add another box to form the lower lip of the bracket. This time, you'll create a box primitive from a polyline:

1. Click the Polyline tool on the Draw toolbar.

2. At the `Specify start point:` prompt, start the polyline from the coordinate 0.5,2.5.

3. Continue the polyline to create a rectangle that is 1 unit in the X axis and 3 units in the Y axis. You should see a rectangular outline of the smaller box to the left, as in Figure 23.5.

4. Click the Extrude tool on the 3D Make control panel or type **EXT**↵.

5. At the `Select objects to extrude:` prompt, pick the polyline and press ↵.

6. At the `Specify height of extrusion or [Direction/Path/taper angle]:` prompt, type **1**↵.

7. The polyline now extrudes in the Z axis to form a bar, as shown in Figure 23.5.

You've now drawn two box primitives by using the Box and Extrude options in the 3D Make control panel. Just for variety's sake, in this exercise you created the smaller box by converting a polyline into a solid, but you could just as easily have used the Box option for that as well. The Extrude option converts polylines, circles, and traces into solids. (Regular lines, 3D lines, 3D Faces, and 3D polylines cannot be extruded.)

TIP If you prefer to work in the 3D Modeling workspace, but need to have ready access to the 2D draw and modify tools, you can open a 2D Draw control panel in the Dashboard. The 2D Draw control panel contains the same tools that you find in the Draw and Modify toolbars. To open it, right click the Dashboard title bar, then select Control Panels ➤ 2D Draw control panel from the shortcut menu. The 2D Draw control panel appears at the top of the dashboard.

Joining Primitives

Now let's see how the two box objects you created are joined. First, you'll move the new box into place, and then you'll join the two boxes to form a single solid:

1. Start the Move command, pick the smaller of the two boxes, and then press ↵.

2. At the `Specify base point or [Displacement] <Displacement>:` prompt, use the Midpoint Osnap override, and pick the middle of the front edge of the smaller box, as shown in the top image in Figure 23.6.

FIGURE 23.6
Moving the smaller box

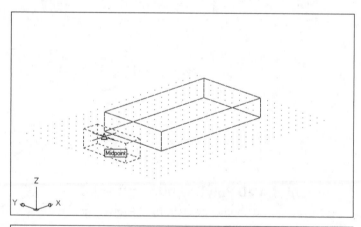

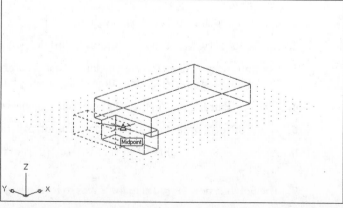

3. At the `Specify second point or <use first point as displacement>:` prompt, use the Midpoint Osnap to pick the middle of the bottom edge of the larger box, as shown in the bottom image in Figure 23.6.

4. Click the Union tool in the 3D Make control panel, choose Modify ➢ Solid Editing ➢ Union, or type **Uni**↵.

5. At the `Select objects:` prompt, pick both boxes and press ↵. Your drawing now looks like Figure 23.7.

FIGURE 23.7

The two boxes joined

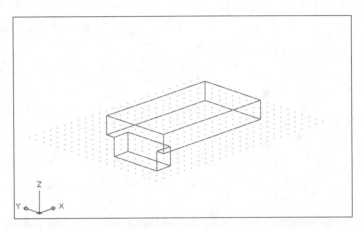

As you can see in Figure 23.7, the form has joined to appear as one object. It also acts like one object when you select it. You now have a composite solid made up of two box primitives.

Now let's place some holes in the bracket. In this next exercise, you will discover how to create negative forms to cut portions out of a solid:

1. Click the Cylinder tool in the 3D Make control panel, type **Cylinder**↵, or choose Draw ➢ Modeling ➢ Cylinder.

2. At the `Specify center point of base or [3P/2P/Ttr/Elliptical]:` prompt, pick a point at the coordinate 9,5.5.

3. At the `Specify base radius or [Diameter]:` prompt, enter **0.25**↵.

TIP As with the Circle command, you can enter **D** to specify a diameter or enter a radius value directly.

4. At the `Specify height or [2Point/Axis endpoint]:` prompt, enter **1.5**↵. The cylinder is drawn.

5. Copy the cylinder 2 units in the negative direction of the Y axis so your drawing looks like Figure 23.8.

You now have two instances of the cylinder primitive, but you still need to define their relationship to the composite solid you created from the two boxes:

1. Choose Modify ➢ Solid Editing ➢ Subtract, type **Su**↵, or click the Subtract tool in 3D Make control panel.

FIGURE 23.8
The cylinders added to
the drawing

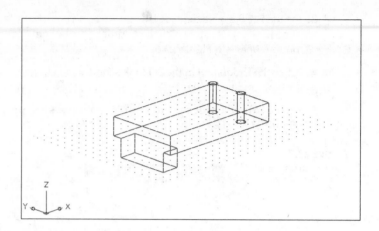

2. At the Select solids and regions to subtract from.. Select objects: prompt, pick the composite solid of the two boxes and press ↵.

3. At the Select solids and regions to subtract.. Select objects: prompt, pick the two cylinders and press ↵. The cylinders have now been subtracted from the bracket.

4. To view the solid, choose View ➤ Hide. You'll see a hidden-line view of the solid, as shown in Figure 23.9.

As you learned in the earlier chapters in Part 4, Wireframe views, such as the one in step 3, are somewhat difficult to decipher. Until you use the Hide command (step 4), you cannot be sure that the subtracted cylinders are in fact holes. Using the Hide command frequently will help you keep track of what's going on with your solid model.

You might also have noticed in step 3 that the cylinders changed shape to conform to the depth of the bracket. You drew the cylinders at a height of 1.5 units, not 1 unit, which is the thickness of the bracket. Having drawn the cylinders taller than needed, you can see that when AutoCAD performed the subtraction, it ignored the portion of the cylinders that doesn't affect the bracket. AutoCAD always discards the portion of a primitive that isn't used in a subtract operation.

FIGURE 23.9
The bracket so far,
with hidden lines
removed

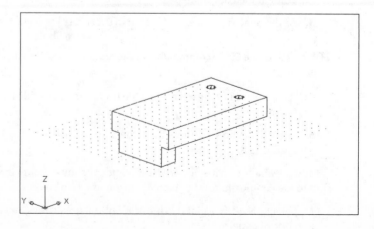

Creating Complex Solids

As you learned earlier, you can convert a polyline into a solid by using the Extrude option in the 3D Make control panel. This process lets you create more-complex shapes than the built-in primitives. In addition to the simple straight extrusion you've already tried, you can also extrude shapes into curved paths, or you can taper an extrusion.

Tapering an Extrusion

Let's look at how you can taper an extrusion to create a fairly complex solid with little effort:

1. Draw a 3 × 3 closed polyline at the top of the current solid. Start near the back-left corner of the bracket at coordinate 3.5,3,1, and then draw the 3 × 3 closed polyline to fit in the top of the composite solid, as shown in Figure 23.10.

WARNING Remember to use the Close option to create the last side of the box.

2. Click the Fillet tool on the Modify toolbar. At the `Select first object or [Undo/Polyline/Radius/Trim/Multiple]:` prompt, type **R**↵ to set the radius of the fillet.

3. At the prompt for the fillet radius, type **0.5**↵.

4. Type **P**↵ to tell the Fillet command that you want to fillet a polyline.

5. Click the polyline. The corners become rounded.

6. Click the Extrude button in the 3D Make control panel or enter **Ext**↵ at the Command prompt.

7. At the `Select objects to extrude:` prompt, pick the polyline you just drew and press ↵.

8. At the `Specify height of extrusion or [Direction/Path/Taper angle] <3.0000>:` prompt, enter **t**↵.

9. At the `Specify angle of taper for extrusion <0>:` prompt, enter **4**↵.

10. At the `Specify height of extrusion or [Direction/Path/Taper angle] <1.0000>:` prompt, enter **3**↵. The extruded polyline looks like Figure 23.11.

FIGURE 23.10
Drawing the 3 × 3 polyline box

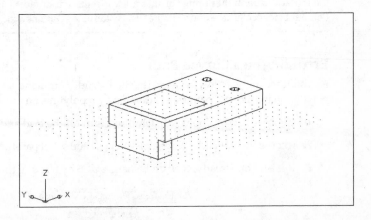

FIGURE 23.11

The extruded polyline

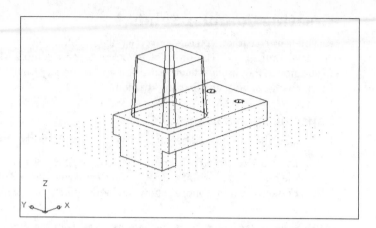

11. Now join the part you just created with the original solid. Choose Modify ➢ Solid Editing ➢ Union, and then select the extruded part and the composite solid just below it. Press ↵ to complete your selection.

TIP In step 9, you can indicate a taper for the extrusion. Specify a taper in terms of degrees from the Z axis, or enter a negative value to taper the extrusion outward. Or press ↵ to accept the default of 0°, to extrude the polyline without a taper.

WHAT ARE ISOLINES?

You might have noticed the message that reads as follows:

```
Current wire frame density: ISOLINES=4
```

This message tells you the current setting for the Isolines system variable, which controls the way curved objects, such as cylinders and holes, are displayed. A setting of 4 causes a cylinder to be represented by four lines with a circle at each end. You can see this in the holes that you've created for the Bracket model in the previous exercise. You can change the Isolines setting by entering **Isolines**↵ at the Command prompt. You then enter a value for the number of lines to use to represent surfaces. This setting is also controlled by the Contour Lines Per Surface option in the Display tab of the Options dialog box.

Extruding on a Curved Path

As you'll see in the following exercise, the Extrude command lets you extrude virtually any polyline shape along a path that is defined by a polyline, an arc, or a 3D polyline:

1. Choose View ➢ Zoom ➢ Extents and turn off the grid and snap modes.

2. Choose View ➢ Hide. This helps you view and select parts of your model in the following steps.

3. If it isn't on already, turn on Dynamic UCS by clicking the DUCS button in the status bar.

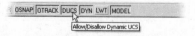

4. Click the Polyline tool in the Draw toolbar, and then place the cursor on the side of the solid as shown in the top left of Figure 23.12. When the cursor is in the correct orientation, use the Midpoint Osnap and select the midpoint of the vertical corner edge shown in Figure 23.12.

5. After you locate the first point, use the direct distance method to draw the polyline shown in the top right of Figure 23.12. Remember that with the direct distance method, you point in the direction you want to go and type the distance and then press ↵.

6. Click the Fillet tool on the Modify toolbar, and then type **R**↵ to set the fillet radius.

7. Enter **0.4**↵ for the fillet radius.

8. Type **P**↵ to select the Polyline option.

9. Click the polyline you drew on the back side of the solid. The second image in Figure 23.12 shows the resulting filleted polyline.

10. Draw a circle with a 0.35-unit radius at the location shown in the bottom image in Figure 23.12.

TIP Figure 23.12 shows a hidden-line view to help you see the polyline and circle more clearly. It shows a lot of extra facets on the curved portion of the model. You can set up AutoCAD so these extra facets don't appear. Open the Options dialog box and click the Show Silhouettes In Wireframe check box on the Display tab.

FIGURE 23.12
Hidden-line view
showing how to set up
your drawing to create
a curved extrusion

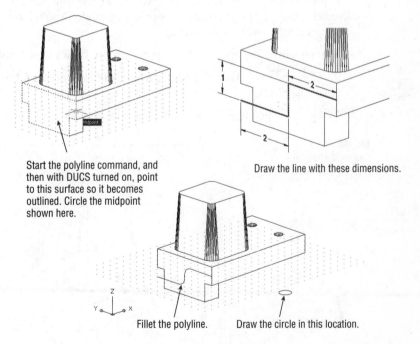

Start the polyline command, and
then with DUCS turned on, point
to this surface so it becomes
outlined. Circle the midpoint
shown here.

Draw the line with these dimensions.

Fillet the polyline.   Draw the circle in this location.

At this point, you've created the components needed to do the extrusion. Next, you'll finish the extruded shape:

1. Click the Sweep button in the 3D Make control panel, click the circle, and then press ↵.

2. At the `Select sweep path or [Alignment/Base point/Scale/Twist]:` prompt, click the polyline curve. AutoCAD pauses a moment and then generates a solid "tube" that follows the path. The tube might not look like a tube because AutoCAD draws extruded solids such as this with four lines showing its profile.

3. Click the Subtract tool in the 3D Make control panel or choose Modify ➢ Solid Editing ➢ Subtract, and then select the composite solid.

4. Press ↵. At the `Select objects:` prompt, click the curved solid and press ↵. The curved solid is subtracted from the square solid. Your drawing will look like Figure 23.13.

In this exercise, you used a curved polyline for the extrusion path, but you can use any type of 2D or 3D polyline, as well as lines and arcs, for an extrusion path.

Revolving a Polyline

When your goal is to draw a circular object, you can use the Revolve command on the 3D Make control panel to create a solid that is revolved, or swept in a circular path. Think of Revolve's action as similar to a lathe that lets you carve a shape from a spinning shaft. In this case, the spinning shaft is a polyline, and rather than carving it, you define the profile and then revolve the profile around an axis.

In the following exercise, you will draw a solid that will form a slot in the tapered solid. I've already created a 2D polyline that is the profile of the slot. You'll use a simple cut and paste to bring the polyline into the bracket drawing:

1. Zoom in to the top of the tapered box, so you have a view similar to Figure 23.14.

2. Open the `rev-shape.dwg` file from the Chapter 23 project folder that you installed from the companion CD.

3. Select the polyline shape, and then choose Edit ➢ Copy With Base Point.

FIGURE 23.13
The solid after subtracting the curve

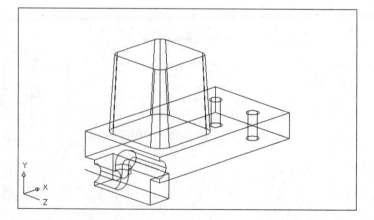

FIGURE 23.14

An enlarged view of the top of the tapered box and pasted polyline

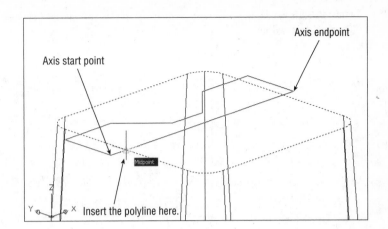

4. At the `Specify base point:` prompt, select the origin of the drawing, which coincides with the grip near the bottom of the shape.

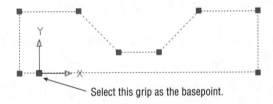

5. Close the `rev-shape.dwg` file without saving it.

6. Back in the Bracket drawing, choose Edit ➤ Paste.

7. Use the Midpoint Osnap to place the polyline at the location shown in Figure 23.14.

8. Click the Revolve tool in the 3D Make control panel or type **Rev**↵ at the Command prompt.

9. At the `Select objects to revolve:` prompt, pick the polyline you just drew and press ↵.

10. When you see the next prompt

    `Specify axis start point or define axis by [Object/X/Y/Z] <Object>:`

    use the Endpoint Osnap override and pick the beginning corner endpoint of the polyline you just added, as shown in Figure 23.14.

11. At the `Specify axis endpoint:` prompt, turn on the Ortho mode (press F8). Then pick a point to the far left of the screen so that the rubber-banding line is parallel with the X axis.

12. At the `Specify angle of revolution or [STart angle] <360>:` prompt, press ↵ to sweep the polyline a full 360°. The revolved form appears, as shown in Figure 23.15.

FIGURE 23.15

The revolved polyline

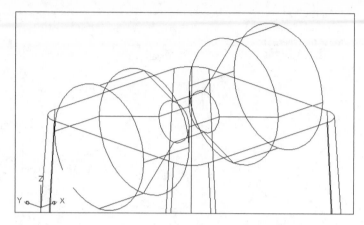

You just created a revolved solid that will be subtracted from the tapered box to form a slot in the bracket. But before you subtract it, you need to make a slight change in the orientation of the revolved solid:

1. Choose Modify ➢ 3D Operations ➢ 3D Rotate. You see the prompt

```
Current positive angle in UCS:  ANGDIR=counterclockwise  ANGBASE=0
Select objects:
```

2. Select the revolved solid and press ↵.

3. At the Specify base point: prompt, use the Midpoint Osnap and click the right side edge of the top surface as shown in Figure 23.16.

FIGURE 23.16

Selecting the points to rotate the revolved solid in 3D space

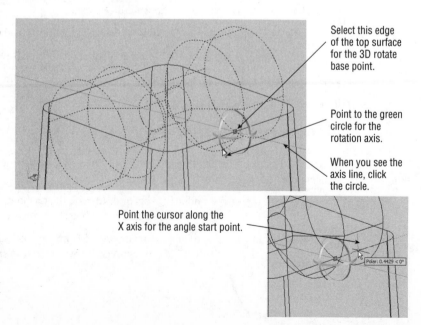

Select this edge of the top surface for the 3D rotate base point.

Point to the green circle for the rotation axis.

When you see the axis line, click the circle.

Point the cursor along the X axis for the angle start point.

4. At the `Pick a rotation axis:` prompt, point to the green rotation grip tool, and when you see a green line appear along the Y axis, click the mouse.

5. At the `Specify angle start point:` prompt, point the cursor in the direction of the X axis and click the mouse.

6. At the `Specify angle end point:` prompt, enter –5↵ for a minus 5 degrees rotation. The solid rotates 5° about the Y axis.

7. Click the Subtract tool in the 3D Make control panel or choose Modify ➢ Solid Editing ➢ Subtract, click the tapered box, and then press ↵.

8. At the `Select objects:` prompt, click the revolved solid and press ↵. Your drawing looks like Figure 23.17.

FIGURE 23.17
The composite solid

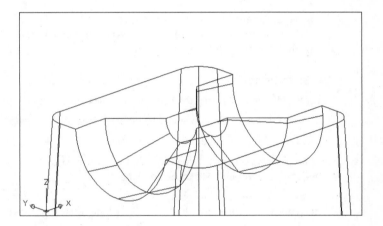

Editing Solids

Basic solid forms are fairly easy to create. Refining those forms requires some special tools. In this section, you'll learn how to use some familiar 2D editing tools, as well as some new tools, to edit a solid. You'll also be introduced to the Slice tool, which lets you cut a solid into two pieces.

Splitting a Solid into Two Pieces

One of the more common solid-editing tools you'll use is the Slice tool. As you might guess from its name, Slice enables you to cut a solid into two pieces. The following exercise demonstrates how it works:

1. Zoom to the previous view.

2. Click the Slice tool in the 3D Make control panel or type **Slice**↵. You may have to expand the 3D Make control panel to find the Slice tool.

3. At the `Select objects to slice:` prompt, click the part you've been working on and press ↵.

TIP In step 3, you could select more than one solid. The Slice command would then slice all the solids through the plane indicated in steps 4 and 5.

4. At the prompt

   ```
   Specify start point of slicing plane or [planar Object/Surface/Zaxis/View/XY/
   YZ/ZX/3points] <3points>:
   ```

   type **XY**↵. This lets you indicate a slice plane parallel to the XY plane.

5. At the `Specify a point on the XY-plane <0,0,0>:` prompt, type **0,0,0.5**↵. This places the slice plane at the Z coordinate of 0.5 units. You can also use the Midpoint Osnap and pick any vertical edge of the rectangular base of the solid.

TIP If you want to delete one side of the sliced solid, you can indicate the side you want to keep by clicking it in step 6, instead of entering **B**↵.

6. At the `Specify a point on desired side or [keep Both sides]:` prompt, type **B**↵ to keep both sides of the solid. AutoCAD will divide the solid horizontally, one-half unit above the base of the part, as shown in Figure 23.18.

THE SLICE OPTIONS

Several options in step 4 of the previous exercise are worth discussing briefly here:

Planar Object   Lets you select an object to define the slice plane.

Surface   Lets you select a surface object to define the shape of a slice (see Chapter 21).

Zaxis   Lets you select two points defining the Z axis of the slice plane. The two points you pick will be perpendicular to the slice plane.

View   Generates a slice plane that is perpendicular to your current view. You are prompted for the coordinate through which the slice plane must pass—usually a point on the object.

XY/YZ/ZX   Pick one of these to determine the slice plane based on the X, Y, or Z axis. You are prompted to pick a point through which the slice plane must pass.

3points   The default; lets you select three points defining the slice plane. Normally, you would pick points on the solid.

FIGURE 23.18
The solid sliced
through the base

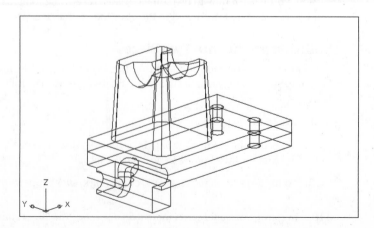

Rounding Corners with the Fillet Tool

Your bracket has a few sharp corners that you might want to round in order to give the bracket a more realistic appearance. You can use the Modify menu's Fillet and Chamfer commands to add these rounded corners to your solid model:

1. Adjust your view of the model so it looks similar to the first image in Figure 23.19.

2. Click the Fillet tool on the Modify toolbar.

3. At the `Select first object or [Polyline/Radius/Trim/Multiple]:` prompt, pick the edge indicated in the first image in Figure 23.19.

4. At the `Enter fillet radius:` prompt, type **0.2**↵.

5. At the `Select an edge or [Chain/Radius]:` prompt, type **C**↵ for the Chain option. Chain lets you select a series of solid edges to be filleted.

6. Select one of the other seven edges at the base of the tapered form and press ↵.

7. Choose View ➢ Hide or type **Hide**↵ to get a better look at your model, as shown in the second image in Figure 23.19.

FIGURE 23.19

Filleting solids

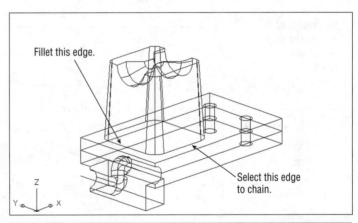

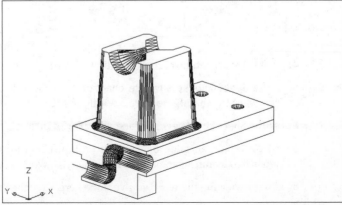

As you saw in step 5, Fillet acts a bit differently when you use it on solids. The Chain option lets you select a set of edges, instead of just two adjoining objects.

Chamfering Corners with the Chamfer Tool

Now let's try chamfering a corner. To practice using Chamfer, you'll add a countersink to the cylindrical hole you created in the first solid:

1. Type **Regen.**↵ to return to a Wireframe view of your model.

2. Click the Chamfer tool on the Modify toolbar or type **Cha.**↵.

3. At this prompt

   ```
   Select first line or [Undo/Polyline/Distance/Angle/Trim/mEthod/Multiple]:
   ```

   pick the edge of the hole, as shown in Figure 23.20. Notice that the top surface of the solid is highlighted and that the prompt changes to `Enter surface selection option [Next/OK (current)] <OK>:`. The highlighting indicates the base surface, which will be used as a reference in step 5. (You could also type **N**↵ to choose the other adjoining surface, the inside of the hole, as the base surface.)

FIGURE 23.20
Picking the edge
to chamfer

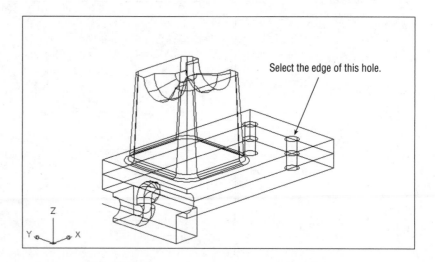

Select the edge of this hole.

4. Press ↵ to accept the current highlighted face.

5. At the `Specify base surface chamfer distance:` prompt, type **0.125.**↵. This indicates that you want the chamfer to have a width of 0.125 across the highlighted surface.

6. At the `Specify other surface chamfer distance <0.1250>:` prompt, type **0.2.**↵.

7. At the `Select an edge or [Loop]:` prompt, click the edges of both holes and then press ↵. When the Chamfer command has completed its work , your drawing will look like Figure 23.21.

8. After reviewing the work you've done here, save the `Bracket.dwg` file.

FIGURE 23.21

The chamfered edges

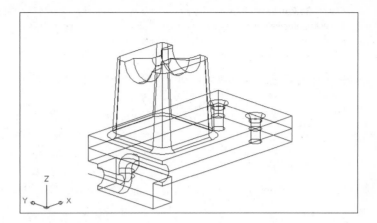

TIP The Loop option in step 7 lets you chamfer the entire circumference of an object. You don't need to use it here because the edge forms a circle. The Loop option is used when you have a rectangular or other polygonal edge you want to chamfer.

Using the Solid Editing Tools

You've added some refinements to the Bracket model by using some standard AutoCAD editing tools. A set of tools is specifically geared toward editing solids. You already used the Union and Subtract tools found in the 3D Make control panel. In this section, you'll explore some of the other tools in that control panel as well as the tools available in the Solid Editing toolbar.

You don't have to perform the exercises described in this section, but reviewing it will show you what's available. When you are more comfortable working in 3D, you may want to come back and experiment with the file called `solidedit.dwg` shown in the figures of this section.

WARNING Many of the features discussed in this section will only work in a parallel projection view. You can switch to a parallel projection view by choosing the 2D Wireframe visual style or by clicking the Parallel Projection tool in the 3D Navigate control panel.

MOVING A SURFACE

You can move any flat surface of a 3D solid using the Move Faces tool in the Solid Editing toolbar. When you click this tool, you are prompted to select faces. Since you can really only select the edge of two joining faces, you must select an edge and then use the Remove option to remove one of the two selected faces from the selection set (see Figure 23.22). Once you've made your selection, press ↵. You can then specify a distance for the move.

After you've selected the surface you want to move, the Move Faces tool acts just like the Move command; you select a base point and a displacement. Notice how the curved side of the model extends its curve to meet the new location of the surface. This shows you that AutoCAD attempts to maintain the geometry of the model when you make changes to the faces.

Move Faces also lets you move entire features, such as the hole in the model. If you look at Figure 23.23, you'll notice that one of the holes has been moved so that it is no longer in line with the other three. This was done by selecting the countersink and the hole while using the Move Faces tool.

FIGURE 23.22

To select the vertical
surface to the far
right of the model,
click the edge, and
then use the Remove
option to remove the
top surface from
the selection.

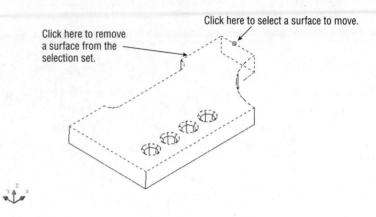

Click here to select a surface to move.

Click here to remove
a surface from the
selection set.

OFFSETTING A SURFACE

Now suppose you want to decrease the radius of the arc in the right corner of the model, and you also want to thicken the model by the same amount as the decrease in the arc radius. To do this, you can use the Offset Faces tool. The Offset Faces tool performs a similar function to the Offset command you used earlier in this book. The difference is that the Offset Faces tool in the Solid Editing toolbar affects 3D solids.

When you click the Offset Faces tool on the Solid Editing toolbar, you are prompted to select faces. As with the Move tool, you must select an edge that will select two faces. If you only want to offset one face, you must use the Remove option to remove one of the faces. In Figure 23.23 an edge is selected. Figure 23.24 shows the effect of the Offset Faces tool when both faces are offset.

FIGURE 23.23

Selecting a surface
to offset

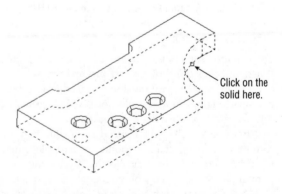

Click on the
solid here.

FIGURE 23.24

The model after off-setting the curved and bottom surfaces

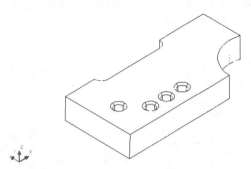

DELETING A SURFACE

Now suppose you've decided to eliminate the curved part of the model altogether. You can delete a surface by using the Delete Faces tool. Once again, you are prompted to select faces. Typically, you really only want to delete one face as in the curved surface in the example model; so you use the Remove option to remove the adjoining face that you do not want to delete before finishing your selection of faces to remove.

When you attempt to delete surfaces, keep in mind that the surface you delete must be recoverable by other surfaces in the model. For example, you cannot remove the top surface of a cube expecting it to turn into a pyramid. That would require the sides to change their orientation, which is not allowed in this operation. You can, on the other hand, remove the top of a box with tapered sides. Then, when you remove the top, the sides converge to form a pyramid.

ROTATING A SURFACE

All the surfaces of the model are parallel or perpendicular to each other. Imagine that your design requires two sides to be at an angle. You can change the angle of a surface by using the Rotate Faces tool:

As with the prior Solid Editing tools, you are prompted to select faces. You must then specify an axis of rotation. You can either select a point or use the default of selecting two points to define an axis of rotation, as shown in Figure 23.25. Once the axis is determined, you can specify a rotation angle. Figure 23.26 shows the result of rotating the two front-facing surfaces 4°.

TAPERING A SURFACE

In an earlier exercise, you saw how to create a new tapered solid by using the Extrude command. But what if you want to taper an existing solid? Here's what you can do to taper an existing 3D solid.

The Taper Faces tool in the Solid Editing toolbar prompts you to select faces. You can select faces as described for the previously discussed Solid Editing tools using the Remove or Add options to select different faces (see Figure 23.27). Press ↵ when you finish your selection, and then indicate the axis from which the taper is to occur. In the model example in Figure 23.27, select two corners defining a vertical axis. Finally, enter the taper angle. Figure 23.28 shows the model tapered at a 4° angle.

FIGURE 23.25
Defining the axis of rotation

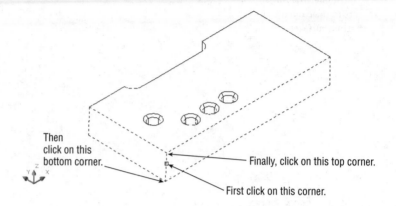

Then click on this bottom corner.

Finally, click on this top corner.

First click on this corner.

FIGURE 23.26
The model after rotating two surfaces

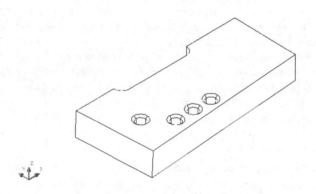

FIGURE 23.27
Selecting the surfaces to taper and indicating the direction of the taper

Select these corners first.

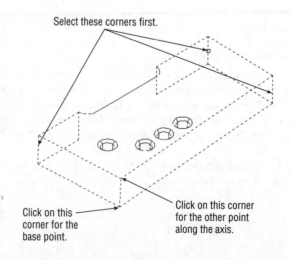

Click on this corner for the base point.

Click on this corner for the other point along the axis.

FIGURE 23.28
The model after taper-
ing the sides

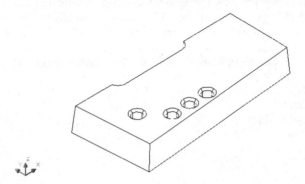

EXTRUDING A SURFACE

You've used the Extrude command to create two of the solids in the Bracket model. The Extrude command requires a closed polyline as a basis for the extrusion. As an alternative, the Solid Editing toolbar offers the Extrude Faces tool, which will extrude a surface of an existing solid.

When you click the Extrude Faces tool on the Solid Editing toolbar, you see the `Select faces or [Undo/Remove]:` prompt. Select an edge or a set of edges, or use the Remove or Add option to select the faces you want to extrude. Press ↵ when you've finished your selection, and then specify a height and taper angle. Figure 23.29 shows the sample model with the front surface extruded and tapered at a 45° angle. You can extrude multiple surfaces at one time if you need to by selecting multiple surfaces.

Aside from those features, the Extrude Faces tool works just like the Extrude command.

TURNING A SOLID INTO A SHELL

In many situations, you'll want your 3D model to be a hollow, rather than solid, mass. The Shell tool lets you convert a solid into a shell.

FIGURE 23.29
The model with a
surface extruded
and tapered

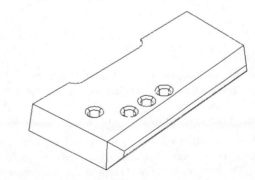

When you click the Shell tool on the Solid Editing toolbar, you are prompted to select a 3D solid. You are then prompted to remove faces. At this point, you can select an edge of the solid to indicate the surface you want removed. The surface you select will be completely removed from the model, exposing the interior of the shell. For example, if you select the front edge of the sample model shown in Figure23.30, the top and front surfaces will be removed from the model, revealing the interior of the solid as shown in Figure 23.31. After selecting the surfaces to remove, you can enter a shell thickness.

FIGURE 23.30
Selecting the edge to
be removed

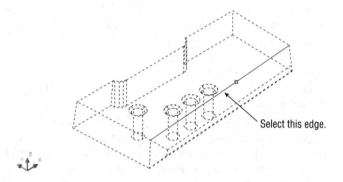

Select this edge.

FIGURE 23.31
The solid model after
using the Shell tool

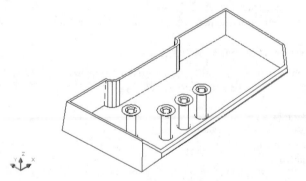

The shell thickness is added to the outside surface of the solid, so when you're constructing your solid with the intention of creating a shell, you need to take this into account.

COPYING FACES AND EDGES

At times, you might want to create a copy of a surface of a solid to analyze its area or to produce another part that mates to that surface. The Copy Faces tool creates a copy of any surface on your model. The copy it produces is a type of object called a *region*. You'll learn more about regions later in this chapter. Right now, let's see how the Copy Faces tool works:

The copies of the surfaces are opaque and can hide objects behind them when you perform a hidden-line removal (choose View ➢ Hide).

Another tool that is similar to Copy Faces is Copy Edges. It works in a similar way, but instead of selecting surfaces as in the Copy Faces tool, you select all the edges you want to copy. The result is a series of simple lines representing the edges of your model. This tool can be useful if you want to convert a solid into a set of 3D Faces. The Copy Edges tool will create a framework onto which you can add 3D Faces.

ADDING SURFACE FEATURES

If you need to add a feature to a flat surface, you can do so with the Imprint tool. An added surface feature can then be colored or extruded. This feature is a little more complicated than some of the other Solid Editing tools, so you might want to try the following exercise to see firsthand how it works.

You'll start by inserting an object that will be the source of the imprint. You will then imprint the main solid model with the object's profile.

1. Choose Insert ➢ Block to open the Insert dialog box.

2. Click Browse; then locate the imprint.dwg file in the \Projects\Chapter23\ folder on the companion CD and select it.

3. In the Insert dialog box, make sure that the Explode check box is selected, and remove the checkmark from the Specify On-Screen check box in the Insertion Point group.

4. Click OK. The block appears in the middle of the solid.

5. Click the Imprint tool.

6. Click the main solid model.

7. Click the inserted solid.

8. At the Delete the source object [Yes/No]<N>: prompt, enter **Y**↵.

You now have an outline of the intersection between the two solids imprinted on the top surface of your model. To help the imprint stand out, try the following steps to change its color:

1. Click the Color Faces tool on the Solid Editing toolbar.

2. Click the imprint from the previous exercise. The imprint and the entire top surface are highlighted.

3. At the Select faces or [Undo/Remove/ALL]: prompt, type **R**↵; then click the outer edge of the top surface to remove it from the selection set.

4. Press ↵ to open the Select Color dialog box.

5. Click the red color sample in the dialog box; then click OK. The imprint is now red.

6. Press ↵ twice to exit the command.

7. To see the full effect of the Color Faces tool, choose the Conceptual or Realistic visual style in the Visual Style control panel. You can also find the visual styles in the View ➢ Visual Styles menu.

If you want to remove an imprint from a surface, use the Clean tool on the Solid Editing toolbar. Click the Clean tool and then click the imprint you want to remove.

USING THE COMMAND LINE FOR SOLID EDITING

The Solid Editing tools are actually options of a single AutoCAD command called Solidedit. If you prefer to use the keyboard, here are some tips on using the Solidedit command. When you first enter **Solid-edit**⏎ at the Command prompt, you see the following prompt:

```
Enter a solids editing option [Face/Edge/Body/Undo/eXit] <eXit>:
```

You can select the Face, Edge, or Body option to edit the various parts of a solid. If you select Face, you see the following prompt:

```
[Extrude/Move/Rotate/Offset/Taper/Delete/Copy/coLor/Undo/eXit] <eXit>:
```

The options from this prompt produce the same results as their counterparts in the Solid Editing toolbar.

If you select Edge at the first prompt, you see the following prompt:

```
Enter an edge editing option [Copy/coLor/Undo/eXit] <eXit>:
```

The Copy option lets you copy a surface, and the Color option lets you add color to a surface.

If you select Body from the first prompt, you'll see the following prompt:

```
[Imprint/seParate solids/Shell/cLean/Check/Undo/eXit] <eXit>:
```

These options also perform the same functions as their counterparts on the Solid Editing toolbar. As you work with this command, you can use the Undo option to undo the last Solidedit option you used without exiting the command.

SEPARATING A DIVIDED SOLID

While editing solids, you can end up with two separate solid forms that were created from one solid, as shown in Figure 23.32. Even though the two solids appear separated, they act like a single object. In these situations, AutoCAD offers the Separate tool in the Solid Editing toolbar. To use it, just click the Separate tool and select the solid that has been separated into two forms.

FIGURE 23.32

When the tall, thin solid is subtracted from the larger solid, the result is two separate forms, yet they still behave as a single object.

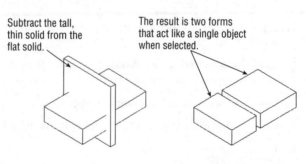

Subtract the tall, thin solid from the flat solid.

The result is two forms that act like a single object when selected.

Separate will separate the two forms into two distinct solids.

Through some simple examples, you've seen how each of the Solid Editing tools works. You aren't limited to using these tools in the way shown in this section, and this book cannot anticipate every situation you might encounter as you create your solid models. These examples are intended as an introduction to these tools, so feel free to experiment with them. You can always use the Undo option to backtrack in case you don't get the results you expect.

TIP   Figure 23.32 is included in the sample figures under the name of `Separate example.dwg` on the companion CD. You can try the Separate tool in this file on your own.

This concludes your tour of the Solid Editing toolbar. Next, you'll learn how to use your 3D solid models to quickly generate 2D working drawings.

Enhancing the 2D Drawing Process

Using solids to model a part—such as the Bracket and the Solidedit examples used in this chapter—might seem a bit exotic, but there are definite advantages to modeling in 3D, even if you want to draw the part in only 2D as a page in a set of manufacturing specs.

The exercises in this section show you how to quickly generate a typical mechanical drawing from your 3D model by using Paper Space and the 3D Make control panel. You will also examine techniques for dimensioning and including hidden lines.

TIP   If your application is architecture, and you've created a 3D model of a building by using solids, you can use the tools described in this section to generate 2D elevation drawings from your 3D solid model.

Drawing a Standard Top, Front, and Right-Side View

One of the more common types of mechanical drawings is the *orthogonal projection*. This style of drawing shows separate top, front, and right-side views of an object. Sometimes a 3D image is also added for clarity. You can derive such a drawing within a few minutes, after you create your 3D solid model. The first step is to select a sheet title block. The title block consists of a border and an area in the lower-right corner for notes and other drawing information.

TIP   If you need to refresh your memory about using Paper Space, refer to Chapter 16.

SETTING UP A TITLE BLOCK LAYOUT

Before you begin the work of setting up your orthogonal views, you'll need to do a little setup. The current Model Space view becomes the default view in a new layout, so start by setting up one orthogonal view in Model Space. Then you'll add a new layout that is based on an AutoCAD template file.

1. Go back to the `Bracket.dwg` file, and if you haven't done so already, save the file by choosing File ➢ Save.

2. In the 3D Navigate control panel, choose Front from the drop-down list. Your view will change to an orthogonal front-side view.

3. Right-click the Layout1 tab, and then select From Template from the shortcut menu.

4. Locate and open the ANSI D -Color Dependent Plot Styles.dwt template.

WARNING If for some reason you do not see a listing of template files in the Create New Drawing dialog box, you will need to set up AutoCAD to look for these files in the right place. Normally, AutoCAD looks in the C:\Documents and Settings\User Name\Local Settings\Application Data\Autodesk\AutoCAD 2007\R17.0\enu\Template folder for template files. Check the Template Drawing File Location listing in the Files tab of the Options dialog box. See Appendix B for details.

5. In the Insert Layout(s) dialog box, click OK. You see the ANSI D title block tab appear at the bottom of the AutoCAD Window.

You've just imported a layout from a template file. Next, you'll make some changes to the layout to make it ready for the orthogonal views.

1. Click the ANSI D title block tab. You see the bracket drawing inside a title block.

2. This title block contains a predefined layout viewport that you don't need for this exercise. Click the inside border of the title block to select the viewport; then press the Delete key.

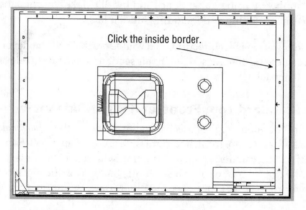

Click the inside border.

3. Choose View ➤ Viewports ➤ 1 Viewport, and then click two diagonal points to add a single rectangular viewport a little larger than the one shown in Figure 23.33.

FIGURE 23.33
Creating the viewport so it is just large enough to contain the view of the bracket

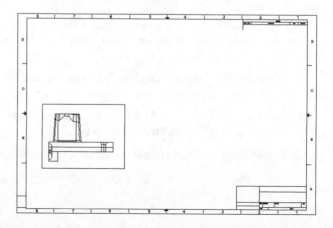

4. Click the viewport border, and then right-click and choose Properties.

5. In the Misc group of the Properties palette, find and select Standard Scale.

6. Click in the Standard Scale drop-down list and select 1:1.

7. Close the Properties palette and press Escape to clear your selection.

You now have a front-side orthogonal view at a scale of 1 to 1. When you create a new view by choosing View ➤ Viewports, the current view in Model Space becomes the default view.

TIP If you're view only shows part of the bracket, you can click on the viewport border then user the viewport's corner grips to adjust its size to include more of the bracket.

CREATING THE ORTHOGONAL VIEWS

Now you are ready to create the other Orthogonal views. The next part will seem simple compared with the steps you had to take to set up the title block and viewport:

1. Choose Draw ➤ Modeling ➤ Setup ➤ View.

2. At the `Enter an option [Ucs/Ortho/Auxiliary/Section]:` prompt, type **O**↵.

3. At the `Specify side of viewport to project:` prompt, place the cursor on the right side of the viewport so that a Midpoint Osnap marker appears, as shown in the first image in Figure 23.34 then click the mouse. A rubber-banding line appears.

4. At the `Specify view center:` prompt, click a point to the right of the viewport, at about half the width of the viewport. The right-side view of the bracket appears, as shown in the second image in Figure 23.34. Click again to adjust the horizontal position of the right-side view.

5. After you're satisfied with the location of the view, press ↵. You don't have to be too precise at this point because you will be able to adjust the view's location later.

6. At the `Specify first corner of viewport:` prompt, click a location below and to the left of the right-side view, as shown in the final image in Figure 23.34.

7. At the `Specify opposite corner of viewport:` prompt, click above and to the right of the view, as shown in the final image in Figure 23.34.

8. At the `Enter view name:` prompt, enter **rightside**↵. Notice that the `Enter an option [Ucs/Ortho/Auxiliary/Section]:` prompt appears again. This enables you to set up another view.

   At this point, you can exit the Setup View tool by pressing ↵, but you need another view. Continue with the following steps to create the top view.

9. Type **O**↵ again, but this time, at the `Specify side of viewport to project:` prompt, click the top edge of the front-view viewport.

10. Follow steps 4 through 7 to create a top view. In step 4, click a point above the viewport instead of to the right.

11. Name this third viewport Top.

12. When you return to the `Enter an option [Ucs/Ortho/Auxiliary/Section]:` prompt, press ↵ to exit the command.

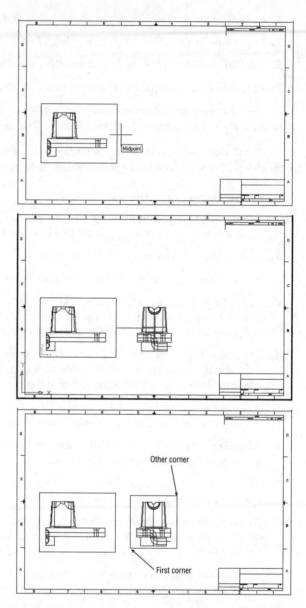

Each new view you create by using the Setup View tool is scaled to match the original view from which it is derived. As you saw in step 3, the view that is generated depends on the side of the viewport you select. If you pick the bottom of the viewport, a bottom view is generated, which looks the same as the top view until you choose View ➤ Hide to display it as a hidden-line view.

Creating an Isometric View

In this section, you will add an Isometric view to your Paper Space layout at a 1-to-1 scale. You can use the Setup View tool to accomplish this, but you'll need to set up a UCS to which the Setup View tool can refer.

The following explains how to set up such a UCS for an Isometric view:

1. Click the Model tab to go to Model Space.

2. Choose View ➢ 3D Views ➢ SE Isometric to display an Isometric view of the model.

3. Choose Tools ➢ New UCS ➢ View to set the UCS to be parallel to the current view plane.

4. Choose Tools ➢ Named UCS to open the UCS dialog box.

5. Rename the current Unnamed UCS to SE Isometric (right-click Unnamed and select Rename, enter the new name, and click OK.).

6. Click the ANSI D title block tab to return to the Layout view of your model.

Notice that even though you changed your view in Model Space, the Paper Space viewports maintain the views as you last left them. Now you're ready to create a viewport showing the same Isometric view you set up in Model Space:

1. Choose Draw ➢ Modeling ➢ Setup ➢ View.

2. At the Enter an option [Ucs/Ortho/Auxiliary/Section]: prompt, type **U**↵.

3. At the Enter an option [Named/World/?/Current] <Current>: prompt, press ↵ to accept the current UCS.

4. At the Enter view scale <1.0000>: prompt, press ↵ to accept the scale of 1.

5. At the Specify view center: prompt, click a point above and to the right of the original viewport. The Isometric view of the model appears, as shown in Figure 23.35. If you don't like the view's location, you can continue to click points until the view's location is just where you want it.

6. Press ↵ when you are satisfied with the view's location.

7. At the Specify first corner of viewport: prompt, place a window around the Isometric view to define the viewport border.

FIGURE 23.35

Adding a viewport for the Isometric view

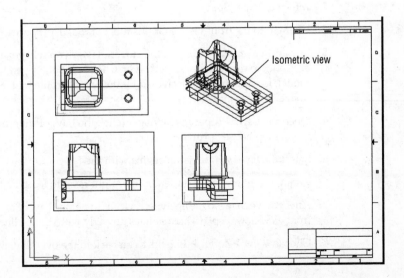

Isometric view

8. Name the view SE Isometric.

9. Press ↵ to exit the View tool.

A lot of steps were involved in creating these views. However, imagine the work involved if you had to create these views manually, and you'll appreciate the power of these few simple tools.

Creating Hidden-Line Views

You aren't quite finished yet. Typically, orthographic projections, such as the top, front, and right-side view, show the hidden portions of the model with dashed lines. For example, the holes toward the right end of the bracket would be shown dashed in the front view. You could set up the view-ports to do a hidden-line removal at plot time, but this would not create the effect you want.

Fortunately, AutoCAD offers the Setup Profile tool to quickly generate a proper Orthographic Projection view of your solid model. Take the following steps to create your first hidden-line view:

1. Go to floating Model Space by double-clicking the lower-left viewport.

2. Choose Draw ➤ Modeling➤ Setup ➤ Profile.

3. Click both halves of the solid model and then press ↵.

4. At the `Display hidden profile lines on separate layer? [Yes/No]<Y>:` prompt, press ↵.

5. At the `Project profile lines onto a plane? <Y>:` prompt, press ↵.

6. At the `Delete tangential edges? <Y>:` prompt, press ↵. AutoCAD will work for a moment, and then the Command prompt will appear with no apparent change to the drawing.

You don't see the effects of the Setup Profile tool yet. You'll need to make the solid model invisible to display the work that was done by the Setup Profile tool. You'll also have to make a few layer changes to get the profile views just right. Here are the steps:

1. Double-click an area outside the viewport or click the Model button on the status bar to return to Paper Space.

2. Zoom in to the front view so it fills most of the display area.

3. Turn off Layer0 (zero). If it is the current layer, you will get a message telling you that you are about to turn off the current layer. Click No. You've just turned off the layer of the solid model, leaving the profile created by the Setup Profile tool. Notice that you see only an image of the front view.

4. Open the Layer Properties Manager (click the Layer Properties Manager tool in the Layers toolbar or choose Format ➤ Layer).

5. Select the layer whose name begins with the *PH* prefix.

6. Change its linetype to Hidden2. You might need to load the hidden-line type.

7. After you've changed the linetype, click OK to exit the Layer Properties Manager dialog box. The front view now displays hidden lines properly with dashed lines, as shown in Figure 23.36.

8. Choose View ➤Zoom ➤ Extents to go back to the overall view of the layout.

FIGURE 23.36
The front view after using the Setup Profile tool

FIGURE 23.36
The front view after using the Setup Profile tool

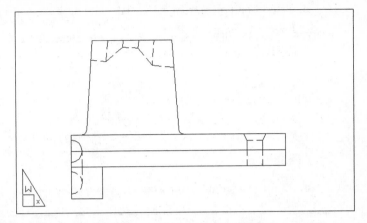

The Setup Profile tool creates a 2D drawing of your 3D model. This 2D drawing is projected onto an imaginary plane that is parallel to the view from which you selected the model while using the Setup Profile tool. To see this clearly, take a look at your model in Model Space:

1. Click the Model tab to go to Model Space.

2. Turn Layer0 back on. You see the projected 2D view next to the 3D model, as shown in Figure 23.37.

Using Visual Styles with a Viewport

In Chapter 20, you saw how you can view your 3D model using visual styles in Model Space. A visual style can give you a more realistic representation of your 3D model, and it can show off more of the details, especially in rounded surfaces. You can also view and plot a visual style in a Layout tab. To do this, you make a viewport active and then turn on the visual style you want to use for that viewport. The following exercise gives you a firsthand look at how this is done:

1. Click the ANSI D title block tab in the lower portion of the AutoCAD window.

2. Double-click inside the viewport with the Isometric view of the model to switch to floating Model Space.

FIGURE 23.37
The projected view next to the 3D solid model

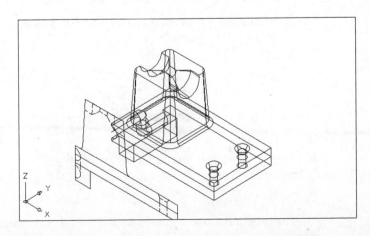

3. Select Conceptual from the Visual Styles drop-down list..

NOTE The view might appear a bit dark because of the black color setting for the object. You can change the color to a lighter one such as cyan or blue to get a better look.

4. Double-click outside the isometric viewport to return to Paper Space.

CREATING A 2D PROJECTION FROM YOUR 3D MODEL

Another tool on the Draw ➤ Modeling ➤ Setup menu creates 2D drawings of 3D solid models. The Drawing tool does nearly the same thing as the Profile tool, with some differences. First, the Setup Drawing tool works only with viewports that are created by the View tool. It automatically turns off the layer on which the solid model resides. So after it has created a 2D view, you can see the results without having to adjust layer settings. Also, unlike the Profile tool, Drawing leaves the 2D drawing objects as individual objects ready to be edited, instead of turning them into blocks.

Finally, the Drawing tool creates layers whose names better describe their purpose. For example, if you use Drawing to create a 2D drawing of the right-side view, you will get layers entitled Rightside-dim, Rightside-hid, and Rightside-vis. These layer names are derived from the View name from which the 2D drawing is derived. Drawing adds the -dim, -hid, and -vis suffixes to the view name to create the layer name. These suffixes are abbreviations for *dimension, hidden,* and *visible.*

You changed the visual style of one viewport without affecting the other viewports. This can really help others visualize your 3D model more clearly.

You'll also want to know how to control the hard-copy output of a shaded view. For this, you use the shortcut menu:

1. Click the Isometric view's viewport border to select it.

2. Right-click to open the shortcut menu, and then point to the Shade Plot option to display a set of Shade Plot options.

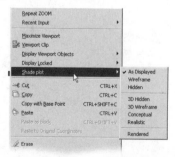

3. Take a moment to study the menu and then click As Displayed.

The As Displayed option plots the viewport as it appears in the AutoCAD window. You use this option to plot the currently displayed visual style. Wireframe plots the viewport as a Wireframe view. Hidden plots the viewport as a Hidden-line view similar to the view you see when you use the Hide command. Below the As Displayed option in the shortcut menu, you see a list of the available visual styles. At the very bottom of the menu, the Rendered option plots the view by using AutoCAD's Render feature described in Chapter 22. You can use the Rendered option to plot ray-traced renderings of your 3D models.

Remember these options on the shortcut menu as you work on your drawings and when you plot. They can be helpful in communicating your ideas, but they can also get lost in the array of tools that AutoCAD offers.

Visualizing Solids

If you're designing a complex object, sometimes it helps to be able to see it in ways that you couldn't in the real world. AutoCAD offers two visualization tools that can really help others understand your design ideas.

If you want to show off the internal workings of a part or an assembly, you can use the X-ray mode, which can be found in the Visual Styles control panel.

Figure 23.38 shows an isometric view of the bracket using the Realistic visual style and the X-ray mode turned on. You can see the internal elements as if the object were semi-transparent. The X-ray mode works with any visual style though it works best with a style that shows some of the surface features such as the Conceptual or Realistic visual styles.

FIGURE 23.38
The bracket displayed using a Realistic visual style and X-ray mode

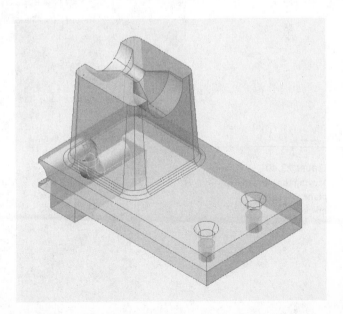

Another tool to help you visualize the internal workings of a design is the sectionplane command. This command creates a plane that defines the location of a cross-section. A sectionplane can also do a bit more than just show a cross-section. Try the following exercise to see how it works.

1. Go to the Bracket.dwg file if it isn't already the current file.

2. Click the Model tab, and then change the color of Layer0 to a light gray so you can see the bracket more clearly when using the Realistic visual style.

3. Select Realistic from the Visual Styles control panel.

4. Enter **sectionplane.⏎** at the Command prompt. You'll see the prompt

   ```
   Select face or any point to locate section line or [Draw section/
   Orthographic]:
   ```

5. Click the front plane of the bracket as shown in Figure 23.39. A plane appears on that surface.

The section plane object can be moved along the solid to give you a real-time view of the section it traverses. To do this, you need to turn on the Live Section feature. To check to see if Live Section is turned on, do the following:

1. Click the section plane, and then right-click. If you see a check mark by the Activate Live Selection option, then you know it is on. If you don't see a check mark, then choose Activate Live Sectioning to turn it on.

FIGURE 23.39
Adding the surface
plane to your bracket

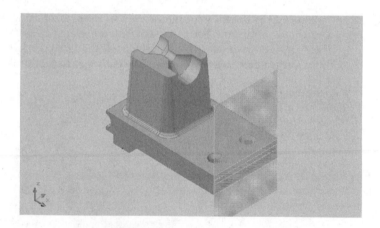

FIGURE 23.40
Moving the surface
plane across the
bracket

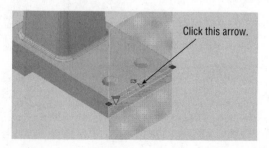

2. Click the triangular grip at the center of the section plane as shown in Figure 23.40.

3. Move the mouse toward the back of the bracket slowly. As you do this, you see the bracket become invisible in the foreground while remaining solid in the background. You also see the section of the bracket at the location of the cursor (see Figure 23.41).

4. When your view looks similar to Figure 23.41, click the mouse.

Now you see only the portion of the bracket behind the section plane plus the cross-section of the plane as shown in Figure 23.41. You can have the section plan display the front portion as a ghosted image by doing the following.

1. With the section plane selected (you should still see its blue grips), right-click and choose Show Cut-Away Geometry. After a moment, the front portion of the bracket appears.

2. Press the Escape key to remove the section plane from the current selection. You can see the entire bracket, including the geometry at the section plane.

You can keep the Show Cut-Away Geometry setting on as you work on your section views or turn it off to help speed things up.

FIGURE 23.41
The surface plane fixed at a location

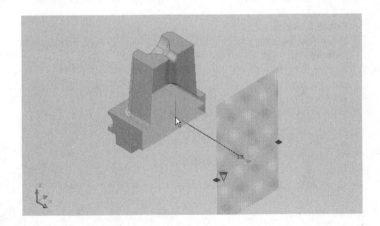

FIGURE 23.42
The entire bracket is displayed with the Show Cut-Away Geometry option turned on

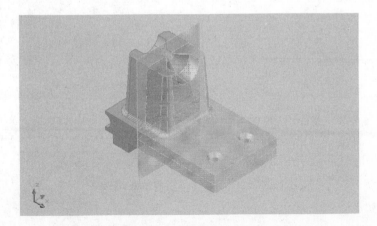

You can also add a jog in the section plane to create a more complex section cut. Here's how it's done.

1. Click the section plane, and then right-click and choose Add Jog To Section.

2. At the `Specify a point on the section line to add jog::` prompt, click the arrow grip at the center of the section plane, the same one you used to move the section plane. After a moment, a jog appears in the section plane.

3. To see the section plane more clearly, press Escape and then click the section plane. (See Figure 23.43.)

4. Click the arrow grip on the back portion of the section plane as shown in Figure 23.43 and drag it toward the right so the jog looks similar to the second panel in Figure 23.43.

5. Press the Escape key to get a clear view of the new section.

As you can see from this example, you can adjust the section using the arrow grips. You can click either the center arrow grip or the endpoint grips to add a jog.

You may have also noticed two other arrows in the section plane. The arrow next to the center arrow grip reverses the side that appears solid, so if you need to get a view from the opposite side, you can reverse the slice with this arrow (see Figure 23.44).

FIGURE 23.43
Moving the jog in the section plane

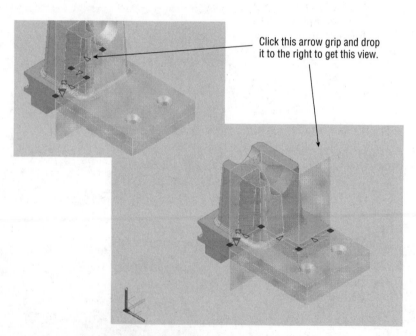

Click this arrow grip and drop it to the right to get this view.

When you click on the other downward-pointing arrow, you see three options for visualizing the section boundary: Section Plane, Section Boundary, and Section Volume.

By using these other settings, you can start to include sections through the sides, back, top, or bottom of the solid. For example, if you click the Section Boundary option, another boundary line appears with grips. To see it clearly, you may have to press Escape and then select the section plane again.

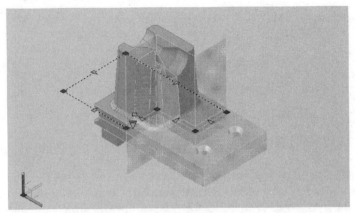

You can then manipulate these grips to show section cuts along those boundaries.

FIGURE 23.44

One arrow reverses the side of the section plane that appears solid. The other arrow presents additional options for the section plane.

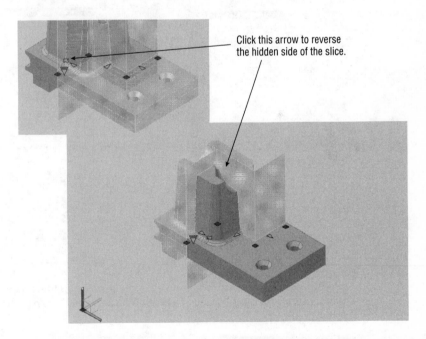

Click this arrow to reverse
the hidden side of the slice.

The Section Volume option displays the boundary of a volume along with grips at the top and bottom of the volume. These grips allow you to create a cut plane from the top or bottom of the solid.

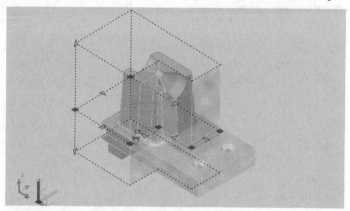

Finally, you can get copy of the solid that is behind or in front of the section plane. Right-click the section plane and choose Generate 2D/3D Section to open the Generate Section/Elevation dialog box. Click the Show Details button to the left to expand the dialog box and display more options.

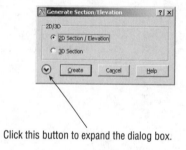

Click this button to expand the dialog box.

If you select 2D Section/Elevation, a 2D image of the section plane is inserted in the drawing in a manner similar to the insertion of a block. You are asked for an insertion point, x and y scale, and rotation angle.

TIP If your application is architectural, you can use a section plane and the 2D Section/Elevation option to get an accurate elevation drawing. Instead of placing the section plane inside the solid, move it away from the solid model and use the 2D Section/Elevation shortcut menu option.

The 3D Section option will create a copy of the portion of the solid that is bounded by the section plane or planes as shown in Figure 23.45.

You can gain access to more detailed settings for the 2D Section/Elevation, 3D Section, and the Live Section Settings by clicking the Section Settings button at the bottom of the Generate Section/ Elevation dialog box. This button opens the Section Settings dialog box, which lists the settings for the section feature.

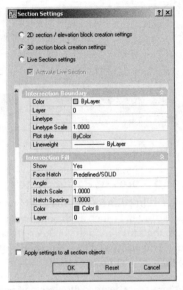

The work you do to find a section is also reflected in the layout views you set up earlier. If you click the ANSI D title block tab to go to the layout, you'll see the section cuts displayed in each of the views.

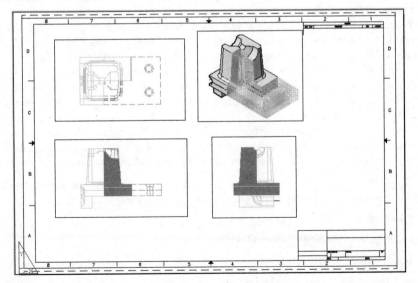

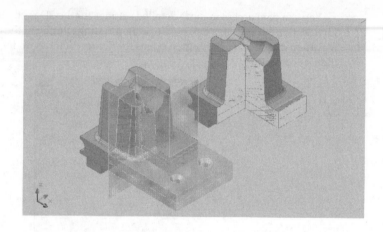

Adding Dimensions and Notes in Paper Space

Although I don't recommend adding dimensions in Paper Space for architectural drawings, it might be a good idea for mechanical drawings such as the one in this chapter. By maintaining the dimensions and notes separate from the actual model, you keep these elements from getting in the way of your work on the solid model. You also avoid the confusion of having to scale the text and dimension features properly to ensure that they will plot at the correct size.

TIP See Chapters 10 and 12 for a more detailed discussion of notes and dimensions.

As long as you set up your Paper Space work area to be equivalent to the final plot size, you can set dimension and text to the sizes you want at plot time. If you want text $\frac{1}{4}$″ high, you set your text styles to be $\frac{1}{4}$″ high.

To include dimensions, just make sure you are in a Layout tab, and then use the dimension commands in the normal way. However, you need to be careful to make sure that full associative dimensioning is turned on. Choose Tools ➤ Options to open the Options dialog box, and then click the User Preferences tab. In the Associative Dimensioning group, click the Make sure the New Dimensions Associative check box is turned on. With associative dimensioning turned on, dimensions in a Layout tab display the true dimension of the object being dimensioned, regardless of the image scale in the viewport.

If you do not have the associative dimensioning option turned on and your viewports are set to a scale other than 1 to 1, you have another option. You can set the Annotation Units option in the Dimension Style dialog box to a proper value. The following steps show you how:

1. Select the Model tab at the bottom of the AutoCAD window, and then choose Dimension ➤ Dimension Style to open the Dimension Style Manager dialog box.

2. Make sure you have selected the style you want to use, and then click Modify to open the Modify Dimension Style dialog box.

3. Click the Primary Units tab.

4. In the Scale Factor input box in the Measurement Scale group, enter the value by which you want your Paper Space dimensions multiplied. For example, if your Paper Space views are

scaled at one-half the actual size of your model, enter **2** in this box to multiply your dimensions' values by two.

TIP To make sure the value you need in step 4 is correct, determine which scale factor you need for your Paper Space drawing to get its actual size; that's the value you need to enter.

5. Click the Apply To Layout Dimensions Only check box. This ensures that your dimension is scaled only while you are adding dimensions in Paper Space. Dimensions added in Model Space are not affected.

6. Click OK to close the Modify Dimension Style dialog box; then click Close in the Dimension Style Manager dialog box.

You've had to complete a lot of steps to get the final drawing, but, compared with having to draw these views by hand, you undoubtedly saved a great deal of time. In addition, as you will see later in this chapter, what you have is more than just a 2D drafted image. With what you created, further refinements are now quite easy.

Using 3D Solid Operations on 2D Drawings

You can apply some of the features described in this chapter to 2D drafting by taking advantage of AutoCAD's region object. *Regions* are two-dimensional objects to which you can apply Boolean operations.

Figure 23.46 shows how a set of closed polyline shapes can be quickly turned into a drawing of a wrench using regions. The shapes at the top of the figure are first converted into regions using the Region tool in the Draw toolbar. Next, the shapes are aligned as shown in the middle of Figure 23.46. Finally, the circles and rectangle are joined with the Union command (choose Modify ➢ Solid Editing ➢ Union, or if you are using LT, choose Modify ➢ Region ➢ Union); then subtract the hexagonal shapes from the shape (choose Modify ➢ Solid Editing ➢ Subtract or if you are using LT, Modify ➢ Region ➢ Subtract). You can use the Region.dwg sample file if you'd like to experiment.

You can use regions to generate complex surfaces that might include holes or unusual bends (see Figure 23.47).

Keep in mind the following:

◆ Regions act like surfaces; when you remove hidden lines, objects behind the regions are hidden.

◆ You can explode regions to edit them. (You can't do this with solids.) However, exploding a region causes the region to lose its surfacelike quality, and objects will no longer hide behind its surface(s).

Finding the Properties of a Solid

All this effort to create a solid model isn't just to create a pretty picture. After your model is drawn and built, you can obtain information about its physical properties. In this section, you will look at a command that lets you gather such information.

TIP LT users can use the Massprop command described here to find the properties of solids that are part of an existing drawing.

You can find the volume, the moment of inertia, and other physical properties of your model by using the Massprop command. These properties can also be recorded as a file on disk so you can modify your model without worrying about losing track of its original properties.

To find the mass properties of a solid, choose Tools ➤ Inquiry ➤ Region/Mass Properties or enter **Massprop**⏎, and then follow the prompts.

FIGURE 23.46

Working with regions in the Region.dwg file

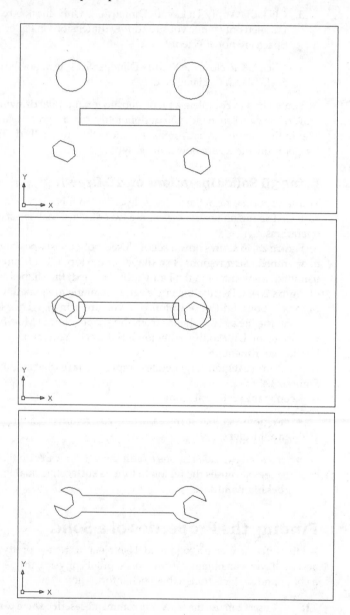

FIGURE 23.47

You can use the regional model to create complex 2D surfaces for use in 3D surface modeling.

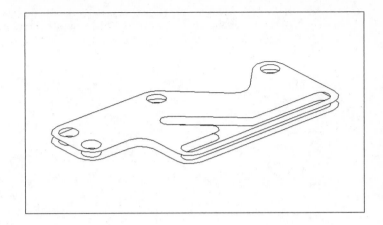

Taking Advantage of Stereolithography

A discussion of solid modeling wouldn't be complete without mentioning stereolithography. This is one of the more interesting technological wonders that have appeared as a by-product of 3D computer modeling. *Stereolithography* is a process that generates resin reproductions of 3D computer solid models. It offers the mechanical designer a method for rapidly prototyping designs directly from AutoCAD drawings. The process requires special equipment that will read computer files in a particular format.

AutoCAD supports stereolithography through the Stlout command. This command generates a .stl file, which can be used with a *Stereolithograph Apparatus* (*SLA*) to generate a model. You must first create a 3D solid model in AutoCAD; then you can use the Export Data dialog box to export your drawing in the STA format. Choose File ➢ Export and make sure the File Of Type drop-down list shows Lithography (*.stl) before you click the Save button.

The AutoCAD 3D solids are translated into a set of triangular-faceted meshes in the .stl file. You can use the Facetres system variable to control the fineness of these meshes. See Chapter 22 for more information on Facetres.

If You Want to Experiment

This chapter has focused on a mechanical project, but you can, of course, use solids to help simplify the construction of 3D architectural forms. If your interest lies in architecture, review the chapter "Architectural Solid Modeling" on the companion CD. There you'll find more exercises focused on solid modeling for building designs.

Part 5

Customization and Integration

In this part:

Chapter 24

Using the Express Tools

You can use a wealth of AutoCAD features to improve your productivity. But even with these aids to efficiency, you can always further automate in certain situations. In this chapter, I'll introduce you to some ways that you can enhance AutoCAD with add-on utilities. You'll also learn how to adapt AutoCAD to fit your particular needs by customizing its menus and toolbars.

First, you'll learn how to load and run the AutoCAD Express tools that are supplied on the AutoCAD distribution CD. By doing so, you'll be prepared to take advantage of the many utilities available from user groups and online services. You'll also see how third-party tools can enhance AutoCAD's role in your workplace. Then you'll learn how you can create keyboard macros and incorporate them into custom menus and toolbars. And, finally, you'll learn how to create custom linetypes and hatch patterns.

Topics in this chapter include the following:

◆ Using Enhancements Straight from the Source

◆ Putting AutoLISP to Work

Using Enhancements Straight from the Source

If you've followed the tutorial in this book, you've already used a few add-on programs that come with AutoCAD, perhaps without even being aware that they were not part of the core AutoCAD program. In this section, I'll introduce you to the AutoCAD Express tools: a set of AutoLISP, ARX, and VBA tools that showcase these powerful customization environments. The best part about the Express tools is that you don't have to know a thing about programming to take advantage of them.

NOTE If you are using LT, you can skip this chapter.

There are so many Express tools that I can't provide step-by-step instructions for all of them. Instead, I'll give you details about some of the more complicated tools and provide shorter descriptions of others.

Adding the Express Toolbars

Although you may have the Express menu in the AutoCAD menu bar, the Express toolbars are not usually installed. Here are the steps to install them:

1. Right-click any docked toolbar, and then choose Customize from the shortcut menu. The Customize User Interface dialog box.

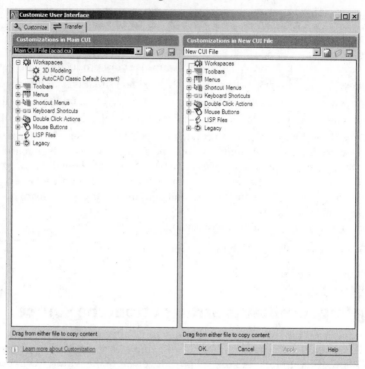

2. Click the Transfer tab at the top of the dialog box.

3. Select Open from the drop-down list right under the Customizations In Main CUI panel.

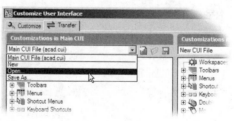

4. Locate and open the `Acetmain.cui` file located in the following folder:

`C:\Documents and Settings\`*User Name*`\Application Data\Autodesk\AutoCAD 2007\R17.0\enu\Support`

5. Note that *User Name* should be your login name for the PC or the name that was used when AutoCAD was installed. Application Data is a hidden folder so you will have to "unhide" it before you can explore to this location. See Appendix A for information on how to do this.

6. Expand the Toolbars list in the panel to the left. You'll see the Express toolbars.

7. In the panel to the right, select Main CUI File (acad.cui) from the drop-down list at the top of the panel.

8. Expand the Toolbars list in the panel to the right.

9. Click one of the toobars in the left column and drag it to the bottom of the Toolbars list in the right column. Do this with each of the toolbars in the left column.

10. Click OK. AutoCAD will reload the current workspace, and the Express toolbars will appear on your screen.

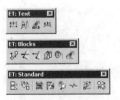

You can close the Express toolbars and later reopen them by right-clicking any docked toolbar and selecting the toolbar from the shortcut menu. You'll be able to recognize the Express toolbars by their ET prefix.

Tools for Managing Layers

In a survey of AutoCAD users, Autodesk discovered that one of the most frequently used features in AutoCAD was the Layer command. As a result, the layer controls in AutoCAD have been greatly improved. Still, there is room for more improvement. The Layers II toolbar discussed in this section isn't really a part of the Express tools, but it is a former set of Express tools that has migrated to the main AutoCAD program.

TIP All the tools discussed in this section have keyboard command equivalents. Check the status bar for the keyboard command name when selecting these tools from the toolbar or drop-down menu.

LOADING THE EXPRESS TOOLS

If you installed AutoCAD by using the Typical Installation option, you might not have installed the AutoCAD Express tools. Fortunately, you can install these utilities separately without having to reinstall the entire program.

Place the AutoCAD 2007 installation CD in your CD drive. When you see the AutoCAD 2007 installation window, make sure the Install option is selected. You'll see a set of numbered steps on the left side of the window. In step 5, Install Supplemental Tools, click the AutoCAD Express Tools option. Follow the installation instructions from there. After you've installed the Express tools, they will appear the next time you open AutoCAD.

USING LAYER WALK TO EXPLORE LAYERS

When you work with a file that has been produced by someone else, you usually have to spend some time becoming familiar with the way layers are set up in that file. This can be a tedious process, but the Layer Walk Express tool can help.

As the name implies, the Layer Walk tool lets you "walk through" the layers of a file, visually isolating each layer as you select the layer's name from a list. You can use Layer Walk to select the layers that you want visible, or you can turn layers on and off to explore a drawing without affecting the current layer settings. To open the LayerWalk dialog box, do the following:

1. Right click on any toolbar, then select Layer II from the shortcut menu.

2. Click the Layer Walk tool from the Layer II toolbar or enter Laywalk↵.

You can click and drag the bottom edge of the dialog box to expand the list so that you can see all the layers in the drawing. When you first open the LayerWalk dialog box, you will see the current visible layers selected. Layers that are off are not selected. Click a single layer, and AutoCAD displays just that layer.

You can use this dialog box to set up layer settings visually by Ctrl+clicking layer names to make them visible. Turn off Restore On Exit to maintain the layer settings you set up in the LayerWalk dialog box or turn it on if you want the drawing to revert to the layer settings before opening the LayerWalk dialog box. Right-click the list of layers to display a set of other options that let you save the layer state and invert the selection.

Changing the Layer Assignment of Objects

In addition to the Layer Walk tool, the Layers II toolbar includes two tools that change the layer assignments of objects: the Layer Match tool and the Change To Current Layer tool.

The Layer Match tool is similar to the Match Properties tool, but is streamlined to operate only on layer assignments. After clicking this tool, select the object or objects you want to change, press ↵, and then select an object whose layer you want to match.

The Change To Current Layer tool changes an object's layer assignment to the current layer. This tool has long existed as an AutoLISP utility, and you'll find that you'll get a lot of use from it.

Controlling Layer Settings through Objects

The remaining Express Layer tools let you make layer settings by selecting objects in the drawing. These tools are easy to use: simply click the tool and then select an object. These tools are so helpful that you might want to consider docking them permanently in your AutoCAD window.

The following list describes each tool:

Layer Isolate/Layer Unisolate   Layer Isolate turns off all the layers except for the layer of the selected object. Layer Unisolate restores the layer settings to the way the drawing was set before you used Layer Isolate.

Layer Freeze   Freezes the layer of the selected object.

Layer Off   Turns off the layer of the selected object.

Layer Lock   Locks the layer of the selected object. A locked layer is visible but cannot be edited.

Layer Unlock   Unlocks the layer of the selected object.

Layer Walk   Lets you dynamically change layer visibility.

Copy Objects To New Layer   Copies an object or set of objects to a different layer.

Tools for Editing Text

It seems that we can never have enough text-editing features. Even in the realm of word processors, we see numerous tools for configuring fonts, paragraphs, tabs, and tables. Some programs even check our grammar. Although we're not trying to write the great American novel in AutoCAD, we are interested in getting our text in the right location, at the right size, and with some degree of style. This often means using a mixture of text- and graphics-editing tools. The following describes some additional tools that will help ease your way through some otherwise difficult editing tasks.

Masking Text Backgrounds   One problem AutoCAD users frequently face is how to get text to read clearly when it is placed over a hatch pattern or other graphic. The Hatch command will hatch around existing text, leaving a clear space behind it. But what about those situations in which you must add text *after* a hatch pattern has been created? Or what about those instances when you need to mask behind text that is placed over a nonhatch object, such as dimension leaders or raster images?

The Text Mask tool addresses this problem by masking the area behind text with a special masking object called a Wipeout.

TIP   The AutoCAD Mtext command offers a background mask option that performs a similar function to the Text Mask tool. While editing text with the Text Formatting toolbar, select the text, right-click, and select Background Mask. You can also turn on the Background Mask through the Properties palette of an Mtext object.

TIP If you want to remove the effects of the Express Text Mask took, choose Express ➢ Text ➢ Unmask Text. This option prompts you to select an object. Select the masked text and press ↵ to delete the mask background.

Adding Linked Text Documents One of the more frustrating and time-consuming aspects to drafting is editing lengthy notes. General notes and specifications change frequently in the life of a project, so editing notes can be a large part of what you do in AutoCAD. Frequently notes are written by someone else, perhaps a specifications writer who doesn't work directly with the drawings.

To help make note editing easier, AutoCAD supplies the Remote Text object. This special object is linked to an external text document. Remote Text objects automatically update their contents when the source document changes.

Using Remote Text is fairly straightforward. Choose Express ➢ Text ➢ Remote Text or type **Rtext**↵ at the Command prompt. Press ↵ when you see the Enter an option[Style/Height/ Rotation/File/Diesel] <File>: prompt, and then locate and select a text file to import.

Express Blocks Tools

Every now and then, you'll want to use objects within a block to trim or extend to, or perhaps you'll want to copy a part of a block to another part of your drawing. In these situations, you can use the following tools. They're fairly simple to use, so the descriptions in this section should be enough to get you started.

You'll find these tools on the Express Blocks toolbar:

Copy Nested Objects Lets you copy single objects within a block. You are allowed to select objects only individually—one click at a time.

Trim To Nested Objects Lets you trim to objects in a block. This tool works just like the standard Trim command with the exception that you must select the cutting edge objects individually.

Extend To Nested Objects Lets you extend to objects in a block. This tool also works like its standard counterpart with the exception that you must select the boundary edge objects you want to extend to individually.

List Xref/Block Properties Displays basic information about an Xref or a block.

Extended Clip In Chapter 7, you saw how to limit the display of an Xref to an L-shaped, rectilinear area. Extended Clip adds the ability to use arcs, circles, and polylines to "clip" the view of an Xref.

Explode Attributes To Text Explodes blocks containing attributes so that the attribute values are converted into plain single-line text.

In addition to the tools on the Express Blocks toolbar, you can access the following tools by choosing Express ➢ Blocks:

Convert Shape To Block Converts a shape object into a block. You can then explode the block to its component objects if needed.

Export Attribute Information Offers a quick way to extract attribute information from a simple text file. You are prompted to select a file location and name and then select the attributes you want to export. The text file is formatted as a tab-delimited file. You can then edit the exported text file and use the Import Attribute Information tool (described next) to update the drawing with the modifications you made to the text file.

Import Attribute Information   Enables you to import changes to the attribute information that has been exported using the Export Attribute Information tool.

Convert Block To Xref   Lets you replace block references in your drawing with Xrefs. For example, you can replace the tub blocks in the apartment plan from earlier tutorials with an Xref of a different tub. When you select this option, the BLOCKTOXREF dialog box opens.

From here, you can select the block you want to replace. You are then asked to select a file that will be the replacing Xref.

Replace Block With Another Block   Replaces one set of block references with another. For example, you can replace the tub block in the apartment plan with the door block, turning all the bathtubs into doors. This tool works in a way similar to the Convert Block To Xref tool.

Express Standard Tools

The Express Standard toolbar seems to be the answer to most AutoCAD users' wish lists. As with many of the Express tools discussed so far, these tools have been floating around in the AutoCAD user community as AutoLISP utilities. Multiple Object Stretch lets you use the crossing polygon selection option to select endpoints and vertexes for stretching. The Move/Copy/Rotate tool combines these three functions into one command. The Break Line Symbol adds the standard break line to your drawing. The Super Hatch tool offers an easy way to create custom hatch patterns. Super Hatch is fairly complex so the next section describes in detail how it can be used.

CREATING CUSTOM HATCH PATTERNS WITH SUPER HATCH

You can access a number of hatch patterns from AutoCAD's Hatch And Gradient dialog box, but at times none of those patterns will fulfill your needs. This is where the Super Hatch tool comes in. With Super Hatch, you can create virtually any hatch pattern you want. You can use objects in your drawing as a basis for a hatch pattern, or you can import bitmap images and use them to form a hatch pattern, such as tiled wallpaper in the Windows Desktop background.

The following exercise shows you how to use Super Hatch:

1. Open the superhatch.dwg file from the companion CD. You'll see a block of an arrow on the left side of the screen and a rectangular area to the right. In this exercise, you'll turn the arrow into a hatch pattern.

2. Click the Super Hatch tool to open the SuperHatch dialog box.

3. Click the Select Existing button to close the SuperHatch dialog box.

4. Click the arrow. It becomes highlighted, and a magenta rectangle encircles the arrow.

At this point, you can indicate the area you want repeated in your pattern. The default is the extents of the selected item as indicated by the magenta rectangle.

5. Click the two points shown in Figure 24.1 to indicate the area that you want repeated. The rectangle changes to reflect the new area. You can repeat the area selection as many times as you need until you get exactly the area you want.

6. Press ↵ to move to the next step.

7. Click the interior of the rectangle to indicate the area you want to hatch. If you have multiple hatch areas, you can continue to select them at this step.

8. Press ↵ to finish your selection of hatch areas. The arrow appears repeated as a pattern within the rectangle, as shown in Figure 24.2.

FIGURE 24.1
Selecting the area
to be repeated

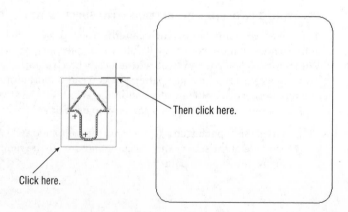

Then click here.

Click here.

FIGURE 24.2
The custom hatch
pattern

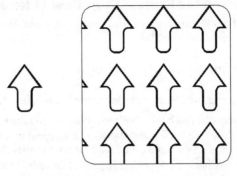

The object you select by using the Select Existing option in the SuperHatch dialog box must be
a block. You can modify that block by using the techniques described in Chapter 7, and the changes
will appear in the hatch pattern as shown in Figure 24.3.

As you can see from the SuperHatch dialog box, you can incorporate Xrefs, blocks, and even image
files into your custom hatch pattern. Each of these options prompts you to insert the object before you
convert it into a hatch pattern. You use the usual insertion method for the type of object you select. For
example, if you choose the Block option, you are prompted for an insertion point, the X and Y scale
factors, and a rotation angle. For image files, you see the same dialog box that you see when you insert
an image file, offering the options for insertion point, scale, and rotation. Figure 24.4 shows a sample
hatch pattern with an image file used instead of an AutoCAD block.

FIGURE 24.3
The custom hatch
pattern after the
arrow block has
been modified to
include the diagonal
hatch pattern

FIGURE 24.4
A custom hatch
pattern using a
bitmap image

Tools on the Express Drop-Down Menu

Most of the Express tools discussed so far are available as options in the AutoCAD menu bar on the Express menu. There are some additional options on the Express menu you won't see in any of the toolbars. You won't want to miss these additional tools. They can greatly enhance your productivity on any type of project.

CONTROLLING SHORTCUTS WITH THE COMMAND ALIAS EDITOR

Throughout this book, I've been showing you the keyboard shortcuts to the AutoCAD commands. In Windows XP, all these shortcuts are stored in a file called Acad.pgp in the C:\Documents and Settings*User Name*\Application Data\Autodesk\AutoCAD 2007\R17.0\enu\Support folder. (Check the Working Support File Search Path option in the Files tab in the Options dialog box to find the exact location for the support files on your system.) In the past, you had to edit this file with a text editor to modify these command shortcuts (otherwise known as command aliases). But to make our lives simpler, Autodesk has supplied the Command Alias Editor, which automates the process of editing, adding, or removing command aliases from AutoCAD.

In addition, the Command Alias Editor lets you store your own alias definitions in a separate file. You can then recall your file to load your own command aliases. Here's how the Command Alias Editor works:

1. Choose Express ➤ Tools ➤ Command Alias Editor to open the AutoCAD Alias Editor dialog box.

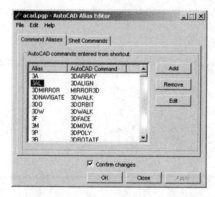

2. As you can see from the button options, you can add, delete, or edit an alias. Click the Add button to open the New Command Alias dialog box.

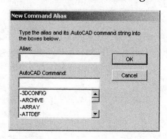

In this dialog box, you enter the desired alias in the Alias input box and then select the command from the AutoCAD Command list box. You can also enter a command or macro name, such as Wipeout, in the input box. When you click the Edit option in the AutoCAD Alias Editor dialog box, you see a dialog box identical to this one with the input boxes already filled in.

3. After you create or edit an alias, click OK to return to the AutoCAD Alias Editor dialog box.

4. Click OK to exit the dialog box. You see a warning message that tells you that you are about to overwrite the Acad.pgp file.

5. Click Yes to update the Acad.pgp file.

If you're a veteran AutoCAD user, you might be accustomed to your own set of command aliases. If so, you might want to create your own .pgp file containing just your custom aliases. Then, whenever you use AutoCAD, open the AutoCAD Alias Editor, choose File ➢ Import, and load your personal .pgp file. From then on, the aliases in your file will be included with those of the standard Acad.pgp file.

Using Extended Clip to Clip a Raster Image to a Curved Shape

In Chapter 7, you saw how you can clip portions of an Xref or a raster image so that only a portion of these objects is visible. One limitation to the Raster Clip option is that you can clip only areas defined by straight lines. You cannot, for example, clip an area defined by a circle or an ellipse.

Extended Clip is designed for those instances when you absolutely need to clip a raster image to a curved area. The following steps show you how it works:

1. Create a clip boundary by using a curved polyline or circle.

2. Choose Express ➢ Modify ➢ Extended Clip.

3. Click the boundary.

4. Click the Xref, block, or image you want to clip.

5. At the

```
Enter maximum allowable error distance for resolution of arc segments <7/16">:
```

6. prompt, press ↵. The Xref, block, or image will clip to the selected boundary.

7. You can erase the boundary you created in step 1 or keep it for future reference.

Extended Clip really doesn't clip to the boundary you created, but instead approximates that boundary by creating a true clip boundary with a series of very short line segments. In fact, the prompt in step 5 lets you specify the maximum allowable distance between the straight line segments it generates and the curve of the boundary you create (see Figure 24.5).

After you've created a boundary by using Extended Clip, you can edit the properties of the boundary by choosing Modify ➢ Clip➢ Xref for Xrefs and blocks or by choosing Modify ➢ Clip ➢ Image for raster images.

FIGURE 24.5

Extended Clip enables you to set the maximum distance from your clip boundary and the one it generates.

Your clip boundary

The clip boundary produced by Extended Clip

USING MAKE LINETYPE TO CREATE A CUSTOM LINETYPE

Most of the time the linetypes provided by AutoCAD are adequate. But if you're looking for that perfect linetype, you can use the Make Linetype tool to create your own. Here's how it works:

1. Open the customltype.dwg sample file from the Figures folder. The sample drawing is made up of simple lines with no polylines, arcs, or circles. When you create your own linetype prototype, make sure the lines are all aligned. Draw a single line and break it to form the segments of the linetype (see Figure 24.6). Also make sure it is drawn to the actual plotted size.

FIGURE 24.6

Creating a custom linetype by using Make Linetype

Click here for the start point.

Click here for the endpoint.

2. Choose Express ➤ Tools ➤ Make Linetype to open the MKLTYPE dialog box. This is a typical file dialog box allowing you to create a new linetype file.

3. Enter **myltype** for the filename, select a location for the file, and then click Save.

4. At the Enter linetype name: prompt, enter **MyLinetype** or any name you want to use to describe the linetype. The name must be a single word.

5. At the Enter linetype description: prompt, enter a description for your linetype. This can be a sentence that best describes your linetype.

6. At the Specify starting point for line definition: prompt, pick one endpoint of the sample linetype.

7. At the Specify ending point for line definition: prompt, pick a point just past the opposite end of the sample linetype. Pick a point past the endpoint of the sample to indicate the gap between the end of the first segment of the linetype and the beginning of the repeating portion as shown in Figure 24.6.

8. At the Select objects: prompt, select the sample linetype lines. When you're done, press ↵. You now have a custom linetype.

If you send your file to someone else, you need to make sure you include your custom linetype files with the drawing file. Otherwise, anything drawn using your custom linetype will appear as a continuous line, and your recipient will get an error message saying that AutoCAD cannot find a linetype resource.

The Make Linetype tool creates a single linetype file for each linetype you create. The linetype file is a simple ASCII text file. If you end up making several linetypes, you can combine your linetype files into one file by using a simple text editor such as Windows Notepad. Don't use WordPad or Word because these programs will introduce special codes to the linetype file.

CREATING CUSTOM SHAPES AS AN ALTERNATIVE TO BLOCKS

Shapes are special types of AutoCAD objects that are similar to blocks. They are usually simple symbols made up of lines and arcs. Shapes take up less memory and can be displayed faster, but they are much less flexible than blocks, and they are not very accurate. You cannot use Object Snaps to snap to specific parts of a shape, nor can you explode shapes. They are best suited for symbols or as components in complex linetypes.

Shapes have always been difficult to create. In the past, you could not create a shape by drawing it. You had to create something called a shape definition by using a special code. A *shape definition* is just an ASCII file that contains a description of the geometry of the shape. Creating such a file was a tedious, arcane process that few users bothered with.

With the introduction of complex linetypes in recent versions of AutoCAD, interest in shapes has revived. To make it easier for users to create shapes, AutoCAD 2007 provides a tool that will create a shape definition file for you based on a line drawing. Try this simple exercise to learn how to create and use a shape:

1. Open the makeshape.dwg sample file from the Chapter 24 folder of the sample project files. This file contains a simple drawing of an upward-pointing arrow. It contains lines and arcs.

2. Choose Express ➢ Tools ➢ Make Shape to open the MKSHAPE dialog box. This is a typical file dialog box that enables you to specify a name and location for your shape definition file.

3. In the File Name input box, enter **Arrow**; then locate the My Documents folder and place your new file there.

4. Click OK to create your file.

5. At the Enter the name of the shape: prompt, enter **Arrow**↵.

6. At the Enter resolution <128>: prompt, enter **512**↵. Shapes are defined with a square matrix of points. All the endpoints of lines and arcs must be on a point within that matrix. At this prompt, you can define the density of that matrix. A higher density will give you a better-looking shape, but you don't want to get carried away with this setting.

7. At the Specify insertion base point: prompt, select the tip of the arrow as shown in Figure 24.7. This will be the insertion point of your shape, which is similar to the insertion point of a block.

8. At the Select objects: prompt, select the entire arrow and then press ↵.

9. You'll see a series of messages telling you what AutoCAD is doing. The last message will tell you whether AutoCAD was successful in creating the shape file, and it will tell you the location and name of the new shape file:

```
Compilation successful.  Output file C:\Documents and Settings\User Name\My
    Documents\Arrow.shx contains 309 bytes.
Shape "ARROW" created.
```

Use the SHAPE command to place shapes in your drawing.

To see how your shape came out, try the following. Here you'll learn how to load and insert a shape:

1. At the Command prompt, type **Load.**↵ to open the Select Shape File dialog box. This is a typical file dialog box.

2. In the My Documents folder, locate the file Arrow.shx and click Open to load it.

3. Now type **Shape.**↵.

4. At the Enter shape name or [?]: prompt, type **Arrow.**↵. Now you'll see the arrow follow the cursor as you move it across the drawing area.

NOTE   If you've forgotten the name of a shape you are loading, you can enter a question mark (?) to see a listing of available shapes.

5. At the Specify insertion point: prompt, click to the right of the original arrow.

6. At the Specify height: prompt, press ↵ to accept the default of 1.

7. At the Specify rotation angle: prompt, enter **45.**↵. The arrow appears at a 45° angle.

FIGURE 24.7

Creating a shape from an existing drawing

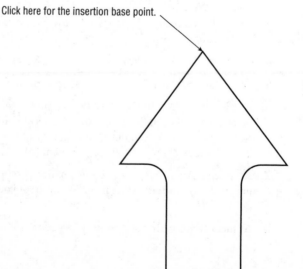

Click here for the insertion base point.

In many ways, a shape acts like a block, but you cannot snap to any of its points. It is also less accurate than a block in its representation, though for some applications this might not be a great concern. Finally, you cannot use complex shapes such as splines or 3D objects for your shape. You can use only lines and arcs.

Still, you might find shapes useful in your application. As mentioned earlier, you can include shapes in linetype definitions. See Chapter 26 for a description on how to create a linetype that includes shapes as part of the line.

TIP You might also notice a tool that converts shapes into AutoCAD blocks. Choose Express ➤ Blocks ➤ Convert Shape To Block, and then select a shape. A prompt asks for a name for the block. You can accept the default name, which is the same name as the shape you are converting.

USING THE EXPRESS SELECTION TOOLS

Sometimes it seems that there aren't enough selection tools available in AutoCAD. In Chapter 2, you learned about the various methods you can use to select groups of objects to build a selection set, which is a set of objects selected for an operation such as a move or copy. The Express tools offer a few more ways to select objects.

The Get Selection Set tool sets up a selection set based on layers or types of objects. When you choose Express ➤ Selection Tools ➤ Get Selection Set, you are prompted to select an object whose layer contains all the objects you want to select. You can press ↵ to create a selection set of all the objects in the drawing. Next, you are prompted to select an object of the type you want. If you press ↵ at the first prompt and then select a line at the second prompt, all the lines in the drawing will be included in a new selection set. You won't see anything happen on the screen, but the next time you use a command that asks you to select objects, you can enter **P**↵ to select the lines.

The other selection tool is Fast Select. When you choose Express ➤ Selection Tools ➤ Fast Select, you are prompted to select an object. After you do so, the object you select plus any object touching it will be selected.

USING DIMSTYLE EXPORT AND DIMSTYLE IMPORT

Most AutoCAD users need to set up their dimension styles only once and then make minor alterations for drawing scale. You can set up your dimension styles in a template file and then use that template whenever you create new drawings. That way, your dimension styles will already be set up the way you want them.

But frequently, you will receive files created by someone else who might not have the same ideas about dimension styles as you do. Normally, this would mean that you have to re-create your favorite settings in a new dimension style. Now with the Express tools, you can export and import dimension styles at any time, saving you the effort of re-creating them.

ATTACHING DATA TO OBJECTS

This set of options is less likely to get as much use as the others you've looked at so far, so I've included a brief description of them here without going into too much detail. They're fairly easy to use, and you shouldn't have any trouble trying them. You can access both tools by choosing Express ➤ Tools:

Attach Xdata Lets you attach extended data to objects. Extended data is usually used only by AutoLISPor ARX applications. You are asked to select the object that will receive the data, and then you are asked for an application name that serves as a tag to tell others who the data belongs to. You can then select a data type. After this is done, you can enter your data.

List Object Xdata Displays extended data that has been attached to an object.

USING FILE TOOLS

AutoCAD has always made extensive use of external files for its operation. Everything from fonts to keyboard shortcuts depends on external files. The Express File tools (choose Express ➤ File Tools) offer options to simplify a few file-related operations. You might find some of these tools helpful on a daily basis, such as Save All Drawings and Close All Drawings. Others, such as Edit Image, might be useful to know about when you need to edit an image. The following is a list of these tools:

Move Backup Files Lets you specify a location for AutoCAD .bak files for the current drawing session.

Convert PLT To DWG Converts HPGL plot files to drawing files. You must first set up AutoCAD or Windows for an HPGL plotter and then specify that HPGL plotter in the Plot or Page Setup dialog box. You must also indicate that you want to plot to a file at the time you produce the plot (select the Plot To File check box in the Printer/Plotter group of the Plot dialog box).

Edit Image Offers a quick way to open and edit an image file that has been inserted into an AutoCAD drawing. Choose Express ➤ File Tools ➤ Edit Image, and then select the image you want to edit. A File dialog box opens, showing the file in a list box. Click Open, and the program associated with the image file type will open the image file.

Redefine Path Lets you redefine the path to external files that are referenced from the current drawing. This includes Xrefs, images, shapes, styles, and Rtext. You can strip a path from a referenced file by using the asterisk option (*) when you see the Enter old directory (use '*' for all), or ? <options>: prompt. When you see the Replace "*" with: prompt, press ↵. If you strip the path in this way, AutoCAD will use the support file search path specified in the Files tab of the Options dialog box. You can specify the type of external file you want to redefine by pressing ↵ at the first prompt. This opens the REDIRMODE dialog box. This dialog box contains a simple check box list of the types of support files whose path you want to redefine.

Update Drawing Property Data Drawing property data can be a handy feature of AutoCAD, but to use it requires some discipline. (See Chapter 19 for more on drawing property data.) For one thing, the amount of data you must enter can be a bit daunting. The Update Drawing Property Data Express tool offers a way to let you quickly add drawing property data by utilizing property data templates. Drawing property data is often the same for a set of drawings, so you can create a template and apply it to similar drawings in a set by using the Update Drawing Property Data tool.

To create a drawing property data template, choose Express ➤ File Tools ➤ Update Drawing Property Data. At the Enter an option [Active template/Edit template/List/Remove/Update] <Update>: prompt, enter E↵ to open the Edit Populate Template dialog box.

Fill in the data and then choose File ➢ Save As. Use the Update option in the Update Drawing Property Data command prompt to apply the template to a drawing or to a set of drawings in a folder.

Save All Drawings   Saves all currently open files. The files remain open for additional editing.

Close All Drawings   Closes all currently open drawings. AutoCAD remains open.

Quick Exit   Closes all currently open drawings and exits AutoCAD. You are asked whether you want to save changes to each file before it is closed.

Revert To Original   Causes a drawing to revert to its last saved state. It does so by closing the file without saving any changes (since the last Save) and then reopening the file.

USING WEB TOOLS

AutoCAD enables you to add URL links to objects. This is a great feature that can help you link drawings to other types of data. The Express Web tools (choose Express ➢ Web Tools) add some enhancements to the URL linking features of AutoCAD:

Show URLs   Displays the URL link attached to an AutoCAD object.

Change URLs   Lets you quickly edit an existing URL of an object. You must still choose Insert ➢ Hyperlink to attach a new URL to an object.

Find And Replace URLs   Replaces a set of existing URLs with a URL of your specification.

Layout Express Tools

AutoCAD includes some Express tools that will help make your work with layouts a lot easier. These tools, found in the Express ➢ Layout Tools menu, address some of the more common operations you will encounter as you work with layouts.

ALIGNING MODEL SPACE OBJECTS WITH LAYOUT OBJECTS

If you ever try to align an object in a layout with objects in a Model Space viewport, you know how difficult it can be. This situation often arises when you accidentally pan or zoom a Model Space viewport, and objects drawn in Paper Space (such as break lines or dimensional notations) become misaligned with the underlying view.

The Align Space tool helps you quickly align objects in a Model Space viewport with objects in the layout Paper Space. Align Space can even rotate a viewport view to align objects that are at an angle. To see firsthand how it works, try the following exercise. You'll align a Plan view of a set of survey data points to a north arrow in Paper Space.

1. Open the `alignspace.dwg` sample file from the companion CD.

2. Choose Express ➢ Layout Tools ➢ Align Space. Notice that the viewport automatically becomes active.

3. At the `FIRST alignment point in MODEL space:` prompt, click the upper endpoint of the north arrow in the viewport, as shown in Figure 24.8.

4. At the `SECOND point in MODEL space or <Return> for none:` prompt, click the endpoint of the bottom end of the north arrow, as shown in Figure 24.8.

FIGURE 24.8

Select these points to align the Model Space north arrow with a Paper Space north arrow.

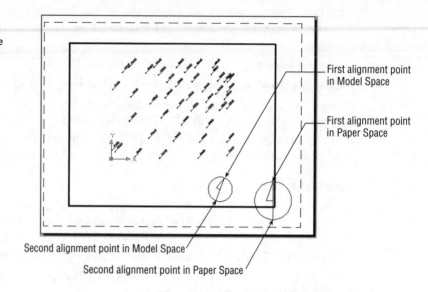

First alignment point in Model Space

First alignment point in Paper Space

Second alignment point in Model Space

Second alignment point in Paper Space

5. At the `FIRST alignment point in PAPER space:` prompt, notice that AutoCAD automatically switches to Paper Space to allow for your next input. Click the upper endpoint of the layout Paper Space north arrow.

6. At the `SECOND alignment point in PAPER space:` prompt, click the lower end of the Paper Space arrow. The two arrows will align, and you will see a message telling you the scale of the viewport.

In this exercise, you can see that the two north arrows are aligned in both scale and direction. The object you are aligning to in Paper Space does not have to be within the area of the viewport either.

If you prefer, you can align a single point without changing the scale or rotation of the viewport by pressing ↵ in step 4 when you see the `SECOND point in MODEL space or <Return> for none:` prompt.

ALIGNING MULTIPLE VIEWPORTS TO A SINGLE VIEWPORT

The Align Space tool lets you align a Model Space object to a Paper Space object, but what if you want to align two Model Space views? For example, suppose you want to overlap two viewports of the same view, with one viewport displaying graphics while the other displays just the power and signal symbols for a small region of the plan.

The Synchronize Viewports tool lets you do just that. It aligns one or more viewports to another "master" viewport. The Synchronize Viewports tool aligns the coordinates in one viewport with the coordinates and scale of another so that the views are matched like pieces of a jigsaw puzzle. To get a better idea of what this means, try the following exercise. Suppose you have an enlarged plan showing a portion of a building. You want to include the grid lines in your plan, but you don't want to have to include other portions of the plan or redraw the grids. Synchronize Viewports can make easy work of this project:

1. Open the `synchronize.dwg` file from the companion CD and then choose Express ➢ Layout Tools ➢ Synchronize Viewports.

2. At the `Select objects:` prompt, click the border of the viewport in the lower-right corner.

3. At the `Select viewports to be aligned to master viewport Select objects:` prompt, click the other two viewports and press ↵. The two viewports will change to show the adjacent areas of the first viewport.

Notice that the three views of the layout combine to show a contiguous Plan view instead of three random views.

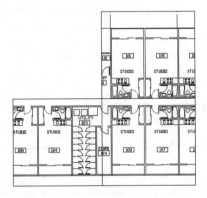

You could use Synchronize Viewports in just this way to piece together parts of a floor plan in a nonrectangular shape.

To finish adding the grid lines, do the following:

1. Double-click in the top viewport and then click the Pan Realtime tool in the Standard toolbar.

2. Shift+click and drag the view downward to bring the grid lines into view. Then Shift+click and drag, and keep the pan motion in an exact vertical direction. Pan downward until you see only the grids and dimensions.

3. Press Esc to exit the Pan tool; then double-click the left viewport, and use the Pan tool to Shift+click and drag the view toward the right. Keep panning until just the grid lines show.

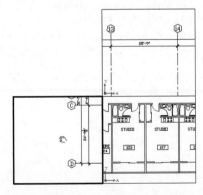

If you've ever tried to do this operation without the aid of the Synchronize Viewports tool, you can see how helpful a tool it is.

FINDING VIEWPORT SCALES AND MERGING LAYOUTS

There are two more fairly simple tools in the Layout Tools category: List Viewport Scale and Merge Layout. List Viewport Scale does just what its name says. Choose Express ➢ Layout Tools ➢ List Viewport Scale and then click a viewport border to display the viewport scale. Merge Layout combines the contents of one layout with another. This tool is handy if you are exporting files to earlier versions of AutoCAD, in which only one layout is possible. Choosing Express ➢ Layout Tools ➢ Merge Layouts opens the LAYOUTMERGE dialog box. This dialog box is a simple list showing the layouts in the current drawing.

You can select the layout that you want merged with the current layout. After you've made your selection and click OK, another dialog box appears that looks identical to the first LAYOUTMERGE dialog box. This time you select the destination layout for the merged layouts.

That covers the Express Layout tools. Like many of the other Express tools, you might find yourself using these tools more than most of the other standard AutoCAD commands, so keep them in mind as you work on the layout of your next set of drawings.

Putting AutoLISP to Work

Most high-end CAD packages offer a macro or programming language to help users customize their systems. AutoCAD has *AutoLISP*, which is a pared-down version of the popular LISP artificial intelligence language.

Don't let AutoLISP scare you. In many ways, an AutoLISP program is just a set of AutoCAD commands that help you build your own features. The only difference is that you have to follow a different set of rules when using AutoLISP. But this isn't so unusual. After all, you had to learn some basic rules about using AutoCAD commands too—how to start commands, for instance, and how to use command options.

If the thought of using AutoLISP is a little intimidating, bear in mind that you don't really need substantial computer knowledge to use this tool. In this section, you will see how to get AutoLISP to help out in your everyday editing tasks, without having to learn the entire programming language.

Loading and Running an AutoLISP Program

Many AutoCAD users have discovered the usefulness of AutoLISP through the thousands of free AutoLISP utilities that are available from web sites and online services. In fact, it's quite common for users to maintain a "toolbox" of their favorite utilities on a disk. But before you can use these utilities, you need to know how to load them into AutoCAD. In the following exercise, you'll load and use a sample AutoLISP utility found on the companion CD:

1. Start AutoCAD and open the 24-unit.dwg file.

2. Choose Tools ➤ Load Application to open the Load/Unload Applications dialog box.

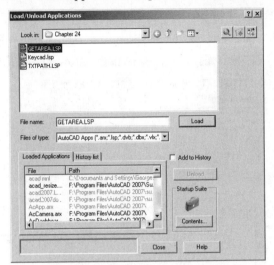

3. Locate and select the GETAREA.LSP file from the companion CD.

4. Click the Load button. The message GETAREA.LSP successfully loaded appears in the message box at the very bottom of the dialog box. If you scroll down the list in the Loaded Applications tab, you also see Getarea.lsp listed there, which tells you that it is loaded.

5. Click Close to close the Load/Unload Applications dialog box.

6. Now enter **getarea**↵.

7. At the Pick point inside area to be calculated: prompt, click inside the unit plan.

8. At the Select location for area note: prompt, pick a point just above the door to the balcony. A label appears, displaying the area of the room in square feet.

You have just loaded and used an AutoLISP utility. As you saw in the Load/Unload Applications dialog box, you can load and try out several other utilities. Next, you'll look more closely at the Load/Unload Applications dialog box.

TIP The functions of some of the more popular AutoLISP utilities have become part of the core AutoCAD program. Tools such as Match Properties and Make Object's Layer Current have been around as AutoLISP utilities since the earliest releases of AutoCAD.

Managing Your AutoLISP and VBA Library

The Load/Unload Applications dialog box gives you plenty of flexibility in managing your favorite AutoLISP utilities. You can also manage your VBA and ARX applications. As you saw in the previous exercise, you can easily find and select utilities by using this dialog box. If you often use a custom application, you can include it in the History List tab of the Load/Unload Applications dialog box, as you'll see in the following steps:

1. Choose Tools ➤ Load Application again to open the Load/Unload Applications dialog box.

2. Click the Add To History check box.

3. Click the History List tab.

4. Select GETAREA.LSP again from the list of applications at the top of the dialog box.

5. Click Load. GETAREA.LSP now appears in the History List tab.

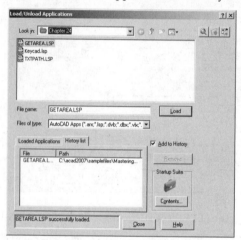

6. Click Close to close the Load/Unload Applications dialog box.

Now when you exit AutoCAD, the dialog box retains the name of the Getarea.lsp utility in the History List tab. When you want to load GETAREA.LSP in a future session, you won't have to hunt it down. You can highlight it in the History List tab and then load it from there. You can add as many items as you want to your History List tab or remove items by highlighting them and clicking the Remove button. The History List tab works with all types of applications that AutoCAD supports.

Loading AutoLISP Programs Automatically

As you start to build a library of AutoLISP and VBA applications, you might find that you use some of them all the time. You can set up AutoCAD to automatically load your favorite applications. To do this, you use the Startup Suite in the Load/Unload Applications dialog box:

1. Choose Tools ➢ Load Applications to open the Load/Unload Applications dialog box.

2. Click the Contents button or the suitcase icon in the Startup Suite group to open the Startup Suite dialog box. This dialog box contains a list box that shows any applications that are to be started whenever AutoCAD starts. You add applications with the Add button at the bottom. If there are applications in the list, you can use the Remove button to remove them.

3. Click the Add button to open the Add File To Startup Suite dialog box. This is a typical file dialog box that enables you to search for and select a file.

4. Locate and select the GETAREA.LSP file in the Chapter 24 folder, and then click Add. The Startup Suite dialog box reappears, and GETAREA.LSP is listed.

5. Click Close, and then click Close again in the Load/Unload Applications dialog box.

From now on, GETAREA.LSP will be loaded automatically whenever you start AutoCAD. You can add several files to the Startup Suite list.

OTHER CUSTOMIZATION OPTIONS

If you are serious about customization, you'll want to know about Autodesk's ObjectARX programming environment that enables Microsoft Visual C++ programmers to develop full applications that work within AutoCAD. ObjectARX enables programmers to create new objects within AutoCAD as well as add functionality to existing objects. ObjectARX is beyond the scope of this book, so to find out more, contact your AutoCAD dealer or visit Autodesk's website at www.autodesk.com.

If you are familiar with Visual Basic, you'll want to know that AutoCAD offers Visual Basic ActiveX Automation as part of its set of customization tools. ActiveX Automation offers the ability to create macros that operate across different applications. It also gives you access to AutoCAD objects through an object-oriented programming environment. Automation is a broad subject, so several chapters on the CD are devoted to this topic.

Creating Keyboard Macros with AutoLISP

You can write some simple AutoLISP programs of your own that create what are called keyboard macros. *Macros*—like script files—are strings of predefined keyboard entries. They are invaluable for shortcuts to commands and options you use frequently. For example, you might often use the Break command to break an object at a single point while editing a particular drawing. Here's a way you can turn this operation into a macro:

1. Close the 24-unit.dwg file without saving it, then open it again, and enter the following text at the Command prompt. Be sure you enter the line exactly as shown here. If you make a mistake while entering this line, you can use the I-beam cursor or arrow keys to go to the location of your error to fix it.

   ```
   (defun C:breakat () (command "break" pause "f" pause "@"))↵
   ```

2. Next, enter **breakat**↵ at the Command prompt. The Break command starts, and you are prompted to select an object.

3. Click the wall on the right side of the unit.

4. At the Specify first break point: prompt, click a point on the wall where you want to create a break, and make sure the Osnap mode is turned off.

5. To see the result of the break, click the wall again. You will see that it has been split into two lines, as shown in Figure 24.9.

You've just written and run your first AutoLISP macro! Let's take a closer look at this very simple program (see Figure 24.10). It starts with an opening parenthesis, as do all AutoLISP programs, followed by the word defun. Defun is an AutoLISP function that lets you create commands; it is followed by the name you want to give the command (Breakat, in this case). The command name is preceded by C:, telling defun to make this command accessible from the command prompt. If the C: were omitted, you would have to start Breakat by using parentheses, as in (Breakat).

FIGURE 24.9
With the grips exposed, you can see that the wall is split into two lines.

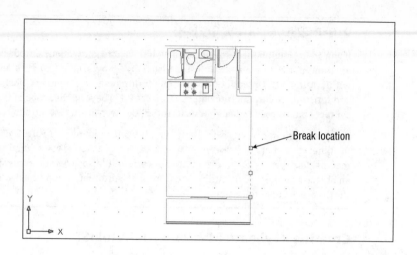

Break location

FIGURE 24.10
Breakdown of the Breakat macro

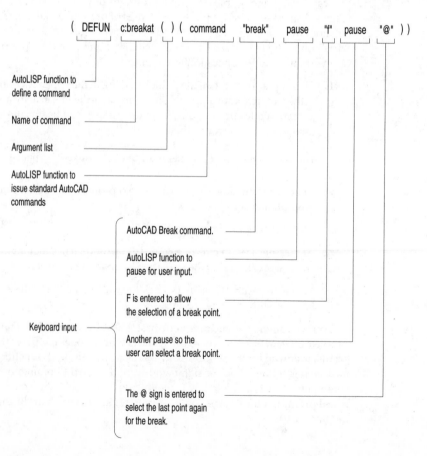

(DEFUN c:breakat ( ) (command "break" pause "f" pause "@"))

AutoLISP function to define a command

Name of command

Argument list

AutoLISP function to issue standard AutoCAD commands

AutoCAD Break command.

AutoLISP function to pause for user input.

F is entered to allow the selection of a break point.

Keyboard input

Another pause so the user can select a break point.

The @ sign is entered to select the last point again for the break.

After the command name is a set of opening and closing parentheses. This set encloses what is called the *argument list*. The details aren't important; just be aware that these parentheses must follow the command name.

Finally, a list of words follows, enclosed by another set of parentheses. This list starts with the word command. Command is an AutoLISP function that tells AutoLISP that whatever follows should be entered just like regular keyboard input. Only one item in the Breakat macro—the word pause—is not part of the keyboard input series. Pause is an AutoLISP function that tells AutoLISP to pause for input. In this particular macro, AutoLISP pauses to let you pick an object to break and the location for the break.

Notice that most of the items in the macro are enclosed in quotation marks. Literal keyboard input must be enclosed in quotation marks in this way. The pause function, on the other hand, does not require quotation marks because it is a proper function, one that AutoLISP can recognize.

Finally, the program ends with a closing parenthesis. All parentheses in an AutoLISP program must be in balanced pairs, so these final two parentheses close the opening parenthesis at the start of the command function as well as the opening parenthesis back at the beginning of the defun function.

Storing AutoLISP Macros as Files

When you create a program at the Command prompt, as you did with the Breakat macro, AutoCAD remembers it only until you exit the current file. Unless you want to re-create this macro the next time you use AutoCAD, save it by copying it into an ASCII text file with an .lsp extension using the Windows Notepad application. Figure 24.11 shows the saved Breakat macro, along with some other macros I use often.

Figure 24.11 shows the contents of a file named Keycad.lsp. This file contains the macro you used previously, along with several others. The other macros are commands that include optional responses. For example, the third item, defun c:corner, causes AutoCAD to start the Fillet command, enter an R⏎ to issue the Radius option, and finally enter a 0 for the fillet radius. Use the Windows Notepad application and copy the listing in Figure 24.11. Give this file the name Keycad.lsp, and be sure you save it as an ASCII file. Then whenever you want to use these macros, you don't have to load each one individually. Instead, you load the Keycad.lsp file the first time you want to use one of the macros, and they're all available for the rest of the session.

After the file is loaded, you can use any of the macros within it just by entering the macro name. For example, entering ptx⏎ will set the point style to the shape of an X.

Macros loaded in this manner will be available to you until you exit AutoCAD. Of course, you can have these macros loaded automatically every time you start AutoCAD by including the Keycad.lsp file in the Startup Suite of the Load/Unload Applications dialog box. That way, you don't have to remember to load it in order to use the macros.

Now that you have some firsthand experience with AutoLISP, I hope these examples will encourage you to try learning more about this powerful tool.

Figure 24.11

The contents of Keycad.lsp

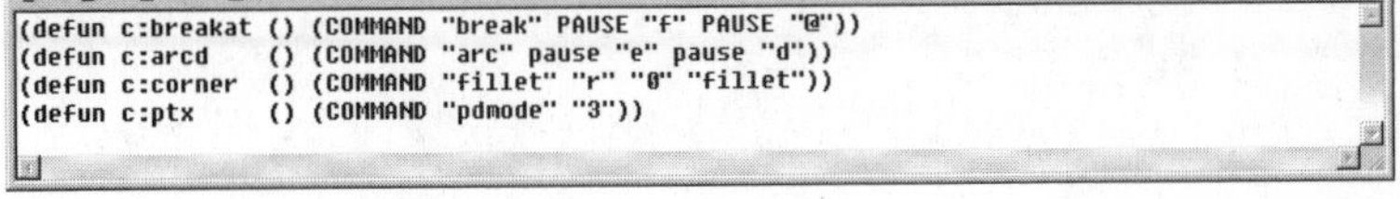

```
Keycad.lsp - Notepad
File  Edit  Search  Help
(defun c:breakat () (COMMAND "break" PAUSE "f" PAUSE "@"))
(defun c:arcd    () (COMMAND "arc" pause "e" pause "d"))
(defun c:corner  () (COMMAND "fillet" "r" "0" "fillet"))
(defun c:ptx     () (COMMAND "pdmode" "3"))
```

If You Want to Experiment

Try to think of some other keyboard macros you would like to create. For example, you might try to create a macro that copies and rotates an object at the same time. This operation is a fairly common one that can be performed using the Grip Edit options, but you can reduce the number of steps needed to copy and rotate by creating a macro. Review the "Creating Keyboard Macros with AutoLISP" section for help.

Here are some hints to get you started:

♦ Use the Copy command to copy an object in place.

♦ Use the same coordinate for the base point and the second point (for example, 0,0).

♦ Use the Last Selection option to rotate the last object selected, which happens to be the original object that was copied.

Chapter 25

Exploring AutoLISP

In the previous chapter, you were introduced to AutoLISP, AutoCAD's macro and programming language. You learned that you can take advantage of this powerful tool without really having to know anything about its internal workings. In this chapter you'll see how you can take more control of AutoLISP and have it do the things you want to do for your own AutoCAD environment. You will learn how to store information such as text and point coordinates, how to create smart macros, and how to optimize AutoLISP's operation on your computer system.

A word of advice as you begin this chapter: be prepared to spend lots of time with your computer—not because programming in AutoLISP is all that difficult, but because it is so addicting! You've already seen how easy it is to use AutoLISP programs. I won't pretend that learning to program in AutoLISP is just as easy as using it, but it really isn't as hard as you might think. And once you've created your first program, you'll be hooked.

Topics in this chapter include the following:

◆ Understanding the Interpreter

◆ Using Arguments and Expressions

◆ Creating a Simple Progam

◆ Selecting Objects with AutoLISP

◆ Controlling the Flow of an AutoLISP Program

◆ Data-Type Conversions

◆ Storing Your Programs as Files

Understanding the Interpreter

You access AutoLISP through the AutoLISP *interpreter*, which is a little like a hand-held calculator. When you enter information at the Command prompt, the interpreter *evaluates* it and then returns an answer. *Evaluating* means performing the instructions described by the information you provide. You could say that evaluation means "find the value of." The information you give the interpreter is like a formula—called an *expression* in AutoLISP.

Let's examine the interpreter's workings in more detail.

1. Start AutoCAD and open a new file called Temp25a. You'll use this file just to experiment with AutoLISP, so don't worry about saving it.

2. At the Command prompt, enter (+ 2 2)↵. The answer, 4, appears on the prompt line. AutoLISP has *evaluated* the formula (+ 2 2) and returned the answer, 4.

By entering information this way, you can perform calculations or even write short programs on the fly.

The plus sign you used in step 2 represents a *function*—an instruction telling the AutoLISP interpreter what to do. In many ways it is like an AutoCAD command. A simple example of a function is the math function, Add, represented by the plus sign. AutoLISP has many built-in functions, and you can create many of your own.

Defining Variables with Setq

Another calculatorlike capability of the interpreter is its ability to remember values. You probably have a calculator that has some memory. This capability allows you to store the value of an equation for future use. In a similar way, the AutoLISP interpreter lets you store values using *variables*.

A variable is like a container that holds a value. That value can change many times in the course of a program's operation. You assign values to variables by using the Setq function. For example, let's assign the numeric value 1.618 to a variable named *Golden*. This value, often referred to as the *golden section*, is the ratio of a rectangular area's height to its width. Aside from having some interesting mathematical properties, the golden section is said to represent a ratio that occurs frequently in nature.

1. At the Command prompt, enter **(setq Golden 1.618)**↵. The value 1.618 appears just below the line you enter. The value of the *Golden* variable is now set to 1.618. Let's check it to make sure.

2. Enter **!Golden**↵ at the Command prompt. As expected, the value 1.618 appears at the prompt.

The exclamation point (!) acts as a special character that extracts the value of an AutoLISP variable at the prompt. From now until you quit AutoCAD, you can access the value of *Golden* at any time, by preceding the variable name with an exclamation point.

In addition to using math formulas as responses to prompts, you can also use values stored as variables. Let's see how we can use the variable *Golden* as the radius for a circle.

1. Click the Circle button on the Draw toolbar.

2. At the Specify center point: prompt, pick a point in the center of your screen.

3. At the **Specify radius of circle or [Diameter]:** prompt, enter **!Golden**↵. A circle appears with the radius of 1.618. Check this using the Properties palette (see Figure 25.1).

FIGURE 25.1

The circle, using the Golden variable as the radius

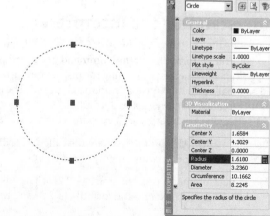

Numbers aren't the only things that can be stored by using Setq. Let's take a look at the variety of other types of data that variables can represent.

Understanding Data Types

WARNING Understanding the various data types and how they differ is important because they can be a source of confusion if not carefully used. Remember that you cannot mix data types in most operations, and quotes and parentheses must always be used in open-and-close pairs.

Variables are divided into several categories called *data types*. Categorizing data into types lets AutoLISP determine precisely how to evaluate the data and keep programs running quickly. Your computer has different ways of storing various types of data, so the use of data types helps AutoLISP communicate with the computer more efficiently. Also, data types aid your programming efforts by forcing you to think of data as having certain characteristics. The following sections describe each of the available data types.

Integers   *Integers* are whole numbers. When a mathematical expression contains only integers, only an integer will be returned. For example, the expression

(/ 2 3)

means two divided by three. (The forward slash is the symbol for the division function.) This expression returns the value 0, because the answer is less than one. Integers are best suited for counting and numbering. The numbers 1, –12, and 144 are all integers.

Real Numbers   *Real numbers,* often referred to as *reals,* are numbers that include decimals. When a mathematical expression contains a real number, a real number will be returned. For example, the expression

(/ 2.0 3)

returns the value 0.66667. Real numbers are best suited in situations that require accuracy. Examples of real numbers are 0.1, 3.14159, and –2.2.

Strings   *Strings* are text values. They are always enclosed in double quotes. Here are some examples of strings: "1", "George", and "Enter a value".

Lists   *Lists* are groups of values enclosed in parentheses. Lists provide a convenient way to store whole sets of values in one variable. There are actually two classes of lists: those meant to be evaluated, and those intended as repositories for data. In the strictest sense, AutoLISP programs are lists, as they are enclosed in parentheses. Here are some examples of lists: (6.0 1.0 0.0), (A B C D), and (setq golden 1.618).

Elements   Finally, there are two basic *elements* in AutoLISP: *atoms* and *lists.* I have already described lists. An atom is an element that cannot be taken apart. Atoms are further grouped into two categories: *numbers* and *symbols.* A number can be a real number or an integer. A symbol, on the other hand, is often a name given to a variable, such as *point1* or *dx2.* As you can see, a symbol can use a number as part of its name; however, its name must always start with a letter. Think of a symbol as a name given to a variable or function as a means of identifying it.

Using Arguments and Expressions

In the previous exercise, you used the Setq function to store variables. The way you used Setq is typical of all functions.

Functions act on *arguments* to accomplish a task. An argument can be a symbol, a number, or a list. A simple example of a function acting on numbers is the addition of 0.618 and 2. In AutoLISP, this function is entered as

```
(+ 0.618 2)
```

which returns the value 2.618.

TIP An expression is actually a list that contains a function and arguments for that function.

This formula—the function followed by the arguments—is called an *expression*. It starts with the left (opening) parenthesis first, then the function, then the arguments, and finally the right (closing) parenthesis.

Arguments can also be expressions, which means you can *nest* expressions. For example, here is how to assign the value returned by 0.618 + 2 to the variable *Golden*:

```
(setq Golden (+ 0.618 2))
```

This is called a *nested expression*. Whenever expressions are nested, the deepest nest is evaluated first, then the next deepest, and so on. In this example, the expression adding 0.618 to 2 is evaluated first. On the next level out, setq assigns the result of the expression (+ 0.168 2) to the variable Golden.

Arguments to functions can also be variables. For example, suppose you use Setq to assign the value 25.4 to a variable called *Mill*. You could then find the result of dividing *Mill* by *Golden*, as follows:

1. Enter **(setq Mill 25.4)**↵ to create a new variable called *Mill*.

2. Next, enter **(/ Mill Golden)**↵. (As mentioned earlier, the forward slash is the symbol for the division function.) This returns the value 15.698393. You can assign this value to yet another variable.

3. Enter **(setq B (/ Mill Golden))**↵ to create a new variable, B. Now you have three variables—*Golden*, *Mill*, and *B*—which are all assigned values that you can later retrieve, either within an AutoCAD command (by entering an ! followed by the variable) or as arguments within an expression.

WATCHING PARENTHESES AND QUOTES

You must remember to close all sets of parentheses when using nested expressions. Take the same care to enter the second quotes in each pair of quotes used to enclose a string.

If you get the prompt showing a parenthesis or set of parentheses followed by the > symbol, for example,

```
(_>
```

you know you have an incomplete AutoLISP expression. This is the AutoLISP prompt. The number of parentheses in the prompt indicates how many parentheses are missing in your expression. If you see this prompt, you must type the closing parenthesis the number of times indicated by the number. AutoCAD will not evaluate an AutoLISP program that has the wrong number of parentheses or quotes.

Using Text Variables with AutoLISP

Our examples so far have shown only numbers being manipulated, but text can also be manipulated in a similar way. Variables can be assigned text strings that can later be used to enter values in commands requiring text input. For text variables, you must enclose text in quotation marks, as in the following example:

```
(setq text1 "This is how text looks in AutoLISP")
```

This example shows a sentence being assigned to the variable *text1*.

Strings can also be *concatenated*, or joined together, to form new strings. Here is an example of how two pieces of text can be added together:

```
(setq text2 (strcat "This is the first part and " "this is the second part"))
```

Here, the AutoLISP function strcat is used to join the two strings. The result is

```
"This is the first part and this is the second part"
```

Strings and numeric values cannot be evaluated together, however. This may seem like a simple rule, but if not carefully considered, it can lead to confusion. For example, it is possible to assign the number 1 to a variable as a text string, by entering

```
(setq foo "1")
```

Later, you might accidentally try to add this string variable to an integer or real number, and AutoCAD will return an error message.

The Setq and the addition and division functions are but three of many functions available to you. AutoLISP offers all the usual math functions, plus many others used to test and manipulate variables. Table 25.1 shows some commonly used math functions.

TABLE 25.1: Math Functions Available in AutoLISP

FUNCTIONS THAT ACCEPT MULTIPLE ARGUMENTS	
Function	**Function**
Add	(+ number number ...)
Subtract	(– number number ...)
Multiply	(* number number ...)
Divide	(/ number number ...)
Find largest number in list	(Max number number ...)
Find smallest number in list	(Min number number ...)
Find the remainder of a division	(Rem number number)

TABLE 25.1: Math Functions Available in AutoLISP *(CONTINUED)*

FUNCTIONS THAT ACCEPT MULTIPLE ARGUMENTS

FUNCTIONS THAT ACCEPT SINGLE ARGUMENTS

Function	Operation
(1 + number)	Add 1 to number
(1 – number)	Subtract 1 from number
(Abs number)	Find the absolute value of number
(Atan angle in radians)	Arc tangent of angle
(Cos angle in radians)	Cosine of angle
(Exp n)	e raised to the nth power
(Expt number n)	Number raised to the nth power
(Gcd integer integer)	Find greatest common denominator
(Log number)	Find natural log of number
(Sin angle in radians)	Sine of angle
(Sqrt number)	Find the square root of number

Storing Points as Variables

Like numeric values, point coordinates can also be stored and retrieved. But since coordinates are actually sets of two or three numeric values, they have to be handled differently. AutoLISP provides the Getpoint function to handle the acquisition of points. Try the following to see how it works.

1. At the Command prompt, enter **(getpoint)**↵. The Command prompt will go blank momentarily.

2. Pick a point near the middle of the screen. In the prompt area, you'll see the coordinate of the point you picked.

Here, Getpoint pauses AutoCAD and waits for you to pick a point. Once you do, it returns the coordinate of the point you pick in the form of a list. The list shows the X, Y, and Z axes enclosed by parentheses.

You can store the coordinates obtained from Getpoint using the Setq function. Try the following to see how this works.

1. Enter **(setq point1 (getpoint))**↵.

2. Pick a point on the screen.

3. Enter **!point1**↵.

Here you stored a coordinate list in a variable called *point1*. You then recalled the contents of *point1* using the !. Notice that the value of the coordinate is in the form of a list with the x, y, and z values appearing as real numbers separated by spaces, instead of the commas you've been used to.

Creating a Simple Program

So far, you have learned how to use AutoLISP to do some simple math and to store values as variables. Certainly, AutoLISP has enormous value with these capabilities alone, but you can do a good deal more. In this section, you'll examine how to combine these three capabilities—math calculations, variables, and lists—to write a simple program for drawing a rectangle.

1. Press F2 to flip to a text display.

2. At the Command prompt, enter **(defun c:rec ()**↵. You will get a new prompt that looks like this:

   (_>

   This is the AutoLISP prompt. It tells you, among other things, that you are in the AutoLISP interpreter. While you see this prompt, you can enter instructions to AutoLISP. You will automatically exit the interpreter when you have finished entering the program. A program is considered complete when you've entered the last parenthesis, thereby balancing all the parentheses in your program.

WARNING   While you're entering lines in AutoLISP, you cannot go back to change a line once you press ↵.

3. Now, very carefully, enter the following several lines. If you make a mistake while typing a line, back up using Backspace and retype the line. Once you press ↵, you cannot go back to fix a line. Each time you enter a line and press ↵, you will see the AutoLISP prompt appear.

TIP   AutoLISP is not *case sensitive*. It doesn't matter if you type entries in upper- or lowercase letters. They will work either way. The only time you must be careful with upper- and lowercase is when you use string data types.

```
(setq Pt1 (getpoint "Pick first corner point:" ))↵
(setq Pt3 (getpoint "Pick opposite corner:" ))↵
(setq Pt2 (list (nth 0 Pt3) (nth 1 Pt1)))↵
(setq Pt4 (list (nth 0 Pt1) (nth 1 Pt3)))↵
(command "Pline" Pt1 Pt2 Pt3 Pt4 "C")↵
) ↵
```

Once you enter the last parenthesis, you return to the standard AutoCAD Command prompt.

4. Check the lines you entered against the listing in step 3, and make sure you entered everything correctly. If you find you made a mistake, start over from the beginning and reenter the program.

TIP   You can use AutoLISP programs transparently, as long as the program doesn't contain an embedded AutoCAD command.

When you are done, you get the message C:REC. This confirms that you have the rectangle drawing program stored in memory. Let's see it in action.

1. Enter **Rec.⏎** at the Command prompt.

2. At the Pick first corner point: prompt, pick a point at coordinate 1,1.

3. At the Pick opposite corner: prompt, pick a point at 6,4. A box appears between the two points you picked (see Figure 25.2).

Dissecting the Rectangle Program

The Rectangle drawing program incorporates all the things you've learned so far. Let's see exactly how it works. First, it finds the two corner coordinates of a rectangle, which it gets from you as input, and then extracts parts of those coordinates to derive the coordinates for the other two corners of the rectangle. Once it knows all four coordinates, the program can draw the lines connecting them. Figure 25.3 illustrates what the Rectangle program does. Next, we'll look at the program in more detail.

FIGURE 25.2
Using the rectangle drawing program

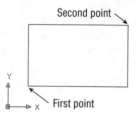

GETTING INPUT FROM THE USER

In the foregoing exercise, you started out with the line

```
(defun c:rec ()
```

You may recall from Chapter 24 that the defun function lets you create commands. The name that follows the defun function is the name of the command as you enter it through the keyboard. The c: tells AutoLISP to make this program act like a command. If the c: is omitted, you would have to enter (rec) to view the program. The set of empty parentheses is for an argument list, which I'll discuss later.

In the next line, the variable *Pt1* is assigned a value for a point you enter using your cursor. Getpoint is the AutoLISP function that pauses the AutoLISP program and allows you to pick a point using your cursor or to enter a coordinate. Once a point is entered, Getpoint returns the coordinate of that point as a list.

Immediately following Getpoint is a line that reads

```
"Pick first corner point:"
```

Getpoint allows you to add a prompt in the form of text. You may recall that when you first used Getpoint, it caused the prompt to go blank. Instead of a blank, you can use text as an argument to the Getpoint function to display a prompt describing what action to take.

FIGURE 25.3

The Rectangle program draws a rectangle by getting two corner points of the rectangle from you and then recombining coordinates from those two points to find the other two points of the rectangle.

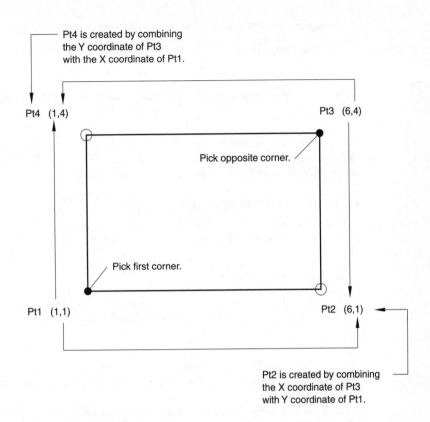

Pt4 is created by combining the Y coordinate of Pt3 with the X coordinate of Pt1.

Pt4 (1,4)   Pt3 (6,4)

Pick opposite corner.

Pick first corner.

Pt1 (1,1)   Pt2 (6,1)

Pt2 is created by combining the X coordinate of Pt3 with Y coordinate of Pt1.

The third line is similar to the second. It uses Getpoint to get the location of another point and then assigns that point to the variable *Pt3*:

```
(setq Pt3 (getpoint "Pick opposite corner:" ))
```

Once AutoLISP has the two corners, it has all the information it needs to find the other two corners of the rectangle.

TAKING APART LISTS

The next thing AutoLISP must do is take *Pt1* and *Pt3* apart to extract their X and Y coordinates and then reassemble those coordinates to get the other corner coordinates. AutoLISP must take the X coordinate from *Pt3*, and the Y coordinate from *Pt1*, to get the coordinate for the lower-right corner of the rectangle (see Figure 25.3). To do this, you use two new functions: Nth and List.

Nth extracts a single element from a list. Since coordinates are lists, Nth can be used to extract an x, y, or z component from a coordinate list. In the fourth line of the program, you see

```
(nth 0 Pt3)
```

Here the zero immediately following the Nth function tells Nth to take element number 0 from the coordinate stored as *Pt3*. Nth starts counting from 0 rather than 1, so the first element of *Pt3* is considered item number 0. This is the x component of the coordinate stored as *Pt3*.

To see firsthand how Nth works, try the following:

1. Enter **!point1.↵**. You see the coordinate list you created earlier using Getpoint.

2. Enter **(nth 0 point1).↵**. You get the first element of the coordinate represented by point1.

Immediately following the first Nth expression is another Nth expression similar to the previous one:

```
(nth 1 Pt1)
```

Here, Nth extracts element number 1, the second element, from the coordinate stored as *Pt1*. This is the y component of the coordinate stored as *Pt1*. If you like, try the previous exercise again, but this time, enter **(nth 1 point1)** and see what value you get.

COMBINING ELEMENTS INTO A LIST

AutoLISP has extracted the x component from *Pt3* and the y component of *Pt1*. They must now be joined together into a new list. This is where the List function comes in. The List expression looks like this:

```
(list (nth 0 pt3) (nth 1 pt1))
```

You know that the first Nth expression extracts an x component and that the second extracts a y component, so the expression can be simplified to look like this:

```
(list X Y)
```

Here X is the value derived from the first Nth expression, and Y is the value derived from the second Nth expression. The List function simply recombines its arguments into another list, in this case another coordinate list.

Finally, the outermost function of the expression uses Setq to create a new variable called *Pt2*, which is the new coordinate list derived from the *List* function. The following is a schematic version of the fourth line of the Rectangle program, so you can see what is going on more clearly.

```
(setq pt2 (list X Y))
```

You can see that *Pt2* is a coordinate list derived from combining the X component from *Pt3* and the Y component from *Pt1*.

Try the following exercise to see how List works.

1. Enter **(list 5 6).↵**. You see the list (5 6) appear in the prompt.

2. Enter **(list (nth 0 point1) (nth 1 point1)).↵**. You see the X and Y coordinates of point1 in a list, excluding the Z coordinate.

The fifth line is similar to the fourth. It creates a new coordinate list using the X value from *Pt1* and the Y value from *Pt2*:

```
(setq Pt4 (list (nth 0 Pt1) (nth 1 Pt3)))
```

The last line tells AutoCAD to draw a polyline through the four points to create a box:

```
(command "Pline" Pt1 Pt2 Pt3 Pt4 "c")
```

The Command function issues the Pline command and then inputs the variables *Pt1* through *Pt4*. Finally, it enters **c** to close the polyline. Note that within this expression, keystroke entries, such as "Pline" and "C", are enclosed in quotes,

GETTING OTHER INPUT FROM THE USER

In your Rectangle program, you were able to prompt the user to pick some points by using the Getpoint function. Several other functions allow you to pause for input and instruct the user what to do. Nearly all these functions begin with the Get prefix.

Table 25.2 shows a list of these Get functions. They accept single values or, in the case of points, a list of two values.

In Getstring, string values are case sensitive. This means that if you enter a lowercase letter in response to Getstring, it will be saved as a lowercase letter; uppercase letters will be saved as uppercase letters. You can enter numbers in response to the Getstring function, but they will be saved as strings and cannot be used in mathematical operations. Also, AutoLISP will automatically add quotes to string values it returns, so you don't have to enter any.

TABLE 25.2: Functions That Pause to Allow Input

FUNCTION	DESCRIPTION
Getint	Allows entry of integer values
Getreal	Allows entry of real values
Getstring	Allows entry of string or text values
Getkword	Allows filtering of string entries through a list of keywords
Getangle	Allows keyboard or mouse entry of angles based on the standard AutoCAD compass points (returns values in radians)
Getorient	Allows keyboard or mouse entry of angles based on Units command setting for angles (returns values in radians)
Getdist	Allows keyboard or mouse entry of distances (always returns values as real numbers, regardless of unit format used)
Getpoint	Allows keyboard or mouse entry of point values (returns values as coordinate lists)
Getcorner	Allows selection of a point by using a window*
Initget	Allows definition of a set of keywords for the Getword function; keywords are strings, as in (initget " Yes No ")

This function requires a base point value as a first argument. This base point defines the first corner of the window. A window appears, allowing you to select the opposite corner.

Just as with Getpoint, all these Get functions allow you to create a prompt by following the function with the prompt enclosed by quotation marks, as in the expression

```
(getpoint "Pick the next point:" )
```

This expression displays the prompt Pick the next point: while AutoCAD waits for your input.

The functions Getangle, Getorient, Getdist, Getcorner, and Getpoint allow you to specify a point from which the angle, distance, or point is to be measured, as in the expression

```
(getangle Pt1 "Pick the next point:" )
```

in which *Pt1* is a previously defined point variable. A rubber-banding line appears from the coordinate defined by *Pt1* (see Figure 25.4).

Once you pick a point, the angle defined by *Pt1* and the point you pick are returned in radians. You can also enter a relative coordinate through the keyboard in the unit system currently being used in your drawing. Getangle and Getdist prompt you for two points if a point variable is not provided. Getcorner always requires a point argument and will generate a window rather than a rubber-banding line (see Figure 25.5).

Selecting Objects with AutoLISP

You can easily create an AutoLISP expression that lets you select a single object and perform some operation on it. Here is an example of a macro that rotates an object 90°:

```
(defun c:r90 () (command "rotate" pause "" pause "90"))
```

In this example, the pause after "rotate" allows you to make a selection. The double quotes that follow act like an ↵, and then another pause allows you to select a rotation point. Finally, a 90 is supplied to tell the Rotate command to rotate your selection 90.

If you load this macro into AutoCAD and run it, you are prompted to select an object. You are then immediately prompted to pick a point for the rotation center. You won't be allowed to continue to select other objects the way you can with most AutoCAD commands.

But what if you want that macro to allow you to make several selections instead of just one? At this point, you almost know enough to create a program to do just that. The only part missing is Ssget.

FIGURE 25.4
Using Getangle

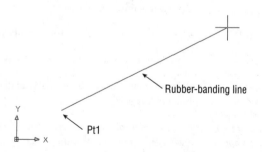

Rubber-banding line

Pt1

FIGURE 25.5
Using Getcorner

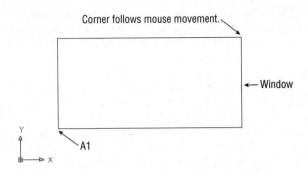

The *Ssget* Function

So far, you know you can assign numbers, text, and coordinates to variables. Ssget is a function that assigns a set of objects to a variable, as demonstrated in the following exercise:

1. Draw a few random lines on the screen.

2. Enter **(setq ss1 (ssget))**↵.

3. At the Select objects: prompt, select the lines using any standard selection method. Notice that you can select objects just as you would at any object-selection prompt.

4. When you are done selecting objects, press ↵. You get the message <Selection set: n> in which n is an alphanumeric value that identifies the selection set.

5. Start the Move command, and at the object-selection prompt, enter **!ss1**↵. The lines you selected previously will be highlighted.

6. Press ↵, and then pick two points to finish the Move command.

In this exercise, you stored a selection set as the variable *ss1*. You can recall this selection set from the Command prompt, using the !, just as you did with other variables.

USING *SSGET* IN AN EXPRESSION

You can also use the *ss1* variable in an AutoLISP expression. For example, the R90 macro in the next exercise lets you select several objects to be rotated 90°:

1. Enter **(defun c:r90 (/ ss1)**↵. The AutoLISP prompt appears.

2. To complete the macro, enter

   ```
   (setq ss1 (ssget))(command "rotate" ss1 "" pause "90"))
   ```

   and press ↵.

3. Enter **r90**↵ to start the macro.

4. At the Select objects: prompt, select a few of the random lines you drew earlier.

5. Press ↵ to confirm your selection, and then pick a point near the center of the screen. The lines you selected rotate 90°.

The defun function tells AutoLISP this is to be a command called r90. A list follows the name of the macro—it's called an *argument list*. We'll look at argument lists a bit later in this chapter.

Following the argument list is the (setq ss1 (ssget)) expression you used in the previous exercise. This is where the new macro stops and asks you to select a set of objects to later be applied to the Rotate command.

The next expression uses the Command function. Command lets you include standard AutoCAD command line input within an AutoLISP program. In this case, the input starts by issuing the Rotate command. It then applies the selection set stored by ss1 to the Rotate command's object-selection prompt. Next, the two " "marks indicate an ↵. The pause lets the user select a base point for the rotation. Finally, the value of 90 is applied to the Rotate command's angle prompt. The entire expression when entered at the Command prompt might look like the following:

```
Command: Rotate↵
Select objects:!ss1↵
Select objects:↵
Specify base point: (pause for input)
Specify rotation angle or [Copy/Reference] <0>: 90↵
```

In this macro, the Ssget function adds flexibility by allowing the user to select as many objects as desired. (You could use the Pause function in place of the variable *ss1*, but with Pause, you cannot anticipate whether the user will use a window, pick points, or select a previous selection set.)

CONTROLLING MEMORY CONSUMPTION WITH LOCAL VARIABLES

Selection sets are memory hogs in AutoLISP. If you create too many of them, you will end up draining AutoLISP's memory reserves. To limit the memory used by selection sets, you can turn them into *local variables*. Local variables are variables that exist only while the program is executing its instructions. Once the program is finished, local variables are discarded.

The vehicle for making variables local is the *argument list*. Let's look again at the set of empty parentheses that immediately follow the program name in the Rectangle program:

```
(defun c:rec () ...)
```

If you include a list of variables between those parentheses, those variables become local. In the new R90 macro you just looked at, the *ss1* selection set variable is a local variable:

WARNING The space after the / in the argument list is very important. Your macro will not work properly without it.

```
(defun c:r90 (/ ss1)...)
```

Notice that the argument list starts with a forward slash, then a space, followed by the list of variables. Once the R90 program is done with its work, any memory assigned to *ss1* can be recovered.

Sometimes you will want a variable to be accessible at all times by all AutoLISP programs. Such variables are known as *global variables*. You can use global variables to store information in the current editing session. You could even store a few selection sets as global variables. To control memory consumption, however, use global variables sparingly.

Controlling the Flow of an AutoLISP Program

A typical task for a program is to execute one function or another depending on some existing condition. This type of operation is often called an *if-then-else conditional statement:* "If a condition is met, then perform computation A, else perform computation B." AutoLISP offers the If function to facilitate this type of operation.

Using the *If* Function

TIP   A common use for the if-then-else statement is to direct the flow of a program in response to a user's Yes or No reply to a prompt. If the user responds with a Yes to the prompt Do you want to continue?, for example, that response can be used in the if-then-else statement to direct the program to go ahead and perform some function, such as erasing objects or drawing a box.

The If function requires two arguments. The first argument must be a value that returns a True or a False—in the case of AutoLISP, *T* for true or *nil* for false. It is like saying "If True then do A." Optionally, you can supply a third argument, which is the action to take if the value returned is nil. ("If True then do A, else do B.")

Here is an example of an If expression:

```
(if Exst (+ a b) (* a b))
```

Here, the value of the *Exst* variable determines which of the two following expressions is evaluated. If *Exst* has a value, it returns T for true; that is, when AutoLISP evaluates *Exst*, the value returned is T. The expression then evaluates the second argument, (+ a b), which is itself an expression. If *Exst* does not have a value or is nil, the expression evaluates the third argument, (* a b).

Several special AutoLISP functions test variables for specific conditions. For example, you can test a number to see if it is equal to, less than, or greater than another number, as in the following:

```
(if (= A B) (+ A B) (* A B))
```

In this expression, if A is equal to B, the second argument is evaluated:

```
(if (> A B) (+ A B) (* A B))
```

In this expression, if A is greater than B, the second argument is evaluated.

The functions that test for T or nil are called *predicates* and *logical operators*. Table 25.3 shows a list of these functions.

TABLE 25.3:   A List of Predicates and Logical Operators

FUNCTION	RETURNS T (TRUE) IF
<	One numeric value is less than another
>	One numeric value is greater than another
<=	One numeric value is less than or equal to another
>=	One numeric value is greater than or equal to another

TABLE 25.3: A List of Predicates and Logical Operators *(CONTINUED)*

FUNCTION	RETURNS T (TRUE) IF
=	Two numeric or string values are equal
/=	Two numeric or string values are not equal
eq	Two values are exactly the same
equal	Two values are the same (approximate)
atom	A symbol represents an atom (as opposed to a list)
listp	A symbol represents a list
minusp	A numeric value is negative
numberp	A symbol is a number, real or integer
zerop	A symbol evaluates to zero
and	All of several expressions or atoms return non-nil
not	A symbol is nil
nul	A list is nil
or	One of several expressions or atoms returns non-nil

Let's see how conditional statements, predicates, and logical operators work together. Suppose you want to write a program that either multiplies two numbers or simply adds the numbers together. You want the program to ask the user which action to take depending on which of the two values is greater.

1. Enter the following program at the Command prompt, just as you did for the Rectangle program.

```
(defun c:mul-add ()↵
(setq A (getreal "Enter first number:" ))↵
(setq B (getreal "Enter second number:" ))↵
(if (< A B) (+ a b) (* a b))↵
)↵
```

2. Now run the program by entering **Mul-add**↵.

3. At the Enter first number: prompt, enter **3**↵.

4. At the Enter second number: prompt, enter **4**↵. The value 7.0 is returned.

5. Try running this program again, but this time enter **4** at the first prompt and **3** at the second prompt. This time, you get the returned value 12.0.

In this program, the first two Setq expressions get two numbers from you. The conditional statement that follows, (< A B), tests to see if the first number you entered is less than the second. If this predicate function returns T for true, (+ a b) is evaluated. If it returns nil for false, (* a b) is evaluated.

You will often find that you need to perform not just one, but several steps depending on some condition. Here is a more complex If expression that evaluates several expressions at once:

```
(if (= A B) (progn (* A B)(+ A B)(- A B) ))
```

In this example, the function Progn tells the If function that several expressions are to be evaluated if (= A B) returns True.

Repeating an Expression

Sometimes you will want your program to repeatedly evaluate a set of expressions until a particular condition is met. If you are familiar with BASIC or Fortran, you know this function as a *loop*.

You can repeat steps in an AutoLISP program by using the While function in conjunction with predicates and logical operators. Like the If function, While's first argument must be one that returns a T or nil. You can have as many other arguments to the While function as you like, just as long as the first argument is a predicate function.

```
(while test (expression 1) (expression 2) (expression 3)...)
```

The While function isn't the only one that will repeat a set of instructions. The Repeat function causes a set of instructions to be executed several times, but unlike While, Repeat requires an integer value for its first argument, as in the following:

```
(Repeat 14 (expression 1)(expression 2)(expression 3)...)
```

In this example, Repeat will evaluate each expression 14 times.

A third function, Foreach, evaluates an expression for each element of a list. The arguments to Foreach are first a variable, then a list whose elements are to be evaluated, and then the expression used to evaluate each element of the list.

```
(foreach var1 ( list1 ) (expression var1))
```

Foreach is a bit more difficult to understand at first, since it involves a variable, a list, and an expression, all working together.

Using Other Built-in Functions

TIP   In many of the examples in this section, you'll see numeric values or lists as arguments. As in all AutoLISP functions, you can use variables as arguments, as long as the variable's value is of the proper data type.

At this point, you have seen several useful programs created with just a handful of AutoLISP functions. Although I can't give you a tutorial showing you how to use every available AutoLISP function, in this final section I'll demonstrate a few more. This is far from a complete list, but it should be enough to get you well on your way to making AutoLISP work for you. Experiment with the functions at your leisure—but remember, using AutoLISP can be addicting!

GEOMETRIC OPERATIONS

These functions are useful for manipulating geometric data. (And don't forget the Get functions listed earlier, in Table 25.2.)

TIP Notice that in some examples an apostrophe precedes a list. This apostrophe tells AutoLISP not to evaluate the list, but to treat it as a repository of data.

Angle Finds the angle between two points, and returns a value in radians. For example,

```
(angle '(6.0 4.0 0.0) '(6.0 5.0 0.0))
```

returns 1.57. This example uses two coordinate lists for arguments, but point variables can also be used.

Distance Finds the distance between two points. The value returned is in base units. Just like Angle, Distance requires two coordinates as arguments. This expression

```
(distance '(6.0 4.0 0.0) '(6.0 5.0 0.0))
```

returns 1.0.

Polar Returns a point in the form of a coordinate list based on the location of a point, an angle, and a distance. This expression

```
(polar '(1.0 1.0 0.0) 1.5708 1.0)
```

returns (0.999996 2.0 0.0). The first argument is a coordinate list; the second is an angle in radians; and the third is a distance in base units. The point must be a coordinate list.

Inters Returns the intersection point of two vectors, with each vector described by two points. The points must be in this order: the first two points define the first vector, and the second two points define the second vector. This expression

```
(inters
'(1.0 4.0 0.0)'(8.0 4.0 0.0)'(5.0 2.0 0.0)'(5.0 9.0 0.0)
)
```

returns (5.0 4.0 0.0). If the intersection point does not lie between either of the two vectors, you can still obtain a point, provided you include a non-nil fifth argument.

STRING OPERATIONS

These functions allow you to manipulate strings. Though you cannot supply strings to the text command directly, you can use the Command function with string variables to enter text, as in the following:

```
(Setq note "This is a test.")
(command "text" (getpoint) "2.0" "0" note)
[This second line does not evaluate properly.  It returns:

Command: (command "text" point "2.0" "0" note )
dtext
Current text style:  "Standard"  Text height:  2.0000
Specify start point of text or [Justify/Style]:
Command: 2.0 Unknown command "2.0".  Press F1 for help.
```

```
Command: 0 Unknown command "0".  Press F1 for help.

Command: This is a test. Unknown command "THIS IS A TEST.".  Press F1 for help.
```

In this example, note is first assigned a string value. Then the command function is used to issue the Text command and place the text in the drawing. Notice the (getpoint) function included to obtain a point location.

Substr   Returns a portion of a string, called a *substring*, beginning at a specified location. This expression

```
(substr "string" 3 4)
```

returns *ring*. The first argument is the string containing the substring to be extracted. The second argument, 3, tells Substr where to begin the new string; this value must be an integer. The third argument, 4, is optional and tells Substr how long the new string should be. Length must also be an integer.

Strcat   Combines several strings, and the result is a string. This expression

```
(strcat string1  string2  etc.…)
```

returns *string1 string2 etc.* In this example, the

```
etc.…
```

indicates you can have as many string values as you want.

Data-Type Conversions

TIP   The Angtos and Rtos functions are especially useful for converting radians to any of the standard angle formats available in AutoCAD. For example, using Angtos you can convert 0.785398 radians to 45d0´ 0˝, or N 45d0´0˝E. Using Rtos you can convert the distance value of 42 to 42.00 or 3´-6˝ (three feet six inches). Be aware that Angtos and Rtos also convert numeric data into strings.

While using AutoLISP, you will often have to convert values from one data type to another. For example, since most angles in AutoLISP must be represented in radians, you must convert them to degrees before you can use them in commands. You can do so using the Angtos function. Angtos will convert a real number representing an angle in radians into a string in the degree format you desire. The following example converts an angle of 1.57 radians into surveyor's units with a precision of four decimal places:

```
(angtos 1.57 4 4)
```

This expression returns N 0d2′44″ E. The first argument is the angle in radians; the second argument is a code that tells AutoLISP which format to convert the angle to; and the third argument tells AutoLISP the degree of precision desired. (The third argument is optional.) The conversion codes for Angtos are as follows:

0 = degrees

1 = degrees/minutes/seconds

2 = grads

3 = radians

4 = surveyor's units

Now that you've seen an example of what the Angtos data-type conversion can do, let's briefly look at other similar functions.

Atof and Atoi Atof converts a string to a real number. This expression

```
(atof "33.334")
```

returns 33.334.

Atoi converts a string to an integer. This expression

```
(atoi "33.334")
```

returns 33.

Itoa and Rtos Itoa converts an integer into a string. The argument must be an integer. This expression

```
(itoa 24)
```

returns 24.

Rtos converts a real number to a string. As with Angtos, a format code and precision value is specified. This expression

```
(rtos 32.3 4 2)
```

returns "2´-8 1/4 \""

NOTE You may notice the \ just after the 1/4 in the returned value. This is an Autolisp symbol that indicates that the following ˝ symbol is part of the string text and not the closing ˝ that indicates the end of the string.

The first argument is the value to be converted; the second argument is the conversion code; and the third argument is the precision value. The codes are as follows:

1 = scientific

2 = decimal

3 = engineering

4 = architectural

5 = fractional

Fix and Float Fix converts a real number into an integer. This expression

```
(fix 3.3334)
```

returns 3.

Float converts an integer into a real number. This expression

    (float 3)

returns 3.0.

Storing Your Programs as Files

When you exit AutoCAD, the Rectangle program will vanish. But just as you were able to save the keyboard shortcuts in Chapter 24, you can create a text file on a disk containing the Rectangle program. That way you will have ready access to it at all times.

To save your programs, open a text editor and enter them through the keyboard just as you entered the Rectangle program, including the first line that contains the defun function. Be sure you save the file with the .LSP filename extension. You can recall your program by choosing Tools ➢ Load Applications, which opens the Load/Unload Applications dialog box.

If you prefer, you can use the manual method for loading AutoLISP programs. This involves the Load AutoLISP function. Just as with all other functions, it is enclosed by parentheses. In Chapter 24, you loaded the GETAREA.LSP file using the Load/Unload Applications dialog box. To use the Load function, instead, to load GETAREA.LSP, you enter the following:

    (Load "getarea")

Load is perhaps one of the simpler AutoLISP functions, since it requires only one argument: the name of the AutoLISP file you want to load. Notice that you do not have to include the .LSP extension.

If the AutoLISP file resides in a folder that isn't in the current path, you need to include the path in the filename, as in the following:

    (Load "C:/AutoCAD2007/Projects/Chapter 24 /getarea")

Notice that the / is used to indicate folders instead of the usual Windows \. The forward slash is used because the backslash has special meaning to AutoLISP in a string value. It tells AutoLISP that a special character follows. If you attempted to use \ in the above example, you would get an error message.

As you might guess, the Load function can be a part of an AutoLISP program. It can also be included as part of a menu to load specific programs whenever you select a menu item. You'll learn more about customizing the menu in the next chapter.

If You Want to Experiment

I hope that you will be enticed into trying some programming on your own and learning more about AutoLISP. For a more detailed look, see The ABCs of AutoLISP on the companion CD. You can also find a wealth of information in the AutoCAD Help window:

1. Choose Help ➢ Additional Resources ➢ Developer Help. The AutoCAD 2007 Developer Help window opens.

2. In the panel on the left, expand the AutoLISP reference listing. You'll see an alphabetic listing of the AutoLISP functions, some of which were discussed in this chapter.

As you work with AutoLISP material in the AutoCAD Help window, you will also see references to Visual LISP. This is a self-contained programming environment for AutoLISP similar to the Visual Basic editor. Visual LISP is an excellent tool if you intend to make extensive use of AutoLISP in your work. Once you understand the basics of AutoLISP, you might want to explore Visual LISP through the tutorial in the AutoCAD Help system. You can find the Visual LISP tutorial by choosing Help ➢ Additional Resources ➢ Developer Help. In the AutoCAD 2007 Help: Developer Documentation window, look under the AutoLISP Tutorial section.

Chapter 26

Customizing Toolbars, Menus, Linetypes, and Hatch Patterns

AutoCAD offers a high degree of flexibility and customization, enabling you to tailor the software's look and feel to your requirements. In this chapter, you will see how to customize AutoCAD so that it integrates more smoothly into your workgroup and office environment.

The first part of the chapter shows how to adapt AutoCAD to fit your particular needs. You will learn how to customize AutoCAD by modifying its menus, and you'll learn how to create custom macros for commands that your workgroup uses frequently.

You'll then take a look at some general issues that arise when you use AutoCAD in an office. In this discussion you might find help with some problems you have encountered when using AutoCAD in your particular work environment. I'll also discuss how to manage AutoCAD projects.

Topics in this chapter include the following:

◆ Using Workspaces

◆ Getting Familiar with the Custom User Interface

◆ Creating Macros in Tools and Menus

◆ Editing Keyboard Shortcuts

◆ Saving, Loading, and Unloading Your Customizations

◆ Understanding the Diesel Macro Language

◆ Creating Custom Linetypes

◆ Creating Hatch Patterns

Using Workspaces

Once you're comfortable with AutoCAD, you may find that you like a certain arrangement of toolbars and palettes or that you have several sets of toolbars that you like to use depending on your type of work. You've already worked with the two workspaces AutoCAD offers out of the box: 3D Modeling and AutoCAD Classic. You can also set up your own custom toolbar arrangements and then save those arrangements for later retrieval using the Workspace feature. Let's take a closer look at how you can customize this feature.

The Workspaces toolbar appears, as shown in Figure 26.1. AutoCAD users will see the Workspaces toobar in its docked position in the upper-left corner of the AutoCAD Window, and LT users will see the floating version. In Chapter 1, you saw how you can use this toolbar to save your AutoCAD window layout. You can save multiple arrangements of toolbars and palettes and then recall them easily by selecting them from the Workspaces toolbar drop-down menu.

FIGURE 26.1

The Workspaces
toolbar

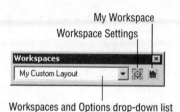

My Workspace

Workspace Settings

Workspaces and Options drop-down list

TIP If you don't have your Workspaces toolbar open already, right-click any toolbar, and then select Workspaces from the shortcut menu.

Click the Workspace Settings tool in the Workspaces toolbar to open the Workspace Settings dialog box, as shown in Figure 26.2.

FIGURE 26.2

The Workspace
Settings dialog box

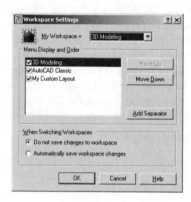

Let's take a moment to look at this dialog box in detail. In Chapter 1, you created a workspace called My Custom Layout by using the Save Current As option in the Workspaces toolbar drop-down list.

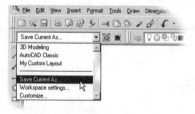

With the Workspace Settings dialog box open, you can see the AutoCAD Classic, 3D Modeling, and the My Custom Layout settings. From here, you can control the behavior of the settings.

The check box next to each setting lets you control whether the item appears in the drop-down list of the Workspaces toolbar. For example, if you remove the check from the My Custom Layout setting, you will only see 3D Modeling and AutoCAD Classic in the drop-down list of the Workspaces toolbar.

The My Workspace = drop-down list lets you select which workspace setting is activated when you click the My Workspace tool in the Workspaces toolbar. You can use this option for your most frequently used workspace settings.

The options in the When Switching Workspaces group at the bottom of the Workspace Settings dialog box let you determine whether workspace changes are saved automatically. For example, if you select Automatically Save Workspace Changes, the next time you switch to a different workspace setting, AutoCAD will save any changes you've made to the current workspace.

The Workspaces toolbar is the easiest customization feature you'll find in AutoCAD, and it can go a long way to help you stay organized. But workspaces are really just the tip of the iceberg when it comes to customizing AutoCAD. In the next section, you'll delve into the *Custom User Interface* feature, or CUI for short, to see how you can customize the AutoCAD menus and toolbars directly.

Getting Familiar with the Custom User Interface

Out of the box, AutoCAD offers a generic arrangement of toolbars, tools, and palettes that works fine for most applications. But the more you use AutoCAD, the more you may find that you tend to use tools that are scattered over several toolbars. You'll probably feel that your work would go easier if you could create a custom set of toolbars and menus to consolidate those tools. If you're to the point of creating custom macros, you might want a way to have easy access to them.

The Customize User Interface is a one-stop location that gives you nearly total control over the menus and toolbars in AutoCAD. With the CUI feature, you can mold the AutoCAD interface to your liking. The main entry point to the CUI is the Customize User Interface dialog box.

The following section introduces you to the CUI by showing you how to add a tool to the Draw toolbar. You'll also get a chance to see how to create an entirely new toolbar and custom tools.

Taking a Quick Customization Tour

The most direct way to adapt AutoCAD to your way of working is to customize the toolbars. AutoCAD offers new users an easy route to customization through the Custom User Interface dialog box. With this dialog box, you can create new toolbars, customize tools, and even create new icons. You can also create keyboard shortcuts.

To get your feet wet, try adding a tool to the Draw toolbar.

1. If it's still open, close the Workspace Settings dialog box.

2. Right-click the Draw toolbar, and then select Customize toward the bottom of the shortcut menu to open the Customize User Interface dialog box, as shown in Figure 26.3. You see four groups in this dialog box: Customizations In All CUI Files, Command List, Preview, and Properties. Notice that you see a view of the Draw toolbar in the Preview group. You also see a list of tools in the Draw toolbar in the Customizations In All CUI Files group.

3. In the Command List group, scroll down the list and locate and select Linear. This is the Linear Dimension command. Notice that when you select Linear, the Properties group displays the properties of the Linear command. The Preview group changes to show the Button Image group, and you see the Linear Dimension icon, as shown in Figure 26.4.

4. Click and drag the Linear listing in the Command List group into the Customizations In All CUI files group, but don't release the mouse button quite yet. As you drag the listing over the tool names in the Customizations In All CUI Files group, you see a bar that tells you where your dragged item will appear.

FIGURE 26.3
The Customize User Interface dialog box

FIGURE 26.4
The Button Image and Preview groups change when you select an element from the Command List group or the Customizations In All CUI Files group.

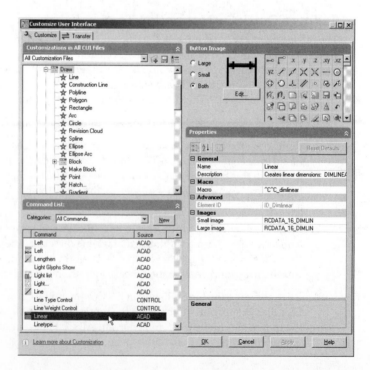

5. Place the bar just below Region and release the mouse button. Linear appears below Region in the list.

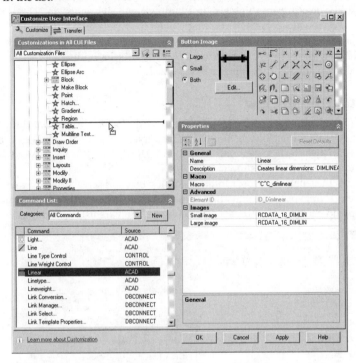

6. Click OK. You'll see some disk activity, and in a moment the Linear tool appears in the Draw toolbar just below the Region tool.

You've just added a command to the Draw toolbar. You can follow these steps to add any command to any toolbar.

Now suppose you've changed you mind and you decide to remove Linear from the Draw toolbar. Here's how it's done:

1. Right-click the Draw toolbar and choose Customize from the shortcut menu.

2. In the Customizations In All CUI Files group of the Customize User Interface dialog box, right-click Linear and choose Delete from the shortcut menu. A warning message appears, asking you if you really want to delete this element.

3. Click Yes.

4. Click OK to close the dialog box.

Now Linear has been removed from the Draw toolbar. As you have just seen, adding tools to a toolbar is a matter of clicking and dragging the appropriate item from one list to another. Deleting a tool is just like deleting anything else in Windows: you right-click and choose Delete.

Before you go too much further, you might want to know a little more about the Customize User Interface dialog box and how it works. You saw briefly how each group displayed different elements of AutoCAD's interface from a listing of toolbar tools to the individual tool's icon. Let's take a look at each group independently to see how it's organized.

Getting the Overall View

When you first opened the Customize User Interface dialog box by right-clicking the Draw toolbar, you saw the Draw toolbar tools listed in the Customizations In All CUI Files group. This group actually lists all the interface elements of AutoCAD, but since you were asked to right-click the Draw menu, that was the one shown.

If you open the Customize User Interface dialog box and scroll down in the Customizations In All CUI Files group, you'll see that all the AutoCAD toolbars are listed. You can see this better by scrolling up and clicking the minus sign next to the Toolbars listing to minimize it.

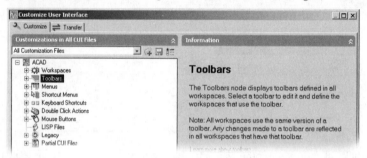

Scroll farther down, and you will also see a menu listing. If you expand this list, you'll see the menus in the menu bar.

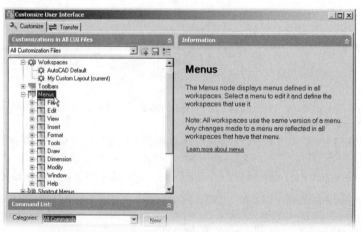

Scroll to the top and you'll see the Workspace settings. Table 26.1 lists all the main items and what they contain.

TABLE 26.1:   The Main Headings in the Customization In All CUI Files Group

ITEM	WHAT IT CONTAINS
Workspaces	The available workspaces currently available
Toolbars	The current toolbars
Menus	The current menubar menus
Shortcut Menus	The menus shown with right-clicks
Keyboard Shortcuts	The current keyboard shortcuts such as Ctrl+C and Ctrl+V
Double-Click Actions	Object dependent double-click action.
Mouse Buttons	The mouse button options such as Shift+click and Ctrl+click
LISP Files	Any custom LISP files that are used with your CUI
Legacy	Any legacy custom items you use such as table or screen menus
Partial CUI Files	Custom CUI files that have been included in the main CUI file

You can customize all the settings. For example, if you want to create new keyboard shortcuts, you can expand the Keyboard Shortcuts listing and add new shortcuts or edit existing ones. Right-click any item to add or delete options. If you click an item, its properties appear in the Properties group where you can modify the item's function. Just as you added the Linear dimension command to the Draw toolbar, you can click and drag a command into one of the menus under the Menus listing to add a command there.

You'll also see some options in the Customizations In All CUI Files title bar. These options give you control over what is displayed in this group. You can also load and save CUI files from here.

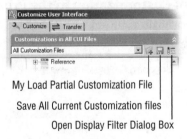

My Load Partial Customization File

Save All Current Customization files

Open Display Filter Dialog Box

You'll learn more about these options later in this chapter.

Finding Commands in the Command List

You've already seen how the Command List group contains all the commands in AutoCAD. You also saw that you can click and drag these items into options in the Customizations In All CUI Files group. This list also contains predefined macros, icons used for toolbars, and something called Control Elements, which are the drop-down lists you see in toolbars. The Layer drop-down list in the Layer toolbar is an example of a *Control Element*. The drop-down lists in the Properties and Styles toolbars are also examples of Control Elements. When you select an item in the Command List group, you will see either its properties in the Properties group or its icon in the Button Image group, or both. The exception to this is the Control Elements, which have no editable feature.

Preview/Button Image/Shortcuts

If you click a toolbar or toolbar tool in the Customizations In All CUI Files group, you will see the Preview or Button Image group. Toolbars display the Preview group, which shows you how the selected toolbar will appear in its floating state. Previews are not editable and are there for your reference.

If you click a tool listing, or *element* as it is called in AutoCAD nomenclature, in the Customizations In All CUI Files group, you will see the Button Image group. This group lets you select an icon for that tool by clicking a list of icons (see Figure 26.5), or you can edit an existing icon or create an entirely new icon. You'll get a chance to see this firsthand later in this chapter.

FIGURE 26.5

The Button Image group

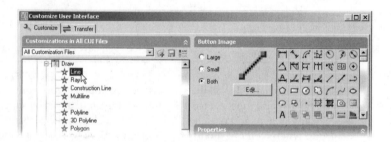

While you are working with the Keyboard Shortcuts in the Customizations In All CUI Files group, this area shows the Shortcuts group, which lists the existing keyboard shortcuts.

Getting to the Core of Customization in the Properties Group

Finally, when you are ready to do some serious customizing, you'll work with the Properties group. The Properties group is set up just like the Properties palette, and it works in the same way. On the left side, you see a listing of options, and to the right of each option is a description or a text input box where you can make changes (see Figure 26.6).

FIGURE 26.6

The Properties group showing the properties for the Line tool

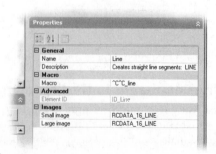

If you go to the Customizations In All CUI Files group and select the Line tool under the Draw toolbar listing, you'll see the properties for that tool in the Properties group, as shown in Figure 26.6.

In the General category, you see the line tool's name. You also see the description that is displayed in the status bar whenever you display its tooltip. You can change this description here in the Properties group, and the description will change in the status bar.

In the Macro category, you see the actual command as it would be entered through the keyboard. The ^C^C that precedes the actual line command input is the equivalent to pressing the Escape key twice. The Advanced category offers information regarding the ID of this particular tool. Finally, the Images category lists the name of the image files used for the Line tool icon. Two icons are listed: one for the large icon version and one for the small icon version of the tool. You'll get a chance to work with the Properties group later in this chapter. Next, you'll try your hand at creating your own custom toolbar.

Creating Your Own Toolbars and Menus

Earlier I mentioned that you can collect your most frequently used tools into a custom toolbar. Now that you've gotten a chance to become familiar with the Customize User Interface dialog box, you can try the following exercise to create your own toolbar.

1. If the Customize User Interface dialog box is not open, right-click the Draw toolbar and choose Customize.

2. In the Customizations In All CUI Files group, scroll to the top of the list.

3. Right-click the Toolbars listing and choose New ➢ Toolbar. You'll see a new toolbar listing appear with the name Toolbar1 highlighted.

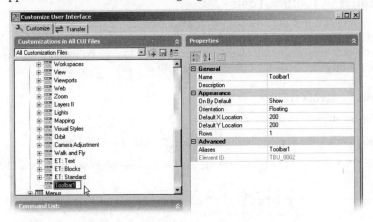

4. Replace Toolbar1 by typing **My Toolbar** to give your toolbar a distinct name. As you type, the name changes. If you decide to change a toolbar name later, right-click a toolbar listing, and then choose Rename.

TIP   You can create custom menus in the same way you create custom toolbars. The only difference is that you right-click the Menus listing in step 3. Once you do that, you can perform the same operations described in the rest of this section to add commands to your custom menu.

You now have a custom toolbar. You'll want to start to populate your toolbar with some commands. You've already seen how this works, but for review, try adding a few commands.

1. In the Command List group, locate the Line tool.

2. Click and drag the Line command to your new toolbar so that you see an arrow pointing to the My Toolbar listing.

3. Release the mouse button. The Line tool appears below My Toolbar.

4. Repeat steps 2 and 3 to add more commands to your toolbar.

5. Click OK to close the Customize User Interface dialog box. AutoCAD will work for a moment and then display the default workspace. In addition, you will see your new custom toolbar appear.

TIP You can delete any tools from your custom toolbar by right-clicking the tool and choosing Delete while in the Customizations In All CUI Files group of the Customize User Interface dialog box. You can also delete your entire toolbar using this method. Take care not to delete any of the existing toolbars you want to keep.

Customizing Toolbar Tools

Now let's move on to more serious customization. Suppose you want to create an entirely new button with its own functions. For example, you might want to create a set of buttons that will insert your favorite symbols. Or you might want to create a toolbar containing a set of tools that open some of the other toolbars that are normally "put away."

CREATING A CUSTOM TOOL

Follow these steps to create a custom tool:

1. Right-click the My Toolbar toolbar, and then choose Customize.

2. In the Command List title bar of the Customize User Interface dialog box, click the New button.

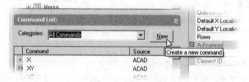

3. In the Properties group, change the Name option to Door.

4. Change Description to Insert a 36 inch door.

5. Change the Macro option to the following:

```
^C^C-insert door;\36;;
```

6. Click and drag the Door element from the Command list into your My Toolbar listing in the Customizations In All CUI Files group.

7. Click OK to close the Customize User Interface dialog box. Now you see your custom button added to your custom toolbar. Notice that its icon is a question mark. This icon is used when no icon has been assigned to the tool.

The series of keystrokes you entered for the macro in step 5 are the same as those you would use to insert the door with the addition of a few special characters. The minus in front of the Insert command tells AutoCAD to bypass the Insert dialog box and use the command line version of the Insert command. The semicolons are equivalent to a ↵ , and the backward slash (\) is a special macro code that tells AutoCAD to pause the macro for user input. In this case, the pause allows you to select the insertion point for the door. The Properties group should look like Figure 26.7.

FIGURE 26.7

The Properties group for your new custom tool that inserts a door block

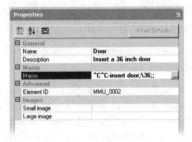

Next, try out the custom tool to make sure it works.

1. Point to the custom tool. You see the Door tooltip, and you also see the description you entered in step 4 appear in the status bar.

2. Click the Door tool. Notice that the door appears in the drawing area at the cursor. It may appear very small since it is being inserted at its default size of 1 unit.

WARNING The Door drawing must be in the default folder or in the Acad search path before the Door button will be inserted. For easy access, you copy the Door.dwg file from the Chapter 4 projects folder to the My Documents folder.

3. Click a location to place the door, and then click a point to set the door rotation. The door appears in the drawing.

In this example, you created a custom tool that inserts the door block. Later in this chapter you'll get a chance to learn more about creating macros for menus and tools. Next, you'll learn how to add a custom icon to your custom tool.

CREATING A CUSTOM ICON

You have all the essential parts of the button defined. Now you just need to create a custom icon to go with your Door button:

1. Right-click the My Toolbar toolbar and choose Customize.

2. In the Customizations In All CUI Files group of the Customize User Interface dialog box, select the Door listing under the My Toolbar option.

3. Take a look at the scroll box in the Button Image group containing the icons.

4. Click any icon image. Notice that the icon appears next to the Door element in the Command list.

5. Click the Edit button to open the Button Editor dialog box. The Button Editor is like a simple drawing program. Across the top are the tools to draw lines, circles, and points, as well as an eraser. Along the right side, you see a color toolbar from which you can choose colors for your icon. In the upper left, you see a preview of your button.

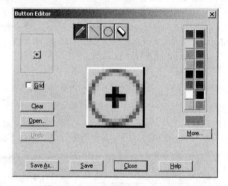

TIP If you prefer, you can use any of the predefined icons in the scroll box to the right of the Button Image group in the Customize User Interface dialog box. Just click the icon you want to use and then click Apply.

6. Before you do anything else, click the Clear button, and then click the Save As button.

7. In the Create File dialog box, create and then open a Custom Icon folder, enter **Door** for the name, and click Save. You now have a blank custom icon in the form of a file called Door.bmp.

8. Draw the door icon shown here. Don't worry if it's not perfect; you can always go back and fix it.

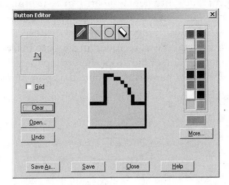

9. Click Save and then click Close.

10. In the Button Image group, scroll the image panel down to the bottom, and then locate and select the door icon you just created.

11. Click OK to close the Customize User Interface dialog box. Now you see your custom icon for the Door tool.

You'll want to know about a number of other options in the Button Editor dialog box. Here is a listing of those options and their purpose:

Grid   Turns a grid on and off in the drawing area. This grid can be an aid in drawing your icon.

Clear   Erases the entire contents of the drawing area.

Undo   Undoes the last operation you performed.

Open   Opens a .bmp file to import an icon. The .bmp file must be small enough to fit in the 16 × 16 pixel matrix provided for icons (24 × 24 for large-format icons).

Pencil/Line/Circle/Erase tools   A row of buttons across the top let you use a pencil for free-hand drawing, or draw a line or circle. You can use the Erase tool to erase areas of the icon.

Color Swatches and More button   Select a color from the column color swatches to the right or click the More button to open the Select Color dialog box for more color options.

Save As   Saves your icon as a .bmp file under a name you enter.

Save   Saves your icon under a name that AutoCAD provides, usually a series of numbers and letters. If you have opened an icon, the icon will be updated under it's original name.

Close   Exits the Button Editor.

Help   Displays helpful information about the features of the Button Editor.

You can continue to add more buttons to build a toolbar of symbols. Of course, you're not limited to a symbols library. You can also incorporate your favorite macros or even AutoLISP routines that you accumulate as you work with AutoCAD. The possibilities are endless.

Creating Macros in Tools and Menus

Combining existing commands into new toolbars can be useful, but you'll get even more benefit from the CUI by creating your own macros. Macros are predefined sets of responses to commands that can help automate your most frequently used processes.

Early on you saw how a macro was included in a tool to insert a door. You added a special set of instructions in the Macro option of the Properties group to perform the door insertion and scale. You also saw how the Line command was formatted as part of a tool.

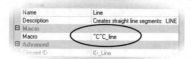

Let's take a closer look at how macros are built. Start by looking at the existing Line tool and how it is formatted.

The Macro option for the Line tool starts with two ^C elements, which are equivalent to pressing the Escape key twice. This cancels any command that is currently operative. The Line command follows, written just as it would be entered through the keyboard. Two Cancels are issued in case you are in a command that has two levels, such as the Edit Vertex option of the Pedit command (Modify ➤ Object ➤ Polyline).

The underscore character (_) that precedes the Line command tells AutoCAD that you are using the English-language version of this command. This feature lets you program non-English versions of AutoCAD by using the English-language command names.

You might also notice that there is no space between the second ^C and the Line command. A space in the line would be the same as ↵. If there were a space between these two elements, ↵ would be entered between the last ^C and the Line command, causing the command sequence to misstep. Another way to indicate ↵ is by using the semicolon, as in the following example:

```
^C^C_LINE;;
```

TIP If a menu macro contains multiple instances of ↵, using semicolons instead of spaces can help make your macro more readable.

In this sample menu option, the Line command is issued, and then an additional ↵ is added. The effect of choosing this option is a line that continues from the last line entered into your drawing. The two semicolons following Line tell AutoCAD to start the Line command and then issue ↵ twice; the first ↵ actually starts the Line command, and then the second ↵ tells AutoCAD to begin a line from the endpoint of the last line entered. (AutoCAD automatically issues a single ↵ at the end of a menu line. In this case, however, you want two instances of ↵, so they must be represented as semicolons.)

Pausing for User Input

Another symbol used in the macro option is the backslash (\); it is used when a pause is required for user input. For example, the sample macro below starts the Arc command and then pauses for your input.

```
^c^c_arc \_e \_d
```

The space between ^c^c_arc and the backslash (\) represents pressing the spacebar. The backslash indicates a pause to enable you to select the starting endpoint for the arc. After you have picked a point, the _e represents the selection of the Endpoint option under the Arc command. A second backslash allows another point selection. Finally, the _d represents the selection of the Direction option. Figure 26.8 illustrates this. If you want the last character in a menu item to be a backslash, you must follow the backslash with a semicolon.

FIGURE 26.8

The execution of the Arc menu item

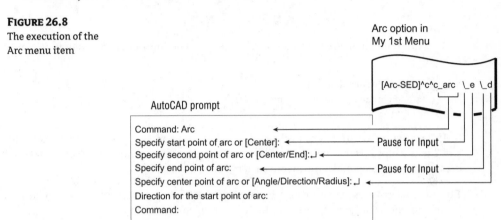

Opening an Expanded Text Box for the Macro Option

As you become more expert at creating macros, you may find the line provided in the Macro option too small for your needs. Fortunately, you can open an expanded text box in which to write longer macros. For example, suppose you want to include the following macro in a tool:

```
(defun c:breakat ()
(command "break" pause "f" pause "@")
)
breakat
```

This example shows the Breakat AutoLISP macro. Everything in this segment is entered just as it would be from the keyboard at the Command prompt. You might find it a bit cumbersome to try to enter this macro in the text box provided by the Macro option in the Properties group of the Customize User Interface dialog box, but if you click the Macro text box, a Browse button appears to the right.

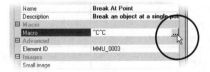

Click the Browse button to open the Long String Editor.

You can then enter the macro and see it clearly. The following shows how it would be entered:

```
^c^c(defun c:breakat ()+
(command "break" pause "f" pause "@")+
);breakat
```

It starts with the usual ^c^c to clear any current commands. The plus sign at the end of lines 1 and 2 tells AutoCAD that the macro continues in the next line without actually breaking it. The break is there to help make the macro easier to read as you enter it.

TIP It's okay to break an AutoLISP program into smaller lines. In fact, it can help you read and understand the program more easily. LT does not support AutoLISP.

LOADING AUTOLISP MACROS

As you become a more advanced AutoCAD user, you might want many of your own AutoLISP macros to load with your custom interface. You can do so by combining all your AutoLISP macros into a single file. Give this file the same name as your menu file but with the .mnl filename extension. Such a file will automatically load with its menu counterpart. For example, say you have a file called Mymenu.mnl containing the Breakat AutoLISP macro. Whenever you load Mymenu.cui, Mymenu.mnl is automatically loaded along with it, giving you access to the Breakat macro. This is a good way to manage and organize any AutoLISP program code you want to include with a menu.

Editing Keyboard Shortcuts

Another area of customization that can be useful is the keyboard shortcut. You probably already know about the standard Ctrl+C and Ctrl+V, which are shortcuts to the Windows Copy and Paste functions. In AutoCAD, Shift+Ctrl+A toggles groups on and off, and Ctrl+1 opens the Properties palette.

You can edit existing keyboard shortcuts or create new ones by opening the Keyboard Shortcuts listing in the Customizations In All CUI Files group of the Customize User Interface dialog box. If you expand this listing, you see Shortcut Keys and Temporary Override keys. These can be expanded to reveal their elements. Select an element to display its properties in the Properties group.

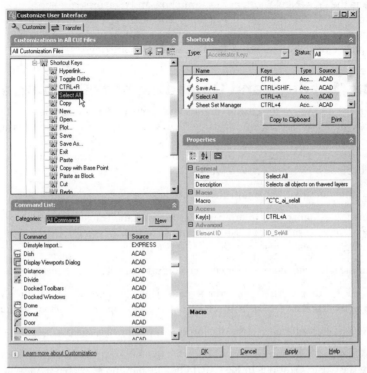

You can click and drag a command from the Command List group into the Shortcut Keys group and then edit its properties to set the shortcut keys you want to use for the command. For example, if you click and drag the Base command from the Command list into the Shortcut Keys list and then select it from that list, you'll see its properties in the Properties group.

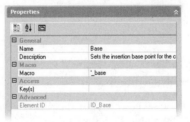

Click the Key(s) option in the Properties group and then click the Browse button that appears to the far right of the Keys option to open the Shortcut Keys dialog box.

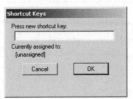

Click in the Press New Shortcut Key input box, and then press the shortcut keys you want to use for this command. For example, if you press Shift+Ctrl+Z, that sequence appears in the input box. If the shortcut you selected is already assigned to another command, you will see a message that says so just below the input box. Click OK, when you are done.

Saving, Loading, and Unloading Your Customizations

You might want to save the custom menus and toolbars that you create with the Customize User Interface dialog box so that you can carry them with you to other computers and load them for ready access.

To save your customization work, you'll need to use the Transfer tab of the Customize User Interface dialog box. Here's how it works.

1. Right-click any toolbar and choose Customize.

2. In the Customize User Interface dialog box, click the Transfer tab. This tab contains two panels: the left panel shows the Customizations In Main CUI group, and the right panel shows a similar group called Customizations In New CUI File.

3. In the left panel, locate your custom component such as a menu or a toolbar.

4. Click and drag it to the appropriate listing in the right panel. In other words, click and drag a custom toolbar from the Toolbars section of the left group to the Toolbars section in the right group.

5. Repeat step 4 for each custom component you have created.

6. When you have copied everything from the left group to the right, click the drop-down list in the Customizations In New CUI File title bar and select Save As.

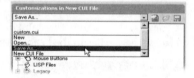

7. In the Save As dialog box, enter a name for your customization file and select a location.

8. Click Save to complete the process.

Your customization will be saved as a .cui file. Once it is saved as a file, you can load it into another copy of AutoCAD by doing the following:

1. Right-click any toolbar and choose Customize.

2. Click the Load Partial Customization File tool in the Customizations In All CUI Files group title bar.

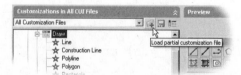

3. In the Open dialog box, locate and select your .cui file, and then click Open.

4. Back in the Customize User Interface dialog box, click OK.

5. If your .cui file contains menus, enter **Workspace**↵↵↵ at the Command prompt. Or if you have the Workspaces toolbar open, select a workspace from the Workspace drop-down list. If it contains toolbars, right-click in a blank area next to an existing docked toolbar, and then select the name of your CUI file and the toolbar.

As an alternative to using the Customize User Interface dialog box, you can use the CUIload command. Enter **Cuiload**↵ at the Command prompt to open the Load/Unload Customizations dialog box.

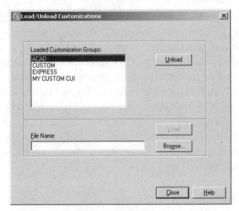

Click the Browse button to locate and select your CUI file. Once you've done this, the name of your file appears in the File Name input box. You can then click the Load button to import it into your AutoCAD session.

Finally, if you want to unload a CUI file, do the following

1. Open the Customize User Interface dialog box.

2. Scroll down to the bottom of the list in the Customizations In All CUI Files group and expand the Partial CUI Files listing.

3. Right-click the partial CUI file you want to unload, and select Unload CUI File.

4. Close the dialog box by clicking OK.

Converting Old Menu Files

If you're an old hand at customization and you've already developed some custom menus in the .MNU or .MNS formats, you can easily convert them into CUI files. Here's how it's done.

1. Right-click any toolbar and choose Customize.

2. In the Customize User Interface dialog box, click the Transfer tab.

3. In the Customizations In New CUI File group to the right, click the drop-down list in the title bar and select Open.

4. In the File Of Type drop-down list toward the bottom of the Open dialog box, select Menu Files.

5. Locate and select your menu file, and then click Open. Your menu file appears in the CUI format in the group to the right.

6. Save your converted menu as a CUI file by following the steps in the previous section.

If you have custom icons in your old menu, AutoCAD will attempt to include them in the new CUI file.

As an alternative to using the Custom User Interface dialog box, you can use the CUIload command described in the previous section.

Understanding the Diesel Macro Language

If you browse through the Acad.mnu file, you'll see many menu options that contain odd-looking text beginning with a dollar sign ($). In some instances, the dollar sign tells AutoCAD to open a shortcut menu. But in many cases, it is used as part of the Diesel macro language. Diesel is one of many macro languages AutoCAD supports, and you can use it to perform some simple operations. Like AutoLISP, Diesel uses parentheses to enclose program code.

In this section, you'll look at the different ways to use Diesel. You'll start by using Diesel directly from the command line. This will show you how a Diesel macro is formatted and will give you a chance to see Diesel in action. Then you'll go on to see how Diesel can be used as part of a menu option to test AutoCAD's current state. In the third section, you'll see how Diesel can be used as part of the menu label to control what is shown in the menu. Finally, you'll learn how Diesel can be used with Field objects to control text in your drawing.

Using Diesel at the Command Line

You can use Diesel at the AutoCAD command line by using a command called Modemacro. The Modemacro command sends information to the status bar. Diesel can be used with Modemacro to perform some simple tasks.

Try the following exercise to experiment with Diesel:

1. At the Command prompt, type **Modemacro**↵.

2. At the Enter new value for MODEMACRO, or . for none <" ">: prompt, enter **$(/,25,2)**↵. You'll see the answer to the equation in the far-left side of the status bar.

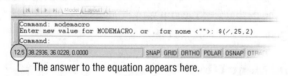

The answer to the equation appears here.

3. To clear the status bar, enter **Modemacro**↵.↵.

The equation you entered in step 2 is referred to as an *expression*. The structure of Diesel expressions is similar to that of AutoLISP. The dollar sign tells AutoCAD that the information that follows is a Diesel expression.

A Diesel expression must include an operator of some sort, followed by the items to be operated on. An *operator* is an instruction to take some specific action, such as adding two numbers or dividing one number by another. Examples of mathematical operators include the plus sign (+) for addition and the forward slash (/) for division.

The operator is often referred to as a *function* and the items to be operated on as the *arguments* to the function, or simply the arguments. So, in the expression (/,25,2), the / is the function, and the 25 and 2 are the arguments. All Diesel expressions, no matter what size, follow this structure and are enclosed by parentheses.

Parentheses are important elements of an expression. All parentheses must be balanced; for each left parenthesis, there must be a right parenthesis.

You can do other things with Diesel besides performing calculations. The Getvar function is an AutoLISP function that you can use to obtain the drawing prefix and name. Try the following to see how Diesel uses Getvar:

1. Type **Modemacro↵** again.

2. Type **$(getvar,dwgprefix)↵**. The location of the current drawing appears in the status bar.

3. Press ↵ to reissue the Modemacro command; then type **$(getvar,dwgname)↵**. Now the name of the drawing appears in the status bar.

In this example, the Getvar function extracts the drawing prefix and name and displays it in the status bar. You can use Getvar to extract any system variable you want. If you've been working through the tutorials in this book, you've seen that virtually all AutoCAD settings are also controlled through system variables. (Appendix C contains a list of all the system variables.) This can be a great tool when you are creating custom menus, because with Getvar, you can "poll" AutoCAD to determine its state. For example, you can find out what command is currently being used. Try the following exercise to see how this works:

1. Click the Line tool in the Draw toolbar.

2. Type **Modemacro↵**. The apostrophe at the beginning of Modemacro lets you use the command while in another command.

3. Type **$(getvar,cmdnames)↵**. The word LINE appears in the status bar, indicating that the current command is the Line command.

Diesel can be useful in a menu when you want an option to perform a specific task depending on which command is currently active.

WARNING LT users cannot use AutoLISP to find the location of AutoCAD resource files. However, you can use the Diesel macro language. For example, to find the log file path, enter **Modemacro** and then **$(getvar,logfilepath)**. The path will be displayed in the far left of the status bar.

Using Diesel in a Custom Menu Macro

So far, you've been experimenting with Diesel through the Modemacro command. To use Diesel in a menu macro requires a slightly different format. You still use the same Diesel format of a dollar sign followed by the expression, but you don't use the Modemacro command to access Diesel. Instead, you use $M=. You can think of $M= as an abbreviation for Modemacro.

Here's a Diesel expression that you can use in a menu macro:

```
^C^C_Blipmode;$M=$(-,1,$(getvar,Blipmode))
```

This menu option turns Blipmode on or off depending on Blipmode's current state. As you might recall, Blipmode is a feature that displays point selections in the drawing area as tiny crosses. These tiny crosses, or *blips* as they are called, do not print and can be cleared from the screen with a redraw. They can be helpful when you need to track your point selections.

In this example, the Blipmode command is invoked, and then the $M= tells AutoCAD that a Diesel expression follows. The expression

```
$(-,1,$(getvar,Blipmode))
```

returns either a 1 or a 0, which is applied to the Blipmode command to turn it either on or off. This expression shows that you can nest expressions. The most deeply nested expression is evaluated first, so AutoCAD evaluates

```
$(getvar,blipmode)
```

to begin with. This returns either a 1 or a 0, depending on whether Blipmode is on or off. Next, AutoCAD evaluates the next level in the expression

```
$(-,1,getvar_result)
```

in which *getvar_result* is either a 1 or a 0. If *getvar_result* is 1, the expression looks like

```
$(-,1,1)
```

which returns a 0. If *getvar_result* is 0, the expression looks like

```
$(-,1,0)
```

which returns a 1. In either case, the end result is that the Blipmode command is assigned a value that is opposite of the current Blipmode setting.

Using Diesel as a Menu Option Label

In the previous example, you saw how to use Diesel in a menu macro to read the status of a command and then return a numeric value to alter that status. You can also use Diesel as part of the menu option name so that the text it displays depends on certain conditions. The following expression shows how to write a menu option name to display the current setting for Blipmode. It includes Diesel code as the menu option label, as follows:

```
$(eval,"Blipmode =" $(getvar,blipmode))
```

TIP When Diesel is used as the menu name, you don't need the $M= code.

Normally, you would just have a menu name, but here you see some Diesel instructions. These instructions tell AutoCAD to display the message Blipmode = 1 or Blipmode = 0 in the menu, depending on the current Blipmode setting.

Here's how it works. You see the familiar $(getvar,blipmode) expression, this time embedded within a different expression. You know that $(getvar,blipmode) returns either a 1 or a 0 depending on whether Blipmode is on or off. The outer expression

```
$(eval,"Blipmode =" getvar_result)
```

displays Blipmode = and then combines this with *getvar_result*, which, as you've learned, will be either 1 or 0. The eval function evaluates any text that follows it and returns its contents. The end result is the appearance of Blipmode = 1 or Blipmode = 0 in the menu, depending on the status of Blipmode. Here's how the option looks in a menu.

You can get even fancier by setting up the menu option label to read Blipmode On or Blipmode Off by using the if Diesel function. Here's that same menu listing with additional Diesel code to accomplish this:

```
$(eval,"Blipmode " $(if,$(getvar,blipmode),"Off","On"))
```

In this example, the simple $(getvar,blipmode) expression is expanded to include the if function. The if function reads the result of $(getvar,blipmode) and then returns the Off or On value depending on whether $(getvar,blipmode) returns a 0 or a 1. Here's a simpler look at the expression:

```
$(if, getvar_result, "Off", "On")
```

If *getvar_result* returns a 1, the if function returns the first of the two options listed after *getvar_result*, which is Off. If *getvar_result* returns a 0, the if function returns On. The second of the two options is optional. Here's how the fancier Blipmode option appears in a menu.

You've really just skimmed the surface of what Diesel can do. To get a more detailed description of how Diesel works, choose Help ➢ Help to open the AutoCAD 2007 Help dialog box. Click the Contents tab, expand the Customization Guide listing, and click the DIESEL listing that appears.

Table 26.2 shows some of the commonly used Diesel functions. Check the AutoCAD Help dialog box for a more detailed list.

TABLE 26.2: A Sample of Diesel Functions. To Indicate True or False, Diesel Uses 1 or 0.

CODE	FUNCTION	EXAMPLE	RESULT	COMMENTS
+	Add	$(+,202,144)	346	
−	Subtract	$(-,202,144)	58	
*	Multiply	$(*,202,144)	29,088	
/	Divide	$(/,202,144)	1.4028	
=	Equal to	$(=,202,144)	0	If numbers are equal, 1 is returned.
<	Less than	$(<,202,144)	0	If the first number is less than the second, 1 is returned.

TABLE 26.2: A Sample of Diesel Functions. To Indicate True or False, Diesel Uses 1 or 0. *(CONTINUED)*

CODE	FUNCTION	EXAMPLE	RESULT	COMMENTS
>	Greater than	$(>,202,144)	1	If the first number is less than the second, 0 is returned.
!	Not equal to	$(!,202,144)	1	If numbers are equal, 0 is returned.
<=	Less than or equal to	$(+,202,144)	0	If the first number is less than or equal to second, 1 is returned.
>=	Greater than or equal to	$(+,202,144)	1	If the first number is less than or equal to the second, 0 is returned.
eq	Equal string	$(eq,"Yes", "No")	0	If both text strings are the same, 1 is returned.
eval	Evaluate text	$(eval,"Here I Am")	Here I Am	Returns text in quotes.
getvar	Get system variable value	$(getvar,ltscale)	Current linetype scale	
if	If/Then	$(if,1,"Yes","No")	Yes	The second argument is returned if the first argument evaluates to 1. Otherwise, the third argument is returned. The third argument is optional.

Using Diesel and Fields to Generate Text

Using Diesel expressions in the status bar or in a menu can be helpful to gather information or to create a more interactive interface, but what if you want the results of a Diesel expression to become part of the drawing? You can employ field objects to do just that.

For example, suppose you want to create a note that shows the scale of the drawing based on the dimension scale. Further, you want the note to automatically update the scale whenever the dimension scale changes. You can add a field object and associate it with a Diesel expression that displays the dimension scale as it relates to the drawing scale. Try the following steps to see how it's done:

A

1. In the Draw toolbar, click the Multiline Text tool and select two points to indicate the text location. The Text Formatting toolbar and Text window appear.

2. Right-click in the Text window and select Insert Field to open the Field dialog box.

3. In the Field Category drop-down list, select Other; then in the Field Names list box, select DieselExpression.

4. Add the following text in the Diesel Expression box to the right. If you need to expand the width of the dialog box, click and drag the right edge of the dialog box.

```
$(eval,"Dimension Scale: 1/")$(/,$(getvar, dimscale),12)$(eval," inch = 1 foot")
```

5. Click OK in the Field dialog box; then click OK in the Text Formatting toolbar. You see the following text displayed in the drawing:

```
Dimension Scale: 1/0.08333333 inch = 1 foot
```

The resulting text might not make sense until you change the dimension scale to a value that represents a scale other than 1-to-1. Here's how to do that:

1. Enter **Dimscale**↵ at the Command prompt.

2. At the `Enter new value for DIMSCALE <1.0000>:` prompt, enter **96**. This is the value for a $1/_8$″ scale drawing.

3. Choose View ➢ Regen or enter **Re**↵. The text changes to read

```
Dimension Scale: 1/8 inch = 1 foot
```

In this example, several Diesel operations were used. The beginning of the expression uses the eval operation to tell AutoCAD to display a string of text:

```
$(eval "Dimension Scale: 1/")
```

The next part tells AutoCAD to get the current value of the Dimscale system variable and divide it by 12:

```
$(/,$(getvar, dimscale),12)
```

Notice that this is a nested expression: `$(getvar,dimscale)` obtains the value of the Dimscale system variable, which is then divided by 12. Finally, the end of the expression adds the final part to the text:

```
$(eval," inch = 1 foot")
```

When it is all put together, you get the text that shows the dimension scale as an architectural scale. Because it is an AutoCAD text object, this text is part of the drawing.

Creating Custom Linetypes

As your drawing needs expand, the standard linetypes might not be adequate for your application. Fortunately, you can create your own. This section explains how to do so.

You'll get an in-depth view of the process of creating linetypes. You'll also learn how to create complex linetypes that cannot be created by using the Express Make Linetype tool.

Viewing Available Linetypes

Although AutoCAD provides the linetypes most commonly used in drafting (see Figure 26.9), the dashes and dots might not be spaced the way you would like, or you might want an entirely new linetype.

TIP AutoCAD stores the linetypes in a file called Acad.lin, which is in ASCII format. When you create a new linetype, you are adding information to this file. Or, if you create a new file containing your own linetype definitions, it too will have the extension .lin. You can edit linetypes as described here, or you can edit them directly in these files.

To create a custom linetype, use the Linetype command. Let's see how this handy command works, by first listing the available linetypes:

1. Open a new AutoCAD file.

2. At the Command prompt, enter **–Linetype**↵. (Don't forget the minus sign at the beginning.)

3. At the Enter an option [?/Create/Load/Set]: prompt, enter **?**↵.

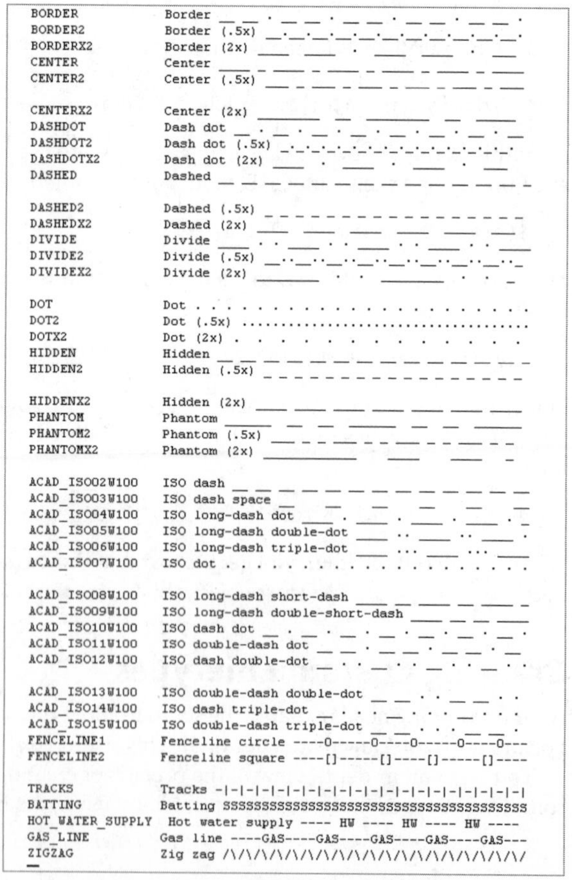

FIGURE 26.9

The lines in this list of standard linetypes were generated with the underscore key (_) and the period (.) and are only rough representations of the actual lines.

4. In the dialog box, locate and double-click `acad.lin` in the listing of available linetype files. You get the list shown in Figure 26.9, which shows the linetypes available in the `Acad.lin` file along with a simple description of each line.

5. You will see a message at the bottom that says Press ENTER to continue:. Do so until you see the command prompt.

Figure 26.9 shows a complete view of the standard linetypes and the ISO and complex linetypes. Figure 26.10 shows how some of the linetypes look in a drawing or when they are plotted.

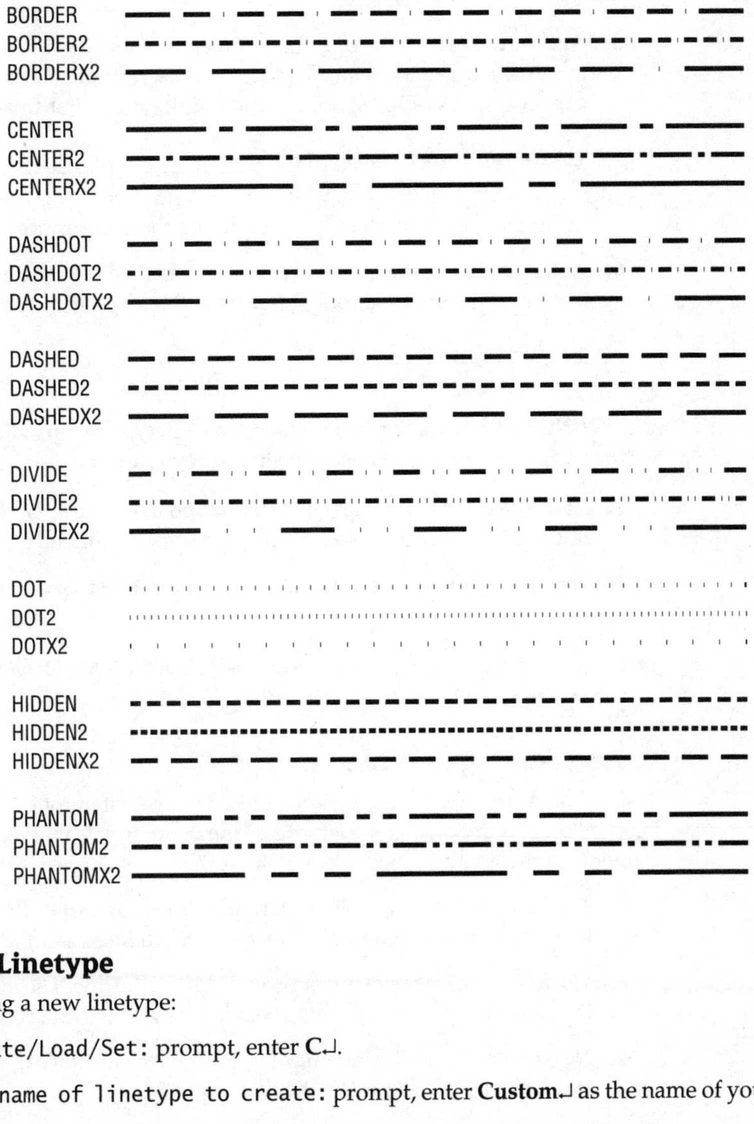

FIGURE 26.10

Some of the more commonly used standard AutoCAD linetypes as they appear when plotted

BORDER
BORDER2
BORDERX2

CENTER
CENTER2
CENTERX2

DASHDOT
DASHDOT2
DASHDOTX2

DASHED
DASHED2
DASHEDX2

DIVIDE
DIVIDE2
DIVIDEX2

DOT
DOT2
DOTX2

HIDDEN
HIDDEN2
HIDDENX2

PHANTOM
PHANTOM2
PHANTOMX2

Creating a New Linetype

Next, let's try creating a new linetype:

1. At the `?/Create/Load/Set:` prompt, enter **C**↵.

2. At the `Enter name of linetype to create:` prompt, enter **Custom**↵ as the name of your new linetype.

3. The dialog box you see next is named Create Or Append Linetype File. You need to enter the name of the linetype file you want to create or add to. If you select the default linetype file, Acad, your new linetype is added to the acad.lin file. If you choose to create a new linetype file, AutoCAD opens a file containing the linetype you create and adds .lin to the filename you supply.

4. Let's assume you want to start a new linetype file. Enter **Newline**↵ in the File Name input box.

TIP If you accept the default linetype file, acad, the prompt in step 5 is Wait, checking if linetype already defined.... This protects you from inadvertently overwriting an existing linetype you want to keep.

5. At the Descriptive text: prompt, enter a text description of your linetype. You can use any keyboard character as part of your description, but the actual linetype can be composed of only a series of lines, points, and blank spaces. For this exercise, enter

    ```
    Custom - My own center line _____ _ _____    ↵
    ```

    using the underscore key (_) to simulate the appearance of your line.

6. At the Enter linetype pattern (on next line): prompt, enter the following numbers, known as the linetype code (after the A that appears automatically):

    ```
    1.0,-.125,.25,-.125↵
    ```

WARNING If you use the Set option of the –Linetype command to set a new default linetype, you will get that linetype no matter what layer you are on.

7. At the New linetype definition saved to file.. Enter an option [?/Create/Load/ Set]: prompt, press ↵ to exit the –Linetype command.

Remember, after you've created a linetype, you must load it in order to use it, as discussed in Chapter 4.

TIP You can also open the acad.lin or other .lin file in Windows Notepad and add the descriptive text and linetype code directly to the end of the file.

Understanding the Linetype Code

In step 6 of the previous exercise, you entered a series of numbers separated by commas. This is the linetype code, representing the lengths of the components that make up the linetype. The separate elements of the linetype code are as follows:

◆ The 1.0 following the A is the length of the first part of the line. (The A that begins the linetype definition is a code that is applied to all linetypes.)

◆ The first –.125 is the blank or broken part of the line. The minus sign tells AutoCAD that the line is *not* to be drawn for the specified length, which is 0.125 units in this example.

◆ Next comes the positive value of 0.25. This tells AutoCAD to draw a line segment 0.25 units long after the blank part of the line.

◆ Finally, the last negative value, –.125, again tells AutoCAD to skip drawing the line for the distance of 0.125 units.

This series of numbers represents the one segment that is repeated to form the line (see Figure 26.11). You can also create a complex linetype that looks like a random broken line, as in Figure 26.12.

FIGURE 26.11
Linetype description with plotted line

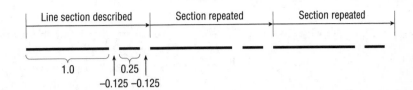

FIGURE 26.12
Random broken line

You might be wondering what purpose the A serves at the beginning of the linetype code. A linetype is composed of a series of line segments and points. The A, which is supplied by AutoCAD automatically, is a code that forces the linetype to start and end on a line segment rather than on a blank space in the series of lines. At times, AutoCAD stretches the last line segment to force this condition, as shown in Figure 26.13.

TIP The values you enter for the line-segment lengths are multiplied by the Ltscale factor; so be sure to enter values for the plotted lengths.

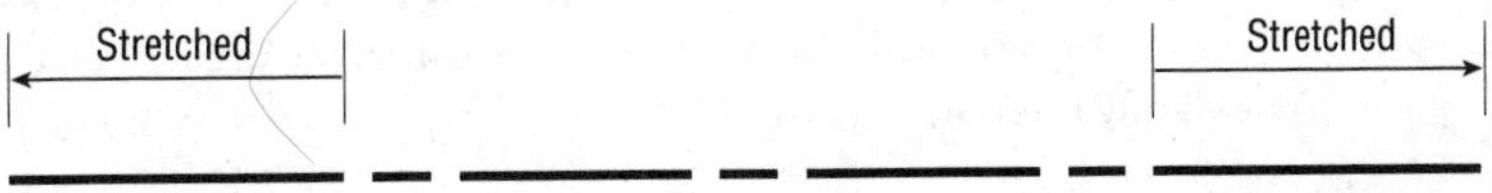

FIGURE 26.13
AutoCAD stretches the beginning and the end of the line as necessary.

As mentioned in the beginning of this section, you can also create linetypes outside AutoCAD by using a word processor or text editor such as Windows Notepad. The standard acad.lin file looks like Figure 26.10, shown earlier in this chapter, with the addition of the code used by AutoCAD to determine the line-segment lengths.

Normally, to use a linetype you have created, you have to load it, through either the Layer or the Linetype dialog box (choose Format ➤ Layers or Format ➤ Linetype). If you use one of your own linetypes frequently, you might want to create a button macro so it will be available as an option on a menu.

Creating Complex Linetypes

A *complex linetype* is one that incorporates text or special graphics. For example, if you want to show an underground gas line in a site plan, you normally show a line with the intermittent word *GAS*, as in Figure 26.14. Fences are often shown with an intermittent circle, square, or X.

For the graphics needed to compose complex linetypes, use any of the symbols in the AutoCAD font files discussed in Chapter 10. Just create a text style by using these symbol fonts, and then specify the appropriate symbol by using its corresponding letter in the linetype description.

To create a linetype that includes text, use the same linetype code described earlier, with the addition of the necessary font file information in brackets. For example, say you want to create the linetype for the underground gas line mentioned previously by using just the letter *G*. You add the following to your Acad.lin file:

```
*Gas_line, -- G -- G -- G --
a,1.0,-0.25, ["G", standard, S=.2, R=0, X=-.1, Y=-.1], -0.25
```

FIGURE 26.14

Samples of complex linetypes

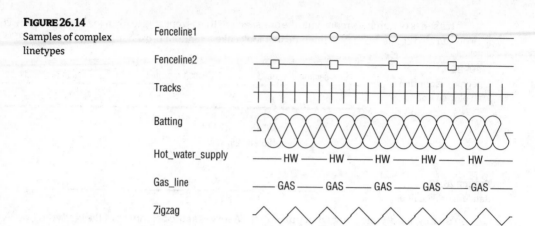

Fenceline1

Fenceline2

Tracks

Batting

Hot_water_supply

Gas_line

Zigzag

The first line servers as a description for anyone looking at this linetype code. The next line is the code itself. Note that the code should not contain spaces. Spaces are used here for clarity.

The information in the square brackets describes the characteristics of the text. The actual text that you want to appear in the line is surrounded by quotation marks. Next are the text style, scale, rotation angle, X displacement, and Y displacement.

WARNING You cannot use the –Linetype command to define complex linetypes. Instead, you must open the Acad.lin file by using a text editor, such as Windows Notepad, and add the linetype information to the end of the file. Make sure you don't duplicate the name of an existing linetype.

You can substitute A for the rotation angle (the R value), as in the following example:

```
a,1.0,-0.25, ["G", standard, S=.2 A=0, X=-.1, Y=-.1], -0.25
```

This has the effect of keeping the text at the same angle, regardless of the line's direction. Notice that in this sample, the X and Y values are a -.1; this will center the Gs on the line. The scale value of .2 will cause the text to be 0.2 units high, so the −.1 is half the height.

In addition to fonts, you can also specify shapes for linetype definitions. Instead of letters, shapes display symbols. Shapes are stored not as drawings, but as definition files, similar to text-font files. In fact, shape files have the same .shx filename extension as text files and are also defined similarly. Figure 26.15 shows some symbols from shape files supplied with the companion CD. The names of the files are shown at the top of each column.

To use a shape in a linetype code, you use the same format as shown previously for text. However, instead of using a letter and style name, you use the shape name and the shape filename, as in the following example:

```
*Capline, ====
a,1.0,-0.25,[CAP,ES.SHX,S=.5,R=0,X=-.1,Y=-.1],-0.25
```

This example uses the CAP symbol from the Es.shx shape file. The symbol is scaled to 0.5 units with 0 rotation and an X and Y displacement of –0.1.

Here is another example that uses the arrow shape:

```
*Arrowline, --|---|---|
a,1.0,-0.25,[ARROW,ES.SHX,S=.5,R=90,X=-.1,Y=-.1],-0.25
```

FIGURE 26.15

Samples of shapes
available on the
companion CD

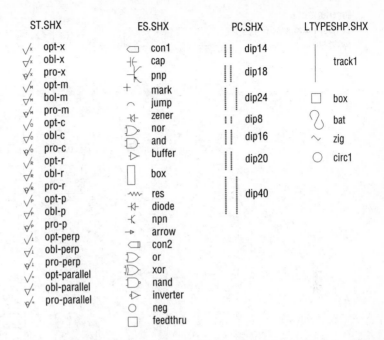

ST.SHX	ES.SHX	PC.SHX	LTYPESHP.SHX
opt-x	con1	dip14	track1
obl-x	cap	dip18	
pro-x	pnp	dip24	box
opt-m	mark	dip8	bat
bol-m	jump	dip16	zig
pro-m	zener	dip20	circ1
opt-c	nor		
obl-c	and	dip40	
pro-c	buffer		
opt-r	box		
obl-r	res		
pro-r	diode		
opt-p	npn		
obl-p	arrow		
pro-p	con2		
opt-perp	or		
obl-perp	xor		
pro-perp	nand		
opt-parallel	inverter		
obl-parallel	neg		
pro-parallel	feedthru		

Just as with the Capline example, the ARROW symbol in this example is scaled to 0.5 units with 0 rotation, and an X and Y displacement of –0.1. Here's what the Arrowline linetype looks like when used with a spline.

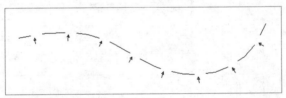

In this example, the Ltype generation option is turned on for the polyline. Note that the arrow from the Es.shx sample shape file is used for the arrow in this linetype.

Creating Hatch Patterns

AutoCAD provides several predefined hatch patterns you can choose from (see Figure 26.16), but you can also create your own. This section demonstrates the basic elements of pattern definition.

Unlike linetypes, hatch patterns cannot be created while you are in an AutoCAD file. The pattern definitions are contained in an external file named Acad.pat. You can open and edit this file with a text editor that can handle ASCII files, such as Windows Notepad. Here is one hatch pattern definition from that file:

```
*square,Small aligned squares
0, 0,0, 0,.125, .125,-.125
90, 0,0, 0,.125, .125,-.125
```

FIGURE 26.16

The standard hatch patterns

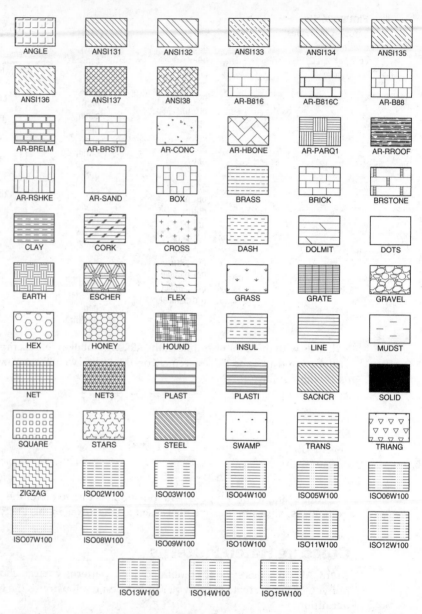

You can see some similarities between pattern descriptions and linetype descriptions. They both start with a line of descriptive text and then give numeric values defining the pattern. However, the numbers in pattern descriptions have a different meaning. This example shows two lines of information. Each line represents a line in the pattern. The first line determines the horizontal line component of the pattern, and the second line represents the vertical component. Figure 26.17 shows the hatch pattern defined in the example.

A pattern is made up of line groups. A *line group* is like a linetype that is arrayed a specified distance to fill the area to be hatched. A line group is defined by a line of code, much as a linetype is defined. In the square pattern, for instance, two lines—one horizontal and one vertical—are used. Each of these lines is duplicated in a fashion that makes the lines appear as boxes when they are combined. Figure 26.18 illustrates this point.

Look at the first line in the definition:

```
0, 0,0, 0,.125, .125,-.125
```

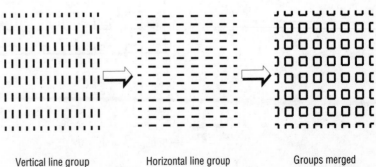

Vertical line group   Horizontal line group   Groups merged
                                                         to form pattern

This example shows a series of numbers separated by commas; it represents one line group. It actually contains four sets of information, separated by blank spaces:

◆ The first component is the 0 at the beginning. This value indicates the angle of the line group, as determined by the line's orientation. In this case, it is 0 for a horizontal line that runs from left to right.

◆ The next component is the origin of the line group, 0,0. This does not mean that the line begins at the drawing origin (see Figure 26.19). It gives you a reference point to determine the location of other line groups involved in generating the pattern.

TIP If you have forgotten the numeric values for the various directions, refer to Chapter 2, which explains AutoCAD's system for specifying angles.

◆ The next component is 0,.125. This determines the distance and direction for arraying the line, as illustrated in Figure 26.20. This value is like a relative coordinate indicating X and Y distances for a rectangular array. It is not based on the drawing coordinates, but on a coordinate system relative to the orientation of the line. For a line oriented at a 0° angle, the code 0,.125 indicates a precisely vertical direction. For a line oriented at a 45° angle, the code 0,.125 represents a 135° direction. In this example, the duplication occurs 90° in relation to the line group, because the X value is 0. Figure 26.21 illustrates this point.

FIGURE 26.19
The origin of
the patterns

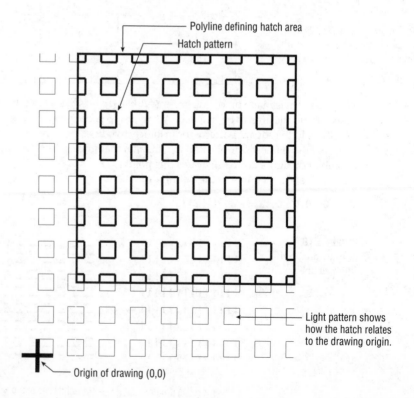

Polyline defining hatch area

Hatch pattern

Light pattern shows
how the hatch relates
to the drawing origin.

Origin of drawing (0,0)

FIGURE 26.20
The distance
and direction
of duplication

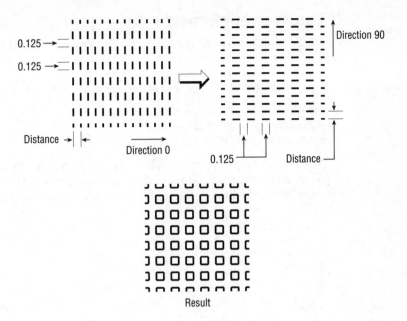

Result

FIGURE 26.21
How the direction of
the line group copy is
determined

The X and Y coordinate values given for the array distance are based on
the orientation of the line group.

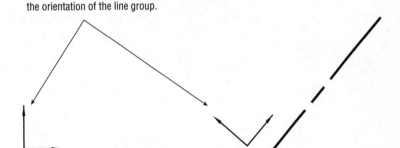

♦ The last component is the actual description of the line pattern. This value is equivalent to
the value given when you create a linetype. Positive values are line segments, and negative
values are blank segments. This part of the line-group definition works exactly as in the linetype definitions you studied in the previous section.

This system of defining hatch patterns might seem somewhat limiting, but you can do a lot with
it. Autodesk managed to come up with 69 patterns—and that was really only scratching the surface.

TIP If you want to include thick lines in your hatch patterns, you have to "build up" line widths
with multiple linetype definitions.

If You Want to Experiment

Creating custom hatch patterns can be a difficult process, so don't be too discouraged if you don't get the pattern you want on your first try. Even for the most experienced AutoCAD user, it can take several passes at writing the hatch pattern code before you can get it right.

Here's a variation on the pattern in the previous hatch pattern exercise:

```
*MYUnknown, Small aligned somethings
0, 0,.0625, 0,.25, .125,-.125
90, .0625,0, 0,.25, .125,-.125
```

Try to guess what this pattern will look like, and then using Windows Notepad, include this pattern at the end of the Acad.pat file in the User Defined Hatch Pattern section. Start AutoCAD and open the Hatch And Gradient dialog box to see if your guess is correct.

Chapter 27

Managing and Sharing Your Drawings

Whether you're a one-person operation working out of your home or one of several hundred AutoCAD users in a large company, file sharing and file maintenance can become the focus of much of your time. In our interconnected world, the volume of messages and files crossing our paths seems to be constantly on the rise. In addition, the Internet has enabled us to be more mobile, adding complexity to our file management tasks.

In this chapter, you'll learn about some of the tools that AutoCAD offers to help you manage your files and the files you share with others. You'll also examine some general issues that arise while using AutoCAD in a workgroup environment. In this discussion, you might find help with some problems you have encountered when using AutoCAD in your particular work environment.

Topics in this chapter include the following:

◆ Sharing Drawings over the Internet

◆ ePublishing Your Drawings

◆ Managing Your Drawings with DesignCenter and the Tool Palettes

◆ Establishing Office Standards

◆ Converting Multiple Layer Settings

Sharing Drawings over the Internet

The Internet has become a major part of the computer industry and everyday life. And the Internet provides AutoCAD users some real, practical benefits through its ability to publish drawings and other documents online. AutoCAD gives you tools that enable you to post drawings on the Internet that others can view and download. In the architecture, engineering, and civil (AEC) industry in particular, this can mean easier access to documents needed by contractors, engineers, cost estimators, and others involved in the design, bidding, and construction of architectural projects. Suppliers of products can post symbol libraries of their products or even 3D solid models.

In this section, you'll learn about the tools AutoCAD provides for publishing and accessing drawings on the Internet (and on any local or wide area network). You'll start by looking at one of the most common uses of the Internet: file transmission.

Sharing Project Files with eTransmit

Perhaps the most common use of the Internet is to send and receive files. Whether you're a one-person office or a member of a 50-person firm, you'll eventually have to share your work with others outside your building. Before eTransmit existed as a feature in AutoCAD, you had to carefully examine what you were sending to make sure you included all the ancillary files needed to view or work on your drawings. Xref, font, and custom linetype files all had to be carefully included with the drawings you sent to consultants or partners in a project, and often something was missed.

By using eTransmit, you can quickly collect all your project drawings into a single archive file, or you can store the files in a separate folder for later processing. This collection of files is included with a report file as a transmittal. Try the following to see how eTransmit works:

1. In AutoCAD, open a file you intend to send to someone; then choose File ➤ eTransmit to open the Create Transmittal dialog box. In the dialog box, you see a tree structure listing of the files that are included in the transmittal. If you need to add more files to the transmittal than are shown in the list, you can click the Add File button to open a file dialog box. To remove files, expand the listed item and remove the checkmark that appears next to the file you want to exclude. You can also use the Files Table tab to view the files as a simple list.

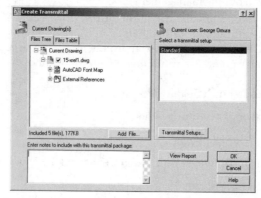

WARNING If you edited the file before choosing File ➤ eTransmit, you will see a message telling you that you must save the drawing before continuing.

2. Click in the Enter Notes To Include With This Transmittal Package input box and enter a description or other note.

3. In the Select A Transmittal Setup group, click the Transmittal Setups button to open the Transmittal Setups dialog box. From here, you can create a new transmittal or rename or modify an existing one.

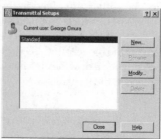

4. Click the Modify button to open the Modify Transmittal Setup dialog box.

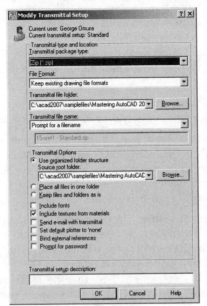

5. In the Transmittal Package Type drop-down list, select the format for your collection of files. You can create a Zip or self-extracting executable archive, or you can save the files in a folder. If you choose the Zip or executable option, you can also add a password by selecting the Prompt For Password check box near the bottom of the dialog box. The person receiving the transmittal file must then enter a password to extract the files. If you choose the Folder option, you can tell AutoCAD where to place the files by using the Browse button. For this exercise, choose the Folder option in the Transmittal Package Type list.

6. Click the Browse button to open the Specify Location Folder dialog box. This is a typical AutoCAD file dialog box that you can use to select a location for your files. You can use the Create New Folder tool to create a new folder for your files. You'll want to keep your transmittal files in a separate location from other files. After you select a location, you return to the Modify Transmittal Setup dialog box.

7. After you've set up your transmittal, click OK. Then click Close in the Transmittal Setups dialog box.

8. Finally, you can preview the report file by clicking the View Report button in the Create Transmittal dialog box.

This report gives you a detailed description of the types of files included in the transmittal. It also alerts you to files that AutoCAD was unable to find but that are required for the drawing.

9. After you've set up the eTransmit options, you can click OK in the Create Transmittal dialog box.

10. If you selected the Zip File option in step 5, you will see the Specify Zip File dialog box. Enter a name and a location for the file and AutoCAD will proceed to collect the files into an archive folder or a Zip file. You can then send the files over the Internet or put them on a removable disk for manual transport.

You probably noticed that you have an option to create additional transmittal setup options in the Transmittal Setups dialog box. That way you can have multiple transmittal options on hand that you don't have to set up each time a different situation arises. For example, you might have the Standard setup configured to create a Zip file and another setup configured to copy the files into a folder. A third setup might be created with a password.

Several options are available for configuring the transmittal setup. The following gives a run-down of those options:

File Format   Lets you select between 2007, exiting file format, and the AutoCAD 2004 and AutoCAD 2000 file formats in case your recipient requires an earlier version.

Transmittal File Name   This option is not available if you select Folder as the transmittal package type. Transmittal File Name lets you determine whether you are prompted for a filename or whether AutoCAD creates a filename for you. Prompt For A File Name is self-explanatory. The other two options, Increment File Name If Necessary and Overwrite If Necessary, offer pre-defined filenames based on the transmittal style and main drawing name.

Use Organized Folder Structure   Preserves the folder structure for the files in the transmittal. This can be important when Xref and other files are located across several folder locations. If the person receiving your files cannot open Xref files properly, try using this option when you resend your transmittal files. This option will create new folders when required for fonts, plot configuration files, and sheet set files. Note that sheet set data files (DTS) are placed in the root folder of the transmittal. Also, AutoCAD will attempt to preserve paths up to one level above the root path of the drawings.

Place All Files In One Folder   This option is self-explanatory.

Keep Files And Folders As Is   Preserves the entire folder structure for the files in the transmittal.

Include Fonts   Tells AutoCAD to include the font files in the transmittal.

Include Textures from Materials   Lets you include bitmap files that are part of a file's material settings.

Send E-Mail With Transmittal   Lets you send an e-mail transmittal with the files included as an attachment. This option streamlines the transmittal process by opening an e-mail dialog box in which you can enter a message and select a recipient for your transmittal.

Set Default Plotter To 'None'   The type of printer you've set up for your files is stored with the drawing file. This option removes any reference to printers or plotters that you have set up for the drawing. By using this option, you can avoid confusion for the person receiving the transmittal drawings.

Bind External References   You can bind external references to the drawings that contain them if it is not important for the recipient to maintain the external references as separate drawings. This can help reduce the number of files in your transmittal, which in turn will reduce any confusion regarding the files you've sent.

Prompt For Password   Gives you the option to password-protect the transmittal file. If you choose this option, you are presented with a dialog box that lets you enter a password and confirm it. The person receiving the transmittal file must then enter the same password to extract the files.

Transmittal Setup Description   Lets you include a brief description of the current transmittal setup.

eTransmit gives you a quick way to package a set of files to be sent to others working on the same project. But you might need to offer a wider distribution of your files. You might want to let others view and plot your drawings from a website without exposing your drawing database to anyone who might visit your site. If this sounds like something you're interested in, you'll want to know about the AutoCAD DWF file format, which lets anyone view AutoCAD files whether they own the program or not. You'll learn more about the DWF file format in the "ePublishing Your Drawings" section later in this chapter.

Protecting AutoCAD Drawing Files

Because AutoCAD drawings specify the methods and materials used to produce an object or a building, the drawings are often treated like legal documents. After an AutoCAD drawing is issued, it is often archived and guarded as a legal record of a design. For this reason, many AutoCAD users are concerned with the possible tampering of drawings that are sent to third parties. Even minor, unauthorized changes to a drawing can have major repercussions to the integrity of a design.

AutoCAD 2007 offers some tools that can help minimize file tampering. The eTransmit feature offers a password-protection option to reduce the possibility of unauthorized tampering of the transmittal files. AutoCAD also offers password protection for individual files as well as a digital signature feature that helps protect both the author of a drawing and the recipient in the event of file tampering.

ADDING PASSWORD PROTECTION TO FILES

The basic type of file protection is the password protection of individual files. AutoCAD offers password protection through the Save Drawing As dialog box and the Options dialog box.

To add a password to a drawing when you save it, do the following:

1. Choose File ➢ Save As to open the Save Drawing As dialog box.

2. Choose Tools ➢ Security Options from the menu in the upper-right corner of the dialog box.

3. In the Security Options dialog box, enter a password or phrase in the input box.

4. Click OK. You are prompted to enter the password again.

5. Enter the password again and click OK to return to the Save Drawing As dialog box.

6. Enter the name and location of your file, and then click Save.

In addition to the Save Drawing As dialog box, you can also add password protection through the Options dialog box:

1. Choose Tools ➢ Options to open the Options dialog box, and then click the Open And Save tab.

2. Click the Security Options button in the File Safety Precautions group to open the Security Options dialog box.

3. Enter your password, select other options as necessary, and then click OK.

As a third option, you can enter **Securityoptions**↵ at the Command prompt to go directly to the Security Options dialog box.

After you've added a password, anyone attempting to open the file will be asked to provide the password before the file can be opened. This includes any attempt to use the file as an Xref or a file insertion.

TIP   After you open a password-protected file and give the password, you can open and close the file repeatedly during that AutoCAD session without having to reenter the password. If you close and reopen AutoCAD, AutoCAD will prompt you for a password the next time you attempt to open the password-protected file.

USING A DIGITAL SIGNATURE

In addition to password protection, you can use a digital signature to authenticate files. A digital signature can't prevent someone from tampering with a file, but it offers a way to validate whether a file has been modified after it has been saved. This protects you in the event that your file is unofficially altered. It also protects the recipient of your file by verifying the file's authenticity and by verifying that it was not altered from the time it left your computer.

The first time you attempt to use the digital signature feature, you see a message telling you that you need a digital ID.

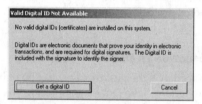

As the message explains, a digital ID is required to use the digital signature feature. AutoCAD uses a digital ID issued by any certificate authority, such as VeriSign, a company that specializes in Internet security. The VeriSign ID is fee based, with prices ranging from about $15 for a basic one-year enrollment to nearly $700 for a professional-level ID. A free 60-day trial is also offered.

The following steps show how to acquire a digital ID:

1. Connect to the Internet. During the process, you will log on to the VeriSign website.

2. From the Windows Taskbar, choose Start ➢ Programs ➢ Autodesk ➢ AutoCAD 2007 ➢ Attach Digital Signatures. Or from AutoCAD, open the Security Options dialog box and click the Digital Signature tab. The Valid Digital ID Not Available warning dialog box appears.

3. Click the Get A Digital ID button. Your web browser opens at the VeriSign page.

4. Select the security services you want and follow the rest of the instructions.

After you've obtained a digital ID, the signature resides in the Registry on your computer. You can then access the digital ID from AutoCAD by using the Digital Signature tab of the Security Options dialog box. Here are the steps:

1. Open the drawing to which you will attach the digital signature, and then open the Security Options dialog box by entering **Securityoptions**↵ at the Command prompt.

2. Click the Digital Signature tab.

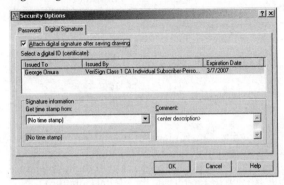

3. Click the Attach Digital Signature After Saving Drawing option to select it. The Signature Information options become available. You can add a date stamp and a brief description.

4. Click OK to exit the dialog box.

The next time you save the file, depending on the level of security you choose during the digital ID setup, you might be prompted for a password. After you enter the password, the file is saved.

The next time the file is opened, you will see the Digital Signature Contents dialog box, which verifies that the drawing has not been tampered with.

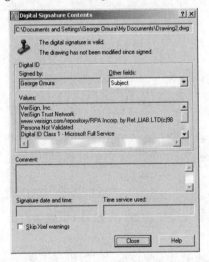

You'll also see a stamp icon in the lower-right corner of the AutoCAD window. You can click this icon at any time to view the digital signature status of the file. You can also issue the Sigvalidate command to view the status. If the file is modified in any way and then saved, a warning message appears at the top of the Validate Digital Signatures dialog box the next time the file is opened.

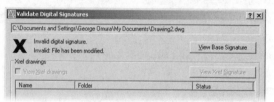

A file containing a digital signature will also display a warning when it is being modified, stating that saving a new version will invalidate the digital signature.

If you need to update a drawing that contains your digital signature, you can do so and then use the Security Options dialog box to reissue the digital signature.

ADDING YOUR DIGITAL SIGNATURE TO MULTIPLE FILES

If you have multiple files to which you would like to attach your digital signature, you'll want to use the Attach Digital Signatures utility. This program runs outside AutoCAD, and it provides a convenient way to attach your digital signature to a set of drawings. Here's how it works:

1. From the Windows Taskbar, choose Start ➢ Programs ➢ Autodesk ➢ AutoCAD 2007 ➢ Attach Digital Signatures to open the Attach Digital Signatures dialog box.

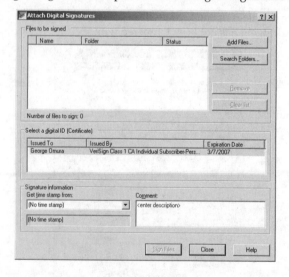

WARNING   If you have not obtained a digital ID, you will see a message telling you that no valid digital IDs are installed on your system. To proceed, you will have to obtain a digital ID from a certificate authority such as VeriSign as described earlier, in "Using a Digital Signature."

2. Click the Add Files button to locate and select files. You can also search for files in a particular folder by clicking the Search Folders button. The files you add appear in the Files To Be Signed list box.

3. If you decide to remove a file from the list box, highlight it and then click Remove. You can also remove all the files from the list by clicking Clear List.

4. The rest of the dialog box is the same as the Digital Signature tab of the Security Options dialog box. You can enter the date and time and a comment for the files you've selected.

5. Click Sign Files when you are sure you have selected the correct files and entered an appropriate comment.

If you exchange AutoCAD drawings regularly with clients and consultants, you'll want to obtain a digital ID and use AutoCAD's digital signature feature. Be aware, however, that because this feature was new in AutoCAD 2004, it works only if you exchange files with others using AutoCAD 2004 or later. In fact, a quick way to remove a digital signature from a file is to save the file in the AutoCAD 2002 or earlier file format.

WARNING   If you intend to use the password feature in conjunction with your digital signature, you must add the signature first before adding the password.

ePublishing Your Drawings

The features discussed so far are intended mostly for exchanging files with others who need to work directly with your AutoCAD files. But there are always associates and clients who need to see only your final drawings and really don't care whether they get AutoCAD files. Or you might be working with people who do not have AutoCAD but still need to view and print your drawings. For those non-AutoCAD end-users, AutoCAD offers the DWF file format.

You can think of the DWF file format as a kind of Adobe Acrobat file for AutoCAD drawings. DWF offers a way to get your plans and design ideas in the hands of more people more easily. With the help of the free Autodesk DWF Viewer—equivalent to the Adobe Viewer for Acrobat documents—DWF files can be viewed using the same types of pan and zoom tools available in AutoCAD, thereby enabling greater detail to be presented in your drawings. In addition, you can embed URL links that can open other documents with a single mouse click. These links can be attached to objects or areas in the drawing.

You can also print DWF files by using your Windows system printer or plotter, all without having AutoCAD installed. A single DWF file can contain multiple drawing "sheets," so you can combine a complete set of drawings into one DWF file.

Exchanging Drawing Sets

Imagine that you are working on a skylight addition to a house and you need to send your drawings to your client for review. In addition to the skylight plans, you want to include some alternate floor plans that your client has asked you to generate. In this exercise, you'll put together a set of drawings that will become a single DWF file that you will send as an e-mail attachment to your client:

1. Open the Sample house.dwg file from the sample files on the companion CD. Notice that the file has several layout tabs, each representing a separate drawing sheet.

2. Choose File ➤ Publish to open the Publish dialog box. Notice that the dialog box lists all the layouts in its main list box, including Model, which is equivalent to the Model Space tab.

(See Chapter 8 for more on layouts.) LT users will not see the Plotter Named In Page Setup option at the bottom of the dialog box.

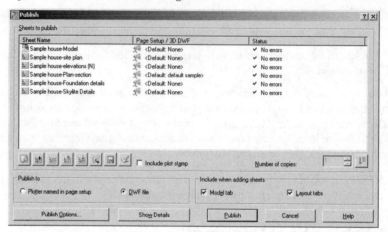

3. In the list box, Ctrl+click Sample House-Model, Sample House-Foundation Details, and Sample House-Skylite Details to select them. You do not want to include these layouts in your DWF file.

4. Right-click and choose Remove or click the Remove Sheets button just below the list of sheets. The items you selected are removed from the list.

At this point, you could go ahead and create a DWF file, but suppose you want to include layouts from a file that is not currently open. The following steps show you how to accomplish this:

1. Right-click and choose Add Sheets or click the Add Sheets button to open the Select Drawings dialog box.

2. Locate and select the `sample house alt.dwg` file. Now you see two new items, Sample House Alt-Model and Sample House Alt-Alternate Plan, in the list box. These are the layout tabs that are in the `sample house alt.dwg` file.

TIP In this last step, the Model tab was imported. You can prevent model tabs from being included in the Sheets To Publish list by turning off the Model Tab option. This option is located in the Include When Adding Sheets group in the lower-right corner of the dialog box.

You have all the sheets that your client needs listed in the list box. Now you're ready to create the DWF file:

1. Save the current list in case you want to reproduce it later. Click the Save Sheet List button. The Save List As dialog box appears, which is a standard file dialog box.

2. Select a location and name for the sheet list and click Save.

3. Back in the Publish dialog box, in the Publish To group at the lower-left of the dialog box, make sure that the DWF File radio button is selected.

4. Click the Publish button. The Select DWF File dialog box appears. This is a standard file dialog box in which you can find a location for your DWF file and also name it. Select a name and location for the DWF file. By default, AutoCAD uses the same name as the current file and the folder location of the current file. You can also set up a default location in the Publish Setup dialog box.

5. Click Select. AutoCAD will display the Processing Background Job message box and spend some time "printing" the selected layouts to a DWF file. The publishing occurs in the background, but you can tell whether it is actually taking place by the plotter icon in the far right of the AutoCAD status bar.

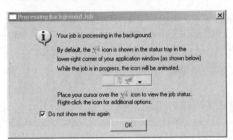
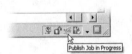

6. When AutoCAD is finished, you'll see the Plot And Publish Complete message bubble in the lower-right corner of the AutoCAD window, indicating that you can view details of the publishing process.

7. Click the link in the bubble that says Click To View Plot And Publish Details. The Plot And Publish Details dialog box appears, offering detailed information about the sheets you published. You can then click the Copy To Clipboard button to export the list to a file as a record. If you want to recall this dialog box later, you can do so by choosing File ➢ View Plot And Publish Details.

You might notice that when you click the Publish button in the previous exercise, AutoCAD behaves as if it is printing the layouts in your list, and that is exactly what it is doing. AutoCAD uses its own DWF printer driver to "print" your drawings to a DWF file. AutoCAD uses the layout settings from the Plot dialog box for each layout to produce the DWF pages.

Other Publish Options

A few more options are available when using the Publish feature. Let's take a moment to review some of the options in the Publish dialog box toolbar:

◆ The Preview tool lets you preview a sheet based on the current settings.

◆ The Add Sheets tool lets you add sheets to the list. The Remove Sheets tool removes a selected item from the list.

◆ The Move Sheet Up and Move Sheet Down tools let you move an item in the list up or down. These are important options because the order of drawings in the list determines the order that the drawings will appear in the Autodesk DWF Viewer. The item at the top of the list appears first, the next one down the list is second, and so on.

◆ The Load Sheet List and Save Sheet List tools let you save and load the list you've compiled, respectively. It is a good idea to save your list in case you need to reproduce the DWF file at some future date.

◆ When the Include Plot Stamp option is turned on, you can use the Plot Stamp Settings tool to specify the data you want to include in the plot stamp. This tool opens the Plot Stamp dialog box. (See Appendix B for more on the Plot Stamp dialog box.)

VIEWING DWF FILES

The Autodesk DWF Viewer offers a fast and simple way to view DWF files, and as I mentioned earlier, it is free. It is installed automatically when you install AutoCAD. Choose Start ➤ Programs ➤ Autodesk ➤ Autodesk DWF Viewer to get it started.

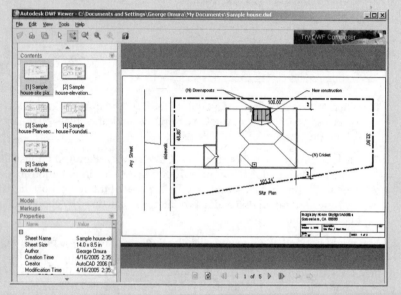

If the person receiving your DWF file does not have a copy of the Autodesk DWF Viewer, send them to the Products page of the Autodesk website (www.autodesk.com) to download their own copy. The download file is relatively small and is easily downloaded even with a slower dial-up connection.

SHORTCUT MENU OPTIONS

If you right-click an item or a set of items in the Publish dialog box list box, you'll see a menu with the standard options mentioned earlier plus some additional options. You'll want to know about a few of these options.

By default, AutoCAD applies the existing layout settings for each layout when it produces the DWF file. These are the settings found in the Plot Or Page Setup dialog box and include settings such as the sheet size, scale, and page orientation. The Change Page Setup option lets you use a different set of layout settings for a selected layout in the list. To use this option, you must have saved a page setup in the Page Setup Or Plot dialog box of the file. (See Chapter 8 for more on the Page Setup dialog box and its options.) You can import a page setup from a different AutoCAD file, or you can assign a page setup to a sheet. Do this by clicking the sheet name and selecting a page setup from the list box that appears in the Page Setup column.

If you happen to have two layouts with the same name, right-click on a layout name, then select the Rename Sheet option on the shortcut menu to rename a layout. The Copy Selected Sheets option will add copies of selected layouts to the list. The copies will have the word *copy* appended to their names. Finally, the last two items in the shortcut menu let you control what is displayed in the list box. Include Layouts When Adding Sheets controls whether layouts are automatically imported from a drawing into the list box. Include Model When Adding Sheets controls whether Model Space views are automatically imported from a drawing into the list box.

The Publish Options Dialog Box

You can set up some additional options by clicking the Publish Options button in the Publish dialog box. You'll then see the Publish Options dialog box.

This dialog box offers options for the location and type of output. The Default Output Location group lets you select the location for DWF files. The General DWF Options group lets you choose between a multisheet DWF file, which combines multiple sheets into one file, or single-sheet DWF files, which creates a file for each sheet. If you choose the Multi-sheet option, you have the added option to specify a default name for your DWF files or to have AutoCAD prompt you for a name each time you create a DWF file. You can also add password protection to the DWF file by using the Password option. The Multi-sheet DWF Options group lets you determine whether you are prompted for a DWF name each time you publish a set or use a predefined filename. At the very bottom of the dialog box in the DWF Data Options group, you have the option to include layer and block information with the DWF file.

Creating a Web-Viewable Drawing

Besides being a great tool for sharing plans, the DWF file format is a good medium for posting drawings on the Web. With DWF, drawings can be viewed on the Web with far more detail than with conventional bitmap graphics. Before the DWF file format, posting drawings on a web page involved capturing bitmap images of drawings and adding them to web pages. Although this method is fairly simple, it allowed for the display of only the crudest of images. Drawings had to be limited in size and resolution to make them easily accessible. If you wanted to add URL links (clickable areas on an image that open other documents), you had to delve into the inner workings of web page design.

TIP URL stands for Uniform Resource Locator and is a standard system for addressing Internet locations on the World Wide Web.

CREATING A DWF FILE BY USING THE PLOT DIALOG BOX

Another way to create DWF files is through the Plot dialog box. If you need to create a DWF file of only a single sheet, you might want to use the Plot dialog box, because it is a simple and familiar procedure.

Open the file that you want to convert to DWF, and then proceed as if you are going to plot the drawing. In the Plot dialog box, select DWF6 ePlot.PC3 from the Name drop-down list in the Printer/Plotter area. Proceed with the plot the normal way. When AutoCAD would normally send the drawing to the printer, you will see a dialog box asking you to enter a name for your plot file and finish with the rest of the plot. You can control the DWF plot as you would any plot.

CONFIGURING THE DWF OUTPUT

In addition to the settings available in the Plot dialog box, you can make some special configuration adjustments to the DWF plotter configuration file. Here is where to find those configuration settings:

1. Choose File ➢ Page Setup Manager to open the Page Setup Manager dialog box, select a setup from the Page Setups list, and then click Modify to open the Page Setup dialog box.

2. Make sure the DWF6ePlot.pc3 configuration file is listed in the Name list box of the Printer/Plotter group.

3. Click the Properties button to the right of the Name drop-down list to open the Plotter Configuration Editor dialog box.

4. Make sure the Device And Document Settings tab is selected; then click the Custom Properties listing in the dialog box.

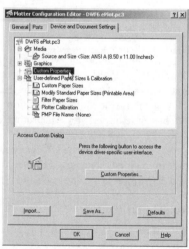

5. Click the Custom Properties button that appears in the lower half of the dialog box to open the DWF6 ePlot Properties dialog box. In this dialog box, you can set the resolution, format, background color, and paper boundary for your DWF file. You can also specify whether to include layer and font information.

6. Click OK after selecting your settings. The Plotter Configuration Editor dialog box reappears. After you've set the custom properties, you can save any new settings in the `DWF6 ePlot.pc3` file, or you can create a new DWF6 PC3 plot configuration file. To save any setting changes, click the Save As button and select the PC3 file in which you want to save the settings.

7. Click OK in the Plotter Configuration Editor dialog box to return to the Page Setup dialog box.

8. Click OK to exit the Page Setup dialog box then close the Page Setup Manager.

TIP   For more information on PC3 plot configuration files, see Chapter 8.

After you select your custom configuration settings in step 5, you needn't open the Plotter Configuration Editor dialog box again the next time you plot a DWF file. If you save your new settings as a new PC3 file, you can select it from the File drop-down list in the Plotter Configuration group. You needn't reenter the custom settings.

You can use either the Publish feature described in the previous section to create single or multiple DWF files or create DWF files directly through the Plot dialog box. You post the output from either method to a website to offer a wide distribution of your drawings. Just create a link to the DWF file from your web page. Be aware that the person attempting to view your DWF file from a web browser will need a copy of the free Autodesk DWF Viewer program that lets you view AutoCAD DWF files. The Autodesk DWF Viewer is automatically installed with AutoCAD 2007.

If you're not that familiar with web page creation, but you want to post your drawings on the Internet, you can use the Publish To Web feature in AutoCAD, discussed next.

Creating a Web Page Containing DWF Files

AutoCAD 2007 offers a tool that will automatically generate a web page containing your DWF files. The Publish To Web Wizard lets you create and edit web pages that contain single or multiple DWF files. You can then place the pages on your web server without any extra work.

To get to the Publish To Web Wizard, choose File ➢ Publish To Web from the AutoCAD menu bar. You can then follow the instructions in the wizard. The Publish To Web Wizard creates all the files needed for the page, including the JavaScript code to enable viewers of the page to drag and drop drawings from the page into their AutoCAD sessions. Figure 27.1 shows a typical listing of the files that were created for a sample web page.

If you feel creative, you can use the Publish To Web Wizard as a starting point to create custom web pages of your drawings, or you can use the pages as is. You can edit the pages by using any number of web programs such as Adobe GoLive or Microsoft FrontPage.

Exchanging DWG Files by Using i-drop

If you need to share your AutoCAD drawings with a lot of people, you can post your files on your website and allow others to download them. This is typically done through a web page by assigning a graphic or a string of text—a *link*—to a file. A person viewing your page can then click the graphic or text to start the download process. You'll learn more about linking in the next section.

FIGURE 27.1

The web page files used for the sample page

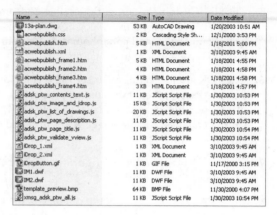

Name	Size	Type	Date Modified
13a-plan.dwg	53 KB	AutoCAD Drawing	1/20/2003 10:51 AM
acwebpublish.css	2 KB	Cascading Style Sh...	12/1/2000 3:53 PM
acwebpublish.htm	5 KB	HTML Document	1/18/2001 5:00 PM
acwebpublish.xml	1 KB	XML Document	3/10/2003 9:45 AM
acwebpublish_frame1.htm	5 KB	HTML Document	1/18/2001 4:55 PM
acwebpublish_frame2.htm	4 KB	HTML Document	1/18/2001 4:58 PM
acwebpublish_frame3.htm	4 KB	HTML Document	1/18/2001 4:58 PM
acwebpublish_frame4.htm	3 KB	HTML Document	1/18/2001 4:57 PM
adsk_ptw_contents_text.js	11 KB	JScript Script File	1/30/2003 10:53 PM
adsk_ptw_image_and_idrop.js	15 KB	JScript Script File	1/30/2003 10:53 PM
adsk_ptw_list_of_drawings.js	20 KB	JScript Script File	1/30/2003 10:53 PM
adsk_ptw_page_description.js	11 KB	JScript Script File	1/30/2003 10:53 PM
adsk_ptw_page_title.js	11 KB	JScript Script File	1/30/2003 10:54 PM
adsk_ptw_validate_vview.js	11 KB	JScript Script File	1/30/2003 10:54 PM
iDrop_1.xml	1 KB	XML Document	3/10/2003 9:45 AM
iDrop_2.xml	1 KB	XML Document	3/10/2003 9:45 AM
iDropButton.gif	1 KB	GIF File	11/17/2000 3:15 PM
IM1.dwf	11 KB	DWF File	3/10/2003 9:45 AM
IM2.dwf	11 KB	DWF File	3/10/2003 9:45 AM
template_preview.bmp	64 KB	BMP File	11/30/2000 4:07 PM
xmsg_adsk_ptw_all.js	11 KB	JScript Script File	1/30/2003 10:54 PM

AutoCAD also offers i-drop, a way to open files directly from a web page. You'll need to know the name of the file you are downloading, but beyond that, the process is quite simple. Try downloading a sample drawing from the Autodesk web page at www.autodesk.com to see how this process works:

1. Connect to your ISP and close all open files in AutoCAD.

2. Open your web browser and go to www.autodesk.com/idrop, then arrange the browser window so you can get a clear view of the AutoCAD window at the same time.

3. In AutoCAD, choose File ➢ New and use the Acad.dwt template to create a new file.

4. Go back to your web browser to the bottom of the autodesk idrop page; then click the chair.

5. Click and drag the chair image from the page into the blank AutoCAD window. Note that when you click on the chair, the cursor changes to a circle with a line through it. That's just telling you that you can't "drop" the image back into itself.

6. When you release the mouse button in the blank AutoCAD window, the file is automatically downloaded and opens in AutoCAD. If you have a file already open in AutoCAD, the downloaded file will be inserted in the open drawing.

The Search The Web tool you used in step 3 is present in all the file dialog boxes that you encounter in AutoCAD. This means that you can import blocks, Xrefs, and even raster image files from websites, as long as you know the names of the files you want to import.

Although you used the AutoCAD Select File dialog box to import a file using i-drop, you can also use your web browser to accomplish the same thing.

TIP You can also click and drag a DWF file from a web page into AutoCAD to download and open a DWG file, provided that a DWG file with the same name as the DWF file exists on the website.

Adding Hyperlinks to Drawings

The Internet gave the world a tool that is so simple yet so powerful that it has permanently altered the way we look at information. Virtually every web page we view contains a hypertext link—a word, a sentence, or an image that takes us to another web page. Such links enable the viewer to explore the content of a web page or gather more information on a particular topic.

AutoCAD offers a similar tool that you can apply to your AutoCAD drawings, called *hyperlinks*. With AutoCAD hyperlinks, you can link any document to an AutoCAD object. Then, with a few clicks of your mouse, you can open these links to view other drawings, text files, spreadsheets, or web pages. After you create a hyperlink in an AutoCAD drawing, you can export the drawing to a DWF file, and that DWF file will also contain the same links. You can then post that DWF file on a web page where others can gain access to those links.

The inclusion of hyperlinks in drawings and DWF files opens a world of new possibilities in the way that you work with drawings. You can link product specifications directly to the objects in the drawing that represent that product. You can also link to extended data beyond the simple symbol or graphic in a drawing, such as a database table or a spreadsheet.

You don't have to limit your links to HTML files containing AutoCAD drawings. You can link to all sorts of web documents, to drawings on your computer or your company network, and even to documents on other sites.

CREATING HYPERLINKS

The following shows you how to add links to a sample floor plan:

1. In AutoCAD, open the file `Houseplan.dwg` in this chapter's folder from the companion CD.

2. Choose Insert ➢ Hyperlink.

3. At the `Select objects:` prompt, click all the hexagonal door symbol, as shown in Figure 27.2.

4. When you're done, press ↵. The Insert Hyperlink dialog box opens (see Figure 27.3).

5. Click the File button on the right side of the dialog box to open the Browse The Web – Select Hyperlink dialog box. It's a typical file dialog box.

6. Locate the `doorsch.dwf` file in the `Projects` subfolder and select it.

7. Click Open. The Insert Hyperlink dialog box reappears. Notice that `doorsch.dwf` appears in the list box at the top of the dialog box.

8. Make sure the Use Relative Path For Hyperlink option is not selected, and then click OK.

FIGURE 27.2

The door symbol in the `Houseplan.dwg` file

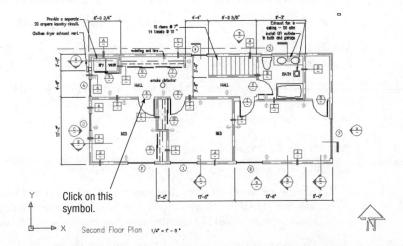

FIGURE 27.3

The Insert Hyperlink dialog box

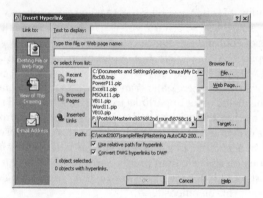

The link you just created is stored with the drawing file. You can then create a DWF file from this drawing, and the link will be preserved in the DWF file.

Now let's see how you can use the link from within the AutoCAD file:

1. Move your cursor over the hexagonal door symbol. Notice that the cursor changes to the Hyperlink icon when it is placed on the symbol. It also shows the name of the file to which the object is linked. This tells you that the object is linked to another document somewhere on your system, on your network, or on the World Wide Web.

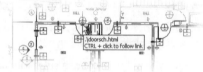

2. Click the hexagonal door symbol to select it.

3. Right-click a blank area of the drawing. In the shortcut menu, choose Hyperlink ➢ Open, to choose the link to the `doorsch.dwf file`. You can also Ctrl+click the door symbol.

Your default web browser opens and displays the file `doorsch.html`.

WARNING   If you installed the sample figures from the companion CD on another drive or folder location, the Hyperlink menu option will reflect that location instead of the one shown in step 3.

You've used the `doorsch.html` file as an example in these exercises, but this could have been a text file, a spreadsheet, a database, or even another AutoCAD file. AutoCAD will start the application associated with the linked file and open the file.

EDITING AND DELETING HYPERLINKS

You can edit or delete a hyperlink by doing the following:

1. Right-click the object whose link you want to edit, and then choose Hyperlink ➢ Edit Hyperlink from the shortcut menu to open the Edit Hyperlink dialog box, which offers the same options as the Insert Hyperlink dialog box (see Figure 27.3, earlier in this chapter).

2. You can now change the link, or you can click the Remove Link button in the lower-left corner of the dialog box to delete the link altogether.

Taking a Closer Look at the Hyperlink Options

You were introduced to the Insert Hyperlink dialog box, shown in Figure 27.3, in the previous exercises. Let's take a moment to study this dialog box in a little more detail.

To specify a file or a website to link to, you can enter either a filename or a website URL in the Type The File Or Web Page Name input box or use the Or Select From List area, which offers a list box and three button options. When you select one of the buttons, the list box changes to offer further, related options.

Recent Files   Displays a list of recently edited AutoCAD files, as illustrated in Figure 27.3. You can then link the object to a file in the list by clicking the filename.

Browsed Pages   Displays a list of websites that you recently visited using your Internet Explorer browser.

Inserted Links   Displays a list of recently inserted links including files or websites.

You can also use the three buttons to the right of the list box to locate specific files, websites, or saved views within the current drawing. As you saw in the exercise, the File button opens the Browse The Web dialog box, which lets you locate and select a file from your computer, from your local area network, or even from an FTP site. This is a typical AutoCAD file dialog box with some additional features.

The buttons in the left column let you select the location of your file search. You can also select a location by using the file navigation tools at the top of the dialog box.

The Web Page button on the right opens a simplified web browser that lets you locate a web page for linking (as shown earlier, in Figure 27.3). In this dialog box, you can use the standard methods for accessing web pages, such as using the Look In drop-down list to select recently visited pages or entering a URL in the Name Or URL input box. The page is then displayed in the main window of the dialog box.

Finally, the Target button in the Insert Hyperlink dialog box opens the Select Place In Document dialog box, which lists the saved views within the drawing that is selected in the Edit Hyperlink list box.

Views are subdivided by layout tab. At the top is the Model Space tab listing, and below that are other layout tab listings. If the current drawing contains saved views, you'll see a plus sign next to the layout tab name. Click the plus sign to display a listing of the views in that layout.

At the very top of the Insert Hyperlink and Edit Hyperlink dialog boxes, you have an input box labeled Text To Display. When a hyperlink is added to an object in AutoCAD, AutoCAD will display a hyperlink icon whenever the cursor passes over the object. You can also include descriptive text that will display along with the icon by entering a description in the Text To Display input box.

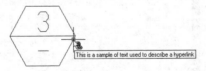

By default, the text is simply the name of the hyperlinked item that you select. You can change the text to provide a better description of the link.

Finally, there is a column of options on the far left of the Insert Hyperlink dialog box, labeled Link To. The top button, Existing File Or Web Page, displays the options discussed so far in this section. The other two buttons change the appearance of the Insert Hyperlink dialog box to offer some different but familiar options.

The View Of This Drawing button changes the display to show just the views that are available in the current drawing. This option performs the same function as the Target button described earlier.

The E-Mail Address button changes the Insert Hyperlink dialog box to enable you to link an e-mail address to an object. Clicking the object will then open your default e-mail application, enabling you to send a message to the address.

Managing Your Drawings with DesignCenter and the Tool Palettes

As you start to build a library of drawings, you'll find that you reuse many components of existing drawing files. Most of the time, you will probably be producing similar types of drawings with some variation, so you'll reuse drawing components such as layer settings, dimension styles, and layouts. It can be a major task just to keep track of all the projects you've worked on. It's especially frustrating when you remember setting up a past drawing in a way that you know would be useful in a current project, but you can't remember that file's name or location.

AutoCAD offers DesignCenter to help you keep track of the documents you use in your projects. You can think of DesignCenter as a kind of super Windows Explorer that is focused on AutoCAD files. DesignCenter lets you keep track of your favorite files and helps you locate files, blocks, and other drawing components. In addition, you can import blocks and other drawing components from one drawing to another by using a simple click and drag. If you've been diligent about setting a unit format for each of your drawings, you can use DesignCenter to import symbols and drawings of different unit formats into a drawing, and the symbols will maintain their proper size. For example, a 90 cm door symbol from a metric drawing can be imported into a drawing in Imperial units, and the DesignCenter will translate the 90 cm metric door size to a 35.43 door.

Getting Familiar with DesignCenter

At first glance, DesignCenter looks a bit mysterious. But it takes only a few mouse clicks to reveal a tool that looks much like Windows Explorer. Try the following steps to get familiar with DesignCenter:

1. Open AutoCAD to a new file, and then click the DesignCenter tool on the Standard toolbar.

   DesignCenter opens as a floating palette (see Figure 27.4).

FIGURE 27.4
DesignCenter opens as a floating palette.

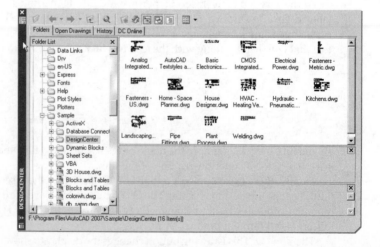

TIP If your DesignCenter view doesn't look like this, with the DesignCenter window divided into two parts, click the Tree View Toggle tool in the DesignCenter toolbar. The Tree view opens on the left side of the DesignCenter window. Click the Home tool to display the contents of the \Sample\DesignCenter folder.

2. Click the Favorites tool in the DesignCenter toolbar.

    DesignCenter displays a listing of the Favorites folder. What you are actually looking at is a view into the C:\Documents and Settings*User Name*\Favorites\Autodesk folder in which *User Name* is your login name. Unless you've already added items to the \Favorites\Autodesk folder, you see a blank view in the right panel. You can add shortcuts to this folder as you work with DesignCenter. You might also see a view showing the tree structure of the files you have open in AutoCAD.

3. Place your cursor in the lower-right corner of the DesignCenter window so that a double-headed diagonal arrow shows; then click and drag the corner out so that you have an enlarged DesignCenter window that looks similar to Figure 27.5. By the way, the view on the right containing the DesignCenter folder is called the Palette view, and the view on the left is called the Tree view.

4. Place your cursor on the border between the Tree view and the Palette view until you see a double-headed cursor. Then click and drag the border to the right to enlarge the Tree view until it covers about one-third of the window.

5. Finally, use the scroll bar at the bottom to adjust your view of the Tree view so you can easily read its contents.

FIGURE 27.5
The components of the DesignCenter palette

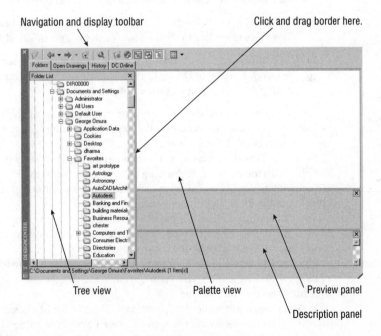

TIP Like the Tool palettes and the Properties palette, DesignCenter has an Auto-hide feature. To use it, click the double-headed arrow icon near the bottom of the DesignCenter title bar. Design-Center will disappear except for the title bar. You can then quickly open DesignCenter by placing the cursor on the title bar.

After you have it set up like this, you can see the similarities between DesignCenter and Windows Explorer. You can navigate your computer or network by using the Tree view, just as you would navigate Windows Explorer. There are a few differences, however, as you'll see in the following exercise:

1. Click the Home tool in the DesignCenter toolbar. The view changes to display the contents of the DesignCenter folder under the \AutoCAD2007\Sample\ folder.

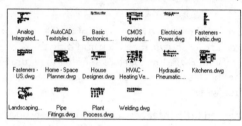

2. Instead of the usual listing of files, you see sample images of each file. These are called *preview icons*.

3. Click the Views tool in the DesignCenter toolbar, and then choose Details from the menu. The Palette view changes to show a detailed list of the files in the DesignCenter folder.

4. Click the Views tool again and then choose Large Icons to return to the previous view. The Views tool is similar to the various View options in Windows Explorer.

5. Click the Basic Electronics.dwg file to select it. You see a preview of the selected file in the Preview panel of DesignCenter. You can adjust the vertical size of the Preview panel by clicking and dragging its top or bottom border.

You can also open and close the Preview panel by clicking the Preview tool in the DesignCenter toolbar. The preview can be helpful if you prefer viewing files and drawing components as a list in the main part of the Palette view.

Below the Preview panel is the Description panel. This panel displays any text information included with the drawing or drawing element selected in the Palette view. To add a description to a drawing that will be visible here, choose File ➤ Properties in AutoCAD; to add a description to a block, use the Block Definition dialog box.

You can open and close this panel by clicking the Description tool in the DesignCenter toolbar. Because the Basic Electronics.dwg file doesn't have a description attached, the description panel shows the message No description found.

Both the Preview and the Description panels can offer help in identifying files that you might be looking for. After you find a file, you can click and drag it into a folder in the Tree view to organize your files into separate folders.

You can also add files to the Favorites folder by right-clicking and then choosing Add To Favorites. The file itself won't be moved to the Favorites folder; instead, a shortcut to the file will be created in the Favorites folder. If you want to work on organizing your Favorites folder, you can open a window to the Favorites folder by right-clicking a file in the Palette view and choosing Organize Favorites. A window to the Favorites folder appears.

Because you'll be working with the sample drawings from the companion CD, go ahead and add the Projects folder to the Favorites folder:

1. Locate the Projects folder (the one created when you installed the sample files from the companion CD) in the left panel Tree view and right-click it.

2. Choose Add To Favorites from the shortcut menu.

3. To go directly to the Favorites folder, click the Favorites tool in the DesignCenter toolbar. The Favorites folder appears in the right panel in Palette view.

4. Double-click the Projects shortcut in the Palette view. You see the contents of the Projects folder.

You can go beyond just looking at file listings. You can look inside files to view their components:

1. In the Palette view, locate the file named 16-unit.dwg in the Chapter 16 folder and double-click it. You see a listing of its components in the Palette view. The Tree view also shows the file highlighted.

2. Double-click the Block listing in the Palette view. Now you see a listing of all the blocks in 16b-unit.dwg.

From here, you can import any of the drawing components from the DesignCenter palette into an open drawing in AutoCAD. But before you try that, try a few other features of the DesignCenter.

Opening and Inserting Files with DesignCenter

By using DesignCenter, you can more easily locate the files you are looking for because you can view thumbnail preview icons. But often that isn't enough. For example, you might want to locate all the files that contain the name of a particular manufacturer in an attribute of a drawing.

After you've found the file you're looking for, you can load it into AutoCAD by right-clicking the filename in the Palette view and then choosing Open In Window. Try it with the following exercise:

1. Click the Up tool in the DesignCenter toolbar twice. This takes you up two levels in the Palette view, from the view of the drawing blocks to the list of filenames.

2. In the Tree view, select the Chapter 12 folder. Then in the Palette view of DesignCenter, locate the 12c-unit.dwg sample.

3. Click and drag 12c-unit.dwg to the AutoCAD 2007 title bar. The drawing appears in the AutoCAD window.

If you want to insert a file into another drawing as a block, you can do so by clicking and dragging the file from the DesignCenter palette view into an open drawing window. You will then be prompted for insertion point, scale, and rotation angle. If you prefer to use the Insert dialog box to insert a drawing from DesignCenter, right-click the filename in the Palette view and then choose Insert As Block. The Insert dialog box opens, offering you the full set of Insert options, as described in Chapter 3.

Finally, you can attach a drawing as an Xref by right-clicking a file in the Palette view of Design-Center and choosing Attach As Xref. The External Reference dialog box opens, offering the insertion point, scale, and rotation options similar to the Insert dialog box. This is the same dialog box described in Chapter 7.

Finding and Extracting the Contents of a Drawing

Aside from the convenience of being able to see thumbnail views of your drawing, DesignCenter might not seem like much of an improvement over Windows Explorer. But DesignCenter goes beyond Windows Explorer in many ways. One of the main features of DesignCenter is that it enables you to locate and extract components of a drawing.

Imagine that you want to find a specific block in a drawing. You remember the name of the block, but you don't remember the drawing you put it in. You can search the contents of drawings by using DesignCenter's Find dialog box. In the following exercise, you will search for a block named Kitchen2-metric among a set of files:

1. In the DesignCenter toolbar, click the Search tool to open the Search dialog box. It looks similar to the Search tool that comes with Windows.

2. Select the drive that contains your Projects folder from the In drop-down list.

3. Select Blocks from the Look For drop-down list. As you can see from the list, you can look for a variety of drawing component types.

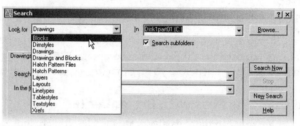

4. Enter **Kitchen2-metric**↵ in the Search For The Name input box then click the Search Now button to start the search. The magnifying glass icon in the lower-right corner will move back and forth, telling you that the Search function is working. After a minute or two, you'll see the name of the block in the window at the bottom of the dialog box.

5. Double-click the block name. DesignCenter displays the block in the Palette view and the file that contains the block in the Tree view.

SEARCH OPTIONS

As you can see from this example, the Search dialog box can be helpful in finding items that are buried in a set of drawings. In the exercise, you searched for a block, but you can search for any named drawing component, including attribute data and text. For example, if you want to find all attributes that contain the name *ABC Manufacturing Company* in your drawings, you can do so with the DesignCenter Search dialog box. Here is a summary of its features:

In Lets you select the drive you want to search.

Look For Options Lets you select the type of item to search for. The options are Blocks, Dimstyles, Drawings, Drawings And Blocks, Hatch Pattern Files, Hatch Patterns, Layers, Layouts, Linetypes, Tablestyles, Textstyles, and Xrefs.

Browse Lets you locate a specific folder to search.

Search Subfolders Lets you determine whether Search searches subfolders in the drive and folder you specify.

Search Now   Starts the search process.

Stop   Cancels the current search.

New Search   Clears all the settings for the current search so you can start fresh on a new search.

Help   Opens the AutoCAD help system to the Search topic.

ADDITIONAL HIDDEN OPTIONS

When you select Drawings from the Look For drop-down list, you see a set of additional tabs in the Search dialog box:

Drawings Tab   Contains two options:

> **Search For The Word(s)**   Lets you specify the text to search for in the Drawing Properties fields.
>
> **In The Field(s)**   Lets you specify the field of the Drawing Properties dialog box to search through, including filename, title, subject, author, and keyword. These are the fields you see when you choose File ➢ Drawing Properties.

Date Modified Tab   Lets you limit search criteria based on dates.

Advanced Tab   Offers three options to further limit your search to specific types of drawing data or to a range of dates:

> **Containing**   Lets you select from a list of data to search for, including block name, block and drawing description, attribute tag, and attribute value.
>
> **Containing Text**   Lets you specify the text to search for in the types of data you select from the Containing option.
>
> **Size Is**   Lets you restrict the search to files greater than or less than the size you specify.

AUTOMATICALLY SCALING BLOCKS AT INSERTION

After you've found the block by using DesignCenter, you can click and drag the block into your open drawing. In the following exercise, you'll do just that, but with a slight twist. The block you've found is drawn in centimeters, but you'll be inserting the Kitchen2-metric block into a drawing named 12c-unit.dwg, which was created in the Imperial measurement system. If you were to insert the Kitchen2-metric block into 12c-unit.dwg, the kitchen would be exactly 2.54 times larger than it should be for 12c-unit.dwg. But as you'll see, DesignCenter takes care of scaling for you. Follow these steps:

1. In AutoCAD, make sure the 12c-unit.dwg sample drawing is loaded if you haven't done so already. You can temporarily close DesignCenter to do this.

2. Back in DesignCenter, click and drag the Kitchen2-metric block from the Palette view into the 12c-unit.dwg window in AutoCAD. The kitchen appears at the appropriate scale.

3. To see that DesignCenter did indeed adjust the scale of the Kitchen2-metric block, click it in the 12c-unit window, and then right-click and choose Properties.

4. Check the Scale X, Scale Y, and Scale Z settings in the Geometry category. Notice that they show .3937 as the scale factor instead of 1.

5. After reviewing the Properties palette, close it.

You might recall from Chapter 3 that you have the opportunity to specify the type of units the drawing is set up for in the Drawing Units dialog box under the Drag-And-Drop Scale drop-down list. DesignCenter uses this information when you drag and drop blocks from DesignCenter into an open drawing. This is how DesignCenter is able to correctly scale a block drawn in metric to a drawing that is drawn in the Imperial format. The same option is offered in the Block Definition dialog box.

Blocks aren't the only type of drawing component you can click and drag from the Palette view. Linetypes, layouts, dimension styles, and text styles can all be imported from files on your computer or network through DesignCenter's Palette view.

Exchanging Data between Open Files

You've seen how you can extract a block from a file stored on your hard disk and place it into an open drawing, but what if you want to copy a block from one open drawing to another open drawing? You change the way the Tree view displays data so that it shows only the files that are loaded in AutoCAD. The following exercise demonstrates how this works:

1. In AutoCAD, make sure that `12c-unit.dwg` is still open; then open the `12c-unit-metric.dwg` file.

2. In DesignCenter, click the Open Drawings tab above the Tree view. The Tree view changes to display only the drawings that are open.

3. Click the plus sign (+) to the left of the `12c-unit.dwg` filename in the Tree view. The list expands to show the components in `12c-unit.dwg`.

4. Click Blocks in the Tree view. The Palette view changes to show a list of blocks available in `12c-unit.dwg`.

5. Locate the Kitchen block in the Palette view.

6. Click and drag Kitchen from the Palette view into the open `12b-unit- metric.dwg` drawing in AutoCAD. You see the block move with the cursor. Once again, DesignCenter has automatically scaled the block to the appropriate size, this time from Imperial to metric.

7. Click anywhere in the drawing to place the Kitchen block.

In this example, you inserted a block from one open drawing into another drawing. If you prefer to use the Insert dialog box, you can right-click the block name in step 6 and choose Insert Block. The Insert dialog box opens, enabling you to set the insertion point, scale, and rotation options.

Just as with drawings, you can see a preview and descriptive text for blocks below the Palette view. In Chapter 4, you had the option to save a preview icon with the block when you first created a block. This is where that preview icon can be really helpful. The preview icon gives you a chance to see what the block looks like when you use DesignCenter to browse through your drawing files. If you don't save a preview icon, you'll see the same block icon that was displayed in the previous Palette view.

You can also add the text description at the time you create the block. Before saving the block, enter a description in the Description input box of the Block Definition dialog box.

If you're updating older drawing files to be used with DesignCenter, you can add text descriptions to blocks by using the Make Block tool in the Draw toolbar. Click the Make Block tool, and then, in the Block Definition dialog box, select the name of a block from the Name drop-down list. Enter the description you want for this block in the Description input box toward the bottom of the Block Definition dialog box. When you're finished, click OK.

Loading Specific Files into DesignCenter

You've seen how you can locate files through the Tree view and Palette view. If you already know the name and location of the file you want to work with, you can use a file dialog box to open files in DesignCenter. Instead of choosing File ➢ Open, you use the Load tool in the DesignCenter toolbar to open the Load dialog box. This is a standard file dialog box that lets you search for files on your computer or network.

If you want to open a file in DesignCenter that you've recently opened, you can use the History tab just above the Tree view. The Tree view closes, and you see a list of the most recent files you've worked on.

Downloading Symbols from DesignCenter Online

Besides enabling you to obtain files and blocks from your computer or network, you can also download symbols directly from Autodesk's DesignCenter Online website. This option offers thousands of ready-to-use symbols for a variety of disciplines. Follow these steps:

1. Connect to the Internet.

2. Click the DC Online tab that appears above the Tree view. The DesignCenter Online symbol categories appear in the Tree view, and the Palette view shows the same categories in a text view.

3. Expand the 2D Architectural listing in the panel to the left to display a set of subcategories.

4. Expand the Bathrooms category, and then click Bath Tubs. The Palette view displays a set of bathtubs.

5. Click on one of the bathtubs. The i-drop icon appears.

6. Click a tub to display an enlarged preview of the tub in the display panel along with a description of the symbol.

7. Click and drag a symbol into the current open drawing. The i-drop cursor appears in the drawing. When you release the mouse button, the symbol appears at the cursor, waiting for you to select an insertion point.

8. Click a location to place the symbol.

9. To return to the opening page of DesignCenter Online, click the DesignCenter Online listing at the top of the Tree view.

Because DesignCenter Online is a website, AutoCAD uses the i-drop feature to bring the symbols into your drawing. As you can see, the list of symbols is fairly extensive. Many of the symbols are samples from third-party vendors that offer expanded symbols libraries.

Customizing the Tool Palettes with DesignCenter

Many AutoCAD users have built their own custom library of symbols and are accustomed to using them in conjunction with custom menus. But creating and editing menus is a bit cumbersome and can become difficult to manage. In Chapter 1, you saw how easy it is to drag and drop a symbol, known as a tool, from the Tool palettes. At first glance, there is no obvious way to add your own tools to the palettes. Adding tools and additional palettes to the Tool palettes is actually fairly simple once you are familiar with DesignCenter. The following exercise shows you how it's done:

1. If it isn't open already, click the Tool Palettes Window tool in the Standard toolbar to open the Tool palettes.

2. Right-click in the Tool palettes and then choose New Palette from the shortcut menu.

3. Enter **My Tool Palette**↵. A new, blank tab is added to the Tool palettes.

4. Go back to DesignCenter, make sure the Folders tab is selected, and click the Home tool.

5. In the Palette view to the right, double-click the Landscaping.dwg file, and then double-click the Blocks icon that appears in the Palette view.

6. Make sure that the Tool palettes are visible behind DesignCenter, and then Ctrl+click Clump Of Trees Or Bushes – Plan And North Arrow.

7. Click and drag the selection to the Tool palettes.

WARNING   If you click a tool in a Tool palette, it is inserted in the current drawing; so take care when clicking around in the Tool palettes.

You've just created a Tool palette and added a symbol. You can continue to add symbols from other drawings to your custom Tool palette. Or, if you have a drawing that contains all the blocks you need for a Tool palette, you can quickly create a Tool palette directly from a file. Here's how that's done.

1. In DesignCenter, go up one folder level so you can select the Landscape.dwg file.

2. Right-click Landscaping.dwg and then choose Create Tool Palette. After a few moments, a new Tool palette called Landscaping appears in the Tool palettes. This new palette contains all the blocks found in the Landscaping.dwg file.

This exercise shows that you can quickly create a palette of all the drawings from a file. You can do the same thing with entire folders of drawings, though you might want to make sure such folders don't contain too many files.

But what if you don't want some of the items in your custom palette? You can remove items easily by using a shortcut menu:

1. In the Landscaping palette, select the top three symbols by right-clicking the tool that is third from the top and then Shift+clicking the top tool. This is a little different from the typical Windows method for selecting items from a list.

2. Right-click and then choose Delete from the shortcut menu. Click OK to confirm the deletion.

You might have noticed the Cut and Copy options in the shortcut menu in step 2. You can use these options to move symbols from one palette to another. For example, instead of deleting the three symbols in step 2, you can choose Cut from the shortcut menu, open another palette, right-click, and choose Paste. The symbols will move to the new palette location. In the next section, you'll see how you can use the Copy and Paste shortcut menu options to make a copy of a tool within the same palette.

CUSTOMIZING A TOOL

Other shortcut menu options let you delete entire palettes or rename tools or palettes. You can also edit the properties of symbols in a palette. The following exercise shows how to use the shortcut menu options to create two scale versions of the same tool:

1. In the Landscaping tab of the Tool palettes, right-click the North Arrow tool and choose Copy from the shortcut menu.

2. Right-click a blank area of the palette and choose Paste. A copy of the North Arrow tool appears in the palette.

3. Right-click the copy of the North Arrow tool, choose Rename from the shortcut menu, and then enter **North Arrow Copy**.

4. Right-click the North Arrow Copy tool and then choose Properties to open the Tool Properties dialog box.

5. Click 1.0000 to the right of the Scale listing and change the value to 4.

6. Click OK, and then click and drag the North Arrow Copy tool into the drawing.

7. Now click and drag the original North Arrow tool into the drawing. Notice that the original North Arrow is smaller than the North Arrow Copy whose scale you changed to 4.

This exercise demonstrates that you can have multiple versions of a tool at different scales. You can then use the tool appropriate to the scale of your drawing. And as you can see from the Tool Properties dialog box, you can modify other tool properties such as color and layer assignments. You can use this feature to set up sets of tools for different scale drawings. For example, you can create a palette of architectural reference symbols for $1/4''$-scale drawings, and you can create another palette for $1/8''$-scale drawings.

ADDING HATCH PATTERNS AND SOLID FILLS

You've seen how you can turn blocks into Tool palette tools, but what about solid fills? In Chapter 1, you saw that sample hatch patterns and solid fills are available in the Tool palettes. Here's how you can add your own:

1. In DesignCenter, use the Tree view to locate the `AutoCAD 2007 Support` folder. In Windows XP, it is typically in

   ```
   C:\Documents and Settings\User Name\Application Data\Autodesk\
   AutoCAD 2007\R17.0\enu\Support
   ```

   (`User Name` is your Windows login name.)

TIP To find out exactly where support files are located, choose Tools ➢ Options to open the Options dialog box. Click the Files tab. Expand the Support File Search Path listing at the top of the list, and then place the cursor on the item just below Support File Search Path. You'll see the path to the Support folder.

2. Double-click the `acad.pat` file shown in the Palette view. AutoCAD will build a list of the patterns and display the list in the Palette view.

3. You can now click and drag a pattern into any Tool palette. You can also click and drag an entire .PAT file into the Tool palette to create a palette of all the patterns in a hatch pattern file.

In this exercise, you used the standard hatch patterns that come with AutoCAD. You can also create your own custom hatch patterns and import them to the Tool palettes by using the method described here. See Chapter 26 for more information on creating custom hatch patterns.

If you want to set up a set of solid fill colors, you can do the following:

1. Click and drag the solid fill pattern from the `Acad.pat` file into the Tool palette.

2. Right-click the new solid fill tool, choose Properties from the shortcut menu, and then select a color from the Color drop-down list in the Tool Properties dialog box.

You can select any color, including colors from the True Color or Color Book tab in the Select Color dialog box that you learned about in Chapter 4. You can also cut and paste an existing solid fill tool to make copies. You can then modify the color property for each copy to get a set of custom solid fill colors.

MANAGING THE TOOL PALETTES

You can perform other types of Tool palettes maintenance operations by using the Customize dialog box. For example, you can change the order of the Tool palette tabs, or you can group tabs into categories that can be turned on or off. The following steps offer a glimpse of what you can do by showing you how to group palettes:

1. To open the Customize dialog box, right-click the Tool palettes and choose Customize Palettes from the shortcut menu.

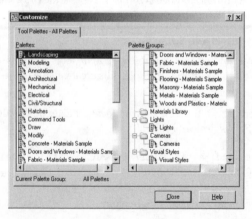

2. Right-click in a blank area of the Palette Groups panel and choose New Group.

3. Enter **My Group** for the new group name.

4. Click and drag My Group to a position just above another group so it is its own group instead of a subgroup.

5. Click and drag Landscaping from the left panel to the right panel just below My Group. You'll see a black bar appear below My Group. Release the mouse button.

6. Click and drag My Tool Palette from the left panel to the right, just below Landscaping.

You've just created a new palette group and moved the two new palettes. You can then view the palettes separately or all together:

1. Click Close to close the Customize dialog box. You see that the Tool palette still displays all the tabs.

2. To display only the new tabs, click the Properties button at the bottom of the palette.

3. Select My Group. Now the Tool palette shows only the two tabs you just created.

You might have noticed that in the Properties menu, you also have the option to show just the new groups or all the palettes. This feature lets you keep the tabs in the Tool palettes organized.

The Tool Palettes tab of the Customize dialog box also lets you change the order of the tabs by clicking and dragging the tab names up or down in the left panel. If you select a palette in the left panel and right-click, you can rename, delete, import, or export a palette.

WARNING   If you use the Export or Import options to move a palette from one computer to another, be aware that you must also import or export the drawings that are the source files for the palette tools.

DesignCenter and Tool palettes offer some great features that will prove invaluable to AutoCAD users. Although these examples show you how to use DesignCenter on a stand-alone computer, you can just as easily perform the same functions across a network or even across the Internet.

This ends our exploration of DesignCenter and Tool palettes. In the next part of this chapter, you'll look at AutoCAD's tools for maintaining layer-naming and other standards throughout an organization and for converting between your own layering system and those of clients or partners.

Establishing Office Standards

Communication is especially important when you are one of many people working on the same project on separate computers. A well-developed set of standards and procedures helps to minimize problems that might be caused by miscommunication. In this section, you'll find some suggestions for setting up these standards.

Establishing Layering and Text Conventions

The issue of CAD standards has always been difficult to resolve. Standardizing layers, dimensions, and text can go a long way toward making file exchange more seamless between different trades, and standards can also make files easier to understand. When everyone follows a standard, the structure of a drawing is more easily understood, and those who have to edit or interpret your work can do so without having to ask a lot of questions.

You have seen how layers can be a useful tool. But they can easily get out of hand when you have free rein over their creation and naming.

With an appropriate layer-naming convention, you can minimize this type of problem (though you might not eliminate it entirely). A too-rigid naming convention can cause as many problems as no convention at all, so it is best to give general guidelines rather than force everyone to stay within narrow limits. As mentioned in Chapter 4, you can create layer names in a way that enables you to group them by using wildcards. AutoCAD allows up to 31 characters in a layer name, so you can use descriptive names.

Lineweights should be standardized in conjunction with colors. If you intend to use a service bureau for your plotting, check with them first; they might require that you conform to their color and lineweight standards.

TIP   If you are an architect, an engineer, or in the construction business, check out some of the CAD layering standards set forth by the American Institute of Architects (AIA) and the Construction Specifications Institute (CSI). The AIA has a website at www.aia.org, and the CSI has a website at www.csinet.org.

Checking Office Standards

WARNING   The Standards command discussed in this section is not available in AutoCAD LT.

AutoCAD offers an open-ended environment that lends itself to easy customization, but this also leaves the door wide open for "on the fly" creation of layer names, dimension styles, and other drawing format options. It's easy to stray from standards, especially when you are under pressure to get a project out on a deadline. So, to help you and your office maintain a level of conformity to office or industry standards, AutoCAD includes the Standards command.

The Standards command lets you quickly compare a drawing against a set of standard layer names, dimension style settings, linetypes, and text styles. A dialog box displays any item that does not conform to the standards you selected. You can then adjust the file to make it conform to your standards.

You can create several sets of standards for different types of files, and you can assign the standards directly to a file so that anyone editing that file can make periodic checks against your office standards while the drawing is being edited.

SETTING UP STANDARDS FILES

The first step in using the Standards command is to set up a file to which other drawing files can be compared. Standards uses an AutoCAD drawing file with a .dws filename extension. Here are the steps you take to create a new DWS standards file.

1. Open AutoCAD and choose File ≻ New.

2. Set up the file with the layers, linetypes, dimension styles, and text styles you will want as your standards.

3. Choose File ≻ Save As.

4. In the Save Drawing As dialog box, choose AutoCAD Drawing Standards (*.dws) from the Files Of Type drop-down list.

5. Choose a convenient folder for the location of your standards file and click Save.

As an alternative to creating a new file, you can open an existing file that contains all the typical settings you will want to use on your projects. You can then delete all the graphics in the file and purge all its blocks and shapes. After you've done this, you can begin at step 3 of the previous exercise to save the file as a DWS standards file.

You can set up as many DWS files as you need for your office. Often a single set of standards is too limiting if your office is involved in a diverse range of projects, so you might want to set up DWS files on a project basis, drawing on a core of generic DWS files.

USING THE STANDARDS COMMAND TO ASSOCIATE STANDARDS

After you've created your DWS standards files, you can begin to check other files for conformity. The next task is to assign your DWS file to the drawing file that you want to check:

1. In AutoCAD, open the file you want to check for standards conformity.

2. Choose Tools ➤ CAD Standards ➤ Configure to open the Configure Standards dialog box. This dialog box contains a list box and a description area. A row of buttons appears vertically between the list box and description.

3. Click the Add Standards File (F3) button in the middle column of the dialog box. It's the one with the plus sign on it.

4. The Select Standards File dialog box opens. This is a typical AutoCAD file dialog box. Notice that the Files Of Type drop-down list shows the Standards (*.dws) file type.

5. Locate and select the standards file that you want to use to check the current file. After a moment, the name of the file you select appears in the list box of the Configure Standards dialog box. On the right side of the dialog box, you see a listing of the items that will be checked whenever you check a file for conformity to the selected standards.

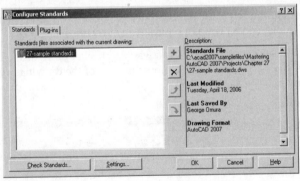

6. Now check the current file against the DWS standards file. Click the Check Standards button in the lower-left corner of the Configure Standards dialog box. AutoCAD pauses while it checks the current file, and then you see the Check Standards dialog box.

If AutoCAD finds a discrepancy between the standards file and the current file, a description of the problem appears at the top of the dialog box. For example, if a dimension style name appears in the current file that is not in the standards file, a message appears indicating that a nonstandard dimension style name exists in the current drawing. If this happens, take the following steps:

1. Below the Problem statement, you see the Replace With list box containing options related to the nonstandard item. You can replace the nonstandard item in your file with an option

in the Replace With list box by selecting the option and clicking the check box to the right of the list. Or you can leave the problem alone for now.

2. Click the Next button in the bottom-right corner of the Check Standards dialog box to move to the next "problem."

3. Repeat steps 1 and 2 until you see the statement Checking is complete in the Problem list box and the Checking Complete dialog box opens to display a summary of the checking results.

In this example, you entered the Check Standards dialog box directly from the Configure Standards dialog box. After you've used the Check Standards dialog box on a file, the DWS standards file is associated with the checked file. You can go directly to the Check Standards dialog box by choosing Tools ➤ CAD Standards ➤ Check during any subsequent editing session.

TIP After you've assigned a DWS standards file to a drawing, you will need to save the drawing, or its association with the DWS file will be lost.

CHECKING STANDARDS FOR MULTIPLE DRAWINGS

The Standards and Check Standards commands are great for checking individual files, but eventually you'll want a method to batch-check a set of files. AutoCAD 2007 provides a utility that does just that. The Batch Standards Checker is a stand-alone utility that audits a set of drawing files and checks them against their associated DWS files. The Batch Standards Checker can also check a set of drawings against a single DWS file of your choice. It then generates an audit report showing any problems it encounters.

Here's how it works:

1. From the Windows Desktop, choose Start ➤ Programs ➤ Autodesk ➤ AutoCAD 2007 ➤ Batch Standards Checker to open the Batch Standards Checker dialog box (see Figure 27.6).

2. Click the Plus button in the middle of the dialog box to open the Batch Standards Checker – File Open dialog box. This is a typical AutoCAD file dialog box.

3. Locate and select the drawings you want to check. You return to the Batch Standards Checker dialog box, and, after a moment, a list of the drawings you selected appears in the Drawings To Check list box.

FIGURE 27.6

The Batch Standards Checker dialog box

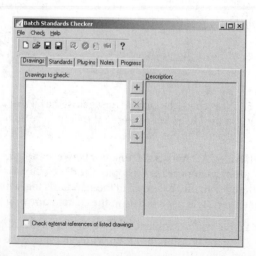

4. Click the Standards tab. This is where you can select the standards file against which your selection will be checked.

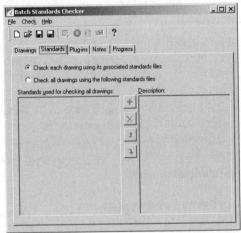

If the drawings you selected in step 3 already have a standards file associated with them, you can use the Check Each Drawing Using Its Associated Standards Files option to check each file. You can then skip to step 7.

5. If you select the Check All Drawings Using The Following Standards Files option, click the plus sign in the middle of the dialog box to open the Batch Standards Checker dialog box.

6. Locate and select a DWS standards file. The file then appears in the Standards Used For Checking All Drawings list box on the left of the Standards tab.

7. Click the Save button at the top of the Batch Standards Checker dialog box.

The Batch Standards Checker file dialog box opens to enable you to specify a Standards Check File name and location. This file will have a `.chx` filename extension. The Batch Standards Checker file is an audit file that stores the drawing list and the list of standards files in the current session. It also stores the results of the audit.

8. After you've specified the location and name of a check file, click the Start Check button.

TIP The CHX file is an XML-based file. XML is a file format designed to allow data exchange over the World Wide Web.

AutoCAD proceeds to check each file listed in the Drawings tab list box. The progress is shown in the Progress tab of the Batch Standards Checker dialog box. If you decide to cancel the audit, you can click the Stop Check button (it looks like a stop sign), which cancels the current audit in progress.

When the checking is finished, the data from the audit is automatically saved in the check file you created in step 7. Then the audit file is opened in your web browser, and you see the results of the audit.

The audit report file displays a number of options in a set of radio buttons:

Overview Displays a simplified view of the problems encountered by the audit. It lists the drawings audited and the number of problems encountered.

Plug-ins Shows the standard plug-ins used to audit the drawings. Autodesk supplies these standard plug-ins, which test for layers, dimension styles, linetypes, and text styles. Third-party developers can create other plug-ins to check for additional problems.

Standards Lists the DWS standards files used for the audit.

Problems Displays a detailed description of the problems encountered in the audit. It gives the drawing name and the specific item name that is a problem. For example, if the audit discovers a nonstandard layer name, the layer name is listed under the drawing name as a nonstandard layer.

Ignored Problems Displays problems that have previously been flagged as problems to ignore. You can flag problems to be ignored by using the Check Standards command within AutoCAD. (See the "Using the Standards Command to Associate Standards" section earlier in this chapter.)

All Displays all the audit information.

REVIEWING PREVIOUSLY SAVED STANDARDS AUDITS

After you've created a check file and completed a standards audit, you can always return to the audit by opening the Batch Standards Checker utility and clicking the Open tool in the toolbar.

This opens the Batch Standards Checker file dialog box, where you can locate and open a previously saved standards check file with the `.chx` filename extension. In this file, you'll see a list of the files that were checked in the Drawings tab and the DWS standards file used in the Standards tab. You can then view the results of the audit by clicking the View Report tool in the toolbar.

This opens a web browser and displays the audit results contained in the standards check file.

Converting Multiple Layer Settings

As AutoCAD files flow in and out of your office, you're likely to find yourself working with layering standards from another system. You might, for example, receive files from an architect who uses the CSI standard for layer names, while your office prefers the AIA standard. If your job involves extensive reworking of such files, you'll want to change the layering system to one you are most familiar with. But converting layer settings is a painstaking and time-consuming process, especially if you have several files that need conversion.

Fortunately, AutoCAD 2007 offers a tool that can make layer conversion from one standard to another much easier. The Layer Translator lets you map "nonstandard" layers (that is, those using a system different from your own) to your own set of standard layers. It can then convert those layers to match your office standards. After you've mapped a set of layers between two files, you can save the map settings in a drawing file. Then any other files you receive that contain the same nonstandard layer settings can be converted to your own layer standards quickly. Let's take a closer look at how the Layer Translator works.

When using the Layer Translator, you must initially match the layers of your incoming file with those of a file whose layers are set up the way you want. Here are the steps to do this:

1. Open the file whose layers you want to convert in AutoCAD, and then choose Tools ➤ CAD Standards ➤ Layer Translator to open the Layer Translator dialog box, which lists the layers from the current file in the Translate From list box.

2. Click the Load button in the Translate To group to open the Select Drawing File dialog box. Locate and select a file that contains the layer settings you want to use for this project. The

file can be a standard DWG file, or it can be a DWS standards file or a DWT template file. After you've opened a file, its layer names appear in the Translate To list box.

3. Select a layer name in the Translate From list, and then select the layer you want to convert it to from the Translate To list box. After you've made your two selections, click the Map button in the middle of the dialog box. You'll see a listing in the Layer Translation Mappings group, showing you the old and new layer names and the layer settings for the conversion (see Figure 27.7).

FIGURE 27.7

The Layer Translator dialog box

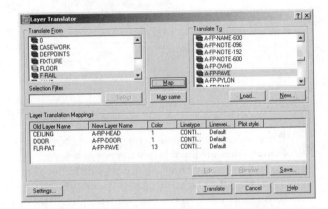

4. Repeat step 3 for all the layers that you want to convert. You can map several layers from the Translate From list to a single layer in the Translate To list if you need to.

5. If there are matching layers in the Translate From and Translate To list boxes, the Map Same button in the middle of the dialog box becomes active. You can then click this button to automatically map layers that have the same names in both the Translate From and the Translate To lists.

After you've completed your layer mapping, you can save the mapping for future use:

1. While still in the Layer Translator dialog box, click the Save button in the Layer Translation Mappings group to open the Save Layer Mappings dialog box. This is a typical AutoCAD file dialog box.

2. Enter a name for your saved settings and click Save. You can save the layer map settings as either a DWS standards file or a DWG file.

3. Click the Translate button, and AutoCAD will proceed to translate the mapped layers.

After you've saved the layer mapping in step 1, you can load the saved layer map settings into the Layer Translator dialog box in future layer translations, saving you the effort of mapping each layer individually each time you want to perform a translation. This will work for incoming files that use the same layer settings, but you'll have to create another layer map settings file for each different layer system you encounter.

To use a saved layer map, click the Load button in the Translate To group of the Layer Translator dialog box, and then select the saved layer map file you saved in step 1. You can have several layer map files for each project involving files with nonstandard layer settings.

Other Layer Translator Options

You'll often come across situations in which the layers in the Translate From list do not correspond directly to those in the Translate To list. For these situations, the Layer Translator offers a few additional options.

If you have difficulty finding a match for layers in the Translate From list, you can create a new layer by clicking the New button in the Translate To group. This opens the New Layer dialog box, in which you can enter the properties for your new layer.

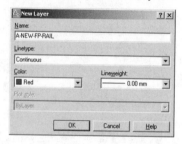

After you create a new layer with this dialog box, it appears in the Translate To list box, enabling you to map Translate From layers to your new layer.

Another option you'll find useful is the Edit button in the Layer Translation Mappings group. You might find that after you've mapped a Translate From layer to a Translate To layer, the Translate To layer is not exactly what you want. You can highlight the mapped layer in the Layer Translation Mappings group list box, and then click Edit to open the Edit Layer dialog box. From here, you can modify the new layer's settings from their original values.

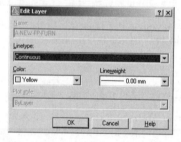

Finally, the Layer Translator offers a set of options that give you some control over the way translations are performed. For example, you can control whether layer colors and linetypes are forced to the ByLayer setting or whether layer assignments for objects in blocks are translated. You can gain access to these options by clicking the Settings button in the lower-left corner of the Layer Translator dialog box. Figure 27.8 shows the Settings dialog box. The options are self-explanatory.

If You Want to Experiment

This chapter has shown you a variety of AutoCAD features that are intended to help improve the work flow on any project you might encounter. Perhaps one of the more important features is the ability to publish to a DWF file format. By using DWF, you can easily exchange drawings with project members, clients, and others who need to view your drawings.

But before others can view the DWF files you create, they need a copy of the Autodesk DWF Viewer. You can obtain a free copy by downloading it from the Autodesk website.

Go to www.autodesk.com and look for the Autodesk DWF View and then download the viewer. The actual download file is called DwfViewerSetup.exe and is approximately 10MB in size. Autodesk grants free use and distribution of the viewer, so you can include copies along with your DWF files.

FIGURE 27.8

The Settings dialog box for the Layer Translator

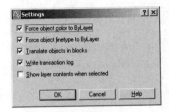

Chapter 28

Keeping a Project Organized with Sheet Sets

It's rare to have a drawing project fit on one sheet. Most CAD projects require multiple sheets, sometimes numbering in the hundreds. With multiple sheets in a project, you often spend a fair amount of time checking cross-references between the drawings and making sure that sheet titles and other information are correct.

Even the smallest project requires some coordination of cross-references between drawings in a set and checking for consistency across sheets. For example, a floor plan of a house will have callout symbols that direct you to a sheet with building elevations, construction details, or door and window schedules. As a CAD user, you eventually spend a lot of time just making sure that you have your set of drawings in the proper order and labeled correctly. Checking a set of drawings for continuity and correctness is a time-consuming job, and errors can easily creep in.

To help make your sheet coordination efforts easier, AutoCAD 2007 offers the Sheet Set Manager. (If you are an LT user, you may be interested in the information presented here, but the Sheet Set Manager is not available in AutoCAD 2007 LT.)

Topics in this chapter include the following:

- ◆ Understanding Sheet Sets

- ◆ Creating a Sheet Set from an Existing Project

- ◆ Managing Title Blocks and Cross-References

- ◆ Customizing Sheet Sets

- ◆ Archiving, Publishing, and eTransmitting Sheet Sets

- ◆ Preparing Your Project Files

Understanding Sheet Sets

The Sheet Set Manager is a tool that keeps track of all the drawings in a project. It also helps maintain the integrity of cross-references between sheets in a set of drawings by automatically updating sheet numbers throughout a set as sheets are added or moved. The Sheet Set Manager won't replace a careful check of a set of drawings before they are released for consumption, but it will reduce the amount of time you spend on coordinating and checking a set of drawings.

Sheet sets and the Sheet Set Manager can be a bit difficult to understand clearly, so in this section you can take a moment to get a better idea of what sheet sets are all about.

Organizing by Reference Files and Sheet Files

To better understand how sheet sets work, it helps to consider the methods used to organize AutoCAD files. One common method for organizing files is to separate drawings into two categories: reference files and sheet files. You can think of *reference files* as the data sources. These are the drawing files that contain the core drawing geometry of a project. For example, they might be the floor plan drawings that contain the paving, finish, ceiling, and power information, all drawn in Model Space.

Sheet files are files that represent the actual printed sheets or pages in the drawing set. Sheet files include title block information as well as the different views of the reference files needed for the sheet. View titles and scale information are also included.

You use one layout tab in the sheet file for each physical sheet that eventually gets printed. The reference files are included as Xrefs in the sheet files with the appropriate views and layers set up for that sheet.

For example, you might have one sheet file called A1 Floor Plan.dwg that has a title block in its layout tab. That layout tab will have a viewport containing a view of an Xref floor plan file. Another sheet file called A2 Enlarged Plan.dwg might contain the same Xref but with a layout tab including multiple viewports to show a more detailed set of views of the plan.

The Sheet Set Manager can take this reference/sheet system of file organization and automate it. Without the Sheet Set Manager, you must create the sheet file, import the reference file, and then add a title block, viewport, and labels to produce a finished sheet. The Sheet Set Manager automates many of the fussy details of creating and maintaining the sheet files.

NOTE The example given here illustrates one way that sheet sets can be used. You don't have to organize your drawings in this way to take advantage of sheet sets. The key point to remember is that the sheet sets focus on drawing layouts as the equivalent to drawing sheets. As long as you set up drawings to use layouts for your final output, you can use sheet sets successfully.

Managing Your Files with Sheet Sets

Sheet sets also serve as a way to gain an overview of your drawing set in a way similar to the table of contents of a book. When you use the Sheet Set Manager, you can view a list of all the drawings in your project and quickly find and open the drawing you need to work on.

You can think of the Sheet Set Manager as a database that contains information about the drawings in the set. It uses a file with the .dst filename extension to store this information. Like a database, this file is updated automatically whenever you make changes to the sheet set. It doesn't wait for you to manually save the sheet set data. In fact, you won't see a File ➢ Save option in the Sheet Set Manager.

The Sheet Set Manager can change multiple drawing files whenever a change affects the entire set. For example, if there is a change in the project information in the title block, you can update all the title blocks in the set by making a single change in the Sheet Set Manager. The Sheet Set Manager can keep track of title block data such as submission dates, drawing titles, people who have worked on the individual drawings, and other title-block–related information.

Finally, the Sheet Set Manager can help simplify the printing of whole sets of drawings by automatically setting up AutoCAD's Publish feature. It can help automate your archiving tasks and help collect all the necessary files to send your set to a different location for editing.

Creating a Sheet Set from an Existing Project

As an introduction to sheet sets, you'll first create a sheet set from an existing set of drawings. You'll then see how your sheet set can be used as a way to keep track of the files in a project.

This example is a small house remodel with some basic drawings. Although the project is small, it will show you the main elements of the Sheet Set Manager.

Using the Create Sheet Set Wizard

The Create Sheet Set Wizard is the main tool you'll use when creating a sheet set. It offers a step-by-step method for setting up new sheet sets, and as with all wizards, you can back up and make changes along the way. Here's how to use it:

1. In AutoCAD, click the Sheet Set Manager tool in the Standard toolbar to open the Sheet Set Manager palette. (You might see the title bar and tabs reversed from the example shown here, depending on whether the palette is located on the left or right side of the AutoCAD window.)

2. Click the drop-down list at the top of the palette and select New Sheet Set to start the Create Sheet Set Wizard.

WARNING   The Sheet Set Manager will not allow you to create a new sheet set unless a drawing is currently open.

3. Click the Existing Drawings radio button and then click Next. The Sheet Set Details screen of the wizard appears.

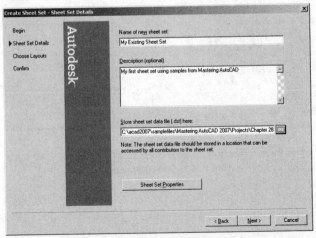

4. Enter **My Existing Sheet Set** for the name of the sheet set.

5. Enter **My first sheet set using samples from Mastering AutoCAD** in the Description text box.

6. Click the Browse button to the right of the Store Sheet Set Data File (.dst) Here text box.

7. Browse to and open the location of the `Sheet Set Sample 1` folder, which is in the `\Projects\ Chapter 28\` folder. This is a folder created when you installed the sample files from the Mastering AutoCAD companion CD.

8. Click Next. The Choose Layouts screen of the wizard appears.

9. Click the Import Options button to open the Import Options dialog box.

10. Make sure all three options have a checkmark; then click OK. You'll learn more about the options in this dialog box in the next section.

11. Click the Browse button and then locate and select the `Sheet Set Sample 1` folder you selected earlier. This is typically located in the `C:\AutoCAD 2007\Projects\Chapter 28` folder. After you've selected the folder, you'll see the list of subfolders in that folder.

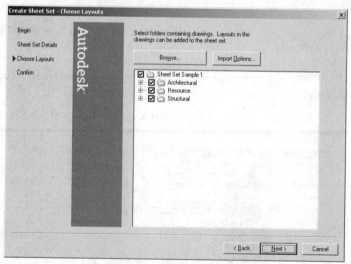

TIP   You can set a default location for your sheet sets by using the Files tab of the Options dialog box. See Appendix A for more on the Options dialog box.

12. Click the plus sign to expand the listings for Architectural and Structural. You see the drawings in those folders. Expand the list for each drawing to see the layouts available in each drawing. You can select and deselect the layouts and drawings to include in the sheet set.

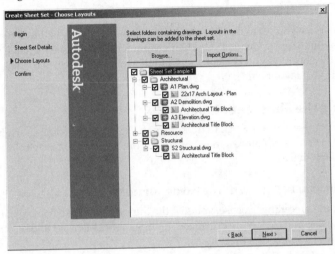

WARNING   Your list may not be in the same order as shown here, but the contents will be basically the same.

13. Remove the checkmark next to the Resource folder shown in the list. You don't want to include the Resource folder because that contains the files used as Xrefs in the Paper Space files. You want to select only the drawings and layouts that represent the sheets in your set.

14. Click Next. You see the last screen of the wizard, which shows you the statistics of your new sheet set. Notice that it shows only the layouts from the selected drawings, because the layouts are really the focus of the Sheet Set Manager. Click Finish to exit the wizard. AutoCAD creates a new sheet set.

15. Select the Sheet List tab in the Sheet Set Manager to view its contents. You see that the Sheet Set Manager now shows a list of the drawings in the Sheet Set Sample 1 folder.

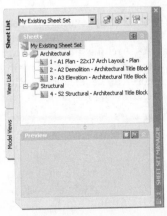

WARNING Your Sheet Set Manager may look slightly taller or narrower than the one shown here, since it can be resized by stretching its borders. The order of the drawings may also be different, but the same drawings will be shown. You can click and drag items in the list to change their order.

The Sheets list you see in the Sheet Set Manager shows you the name of the existing drawing files with the layout name appended. This helps you identify both the filename and the layout associated with the sheet. As you become more familiar with the Sheet Set Manager, you can choose to display only the layout name.

Exploring the Sheet Set Manager

Although you have more work to do before the sheet set becomes a useful tool, it's complete enough that you can explore some features of the Sheet Set Manager before you add the resource drawings.

FORMATTING SHEET SETS WITH THE IMPORT OPTIONS

In step 9 of the preceding exercise, you saw the Import Options dialog box. This dialog box lets you control how files and folders are organized in the Sheet Set Manager and how the sheets are assigned names. Here is a listing of these options:

Prefix Sheet Titles With File Name The Sheet Set Manager displays only the layout names in its Sheet List. With this option turned on, the Sheet Set Manager will add the name of the file containing the layout as a prefix to the sheet name. If you want only the layout name to appear in the Sheets list, turn off this option.

Create Subsets Based On Folder Structure If you set up your file structure to separate your project folder into subfolders (such as architectural, mechanical, structural, and civil), you can retain that structure in the Sheet Set Manager by turning on this option. Turn off this option if you want the Sheet Set Manager to display all the sheets in your project in a single column with no subfolders.

Ignore Top Level Folder When you select a project folder containing your drawings for the sheet set, and subfolders are used to keep separate categories of drawings organized, this option will cause the Sheet Set Manager to ignore the top-level folder and display only the subfolders. This is useful if you have one main folder that contains subfolders of your drawings.

The sample folders you used for the previous exercise were set up to demonstrate how these options work. All the options were turned on. As a result, the Sheet Set Manager displayed the sheets with two main categories, Architectural and Structural, reflecting the folder structure of the sample project files. It also did not display the main folder called Sheet Set Sample 1 because you turned on the Ignore Top Level Folder option. Finally, the sheet names showed the layout names appended to the drawing filenames because the Prefix Sheet Titles With File Name option was turned on.

SETTING THE SHEET SET PROPERTIES

In the Sheet Set Details screen of the Create Sheet Set Wizard, you saw a button labeled Sheet Set Properties. If you click this button, the Sheet Set Properties dialog box opens, showing you some of the settings that are part of your new sheet set.

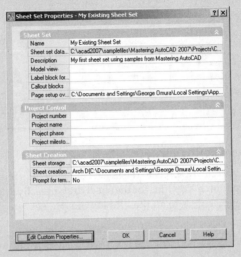

Much of this information describes the location of the files that the Sheet Set Manager will use as you work with sheet sets. Also note that there is an Edit Custom Properties button at the bottom of the dialog box. This enables you to add or edit some of the properties of the sheet set. This information can be edited in the Sheet Set Manager, as you'll see later.

PREVIEWING AND OPENING DRAWINGS IN THE SHEET SET MANAGER

You can view quite a bit of information about the drawings in your list. You can also open a file just by double-clicking its name in the Sheet List. Here's how:

1. Select 1 - A1 Plan - 22 x17 Arch Layout - Plan from the Sheet List. The Details group at the bottom of the palette displays a description of the sheet, including the name, location, and size of the file that contains the sheet.

2. Click the Preview button in the title bar of the Details group. The description changes into a thumbnail view of the drawing.

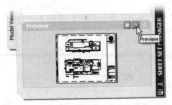

3. Double-click the 1 - A1 Plan - 22 x17 Arch Layout - Plan listing. AutoCAD opens the drawing.

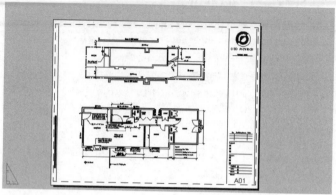

ADDING THE RESOURCE DRAWINGS

Now add the resource drawings to the Sheet Set Manager's Sheet List. Remember that the resource drawings are the source Xref files for the sheet drawings. By adding them to the Sheet Set Manager, you will have ready access to all the files in your project:

1. Select the Model Views tab in the Sheet Set Manager. The palette changes to show the Locations list. Right now, nothing is shown except for the Add New Location listing.

NOTE   You might recall that earlier in the "Using the Create Sheet Set Wizard" section, I asked you not to include the Resource folder. That's because the Sheet Set Wizard will attempt to create a sheet from all the files in your selection. You don't want to include your resource files as sheets, but you do want to include them as resources.

2. Double-click the Add New Location listing. A standard file dialog box opens.

3. Locate and select the Resource subfolder under the Sheet Set Sample 1 folder that you've been using; then click Open. The Sheet Set Manager palette displays the list of drawings in that folder.

4. Double-click the plans.dwg listing. The plans file opens, showing you the source drawing for the 1 - A1 Plan drawing.

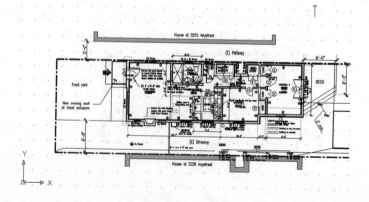

Your sheet set now contains a list of all the files in the project. You can now use the Sheet Set Manager to keep track of your AutoCAD files as the project progresses. If you need to plot all your sheets, archive them, or move them, you can do so with relative ease by using options described toward the end of this chapter.

Adding New Sheets to Your Sheet Set

Now that you've created a sheet set from an existing project, as the project continues you'll want to use the Sheet Set Manager to create any new sheets that you want to add to your set. This will ensure that the Sheet Set Manager knows about all the files in the project at all times.

But before you start to add new sheets, you'll need to do a bit of setup. You'll need to make sure that the Sheet Set Manager knows which template file to use for any new sheet drawings you add to the set.

POINTING TO A SHEET TEMPLATE

The following exercise will show you how to tell the Sheet Set Manager which template file to use for new sheets:

1. Select the Sheet List tab of the Sheet Set Manager.

2. Right-click the My Existing Sheet Set listing at the top of the Sheets list; then select Properties. The Sheet Set Properties dialog box opens. (See the "Setting the Sheet Set Properties" sidebar earlier in this chapter.) You see three groups of listings: Sheet Set, Project Control, and Sheet Creation. The Sheet Set group offers information about the current sheets and sheet set. The Project Control group lets you add information regarding the sheet set such as the project name, number, and milestones. The Sheet Creation group lists information about new sheets.

3. Click the Sheet Creation Template option, in the Sheet Creation group. If you can't read the names of the options, hover your cursor over the name and the full option name will appear as a tooltip. A Browse button appears to the right of the option.

4. Click the Browse button to open the Select Layout As Sheet Template dialog box.

   Notice that the Drawing Template File Name text box shows the location of the current default file from which a new sheet will be derived. That default location is as follows:

   ```
   C:\Documents and Settings\User Name\Local Settings
   \Application Data\Autodesk\AutoCAD 2007\R17.0\enu
   \Template\SheetSets\Architectural Imperial.dwt
   ```

TIP You can change the default location for sheet set templates in the Files tab of the Options dialog box (choose Tools ➢ Options). In the Files tab, expand the list for Template Settings, select Sheet Set Template File Location, click Browse, and then locate and select your sheet set template file location.

   Also note that a layout name is listed in the Select A Layout To Create New Sheets list box.

5. Continue to select a template file. Click the Browse button to the far right of the Drawing Template File Name text box to open the Select Drawing dialog box. This is a standard file dialog box.

6. Browse to the \Chapter 28\Sheet Set Sample 1\Resource folder, select the 22 × 17 Arch.dwt file, and then click Open. This is the template file used for the sheet drawings of the set you've been working with.

7. Back in the Select Layout As Sheet Template dialog box, select Architectural Title Block from the Select A Layout To Create New Sheets list; then click OK. Click OK in the Sheet Set Properties dialog box.

8. You see a confirmation window asking whether you want to apply the change you made to all nested subsets. Click Yes.

You've just set up your sheet set to "point" to a custom template that contains the title block for any new sheet files you might create. The last step points out a feature you'll want to be aware of.

In this exercise, you set the 22 x 17 Arch.dwt template file to be the file the Sheet Set Manager uses for all new drawings. If you prefer, you can set up the Sheet Set Manager to use different template files for new sheets in the sheet subsets. For example, you can have one template for the Architectural subset and a different one for the Structural subset if they require different title blocks.

To set up the template for the subsets, follow the steps in the previous exercise, but instead of right-clicking the My Existing Sheet Set listing, select the subset name. In the Sheet Set Sample 1 sheet set, the name would be Architectural or Structural.

Another option is to turn on the Prompt For Template option near the bottom of the Sheet Set Properties dialog box. As the option name indicates, it prompts you for a template file whenever you create a new sheet.

ADDING A NEW SHEET

Now you're ready to create new sheets that are based on the same title block as the other existing sheets in the set:

1. In the Sheet Set Manager palette, right-click the Architectural subset listing and select New Sheet to add a sheet under this heading. The New Sheet dialog box opens.

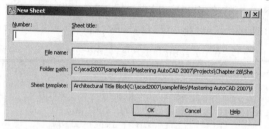

2. In the Number text box, enter **A4**, and in the Sheet Title text box enter **Details**. Notice that as you type, the File Name text box is automatically filled in. You can enter a different sheet title if you like.

3. Click OK to finish creating your new sheet. You'll see your new sheet appear in the Sheets list of the Sheet Set Manager palette.

4. Double-click the A4 - Details listing in the Sheets list. The A4 Details drawing opens to the layout tab. Notice that the layout tab has been given the name A4 Details.

5. After reviewing these steps, you can close all the drawings and the Sheet Set Manager.

Before you added the new A4 Details sheet, the Sheet Set Manager had only been collecting data about your sheet set and displaying that data in the palette. It hadn't actually created any new files. In the preceding exercise, the Sheet Set Manager created the A4 Details file, though it didn't open it until you double-clicked it in step 4.

Now that the A4 sheet has been created, you can edit it as you would any other drawing to include Xref files, blocks, or other drawing data. You can then create a viewport in the layout to lay out the sheet the way you want.

TIP Besides keeping track of existing and new drawing files in a project, the Sheet Set Manager can help you with plotting, archiving, and publishing your set. See the "Archiving, Publishing, and eTransmitting Sheet Sets" section later in this chapter.

In a large project with many sheets, managing title block information can be a lot of work. In the next section, you'll look at some other sheet set features that can automate much of the work of maintaining title block information. You'll also learn how the Sheet Set Manager can simplify the creation of callout bubbles and cross-references between drawings.

Managing Title Blocks and Cross-References

You've just seen that at a basic level, you can use the Sheet Set Manager to keep track of files in a set of drawings. But other features can help reduce the time it takes to create and maintain sheets. In this section, you'll look at some of the more advanced sheet set features by creating a sheet set that is based on an existing one.

The Sheet Set Manager can use specially designed template files to automate the creation and management of your sheets. You can include fields (see Chapter 11 for more on fields) that are "sheet set aware," enabling the Sheet Set Manager to automatically update text whenever there is a change in the sheet set. In addition, the Sheet Set Manager can use blocks with field attributes to automate the process of adding drawing titles and reference symbols, called *callout blocks* in the Sheet Set Manager. You can customize these templates and callout blocks to fit your particular style of drawing and method of organization.

Creating a New Sheet Set Based on an Existing One

To see firsthand how the Sheet Set Manager can help you manage title blocks and cross-references, you'll create a new sheet set based on an existing sample sheet set already created by Autodesk. You'll use a sample sheet set that is found in the user template folder for new AutoCAD 2007 installations. This sample sheet set uses a template file that has the title block and callout blocks already set up and available for use.

Just as before, you'll start by opening the Create Sheet Set Wizard. Follow these steps:

1. If it isn't already open, click the Sheet Set Manager tool in the Standard toolbar.

2. Open a new, blank file, then click the drop-down list at the top of the palette and select New Sheet Set to start the Create Sheet Set Wizard.

3. Make sure that the An Example Sheet Set radio button is selected and click Next. The Sheet Set Example screen appears. Here you can select from the standard sheet set examples provided by Autodesk, or if you have a custom sheet set or sheet sets from a third party, you can use the Browse To Another Sheet Set To Use As An Example option.

4. Make sure the Select A Sheet Set To Use As An Example radio button is selected. Then select Architectural Imperial Sheet Set from the list box and click Next. The Sheet Set Details screen appears.

5. Enter **My Sheet Set** in the Name Of New Sheet Set input box. You also have the opportunity to add a description of the sheet set in the Description box. The Store Sheet Set Data File (.dst) Here option lets you determine where the sheet set data file is stored. You can see the current location by placing the cursor over the input box. A tooltip displays the path to the location. This tooltip is useful if the path is too long to read from the input box.

6. Click the Browse button to the right of the Store Sheet Set Data File input box and browse to the location of the sample files for this chapter. Typically, this location is \Chapter 28\ Sheet Set Sample 2.

7. Back in the Sheet Set Details screen of the Create Sheet Set Wizard, click Next. The Confirm screen appears. This screen lets you review the settings before you confirm the creation of your sheet set. You've seen this information in the Sheet Set Properties dialog box.

8. Click the Finish button to create your new sheet set. Now you see a list of predefined sheet categories in the Sheet List tab of the Sheet Set Manager.

Now if you check your sample file folder, \Projects\Chapter 28\Sheet Set Sample 2, you'll find the My Sheet Set.dst file that you've just created. As you've seen in prior steps, this file holds the information regarding the location of the files and custom settings for your sheet set.

In the first sheet set you created, you created a sheet set from drawings that already had Xrefs and views set up for the sheets. The next section shows you how to use the Sheet Set Manager to create a sheet from scratch including views and Xrefs.

Building a Set of Drawings

The sheet set you just created is like the framework of your set of plans. It is not the actual set of drawings, but rather a structure onto which you can start to build your set of drawings. The Sheet Set Manager manages the coordination and continuity of the set as you add sheets to the set.

To see how these drawing components are managed by the Sheet Set Manager, you'll create some sheets from existing Model Space files. Start by adding a couple of floor plans to the sheet set.

You'll use the resource drawings that you saw in the first set of exercises in this chapter as the basis for the new sheets.

SETTING UP SOME VIEWS

The Sheet Set Manager uses drawing views to help simplify the creating of viewports within a sheet, so you'll start by creating some views in a plan drawing. These views will define the areas and layer settings that will be needed later when you create the plan sheets. Follow these steps:

1. Open the plans.dwg file from the Chapter 28\Sheet Set Sample 2\Resource folder. You see two plans of the house. The top plan is a floor plan, and the lower plan is a combination of a floor plan and a site plan.

2. Click the Layer Properties Manager tool.

3. Click the Layer States Manager tool in the upper-left side of the Layer Properties Manager dialog box.

4. In the Layer States Manager dialog box, select Plan_site from the list box and then click the Restore button.

5. Click OK in the Layer Properties Manager dialog box.

You've just restored a layer state that shows all the appropriate layers for the site plan. Next you'll save a view of just the site plan, which you will use a bit later when you create the site plan sheet:

1. Choose View ➢ Named Views to open the View Manager dialog box.

2. Make sure that Current is selected in the list to the left. Then click the New button on the right side of the dialog box.

3. In the New View dialog box, enter **Site Plan** for the View name. Click the Define View Window button. The dialog box temporarily closes to enable you to select a window to define the view area.

4. Place a selection window around the area shown in Figure 28.1. Press ⏎ when you are satisfied with the boundary selection.

5. Back in the New View dialog box, make sure that the Save Layer Snapshot With View option is turned on; then click OK.

6. Click OK in the View Manager dialog box to close it.

TIP If you need to adjust the view area, open the View Manager dialog box again, select the view name from the list box, and click the Define View Window button. The dialog box will temporarily close, and the drawing will display with the view area highlighted. You can then re-select the view area with a selection window.

You've just created a view for the site plan. Now create another view for the floor plan:

1. Click the Layer Properties Manager tool again. Then click the Layer States Manager tool in the upper-left side of the Layer Properties Manager dialog box.

2. In the Layer States Manager dialog box, select Plan_finish from the list box; then click the Restore button.

FIGURE 28.1
Selecting the
view area

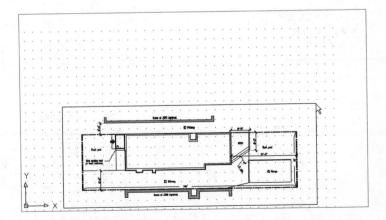

3. Click OK in the Layer Properties Manager dialog box to close it.

4. Choose View ➢ Named Views to open the View Manager dialog box.

5. Make sure that Current is selected in the left panel. Then click the New button on the right side of the dialog box.

6. In the New View dialog box, enter **Floor Plan** for the View name. Click the Define View Window button. Then place a selection window around the area shown in Figure 28.2. Press ↵ when you are satisfied with the area you've selected.

7. Back in the New View dialog box, click OK. Then click OK in the View Manager dialog box to close it.

8. Choose File ➢ Save to save the changes you've just made, and then close the `plans.dwg` file.

If you know that you want to use other views for your sheets, you can continue to define more views. But for this exercise, let's move on to actually creating a sheet from the views you just created.

CREATING A SHEET

Now that you have some views defined, you're ready to create a sheet for those views:

1. If it isn't already open, click the Sheet Set Manager tool in the Standard toolbar.

2. Select Architectural from the list; then right-click and select New Sheet to open the New Sheet dialog box.

3. Enter **A1** in the Number input box. This defines the sheet number that will appear in the lower-right corner of the sheet. Notice that as you type, your entry appears in both the Number input box and the File Name input box.

4. Enter **Site Plan and Floor Plan** in the Sheet Title input box. Again, notice that as you type, your entry appears in both the Sheet Title input box and the File Name input box.

5. Click OK. AutoCAD creates a new file called `A1 - Site Plan and Floor Plan`, and you see the new drawing name appear as a subhead below Architectural in the Sheet Set Manager.

6. Double-click the A1 - Site Plan And Floor Plan listing. The sheet appears in AutoCAD.

FIGURE 28.2
Selecting the view area

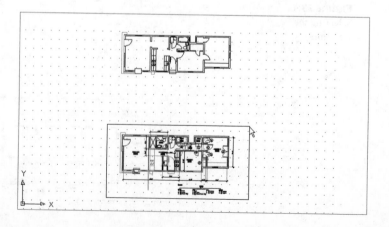

If you look closely, you'll notice that the sheet number is already in place in the lower-right corner of the drawing. The Sheet Set Manager was able to apply the sheet number you entered in step 3 to the new sheet because the template uses a field for the sheet number text. You'll learn how to add such a field to your own title block later in this chapter. For now, you'll add the views you created in the plans.dwg file to this new sheet.

ADDING YOUR VIEWS TO THE NEW SHEET

You've created views in your plans.dwg resource drawing, and you've created a new sheet for the Plan views. The next step is to insert those saved views into the sheet.

Start by adding the resource drawings to the sheet set:

1. Click the Model Views tab, and then double-click the Add New Location listing in the Locations list.

2. Browse to and open the \Chapter28\Sheet Set Sample 2\Resource folder and open it. The files in the Resource folder appear in the list of resource drawings.

With the resource files added to the Sheet Set Manager, you can add a view to the A1 sheet from the plans.dwg file you worked on earlier:

1. Click the plus sign next to the plans.dwg listing. The list expands to show the Site Plan and Floor Plan views you created earlier in this chapter.

2. Make sure the A1 Site Plan And Floor Plan drawing is the current one; then select Site Plan from the list, right-click, and choose Place On Sheet. Don't click your mouse yet, but as you move the cursor over the A1 - Site Plan And Floor Plan layout, you see the Site Plan view of plans.dwg along with a title bubble, all following the cursor. You can also click and drag the Site Plan view from the list into the sheet to get the same result.

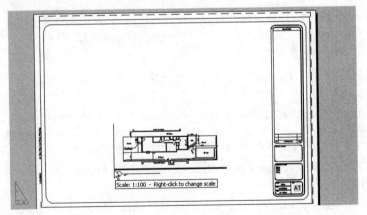

3. Right-click in the Layout view to display a list of drawing scales.

4. Select $1/8'' = 1'$ from the list.

5. Place the view in the top half of the layout and click. The Site Plan view is placed in the layout along with a title bubble, drawing scale, and view title.

6. Back in the Sheet Set Manager, select Floor Plan from the list; then right-click and select Place On Sheet.

7. Right-click in the Layout view and then select $^1/_4˝ = 1´$ from the list.

8. Place the view in the lower half of the layout and click. The Floor Plan view is placed in the layout along with a title bubble, drawing scale, and view title.

9. Zoom in to the title bubble for the Site Plan view. Notice that it already has the proper view name and scale.

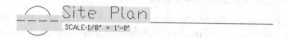

In the preceding exercise, the Sheet Set Manager performed several steps that you could have done "manually" with much more effort. It imported the plans.dwg file as an Xref into the A1 - Site Plan And Floor Plan layout. It then created a viewport in the layout, scaled the layout view according to your selections in steps 4 and 7, and finally added a title bubble and the title and scale for each view.

EDITING THE VIEW NUMBERS

You need to take care of one more item for this sheet. Although the view names and scales have been provided by the Sheet Set Manager, you still need the view numbers. Right now they are just three dashes. Follow these steps:

1. In the Sheet Set Manager, select the Sheet Views tab.

2. Expand the list, and select Site Plan; then right-click and select Rename & Renumber to open the Rename & Renumber View dialog box.

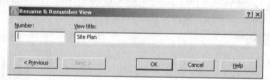

3. Enter **1** in the Number input box. Notice that the name of the view is available for editing as well.

4. Click the Next or Previous button, whichever is available for selection. This advances the data in the dialog box to the next view, which is the Floor Plan view. Enter **2** in the Number input box. Once again, you see the name of the view.

5. Click OK; then choose View ➢ Regen. Now the title bubbles change to show the numbers 1 and 2 for the two views.

The final task is to hide the viewport borders. You can do this by creating a layer just for the viewports and then turning off that layer:

1. Use the Layer Properties Manager to create a layer called Viewport.

2. Turn the Viewport layer off, and click OK to close the Layer Properties Manager.

3. Select the two viewports. Select Viewport from the Layer drop-down list in the Layers toolbar. You'll see a warning message telling you that the layer you have assigned to the selected objects is frozen or turned off. Click OK. The viewports disappear.

Adding the view numbers is important for two reasons. The obvious one is so you have a number you can refer to when referencing this plan sheet in the future. But the Sheet Set Manager also keeps track of this view number so that later, when you start to add callout blocks to your drawing set, the Sheet Set Manager knows which view goes with the callout block you are adding. The next section will show you how this works.

Adding Callout Blocks as Cross-Reference Symbols

As mentioned earlier, in the process of building a set of drawings, you will have to add cross-reference symbols. One common type of cross-reference indicates an elevation view of a building from a floor plan.

In a typical set of architectural drawings, you will have a sheet or several sheets that show the sides of a building. The most common views are the north, south, east, and west sides of a building. Elevation drawings are used to indicate window locations, wall finishes, building heights, floor levels, and other key elements in the design. Reference symbols, called callout blocks in AutoCAD, are placed in the floor plan and tell the viewer which sheet contains these elevation drawings and show where the view is taken in relation to the plan.

In this section, you'll learn how to set up an Elevation view and place callout blocks in the floor plan that show which sheet contains the elevation. You'll see how callout blocks are tied to sheet numbers so that even if a sheet number changes, the callout block will always indicate the right sheet number.

You'll use a sheet set similar to the one you just started, but with a few additions to save some work for you. The My Sheet Set 1.dst sheet set has the A1 Site Plan And Floor Plan sheet already created and an additional sheet A2 Elevation Plan. This additional sheet contains two Elevation views. These Elevation views were created in the same way as the Plan views in the previous exercise, so no method was used to create them that you haven't already been shown.

In the following steps, you'll add a callout block to the A1 sheet that references the A2 sheet. Along the way, you'll become familiar with some of the other features of the Sheet Set Manager.

Start by closing the current sheet set and the files associated with it:

1. In the Sheet Set Manager, select the Sheet List tab.

2. Right-click My Sheet Set from the list; then click Close Sheet Set.

3. Close and save any drawing that might be open except for the blank default drawing file.

Next, open the sample sheet set:

1. Click Open from the drop-down list. Then in the Open Sheet Set dialog box, locate and select My Sheet 1.dst in the Chapter 28\Sheet Set Sample 3 folder. Click Open in the Open Sheet Set dialog box.

2. Make sure that the Sheet List tab is selected; then double-click A1 Site Plan And Floor Plan and A2 Elevations to open these two files.

Now go ahead and add the callout symbol to the A1 sheet:

1. In the Sheet List tab of the Sheet Set Manager, double-click the A1 sheet again. Because it's already open, double-clicking the A1 sheet makes it the current drawing file.

2. Enlarge your view of the floor plan so it looks similar to Figure 28.3.

FIGURE 28.3
Enlarge your view and place the callout block as shown.

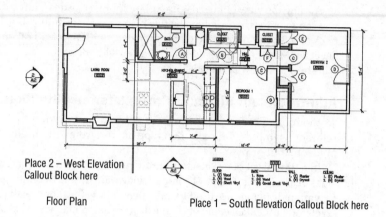

Place 2 – West Elevation Callout Block here

Floor Plan

Place 1 – South Elevation Callout Block here

3. Click the Sheet Views tab; then select and right-click 1 - South Elevation.

4. Choose Place Callout Block ➤ Elev Indicator Ext - Up from the shortcut menu. As you move the cursor into the drawing area, you'll see a symbol appear at the cursor. This is the callout block for the exterior elevation.

5. Position the callout block as shown in Figure 28.3 and click. Notice that the callout block already shows the appropriate drawing number and sheet number.

6. Right-click 2 - West Elevation and choose Place Callout Block ➤ Elev Indicator Ext - Right from the shortcut menu.

7. Place this callout block to the left of the floor plan, as shown in Figure 28.3.

When you inserted the callout blocks in steps 4 through 7, the Sheet Set Manager automatically added the appropriate sheet and view number to the block, saving you the effort of checking which drawing contained the Elevation view and making sure the numbers between the callout block and view matched.

TIP Later, when you learn how to create your own custom callout blocks, you'll learn about the hyperlink feature. The callout blocks you just added have this feature turned on, so if you Ctrl+click the text of either of the callout blocks, AutoCAD will open the drawing containing the view that the callout block references, namely, the A2 Elevation drawing.

Editing Sheet Numbers and Title Block Information

Now suppose that you need to change the sheet number of the elevation sheet from A2 to A3 to make room for a demolition plan. The following exercise demonstrates how the Sheet Set Manager can make quick work of such a change:

1. In the Sheet Set Manager, select the Sheet List tab.

2. Right-click the A2 Elevations sheet listing and choose Rename & Renumber.

3. In the Rename & Renumber Sheet dialog box, change the number from A2 to A3; then click OK.

4. Choose View ➢ Regen. Notice that the Elevation callout blocks you added earlier now show the new sheet number for the Elevation sheet.

5. Double-click A3 Elevations from the Sheet List tab; then choose View ➢ Regen. If you look at the sheet number in the lower-right corner of the drawing, you'll see that it has changed to A3.

As you can see from this exercise, the drawing numbers are coordinated through settings within the Sheet Set Manager as long as you use the callout symbols from the Sheet Set Manager.

Drawing numbers aren't the only part that can be managed through the Sheet Set Manager. You have two sheets in the set now, but they were created without regard for the client name and address in the title block. You'll need to go back and add this information to the sheets. Here's a quick way to do it:

1. In the Sheets list of the Sheet Set Manager, right-click My Sheet Set 1 at the top of the list box; then choose Properties to open the Sheet Set Properties dialog box.

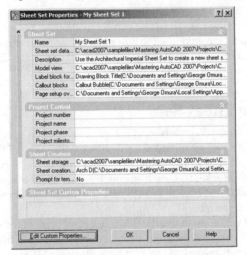

2. Scroll down to the lower half of the Sheet Set Properties dialog box where you see a set of options labeled Sheet Set Custom Properties. Click the Project Address 1 label and enter **444 Crescent Way** for the first line of the address. Or, you can add anything you like. You may need to widen the first column to read the label, or hover over the label to see a tooltip showing the full label.

3. In the next option, Project Address 2, enter **Big Bear, Ca**.

4. Enter **Smith Residence** for the Project Name.

5. Finally, leave the Client, Project Number, and Project Address 3 options blank; then click OK.

6. Zoom in to the lower-right corner of the sheet so you can clearly see the title block information; then click View ➢ Regen to display the changes in the current sheet.

The changes you made in this exercise affect all the existing sheets in the set. Also, if you add new sheets, they will display the new address and project name.

Closing a Sheet Set

By now, you have two sheet sets open: the one you created from an existing set of drawings, and the one you opened for the latest set of exercises. In the next section, you'll look at customizing sheet sets. You won't need both sheet sets open. Close the one you've been working on by following these steps:

1. Click the drop-down list at the top of the Sheet Set Manager.

2. Right-click My Sheet Set 1 and select Close Sheet Set.

3. In preparation for the next section, close all the drawings that are open in AutoCAD except for the 22 ×17 Arch.dwt file and leave the Sheet Set Manager open. You'll need the 22 ×17 Arch.dwt file for a later exercise so if it is not open, open it now.

WARNING   Closing a sheet set doesn't automatically close the drawings associated with it.

As you can see, you can have multiple sheet sets open at any one time. This feature can facilitate the movement of drawing data from one project to another. For example, you might want to borrow construction details from one set to add to a new set. You can use the Sheet Set Manager to locate the detail sheet from the prior project and then cut and paste drawing data from that drawing into a drawing in your most current project.

Customizing Sheet Sets

In the preceding section, you created and used a sheet set that was based on a "canned" sheet set from Autodesk. That sheet set included a title block with many of the field text objects already embedded in the title block so you could take advantage of the Sheet Set Manager's ability to control the text in the title block. The view title bubbles and callout blocks were also supplied, and they also contained the field text objects to automate the insertion of view names and coordination of callout cross-reference numbers.

But not everyone will want to use the title blocks and symbols offered in the Autodesk samples. You aren't limited to using the "canned" sheet set from Autodesk. In this section, you'll look at how to customize your own title block to work with the Sheet Set Manager. You'll also learn how to create custom view titles and callout blocks.

Customizing a Title Block

To begin your exploration of sheet set customization, you'll add field objects to the sample title block you used in the beginning of this chapter. Remember that that first project was an existing set of drawings that wasn't set up to take full advantage of all the sheet set features that you saw in the latest set of exercises. The title block in that early exercise contained some attributes that could be used to include text information, but the title block was not "sheet set aware." To prepare a title block for use with the Sheet Set Manager, you'll need to convert those attribute values into field objects. This entails editing the title block and saving it as the template file for the sheet set.

WARNING In this section, I use the terms *title block* and *AutoCAD block*, which might cause some confusion. *Title block* is a standard drafting term meaning the drawing border and drawing title information, including a business logo and other textual information about the drawing. *AutoCAD block* refers to the type of AutoCAD object known as a *block* that is a collection of objects combined into one object. See Chapter 4 for more on AutoCAD blocks.

SETTING UP SHEET NUMBERS AND TITLES

The first thing you'll do is set up the title block to create a "sheet set aware" number and title. This will enable the Sheet Set Manager to control the number and title that appears in the title block, as you saw in earlier exercises.

You could just open the template file and start editing the title block without involving the Sheet Set Manager in any way. But in the following set of exercises, you'll edit the template file with a little help from the Sheet Set Manager. By using the Sheet Set Manager while editing your template file, you'll be able to get instant feedback on your edits.

Start by creating a new sheet in the sheet set that you created in the beginning of this chapter. You'll use this new sheet to edit the title block. Follow these steps:

1. If it's closed, open the My Existing Sheet Set sheet set. Remember that this was the first sheet set in the \Chapter 28\Sheet Set Sample 1 folder.

2. In the Sheets list, right-click the sheet set name at the top of the list and choose New Sheet.

3. In the New Sheet dialog box, enter **000** for the sheet number and enter **Template Edit** for the sheet title. Then click OK. The sheet number and title can be anything because this is not a sheet you will save.

4. In the Sheet Set Manager, double-click the 000 - Template Edit listing. The sheet you just created appears in the AutoCAD window.

Remember that a new file based on a template is really just a copy of the template. As I mentioned earlier, the title block is an AutoCAD block that contains attribute definitions. To edit those definitions, you'll need to explode the block:

1. Click the title block to select it.

2. Click the Explode tool in the Modify toolbar.

Now you're ready to start editing the attribute definitions. Start by editing the definition for the sheet number in the lower-right corner of the title block:

1. Locate the attribute definition in the lower-right corner of the title block that shows a large *No.* and double-click it. This is the attribute definition for the sheet number. The Edit Attribute Definition dialog box opens.

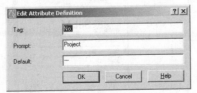

2. Double-click in the Default text box. Then right-click it and choose Insert Field to open the Field dialog box.

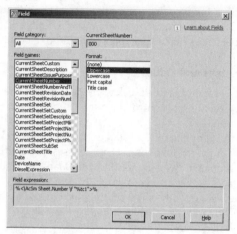

3. Select SheetSet from the Field Category drop-down list in the upper-left corner of the dialog box.

4. In the Field Names list box, select CurrentSheetNumber.

5. In the Format list box, select Uppercase. Then click OK.

6. Back in the Edit Attribute Definition dialog box, notice that the Default text box now shows 000, the number you assigned to this drawing. This tells you that your field attribute is working properly because the default value shows the current sheet number. The gray background of the text tells you that the text is a field.

7. Click OK to exit the Edit Attribute Definition dialog box.

8. Press ↵ to exit the attribute editing mode.

As you saw in step 6, you received instant feedback when you assigned the CurrentSheet Number attribute field to the attribute definition. The default value changed to the sheet number of the current drawing.

Next, you'll make a similar change to add the project name to the title block:

1. Zoom in to the area of the title block that shows the project information.

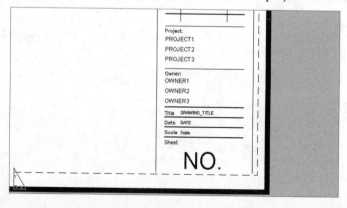

2. Double-click the DRAWING_TITLE attribute definition just below the OWNER3 attribute definition.

3. As in the preceding exercise, select the Default value, right-click, and choose Insert Field.

4. Select CurrentSheetTitle from the Field Names list, and select Title Case from the Format list.

5. Click OK. Notice that now the Default value is the current sheet title, Template Edit.

6. Click OK to accept the changes in the Edit Attribute Definition dialog box.

7. Press ↵ to exit the attribute editing mode.

These two exercises demonstrate how you can add a field object to an attribute definition and have those definitions give you immediate feedback about their association to the sheet set. In the first case, you saw that the default sheet number in the Edit Attribute Definition dialog box reflected the current sheet number. In the second exercise, you saw that the sheet title appeared.

ADDING CUSTOM SHEET SET PROPERTIES

You've added two of the standard sheet set fields to the title block. The standard fields are the ones that appear in the Field Names list in the Field dialog box. But what if you want to add custom sheet set fields that aren't on the list? You can create your own field categories in the Sheet Set Manager. In the following set of exercises, you'll create some custom fields in the Sheet Set Manager properties dialog box and then go on to add those fields to your title block.

First, set up some new custom fields:

1. In the Sheet Set Manager, right-click My Existing Sheet Set at the top of the Sheets list and choose Properties.

2. At the bottom of the Sheet Set Properties dialog box, click the Edit Custom Properties button to open the Custom Properties dialog box.

3. Click the Add button to open the Add Custom Property dialog box.

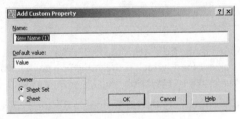

4. In the Name text box, enter **Project 1**. This will be the first line for the project information area in the title block.

5. In the Default Value text box, enter **Project Line 1**.

6. In the Owner group at the bottom of the dialog box, make sure Sheet Set is selected. This tells the Sheet Set Manager that this value applies to all the sheets in the set, not just the individual sheets.

7. Click OK to return to the Custom Properties dialog box.

8. Repeat steps 3 through 7 to add two more custom properties called Project 2 and Project 3, with the values Project Line 2 and Project Line 3.

9. After you've created the three custom properties, click OK to close the Custom Properties dialog box and then click OK in the Sheet Set Properties dialog box.

You've created some custom properties. Now include those properties in your title block:

1. Pan up to the area in the title block that shows the project information.

2. Double-click the Project 1 attribute definition. In the Edit Attribute Definition dialog box, highlight the Default text box, right-click, and choose Insert Field.

3. In the Field Names list box, select CurrentSheetSetCustom.

4. Open the Custom Property Name drop-down list near the bottom of the dialog box and select Project1. Notice that all the custom properties you created are listed here.

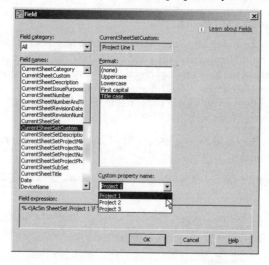

5. Click OK to return to the Edit Attribute Definition dialog box. Notice that the default field value shows Project Line 1, which is the value you gave for the default value for the custom properties in the previous exercise.

6. Click OK, and then repeat steps 2 through 5 for the Project 2 and Project 3 attribute definitions.

7. Press ↵ to exit the attribute edit mode.

SAVING YOUR NEW TITLE BLOCK AS A TEMPLATE

You've just seen how to include custom sheet set properties in your title block. Now you're ready to convert your newly edited title block back into the template file you are using for this sheet set. First, you need to turn your exploded title block back into an AutoCAD block object:

1. Zoom out so you can see all the title block.

2. Click the Make Block tool in the Draw toolbar.

3. Select 22 × 17ArchBlock from the Name drop-down list.

4. Click the Select Objects button and select the entire title block.

5. Make sure that the Convert To Block radio button is selected in the Objects group.

6. Click OK. You'll see a warning message telling you that you are about to redefine the 22 × 17ArchBlock block. Click Yes.

7. The Edit Attributes dialog box opens. You don't need to change anything here, so click OK.

TAKING ADVANTAGE OF OTHER FIELD OPTIONS

As you learned in Chapter 11, you can add field objects directly to a drawing if you want drawing data to appear as text. For example, you can add field text directly in a drawing layout to provide information about the author of a drawing, the date the drawing was printed, or the scale to which the layout is set for plotting.

This information can be included in small print on the border of the drawing to aid others when they need to know more about the drawing's origin. You can either add the field directly to the drawing by using the Field command or include it in Mtext or Dtext as part of a paragraph or sentence. Here is a listing of field options from the Field Category list of the Field dialog box to help you get an idea of what you can include as text in a sheet:

Date & Time Lets you add a date and time "stamp" to your drawing. You can select from a variety of date and time styles or show only a date or only a time.

Document Lets you add data from the drawing properties that are stored in AutoCAD by using the Dwgprops command (choose File ➤ Drawing Properties). This includes information such as the author, filename and size, comments, title, and subject.

Linked Lets you add a hyperlink to another file.

Objects Lets you include the name or property of an object. For example, you can add a block name as a field text label, or you can add the layer of an object.

Other Lets you add Diesel expressions or system variable values as field text.

Plot Lets you display plot settings as text in your drawing. This can be useful to help others determine how a drawing was plotted.

SheetSet Offers options to help automate many of the labeling chores you normally do when creating sheets.

You'll notice that the title block now shows the sheet number 000, and if you look closely, you'll also see that the sheet title shows Template Edit. These are the name and number you assigned to this sheet when you first created it.

The next task is to save the file as the template file for the current sheet set:

1. Right-click in the layout tab labeled 000 Template Edit and then choose Rename.

2. Rename the layout to My Title Block.

3. Choose File ➤ Save As. In the Save Drawing As dialog box, select AutoCAD Drawing Template (*.dwt) from the File Of Type drop-down list.

4. Browse to the location of the template file for this sheet set and select 22×17 Arch.dwt and click Save. Typically, this location is C:\AutoCAD 2007\Projects\Chapter 28\Sheet Set Sample 1\Resource. Click Yes at the warning message box.

5. Click OK in the Template Description dialog box.

TIP Normally, at this point you could close the newly saved template file and remove the 000 - Template Edit sheet from the Sheets list, but you'll use this file again later when you create other components of the sheet set.

TESTING THE NEW TEMPLATE

Now you can test the new template to make sure it is working. You'll start by creating a new sheet to check whether the sheet number and title appear correctly:

1. Right-click My Existing Sheet Set and choose New Sheet.

2. Enter **A5** for the number and **Schedules** for the title; then click OK.

3. Double-click A5 - Schedules from the Sheets list of the Sheet Set Manager to open it. The sheet shows A5 for the number and Schedules for the title.

You also added some new custom sheet set properties. Do the following to see if they are working properly:

1. Right-click My Existing Sheet Set at the top of the Sheets list in the Sheet Set Manager; then choose Properties.

2. Toward the bottom of the Sheet Set Properties dialog box, change the value for Project1 to John Smith Residence.

3. Change the value for Project 2 to 123 Anystreet. Change the value for Project 3 to Roseville, California.

4. Click OK.

5. Choose View ➢ Regen. The title block now shows the new project information you just edited.

You've customized the title block with custom properties and a "sheet set aware" number and title. Armed with this information, you can customize any title block to take full advantage of the sheet set features.

You can include a lot of information in the title block through the Sheet Set field option. Table 28.1 gives you a rundown of the sheet set options to help you decide what you might want to include.

Creating Custom View Labels and Callout Blocks

In the earlier section "Managing Title Blocks and Cross-References," you learned how to create a new sheet set from an existing one. You saw that the Sheet Set Manager was able to automatically create a viewport and add a view label, including a view number bubble, view title, and the scale for the view. Just like the title block, the view label you used in the "Adding Your Views to the New Sheet" section was a block with field attribute values. You can create your own view label block or edit an existing one by using the methods you've already seen for the title block. Callout blocks are also created and edited in the same way.

TABLE 28.1:   The Field Options Available for Sheet Sets

FIELD NAME	PURPOSE
CurrentSheetCustom	Displays custom sheet data. Custom sheet data can be added and edited through the Sheet Set Properties dialog box.
CurrentSheetDescription	Displays the description for the current sheet found in the properties for the sheet. Select the sheet name from the Sheet Set Manager's Sheet List tab, right-click, and choose Properties.
CurrentSheetNumber	Displays the current sheet number.
CurrentSheetNumberAndTitle	Displays the sheet number and title combined into one line of text.
CurrentSheetSet	Displays the name of the current sheet set.
CurrentSheetSetCustom	Displays a custom value for the current sheet set.
CurrentSheetSetDescription	Displays the sheet set description, which can be found in the Sheet Set Properties dialog box.
CurrentSheetSetSubSet	Displays the name of a subset of the current sheet set.
CurrentSheetTitle	Displays the current sheet title.
SheetSet	Displays any standard sheet set value (such as sheet number and title, sheet title, sheet number, or sheet description) from any sheet in the sheet set.
SheetSetPlaceholder	Displays standard sheet set values from within callout blocks.
SheetView	Displays sheet set view data such as view title, view number, or view scale.
CurrentSheetCategory	Displays a category field.
CurrentSheetIssuePurpose	Displays an Issue Purpose field.
CurrentSheetRevisionDate	Displays revision date field.
CurrentSheetRevisionNumber	Displays revision number field.
CurrentSheetProjectMilestone	Displays a project milestone field.
CurrentSheetProjectName	Displays category field.
CurrentSheetProjectNumber	Displays project number field.
CurrentSheetProjectPhase	Displays a project phase field.

CREATING THE COMPONENTS OF YOUR VIEW LABEL

In this section, you'll create a custom view label. This will help you to understand which field attributes are used for the view label. You will also learn how to set up the Sheet Set Manager to use your custom block.

Just as with the title block, you could create the view label block in AutoCAD without using the Sheet Set Manager, but using it helps simplify your work and also helps verify that you are on the right track. You'll start by going back to the template file you edited earlier, and then you'll create the graphics and attribute definitions for your custom view label.

1. Return to the 22 × 17 Arch.dwt file that you updated in the earlier exercise. You'll add the view label block to this drawing.

2. Make sure the current layer is set to 0; then draw a circle with a 0.25″ diameter.

3. Add a line to the right of the circle that is 1″ long, as shown in Figure 28.4.

FIGURE 28.4
Beginning to create
the view label block

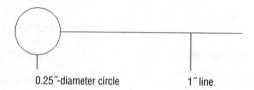

0.25″-diameter circle   1″ line

4. Choose Draw ➢ Block ➢ Define Attributes to open the Attribute Definition dialog box.

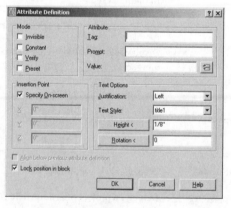

5. Enter **ViewNumber** in the Tag text box and **View Number** in the Prompt text box.

6. Click the Insert Field button to the right of the Value text box to open the Field dialog box.

7. Select SheetSet in the Field Category drop-down list; then select SheetSetPlaceholder from the Field Names list.

8. Select ViewNumber from the Placeholder Type list and Uppercase from the Format list.

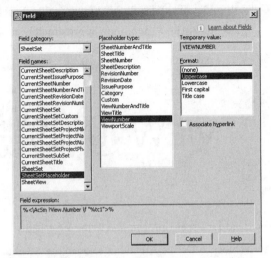

You've just added the field that this block will need for the view number. Next you'll need to make sure the text is formatted correctly.

9. Click OK to return to the Attribute Definition dialog box. Set the Justification value in the Text Options group to Middle, and set the Height value to 0.15.

10. Turn on the Preset option in the Mode group.

WARNING   If you don't turn on this option, you will be prompted for the attribute value when the view is inserted, even though the Sheet Set Manager supplies these values automatically.

11. Click OK; then use the Center Osnap to place the attribute definition in the center of the circle. You now see VIEWNUMBER in large letters centered on the circle.

TIP   If you forgot a setting in the previous steps, you can always go back and use the Properties palette to modify the attribute definition settings. Select the attribute definition, right-click, and choose Properties.

Next you need to add the view title and scale. The steps to add these parts of the view label are the same as for the view number that you just added. You first create an attribute definition by using the Insert Field option for the attribute value. The only difference is the location and text options for the attribute definition. Here are the steps:

1. Choose Draw ➢ Block ➢ Define Attributes to open the Attribute Definition dialog box. Enter **ViewTitle** in the Tag text box and **View Title** in the Prompt text box.

2. Click the Insert Field button to the right of the Value text box to open the Fields dialog box. Select SheetSet in the Field Category drop-down list, and select SheetSetPlaceholder from the Field Names list.

3. Select ViewTitle from the Placeholder Type list and Title Case from the Format list.

4. Click OK; then in the Attribute Definition dialog box, set Justification to Left and Height to 0.15. Also make sure that the Preset option in the Mode group is turned on.

5. Click OK, and place the attribute definition approximately as shown in Figure 28.5.

FIGURE 28.5

The parts of the view label block

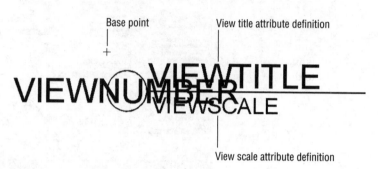

Finally, you need to add the scale information to the View Title:

1. Choose Draw ➢ Block ➢ Define Attributes to open the Attribute Definition dialog box a third time. Enter **ViewScale** in the Tag text box and **View Scale** in the Prompt text box.

2. Click the Insert Field button to the right of the Value text box to open the Fields dialog box. Make sure that Sheet Sets is selected in the Field Category drop-down list and that SheetSetPlaceholder is selected in the Field Names list.

3. Select ViewportScale from the Placeholder Type list and select #″ = 1′-0″ from the Format list.

4. Click OK to exit the Field dialog box.

5. Set the Justification value in the Text Options group to Left, set the Height value to 0.1, and turn on the Preset option.

6. Click OK; then place the View Scale attribute definition approximately as shown in Figure 28.5.

TURNING THE COMPONENTS INTO A BLOCK

You have all the attribute definitions you'll need. The next task is to turn the whole thing into a block:

1. Choose Make Block from the Draw toolbar.

2. In the Block Definition dialog box, enter **ViewTitle** for the block name.

3. Click the Select Objects button. Select all the objects you created in this set of exercises, including the circle and line that you started with.

4. Click the Pick Insertion Base Point button and select the point indicated in Figure 28.5. This is important because the insertion point of the block will coincide with the lower-left corner of the viewport that the Sheet Set Manager creates when adding views to a sheet.

5. Click OK to finish the block. The block is now a part of your template file. All you need to do is save it to have the block available to the Sheet Set Manager.

6. If the ViewTitle block remains in the drawing, erase it and then zoom out so you see the entire layout.

7. Choose File ➢ Save to save the template file, which now includes your ViewTitle block.

You might notice that in step 5, the text in the block obscures the circle and line graphic. Fields always show a gray background to distinguish them from other types of text. The gray background does not print, so even though it appears to cover the line and circle, the fields will not interfere with the printing of those objects.

INCLUDING YOUR VIEW LABEL IN THE SHEET SET

You need to complete one more task to let the Sheet Set Manager know that your ViewTitle block is available. To do this, you need to open the Sheet Set Manager Preferences dialog box and "point" to the ViewTitle block. Here's how that's done:

1. Right-click My Existing Sheet Set from the Sheets list and choose Properties.

2. In the Sheet Set Properties dialog box, click the Label Block For Views listing in the Sheet Set group.

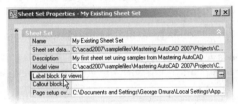

3. Click the Browse button to the far right of the Label Block For Views listing.

4. In the Select Block dialog box, click the Browse button to the far right of the Enter The Drawing File Name text box. In the Select Drawing dialog box, locate and select the 22 × 17 Arch.dwt template file you've been working with for this sheet set. Remember to choose AutoCAD Drawing Template (*.dwt) in the File Of Type drop-down list at the bottom of the Select Drawing dialog box.

5. Back in the Select Block dialog box, click the Choose Blocks In The Drawing File radio button. Select ViewTitle from the list box just below the option. Click OK after you've made the selection, and then click OK in the Sheet Set Properties dialog box.

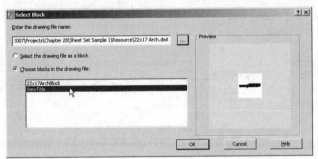

Remember that you created the ViewTitle block inside the 22 × 17 Arch.dwt template file, so when you saved that file, the block became a part of that template file. In steps 4 and 5, you selected the template file and then selected the block within that file. If you prefer, you can save your view title blocks as individual files. If you choose this route, make sure you select the Select The Drawing File As A Block option in step 4.

TIP   If you would rather use a drawing as a block, you do not have to turn the circle-and-line draw-ing and attribute definitions into a block. Leave them "unblocked" in the file, and save the file with a name indicating that it is a file for the view title. Also make sure you specify a base point for the drawing by using the Base command (choose Draw ➢ Block ➢ Base).

Now you're ready to test the block by adding a sheet and inserting a view. Remember that the Sheet Set Manager uses views to determine the contents of new viewports. Follow these steps:

1. Right-click My Existing Sheet Set from the Sheets list and choose New Sheet.

2. Enter **001** for the number and **View Test** for the sheet name; then click OK.

3. Double-click the 001 View Test listing in the Sheets list of the Sheet Set Manager to open the file.

4. Click the Model Views tab of the Sheet Set Manager; then expand the list for the elevations.dwg listing.

5. Right-click South Elevation from the list and choose Place On Sheet.

6. Right-click the layout drawing area and choose $1/_8$" = 1'. Click in the layout to place the view. The view appears along with the view title block you created in the beginning of this section.

You've seen how to create a custom view label block. The process for creating a callout block is basically the same.

CREATING A CALLOUT BLOCK

You might recall that you were able to insert a callout block in a Plan view that was linked to an ele-vation drawing on another sheet. You can create a custom callout block by using the same steps you used to create the view title block in the preceding section. The only difference is that you select a different set of field values for the attribute definitions of the block.

A callout block typically shows a circle with a view number on top and a sheet number on the bottom, as shown in Figure 28.6.

Figure 28.7 shows an exploded version of the callout block with the attribute definitions labeled with the appropriate field values. Those field values are found under the SheetSetPlaceholder field names in the Field dialog box.

FIGURE 28.6

A typical callout block inserted in a drawing

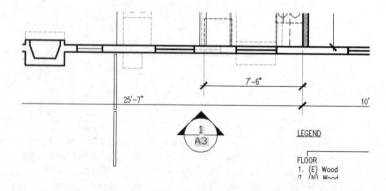

FIGURE 28.7

The attribute defini-
tions of a callout block
and their associated
field values

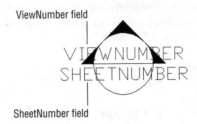

ViewNumber field

SheetNumber field

In addition, you will want to turn on the Associate Hyperlink option in the Field dialog box.

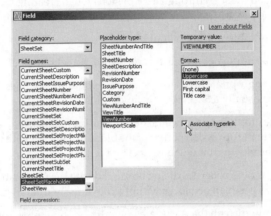

With this option turned on, a hyperlink is created between the callout block and the view associated with it. This hyperlink will enable you to go directly to the sheet and the view being referenced by the callout block just by Ctrl+clicking the field value within the callout block.

Just as with the view title block, you can include the callout block inside the template file, or you
can create individual files for each of your callout blocks. You can also have several callout blocks
for different purposes.

For example, in the My Sample Sheet Set you created toward the beginning of this chapter, you
saw that several callout blocks were available in the View List shortcut menu.

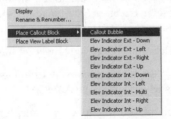

In that example, there was a callout block for the arrow directions. You can create a similar set
of callout blocks for your drawings. You can also include callout blocks for details and finishes. You
can even invent some uses on your own.

TIP If you like the callout blocks and label blocks that are already available in the My Sample Sheet Set exercise, you can find them as blocks in the template file that was used for that project. The location of that template file is `C:\Documents and Settings\`*User Name*`\Local Settings\ Application Data\Autodesk\AutoCAD 2007\R17.0\enu\Template\ SheetSets\ Architectural Imperial.dwt`. You can customize the graphics for that template file and use them for your own projects.

REVIEWING THE STEPS FOR CREATING CUSTOM CALLOUT AND VIEW LABEL BLOCKS

The callout block and view label feature will save you a lot of time when you are building your set of drawings, but you must go through a lot of steps when creating them. To help you get a better overall grasp of the process, here is a checklist of the general steps you need to take:

- Create the graphics for the callout blocks.

- Create the attribute definitions for the text in the callout blocks.

- Assign the appropriate fields for the attribute definition values. For callout blocks and view titles, this is usually a SheetSetPlaceholder field.

- Convert the graphics and attribute definitions into a block. Place the insertion point of view title blocks in the upper-left corner of the block to coincide with the location of the lower-left corner of the viewport it will be associated with.

- Use the Sheet Set Properties dialog box to indicate the file location of your callout and view title blocks. These can be blocks within a file or individual files.

Also remember to turn on the Associate Hyperlink option when selecting the fields for your callout blocks.

Archiving, Publishing, and eTransmitting Sheet Sets

The sheet sets feature is a great way to keep your project files organized while you are creating your drawings. You can also use the Sheet Set Manager to turn your set into a package that can be easily sent to others who might need to work on the drawings or view them. Or you can use the Sheet Set Manager to create an archive of your set for safekeeping at the end of the project.

You might have noticed that the Sheet Set shortcut menu contains several options. Right-click the main title of your sheet set in the Sheet Set Manager's Sheets list, and you see the Archive, Publish, and eTransmit options:

- The Archive option lets you collect your sheet set files into a Zip archive file.

- The Publish option offers a convenient way to convert your set into a format that can be easily read by others who do not have AutoCAD.

- The eTransmit option offers a way to easily transport your sheet set to others who might need to work on the set.

In this section, you'll take a closer look at these three sets of features for sharing your sheet set.

Archiving Your Sheet Set

One of the more important housekeeping jobs you'll do is archiving completed projects. If you organize your projects by folders, you could archive the entire folder for a project, but in so doing, you could be archiving many files that are really not part of the set.

The sheet set Archive option lets you be more selective about the files you archive. You can exclude files in the sheet set or include other files that are not necessarily AutoCAD drawings.

When you are ready to archive your sheet set, save all the files in your archive and then open the Archive dialog box by doing the following:

1. Right-click the name of your sheet set in the Sheets list of the Sheet Set Manager.

2. Choose Archive from the shortcut menu to open the Archive A Sheet Set dialog box.

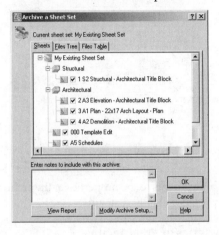

The Archive A Sheet Set dialog box has three tabs. The Sheets tab shows you the name of the sheets that will be archived. The check boxes by the sheet names indicate the sheets that will be archived. If you decide that you want to leave a sheet out of the archive, you can remove the checkmark. The unchecked file and its associated Xref will not be archived.

The Files Tree tab offers a slightly different view of the archive. Instead of just showing you the sheet names, the Files Tree tab shows you the actual filenames that will be archived. These include support files such as the Sheet Set data file and the template file associated with the sheet set.

The Files Table tab shows you even more detail about the files that will be archived, such as the path, the AutoCAD version, and similar information; it also includes information on the resource files that are Xrefs in the sheet files.

In both the Files Tree and Files Table tabs, the Add A File button enables you to include other files with the archive that are not necessarily AutoCAD related but are part of the overall project. You can use this option to include Excel or Word documents that represent correspondence or worksheets.

MODIFYING THE ARCHIVE SETUP

By default, the sheet set Archive feature saves files in the .zip archive format. You can change the way the archives are saved, as well as the location of the archive, the archive name, and several other settings through the Modify Archive Setup dialog box.

Click the Modify Archive Setup button in the Archive A Sheet Set dialog box to open the Modify Archive Setup dialog box.

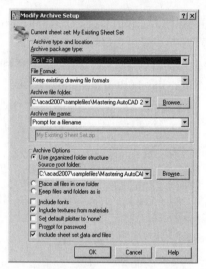

Here you can make adjustments to the properties of the archive file, including the type of file to create and whether to preserve the file structure.

SAVING THE VITAL STATISTICS OF YOUR ARCHIVE

You can also view and save pertinent information about your archived sheet set by clicking the View Report button in the Archive A Sheet Set dialog box. Clicking this button opens the View Archive Report dialog box.

You can view the vital statistics regarding your sheet set archive. You also have the option to save the information in a file by clicking the Save As button. This opens a standard save file dialog box enabling you to assign a name and location for the information file. It is stored as a plain-text file with the .txt filename extension.

Batch Plotting and Publishing Your Sheet Set

Another advantage to using sheet sets is that you can print all the sheets in a set at once and in the background. The Publish option in the Sheet Set shortcut menu enables you to turn the Sheet Set Manager into a batch plot utility.

When you right-click the sheet set title in the Sheets list of the Sheet Set Manager, you'll see the Publish option. Click Publish, and another set of options appears, offering several plotting and publishing options.

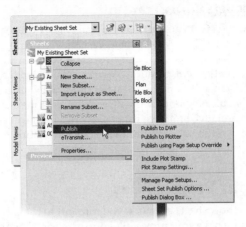

The following list gives a rundown of these options. More detailed descriptions of these options are offered in Chapters 7 and 27. See Appendix B for more on plot stamps.

Publish To DWF   Publishes your sheet set to a DWF file. This option uses the Publish command's current default settings for the Publish feature and the Sheet Set Publish Options command. Before you use this option, make sure your settings are correct by using the Sheet Set Publish Options command in the Sheet Set shortcut menu.

Publish To Plotter   Sends your sheet set to a printer or plotter. This option uses the Publish current default settings for the Publish feature and the Sheet Set Publish Options command. Before you use this option, make sure your settings are correct by choosing Publish ➤ Sheet Set Publish in this shortcut menu.

Publish Using Page Setup Override   Enables you to override the default layout settings in your sheets with a named page setup. See Chapter 8 for more on page setups. This can help to unify the plotter settings for all the sheets in your sheet set.

Include Plot Stamp   Turns on the plot stamp feature in AutoCAD. When this option is turned on, a checkmark appears next to it in the shortcut menu. See Appendix B for more on plot stamps.

Plot Stamp Settings   Opens the Plot Stamp dialog box. You can then make setting changes to your plot stamps. See Appendix B for more on plot stamps.

Manage Page Setups   Lets you edit or create a page setup that you want to apply to your sheets as they are published. When you click this option, you see the Page Setup Manager dialog box, which is the same dialog box that you see when you right-click a layout tab and choose Page Setup Manager. See Chapter 8 for more on page setups.

Sheet Set Publish Options   Opens the Sheet Set Publish Options dialog box, which is essentially the same as the Publish Options dialog box described in Chapter 27. This dialog box lets you set the type of DWF file to create, the file location, and security options.

Publish Dialog Box   Opens the Publish dialog box and populates the Sheets To Publish list with the sheets in the sheet set. See Chapter 27 for more on the Publish dialog box.

Packaging Sheet Sets with eTransmit

In Chapter 27, you learned that you can use the eTransmit feature to package a set of AutoCAD files into a Zip file in order to send the files to someone else who might need to edit them. eTransmit is similar to the sheet set Archive feature, but it also makes sure that all the supporting files, including fonts, font maps, and plotter configuration files, are included in the Zip file.

When you select eTransmit from the Sheet Set shortcut menu, the list of files to include in the eTransmit file is automatically populated with the files from the current sheet set. This means that you don't have to "manually" build the list of drawings for the eTransmit file.

If you need to make setting changes for the eTransmit feature, you can do so by selecting the Transmittal Setups option in the Sheet Set shortcut menu.

Preparing Your Project Files

Now that you've seen how sheet sets work, you can start to use them on your own projects. Sheet sets work best when you have your project files organized and have some additional files prepared and on hand. Here's a checklist of things to keep in mind when you start to use sheet sets:

◆ Organize your files so that when you import your project into a sheet set, they will be automatically organized by discipline or sheet number.

◆ Use only one layout per sheet set drawing file. The Sheet Set Manager only uses one drawing per sheet and one layout per drawing.

◆ Create a template file containing the title block that you want to use for your project. Make sure to include any sheet set fields that you want to use in the title block attribute definitions. You can also include your callout blocks in the template file for convenience.

◆ Since all the sheets in your project will most likely be printed on the same size sheet with the same plot specifications, it helps to create a sheet setup that you can apply to all your sheets. You can store the sheet setup in any drawing file and then use the Sheet Set Properties option to locate that file to assign the page setup to the entire sheet set.

If You Want to Experiment

The Sheet Set Manager is not the most flashy feature in AutoCAD, but it can be a real time-saver, especially when you're working on large projects with hundreds of files. But you don't have to be producing the drawings for the Sears Tower to take advantage of sheet sets. Even small projects can benefit from this feature.

For practice, you can go back to your original sheet set file and create a detail bubble callout block:

1. Return to the 22 × 17 Arch.dwt file.

2. Make sure the current layer is set to 0, and then draw a circle with a 0.25″ diameter.

3. Add a horizontal line through the center of the circle, as shown in Figure 28.7, earlier in this chapter.

4. Choose Draw ➢ Block ➢ Define Attributes to open the Attribute Definition dialog box.

5. Enter **ViewNumber** in the Tag text box and **View Number** in the Prompt text box.

6. Click the Insert Field button to the right of the Value text box to open the Field dialog box.

7. Select SheetSet in the Field Category drop-down list; then select SheetSetPlaceholder from the Field Names list.

8. Select ViewNumber from the Placeholder Type list and Uppercase from the Format list; then click OK.

9. Set the Justification value to Middle and the Height value to 0.1; then click OK in the Attribute Definition dialog box.

10. Place the attribute definition in the top half of the circle, as shown in Figure 28.8.

FIGURE 28.8
The components of a
detail callout block

11. Repeat steps 4 through 10, but this time, in step 8, select SheetNumber from the Placeholder Type list.

You have all the parts ready for the new callout block. The next step is to turn it into a block and save the template file:

1. Turn the circle, line, and attribute definitions into a block called DetailBbl.

2. If the DetailBbl block remains in the drawing, erase it and then change the view so it shows the entire drawing.

3. Save the 22 × 17 Arch.dwt file.

The final task is to tell the Sheet Set Manager that you have an additional callout block that you want to use with the sheet set.

1. In the Sheet Set Manager, right-click My Existing Sheet Set and choose Properties.

2. In the Sheet Set group, click the Callout Blocks listing; then click the Browse button to the far right of the listing.

3. In the List Of Blocks dialog box, click the Add button. In the Select Block dialog box, click the Browse button and locate and select the 22 × 17 Arch.dwt template file.

4. Back in the Select Block dialog box, click the Choose Blocks In The Drawing File radio button and select DetailBbl.

5. Click OK; then click OK again in the List Of Blocks dialog box and the Sheet Set Properties dialog box.

Now when you click the Sheet Views tab in the Sheet Set Manager, and you right-click a view, you'll see your new block in the Place Callout Block cascading menu.

TIP If you want to repeat the exercises in this chapter, you can reset the sheet set sample folders to their original state by copying the sheet set sample folders from the \Chapter 28\Backup folder into the \Chapter 28 folder.

Appendix A

Installing and Setting Up AutoCAD

This appendix gives you information on installing AutoCAD 2007 on your system and describes the system parameters that you will want to set to configure AutoCAD to meet the needs of your operating environment. Throughout this appendix, the system variable associated with a setting, when available, is included at the end of an option description, enclosed in brackets. System variables are settings that enable you to control AutoCAD's behavior when using commands and features. You'll find a detailed description of the AutoCAD system variables in Appendix C.

Before Installing AutoCAD

Before you begin the installation process, be sure you have at least 750MB of free disk space on the drive on which you intend to install AutoCAD. You will also want at least an additional 100MB of free disk space for AutoCAD temporary files and swap files, plus another 20MB for the tutorial files you will create.

For 2D work, you will also need Windows XP (Professional or Tablet edition), Internet Explorer 6 with Service Pack 1, a Pentium IV-CPU or better, at least 512MB of RAM, and a video card that supports at least a 1024 × 768 resolution and TrueColor.

For serious 3D work, Autodesk recommends 2GB of RAM, 2GB of free disk space not including the AutoCAD installation, and a 128MB or greater OpenGL®-capable workstation class graphics card. Autodesk has a list of certified graphics cards for 3D modeling. This list is always being updated so check the Autodesk website for the latest information.

Finally, have your AutoCAD vendor's name and phone number ready. You will be asked to enter this information during the installation. Single-user systems have a 30-day grace period, so you can install and use AutoCAD without entering your authorization code right away. You can obtain an authorization code by fax, by phone, or over the Internet as indicated when you first start AutoCAD. The trial software that comes with this book cannot be authorized, so be sure that you have a good block of free time to study AutoCAD before you install it.

Proceeding with the Installation

AutoCAD 2007 installs like most other Windows programs, but you'll want to know a few things before you start. This section provides some information that can be helpful as you begin your installation.

Installing the AutoCAD Software

Installing AutoCAD is simple and straightforward; AutoCAD uses an installation wizard like most other Windows programs. Here are some guidelines to follow during the installation process:

- Before you start, make sure you have enough disk space and also make sure that no other programs are running. You will also need your AutoCAD serial number. These items are usually on the package label. If you are installing the trial version from the companion CD, use the serial number 000-00000000.

- Typically, the AutoCAD installation program starts automatically when you insert the AutoCAD 2007 CD into your computer, but in the event that it doesn't, do the following:

   1. In Windows, choose Start ➢ Run to open the Run dialog box.

   2. In the Open box, enter **D:setup**. Enter the letter of your CD drive in place of the *D* in this example. Click OK when you are ready. You see the AutoCAD 2007 Master Setup dialog box.

- You'll see a row of tabs at the top of the Install dialog box labeled, Documentation and Support. Select the Install tab and select Stand Alone Installation. The rest of the dialog box will change to show the Install options. Click Install under Install AutoCAD 2007.

- After the installation starts, follow the directions in the installation wizard. In the Personal Information screen, you are asked for your name, company, and AutoCAD vendor's name and telephone number. This information will be displayed on the opening AutoCAD screen, so don't enter anything you'll regret later.

- You are also asked to select the location for your AutoCAD files. The tutorials in this book assume that you have AutoCAD on drive C and in a folder called \Program Files\Autodesk\AutoCAD 2007\—these are the defaults during the installation.

- You are given the choice of Typical or Custom installation. Choose Typical.

- You are also asked if you want to install the Express tools and sample files. Go ahead and install them.

- If you don't have enough disk space, the installation wizard will let you know exactly how much room you need on each drive involved in the installation. You can take steps to make more room by using Windows Explorer or the Windows Disk Cleanup utility. If you do this, make sure you close those programs when you've finished making room and before you return to the AutoCAD setup.

After the installation is complete, you will see the AutoCAD 2007 Setup dialog box, which might ask whether you want to restart your computer. It's usually better to restart your computer immediately after installing AutoCAD, if it requests that you do so.

Configuring AutoCAD

In this section, you will learn how to configure AutoCAD to work the way you want it to work. You can configure AutoCAD at any time during an AutoCAD session by using the Options dialog box.

The tutorials in this book assume that you are using the default Options settings. As you become more familiar with the workings of AutoCAD, you might want to adjust the way AutoCAD works, using the Options dialog box. You can also set many of the options in the Options dialog box through system variables.

Choose Tools ≻ Options or type **options.⏎** at the Command prompt to open the Options dialog box, which has the following tabs and settings.

TIP   Many of the options in the Options dialog box show an AutoCAD file icon. This icon indicates that the option's setting is saved with the file, as opposed to being saved as part of AutoCAD's default settings.

The Files Tab

You use the options on the Files tab to tell AutoCAD where to place or find files it needs to operate. It uses a hierarchical list, similar to the one presented by Windows Explorer. You first see the general topics in the Search Paths, File Names, And File Locations list box. You can expand any item in the list by clicking its plus sign.

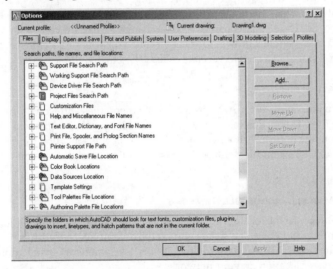

The following explanations describe each item in the list box. Chances are you won't have to use most of them, but you might change others occasionally.

TIP   The related system variable is shown in brackets at the end of the description of each item.

SUPPORT FILE SEARCH PATH

AutoCAD relies on external files for many of its functions. Menus, text fonts, linetypes, and hatch patterns are a few examples of features that rely on external files. The Support File Search Path item tells AutoCAD where to look for these files. You can add folder paths to this listing by clicking the Add button and entering a new path or using the Browse button. It's probably not a good idea to delete any of the existing items under this heading unless you really know what you are doing.

If you are familiar with using environment variables, you can include them in the search paths.

WORKING SUPPORT FILE SEARCH PATH

The Working Support File Search Path item contains a read-only list of the support file search path for the current session, including any special settings that might be included with command switches and environment settings.

DEVICE DRIVER FILE SEARCH PATH

The Device Driver File Search Path item locates the device drivers for AutoCAD. *Device drivers* are applications that enable AutoCAD to communicate directly with the printers, plotters, and input devices. In most cases, you do not have to do anything with this setting.

PROJECT FILES SEARCH PATH

Eventually, a consultant or other AutoCAD user will provide you with files that rely on Xrefs or raster images. Often, such files will expect the Xref or raster image to be in a particular folder. When such files are moved to another location with a different folder system, Xref-dependent files will not be able to find their Xrefs. The Project Files Search Path item enables you to specify a folder where Xrefs or other dependent files are stored. If AutoCAD is unable to find an Xref or other file, it will look in the folder you specify in this listing.

To specify this folder, highlight Project Files Search Path and then click the Add button. AutoCAD suggests `Project1` as the folder name. You can change the name if you prefer. Click the plus sign next to `Project1`, and then click Browse to select a location for your project file search path. The project file search path is stored in a system variable called Projectname [Projectname].

CUSTOMIZATION FILES

If you are customizing AutoCAD with your own menu files and icons, you can use this setting to locate your files. This option makes if convenient to keep your customization files in a place that is separate from the built-in AutoCAD files. You can specify a location for the main customization files like your CUI menu files, enterprise customization files for files you want to share, and your custom icons.

HELP AND MISCELLANEOUS FILE NAMES

This item lets you set the location of a variety of support files including menu, help, automatic save, log, and configuration files. It also lets you set the default Internet address for the Launch Browser button on the AutoCAD Standard toolbar. If you have a network installation, you can also set the License Manager location on your network.

TEXT EDITOR, DICTIONARY, AND FONT FILE NAMES

Use this item to set the location of the text editor [mtexted], the Custom and Standard dictionaries [Dctmain, Dctust], and the alternate font and font mapping files [Fontalt]. Chapter 10 describes these tools in more detail.

PRINT FILE, SPOOLER, AND PROLOG SECTION NAMES

You can specify a print filename other than the default that is supplied by AutoCAD whenever you plot to a file. The Spooler option lets you specify an application intended to read and plot a plot file. The Prolog option is intended for PostScript export. It lets you specify the Prolog section from the `Acad.psf` file that you want AutoCAD to include with exported Encapsulated PostScript files. See Appendix B and Chapter 19 for more information on exporting PostScript files and the `Acad.psf` file [Psprolog].

PRINTER SUPPORT FILE PATH

Several support files are associated with the AutoCAD printing and plotting system. This item enables you to indicate where you want AutoCAD to look for these files.

AUTOMATIC SAVE FILE LOCATION

You can indicate the location for AutoCAD's automatic save file by using this item [Savefilepath].

COLOR BOOK LOCATIONS

This item lets you specify the locations for the PANTONE color book. This is an optional installation item so if the PANTONE color books are not installed, you can install them through your AutoCAD 2007 Installation CD.

DATA SOURCES LOCATION

This item lets you specify the location for ODBC (Open Database Connectivity) Data Link files for linking AutoCAD drawings to database files.

TEMPLATE SETTINGS

When you select the Use A Template option in the Create New Drawing dialog box, AutoCAD looks at this setting for the location of template files. You can modify this setting, but chances are you won't need to.

TOOL PALETTES FILE LOCATIONS

This item lets you specify a location for your custom Tool palettes resource files. When you create custom palettes, AutoCAD will store its data regarding those palettes in this location.

AUTHORING PALETTE FILE LOCATIONS

If you are creating custom dynamic blocks, you can designate a folder location where you keep your custom block settings and files.

LOG FILE LOCATION

With this item, you can indicate where log files are to be placed [Logfilepath].

PLOT AND PUBLISH LOG FILE LOCATION

With this item, you can indicate where Plot and Publish log files are to be placed [Logfilepath].

TEMPORARY DRAWING FILE LOCATION

AutoCAD creates temporary files to store portions of your drawings as you work on them. You usually don't have to think about these temporary files unless they start crowding your hard disk or unless you are working on a particularly large file on a system with little memory. This item lets you set the location for temporary files. The default location is the C:\Documents and Settings\ User Name\Local Settings\Temp\ folder. User Name is your login name. If you have a hard disk that has lots of room and is very fast, you might want to change this setting to a location on that drive to improve performance [Tempprefix, read-only].

TEMPORARY EXTERNAL REFERENCE FILE LOCATION

If you are on a network and you foresee a situation in which another user will want to open an Xref of a file you are working on, you can set the Demand Load Xrefs setting in the Open And Save tab to Enabled With Copy. This causes AutoCAD to make and use a copy of any Xref that is currently loaded. This way, others can open the original file. The Temporary External Reference File Location lets you specify the folder where AutoCAD will store this copy of an Xref [Xloadpath].

TEXTURE MAPS SEARCH PATH

This item specifies the location for AutoCAD Render texture maps. In most cases, you won't have to change this setting. You can, however, add a folder name to this item for your own texture maps as you acquire or create them.

I-DROP ASSOCIATED FILE LOCATION

This is where you specify the location of files imported to your computer through the i-drop function in AutoCAD. By default, no location is specified, so the i-drop imported DWG file is placed in the same folder location as the current drawing.

NOTE While in AutoCAD, you might want to quickly find the location of a resource file such as a log file or the automatic save file. You can do so by using the system variable associated with the resource. For example, to quickly find the location of the log file path, enter **logfilepath.**⏎ at the Command prompt. For the automatic save file, enter **savefilepath.**⏎. LT users can employ the Modemacro command as in **Modemacro.**⏎**$(getvar,logfilepath).**⏎ or **Modemacro.**⏎**$(getvar,savefilepath).**⏎. See Chapter 26 for more on Modemacro.

The Display Tab

The settings on this tab let you control the appearance of AutoCAD. You can make AutoCAD look completely different with these settings if you choose. Scroll bars, fonts, and colors are all up for grabs.

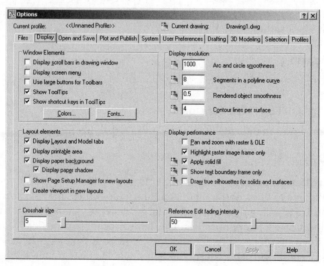

THE WINDOW ELEMENTS GROUP

These options control the general settings for AutoCAD windows:

Display Scroll Bars In Drawing Window Lets you turn the scroll bars on and off. If you have a small monitor with low resolution, you might want to turn the scroll bars off for a larger drawing area.

Display Screen Menu   Turns on the old AutoCAD Format Screen menu that once appeared on the right side of the screen. If you really must have it displayed, this is where you can turn it back on.

Use Large Buttons For Toolbars   Controls whether large icon buttons are used in toolbars.

Show ToolTips   Controls whether tooltips are shown when you hover the mouse over tools.

Show Shortcut Keys In ToolTips   Controls whether shortcut keys are displayed in tooltips.

Colors   Opens a dialog box that lets you set the color for the various components of the AutoCAD window. This is where you can change the background color of the drawing area if you find that black doesn't work for you.

Fonts   Opens a dialog box that lets you set the fonts of the AutoCAD window. You can select from the standard set of Windows fonts available in your system.

THE DISPLAY RESOLUTION GROUP

These options control the way objects are displayed in AutoCAD. You can choose between display accuracy and speed:

Arc And Circle Smoothness   Controls the appearance of arcs and circles, particularly when you zoom in on them. In some instances, arcs and circles will appear to be octagons, even though they will plot as smooth arcs and circles. If you want arcs and circles to appear smoother, you can increase this setting. An increase will also increase memory use. This setting is also controlled by the Viewres system variable [Viewres].

Segments In A Polyline Curve   Controls the smoothness of polyline curves. Increase the value to make curved polylines appear smoother and less segmented. Decrease the value for improved display performance. This option is also set by the Splinesegs system variable [Splinesegs].

Rendered Object Smoothness   Controls the smoothness of curved solids when they are rendered or shaded. Values can range from 0.01 to 10 [Facetres].

Contour Lines Per Surface   Lets you set the number of contour lines used to represent solid, curved surfaces. Values can range from 0 to 2047 [Isolines].

THE LAYOUT ELEMENTS GROUP

These options control the display of elements in the Paper Space Layout tabs. See Chapters 8 and 16 for more information. Most of these options are self-explanatory. The Show Page Setup Manager For New Layouts option opens the Page Setup Manager dialog box whenever a layout is first opened. The Create Viewport In New Layouts option automatically creates a viewport in a layout when it is first opened.

THE DISPLAY PERFORMANCE GROUP

You can adjust a variety of display-related settings from this group:

Pan And Zoom With Raster & OLE   Controls the way raster images react to real-time pans and zooms. If this option is selected, raster images move with the cursor. Turn this option off for better performance [Rtdisplay].

Highlight Raster Image Frame Only   Determines how raster images appear when selected. Turn this option on for better performance [Imagehlt].

Apply Solid Fill   Controls the display of filled objects such as wide polylines and areas filled with the solid hatch pattern. This option is also controlled by the Fillmode system variable. See

Chapter 18 for more information on filled polylines and the solid hatch pattern. Turn this option off for better performance [Fillmode].

Show Text Boundary Frame Only   Controls the way text is displayed. Turn this option on to display text as rectangular boundaries [Qtextmode].

Draw True Silhouettes For Solids And Surfaces   Controls whether surface meshes for solid models are displayed. Turn this option off for better performance [Dispsilh].

THE CROSSHAIR SIZE SLIDER

This slider controls the size of the crosshair cursor. You can set this to 100 percent to simulate the full-screen crosshair cursor of earlier versions of AutoCAD [Cursorsize].

THE REFERENCE EDIT FADING INTENSITY SLIDER

This slider controls the display of nonselected objects during in-place reference editing. See Chapter 7 for more information on in-place reference editing [Xfadectl].

The Open And Save Tab

The Open And Save tab offers general file-related options such as the frequency of the Automatic Save and the default file version for the Save and Save As options.

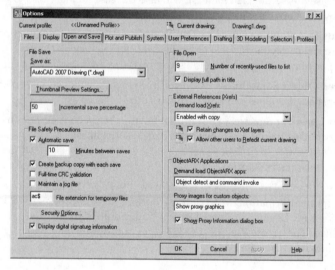

THE FILE SAVE GROUP

You can control how AutoCAD saves files by using the options in this group:

Save As   This drop-down list lets you set the default file type for the File ➢ Save and the File ➢ Save As options. If you are working in an environment that requires Release 14 files as the standard file type, for example, you can use this option to select Release 14 as the default file type. You can also set up AutoCAD to save DXF files by default.

Thumbnail Preview Settings   Lets you determine whether a preview image is saved with a drawing. Preview images are used in the AutoCAD File dialog box and in DesignCenter to let you preview a file before opening it [Rasterpreview]. You can also control the display of the sheet set preview [Updatethumbnail].

Incremental Save Percentage   Controls the degree to which the Incremental Save feature is used whenever you choose File ➤ Save or File ➤ Save As. An incremental save improves the time it takes to save a file to disk, but it also makes the file size larger. If you have limited disk space, you can set this value to 25. A value of 0 turns off incremental save altogether, but will reduce AutoCAD performance. This option is also controlled through the Isavepercent system variable [Isavepercent].

THE FILE SAFETY PRECAUTIONS GROUP

These options control the automatic backup features of AutoCAD:

Automatic Save   Offers control over the Automatic Save features. You can turn it on or off by using the check box or set the frequency at which files are saved by using the Minutes Between Saves input box. You can set the location for the automatic save files by using the Automatic Save File Location listing in the Files tab of the Options dialog box. You can also set the frequency of automatic saves through the Savetime system variable [Savefilepath, Savefile].

Create Backup Copy With Each Save   Lets you determine whether a BAK file is saved along with every save you perform. You can turn this option off to conserve disk space. You can also use the Isavebak system variable to turn this option on or off [Isavebak, Tempprefix].

Full-Time CRC Validation   Controls the cyclic redundancy check feature, which checks for file errors whenever AutoCAD reads a file. This feature is helpful in troubleshooting hardware problems in your system.

Maintain A Log File   Lets you record the data in the AutoCAD Text window. See Chapter 19 for more on this feature. You can set the location for log files in the Files tab of the Options dialog box [Logfilemode, Logfilename].

File Extension For Temporary Files   Lets you set the filename extension for AutoCAD temporary files. These are files AutoCAD uses to store drawing data temporarily as you work on a file. If you are working on a network where temporary files from multiple users might be stored in the same folder, you might want to change this setting to identify your temporary files.

Security Options   Opens the Security Options dialog box, in which you can either password-protect a file or add a digital signature. See Chapter 27 for more on these features.

Display Digital Signature Information   When a file containing a digital signature is opened, this option will display a warning message alerting you to the presence of the signature [Sigwarn]. See Chapter 27 for more on the digital signature feature.

THE FILE OPEN GROUP

You can control how AutoCAD displays filenames in the File menu or the drawing title bar:

Number Of Recently-Used Files To List   This input box lets you specify the number of files listed in the File menu history list. The default is 9, but you can enter a value from 0 to 9.

Display Full Path In Title   Just as its name indicates, this option controls whether the full path is included in the title bar with a drawing's name.

THE EXTERNAL REFERENCES (XREFS) GROUP

These options let you control memory and layer features of Xrefs:

Demand Load Xrefs   Lets you turn on the Demand Load feature of Xrefs. Demand Load helps to improve the performance of files that use Xrefs by loading only those portions of an Xref drawing that are required for the current open drawing. This option is a drop-down list with three options: Disabled turns off demand loading, Enabled turns on demand loading, and Enabled With Copy turns on demand loading by using a copy of the Xref source file. This last option enables others on a network to edit the Xref source file while you're working on a file that also uses the file [Xloadctl].

Retain Changes To Xref Layers   Lets you save layer settings of Xref files in the current drawing. This does not affect the source Xref file. With this setting turned off, the current file will import the layer settings of the Xref file when it loads that file. This setting is also controlled by the Visretain system variable [Visretain].

Allow Other Users To Refedit Current Drawing   Lets you specify whether others can simultaneously edit a file that you are editing. This option is intended to enable others to use the Modify ➢ Xref And Block Editing option (the Refedit command) on files that you currently have loaded in AutoCAD [Xedit].

THE OBJECTARX APPLICATIONS GROUP

AutoCAD allows users and third-party developers to create custom objects that usually require the presence of a custom ObjectARX application to support the object. These options control the way AutoCAD treats custom objects and their related ObjectARX applications:

Demand Load ObjectARX Apps   Controls when a supporting third-party application is loaded if a custom object is present in a file. This option offers several settings that you can select from a drop-down list. The available settings are Disable Load On Demand, Custom Object Detect, Command Invoke, and Object Detect And Command Invoke. Disable Load On Demand prevents AutoCAD from loading third-party applications when a custom object is present. Some standard AutoCAD commands will not work if you select Disable Load On Demand because AutoCAD itself uses ObjectARX applications. Custom Object Detect causes AutoCAD to automatically load an ARX application if a custom object is present. Command Invoke loads a custom application when you invoke a command from that application. The Object Detect And Command Invoke option loads an ARX application when either a custom object is present or when you invoke a command from that application [Demandload].

Proxy Images For Custom Objects   Offers a drop-down list with three settings that control the display of custom objects when the objects supporting ARX applications are not present on your system. Do Not Show Proxy Graphics turns off the display of custom objects. Show Proxy Graphics displays the custom object. Show Proxy Bounding Box shows a bounding box in place of the custom object.

Show Proxy Information Dialog Box   Lets you determine whether the Show Proxy Information warning dialog box is used. When this option is selected, the Show Proxy Information warning appears when a drawing with custom objects is opened but the objects' associated ARX application cannot be found by AutoCAD [Proxynotice].

The Plot And Publish Tab

The Plot And Publish tab in the Options dialog box offers settings related to printing and plotting. See Chapter 8 and Appendix B for a description of these options.

The System Tab

These options in the System tab offer control over some of AutoCAD's general interface settings such as display drivers and pointing devices.

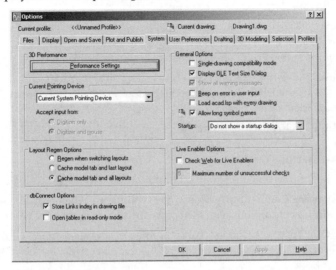

THE 3D PERFORMANCE GROUP

Clicking the Performance Settings button in this group displays a variety of settings to help you fine-tune the performance of your 3D graphics. When you click this option, the Adaptive Degradation And Performance Tuning dialog box opens. Adaptive degradation refers to the way AutoCAD's display behaves as you change views such as camera or orbital. AutoCAD will degrade the view to keep up with real-time changes in a view, thus the term "adaptive degradation." You can control just how the view degrades using these options. The Hardware And Performance Tuning section gives you information about your current graphic system and allows you to make setting changes. See the "Adjusting AutoCAD's 3D Graphics System" section later in this appendix.

THE CURRENT POINTING DEVICE GROUP

You can choose the type of pointing device you want to use with AutoCAD through the options in this group. The drop-down list offers Current System Pointing Device and Wintab Compatible Digitizer ADI 4.2 – by Autodesk. If you want to use the default Windows pointing device, choose Current System Pointing Device. If you have a digitizer that uses the Wintab driver, you can select Wintab Compatible Digitizer.

You can further limit AutoCAD's use to the Wintab Compatible Digitizer by selecting the Digitizer Only radio button. If you select the Digitizer And Mouse radio button, AutoCAD will accept input from both devices.

THE LAYOUT REGEN OPTIONS GROUP

This set of radio buttons enables you to specify how regens are applied when working with layout tabs:

Regen When Switching Layouts   This causes AutoCAD to force a regen when you select a Layout or Model tab. Use this option when your computer is limited in RAM.

Cache Model Tab And Last Layout This causes AutoCAD to suppress regens when switching to the Model tab or the most recently opened Layout tab. Other layouts will regen when selected.

Cache Model Tab And All Layouts This causes AutoCAD to suppress regens when selecting any Layout tabs or the Model tab.

THE DBCONNECT OPTIONS GROUP

The check boxes in this group offer controls over the dbConnect feature:

Store Links Index In Drawing File Lets you specify where database link data is stored. If this check box is selected, link data is stored in the drawing that is linked to a database. This increases file size and file-loading time.

Open Tables In Read-Only Mode Lets you limit access to database files.

THE GENERAL OPTIONS GROUP

This set of check boxes enables you to set options related to the general operation of AutoCAD:

Single-Drawing Compatibility Mode Lets you control whether AutoCAD allows you to open multiple documents or limits you to a single document, as in earlier versions of AutoCAD [Sdi].

Display OLE Text Size Dialog Lets you control the display of the OLE Text Size dialog box, which normally appears when you insert OLE text objects into an AutoCAD drawing by choosing Edit ➢ Paste.

Show All Warning Messages If you turn off a warning message with the Don't Display This Warning Again option, this option enables you to turn all warning messages back on. If no warning messages have been turned off, this option is grayed out.

Beep On Error In User Input Turns on an alarm beep that sounds whenever there is an input error.

Load Acad.lsp With Every Drawing Lets you determine whether an Acad.lsp file is loaded with every drawing. If you are used to using an Acad.lsp file with your AutoCAD system, you can select this option; otherwise, AutoCAD will load only the Acaddoc.lsp file [Acadlspasdoc].

Allow Long Symbol Names Enables you to use long names for items such as layer, block, linetype, and text-style names. With this option turned on, you can enter as many as 255 characters for names [Extnames].

Startup This drop-down list lets you determine whether AutoCAD displays the AutoCAD Startup dialog box when you first start AutoCAD or whether the Create New Drawing dialog box opens when you choose File ➢ New. If Show Startup Dialog Box is selected, these dialog boxes appear. Otherwise, AutoCAD automatically opens a default blank file based on the last template file used, and the Select Template dialog box appears when you choose File ➢ New.

THE LIVE ENABLER OPTIONS GROUP

Since AutoCAD 14, third-party developers have had the ability to create custom objects, also known as *proxy objects*, through a programming tool known as ObjectARX. When this feature was first introduced, you had to have the third-party application installed on your computer in order to view or edit such custom objects. *Object enablers* are small programs, like plug-ins to AutoCAD, that enable you to view and edit custom third-party objects without having the full third-party application present. These object enablers might be available on the Web for free download if the third-party producer has posted them.

Check Web For Live Enablers   By selecting this option, AutoCAD will look for enablers over the Internet. For example, if you receive a file created in Architectural Desktop that contains a custom object, AutoCAD can automatically go to the Autodesk website and download the Architectural Desktop Object Enabler so that you can edit and view the file. The Live Enabler options let you control how the Object Enabler feature is engaged when AutoCAD encounters custom objects.

Maximum Number Of Unsuccessful Checks   This option lets you specify the number of times AutoCAD checks the Internet for object enablers after an attempt to make a connection has failed.

The User Preferences Tab

The options in the User Preferences tab enable you to adjust the way AutoCAD reacts to user input.

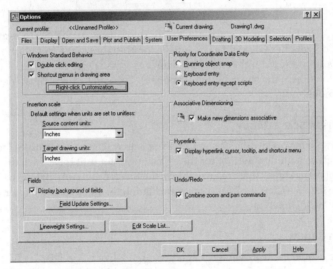

THE WINDOWS STANDARD BEHAVIOR GROUP

These settings enable you to control how AutoCAD reacts to keyboard accelerators and mouse right-clicks:

Double Click Editing   Controls whether a double-click on an object automatically starts an editing command for the object. If this option is turned off, double-clicking objects has no affect. [Dblclkedit].

Shortcut Menus In Drawing Area   Lets you see the shortcut menu when you right-click. When this check box is not selected, AutoCAD responds to a right-click with an ↵ [Shortcutmenu].

Right-Click Customization Opens the Right-Click Customization dialog box, which offers further options for the behavior of the right-click in AutoCAD.

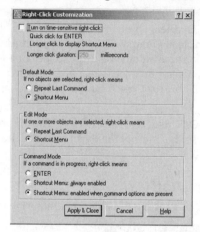

The Turn On Time-Sensitive Right-Click option causes AutoCAD to respond differently depending on whether you right-click quickly or hold the right mouse button down momentarily. With this option, a rapid right-click issues an ↵ as if you press the Enter key. If you hold the right mouse button down, the shortcut menu appears. You can further adjust the time required to hold down the mouse button.

THE INSERTION SCALE GROUP

These settings control how the DesignCenter or i-drop feature determines the scale of blocks when blocks are given a unitless setting for their DesignCenter unit type. Each drop-down list offers the standard set of unit types that are available in the Block Definition dialog box under the Insert Units drop-down list. See Chapter 7 for more information on blocks and Chapter 27 for information on DesignCenter [Insunits].

THE FIELDS GROUP

These settings offer control over the display and refresh of fields. Display Background Of Fields lets you control the display of the gray background on fields. This background lets you see at a glance which text object in a drawing is a field. The background does not print. Clicking the Field Update Settings button opens a dialog box that lets you select the action that updates fields.

THE PRIORITY FOR COORDINATE DATA ENTRY GROUP

These options control the way AutoCAD responds to coordinate input:

Running Object Snap Forces AutoCAD to use Running Osnaps at all times [Osnapcoord].

Keyboard Entry Enables you to use keyboard entry for coordinate input.

Keyboard Entry Except Scripts Enables you to use keyboard entry for coordinate input, except in scripts [Osnapcoord].

THE ASSOCIATIVE DIMENSIONING GROUP

This area has one option, Make New Dimensions Associative, which you can toggle on or off. This option lets you control whether AutoCAD uses the true associative dimension feature. With true associative dimension, a dimension will follow changes to an object whenever the object is edited. In the old method, you have to include a dimension definition point during the editing process in order to have the dimension follow changes in an object.

THE HYPERLINK GROUP

The one option in this group turns on or off the display of the Hyperlink cursor, tooltip, and shortcut menu.

THE UNDO/REDO GROUP

Controls how Undo and Redo react with the Zoom and Pan commands.

LINEWEIGHT SETTINGS

Click the Lineweight Settings button to open the Lineweight Settings dialog box. See Chapters 8 and 15 for more information about the Lineweight Settings dialog box.

EDIT SCALE LIST

Click the Edit Scale List button to open the Edit Scale List dialog box. You can add your own custom scales, which will appear in the Plot dialog box.

The Drafting Tab

The Drafting tab offers settings that relate to the drawing cursor, including the AutoSnap and AutoTrack features.

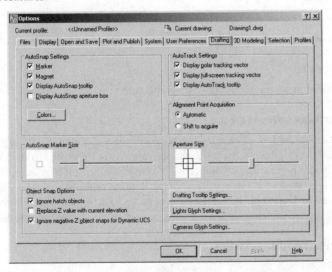

THE AUTOSNAP SETTINGS GROUP

The options in this group control the AutoSnap features that are engaged when you use osnaps:

Marker   Turns on the small, square graphic that appears on the osnap location. If you prefer not to see this marker, clear this check box [Autosnap].

Magnet   Causes the osnap cursor to "jump to" an osnap location as the cursor moves close to that location [Autosnap].

Display AutoSnap Tooltip   Controls the display of the Osnap tooltip [Autosnap].

Display AutoSnap Aperture Box   Displays a square over the cursor whenever osnaps are active. If you are familiar with earlier versions of AutoCAD, you'll recognize the Aperture Box as the graphic used to indicate osnaps before the AutoSnap feature was introduced [Apbox].

Colors   Lets you determine the color for the AutoSnap marker. Opens the Drawing Window Colors dialog box.

THE AUTOSNAP MARKER SIZE SLIDER

Move the slider to control the size of the AutoSnap marker.

THE AUTOTRACK SETTINGS GROUP

These options offer control over the tracking vector used for Polar Tracking and Osnap Tracking:

Display Polar Tracking Vector   Turns the Polar Tracking vector on or off [Trackpath].

Display Full-Screen Tracking Vector   Lets you control whether the tracking vector appears across the full width of the drawing window or stops at the cursor location or the intersection of two tracking vectors [Trackpath].

Display AutoTrack Tooltip   Turns the Osnap Tracking tooltip on or off [Autosnap].

THE ALIGNMENT POINT ACQUISITION GROUP

This option lets you determine the method for acquiring Osnap Tracking alignment points.

THE APERTURE SIZE SLIDER

Move the slider to set the size of the osnap aperture pickbox [Aperture].

THE OBJECT SNAP OPTIONS GROUP

This group offers the Ignore Hatch Objects and Replace Z Value With Current Elevation options. When Ignore Hatch Objects is turned off, object snaps will attempt to snap to geometry within hatch patterns. When turned on, Replace Z Value With Current Elevation causes AutoCAD to use the current UCS default Z value instead of the Z value of the selected point. Ignore Negative Z Object Snaps For Dynamic UCS causes object snaps to ignore locations with negative Z values while using the DUCS feature.

THE DRAFTING TOOLTIP SETTINGS

Give you control over the color, size, and transparency of tooltips.

THE LIGHT GLYPH SETTINGS

Give you control over the color and size of the spot and point light glyphs.

THE CAMERA GLYPH SETTINGS

Give you control over the color and size of the camera glyph.

The 3D Modeling Tab

The options on this tab control the behavior and display of your drawing when you are working in 3D modes. You can adjust the appearance of the crosshairs and the UCS icon. You can specify the default method for displaying 3D objects, and you can specify the default settings for Walk And Fly and Animation features.

3D CROSSHAIRS

These settings control the behavior and appearance of the cross hair cursor when viewing your drawing in 3D.

Show Z Axis In Crosshairs   Displays the Z axis in the crosshairs.

Label Axes In Standard Crosshairs   Displays the X, Y, and Z axis labels on the crosshairs.

Show Labels For Dynamic UCS   Displays the axis labels during the use of Dynamic UCS regardless of the Label Axes In Standard Crosshairs setting.

Crosshair Labels   Lets you select from three label styles: Use X, Y, Z; Use N, E, z; Use Custom Labels. If you select Use Custom Labels, you can enter the labels you want to display for the X, Y, and Z axes in the boxes provided.

DISPLAY UCS ICON

These three options pretty much explain themselves. Each option determines when the UCS icon is displayed. By default, they are all turned on, so the UCS icon always displays.

DYNAMIC INPUT

When turned on, the Show Z Field For Pointer Input option will offer a Z coordinate for input when using the Dynamic Input mode.

3D OBJECTS

These settings affect the display of 3D objects. Visual Style While Creating 3d Objects is self-explanatory. Deletion Control While Creating 3D Objects lets you determine whether defining objects used to create 3D objects are saved or deleted.

The U and V isoline settings let you set the number of isolines on 3D solids and surface meshes. Isolines are the lines you see on a mesh or solid that help you visualize their shape. You see them in wireframe and realistic visual styles.

3D NAVIGATION

If you want to adjust the way AutoCAD behaves when you are navigating a 3D view, these settings will help. Reverse Mouse Wheel Zoom is self-explanatory. The remaining two buttons give you control over the behavior of the Walk And Fly feature and the Animation settings.

Walk And Fly Settings Click this button to open the Walk And Fly Settings dialog box.

When you first start the 3DWalk or 3DFly feature, you see an instructional window that tells you how to use the feature. You use the options in the Settings group of the Walk And Fly Settings dialog box to specify when that instructional window appears. After using these features a few times, you may find the instructional window annoying and turn it off. You can turn it back on in this dialog box. You can also set the Position Locator window to automatically appear or not appear.

The Current Drawing Settings group lets you set the step size and steps per second when "walking" or "flying" through your model. These are the same settings that you see in the Navigate control panel for Step Size and Steps Per Second.

Animation Settings Click this button to open the Animation Settings dialog box. Here you can control the default visual style, resolution, frame rate, and animation file format when using the Motion Path Animation (anipath) feature.

The Selection Tab

The options in the Selection tab of the Options dialog box control the way you select objects in AutoCAD. You can also make adjustments to the Grips feature.

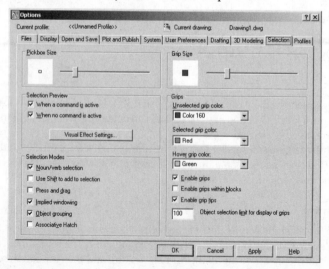

THE PICKBOX SIZE SLIDER

Lets you adjust the size of the pickbox [Pickbox].

THE GRIP SIZE SLIDER

Lets you adjust the size of grips [Gripsize].

THE SELECTION PREVIEW GROUP

Lets you control the behavior of the selection preview when you hover over objects. Click the Visual Effect Settings button to fine-tune the visual effects of the object selection, including the color and pattern of auto select windows.

THE SELECTION MODES GROUP

Lets you control the degree to which AutoCAD conforms to standard graphical user interface (GUI) methods of operation:

Noun/Verb Selection Makes AutoCAD work more like other Windows programs by letting you select objects before you choose an action or command [Pickfirst].

Use Shift To Add To Selection Lets you use the standard GUI method of holding down the Shift key to select multiple objects. When the Shift key is not held down, only the single object picked or the group of objects indicated with a window will be selected. Previously selected objects are deselected, unless the Shift key is held down during selection. To turn this feature on by using system variables, set Pickadd to 0 [Pickadd].

Press And Drag Lets you use the standard GUI method for placing window selections. First, click and hold down the Pick button on the first corner of the window; then, while holding down the Pick button, drag the other corner of the window into position. When the other corner is in place, you let go of the Pick button to finish the window. This setting applies to both Verb/Noun and Noun/Verb operations. In the system variables, set Pickdrag to 1 for this option [Pickdrag].

Implied Windowing Causes a window or crossing window to start automatically if no object is picked at the `Select objects:` prompt. This setting has no effect on the Noun/Verb setting. In the system variables, set Pickauto to 1 for this option [Pickauto].

Object Grouping Lets you select groups as single objects [Pickstyle].

Associative Hatch Lets you select both a hatch pattern and its associated boundary by using a single pick [Pickstyle].

THE GRIPS GROUP

These options control the Grips feature:

Unselected Grip Color Lets you select a color for grips that are exposed but not selected [Gripcolor].

Selected Grip Color Lets you set the color for grips that are exposed and selected [Griphot].

Hover Grip Color Lets you set the color for grips when the cursor hovers over the grip [Griphover].

Enable Grips Turns on grips.

Enable Grips Within Blocks Turns on the display of grips within blocks. Although you cannot edit grips within blocks, you can use grips within blocks as selection points [Gripblock].

Enable Grip Tips   Turns on the display of grip tooltips for custom objects that have them [Griptips].

Object Selection Limit For Display Of Grips   Controls the display of grips based on the number of objects selected. If set to 1, grips are not displayed if more than one object is selected. You can select a range from 1 to 32,767. The default is 100 [Gripobjlimit].

The Profiles Tab

In Windows XP Professional, a user profile is saved for each login name. Depending on the login name you use, you can have a different Windows setup. The Profiles tab offers a similar function for AutoCAD users. You can store different settings from the Options dialog box in a profile and recall them at any time. You can also save them to a file with the .arg extension and then take that file to another system. It's a bit like being able to take your Options settings with you wherever you go.

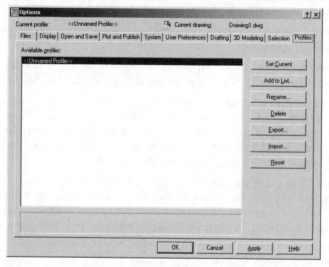

The main part of the Profiles tab displays a listing of available profiles. The default profile is shown as <<Unnamed Profile>>. As you add more profiles, they will appear in the list.

To create a new profile, highlight a profile name from the list and then click Add To List. The Add Profile dialog box opens, enabling you to enter a profile name and a description of the profile. The description appears in the box below the list on the Profiles tab whenever that profile is selected.

After you've created a new profile, you can modify the settings on the other tabs of the Options dialog box, and the new settings will be associated with the new profile. Profiles will store the way menus are set up, so you can use them as an aid to managing both your own custom schemes and third-party software. Here is a brief description of the options on the Profiles tab:

Set Current   Installs the settings from the selected profile.

Add To List   Creates a new profile.

Rename   Enables you to rename a profile and change its description.

Delete   Removes the selected profile from the list.

Export   Lets you save a profile to a file.

Import   Imports a profile that has been saved to a file.

Reset   Resets the values for a selected profile to its default settings.

Configuring the Tablet Menu Area

If you own a digitizing tablet and you would like to use it with the AutoCAD tablet menu template, you must configure your tablet menu. You can open the `Tablet.dwg` file in the `Sample` folder of the `AutoCAD 2007` folder and print the tablet menu template drawing to a size that will fit your digitizing tablet. Then do the following:

1. Securely fasten your tablet menu template to the tablet. Be sure the area covered by the template is completely within the tablet's active drawing area.

2. Choose Tools ➢ Tablet ➢ Configure. The following prompt appears:

```
Enter number of tablet
menus desired (0-4) <0>:
```

Enter **4**↵. For the next series of prompts, you will be locating the four tablet menu areas, starting with menu area 1 (see Figure A.1).

FIGURE A.1

How to locate the tablet menu areas

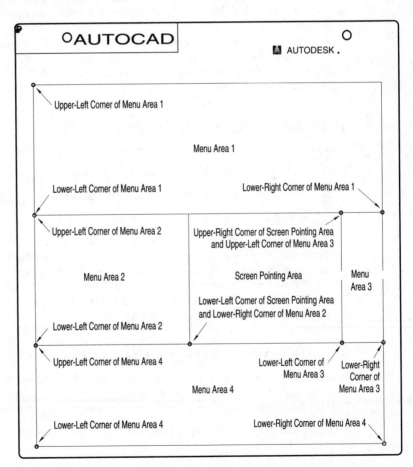

3. Follow the instructions provided by the Command prompt.

4. When you are asked if you want to respecify the fixed screen-pointing area, enter **Y**↵, and then select the corners of the pointing area as indicated by the prompts.

Turning On the Noun/Verb Selection Method

If, for some reason, the Noun/Verb Selection method is not available, follow these steps to turn it on:

1. Choose Tools ➢ Options. Then, in the Options dialog box, click the Selection tab.

2. In the Selection Modes group, click the Noun/Verb Selection check box.

3. Click OK.

You should now see a small square at the intersection of the crosshair cursor. This square is actually a pickbox superimposed on the cursor. It tells you that you can select objects, even while the Command prompt appears at the bottom of the screen and no command is currently active. As you saw earlier, the square will momentarily disappear when you are in a command that asks you to select points.

You can also turn on Noun/Verb Selection by entering ' **Pickfirst**↵ at the Command prompt. At the Enter new value for PICKFIRST <0>: prompt, enter **1**↵. (Entering **0** turns the Pickfirst function off.) The Pickfirst system variable is stored in the AutoCAD configuration file. See Appendix C for more on system variables.

Turning On the Grips Feature

If, for some reason, the Grips feature is not available, follow these steps to turn it on:

1. Choose Tools ➢ Options. Then in the Options dialog box, click the Selection tab.

2. In the Grips group, click the Enable Grips check box.

3. Click OK, and you are ready to proceed.

The Selection tab of the Options dialog box also lets you specify whether grips appear on objects that compose a block (see Chapter 4 for more on blocks), as well as set the grip color and size. You can also set these options by using the system variables described in Appendix C.

You can also turn the Grips feature on and off by entering ' **Grips**↵. At the Enter new value for GRIPS <0>: prompt, enter **1** to turn grips on or **0** to turn grips off. Grips is a system variable that is stored in the AutoCAD configuration file.

Setting Up the Tracking Vector Feature

If AutoCAD does not display a tracking vector as described in the early chapters of this book or if the tracking vector does not behave as described, chances are this feature has been turned off or altered. Take the following steps to configure the tracking vector so that it behaves as described in this book:

1. Open the Options dialog box by choosing Tools ➢ Options.

2. Click the Drafting tab.

3. Click all three options in the AutoTrack Settings group.

4. Make sure that the Marker, Magnet, and Display AutoSnap Tooltip check boxes are selected in the AutoSnap Settings group.

5. Make sure the Automatic radio button in the Alignment Point Acquisition group is selected.

6. Click OK to exit the dialog box.

Adjusting AutoCAD's 3D Graphics System

You can adjust the performance of AutoCAD's 3D graphics system through the Adaptive Degradation And Performance Tuning dialog box. To open this dialog box, click the System tab in the Options dialog box, and then click the Performance Settings button in the 3D Performance group.

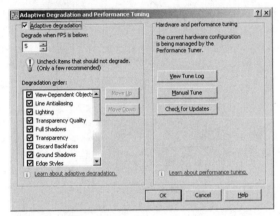

This dialog box offers control over the way AutoCAD displays 3D models when you use the 3D Orbit tool or when you are using a visual style. Here is a listing of the options for the Adaptive Degradation And Performance Tuning dialog box.

The Adaptive Degradation Group

The 3D navigation tools enable you to adjust your view in real time, which places high demands on your display system. To maintain the smoothness of the real-time update of your 3D views, AutoCAD will degrade the display while performing the view transformations.

The options in the Adaptive Degradation group let you set the level to which the view is degraded while you are navigating your model in real time. You can turn this feature off completely by unchecking the Adaptive Degradation check box. If you prefer, you can determine the specific feature to be degraded on an individual basis by removing the check box next to an item name in the Degradation Order list box. The Degrade When Fps Is Below setting lets you set when, in frames per second, the degradation takes effect.

The Hardware and Performance Tuning Group

The Hardware And Performance Tuning group lets you view and adjust your display system's performance. The View Tune Log button displays the vital statistics for your display system. The Manual Tune button opens the Manual Performance Tuning dialog box. The Check For Updates button takes you to the Autodesk website to allow you to see if new drivers are available for your graphics display card.

The Manual Performance Tuning Dialog Box

When you click the Manual Tune button, the Manual Performance Tuning dialog box opens.

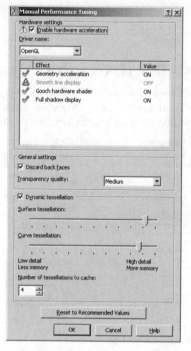

The Hardware Settings group lets you determine whether to use hardware acceleration. If you turn on Hardware Acceleration, the Driver Name option becomes available, and the available features for the selected type of acceleration are displayed in the list box.

The General Settings group offers two options:

Discard Back Faces   In most 3D rendering systems, surfaces have just one visible side. The back sides of surfaces are invisible. This doesn't matter for objects such as cubes and spheres because you see only one side of a surface at any given time; but in some situations, you can see both sides of a surface, such as a single surface used as a wall.

If your drawing is composed of mostly closed objects such as cubes and spheres and you will see only one surface, you can select the Discard Back Faces check box to improve system performance. If you have many single surfaces that will be viewed from both sides, you will want to leave this option turned off.

Transparency Quality   This option lets you control the visual quality of transparent objects in your model when viewing your model in a realistic visual style. You can set transparency to a high-, medium-, or low-quality level. Low-quality levels will show transparent objects with a "screen door" effect, whereas medium and high options will give transparent objects a smoother appearance. The low-quality level allows faster view changes.

The options in the Dynamic Tessellation group determine the smoothness of 3D objects when you use a visual style other than a wireframe or hidden view. To simulate smoothness, the graphic system divides curved surfaces into triangles called *tessellations*. You can turn all these features on or off by using the check box next to the group title:

Surface Tessellation   Controls the amount of detail shown for surfaces. Greater detail requires more surface tessellation, which in turn requires more system memory.

Curve Tessellation   Controls the amount of detail shown for curved surfaces. Greater detail requires more surface tessellation, which in turn requires more system memory.

Number Of Tessellations To Cache   Controls the number of tessellations that are cached. A *cache* is a part of memory reserved to store frequently used data. AutoCAD will always cache one tessellation. Caching two tessellations will improve the appearance and performance of 3D objects when you use multiple viewports.

Finding Hidden Folders That Contain AutoCAD Files

Many of AutoCAD's features rely on external files to store settings and other resources. Many of these files reside in hidden folders. These folders are:

```
C:\Documents and Settings\User Name\Application Data\Autodesk\AutoCAD 2007\R17.0\enu
C:\Documents and Settings\All Users\Application Data\Autodesk\AutoCAD 2007\R17.0\enu
```

If you attempt to user Explorer to browse to these locations, you may not find the \Application Data folder. You can "unhide" this folder by doing the following:

1. Right-click the Start button in the lower-left corner of your screen, and then choose Explore to open Windows Explorer.

2. Choose Tools ➢ Folder Options from the menu bar.

3. In the Folder Options dialog box, select the View tab.

4. In the Advanced Settings list, look for the Hidden Files And Folders option. You will see two radio buttons just below this option.

5. Select the Show Hidden Files And Folders radio button.

6. Click OK to close the Folder Options dialog box.

After you've done this, the Application Data folder will be visible, and you will be able to browse to AutoCAD folders that are found there. Once you are able to explore these folders, you might want to create a shortcut to them (right-click the folder and choose Create Shortcut) and then place the shortcut on your desktop or other convenient location. That way you can get to these folders without having to navigate through several layers of folders.

Appendix B

Hardware and Software Tips

Because some of the items that make up an AutoCAD system are not found on the typical desktop system, I have provided this appendix to help you understand some of them. This appendix also discusses ways you can improve AutoCAD's performance through software and hardware.

The Graphics Display

There are two issues to consider concerning the graphics display: *resolution* and *performance*. Fortunately, nearly all computers sold today have display systems that are more than adequate for AutoCAD, thanks to the popularity of 3D games. You do need to make sure that your resolution is set to at least 1024 × 768, preferably higher. The higher your resolution, the more detail you'll be able to see in your drawings.

If you have an older system that needs a graphics display upgrade, you will want to consider the following factors in choosing a new display:

PCI Express Graphics Cards   Contemporary motherboards use high-speed PCI Express (PCIe) slots that offer the fastest video throughput available. Check that yours is a system of this type. If you are only doing 2D work, you can get by with an older AGP (Accelerated Graphics Port) graphics card. Windows XP also provides options for using multiple monitors, an approach that has been popular among AutoCAD users. Multiple monitors enable AutoCAD users to view multiple or large documents more easily.

If you want to take full advantage of AutoCADs new 3D features, you will want one of the Autodesk certified graphics cards in your system. Here is a list of certified cards as of this writing:

- ATI FireGL (V3100, V3200, V5000, V5100, V7100, V7300, V7350, X1, X2 AGP Pro, X3-256)
- ATI Mobility FireGL (T2, V3200)
- Nvidia Quadro FX (1000, 1100, 1300, 1400, 3000, 3400/4400, 4500, 500, 540, 600, 700)
- Nvidia Quadro4 (700XGL, 750 XGL, 900 XGL, 980 XGL)
- NEC TE6

Even if you already have one of these cards, make sure you have the latest drivers. You can go to the Autodesk web page and download the appropriate driver by doing the following:

Choose Tools ➢ Options and select the System tab. Click the Performance Settings button, and then in the Adaptive Degradation And Performance Tuning dialog box, click the Check For Updates button. The Autodesk AutoCAD Certified Hardware XML Database page opens. You can locate driver updates on this page.

Pointing Devices

Our basic means of communicating with computers is the keyboard and pointing device. Most likely, you will use a mouse, but if you are still in the market for a pointing device, choose an input device that generates smooth cursor movement. Some of the lesser-quality input devices cause erratic movement. Because AutoCAD relies on precise input, you might want to upgrade to an optical mouse, which is less likely to wear out or accumulate dirt in its mechanism.

If you need to trace large drawings, you might want to consider a digitizing tablet. It is usually a rectangular object with a penlike *stylus* or a device called a *puck,* which resembles a mouse. It has a smooth surface on which to draw. The most common size is 4″ × 5″, but digitizing tablets are available in sizes up to 60″ × 70″. The tablet gives a natural feel to drawing with the computer because the movement of the stylus or puck is directly translated into cursor movement.

AutoCAD supports Wintab-compatible digitizers. If your digitizer has a Wintab driver, you can use your digitizer as both a tracing device (to trace drawings on a tablet) and a general pointing device for Windows to choose program menu items.

Your Wintab digitizer must be installed and configured under Windows. Make sure it is working in Windows before enabling it in AutoCAD, or you will not be able to use the digitizer as a pointing device (mouse). To enable the digitizer in AutoCAD, choose Tools ➢ Options to open the Options dialog box and click the System tab. Open the Current Pointing Device drop-down list and select Wintab-Compatible Digitizer ADI 4.2 – by Autodesk, Inc.

Output Devices

Output options vary greatly in quality and price. Quality and paper size are the major considerations for printers. Nearly all printers give accurate drawings, but some produce better line quality than others. Some plotters give merely acceptable results, while others are quite impressive in their speed, color, and accuracy.

AutoCAD can use the Windows XP or Windows 2000 system printer, so any device that Windows supports is also supported by AutoCAD. You can also plot directly to an output device, although Autodesk recommends that you set up your plotter or printer through Windows and then select the device from the Plot Configuration group in the Plot Device tab of the Plot dialog box or the Page Setup dialog box.

So many types of printers are available these days that it has become more difficult to choose the right printer for your application. This section describes the broad categories of printers available and how they relate to AutoCAD. You will also want to consider the other uses for your printer, such as word-processing or color graphics. Here are a few printing options:

Laser Printers   Laser printers produce high-quality line-work output. The standard office laser printer is usually limited to 8.5″ × 14″ paper; however, 11″ × 17″laser printers for graphics and CAD work are now becoming affordable and are commonly used for proof plots. Resolution and speed are the major considerations if you are buying a laser printer. An output of 300dpi (dots per inch) produces acceptable plots, but 600dpi is fast becoming the standard. You should also look for a laser printer with sufficient built-in memory to improve spooling and plotting speeds.

Color Ink-Jet Printers   These printers offer speed and quality output. Some color ink-jet printers even accept 19″ 22″ paper. Because ink-jet printers are competitively priced, they can offer the best solution for low-cost check plots. And the 19″ × 22″ paper size is quite acceptable for half-size plots, a format that many architects and engineers are using now.

PostScript Printers   If you want to use a PostScript device to output your drawings, the best method is to use File ➢ Export or the Psout command. These options convert your drawing into a true PostScript file. You can then send your file to a PostScript printer or typesetting machine. This can be especially useful for printed circuit board (PCB) layout that requires photo negatives for output. If you are an architect who needs presentation-quality drawings, you might want to consider using the Encapsulated PS (*.eps) option in the Export Data dialog box. Often service bureaus that offer a raster plotter service can produce E-size PostScript output from a PostScript file. The uses of this option are really quite open-ended.

Another option is to export your drawing to an illustration program such as Adobe Illustrator and make any refinements to your drawing there. You can save files in the AutoCAD 2007 DXF file format or use the File ➢ Export option to export files to the Windows metafile format. Most illustration programs accept either of these formats.

Plotters   Printer technology has changed significantly since the early versions of AutoCAD. This is especially true in the area of large format plotters. Output devices intended for CAD were once dominated by pen plotters, but now color ink-jet plotters and printers are commonplace. Ink-jet technology offers far greater flexibility and speed, giving you many more options in the look of your output.

You can also find laser or electrostatic plotters at a much higher price. Ink-jet plotters offer the best value; they are fast and fairly inexpensive compared with the older pen plotters they supersede. For a bit more expense, you can step up to a color plotter.

If you need large plots but can't afford a large plotter, many blueprint companies and even some copy centers offer plotting as a service. This can be a good alternative to purchasing your own plotter. Check with your local blueprinter or CAD service bureau.

Fine-Tuning the Appearance of Output

In Chapter 8, you were introduced to the printing and plotting features in AutoCAD. You learned about the AutoCAD features you can use to control the appearance of your output, including layouts and lineweights. This section covers some of the finer points of printer and plotter setup. You'll find information on controlling how lines overlap, how to include more media sizes, adding plot stamps, adjusting the aspect ratio or your printer, and more.

Making Detailed Adjustments with the Printer/Plotter Configuration Options

If you open the Plot dialog box or the Page Setup dialog box, you'll see the option groups that offer control over how your plotter or printer works.

These groups seem innocent enough, but behind two of these groups lies a vast set of options that can be quite intimidating. You've already seen in Chapter 8 how the Plot Style Table options work. This section covers the options available when you click the Properties button in the Printer/Plotter group.

The Printer/Plotter Configuration options enable you to adjust those printer or plotter settings that you might want to change only occasionally. These settings are fairly technical and include such items as the port your printer is connected to, the quality of bitmap image printing, custom paper sizes, and printer calibration, which lets you adjust your plotter for any size discrepancies in output. You won't be using most of these settings often, but you should know that they exist just in case you encounter a situation in which you need to make some subtle change to your printer's configuration. You can also use these options to create multiple configurations of the same plotter for quick access to custom settings.

All the settings in this group are stored in a file with the `.pc3` filename extension. You can store and recall any number of configuration files for situations that call for different plotter settings. PC3 files are normally stored in the `Plotters` folder under the `C:\Documents and Settings\`*User Name*`\Application Data\Autodesk\AutoCAD 2007\R17.0\enu\`folder. *User Name* is your login name. You can access this folder by choosing File ➤ Plotter Manager from the AutoCAD menu bar.

The Printer/Plotter group in the Plot And Page Setup dialog box offers a drop-down list from which you can select a printer or file output configuration. If a PC3 file exists for a plotter configuration, the drop-down list will display it, and the list will display any Windows system printer. After you've selected an output device from the list, you can click the Properties button to access the Plotter Configuration Editor dialog box.

TIP You can configure AutoCAD to create bitmap files in the most common file formats (such as TIFF, Targa, and PCX) or to create Autodesk's DWF file format for the Internet. After you've configured AutoCAD for these types of output, this is where you select the file output type.

The Plotter Configuration Editor dialog box has three tabs: General, Ports, and Device And Document Settings. The General tab displays a list of Windows drivers that this configuration uses, if any, and there is a space for your own comments.

TIP You can access and edit the plotter configuration settings without opening AutoCAD. To do this, locate the PC3 file in the `Plotters` subfolder under the `C:\Documents and Settings\`*User Name*`\Application Data\Autodesk\AutoCAD 2007\R17.0\enu\Plotters` folder (*User Name* is your login name), and double-click it.

The Ports tab lets you specify where your plotter data is sent. This is where you should look if you are sending your plots to a network plotter or if you decide to create plot files. You can also select the AutoSpool feature, which enables you to direct your plot to an intermediate location for distribution to the appropriate output device.

The Device And Document Settings tab is the main part of this dialog box. It offers a set of options ranging from OLE output control to custom paper sizes. The main list box offers options in a hierarchical list, similar to a listing in Windows Explorer. Toward the bottom of the dialog box are the Import, Save As, and Defaults buttons. These buttons let you import configuration settings from earlier versions of AutoCAD, save the current settings as a file, or return the settings to their default values.

The list has four main categories: Media, Graphics, Custom Properties, and User-Defined Paper Sizes & Calibration. Not all the options under these categories are available for all plotters. When you select an item from this list, the area just below the list displays the options associated with that item. The following describes each category and its options, using the Xerox Engineering Systems XES8855 as an example.

THE MEDIA CATEGORY

Some plotters, such as the Xerox Engineering Systems 8800 series, offer options for the source and size of printer media and for the media type. If the Source And Size option is available, the dialog box offers a listing of the source, such as sheet feed or roll, and the sheet size. The Media Type option lets you choose from bond, vellum, or glossy paper or any other medium that is specifically controlled by the plotter. Duplex Printing, when available, controls options for double-sided printing in printers that support this feature. Media Destination, when available, lets you select a destination for output such as collating or stapling in printers that support such features.

THE PHYSICAL PEN CONFIGURATION CATEGORY (SHOWN ONLY FOR PEN PLOTTERS)

Pen plotters have features that diverge from the typical laser or ink-jet printers or plotters. When these options are present, they let you control some of the ways that AutoCAD generates data for pen plotters. Here is a listing of those pen plotter feature settings:

Prompt For Pen Swapping   Stops the plotter to enable you to switch pens. This feature is designed primarily for single-pen plotters.

Area Fill Correction   Tells AutoCAD to compensate for pen width around the edges of a solid-filled area in order to maintain dimensional accuracy of the plot.

Pen Optimization Level   Sets how AutoCAD sorts pen movement for optimum speed. AutoCAD does a lot of preparation before sending your drawing to the plotter. If you are using a pen plotter, one of the things it does is optimize the way it sends vectors to your plotter, so your plotter doesn't waste time making frequent pen changes and moving from one end of the plot to another just to draw a single line.

Physical Pen Characteristics   Lets you assign plotter pen numbers to AutoCAD colors, adjust the speed of individual pens, and assign pen widths.

THE GRAPHICS CATEGORY

These settings give you control over both vector and raster output from your plotter. The Vector Graphics settings let you control resolution and color depth, as well as the method for creating shading. If you want to configure your printer for virtual pens, select 255 Virtual Pens under the Color Depth option.

The Raster And Shaded/Rendered Viewports slider gives you control over the quality of any bitmap images. If this slider is placed all the way to the left, raster images will not be plotted. As you move the slider to the right, the raster image quality increases, the speed of printing decreases, and memory requirements increase. The OLE slider controls the quality of OLE linked or embedded files. With the slider all the way to the left, OLE objects will not be printed. As you move the slider farther to the right, OLE image quality and memory requirements increase while speed is reduced.

The Trade-Off slider lets you choose how the Raster and OLE sliders improve speed. You can choose between lower resolution and fewer colors.

For printers and plotters that support TrueType fonts, the TrueType Text options enable you to select between plotting text as graphics or as TrueType text.

THE CUSTOM PROPERTIES CATEGORY

Select Custom Properties from the Device And Document Settings tab, and you'll see the Custom Properties button appear in the lower part of the dialog box. This button gives you access to the same printer or plotter settings that are available from the Windows system printer settings. You can also access these settings by choosing Start ➤ Printers And Faxes, right-clicking the desired printer, and choosing Properties from the shortcut menu.

TIP   The options offered through the Custom Properties button often duplicate many of the items in the Device And Documents tab. If an option is not accessible from the Device And Documents tab, select the options under Custom Properties.

THE INITIALIZATION STRING

Some plotters require preinitialization and postinitialization codes, in the form of ASCII text strings, to get the plotter's attention. If you have such a plotter, this option lets you enter those strings.

USER-DEFINED PAPER SIZES & CALIBRATION

The options in the User-Defined Paper Sizes & Calibration category offer some of the more valuable options in this dialog box. In particular, the Plotter Calibration option can be useful in ensuring the accuracy of your plots.

Plotter Calibration

If your printer or plotter is not producing an accurate plot, focus on the Plotter Calibration option. If your plotter stretches or shrinks your image in one direction or another, this option lets you adjust the width and height of your plotter's output. To use it, click Plotter Calibration.

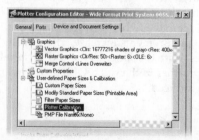

A button Calibrate Plotter button appears. Click this button to start the Calibrate Plotter Wizard. You are asked first to select a paper size and then to select a width and height for a rectangle that will be plotted with your printer. Figure B.1 shows the wizard screen that asks for the rectangle size.

You can use the Calibrate Plotter Wizard to plot a sample rectangle of a specific size. You then measure the rectangle and check its actual dimensions against the dimensions that you entered. If there are any discrepancies between the plotted dimensions and the dimensions you specified, you can enter the actual plotted size and print another test rectangle. You can repeat this process until your plotted rectangle exactly matches the dimensions entered into the wizard.

FIGURE B.1

The Calibrate Plotter Wizard lets you adjust the width and height scaling of your plotter output in order to fine-tune the accuracy of your plots.

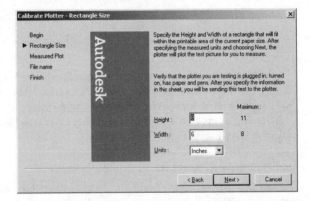

Toward the end of the Calibrate Plotter Wizard's steps, you'll be asked to give a name for a Plot Model Parameter (PMP) file that will store your calibration data. The PMP file also stores any custom paper size information that you input from other parts of the User-Defined Paper Sizes & Calibration options. This file is then associated with the PC3 file that stores your plotter configuration data.

If you have more than one PC3 file for your plotter, you can associate the PMP file with your other PC3 files by using the PMP File Name option in the Device And Document Settings tab. You need only one calibration file for each plotter or printer you are using. This option appears under the User-Defined Paper Sizes & Calibration category.

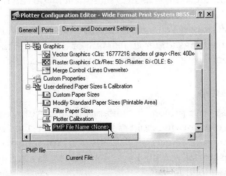

To associate a PMP file with a PC3 plotter configuration file, select the PC3 file from the Name drop-down list in the Printer/Plotter section of the Plot dialog box. Click the Properties button, and then, in the Device And Document Settings tab, click the PMP File Name listing. The PMP options appear in the bottom of the dialog box. Click the Attach button, and then select the PMP file from the Open dialog box. Click OK. You'll see that the PMP file has been added to the PMP filename listing.

Custom Paper Sizes

Some plotters offer custom paper sizes. This feature is usually available for printers and plotters that you've set up to use the AutoCAD drivers instead of the Windows system drivers. If your plotter offers this option, you'll see a list box and a set of buttons when you select Custom Paper Sizes.

Clicking the Add button starts the Custom Paper Size Wizard, which lets you set the sheet size and margin, as well as the paper source. This information is then saved in a PMP file. You are asked to provide a specific name for the custom paper size, which will be listed in the Custom Paper Size list box.

After you've created a custom paper size, you can edit or delete it by clicking the Edit or Delete button in the Custom Paper Sizes options.

Modify Standard Paper Size

The last item in the Device And Document Settings tab is the Modify Standard Paper Size option. If this option is available, you can adjust the margins of a standard paper size.

TIP If you are using an older pen plotter, you will see the Physical Pen Configuration options in the Device And Document Settings tab. These additional options give you control over pen speed, pen optimization, and area fill correction.

IMPORT, SAVE AS, AND DEFAULTS

The Import, Save As, and Defaults buttons at the bottom of the Plotter Configuration Editor let you import or save your plotter settings as PC3 files, which you can then load from the Plot Device tab of the Plot dialog box and the Page Setup dialog box, as described earlier in this appendix. The Import button lets you import PCP and PC2 files from earlier versions of AutoCAD. Save As lets you save your current settings under an existing or a new PC3 filename. The Defaults button restores the default settings, if any, for the current plotter configuration.

Adding a Plot Stamp

To help cross-reference your printer or plotter output to AutoCAD drawing files, it's a good idea to add a *plot stamp* to your drawings that identifies the date, the time, and the filename of the drawing that generated your plot. To accomplish this, the Plot Stamp feature lets you imprint data onto your plotted drawings, usually in the lower-left corner. In addition, Plot Stamp lets you keep a record of your plots in a log file.

To use Plot Stamp, type **Plotstamp**↵ at the AutoCAD Command prompt. You can also turn on the Plot Stamp On option in the Plot dialog box and then click the Plot Stamp Settings button that appears to the right of the option. The Plot Stamp dialog box opens (see Figure B.2).

The Plot Stamp dialog box offers several options that let you determine what to include in the stamp.

TIP If the options are grayed out, click the Save As button to save Plot Stamp settings under a new file.

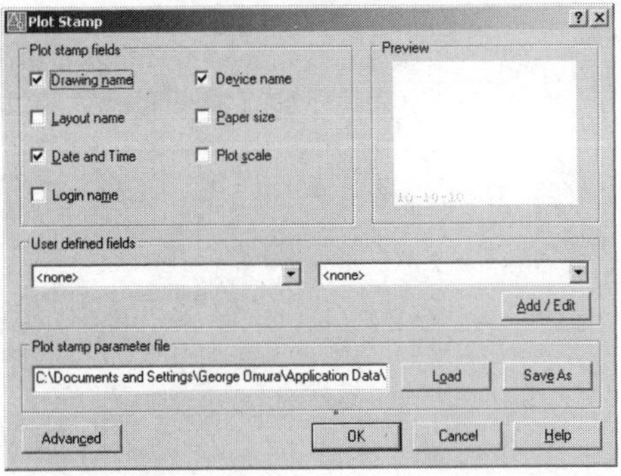

FIGURE B.2

The Plot Stamp
dialog box

The Plot Stamp Fields group lets you include seven predefined options in your stamp, including drawing, layout, and output device name. The User Defined Fields group lets you add custom text to the stamp. To use this feature, click the Add/Edit button in the User Defined Fields group. The User Defined Fields dialog box opens, as shown in Figure B.3.

You can use the Add, Edit, or Delete button to add or make changes to the user-defined fields. After you've added a field, it will appear in both the list boxes in the User Defined Fields group of the Plot Stamp dialog box.

To control the location, orientation, font, and font size of the plot stamp, click the Advanced button in the lower-left corner of the Plot Stamp dialog box to open the Advanced Options dialog box, shown in Figure B.4.

This dialog box lets you specify the orientation of the stamp on the page as well as the exact location of the stamp in relation to either the printable area or the paper border. In addition, you can specify whether to save a record of your plotting activities in a log file by using the Log File Location group.

Controlling How Lines Overlap

Some output devices let you control how overlapping lines and shaded areas affect one another, a feature known as *merge control*. In versions of AutoCAD prior to 2000, merge control was handled through additional commands such as Hpconfig or OCEconfig. AutoCAD 2007 includes merge control as part of the Plotter Configuration Editor dialog box.

You can gain access to merge control by opening the Plotter Configuration Editor and, in the Graphics area of the Device And Document Settings tab, clicking the plus sign next to Graphics to expand the list of Graphics options.

If your device supports merge control, you will see it listed under Graphics as shown in Figure B.5.

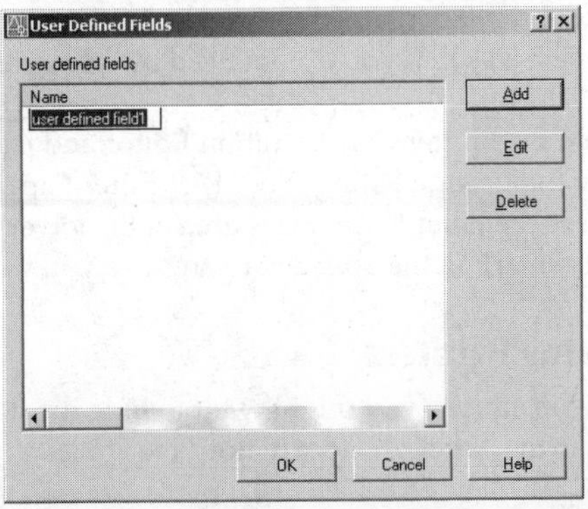

FIGURE B.3

The User Defined
Fields dialog box

FIGURE B.4

The Advanced Options dialog box

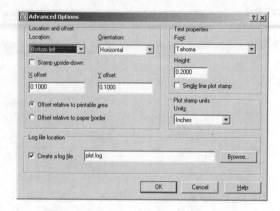

FIGURE B.5

The location of the Merge Control setting in the Plotter Configuration Editor

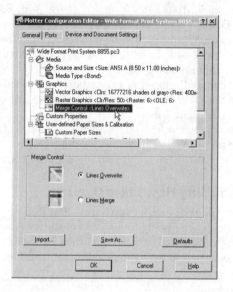

Filtering Paper Sizes

AutoCAD displays all the available paper sizes for a selected output device in the Page Setup dialog box or the Plot dialog box. For some plotters, the list can be a bit overwhelming. You can filter out paper sizes that you do not need by using the Filter Paper Sizes option in the Plotter Configuration Editor.

Open the Plotter Configuration Editor and click the plus sign next to the User-Defined Paper Sizes & Calibration listing. You'll see Filter Paper Sizes as an option. After you select this option, you'll see the Filter Paper Sizes area in the lower half of the Plotter Configuration Editor. Remove the checkmark in the box next to any size you won't need.

Filtering Printers

In some instances, you might want to hide the Windows system printer from the list of printers shown in the AutoCAD Plot dialog box. For example, there might be several shared system printers on a network that are not intended for AutoCAD use, so you would not want those printers to appear in your list of available printers. You can do this by turning on the Hide System Printers option at the bottom of the General Plot Options group in the Plot And Publish tab of the Options dialog box (choose Tools ➤ Options). This limits the selection of printers and plotters to those that have a PC3 plotter configuration. You can further limit the plotter selections by moving any unneeded PC3 file out of the AutoCAD Plotters folder and into another folder for storage.

Controlling the Plot Preview Background Color

If you prefer to use a color other than white for the plot preview background, you can set the plot preview background color by using the Color Options dialog box:

1. Choose Tools ➤ Options to open the Options dialog box.

2. Select the Display tab.

3. In the Windows Elements group, click the Colors button to open the Drawing Window Colors dialog box.

4. Select Plot Preview from the Context list.

5. Select a color from the Color drop-down list.

6. Click the Apply & Close button.

Controlling the Windows Metafile Background Color

If you prefer using the Windows metafile file type to export AutoCAD drawings to other programs, you can control the background color of your exported file. The AutoCAD Wmfbkgnd system variable lets you control the background color of exported Windows metafiles. Wmfbkgnd offers two settings: off generates a transparent background, and on generates the background color of the current view. The initial default value is off.

Fine-Tuning PostScript File Export

AutoCAD provides the PostScript user with a great deal of control over the formatting of the PostScript file that is output with the File ➤ Export and Psout commands. The options range from font-substitution mapping to custom PostScript prologue data.

However, you need to master the PostScript programming language to take full advantage of AutoCAD PostScript output. Most of this control is offered through a file named Acad.psf. This is the master support file for the Psout command. You can customize the PostScript file created by Psout by making changes in the Acad.psf file. Acad.psf is divided into sections that affect various parts of the PostScript output. Each section begins with a title preceded by an asterisk: the *fonts section lets you control font substitution, for example.

You will also want to know about the Psprolog system variable, which instructs Psout to include your custom prologue statement in its PostScript output. You add your custom prologue to the Acad.psf file by using a text editor. The prologue should begin with a section heading that you devise. The heading can say anything, but it must begin with an asterisk like all the other section headings. Everything following the heading, up to the next heading or the end of the file, and excluding comments, will be included in the Psout output file.

> **TIP** A complete discussion of Psout PostScript support is beyond the scope of this book. If you are interested in learning more, consult the PostScript section of the AutoCAD Customization manual.

You can also add a PostScript plotter to the plotter configuration. When you do this, AutoCAD plots the drawing as a series of vectors, just like any other plotter. If you have any filled areas in your drawing and you are plotting to a PostScript file, the vectors that are used to plot those filled areas can greatly increase plot-file size and the time it takes to plot your PostScript file.

Memory and AutoCAD Performance

Next to your computer's CPU, memory has the greatest impact on AutoCAD's speed. How much you have, and how you use it, can make a big difference in whether you finish that rush job on schedule or work late nights trying. This section will clarify some basic points about memory and how AutoCAD uses it.

AutoCAD is a virtual memory system. This means that when your RAM resources reach their limit, part of the data stored in RAM is temporarily moved to your hard disk to make more room in RAM. This temporary storage of RAM to your hard disk is called *virtual memory paging*. Through memory paging, AutoCAD will continue to run, even though your work might exceed the capacity of your RAM. The Windows operating system manages this virtual memory paging. If you have several programs open at once, Windows will determine how much memory to allocate to each program. AutoCAD always attempts to store as much of your drawing in RAM as possible. When the amount of RAM required for a drawing exceeds the amount of physical RAM in your system, Windows will page parts of the data stored in RAM to the hard disk. Your drawing size, the number of files you have open in AutoCAD, and the number of programs you have open under Windows will affect how much RAM you have available. For this reason, if your AutoCAD editing session is slowing down, try closing other applications you might have open or closing files that you are no longer using. This will free up more memory for AutoCAD and the drawing file.

AutoCAD and Your Hard Disk

You will notice that AutoCAD slows down when paging occurs. If this happens frequently, the best thing you can do is add more RAM. But you can also improve the performance of AutoCAD under these conditions by ensuring that you have adequate hard-disk space and that free hard-disk space has been *defragmented* or *optimized*. A defragmented disk will offer faster access, thereby improving paging speed.

Windows dynamically allocates swap-file space. However, make sure that there is enough free space on your hard disk to allow Windows to set up the space. A good guideline is to allow enough space for a swap file that is twice the size of your RAM capacity. If you have the minimum 512MB of RAM, you need to allow space for a 1024MB swap file (at a minimum). This will give your system 1024MB of virtual memory. Also consider setting the minimum and maximum swap file space to be equal.

Fast, high-capacity hard disks are fairly inexpensive, so even if you are not running out of space, you might want to consider adding another hard disk with as much capacity as you can afford. In fact, you can greatly improve your system speed by upgrading from an old hard drive to a new one. Consider upgrading to an SATA or SATA2 hard drive controller and drive. You might also consider a Raid0 hard drive setup if your system supports it. Raid0 can greatly improve the speed of your system by dividing hard drive access between two drives. Such a system can nearly double access speeds.

Keep Your Hard Disk Clean

If you are not in the habit of emptying your Recycle Bin, you want to get into the habit of doing so. Every file that you "delete" using Windows Explorer is actually passed to the Recycle Bin. You need to clear this out regularly. If you are a regular Internet user, check your Internet cache folder for unnecessary files. You can employ one of the many hard-disk cleaning utilities to do this. Finally, it is a good idea to perform regular maintenance on your hard disk to keep it clear of fragmentation and unused files. The Tools tab of the Properties dialog box for your hard disk offers error-checking and defragmenting options.

AutoCAD Tools to Improve Memory Use

AutoCAD offers some tools to help make your use of system memory more efficient. Partial Open and the Spatial and Layer indexes let you manage the memory use of large drawings and multiple open files by reducing the amount of a file that is loaded into memory. Using these tools, you can have AutoCAD open only those portions of a file that you want to work on.

Using Partial Open to Conserve Memory and Improve Speed

Use the Partial Open option in the File dialog box when you know you are going to work on only a small portion or a particular set of layers of a large drawing. Choose File ➢ Open, and then locate and select the file you want to open. At the bottom-right corner of the dialog box, click the down arrow next to the Open button, and select Partial Open to open the Partial Open dialog box. Note that this option is available only for files created and edited in AutoCAD 2000 and later.

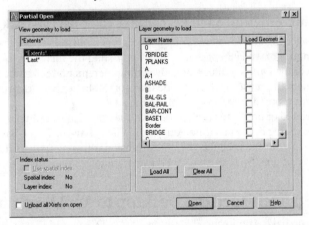

You can use this dialog box to open specific views of your drawing by selecting the view name from the View Geometry To Load list box. Only the geometry displayed in the selected view will be loaded into memory. This does not limit you to only that view as you edit the drawing. Subsequent views will cause AutoCAD to load the geometry of those views as needed.

You can further limit the amount of a drawing that is loaded into memory by selecting only those layers you want to work with. Place a checkmark next to the layers you want in the Layer Geometry To Load list box.

After a file is opened by using the Partial Open option, you can always make further adjustments by choosing File ➢ Partial Load. This opens the Partial Load dialog box, which offers the same options as the Partial Open dialog box. The Partial Load dialog box is not available for files that are opened normally without using the Partial Open option.

Using Spatial and Layer Indexes to Conserve Memory

The Spatial and Layer indexes are lists that keep a record of geometry in a drawing. A *Spatial index* lists a drawing's geometry according to the geometry's location in space. A *Layer index* lists the drawing's geometry according to layer assignments. These indexes offer more-efficient memory use and faster loading times for drawings that are being used as Xrefs. They take effect only when Demand Load is turned on. (See Chapter 7 for more on Demand Load.) The Layer index enables AutoCAD to load only those layers of an Xref that are not frozen. AutoCAD uses the Spatial index to load only objects in an Xref that are within the boundary of a clipped Xref.

You can turn on the Spatial and Layer indexes for a file through the Indexctl system variable. Indexctl has four settings:

◆ 0 is the default. This turns off Spatial and Layer indexing.

◆ 1 turns on Layer indexing.

◆ 2 turns on Spatial indexing.

◆ 3 turns on both Layer and Spatial indexing.

To use the Indexctl system variable, type **Indexctl**↵. Then, at the Enter new value for INDEXCTL <0>: prompt, enter the number of the setting option you want to use.

TIP The Partial Open option in the Select File dialog box includes the Index Status button group, which offers information on the index status of a drawing. If the drawing you're opening has Spatial or Layer indexing turned on, you can use it by selecting the Spatial Index check box.

Using the Incremental Save Percentage to Conserve Disk Space

If your disk is getting crowded and you need to squeeze as many files as you can onto it, you can reduce the amount of wasted space in a file by adjusting the Incremental Save value in the Open And Save tab of the Options dialog box. By setting Incremental Save to a lower value, you can reduce the size of files to some degree. The trade-off is slower performance when saving files. See Appendix A for more information on this setting.

Another related option is to turn off the BAK file option, also located in the Open And Save tab of the Options dialog box. Each time you choose File ➢ Save or File ➢ Save As, AutoCAD creates a backup copy of your file with the .bak file extension. When you turn off the Create Backup Copy With Each Save option, BAK files are not created, thereby saving disk space.

Setting Up Architectural Desktop to Act Like Standard AutoCAD

Many users who have Architectural Desktop 2007 (ADT) would like to use this book to learn AutoCAD 2007. However, the interface to ADT is quite different from the standard AutoCAD interface. Still, underneath the ADT menus and palettes lies the basic AutoCAD program discussed in this book. If you have Architectural Desktop 2007, the following instructions show you how to set up a shortcut on your Windows Desktop to launch standard AutoCAD 2007.

1. Make a copy of the ADT windows desktop shortcut. Right-click the Architectural Desktop 2007 shortcut and choose Copy.

2. Right-click a blank spot on the Desktop and choose Paste.

3. Right-click the copy of the ADT shortcut and choose Properties.

4. In the Target text box, change the value to read as follows:

```
"C:\Program Files\Autodesk Architectural Desktop 2007\acad.exe" /t "acad.dwt"
/p "Standard AutoCAD"
```

The /t is a command switch that tells AutoCAD to use a specific template file, which in this case is acad.dwt. The /p is a command switch that tells AutoCAD to use the Standard AutoCAD profile when starting AutoCAD. Note that the Standard AutoCAD profile does not exist. AutoCAD will create it when you attempt to start AutoCAD from the shortcut. Click Apply after you've made the change to the Target text box.

5. Click the Change Icon button, and then click the Browse button in the Change Icon dialog box. From here, you can select a different icon from the Change Icon dialog box.

6. Click OK to exit the Shortcut Properties dialog box. Then right-click the shortcut copy again and choose Rename.

7. Rename the shortcut to **AutoCAD 2007**.

Double-click your new AutoCAD 2007 Desktop shortcut to start AutoCAD 2007. You will see a warning message that the Standard AutoCAD profile does not exist and that AutoCAD will create it using the default AutoCAD settings. Once AutoCAD has started, the title bar will still show Autodesk Architectural Desktop 2007, but the program will behave like standard AutoCAD 2007. You can still start the full version of Architectural Desktop by using the Architectural Desktop 2007 shortcut or if you launch AutoCAD by double-clicking an AutoCAD file.

When Things Go Wrong

AutoCAD is a complex program, and at times AutoCAD doesn't behave in a way you expect. If you run into problems, chances are they won't be insurmountable. Here are a few tips on what to do when AutoCAD doesn't work the way you expect.

Starting Up or Opening a File

The most common reason you'll have difficulty opening a file is a lack of free disk space. If you encounter errors attempting to open files, check whether you have adequate free disk space on all your drives.

If you've recently installed AutoCAD but you cannot start it, you might have a configuration problem. Before you panic, try reinstalling AutoCAD from scratch. Particularly if you are installing the CD version, this does not take long. (See Appendix A for installation instructions.) Before you reinstall AutoCAD, use the Uninstall program to remove the current version of AutoCAD. After you've uninstalled AutoCAD, delete the AutoCAD 2007 folder from the Program Files folder and also delete the AutoCAD 2007 folders under the following two locations:

```
C:\Documents and Settings\UserName\Application Data\Autodesk
C:\Documents and Settings\UserName\Local Settings\Application Data\Autodesk
```

Make sure you have your authorization code, serial number, and CD key handy. Make sure that you've closed all other programs when you run the AutoCAD installation. As a final measure, restart your computer when you've completed the installation.

Restoring Corrupted Files

Hardware failures can result in data files becoming corrupted. When this happens, AutoCAD is unable to open the drawing file. Fortunately, there is hope for damaged files. In most cases, AutoCAD will run through a file-recovery routine automatically the next time you open AutoCAD after a crash. You'll see a panel on the left side of the AutoCAD window listing files that are available for recovery, including .bak files. You can double-click the file you want to recover and then save it.

If you have a file you know is corrupted, but it doesn't appear in the panel described in the previous paragraph, you can start the file-recovery utility by choosing File ➢ Drawing Utilities ➢ Recover. This opens the Select File dialog box, enabling you to select the file you want to recover. After you enter the name, AutoCAD goes to work. You'll see a series of messages, most of which have little meaning to the average user. Then the recovered file is opened. You might lose some data, but a partial file is better than no file at all, especially when the file represents several days of work.

Another possibility is to attempt to recover your drawing from the BAK file—the last saved version before your drawing was corrupted. Rename the drawing BAK file to a DWG file with a different name, and then open it. The drawing will contain only what was in your drawing when it was previously saved.

If you want to restore a file that you've just been working on, you can check the alphanumeric file with the .SV$ file name extension. This is the file AutoCAD uses to store your drawing during automatic saves. Change the .sv$ filename extension to .dwg, and then open the file.

In some situations, a file is so badly corrupted it cannot be restored. By backing up frequently, you can minimize the inconvenience of such an occurrence. You might also want to consider a third-party utility that performs regular disk maintenance.

Troubleshooting Other Common Problems

AutoCAD is a large, complex program, so you are bound to encounter some difficulties from time to time. This section covers a few of the more common problems experienced while using AutoCAD.

You can see but cannot select objects in a drawing someone else has worked on. This might be happening because you have a Paper Space view instead of a Model Space view. To make sure you're in Model Space, type **Tilemode↵** and then type **1↵**. Or you can turn on the UCS icon (by typing **Ucsicon↵On↵**). If you see the triangular UCS icon in the lower-left corner, you are in Paper Space. You must go to Model Space before you can edit the drawing. Another item to check is the layer lock setting. If a layer is locked, you won't be able to edit objects on that layer.

Grips do not appear when objects are selected. Make sure the Grips feature is enabled (choose Tools ➢ Grips). See Appendix A for details.

Selecting objects doesn't work as described in this book. Check the Selection settings to make sure they are set the same way as the exercise specifies. See Chapter 2 for details. Also check the Selection tab in the Options dialog box (choose Tools ➢ Options). See Appendix A for more on the Selection tab of the Options dialog box.

Text appears in the wrong font style, or an error message says AutoCAD cannot find font files. When you are working on files from another company, it's not uncommon that you will encounter a file that uses special third-party fonts that you do not have. You can usually substitute standard AutoCAD fonts for any fonts you don't have without adverse effects. AutoCAD automatically displays a dialog box that lets you select font files for the substitution. You can either choose a font file or press the Esc key to ignore the message. (See Chapter 10 for more on font files.) If you choose to ignore the error message, you might not see some of the text that would normally appear in the drawing.

You can't import DXF files.   Various problems can occur during the DXF import, the most common of which is that you are trying to import a DXF file into an existing drawing rather than a new drawing. Under some conditions, you can import a DXF file into an existing drawing by using the Dxfin command, but AutoCAD might not import the entire file.

To ensure that your entire DXF file is safely imported, choose File ➢ Open and select *.DXF from the File Type drop-down list. Then import your DXF file.

If you know the DXF file you are trying to import is in the ASCII format and not a binary .DXF, take a look at the file with a text editor. If it contains odd-looking lines of characters, chances are the file is damaged or contains extra data that AutoCAD cannot understand. Try deleting the odd-looking lines of characters, and then import the file again. (Make a backup copy of the file before you attempt this.)

A file cannot be saved to disk.   Frequently, a hard disk will fill up quickly during an editing session. AutoCAD can generate temporary and swap files many times larger than the file you are editing. This might leave you with no room to save your file. If this happens, you can empty the Recycle Bin to clear some space on your hard disk or delete old AutoCAD BAK files you don't need. *Do not delete temporary AutoCAD files.*

The keyboard shortcuts for commands are not working.   If you are working on an unfamiliar computer, chances are the keyboard shortcuts (or command aliases) have been altered. The command aliases are stored in the Acad.pgp file. Use the Windows Search utility to locate this file and make sure that the Acad.pgp file is in the C:\Documents and Settings*User Name*\ Application Data\Autodesk\AutoCAD 2007\R17.0\enu\Support folder.

Plots come out blank.   Check the scale factor you are using for your plot. Often, a blank plot means your scale factor is making the plot too large to fit on the sheet. Try plotting with the Scale To Fit option. If you get a plot, you know your scale factor is incorrect. See Chapter 8 for more on plotting options. Check your output before you plot by using the Full Preview option in the Plot Configuration dialog box.

You cannot get your drawing properly oriented on the sheet.   If you want to change the orientation of your drawing on a plotted sheet, and the Plot Configuration orientation options don't seem to work, try rotating the UCS to align with your desired plot view and then type **Plan**↵. Adjust the view to display what you want plotted, and then use the View command (choose View ➢ Named Views) to save this view. When you are ready to plot, use the View option in the Plot Configuration dialog box and plot the saved view, instead of rotating the plot.

Dimensions appear as objects or lines and text and do not act as described in this book. The Dimassoc system variable has been set to 0 or was 0 when the dimension was created. Another possibility is that the dimension was reduced to its component objects by using the Explode command. Make sure Dimassoc is on by typing **Dimassoc**↵**2**↵. Unfortunately, an exploded dimension or one that was created with Dimassoc turned off cannot be converted to a true dimension object. You must redraw the dimension.

A file containing an Xref appears to be blank or parts are missing.   AutoCAD cannot find the Xref file. Use the Xref Manager dialog box (choose Insert ➢ Xref Manager) to reestablish a connection with the Xref file. After the Xref Manager dialog box is open, select the missing Xref from the list, and then click the Browse button and locate and select the file by using the Browse dialog box.

As you draw, little marks appear on your screen where you have selected points.   The Blipmode system variable is on. Turn it off by typing **Blipmode**↵**off**↵.

A file you want to open is read-only, even though you know no one else on the network is using the file. Every now and then, you might receive a file that you cannot edit because it is read-only. This frequently happens with files that have been archived to a CD. If you have a file that is read-only, try the following:

1. Locate the read-only file with Windows Explorer and right-click its filename.

2. Choose Properties from the shortcut menu to open the Properties dialog box.

3. Click the General tab.

4. Click the Read-Only check box to remove the check.

Tracking vectors do not appear in the drawing as described in this book. Make sure that the AutoTrack features are turned on. See the discussion of the Drafting tab in the Options dialog box in Appendix A.

The Hyperlink icon does not appear as described in Chapter 27. Make sure the Hyperlink options are turned on in the User Preferences tab in the Options dialog box.

When you open new files, the drawing area is not the same as described in this book. Make sure you're using the correct default unit style for new drawings. In the Create New Drawing dialog box, click the Start From Scratch button and select the appropriate unit style from the Default Settings button group. If you are using feet and inches, select Imperial (feet and inches). If you are using metric measurements, select Metric. AutoCAD will use the Acad.dwt file template for new Imperial measurement drawings and the Acadiso.dwt template for metric measurement drawings. You can also use the Measureinit system variable to set the default unit style.

When you offset polylines, such as rectangles or polygons, the offset object has extra line segments or rounded corners. Set the Offsetgap system variable to 0. Offsetgap controls the behavior of the line segments of offset polylines. When Offsetgap is set to 0, the individual line segments of a polyline are extended to join end to end. When Offsetgap is set to 1, the line segments retain their original length and are joined with an arc. If Offsetgap is set to 2, the line segments retain their original length and are joined by a straight-line segment.

Your older AutoCAD file contains filled areas that were once transparent, but in AutoCAD 2007 the text and line work are obscured by solid fills. Earlier versions of AutoCAD let you adjust the Merge Control feature of your plotter, which in turn allowed solid filled areas to appear transparent. The Merge Control feature is still available, but it has been moved to the Plotter Configuration Editor. See the section on merge control earlier in this appendix for more information.

Another option is to use the Draworder command to move the solid filled area "behind" other objects in the drawing. See Chapter 14 for more on the Draworder command.

Filled, non-TrueType fonts appear to have extraneous lines around the edges. If your font looks distorted and lines appear around the edges, it may be due to a setting in the plot style table. Open the plot style table for your drawing (see Chapter 9) and make sure the Line End Style setting for the text's layer or plot style is set to Use Object End Style.

Appendix C

System and Dimension Variables

System variables let you fine-tune your AutoCAD environment. Dimension variables govern the specific dimensioning functions of AutoCAD.

You set a system variable by entering the variable name at the Command prompt. Or, if you are in the middle of another command, you can set a system variable by entering the variable name preceded by an apostrophe. For example, if you are drawing a series of line segments, you can enter ´Snapang↵ at the Specify next point or [Undo]: prompt to change the Snapang system variable on the fly. You can also access these variables through the AutoLISP interpreter by using the Getvar and Setvar functions, as well as through ActiveX automation. LT users can use the Modemacro command and the Diesel macro language to obtain information from the system variables. (See Chapter 26 for more on Modemacro and Diesel.)

This appendix is divided into two major sections; the first concerns setting system variables, and the second concerns setting dimension variables. This division is somewhat artificial, because as far as AutoCAD is concerned, there is no difference between system variables and dimension variables—you use both types of variables the same way. But because the set of dimension variables is quite extensive, I've separated them here for clarity.

At the end of this appendix, you will also find a detailed description of the Dimension Style dialog boxes. They are presented here to supplement the main discussion of dimensions in Chapter 12.

Setting System Variables

Table C.1 lists the variables and indicates whether they are read-only or adjustable. Most of these variables have counterparts in other commands, as listed in the table. For example, you can adjust Angdir and Angbase by using the Ddunits command (choose Format ➤ Units). Many, such as Highlight and Expert, do not have equivalent commands. You must adjust these at the command line (or through AutoLISP).

TABLE C.1: System Variables. Items Marked with an Asterisk Were Added in AutoCAD 2006. Items Marked with Two Asterisks Are New in AutoCAD 2007.

VARIABLE NAME	ASSOCIATED COMMAND	WHERE SAVED	USE
3ddwfprec**	3ddwf	With drawing	Controls the precision of 3ddwf publishing; 1 = 1, 2 = 0.5, 3 = 0.2 4 = 0.1, 5 = 0.01, and 6 = 0.001

TABLE C.1: System Variables. Items Marked with an Asterisk Were Added in AutoCAD 2006. Items Marked with Two Asterisks Are New in AutoCAD 2007. *(CONTINUED)*

VARIABLE NAME	ASSOCIATED COMMAND	WHERE SAVED	USE
Acadlspasdoc	Options	Registry	Controls the loading of the Acad.lsp file when present: 0 = load only into first drawing (initial value); 1 = into every opened drawing.
Acadprefix (read-only)	Options	NA	Indicates the AutoCAD environment setting.
Acadver	NA	NA	Indicates the AutoCAD version number.
Acisoutver	Acisout	With drawing	Controls ACIS version of SAT files.
Adcstate (read-only)	NA	Registry	Indicates the current display state of the AutoCAD DesignCenter: 0 = closed; 1 = opened.
Aflags	Units	NA	Controls attribute mode settings: 1 = invisible; 2 = constant; 4 = verify; 8 = preset.
Angbase	Units	With drawing	Controls direction of 0 angle relative to the current UCS.
Angdir	Units	With drawing	Controls positive direction of angles: 0 = counterclockwise; 1 = clockwise.
Apbox	Draw, Edit	Registry	Displays AutoSnap aperture box when AutoSnap is activated: 0 = off; 1 = on.
Aperture	Draw, Edit	Registry	Sets size of Osnap cursor in pixels.
Apstate (read-only)	Bedit	NA	Indicates whether the Block Authoring Palettes window is open: 0 = closed, 1 = open.
Area (read-only)	Area	NA	Displays last area calculation; use with Setvar or AutoLISP's Getvar function.
Assiststate	Quick Help	NA	Controls the display of the Info palette Quick Help: 0 = off; 1 = on.
Attdia	Insert/Attribute	With drawing	Controls the Attribute dialog box: 0 = no dialog box; 1 = dialog box.
Attmode	Attdisp	With drawing	Controls attribute display mode: 0 = off; 1 = normal; 2 = on.
Attreq	Insert	With drawing	Controls the prompt for attributes: 0 = no prompt or dialog box for attributes (attributes use default values); 1 = normal prompt or dialog box upon attribute insertion.

TABLE C.1:   System Variables. Items Marked with an Asterisk Were Added in AutoCAD 2006. Items Marked with Two Asterisks Are New in AutoCAD 2007. *(CONTINUED)*

VARIABLE NAME	ASSOCIATED COMMAND	WHERE SAVED	USE
Auditctl	Config	Registry	Controls whether an audit file is created: 0 = disable; 1 = enable creation of ADT file.
Aunits	Units	With drawing	Controls angular units: 0 = decimal degrees; 1 = degrees-minutes-seconds; 2 = grads; 3 = radians; 4 = surveyor's units.
Auprec	Units	With drawing	Controls the precision of angular units determined by decimal place.
Autosnap	Draw, Edit	Registry	Controls AutoSnap display and features: 0 = everything off; 1 = marker on; 2 = Snaptip on; 4 = magnet on.
Backgroundplot	Plot, Publish	Registry	Controls the background plot feature: 0 = off; 1 = background for Plot but not Publish; 2 = background for Publish but not Plot; 4 = background for both Plot and Publish.
Backz (read-only)	Dview	With drawing	Displays distance from Dview target to back clipping plane.
Bactioncolor*	Bedit	Registry	Controls the color of Actions in the Block Editor. Values can be index colors from 1 to 255 or RGB colors specified as RGB:CCC, CCC,CCC; CCC is a value from 1 to 255.
Bdependencyhighlight	Bedit	Registry	Controls the highlighting of dependent objects when Actions or parameters are selected; 1 = highlight on; 0 = highlight off.
Bgripobjcolor*	Bedit	Registry	Sets the color of grips in the Block Editor. See Bactioncolor for settings.
Bgropobjsize*	Bedit	Registry	Sets the display size of grips. Values can be from 1 to 255.
Bindtype	Xref	*NA*	Controls the way Xref names are handled when bound to a file: 0 = maintain Xref filename prefix (initial value); 1 = remove Xref filename prefix.
Blipmode	*NA*	With drawing	Controls appearance of blips: 0 = off; 1 = on.

TABLE C.1: System Variables. Items Marked with an Asterisk Were Added in AutoCAD 2006. Items Marked with Two Asterisks Are New in AutoCAD 2007. *(CONTINUED)*

VARIABLE NAME	ASSOCIATED COMMAND	WHERE SAVED	USE
Blockeditlock*	Bedit	Registry	Locks the Block Editor from use; 0 = not locked; 1 = locked.
Blockeditor* (read-only)	Bedit	NA	Indicates if the Block Editor is open; 0 = not open; 1 = open.
Bparametercolor*	Bedit	Registry	Controls the color of parameters in the Block Editor. See Bactioncolor for settings.
Bparameterfont*	Bedit	Registry	Controls the fonts used for parameters. TrueType or AutoCAD SHX fonts can be specified. Include the SHX file extension for SHX fonts.
Bparametersize*	Bedit	Registry	Controls the parameter text sizes relative to the screen. Accepts intigers from 1 to 255.
Btmarkdisplay*	Bedit	Registry	Controls the display of value set markers; 0 = not displayed; 1 = displayed.
Bvmode*	Bedit	NA	Controls how "invisible" objects are displayed; 0 = not visible; 1 = grayed out.
Calcinput*	Dialog box Input Boxes	Registry	Controls whether mathematical expressions are evaluated when entered in input boxes; 0 = not evaluated; 1 = evaluated by pressing the END key.
Cameradisplay**	Camera	With drawing	Controls the display of camera glyphs; 0 = not displayed, 1 = displayed.
Cameraheight**	Camera	With drawing	Controls the default height for new cameras.
Cdate (read-only)	Time	NA	Displays calendar date/time read from system date (YYYY MMDD.HHMMSSMSEC).
Cecolor	Color	With drawing	Controls current default color assigned to new objects.
Celtscale	NA	With drawing	Controls current linetype scale for individual objects.
Celtype	Linetype	With drawing	Controls current default linetype assigned to new objects.

TABLE C.1: System Variables. Items Marked with an Asterisk Were Added in AutoCAD 2006. Items Marked with Two Asterisks Are New in AutoCAD 2007. *(CONTINUED)*

VARIABLE NAME	ASSOCIATED COMMAND	WHERE SAVED	USE
Celweight	Lineweight	With drawing	Controls the default lineweight for new objects: −1 = Bylayer; −2 = Byblock; −3 = default as set by Lwdefault. Specific lineweight values can also be entered in millimeters.
Centermt*	Mtext	User settings	Controls how the Mtext bounding box behaves; 0 = one corner remains stationary while other corner moves; 1 = center remains stationary while both corners move.
Chamfera	Chamfer	With drawing	Controls first chamfer distance.
Chamferb	Chamfer	With drawing	Controls second chamfer distance.
Chamferc	Chamfer	With drawing	Controls chamfer distance for Angle option.
Chamferd	Chamfer	With drawing	Controls chamfer angle for Angle option.
Chammode	Chamfer	*NA*	Controls method of chamfer: 0 = use two distances; 1 = use distance and angle.
Circlerad	Circle	*NA*	Controls the default circle radius: 0 = no default.
Clayer	Layer	With drawing	Sets the current layer.
Cleanscreenstate (read-only)	Cleanscreen	*NA*	Reports the status of the clean screen feature; 0 = off, 1 = on
Clistate* (read-only)	Command Window	*NA*	Indicates whether the command window is hidden or displayed; 0 = hidden; 1 = displayed.
Cmaterial**	Material	With drawing	Controls the default material for new objects; value can be Bylayer or the name of an existing material in the drawing.

TABLE C.1:   System Variables. Items Marked with an Asterisk Were Added in AutoCAD 2006. Items Marked with Two Asterisks Are New in AutoCAD 2007. *(CONTINUED)*

VARIABLE NAME	ASSOCIATED COMMAND	WHERE SAVED	USE
Cmdactive (read-only)	NA	NA	Displays whether a command, script, or dialog box is active: 1 = command active; 2 = transparent command active; 4 = script active; 8 = dialog box active (values are cumulative, so 3 = command and transparent command are active).
Cmddia	NA	Registry	Controls use of dialog boxes for some commands: 0 = don't use dialog box; 1 = use dialog box.
Cmdecho	Autolisp	NA	With AutoLISP, controls display of prompts from embedded AutoCAD commands: 0 = no display of prompt; 1 = display prompts.
Cmdhistoryinputmax*	NA	Registry	Sets the maximum number of command input values stored for later retrieval from the shortcut menu.
Cmdnames (read-only)	NA	NA	Displays the English name of the currently active command.
Cmljust	Mline	With drawing	Sets method of justification for multilines: 0 = top; 1 = middle; 2 = bottom.
Cmlscale	Mline	With drawing	Sets scale factor for multiline widths: a 0 value collapses the multiline to a single line; a negative value reverses the justification.
Cmlstyle	Mline	With drawing	Displays current multiline style by name.
Compass	3dorbit	NA	Controls the display of the 3D compass: 0 = off (initial value); 1 = on.
Coords	F6, Ctrl+D	With drawing	Controls coordinate readout: 0 = coordinates displayed only when points are picked; 1 = absolute coordinates dynamically displayed as cursor moves; 2 = distance and angle displayed during commands that accept relative distance input.
Cplotstyle	Plot, Pagesetup	With drawing	Controls the default plot style for new objects. Startup values are ByLayer, ByBlock, Normal, and User Defined.

TABLE C.1: System Variables. Items Marked with an Asterisk Were Added in AutoCAD 2006. Items Marked with Two Asterisks Are New in AutoCAD 2007. *(CONTINUED)*

VARIABLE NAME	ASSOCIATED COMMAND	WHERE SAVED	USE
Cprofile (read-only)	Options	Registry	Displays the current profile name.
Crossingareacolor*	Object Selection	Registry	Sets the color for the crossing window. Use the AutoCAD ACI color numbers. Selectionarea must be on for this system variable to work.
Cshadow**	Visualstyles	With drawing	Controls the shadow display of 3D objects; 0 = cast and receive shadows, 1 = cast shadows, 2 = receive shadows, 3 = ignore shadows.
Ctab (read-only)	(tabs)	With drawing	Displays the name of the current tab.
Ctablestyle	Table	With drawing	Controls the name of the current table style.
Cursorsize	*NA*	Registry	Determines size of crosshairs as a percentage of the screen size (1–100).
Cvport (read-only)	Vports	With drawing	Displays ID number of current viewport.
Dashboardstate**	Dashboard	*NA*	Reports the Dashboard window status; 0 = not active, 1 = active
Date (read-only)	Time	*NA*	Displays date and time in Julian format.
Dblclkedit**	Double-click	Registry	Controls whether a double-click issues a command or macro; 0 = disabled, 1 = enabled
Dbmod (read-only)	*NA*	*NA*	Displays drawing modification status: 1 = object database modified; 2 = symbol table modified; 4 = database variable modified; 8 = window modified; 16 = view modified.
Dctcust	Spell	Registry	Sets default custom spelling dictionary filename, including path.
Dctmain	Spell	Registry	Sets default main spelling dictionary filename; requires specific keywords for each language. See AutoCAD Help for complete list of keywords.

TABLE C.1: System Variables. Items Marked with an Asterisk Were Added in AutoCAD 2006. Items Marked with Two Asterisks Are New in AutoCAD 2007. *(CONTINUED)*

VARIABLE NAME	ASSOCIATED COMMAND	WHERE SAVED	USE
Defaultlighting**	Lighting	With drawing	Controls the default lighting in the current viewport, 0 = automatically turns off when other lights are turned on, 1 = on
Defaultlightingtype**	Lighting	With drawing	Determines the type of default light used; 0 = old, single distant light, 1 = new dual distant light.
Deflplstyle	Plotstyle	With drawing	Sets the default plot style for new layers.
Defplstyle	Plotstyle	Registry	Sets the default plot style for new objects.
Delobj	NA	With drawing	Controls whether source objects used to create new objects are retained: 0 = delete objects; 1 = retain objects.
Demandload	NA	Registry	Controls loading of third-party applications required for custom objects in drawing (0–3).
Diastat (read-only)	NA	NA	Displays how last dialog box was exited: 0 = Cancel; 1 = OK.
Dispsilh	All curved solids	With drawing	Controls silhouette display of curved 3D solids: 0 = no silhouette; 1 = silhouette curved solids.
Distance	Dist	NA	Displays last distance calculated by Dist command.
Donutid	Donut	NA	Controls default inside diameter of a donut.
Donutod	Donut	NA	Controls default outside diameter of a donut.
Dragmode	NA	With drawing	Controls dragging: 0 = no dragging; 1 = if requested; 2 = automatic drag.
Dragp1	NA	Registry	Controls regeneration-drag input sampling rate.
Dragp2	NA	Registry	Controls fast-drag input sampling rate.
Dragvs**	Visualstyle	With drawing	Controls the visual style when creating 3D objects. Use a period (.) to specify the current visual style or enter the name of a visual style that exists in the current drawing.

TABLE C.1: System Variables. Items Marked with an Asterisk Were Added in AutoCAD 2006. Items Marked with Two Asterisks Are New in AutoCAD 2007. *(CONTINUED)*

VARIABLE NAME	ASSOCIATED COMMAND	WHERE SAVED	USE
Draworderctl	Draworder	With drawing	Controls the level of functionality offered by the Draworder command: 0 = regen required to display draw order; 1 = draw order display is immediate; 2 = adds inheritance to objects with draw order; 3 = full Draworder functionality (1 and 2 combined).
Drstate* (read-only)	*NA*	*NA*	Indicates whether the Drawing Recovery window is open; 0 = not open; 1 = open.
Dtexted*	Dtext	Registry	Controls Dtext behavior; 0 = in-place editing; 1 = opens dialog box for editing as in previous versions of AutoCAD.
Dwfframe**	Xref dwf	With drawing	Controls the display of a DWF frame; 0 = no frame, 1 = frame is visible and plots, 2 frame is visible but does not plot.
Dwfosnap**	Xref dwf	Registry	Controls the ability to snap to DWF geometry; 0 = disabled, 1 enabled.
Dwgcheck	*NA*	Registry	Controls the display of a warning dialog box indicating that a drawing was last edited in a program other than AutoCAD: 0 = suppress dialog box; 1 = display dialog box when needed.
Dwgcodepage (read-only)	*NA*	With drawing	Displays code page of drawing (see Syscodepage).
Dwgname (read-only)	Open	*NA*	Displays drawing name and drive/folder, if specified by user.
Dwgprefix (read-only)	*NA*	*NA*	Displays drive and folder of current file.
Dwgtitled (read-only)	*NA*	*NA*	Displays whether a drawing has been named: 0 = untitled; 1 = named by user.
Dyndigrip*	Dynamic Input	Registry	Controls how dimensions are displayed while grip editing. Values can be the sum of the following for combined settings: 0 = none; 1 = resulting dimension ; 2 = change in dimension; 4 = absolute angle ; 8 = change in angle; 16 = arc radius; 31 = all settings on.

TABLE C.1: System Variables. Items Marked with an Asterisk Were Added in AutoCAD 2006. Items Marked with Two Asterisks Are New in AutoCAD 2007. *(CONTINUED)*

VARIABLE NAME	ASSOCIATED COMMAND	WHERE SAVED	USE
Dyndivis*	Dynamic Input	User settings	Controls the number of dimensions that are visible while grip editing; 0 = first dimension in prompt order; 1 = first two dimensions; 2 = all dimensions allowed by the Dyndigrip setting.
Dynmode*	Dynamic Input	User settings	Controls the overall behavior of Dynamic Input; 0 = off; 1 = prompt input only; 2 = dimensions only; 3 = both prompt and dimension input. Negative values can be used and toggled on or off using the F12 key.
Dynpicoords*	Dynamic Input	User settings	Controls whether Dynamic Input uses relative or absolute coordinates; 0 = relative; 1 = absolute.
Dyniformat*	Dynamic Input	User settings	Controls whether Dynamic Input uses polar or Cartesian coordinates; 0 = polar; 1 = Cartesian.
Dynpivis*	Dynamic Input	User settings	Controls when keyboard input is displayed; 0 = when you type; 1 = automatically when prompted for input; 2 = always.
Dynprompt*	Dynamic Input	User settings	Controls the display of prompts; 0 = no display; 1 = display.
Dyntooltips*	Dynamic Input	User settings	Controls the extent of tooltip display; 0 = Dynamic Input fields only; 1 = all tooltips.
Edgemode	Trim, Extend	Registry	Controls how trim and extend boundaries are determined: 0 = boundaries defined by object only; 1 = boundaries defined by objects and their extension.
Elevation	Elev	With drawing	Controls current 3D elevation relative to current UCS.
Enterprisemenu*	Custom User Interfact (CUI)	Registry	Displays the CUI filename and path.
Errno (read-only)	Autolisp	*NA*	Displays Autolisp error code.

TABLE C.1: System Variables. Items Marked with an Asterisk Were Added in AutoCAD 2006. Items Marked with Two Asterisks Are New in AutoCAD 2007. *(CONTINUED)*

VARIABLE NAME	ASSOCIATED COMMAND	WHERE SAVED	USE
Expert	*NA*	*NA*	Controls prompts, depending on level of user's expertise: 0 = normal prompts; 1 = suppresses `About to regen` and `Really want to turn the \current layer off` prompts; 2 = suppresses `Block already defined` and `A drawing with this name already exists` prompts for Block command; 3 = suppresses `An item with this name already exists` prompt for the Linetype command; 4 = suppresses `An item with this name already exists` prompt for the UCS/Save and Vports/Save options; 5 = suppresses `An item with this name already exists` prompt for Dim/Save and Dim/Override commands.
Explmode	Explode	With drawing	Controls whether blocks inserted with different x, y, and z values are exploded: 0 = blocks are not exploded; 1 = blocks are exploded.
Extmax (read-only)	Zoom	With drawing	Displays upper-right corner coordinate of Extents view.
Extmin (read-only)	Zoom	With drawing	Displays lower-left corner coordinate of Extents view.
Extnames	Options	With drawing	Controls the length of names for named objects in AutoCAD: 0 = limit names to 31 characters; 1 = allow up to 255 characters.
Facetratio	Shade, Hide	*NA*	Controls aspect ratio of faceting of curved 3D surfaces. Value is 0 or 1; 1 increases the density of the mesh.
Facetres	Shade, Hide	With drawing	Controls appearance of smooth, curved, 3D surfaces when shaded or hidden. Value can be between 0.01 and 10. The higher the number, the more faceted (and smoother) the curved surface, and the longer the time needed for shade and hidden-line removal.
Fielddisplay	Field	Registry	Controls the gray, non-plotting background of fields: 0 = no background; 1 = background.

TABLE C.1: System Variables. Items Marked with an Asterisk Were Added in AutoCAD 2006. Items Marked with Two Asterisks Are New in AutoCAD 2007. *(CONTINUED)*

VARIABLE NAME	ASSOCIATED COMMAND	WHERE SAVED	USE
Fieldeval*	Field	With drawing	Controls the way fields are updated. Values can be added for combined features: 0 = no update; 1 = on open; 2 = on save; 4 = on plot; 8 = on use of eTransmit; 16 = on regen.
Filedia	Dialog box	Registry	Specifies whether a file dialog box is used by default: 0 = don't use unless requested with a ~ (a tilde); 1 = use whenever possible.
Filletrad	Fillet	With drawing	Controls fillet radius.
Fillmode	Fill	With drawing	Controls fill status: 0 = off; 1 = on.
Fontalt	Open, Dxfin, other File ➢ Import options	Registry	Lets you specify an alternative font when AutoCAD cannot find the font associated with a file. If no font is specified for Fontalt, AutoCAD displays a warning message and a dialog box in which you manually select a font.
Fontmap		Registry	Similar to Fontalt, but lets you designate a set of font substitutions through a font-mapping file. Example line from mapping file: `romans: C:\WINDOWS\FONTS\times.ttf`. This substitutes Romans font with Times TrueType font. Font-mapping file can be any name, with extension .fmp.
Frontz (read-only)	Dview	With drawing	Controls front clipping plane for current viewport; use with Viewmode system variable.
Fullopen (read-only)	Open	*NA*	Displays whether the current drawing is fully or partially opened.
Fullplotpath*	Plot Spool	Registry	Controls whether the full plot path is sent to the plot spooler; 0 = send only the drawing filename; 1 = send full path.
Gfang	Bhatch	With drawing	Controls the gradient fill angle.

TABLE C.1: System Variables. Items Marked with an Asterisk Were Added in AutoCAD 2006. Items Marked with Two Asterisks Are New in AutoCAD 2007. *(CONTINUED)*

VARIABLE NAME	ASSOCIATED COMMAND	WHERE SAVED	USE
Gfclr1	Bhatch	With drawing	Controls the gradient fill color #1. Values can be index colors from 1 to 255 or RGB colors specified as RGB:CCC,CCC,CCC; CCC is a value from 1 to 255.
Gfclr2	Bhatch	With drawing	Controls the gradient fill color #2. See Gfclr1 for settings.
Gfclrlum	Bhatch	With drawing	In single-color gradients, controls the shade of the noncolor end of the gradient.
Gfclrstate	Bhatch	With drawing	Controls whether gradient is one or two color. 0 = two color; 1 = single color.
Gfname	Bhatch	With drawing	Controls the gradient pattern. Values are from 1 to 7. See Gradient tab of Hatch And Gradient dialog box for the patterns. Patterns are numbered from top to bottom, left to right starting with 1.
Gfshift	Bhatch	Not saved	Controls whether gradient fills are centered: 0 = centered; 1 = shifted up and to the left.
Griddisplay**	Grid	With drawing	Controls whether grids are restricted to the drawing limits or not; 0 = restrict to limits, 1 = no restriction
Gridmajor**	Grid	With drawing	Sets the interval of major grid lines for all but 2D wireframe visual styles.
Gridmode	Grid	With drawing	Controls grid: 0 = off; 1 = on.
Gridunit	Grid	With drawing	Controls grid spacing.
Gripblock	Grips	Registry	Controls display of grips in blocks: 0 = show insertion point grip only; 1 = show grips of all objects in block.
Gripcolor	Grips	Registry	Controls color of unselected grips. Choices are integers from 1 to 255; default is 5.
Gripdyncolor**	Grips	Registry	Sets the color of grips for dynamic blocks. Index color range from 1 to 255.

TABLE C.1: System Variables. Items Marked with an Asterisk Were Added in AutoCAD 2006. Items Marked with Two Asterisks Are New in AutoCAD 2007. *(CONTINUED)*

VARIABLE NAME	ASSOCIATED COMMAND	WHERE SAVED	USE
Griphot	Grips	Registry	Controls color of hot grips. Choices are integers from 1 to 255; default is 1.
Griphover	Grips	Registry	Controls the color of a grip when the cursor hovers over the grip. Values are index colors from 1 to 255; default is 3.
Gripobjlimit	Grips	Registry	Controls the display of grips based on the number of objects selected. If set to 1, grips are not displayed if more than one object is selected. Range is from 1 to 32,767; default is 100.
Grips	Grips	Registry	Controls use of grips: 0 = grips disabled; 1 = grips enabled (default).
Gripsize	Grips	Registry	Controls grip size (in pixels), from 1 to 255; default is 3.
Griptips	Grips	Registry	Controls the display of grip tips for custom objects: 0 = no grip tips, 1 = grip tips; default is 1.
Gtauto**	Grips	Registry	Controls the display of grip tools; 0 = not displayed automatically, 1 = displayed automatically
Gtdefault**	3Dmove, 3Drotate	Registry	Controls whether the 3D versions of Move and Rotate automatically start when in a 3D view; 0 = Move and Rotate start, 1 = 3Dmove and 3Drotate start.
Gtlocation**	Grip	Registry	Sets the location for grip tools; 0 = same as UCS icon, 1 = aligned with the last selected object.
Halogap**	Hide	With drawing	Sets the gap between 3D objects and the objects they hide as a percentage of 1. Valid only for 2D views.
Handles (read-only)	*NA*	With drawing	Displays status of object handles: 0 = off; 1 = on.
Hideprecision	Hide, Shade, Hlsettings	*NA*	Controls the Hide/Shade precision accuracy: 0 = single precision; 1 = double precision.

TABLE C.1: System Variables. Items Marked with an Asterisk Were Added in AutoCAD 2006. Items Marked with Two Asterisks Are New in AutoCAD 2007. *(CONTINUED)*

VARIABLE NAME	ASSOCIATED COMMAND	WHERE SAVED	USE
Hidetext**	Hide, Text, Dtext, Mtext	With drawing	Sets whether text is processed during the Hide command; Off = text not hidden, On = Text is hidden but does not hide other objects.
Highlight	Select	*NA*	Controls whether objects are highlighted when selected: 0 = none; 1 = highlighting.
Hpang	Hatch	*NA*	Sets default hatch pattern angle.
Hpassoc	Hatch	Registry	Controls associative property of hatch pattern: 0 = not associative; 1 = associative; default = 1.
Hpbound	Hatch	Registry	Controls type of object created by Hatch and Boundary commands: 0 = region; 1 = polyline.
Hpdouble	Hatch	*NA*	Sets default hatch doubling for user-defined hatch pattern: 0 = no doubling; 1 = doubling at 90 .
Hpdraworder	Hatch	*NA*	Controls the draw order of hatches: 0 = no draw order; 1 = send hatch to back of all objects; 2 = bring to front of all objects; 3 = behind boundary; 4 = in front of boundary.
Hpgaptol	Hatch	Registry	Controls the gap tolerance for hatch boundaries. Values are from 0 to 5000. When the value is 0, the hatch requires a completely closed outline with no gaps.
Hpinherit*	Hatch	With drawing	Controls how the hatch origin is determined when using the hatch Inherit Properties option; 0 = hporigin; 1 = origin of source hatch pattern.
Hpname	Hatch	*NA*	Sets default hatch pattern name; use a period (.) to set to no default.
Hpobjwarning*	Hatch	Registry	Sets the maximum number of boundary objects that can be selected before a warning is issued.
Hporigin*	Hatch	Drawing	Controls the hatch origin point.

TABLE C.1:   System Variables. Items Marked with an Asterisk Were Added in AutoCAD 2006. Items Marked with Two Asterisks Are New in AutoCAD 2007. *(CONTINUED)*

VARIABLE NAME	ASSOCIATED COMMAND	WHERE SAVED	USE
Hporiginmode*	Hatch	Registry	Controls how the hatch origin is determined; 0 = Hporigin; 1–5 = use extent of rectangular boundary of hatch; 1 is the bottom left, 2 is bottom right, 3 is top left, 4 is top right, and 5 is center.
Hpscale	Hatch	*NA*	Sets default scale for hatch patterns; cannot be 0.
Hpseparate*	Hatch	Registry	Controls whether separate hatch objects are created when separate areas are selected. 0 = single hatch object; 1 = one hatch object per boundary area.
Hpspace	Hatch	*NA*	Sets default line spacing for user-defined hatch pattern; cannot be 0.
Hyperlinkbase	Hyperlink	With drawing	Sets the base location for hyperlink addresses. If left blank, the drawing path is used.
Imagehlt	Options	Registry	Controls highlighting of raster images: 0 = frame only; 1 = entire image.
Impliedface**	3D objects	Registry	Allows the selection of implied faces; 0 = not selectable, 1 = selectable.
Indexctl	*NA*	With drawing	Controls whether Layer and Spatial indexes are created and saved in drawings: 0 = no index; 1 = Layer index; 2 = Spatial index; 3 = both.
Inetlocation	Browser	Registry	Stores the Internet location used by the Browser command.
Inputhistorymode*	Input History	Registry	Controls the display of the input history; 0 = none; 1 = displayed in command line or Dyanamic Input through Up and Down arrow keys; 2 = through shortcut menu for all commands; 4 = through shortcut menu for current command; 8 = display markers for recent input of points.
Insbase	Base	With drawing	Controls insertion base point of current drawing.

TABLE C.1: System Variables. Items Marked with an Asterisk Were Added in AutoCAD 2006. Items Marked with Two Asterisks Are New in AutoCAD 2007. *(CONTINUED)*

VARIABLE NAME	ASSOCIATED COMMAND	WHERE SAVED	USE
Insname	Insert	*NA*	Sets default block or filename for Insert command; enter a period (.) to set to no default.
Insunits	Units	With drawing	Sets the units value for the DesignCenter insert: 0 = unitless; 1 = inches; 2 = feet; 3 = miles; 4 = millimeters; 5 = centimeters; 6 = meters; 7 = kilometers; 8 = microinches; 9 = mils; 10 = yards; 11 = angstroms; 12 = nanometers; 13 = microns; 14 = decimeters; 15 = decameters; 16 = hectometers; 17 = gigameters; 18 = astronomical units; 19 = light years; 20 = parsecs.
Insunitsdefsource	Units	Registry	Sets the default source units. Values are the same as for Insunits.
Insunitsdeftarget	Units	Registry	Sets the default target units. Values are the same as for Insunits.
Intelligentupdate*	Display	Registry	Controls the display refresh rate in frames per second. Affects scripts and AutoLISP graphic routines.
Interferecolor**	Interfere	With drawing	Sets the color of the interference object. Can be 1 to 255 index color or RGB in the format RGB:000,000,000.
Interfereobjvs**	Interfere	With drawing	Sets the visual style for interference objects.
Interferevpvs**	Interfere	With drawing	Sets the visual style for viewport during the interfere command.
Intersectioncolor	Hide	With drawing	Controls the color of the intersection of 3D surfaces when Hide or Hidden Shademode are used. The interesting surfaces are displayed by "intersection polylines." 0 = Byblock; 256 = Bylayer; 257 = entity color; 1 through 255 = AutoCAD index color. Intersectioncolor is valid only when the Intersectiondisplay system variable is set to 1; default = 257.

TABLE C.1: System Variables. Items Marked with an Asterisk Were Added in AutoCAD 2006. Items Marked with Two Asterisks Are New in AutoCAD 2007. *(CONTINUED)*

VARIABLE NAME	ASSOCIATED COMMAND	WHERE SAVED	USE
Intersectiondisplay	Hide	With drawing	Controls whether the intersection of 3D surfaces are displayed with a line, called an intersection polyline: 0 = no intersection polyline; 1 = display intersection polyline; default = 0.
Isavebak	Save	Registry	Controls the creation of BAK files: 0 = no BAK file created; 1 = BAK file created.
Isavepercent	Save	Registry	Determines whether to do a full or an incremental save based on the amount of wasted space tolerated in a drawing file: (0–100).
Isolines	Curved solids	With drawing	Specifies the number of lines on a solid's surface to help visualize its shape.
Lastangle (read-only)	Arc	*NA*	Displays ending angle for last arc drawn.
Lastpoint	*NA*	*NA*	Sets or displays coordinate normally referenced by @.
Lastprompt	*NA*	*NA*	Saves last string echoed to the command line.
Latitude**	Geographicloation	With drawing	Sets the latitude of the drawing in decimal format.
Layerfilteralert*	Layer	Registry	Deletes layer filters when they become too numerous. 0 = off; 1 = delete when Layer Manager is opened without warning; 2 = display a warning and offer options when Layer Manager is opened; 3 = display a warning and offer options when drawing is opened.
Layoutregenctl	Options	Registry	Controls the way regens occur when switching between Model/Layout tabs: 0 = regen at each tab selection; 1 = no regen for Model tab or last used Layout tab; 2 = after initial opening of tabs, no regens while switching between tabs.

TABLE C.1: System Variables. Items Marked with an Asterisk Were Added in AutoCAD 2006. Items Marked with Two Asterisks Are New in AutoCAD 2007. *(CONTINUED)*

VARIABLE NAME	ASSOCIATED COMMAND	WHERE SAVED	USE
Legacyctrlpick**	Ctrl+left click	Registry	Sets the behavior of Ctrl+left-click; 0 = select 3D subobjects, 1 = cycle selection of overlapping objects.
Lenslength (read-only)	Dview	With drawing	Displays focal length of lens used for perspective display.
Lightglyphdisplay**	Lights	Drawing	Sets the display of light glyphs; 0 = off, 1 = on.
Lightliststate** (read-only)	Lightlist	*NA*	Reports whether the lights in Model palette are open or closed; 0 = closed, 1 = open
Limcheck	Limits	With drawing	Controls limit checking: 0 = no checking; 1 = checking.
Limmax	Limits	With drawing	Controls coordinate of drawing's upper-right limit.
Limmin	Limits	With drawing	Controls coordinate of drawing's lower-left limit.
Lispinit	Load	Registry	Preserves AutoLISP-defined functions and variables beyond current drawing session: 0 = AutoLISP variables preserved; 1 = AutoLISP functions valid for current session only.
Locale (read-only)	*NA*	*NA*	Displays ISO language code used by your version of AutoCAD.
Localrootprefix (read-only)	Options	Registry	Displays file path for support and custom files. If entered at the Command prompt through AutoLISP as in (getvar "localrootprefix"), the full path is displayed.
Lockui*	AutoCAD Window	Registry	Locks location and size of toolbars and other windows. 0 = not locked; 1 = docked toolbars are locked; 2 = docked windows are locked; 4 = floating toolbars are locked; 8 = floating windows are locked.
Loftang1**	Loft	With drawing	Sets the draft angle from the first cross-section of a loft.
Loftang2**	Loft	With drawing	Sets the draft angle from the last cross-section of a loft.

TABLE C.1: System Variables. Items Marked with an Asterisk Were Added in AutoCAD 2006. Items Marked with Two Asterisks Are New in AutoCAD 2007. *(CONTINUED)*

VARIABLE NAME	ASSOCIATED COMMAND	WHERE SAVED	USE
Loftmag1**	Loft	With drawing	Sets the draft angle magnitude of the first cross-section of a loft.
Loftmag2**	Loft	With drawing	Sets the draft angle magnitude of the last cross-section of a loft.
Loftnormals**	Loft	With drawing	Controls whether normals of cross-sections are used for a loft. Ignored if a path or guide is specified. 0 = ruled, 1 = smooth, 2 = first normal, 3 = last normal, 4 = both ends normal, 5 = all normal, 6 = Use draft angle and magnitude (loftang1,2 and loftmag1,2).
Loftparam**	Loft	With drawing	Controls the direction of lofts; 1 = No Twist - minimize twist between cross-sections, 2 = Align Direction - align to start end end of cross-sections, 4 = Simplify - straight between cross-sections, 8 = Closed - Loop back to first cross-section.
Logfilemode	*NA*	Registry	Determines whether log file is recorded: 0 = log file off; 1 = log file on.
Logfilename (read-only)	*NA*	Registry	Specifies name/path of log file.
Logfilepath	Options	Registry	Sets the path for the log file.
Loginname (read-only)	*NA*	*NA*	Displays user's login name.
Longitude	Geographiclocation	With drawing	Longitude of model in decimal format.
Ltscale	Ltscale	With drawing	Controls the global linetype scale factor.
Lunits	Units	With drawing	Controls unit styles: 1 = scientific; 2 = decimal; 3 = engineering; 4 = architectural; 5 = fractional.
Luprec	Units	With drawing	Controls unit accuracy by decimal place or size of denominator.
Lwdefault	Lineweight	Registry	Sets the default lineweight. Values are specified in millimeters (25 = 0.25mm).

TABLE C.1: System Variables. Items Marked with an Asterisk Were Added in AutoCAD 2006. Items Marked with Two Asterisks Are New in AutoCAD 2007. *(CONTINUED)*

VARIABLE NAME	ASSOCIATED COMMAND	WHERE SAVED	USE
Lwdisplay	Lineweight	With drawing	Determines whether lineweights are displayed: 0 = not displayed; 1 = displayed.
Lwunits	Lineweight	Registry	Sets the display of lineweight units: 0 = inches; 1 = millimeters.
Matstate** (read-only)	Materials	*NA*	Reports the status of the Materials palette; 0 = closed, 1 = open
Maxactvp	Viewports, Vports	With drawing	Controls maximum number of viewports to regenerate at one time.
Maxobjmem	*NA*	*NA*	Specifies the amount of virtual memory that can be used before AutoCAD starts paging a drawing out to disk.
Maxsort	*NA*	Registry	Controls maximum number of items to be sorted when a command displays a list.
Mbuttonpan	Options	Registry	Determines the behavior of the pointing device's wheel or third button: 0 = behavior determined by menu file; 1 = click-and-drag panning.
Measureinit	Open	Registry	Sets the unit style for new drawings. Determines whether metric or Imperial template file should be used. Determines which default linetype and hatch pattern files should be used: 0 = Imperial; 1 = metric.
Measurement	Bhatch, Linetype	With drawing	Sets drawing units as Imperial or metric: 0 = Imperial; 1 = metric.
Menuctl	*NA*	Registry	Controls whether side menu changes in response to a command name entered from the keyboard: 0 = no response; 1 = menu response.
Menuecho	*NA*	*NA*	Controls messages and Command prompt display from commands embedded in menu: 0 = display all messages; 1 = suppress menu item name; 2 = suppress Command prompts; 4 = disable toggle of menu echo; 8 = debugging aid for Diesel expressions.

TABLE C.1: System Variables. Items Marked with an Asterisk Were Added in AutoCAD 2006. Items Marked with Two Asterisks Are New in AutoCAD 2007. *(CONTINUED)*

VARIABLE NAME	ASSOCIATED COMMAND	WHERE SAVED	USE
Menuname (read-only)	Menu	With drawing	Displays name of current menu file.
Mirrtext	Mirror	With drawing	Controls mirroring of text: 0 = disabled; 1 = enabled.
Modemacro	*NA*	*NA*	Controls display of user-defined text in status line.
Msmstate** (read-only)	Markup Set Mgr	*NA*	Reports the status of the Markup Set Manager; 0 = closed, 1 = open.
Msolescale	OLE	With drawing	Sets the scale of OLE objects that include text. If the value is 0, scale is set by the Dimscale value.
Mtexted	Mtext	Registry	Controls name of program used for editing Mtext objects.
Mtextfixed	Mtext	Registry	Controls how text in the Multiline Text Editor is displayed: 0 = AutoCAD attempts to display the text as closely as possible to the actual size and appearance in the drawing; 1 = text is displayed in a fixed size and location based on the last size and position.
Mtjigstring	Mtext	Registry	Controls the display of the sample text that is displayed when placing the text boundary for Mtext. The default is abc, but can be set to anything up to 10 characters. Enter a period (.) for no display.
Mydocumentsprefix (read-only)	Options	Registry	Displays the full path for the current user's My Documents folder.
Nfwstate	New Feature Workshop	Registry	Turns the New Feature Workshop on or off: 0 = off and not displayed in Help; 1 = on and displayed in Help.
Nodename	*NA*	Registry	Controls the filename extension for AutoCAD temporary files.
Nomutt	*NA*	*NA*	Suppresses message display (muttering): 0 = normal display; 1 = suppress messages.

TABLE C.1: System Variables. Items Marked with an Asterisk Were Added in AutoCAD 2006. Items Marked with Two Asterisks Are New in AutoCAD 2007. *(CONTINUED)*

VARIABLE NAME	ASSOCIATED COMMAND	WHERE SAVED	USE
Northdirection**	Geographiclocation	With drawing	Sets the north direction in a model. This value is affected by Aunits and Auprec.
Obscuredcolor	Hide, Shade, Hlsettings	With drawing	Controls the color of obscured lines in hidden or shaded views: 0 and 256 = object color; 1 through 255 = AutoCAD color index. This feature is disabled when Obscuredltype is set to 0.
Obscuredltype	Hide, Shade, Hlsettings	With drawing	Controls the linetype of obscured lines in hidden or shaded 3D views: 0 = obscured lines are not displayed (default); 1 = solid line; 2 through 11 = various dashed and dotted lines.
Offsetdist	Offset	*NA*	Controls default offset distance.
Offsetgaptype	Offset	Registry	Controls how polyline line segments are joined when offset: 0 = extend line segments to join ends; 1 = keep line segments the same length and join endpoints with arcs; 2 = keep line segments the same length and join endpoints with lines.
Oleframe	OLE	With drawing	Controls the display of the frame around OLE objects: 0 = no frame; 1 = frame displays and plots; 2 = frame displays but does not plot.
Olehide	*NA*	Registry	Controls display of OLE objects.
Olequality	Options	Registry	Controls the quality of OLE objects: 0 = line art; 1 = text; 2 = graphics; 3 = photograph; 4 = high-quality photograph.
Olestartup	Options	With drawing	Determines whether the source application of an OLE object is loaded when the OLE object is plotted: 0 = no load; 1 = load.
Opmstate (read-only)	Properties	Registry	Displays the current state of the Properties palette: 0 = not open; 1 = open.
Orthomode	F8, Ortho	With drawing	Controls Ortho mode: 0 = off; 1 = on.

TABLE C.1: System Variables. Items Marked with an Asterisk Were Added in AutoCAD 2006. Items Marked with Two Asterisks Are New in AutoCAD 2007. *(CONTINUED)*

VARIABLE NAME	ASSOCIATED COMMAND	WHERE SAVED	USE
Osmode	Osnap	With drawing	Sets current default Osnap mode: 0 = none; 1 = endpoint; 2 = midpoint; 4 = center; 8 = node; 16 = quadrant; 32 = intersection; 64 = insert; 128 = perpendicular; 256 = nearest; 512 = quick. If more than one mode is required, enter the sum of those modes.
Osnapcoord	Osnap	Registry	Controls whether coordinates entered at the command line use running object snaps: 0 = Running Osnaps settings override; 1 = keyboard entry overrides; 2 = keyboard entry overrides, except in scripts.
Osnaphatch	Hatch, Osnap	With drawing	Controls how osnap behaves with hatches: 0 = osnap ignores hatches; 1 = osnap does not ignore hatches.
Osnapnodelegacy*	Mtext, Osnap	With drawing	Controls how osnaps behave with Mtext bounding box grips: 0 = osnap recognizes Mtext grips; 1 = osnap ignores Mtext grips.
Osnapz*	Osnaps	NA	Controls the Z value of osnap selections; 0 = use Z of selected point; 1 = use current Z of current UCS.
Osoptions	Osnaps	Registry	Controls the suppression of osnaps on hatch objects and objects with negative Z coordinate values for DUCS; 0 = operate on hatches and –Z coordinates, 1 = ignore hatches, 2 = ignore –Z coordinates.
Paletteopaque	Toolpalettes	Registry	Controls the transparency of palettes that offer transparency. Availability of transparency depends on the operating system and whether hardware accelerators are in use. 0 = turned on by user; 1 = off by user; 2 = on by user but unavailable; 3 = off by user but unavailable.
Paperupdate	Plot	Registry	Controls the display of paper size warning message: 0 = display warning if the paper size in a Paper Space layout is not supported by the specified plotter; 1 = adjust paper size to conform with plotter configuration.

TABLE C.1: System Variables. Items Marked with an Asterisk Were Added in AutoCAD 2006. Items Marked with Two Asterisks Are New in AutoCAD 2007. *(CONTINUED)*

VARIABLE NAME	ASSOCIATED COMMAND	WHERE SAVED	USE
Pdmode	Ddptype	With drawing	Controls type of symbol used as a point during Point command.
Pdsize	Point	With drawing	Controls size of symbol set by Pdmode.
Peditaccept	Pedit	Registry	Controls the display of the `Object selected is not a polyine` prompt when selecting nonpolyline object with the Pedit command: 0 = prompt; 1 = no prompt.
Pellipse	Ellipse	With drawing	Controls type of object created with Ellipse command: 0 = true NURBS ellipse; 1 = polyline representation of ellipse.
Perimeter (read-only)	Area, List	*NA*	Displays last perimeter value derived from Area and List commands.
Perspective**	Perspective	With drawing	Sets the perspective view in Model Space. 0 = off, 1 = on. Does not affect 2D Wireframe views.
Pfacevmax (read-only)	Pface	*NA*	Displays maximum number of vertices per face. (PFaces are 3D surfaces designed for use by third-party software producers and are not designed for end-users.)
Pickadd	Select	Registry	Determines how items are added to a selection set: 0 = only most recently selected item(s) become selection set (to accumulate objects in a selection set, hold down Shift while selecting); 1 = selected objects accumulate in a selection set as you select them (hold down Shift while selecting items to remove those items from the selection set).
Pickauto	Select	Registry	Controls automatic window at `Select objects:` prompt: 0 = window is disabled; 1 = window is enabled.
Pickbox	Select	Registry	Controls size of object-selection pickbox (in pixels).

TABLE C.1: System Variables. Items Marked with an Asterisk Were Added in AutoCAD 2006. Items Marked with Two Asterisks Are New in AutoCAD 2007. *(CONTINUED)*

VARIABLE NAME	ASSOCIATED COMMAND	WHERE SAVED	USE
Pickdrag	Select	Registry	Controls how selection windows are used: 0 = click each corner of the window; 1 = Shift+click and hold on first corner, and then drag and release for the second corner.
Pickfirst	Select	Registry	Controls whether you can pick object(s) before you select a command: 0 = disabled; 1 = enabled.
Pickstyle	Group, Hatch	With drawing	Controls whether groups and/or associative hatches are selectable: 0 = neither are selectable; 1 = groups only; 2 = associative hatches only; 3 = both groups and associative hatches.
Platform (read-only)	*NA*	*NA*	Identifies the version of AutoCAD being used.
Plinegen	Pline, Pedit	With drawing	Controls how polylines generate linetypes around vertices: 0 = linetype pattern begins and ends at vertices; 1 = linetype patterns ignore vertices and begin and end at polyline beginning and ending.
Plinetype	Pline	Registry	Controls whether AutoCAD creates optimized 2D polylines and/or converts existing polylines to optimized polylines: 0 = polylines in existing drawings are not converted, and new polylines are not optimized; 1 = polylines in existing drawings are not converted, but new polylines are optimized; 2 = polylines in existing drawings are not converted, and new polylines are optimized.
Plinewid	Pline	With drawing	Controls default polyline width.
Plotoffset	Plot	Registry	Controls whether the plot offset is relative to the edge of paper or printable area: 0 = printable area; 1 = edge of paper.
Plotrotmode	Plot	Registry	Controls orientation of your plotter output.
Plquiet	*NA*	Registry	Controls the display of dialog boxes for batch plotting and scripts: 0 = display dialog boxes; 1 = do not display dialog boxes.

TABLE C.1: System Variables. Items Marked with an Asterisk Were Added in AutoCAD 2006. Items Marked with Two Asterisks Are New in AutoCAD 2007. *(CONTINUED)*

VARIABLE NAME	ASSOCIATED COMMAND	WHERE SAVED	USE
Polaraddang	Dsettings	Registry	Sets the value of the Additional Angle setting of the Polar Snap tab of the Drafting Settings dialog box. You can enter as many as 10 angles of 25 characters each separated by semicolons.
Polarang	Dsettings	Registry	Sets the Increment Angle setting of the Polar Snap tab of the Drafting Settings dialog box.
Polardist	Dsettings	Registry	Sets the Polar Snap distance.
Polarmode	Dsettings, Options	With drawing	Sets Polar and Object Snap Tracking settings. The value is the sum of four pairs of codes as follows. Polar angle measurement: 0 = absolute; 1 = relative. Object Snap Tracking: 0 = orthogonal only; 2 = use Polar Tracking settings. Use additional Polar Tracking angles: 0 = no; 4 = yes. Acquire Object Snap Tracking points (Options dialog box): 0 = automatically; 8 = Shift to acquire.
Polysides	Polygon	*NA*	Controls the default number of sides for a polygon.
Popups (read-only)	*NA*	*NA*	Displays whether the current system supports drop-down menus: 0 = no; 1 = yes.
Previeweffect*	Object Selection	Registry	Controls the visual effect of hovering over objects (preview selection). 0 = dashed lines; 1 = thickened lines; 2 = dashed and thickened lines
Previewfilter*	Object Selection	Registry	Controls the type of object that is highlighted when the cursor hovers over it; 0 = no exclusion; 1 = excluded locked layers; 2 = excludes xrefs; 4 = excludes tables; 8 = excludes mtext; 16 = excludes hatches; 32 = excludes groups.
Product (read-only)	AutoCAD	*NA*	Displays product name.
Program (read-only)	AutoCAD	*NA*	Reports the program name.

TABLE C.1:   System Variables. Items Marked with an Asterisk Were Added in AutoCAD 2006. Items Marked with Two Asterisks Are New in AutoCAD 2007. *(CONTINUED)*

VARIABLE NAME	ASSOCIATED COMMAND	WHERE SAVED	USE
Projectname	Options	Registry	Assigns a project name to a drawing. The project name can be associated with one or more folders.
Projmode	Trim, Extend	Registry	Controls how the Trim and Extend commands affect objects in 3D: 0 = objects must be coplanar; 1 = trims/extends based on a plane parallel to the current UCS; 2 = trims/extends based on a plane parallel to the current view plane.
Proxygraphics	*NA*	With drawing	Controls whether images of proxy objects are stored in a drawing: 0 = images not stored; 1 = images saved.
Proxynotice	*NA*	Registry	Issues a warning to the user when a proxy object is created, i.e., when user opens a drawing containing custom objects created using an application that is not loaded: 0 = no warning; 1 = warning displayed.
Proxyshow	*NA*	Registry	Specifies whether and how proxy objects are displayed: 0 = no display; 1 = graphic display of all proxy objects; 2 = only bounding box shown.
Proxywebsearch	Options	Registry	Controls whether AutoCAD searches the Web for Object Enablers: 0 = prevent search; 1 = search Web for Object Enablers if there is an Internet connection; 2 = specify the number of attempts to find Object Enablers.
Psltscale	Pspace	With drawing	Controls Paper Space linetype scaling.
Psolheight**	Polysolid	With drawing	Controls the default height of a polysolid.
Psolwidth**	Polysolid	With drawing	Controls the default width of a polysolid.

TABLE C.1: System Variables. Items Marked with an Asterisk Were Added in AutoCAD 2006. Items Marked with Two Asterisks Are New in AutoCAD 2007. *(CONTINUED)*

VARIABLE NAME	ASSOCIATED COMMAND	WHERE SAVED	USE
Psquality	PsIn	Registry	Controls how images are generated in AutoCAD with the PsIn command. Value is an integer: 0 = only bounding box is drawn; >0 = number of pixels per AutoCAD drawing unit; <0 = outline with no fills, and absolute value of setting determines pixels per drawing units.
Pstylemode	Options	Drawing	Determines the type of plot styles used in new or imported drawings: 0 = color plot styles; 1 = named plot styles.
Pstylepolicy	NA	Registry	Determines whether object colors are associated with its plot style: 0 = no association; 1 = association.
Psvpscale	Vports	NA	Sets the default view scale factor for new viewports in paper space. The value is a ratio between the model space scale and the paper space scale. Values must be positive real: 0 = scale to fit.
Publishallsheets	Publish	Registry	Controls the content of the Publish dialog box list box; 0 = current document only, 1 = all open documents.
Pucsbase	Ucsman	With drawing	Stores the name of a UCS that you want to use as the base for orthographic UCS settings. Paper Space only.
Qcstate* (read-only)	QuickCalc	NA	Indicates whether QuickCalc is active; 0 = not active; 1 = active.
Qtextmode	Qtext	With drawing	Controls the quick text mode: 0 = off; 1 = on.
Rasterdpi	Plot	Registry	Controls the conversion from millimeters or inches to dots per inch when working with dimensionless output such as the raster plotter option. Acceptable value range is 100 to 32,767dpi.
Rasterpercent	Plot	Registry	Sets the percentage amount of virtual memory allocated to printing raster images.

TABLE C.1: System Variables. Items Marked with an Asterisk Were Added in AutoCAD 2006. Items Marked with Two Asterisks Are New in AutoCAD 2007. *(CONTINUED)*

VARIABLE NAME	ASSOCIATED COMMAND	WHERE SAVED	USE
Rasterpreview	Save	Registry	Controls whether raster preview images are saved with the drawing and sets the format type: 0 = no preview image created; 1 = BMP preview image.
Rasterthreshold	Plot	Registry	Sets the threshold of memory in megabytes beyond which the system memory will be checked. Plot will be aborted if the raster size exceeds available memory.
Recoverymode*	Drawing Recovery	Registry	Controls how the Drawing Recovery feature behaves after a system failure; 0 = recovery information is not recorded; 1 = recovery information is recorded but the recovery window is not displayed; 2 = recovery information is recorded and recovery window is displayed at startup.
Refeditname (read-only)	Refedit	*NA*	Displays the current reference-editing state of a drawing.
Regenmode	Regenauto	With drawing	Controls Regenauto mode: 0 = off; 1 = on.
Re-init	Reinit	*NA*	Reinitializes I/O ports, digitizers, display, plotter, and ACAD.PGP: 1 = digitizer port; 2 = plotter port; 4 = digitizer; 8 = display; 16 = PGP file reload.
Rememberfolders	*NA*	Registry	Controls the default folder displayed in file dialog boxes. 0 = use Start In Path specification from AutoCAD icon; 1 = last used path.
Renderprefsstate** (read-only)	*Render*	*NA*	Returns the Render Settings palette status; 0 = closed, 1 = open.
Reporterror	*NA*	Registry	Controls whether errors can be reported to Autodesk as they occur: 0 = no error report; 1 = error report message is displayed with option to send error report to Autodesk.
Roamablerootprefix (read-only)	*NA*	Registry	Displays the full path name for customizable support files for roaming profiles.

TABLE C.1: System Variables. Items Marked with an Asterisk Were Added in AutoCAD 2006. Items Marked with Two Asterisks Are New in AutoCAD 2007. *(CONTINUED)*

VARIABLE NAME	ASSOCIATED COMMAND	WHERE SAVED	USE
Rtdisplay	Rtpan, Rtzoom	Registry	Controls display of raster images during real-time Pan and Zoom.
Savefile (read-only)	Autosave	Registry	Displays filename that is autosaved.
Savefilepath	*NA*	Registry	Specifies the folder location for automatic save files.
Savename (read-only)	Save	*NA*	Displays user filename under which file is saved.
Savetime	Autosave	Registry	Controls time interval between automatic saves, in minutes: 0 = disable automatic save.
Screenboxes (read-only)	Menu	Registry	Displays number of slots or boxes available in side menu.
Screenmode (read-only)	*NA*	Registry	Displays current display mode: 0 = text; 1 = graphics; 2 = dual screen.
Screensize (read-only)	*NA*	*NA*	Displays current viewport size in pixels.
SDI	*NA*	Registry	Determines whether AutoCAD allows multiple documents or limits user to single document editing: 0 = multiple documents; 1 = single document; 2 = single documents because loaded third-party application does not support multiple documents (read-only); 3 = same as 2 with SDI set to 1 by user.
Selectionarea*	Object Selection	Registry	Controls whether a shaded area is displayed with selection windows, including crossing and polygon windows. 0 = off; 1 = on
Selectionareaopacity*	Object Selection	Registry	Controls the opacity of the shaded area of a selection window. Range is from 0 to 100 with low values being more transparent.
Selectionpreview*	Object Selection	Registry	Controls object's selection preview when the cursor hovers over an object; 0 = off; 1 = preview when no command is active; 2 = preview when Command prompts to select object.

TABLE C.1: System Variables. Items Marked with an Asterisk Were Added in AutoCAD 2006. Items Marked with Two Asterisks Are New in AutoCAD 2007. *(CONTINUED)*

VARIABLE NAME	ASSOCIATED COMMAND	WHERE SAVED	USE
Shadedge	Shade	With drawing	Controls how drawing is shaded: 0 = faces shaded, no edge highlighting; 1 = faces shaded, edge highlighting; 2 = faces not filled, edges in object color; 3 = faces in object color, edges in background color.
Shadedif	Shade	With drawing	Sets difference between diffuse reflective and ambient light. Value represents percentage of diffuse reflective light.
Shadowplanelocation**	Vsshadow	With drawing	Sets the location on the Z axis of an invisible ground plane used to display shadows.
Shortcutmenu	Right-click	Registry	Controls the Default, Edit, and Command mode shortcut menus. For multiple options, use the sum of option values: 0 = restore R14 behavior; 1 = Default mode shortcut enabled; 2 = Edit mode shortcut enabled; 4 = Command mode shortcut enabled; 8 = Command mode shortcut enabled only when options are shown in command line.
Showhist**	3D Solids	With drawing	Controls the Show History property of 3D solids; 0 = do not show history, 1 = show history unless set differently for individual solids, 2 = show history of all solids.
Showlayerusage*	Layer	Registry	Controls the display of the Layer Usage icon in the Layer Properties Manager. This icon indicates whether a layer is in use; 0 = off; 1 = on.
Shpname	Shape	*NA*	Controls default shape name.
Sigwarn	Sigvalidate	Registry	Controls whether the digital signature warning message is displayed when a file containing a digital signature is opened: 0 = warning appears only if a digital signature is present and is not valid; 1 = warning appears if digital signature is present.
Sketchinc	Sketch	With drawing	Controls sketch record increment.
Skpoly	Sketch	With drawing	Controls whether the Sketch command uses regular lines or polylines: 0 = line; 1 = polyline.

TABLE C.1:   System Variables. Items Marked with an Asterisk Were Added in AutoCAD 2006. Items Marked with Two Asterisks Are New in AutoCAD 2007. *(CONTINUED)*

VARIABLE NAME	ASSOCIATED COMMAND	WHERE SAVED	USE
Snapang	Snap	With drawing	Controls snap and grid angle.
Snapbase	Snap	With drawing	Controls snap, grid, and hatch pattern origin.
Snapisopair	Snap	With drawing	Controls isometric plane: 0 = left; 1 = top; 2 = right.
Snapmode	F9, Snap	With drawing	Controls snap toggle: 0 = off; 1 = on.
Snapstyl	Snap	With drawing	Controls snap style: 0 = standard; 1 = isometric.
Snaptype	Snap	Registry	Controls whether polar or grid snap is current: 0 = grid snap; 1 = polar snap.
Snapunit	Snap	With drawing	Controls snap spacing given in x and y values.
Solidcheck	Solidedit	*NA*	Controls solid validation for 3D solids in current session: 0 = off; 1 = on.
Solidhist**	3D Solids	With drawing	Controls whether 3D solid history is retained; 0 = discard history, 1 = record history.
Sortents	*NA*	Registry	Controls whether objects are sorted based on their order in database: 0 = disabled; 1 = sort for object selection; 2 = sort for object snap; 4 = sort for redraws; 8 = sort for Mslide; 16 = sort for regen; 32 = sort for plot; 64 = sort for Psout.
Splframe		With drawing	Controls display of spline vertices, defining mesh of a surface-fit mesh, and display of "invisible" edges of 3D Faces: 0 = no display of spline vertices, display only fit surface of a smoothed 3D Mesh, and no display of "invisible" edges of 3D Face; 1 = spline vertices are displayed, only defining mesh of a smoothed 3D Mesh is displayed, "invisible" edges of 3D Face are displayed.

TABLE C.1:   System Variables. Items Marked with an Asterisk Were Added in AutoCAD 2006. Items Marked with Two Asterisks Are New in AutoCAD 2007. *(CONTINUED)*

VARIABLE NAME	ASSOCIATED COMMAND	WHERE SAVED	USE
Splinesegs	Pline, Pedit	With drawing	Controls number of line segments used for each spline patch.
Splinetype	Pline, Pedit	With drawing	Controls type of spline curve generated by Pedit spline: 5 = quadratic B-spline; 6 = cubic B-spline.
Ssfound (read-only)	Sheet Set Manager	NA	Displays the location of a sheet set after a search for sheet sets.
Sslocate	Sheet Set Manager	User settings	Controls whether sheet sets are automatically located and opened when a drawing associated with a sheet set is opened: 0 = do not open sheet set; 1 = open sheet set. Ssmautoopen must also be set to 1.
Ssmautoopen	Sheet Set Manager	User settings	Controls whether the Sheet Set Manager is opened when a drawing associated with a sheet set is opened: 0 = do not open sheet set; 1 = open sheet set. Sslocate must also be set to 1.
Ssmpolltime**	Sheet Set Manager	Registry	Sets the time in seconds between automatic refreshes of sheet set status data. Values from 20 to 600 are valid. See Ssmsheetstatus.
Ssmsheetstatus**	Sheet Set Manager	Registry	Sets how sheet set status data is refreshed; 0 = No automatic refresh, 1 = refresh when sheet set is loaded/updated, 2 = refresh when sheet set is loaded/updated or at Ssmpolltime interval.
Ssmstate (read-only)	Sheet Set Manager	NA	Shows whether the Sheet Set Manager is open: 0 = not open; 1 = open.
Standardsviolations	Standards	Registry	Controls whether user is notified when a file contains standards violations: 0 = no notification; 1 = notification when standards violations occur; 2 = notification via icon in status bar.

TABLE C.1: System Variables. Items Marked with an Asterisk Were Added in AutoCAD 2006. Items Marked with Two Asterisks Are New in AutoCAD 2007. *(CONTINUED)*

VARIABLE NAME	ASSOCIATED COMMAND	WHERE SAVED	USE
Startup	New/Qnew	Registry	Controls whether the Startup dialog box appears when AutoCAD is first opened. Also controls whether the Create New Drawing dialog box appears when a new document is created by choosing File ➤ New. 0 = displays Select Template dialog box for File ➤ New, opens AutoCAD with no Startup dialog box; 1 = displays Create New Drawing or Startup dialog box.
Stepsize**	Walk/Fly	With drawing	Sets the step size on Walk or Fly mdoe.
Stepspersec**	Walk/Fly	With drawing	Sets the number of steps per second in Walk or Fly mode.
Sunpropertiesstate** (read-only)	Sun Properties	NA	Reports the status of the Sun Properties palette, 0 = closed, 1 = open.
Sunstatus**	Sun Properties	With drawing	Turns the sun on or off; 0 = off, 1 = on
Surftab1		With drawing	Controls number of facets in the *m* direction of meshes.
Surftab2	ERevsurf, Edgesurf	With drawing	Controls number of facets in the *n* direction of meshes.
Surftype	Pedit	With drawing	Controls type of surface fitting used by the Pedit command's Smooth option: 5 = quadratic B-spline surface; 6 = cubic B- spline surface; 8 = Bezier surface.
Surfu	3Dmesh	With drawing	Controls surface density in the *m* direction.
Surfv	3Dmesh	With drawing	Controls surface density in the *n* direction.
Syscodepage (read-only)	*NA*	*NA*	Displays system code page specified in Acad.xmx.
Tableindicator*	Tables	User settings	Controls the display of row numbers and column letters when editing table entries; 0 = off; 1 = on.

TABLE C.1: System Variables. Items Marked with an Asterisk Were Added in AutoCAD 2006. Items Marked with Two Asterisks Are New in AutoCAD 2007. *(CONTINUED)*

VARIABLE NAME	ASSOCIATED COMMAND	WHERE SAVED	USE
Tabmode	Tablet	*NA*	Controls tablet mode: 0 = off; 1 = on.
Target (read-only)	Dview	With drawing	Displays coordinate of perspective target point.
Tbcustomize	Customize	Registry	Controls whether toolbars can be customized: 0 = customize disabled for toolbars; 1 = customize enabled.
Tdcreate (read-only)	Time	With drawing	Displays time and date of file creation in Julian format.
Tdindwg (read-only)	Time	With drawing	Displays total editing time in days and decimal days.
Tducreate (read-only)	Time	With drawing	Displays the time and date that a drawing was created.
Tdupdate (read-only)	Time	With drawing	Displays time and date of last file update in Julian format.
Tdusrtimer (read-only)	Time	With drawing	Displays user-controlled elapsed time in days and decimal days.
Tduupdate (read-only)	Time	With drawing	Displays the time and date of last update or save.
Tempoverrides*	Drafting Settings	Registry	Controls the drafting settings' temporary override key function; 0 = off; 1 = on.
Tempprefix (read-only)	*NA*	*NA*	Displays location for temporary files.
Texteval	*NA*	*NA*	Controls interpretation of text input: 0 = AutoCAD takes all text input literally; 1 = AutoCAD interprets "(" and "!" as part of an AutoLISP expression, unless either the Text or Dtext command is active.
Textfill	Text	Registry	Controls display of Bitstream, TrueType, and PostScript Type 1 fonts: 0 = outlines; 1 = filled.
Textqlty	Text	With drawing	Controls resolution of Bitstream, TrueType, and PostScript Type 1 fonts: values from 1.0 to 100.0. The lower the value, the lower the output resolution. Higher resolutions improve font quality but decrease display and plot speeds.

TABLE C.1: System Variables. Items Marked with an Asterisk Were Added in AutoCAD 2006. Items Marked with Two Asterisks Are New in AutoCAD 2007. *(CONTINUED)*

VARIABLE NAME	ASSOCIATED COMMAND	WHERE SAVED	USE
Textsize	Text, Dtext	With drawing	Controls default text height.
Textstyle	Text, Dtext	With drawing	Controls default text style.
Thickness	Elev	With drawing	Controls default 3D thickness of object being drawn.
Tilemode	Mspace, Pspace	With drawing	Controls Paper Space and viewport access: 0 = Paper Space and viewport objects enabled; 1 = strictly Model Space.
Timezone**	Geographiclocation	With drawing	Sets the time zone.
Tootipmerge**	Tooltip	User settings	Controls merged tooltips; 0 = not merged, 1 = merged.
Tooltips	Icon tool palettes	Registry	Controls display of tool tips: 0 = off; 1 = on.
Tpstate (read-only)	Toolpalettes	*NA*	Tells whether the Tool Palettes window is active. 0 = not active, 1 = active
Tracewid	Trace	With drawing	Controls trace width.
Trackpath	Options	Registry	Controls the display of the tracking vector: 0 = full screen; 1 = only between alignment points; 2 = no Polar Tracking vector; 3 = no Polar or Object Snap Tracking vector.
Trayicons	*NA*	Registry	Controls the display of the AutoCAD tray icons in the lower-right corner of the AutoCAD window: 0 = no display; 1 = display.
Traynotify	*NA*	Registry	Controls the display of service notifications in the AutoCAD tray: 0 = no notification; 1 = notification.
Traytimeout	*NA*	Registry	Controls how long tray notifications are displayed. Values from 0 to 10 are valid.

TABLE C.1: System Variables. Items Marked with an Asterisk Were Added in AutoCAD 2006. Items Marked with Two Asterisks Are New in AutoCAD 2007. *(CONTINUED)*

VARIABLE NAME	ASSOCIATED COMMAND	WHERE SAVED	USE
Treedepth	Treestat	With drawing	Controls depth of tree-structured Spatial index affecting speed of AutoCAD database search. First two digits are for Model Space nodes; second two digits are for Paper Space nodes. Use positive integers for 3D drawings and negative integers for 2D drawings. Negative values can improve speed of 2D operation.
Treemax	Regen, Treedepth	Registry	Limits memory use during regens by limiting maximum number of nodes in Spatial index created with the Treedepth command.
Trimmode	Chamfer, Fillet	Registry	Controls whether lines are trimmed during the Chamfer and Fillet commands: 0 = no trim; 1 = trim (as with pre-Release-13 versions of AutoCAD).
Tspacefac	Mtext	*NA*	Sets multiline text line spacing as a percentage of text height. Valid range is between 0.25 and 4.0.
Tspacetype	Mtext	*NA*	Controls multiline text line spacing quality: 1 = use tallest letter for basis of line spacing; 2 = use text height specification as basis of line spacing.
Tstackalign	Mtext	With drawing	Controls text alignment for stacked text: 0 = bottom; 1 = center; 2 = top.
Tstacksize	Mtext	With drawing	Sets stacked fraction text height as percent of normal text height. Valid range is 1 to 127.
Ucsaxisang	Ucs	Registry	Sets the default rotation angle for X, Y, or Z axis option of UCS command.
Ucsbase	Ucs	With drawing	Sets the name of the UCS used as a basis for orthographic UCS options.
Ucsfollow	Ucs	With drawing	Controls whether AutoCAD automatically changes to Plan view of UCS while in Model Space: 0 = UCS change does not affect view; 1 = UCS change causes view to change with UCS.

TABLE C.1: System Variables. Items Marked with an Asterisk Were Added in AutoCAD 2006. Items Marked with Two Asterisks Are New in AutoCAD 2007. *(CONTINUED)*

VARIABLE NAME	ASSOCIATED COMMAND	WHERE SAVED	USE
Ucsaxisang**	UCS	Registry	Sets the default rotation angle for the X, Y, or Z axis in the UCS command. Valid values are: 5, 10, 15, 18, 22.5, 30, 45, 90, and 180.
Ucsbase**	UCS	With drawing	Stores the name of the UCS used as a basis for orthographic UCS settings. Any existing, named UCS can be used.
Ucsdetect**	UCS	With drawing	Controls whether DUCS is active; 0 = not active, 1 = active.
Ucsfollow	UCS	With drawing	Determines whether a plan view is automatically produced following a UCS selection. 0 = no view change, 1 = change view to plan of new UCS.
Ucsicon	Ucsicon	With drawing	Controls UCS icon: 1 = on; 2 = UCS icon appears at origin.
Ucsname (read-only)	Ucs	With drawing	Displays name of current UCS.
Ucsorg (read-only)	Ucs	With drawing	Displays origin coordinate for current UCS relative to World Coordinate System.
Ucsortho	Ucs	With drawing	Controls whether the UCS follows orthographic views: 0 = does not follow; 1 = follows orthographic view.
Ucsview	View	With drawing	Controls whether a UCS is saved with a named view: 0 = not saved; 1 = saved.
Ucsvp	Vport	With drawing	Controls whether the UCS follows the orientation of a new viewport: 0 = current UCS; 1 = follow orientation of viewport view.
Ucsxdir (read-only)	Ucs	With drawing	Displays *x* direction of current UCS relative to World Coordinate System.
Ucsydir (read-only)	Ucs	With drawing	Displays *y* direction of current UCS relative to World Coordinate System.

TABLE C.1: System Variables. Items Marked with an Asterisk Were Added in AutoCAD 2006. Items Marked with Two Asterisks Are New in AutoCAD 2007. *(CONTINUED)*

VARIABLE NAME	ASSOCIATED COMMAND	WHERE SAVED	USE
Undoctl (read-only)	Undo	*NA*	Displays current state of Undo feature: 1 = Undo enabled; 2 = only one command can be undone; 4 = Autogroup mode enabled; 8 = group is currently active.
Undomarks (read-only)	Undo	*NA*	Displays number of marks placed by Undo command.
Unitmode	Units	With drawing	Controls how AutoCAD displays fractional, foot-and-inch, and surveyor's angles: 0 = industry standard; 1 = AutoCAD input format.
Updatethumbnail	Sheet Set Manager	With drawing	Controls the display of the Sheet Set Manager preview thumbnail: 0 = no updates; 1 = update model view thumbnail; 2 = update sheet view thumbnail; 4 = update sheet thumbnail; 8 = update thumbnails when sheets are edited or created; 16 = update when drawing is saved.
Useri1–Useri5	Autolisp, Diesel	With drawing	Indicates five user variables capable of storing integer values.
Userr1–Userr5	Autolisp, Diesel	With drawing	Indicates five user variables capable of storing real values.
Users1–Users5	Autolisp, Diesel	With drawing	Indicates five user variables capable of storing string values.
Viewctr (read-only)	*NA*	With drawing	Displays center of current view in coordinates.
Viewdir (read-only)	Dview	With drawing	Displays camera-viewing direction in coordinates.
Viewmode (read-only)	Dview	With drawing	Displays view-related settings for current viewport: 1 = perspective on; 2 = front clipping on; 4 = back clipping on; 8 = UCS follow on; 16 = front clip not at a point directly in front of the viewer's eye.
Viewsize (read-only)	*NA*	With drawing	Displays height of current view in drawing units.

TABLE C.1:   System Variables. Items Marked with an Asterisk Were Added in AutoCAD 2006. Items Marked with Two Asterisks Are New in AutoCAD 2007. *(CONTINUED)*

VARIABLE NAME	ASSOCIATED COMMAND	WHERE SAVED	USE
Viewtwist (read-only)	Dview	With drawing	Displays twist angle for current viewport.
Visretain	Layer	With drawing	Controls whether layer setting for Xrefs is retained: 0 = current layer color, linetype, and visibility settings retained when drawing is closed; 1 = layer settings of Xref drawing always renewed when file is opened.
Vpmaximizedstate (read-only)	Vpmax	*NA*	Indicates whether a viewport is maximized: 0 = not maximized; 1 = maximized.
Vsbackgrounds**	Visual Style	With drawing	Turns on backgrounds in the visual style for the current viewport. 0 = off, 1 = on.
Vsedgecolor**	Visual Style	With drawing	Sets the edge color for the current visual style.
Vsedgejitter**	Visual Style	With drawing	Sets the degree of jitter for the current visual style; 1 = low, 2 = medium, 3 = high.
Vsedgeoverhang**	Visual Style	With drawing	Sets the line extension for the current visual style; From 1 to 100 pixels.
Vsedges**	Visual Style	With drawing	Set the type of edges to display for the current visual style; 0 = no edges, 1 = display isolines, 2 = display facet edgets.
Vsedgesmooth**	Visual Style	With drawing	Sets the minimum angle at which edges are displayed; a range from 0 to 180.
Vsfacecolormode**	Visual Style	With drawing	Sets the method to calculate face colors as affected by view angle; 0 = Normal - does not apply color modifier, 1 Monochrome - displays color set in vsmonocolor, 2 = Tint = use vsmonocolor setting to shade faces, 3 = Desaturate - Soften color through desaturation.
Vsfacehighlight**	Visual Style	With drawing	Sets the specular highlight of objects that have no material assignment; range from −100 to 100.
Vsfaceopacity**	Visual Style	With drawing	Sets the opacity of faces; range from −100 to 100.

TABLE C.1:   System Variables. Items Marked with an Asterisk Were Added in AutoCAD 2006. Items Marked with Two Asterisks Are New in AutoCAD 2007. *(CONTINUED)*

VARIABLE NAME	ASSOCIATED COMMAND	WHERE SAVED	USE
Vsfacestyle**	Visual Style	With drawing	Sets the face style; 0 = no style, 1 = Real - realistic style, 2 = Gooch - Cool to warm colors to indicate depth.
Vshalogap**	Visual Style	With drawing	Sets the gap between 3D objects and the objects they hide. Range from 0 to 100.
Vshideprecision**	Visual Style	NA	Sets the accuracy of hide and shade.
Vsintersectioncolor**	Visual Style	With drawing	Sets the color of intersection edges in visual styles; 0 = byblock, 256 = bylayer, 257 = byentity, 1 to 255 index color or RGB and Color Book.
Vsintersectionedges**	Visual Style	With drawing	Controls the display of intersection edges in visual styles; 0 = off, 1 = on. See Intersectiondisplay for 2D Wireframe.
Vsintersectionltype**	Visual Style	With drawing	Sets the linetype for intersection edges in visual styles; 0 = off, 1 = solid, 2 = dashed, 3 = dotted, 4 = short dash, 5 = medium dash, 6 = long dash, 7 = double short dash, 8 = double medium dash, 9 = double long dash, 10 = medium long dash, 11 = sparse dot.
Vsisoontop**	Visual Style	With drawing	Display isolines on shaded objects in visual style; 0 = off, 1 = on.
Vslightingquality**	Visual Style	With drawing	Sets the smoothing quality for visual style; 0 = show facets, 1 = smooth.
Vsmaterialmode**	Visual Style	With drawing	Controls the display of materials in visual styles; 0 = no materials, 1 = display materials but no texture, 2 display materials and textures.
Vsmax (read-only)	*NA*	With drawing	Displays coordinates of upper-right corner of virtual screen.
Vsmin (read-only)	*NA*	With drawing	Displays coordinates of lower-left corner of virtual screen.
Vsmonocolor**	Visual Style	With drawing	Sets the monochrome and tint color for visual styles.

TABLE C.1: System Variables. Items Marked with an Asterisk Were Added in AutoCAD 2006. Items Marked with Two Asterisks Are New in AutoCAD 2007. *(CONTINUED)*

VARIABLE NAME	ASSOCIATED COMMAND	WHERE SAVED	USE
Vsobscuredcolor**	Visual Style	With drawing	Sets the color for obscured lines in visual styles.
Vsobscurededges**	Visual Style	With drawing	Controls the display of hidden edges; 0 = off, 1 = on
Vsobscuredltype**	Visual Style	With drawing	Controls the linetype of hidden lines in visual styles. See Vsintersectionltype for settings.
Vsshadows**	Visual Style	With drawing	Determines whether visual style displays shadows; 0 = no shadows, 1 = ground shadows only, 2 = full shadows.
Vssilhedges**	Visual Style	With drawing	Controls the display of silhouette edges in visual styles; 0 = off, 1 = on.
Vssilhwidth**	Visual Style	With drawing	Sets the width of silhouette edges in pixels; range from 1 to 25.
Vsstate** (read-only)	Visual Style	NA	Reports the status of the Visual Styles palette. 0 = off, 1 = on.
Vtduration*	Zoom and Pan	Registry	Controls the duration of zoom or pan transitions. Range is from 0 to 5000 milliseconds.
Vtenable*	Zoom and Pan	Registry	Controls the View Transition feature for pan/zoom, rotation, and scripts. Values from 0 to 7 are valid. 0 = off; 1 = pan/zoom only; 2 = rotation only; 3 = pan/zoom and rotation; 4 = scripts only; 5 pan/zoom and scripts; 6 = rotation and scripts; 7 = all.
Vtfps*	Zoom and Pan	Registry	Controls the view transition smoothness in frames per second, from 1 to 30.
Whiparc	NA	Registry	Controls the tessellation of circles and arcs: 0 = tessellated; 1 = not tessellated.
Whipthread**	Zoom	Registry	In multiprocessor PCs, sets whether additional processor is used to improve display speed. 0 = no additional processing, 1 = Regens processed, 2 Redraws processed, 3 Regens and Redraws processed.

TABLE C.1: System Variables. Items Marked with an Asterisk Were Added in AutoCAD 2006. Items Marked with Two Asterisks Are New in AutoCAD 2007. *(CONTINUED)*

VARIABLE NAME	ASSOCIATED COMMAND	WHERE SAVED	USE
Windowareacolor*	Window Selection	Registry	Controls the color for window selection with a range of 1 to 255. Selectionarea must be on.
Wmfbkgnd	Export, Cut	*NA*	Sets the way backgrounds and borders are generated in exported Windows metafiles: 0 = transparent backgrounds, no borders; 1 = background same as AutoCAD background, border is reverse color of background.
Wmfforegrnd	Options	*NA*	Controls the appearance of Windows metafile export from AutoCAD: 0 = ensures foreground color is darker than background; 1 = ensures background color is darker than foreground. This feature takes effect only if Wmfgkgrnd is set to 0.
Worlducs (read-only)	UCS	*NA*	Displays status of WCS: 0 = current UCS is not WCS; 1 = current UCS is WCS.
Worldview	Dview, Vpoint	With drawing	Controls whether the Dview and Vpoint commands operate relative to UCS or WCS: 0 = current UCS is used; 1 = WCS is used.
Writestat (read-only)	*NA*	*NA*	Displays the current drawing's read/write status: 0 = read-only; 1 = drawing can be written to.
Wscurrent* (read-only)	Workspace	NA	Indicates the current workspace name.
Xclipframe	Xref	With drawing	Controls visibility of Xref clipping boundaries: 0 = clipping boundary is not visible; 1 = boundary is visible.
Xedit	Options	With drawing	Controls Refedit availability of current drawing: 0 = not available for in-place Xref editing; 1 = available for in-place Xref editing.
Xfadectl	Options	*NA*	Controls fading intensity in percent value for objects not selected while using Refedit (in-place Xref editing). Valid range is 0 to 90.

TABLE C.1: System Variables. Items Marked with an Asterisk Were Added in AutoCAD 2006. Items Marked with Two Asterisks Are New in AutoCAD 2007. *(CONTINUED)*

VARIABLE NAME	ASSOCIATED COMMAND	WHERE SAVED	USE
Xloadctl	Xref, Xclip	Registry	Controls Xref demand loading, and creation of copies of original Xref: 0 = no demand loading allowed, entire Xref drawing is loaded; 1 = demand loading allowed, and original Xref file is kept open; 2 = demand loading allowed, using a copy of Xref file stored in AutoCAD temp files folder.
Xloadpath	Xref	Registry	Creates a path for storing temporary copies of demand-loaded Xref files.
Xrefctl	Xref	Registry	Controls whether Xref log files are written: 0 = no log files; 1 = log files written.
Xrefnotify	Xref	Registry	Determines whether notification appears in the AutoCAD tray for updated or missing Xrefs: 0 = no notification; 1 = notification that current drawing contains Xrefs (if Xrefs are missing, a yellow alert icon is displayed); 2 = same as 1 notification and includes a balloon message.
Xreftype	Time	Registry	Controls whether the default Xref type is Attach or Overlay: 0 = Attach; 1 = Overlay.
Zoomfactor	Mouse wheel	Registry	Controls the amount of zoom applied to a drawing when the mouse wheel is turned. Valid range is between 3 and 100. Default is 10.
Zoomwheel**	Mouse wheel	Registry	Controls the direction of the zoom when using the wheel mouse; 0 = wheel forward - zoom in, 1 = wheel forward - zoom out.

Setting Dimension Variables

Chapter 12 discussed the options for dimensioning available through the Dimension Style and other dialog boxes and mentioned that most of these options have equivalent system variables. Later in this appendix you'll find a complete discussion of all elements of the Dimension Style dialog box and how to use it.

This section provides further information about the dimension variables. For starters, Table C.2 lists each variable, its default status, and a brief description of what it does. You can get a similar listing by entering **–Dimstyle.** at the Command prompt, and then typing **ST** to select the Status option. Alternatively, you can use the AutoCAD Help system. This section also discusses a few system variables that do not appear in the Dimension Style dialog box.

TABLE C.2: Dimension Variables

DIMENSION VARIABLE	DEFAULT SETTING	DESCRIPTION
General Dimension Controls		
Dimaso	On	Turns partial associative dimension on and off (obsolete).
Dimassoc	2	Turns true associative dimension on and off: 0 = exploded dimension; 1 = pre-2002 associative dimensions; 2 = fully associative dimensions.
Dimsho	On	Updates dimensions dynamically while dragging.
Dimstyle	Standard	Indicates name of current dimension style.
Dimtmove	0	Sets the way dimension text behaves when moved: 0 = move dimension line with text; 1 = add leader and move text freely; 2 = no leader and move text freely.
Dimupt	Off	Controls user positioning of text during dimension input: 0 = automatic text positioning; 1 = user-defined text positioning allowed.
Scale		
Dimasz	0.18 (approx. $^3/_{16}''$)	Indicates arrow size.
Dimcen	0.09 (approx. $^3/_{32}''$)	Indicates center mark size.
Dimlfac	1.0000	Multiplies measured distance by a specified scale factor.
Dimscale	1.0000	Indicates overall scale factor of dimensions.
Dimtsz	0″	Indicates tick size.
Dimtxt	0.18 (approx. $^3/_{16}''$)	Indicates text height.
Offsets		
Dimdle	0″	Indicates the amount the dimension line extends beyond the extension line.

TABLE C.2: Dimension Variables (*CONTINUED*)

Dimension Variable	Default Setting	Description
Dimdli	0.38 (approx. $^3/_8$″)	Indicates the dimension line offset for continuation or base.
Dimexe	0.18 (approx. $^3/_{16}$″)	Indicates the amount the extension line extends beyond the dimension line.
Dimexo	0.0625 or $^1/_{16}$″	Indicates extension line origin offset.
Tolerances		
Dimalttz	0	Controls zero suppression of tolerance values: 0 = leave out zero feet and inches; 1 = include zero feet and inches; 2 = include zero feet; 3 = include zero inches; 4 = suppress leading zeros in decimal dimensions; 8 = suppress leading zeros in decimal dimensions.
Dimdec	4	Sets decimal place for primary tolerance values.
Dimlim	Off	When on, shows dimension limits.
Dimtdec	4	Sets decimal place for tolerance values.
Dimtm	0″	Indicates minus tolerance.
Dimtol	Off	When on, shows dimension tolerances.
Dimtolj	1	Controls vertical location of tolerance values relative to nominal dimension: 0 = bottom; 1 = middle; 2 = top.
Dimtp	0″	Indicates plus tolerance.
Dimtzin	0	Controls zero suppression in tolerance values: 0 = leave out zero feet and inches; 1 = include zero feet and inches; 2 = include zero feet; 3 = include zero inches; 4 = suppress leading zeros in decimal dimensions; 8 = suppress leading zeros in decimal dimensions; 12 = suppress leading and trailing zeros in decimal dimensions.
Rounding		
Dimazin	0	Controls zero suppression for angular dimensions: 0 = display all zeros; 1 = suppress leading zeros; 2 suppress trailing zeros; 3 = suppress all zeros.
Dimrnd	0″	Indicates a rounding value.

TABLE C.2:   Dimension Variables *(CONTINUED)*

DIMENSION VARIABLE	DEFAULT SETTING	DESCRIPTION
Dimzin	0	Controls zero suppression dimension text: 0 = leave out zero feet and inches; 1 = include zero feet and inches; 2 = include zero feet; 3 = include zero inches; 4 = suppress leading zeros in decimal dimensions; 8 = suppress leading zeros in decimal dimensions; 12 = suppress leading and trailing zeros in decimal dimensions.
Dimension Arrow & Text Control		
Dimadec	−1	Controls the number of decimal places shown for angular dimension text: 1 = uses the value set by Dimdec dimension variable; 0–8 = specifies the actual number of decimal places to be shown.
Dimatfit	3	Controls the way text and arrows are placed when there is not enough room to fit both within extension lines: 0 = place both outside extension lines; 1 = move arrows first; 2 = move text first; 3 = move either text or arrows, whichever is best fit.
Dimaunit	0	Controls angle format for angular dimensions; settings are the same as for Aunits system variable.
Dimblk	" "	Predefined or user-defined arrow block name. You can enter a user-defined block name or one of the following: _DOT, _DOTSMALL, _DOTBLANK, _ORIGIN, _ORIGIN2, _OPEN, _OPEN90, _OPEN30, _CLOSED, _SMALL, _OBLIQUE, _BOXFILLED, _BOXBLANK, _CLOSEDBLANK, _DATUMFILLED, _DATUMBLANK, _INTEGRAL, ARCHTICK.
Dimblk1	" "	Predefined or user-defined arrow block name for first end of dimension line used with Dimsah. See Dimblk for valid options.
Dimblk2	" "	Predefined or user-defined arrow block name for second end of dimension line used with Dimsah. See Dimblk for valid options.
Dimldrblk	" "	Sets the leader arrow type.
Dimdsep	. (period)	User-defined separator for decimals when dimension units are set to decimal.

TABLE C.2: Dimension Variables *(CONTINUED)*

DIMENSION VARIABLE	DEFAULT SETTING	DESCRIPTION
Dimfit	3	Controls location of text and arrows for extension lines, if space is not available for both: 0 = text and arrows placed outside; 1 = text has priority, arrows are placed outside extension lines; 2 = arrows have priority; 3 = AutoCAD chooses between text and arrows, based on best fit; 4 = a leader is drawn from dimension line to dimension text when space for text not available; 5 = no leader.
Dimfrac	0	Sets the fraction format for architectural and fractional formats: 0 = vertical; 1 = diagonal; 2 = not stacked.
Dimgap	$\frac{1}{16}$″ or 0.09″	Controls distance between dimension text and dimension line.
Dimjust	0	Controls horizontal dimension text position: 0 = centered between extension lines; 1 = next to first extension line; 2 = next to second extension line; 3 = above and aligned with the first extension line; 4 = above and aligned with second extension line.
Dimldrblk	0	Sets the arrow type for leaders: 0 = standard closed filled arrow; (period) = no arrow. See Dimblk for valid options.
Dimlunit	Off	Sets unit style for all dimension types except angular: 1 = Scientific; 2 = Decimal; 3 = Engineering; 4 = Architectural; 5 = Fractional; 6 = Windows Desktop.
Dimsah	Off	Allows use of two different arrowheads on a dimension line. See Dimblk1 and Dimblk2.
Dimtfac	1.0″	Controls scale factor for dimension tolerance text.
Dimtad	0	When on, places text above the dimension line.
Dimtfill	0	Sets the background for dimension text. 0 = no background, 1 = background of drawing, 2 = background set by Dimtfillclr.
Dimtfillclr	0	Sets the color for text background in dimensions, 0 = byblock, 256 = bylayer. Also use index or true color.
Dimtih	On	When on, text inside extensions is horizontal.
Dimtix	Off	Forces text between extensions.

TABLE C.2:   Dimension Variables *(CONTINUED)*

DIMENSION VARIABLE	DEFAULT SETTING	DESCRIPTION
Dimtoh	On	When on, text outside extensions is horizontal.
Dimtvp	0	Controls text's vertical position based on numeric value.
Dimtxsty	Standard	Controls text style for dimension text.
Dimunit	2	Controls unit style for all dimension style groups except angular. Settings are same as for Lunit system variable.
Dimension & Extension Line Control		
Dimarcsym	0	Controls the arc symbol placement; 0 = before dimension text, 1 = above dimension text, 2 = suppress arc length symbol.
Dimfxl	1.0000	Sets the length of extension lines between origin and dimension line in drawing units.
Dimfxlon	Off	Turns on fixed-length extension lines.
Dimjogang	45 (90 for metric)	Sets the angle for the jog line in jogged radius dimensions.
Dimltex1	" "	Sets the linetype for the first extension line.
Dimltex2	" "	Sets the linetype for the second extension line.
Dimsd1	Off	When on, suppresses the first dimension line.
Dimsd2	Off	When on, suppresses the second dimension line.
Dimse1	Off	When on, suppresses the first extension line.
Dimse2	Off	When on, suppresses the second extension line.
Dimsoxd	Off	When on, suppresses dimension lines outside extension lines.
Dimtofl	Off	When on, forces a dimension line between extension lines.
Alternate Dimension Options		
Dimalt	Off	When on, alternate units selected are shown.

TABLE C.2: Dimension Variables *(CONTINUED)*

DIMENSION VARIABLE	DEFAULT SETTING	DESCRIPTION
Dimaltd	2	Indicates alternate unit decimal places.
Dimaltf	25.4000	Indicates alternate unit scale factor.
Dimalttd	2	Indicates alternate unit tolerance decimal places.
Dimaltu	2	Indicates alternate unit style. See Lunits system variable for values.
Dimaltz	0	Controls the suppression of zeros for alternate dimension values.
Dimapost	" "	Adds suffix to alternate dimension text.
Dimpost	" "	Adds suffix to dimension text.
Colors and Lineweights		
Dimclrd	0 or ByBlock	Controls color of dimension lines and arrows.
Dimclre	0 or ByBlock	Controls color of dimension extension lines.
Dimclrt	0 or ByBlock	Controls color of dimension text.
Dimlwd	ByBlock	Controls the lineweight of dimension lines. Valid values are ByLayer, ByBlock, or integer representing 100th millimeter.
Dimlwe	ByBlock	Controls the lineweight of extension lines. Valid values are ByLayer, ByBlock, or integer representing 100th millimeter.

Finally, for those of you who might want to write macros, scripts, or AutoLISP programs to control dimension styles, you'll learn about using two options of the Dimstyle command to set and recall dimension styles from the command line: — **Dimstyle⏎S⏎** and **–Dimstyle⏎R⏎**.

If you want to change a setting through the command line instead of through the Dimension Style dialog box, you can enter the system variable name at the Command prompt.

Storing Dimension Styles through the Command Line

After you set the dimension variables as you like, you can save the settings by using the Dimstyle command. The Dimstyle/Save command records all the current dimension variable settings (except Dimassoc) with a name you specify. Follow these steps:

1. At the Command prompt, enter **–Dimstyle⏎**.

2. At the [Save/Restore/Status/Variables/Apply/?] <Restore>: prompt, press ⏎.

3. When the `Enter name for new dimension style or [?]:` prompt appears, you can enter a question mark (**?**) to get a listing of any dimension styles currently saved, or you can enter a name under which you want the current settings saved.

For example, suppose you change some of your dimension settings through dimension variables instead of through the Dimension Style dialog box, as shown in the following list:

Dimtsz	0.044
Dimtad	On
Dimtih	Off
Dimtoh	Off

These settings are typical for an Architectural style of dimensioning; you might save them under the name My Architectural, as you did in an exercise in Chapter 12. Then suppose you change other dimension settings for dimensions in another format—surveyor's dimensions on a site plan, for example. You might save them with the name Survey, again using the Save option of the Dimstyle command. When you want to return to the settings you used for your architectural drawing, use the Restore option of the Dimstyle command, described in the next section.

Restoring a Dimension Style from the Command Line

To restore a dimension style you've saved by using the Dimstyle Save option, follow these steps:

1. At the Command prompt, enter **–Dimstyle**↵.

2. At the `[Save/Restore/STatus/Variable/Apply/?] <Restore>:` prompt, press ↵.

3. At the following prompt

```
Enter dimension style name, [?] or <select dimension>:
```

you have three options: enter a question mark (**?**) to get a listing of saved dimension styles; enter the name of a style, such as Arch, if you know the name of the style you want; or use the cursor to select a dimension on the screen whose style you want to match.

Notes on Metric Dimensioning

The AutoCAD user community is worldwide, and many of you might be using the metric system in your work. As long as you are not mixing Imperial (feet and inches) and metric measurements, using the metric version of AutoCAD is fairly easy. In the Drawing Units dialog box (choose Format ➢ Units), set your measurement system to decimal, and set the Units To Scale Inserted Content option to the appropriate metric option; then draw distances in millimeters or centimeters. At plot time, select the MM radio button (millimeters) under Paper Size and Paper Units in the Plot dialog box.

If your drawings are to be in both Imperial and metric measurements, you will be concerned with several settings, as follows:

Dimlfac Sets the scale factor for dimension values. The dimension value will be the measured distance in AutoCAD units times this scale factor. Set Dimlfac to 25.4 if you have drawn in inches but want to dimension in millimeters. The default is 1.0000. If you want to scale dimension values from millimeters to inches, use a value of 0.03937.

Dimalt Turns the display of alternate dimensions on or off. Alternate dimensions are dimension text added to your drawing, in addition to the standard dimension text.

Dimaltf Sets the scale factor for alternate dimensions (that is, to metric from Imperial). The default is 25.4, which is the millimeter equivalent of 1″. If you are using metric ISO units, the default will be 0.03937, which is the inch equivalent of 1 mm.

Dimaltd Sets the number of decimal places displayed in the alternate dimensions.

Dimapost Adds a suffix to alternate dimensions, as in 4.5 mm.

USING THE AUTOCAD METRIC TEMPLATE

If you prefer, you can use the metric template drawing supplied by AutoCAD:

1. Choose File ➢ New. If you see the Select Template dialog box, go to step 2; otherwise skip to step 3.

2. Select the Acadiso.dwt file and click Open. You can also select acadISO – Named Plot Styles.dwt if you want to use a named plot style.

3. In the Create New Drawing dialog box, click the Template button. Then select the filename Acadiso.dwt and click OK to open the template. You can also select ACADISO – Named Plot Style.DWT if you want to use a named plot style.

These templates are set up for metric/ISO standard drawings.

You can also click the Metric radio button in the Start From Scratch option of the Create New Drawing dialog box. When you do so, subsequent new files will be set to metric by default.

If the AutoCAD 2007 Startup dialog box does not appear when you open AutoCAD or if you don't see the Create New Drawing dialog box when you choose File ➢ New, you can turn these dialog boxes on by using the Startup option in the System tab of the Options dialog box. Choose Tools ➢ Options, and then click the System tab in the Options dialog box. In the General Options group, select Show Startup Dialog Box from the Startup drop-down list.

Taking a Closer Look at the Dimension Style Dialog Boxes

As you saw in Chapter 12, you can control the appearance and format of dimensions through dimension styles. You can create new dimension styles or edit existing ones. This section describes all the components of the dialog boxes you use to create and maintain dimension styles.

The Dimension Style Manager Dialog Box

The Dimension Style Manager dialog box is the gateway to dimension styles. With this dialog box, you can create a new dimension style, edit existing dimension styles, or make an existing dimension style current. To open the Dimension Style Manager dialog box, choose Dimension ➢ Dimension Style.

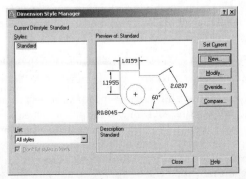

TIP You can use the DesignCenter to import dimension styles from one drawing into another.

The following sections describe the options in the Dimension Style Manager dialog box.

PREVIEW OF *STANDARD*

The image you see in the right half of the Dimension Style Manager dialog box gives you a preview of your dimension style. It shows a sample of most of the types of dimensions you'll use, formatted the way you specified when you created or modified your dimension style.

THE STYLES LIST BOX

The Styles list box displays the available dimension styles. You can highlight the dimension style names in the Styles list box to indicate a style to be used with the Set Current, New, Modify, and Override options. You can also right-click a style name and then rename or delete the selected style.

THE LIST DROP-DOWN LIST

The List drop-down list lets you control what is listed in the Styles list box. You can display either all the styles available or only the styles in use in the drawing.

DON'T LIST STYLES IN XREFS

The Don't List Styles In Xrefs check box lets you specify whether dimension styles in Xrefs are listed in the Styles list box.

THE SET CURRENT BUTTON

The Set Current button lets you set the dimension style highlighted in the Styles list box to be current.

THE NEW BUTTON

The New button lets you create a new dimension style. The New button will use the dimension style that is highlighted in the Styles list box as the basis for the new style. Clicking the New button opens the Create New Dimension Style dialog box.

In the Create New Dimension Style dialog box, you can enter the name for your new dimension style. You can also select the source dimension style on which your new dimension style will be based.

New Style Name Lets you specify the name for your new dimension style.

Start With Lets you select an existing style on which to base your new dimension style.

Use For Lets you choose a dimension type for your new dimension style. For a completely new dimension style, use the All Dimensions option in the Use For drop-down list. If you want to modify the specifications for a particular dimension type of an existing dimension style, select a dimension type from this list. Your modified dimension type will appear in the Styles list box under the main style you specify in the Start With drop-down list. After you've modified a dimension type, the new type will be applied to any new dimensions.

After you've entered your options in the Create New Dimension Style dialog box, click Continue. You see the New Dimension Style dialog box described in the next section. When you are finished setting up your new style, you will see it listed in the Styles list box.

THE MODIFY BUTTON

The Modify button lets you modify the dimension style that is selected in the Styles list box. Clicking this option opens the Modify Dimension Style dialog box described in the next section.

THE OVERRIDE BUTTON

The Override button lets you create a temporary dimension style based on an existing style. You might want to use this option if you need to create a dimension that differs only slightly from an existing style.

To use the Override option, select a style from the Styles list box and then click Override. You'll see the Override Current Style dialog box described in the next section. After you create an override, you'll see it listed as <style overrides> in the Styles list box right under the style you used to create the override.

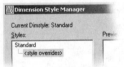

The override then becomes the default dimension style until you select another one from the Styles list. When you select a different style to be current, you will see a message telling you that the unsaved style will be discarded. To save an override style, select the override from the Styles list box and click New. Then click Continue in the Create New Dimension Style dialog box, and click OK in the New Dimension Style dialog box. You can also merge the Override style with its source style by right-clicking the <style overrides> listing and selecting Save To Current Style.

THE COMPARE BUTTON

The Compare button lets you compare the differences between two dimension styles. When you click the Compare button, the Compare Dimension Styles dialog box opens.

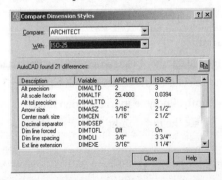

You can select the two styles you want to compare from the Compare and With drop-down lists. The differences will appear in the list box. Just above the upper-right corner of the list box is a Copy button; this copies the contents of the list box to the Windows Clipboard, enabling you to save the comparison to a word-processed document.

The New/Modify/Override Dimension Style Dialog Box

When you click the New button in the Dimension Style Manager dialog box and then click Continue in the Create New Dimension Style dialog box, the New Dimension Style dialog box opens.

You will also see this same dialog box under a different name when you select the Modify or Override button in the Dimension Style Manager dialog box. The options in this dialog box let you determine all the characteristics of your dimension style. This section provides detailed descriptions of each available option.

TIP The equivalent dimension style variables are shown in brackets at the end of the description of each option.

THE LINES TAB

The options in this tab give you control over the appearance of dimension and extension lines. Figure C.1 shows an example of some of the dimension components that are affected by these options. The value you enter here for distances should be in final plot sizes and will be multiplied by the dimension scale value in the Fit tab to derive the actual extension distance in the drawing.

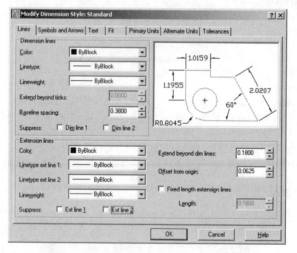

The Dimension Lines Group

The following options let you control the general behavior and characteristics of the dimension lines:

Color Lets you set the color of the dimension line [Dimclrd].

Linetype Lets you set the linetype for dimension lines.

Lineweight Lets you set the lineweight for dimension lines [Dimlwd].

Extend Beyond Ticks   Lets you set the distance that the dimension line extends beyond the extension lines. The value you enter here should be in final plot sizes and will be multiplied by the dimension scale value in the Fit tab to derive the actual extension distance in the drawing [Dimdle].

Baseline Spacing   Lets you specify the distance between stacked dimensions [Dimdli, Dimbaseline].

Suppress   Check boxes let you suppress the dimension line on either side of the dimension text [DimLine1, DimLine2].

FIGURE C.1

Examples of how some of the options in the Lines tab affect dimensions

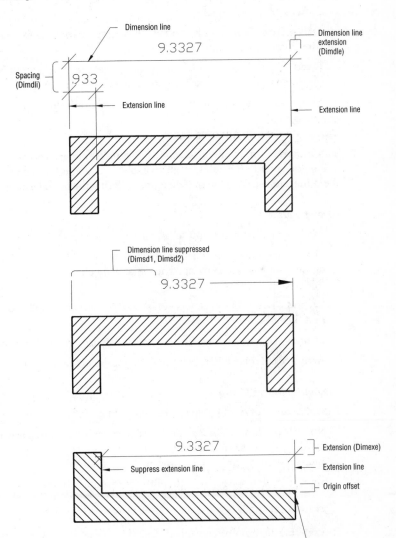

The Extension Lines Group

The following options let you control the general behavior and characteristics of the extension lines:

Color   Lets you set the color for extension lines [Dimclre].

Linetype Ext Line 1   Controls the linetype for the first extension line.

Linetype Ext Line 2   Controls the linetype for the second extension line.

Lineweight   Lets you set the lineweight for extension lines [Dimlwe].

Extend Beyond Dim Lines   Lets you set the distance that extension lines extend beyond dimension lines [Dimexe].

Offset From Origin   Lets you set the distance from the extension line to the object being dimensioned [Dimexo].

Fixed Length Extension Lines   Lets you set the extension lines to a fixed length. The Length input box provides a space to enter the length you want.

Suppress   Check boxes let you suppress one or both extension lines [Ext Line1, Ext Line2].

THE SYMBOLS AND ARROWS TAB

The options in this tab give you control over the appearance of arrowheads and center marks. The value you enter in this tab for distances should be in final plot sizes and will be multiplied by the dimension scale value in the Fit tab to derive the actual extension distance in the drawing.

Arrowheads

The following options let you select the type and sizes of arrowheads for dimensions and leaders:

First   Drop-down list lets you select the type of arrowhead to use on dimension lines. By default, the second arrowhead automatically changes to match the arrowhead you specify for this setting [Dimblk1].

Second   Drop-down list lets you select a different arrowhead from the one you select for first [Dimblk2].

Leader   Drop-down list lets you specify an arrowhead for leader notes [Dimldrblk].

Arrow Size   Lets you specify the size for the arrowheads [Dimasz].

The Center Marks Group

The following options let you set the center mark for radius and diameter dimensions:

None/Mark/Line   These radio buttons let you select the type of center mark used in radius and diameter dimensions. The Mark option draws a small cross mark, Line draws a cross mark and center lines, and None draws nothing [Dimcen].

Size   Lets you specify the size of the center mark [Dimcen].

The Arc Length Symbol Group

This set of radio buttons controls the display of the arc-length symbol in arc-length dimensions.

Preceding Dimension Text   Places the symbol before the dimension text.

Above Dimension Text   Places the symbol above the dimension text.

None   No symbol.

The Radius Dimension Jog Group

You can set the angle of the radius dimension jog with this setting. The radius dimension jog is the short line in the radius dimension that indicates that the dimension is measured to a point out of view.

THE TEXT TAB

The options in the Text tab give you control over the appearance of the dimension text. You can set the text style and default location of text in relation to the dimension line. If the text style you select for your dimension text has a height value of 0, you can set the text height from this tab.

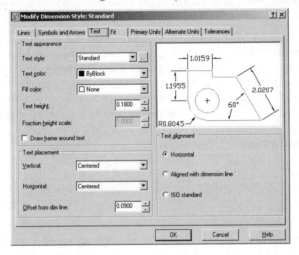

The Text Appearance Group

The following options give you control over the appearance of text:

Text Style   Drop-down list lets you select an existing text style for your dimension text. You can also create a new style for your dimension text by clicking the Browse button [Dimtxsty].

Text Color   Drop-down list lets you select a color for your dimension text [Dimclrt].

Fill Color   Drop-down list lets you select a color for your dimension background.

Text Height   Lets you specify a text height for dimension text. This option is valid only for text styles with 0 height [Dimtxt].

Fraction Height Scale   Lets you specify a scale factor for the height of fractional text. This option is available only when Architectural or Fractional is selected in the Primary Units tab [Dimtfac].

Draw Frame Around Text   Check box draws a rectangle around the dimension text when selected [Dimgap].

The Text Placement Group

The following options give you control over the placement of text, including the ability to specify the distance of text from the dimension line:

Vertical   Drop-down list lets you set the vertical position of the text in relation to the dimension line. The options are Centered, Above, Outside, and JIS. Centered places the text in line with the dimension line. The dimension line is broken to accommodate the text. Above places the text above the dimension line, leaving the dimension line unbroken. Outside places the text away from the dimension line at a location farthest from the object being dimensioned. JIS places the text in conformance with the Japanese Industrial Standards [Dimtad].

Horizontal   Drop-down list lets you set the location of the text in relation to the extension lines. The options are Centered, At Ext Line 1, At Ext Line 2, Over Ext Line 1, and Over Ext Line 2. Centered places the text between the two extension lines. At Ext Line 1 places the text next to the first extension line but still between the two extension lines. At Ext Line 2 places the text next to the second extension line but still between the two extension lines. Over Ext Line 1 places the text above the first extension line and aligned with the first extension line. Over Ext Line 2 places the text above the second extension line and aligned with the second extension line [Dimjust].

Offset From Dim Line   Lets you determine the distance from the baseline of text to the dimension line when text is placed above the dimension line. It also lets you set the size of the gap between the dimension text and the endpoint of the dimension line when the text is in line with the dimension line. You can use this option to set the margin around the text when the dimension text is in a centered position that breaks the dimension line into two segments [Dimgap].

The Text Alignment Group

The following options give you control over the alignment of text in relation to the dimension line:

Horizontal   Keeps the text in a horizontal orientation, regardless of the dimension line orientation.

Aligned With Dimension Line   Aligns the text with the dimension line.

ISO Standard   Aligns the text with the dimension line when it is between the extension lines; otherwise the text is oriented horizontally [Dimtih, Dimtoh].

THE FIT TAB

The options in the Fit tab let you fine-tune the behavior of the dimension text and arrows under special conditions. For example, you can select an optional placement for text and arrows when there isn't enough room for them between the extension lines.

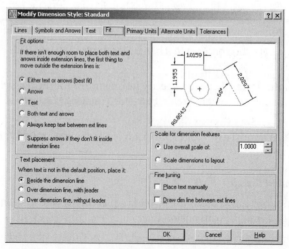

The Fit Options Group

The Fit Options radio buttons let you determine which dimension component is moved when there isn't enough room between the extension lines for either or both the text or the arrows.

Either Text Or Arrows (Best Fit)   Automatically determines whether only text, only arrows, or both text and arrows will fit between the extension lines and then places them accordingly. For example, if there isn't enough room for both text and arrows, and the text is wider than the two arrows combined, the text will be placed outside the extension lines. If the width of the arrows is greater than the width of the text, the arrows will be moved outside the extension lines. If the gap between the extension lines is too narrow for either the text or arrows, both the arrows and the text will be moved outside the extension lines [Dimatfit].

Arrows   Moves the arrows outside the extension lines when there isn't enough room for both arrows and text between the extension lines. If the gap between the extension lines is too narrow for either the text or the arrows, both the arrows and the text will be moved outside the extension lines [Dimatfit].

Text   Moves the text outside the extension line when there isn't enough room for both arrows and text between the extension lines. If the gap between the extension lines is too narrow for either the text or the arrows, both the arrows and the text will be moved outside the extension lines [Dimatfit].

Both Text And Arrows   Moves both the text and the arrows outside the extension line when there isn't enough room for both arrows and text between the extension lines [Dimatfit].

Always Keep Text Between Ext Lines   Places the text between the extension lines, regardless of whether the text will fit there [Dimtix].

Suppress Arrows If They Don't Fit Inside Extension Lines   Removes the arrows entirely if they don't fit between the extension lines [Dimsoxd].

The Text Placement Group

The Text Placement radio buttons determine how the dimension text will behave when it is moved from its default location:

Beside The Dimension Line   Keeps the text in its normal location relative to the dimension line [Dimtmove].

Over Dimension Line, With Leader   Lets you move the dimension text, independent of the dimension line. A leader is added between the dimension line and the text [Dimtmove].

Over Dimension Line, Without Leader   Lets you move the dimension text, independent of the dimension line. No leader is added [Dimtmove].

The Scale For Dimension Features Group

These options offer control over the scale of the dimension components. You can set a fixed scale, or you can allow the dimension components to be scaled depending on the Paper Space viewport in which they are displayed:

Use Overall Scale Of   Radio button and input box let you determine the scale of the dimension components. All the settings in the Dimension Style dialog box will be scaled to the value you set in the input box if this radio button is selected [Dimscale].

Scale Dimensions To Layout Will scale all the dimension components to the scale factor assigned to the Paper Space viewport in which the drawing appears [Dimscale].

The Fine Tuning Group

The following two check boxes offer miscellaneous settings for dimension text and dimension lines:

Place Text Manually Enables you to manually place the dimension text horizontally along the dimension line when you are inserting dimensions in your drawing [Dimupt].

Draw Dim Line Between Ext Lines Forces AutoCAD to draw a dimension line between the extension lines no matter how narrow the distance is between the extension lines [Dimtofl].

THE PRIMARY UNITS TAB

The options in the Primary Units tab let you set the format and content of the dimension text, including the unit style for linear and angular dimensions.

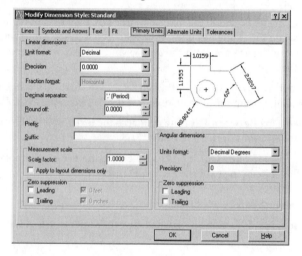

The Linear Dimensions Group

The following options give you control over the unit style and the formatting of dimension text for linear dimensions:

Unit Format Drop-down list lets you determine the unit style of the dimension text. The options are Scientific, Decimal, Engineering, Architectural, Fractional, and Windows Desktop. You must set this option independent of the overall drawing units setting (choose Format ➢ Units) if you want the dimension text to appear in the appropriate style [Dimunit].

Precision Drop-down list lets you set the precision of the dimension text. This option will round off the dimension text to the nearest precision value you set. It does not affect the actual precision of the drawing [Dimdec].

Fraction Format Drop-down list is available only for Architectural and Fractional unit formats. This option lets you select between vertically stacked, diagonally stacked, and horizontal fractions [Dimfrac].

Decimal Separator   Drop-down list lets you select a decimal separator for dimension unit formats that display decimals. You can choose a period, a comma, or a space. If you want to use a dimension separator not included in the list, you can use the Dimsep system variable to specify a custom dimension separator [Dimsep].

Round Off   Lets you determine the degree of rounding applied to dimensions. For example, you can set this option to 0.25 to round off dimensions to the nearest .25 or $1/4$ of a unit [Dimrnd].

Prefix   Lets you include a prefix for all linear dimension text. For example, if you want all your linear dimension text to be preceded by the word *Approximately,* you can enter **Approximately** in this input box. Control codes can be used for special characters. See Chapter 10 for more information on character codes [Dimpost].

Suffix   Lets you include a suffix for all linear dimension text. Control codes can be used for special characters. See Chapter 10 for more information on character codes [Dimpost].

The Measurement Scale Group

This group offers options that can convert dimension values to different scale factors. For example, dimensions in Imperial units can be scaled to metric, and vice versa. The options are as follows:

Scale Factor   Lets you set a scale factor for the dimension text. This option will scale the value of the dimension text to the value you enter. For example, if you want your dimensions to display distances in centimeters, even though the drawing was created in inches, you can enter 2.54 for this option. Your dimension text will then display dimensions in centimeters. Conversely, if you want your dimension text to show dimensions in inches, even though you've created your drawing using centimeters, you enter 0.3937 (the inverse of 2.54) for this option [Dimlfac].

Apply To Layout Dimensions Only   Causes AutoCAD to apply the measurement scale factor to Paper Space layouts only. With this check box selected, the Dimlfac dimension variable gives a negative value [Dimlfac].

The Zero Suppression Group

Lets you suppress zeros so they do not appear in the dimension text. For dimensions other than architectural, you can suppress leading and trailing zeros. For example, 0.500 becomes .500 if you suppress leading zeros. It becomes 0.5 if you suppress trailing zeros. For architectural dimensions, you can suppress zero feet or zero inches, although typically you would not suppress zero inches [Dimzin].

The Angular Dimensions Group

The following options enable you to format angle dimensions:

Units Format   Drop-down list lets you select a format for angular dimensions. The options are Decimal Degrees, Degrees Minutes Seconds, Gradians, and Radians [Dimaunit].

Precision   Lets you set the precision for the angular dimension text [Dimadec].

Zero Suppression   Lets you suppress leading or trailing zeros in angular dimensions [Dimazin].

THE ALTERNATE UNITS TAB

The Alternate Units tab lets you apply a second set of dimension text for linear dimensions. This second set of text can be used for alternate dimension styles or units. Typically, alternate units are used to display dimensions in metric if your main dimensions are in feet and inches.

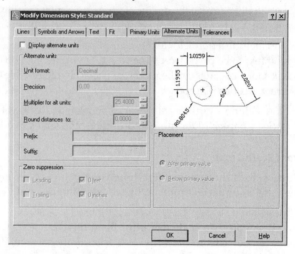

Click the Display Alternate Units check box to turn on alternate units. This causes AutoCAD to include an additional dimension text in the format you specify in the Alternate Units tab [Dimalt].

The Alternate Units Group

The following options offer control over the unit style and the formatting of dimension text for linear dimensions:

Unit Format   Drop-down list lets you determine the unit style of the dimension text. The options are Scientific, Decimal, Engineering, Architectural Stacked, Fractional Stacked, Architectural, Fractional, and Windows Desktop. You must set this option independent of the overall drawing units setting (choose Format ➤ Units) if you want the dimension text to appear in the appropriate style [Dimaltu]. You can adjust the size of fractions relative to the main dimension text by using the Dimfac dimension variable.

Precision   Drop-down list lets you set the precision of the dimension text. This option will round off the dimension text to the nearest precision value you set. It does not affect the actual precision of the drawing [Dimaltd].

Multiplier For Alt Units   Lets you set a multiplier value for the dimension text. This option will multiply the value of the dimension text by the value you enter. For example, if you want your alternate dimensions to display distances in centimeters even though the drawing was created in inches, you can enter 2.54 for this option. Your alternate dimension text will then display dimensions in centimeters. Conversely, if you want to have your alternate dimension text show dimensions in inches, even though you've created your drawing by using centimeters, you enter 0.3937 (the inverse of 2.54) for this option [Dimaltf].

Round Distances To   Lets you determine the degree of rounding applied to alternate dimensions. For example, you can set this option to 0.25 to round off dimensions to the nearest .25 or $1/4$ of a unit [DImaltrnd].

Prefix   Lets you include a prefix for all linear alternate dimension text. For example, if you want all linear dimension text to be preceded by the word *Approximately*, you can enter **Approximately** in the Prefix input box. Control codes can be used for special characters. See Chapter 10 for more information on character codes [Dimpost].

Suffix   Lets you include a suffix for all linear alternate dimension text. Control codes can be used for special characters. See Chapter 10 for more information on character codes [Dimapost].

The Zero Suppression Group

The check boxes in this group let you suppress zeros so they do not appear in the alternate dimension text. For dimensions other than architectural, you can suppress leading and trailing zeros. For example, 0.500 becomes .500 if you suppress leading zeros. It becomes 0.5 if you suppress trailing zeros. For architectural dimensions, you can suppress zero feet or zero inches, though typically you would not suppress zero inches [Dimaltz].

The Placement Group

The following options let you determine the location for the alternate units:

After Primary Value   Places the alternate dimension text behind and aligned with the primary dimension text [Dimapost].

Below Primary Value   Places the alternate dimension text below the primary dimension text and above the dimension line [Dimapost].

THE TOLERANCES TAB

The options in the Tolerances tab offer the inclusion and formatting of tolerance dimension text.

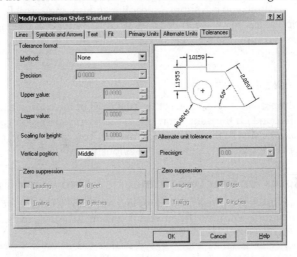

The Tolerance Format Group

The following options offer control over the format of tolerance dimension text:

Method   Lets you turn on and set the format for the tolerance dimension text. The options are None, Symmetrical, Deviation, Limits, and Basic. None turns off the tolerance dimension text.

Symmetrical adds a plus/minus tolerance dimension. This is a single dimension preceded by a plus/minus sign. Deviation adds a stacked tolerance dimension showing separate upper and lower tolerance values. The Limits option replaces the primary dimension with a stacked dimension showing maximum and minimum dimension values. The Basic option draws a box around the primary dimension value. If an alternate dimension is used, the box encloses both primary and alternate dimension text [Dimtol, Dimlim, (minus) Dimgap].

Precision Drop-down list lets you set the precision of the tolerance dimension text. This option will round off the dimension text to the nearest precision value you set. It does not affect the actual precision of the drawing [Dimtdec].

Upper Value Lets you set the upper tolerance value for the Symmetrical, Deviation, and Limits tolerance methods [Dimtp].

Lower Value Lets you set the lower tolerance value for the Deviation and Limits tolerance methods [Dimtm].

Scaling For Height Lets you adjust the size for the tolerance dimension text as a proportion of the primary dimension text height [Dimtfac].

Vertical Position Lets you determine the vertical position of the tolerance text. The options are Top, Middle, and Bottom. The Top option aligns the top tolerance value of a stacked pair of values with the primary dimension text. Middle aligns the gap between stacked tolerance values with the primary dimension text. Bottom aligns the bottom value of two stacked tolerance values with the primary dimension text [Dimtolj].

The Zero Suppression Groups

Lets you suppress zeros so they do not appear in the tolerance dimension text. For dimensions other than architectural, you can suppress leading and trailing zeros. For example, 0.500 becomes .500 if you suppress leading zeros. It becomes 0.5 if you suppress trailing zeros. For architectural dimensions you can suppress zero feet or zero inches, though typically you would not suppress zero inches [Dimtzin].

The Alternate Unit Tolerance Group

The Precision drop-down list lets you set the precision of the alternate tolerance dimension text. This option will round off the dimension text to the nearest precision value you set. It does not affect the actual precision of the drawing [Dimalttd]. You can also control zero suppression (see "The Zero Suppression Group" mentioned previously).

Drawing Blocks for Your Own Dimension Arrows and Tick Marks

If you don't want to use the arrowheads supplied by AutoCAD for your dimension lines, you can create a block of the arrowheads or tick marks you want, to be used in the Arrowheads group of the Dimension Styles/Geometry dialog box.

TIP To access the Arrowhead options, open the Symbols And Arrows tab of the New, Modify, Or Override Dimension Style dialog box.

For example, suppose you want a tick mark that is thicker than the dimension lines and extensions. You can create a block of the tick mark on a layer you assign to a thick pen weight and then assign that block to the Arrowhead setting. To do so, choose Dimension ➤ Styles from the menu bar to open the Dimension Styles dialog box; then select a style from the Style list and click the Modify button. In the Symbols And Arrows tab, select User Arrow from the First drop-down list in the Arrowheads group. In the User Arrow dialog box, enter the name of your arrow block.

When you draw the arrow block, make it 1 unit long. The block's insertion point will be used to determine the point of the arrow that meets the extension line, so make sure you place the insertion point at the tip of the arrow. Because the arrow on the right side of the dimension line will be inserted with a zero rotation value, create the arrow block so that it is pointing to the right (see Figure C.2). The arrow block is rotated 180° for the left side of the dimension line.

If you want a different type of arrow at both ends of the dimension line, create a block for each arrow. Then, in the Dimension Styles/Geometry dialog box, choose User in the drop-down list for the first arrowhead and enter the name of one block. Then choose User in the drop-down list for the second arrowhead and enter the name of the other block.

FIGURE C.2

The orientation and size of a block used in place of the default arrow

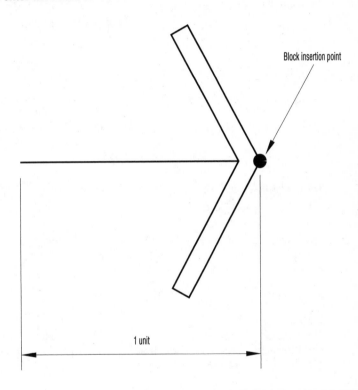

Block insertion point

1 unit

Appendix D

New Features

It has only been a year since Autodesk last offered a new version of AutoCAD, so you might think that AutoCAD 2007 contains only minor changes. But there are many significant additions to this latest offering as well as numerous smaller changes. This appendix provides an overview of these additions, as well as new and updated commands.

AutoCAD 2007 has a completely new 3D feature set. Every aspect of 3D has been reworked to make it easier for you to create, edit, and present your ideas in 3D. Even the way you access tools for 3D modeling has been enhanced through a new tool palette called the Dashboard (see Figure D.1). Most of the major 3D features are covered in Part 4 of this book, but to get a quick rundown of these new features, you can review the following sections.

Creating 3D Objects

AutoCAD offers the basic 3D solid primitives: box, wedge, cylinder, cone, sphere, pyramid and torus. These are shapes that you can combine to build more complex forms. A new 3D solid called *polysolid* lets you create wall-like structures. Another command called Sweep lets you extrude a 2D shape along a path to form a tube or a non-linear extrusion. Sweep can be used in conjunction with Helix to form 3D springs or other coiled shapes. *Presspull* will turn a 2D shape into a 3D object using a press and pull motion as shown in Figure D.2. You can press a 2D shape into an existing solid to form a depression or pull the shape to form a solid.

FIGURE D.1
The Dashboard gives you access to the new 3D functions.

Besides 3D solids, you can create complex surfaces. At the basic level, you can create a plane surface using the Planesurf command. This is a flat, rectangular surface that can be used in a variety of ways in your 3D model. Other more complex surfaces can be formed using the Loft and Sweep commands. With Loft, you can create a sheetlike surface that follows the contours of a series of 2D objects (see Figure D.3). For example, you can take a drawing of geographic contours and then use Loft to create a 3D surface of the contours.

3D surfaces can be turned into 3D solids using the Thicken command. You only need to supply a thickness value. If you have older drawings that contain objects whose thickness property is greater than zero, another command called Convtosurface will convert such objects to the new 3D surface objects. This can be useful in converting older 3D AutoCAD surface models into solids for more advanced editing. Another command called Convtosolid will convert a polyline into a solid. The polyline must have a width and thickness property greater than zero.

You can also use 3D surface objects to slice 3D solids. You can use a 3D surface plane to create a flat slice or use a more complex 3D surface to contour the surface of a solid.

Editing 3D Objects

3D objects can be grip edited in a variety of ways. When you click a 3D solid, you will see square grips appear at key points such as corners or edges. The square grips let you move the location of the feature associated with the grip. You will also see arrow grips that allow you to adjust the overall dimension of a solid. Ctrl+clicking a solid displays even more grips for surfaces and edges.

FIGURE D.2
Presspull can convert 2D objects as shown on the left into 3D solids as shown on the right.

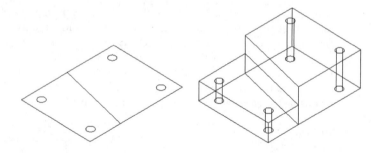

FIGURE D.3
Loft lets you create complex surfaces.

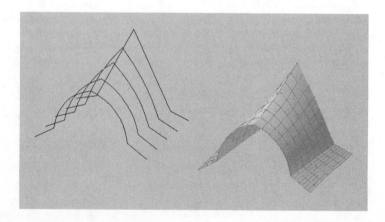

FIGURE D.4

The Grip tool lets you restrain the motion of a grip along the X, Y, or Z axis.

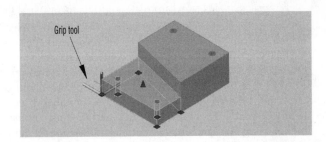

Grip tool

In addition to the square and arrow grips, you can use grip tools to limit motion to the X, Y, or Z axis. The Grip tool is a graphical tool that looks similar to the UCS icon (see Figure D.4).

In the past, you had to become familiar with the User Coordinate System to really do any useful work in 3D. The Dynamic UCS (DUCS) is a new feature that automatically orients your coordinate system to the surface of a 3D giving you better 3D control. The DUCS can be turned on or off using the DUCS button in the status bar.

2D objects can be used to shape the surface of 3D solids using the Presspull command. For example, you can draw a line across a surface and then use Presspull to press or pull the surface subdivision created by the line. This works with arcs, circles, splines, and other 2D objects as well.

You can use 3D surface objects in conjunction with the Slice command to "sculpt" the surface of a 3D solid. This is significant because using tools such as Loft and Sweep, you can create complex, free-form 3D surfaces like the bodywork of a car or the contours of hillside. Such surfaces can then be applied to a 3D solid using the Slice command.

The AutoCAD grid has been updated to offer better functionality with 3D modeling (see Figure D.5). Using a 3D visual style (see the "Visualizing 3D" section next), the grid appears as lines rather than as the dots of the old style grid. Grids also display subdivisions that dynamically change depending on the zoom factor of your view.

Visualizing 3D

The 3D rendering side of AutoCAD is now easier to use. If you are familiar with Autodesk Viz or Max, you will feel more at home with AutoCAD. The same Point, Distant, spotlight, and sun are still available through a simplified interface. Materials can now be created and applied through an Autodesk Viz-like Materials palette.

FIGURE D.5

The AutoCAD grid as it appears in a 3D view.

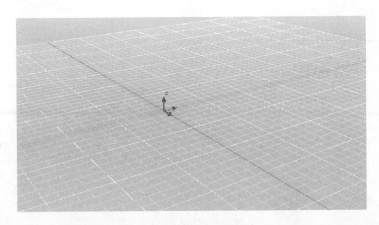

The old Shade modes have been replaced with visual styles, which allow you to set the degree of realism applied to your 3D model as you work. It is easy to go from a 2D wireframe to a more realistic view so you can "spot check" your model as you work. You can also customize visual styles to produce the look you want, including a hand-sketched look. An Xray mode (Vsfaceopacity command) has also been included to allow you to see through to the internal structure of a 3D solid (see Figure D.6).

Getting around in your model has been enhanced with a set of viewing tools. The Constrained Orbit tool, otherwise known as the 3Dorbit command, lets you rotate your view around an object in any direction. The Walk and Fly tools (3Dwalk command) let you navigate through your model using familiar controls similar to those found in PC games. Views now become camera objects that can be controlled through the Properties palette. You can now set the focal length, clip planes, and other properties. Views also can be saved with special properties, including background colors and layer settings. A preview window lets you see exactly what the camera sees as you make changes to a camera's location.

Cutaway drawings of 3D models are now possible with the Sectionplane command. You can cut a single section through a 3D solid, or you can jog a section plane for a more complex view. You can also include section planes from several sides of an object. Section planes can show hidden portions of a section as a ghosted image, and you can create 2D and 3D copies of sections (see Figure D.7). Sectionplane does not affect the 3D solid to which it is applied. It only displays hidden portions of the solid.

FIGURE D.6
A solid viewed with
Xray mode turned on

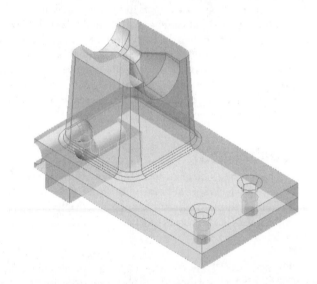

FIGURE D.7
Cutaway drawings
can be created using
the Sectionplane
command.

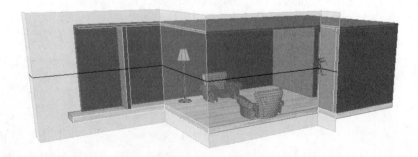

For rendering, AutoCAD uses the same Mental Ray Rendering system used in Autodesk Viz, so you can get a wide range of rendering styles from schematic to realistic. Global Illumination is a feature that gives architectural interior views more realistic lighting effects, as shown in Figure D.8.

And finally, AutoCAD includes a basic animation tool that will generate an animated walkthrough of your model. The Anipath command lets you set a path for both the camera and target and also gives you control over frames per second and total duration. You can set the rendering level from simple wireframe to fully rendered frames. You can also choose the file type. Animation paths can be lines, arcs, or polylines. You also have a choice of a point if you want to keep the camera or target at a stationary location.

Other Updates

Besides the new 3D features, AutoCAD 2007 offers some new enhancements to external references and file export. The External Reference feature has gotten a face lift with the External References palette. Through the palette interface, you can load AutoCAD drawings as external references, as well as bitmap images and Autodesk DWF files. A Details section in the External References palette gives you more detailed information about the Xref files attached to a drawing.

Another new feature is one that takes a little digging to find. AutoCAD now supplies a PDF plotter driver so you can create PDF files directly in AutoCAD. Use the Add-A-Plotter Wizard to install the Autodesk ePlot (PDF) plotter driver. Once installed, you can select the DWG to PDF.pc3 plotter from the Printer/Plotter option of the Plot dialog box. See Chapter 19 for more information on the Add-A-Plotter wizard and Chapter 8 for more on printing and plotting.

If you an AutoCAD subscription member, you can use the Autodesk Vault to store and share drawing data with other members of your design team. Autodesk Vault is a feature that allows you to store data on an Autodesk server. It is secure and password protected.

FIGURE D.8

A rendered interior view using Global Illumination

Finally, the Autodesk DWF file format has been enhanced and now supports 3D models. With the included DWF viewer, 3D models can be rotated and sliced. Dimensions can also be listed.

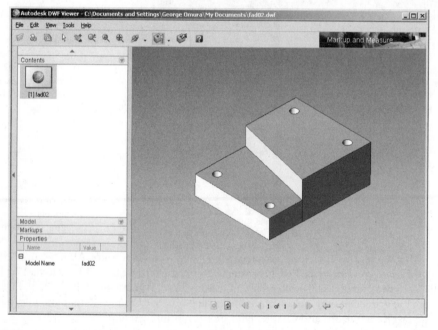

Index

Note to the Reader: Throughout this index **boldfaced** page numbers indicate primary discussions of a topic. *Italicized* page numbers indicate illustrations.

H

Halfwidth polyline option, 601, *602*
Halogap system variable, 1080
Handles system variable, 1080
hard clip limits, **301–302**, *301*
hard disk drives, 642, **1060–1061**
Hardware And Performance
   Tuning Group settings, 1045
Hatch And Gradient dialog box,
   239–240, *239*
      for gradients, **252–253**, *252–253*
      More Options, **250–252**, *250*
      for object area, 637–638
      options in, **249–250**
      for position, *241*, 242–243
      for solid fills, 628
      tips for, **254**
Hatch Edit dialog box, 247–248
Hatch Pattern Palette dialog box,
   242–243, *242*, 248–250, 628
hatch patterns, **238**
      adding, **239–240**
      additional features, **250–252**
      for area of objects, **637–638**, *638*
      creating, **938–941**, *938–941*
      Express Tools for, **865–867**,
         866–867
      for gradients, **252–253**, *252–253*
      layers for, 239
      matching, **255**
      modifying, **247–249**, *248–249*
      position of, **240–243**, *241–243*
      predefined, 242–243, *244*
      size of, **246–247**
      and space planning, **254–257**, *256*
      standard, *938*
      tips for, **254**
      for Tool Palettes, **971–972**
Hatch tool, 35, *35*, 239, 628
height
      cameras, 797
      dimension text, **393–394**, 1125
      shapes, 872
      text, **334–336**, *335*, 351, 356, 438
Height option, 797
helicoils, 740–741, *740*
Helix tool, 738–739, *739–740*
help
      for commands, **70–74**, *70–73*
      context-sensitive, **72**
      in DesignCenter searches, 967
      for Diesel, 929
      for groups, 147

for icons, 919
      sources of, **72–73**
Help dialog box, 929
Help feature in DesignCenter, 967
help files, location of, 1026
Help for Autodesk Subscription
   Users option, 72
Help menu
      Additional Resources menu,
         905–906
      Help command, 70
      New Features Workshop
         command, 4
Help menu Info Palette
   command, 72
hexagons, dimensioning, **420–425**,
   421–425
Hidden Files And Folders
   option, 1047
hidden folders, **1047**
hidden lines
      in 3D models, 818
      in curved extrusions, 821, *821*
      in viewports, **842–843**, *843*
HIDDEN linetypes, *170*, 933
Hidden option
      in plotting, 287
      for spheres, 694, *695*
Hide command, 289, 818
Hide System Printers option,
   304, 1059
Hideprecision system variable, 1080
Hidetext system variable, 1081
hiding
      by masking, 551
      in plotting, 289
Highlight options for groups, 145
Highlight Interference option, 734
Highlight Interfering Pair
   option, 734
Highlight Raster Image Frame
   Only option, 1029
Highlight system variable, 366, 1081
highlighting selected objects, 53, *53*
history
      of commands, 74, *74*
      of recent files, 969
History tab, 969
Home dimension text option, 406
Hor Xline option, 211
Horizontal Cell Margin option, 377
horizontal dimensions, **400–401**,
   400, 1126
horizontal lines, 40

horizontal Xlines, 211
hot grips, 63, *63*, 65
Hot_water_supply linetype, *170*, *936*
hotspots of spotlights, 779, *779*
How To Apply option, 522
Hpang system variable, 1081
Hpassoc system variable, 1081
Hpbound system variable, 1081
Hpdouble system variable, 1081
Hpdraworder system variable, 1081
Hpgaptol system variable, 1081
HPGL plot files, 655
Hpinherit system variable, 1081
Hpname system variable, 1081
Hpobjwarning system variable, 1081
Hporigin system variable, 1081
Hporiginmode system variable, 1082
Hpscale system variable, 1082
Hpseparate system variable, 1082
Hpspace system variable, 1082
Hyperlink icon, missing, 1066
Hyperlink menu, Open
   command, 960
Hyperlink option, 127
Hyperlinkbase system variable, 1082
hyperlinks, **958–959**
      creating, **959–960**, *959–960*
      editing and deleting, **960**
      options for, **961–962**, 1037
hyphens (-)
      in AutoLISP, 889
      with calculator, 536
      in Diesel, 929
      for keyboard commands, 25
      in linetype patterns, 934
      for macros, 917
      with tables, 382
      in units, 83

I

I command, 441
i-drop
      for file exchange, **957–958**
      file location for, 1028
Iad command, 481
iat command, 477
Icl command, 480
icons
      creating, **918–919**, *918–919*
      descriptions for, 16, *16*
      for UCS, 10, 543, 704, **712**
ID command, 635
if code in Diesel, 930

What's on the CD

This CD offers valuable resources, including a 30-day trial copy of AutoCAD 2007, bonus chapters, add-ons, utilities, the DWG, and other files needed for the book's exercises, and more. Specifically, you'll find:

AutoCAD 2007 Trial lets you try the new features covered in this book and practice the tutorials. This trial version is fully functional but expires after 30 days of use and includes the Autodesk Express Viewer.

Project Files from the exercises in the book are included so you can easily study any topic at any time.

VBA and Active X chapters discuss how Microsoft Visual Basic or Excel interact with AutoCAD. The chapters also show you how to use the VBA programming language and user interface tools to build user-friendly front ends to your AutoCAD applications. The AutoCAD object model is also introduced, and source code for all the program examples is included.

Architectural Solid Modeling chapter covers more advanced 3D modeling topics. This chapter will teach you how to become a 3D pro with more detailed information on how to accurately model your designs.

"Working with External Databases" chapter shows how to use the AutoCAD dbConnect Man-ager to link database files to AutoCAD drawings. This way, you can use a database program's more sophisticated software tools to analyze the nongraphic data you need to work with in your design projects.

2D and 3D parts library includes kitchen cabinets, furniture, trees, and people

Wiley Publishing, Inc.
End-User License Agreement

R.C.L.

MARS 2007

A A11